Marketing

An Introduction

MyMarketingLab™

MyMarketingLab is an online assessment and preparation solution for courses in Principles of Marketing, Marketing Management, Consumer Behavior, Advertising, and Professional Selling that helps you actively study and prepare material for class. Chapter-by-chapter activities, including study plans, focus on what you need to learn and to review in order to succeed.

Visit **www.mymktlab.com** to learn more.

Marketing

An Introduction Eleventh Edition

 GARY ARMSTRONG
University of North Carolina

 PHILIP KOTLER
Northwestern University

PEARSON

Boston   Columbus   Indianapolis   New York   San Francisco
Upper Saddle River   Amsterdam   Cape Town   Dubai   London
Madrid   Milan   Munich   Paris   Montreal   Toronto   Delhi   Mexico City
São Paulo   Sydney   Hong Kong   Seoul   Singapore   Taipei   Tokyo

Library of Congress Cataloging-in-Publication Data
Armstrong, Gary (Gary M.)
    Marketing : an introduction / Gary Armstrong, Philip Kotler.—11th ed.
        p. cm.
    Includes bibliographical references and index.
    ISBN-13: 978-0-13-274403-4
    ISBN-10: 0-13-274403-1
1. Marketing. I. Kotler, Philip. II. Title.
    HF5415.K625 2013
    658.8--dc23   2011042944

Editorial Director: Sally Yagan
Acquisitions Editor: Erin Gardner
Editorial Project Manager: Meeta Pendharkar
Editorial Assistant: Anastasia Greene
Director of Marketing: Maggie Moylan
Executive Marketing Manager: Anne Fahlgren
Senior Managing Editor: Judy Leale
Senior Production Project Manager: Karalyn Holland
Senior Operations Supervisor: Arnold Villa
Operations Specialist: Cathleen Petersen
Creative Director: Blair Brown
Senior Art Director/Supervisor: Janet Slowik

Interior Designer: Karen Quigley
Cover Art: David Benton/Robert Adrian Hillman/
    Shutterstock Images
Senior Media Project Manager: Denise Vaughn
Media Project Manager, Production: Lisa Rinaldi
Full-Service Project Management: S4Carlisle
    Publishing Services
Composition: S4Carlisle Publishing Services
Printer/Binder: Courier/Kendallville
Cover Printer: Lehigh-Phoenix Color/Hagerstown
Text Font: 10/12 Times LT Std

Credits and acknowledgments borrowed from other sources and reproduced, with permission, in this textbook appear on the appropriate page within the text.

Microsoft and/or its respective suppliers make no representations about the suitability of the information contained in the documents and related graphics published as part of the services for any purpose. All such documents and related graphics are provided "as is" without warranty of any kind. Microsoft and/or its respective suppliers hereby disclaim all warranties and conditions with regard to this information, including all warranties and conditions of merchantability, whether express, implied or statutory, fitness for a particular purpose, title and non-infringement. In no event shall Microsoft and/or its respective suppliers be liable for any special, indirect or consequential damages or any damages whatsoever resulting from loss of use, data or profits, whether in an action of contract, negligence or other tortious action, arising out of or in connection with the use or performance of information available from the services.

The documents and related graphics contained herein could include technical inaccuracies or typographical errors. Changes are periodically added to the information herein. Microsoft and/or its respective suppliers may make improvements and/or changes in the product(s) and/or the program(s) described herein at any time. Partial screen shots may be viewed in full within the software version specified.

Microsoft® and Windows® are registered trademarks of the Microsoft Corporation in the U.S.A. and other countries. This book is not sponsored or endorsed by or affiliated with the Microsoft Corporation.

Many of the designations by manufacturers and sellers to distinguish their products are claimed as trademarks. Where those designations appear in this book, and the publisher was aware of a trademark claim, the designations have been printed in initial caps or all caps.

10 9 8 7 6 5 4 3 2 1
ISBN 13: 978-0-13-274403-4
ISBN 10:   0-13-274403-1

To Kathy, Betty, Mandy, Matt, KC, Keri,
Delaney, Molly, Macy, and Ben; Nancy, Amy, Melissa, and Jessica

About the Authors

As a team, Gary Armstrong and Philip Kotler provide a blend of skills uniquely suited to writing an introductory marketing text. Professor Armstrong is an award-winning teacher of undergraduate business students. Professor Kotler is one of the world's leading authorities on marketing. Together they make the complex world of marketing practical, approachable, and enjoyable.

GARY ARMSTRONG is Crist W. Blackwell Distinguished Professor Emeritus of Undergraduate Education in the Kenan-Flagler Business School at the University of North Carolina at Chapel Hill. He holds undergraduate and master's degrees in business from Wayne State University in Detroit, and he received his Ph.D. in marketing from Northwestern University. Dr. Armstrong has contributed numerous articles to leading business journals. As a consultant and researcher, he has worked with many companies on marketing research, sales management, and marketing strategy.

Professor Armstrong's first love has always been teaching. His long-held Blackwell Distinguished Professorship is the only permanently endowed professorship for distinguished undergraduate teaching at the University of North Carolina at Chapel Hill. He has been very active in the teaching and administration of Kenan-Flagler's undergraduate program. His administrative posts have included Chair of Marketing, Associate Director of the Undergraduate Business Program, Director of the Business Honors Program, and many others. Through the years, he has worked closely with business student groups and has received several campus-wide and Business School teaching awards. He is the only repeat recipient of the school's highly regarded Award for Excellence in Undergraduate Teaching, which he received three times. Most recently, Professor Armstrong received the UNC Board of Governors Award for Excellence in Teaching, the highest teaching honor bestowed by the 16-campus University of North Carolina system.

PHILIP KOTLER is S. C. Johnson & Son Distinguished Professor of International Marketing at the Kellogg School of Management, Northwestern University. He received his master's degree at the University of Chicago and his Ph.D. at M.I.T., both in economics. Dr. Kotler is author of *Marketing Management* (Pearson Prentice Hall), now in its fourteenth edition and the world's most widely used marketing textbook in graduate schools of business worldwide. He has authored dozens of other successful books and has written more than 100 articles in leading journals. He is the only three-time winner of the coveted Alpha Kappa Psi award for the best annual article in the *Journal of Marketing*.

Professor Kotler was named the first recipient of two major awards: the Distinguished Marketing Educator of the Year Award, given by the American Marketing Association, and the Philip Kotler Award for Excellence in Health Care Marketing, presented by the Academy for Health Care Services Marketing. His numerous other major honors include the Sales and Marketing Executives International Marketing Educator of the Year Award; the European Association of Marketing Consultants and Trainers Marketing Excellence Award; the Charles Coolidge Parlin Marketing Research Award; and the Paul D. Converse Award, given by the American Marketing Association to honor "outstanding contributions to science in marketing." A recent *Forbes* survey ranks Professor Kotler in the top 10 of the world's most influential business thinkers. And in a recent *Financial Times* poll of 1,000 senior executives across the world, Professor Kotler was ranked as the fourth "most influential business writer/guru" of the twenty-first century.

Dr. Kotler has served as chairman of the College on Marketing of the Institute of Management Sciences, a director of the American Marketing Association, and a trustee of the Marketing Science Institute. He has consulted with many major U.S. and international companies in the areas of marketing strategy and planning, marketing organization, and international marketing. He has traveled and lectured extensively throughout Europe, Asia, and South America, advising companies and governments about global marketing practices and opportunities.

Brief Contents

Contents

4 Managing Marketing Information to Gain Customer Insights 94

5 Understanding Consumer and Business Buyer Behavior 126

**PART 3 ➤ DESIGNING A CUSTOMER-DRIVEN STRATEGY
AND MIX 162**

Customer-Driven Marketing Strategy: Creating Value for Target Customers 162

Products, Services, and Brands: Building Customer Value 194

8 Developing New Products and Managing the Product Life Cycle 228

9 Pricing: Understanding and Capturing Customer Value 254

11 Retailing and Wholesaling   322

12 Communicating Customer Value: Advertising and Public Relations   354

PART 4 ▶ EXTENDING MARKETING 450

15 The Global Marketplace 450

16 Sustainable Marketing: Social Responsibility and Ethics   478

Preface

The Eleventh Edition of
Marketing: An Introduction

On the Road to Learning Marketing!

Top marketers all share a common goal: putting consumers at the heart of marketing. Today's marketing is all about creating customer value and building profitable customer relationships in a fast-changing, high-tech, global marketing environment. It starts with understanding consumer needs and wants, deciding which target markets the organization can serve best, and developing a compelling value proposition by which the organization can attract, keep, and grow targeted consumers. If the organization does these things well, it will reap the rewards in terms of market share, profits, and customer equity. In the eleventh edition of *Marketing: An Introduction,* you'll see how *customer value*—creating it and capturing it—drives every good marketing strategy.

Marketing: An Introduction makes the road to learning and teaching marketing more productive and enjoyable than ever. The eleventh edition's streamlined approach strikes an effective balance between depth of coverage and ease of learning. Unlike more abbreviated texts, it provides complete and timely coverage of all the latest marketing thinking and practice. Unlike longer, more complex texts, its moderate length makes it easy to digest in a given semester or quarter.

Marketing: An Introduction's approachable organization, style, and design are well suited to beginning marketing students. The eleventh edition's learning design—with integrative *Road to Marketing* features at the start and end of each chapter plus insightful author comments throughout—helps students to learn, link, and apply important concepts. Its simple organization and writing style present even the most advanced topics in an approachable, exciting way. The eleventh edition brings marketing to life with deep and relevant examples and illustrations throughout. And when combined with MyMarketingLab, our online homework and personalized study tool, *Marketing: An Introduction* ensures that students will come to class well prepared and leave class with a richer understanding of basic marketing concepts, strategies, and practices. So fasten your seat belt and let's get rolling down the road to learning marketing!

The Marketing Journey:
Five Major Customer Value Themes

The eleventh edition of *Marketing: An Introduction* builds on five major value themes.

1. ***Creating value** for **customers in order to capture value** from **customers in return.*** Today's marketers must be good at *creating customer value* and *managing customer relationships*. Outstanding marketing companies understand the marketplace and customer needs, design value-creating marketing strategies, develop integrated marketing programs that deliver value and satisfaction, and build strong customer relationships. In return, they capture value from customers in the form of sales, profits, and customer equity.

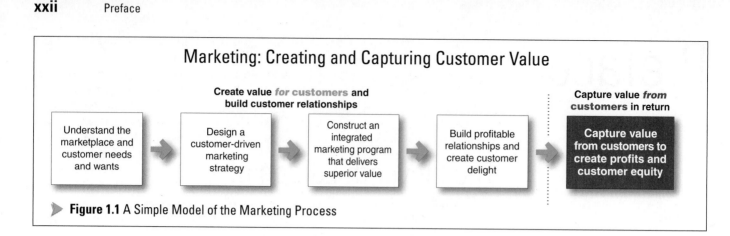

Figure 1.1 A Simple Model of the Marketing Process

This innovative customer value *framework* is introduced at the start of Chapter 1 in a five-step marketing process model, which details how marketing *creates* customer value and *captures* value in return. The framework is carefully explained in the first two chapters and then integrated throughout the remainder of the text.

2. ***Building and managing strong brands to create brand equity.*** Well-positioned brands with strong brand equity provide the basis upon which to build profitable customer relationships. Today's marketers must position their brands powerfully and manage them well to create valued customer brand experiences. The eleventh edition provides a deep focus on brands, anchored by a Chapter 7 section on Branding Strategy: Building Strong Brands.

3. ***Measuring and managing return on marketing.*** Especially in uncertain economic times, marketing managers must ensure that their marketing dollars are being well spent. In the past, many marketers spent freely on big, expensive marketing programs, often without thinking carefully about the financial returns on their spending. But all that has changed rapidly. "Marketing accountability"—measuring and managing return on marketing investments—has now become an important part of strategic marketing decision making. This emphasis on marketing accountability is addressed throughout the eleventh edition.

4. ***Harnessing new marketing technologies.*** New digital and other high-tech marketing developments are dramatically changing how consumers and marketers relate to one another. The eleventh edition thoroughly explores the new technologies impacting marketing, from digital relationship-building tools in Chapter 1 to new digital and online marketing technologies in Chapters 12 and 14 to the exploding use of online social networks and consumer-generated marketing in Chapters 1, 5, 12, 13, and 14—and about everywhere else in the text.

5. ***Sustainable marketing around the globe.*** As technological developments make the world an increasingly smaller and more fragile place, marketers must be good at marketing their brands globally and in sustainable ways. New material throughout the eleventh edition emphasizes the concepts of global marketing and sustainable marketing—meeting the present needs of consumers and businesses while also preserving or enhancing the ability of future generations to meet their needs. The eleventh edition integrates global marketing and sustainability topics throughout the text. It then provides focused coverage on each topic in Chapters 15 and 16, respectively.

What's New in the Eleventh Edition?

We've thoroughly revised the eleventh edition of *Marketing: An Introduction* to reflect the major trends and forces that are impacting marketing in this era of customer value and relationships. Here are just some of the changes you'll find in this edition.

● The eleventh edition continues to build on and extend the innovative **customer-value framework** from previous editions. The customer value model presented in the first chapter is fully integrated throughout the remainder of the book, offering a clear and comprehensive customer-value approach.

- Every chapter of the eleventh edition features revised and expanded discussions of the explosive impact of exciting **new marketing technologies** on consumers and marketers. More than any other development, new digital marketing and online technologies are now affecting the ways in which marketers and customers learn about and relate to one another—from online social networks and communities discussed in Chapters 1, 5, and 14; to "Webnography" research tools in Chapter 4, neuromarketing in Chapter 5, and location-based marketing in Chapter 7; to Internet and mobile marketing and other new communications technologies in Chapters 1, 12, 14, and elsewhere.

- Throughout the eleventh edition, you will find revised coverage of the rapidly **changing nature of customer relationships** with companies and brands. Today's marketers are creating deep consumer involvement and a sense of customer community surrounding their brands—making brands a meaningful part of consumers' conversations and lives. Today's new relationship-building tools include everything from Web sites, blogs, in-person events, and video sharing to online communities and social networks such as Facebook, YouTube, Twitter, or a company's own social networking sites. For just a few examples, see Chapter 1 (the section on the Changing Nature of Customer Relationships), Chapter 4 (qualitative approaches to gaining deeper customer insights), Chapter 5 (managing online influence and marketing through social networks), Chapter 8 (customer-driven new product development and co-creation), Chapter 12 (the shift toward more personalized, interactive communications), and Chapter 14 (online social networks, customer communities, and interactive digital media).

- The eleventh edition contains substantial new material on the continuing trend toward two-way interactions between customers and brands, including such topics as **customer-managed relationships**, **crowdsourcing**, **customer co-creation**, and **consumer-generated marketing**. Today's more empowered customers are giving as much as they get in the form of two-way relationships (Chapter 1), a more active role in providing customer insights (Chapter 4), crowdsourcing and co-creating new products (Chapter 7), consumer-generated marketing content (Chapters 1 and 12), developing or passing along brand messages (Chapters 1, 5, 7, and 12), interacting in customer communities (Chapters 5, 12, and 14), and other developments.

- New coverage in every chapter of the eleventh edition shows how companies and consumers are dealing with **marketing in an uncertain economy** in the aftermath of the recent Great Recession. Starting with a section and feature in Chapter 1 and continuing with new sections, discussions, and examples integrated throughout the text, the eleventh edition shows how now, even as the economy recovers, marketers must focus on creating customer value and sharpening their value propositions in this era of more sensible consumption.

- New material throughout the eleventh edition highlights the increasing importance of **sustainable marketing**. The discussion begins in Chapter 1 and ends in Chapter 16, which pulls marketing together under a sustainable marketing framework. In between, frequent discussions and examples show how sustainable marketing calls for socially and environmentally responsible actions that meet both the immediate and the future needs of customers, companies, and society as a whole.

- The eleventh edition provides new discussions and examples of the growth in **global marketing**. As the world becomes a smaller, more competitive place, markets face new global marketing challenges and opportunities, especially in fast-growing emerging markets such as China, India, Brazil, Africa, and others. You'll find much new coverage of global marketing throughout the text, starting in Chapter 1. The topic is discussed fully in Chapter 15.

- The eleventh edition provides revised and expanded coverage of the developments in the fast-changing areas of **integrated marketing communications** *and* **direct and online marketing**. It tells how marketers are blending the new digital and direct technologies—everything from Internet and mobile marketing to blogs, viral videos, and online social networks—with traditional media to create more targeted, personal, and interactive customer relationships. In this way, *Marketing: An Introduction* provides more current or encompassing coverage of these exciting developments than any text on the market.

- The eleventh edition continues to improve on its **innovative learning design**. The text's active and integrative presentation includes learning enhancements such as annotated chapter-opening stories, a chapter-opening objective outline, and explanatory author comments on major chapter sections and figures. Figures annotated with author comments help students to simplify and organize chapter material. End-of-chapter features help to summarize important chapter concepts and highlight important themes, such as marketing technology, ethics, and financial marketing analysis. This innovative learning design facilitates student understanding and eases learning.
- **Appendix 1—Company Cases** provides 16 **NEW** company cases by which students can apply what they learn to actual company situations. The eleventh edition also features many new video cases, with brief end-of-chapter summaries and discussion questions. A **newly revised Appendix 2—Marketing Plan** presents a brand new marketing plan by which students can apply text concepts to a hypothetical brand and situation.
- Finally, most of the chapter-opening stories and Marketing at Work features in the text are either new to the eleventh edition or revised for currency.

Real Travel Experiences: Marketing at Work

Marketing: An Introduction, eleventh edition, guides new marketing students down the intriguing, discovery-laden road to learning marketing in an applied and practical way. The text takes a practical marketing-management approach, providing countless in-depth, real-life examples and stories that bring the marketing journey to life. Every chapter contains a *First Stop* opening story and *Marketing at Work* features that reveal the drama of modern marketing. Students learn how:

- Giant social network Facebook promises to become one of the world's most powerful and profitable online marketers—but it's just getting started.
- Small fast-food burger chain In-N-Out creates customer delight that has its customers telling others, "There's In-N-Out, and then there's everyone else."
- Domino's Pizza turned a five-year revenue slide into a fresh, hot turnaround by simply listening to customers and using their insights to develop better products and marketing.
- Apple's deep understanding of consumer behavior engenders an intense loyalty in the hearts of Apple customers and creates stunning sales and profit for the company.
- Dunkin' Donuts successfully targets the "Dunkin' Tribe"—not the Starbucks snob but the average Joe.
- Walmart, the world's largest retailer, and Amazon.com, the planet's largest online merchant, are fighting it out online on price.
- Dollar General has become one of today's hottest retailers by matching the economic times—its "Save time. Save money. Every day." slogan isn't just for show.
- Netflix stays atop the changing video entertainment distribution industry by disintermediating itself before competitors can do it.
- The explosion of the Internet, mobile devices, and other technologies has some marketers asking: "Who needs face-to-face selling anymore?"
- Under its Sustainable Living Plan, Unilever plans to double its size by 2020 while at the same time reducing its impact on the planet.
- For Coca-Cola, marketing in Africa is like "sticking its hand into a bees' nest to get some honey."
- Google's odyssey into mainland China—and back out again—vividly illustrates the prospects and perils of going global.

More than ever before, the eleventh edition of *Marketing: An Introduction* makes teaching and learning marketing easier, more effective, more practical, and more enjoyable.

Marketing Journey Travel Aids

A wealth of chapter-opening, within-chapter, and end-of-chapter learning devices helps you to learn, link, and apply major concepts.

- *Chapter-opening Road Maps.* The active and integrative opening spread in each chapter features an *Objective Outline* that outlines chapter contents and learning objectives, a brief *Previewing the Concepts* section that introduces chapter concepts, and a *First Stop* opening vignette—an engaging, deeply developed, illustrated, and annotated marketing story that introduces the chapter material and sparks your interest.
- *Author comments and figure annotations.* Throughout the chapter, author comments ease and enhance your learning by introducing and explaining major chapter sections and figures.
- *Marketing at Work highlights.* Each chapter contains two highlight features that provide an in-depth look at real marketing practices of large and small companies.
- *Rest Stop: Reviewing the Concepts.* Sections at the end of each chapter summarize key chapter concepts and provide questions, exercises, and cases by which students can review and apply what they've learned. The *Chapter Review and Key Terms* section reviews major chapter concepts and links them to chapter objectives. It also provides a helpful listing of chapter key terms by order of appearance with page numbers that facilitate easy reference.
- *Discussion and Critical Thinking questions and exercises.* Sections at the end of each chapter help students to keep track of and apply what they've learned in the chapter.
- *Minicases and Applications:* Brief *Marketing Technology, Marketing Ethics,* and *Marketing by the Numbers* sections at the end of each chapter provide short application cases that facilitate discussion of current issues and company situations in areas such as marketing technology, ethics, and financial marketing analysis. A *Video Case* section contains short vignettes with discussion questions to be used with a set of mostly new 4- to 7-minute videos that accompany the eleventh edition. An end-of-chapter *Company Cases* section identifies which of the all-new company cases found in Appendix 1 are best for use with each chapter.

Additional marketing travel aids include the following.

- *Company Cases.* Appendix 1 contains 16 all-new company cases that help you to apply major marketing concepts to real company and brand situations.
- *Marketing Plan.* Appendix 2 contains a brand new sample marketing plan that helps you to apply important marketing planning concepts.
- *Marketing by the Numbers.* An innovative Appendix 3 provides you with a comprehensive introduction to the marketing financial analysis that helps to guide, assess, and support marketing decisions.

More than ever before, the eleventh edition of *Marketing: An Introduction* provides an effective and enjoyable total package for moving students down the road to learning marketing!

A Total Teaching and Learning Package

A successful marketing course requires more than a well-written book. Today's classroom requires a dedicated teacher and a fully integrated teaching system. A total package of teaching and learning supplements extends this edition's emphasis on effective teaching and learning. The following aids support the eleventh edition of *Marketing: An Introduction.*

Videos

The video library for the eleventh edition contains 16 exciting new segments, specially produced for use with this text. All segments are on the DVD, which can be ordered using the ISBN: **0-13-274423-6,** and in the MyMarketingLab. Here are just a few of the videos that are offered:

OXO's Strategic Market Planning

Dominos' Product Revamp due to Market Intelligence

HSN in the Changing Marketplace

Ecoist's Brilliant Business Strategy

MyMarketingLab

MyMarketingLab is an online assessment and preparation solution for courses in Principles of Marketing, Marketing Management, Consumer Behavior, Advertising, Integrated Marketing Communication, and Sales Management that helps you actively study and prepare for class. Chapter-by-chapter activities help you focus on what to learn and review in order to succeed. Visit www.mymktlab.com to learn more.

More Valuable Resources

CourseSmart

CourseSmart eTextbooks were developed for students looking to save on required or recommended textbooks. Students simply select their eText by title or author and purchase immediate access to the content for the duration of the course using any major credit card. With a CourseSmart eText, students can search for specific keywords or page numbers, take notes online, print out reading assignments that incorporate lecture notes, and bookmark important passages for later review. For more information or to purchase a Course-Smart eTextbook, visit www.coursesmart.com.

Acknowledgments

No book is created only by its authors. We greatly appreciate the valuable contributions of several people who helped make this new edition possible. As always, we owe very special thanks to Keri Jean Miksza for her dedicated and valuable help in *all* phases of the project, and to her husband Pete and little daughter Lucy for all the support they provided Keri during this often-hectic project.

We thank Andy Norman of Drake University for his skillful development of company and video cases, the Marketing Plan appendix, and selected marketing stories; and Lew Brown of the University of North Carolina at Greensboro for his able assistance in helping prepare selected marketing stories and highlights. We also thank Laurie Babin of the University of Louisiana at Monroe for her dedicated efforts in preparing end-of-chapter materials and keeping our Marketing by the Numbers appendix fresh.

Many reviewers at other colleges and universities provided valuable comments and suggestions for this and previous editions. We are indebted to all the reviewers and colleagues for their thoughtful inputs. Some of the current reviewers include:

ELEVENTH EDITION REVIEWERS

Keith Starcher, *Indiana Wesleyan University*
Datha Damron-Martinez, *Truman State University*
Linda Coleman, *Salem State University*
Karen Halpern, *South Puget Sound Community College*
Thomas Voigt, *Judson University*

Sylvia Clark, *St. John's University*
Jan Hardesty, *University of Arizona*
Mary Conran, *Temple University*
Erika Matulich, *University of Tampa*
Marc Newman, *Hocking College*

TENTH EDITION REVIEWERS

George Bercovitz, *York College*
Sylvia Clark, *St. John's University*
Datha Damron-Martinez, *Truman State University*
Ivan Filby, *Greenville College*
John Gaskins, *Longwood University*
Karen Halpern, *South Puget Sound Community College*
Jan Hardesty, *University of Arizona*
Hella-Ilona Johnson, *Olympic College*
Marc Newman, *Hocking College*

Vic Piscatello, *University of Arizona*
William M.Ryan, *University of Connecticut*
Elliot Schreiber, *Drexel University*
Robert Simon, *University of Nebraska, Lincoln*
John Talbott, *Indiana University*
Rhonda Tenenbaum, *Queens College*
Tom Voigt, *Judson University*
Terry Wilson, *East Stroudsburg University*

We also owe a great deal to the people at Pearson Prentice Hall who helped develop this book. Project Manager Meeta Pendharkar provided valuable assistance in managing the many facets of this complex revision project. Senior Art Director Janet Slowik developed the eleventh edition's exciting design, and Senior Production Project Manager Karalyn Holland helped guide the book through the complex production process. We'd also like to thank Sally Yagan, Judy Leale, Erin Gardner, Anne Fahlgren, and Anastasia Greene. We are proud to be associated with the fine professionals at Pearson Prentice Hall. We also owe a mighty debt of gratitude to Project Editor Roxanne Klaas and the fine team at S4Carlisle Publishing Services.

Finally, we owe many thanks to our families for all of their support and encouragement—Kathy, Betty, Mandy, Matt, KC, Keri, Delaney, Molly, Macy, and Ben from the Armstrong clan and Nancy, Amy, Melissa, and Jessica from the Kotler family. To them, we dedicate this book.

Gary Armstrong
Philip Kotler

Marketing

An Introduction

1 Marketing
Creating and Capturing Customer Value

CHAPTER ROAD MAP

Objective Outline

▶ **OBJECTIVE 1** **Define marketing and outline the steps in the marketing process.** What Is Marketing? (4–6)

▶ **OBJECTIVE 2** **Explain the importance of understanding customers and the marketplace and identify the five core marketplace concepts.** Understanding the Marketplace and Customer Needs (6–8)

▶ **OBJECTIVE 3** **Identify the key elements of a customer-driven marketing strategy and discuss the marketing management orientations that guide marketing strategy.** Designing a Customer-Driven Marketing Strategy (9–12); Preparing an Integrated Marketing Plan and Program (12–13)

▶ **OBJECTIVE 4** **Discuss customer relationship management and identify strategies for creating value *for* customers and capturing value *from* customers in return.** Building Customer Relationships (13–20); Capturing Value from Customers (20–23)

▶ **OBJECTIVE 5** **Describe the major trends and forces that are changing the marketing landscape in this age of relationships.** The Changing Marketing Landscape (23–29)

Previewing the Concepts

Fasten your seatbelt! You're about to begin an exciting journey toward learning about marketing. This chapter introduces you to the basic concepts of marketing. We start with the question: What is marketing? Simply put, marketing is managing profitable customer relationships. The aim of marketing is to create value for customers and capture value from customers in return. Next we discuss the five steps in the marketing process—from understanding customer needs, to designing customer-driven marketing strategies and integrated marketing programs, to building customer relationships and capturing value for the firm. Finally, we discuss the major trends and forces affecting marketing in this age of customer relationships. Understanding these basic concepts and forming your own ideas about what they really mean to you will provide a solid foundation for all that follows.

Let's start with a good story about marketing in action at JetBlue, an airline with an evangelistic zeal for creating customer-satisfying experiences. JetBlue has a deep passion for building customer value and relationships. In return, delighted customers reward the airline with their loyalty and can't wait to tell others about their JetBlue experiences. You'll see this theme of creating customer value in order to capture value in return repeated throughout the first chapter and the remainder of the text.

NOT A TAGLINE. A PROMISE.

jetBlue™ YOU ABOVE ALL™

▲ **JetBlue creates first-rate, customer-satisfying experiences. Its slogan—JetBlue: YOU ABOVE ALL—tells customers that they are at the very heart of JetBlue's strategy and culture.**

JetBlue Airways

First Stop

JetBlue: A Deep Passion for Creating Customer Value and Relationships

There's an old adage in the airline industry: "You're not flying planes, you're flying people." These days, however, it seems that many big airlines overlook the people factor. Instead, they focus on moving their human cargo as efficiently as possible while charging as much as the traffic will bear. The American Customer Satisfaction Index rates the airline industry second-to-last among 47 industries in customer satisfaction, tied with perennial cellar-dweller cable and satellite TV services.

Not so at JetBlue Airways, however. From the very beginning, young JetBlue (little more than a decade old) has built a reputation for creating first-rate, customer-satisfying experiences. Its slogan—JetBlue: YOU ABOVE ALL—tells the JetBlue faithful that they are at the very heart of the company's strategy and culture. "We are a customer service company that just happens to fly airplanes," says JetBlue's director of customer experience and analysis.

At JetBlue, customer care starts with basic amenities that exceed customer expectations, especially for a low-cost carrier. JetBlue's well-padded, leather-covered coach seats allow three inches more legroom than the average airline seat. Although the airline doesn't serve meals, it offers the best selection of free beverages and snacks to be found at 30,000 feet (including unexpected treats such as Terra Blues chips, Immaculate Baking's Chocobillys cookies, and Dunkin' Donuts coffee). Every JetBlue seat has its own LCD entertainment system, complete with free 36-channel DirecTV and 100+ channels of SiriusXM Radio. JetBlue rounds out the amenities with free Wi-Fi in terminals, and starting in 2012 it plans to offer free broadband wireless onboard every flight.

Such tangibles help keep JetBlue travelers satisfied. But JetBlue CEO David Barger knows that the tangibles are only a small part of what really makes JetBlue special. "The hard product—airplanes, leather seats, satellite TVs—as long as you have a checkbook, ...can be replicated," says Barger. "It's the JetBlue *culture* that can't be replicated. The *human* side of the equation is the most important part of what we're doing." It's that JetBlue culture—the near-obsessive focus on the customer flying experience—that creates not just satisfied JetBlue customers, but *delighted* ones.

At JetBlue, developing a customer-centered corporate culture starts with hiring quality people whose personal values match JetBlue's values—from work-at-home part-time call center reservationists to baggage handlers to flight attendants and even pilots. By the time JetBlue employees are onboard and trained, they not only *know* the company's core values—safety, integrity, caring, passion, and fun—they *live* them. It's those heartfelt values that result in outstanding customer experiences. And the outstanding customer experiences make JetBlue's customers the most satisfied and loyal in the industry.

Whereas passengers on most competing airlines regard flying as an experience just to be tolerated, many JetBlue customers actually look forward to flying. And customers themselves spread the good word about JetBlue with evangelistic zeal. In fact, when it comes to *social*

> When JetBlue Airways tells customers "YOU ABOVE ALL," the company really means it. As a result, JetBlue customers are the most satisfied and loyal of any in the airline industry. They can't wait to tell others about their outstanding JetBlue experiences.

currency—how avidly people relate to and share a brand with friends, family, or their online and offline social networks—JetBlue is the strongest brand in the nation, outperforming even much-talked-about Apple. "People love to talk about JetBlue because the experience is so unexpected," says one analyst, "especially given the 'value' price."

Throughout its history, in ads and promotions, JetBlue has often let its customers do the talking. For example, its "Experience Jet-Blue" Web site features authentic testimonials from some of the airline's most devoted fans (found through Twitter and Facebook). The customers give glowing first-person accounts about why they like flying JetBlue. "It's like an open bar for snacks," says one customer. "They're constantly walking around offering it, so I'm never thirsty or hungry." Another JetBlue fan, a 6'3" woman from Portland, Oregon, likes the seating: "I can stretch and sit crosslegged—no black-and-blue knees," she says. "The customer service is above and beyond," declares a third customer, a small business owner from Boston. "Jet-Blue is very similar to flying first class."

In a former advertising campaign called "Sincerely, JetBlue," actual customers gave voice to even deeper JetBlue experiences. In one ad, for example, customer Melissa confided, "Let me tell you, I wanted not to like you, if only because everyone seems to love you. I got on a flight with a pen and paper, waiting to take down every irritating detail." But, she continued, "two flights later, I was staring at the same blank piece of paper. You've done nothing wrong and everything more than right, if that's possible." After detailing all the right things the airline does, she mock-lamented, "JetBlue, I wanted not to like you but it can't be done—at all. Sincerely, Melissa Mc-Call, Portland, Oregon."

In other "Sincerely, JetBlue" ads, customers recounted specific service heroics by dedicated JetBlue employees. For example, customer Brian related how a JetBlue flight attendant dashed from the plane just before takeoff to retrieve a brand-new iPod he'd left in a rental car. Ann recounted how, when her JetBlue flight was delayed by a snowstorm, the airline eased the long wait by providing pizza and even a live band. "My [three-year-old] son was dancing. I was dancing," she remembers. "It made a horrible experience really nice." And the Steins from Darien, Connecticut, told about the time they arrived late at night for a family vacation in Florida with their three very tired small children only to learn that their hotel wouldn't take them in. Jason Stein recalled, "Out of nowhere we heard a voice from behind us, go ahead, take my room." His wife Nancy continued: "A superhero in a JetBlue pilot's uniform, who sacrificed his room graciously, saved our night. And we slept like babies. Thank you, JetBlue. Sincerely, Nancy and Jason Stein."

Being good to customers has been good for JetBlue. Last year, it reported record revenues of $3.8 billion, a 70 percent increase over the past five years. Even during the recent Great Recession, as most competing airlines were cutting routes, retiring aircraft, laying off employees, and losing money, JetBlue was adding planes, expanding into new cities, hiring thousands of new employees, and turning profits.

Perhaps even more important to future success, customers continue to adore their JetBlue. For six straight years, the customer-centered company has topped the J.D. Powers customer satisfaction rankings among major U.S. airlines. For the past two years, JetBlue has received the airline industry's highest customer loyalty scores in the respected Satmetrix Net Promoter rankings. Sixty percent of customers rated JetBlue 9 or 10 on a zero-to-ten point scale indicating the likelihood that they would recommend JetBlue to others, an astonishing 45 points higher than the industry average.

So, JetBlue really means it when it tells customers, YOU ABOVE ALL. "We have sought to reinvent the traditional airline customer service model, to prove that it can be done the right way and done well," says CEO Barger. JetBlue's senior VP of marketing agrees. "YOU ABOVE ALL gets us back to our DNA, our original mission, bringing humanity back to air travel."[1]

T oday's successful companies have one thing in common: Like JetBlue, they are strongly customer focused and heavily committed to marketing. These companies share a passion for understanding and satisfying customer needs in well-defined target markets. They motivate everyone in the organization to help build lasting customer relationships based on creating value.

Customer relationships and value are especially important today. Facing dramatic technological changes and deep economic, social, and environmental challenges, today's customers are spending more carefully and reassessing their relationships with brands. In turn, it's more important than ever to build strong customer relationships based on real and enduring value.

What Is Marketing?

Marketing, more than any other business function, deals with customers. Although we will soon explore more-detailed definitions of marketing, perhaps the simplest definition is this one: *Marketing is managing profitable customer relationships.* The twofold goal of marketing is to attract new customers by promising superior value and to keep and grow current customers by delivering satisfaction.

For example, McDonald's fulfills its "i'm lovin' it" motto by being "our customers' favorite place and way to eat" the world over, giving it a market share greater than that of its nearest three competitors combined. Walmart has become the world's largest retailer—and the world's largest company—by delivering on its promise, "Save Money. Live Better."[2]

Sound marketing is critical to the success of every organization. Large for-profit firms, such as Google, Target, Procter & Gamble, Toyota, and Microsoft, use marketing. But so do not-for-profit organizations, such as colleges, hospitals, museums, symphony orchestras, and even churches.

You already know a lot about marketing—it's all around you. Marketing comes to you in the good old traditional forms: You see it in the abundance of products at your nearby shopping mall and the ads that fill your TV screen, spice up your magazines, or stuff your mailbox. But in recent years, marketers have assembled a host of new marketing approaches, everything from imaginative Web sites and online social networks to cell phone apps. These new approaches do more than just blast out messages to the masses. They reach you directly and personally. Today's marketers want to become a part of your life and enrich your experiences with their brands—to help you *live* their brands.

At home, at school, where you work, and where you play, you see marketing in almost everything you do. Yet, there is much more to marketing than meets the consumer's casual eye. Behind it all is a massive network of people and activities competing for your attention and purchases. This book will give you a complete introduction to the basic concepts and practices of today's marketing. In this chapter, we begin by defining marketing and the marketing process.

Marketing Defined

What *is* marketing? Many people think of marketing as only selling and advertising. We are bombarded every day with TV commercials, catalogs, sales calls, and e-mail pitches. However, selling and advertising are only the tip of the marketing iceberg.

Today, marketing must be understood not in the old sense of making a sale—"telling and selling"—but in the new sense of *satisfying customer needs*. If the marketer understands consumer needs; develops products that provide superior customer value; and prices, distributes, and promotes them effectively, these products will sell easily. In fact, according to management guru Peter Drucker, "The aim of marketing is to make selling unnecessary."[3] Selling and advertising are only part of a larger *marketing mix*—a set of marketing tools that work together to satisfy customer needs and build customer relationships.

Broadly defined, marketing is a social and managerial process by which individuals and organizations obtain what they need and want through creating and exchanging value with others. In a narrower business context, marketing involves building profitable, value-laden exchange relationships with customers. Hence, we define **marketing** as the process by which companies create value for customers and build strong customer relationships in order to capture value from customers in return.[4]

Marketing
The process by which companies create value for customers and build strong customer relationships in order to capture value from customers in return.

The Marketing Process

▶ **Figure 1.1** presents a simple, five-step model of the marketing process. In the first four steps, companies work to understand consumers, create customer value, and build strong customer relationships. In the final step, companies reap the rewards of creating superior customer value. By creating value *for* consumers, they in turn capture value *from* consumers in the form of sales, profits, and long-term customer equity.

Create value *for customers* and
build customer relationships

| Understand the marketplace and customer needs and wants | → | Design a customer-driven marketing strategy | → | Construct an integrated marketing program that delivers superior value | → | Build profitable relationships and create customer delight | → | Capture value *from customers* in return — Capture value from customers to create profits and customer equity |

This important figure shows marketing in a nutshell! By creating value *for* customers, marketers capture value *from* customers in return. This five-step process forms the marketing framework for the rest of the chapter and the remainder of the text.

Figure 1.1 A Simple Model of the Marketing Process

In this chapter and the next, we will examine the steps of this simple model of marketing. In this chapter, we review each step but focus more on the customer relationship steps—understanding customers, building customer relationships, and capturing value from customers. In Chapter 2, we look more deeply into the second and third steps—designing marketing strategies and constructing marketing programs.

Understanding the Marketplace and Customer Needs

Author Comment ▶
Marketing is all about creating value for customers. So, as the first step in the marketing process, the company must fully understand consumers and the marketplace in which it operates.

As a first step, marketers need to understand customer needs and wants and the marketplace in which they operate. We examine five core customer and marketplace concepts: (1) *needs, wants, and demands*; (2) *market offerings (products, services, and experiences)*; (3) *value and satisfaction*; (4) *exchanges and relationships*; and (5) *markets*.

Customer Needs, Wants, and Demands

Needs
States of felt deprivation.

The most basic concept underlying marketing is that of human needs. Human **needs** are states of felt deprivation. They include basic *physical* needs for food, clothing, warmth, and safety; *social* needs for belonging and affection; and *individual* needs for knowledge and self-expression. Marketers did not create these needs; they are a basic part of the human makeup.

Wants
The form human needs take as they are shaped by culture and individual personality.

Wants are the form human needs take as they are shaped by culture and individual personality. An American *needs* food but *wants* a Big Mac, french fries, and a soft drink. A person in Papua, New Guinea, *needs* food but *wants* taro, rice, yams, and pork. Wants are shaped by one's society and are described in terms of objects that will satisfy those needs. When backed by buying power, wants become **demands**. Given their wants and resources, people demand products with benefits that add up to the most value and satisfaction.

Demands
Human wants that are backed up by buying power.

Outstanding marketing companies go to great lengths to learn about and understand their customers' needs, wants, and demands. They conduct consumer research and analyze mountains of customer data. Their people at all levels—including top management—stay close to customers. For example, Kroger chairman and CEO David Dillon regularly dons blue jeans and roams the aisles of local Kroger supermarkets, blending in with and talking to other shoppers. He wants to see his stores through customers' eyes and understand why they make the choices they do. Similarly, to stay closer to customers, successful Ford CEO Alan Mulally has been known to spend time selling cars at Ford dealerships.[5]

Market Offerings—Products, Services, and Experiences

Market offerings
Some combination of products, services, information, or experiences offered to a market to satisfy a need or want.

Consumers' needs and wants are fulfilled through **market offerings**—some combination of products, services, information, or experiences offered to a market to satisfy a need or a want. Market offerings are not limited to physical *products*. They also include *services*—activities or benefits offered for sale that are essentially intangible and do not result in the ownership of anything. Examples include banking, airline, hotel, retailing, and home repair services.

More broadly, market offerings also include other entities, such as *persons, places, organizations, information,* and *ideas.* For example, the "Pure Michigan" campaign markets

Explore nature. There are surprises everywhere.

DiscoverTheForest.org

▲ **Market offerings are not limited to physical products. Here, with Shrek's help, the U.S. Forest Service markets the idea of reconnecting young people with exploring the joys of nature firsthand.**

Courtesy of US Forest Service. Shrek® 2011 DreamWorks Animation, LLC, used with permission of DreamWorks Animation LLC.

the state of Michigan as a tourism destination that "lets unspoiled nature and authentic character revive your spirits." ▶ And the U.S. Forest Service's "Reconnecting Kids with Nature" campaign markets the idea of encouraging urban young people to explore the joys of nature firsthand. Its DiscoverTheForest.org Web site helps children and their parents figure out where to go outdoors and what to do there.[6]

Many sellers make the mistake of paying more attention to the specific products they offer than to the benefits and experiences produced by these products. These sellers suffer from **marketing myopia**. They are so taken with their products that they focus only on existing wants and lose sight of underlying customer needs.[7] They forget that a product is only a tool to solve a consumer problem. A manufacturer of quarter-inch drill bits may think that the customer needs a drill bit. But what the customer *really* needs is a quarter-inch hole. These sellers will have trouble if a new product comes along that serves the customer's need better or less expensively. The customer will have the same *need* but will *want* the new product.

Marketing myopia
The mistake of paying more attention to the specific products a company offers than to the benefits and experiences produced by these products.

Smart marketers look beyond the attributes of the products and services they sell. By orchestrating several services and products, they create *brand experiences* for consumers. For example, you don't just visit Walt Disney World Resort; you immerse yourself and your family in a world of wonder, a world where dreams come true and things still work the way they should. You're "in the heart of the magic!" says Disney.

Even a seemingly functional product becomes an experience. HP recognizes that a personal computer is much more than just a cold collection of wires and electrical components. It's an intensely personal user experience. As noted in one HP ad, "There is hardly anything that you own that is *more* personal. Your personal computer is your backup brain. It's your life. . . . It's your astonishing strategy, staggering proposal, dazzling calculation." It's your connection to the world around you. HP's recent "Everybody On" marketing campaign doesn't talk much about technical specifications. Instead, it celebrates how HP's technologies help create seamless connections in today's "instant-on world."[8]

Customer Value and Satisfaction

Consumers usually face a broad array of products and services that might satisfy a given need. How do they choose among these many market offerings? Customers form expectations about the value and satisfaction that various market offerings will deliver and buy accordingly. Satisfied customers buy again and tell others about their good experiences. Dissatisfied customers often switch to competitors and disparage the product to others.

Marketers must be careful to set the right level of expectations. If they set expectations too low, they may satisfy those who buy but fail to attract enough buyers. If they set expectations too high, buyers will be disappointed. Customer value and customer satisfaction are key building blocks for developing and managing customer relationships. We will revisit these core concepts later in the chapter.

Exchanges and Relationships

Exchange
The act of obtaining a desired object from someone by offering something in return.

Marketing occurs when people decide to satisfy their needs and wants through exchange relationships. **Exchange** is the act of obtaining a desired object from someone by offering something in return. In the broadest sense, the marketer tries to bring about a response to some market offering. The response may be more than simply buying or trading products and services. A political candidate, for instance, wants votes; a church wants membership; an orchestra wants an audience; and a social action group wants idea acceptance.

Marketing consists of actions taken to create, maintain, and grow desirable exchange *relationships* with target audiences involving a product, service, idea, or other object. Companies want to build strong relationships by consistently delivering superior customer value. We will expand on the important concept of managing customer relationships later in the chapter.

Markets

Market
The set of all actual and potential buyers of a product or service.

The concepts of exchange and relationships lead to the concept of a market. A **market** is the set of actual and potential buyers of a product or service. These buyers share a particular need or want that can be satisfied through exchange relationships.

Marketing means managing markets to bring about profitable customer relationships. However, creating these relationships takes work. Sellers must search for buyers, identify their needs, design good market offerings, set prices for them, promote them, and store and deliver them. Activities such as consumer research, product development, communication, distribution, pricing, and service are core marketing activities.

Although we normally think of marketing as being carried out by sellers, buyers also carry out marketing. Consumers market when they search for products, interact with companies to obtain information, and make their purchases. In fact, today's digital technologies, from Web sites and online social networks to smartphones, have empowered consumers and made marketing a truly interactive affair. Thus, in addition to customer relationship management, today's marketers must also deal effectively with *customer-managed relationships*. Marketers are no longer asking only "How can we reach our customers?" but also "How should our customers reach us?" and even "How can our customers reach each other?"

▶ **Figure 1.2** shows the main elements in a marketing system. Marketing involves serving a market of final consumers in the face of competitors. The company and competitors research the market and interact with consumers to understand their needs. Then they create and send their market offerings and messages to consumers, either directly or through marketing intermediaries. Each party in the system is affected by major environmental forces (demographic, economic, natural, technological, political, and social/cultural).

Each party in the system adds value for the next level. The arrows represent relationships that must be developed and managed. Thus, a company's success at building profitable relationships depends not only on its own actions but also on how well the entire system serves the needs of final consumers. Walmart cannot fulfill its promise of low prices unless its suppliers provide merchandise at low costs. And Ford cannot deliver a high-quality car-ownership experience unless its dealers provide outstanding sales and service.

Arrows represent relationships that must be developed and managed to create customer value and profitable customer relationships.

▶ **Figure 1.2** A Modern Marketing System

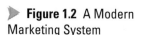
Each party in the system adds value. Walmart cannot fulfill its promise of low prices unless its suppliers provide low costs. Ford cannot deliver a high quality car-ownership experience unless its dealers provide outstanding service.

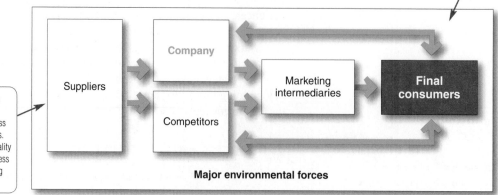

Author Comment ▶

Once the company fully understands its consumers and the marketplace, it must decide which customers it will serve and how it will bring them value.

Marketing management
The art and science of choosing target markets and building profitable relationships with them.

Designing a Customer-Driven Marketing Strategy

Once it fully understands consumers and the marketplace, marketing management can design a customer-driven marketing strategy. We define **marketing management** as the art and science of choosing target markets and building profitable relationships with them. The marketing manager's aim is to find, attract, keep, and grow target customers by creating, delivering, and communicating superior customer value.

To design a winning marketing strategy, the marketing manager must answer two important questions: *What customers will we serve (what's our target market)?* and *How can we serve these customers best (what's our value proposition)?* We will discuss these marketing strategy concepts briefly here and then look at them in more detail in Chapters 2 and 6.

Selecting Customers to Serve

The company must first decide *whom* it will serve. It does this by dividing the market into segments of customers (*market segmentation*) and selecting which segments it will go after (*target marketing*). Some people think of marketing management as finding as many customers as possible and increasing demand. But marketing managers know that they cannot serve all customers in every way. By trying to serve all customers, they may not serve any customers well. Instead, the company wants to select only customers that it can serve well and profitably. For example, Nordstrom profitably targets affluent professionals; Dollar General profitably targets families with more modest means.

Ultimately, marketing managers must decide which customers they want to target and on the level, timing, and nature of their demand. Simply put, marketing management is *customer management* and *demand management*.

Choosing a Value Proposition

The company must also decide how it will serve targeted customers—how it will *differentiate and position* itself in the marketplace. A brand's *value proposition* is the set of benefits or values it promises to deliver to consumers to satisfy their needs. Facebook helps you "connect and share with the people in your life," whereas YouTube "provides a place for people to connect, inform, and inspire others across the globe." BMW promises "the ultimate driving machine," whereas the diminutive Smart car suggests that you "Open your mind to the car that challenges the status quo."

Such value propositions differentiate one brand from another. They answer the customer's question, "Why should I buy your brand rather than a competitor's?" Companies must design strong value propositions that give them the greatest advantage in their target markets. ▶ For example, the smart car is positioned as compact, yet comfortable; agile, yet economical; and safe, yet ecological. It offers a "guilt-free, 95% recyclable way to go from your driveway to virtually anywhere."

Marketing Management Orientations

Marketing management wants to design strategies that will build profitable relationships with target consumers. But what *philosophy* should guide these marketing strategies? What weight should be given to the interests of customers, the organization, and society? Very often, these interests conflict.

smart
open your mind.

It's a fuel-efficient fan favorite. Chalk it up to the smart fortwo's innate charm. Superb Mercedes-Benz engineering. Vast amounts of head and legroom. Exceptional safety ratings. And of course, its EPA-estimated 41 mpg highway. The smart fortwo is the guilt-free, 95% recyclable way to go from your driveway to virtually anywhere. And every mile, every turn, every stop along the way is fun. Sorry, big guy. Efficiency is in these days. smartusa.com

▲ **Value propositions: The smart car suggests that you "open your mind"—"Sorry, big guy. Efficiency is in these days."**

smartUSA

There are five alternative concepts under which organizations design and carry out their marketing strategies: the *production*, *product*, *selling*, *marketing*, and *societal marketing concepts*.

The Production Concept

Production concept
The idea that consumers will favor products that are available and highly affordable; therefore, the organization should focus on improving production and distribution efficiency.

The **production concept** holds that consumers will favor products that are available and highly affordable. Therefore, management should focus on improving production and distribution efficiency. This concept is one of the oldest orientations that guides sellers.

The production concept is still a useful philosophy in some situations. For example, both personal computer maker Lenovo and home appliance maker Haier dominate the highly competitive, price-sensitive Chinese market through low labor costs, high production efficiency, and mass distribution. However, although useful in some situations, the production concept can lead to marketing myopia. Companies adopting this orientation run a major risk of focusing too narrowly on their own operations and losing sight of the real objective—satisfying customer needs and building customer relationships.

The Product Concept

Product concept
The idea that consumers will favor products that offer the most quality, performance, and features; therefore, the organization should devote its energy to making continuous product improvements.

The **product concept** holds that consumers will favor products that offer the most in quality, performance, and innovative features. Under this concept, marketing strategy focuses on making continuous product improvements.

Product quality and improvement are important parts of most marketing strategies. However, focusing *only* on the company's products can also lead to marketing myopia. For example, some manufacturers believe that if they can "build a better mousetrap, the world will beat a path to their doors." But they are often rudely shocked. Buyers may be looking for a better solution to a mouse problem but not necessarily for a better mousetrap. The better solution might be a chemical spray, an exterminating service, a house cat, or something else that suits their needs even better than a mousetrap. Furthermore, a better mousetrap will not sell unless the manufacturer designs, packages, and prices it attractively; places it in convenient distribution channels; brings it to the attention of people who need it; and convinces buyers that it is a better product.

The Selling Concept

Selling concept
The idea that consumers will not buy enough of the firm's products unless the firm undertakes a large-scale selling and promotion effort.

Many companies follow the selling concept, which holds that consumers will not buy enough of the firm's products unless it undertakes a large-scale selling and promotion effort. The **selling concept** is typically practiced with unsought goods—those that buyers do not normally think of buying, such as insurance or blood donations. These industries must be good at tracking down prospects and selling them on a product's benefits.

Such aggressive selling, however, carries high risks. It focuses on creating sales transactions rather than on building long-term, profitable customer relationships. The aim often is to sell what the company makes rather than making what the market wants. It assumes that customers who are coaxed into buying the product will like it. Or, if they don't like it, they will possibly forget their disappointment and buy it again later. These are usually poor assumptions.

The Marketing Concept

Marketing concept
A philosophy in which achieving organizational goals depends on knowing the needs and wants of target markets and delivering the desired satisfactions better than competitors do.

The **marketing concept** holds that achieving organizational goals depends on knowing the needs and wants of target markets and delivering the desired satisfactions better than competitors do. Under the marketing concept, customer focus and value are the *paths* to sales and profits. Instead of a product-centered *make and sell* philosophy, the marketing concept is a customer-centered *sense and respond* philosophy. The job is not to find the right customers for your product but to find the right products for your customers.

▶ **Figure 1.3** contrasts the selling concept and the marketing concept. The selling concept takes an *inside-out* perspective. It starts with the factory, focuses on the company's existing products, and calls for heavy selling and promotion to obtain profitable sales. It focuses primarily on customer conquest—getting short-term sales with little concern about who buys or why.

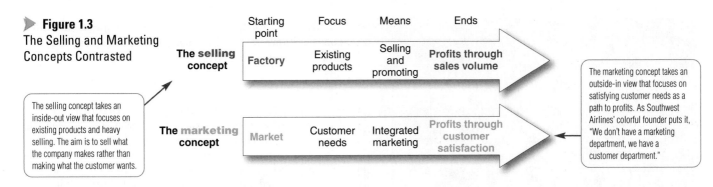

Figure 1.3
The Selling and Marketing Concepts Contrasted

The selling concept takes an inside-out view that focuses on existing products and heavy selling. The aim is to sell what the company makes rather than making what the customer wants.

The marketing concept takes an outside-in view that focuses on satisfying customer needs as a path to profits. As Southwest Airlines' colorful founder puts it, "We don't have a marketing department, we have a customer department."

In contrast, the marketing concept takes an *outside-in* perspective. As Herb Kelleher, the colorful founder of Southwest Airlines, puts it, "We don't have a marketing department; we have a customer department." The marketing concept starts with a well-defined market, focuses on customer needs, and integrates all the marketing activities that affect customers. In turn, it yields profits by creating relationships with the right customers based on customer value and satisfaction.

Implementing the marketing concept often means more than simply responding to customers' stated desires and obvious needs. *Customer-driven* companies research customers deeply to learn about their desires, gather new product ideas, and test product improvements. Such customer-driven marketing usually works well when a clear need exists and when customers know what they want.

In many cases, however, customers *don't* know what they want or even what is possible. As Henry Ford once remarked, "If I'd asked people what they wanted, they would have said faster horses."[9] For example, even 20 years ago, how many consumers would have thought to ask for now-commonplace products such as tablet computers, smartphones, digital cameras, 24-hour online buying, and GPS systems in their cars? Such situations call for *customer-driving* marketing—understanding customer needs even better than customers themselves do and creating products and services that meet both existing and latent needs, now and in the future. As an executive at 3M put it, "Our goal is to lead customers where they want to go before *they* know where they want to go."

The Societal Marketing Concept

Societal marketing concept
The idea that a company's marketing decisions should consider consumers' wants, the company's requirements, consumers' long-run interests, and society's long-run interests.

The **societal marketing concept** questions whether the pure marketing concept overlooks possible conflicts between consumer *short-run wants* and consumer *long-run welfare*. Is a firm that satisfies the immediate needs and wants of target markets always doing what's best for its consumers in the long run? The societal marketing concept holds that marketing strategy should deliver value to customers in a way that maintains or improves both the consumer's *and society's* well-being. It calls for *sustainable marketing*, socially and environmentally responsible marketing that meets the present needs of consumers and businesses while also preserving or enhancing the ability of future generations to meet their needs.

Even more broadly, many leading business and marketing thinkers are now preaching the concept of *shared value,* which recognizes that societal needs, not just economic needs, define markets.[10]

The concept of shared value focuses on creating economic value in a way that also creates value for society. A growing number of companies known for their hard-nosed approach to business—such as GE, Google, IBM, Intel, Johnson & Johnson, Nestlé, Unilever, and Walmart—have already embarked on important efforts to create shared economic and societal value by rethinking the intersection between society and corporate performance. They are concerned not just with short-term economic gains, but with the well-being of their customers, the depletion of natural resources vital to their businesses, the viability of key suppliers, and the economic well-being of the communities in which they produce and sell. One prominent marketer calls this *Marketing 3.0.* "Marketing 3.0 organizations are values-driven," he says. "I'm not talking about being value-driven. I'm talking about 'values' plural, where values amount to caring about the state of the world."

▲ **The societal marketing concept: According to UPS, social responsibility "isn't just good for the planet. It's good for business."**

AP Images/Cheryl Gerber

As ▶ **Figure 1.4** shows, companies should balance three considerations in setting their marketing strategies: company profits, consumer wants, *and* society's interests. ▶ UPS does this well.[11]

UPS seeks more than just short-run sales and profits. Its three-pronged corporate sustainability mission stresses *economic prosperity* (profitable growth through a customer focus), *social responsibility* (community engagement and individual well-being), and *environmental stewardship* (operating efficiently and protecting the environment). Whether it involves greening up its operations or urging employees to volunteer time in their communities, UPS proactively seeks opportunities to act responsibly. For example, UPS employees have volunteered millions of hours to United Way's Live United campaign to improve the education, income, and health of the nation's communities. UPS knows that doing what's right benefits both consumers and the company. By operating efficiently and acting responsibly, it can "meet the needs of the enterprise . . . while protecting and enhancing the human and natural resources that will be needed in the future." Social responsibility "isn't just good for the planet," says the company. "It's good for business."

Author Comment ▶

The customer-driven marketing strategy discussed in the previous section outlines which customers the company will serve (the target market) and how it will serve them (the value proposition). Now, the company develops marketing plans and programs—a marketing mix—that will actually deliver the intended customer value.

Preparing an Integrated Marketing Plan and Program

The company's marketing strategy outlines which customers it will serve and how it will create value for these customers. Next, the marketer develops an integrated marketing program that will actually deliver the intended value to target customers. The marketing program builds customer relationships by transforming the marketing strategy into action. It consists of the firm's *marketing mix*, the set of marketing tools the firm uses to implement its marketing strategy.

The major marketing mix tools are classified into four broad groups, called the *four Ps* of marketing: product, price, place, and promotion. To deliver on its value proposition, the firm must first create a need-satisfying market offering (product). It must then decide how much it will charge for the offering (price) and how it will make the offering available to target consumers (place). Finally, it must communicate with target customers about the offering and persuade them of its merits (promotion). The firm must blend each marketing mix tool into a comprehensive *integrated marketing program* that communicates and delivers the intended value to chosen customers. We will explore marketing programs and the marketing mix in much more detail in later chapters.

▶ **Figure 1.4** The Considerations Underlying the Societal Marketing Concept

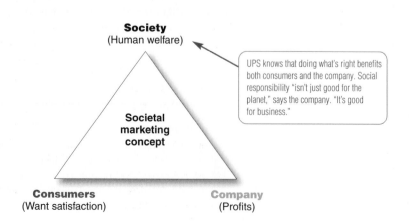

Society
(Human welfare)

UPS knows that doing what's right benefits both consumers and the company. Social responsibility "isn't just good for the planet," says the company. "It's good for business."

Societal marketing concept

Consumers
(Want satisfaction)

Company
(Profits)

SPEED BUMP | LINKING THE CONCEPTS

Stop here for a moment and stretch your legs. What have you learned so far about marketing? For the moment, set aside the more formal definitions we've examined and try to develop your own understanding of marketing.

- In *your own words*, what *is* marketing? Write down *your* definition. Does your definition include such key concepts as customer value and relationships?
- What does marketing *mean* to you? How does it affect your daily life?
- What brand of athletic shoes did you purchase last? Describe your relationship with Nike, Adidas, Reebok, Converse, New Balance, or whatever brand of shoes you purchased.

Author Comment ▶
Doing a good job with the first three steps in the marketing process sets the stage for step four, building and managing customer relationships.

Building Customer Relationships

The first three steps in the marketing process—understanding the marketplace and customer needs, designing a customer-driven marketing strategy, and constructing a marketing program—all lead up to the fourth and most important step: building and managing profitable customer relationships.

Customer Relationship Management

Customer relationship management is perhaps the most important concept of modern marketing. Some marketers define it narrowly as a customer data management activity (a practice called *CRM*). By this definition, it involves managing detailed information about individual customers and carefully managing customer *touchpoints* to maximize customer loyalty. We will discuss this narrower CRM activity in Chapter 4, when dealing with marketing information.

Most marketers, however, give the concept of customer relationship management a broader meaning. In this broader sense, **customer relationship management** is the overall process of building and maintaining profitable customer relationships by delivering superior customer value and satisfaction. It deals with all aspects of acquiring, keeping, and growing customers.

Customer relationship management
The overall process of building and maintaining profitable customer relationships by delivering superior customer value and satisfaction.

Relationship Building Blocks: Customer Value and Satisfaction
The key to building lasting customer relationships is to create superior customer value and satisfaction. Satisfied customers are more likely to be loyal customers and give the company a larger share of their business.

Customer-perceived value
The customer's evaluation of the difference between all the benefits and all the costs of a marketing offer relative to those of competing offers.

Customer Value. Attracting and retaining customers can be a difficult task. Customers often face a bewildering array of products and services from which to choose. A customer buys from the firm that offers the highest **customer-perceived value**—the customer's evaluation of the difference between all the benefits and all the costs of a market offering relative to those of competing offers. Importantly, customers often do not judge values and costs "accurately" or "objectively." They act on *perceived* value.

To some consumers, value might mean sensible products at affordable prices. To other consumers, however, value might mean paying more to get more. For example, a top-of-the-line Weber Summit E-670 barbecue grill carries a suggested retail price of $2,600, more than five times the price of competitor Char-Broil's best grill. According to Weber, the stainless steel Summit grill "embraces true grilling luxury with the highest quality materials, exclusive features, and stunning looks." However, Weber's marketing also suggests that the grill is a real value, even at the premium price. For the money, you get practical features such as all-stainless steel construction, spacious cooking and work areas, lighted control knobs, a tuck-away motorized rotisserie system, and an LED tank scale that lets you know how much propane you have left in the tank. Is the Weber Summit grill worth the premium price compared to less expensive grills? To many consumers, the answer is no. But to the target segment of affluent, hard-core grillers, the answer is "yes."[12]

Customer satisfaction
The extent to which a product's perceived performance matches a buyer's expectations.

Customer Satisfaction. Customer satisfaction depends on the product's perceived performance relative to a buyer's expectations. If the product's performance falls short of expectations, the customer is dissatisfied. If performance matches expectations, the customer is satisfied. If performance exceeds expectations, the customer is highly satisfied or delighted.

Outstanding marketing companies go out of their way to keep important customers satisfied. Most studies show that higher levels of customer satisfaction lead to greater customer loyalty, which in turn results in better company performance. Smart companies aim to delight customers by promising only what they can deliver and then delivering more than they promise. Delighted customers not only make repeat purchases but also become willing marketing partners and "customer evangelists" who spread the word about their good experiences to others (see Marketing at Work 1.1).

For companies interested in delighting customers, exceptional value and service become part of the overall company culture. For example, year after year, Ritz-Carlton ranks at or near the top of the hospitality industry in terms of customer satisfaction. ▶ Its passion for satisfying customers is summed up in the company's credo, which promises that its luxury hotels will deliver a truly memorable experience—one that "enlivens the senses, instills well-being, and fulfills even the unexpressed wishes and needs of our guests."[13]

Check into any Ritz-Carlton hotel around the world, and you'll be amazed by the company's fervent dedication to anticipating and meeting even your slightest need. Without ever asking, they seem to know that you're allergic to peanuts and want a king-size bed, a non-allergenic pillow, the blinds open when you arrive, and breakfast with decaffeinated coffee in your room. Each day, hotel staffers—from those at the front desk to those in maintenance and housekeeping—discreetly observe and record even the smallest guest preferences. Then, every morning, each hotel reviews the files of all new arrivals who have previously stayed at a Ritz-Carlton and prepares a list of suggested extra touches that might delight each guest.

Once they identify a special customer need, Ritz-Carlton employees go to legendary extremes to meet it. For example, to serve the needs of a guest with food allergies, a Ritz-Carlton chef in Bali located special eggs and milk in a small grocery store in another country and had them delivered to the hotel. In another case, when the hotel's laundry service failed to remove a stain on a guest's suit before the guest departed, the hotel manager traveled to the guest's house and personally delivered a reimbursement check for the cost of the suit. According to one Ritz-Carlton manager, if the chain gets hold of a picture of a guest's pet, it will make a copy, have it framed, and display it in the guest's room in whatever Ritz-Carlton the guest visits. As a result of such customer service heroics, an amazing 95 percent of departing guests report that their stay has been a truly memorable experience. More than 90 percent of Ritz-Carlton's delighted customers return.

▲ **Customer satisfaction:** Ritz-Carlton's passion for satisfying customers is summed up in its Credo, which promises a truly memorable experience—one that "enlivens the senses, instills well-being, and fulfills even the unexpressed wishes and needs of our guests."

Tim Draper/DK Images

However, a company doesn't have to be a luxury hotel chain with over-the-top service to create customer delight. Customer satisfaction "has a lot more to do with how well companies deliver on their basic, even plain-vanilla promises than on how dazzling the service experience might be," says one expert. "To win [customers'] loyalty, forget the bells and whistles and just solve their problems."[14]

Although a customer-centered firm seeks to deliver high customer satisfaction relative to competitors, it does not attempt to *maximize* customer satisfaction. A company can always increase customer satisfaction by lowering its price or increasing its services. But this may result in lower profits. Thus, the purpose of marketing is to generate customer value profitably. This requires a very delicate balance: The marketer must continue to generate more customer value and satisfaction but not "give away the house."

MARKETING AT WORK | 1.1

In-N-Out Burger: The Power of Customer Delight

In-N-Out Burger opened its first restaurant in Baldwin Park, California, in 1948. It was a simple affair, with two drive-through lanes, a walk-up window, outdoor seating, and a menu that boasted only burgers, shakes, fries, and soft drinks. That was a pretty standard format for the time. In fact, another California burger stand fitting about the same description was opened that same year just 45 minutes away by the McDonald brothers. Today, however, In-N-Out is pretty much the exact opposite of McDonald's. Whereas McDonald's now operates more than 32,700 stores worldwide and pulls in more than $79 billion in annual systemwide sales, In-N-Out has less than 270 stores in five states (California, Nevada, Utah, Arizona, and Texas) and about $465 million in annual sales.

But In-N-Out Burger never wanted to be another McDonald's. And despite its smaller size—or perhaps because of it—In-N-Out's customers like the regional chain just the way it is. When it comes to customer satisfaction—make that customer *delight*—In-N-Out beats McDonald's hands down. It regularly posts the highest customer satisfaction scores of any fast-food restaurant in its market area. Just about anyone who's been to In-N-Out thinks it makes the best burger they've ever had.

In-N-Out has earned an almost cult-like following by doing something unthinkable: not changing. From the start, the chain has focused tenaciously on customer well-being. Its founding philosophy is as strongly held today as it was when the first In-N-Out Burger opened its doors: "Give customers the freshest, highest quality foods you can buy and provide them with friendly service in a sparkling clean environment."

Unlike McDonald's or Burger King, which introduce a seemingly unending stream of new menu items, In-N-Out's simple menu never changes. Instead, In-N-Out still focuses on what it does well: making really good hamburgers, really good fries, and really good shakes—that's it. The burgers are made from 100 percent pure, fresh beef with no additives, fillers, or preservatives. Potatoes and other fresh vegetables are hand cut daily at every restaurant, and shakes are made from—yes—real ice cream. In an industry increasingly enamored with technologies like cryogenically frozen ingredients and off-site food preparation, you won't find a single freezer, heat lamp, or microwave oven at an In-N-Out. Every meal is custom-made with fresh ingredients. "We serve every customer, one burger at a time," says one restaurant manager.

Although the menu might seem limited, In-N-Out employees will gladly customize a burger to each customer's tastes. In fact, over the years a "secret menu" has emerged for customers who know the right code words (which aren't advertised or posted on the menu board). So a customer in the know might order a "Double-Double Animal Style" (double burger and double cheese, with pickles, grilled onions, extra spread, and fried mustard). Ordering a 4×4 gets you four beef patties and four slices of cheese, and a "grilled cheese" is an In-N-Out cheeseburger without the meat. Knowing the secret menu makes regulars feel even more special.

It's not just In-N-Out's food that pleases customers. The chain also features friendly and well-trained employees. In-N-Out treats its employees very well. It pays new part-time staff $10 an hour to start and gives them regular pay raises. Part-timers also get paid vacations. General managers make at least $100,000 a year plus bonuses and a full-benefit package that rivals anything in the corporate world. Managers who meet goals are sent on lavish trips with their spouses, often to Europe in first-class seats. Managers are also promoted from within—80 percent of In-N-Out managers started at the very bottom. As a result, In-N-Out has one of the lowest turnover rates in an industry famous for high turnover.

Happy, motivated employees help to create loyal, satisfied customers. In fact, words like *loyal* and *satisfied* don't do justice to how customers feel about In-N-Out Burger. *Delighted* or even *fanatically loyal* might say it better. The restaurant chain has developed an unparalleled cult following. When a new In-N-Out first opens, the line of cars often stretches out a mile or more, and people stand in line for an hour to get a burger, fries, and a shake. Fans have been known to camp overnight to be first in line. When the first Arizona store opened in Scottsdale, people waited in line for as long as four hours while news helicopters buzzed above the parking lot.

Ardent fans willingly go out of their way to satisfy an In-N-Out Burger craving. Jeff Rose, a financial planner from Carbondale, Illinois, always stops at In-N-Out first when he visits his mother in Las Vegas. "You have to pass it when you drive to her house," he says in his own defense. But how does he

▲ In-N-Out Burger delights customers by focusing on friendly service and what it does well: making really good hamburgers, really good fries, and really good shakes—that's it.

Peter Bennett/Ambient Images/Newscom

explain that he once paid an extra $40 in cab fare to visit an In-N-Out on the way to the San Diego airport?

In-N-Out doesn't spend much on advertising—it doesn't have to. Other than a small promotional budget for local billboards and some radio ads, when it comes to getting the word out, In-N-Out lets its customers do its heavy lifting. Loyal customers are true apostles for the brand. They proudly wear In-N-Out T-shirts and slap In-N-Out bumper stickers on their cars. Rabid regulars drag a constant stream of new devotees into In-N-Out restaurants, an act often referred to as "the conversion." They can't wait to pass along the secret menu codes and share the sublime pleasures of diving into a 4×4 Animal Style. "When you tell someone else what 'animal style' means," says an analyst, "you feel like you're passing on a secret handshake. People really get into the whole thing."

In-N-Out doesn't use paid endorsers, but word-of-mouth regularly flows from the mouths of A-list celebrities. When former *Tonight Show* host Conan O'Brien once asked Tom Hanks what he recommended doing in Los Angeles, Hanks replied, "One of the truly great things about Los Angeles is In-N-Out Burger." PGA golf star Phil Mickelson talked about the chain so much that whenever he hit a losing streak, sportswriters began suggesting that he cut back on the Double-Doubles. Once, when celebrity socialite Paris Hilton was pulled over and charged with driving under the influence, her excuse was that she was on

her way to satisfy an "In-N-Out urge" (a term originating from fans cutting the "B" and the "r" off from the company name on bumper stickers).

In-N-Out Burger is privately owned and doesn't release sales and profit figures. But if the long lines snaking out the door at lunchtime are any indication, the chain is doing very well financially. In-N-Out's average sales per store are double the industry average and well ahead of leaders McDonald's and Burger King. "The more chains like McDonald's and Burger King change and expand, the more In-N-Out sticks to its guns," says the analyst. "In a way, it symbolizes the ideal American way of doing business: Treating people well, focusing on product quality, and being very successful." In-N-Out's customers couldn't agree more. When it comes to fast-food chains, delighted customers will tell you, "There's In-N-Out, and then there's everyone else."

Sources: Stacy Perman, "In-N-Out Burger's Marketing Magic," *Businessweek*, April 24, 2009, accessed at www.businessweek.com; Stacy Perman, "The Secret Sauce at In-N-Out Burger," *Businessweek*, April 20, 2009, p. 68; Dan Macsai, "The Sizzling Secrets of In-N-Out Burger," *Fast Company*, April 22, 2009, accessed at www.fastcompany.com; Michael Rigert, "In-N-Out Fans Come Out En Masse for Orem Opening," *Daily Herald* (*Orem*), November 20, 2009; Gil Rudawsky, "Is In-N-Out Burger Moving East?" *Daily Finance*, May 26, 2010, accessed at www.dailyfinance.com; Nancy Luna, "Attack of the Double-Double," *D Magazine*, March 2011, p. 54; and www.in-n-out.com, accessed November 2011.

Customer Relationship Levels and Tools

Companies can build customer relationships at many levels, depending on the nature of the target market. At one extreme, a company with many low-margin customers may seek to develop *basic relationships* with them. For example, Nike does not phone or call on all of its consumers to get to know them personally. Instead, Nike creates relationships through brand-building advertising, public relations, and its numerous Web sites and apps. At the other extreme, in markets with few customers and high margins, sellers want to create *full partnerships* with key customers. For example, Nike sales representatives work closely with the Sports Authority, Dick's Sporting Goods, Foot Locker, and other large retailers. In between these two extremes, other levels of customer relationships are appropriate.

Beyond offering consistently high value and satisfaction, marketers can use specific marketing tools to develop stronger bonds with customers. For example, many companies offer *frequency marketing programs* that reward customers who buy frequently or in large amounts. Airlines offer frequent-flyer programs, hotels give room upgrades to their frequent guests, and supermarkets give patronage discounts to "very important customers." For example, JetBlue Airways offers its TrueBlue members frequent-flyer points they can use on any seat on any JetBlue flight with no blackout dates. ▶ JetBlue promises its members "More award flights. More points. More to love." The airline's "Be True" marketing campaign even highlights real TrueBlue members who are nominated by JetBlue crewmembers for their TrueBlue dedication to inspiring causes.

Other companies sponsor *club marketing programs* that offer members special benefits and create member communities. For example, buy one of those Weber grills and you can join the Weber Nation—"the site for real people who love their Weber grills."

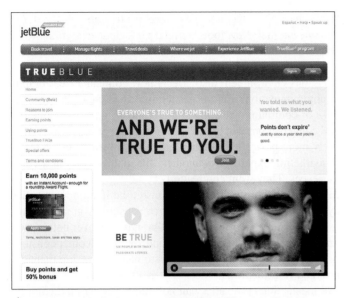

▲ **Frequency marketing programs: JetBlue Airways offers its TrueBlue members "More to love." It even features real TrueBlue members in its "Be True" marketing campaign.**

JetBlue Airways

Membership gets you exclusive access to online grilling classes, an interactive recipe box, grilling tips and 24/7 telephone support, audio and video podcasts, straight-talk forums for interacting with other grilling fanatics, and even a chance to star in a Weber TV commercial. "Become a spatula-carrying member today," says Weber.[15]

The Changing Nature of Customer Relationships

Significant changes are occurring in the ways companies relate to their customers. Yesterday's companies focused on mass marketing to all customers at arm's length. Today's companies are building deeper, more direct, and lasting relationships with more carefully selected customers. Here are some important trends in the way companies and customers are relating to one another.

Relating with More Carefully Selected Customers

Few firms today still practice true mass marketing—selling in a standardized way to any customer who comes along. Today, most marketers realize that they don't want relationships with every customer. Instead, they target fewer, more profitable customers. "Not all customers are worth your marketing efforts," states one analyst. "Some are more costly to serve than to lose."[16]

Many companies now use customer profitability analysis to pass up or weed out losing customers and target winning ones for pampering. One approach is to preemptively screen out potentially unprofitable customers. Progressive Insurance does this effectively. It asks prospective customers a series of screening questions to determine if they are right for the firm. If they're not, Progressive will likely tell them, "You might want to go to Allstate." A marketing consultant explains: "They'd rather send business to a competitor than take on unprofitable customers." Screening out unprofitable customers lets Progressive provide even better service to potentially more profitable ones.[17]

But what should the company do with unprofitable customers that it already has? ▶ If it can't turn them into profitable ones, the company may want to dismiss those customers who are too unreasonable or that cost more to serve than they are worth. "Save your company by firing your customers," advises one marketer. "Well, not all your customers—just the ones who ask for more than they give." Adds another marketer, "Firing the customers you can't possibly please gives you the bandwidth and resources to coddle the ones that truly deserve your attention and repay you with referrals, applause, and loyalty."[18] Consider this example:

▲ **Marketers don't want relationships with every possible customer. In fact, a company might want to "fire" customers that cost more to serve than to lose.**

> Sprint recently sent out letters to about 1,000 people to inform them that they had been summarily dismissed—but the recipients were Sprint *customers*, not employees. For about a year, the wireless-service provider had been tracking the number and frequency of support calls made by a group of high-maintenance users. According to a Sprint spokesperson, "in some cases, they were calling customer care hundreds of times a month . . . on the same issues, even after we felt those issues had been resolved." Ultimately, the company determined it could not meet the needs of this subset of subscribers and, therefore, waived their termination fees and cut off their service. Such "customer divestment" practices were once considered an anomaly. But new segmentation approaches and technologies have made it easier to focus on retaining the right customers and, by extension, showing problem customers the door.

Relating More Deeply and Interactively

Beyond choosing customers more selectively, companies are now relating with chosen customers in deeper, more meaningful ways. Rather than relying on one-way, mass-media messages only, today's marketers are incorporating new, interactive approaches that help build targeted, two-way customer relationships.

Interactive Customer Relationships. New technologies have profoundly changed the ways in which people relate to one another. New tools for relating include everything from e-mail, Web sites, blogs, cell phones, and video sharing to online communities and social networks, such as Facebook, YouTube, and Twitter.

This changing communications environment also affects how companies and brands relate to customers. The new communications approaches let marketers create deeper customer involvement and a sense of community surrounding a brand—to make the brand a meaningful part of consumers' conversations and lives. "Becoming part of the conversation between consumers is infinitely more powerful than handing down information via traditional advertising," says one marketing expert. Says another, "People today want a voice and a role in their brand experiences. They want co-creation."[19]

At the same time that the new technologies create relationship-building opportunities for marketers, however, they also create challenges. They give consumers greater power and control. Today's consumers have more information about brands than ever before, and they have a wealth of platforms for airing and sharing their brand views with other consumers. Thus, the marketing world is now embracing not only customer relationship management, but also **customer-managed relationships**.

Customer-managed relationships
Marketing relationships in which customers, empowered by today's new digital technologies, interact with companies and with each other to shape their relationships with brands.

Greater consumer control means that companies can no longer rely on marketing by *intrusion*. Instead, marketers must practice marketing by *attraction*—creating market offerings and messages that involve consumers rather than interrupt them. Hence, most marketers now augment their mass-media marketing efforts with a rich mix of direct marketing approaches that promote brand-consumer interaction.

For example, many brands are creating dialogues with consumers via their own or existing *online social networks*. To supplement their traditional marketing campaigns, companies now routinely post their latest ads and made-for-the-Web videos on video-sharing sites. They join social networks. Or they launch their own blogs, online communities, or consumer-generated review systems, all with the aim of engaging customers on a more personal, interactive level.

Take Twitter, for example. Organizations ranging from Dell, JetBlue Airways, and Dunkin' Donuts to the Chicago Bulls, NASCAR, and the Los Angeles Fire Department have created Twitter pages and promotions. They use "tweets" to start conversations with Twitter's more than 200 million registered users, address customer service issues, research customer reactions, and drive traffic to relevant articles, Web sites, contests, videos, and other brand activities. For example, Dell monitors Twitter-based discussions and responds quickly to individual problems or questions. Tony Hsieh, CEO of the Zappos family of companies, who has more than 1.7 million Twitter followers, says that Twitter lets him give customers "more depth into what we're like, and my own personality." Another marketer notes that companies can "use Twitter to get the fastest, most honest research any company ever heard—the good, bad, and ugly—and it doesn't cost a cent."[20]

Similarly, almost every company has something going on Facebook these days. Starbucks has more than 20 million Facebook "fans"; Coca-Cola has more than 23 million. Social media such as Facebook, YouTube, Twitter, and e-mail can get consumers involved with and talking about a brand. For example, ice cream retailer Cold Stone Creamery uses all of these media to engage customers:[21]

▲ **Online social networks: Cold Stone Creamery uses a variety of social media to engage customers on a more personal, interactive level. Its Facebook page constitutes a modern-day, online version of an ice cream social.**

Kahala Corp.

On YouTube, Cold Stone posts footage from events like its annual "World's Largest Ice Cream Social," which benefits Make-A-Wish Foundation. ▶ Cold Stone's Facebook page, with more than 1.4 million friends, constitutes a modern-day, online version of an ice cream social. Fans can post pictures of their favorite Cold Stone experiences, exchange views with the company and fellow ice cream lovers, learn about new flavors and happenings, or send a Cold Stone eGift—a cone, milkshake, or just a dollar amount—to a friend who needs a lift. Social media help build both customer relationships and sales. In response to a recent 2-for-$5 coupon campaign using e-mail and Facebook, fans printed more than 500,000 coupons in just three weeks, redeeming an amazing 14 percent of them. A new-summer-flavors contest drew 4,000 entrants and 66,000 new fans in just eight weeks. According to Cold Stone, every social media campaign so far has brought a spike in store traffic and sales. More than half of the company's advertising budget is now dedicated to non-traditional activities like social media.

Most marketers are still learning how to use social media effectively. The problem is to find unobtrusive ways to enter consumers' social conversations with engaging and relevant brand messages. Simply posting a humorous video, creating a social network page, or hosting a blog isn't enough. Successful social network marketing means making relevant and genuine contributions to consumer conversations. "Nobody wants to be friends with a brand," says one online marketing executive. "Your job [as a brand] is to be part of other friends' conversations."[22]

Consumer-generated marketing

Brand exchanges created by consumers themselves—both invited and uninvited—by which consumers are playing an increasing role in shaping their own brand experiences and those of other consumers.

Consumer-Generated Marketing. A growing part of the new customer dialogue is **consumer-generated marketing**, by which consumers themselves are playing a bigger role in shaping their own brand experiences and those of others. This might happen through uninvited consumer-to-consumer exchanges in blogs, video-sharing sites, and other digital forums. But increasingly, companies are *inviting* consumers to play a more active role in shaping products and brand messages.

Some companies ask consumers for new product ideas. For example, Coca-Cola's Vitaminwater brand recently set up a Facebook app to obtain consumer suggestions for a new flavor, promising to manufacture and sell the winner ("Vitaminwater was our idea; the next one will be yours."). The new flavor—Connect (black cherry-lime with vitamins and a kick of caffeine)—was a big hit. In the process, Vitaminwater doubled its Facebook fan base to more than one million.[23]

Other companies are inviting customers to play an active role in shaping ads. For example, PepsiCo, Southwest Airlines, MasterCard, Unilever, H. J. Heinz, and many other companies have run contests for consumer-generated commercials that have been aired on national television. For the past several years, PepsiCo's Doritos brand has held a "Crash the Super Bowl" contest in which it invites 30-second ads from consumers and runs the best ones during the game. The consumer-generated ads have been a huge success. Last year, PepsiCo added the PepsiMax brand to the contest and consumers submitted nearly 5,600 entries. The winning fan-produced ad for Doritos (called "Pug Attack") tied for number one with Bud Light's agency-produced "Dog sitter" ad in the *USA Today* Ad Meter ratings, earning the creator a $1,000,000 cash prize from PepsiCo. The ad cost only about $500 to make. In all, PepsiCo placed two consumer-made Doritos ads and two PepsiMax ads in the top 10 out of 61 Super Bowl ads.[24]

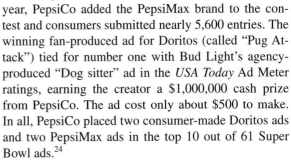

However, harnessing consumer-generated content can be a time-consuming and costly process, and companies may find it difficult to glean even a little gold from all the garbage. For example, when Heinz invited consumers to submit homemade ads for its ketchup on its YouTube page, it ended up sifting through more than 8,000 entries, of which it posted nearly 4,000. Some of the amateur ads were very good—entertaining and potentially effective. Most, however, were so-so at best, and others were downright dreadful. In one ad, a contestant chugged ketchup straight from the bottle. In

▲ Harnessing consumer-generated marketing: When H. J. Heinz invited consumers to submit homemade ads for its ketchup brand on YouTube, it received more than 8,000 entries—some very good but most only so-so or even downright dreadful.

AJ Mast/Redux Pictures

another, the would-be filmmaker brushed his teeth, washed his hair, and shaved his face with Heinz's product.[25]

Consumer-generated marketing, whether invited by marketers or not, has become a significant marketing force. Through a profusion of consumer-generated videos, reviews, blogs, and Web sites, consumers are playing an increasing role in shaping their own brand experiences. Beyond creating brand conversations, customers are having an increasing say about everything from product design, usage, and packaging to pricing and distribution. Brands need to accept and embrace the emergence of consumer power. Says one analyst, "Humans, formerly known as either consumers or couch potatoes, are now creators and thought leaders, passive no more."[26]

Partner Relationship Management

Author Comment ▶
Marketers can't create customer value and build customer relationships by themselves. They must work closely with other company departments and partners outside the firm.

Partner relationship management
Working closely with partners in other company departments and outside the company to jointly bring greater value to customers.

When it comes to creating customer value and building strong customer relationships, today's marketers know that they can't go it alone. They must work closely with a variety of marketing partners. In addition to being good at *customer relationship management*, marketers must also be good at **partner relationship management**—working closely with others inside and outside the company to jointly bring more value to customers.

Traditionally, marketers have been charged with understanding customers and representing customer needs to different company departments. However, in today's more connected world, every functional area in the organization can interact with customers. The new thinking is that—no matter what your job is in a company—you must understand marketing and be customer focused. Rather than letting each department go its own way, firms must link all departments in the cause of creating customer value.

Marketers must also partner with suppliers, channel partners, and others outside the company. Marketing channels consist of distributors, retailers, and others who connect the company to its buyers. The *supply chain* describes a longer channel, stretching from raw materials to components to final products that are carried to final buyers. Through *supply chain management*, companies today are strengthening their connections with partners all along the supply chain. They know that their fortunes rest on more than just how well they perform. Success at delivering customer value rests on how well their entire supply chain performs against competitors' supply chains.

Capturing Value from Customers

Author Comment ▶
Look back at Figure 1.1. In the first four steps of the marketing process, the company creates value *for* target customers and builds strong relationships with them. If it does that well, it can capture value *from* customers in return in the form of loyal customers who buy and continue to buy the company's brands.

The first four steps in the marketing process outlined in Figure 1.1 involve building customer relationships by creating and delivering superior customer value. The final step involves capturing value in return in the form of sales, market share, and profits. By creating superior customer value, the firm creates highly satisfied customers who stay loyal and buy more. This, in turn, means greater long-run returns for the firm. Here, we discuss the outcomes of creating customer value: customer loyalty and retention, share of market and share of customer, and customer equity.

Creating Customer Loyalty and Retention

Good customer relationship management creates customer satisfaction. In turn, satisfied customers remain loyal and talk favorably to others about the company and its products. Studies show big differences in the loyalty of customers who are less satisfied, somewhat satisfied, and completely satisfied. Even a slight drop from complete satisfaction can create an enormous drop in loyalty. Thus, the aim of customer relationship management is to create not only customer satisfaction but also customer delight.

The recent Great Recession and the economic uncertainty that followed it put strong pressures on customer loyalty. It created a new consumer spending sensibility that will last well into the future. Recent studies show that, even in an improved economy, 55 percent of U.S. consumers say they would rather get the best price than the best brand. Some 50 percent of consumers now purchase store brands "all the time" as part of their regular shopping behavior, up from just 12 percent in the early 1990s. Nearly two-thirds say they will now shop at a different store with lower prices even if it's less convenient. Research also shows that it's five times cheaper to keep an old customer than acquire a new one. Thus, companies today must shape their value propositions even more carefully and treat their profitable customers well to keep them loyal.[27]

Losing a customer means losing more than a single sale. It means losing the entire stream of purchases that the customer would make over a lifetime of patronage. For example, here is a classic illustration of **customer lifetime value:**

Customer lifetime value
The value of the entire stream of purchases a customer makes over a lifetime of patronage.

▲ Customer lifetime value: To keep customers coming back, Stew Leonard's has created the "Disneyland of dairy stores." Rule #1— The customer is always right. Rule #2—If the customer is ever wrong, reread Rule #1.

Stew Leonard's

Stew Leonard, who operates a highly profitable four-store supermarket in Connecticut and New York, once said that he sees $50,000 flying out of his store every time he sees a sulking customer. Why? Because his average customer spends about $100 a week, shops 50 weeks a year, and remains in the area for about 10 years. If this customer has an unhappy experience and switches to another supermarket, Stew Leonard's has lost $50,000 in lifetime revenue. The loss can be much greater if the disappointed customer shares the bad experience with other customers and causes them to defect.

To keep customers coming back, Stew Leonard's has created what the *New York Times* has dubbed the "Disneyland of Dairy Stores," complete with costumed characters, scheduled entertainment, a petting zoo, and animatronics throughout the store. From its humble beginnings as a small dairy store in 1969, Stew Leonard's has grown at an amazing pace. It's built 29 additions onto the original store, which now serves more than 300,000 customers each week. This legion of loyal shoppers is largely a result of the store's passionate approach to customer service. ▶ "Rule #1: The customer is always right. Rule #2: If the customer is ever wrong, re-read rule #1."[28]

Stew Leonard's is not alone in assessing customer lifetime value. Lexus, for example, estimates that a single satisfied and loyal customer is worth more than $600,000 in lifetime sales. And the estimated lifetime value of a young mobile phone consumer is $26,000.[29] In fact, a company can lose money on a specific transaction but still benefit greatly from a long-term relationship. This means that companies must aim high in building customer relationships. Customer delight creates an emotional relationship with a brand, not just a rational preference. And that relationship keeps customers coming back.

Growing Share of Customer

Beyond simply retaining good customers to capture customer lifetime value, good customer relationship management can help marketers increase their **share of customer**—the share they get of the customer's purchasing in their product categories. Thus, banks want to increase "share of wallet." Supermarkets and restaurants want to get more "share of stomach." Car companies want to increase "share of garage," and airlines want greater "share of travel."

Share of customer
The portion of the customer's purchasing that a company gets in its product categories.

To increase share of customer, firms can offer greater variety to current customers. Or they can create programs to cross-sell and up-sell to market more products and services to existing customers. For example, Amazon.com is highly skilled at leveraging relationships with its 90 million customers to increase its share of each customer's spending budget:[30]

Originally an online bookseller, Amazon.com now offers customers music, videos, consumer electronics, toys, office products, home improvement items, lawn and garden products, apparel and accessories, jewelry, tools, and even groceries. In addition, based on each customer's purchase and search history, the company recommends related products that might be of interest. This recommendation system influences up to 30 percent of all sales. Amazon.com's ingenious Amazon Prime two-day shipping program has also help boost the online giant's share of customers' wallets. For an annual fee of $79, Prime members receive delivery of all their purchases within two days, whether it's a single paperback book or a 60-inch HDTV. "Amazon Prime may be the most ingenious and effective customer loyalty program in all of e-commerce, if not retail in general," says one analyst. "It converts casual shoppers, who gorge on the gratification of having purchases reliably appear two days after the order, into Amazon addicts." As a result, after signing up for Prime, shoppers more than double their annual Amazon .com purchases. The shipping program is responsible for an estimated 20 percent of Amazon's U.S. sales.

Building Customer Equity

We can now see the importance of not only acquiring customers but also keeping and growing them. The value of a company comes from the value of its current and future customers. Customer relationship management takes a long-term view. Companies want not only to create profitable customers but also "own" them for life, earn a greater share of their purchases, and capture their customer lifetime value.

What Is Customer Equity?

Customer equity
The total combined customer lifetime values of all of the company's customers.

The ultimate aim of customer relationship management is to produce high *customer equity*.[31] **Customer equity** is the total combined customer lifetime values of all of the company's current and potential customers. As such, it's a measure of the future value of the company's customer base. Clearly, the more loyal the firm's profitable customers, the higher its customer equity. Customer equity may be a better measure of a firm's performance than current sales or market share. Whereas sales and market share reflect the past, customer equity suggests the future. ▶ Consider Cadillac:[32]

▲ **Managing customer equity: To increase customer lifetime value and customer equity, Cadillac needs to make the Caddy cool again by targeting a younger generation of customers.**

Transstock/Terra/Corbis

In the 1970s and 1980s, Cadillac had some of the most loyal customers in the industry. To an entire generation of car buyers, the name *Cadillac* defined American luxury. Cadillac's share of the luxury car market reached a whopping 51 percent in 1976, and based on market share and sales, the brand's future looked rosy. However, measures of customer equity would have painted a bleaker picture. Cadillac customers were getting older (average age 60) and average customer lifetime value was falling. Many Cadillac buyers were on their last cars. Thus, although Cadillac's market share was good, its customer equity was not.

Compare this with BMW. Its more youthful and vigorous image didn't win BMW the early market share war. However, it did win BMW younger customers (average age about 40) with higher customer lifetime values. The result: In the years that followed, BMW's market share and profits soared while Cadillac's fortunes eroded badly. In recent years, Cadillac has struggled to make the Caddy cool again by targeting a younger generation of consumers. The moral: Marketers should care not just about current sales and market share. Customer lifetime value and customer equity are the name of the game.

Building the Right Relationships with the Right Customers

Companies should manage customer equity carefully. They should view customers as assets that need to be managed and maximized. But not all customers, not even all loyal customers, are good investments. Surprisingly, some loyal customers can be unprofitable, and some disloyal customers can be profitable. Which customers should the company acquire and retain?

The company can classify customers according to their potential profitability and manage its relationships with them accordingly. ▶ **Figure 1.5** classifies customers into one of four relationship groups, according to their profitability and projected loyalty.[33] Each group requires a different relationship management strategy. *Strangers* show low potential

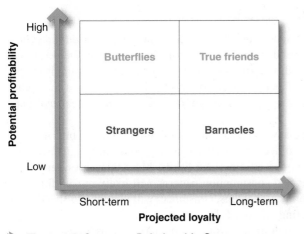

Figure 1.5 Customer Relationship Groups

profitability and little projected loyalty. There is little fit between the company's offerings and their needs. The relationship management strategy for these customers is simple: Don't invest anything in them.

Butterflies are potentially profitable but not loyal. There is a good fit between the company's offerings and their needs. However, like real butterflies, we can enjoy them for only a short while and then they're gone. An example is stock market investors who trade shares often and in large amounts but who enjoy hunting out the best deals without building a regular relationship with any single brokerage company. Efforts to convert butterflies into loyal customers are rarely successful. Instead, the company should enjoy the butterflies for the moment. It should create satisfying and profitable transactions with them, capturing as much of their business as possible in the short time during which they buy from the company. Then, it should cease investing in them until the next time around.

True friends are both profitable and loyal. There is a strong fit between their needs and the company's offerings. The firm wants to make continuous relationship investments to delight these customers and nurture, retain, and grow them. It wants to turn true friends into *true believers*, who come back regularly and tell others about their good experiences with the company.

Barnacles are highly loyal but not very profitable. There is a limited fit between their needs and the company's offerings. An example is smaller bank customers who bank regularly but do not generate enough returns to cover the costs of maintaining their accounts. Like barnacles on the hull of a ship, they create drag. Barnacles are perhaps the most problematic customers. The company might be able to improve their profitability by selling them more, raising their fees, or reducing service to them. However, if they cannot be made profitable, they should be "fired."

The point here is an important one: Different types of customers require different relationship management strategies. The goal is to build the *right relationships* with the *right customers*.

SPEED BUMP | LINKING THE CONCEPTS

We've covered a lot of territory. Again, slow down for a moment and develop *your own* thoughts about marketing.

- In *your own words*, what *is* marketing and what does it seek to accomplish?
- How well does Lexus manage its relationships with customers? What customer relationship management strategy does it use? What relationship management strategy does Walmart use?
- Think of a company for which you are a *true friend*. What strategy does this company use to manage its relationship with you?

Author Comment ▶
Marketing doesn't take place in a vacuum. Now that we've discussed the five steps in the marketing process, let's examine how the ever-changing marketplace affects both consumers and the marketers who serve them. We'll look more deeply into these and other marketing environment factors in Chapter 3.

The Changing Marketing Landscape

Every day, dramatic changes are occurring in the marketplace. Richard Love of HP observed, "The pace of change is so rapid that the ability to change has now become a competitive advantage." Yogi Berra, the legendary New York Yankees catcher and manager, summed it up more simply when he said, "The future ain't what it used to be." As the marketplace changes, so must those who serve it.

In this section, we examine the major trends and forces that are changing the marketing landscape and challenging marketing strategy. We look at five major developments: the uncertain economic environment, the digital age, rapid globalization, the call for more ethics and social responsibility, and the growth of not-for-profit marketing.

The Changing Economic Environment

Beginning in 2008, the United States and world economies experienced the Great Recession, a stunning economic meltdown unlike anything since the Great Depression of the 1930s. The stock market plunged, and trillions of dollars of market value simply evaporated. The financial crisis left shell-shocked consumers short of both money and confidence as they faced losses in income, a severe credit crunch, declining home values, and rising unemployment.

The Great Recession caused many consumers to rethink their spending priorities and cut back on their buying. After two decades of overspending, consumers tightened their purse strings and changed their buying attitudes and habits. More than just a temporary change, the new consumer values and consumption patterns will likely remain for many years to come. Even as the economy strengthens, consumers will continue to spend more carefully and sensibly (see Marketing at Work 1.2).

In response, companies in all industries—from discounters such as Target to luxury brands such as Lexus—have aligned their marketing strategies with the new economic realities. More than ever, marketers are emphasizing the *value* in their value propositions. They are focusing on value-for-the-money, practicality, and durability in their product offerings and marketing pitches.

▲ In the current economic environment, companies must emphasize the value in their value propositions. Target has shifted the balance more toward the "Pay Less" half of its "Expect More. Pay Less" positioning.

Justin Sullivan/Getty Images

For example, for years discount retailer Target focused increasingly on the "Expect More" side of its "Expect More. Pay Less." value proposition. It's carefully cultivated "upscale-discounter" image successfully differentiated it from Walmart's more hard-nosed "lowest price" position. But when the economy soured, many consumers worried that Target's trendier assortments and hip marketing also meant higher prices, and Target's performance slipped. ▶ So Target has shifted its balance more toward the "Pay Less" half of the slogan, making certain that its prices are in line with Walmart's and that customers know it. Although still trendy, Target's marketing now also features more practical price and savings appeals. "We let too much space drift between 'Expect More' and 'Pay Less,'" says Target's chief marketing officer. Target's latest "Life's A Moving Target" campaign seems to have found the right balance between the two sides of its positioning. "We believe we've negated the price perception issues," says the executive.[34]

At the other extreme, even luxury brands are adding value to their buying equations. For example, for years Lexus has emphasized status and performance. Its pre-Christmas ads typically feature a loving spouse giving his or her significant other a new Lexus wrapped in a big red bow. Lexus is still running those ads, but it's also hedging its bets by running other ads with the tagline "lowest cost of ownership," referring to Lexus' decent fuel economy, durability, and high resale value.

In adjusting to the new economy, companies may be tempted to cut their marketing budgets and slash prices in an effort to coax more frugal customers into opening their wallets. However, although cutting costs and offering selected discounts can be important marketing tactics, smart marketers understand that making cuts in the wrong places can damage long-term brand images and customer relationships. The challenge is to balance the brand's value proposition with the current times while also enhancing its long-term equity.

"A recession creates winners and losers just like a boom," notes one economist. "When a recession ends, when the road levels off and the world seems full of promise once more, your position in the competitive pack will depend on how skillfully you managed [during the tough times]."[35] Thus, rather than slashing prices in difficult times, many marketers held the line on prices and instead explained why their brands were worth it. And rather than cutting their marketing budgets, companies such as McDonald's, Hyundai, and General Mills maintained or actually increased their marketing spending, leaving them

| **MARKETING AT WORK** | 1.2 |

A New Era of More Sensible Consumption

The Great Recession of 2008 to 2009 and its aftermath hit American consumers hard. The housing bust, credit crunch, high unemployment, and plunging stock market blew away the savings and confidence of consumers who for years operated on a buy-now, pay-later philosophy, chasing bigger homes, bigger cars, and better brands. The new economic realities forced consumers to bring their excessive consumption back in line with their incomes and rethink buying priorities. People across all income segments reined in their spending, postponed big purchases, searched for bargains, and hunkered down to weather the worst economic crisis since the Great Depression rocked the worlds of their parents or grandparents.

Today, as the world moves into the postrecession era, consumer incomes and spending are again on the rise. However, even as the economy strengthens, rather than reverting to their old free-spending ways, Americans are now showing an enthusiasm for frugality not seen in decades. Sensible consumption has made a comeback, and it might be here to stay. The behavioral shift isn't simply about spending less. The new consumption ethic emphasizes simpler living and more value for the dollar. It focuses on living with less, fixing something yourself instead of buying a new one, packing a lunch instead of eating out, spending more time in discount chains, or trading down to store brands. Despite their rebounding means, consumers are now clipping more coupons, swiping their credit cards less, and putting more in the bank.

For example, not that long ago, yoga teacher Gisele Sanders shopped at the Nordstrom in Portland, Oregon, and didn't think twice about dropping $30 for a bottle of Chianti to go with dinner. That was before the recession, when her husband, a real estate agent, began to feel the brunt of slowing home sales. Now, even with the improved economy, Sanders picks up grocery-store wine at $10 or less per bottle, shops for used clothes, and takes her mother's advice about turning down the thermostat during winter. "It's been a long time coming," she said. "We were so off the charts before."

Such new-found buying sensibilities are more than just a fad—most experts agree that the impact of the Great Recession will last well into the future. "It is a whole reassessment of values," says a retailing consultant. "We had just been shopping until we drop, and consuming and buying it all, and replenishing before things wear out. People [have learned] again to say, 'No, not today.'"

The pain of the Great Recession moved many consumers to reconsider their very definition of the good life, changing the way they buy, sell, and live in a postrecession society. "People are finding happiness in old-fashioned virtues—thrift, savings, do-it-yourself projects, self-improvement, hard work, faith, and community—and in activities and relationships outside

the consumer realm," says John Gerzema, chief insights officer for ad agency Young & Rubicam, which maintains one of the world's largest databases of information about consumer attitudes. In what Gerzema calls the "spend shift," consumers have become uneasy with debt and excess spending and skeptical of materialistic values. "From now on, our purchases will be more considered. We are moving from mindless to mindful consumption."

Most consumers see the new frugality as a good thing. One recent survey showed that 78 percent of people believe the recession has changed their spending habits for the better. In another survey, 79 percent of consumers agreed with the statement, "I feel a lot smarter now about the way I shop versus two years ago." Some 65 percent of Americans feel that "since the recession I realize I am happier with a simpler more down-to-basic lifestyle." According to a researcher, "They look at their old spending habits and are a bit embarrassed by their behavior. So while consumption may [not] be as carefree and fun as it was before, consumers seem to like their new outlook, mindfulness, and strength."

For example, in Maine, Sindi Card says her husband's job is now secure. However, because the couple has two sons in college, even in the more buoyant economy, she fixed her broken 20-year-old clothes dryer herself. It was a stark change from the past, when she would have taken the old model to the dump and had a new one delivered. With help from an appliance-repair Web site, she saved hundreds of dollars. "We all need to find a way to live within our means," she said.

The new, more practical spending values don't mean that people have resigned themselves to lives of deprivation. As the

▲ Even as the economy strengthens, rather than reverting to their old free-spending ways, Americans are now showing an enthusiasm for frugality not seen in decades. More sensible spending might be here to stay.

igor kisselev/Shutterstock.com

economy has improved, consumers are indulging in luxuries and bigger-ticket purchases again, just more sensibly. "We're seeing an emergence in what we call 'conscious recklessness,' where consumers actually plan out frivolous or indulgent spending," says the researcher. It's like someone on a diet who saves up calories by eating prudently during the week and then lets loose on Friday night. But "people are more mindful now and aware of the consequences of their (and others') spending. So luxury is [again] on the 'to-do' list, but people are taking a more mindful approach to where, how, and on what they spend."

What does the new era of consumer spending mean to marketers? Whether it's for everyday products like cereal and detergents or expensive luxuries like Starbucks coffee or diamonds, marketers must clearly spell out their value propositions: what it is that makes their brands worth a customer's hard-earned money. Frugality is in; value is under scrutiny. For companies, it's not about cutting costs and prices. Instead, they must use a different approach to reach today's more pragmatic consumers: Forego the flash and prove your products' worth. According to Starbucks CEO Howard Schultz:

> There's been a real sea change in consumer behavior. And [companies] must appeal to the consumer in a different way today than they did two or three years ago. And it's not all based on value.

Cutting prices or putting things on sale is not sustainable business strategy. . . . You can't cut enough costs to save your way to prosperity. I think the question is, What is your relevancy to the new life of the consumer, who is more discriminating about what they're going to spend money on?"

Even diamond marketer De Beers has adjusted its long-standing "A diamond is forever" value proposition to these more sensible times. One ad, headlined "Here's to Less," makes that next diamond purchase seem—what else—downright practical. "Our lives are filled with things. We're overwhelmed by possessions we own but do not treasure. Stuff we buy but never love. To be thrown away in weeks rather than passed down for generations. Perhaps we will be different now. Perhaps now is an opportunity to reassess what really matters. After all, if everything you ever bought her disappeared overnight, what would she truly miss? A diamond is forever."

Sources: Extracts, quotes, and other information from Mark Dolliver, "Will Traumatized Consumers Ever Recover?" *Adweek*, March 22, 2010, accessed at www.adweek.com; Leigh Buchanan, "Decoding the New Consumer," *Inc.,* September 2010, pp. 159–160; Dan Sewell, "New Frugality Emerges," *Washington Times*, December 1, 2008; John Gerzema, "How U.S. Consumers Are Steering the Spend Shift," *Advertising Age*, October 11, 2010, p. 26; and "Howard Schultz, I'm Getting a Second Shot," *Inc.,* April 2011, pp. 52–53.

stronger when the economy strengthened. The goal in uncertain economic times is to build market share and strengthen customer relationships at the expense of competitors who cut back.

The Digital Age

The explosive growth in digital technology has fundamentally changed the way we live—how we communicate, share information, learn, shop, and access entertainment. In turn, it has had a major impact on the ways companies bring value to their customers. ▶ For better or worse, technology has become an indispensable part of our lives:[36]

> Karl and Dorsey Gude of East Lansing, Michigan, can remember simpler mornings not too long ago. They sat together and chatted as they ate breakfast and read the newspaper and competed only with the television for the attention of their two teenage sons. That was so last century. Today, Karl wakes around 6:00 AM to check his work e-mail and his Facebook and Twitter accounts. The two boys, Cole and Erik, start each morning with text messages, video games, and Facebook. Dorsey cracks open her laptop right after breakfast. The Gudes' sons sleep with their phones next to their beds, so they start the day with text messages in place of alarm clocks. Karl, an instructor at Michigan State University, sends texts to his two sons to wake them up. "We use texting as an in-house intercom," he says. "I could just walk upstairs, but they always answer their texts." This is morning in the Internet age. After six to eight hours of network deprivation—also known as sleep—people are increasingly waking up and lunging for cell phones and laptops, sometimes even before swinging their legs to the floor and tending to more biologically current activities.

The digital age has provided marketers with exciting new ways to learn about and track customers and create products and services tailored to individual customer needs. Digital technology has also brought a new wave of communication, advertising, and relationship

▲ **In this digital age, for better or worse, technology has become an indispensable part of our lives. The technology boom provides exciting new opportunities for marketers.**

David Sacks/The Image Bank/Getty Images

Internet
A vast public web of computer networks that connects users of all types all around the world to each other and to an amazingly large information repository.

building tools—ranging from online advertising and video-sharing tools to online social networks and mobile phone apps. The digital shift means that marketers can no longer expect consumers to always seek them out. Nor can they always control conversations about their brands. The new digital world makes it easy for consumers to take marketing content that once lived only in advertising or on a brand Web site with them wherever they go and share it with friends. More than just add-ons to traditional marketing channels, the new digital media must be fully integrated into the marketer's customer-relationship-building efforts.

The most dramatic digital technology is the **Internet**. Almost 85 percent of the U.S. population now has Internet access. On a typical day, 62 percent of American adults check their e-mail, 49 percent use Google or another search engine to find information, 43 percent get the news, 38 percent keep in touch with friends on social-networking sites such as Facebook and LinkedIn, and 23 percent watch a video on a video-sharing site such as YouTube. And by 2020, many experts believe, the Internet will be accessed primarily via a mobile device operated by voice, touch, and even thought or "mind-controlled human-computer interaction."[37]

Online marketing is now the fastest-growing form of marketing. These days, it's hard to find a company that doesn't use the Web in a significant way. In addition to the click-only dot-coms, most traditional brick-and-mortar companies have now become *click-and-mortar* companies. They have ventured online to attract new customers and build stronger relationships with existing ones. Today, more than 75 percent of American online users use the Internet to shop. Last year, consumer online retail spending topped $143 billion, up more than 11 percent over the previous year.[38] Business-to-business (B-to-B) online commerce is also booming.

Thus, the technology boom is providing exciting new opportunities for marketers. We will explore the impact of digital marketing technologies in future chapters, especially Chapter 14.

The Growth of Not-for-Profit Marketing

In recent years, marketing has also become a major part of the strategies of many not-for-profit organizations, such as colleges, hospitals, museums, zoos, symphony orchestras, and even churches. The nation's not-for-profits face stiff competition for support and membership. Sound marketing can help them attract membership, funds, and support.[39]

For example, not-for-profit St. Jude Children's Research Hospital has a special mission: "Finding cures. Saving children." Named the most-trusted charity in the nation by Harris Interactive, St. Jude serves some 5,700 patients each year and is the nation's top children's cancer hospital. What's even more special is that St. Jude does not deny any child treatment for financial reasons—families never have to pay for treatment not covered by insurance. So how does St. Jude support its $1.6 million daily operating budget? By raising funds through powerhouse marketing:[40]

This past winter, St. Jude Children's Hospital was about as ever-present as Santa Claus. It was in public service announcements (PSAs), in the press box on the lapel pins of Fox Sports announcers, on air with "American Chopper" on the Discovery Channel, in holiday gift cards, in Facebook news feeds, at the checkout at Target, and at the Domino's pizza counter. None of this happened by chance. Rather, it resulted from high-powered marketing. St. Jude targets a broad cross-section of consumers using a mix of event marketing, celebrity star power, and corporate partnerships. Fundraising efforts include everything from PSAs and a sophisticated Internet presence to Trike-a-thons and Math-a-thons to an Up 'Til Dawn student challenge and a Dream Home Giveaway. The result is a pervasive brand that brings in hundreds of millions of dollars each year—$692 million last year alone—from preschoolers and professionals to eighth-graders and 80-year-olds.

▲ **Not-for-profit marketing: St. Jude aggressively markets its powerful mission—"Finding Cures. Saving Children."**

AP Images/PRNewsFoto/St. Jude Children's Research Hospital

St. Jude counts Target, Domino's, Williams-Sonoma, Regal Cinemas, and Expedia among the more than 50 partners that participate in its annual Thanks and Giving campaign, ▶ which asks consumers to "give thanks for the healthy kids in your life, and give to those who are not." Companies ask for dollar add-ons at the register, donate a portion of sales during specified times, or promote specific products that benefit St. Jude. St. Jude makes full use of every connection. For example, when Fox Sports named St. Jude its charity partner last year, St. Jude invited on-air talent to its Memphis campus to meet with patient families. ("When people set foot on this campus, it forever changes their lives, and they want to do more," says St. Jude's chief marketing officer.) It created PSAs featuring Fox Sports personalities, along with Game Day Give Back, which encouraged consumers to host football-viewing parties to benefit St. Jude. An 11-year-old St. Jude patient even went head to head with "Fox NFL Sunday" co-host Terry Bradshaw, picking the week's winners throughout the season and participating in Fox Sports' Super Bowl pre-game show.

Government agencies have also shown an increased interest in marketing. For example, the U.S. military has a marketing plan to attract recruits to its different services, and various government agencies are now designing *social marketing campaigns* to encourage energy conservation and concern for the environment or discourage smoking, excessive drinking, and drug use. Even the once-stodgy U.S. Postal Service has developed innovative marketing to sell commemorative stamps, promote its priority mail services, and lift its image as a contemporary and competitive organization. In all, the U.S. government is the nation's 33rd largest advertiser, with an annual advertising budget of more than $1 billion.[41]

Rapid Globalization

As they are redefining their customer relationships, marketers are also taking a fresh look at the ways in which they relate with the broader world around them. Today, almost every company, large or small, is touched in some way by global competition. A neighborhood florist buys its flowers from Mexican nurseries, and a large U.S. electronics manufacturer competes in its home markets with giant Korean rivals. A fledgling Internet retailer finds itself receiving orders from all over the world at the same time that an American consumer-goods producer introduces new products into emerging markets abroad.

American firms have been challenged at home by the skillful marketing of European and Asian multinationals. Companies such as Toyota, Nokia, Nestlé, and Samsung have often outperformed their U.S. competitors in American markets. Similarly, U.S. companies in a wide range of industries have developed truly global operations, making and selling their products worldwide. Quintessentially American McDonald's now serves 58 million customers daily in more than 32,000 local restaurants in 117 countries worldwide—66 percent of its corporate revenues come from outside the United States. Similarly, Nike markets in more than 180 countries, with non-U.S. sales accounting for 65 percent of its worldwide sales.[42] Today, companies are not just selling more of their locally produced goods in international markets; they are also sourcing more supplies and components abroad.

Thus, managers in countries around the world are increasingly taking a global, not just local, view of the company's industry, competitors, and opportunities. They are asking: What is global marketing? How does it differ from domestic marketing? How do global competitors and forces affect our business? To what extent should we "go global"? We will discuss the global marketplace in more detail in Chapter 15.

Sustainable Marketing— The Call for More Social Responsibility

Marketers are reexamining their relationships with social values and responsibilities and with the very Earth that sustains us. As the worldwide consumerism and environmentalism movements mature, today's marketers are being called on to develop *sustainable marketing*

Sustainable marketing: Patagonia believes in "using business to inspire solutions to the environmental crisis." It backs these words by pledging at least 1 percent of its sales or 10 percent of its profits, whichever is greater, to the protection of the natural environment.

Patagonia, Inc.

practices. Corporate ethics and social responsibility have become hot topics for almost every business. And few companies can ignore the renewed and very demanding environmental movement. Every company action can affect customer relationships. Today's customers expect companies to deliver value in a socially and environmentally responsible way.

The social-responsibility and environmental movements will place even stricter demands on companies in the future. Some companies resist these movements, budging only when forced by legislation or organized consumer outcries. Forward-looking companies, however, readily accept their responsibilities to the world around them. They view sustainable marketing as an opportunity to do well by doing good. They seek ways to profit by serving immediate needs and the best long-run interests of their customers and communities.

Some companies, such as Patagonia, Ben & Jerry's, Timberland, Method, and others, practice *caring capitalism*, setting themselves apart by being civic minded and responsible. They build social responsibility and action into their company value and mission statements. For example, when it comes to environmental responsibility, ▶ outdoor gear marketer Patagonia is "committed to the core." "Those of us who work here share a strong commitment to protecting undomesticated lands and waters," says the company's Web site. "We believe in using business to inspire solutions to the environmental crisis." Patagonia backs these words with actions. Each year it pledges at least 1 percent of its sales or 10 percent of its profits, whichever is greater, to the protection of the natural environment.[43] We will revisit the topic of sustainable marketing in greater detail in Chapter 16.

Author Comment ▶
Remember Figure 1.1 outlining the marketing process? Now, based on everything we've discussed in this chapter, we'll expand that figure to provide a road map for learning marketing throughout the remainder of this text.

So, What Is Marketing? Pulling It All Together

At the start of this chapter, Figure 1.1 presented a simple model of the marketing process. Now that we've discussed all the steps in the process, ▶ **Figure 1.6** presents an expanded model that will help you pull it all together. What is marketing? Simply put, marketing is the process of building profitable customer relationships by creating value for customers and capturing value in return.

The first four steps of the marketing process focus on creating value for customers. The company first gains a full understanding of the marketplace by researching customer needs and managing marketing information. It then designs a customer-driven marketing strategy based on the answers to two simple questions. The first question is "What consumers will we serve?" (market segmentation and targeting). Good marketing companies know that they cannot serve all customers in every way. Instead, they need to focus their resources on the customers they can serve best and most profitably. The second marketing strategy question is "How can we best serve targeted customers?" (differentiation and positioning). Here, the marketer outlines a value proposition that spells out what values the company will deliver to win target customers.

With its marketing strategy chosen, the company now constructs an integrated marketing program—consisting of a blend of the four marketing mix elements—the four Ps—that transforms the marketing strategy into real value for customers. The company develops product offers and creates strong brand identities for them. It prices these offers to create real customer value and distributes the offers to make them available to target consumers. Finally, the company designs promotion programs that communicate the value proposition to target customers and persuade them to act on the market offering.

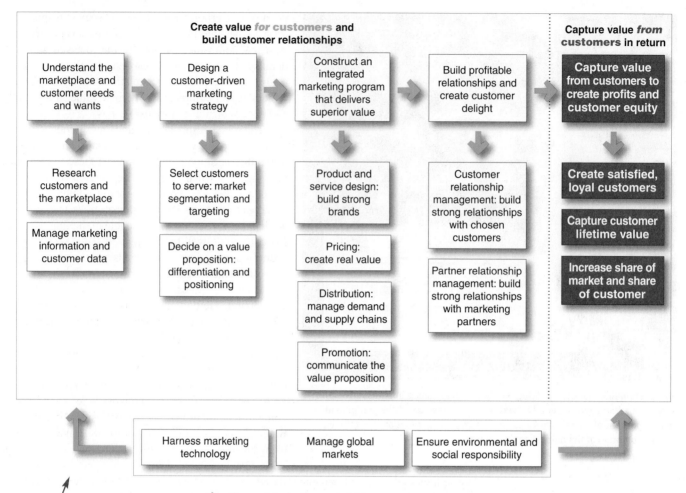

Figure 1.6 An Expanded Model of the Marketing Process

This expanded version of Figure 1.1 at the beginning of the chapter provides a good road map for the rest of the text. The underlying concept of the entire text is that marketing creates value *for* customers in order to capture value *from* customers in return.

Perhaps the most important step in the marketing process involves building value-laden, profitable relationships with target customers. Throughout the process, marketers practice customer relationship management to create customer satisfaction and delight. In creating customer value and relationships, however, the company cannot go it alone. It must work closely with marketing partners both inside the company and throughout its marketing system. Thus, beyond practicing good customer relationship management, firms must also practice good partner relationship management.

The first four steps in the marketing process create value *for* customers. In the final step, the company reaps the rewards of its strong customer relationships by capturing value *from* customers. Delivering superior customer value creates highly satisfied customers who will buy more and buy again. This helps the company capture customer lifetime value and greater share of customer. The result is increased long-term customer equity for the firm.

Finally, in the face of today's changing marketing landscape, companies must take into account three additional factors. In building customer and partner relationships, they must harness marketing technology, take advantage of global opportunities, and ensure that they act in an environmentally and socially responsible way.

Figure 1.6 provides a good road map to future chapters of this text. Chapters 1 and 2 introduce the marketing process, with a focus on building customer relationships and capturing value from customers. Chapters 3 through 5 address the first step of the marketing process—understanding the marketing environment, managing marketing information, and understanding consumer and business buyer behavior. In Chapter 6, we look more deeply into the two major marketing strategy decisions: selecting which customers to serve (segmentation and targeting) and determining a value proposition (differentiation and positioning). Chapters 7 through 14 discuss the marketing mix variables, one by one. The final two chapters examine special marketing considerations: global marketing and sustainable marketing.

REST STOP | REVIEWING THE CONCEPTS

MyMarketingLab

Now that you have completed the chapter, return to www.mymktlab.com to experience and apply the concepts and to explore the additional study materials for this chapter.

CHAPTER REVIEW AND KEY TERMS

Objectives Review

Today's successful companies—whether large or small, for-profit or not-for-profit, domestic or global—share a strong customer focus and a heavy commitment to marketing. The goal of marketing is to build and manage profitable customer relationships.

> **OBJECTIVE 1 Define marketing and outline the steps in the marketing process.** (pp 4–6)

Marketing is the process by which companies create value for customers and build strong customer relationships in order to capture value from customers in return.

The marketing process involves five steps. The first four steps create value *for* customers. First, marketers need to understand the marketplace and customer needs and wants. Next, marketers design a customer-driven marketing strategy with the goal of getting, keeping, and growing target customers. In the third step, marketers construct a marketing program that actually delivers superior value. All of these steps form the basis for the fourth step, building profitable customer relationships and creating customer delight. In the final step, the company reaps the rewards of strong customer relationships by capturing value *from* customers.

> **OBJECTIVE 2 Explain the importance of understanding customers and the marketplace and identify the five core marketplace concepts.** (pp 6–8)

Outstanding marketing companies go to great lengths to learn about and understand their customers' *needs*, *wants*, and *demands*. This understanding helps them to design want-satisfying market offerings and build value-laden customer relationships by which they can capture *customer lifetime value* and greater *share of customer*. The result is increased long-term *customer equity* for the firm.

The core marketplace concepts are needs, wants, and demands; market offerings (products, services, and experiences); value and satisfaction; exchange and relationships; and markets. Wants are the form taken by human needs when shaped by culture and individual personality. When backed by buying power, wants become demands. Companies address needs by putting forth a value proposition, a set of benefits that they promise to consumers to satisfy their needs. The value proposition is fulfilled through a market offering, which delivers customer value and satisfaction, resulting in long-term exchange relationships with customers.

> **OBJECTIVE 3 Identify the key elements of a customer-driven marketing strategy and discuss the marketing management orientations that guide marketing strategy.** (pp 9–13)

To design a winning marketing strategy, the company must first decide *whom* it will serve. It does this by dividing the market into segments of customers (*market segmentation*) and selecting which segments it will cultivate (*target marketing*). Next, the company must decide *how* it will serve targeted customers (how it will *differentiate and position* itself in the marketplace).

Marketing management can adopt one of five competing market orientations. The *production concept* holds that management's task is to improve production efficiency and bring down prices. The *product concept* holds that consumers favor products that offer the most in quality, performance, and innovative features; thus, little promotional effort is required. The *selling concept* holds that consumers will not buy enough of an organization's products unless it undertakes a large-scale selling and promotion effort. The *marketing concept* holds that achieving organizational goals depends on determining the needs and wants of target markets and delivering the desired satisfactions more effectively and efficiently than competitors do.

The *societal marketing concept* holds that generating customer satisfaction *and* long-run societal well-being through sustainable marketing strategies is key to both achieving the company's goals and fulfilling its responsibilities.

▷ **OBJECTIVE 4** Discuss customer relationship management and identify strategies for creating value *for* customers and capturing value *from* customers in return. (pp 13–23)

Broadly defined, *customer relationship management* is the process of building and maintaining profitable customer relationships by delivering superior customer value and satisfaction. The aim of customer relationship management is to produce high *customer equity,* the total combined customer lifetime values of all of the company's customers. The key to building lasting relationships is the creation of superior *customer value* and *satisfaction.*

Companies want not only to acquire profitable customers but also build relationships that will keep them and grow "share of customer." Different types of customers require different customer relationship management strategies. The marketer's aim is to build the *right relationships* with the *right customers.* In return for creating value *for* targeted customers, the company captures value *from* customers in the form of profits and customer equity.

In building customer relationships, good marketers realize that they cannot go it alone. They must work closely with marketing partners inside and outside the company. In addition to being good at customer relationship management, they must also be good at *partner relationship management.*

▷ **OBJECTIVE 5** Describe the major trends and forces that are changing the marketing landscape in this age of relationships. (pp 23–29)

Dramatic changes are occurring in the marketing arena. The Great Recession left many consumers short of both money and confidence, creating a new age of consumer frugality that will last well into the future. More than ever, marketers must now emphasize the *value* in their value propositions. The challenge is to balance a brand's value proposition with current times while also enhancing its long-term equity.

The boom in digital technology has created exciting new ways to learn about and relate to individual customers. It has also allowed new approaches by which marketers can target consumers more selectively and build closer, two-way customer relationships in the digital era.

In an increasingly smaller world, many marketers are now connected *globally* with their customers and marketing partners. Today, almost every company, large or small, is touched in some way by global competition. Today's marketers are also reexamining their ethical and societal responsibilities. Marketers are being called to take greater responsibility for the social and environmental impact of their actions. Finally, in recent years, marketing also has become a major part of the strategies of many not-for-profit organizations, such as colleges, hospitals, museums, zoos, symphony orchestras, and even churches.

Pulling it all together, as discussed throughout the chapter, the major new developments in marketing can be summed up in a single word: *relationships*. Today, marketers of all kinds are taking advantage of new opportunities for building relationships with their customers, their marketing partners, and the world around them.

Key Terms

Objective 1
Marketing (p 5)

Objective 2
Needs (p 6)
Wants (p 6)
Demands (p 6)
Market offerings (p 6)
Marketing myopia (p 7)
Exchange (p 7)
Market (p 8)

Objective 3
Marketing management (p 9)
Production concept (p 10)
Product concept (p 10)
Selling concept (p 10)
Marketing concept (p 10)
Societal marketing concept (p 11)

Objective 4
Customer relationship management (p 13)
Customer-perceived value (p 13)

Customer satisfaction (p 14)
Customer-managed relationships (p 18)
Consumer-generated marketing (p 19)
Partner relationship management
    (p 20)
Customer lifetime value (p 21)
Share of customer (p 21)
Customer equity (p 22)

Objective 5
Internet (p 27)

DISCUSSION AND CRITICAL THINKING

Discussion Questions

1. Define marketing and discuss how it is more than just "telling and selling." (AACSB: Communication; Reflective Thinking)
2. Marketing has been criticized because it "makes people buy things they don't really need." Refute or support this accusation. (AACSB: Communication; Reflective Thinking)
3. What is a market offering and why should marketers avoid focusing on just their offering to potential buyers? (AACSB: Communication; Reflective Thinking)
4. What is a customer-driven marketing strategy and how can a company design one? (AACSB: Communication)
5. When implementing customer relationship management, why might a business desire fewer customers over more customers? Shouldn't the focus of marketing be to acquire as many customers as possible? (AACSB: Communication; Reflective Thinking)
6. Discuss trends impacting marketing and the implications of these trends on how marketers deliver value to customers. (AACSB: Communication)

Critical Thinking Exercises

1. Form a small group of three or four students. Discuss a need or want you have that is not adequately satisfied by any offerings currently in the marketplace. Think of a product or service that will satisfy that need or want. Describe how you will differentiate and position your offering in the marketplace and develop the marketing program for your offering. Present your ideas to the other groups. (AACSB: Communication; Reflective Thinking)
2. Consider a product that you use or a retailer you patronage frequently. Estimate how much you are worth to the retailer or manufacturer of the brand you prefer if you remain loyal to that marketer for the rest of your life (your customer lifetime value). What factors should you consider when deriving an estimate of your lifetime value to the company? How can the company increase your lifetime value? (AACSB: Communication; Reflective Thinking; Analytic Reasoning)
3. Learn about careers in marketing at http://careers-in-marketing.com/. Interview someone who works in one of the marketing jobs described on this Web site and ask him or her the following questions:
   a. What does your job entail?
   b. How did you get to this point in your career? Is this what you thought you'd be doing when you grew up? What influenced you to get into this field?
   c. What education is necessary for this job?
   d. What advice can you give to college students?
   e. Add one additional question that you create.

   Write a brief report of the responses to your questions and explain why you would or would not be interested in working in this field. (AACSB: Communication; Reflective Thinking)

MINICASES AND APPLICATIONS

Marketing Technology Apple and Adobe—Flash Clash

Apple's iDevices— iPods, iPhones, and iPads—are wildly popular. But where's the flash? Adobe Flash, that is. Adobe's Flash, the long-standing multimedia platform behind approximately 75 percent of the animated and streaming audio and video on the Internet, is not supported by Apple's devices. Many purchasers were disappointed after spending hundreds of dollars on sleek iPads only to realize they couldn't play their favorite Internet game or watch that funny video on their device. And they still can't, even with the second generation device, the iPad2. It seems Apple's late founder and CEO, Steve Jobs, didn't like Flash and would not support it on Apple's devices. Instead, app developers must conform to Apple's operating system and existing applications on the Web must convert to HTML5 to play on an Apple product. Adobe's co-founders claim Apple is "undermining the next chapter of the Web" and bloggers exclaim this is not just an "Adobe/Apple problem . . . but an Apple/World problem."

1. Does Apple appear to embrace the marketing concept? (AACSB: Communication; Reflective Thinking; Technology)
2. Research the controversy surrounding this issue and debate whether Apple did the right thing for its customers by not including the ubiquitous Adobe Flash software on Apple's products. (AACSB: Communication; Reflective Thinking)

Marketing Ethics   Marketing a Killer Product

Sixty years ago, about 45 percent of Americans smoked cigarettes, but now the smoking rate is less than 20 percent. This decline results from knowledge of the potential health dangers of smoking and from marketing restrictions for this product. Although smoking rates are declining in most developed nations, more and more consumers in developing nations, such as Russia and China, are puffing away. Smoker rates in some countries run as high as 40 percent. Developing nations account for more than 70 percent of world tobacco consumption and marketers are fueling this growth. Most of these nations do not have the restrictions prevalent in developed nations, such as advertising bans, warning labels, and distribution restrictions. Consequently, predictions are that one billion people worldwide will die this century from smoking-related ailments.

1. Given the extreme health risks, should marketers stop selling cigarettes even though they are legal and demanded by consumers? Should cigarette marketers continue to use marketing tactics that are restricted in one country in other countries where they are not restricted? (AACSB: Communication; Ethical Reasoning)
2. Research the history of cigarette marketing in the United States. Are there any new restrictions with respect to marketing this product? (AACSB: Communication; Reflective Thinking)

Marketing by the Numbers   Marketing Expenditures and Salaries

Marketing is expensive! A 30-second advertising spot during the Super Bowl costs more than $3 million, and that doesn't include the $500,000 or more to produce the commercial. Anheuser-Busch usually purchases multiple spots each year. Similarly, sponsoring one car during one NASCAR race costs $500,000. But Sprint, the sponsor of the popular Sprint Cup, pays much more than that. And many marketers sponsor more than one car in more than one race. Want customers to order your product by phone? That will cost you $8 to $13 per order. Or how about a sales representative calling on customers? About $100 per sales call, and that's if the rep doesn't have to get on an airplane and stay in a hotel, which can be very costly considering some companies have thousands of sales reps calling on thousands of customers. And that $1-off coupon for Tropicana orange juice that you got in the Sunday newspaper? It costs Tropicana more than $1 when you redeem it at the store. These are all examples of just one marketing element—promotion. Marketing costs also include the costs of product research and development, the costs

of distributing products to buyers, and the costs of all the employees working in marketing.

1. Select a publicly traded company and research how much was spent on marketing activities in the most recent year of available data. What percentage of sales does marketing expenditures represent for the company? Have these expenditures increased or decreased over the past five years? Write a brief report of your findings. (AACSB Communication; Analytic Reasoning)
2. Search the Internet for salary information regarding jobs in marketing from a Web site such as www.marketingsalaries.com/home/national_averages.htm?function=# or a similar Web site. What is the national average for five different jobs in marketing? How do the averages compare in different areas of the country? Write a brief report on your findings. (AACSB: Communication; Use of IT; Reflective Thinking)

Video Case   Zappos

These days, online retailers are a dime a dozen, and many don't make a lasting impact. Yet, in only a short time, Zappos has become a billion dollar e-tailer and an important part of the Amazon.com empire. How did Zappos hit the dot-com jackpot? By providing its customers with some of the best service available anywhere. Zappos showers its customers with such perks as free shipping both ways, surprise upgrades to overnight service, a 365-day return policy, and a call center that is always open. Customers are also delighted by employees who are empowered to spontaneously hand out rewards based on unique needs.

With such attention to customer service, it's no surprise that Zappos has an almost cult-like following of repeat customers.

However, remaining committed to the philosophy that the customer is always right can be challenging. This video highlights some of the dilemmas that can arise from a highly customer-centric strategy. Zappos also demonstrates the ultimate rewards they receive from keeping that commitment.

After viewing the video featuring Zappos, answer the following questions:

1. How would you describe Zappos' market offering?
2. What is Zappos' value proposition? How does it relate to its market offering?
3. How does Zappos build long-term customer relationships?

Company Cases   1 Converse / 4 Meredith / 10 Pandora

See Appendix 1 for cases appropriate for this chapter. **Case 1, Converse: Shaping the Customer Experience.** Converse continues to provide customers with the authentic experience they desire by allowing them to shape that experience. **Case 4, Meredith: Thanks to Good Marketing Information, Meredith *Knows* Women.** Through its massive database and expertise in managing information, Meredith builds and maintains strong relationships with women. **Case 10: Pandora: Disintermediator or Disintermediated?** Using an ingenious mathematical algorithm, music service Pandora knows exactly what customers want to hear.

2

Company and Marketing Strategy
Partnering to Build Customer Relationships

CHAPTER ROAD MAP

Objective Outline

▷ **OBJECTIVE 1 Explain company-wide strategic planning and its four steps.** Company-Wide Strategic Planning: Defining Marketing's Role (38–41)

▷ **OBJECTIVE 2 Discuss how to design business portfolios and develop growth strategies.** Designing the Business Portfolio (41–46)

▷ **OBJECTIVE 3 Explain marketing's role in strategic planning and how marketing works with its partners to create and deliver customer value.** Planning Marketing: Partnering to Build Customer Relationships (46–48)

▷ **OBJECTIVE 4 Describe the elements of a customer-driven marketing strategy and mix and the forces that influence it.** Marketing Strategy and the Marketing Mix (48–54)

▷ **OBJECTIVE 5 List the marketing management functions, including the elements of a marketing plan, and discuss the importance of measuring and managing return on marketing investment.** Managing the Marketing Effort (54–58); Measuring and Managing Return on Marketing Investment (58–59)

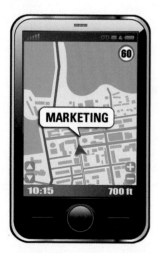

Previewing the Concepts

In the first chapter, we explored the marketing process by which companies create value for consumers in order to capture value from them in return. In this leg of the journey, we dig deeper into steps two and three of that process: designing customer-driven marketing strategies and constructing integrated marketing programs. First, we look at the organization's overall strategic planning, which guides marketing strategy and planning. Next, we discuss how, guided by the strategic plan, marketers partner closely with others inside and outside the firm to create value for customers. We then examine marketing strategy and planning—how marketers choose target markets, position their market offerings, develop a marketing mix, and manage their marketing programs. Finally, we look at the important step of measuring and managing return on marketing investment (marketing ROI).

Let's begin by looking at McDonald's and a good company and marketing strategy story. When it burst onto the scene more than 50 years ago, McDonald's perfected the modern fast-food concept and grew rapidly. By the turn of the twenty-first century, however, McDonald's once-shiny Golden Arches seemed to be losing some of their luster. But thanks to a new customer-focused strategic blueprint—called the "Plan to Win"—McDonald's launched an amazing turnaround that once again has both customers and the company humming the chain's catchy jingle, "i'm lovin' it."

First Stop

McDonald's: A Customer-Focused "Plan to Win" Strategy

▲ McDonald's new customer-focused strategy—called the "Plan to Win"—got the company back to the profitable basics of creating exceptional customer experiences.

Jb Reed/Bloomberg/Getty Images

More than half a century ago, Ray Kroc, a 52-year-old salesman of milk-shake-mixing machines, set out on a mission to transform the way Americans eat. In 1955, Kroc discovered a string of seven restaurants owned by Richard and Maurice McDonald. He saw the McDonald brothers' fast-food concept as a perfect fit for America's increasingly on-the-go, time-squeezed, family-oriented lifestyles. Kroc bought the small chain for $2.7 million, and the rest is history.

From the start, Kroc preached a motto of QSCV—quality, service, cleanliness, and value. These goals became mainstays in McDonald's corporate and marketing strategy. By applying these values, the company perfected the fast-food concept—delivering convenient, good-quality food at affordable prices.

McDonald's grew quickly to become the world's largest fast-feeder. The fast-food giant's more than 32,700 restaurants worldwide now serve 64 million customers each day, racking up systemwide sales of more than $77 billion annually. The Golden Arches are one of the world's most familiar symbols; other than Santa Claus, no character in the world is more recognizable than Ronald McDonald.

In the mid-1990s, however, McDonald's fortunes began to turn. The company appeared to fall out of touch with customers. Americans were looking for fresher, better-tasting food and more contemporary atmospheres. They were also seeking healthier eating options. In a new age of health-conscious consumers and $5 lattes at Starbucks, McDonald's strategy seemed a bit out of step with the times. One analyst sums it up this way:

McDonald's was struggling to find its identity amid a flurry of new competitors and changing consumer tastes. The company careened from one failed idea to another. It tried to keep pace by offering pizza, toasted deli sandwiches, and the Arch Deluxe, a heavily advertised new burger that flopped. It bought into nonburger franchises like Chipotle and Boston Market. It also tinkered with its menu, no longer toasting the buns, switching pickles, and changing the special sauce on Big Macs. None of these things worked. All the while, McDonald's continued opening new restaurants at a ferocious pace, as many as 2,000 per year. The new stores helped sales, but customer service and cleanliness declined because the company couldn't hire and train good workers fast enough. Meanwhile, McDonald's increasingly became a target for nutritionists and social activists, who accused the chain of contributing to the nation's obesity epidemic with "super size" French fries and sodas as well as Happy Meals that lure kids with the reward of free toys.

> Fast-food giant McDonald's knows the importance of good strategic and marketing planning. Thanks to its new customer-focused strategic blueprint—called the Plan to Win—customers and the company alike are once again humming the chain's catchy jingle, "i'm lovin' it."

Although McDonald's remained the world's most visited fast-food chain, the once-shiny Golden Arches lost some of their luster. Sales growth slumped, and its market share fell by more than 3 percent between 1997 and 2003. In 2002, the company posted its first-ever quarterly loss. In the face of changing customer value expectations, the company had lost sight of its fundamental value proposition. "We got distracted from the most important thing: hot, high-quality food at a great value at the speed and convenience of McDonald's," says current CEO Jim Skinner. The company and its strategy needed to adapt.

In early 2003, a troubled McDonald's announced a new strategic blueprint—what it now calls its "Plan to Win." At the heart of this strategic plan was a new mission statement that refocused the company on its customers. According to the analyst:

> The company's mission was changed from "being the world's best quick-service restaurant" to "being our customers' favorite place and way to eat." The Plan to Win lays out where McDonald's wants to be and how it plans to get there, all centered on five basics of an exceptional customer experience: people, products, place, price, and promotion. While the five Ps smack of corny corporate speak, company officials maintain that they have profoundly changed McDonald's strategic direction and priorities. The plan, and the seemingly simple shift in mission, forced McDonald's and its employees to focus on quality, service, and the restaurant experience rather than simply providing the cheapest, most convenient option to customers. The Plan to Win—which barely fits on a single sheet of paper—is now treated as sacred inside the company.

Under the Plan to Win, McDonald's got back to the basic business of taking care of customers. The goal was to get "better, not just bigger." The company halted rapid expansion and instead poured money back into improving the food, the service, the atmosphere, and marketing at existing outlets. McDonald's redecorated its restaurants with clean, simple, more-modern interiors and amenities such as live plants, Wi-Fi access, and flat-screen TVs showing cable news. Play areas in some new restaurants now feature video games and even stationary bicycles with video screens. To make the customer experience more convenient, McDonald's stores now open earlier to extend breakfast hours and stay open longer to serve late-night diners—more than one-third of McDonald's restaurants are now open 24 hours a day.

A reworked menu, crafted by Chef Daniel Coudreaut, a Culinary Institute of America graduate and former chef at the Four Seasons in Dallas, now provides more choice and variety, including healthier options, such as Chicken McNuggets made with white meat, a line of Snack Wraps, low-fat "milk jugs," apple slices, Premium Salads, and the Angus burger. Within only a year of introducing its Premium Salads, McDonald's became the world's largest salad seller. The company also launched a major multifaceted education campaign that underscores the important interplay between eating right and staying active.

McDonald's rediscovered dedication to customer value sparked a remarkable turnaround. Since announcing its Plan to Win, McDonald's sales have increased by more than 40 percent, and profits have more than tripled. In 2008, when the stock market lost one-third of its value—the worst loss since the Great Depression—McDonald's stock gained nearly 6 percent, making it one of only two companies in the Dow Jones Industrial Average whose share price rose during that year (the other was Walmart). From 2008 through the end of 2010, as the economy and the restaurant industry as a whole struggled, McDonald's outperformed its competitors by a notable margin. Despite the tough times, McDonald's achieved a lofty 12.7 percent three-year compound annual total return to investors versus the S&P 500 average of −2.9 percent.

Thus, McDonald's now appears to have the right strategy for the times. Now, once again, when you think McDonald's, you think convenience and value. The contemporary menu features iconic favorites along with new products that today's consumer wants—whether it's Premium Salads, snack wraps, Angus Burgers, or McCafé coffees and smoothies. And that has customers and the company alike humming the chain's catchy jingle, "i'm lovin' it."[1]

MyMarketingLab

Visit www.mymktlab.com to find activities that help you learn and review in order to succeed in this chapter.

L ike McDonald's, outstanding marketing organizations employ strongly customer-driven marketing strategies and programs that create customer value and relationships. These marketing strategies and programs, however, are guided by broader company-wide strategic plans, which must also be customer focused. To understand the role of marketing, we must first understand the organization's overall strategic planning process.

Author Comment ▶
Company-wide strategic planning guides the company's marketing strategy and planning. Like marketing strategy, the company's broader strategy must also be customer focused.

Company-Wide Strategic Planning: Defining Marketing's Role

Each company must find the game plan for long-run survival and growth that makes the most sense given its specific situation, opportunities, objectives, and resources. This is the focus of **strategic planning**—the process of developing and maintaining a strategic fit between the organization's goals and capabilities and its changing marketing opportunities.

Strategic planning sets the stage for the rest of planning in the firm. Companies usually prepare annual plans, long-range plans, and strategic plans. The annual and long-range plans deal with the company's current businesses and how to keep them going. In contrast,

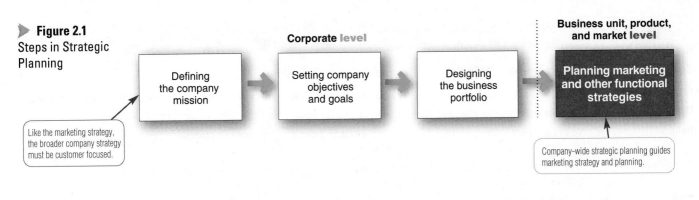

Figure 2.1
Steps in Strategic
Planning

Like the marketing strategy, the broader company strategy must be customer focused.

Corporate level

Defining the company mission → Setting company objectives and goals → Designing the business portfolio →

Business unit, product, and market level

Planning marketing and other functional strategies

Company-wide strategic planning guides marketing strategy and planning.

Strategic planning

The process of developing and maintaining a strategic fit between the organization's goals and capabilities and its changing marketing opportunities.

the strategic plan involves adapting the firm to take advantage of opportunities in its constantly changing environment.

At the corporate level, the company starts the strategic planning process by defining its overall purpose and mission (see ▶ **Figure 2.1**). This mission is then turned into detailed supporting objectives that guide the entire company. Next, headquarters decides what portfolio of businesses and products is best for the company and how much support to give each one. In turn, each business and product develops detailed marketing and other departmental plans that support the company-wide plan. Thus, marketing planning occurs at the business-unit, product, and market levels. It supports company strategic planning with more detailed plans for specific marketing opportunities.

Defining a Market-Oriented Mission

Mission statement

A statement of the organization's purpose—what it wants to accomplish in the larger environment.

An organization exists to accomplish something, and this purpose should be clearly stated. Forging a sound mission begins with the following questions: What *is* our business? Who is the customer? What do consumers value? What *should* our business be? These simple-sounding questions are among the most difficult the company will ever have to answer. Successful companies continuously raise these questions and answer them carefully and completely.

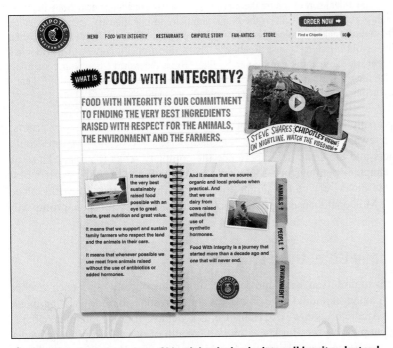

Many organizations develop formal mission statements that answer these questions. A **mission statement** is a statement of the organization's purpose—what it wants to accomplish in the larger environment. A clear mission statement acts as an "invisible hand" that guides people in the organization.

Some companies define their missions myopically in product or technology terms ("We make and sell furniture" or "We are a chemical-processing firm"). But mission statements should be *market oriented* and defined in terms of satisfying basic customer needs. Products and technologies eventually become outdated, but basic market needs may last forever. For example, Facebook doesn't define itself as just an online social network. Its mission is to "give people the power to share and make the world more open and connected." Likewise, Chipotle's mission isn't to sell burritos. ▶ Instead, the restaurant promises "Food with Integrity," highlighting its commitment to the immediate and long-term welfare of customers and the environment. Chipotle serves natural, sustainable, local ingredients raised "with respect for the animals, the environment, and the farmers." ▶ **Table 2.1** provides several other examples of product-oriented versus market-oriented business definitions.[2]

▲ Market-oriented missions: Chipotle's mission isn't to sell burritos. Instead, it promises "Food with Integrity," highlighting its commitment to good food made from natural, local, and sustainably raised ingredients.

© Chipotle Mexican Grill, Inc.

▶ **Table 2.1**	Market-Oriented Business Definitions	
Company	**Product-Oriented Definition**	**Market-Oriented Definition**
Facebook	We are an online social network.	We give people the power to share and make the world more open and connected.
General Mills	We make consumer food products.	We nourish lives by making them healthier, easier, and richer.
Hulu	We are an online video service.	We help people find and enjoy the world's premium video content when, where, and how they want it.
Home Depot	We sell tools and home repair and improvement items.	We empower consumers to achieve the homes of their dreams.
NASA	We explore outer space.	We reach for new heights and reveal the unknown so that what we do and learn will benefit all humankind.
Nike	We sell athletic shoes and apparel.	We bring inspiration and innovation to every athlete* in the world. (*If you have a body, you are an athlete.)
Revlon	We make cosmetics.	We sell lifestyle and self-expression; success and status; memories, hopes, and dreams.
Ritz-Carlton Hotels & Resorts	We rent rooms.	We create the Ritz-Carlton experience—one that enlivens the senses, instills well-being, and fulfills even the unexpressed wishes and needs of our guests.
Walmart	We run discount stores.	We deliver low prices every day and give ordinary folks the chance to buy the same things as rich people. "Save Money. Live Better."

Mission statements should be meaningful and specific yet motivating. They should emphasize the company's strengths in the marketplace. Too often, mission statements are written for public relations purposes and lack specific, workable guidelines. Says marketing consultant Jack Welch:[3]

> Few leaders actually get the point of forging a mission with real grit and meaning. [Mission statements] have largely devolved into fat-headed jargon. Almost no one can figure out what they mean. [So companies] sort of ignore them or gussy up a vague package deal along the lines of: "our mission is to be the best fill-in-the-blank company in our industry." [Instead, Welch advises, CEOs should] make a choice about how your company will win. Don't mince words! Remember Nike's old mission, "Crush Reebok"? That's directionally correct. And Google's mission statement isn't something namby-pamby like "To be the world's best search engine." It's "To organize the world's information and make it universally accessible and useful." That's simultaneously inspirational, achievable, and completely graspable.

Finally, a company's mission should not be stated as making more sales or profits; profits are only a reward for creating value for customers. Instead, the mission should focus on customers and the customer experience the company seeks to create. Thus, as discussed in our chapter-opening story, McDonald's mission isn't "to be the world's best and most profitable quick-service restaurant"; it's "to be our customers' favorite place and way to eat." If McDonald's accomplishes this customer-focused mission, profits will follow.

Setting Company Objectives and Goals

The company needs to turn its mission into detailed supporting objectives for each level of management. Each manager should have objectives and be responsible for reaching them. For example, most Americans know H. J. Heinz for its ketchup—it sells more than 650 billion bottles of ketchup each year. But Heinz owns a breadth of other food products under a variety of brands, ranging from Heinz and Ore-Ida to Classico. Heinz ties this diverse product portfolio together under this mission: "As the trusted leader in nutrition and wellness, Heinz—the original Pure Food Company—is dedicated to the sustainable health of people, the planet, and our company."

NO ONE GROWS KETCHUP LIKE HEINZ.

That's because every red, ripe tomato in every bottle is grown only from Heinz seeds.
It's what helps us deliver the uniquely thick, rich flavor that America loves.

HEINZ. GROWN, NOT MADE.™

Learn more at www.heinzketchup.com.

▲ Heinz's overall objective is to build profitable customer relationships by developing foods "superior in quality, taste, nutrition, and convenience" that embrace its nutrition and wellness mission.

© 2007 H.J. Heinz Co., L.P.

Business portfolio
The collection of businesses and products that make up the company.

Portfolio analysis
The process by which management evaluates the products and businesses that make up the company.

This broad mission leads to a hierarchy of objectives, including business objectives and marketing objectives. ▶ Heinz's overall objective is to build profitable customer relationships by developing foods "superior in quality, taste, nutrition, and convenience" that embrace its nutrition and wellness mission. It does this by investing heavily in research. However, research is expensive and must be funded through improved profit, so improving profits becomes another major objective for Heinz. Profits can be improved by increasing sales or reducing costs. Sales can be increased by improving the company's share of domestic and international markets. These goals then become the company's current marketing objectives.

Marketing strategies and programs must be developed to support these marketing objectives. To increase its market share, Heinz might broaden its product lines, increase product availability and promotion in existing markets, and expand into new markets. For example, last year Heinz added breakfast products to its Weight Watchers Smart Ones brand. And it experienced double-digit growth in emerging global markets, which now contribute 30 percent of total sales growth.[4]

These are Heinz's broad marketing strategies. Each broad marketing strategy must then be defined in greater detail. For example, increasing the product's promotion may require more advertising and public relations efforts; if so, both requirements will need to be spelled out. In this way, the firm's mission is translated into a set of objectives for the current period.

Designing the Business Portfolio

Guided by the company's mission statement and objectives, management now must plan its business portfolio—the collection of businesses and products that make up the company. The best **business portfolio** is the one that best fits the company's strengths and weaknesses to opportunities in the environment.

Most large companies have complex portfolios of businesses and brands. Strategic and marketing planning for such business portfolios can be a daunting but critical task. For example, ESPN's portfolio consists of more than 50 business entities, ranging from multiple ESPN cable channels to ESPN Radio, ESPN.com, *ESPN The Magazine*, and even ESPN Zone sports-themed restaurants (see Marketing at Work 2.1). In turn, ESPN is just one unit in the even broader, more complex portfolio of its parent company, The Walt Disney Company. The Disney portfolio includes its many Disney theme parks and resorts; Disney studio entertainment (movie, television, and theatrical production companies such as Walt Disney Pictures, Pixar, Touchstone Pictures, and Hollywood Pictures); Disney consumer products (from apparel and toys to interactive games); and a sizable collection of broadcast, cable, radio, and Internet media businesses (including ESPN and the ABC Television Network).

Business portfolio planning involves two steps. First, the company must analyze its *current* business portfolio and determine which businesses should receive more, less, or no investment. Second, it must shape the *future* portfolio by developing strategies for growth and downsizing.

Analyzing the Current Business Portfolio

The major activity in strategic planning is business **portfolio analysis**, whereby management evaluates the products and businesses that make up the company. The company will want to put strong resources into its more profitable businesses and phase down or drop its weaker ones.

Management's first step is to identify the key businesses that make up the company, called *strategic business units* (SBUs). An SBU can be a company division, a product line within a division, or sometimes a single product or brand. The company next assesses the

MARKETING AT WORK 2.1

ESPN: A Real Study in Strategic and Marketing Planning

When you think about ESPN, you probably think of it as a cable TV network, or a magazine, or maybe a Web site. ESPN is all of those things. But over the years, ESPN has grown to become much more. Thanks to stellar strategic and marketing planning, the brand now consists of a vast array of sports-entertainment entities.

In 1979, entrepreneur Bill Rasmussen took a daring leap and founded the around-the-clock sports network ESPN (Entertainment and Sports Programming Network). Two years later, George Bodenheimer took a job in ESPN's mailroom. The rest, as they say, is history. Despite many early skeptics, Bodenheimer (who rose through the ranks to become ESPN's energetic president) currently presides over a multibillion dollar sports empire. Here's a brief summary of the incredible variety of entities now tied together under the ESPN brand.

Television: From its original groundbreaking cable network—ESPN, which now serves more than 100 million households—the ESPN brand has sprouted five additional networks—ESPN2, ESPN Classic, ESPNEWS, ESPNU, ESPN Deportes (Spanish-language), plus ESPN International (46 international networks around the world serving fans in more than 200 countries on every continent). ESPN also produces the sports programming on ABC, dubbed "ESPN on ABC," and is the home of the NBA Finals, NASCAR, college football, college basketball, World Cup Soccer, the IndyCar 500, the Little League World Series, and more.

One of the pioneers in high-definition TV broadcasting, ESPN outbid the major broadcast networks to capture the rights to air college football's Bowl Championship Series (BCS) beginning in 2011. Paying a reported $500 million for those rights, ESPN settled a decade-long argument over whether cable TV had the mass appeal necessary to support major sports events.

Radio: Sports radio is thriving, and ESPN operates the largest sports radio network, with 750 U.S. affiliates and more than 350 full-time stations plus Spanish-language ESPN Deportes in major markets. Overseas, ESPN has radio and syndicated radio programs in 11 countries.

Digital: ESPN.com is one of the world's leading sports Web sites. And ESPNRadio.com is the most listened-to online sports destination, with 35 original podcasts each week. ESPN3, a broadband sports network available at no cost to fans who receive their high-speed Internet connection from an affiliated service provider, delivers more than 3,500 live sporting events each year. It also provides on-demand video from ESPN's other networks plus exclusive content and video games. ESPN also delivers mobile sports content via all major U.S. wireless providers—including

real-time scores, stats, late-breaking news, video-on-demand, and even live TV. ESPN recently extended the brand further through an agreement with YouTube, featuring an ESPN channel of ad-supported short-form sports content and highlights.

Publishing: When ESPN first published *ESPN The Magazine* in 1998, critics gave it little chance against the mighty sports magazine *Sports Illustrated*. Yet, with its bold look, bright colors, and unconventional format, the ESPN publication now serves more than 2 million subscribers and continues to grow, as compared with *SI's* stagnant 3.3 million subscribers. ESPN also publishes books through its ESPN Books division, including 11 new titles last year.

▲ **ESPN is more than just cable networks, publications, and other media. To consumers, ESPN is synonymous with sports entertainment, inexorably linked with consumers' sports memories, realities, and anticipations.**

x05/ZUMA Press/Newscom

As if all this weren't enough, ESPN also manages events, including the X Games, Winter X Games, ESPN Outdoors (featuring the Bassmaster Classic), the Skins Games, the Jimmy V Classic, and several football bowl games. It also develops ESPN-branded consumer products and services, including CDs, DVDs, video games, apparel, and even golf schools. If reading all this makes you hungry, you may be near an ESPN Zone, which includes a sports-themed restaurant, interactive games, and sports-related merchandise sales. You'll now find ESPN content in airports and on planes, in health clubs, and even on gas station video panels.

Managing this successful and growing brand portfolio is no easy proposition, but ESPN has been more than up to the task. What ties it all together? The brand's customer-focused mission: "To serve sports fans wherever sports are watched, listened to, discussed, debated, read about, or played." To most consumers, ESPN is a unified brand experience—a meaningful part of their lives that goes well beyond the cable networks, publications, and other entities it comprises.

ESPN is synonymous with sports entertainment, inexorably linked with consumers' sports memories, realities, and anticipations. No matter what your sport or where you are, ESPN probably plays a prominent part in the action. To fans around the world, ESPN means sports. Tech savvy, creative, and often irreverent, the well-managed, ever-extending brand portfolio continues to build meaningful customer experiences and relationships. If it has to do with your life and sports—large or small—ESPN covers it for you, anywhere you are 24/7.

ESPN president George Bodenheimer notes that ESPN's flagship show, *SportsCenter*, is locally produced in 13 locales and eight languages around the globe. "The sun never sets on *SportsCenter,*" he boasts. Perhaps the company should rename ESPN to stand for Every Sport Possible—Now.

Source: See Mark Veverka, "ESPN Stays in Tech Vanguard," *Barron's,* February 14, 2011, p. 24; and information from http://espn.go.com/mediakit/ overview/about_espn.html, http://espnmediazone3.com/wpmu/, and www.espn .com, accessed November 2011.

---

attractiveness of its various SBUs and decides how much support each deserves. When designing a business portfolio, it's a good idea to add and support products and businesses that fit closely with the firm's core philosophy and competencies.

The purpose of strategic planning is to find ways in which the company can best use its strengths to take advantage of attractive opportunities in the environment. For this reason, most standard portfolio analysis methods evaluate SBUs on two important dimensions: the attractiveness of the SBU's market or industry and the strength of the SBU's position in that market or industry. The best-known portfolio-planning method was developed by the Boston Consulting Group, a leading management consulting firm.[5]

The Boston Consulting Group Approach

Using the now-classic Boston Consulting Group (BCG) approach, a company classifies all its SBUs according to the **growth-share matrix**, as shown in ▶ **Figure 2.2**. On the vertical axis, *market growth rate* provides a measure of market attractiveness. On the horizontal axis, *relative market share* serves as a measure of company strength in the market. The growth-share matrix defines four types of SBUs:

Growth-share matrix
A portfolio-planning method that evaluates a company's SBUs in terms of its market growth rate and relative market share.

1. *Stars.* Stars are high-growth, high-share businesses or products. They often need heavy investments to finance their rapid growth. Eventually their growth will slow down, and they will turn into cash cows.
2. *Cash cows.* Cash cows are low-growth, high-share businesses or products. These established and successful SBUs need less investment to hold their market share. Thus, they produce a lot of the cash that the company uses to pay its bills and support other SBUs that need investment.
3. *Question marks.* Question marks are low-share business units in high-growth markets. They require a lot of cash to hold their share, let alone increase it. Management has to think hard about which question marks it should try to build into stars and which should be phased out.
4. *Dogs.* Dogs are low-growth, low-share businesses and products. They may generate enough cash to maintain themselves but do not promise to be large sources of cash.

Figure 2.2 The BCG Growth-Share Matrix

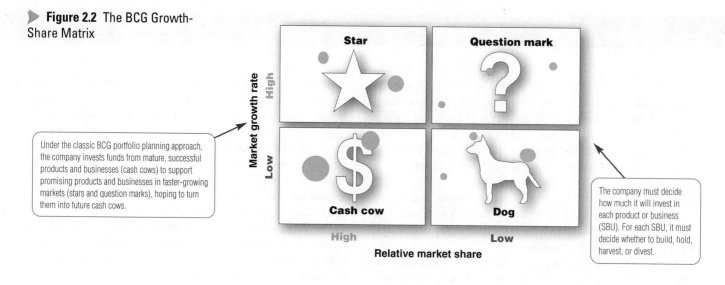

Under the classic BCG portfolio planning approach, the company invests funds from mature, successful products and businesses (cash cows) to support promising products and businesses in faster-growing markets (stars and question marks), hoping to turn them into future cash cows.

The company must decide how much it will invest in each product or business (SBU). For each SBU, it must decide whether to build, hold, harvest, or divest.

The 10 circles in the growth-share matrix represent the company's 10 current SBUs. The company has two stars, two cash cows, three question marks, and three dogs. The areas of the circles are proportional to the SBU's dollar sales. This company is in fair shape, although not in good shape. It wants to invest in the more promising question marks to make them stars and maintain the stars so that they will become cash cows as their markets mature. Fortunately, it has two good-sized cash cows. Income from these cash cows will help finance the company's question marks, stars, and dogs. The company should take some decisive action concerning its dogs and its question marks.

Once it has classified its SBUs, the company must determine what role each will play in the future. It can pursue one of four strategies for each SBU. It can invest more in the business unit to *build* its share. Or it can invest just enough to *hold* the SBU's share at the current level. It can *harvest* the SBU, milking its short-term cash flow regardless of the long-term effect. Finally, it can *divest* the SBU by selling it or phasing it out and using the resources elsewhere.

As time passes, SBUs change their positions in the growth-share matrix. Many SBUs start out as question marks and move into the star category if they succeed. They later become cash cows as market growth falls, and then finally die off or turn into dogs toward the end of their life cycle. The company needs to add new products and units continuously so that some of them will become stars and, eventually, cash cows that will help finance other SBUs.

Problems with Matrix Approaches

The BCG and other formal methods revolutionized strategic planning. However, such centralized approaches have limitations: They can be difficult, time-consuming, and costly to implement. Management may find it difficult to define SBUs and measure market share and growth. In addition, these approaches focus on classifying *current* businesses but provide little advice for *future* planning.

Because of such problems, many companies have dropped formal matrix methods in favor of more customized approaches that better suit their specific situations. Moreover, unlike former strategic-planning efforts that rested mostly in the hands of senior managers at company headquarters, today's strategic planning has been decentralized. Increasingly, companies are placing responsibility for strategic planning in the hands of cross-functional teams of divisional managers who are close to their markets.

For example, consider The Walt Disney Company. ▶ Most people think of Disney as theme parks and wholesome family entertainment. But in the mid-1980s, Disney set up a powerful, centralized strategic planning group to guide its direction and growth. Over the next two decades, the strategic planning group turned The Walt Disney Company into a huge and diverse collection of media and entertainment businesses. As discussed earlier in the chapter, the sprawling company grew to include everything from

Managing the business portfolio: Most people think of Disney as theme parks and wholesome family entertainment. However, over the past two decades, it has become a sprawling collection of media and entertainment businesses that requires big doses of the famed "Disney Magic" to manage.

Martin Beddall/Alamy

theme resorts and film studios (Walt Disney Pictures, Touchstone Pictures, Hollywood Pictures, Pixar, and others) to media networks (ABC Television plus ESPN, Disney Channel, parts of A&E and History Channel, and a half dozen others) to consumer products and a cruise line.

The newly transformed company proved hard to manage and performed unevenly. To improve performance, Disney disbanded the centralized strategic planning unit, decentralizing its functions to Disney division managers. As a result, Disney retains its position at the head of the world's media conglomerates. And despite recently facing "the weakest economy in our lifetime," Disney's sound strategic management of its broad mix of businesses has helped it fare better than rival media companies.[6]

Developing Strategies for Growth and Downsizing

Beyond evaluating current businesses, designing the business portfolio involves finding businesses and products the company should consider in the future. Companies need growth if they are to compete more effectively, satisfy their stakeholders, and attract top talent. At the same time, a firm must be careful not to make growth itself an objective. The company's objective must be to manage "profitable growth."

Marketing has the main responsibility for achieving profitable growth for the company. Marketing needs to identify, evaluate, and select market opportunities and establish strategies for capturing them. One useful device for identifying growth opportunities is the **product/market expansion grid**, shown in ▶ **Figure 2.3**.[7] We apply it here to performance sports apparel maker Under Armour. Only 15 years ago, Under Armour introduced its innovative line of comfy, moisture-wicking shirts and shorts. Since then, it has grown rapidly in its performance-wear niche. Over just the past five years, Under Armour's sales more than doubled and profits grew 25 percent. Looking forward, the company must look for new ways to keep growing.[8]

First, Under Armour might consider whether the company can achieve deeper **market penetration**—making more sales without changing its original product. It can spur growth through marketing mix improvements—adjustments to its product design, advertising, pricing, and distribution efforts. For example, Under Armour offers an ever-increasing range of styles and colors in its original apparel lines. It recently boosted its promotion spending in an effort to drive home its "performance and authenticity" positioning. The company also added direct-to-consumer distribution channels, including its own retail stores, Web site, and toll-free call center. Direct-to-consumer sales grew almost 60 percent last year and now account for more than 23 percent of total revenues.

Second, Under Armour might consider possibilities for **market development**—identifying and developing new markets for its current products. Under Armour could

Product/market expansion grid
A portfolio-planning tool for identifying company growth opportunities through market penetration, market development, product development, or diversification.

Market penetration
Company growth by increasing sales of current products to current market segments without changing the product.

Market development
Company growth by identifying and developing new market segments for current company products.

▶ **Figure 2.3** The Product/Market Expansion Grid

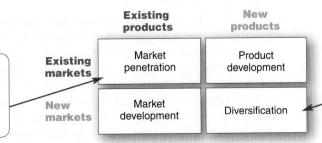

	Existing products	New products
Existing markets	Market penetration	Product development
New markets	Market development	Diversification

Companies can grow by better penetrating current markets with current products. For example, Under Armour offers an ever-increasing range of styles, has boosted its promotion spending, and recently added new direct distribution channels.

Through diversification, companies can grow by starting up or buying businesses outside their current product/markets. For example, Under Armour can begin making and marketing fitness equipment. But it must be careful not to overextend its positioning.

▲ **Growth: Under Armour has grown at a blistering rate under its multipronged growth strategy.**

Larry French/Stringer/Getty Images

Product development
Company growth by offering modified or new products to current market segments.

Diversification
Company growth through starting up or acquiring businesses outside the company's current products and markets.

Author Comment ▶
Marketing can't go it alone in creating customer value. Under the company-wide strategic plan, it must work closely with other departments to form an effective internal company value chain. It must also work with other companies in the marketing system to create an external value delivery network that jointly serves customers.

review new *demographic markets*. ▶ For instance, the company recently stepped up its emphasis on women consumers and predicts that its women's apparel business will someday be larger than its men's apparel business. The Under Armour "Athletes Run" advertising campaign includes a 30-second "women's only" spot. Under Armour could also pursue new *geographical markets*. For example, the brand has announced its intentions to expand internationally.

Third, Under Armour could consider **product development**—offering modified or new products to current markets. For example, after years of pitting cotton as the enemy of its sweat-absorbing synthetic materials, Under Armour recently introduced its own cotton-based line. Recognizing that many consumers simply like the feel of cotton and wear it in casual settings, the company wants a piece of the 80 percent of the active apparel market captured by cotton products. Under Armour claims that its own blend—called Charged Cotton—dries five times faster than normal cotton. "Mother nature made it," claims one ad. "We made it better."

Finally, Under Armour might consider **diversification**—starting up or buying businesses beyond its current products and markets. For example, it could move into nonperformance leisurewear or begin making and marketing Under Armour fitness equipment. When diversifying, companies must be careful not to overextend their brands' positioning.

Companies must not only develop strategies for growing their business portfolios but also strategies for *downsizing* them. There are many reasons that a firm might want to abandon products or markets. The firm may have grown too fast or entered areas where it lacks experience. The market environment might change, making some products or markets less profitable. For example, in difficult economic times, many firms prune out weaker, less-profitable products and markets to focus their more limited resources on the strongest ones. Finally, some products or business units simply age and die.

When a firm finds brands or businesses that are unprofitable or that no longer fit its overall strategy, it must carefully prune, harvest, or divest them. For example, in recent years, GM has pruned several underperforming brands from its portfolio, including the Oldsmobile, Pontiac, Saturn, and Hummer car brands and the Goodwrench parts line. Similarly, Ford recently shed its Mercury brand and sold off Jaguar, Land Rover, and Volvo. Weak businesses usually require a disproportionate amount of management attention. Managers should focus on promising growth opportunities, not fritter away energy trying to salvage fading ones.

Planning Marketing:
Partnering to Build Customer Relationships

The company's strategic plan establishes what kinds of businesses the company will operate and its objectives for each. Then, within each business unit, more detailed planning takes place. The major functional departments in each unit—marketing, finance, accounting, purchasing, operations, information systems, human resources, and others—must work together to accomplish strategic objectives.

Marketing plays a key role in the company's strategic planning in several ways. First, marketing provides a guiding *philosophy*—the marketing concept—that suggests the company strategy should revolve around building profitable relationships with important consumer groups. Second, marketing provides *inputs* to strategic planners by helping to identify attractive market opportunities and assessing the firm's potential to take advantage of them. Finally, within individual business units, marketing designs *strategies* for reaching the unit's objectives. Once the unit's objectives are set, marketing's task is to help carry them out profitably.

Customer value is the key ingredient in the marketer's formula for success. However, as noted in Chapter 1, although marketing plays a leading role, it alone cannot produce superior value for customers. It can be only a partner in attracting, keeping, and growing customers. In addition to *customer relationship management*, marketers must also practice *partner relationship management*. They must work closely with partners in other company departments to form an effective internal *value chain* that serves customers. Moreover, they must partner effectively with other companies in the marketing system to form a competitively superior external *value delivery network*. We now take a closer look at the concepts of a company value chain and a value delivery network.

Partnering with Other Company Departments

Value chain

The series of internal departments that carry out value-creating activities to design, produce, market, deliver, and support a firm's products.

Each company department can be thought of as a link in the company's internal **value chain**.[9] That is, each department carries out value-creating activities to design, produce, market, deliver, and support the firm's products. The firm's success depends not only on how well each department performs its work but also on how well the various departments coordinate their activities.

For example, Walmart's goal is to create customer value and satisfaction by providing shoppers with the products they want at the lowest possible prices. Marketers at Walmart play an important role. They learn what customers need and stock the stores' shelves with the desired products at unbeatable low prices. They prepare advertising and merchandising programs and assist shoppers with customer service. Through these and other activities, Walmart's marketers help deliver value to customers.

However, the marketing department needs help from the company's other departments. Walmart's ability to help you "Save Money. Live Better." depends on the purchasing department's skill in developing the needed suppliers and buying from them at low cost. Walmart's information technology department must provide fast and accurate information about which products are selling in each store. And its operations people must provide effective, low-cost merchandise handling.

A company's value chain is only as strong as its weakest link. Success depends on how well each department performs its work of adding customer value and on how the company coordinates the activities of various departments. ▶ At Walmart, if purchasing can't obtain the lowest prices from suppliers, or if operations can't distribute merchandise at the lowest costs, then marketing can't deliver on its promise of unbeatable low prices.

Ideally, then, a company's different functions should work in harmony to produce value for consumers. But, in practice, interdepartmental relations are full of conflicts and misunderstandings. The marketing department takes the consumer's point of view. But when marketing tries to develop customer satisfaction, it can cause other departments to do a poorer job *in their terms*. Marketing department actions can increase purchasing costs, disrupt production schedules, increase inventories, and create budget headaches. Thus, other departments may resist the marketing department's efforts.

Yet marketers must find ways to get all departments to "think consumer" and develop a smoothly functioning value chain. One marketing expert puts it this way: "True market orientation does not mean becoming marketing-driven; it means that the entire company obsesses over creating value for the customer and views itself as a bundle of processes

▲ The value chain: Walmart's ability to help you "Save Money. Live Better." by offering the right products at lower prices depends on the contributions of people in all of the company's departments.

that profitably define, create, communicate, and deliver value to its target customers. . . . Everyone must do marketing regardless of function or department."[10] Thus, whether you're an accountant, an operations manager, a financial analyst, an IT specialist, or a human resources manager, you need to understand marketing and your role in creating customer value.

Partnering with Others in the Marketing System

In its quest to create customer value, the firm needs to look beyond its own internal value chain and into the value chains of its suppliers, distributors, and, ultimately, its customers. Again, consider McDonald's. People do not swarm to McDonald's only because they love the chain's hamburgers. Consumers flock to the McDonald's *system*, not only to its food products. Throughout the world, McDonald's finely tuned value delivery system delivers a high standard of QSCV—quality, service, cleanliness, and value. McDonald's is effective only to the extent that it successfully partners with its franchisees, suppliers, and others to jointly create "our customers' favorite place and way to eat."

More companies today are partnering with other members of the supply chain—suppliers, distributors, and, ultimately, customers—to improve the performance of the customer **value delivery network**. Competition no longer takes place only between individual competitors. Rather, it takes place between the entire value delivery networks created by these competitors. Thus, Toyota's performance against Ford depends on the quality of Toyota's overall value delivery network versus Ford's. Even if Toyota makes the best cars, it might lose in the marketplace if Ford's dealer network provides more customer-satisfying sales and service.

Value delivery network
The network made up of the company, its suppliers, its distributors, and, ultimately, its customers who partner with each other to improve the performance of the entire system.

SPEED BUMP | LINKING THE CONCEPTS

Pause here for a moment to apply what you've read in the first part of this chapter.

- Why are we talking about company-wide strategic planning in a marketing text? What *does* strategic planning have to do with marketing?
- What is McDonald's strategy and mission? What role does marketing play in helping McDonald's to accomplish its strategy and mission?
- What roles do other McDonald's departments play and how can the company's marketers partner with these departments to maximize overall customer value?

Author Comment ▶
Now that we've set the context in terms of company-wide strategy, it's time to discuss customer-driven marketing strategies and programs.

Marketing strategy
The marketing logic by which the company hopes to create customer value and achieve profitable customer relationships.

Marketing Strategy and the Marketing Mix

The strategic plan defines the company's overall mission and objectives. Marketing's role is shown in ▶ **Figure 2.4**, which summarizes the major activities involved in managing a customer-driven marketing strategy and the marketing mix.

Consumers are in the center. The goal is to create value for customers and build profitable customer relationships. Next comes **marketing strategy**—the marketing logic by which the company hopes to create this customer value and achieve these profitable relationships. The company decides which customers it will serve (segmentation and targeting) and how (differentiation and positioning). It identifies the total market and then divides it into smaller segments, selects the most promising segments, and focuses on serving and satisfying the customers in these segments.

Guided by marketing strategy, the company designs an integrated *marketing mix* made up of factors under its control—product, price, place, and promotion (the four Ps). To find the best marketing strategy and mix, the company engages in marketing analysis, planning, implementation, and control. Through these activities, the company watches and adapts to the actors and forces in the marketing environment. We will now look briefly at each activity. In later chapters, we will discuss each one in more depth.

Figure 2.4 Managing Marketing Strategies and the Marketing Mix

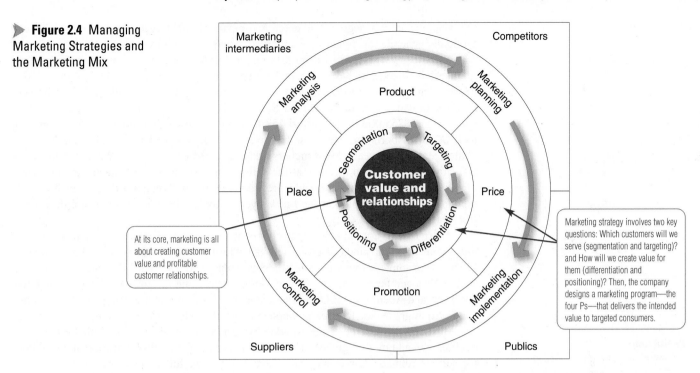

At its core, marketing is all about creating customer value and profitable customer relationships.

Marketing strategy involves two key questions: Which customers will we serve (segmentation and targeting)? and How will we create value for them (differentiation and positioning)? Then, the company designs a marketing program—the four Ps—that delivers the intended value to targeted consumers.

Customer-Driven Marketing Strategy

As emphasized throughout Chapter 1, to succeed in today's competitive marketplace, companies must be customer centered. They must win customers from competitors and then keep and grow them by delivering greater value. But before it can satisfy customers, a company must first understand customer needs and wants. Thus, sound marketing requires careful customer analysis.

Companies know that they cannot profitably serve all consumers in a given market—at least not all consumers in the same way. There are too many different kinds of consumers with too many different kinds of needs. Most companies are in a position to serve some segments better than others. Thus, each company must divide up the total market, choose the best segments, and design strategies for profitably serving chosen segments. This process involves *market segmentation*, *market targeting*, *differentiation*, and *positioning*.

Market Segmentation

The market consists of many types of customers, products, and needs. The marketer must determine which segments offer the best opportunities. Consumers can be grouped and served in various ways based on geographic, demographic, psychographic, and behavioral factors. The process of dividing a market into distinct groups of buyers who have different needs, characteristics, or behaviors, and who might require separate products or marketing programs, is called **market segmentation**.

Every market has segments, but not all ways of segmenting a market are equally useful. For example, Tylenol would gain little by distinguishing between low-income and high-income pain relief users if both respond the same way to marketing efforts. A **market segment** consists of consumers who respond in a similar way to a given set of marketing efforts. In the car market, for example, consumers who want the biggest, most comfortable car regardless of price make up one market segment. Consumers who care mainly about price and operating economy make up another segment. It would be difficult to make one car model that was the first choice of consumers in both segments. Companies are wise to focus their efforts on meeting the distinct needs of individual market segments.

Market Targeting

After a company has defined its market segments, it can enter one or many of these segments. **Market targeting** involves evaluating each market segment's attractiveness and

Market segmentation

Dividing a market into distinct groups of buyers who have different needs, characteristics, or behaviors, and who might require separate products or marketing programs.

Market segment

A group of consumers who respond in a similar way to a given set of marketing efforts.

Market targeting

The process of evaluating each market segment's attractiveness and selecting one or more segments to enter.

selecting one or more segments to enter. A company should target segments in which it can profitably generate the greatest customer value and sustain it over time.

A company with limited resources might decide to serve only one or a few special segments or market niches. Such nichers specialize in serving customer segments that major competitors overlook or ignore. For example, Ferrari sells only 1,500 of its very high-performance cars in the United States each year but at very high prices—from an eye-opening $255,000 for its Ferrari 458 Italia to an astonishing more than $2 million for its FXX super sports car, which can be driven only on race tracks (it usually sells 10 in the United States each year). Most nichers aren't quite so exotic. White Wave, the maker of Silk Soymilk, has found its niche as the nation's largest soy milk producer. And profitable low-cost airline Allegiant Air avoids direct competition with major airline rivals by targeting smaller, neglected markets and new flyers. Nicher Allegiant "goes where they ain't" (see Marketing at Work 2.2).

Alternatively, a company might choose to serve several related segments—perhaps those with different kinds of customers but with the same basic wants. Abercrombie & Fitch, for example, targets college students, teens, and kids with the same upscale, casual clothes and accessories in three different outlets: the original Abercrombie & Fitch, Hollister, and Abercrombie. Or a large company (for example, car companies like Honda and Ford) might decide to offer a complete range of products to serve all market segments.

Most companies enter a new market by serving a single segment; if this proves successful, they add more segments. For example, Nike started with innovative running shoes for serious runners. Large companies eventually seek full market coverage. Nike now makes and sells a broad range of sports products for just about anyone and everyone, with the goal of "helping athletes at every level of ability reach their potential."[11] It designs different products to meet the special needs of each segment it serves.

Market Differentiation and Positioning

After a company has decided which market segments to enter, it must determine how to differentiate its market offering for each targeted segment and what positions it wants to occupy in those segments. A product's *position* is the place it occupies relative to competitors' products in consumers' minds. Marketers want to develop unique market positions for their products. If a product is perceived to be exactly like others on the market, consumers would have no reason to buy it.

Positioning is arranging for a product to occupy a clear, distinctive, and desirable place relative to competing products in the minds of target consumers. Marketers plan positions that distinguish their products from competing brands and give them the greatest advantage in their target markets.

BMW is "The ultimate driving machine"; Audi promises "Truth in Engineering." Neutrogena is "#1 Dermatologist Recommended"; ▶ Burt's Bees offers "Earth friendly natural personal care products for The Greater Good." At McDonald's you'll be saying "i'm lovin' it"; at Burger King you can "Have it your way." Such deceptively simple statements form the backbone of a product's marketing strategy. For example, McDonald's designs its entire worldwide integrated marketing campaign—from television and print commercials to its Web sites—around the "i'm lovin' it" positioning.

In positioning its brand, a company first identifies possible customer value differences that provide competitive advantages on which to build the position. A company can offer greater customer value by either charging lower prices than competitors or offering more benefits to justify higher prices. But if the company *promises* greater value, it must then *deliver* that greater value. Thus, effective positioning begins with **differentiation**—actually *differentiating* the company's market offering so that it gives consumers more value. Once the

Positioning
Arranging for a product to occupy a clear, distinctive, and desirable place relative to competing products in the minds of target consumers.

Differentiation
Actually differentiating the market offering to create superior customer value.

▲ Burt's Bees offers "Earth friendly natural personal care products for The Greater Good." Such deceptively simple statements form the backbone of a product's marketing strategy.
BURT'S BEES® is a registered trademark of The Clorox Company. Used with permission.

MARKETING AT WORK   2.2

Nicher Allegiant Air: "Going Where They Ain't"

In July 2001, Maurice Gallagher wanted to start a new airline. Conventional wisdom suggested that, to be successful, a new airline needed to follow the JetBlue model: Invest a lot of cash and fly from a large urban hub with lots of brand-new planes. It needed to meet competitors head-on, wresting frequent flyers from rival airlines in the hypercompetitive commercial airspace. Unfortunately, Gallagher didn't have much cash, and he had only one aging, gas-guzzling, 150-seat MD-80 airplane. So he needed to find a different model—one that let him find his own special uncontested niche in the chronically overcrowded skies.

The result is Allegiant Air, arguably today's most successful American airline. Over the past six years, as other airlines struggled through the worst recession in recent history, Allegiant has seen six straight years of profits—something no other airline can claim. Last year alone, Allegiant's revenue soared 19 percent, with operating margins of 16 percent, more than double the industry average. As other airlines have cut back, the budding Allegiant Air launched 23 new routes and ended the year with 52 planes.

So, what makes Allegiant different? In an industry littered with failing low-cost initiatives, "we needed a strategy that was low-cost and could make money from day one," says Gallagher. "Slowly, we figured it out: Go where they ain't." By "go where they ain't," Gallagher means a new kind of airline—one that finds a whole new way to serve a customer niche now neglected by major competitors. According to one analyst, unlike other airlines, Allegiant "eschews business travelers, daily flights, even service between major cities." Allegiant is the "un-airline."

First, Allegiant looks for uncontested turf—routes neglected by larger, more established competitors. In their efforts to cut costs, the major airlines have abandoned many smaller markets, and Allegiant has moved in to fill the gap. It began by connecting its home city, Las Vegas—and later other popular tourist destinations such as Los Angeles, Orlando, and Phoenix—with dozens of otherwise empty airports in smaller cities such as Fresno, California; Bozeman, Montana; Peoria, Illinois; and Toledo, Ohio. These smaller markets around cities not served by any other scheduled airline welcome Allegiant with open arms and runways. "These small cities have been neglected over the years," Gallagher notes. "We're the circus coming to town, but we don't ever leave." As a result of flying where other airlines don't, Allegiant has direct competition on only 7 of its 136 routes.

Second, Allegiant doesn't just target the usual frequent business and leisure flyers coveted by rival airlines. Instead, rather than trying to steal competitors' passengers, Allegiant also targets customers who might not otherwise fly—those who are used to driving an hour or two to some vacation spot but now want to go on a real vacation. Allegiant's idea is to entice that person in Peoria, who doesn't fly all that much, to get off the couch and take a weekend vacation at a more distant destination, such as Las Vegas or Orlando. Allegiant also offers charter flights, so the local Kiwanis Club can charter a plane and take its members and their families on a group vacation.

To entice these more-reluctant travelers, Allegiant offers rock-bottom fares and direct flights. It "provides a complete travel experience with great value and without all the hassle," says the airline. Allegiant lures passengers on board with really low teaser fares—as low as $9. Of course, you have to pay extra to book online or phone a call center. You also have to pay to check your bags, for priority boarding, or for a reserved seat. But add it all up, and you'll still pay less than you would for a ticket on a competing airline. And Allegiant's à la carte pricing structure provides psychological advantages. "If I tried to charge you $110 up front, you wouldn't pay it," observes

▲ **Nichers: Profitable low-cost airline Allegiant Air avoids direct competition with major airline rivals by targeting smaller, neglected markets and new flyers. Allegiant "goes where they ain't."**

Brockton Creative Group and Allegiant Travel Company; (beach photo) Devon Stephens/ iStockphoto.com

Gallagher. "But if I sell you a $75 ticket and you self-select the rest, you will."

What's more, Allegiant doesn't just sell airline tickets. It also encourages customers to buy an entire vacation package at its Web site. Last year, it sold 400,000 hotel rooms, along with extras such as rental cars, show tickets, and even beach towels and suntan oil. These extra revenues per passenger comprise nearly one-third of the company's business.

To support its lower fares, Allegiant prides itself on being one of the industry's lowest-cost, most-efficient operators. Even though its old MD-80 airplanes slurp gas, Allegiant buys used ones for as little as $4 million, a tenth of what it costs Southwest to buy a new 737. And rather than running three-times-a-day service to its smaller markets, Allegiant offers about three flights a week. Passengers don't seem to mind the less-frequent service, especially since they can fly nonstop. Whereas flying Allegiant nonstop from Peoria to Las Vegas takes a little less than seven hours, the same trip using other airlines with connecting flights might take 19 hours—and you pay more for the ticket.

Less frequent flights make for more efficient use of Allegiant's fleet. For example, the low-cost airline serves 40 destinations from Las Vegas with only 14 planes, with an average occupancy of 90 percent. Greater efficiency results in higher margins, despite lower fares.

Under its "go where they ain't" strategy, nicher Allegiant is thriving in an otherwise supercompetitive airline environment. Whereas the major airlines are battling it out with one another for the same passengers in major markets, Allegiant has found its own uncluttered space. In a mature industry that's struggling just to stay in the air, Allegiant has found a profitable place to land. According to Gallagher, Allegiant Air has identified 300 more potential routes in the United States, Canada, Mexico, and the Caribbean. And it recently agreed to acquire 18 more MD-80s from another airline.

"They're very much one of a kind," says an airline analyst. Forget talk about milking secondary markets, cutting costs, or flying all-but-vintage airplanes. "The truth is, [Allegiant Air] is a totally new business model."

Sources: Quotes and other information from Jerome Greer Chandler, "Pledging Allegiant Ascendance of the Un-Airline," *Air Transport World*, February 2010, p. 60; Greg Lindsay, "Flying for Fun and Profit," *Fast Company,* September 2009, p. 48; Charisse Jones, "Airline Caters to Passengers in Small Communities Rather than Business Travelers," *USA Today*, October 19, 2009; "Allegiant Air's Success Comes with No Frills," Morning Edition, National Public Radio, April 17, 2009; "Allegiant Air Named Top-Performing Low-Cost Airline by Aviation Week," *PR Newswire*, July 21, 2010; Andrew Compart, "Double Vision," *Aviation Week*, February 14, 2011, p. 41; and www.allegiantair.com, November 2011.

company has chosen a desired position, it must take strong steps to deliver and communicate that position to target consumers. The company's entire marketing program should support the chosen positioning strategy.

Developing an Integrated Marketing Mix

Marketing mix
The set of tactical marketing tools—product, price, place, and promotion—that the firm blends to produce the response it wants in the target market.

After determining its overall marketing strategy, the company is ready to begin planning the details of the **marketing mix**, one of the major concepts in modern marketing. The marketing mix is the set of tactical marketing tools that the firm blends to produce the response it wants in the target market. The marketing mix consists of everything the firm can do to influence the demand for its product. The many possibilities can be collected into four groups of variables—the four Ps. ▶ **Figure 2.5** shows the marketing tools under each P.

- *Product* means the goods-and-services combination the company offers to the target market. Thus, a Ford Escape consists of nuts and bolts, spark plugs, pistons, headlights, and thousands of other parts. Ford offers several Escape models and dozens of optional features. The car comes fully serviced and with a comprehensive warranty that is as much a part of the product as the tailpipe.
- *Price* is the amount of money customers must pay to obtain the product. For example, Ford calculates suggested retail prices that its dealers might charge for each Escape. But Ford dealers rarely charge the full sticker price. Instead, they negotiate the price with each customer, offering discounts, trade-in allowances, and credit terms. These actions adjust prices for the current competitive and economic situations and bring them into line with the buyer's perception of the car's value.

Figure 2.5 The Four Ps of the Marketing Mix

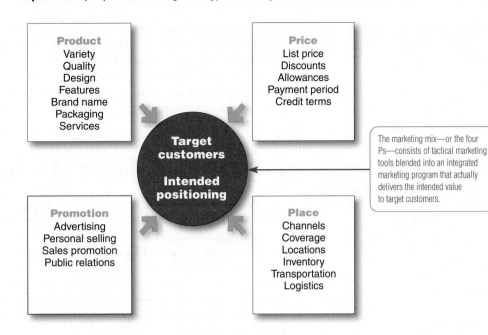

- *Place* includes company activities that make the product available to target consumers. Ford partners with a large body of independently owned dealerships that sell the company's many different models. Ford selects its dealers carefully and strongly supports them. The dealers keep an inventory of Ford automobiles, demonstrate them to potential buyers, negotiate prices, close sales, and service the cars after the sale.
- *Promotion* refers to activities that communicate the merits of the product and persuade target customers to buy it. Ford spends more than $1.5 billion each year on U.S. advertising to tell consumers about the company and its many products.[12] Dealership salespeople assist potential buyers and persuade them that Ford is the best car for them. Ford and its dealers offer special promotions—sales, cash rebates, and low financing rates—as added purchase incentives.

An effective marketing program blends each marketing mix element into an integrated marketing program designed to achieve the company's marketing objectives by delivering value to consumers. The marketing mix constitutes the company's tactical tool kit for establishing strong positioning in target markets.

Some critics think that the four Ps may omit or underemphasize certain important activities. For example, they ask, "Where are services?" Just because they don't start with a *P* doesn't justify omitting them. The answer is that services, such as banking, airline, and retailing services, are products too. We might call them *service products*. "Where is packaging?" the critics might ask. Marketers would answer that they include packaging as one of many product decisions. All said, as Figure 2.5 suggests, many marketing activities that might appear to be left out of the marketing mix are subsumed under one of the four Ps. The issue is not whether there should be four, six, or ten Ps so much as what framework is most helpful in designing integrated marketing programs.

There is another concern, however, that is valid. It holds that the four Ps concept takes the seller's view of the market, not the buyer's view. From the buyer's viewpoint, in this age of customer value and relationships, the four Ps might be better described as the four Cs:[13]

4Ps	4Cs
Product	Customer solution
Price	Customer cost
Place	Convenience
Promotion	Communication

Thus, whereas marketers see themselves as selling products, customers see themselves as buying value or solutions to their problems. And customers are interested in more than just the price; they are interested in the total costs of obtaining, using, and disposing of a product. Customers want the product and service to be as conveniently available as possible. Finally, they want two-way communication. Marketers would do well to think through the four Cs first and then build the four Ps on that platform.

Author Comment ▶
So far we've focused on the *marketing* in marketing management. Now, let's turn to the *management*.

Managing the Marketing Effort

In addition to being good at the *marketing* in marketing management, companies also need to pay attention to the *management*. Managing the marketing process requires the four marketing management functions shown in ▶ **Figure 2.6**—*analysis*, *planning*, *implementation*, and *control*. The company first develops company-wide strategic plans and then translates them into marketing and other plans for each division, product, and brand. Through implementation, the company turns the plans into actions. Control consists of measuring and evaluating the results of marketing activities and taking corrective action where needed. Finally, marketing analysis provides information and evaluations needed for all the other marketing activities.

Marketing Analysis

SWOT analysis
An overall evaluation of the company's strengths (S), weaknesses (W), opportunities (O), and threats (T).

Managing the marketing function begins with a complete analysis of the company's situation. The marketer should conduct a **SWOT analysis** (pronounced "swat" analysis), by which it evaluates the company's overall strengths (S), weaknesses (W), opportunities (O), and threats (T) (see ▶ **Figure 2.7**). Strengths include internal capabilities, resources, and positive situational factors that may help the company serve its customers and achieve its objectives. Weaknesses include internal limitations and negative situational factors that may interfere with the company's performance. Opportunities are favorable factors or trends in the external environment that the company may be able to exploit to its advantage. And threats are unfavorable external factors or trends that may present challenges to performance.

The company should analyze its markets and marketing environment to find attractive opportunities and identify environmental threats. It should analyze company strengths and weaknesses as well as current and possible marketing actions to determine which opportunities it can best pursue. The goal is to match the company's strengths to attractive opportunities in the environment, while simultaneously eliminating or overcoming the weaknesses

▶ **Figure 2.6** Managing Marketing: Analysis, Planning, Implementation, and Control

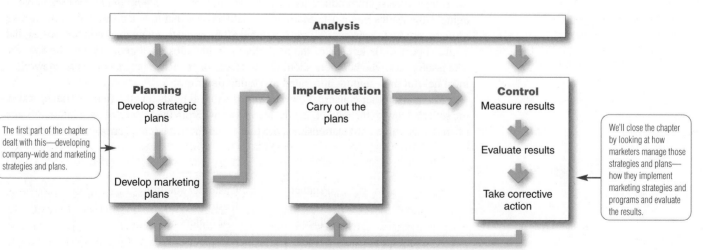

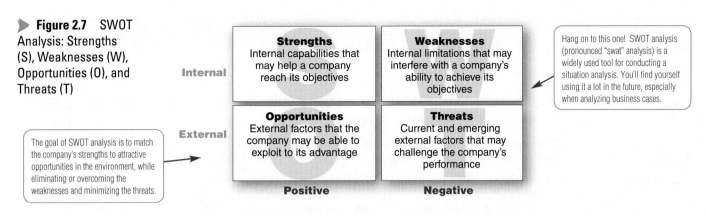

▶ Figure 2.7 SWOT Analysis: Strengths (S), Weaknesses (W), Opportunities (O), and Threats (T)

The goal of SWOT analysis is to match the company's strengths to attractive opportunities in the environment, while eliminating or overcoming the weaknesses and minimizing the threats.

and minimizing the threats. Marketing analysis provides inputs to each of the other marketing management functions. We discuss marketing analysis more fully in Chapter 3.

Marketing Planning

Through strategic planning, the company decides what it wants to do with each business unit. Marketing planning involves choosing marketing strategies that will help the company attain its overall strategic objectives. A detailed marketing plan is needed for each business, product, or brand. What does a marketing plan look like? Our discussion focuses on product or brand marketing plans.

▶ **Table 2.2** outlines the major sections of a typical product or brand marketing plan. (See Appendix 2 for a sample marketing plan.) The plan begins with an executive summary that quickly reviews major assessments, goals, and recommendations. The main section of the plan presents a detailed SWOT analysis of the current marketing situation as well as potential threats and opportunities. The plan next states major objectives for the brand and outlines the specifics of a marketing strategy for achieving them.

A *marketing strategy* consists of specific strategies for target markets, positioning, the marketing mix, and marketing expenditure levels. It outlines how the company intends to create value for target customers in order to capture value in return. In this section, the planner explains how each strategy responds to the threats, opportunities, and critical issues spelled out earlier in the plan. Additional sections of the marketing plan lay out an action program for implementing the marketing strategy along with the details of a supporting *marketing budget*. The last section outlines the controls that will be used to monitor progress, measure return on marketing investment, and take corrective action.

Marketing Implementation

Marketing implementation
Turning marketing strategies and plans into marketing actions to accomplish strategic marketing objectives.

Planning good strategies is only a start toward successful marketing. A brilliant marketing strategy counts for little if the company fails to implement it properly. **Marketing implementation** is the process that turns marketing *plans* into marketing *actions* to accomplish strategic marketing objectives. Whereas marketing planning addresses the *what* and *why* of marketing activities, implementation addresses the *who*, *where*, *when*, and *how*.

Many managers think that "doing things right" (implementation) is as important as, or even more important than, "doing the right things" (strategy). The fact is that both are critical to success, and companies can gain competitive advantages through effective implementation. One firm can have essentially the same strategy as another, yet win in the marketplace through faster or better execution. Still, implementation is difficult—it is often easier to think up good marketing strategies than it is to carry them out.

In an increasingly connected world, people at all levels of the marketing system must work together to implement marketing strategies and plans. At John Deere, for example, marketing implementation for the company's residential, commercial, agricultural, and industrial equipment requires day-to-day decisions and actions by thousands of people

▶ **Table 2.2**	Contents of a Marketing Plan

Section	Purpose
Executive summary	Presents a brief summary of the main goals and recommendations of the plan for management review, helping top management find the plan's major points quickly.
Current marketing situation	Describes the target market and the company's position in it, including information about the market, product performance, competition, and distribution. This section includes the following: ● A *market description* that defines the market and major segments and then reviews customer needs and factors in the marketing environment that may affect customer purchasing. ● A *product review* that shows sales, prices, and gross margins of the major products in the product line. ● A review of *competition* that identifies major competitors and assesses their market positions and strategies for product quality, pricing, distribution, and promotion. ● A review of *distribution* that evaluates recent sales trends and other developments in major distribution channels.
Threats and opportunities analysis	Assesses major threats and opportunities that the product might face, helping management to anticipate important positive or negative developments that might have an impact on the firm and its strategies.
Objectives and issues	States the marketing objectives that the company would like to attain during the plan's term and discusses key issues that will affect their attainment.
Marketing strategy	Outlines the broad marketing logic by which the business unit hopes to create customer value and relationships and the specifics of target markets, positioning, and marketing expenditure levels. How will the company create value for customers in order to capture value from customers in return? This section also outlines specific strategies for each marketing mix element and explains how each responds to the threats, opportunities, and critical issues spelled out earlier in the plan.
Action programs	Spells out how marketing strategies will be turned into specific action programs that answer the following questions: *What* will be done? *When* will it be done? *Who* will do it? *How* much will it cost?
Budgets	Details a supporting marketing budget that is essentially a projected profit-and-loss statement. It shows expected revenues and expected costs of production, distribution, and marketing. The difference is the projected profit. The budget becomes the basis for materials buying, production scheduling, personnel planning, and marketing operations.
Controls	Outlines the controls that will be used to monitor progress, allow management to review implementation results, and spot products that are not meeting their goals. It includes measures of return on marketing investment.

both inside and outside the organization. Marketing managers make decisions about target segments, branding, product development, pricing, promotion, and distribution. They talk with engineering about product design, with manufacturing about production and inventory levels, and with finance about funding and cash flows. They also connect with outside people, such as advertising agencies to plan ad campaigns and the news media to obtain publicity support. The sales force urges and supports John Deere dealers and large retailers like Lowe's in their efforts to convince residential, agricultural, and industrial customers that "Nothing Runs Like a Deere."

Marketing Department Organization

The company must design a marketing organization that can carry out marketing strategies and plans. If the company is very small, one person might do all the research, selling, advertising, customer service, and other marketing work. As the company expands, however, a marketing department emerges to plan and carry out marketing activities. In large companies, this department contains many specialists—product and market managers, sales

▲ **Marketers must continually plan their analysis, implementation, and control activities.**

PM Images/Stone/Getty Images

managers and salespeople, market researchers, and advertising experts, among others.

To head up such large marketing organizations, many companies have now created a *chief marketing officer* (or CMO) position. This person heads up the company's entire marketing operation and represents marketing on the company's top management team. The CMO position puts marketing on equal footing with other C-level executives, such as the chief operating officer (COO) and the chief financial officer (CFO).[14]

Modern marketing departments can be arranged in several ways. The most common form of marketing organization is the *functional organization*. Under this organization, different marketing activities are headed by a functional specialist—a sales manager, an advertising manager, a marketing research manager, a customer service manager, or a new product manager. A company that sells across the country or internationally often uses a *geographic organization*. Its sales and marketing people are assigned to specific countries, regions, and districts. Geographic organization allows salespeople to settle into a territory, get to know their customers, and work with a minimum of travel time and cost. Companies with many very different products or brands often create a *product management organization*. Using this approach, a product manager develops and implements a complete strategy and marketing program for a specific product or brand.

For companies that sell one product line to many different types of markets and customers who have different needs and preferences, a *market* or *customer management organization* might be best. A market management organization is similar to the product management organization. Market managers are responsible for developing marketing strategies and plans for their specific markets or customers. This system's main advantage is that the company is organized around the needs of specific customer segments. Many companies develop special organizations to manage their relationships with large customers. For example, companies such as P&G and Stanley Black & Decker have created large teams, or even whole divisions, to serve large customers, such as Walmart, Target, Safeway, or Home Depot.

Large companies that produce many different products flowing into many different geographic and customer markets usually employ some *combination* of the functional, geographic, product, and market organization forms.

Marketing organization has become an increasingly important issue in recent years. More and more, companies are shifting their brand management focus toward *customer management*—moving away from managing only product or brand profitability and toward managing customer profitability and customer equity. They think of themselves not as managing portfolios of brands but as managing portfolios of customers. And rather than managing the fortunes of a brand, they see themselves as managing customer–brand experiences and relationships.

Marketing Control

Marketing control

Measuring and evaluating the results of marketing strategies and plans and taking corrective action to ensure that the objectives are achieved.

Because many surprises occur during the implementation of marketing plans, marketers must practice constant **marketing control**—evaluating the results of marketing strategies and plans and taking corrective action to ensure that the objectives are attained. Marketing control involves four steps. Management first sets specific marketing goals. It then measures its performance in the marketplace and evaluates the causes of any differences between expected and actual performance. Finally, management takes corrective action to close the gaps between goals and performance. This may require changing the action programs or even changing the goals.

Operating control involves checking ongoing performance against the annual plan and taking corrective action when necessary. Its purpose is to ensure that the company achieves the sales, profits, and other goals set out in its annual plan. It also involves determining the profitability of different products, territories, markets, and channels. *Strategic control* involves looking at whether the company's basic strategies are well matched to its opportunities. Marketing strategies and programs can quickly become outdated, and each company should periodically reassess its overall approach to the marketplace.

Measuring and Managing Return on Marketing Investment

Author Comment ▶

Measuring return on marketing investment has become a major marketing emphasis. But it can be difficult. For example, a Super Bowl ad reaches more than 100 million consumers but may cost as much as $3 million for 30 seconds of airtime. How do you measure the specific return on such an investment in terms of sales, profits, and building customer relationships? We'll look at this question again in Chapter 12.

Marketing managers must ensure that their marketing dollars are being well spent. In the past, many marketers spent freely on big, expensive marketing programs, often without thinking carefully about the financial returns on their spending. They believed that marketing produces intangible creative outcomes, which do not lend themselves readily to measures of productivity or return. But in today's more constrained economy, all that is changing:[15]

> For years, corporate marketers have walked into budget meetings like neighborhood junkies. They couldn't always justify how well they spent past handouts or what difference it all made. They just wanted more money—for flashy TV ads, for big-ticket events, for, you know, getting out the message and building up the brand. But those heady days of blind budget increases are fast being replaced with a new mantra: measurement and accountability. Marketing's days as a soft science are officially over. In its place, the concept of marketing performance—the practice of measuring, learning from, and improving upon marketing strategies and tactics over time—is taking hold. More companies are now working to connect the dots between marketing activities and results than ever before.

Almost half of the companies in one recent study reported that marketing measurement—including all the ways that companies measure the impact of marketing activities—is a top priority within marketing and at corporate levels. Three-fourths of the companies reported that they are linking marketing performance measurement to financial results, and more than half are using marketing measurement to drive improvements in marketing strategy.[16]

Return on marketing investment (or marketing ROI)
The net return from a marketing investment divided by the costs of the marketing investment.

One important marketing performance measure is **return on marketing investment** (or **marketing ROI**). *Marketing ROI* is the net return from a marketing investment divided by the costs of the marketing investment. It measures the profits generated by investments in marketing activities.

Marketing ROI can be difficult to measure. In measuring financial ROI, both the *R* and the *I* are uniformly measured in dollars. For example, when buying a piece of equipment, the productivity gains resulting from the purchase are fairly straightforward. As of yet, however, there is no consistent definition of marketing ROI. For instance, returns like advertising and brand-building impact aren't easily put into dollar returns.

One recent survey found that although two-thirds of companies have implemented return on marketing investment programs in recent years, only 22 percent of companies report making good progress in measuring marketing ROI. Another study found that less than one-fourth of companies believed they are excelling at measuring their marketing performance. The major problem is figuring out what specific measures to use and obtaining good data on these measures.[17]

A company can assess marketing ROI in terms of standard marketing performance measures, such as brand awareness, sales, or market share. ▶ Many companies are assembling such measures into *marketing dashboards*—meaningful sets of marketing performance measures in a single display used to monitor strategic marketing performance. Just

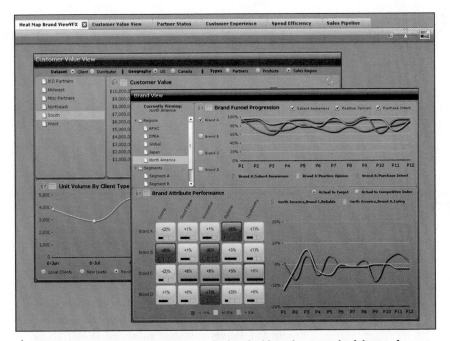

▲ **Many companies are assembling marketing dashboards—meaningful sets of marketing performance measures in a single display used to set and adjust their marketing strategies.**

as automobile dashboards present drivers with details on how their cars are performing, the marketing dashboard gives marketers the detailed measures they need to assess and adjust their marketing strategies. For example, VF Corporation uses a marketing dashboard to track the performance of its 30 lifestyle apparel brands—including Wrangler, Lee, The North Face, Vans, Nautica, 7 For All Mankind, and others. VF's marketing dashboard tracks brand equity and trends, share of voice, market share, online sentiment, and marketing ROI in key markets worldwide, not only for VF brands but also for competing brands.[18]

Increasingly, however, beyond standard performance measures, marketers are using customer-centered measures of marketing impact, such as customer acquisition, customer retention, customer lifetime value, and customer equity. These measures capture not only current marketing performance but also future performance resulting from stronger customer relationships. ▶ **Figure 2.8** views marketing expenditures as investments that produce returns in the form of more profitable customer relationships.[19] Marketing investments result in improved customer value and satisfaction, which in turn increases customer attraction and retention. This increases individual customer lifetime values and the firm's overall customer equity. Increased customer equity, in relation to the cost of the marketing investments, determines return on marketing investment.

Regardless of how it's defined or measured, the marketing ROI concept is here to stay. "In good times and bad, whether or not marketers are ready for it, they're going to be asked to justify their spending with financial data," says one marketer. Adds another, marketers "have got to know how to count."[20]

▶ **Figure 2.8** Return on Marketing Investment

Source: Adapted from Roland T. Rust, Katherine N. Lemon, and Valerie A. Zeithaml, "Return on Marketing: Using Consumer Equity to Focus Marketing Strategy," *Journal of Marketing*, January 2004, p. 112.

Beyond measuring return on marketing investment in terms of standard performance measures such as sales or market share, many companies are using customer-relationship measures, such as customer satisfaction, retention, and equity. These are more difficult to measure but capture both current and future performance.

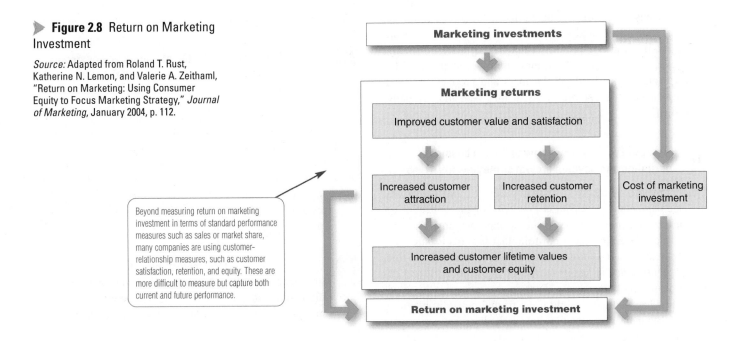

REST STOP	REVIEWING THE CONCEPTS

MyMarketingLab

Now that you have completed the chapter, return to www.mymktlab.com to experience and apply the concepts and to explore the additional study materials for this chapter.

CHAPTER REVIEW AND KEY TERMS

Objectives Review

In Chapter 1, we defined *marketing* and outlined the steps in the marketing process. In this chapter, we examined company-wide strategic planning and marketing's role in the organization. Then we looked more deeply into marketing strategy and the marketing mix and reviewed the major marketing management functions. So you've now had a pretty good overview of the fundamentals of modern marketing.

OBJECTIVE 1 Explain company-wide strategic planning and its four steps. (pp 38–41)

Strategic planning sets the stage for the rest of the company's planning. Marketing contributes to strategic planning, and the overall plan defines marketing's role in the company.

Strategic planning involves developing a strategy for long-run survival and growth. It consists of four steps: (1) defining the company's mission, (2) setting objectives and goals, (3) designing a business portfolio, and (4) developing functional plans. The company's *mission* should be market oriented, realistic, specific, motivating, and consistent with the market environment. The mission is then transformed into detailed *supporting goals and objectives*, which in turn guide decisions about the business portfolio. Then each business and product unit must develop *detailed marketing plans* in line with the company-wide plan.

OBJECTIVE 2 Discuss how to design business portfolios and develop growth strategies. (pp 41–46)

Guided by the company's mission statement and objectives, management plans its *business portfolio*, or the collection of businesses and products that make up the company. The firm wants to produce a business portfolio that best fits its strengths and weaknesses to opportunities in the environment. To do this, it must analyze and adjust its *current* business portfolio and develop *growth* and *downsizing* strategies for adjusting the *future* portfolio. The company might use a formal portfolio-planning method. But many companies are now designing more-customized portfolio-planning approaches that better suit their unique situations.

OBJECTIVE 3 Explain marketing's role in strategic planning and how marketing works with its partners to create and deliver customer value. (pp 46–48)

Under the strategic plan, the major functional departments—marketing, finance, accounting, purchasing, operations, information systems, human resources, and others—must work together to accomplish strategic objectives. Marketing plays a key role in the company's strategic planning by providing a *marketing concept philosophy* and *inputs* regarding attractive market opportunities. Within individual business units, marketing designs *strategies* for reaching the unit's objectives and helps to carry them out profitably.

Marketers alone cannot produce superior value for customers. Marketers must practice *partner relationship management*, working closely with partners in other departments to form an effective *value chain* that serves the customer. And they must also partner effectively with other companies in the marketing system to form a competitively superior *value delivery network*.

OBJECTIVE 4 Describe the elements of a customer-driven marketing strategy and mix and the forces that influence it. (pp 48–54)

Customer value and relationships are at the center of marketing strategy and programs. Through market segmentation, targeting, differentiation, and positioning, the company divides the total market into smaller segments, selects segments it can best serve, and decides how it wants to bring value to target consumers in the selected segments. It then designs an *integrated marketing mix* to produce the response it wants in the target market. The marketing mix consists of product, price, place, and promotion decisions (the four Ps).

OBJECTIVE 5 List the marketing management functions, including the elements of a marketing plan, and discuss the importance of measuring and managing return on marketing investment. (pp 54–59)

To find the best strategy and mix and to put them into action, the company engages in marketing analysis, planning, implementation, and control. The main components of a *marketing plan* are the executive summary, the current marketing situation, threats and opportunities, objectives and issues, marketing strategies, action programs, budgets, and controls. Planning good strategies is often easier than carrying them out. To be successful, companies must also be effective at *implementation*—turning marketing strategies into marketing actions.

Marketing departments can be organized in one or a combination of ways: *functional marketing organization, geographic organization, product management organization*, or *market management organization*. In this age of customer relationships, more and more companies are now changing their organizational focus from product or territory management to customer relationship management. Marketing organizations carry out *marketing control*, both operating control and strategic control.

Marketing managers must ensure that their marketing dollars are being well spent. In a tighter economy, today's marketers face growing pressures to show that they are adding value in line with their costs. In response, marketers are developing better measures of *return on marketing investment*. Increasingly, they are using customer-centered measures of marketing impact as a key input into their strategic decision making.

Key Terms

Objective 1
Strategic planning (p 38)
Mission statement (p 39)

Objective 2
Business portfolio (p 41)
Portfolio analysis (p 41)
Growth-share matrix (p 43)
Product/market expansion grid (p 45)
Market penetration (p 45)
Market development (p 45)

Product development (p 46)
Diversification (p 46)

Objective 3
Value chain (p 47)
Value delivery network (p 48)

Objective 4
Marketing strategy (p 48)
Market segmentation (p 49)
Market segment (p 49)

Market targeting (p 49)
Positioning (p 50)
Differentiation (p 50)
Marketing mix (p 52)

Objective 5
SWOT analysis (p 54)
Marketing implementation (p 55)
Marketing control (p 57)
Return on marketing investment
    (marketing ROI) (p 58)

DISCUSSION AND CRITICAL THINKING

Discussion Questions

1. Explain what is meant by a *market-oriented* mission statement and discuss the characteristics of effective mission statements. (AACSB: Communication)
2. Describe the business portfolio planning process and the role marketing plays in the process. (AACSB: Communications)
3. Explain why it is important for all departments of an organization—marketing, accounting, finance, operations management, human resources, and so on—to "think consumer." Why is it important that even people who are not in marketing understand it? (AACSB: Communication)

4. Explain the roles of market segmentation, market targeting, differentiation, and positioning in implementing an effective marketing strategy. (AACSB: Communication)
5. Define each of the four Ps. What insights might a firm gain by considering the four Cs rather than the four Ps? (AACSB: Communication; Reflective Thinking)
6. Discuss the four marketing management functions. (AACSB: Communication)

Critical Thinking Exercises

1. In a small group, give an example of how Red Bull Energy drink makers can grow by applying each of the product/market expansion grid strategies. Be sure to name and describe each strategy and discuss how the company can use each strategy to grow. (AACSB: Communication; Reflective Thinking)
2. Marketers are increasingly held accountable for demonstrating marketing success. Research the various marketing metrics, in addition to those described in the chapter and

Appendix 3, used by marketers to measure marketing performance. Write a brief report of your findings. (AACSB: Communication; Reflective Thinking)
3. Explain the role of a chief marketing officer (CMO). Learn more about this C-level executive position and find an article that describes the importance of this position, the characteristics of an effective CMO, and any issues surrounding this position. (AACSB: Communication; Reflective Thinking)

MINICASES AND APPLICATIONS

Marketing Technology   It's All in the Clouds

Cloud computing is the future and Apple is helping shape that future. Apple's iCloud service allows Apple device users to store their music, videos, pictures, and books on Apple's servers. No more syncing devices with computers or cumbersome transferring to iPods, iPhones, and iPads, because users will be able to access all of their collections from any device. That's because nothing will be stored on users' devices—it will be in the 'cloud.' For $25 a year, users remotely access copies of their songs that will work with any computer and any Apple mobile device but not sync with any other mobile device, such as a Blackberry or Android tablet.

Apple is taking on Amazon.com and Google, whose similar services require tedious uploading of files by customers.

1. Explain which product/market expansion grid strategy Apple is pursuing by introducing the iCloud service. How is Apple differentiating its new product from those offered by competitors? (AACSB: Communication; Reflective Thinking)
2. Conduct a SWOT analysis of Apple, identifying the factors likely to influence whether the iCloud service will succeed. (AACSB: Communication; Reflective Thinking)

Marketing Ethics   Toning Shoes

With 64 percent of the women in the United States overweight or obese and less than half participating in regular physical activity, athletic shoe marketers saw an opportunity: "toning shoes." The marketers tout these shoes as revolutionary—you can tone your muscles, lose weight, and improve your posture just by wearing them and going about your daily business. The claims are based on shoemaker-sponsored studies, but the Podiatric Medical Association agrees that toning shoes have some health value. They purportedly perform their magic by destabilizing a person's gait, making leg muscles work harder. Consumers, particularly women, are buying it. Toning shoe sales by Sketchers, Reebok, and other producers are soaring.

However, these shoes have their critics, who claim a shoe that comes with an instruction booklet and an educational DVD to explain proper usage should wave warning flags to consumers. Some doctors claim the shoes are dangerous, causing

strained Achilles tendons or worse—one wearer actually broke her ankle while wearing them. A study by the American Council on Exercise found no benefit in toning shoes over regular walking or other exercise. Noticeably absent from the toning shoe feeding frenzy is Nike, who thinks it's all hype. This leader in the women's shoe market, however, is losing market share to competitors.

1. Should these shoemakers capitalize on consumers who want to be fit without doing the work to achieve that goal? Do you think that basing claims on research sponsored by the company is ethical? Explain. (AACSB: Communication; Ethical Reasoning)
2. Should Nike have entered this product category instead of giving up market share to competitors? Explain. (AACSB: Communication; Ethical Reasoning)

Marketing by the Numbers   Marketing Performance Assessment

Appendix 3, Marketing by the Numbers, discusses other marketing profitability metrics beyond the return on marketing investment (marketing ROI) measure described in this chapter.

Consider the following profit-and-loss statements for two businesses. Review Appendix 3 and answer the following questions.

Business A		
Net Sales		$800,000,000
Cost of goods sold		375,000,000
Gross Margin		$425,000,000
Marketing Expenses		
Sales expenses	$70,000,000	
Promotion expenses	30,000,000	
		100,000,000
General and Administrative Expenses		
Marketing salaries and expenses	$10,000,000	
Indirect overhead	80,000,000	90,000,000
Net profit before income tax		$235,000,000

Business B		
Net Sales		$900,000,000
Cost of goods sold		400,000,000
Gross Margin		$500,000,000
Marketing Expenses		
Sales expenses	$90,000,000	
Promotion expenses	50,000,000	140,000,000
General and Administrative Expenses		
Marketing salaries and expenses	$ 20,000,000	
Indirect overhead	100,000,000	120,000,000
Net profit before income tax		$240,000,000

1. Calculate marketing return on sales (or marketing ROS) and marketing return on investment (or marketing ROI) for both companies as described in Appendix 3. (AACSB: Communication; Analytic Thinking)

2. Which company is doing better overall and with respect to marketing? Explain. (AACSB: Communication; Analytic Reasoning; Reflective Thinking)

Video Case   OXO

You might know OXO for its well-designed, ergonomic kitchen gadgets. But OXO's expertise at creating hand-held tools that look great *and* work well has prompted the company to expand into products for bathrooms, garages, offices, babies' rooms, and even medicine cabinets. In the past, this award-winning manufacturer has managed to move its products into almost every home in the United States by relying on a consistent, sometimes nontraditional, marketing strategy.

However, in a highly competitive and turbulent market, OXO has focused on evaluating and modifying its marketing strategy in order to grow the brand. This video demonstrates how OXO is using strategic planning to ensure that its marketing strategy results in the best marketing mix for the best and most profitable customers.

After viewing the video featuring OXO, answer the following questions:

1. What is OXO's mission?
2. What are some of the market conditions that have led OXO to reevaluate its marketing strategy?
3. How has OXO modified its marketing mix? Are these changes in line with its mission?

Company Cases   2 Trap-Ease America / 8 Samsung / 14 eBay

See Appendix 1 for cases appropriate for this chapter. **Case 2, Trap-Ease America: The Big Cheese of Mousetraps.** A company creates a "better mousetrap" only to learn that launching a new product takes more than a great product. **Case 8, Samsung: From Gallop to Run.** By completely overhauling its business and marketing strategies, Samsung becomes the world's largest consumer electronics manufacturer. **Case 14, eBay: Fixing an Online Marketing Pioneer.** Once the biggest online retailer, eBay alters its marketing strategy to alleviate growing pains.

3

Analyzing the Marketing
Environment

CHAPTER ROAD MAP

Objective Outline

Previewing the Concepts

So far, you've learned about the basic concepts of marketing and the steps in the marketing process for building profitable relationships with targeted consumers. Next, we'll begin digging deeper into the first step of the marketing process—understanding the marketplace and customer needs and wants. In this chapter, you'll see that marketing operates in a complex and changing environment. Other actors in this environment—suppliers, intermediaries, customers, competitors, publics, and others—may work with or against the company. Major environmental forces—demographic, economic, natural, technological, political, and cultural—shape marketing opportunities, pose threats, and affect the company's ability to build customer relationships. To develop effective marketing strategies, you must first understand the environment in which marketing operates.

To start, let's look at YouTube, the Internet video-sharing giant that burst onto the scene only a few short years ago. Today, viewers around the globe watch more than 2 billion videos a day on YouTube, giving it a 43 percent share of the online video market. To stay on top and grow profitably, however, YouTube will have to adapt nimbly to the fast-changing marketing environment.

▲ **YouTube worked with Kraft's Philadelphia Cream Cheese brand to create an effective YouTube-based campaign built around the Real Women of Philadelphia YouTube channel, which featured Food Network chef Paula Deen.**

Jarrod Weaton/Weaton Digital, Inc.

First Stop

YouTube: Adapting to the Fast-Changing Marketing Environment

Some 2,500 years ago, Greek philosopher Heraclitus observed, "Change is the only constant." That statement holds especially true today in the turbulent video entertainment industry. Today's environment is a far cry from the old days of finding video entertainment only on your TV from schedules set by the networks. Instead, consumers now face a bewildering array of choices about what they watch, as well as how, when, and where. But if the fast-changing video environment sometimes befuddles consumers, it's doubly daunting for companies that serve them.

Perhaps no company has navigated this changeable marketing environment better than Google-owned YouTube. YouTube's mission is to provide a distribution platform by which people can discover, watch, and share video entertainment. YouTube is now so pervasive that it's hard to believe the first video was uploaded on the site only a few short years ago in 2005. Today, viewers around the world watch more than 2 billion videos on YouTube each day and upload more than 35 hours of new video to the site every minute of every day. YouTube now captures a 43 percent share of the online video market and is the third-most visited Web site on the Internet, trailing only Google (its parent company) and Facebook.

Rather than simply surviving in its chaotic environment, YouTube is thriving in it, leading the way in shaping how video is produced, distributed, and monetized. For the first several years, YouTube's revenues barely covered costs. Recently, however, the video-sharing site has reached the Valhalla of dot-coms. Not only is it generating mind-numbing traffic, it's also making money; last year, income reached nearly $1 billion.

YouTube began as a place where regular folks could upload low-quality homemade video clips. But as the video industry has bolted forward, YouTube has adapted quickly. For example, to compete with new video-streaming competitors such as Netflix and Hulu, in 2008 YouTube created a section called "Shows," which provides access to an ever-expanding list of full-length films and television episodes accompanied by advertisements.

But more than just reacting to changes in the environment, YouTube wants to lead those changes. So rather than simply providing more access to traditional Hollywood-type content, YouTube created its Partner Program, which encourages aspiring Web video producers to create original new content for YouTube. In all, more than 10,000 partners now participate in the Partner Program, producing new content and sharing the revenue that YouTube generates from ads that accompany their videos. As just one example, partner Mark Douglas produces *Key of Awesome*, a musical comedy series that spoofs celebrities and the pop culture. It's now the second-most-viewed Web series on YouTube. One Ke$ha parody has an incredible 75 million views, two and one-half times as many views as the original Ke$ha video that it parodies.

With all the channels now available on broadcast and cable television, you'd think there would be little need for even more video content. But YouTube sees things differently. It plans to employ the power of its vast social network by creating thousands, if not hundreds of thousands, of channels. YouTube wants to be a home for special-interest channels that have no place on

> Video-sharing giant YouTube dwarfs its competitors, capturing a 43 percent share of the online video market. But to stay on top, it will have to adapt nimbly to the turbulent marketing environment.

network or cable TV. The aim is to provide something for everyone. "On cable, there is no kitesurfing channel, no skiing channel, no piano channel," says YouTube CEO Salar Kamangar, an avid kitesurfer, skier, and pianist. "So . . . we're helping define a new way for content creators to reach an audience, and all the topics [an individual might] care about suddenly have a home."

Creating innovative content in the topsy-turvy video environment presents a big challenge. But finding new and better ways to *distribute* that content might be an even bigger one. YouTube's favorite distribution playground has been the Internet on PCs. It has also expanded into mobile with a popular app that gives people on the go full access to YouTube. But with technology exploding, that model doesn't go far enough anymore. One YouTube executive sums up the company's broader distribution ambitions this way: "YouTube is emerging as the first global TV station, the living room for the world," taking video to people wherever they are, whenever they want it.

To become the living room for the world, however, YouTube needs to be on every available screen—especially the big one in people's living rooms. Ultimately, in addition to having people access YouTube via their PCs, tablets, and phones, YouTube wants people to watch YouTube the same way they watch TV. The stakes are huge. The average YouTube session lasts only 15 minutes, whereas the average television watcher spends five hours a day in front of the television. To that end, YouTube is working feverishly to create an experience on the big screen that will attract more people and keep them watching longer. For example, it's creating Personalized Channels, dynamic streams of videos adjusted to an individual's viewing patterns, much as Pandora radio creates personalized music stations.

At the same time that YouTube is changing the way it produces and distributes video content, it's also trying to figure out the best way to monetize (or make money on) that content in an era when consumers still think that everything on the Internet should be free. To that end, YouTube is developing an advertising model that's built around the way people use the site, a model that best suits the needs of users, content providers, advertisers, and its own bottom line.

For example, YouTube worked with Kraft Food's Philadelphia Cream Cheese brand to create an effective YouTube-based campaign. Recognizing that YouTube is a haven for how-to videos, the brand came up with a "Real Women of Philadelphia" (RWoP) community Web site, starring Food Network chef Paula Deen. The site revolves around YouTube-hosted videos, including Paula Deen videos posted by Kraft, "how-to" recipe videos, and cooking contests that invite users to submit their own cooking videos via YouTube.

On opening day of the first season, Kraft placed a commercial for RWoP featuring Paula Deen on YouTube's home page for $375,000. The goal was to drive traffic to the RWoP site and The Philadelphia Channel on YouTube. Although $375,000 might seem expensive, the Paula Deen commercial on YouTube was seen by 51 million people, making it much cheaper than an ad with comparable reach on prime-time television. More important, ten million people viewed the ad all the way through, and 100,000 people clicked through to the RWoP Web site. Ultimately, RWoP helped boost the brand's revenue by 5 percent, its first real sales lift in five years. "You look at those numbers; they almost don't even make sense," says Philadelphia's brand manager. "It's bigger than TV."

What does the future hold for YouTube? Stay tuned. But to remain on top, the company will have to be nimble in adapting to the ever-changing marketing environment—or better, in leading the change. To repeat the words of Heraclitus, change will be the only constant. A respected current marketing thinker puts it a little differently: "In five years, if you're still in the same business you're in now, you're going to be out of business."[1]

MyMarketingLab

Visit www.mymktlab.com to find activities that help you learn and review in order to succeed in this chapter.

Marketing environment
The actors and forces outside marketing that affect marketing management's ability to build and maintain successful relationships with target customers.

Microenvironment
The actors close to the company that affect its ability to serve its customers—the company, suppliers, marketing intermediaries, customer markets, competitors, and publics.

Macroenvironment
The larger societal forces that affect the microenvironment—demographic, economic, natural, technological, political, and cultural forces.

A company's **marketing environment** consists of the actors and forces outside marketing that affect marketing management's ability to build and maintain successful relationships with target customers. Like YouTube, companies constantly watch and adapt to the changing environment—or, in many cases, lead those changes.

More than any other group in the company, marketers must be environmental trend trackers and opportunity seekers. Although every manager in an organization should watch the outside environment, marketers have two special aptitudes. They have disciplined methods—marketing research and marketing intelligence—for collecting information about the marketing environment. They also spend more time in customer and competitor environments. By carefully studying the environment, marketers can adapt their strategies to meet new marketplace challenges and opportunities.

The marketing environment consists of a *microenvironment* and a *macroenvironment*. The **microenvironment** consists of the actors close to the company that affect its ability to serve its customers—the company, suppliers, marketing intermediaries, customer markets, competitors, and publics. The **macroenvironment** consists of the larger societal forces that affect the microenvironment—demographic, economic, natural, technological, political, and cultural forces. We look first at the company's microenvironment.

The Microenvironment

Author Comment ▶
The microenvironment includes all the actors close to the company that affect, positively or negatively, its ability to create value for and relationships with customers.

Marketing management's job is to build relationships with customers by creating customer value and satisfaction. However, marketing managers cannot do this alone. ▶ **Figure 3.1** shows the major actors in the marketer's microenvironment. Marketing success requires building relationships with other company departments, suppliers, marketing intermediaries, competitors, various publics, and customers, which combine to make up the company's value delivery network.

The Company

In designing marketing plans, marketing management takes other company groups into account—groups such as top management, finance, research and development (R&D), purchasing, operations, and accounting. All of these interrelated groups form the internal environment. Top management sets the company's mission, objectives, broad strategies, and policies. Marketing managers make decisions within the broader strategies and plans made by top management. Then, as we discussed in Chapter 2, marketing managers must work closely with other company departments. With marketing taking the lead, all departments—from manufacturing and finance to legal and human resources—share the responsibility for understanding customer needs and creating customer value.

Suppliers

Suppliers form an important link in the company's overall customer value delivery network. They provide the resources needed by the company to produce its goods and services. Supplier problems can seriously affect marketing. Marketing managers must watch supply availability and costs. Supply shortages or delays, labor strikes, natural disasters, and other events can cost sales in the short run and damage customer satisfaction in the long run. Rising supply costs may force price increases that can harm the company's sales volume.

Most marketers today treat their suppliers as partners in creating and delivering customer value. For example, cosmetics maker L'Oréal knows the importance of building close relationships with its extensive network of suppliers, who supply everything from polymers and fats to spray cans and packaging to production equipment and office supplies:[2]

> L'Oréal is the world's largest cosmetics manufacturer, with 23 brands in 130 countries ranging from Maybelline and Kiehl's to Lancôme and Redken. The company's supplier network is crucial to its success. As a result, L'Oréal treats suppliers as respected partners. On the one hand,

▶ **Figure 3.1** Actors in the Microenvironment

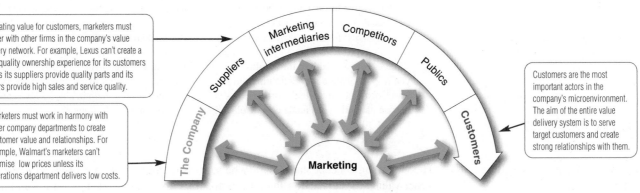

▲ L'Oréal builds long-term supplier relationships based on mutual benefit and growth. It "wants to make L'Oréal a top performer and one of the world's most respected companies. Being respected also means being respected by our suppliers."

TEH ENG KOON/AFP/Getty Images and PR NEWSWIRE/Newscom

Marketing intermediaries
Firms that help the company to promote, sell, and distribute its goods to final buyers.

the company expects a lot from suppliers in terms of design innovation, quality, and sustainability. On the other hand, L'Oréal works closely with suppliers to help them meet its exacting standards. According to the company's supplier Web site, it treats suppliers with "fundamental respect for their business, their culture, their growth, and the individuals who work there. Each relationship is based on . . . shared efforts aimed at promoting growth and mutual profits that make it possible for suppliers to invest, innovate, and compete." ▶ As a result, more than 75 percent of L'Oréal's supplier-partners have been working with the company for 10 years or more and the majority of them for several decades. Says the company's head of purchasing, "The CEO wants to make L'Oréal a top performer and one of the world's most respected companies. Being respected also means being respected by our suppliers."

Marketing Intermediaries

Marketing intermediaries help the company promote, sell, and distribute its products to final buyers. They include resellers, physical distribution firms, marketing services agencies, and financial intermediaries. *Resellers* are distribution channel firms that help the company find customers or make sales to them. These include wholesalers and retailers who buy and resell merchandise. Selecting and partnering with resellers is not easy. No longer do manufacturers have many small, independent resellers from which to choose. They now face large and growing reseller organizations, such as Walmart, Target, Home Depot, Costco, and Best Buy. These organizations frequently have enough power to dictate terms or even shut smaller manufacturers out of large markets.

Physical distribution firms help the company stock and move goods from their points of origin to their destinations. *Marketing services agencies* are the marketing research firms, advertising agencies, media firms, and marketing consulting firms that help the company target and promote its products to the right markets. *Financial intermediaries* include banks, credit companies, insurance companies, and other businesses that help finance transactions or insure against the risks associated with the buying and selling of goods.

Like suppliers, marketing intermediaries form an important component of the company's overall value delivery network. In its quest to create satisfying customer relationships, the company must do more than just optimize its own performance. It must partner effectively with marketing intermediaries to optimize the performance of the entire system.

Thus, today's marketers recognize the importance of working with their intermediaries as partners rather than simply as channels through which they sell their products. For example, when Coca-Cola signs on as the exclusive beverage provider for a fast-food chain, such as McDonald's, Wendy's, or Subway, it provides much more than just soft drinks. It also pledges powerful marketing support.[3]

Coca-Cola assigns cross-functional teams dedicated to understanding the finer points of each retail partner's business. It conducts a staggering amount of research on beverage consumers and shares these insights with its partners. It analyzes the demographics of U.S. zip code areas and helps partners determine which Coke brands are preferred in their areas. Coca-Cola has even studied the design of drive-through menu boards to better understand which layouts, fonts, letter sizes, colors, and visuals induce consumers to order more food and drink. Based on such insights, the Coca-Cola Food Service group develops marketing programs and merchandising tools that help its retail partners improve their beverage sales and profits. Its Web site, www.CokeSolutions.com, provides retailers with a wealth of information, business solutions, and merchandising tips. "We know that you're passionate about delighting guests and enhancing their real experiences on every level," says Coca-Cola to its retail partners. "As your partner, we want to help in any way we can." Such intense partnering has made Coca-Cola a runaway leader in the U.S. fountain soft-drink market.

Competitors

The marketing concept states that, to be successful, a company must provide greater customer value and satisfaction than its competitors do. Thus, marketers must do more than simply adapt to the needs of target consumers. They also must gain strategic advantage by positioning their offerings strongly against competitors' offerings in the minds of consumers.

No single competitive marketing strategy is best for all companies. Each firm should consider its own size and industry position compared to those of its competitors. Large firms with dominant positions in an industry can use certain strategies that smaller firms cannot afford. But being large is not enough. There are winning strategies for large firms, but there are also losing ones. And small firms can develop strategies that give them better rates of return than large firms enjoy.

Publics

Public

Any group that has an actual or potential interest in or impact on an organization's ability to achieve its objectives.

The company's marketing environment also includes various publics. A **public** is any group that has an actual or potential interest in or impact on an organization's ability to achieve its objectives. We can identify seven types of publics:

- *Financial publics.* This group influences the company's ability to obtain funds. Banks, investment analysts, and stockholders are the major financial publics.
- *Media publics.* This group carries news, features, and editorial opinion. It includes newspapers, magazines, television stations, and blogs and other Internet media.
- *Government publics.* Management must take government developments into account. Marketers must often consult the company's lawyers on issues of product safety, truth in advertising, and other matters.
- *Citizen-action publics.* A company's marketing decisions may be questioned by consumer organizations, environmental groups, minority groups, and others. Its public relations department can help it stay in touch with consumer and citizen groups.
- *Local publics.* This group includes neighborhood residents and community organizations. Large companies usually create departments and programs that deal with local community issues and provide community support. ▶ For example, the P&G Tide Loads of Hope program recognizes the importance of community publics. It provides mobile laundromats and loads of clean laundry to families in disaster-stricken areas. P&G washes, dries, and folds clothes for these families for free because "we've learned [that] sometimes even the littlest things can make a difference."[4]
- *General public.* A company needs to be concerned about the general public's attitude toward its products and activities. The public's image of the company affects its buying.
- *Internal publics.* This group includes workers, managers, volunteers, and the board of directors. Large companies use newsletters and other means to inform and motivate their internal publics. When employees feel good about the companies they work for, this positive attitude spills over to the external publics.

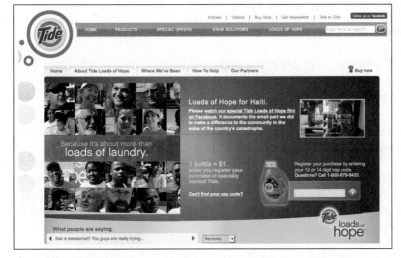

▲ **Publics: P&G's Tide Loads of Hope program recognizes the importance of community publics. It washes, dries, and folds loads of clothes for families struck by local disasters.**

The Procter & Gamble Company

A company can prepare marketing plans for these major publics as well as for its customer markets. Suppose the company wants a specific response from a particular public, such as goodwill, favorable word of mouth, or donations of time or money. The company would have to design an offer to this public that is attractive enough to produce the desired response.

Customers

As we've emphasized throughout, customers are the most important actors in the company's microenvironment. The aim of the entire value delivery network is to serve target customers and create strong relationships with them. The company might target any or all five types of customer markets. *Consumer markets* consist of individuals and households that buy goods and services for personal consumption. *Business markets* buy goods and services for further processing or use in their production processes, whereas *reseller markets* buy goods and services to resell at a profit. *Government markets* consist of government agencies that buy goods and services to produce public services or transfer the goods and services to others who need them. Finally, *international markets* consist of these buyers in other countries, including consumers, producers, resellers, and governments. Each market type has special characteristics that call for careful study by the seller.

The Macroenvironment

The company and all of the other actors operate in a larger macroenvironment of forces that shape opportunities and pose threats to the company. ▶ **Figure 3.2** shows the six major forces in the company's macroenvironment. In the remaining sections of this chapter, we examine these forces and show how they affect marketing plans.

The Demographic Environment

Demography is the study of human populations in terms of size, density, location, age, gender, race, occupation, and other statistics. The demographic environment is of major interest to marketers because it involves people, and people make up markets. The world population is growing at an explosive rate. It now exceeds 6.9 billion people and is expected to grow to more than 8 billion by the year 2030.[5] The world's large and highly diverse population poses both opportunities and challenges.

Demography
The study of human populations in terms of size, density, location, age, gender, race, occupation, and other statistics.

Changes in the world demographic environment have major implications for business. Thus, marketers keep a close eye on demographic trends and developments in their markets. They analyze changing age and family structures, geographic population shifts, educational characteristics, and population diversity. Here, we discuss the most important demographic trends in the United States.

The Changing Age Structure of the Population

The U.S. population currently stands at more than 311 million and may reach almost 364 million by 2030.[6] The single most important demographic trend in the United States is the changing age structure of the population. The U.S. population contains several generational groups. Here, we discuss the three largest groups—the baby boomers, Generation X, and the Millennials—and their impact on today's marketing strategies.

Baby boomers
The 78 million people born during the years following World War II and lasting until 1964.

The Baby Boomers. The post–World War II baby boom produced 78 million **baby boomers**, who were born between 1946 and 1964. Over the years, the baby boomers have been one of the most powerful forces shaping the marketing environment. The youngest

▶ **Figure 3.2** Major Forces in the Company's Macroenvironment

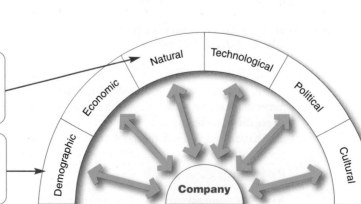

Concern for the natural environment has spawned a so-called green movement in industries ranging from PCs to diesel locomotives. For example, last year HP recovered and recycled 200 million pounds of electronics globally, equivalent to 800 jumbo jets.

Changing demographics mean changes in markets, which in turn require changes in marketing strategies. For example, Merrill Lynch now targets aging baby boomers to help them overcome the hurdles to retirement planning.

Marketers also want to be socially responsible citizens in their markets and communities. For example, shoe brand TOMS was *founded* on a cause: "No complicated formulas. It's simple," says the company's founder. "You buy a pair of TOMS and I give a pair to a child on your behalf."

boomers are now in their mid-forties; the oldest are in their sixties and entering retirement. The maturing boomers are rethinking the purpose and value of their work, responsibilities, and relationships.

After years of prosperity, free spending, and saving little, the Great Recession hit many baby boomers hard, especially the preretirement boomers. A sharp decline in stock prices and home values ate into their nest eggs and retirement prospects. As a result, many boomers are now spending more carefully and planning to work longer.

However, although some might be feeling the postrecession pinch, the baby boomers are still the wealthiest generation in U.S. history. Today's baby boomers account for about 25 percent of the U.S. population but control an estimated 80 percent of the nation's personal wealth. The 50-plus consumer segment now accounts for nearly half of all discretionary consumer spending.[7] As they reach their peak earning and spending years, the boomers will continue to constitute a lucrative market for financial services, new housing and home remodeling, new cars, travel and entertainment, eating out, health and fitness products, and just about everything else.

It would be a mistake to think of the older boomers as phasing out or slowing down. Today's boomers think young no matter how old they are. One study showed that boomers, on average, see themselves 12 years younger than they actually are. And rather than viewing themselves as phasing out, they see themselves as entering new life phases. The more active boomers—sometimes called zoomers, or baby boomers with zip—have no intention of abandoning their youthful lifestyles as they age. "It is time to throw out the notion that the only things marketable to [the older boomers] are chiropractic mattresses, arthritis drugs, and [staid] cruises," says one marketer. "Boomers have sought the fountain of youth through all stages of life and have incorporated aspects of play and fun into everything from careers to cars."[8]

Perhaps no one is targeting the baby boomers more fervently than the financial services industry. Collectively, the baby boomers have earned $3.7 trillion, more than twice as much as members of the prior generation. They'll also be inheriting $14 to $20 trillion during the next 20 years as their parents pass away. Thus, especially in the aftermath of the Great Recession, the boomers will need lots of money management help as they approach retirement. Merrill Lynch recently launched a marketing campaign aimed at helping boomers with retirement planning:[9]

> Most retirement ads from financial institutions show attractive older couples on the beach enjoying their idyllic golden years. In contrast, the Merrill Lynch retirement planning campaign talks about now—about the hurdles that people face in getting ready for their retirement. Themed "help2retire _____" (read "help2retire blank"), the campaign encourages 50-plus-year-olds to "fill in the blank" with aspects of their current working and financial lives that they'd like to resolve so they can focus on what matters most in retirement planning. Different ads suggest words such as help2retire Hassles, or Cold Feet, or Guesswork. Merrill Lynch research shows that recession-tempered boomers are cautiously optimistic about retirement but need help planning for it. Merrill wants to provide that help in the form of personalized financial advice. Merrill is approaching the topic from both a rational and an emotional standpoint. It's not just about "the numbers" but also about "life goals." Says the head of Merrill Lynch's Wealth Management: "It's not just about aspiring to get a second home in a warm location [anymore]. It's about spending more time with your family and friends and relieving the anxiety around the guesswork that so many [boomers] are feeling."

Generation X. The baby boom was followed by a *birth dearth*, creating another generation of 49 million people born between 1965 and 1976. Author Douglas Coupland calls them **Generation X** because they lie in the shadow of the boomers and lack obvious distinguishing characteristics.

Considerably smaller that the boomer generation that precedes them and the Millennials who follow, the Generation Xers are a sometimes overlooked consumer group. Although they seek success, they are less materialistic than the other groups; they prize experience, not acquisition. For many of the Gen Xers who are parents, family comes first—both children and their aging parents—and career second. From a marketing standpoint, the Gen

Generation X
The 49 million people born between 1965 and 1976 in the "birth dearth" following the baby boom.

▲ **Targeting Gen Xers:** Virginia tourism now aims its well-known "Virginia is for Lovers" campaign at Gen Xer families, who want new experiences close to home. "Love: It's at the heart of every Virginia vacation."

Virginia Tourism Corporation

Xers are a more skeptical bunch. They tend to research products before they consider a purchase, prefer quality to quantity, and tend to be less receptive to overt marketing pitches.

The Gen Xers have now grown up and are taking over. They are increasingly displacing the lifestyles, culture, and values of the baby boomers. They are moving up in their careers, and many are proud homeowners with young, growing families. They are the most educated generation to date, and they possess hefty annual purchasing power. They spend 62 percent more on housing, 50 percent more on apparel, and 27 percent more on entertainment than the average. However, like the baby boomers, the Gen Xers now face growing economic pressures. Like almost everyone else these days, they are spending more carefully.[10]

Still, with so much potential, many brands and organizations are focusing on Gen Xers as a prime target segment. ▶ For example, the Virginia Tourism Corporation, the state's tourism arm, is now targeting Gen X families:[11]

Virginia's 40-year romance with the baby boomer generation is waning. The Virginia Tourism Corporation (VTC), best known for its enduring "Virginia is for Lovers" campaign, is now wooing a new audience: Generation X. They're younger and more adventuresome, and they spend more money on travel in Virginia. VTC research showed that Generation X households contribute about 45 percent of the $19.2 billion spent on travel in Virginia each year. Whereas boomers are mostly done with child rearing and lean toward more exotic travel locations farther from home, "the Generation Xers are new families who need new experiences close to home," says Alisa Bailey, CEO and president of VTC. "They want beaches, good places to relax, warm, friendly people. They love amusement and theme parks, and they want places that are good for what we call soft adventure, like canoeing, and hiking." The "Virginia is for Lovers" slogan hasn't changed. But marketing now targets a younger market, showing more Gen X families. It also uses more Generation X-oriented media, such as Facebook, Twitter, and blogs.

Millennials (or Generation Y)

The 83 million children of the baby boomers born between 1977 and 2000.

Millennials. Both the baby boomers and Gen Xers will one day be passing the reins to the **Millennials** (also called **Generation Y** or the echo boomers). Born between 1977 and 2000, these children of the baby boomers number 83 million or more, dwarfing the Gen Xers and becoming larger even than the baby boomer segment.[12] In the postrecession era, the Millennials are the most financially strapped generation. Facing higher unemployment and saddled with more debt, many of these young consumers have near-empty piggy banks. Still, because of their numbers, the Millennials make up a huge and attractive market, both now and in the future.

One thing that all Millennials have in common is their utter fluency and comfort with digital technology. They don't just embrace technology; it's a way of life. The Millennials were the first generation to grow up in a world filled with computers, mobile phones, satellite TV, iPods and iPads, and online social networks. As a result, they engage with brands in an entirely new way, such as with mobile or social media. "They tend to expect one-to-one communication with brands," says one analyst, "and embrace the ability to share the good and bad about products and services with friends and strangers."[13]

Rather than having mass marketing messages pushed at them, the Millennials prefer to seek out information and engage in two-way brand conversations. Thus, reaching them effectively requires creative marketing approaches. ▶ For example, consider Keds, the 95-year-old sneaker brand, which recently launched an integrative marketing campaign aimed at reintroducing the iconic brand to young Millennial consumers.[14]

The Keds campaign—called "How Do You Do?"—engages the Millennials firsthand through print ads, a micro Web site, YouTube videos, Twitter, Facebook, brand ambassadors, artists,

Targeting Millennials: The Keds "How Do You Do?" campaign urges young Millennial consumers to engage, create, and collaborate, portraying Keds sneakers as a canvas to express that creativity.

Xiao Chang/The Daily Pennsylvanian

and a mobile campus tour. At the heart of the campaign is a 32-foot white Keds shoebox on wheels, which is making a cross-country tour of college campuses. The arts-based campaign urges Millennials to engage, create, and collaborate, emphasizing Keds sneakers as a canvas for expressing that creativity. Inside the mobile shoebox, visitors can watch videos about the local artists, retail outlets, and charity organizations that Keds is working with in each city. They can also see a gallery of locally inspired Keds shoes or even use a touch-screen kiosk to customize and purchase their own sneakers at the Keds Web site. Other campaign elements expand on the "How Do You Do?" campaign slogan. As it tours from city to city, the campaign asks Millennials questions to tweet about, such as "How Do You Do Austin?" or "How Do You Do Inspiration?" or, simply, "How Do You Do Keds?" "We really feel that what's important to this consumer is to engage with a brand and experience [it] firsthand," says Keds president Kristin Kohler.

Generational Marketing. Do marketers need to create separate products and marketing programs for each generation? Some experts warn that marketers need to be careful about turning off one generation each time they craft a product or message that appeals effectively to another. Others caution that each generation spans decades of time and many socioeconomic levels. For example, marketers often split the baby boomers into three smaller groups—leading-edge boomers, core boomers, and trailing-edge boomers—each with its own beliefs and behaviors. Similarly, they split the Millennials into teens and young adults.

Thus, marketers need to form more precise age-specific segments within each group. More important, defining people by their birth date may be less effective than segmenting them by their lifestyle, life stage, or the common values they seek in the products they buy. We will discuss many other ways to segment markets in Chapter 6.

The Changing American Family

The traditional household consists of a husband, wife, and children (and sometimes grandparents). Yet, the once American ideal of the two-child, two-car suburban family has lately been losing some of its luster.

In the United States today, married couples with children represent only 21 percent of the nation's 117 million households, married couples without children represent 30 percent, and single parents are another 17 percent. A full 32 percent are nonfamily households—singles living alone or adults of one or both sexes living together.[15] More people are divorcing or separating, choosing not to marry, marrying later, or marrying without intending to have children. Marketers must increasingly consider the special needs of nontraditional households because they are now growing more rapidly than traditional households. Each group has distinctive needs and buying habits.

The number of working women has also increased greatly, growing from under 40 percent of the U.S. workforce in the late 1950s to 59 percent today. Both husband and wife work in 59 percent of all married-couple families. Meanwhile, more men are staying home with their children and managing the household while their wives go to work. According to one estimate, the number of stay-at-home dads reached nearly 2 million last year, or one in every 15 fathers.[16]

The significant number of women in the workforce has spawned the child day-care business and increased the consumption of career-oriented women's clothing, convenience foods, financial services, and time-saving services. Royal Caribbean targets time-crunched working moms with budget-friendly family vacations that are easy to plan and certain to wow the family. Royal Caribbean estimates that, although vacations are a joint decision, 80 percent of all trips are planned and booked by women—moms who are pressed for time, whether they work or not. "We want to make sure that you're the hero, that when your family comes on our ship, it's going to be a great experience for all of them," says a senior marketer at Royal Caribbean, "and that you, mom, who has done all the planning and scheduling, get to enjoy that vacation."[17]

Geographic Shifts in Population

This is a period of great migratory movements between and within countries. Americans, for example, are a mobile people, with about 15 percent of all U.S. residents moving each year. Over the past two decades, the U.S. population has shifted toward the Sunbelt states. The West and South have grown, whereas the Midwest and Northeast states have lost population.[18] Such population shifts interest marketers because people in different regions buy differently. For example, people in the Midwest buy more winter clothing than people in the Southeast.

Also, for more than a century, Americans have been moving from rural to metropolitan areas. In the 1950s, they made a massive exit from the cities to the suburbs. Today, the migration to the suburbs continues. And more and more Americans are moving to *micropolitan areas*, small cities located beyond congested metropolitan areas, such as Bozeman, Montana; Natchez, Mississippi; and Torrington, Connecticut. These smaller micros offer many of the advantages of metro areas—jobs, restaurants, diversions, community organizations—but without the population crush, traffic jams, high crime rates, and high property taxes often associated with heavily urbanized areas.[19]

The shift in where people live has also caused a shift in where they work. For example, the migration toward micropolitan and suburban areas has resulted in a rapid increase in the number of people who *telecommute*—work at home or in a remote office and conduct their business by phone or the Internet. This trend, in turn, has created a booming SOHO (small office/home office) market. An increasing number of people are working from home with the help of electronic conveniences such as PCs, smartphones, and broadband Internet access. One recent study estimates that more than one-half of American businesses now support some kind of telecommuting program, and 8.1 million Americans work solely from home.[20]

Many marketers are actively courting the lucrative telecommuting market. ▶ For example, WebEx, the Web-conferencing division of Cisco, helps connect people who telecommute or work remotely. With WebEx, people can meet and collaborate online via computer or smartphone, no matter what their work location. "All you need to run effective online meetings is a browser and a phone," says the company. With WebEx, people working anywhere can interact with other individuals or small groups to make presentations, exchange documents, and share desktops, complete with audio and full-motion video.[21]

▲ Cisco targets the growing telecommuter market with WebEx, which lets people meet and collaborate online, no matter what their work location.

© 2011 Cisco Systems, Inc.

A Better-Educated, More White-Collar, More Professional Population

The U.S. population is becoming better educated. For example, in 2009, 87 percent of the U.S. population over age 25 had completed high school and 30 percent had completed college, compared with 69 percent and 17 percent, respectively, in 1980. Moreover, nearly two-thirds of high school graduates now enroll in college within 12 months of graduating.[22] The workforce also is becoming more white collar. Job growth is now strongest for professional workers and weakest for manufacturing workers. Between 2008 and 2018, the number of professional workers is expected to increase 17 percent, while manufacturing workers are expected to decline more than 24 percent.[23] The rising number of educated professionals will affect not just what people buy but also how they buy.

Increasing Diversity

Countries vary in their ethnic and racial makeup. At one extreme is Japan, where almost everyone is Japanese. At the other extreme is the United States, with people from virtually all national origins. The United States has often been called a melting pot, where diverse groups from many nations and cultures have melted into a single, more homogenous whole. Instead, the United States seems to have become more of a "salad bowl" in which various groups have mixed together but have maintained their diversity by retaining and valuing important ethnic and cultural differences.

Marketers now face increasingly diverse markets, both at home and abroad, as their operations become more international in scope. The U.S. population is about 65 percent white, with Hispanics at about 16 percent and African Americans at about 13 percent. The U.S. Asian American population now totals 4.6 percent of the total U.S. population, with the remaining 1.8 percent being American Indian, Eskimo, Aleut, or people of two or more races. Moreover, more than 34 million people living in the United States—more than 13 percent of the population—were born in another country. The nation's ethnic populations are expected to explode in coming decades. By 2050, Hispanics will be an estimated 30 percent of the population, African Americans will hold steady at about 13 percent, and Asians will increase to 7.8 percent.[24]

Most large companies, from P&G, Walmart, Allstate, and Bank of America to Levi Strauss and Harley-Davidson, now target specially designed products, ads, and promotions to one or more of these groups. For example, Harley-Davidson recently launched a print and online campaign celebrating the dedication and pride of Hispanic Harley riders, or Harlistas, and their relationships with the brand. Harley even invited Hispanic riders to share their own experiences about what being a part of the Harlista community means to them. It showcases the passion and commitment of Harlistas in a documentary—*Harlistas: An American Journey*—directed by an award-winning director. "Being a Harlista," says one ad, "is about living fearlessly, overcoming obstacles, and experiencing the camaraderie of the open road." In addition, Harley-Davidson has long been a supporter of the Latin Billboard Music Awards, Lowrider Tours, Los Angeles' Fiesta Broadway, and one of the largest Hispanic motorcycle clubs in the United States, the Latin American Motorcycle Association (LAMA).[25]

Diversity goes beyond ethnic heritage. For example, another attractive diversity segment is the 54 million U.S. adults with disabilities—a market larger than African Americans or Hispanics—representing more than $220 billion in annual spending power. Most individuals with disabilities are active consumers. For example, one study found that the segment spends $13.6 billion on 31.7 million business or leisure trips every year. And if certain needs were met, the amount spent on travel could double to $27 billion annually.[26]

▲ Targeting consumers with disabilities: Samsung features people with disabilities in its mainstream advertising and signs endorsement deals with Paralympic athletes.

GEPA/Imago/Icon SMI/Newscom

How are companies trying to reach consumers with disabilities? Many marketers now recognize that the worlds of people with disabilities and those without disabilities are one in the same. Marketers such as McDonald's, Verizon Wireless, Nike, Samsung, and Honda have featured people with disabilities in their mainstream marketing. ▶ For instance, Samsung and Nike sign endorsement deals with Paralympic athletes and feature them in advertising.

Many major companies also explicitly target gay and lesbian consumers. According to one estimate, the 6 to 7 percent of U.S. adults who identify themselves as lesbian, gay, bisexual, and transgender (LGBT) have buying power of over $743 billion.[27] As a result of TV shows such as *Modern Family* and *Glee,* movies like *Brokeback Mountain* and *The Kids Are All Right,* and openly gay celebrities and public figures such as Neil Patrick Harris, Ellen DeGeneres, David Sedaris, and Congressman Barney Frank, the LGBT community has increasingly emerged into the public eye.

A number of media now provide companies with access to this market. For example, Planet Out Inc., a leading global media and entertainment company that exclusively serves the LGBT community, offers several successful magazines (*Out, The Advocate, Out Traveler*) and Web sites (Gay.com and PlanetOut.com). In addition, media giant Viacom's MTV Networks offer LOGO, a cable television network aimed at gays and lesbians and their friends and family. LOGO is now available in 46 million U.S. households. The network also manages seven LGBT Web sites such as 365GAY.com and AfterEllen.com. More than 100 mainstream marketers have advertised on LOGO, including Ameriprise Financial, Anheuser-Busch, Continental Airlines, Dell, Levi Strauss, eBay, J&J, Orbitz, Sears, Sony, and Subaru.

Companies in a wide range of industries are now targeting the LGBT community with gay-specific marketing efforts. For example, American Airlines has a dedicated LGBT sales team, sponsors gay community events, and offers a special gay-oriented Web site (www.aa.com/rainbow) that features travel deals, an e-newsletter, podcasts, and a gay events calendar. The airline's focus on gay consumers has earned it double-digit revenue growth from the LGBT community each year for more than a decade.[28]

As the population in the United States grows more diverse, successful marketers will continue to diversify their marketing programs to take advantage of opportunities in fast-growing segments.

SPEED BUMP | LINKING THE CONCEPTS

Pull over here and think about how deeply these demographic factors impact all of us and, as a result, marketing strategies.

- Apply these demographic developments to your own life. Give some specific examples of how changing demographic factors affect you and your buying behavior.
- Identify a specific company that has done a good job of reacting to the shifting demographic environment—generational segments (baby boomers, Gen Xers, or Millennials), the changing American family, and increased diversity. Compare this company to one that's done a poor job.

Author Comment ▶
The economic environment can offer both opportunities and threats. For example, in the postrecession era of more sensible consumer spending, "value" has become the marketing watchword.

Economic environment
Economic factors that affect consumer purchasing power and spending patterns.

The Economic Environment

Markets require buying power as well as people. The **economic environment** consists of economic factors that affect consumer purchasing power and spending patterns. Marketers must pay close attention to major trends and consumer spending patterns both across and within their world markets.

Nations vary greatly in their levels and distribution of income. Some countries have *industrial economies*, which constitute rich markets for many different kinds of goods. At the other extreme are *subsistence economies*; they consume most of their own agricultural and industrial output and offer few market opportunities. In between are *developing economies* that can offer outstanding marketing opportunities for the right kinds of products.

Consider India with its population of more than 1.1 billion people. In the past, only India's elite could afford to buy a car. In fact, only one in seven Indians currently owns one. But recent dramatic changes in India's economy have produced a growing middle class and rapidly rising incomes. Now, to meet the new demand, European, North American, and Asian automakers are introducing smaller, more-affordable vehicles in India. But they'll have to find a way to compete with India's Tata Motors, which markets the least expensive car ever in the world, the Tata Nano. Dubbed "the people's car," the Nano sells for just over 100,000 rupees (about US$2,500). It can seat four passengers, gets 50 miles per gallon, and travels at a top speed of 60 miles per hour. The ultralow-cost car is designed to be India's Model T—the car that puts the developing nation on wheels. ▶ "Can you imagine a car within the reach of all?" asks a Nano advertisement. "Now you can," comes the answer. Tata hopes to sell one million of these vehicles per year.[29]

Changes in Consumer Spending

Economic factors can have a dramatic effect on consumer spending and buying behavior. For example, until fairly recently, American consumers spent freely, fueled by income growth, a boom in the stock market, rapid increases in housing values, and other economic

Can you imagine a car within the reach of all?

Can you fit your family into the smallest of cars? Without a squeeze?

now you can.

Can you feel the safety of a big car? In a car nearly half its size?

Can you find more miles in your every litre? Almost as much as a two wheeler?

Can you make a difference to the environment? By hurting it the least?

Can you imagine a car that will change the world? Again.

nano

TATA MOTORS

▲ **Economic environment: To capture India's growing middle class, Tata Motors introduced the small, affordable Tata Nano. "Can you imagine a car within the reach of all?" asks this advertisement. "Now you can."**
Tata Motors Limited

Author Comment ▶
Today's enlightened companies are developing *environmentally sustainable* strategies in an effort to create a world economy that the planet can support indefinitely.

Natural environment
Natural resources that are needed as inputs by marketers or that are affected by marketing activities.

good fortunes. They bought and bought, seemingly without caution, amassing record levels of debt. However, the free spending and high expectations of those days were dashed by the Great Recession of 2008/2009.

As a result, as discussed in Chapter 1, consumers have now adopted a back-to-basics sensibility in their lifestyles and spending patterns that will likely persist for years to come. They are buying less and looking for greater value in the things that they do buy. In turn, *value marketing* has become the watchword for many marketers. Marketers in all industries are looking for ways to offer today's more financially frugal buyers greater value—just the right combination of product quality and good service at a fair price.

You'd expect value pitches from the sellers of everyday products. For example, as Target has shifted emphasis toward the "Pay Less" side of its "Expect More. Pay Less." slogan, the once-chic headlines at the Target.com Web site have been replaced by more practical appeals such as "Our lowest prices of the season," "Fun, sun, save," and "Free shipping, every day." However, these days, even luxury-brand marketers are emphasizing good value. For instance, upscale car brand Infiniti now promises to "make luxury affordable."

Income Distribution

Marketers should pay attention to *income distribution* as well as income levels. Over the past several decades, the rich have grown richer, the middle class has shrunk, and the poor have remained poor. The top 5 percent of American earners get nearly 22 percent of the country's adjusted gross income, and the top 20 percent of earners capture almost 50 percent of all income. In contrast, the bottom 40 percent of American earners get just 12.6 percent of the total income.[30]

This distribution of income has created a tiered market. Many companies—such as Nordstrom and Neiman Marcus—aggressively target the affluent. Others—such as Dollar General and Family Dollar—target those with more modest means. In fact, dollar stores are now the fastest-growing retailers in the nation. Still other companies tailor their marketing offers across a range of markets, from the affluent to the less affluent. For example, Ford offers cars ranging from the low-priced Ford Fiesta, starting at $13,200, to the luxury Lincoln Navigator SUV, starting at $57,630.

Changes in major economic variables, such as income, cost of living, interest rates, and savings and borrowing patterns, have a large impact on the marketplace. Companies watch these variables by using economic forecasting. Businesses do not have to be wiped out by an economic downturn or caught short in a boom. With adequate warning, they can take advantage of changes in the economic environment.

The Natural Environment

The **natural environment** involves the natural resources that are needed as inputs by marketers or that are affected by marketing activities. Environmental concerns have grown steadily over the past three decades. In many cities around the world, air and water pollution have reached dangerous levels. World concern continues to mount about the possibilities of global warming, and many environmentalists fear that we soon will be buried in our own trash.

Marketers should be aware of several trends in the natural environment. The first involves growing shortages of raw materials. Air and water may seem to be infinite resources, but some groups see long-run dangers. Air pollution chokes many of the world's large cities, and water shortages are already a big problem in some parts of the United States and the world. By 2030, more than one in three people in the world will not have enough water to drink.[31] Renewable resources, such as forests and food, also have to be used wisely. Nonrenewable resources, such as oil, coal, and various minerals, pose a serious problem. Firms making products that require these scarce resources face large cost increases, even if the materials remain available.

A second environmental trend is *increased pollution*. Industry will almost always damage the quality of the natural environment. Consider the disposal of chemical and nuclear wastes; the dangerous mercury levels in the ocean; the quantity of chemical pollutants in the soil and food supply; and the littering of the environment with nonbiodegradable bottles, plastics, and other packaging materials.

A third trend is *increased government intervention* in natural resource management. The governments of different countries vary in their concern and efforts to promote a clean environment. Some, such as the German government, vigorously pursue environmental quality. Others, especially many poorer nations, do little about pollution, largely because they lack the needed funds or political will. Even richer nations lack the vast funds and political accord needed to mount a worldwide environmental effort. The general hope is that companies around the world will accept more social responsibility and that less expensive devices can be found to control and reduce pollution.

In the United States, the Environmental Protection Agency (EPA) was created in 1970 to create and enforce pollution standards and conduct pollution research. In the future, companies doing business in the United States can expect continued strong controls from government and pressure groups. Instead of opposing regulation, marketers should help develop solutions to the material and energy problems facing the world.

Concern for the natural environment has spawned the so-called green movement. Today, enlightened companies go beyond what government regulations dictate. They are developing strategies and practices that support **environmental sustainability**—an effort to create a world economy that the planet can support indefinitely.

Environmental sustainability
Developing strategies and practices that create a world economy that the planet can support indefinitely.

Many companies are responding to consumer demands with more environmentally responsible products. Others are developing recyclable or biodegradable packaging, recycled materials and components, better pollution controls, and more energy-efficient operations. For example, PepsiCo—which owns brands ranging from Frito-Lay and Pepsi to Quaker, Gatorade, and Tropicana—is working to dramatically reduce its environmental footprint.[32]

PepsiCo markets hundreds of products that are grown, produced, and consumed worldwide. Making and distributing these products requires water, electricity, and fuel. In 2007, the company set as its goal to reduce water consumption by 20 percent, electricity consumption by 20 percent, and fuel consumption by 25 percent per unit of production by 2015. It's already well on its way to meeting these goals. ▶ For example, a solar-panel field now generates power for three-quarters of the heat used in Frito-Lay's Modesto, California, SunChips plant and SunChips themselves come in the world's first 100 percent compostable package. A wind turbine now supplies more than two-thirds of the power at PepsiCo's beverage plant in Mamandur, India. On the packaging front, PepsiCo recently introduced new half-liter bottles of its Lipton iced tea, Tropicana juice, Aquafina Flavor-Splash, and Aquafina Alive beverages that contain 20 percent less plastic than the original packaging. Aquafina has trimmed the amount of plastic used in its bottles by 35 percent since 2002, saving 50 million pounds of plastic annually.

▲ **Environmental sustainability: PepsiCo is working to reduce its environmental footprint. For example, a solar-panel field now generates three-quarters of the heat used in Frito-Lay's Modesto, California, SunChips plant and SunChips themselves come in the world's first 100 percent compostable package.**

AP Images/Mary Altaffer

Companies today are looking to do more than just good deeds. More and more, they are recognizing the link between a healthy ecology and a healthy economy. They are learning that environmentally responsible actions can also be good business.

Author Comment ▶

Technological advances are perhaps the most dramatic forces affecting today's marketing strategies. Just think about the tremendous impact of the Web—which emerged in the mid-1990s—on marketing. You'll see examples of the fast-growing world of online marketing throughout every chapter, and we'll discuss it in detail in Chapter 14.

Technological environment

Forces that create new technologies, creating new product and market opportunities.

The Technological Environment

The **technological environment** is perhaps the most dramatic force now shaping our destiny. Technology has released such wonders as antibiotics, robotic surgery, miniaturized electronics, smartphones, and the Internet. It also has released such horrors as nuclear missiles, chemical weapons, and assault rifles. It has released such mixed blessings as the automobile, television, and credit cards. Our attitude toward technology depends on whether we are more impressed with its wonders or its blunders.

New technologies can offer exciting opportunities for marketers. For example, what would you think about having tiny little transmitters implanted in all the products you buy, which would allow tracking of the products from their point of production through use and disposal? On the one hand, it would provide many advantages to both buyers and sellers. On the other hand, it could be a bit scary. Either way, it's already happening:

> Envision a world in which every product contains a tiny transmitter, loaded with information. As you stroll through supermarket aisles, shelf sensors detect your selections and beam ads to your shopping cart screen, offering special deals on related products. As your cart fills, scanners detect that you might be buying for a dinner party; the screen suggests a wine to go with the meal you've planned. When you leave the store, exit scanners total up your purchases and automatically charge them to your credit card. At home, readers track what goes into and out of your pantry, updating your shopping list when stocks run low. For Sunday dinner, you pop a Butterball turkey into your "smart oven," which follows instructions from an embedded chip and cooks the bird to perfection. Seem far-fetched? Not really. In fact, it might soon become a reality, thanks to radio-frequency identification (RFID) transmitters that can be embedded in the products you buy.

Many firms are already using RFID technology to track products through various points in the distribution channel. ▶ For example, Walmart has strongly encouraged suppliers shipping products to its distribution centers to apply RFID tags to their pallets. So far, more than 600 Walmart suppliers are doing so. And clothing retailer American Apparel uses RFID to manage inventory in many of its retail stores. Every stocked item carries an RFID tag, which is scanned at the receiving docks as the item goes into inventory. American Apparel puts only one of each item on the store floor at a time. When the item is sold, a point-of-sale RFID reader alerts the inventory system and prompts employees to bring a replacement onto the floor. Another RFID reader located between the stockroom and the store floor checks to see that this was done. In all, the system creates inventory efficiencies and ensures that the right items are always on the sales floor. As a result, American Apparel stores with RFID systems average 14 percent higher sales but 15 percent lower stockroom inventories than other stores. And the chain's RFID stores require 20 to 30 percent fewer staff because employees don't have to spend five or more hours a day doing manual inventory checks.[33]

▲ **Technological environment: Envision a world in which every product contains a transmitter loaded with information. In fact, it's already happening on the back of RFID product labels like this one at Walmart.**

Marc F. Henning/Alamy

The technological environment changes rapidly. Think of all of today's common products that were not available 100 years ago—or even 30 years ago. Abraham Lincoln did not know about automobiles, airplanes, radios, or the electric light. Woodrow Wilson did not know about television, aerosol cans, automatic dishwashers, air conditioners, antibiotics, or computers. Franklin Delano Roosevelt did not know about xerography, synthetic detergents, birth control pills, jet engines, or earth satellites. John F. Kennedy did not know about PCs, cell phones, the Internet, or Google.

New technologies create new markets and opportunities. However, every new technology replaces an older technology. Transistors hurt the vacuum-tube industry, digital photography hurt the film business, and MP3 players and digital downloads are hurting the CD business. When old industries fought or ignored new technologies, their businesses declined. Thus, marketers should watch the technological environment closely. Companies that do not keep up will soon find their products outdated. If that happens, they will miss new product and market opportunities.

As products and technology become more complex, the public needs to know that these items are safe. Thus, government agencies investigate and ban potentially unsafe products. In the United States, the Food and Drug Administration (FDA) has created complex regulations for testing new drugs. The Consumer Product Safety Commission (CPSC) establishes safety standards for consumer products and penalizes companies that fail to meet them. Such regulations have resulted in much higher research costs and longer times between new product ideas and their introduction. Marketers should be aware of these regulations when applying new technologies and developing new products.

The Political and Social Environment

Marketing decisions are strongly affected by developments in the political environment. The **political environment** consists of laws, government agencies, and pressure groups that influence or limit various organizations and individuals in a given society.

Legislation Regulating Business

Even the strongest advocates of free-market economies agree that the system works best with at least some regulation. Well-conceived regulation can encourage competition and ensure fair markets for goods and services. Thus, governments develop *public policy* to guide commerce—sets of laws and regulations that limit business for the good of society as a whole. Almost every marketing activity is subject to a wide range of laws and regulations.

Legislation affecting business around the world has increased steadily over the years. The United States and many other countries have many laws covering issues such as competition, fair trade practices, environmental protection, product safety, truth in advertising, consumer privacy, packaging and labeling, pricing, and other important areas (see Table 3.1).

Understanding the public policy implications of a particular marketing activity is not a simple matter. In the United States, there are many laws created at the national, state, and local levels, and these regulations often overlap. For example, aspirins sold in Dallas are governed by both federal labeling laws and Texas state advertising laws. Moreover, regulations are constantly changing; what was allowed last year may now be prohibited, and what was prohibited may now be allowed. Marketers must work hard to keep up with changes in regulations and their interpretations.

Business legislation has been enacted for a number of reasons. The first is to *protect companies* from each other. Although business executives may praise competition, they sometimes try to neutralize it when it threatens them. Therefore, laws are passed to define and prevent unfair competition. In the United States, such laws are enforced by the FTC and the Antitrust Division of the Attorney General's office.

The second purpose of government regulation is to *protect consumers* from unfair business practices. Some firms, if left alone, would make shoddy products, invade consumer privacy, mislead consumers in their advertising, and deceive consumers through their packaging and pricing. Unfair business practices have been defined and are enforced by various agencies.

The third purpose of government regulation is to *protect the interests of society* against unrestrained business behavior. Profitable business activity does not always create a better quality of life. Regulation arises to ensure that firms take responsibility for the social costs of their production or products.

International marketers will encounter dozens, or even hundreds, of agencies set up to enforce trade policies and regulations. In the United States, Congress has established federal regulatory agencies, such as the FTC, the FDA, the Federal Communications Commission, the Federal Energy Regulatory Commission, the Federal Aviation Administration, the Consumer Product Safety Commission, the Environmental Protection Agency, and hundreds of others. Because such government agencies have some discretion in enforcing the laws, they can have a major impact on a company's marketing performance.

New laws and their enforcement will continue to increase. Business executives must watch these developments when planning their products and marketing programs. Marketers

> **Table 3.1** | Major U.S. Legislation Affecting Marketing

Legislation	Purpose
Sherman Antitrust Act (1890)	Prohibits monopolies and activities (price fixing, predatory pricing) that restrain trade or competition in interstate commerce.
Federal Food and Drug Act (1906)	Created the Food and Drug Administration (FDA). It forbids the manufacture or sale of adulterated or fraudulently labeled foods and drugs.
Clayton Act (1914)	Supplements the Sherman Act by prohibiting certain types of price discrimination, exclusive dealing, and tying clauses (which require a dealer to take additional products in a seller's line).
Federal Trade Commission Act (1914)	Established the Federal Trade Commission (FTC), which monitors and remedies unfair trade methods.
Robinson-Patman Act (1936)	Amends the Clayton Act to define price discrimination as unlawful. Empowers the FTC to establish limits on quantity discounts, forbid some brokerage allowances, and prohibit promotional allowances except when made available on proportionately equal terms.
Wheeler-Lea Act (1938)	Makes deceptive, misleading, and unfair practices illegal regardless of injury to competition. Places advertising of food and drugs under FTC jurisdiction.
Lanham Trademark Act (1946)	Protects and regulates distinctive brand names and trademarks.
National Traffic and Safety Act (1958)	Provides for the creation of compulsory safety standards for automobiles and tires.
Fair Packaging and Labeling Act (1966)	Provides for the regulation of packaging and the labeling of consumer goods. Requires that manufacturers state what the package contains, who made it, and how much it contains.
Child Protection Act (1966)	Bans the sale of hazardous toys and articles. Sets standards for child resistant packaging.
Federal Cigarette Labeling and Advertising Act (1967)	Requires that cigarette packages contain the following statement: "Warning: The Surgeon General Has Determined That Cigarette Smoking Is Dangerous to Your Health."
National Environmental Policy Act (1969)	Establishes a national policy on the environment. The 1970 Reorganization Plan established the Environmental Protection Agency (EPA).
Consumer Product Safety Act (1972)	Establishes the Consumer Product Safety Commission and authorizes it to set safety standards for consumer products as well as exact penalties for failing to uphold those standards.
Magnuson-Moss Warranty Act (1975)	Authorizes the FTC to determine rules and regulations for consumer warranties and provides consumer access to redress, such as the class action suit.
Children's Television Act (1990)	Limits the number of commercials aired during children's programs.
Nutrition Labeling and Education Act (1990)	Requires that food product labels provide detailed nutritional information.
Telephone Consumer Protection Act (1991)	Establishes procedures to avoid unwanted telephone solicitations. Limits marketers' use of automatic telephone dialing systems and artificial or prerecorded voices.
Americans with Disabilities Act (1991)	Makes discrimination against people with disabilities illegal in public accommodations, transportation, and telecommunications.
Children's Online Privacy Protection Act (2000)	Prohibits Web sites or online services operators from collecting personal information from children without obtaining consent from a parent and allowing parents to review information collected from their children.
Do-Not-Call Implementation Act (2003)	Authorizes the FTC to collect fees from sellers and telemarketers for the implementation and enforcement of a National Do-Not-Call Registry.
CAN-SPAM Act (2003)	Regulates the distribution and content of unsolicited commercial e-mail.
Financial Reform Law (2010)	Creates the Bureau of Consumer Financial Protection, which writes and enforces rules for the marketing of financial products to consumers. It is also responsible for enforcement of the Truth-in-Lending Act, the Home Mortgage Disclosure Act, and other laws designed to protect consumers.

need to know about the major laws protecting competition, consumers, and society. They need to understand these laws at the local, state, national, and international levels.

Increased Emphasis on Ethics and Socially Responsible Actions

Written regulations cannot possibly cover all potential marketing abuses, and existing laws are often difficult to enforce. However, beyond written laws and regulations, business is also governed by social codes and rules of professional ethics.

Socially Responsible Behavior. Enlightened companies encourage their managers to look beyond what the regulatory system allows and simply "do the right thing." These socially responsible firms actively seek out ways to protect the long-run interests of their consumers and the environment.

The recent rash of business scandals, as well as increased concerns about the environment, have created fresh interest in the issues of ethics and social responsibility. Almost every aspect of marketing involves such issues. Unfortunately, because these issues usually involve conflicting interests, well-meaning people can honestly disagree about the right course of action in a given situation. Thus, many industrial and professional trade associations have suggested codes of ethics. And more companies are now developing policies, guidelines, and other responses to complex social responsibility issues.

The boom in Internet marketing has created a new set of social and ethical issues. Critics worry most about online privacy issues. There has been an explosion in the amount of personal digital data available. Users, themselves, supply some of it. They voluntarily place highly private information on social-networking sites, such as Facebook or LinkedIn, or on genealogy sites that are easily searched by anyone with a computer or a smart phone.

However, much of the information is systematically developed by businesses seeking to learn more about their customers, often without consumers realizing that they are under the microscope. Legitimate businesses track consumers' Internet browsing and buying behavior and collect, analyze, and share digital data from every move consumers make at their Web sites. Critics worry that these companies may now know *too* much and might use digital data to take unfair advantage of consumers. Although most companies fully disclose their Internet privacy policies and most try to use data to benefit their customers, abuses do occur. As a result, consumer advocates and policymakers are taking action to protect consumer privacy. In Chapter 16, we discuss these and other societal marketing issues in greater depth.

Cause-Related Marketing. To exercise their social responsibility and build more positive images, many companies are now linking themselves to worthwhile causes. These days, every product seems to be tied to some cause. Buy a pink mixer from KitchenAid and support breast cancer research. Purchase a special edition bottle of Dawn dishwashing detergent, and P&G will donate a dollar to help rescue and rehabilitate wildlife affected by oil spills. Go to Staples' DoSomething101 Web site or Facebook page and fill a virtual backpack with essential school supplies needed by school children living in poverty. Pay for these purchases with the right charge card and you can support a local cultural arts group or help fight heart disease.

In fact, some companies are founded entirely on cause-related missions. Under the concept of "values-led business" or "caring capitalism," their mission is to use business to make the world a better place. For example, TOMS Shoes was founded as a for-profit company—it wants to make money selling shoes. But the company has an equally important not-for-profit mission—putting shoes on the feet of needy children around the world. For every pair of shoes you buy from TOMS, the company will give another pair to a child in need on your behalf.

Cause-related marketing has become a primary form of corporate giving. It lets companies "do well by doing good" by linking purchases of the company's products or services with benefiting worthwhile causes or charitable organizations. ▶ At TOMS Shoes, the "do well" and "do good" missions go hand in hand. Beyond being socially admirable, the buy-one-give-one-away concept is also a good business proposition. "Giving not only makes you feel good, but it actually is a very good business strategy," says TOMS founder

▲ **Cause-related marketing: TOMS Shoes pledges: "No complicated formulas, it's simple . . . you buy a pair of TOMS and we give a pair to a child on your behalf." Here, TOMs founder and CEO Blake Mycoskie gives out shoes in Argentina.**

AP Images/PRNewsFoto/TOMS Shoes

Blake Mycoskie. "Business and charity or public service don't have to be mutually exclusive. In fact, when they come together, they can be very powerful."[34]

Companies now sponsor hundreds of cause-related marketing campaigns each year. Many are backed by large budgets and a full complement of marketing activities. For example, PepsiCo's Pepsi Refresh Project awards tens of millions of dollars in grants to fund "refreshing ideas that will change the world." PepsiCo promotes the program with a full-blown multimedia campaign. More than a mere add-on cause-related marketing campaign, Pepsi Refresh puts social responsibility at the heart of Pepsi's positioning (see Marketing at Work 3.1).

Cause-related marketing has stirred some controversy. Critics worry that cause-related marketing is more a strategy for selling than a strategy for giving—that "cause-related" marketing is really "cause-exploitative" marketing. Thus, companies using cause-related marketing might find themselves walking a fine line between increased sales and an improved image and facing charges of exploitation. For example, following the 2011 Japanese tsunami disaster, Microsoft's Bing search engine created a backlash when it posted a message on Twitter offering to donate $1 to Japan's relief efforts each time someone forwarded its message. The tweet set off a firestorm of complaints from Twitter users, who accused Bing of using the tragedy as a marketing opportunity. Microsoft quickly apologized.[35]

However, if handled well, cause-related marketing can greatly benefit both the company and the cause. The company gains an effective marketing tool while building a more positive public image. The charitable organization or cause gains greater visibility and important new sources of funding and support. Spending on cause-related marketing in the United States skyrocketed from only $120 million in 1990 to more than $1.7 billion in 2011.[36]

The Cultural Environment

The **cultural environment** consists of institutions and other forces that affect a society's basic values, perceptions, preferences, and behaviors. People grow up in a particular society that shapes their basic beliefs and values. They absorb a worldview that defines their relationships with others. The following cultural characteristics can affect marketing decision making.

The Persistence of Cultural Values

People in a given society hold many beliefs and values. Their core beliefs and values have a high degree of persistence. For example, most Americans believe in individual freedom, hard work, getting married, and achievement and success. These beliefs shape more specific attitudes and behaviors found in everyday life. *Core* beliefs and values are passed on from parents to children and are reinforced by schools, churches, business, and government.

Secondary beliefs and values are more open to change. Believing in marriage is a core belief; believing that people should get married early in life is a secondary belief. Marketers have some chance of changing secondary values but little chance of changing core values. For example, family-planning marketers could argue more effectively that people should get married later than not getting married at all.

Shifts in Secondary Cultural Values

Although core values are fairly persistent, cultural swings do take place. Consider the impact of popular music groups, movie personalities, and other celebrities on young people's hairstyle and clothing norms. Marketers want to predict cultural shifts to spot new

Author Comment ▶
Cultural factors strongly affect how people think and how they consume. So marketers are keenly interested in the cultural environment.

Cultural environment
Institutions and other forces that affect society's basic values, perceptions, preferences, and behaviors.

MARKETING AT WORK   3.1

The Pepsi Refresh Project: What Does Your Brand Care About?

It seems that almost every brand is supporting some worthy cause these days, from promoting healthful living to curing cancer to ending poverty or world hunger. But the Pepsi Refresh Project is no mere cause-related marketing effort, added on to pay token homage to a borrowed cause. Instead, the Pepsi Refresh Project makes "doing good" a major element of the Pepsi brand's mission and positioning. Supported by a large budget and full complement of marketing activities, Pepsi Refresh promotes the concept of social responsibility as much as it promotes the Pepsi brand itself.

Through the Pepsi Refresh campaign, PepsiCo redefines its flagship brand not just as a soft drink but as an agent for world change. The project awards millions of dollars in grants to fund hundreds of worthwhile ideas by individuals and communities that will "refresh the world." "What do you care about?" asks one Pepsi Refresh ad. "Maybe it's green spaces. Or educational comic books. Maybe it's teaching kids to rock out. The Pepsi Refresh Project: Thousands of ideas. Millions in grants."

To obtain a Pepsi Refresh grant ranging from $5,000 to $250,000, individuals and organizations go to the campaign's refresheverything.com Web site and propose ideas for how to make the world a better place. Then, consumers vote at the site for their favorite projects and Pepsi funds the winners. Last year, Pepsi accepted 1,000 proposals each month in six different areas: health, arts and culture, food and shelter, the planet, neighborhoods, and education. In all, it awarded $20 million to fund nearly 1,000 projects.

The Pepsi Refresh Project not only delivers a new kind of social responsibility brand message, it delivers that message in a whole new, more social way. To engage people with the project, Pepsi is spreading the "do good" message though an integrated campaign that makes heavy use of big social networks like Facebook, Twitter, and YouTube. It has also collaborated with Hulu to sponsor its first original series, the reality show "If I Can Dream." The Pepsi Refresh Project has even partnered with *Spin* magazine, music festival South by Southwest, and two indie bands in a Web-based contest where music lovers vote between the two for their favorite band. Rock band Metric beat out Broken Social Scene for a $100,000 grant that it gave to the Women's Funding Network.

Unlike many other cause-related marketing campaigns, Pepsi Refresh is not just an add-on that links a brand to a cause that is only peripherally relevant to the brand message. Rather, Pepsi Refresh is a fully integrated marketing campaign wrapped around Pepsi's unified "refresh your world" brand message. Beyond social media, the Pepsi Refresh Project utilizes spot ads on the major TV networks and cable channels, print ads, and a major PR effort. The campaign also employs a host of celebrity endorsers. Among others, Pepsi has recruited Demi Moore; NFL players Mark Sanchez, DeMarcus Ware, and Drew Brees; and NASCAR

veterans Jeff Gordon, Dale Earnhardt, Jr., and Jimmie Johnson to apply for grants and act as spokespeople in broadcast ads.

The projects funded by the Pepsi Refresh Project so far are almost too numerous to list. Many of the grant awards have been given to everyday people just trying to improve their own little corners of the world. For example, Jeanne Acutanza from Kirkland, Washington, received $5,000 that helped her children's school grow a sustainable garden and give the harvest to local food banks. Calvin Cannon got $5,000 for his Clothe the N.A.K.E.D. Prom Date project, which sponsored upstanding low-income young men in Shelbyville, Tennessee, by paying for their tuxedo rentals for the prom. And the Associates of Redlands Bowl received $25,000 to support performing arts in their community of Redlands, California. "I'm proud of every idea we're supporting," says Pepsi CEO Indra Nooyi, "but it's the simplicity of [these ideas that's] so innovative. You would never have thought that one simple thing could bring about [such] a big change in a community."

▲ Cause-related marketing: The Pepsi Refresh Project isn't just an add-on that pays token homage to a borrowed cause. It makes "doing good" a major element of Pepsi's mission and positioning.

Pepsi-Cola Company. Martin Wonnacott/Cake-Factory.

All of this "doing good" is admirable, but does it help sell Pepsi? After all, at the end of the day, Pepsi is in the soft drink business. In that regard, the Pepsi Refresh Project has had its share of doubters. As one social marketer states, "This is big, new, getting a lot of attention. It's impactful; it's innovative. [But] what the industry is talking about now is, is this a gamble that was worth taking in terms of a lift in sales? That's the holy grail."

After the first year of the Pepsi Refresh Project, the "sales lift" question was very much open to debate. During 2010, Pepsi and Diet Pepsi sales volumes dropped 4.8 percent and 5.2 percent, respectively, compared with a more modest industrywide decline of 0.5 percent. Perhaps more important, Pepsi-Cola, the perennial number two soft drink brand behind Coca-Cola, dropped to number three behind Diet Coke. Even as its numbers dip, however, PepsiCo is not retreating from the good-works Pepsi Refresh Project. In fact, the company steadfastly insists that the project has surpassed its expectations. "It's a long-term play," says a Pepsi spokesperson. As a result, PepsiCo not only continued the campaign for a second year but also expanded it to other countries.

As evidence of the campaign's success, Pepsi points to impressive results in the social media. Last year, consumers cast 75 million votes in awarding the $20 million in grant funds. The number of Pepsi Facebook fans quadrupled to more than 1 million in just eight months. And whereas Pepsi used to get a Twitter tweet every five minutes or so, it now receives more tweets per minute than a person can read. PepsiCo has also developed a return-on-investment scorecard that ties different elements of the Pepsi Refresh campaign back to the health of the brand.

Based on that harder analysis, the company is holding steady on its large Pepsi Refresh Project budget at the same time that it is boosting other mass-media spending for the brand.

Beyond the more tangible returns, the Pepsi Refresh Project has drawn wide attention and praise. For example, PepsiCo was named by ad industry publication *Advertising Age* as last year's runner-up "Marketer of the Year." PepsiCo CEO Nooyi received the Ad Council's Public Service Award for her commitment to social responsibility. And Pepsi bottlers assert that Refresh is a clear winner in terms of clout gained with local communities.

Regardless of where the Pepsi Refresh Project goes from here, PepsiCo and other observers will learn much from this sweeping, first-of-its-kind social responsibility campaign. Ana Maria Irazabal, director of marketing for Pepsi, wants the campaign to become the model of the future. "We want people to be aware that every time you drink a Pepsi you are actually supporting the Pepsi Refresh Project and ideas that are going to move this country forward. We may be the first to do something like this, but hopefully, we're not the last."

Sources: Mike Esterl, "Pepsi Thirsty for a Comeback," *Wall Street Journal*, March 18, 2011, p. B5; Natalie Zmuda, "Pass or Fail, Pepsi's Refresh Will Be Case for Marketing Textbooks," *Advertising Age*, February 8, 2010, p. 1; Zmuda, "Who Are the Big Pepsi Refresh Winners? Local Bottlers and Community Groups," *Advertising Age*, November 1, 2010, p. 2; Zmuda, "Pepsi Expands Refresh Project: Social-Media Experiment Becomes Full-Blown Global Marketing Strategy," *Advertising Age*, September 7, 2010, accessed at www.adage.com; Stuart Elliott, "Pepsi Invites the Public to Do Good," *New York Times*, January 31, 2010, p. B6; Zmuda, "How Pepsi Blinked, Fell Behind Diet Coke," *Advertising Age*, March 21, 2011, pp. 1, 6; and www.refresheverything.com, accessed June 2011.

opportunities or threats. The major cultural values of a society are expressed in people's views of themselves and others, as well as in their views of organizations, society, nature, and the universe.

People's Views of Themselves. People vary in their emphasis on serving themselves versus serving others. Some people seek personal pleasure, wanting fun, change, and escape. Others seek self-realization through religion, recreation, or the avid pursuit of careers or other life goals. Some people see themselves as sharers and joiners; others see themselves as individualists. People use products, brands, and services as a means of self-expression, and they buy products and services that match their views of themselves.

Marketers can target their products and services based on such self-views. For example, TOMS Shoes appeals to people who see themselves as part of the broader world community. In contrast, Kenneth Cole shoes appeal to fashion individualists. In its ads, the company declares, "We all walk in different shoes," asserting that Kenneth Cole represents "25 years of nonuniform thinking."

People's Views of Others. People's attitudes toward and interactions with others shift over time. In recent years, some analysts have voiced concerns that the Internet age would result in diminished human interaction, as people buried their heads in their computers or e-mailed and texted rather than interacting personally. Instead, today's digital technologies seem to have launched an era of what one trend watcher calls *mass mingling*. ➤ Rather than interacting less, people are using online social media and mobile communications to connect more than ever. And, often, more online and mobile interactions result in more offline mingling:[37]

▲ **Mass mingling: Rather than diminishing human interaction, today's social media and mobile communications are causing people to increasingly tap into their networks of friends.**

Donald Miralle/Taxi/Getty Images

More people than ever [are] living large parts of their lives online. Yet, those same people also mingle, meet up, and congregate more often with other "warm bodies" in the offline world. In fact, social media and mobile communications are fueling a *mass mingling* that defies virtually every cliché about diminished human interaction in our "online era." Ironically, the same technology that was once condemned for turning entire generations into mobile gaming zombies and avatars is now deployed to get people *out* of their homes.

Basically, the more [people] date and network and twitter and socialize online, the more likely they are to eventually meet up with friends and followers in the real world. Thanks to social networking services such as Facebook (whose more than 500 million fans spend more than 700 *billion* minutes a month on the site), people are developing more diverse social networks, defying the notion that technology pulls people away from social engagement. Rather than being more isolated, people today are increasingly tapping into their networks of friends.

This new way of interacting strongly affects how companies market their brands and communicate with customers. "Consumers are increasingly tapping into their networks of friends, fans, and followers to discover, discuss, and purchase goods and services in ever-more sophisticated ways," says one analyst. "As a result, it's never been more important for brands to make sure they [tap into these networks] too."[38]

People's Views of Organizations. People vary in their attitudes toward corporations, government agencies, trade unions, universities, and other organizations. By and large, people are willing to work for major organizations and expect them, in turn, to carry out society's work.

The past two decades have seen a sharp decrease in confidence in and loyalty toward America's business and political organizations and institutions. In the workplace, there has been an overall decline in organizational loyalty. Waves of company downsizings bred cynicism and distrust. In just the last decade, major corporate scandals, rounds of layoffs resulting from the recent recession, the financial meltdown triggered by Wall Street bankers' greed and incompetence, and other unsettling activities have resulted in a further loss of confidence in big business. Many people today see work not as a source of satisfaction but as a required chore to earn money to enjoy their nonwork hours. This trend suggests that organizations need to find new ways to win consumer and employee confidence.

People's Views of Society. People vary in their attitudes toward their society—patriots defend it, reformers want to change it, and malcontents want to leave it. People's orientation to their society influences their consumption patterns and attitudes toward the marketplace. American patriotism has been increasing gradually for the past two decades. It surged, however, following the September 11, 2001, terrorist attacks and the Iraq war. For example, the summer following the start of the Iraq war saw a surge of pumped-up Americans visiting U.S. historic sites, ranging from the Washington, DC monuments, Mount Rushmore, the Gettysburg battlefield, and the *USS Constitution* ("Old Ironsides") to Pearl Harbor and the Alamo. Following these peak periods, patriotism in the United States still remains high. A recent global survey on "national pride" found Americans tied for number one among the 17 democracies polled.[39]

Marketers respond with patriotic products and promotions, offering everything from floral bouquets to clothing with patriotic themes. Although most of these marketing efforts are tasteful and well received, waving the red, white, and blue can prove tricky. Except in cases where companies tie product sales to charitable contributions, such flag-waving promotions can be viewed as attempts to cash in on triumph or tragedy. Marketers must take care when responding to such strong national emotions.

People's Views of Nature. People vary in their attitudes toward the natural world—some feel ruled by it, others feel in harmony with it, and still others seek to master it. A long-term trend has been people's growing mastery over nature through technology and the belief that nature is bountiful. More recently, however, people have recognized that nature is finite and fragile; it can be destroyed or spoiled by human activities.

This renewed love of things natural has created a 63-million-person "lifestyles of health and sustainability" (LOHAS) market, consumers who seek out everything from natural, organic, and nutritional products to fuel-efficient cars and alternative medicine. This segment spends nearly $300 billion annually on such products.[40]

Tom's of Maine caters to such consumers with sustainable, all-natural personal care products—toothpaste, deodorant, mouthwash, and soap—made with no artificial colors, flavors, fragrances, or preservatives.[41] The products are also "cruelty-free" (no animal testing or animal ingredients). Tom's makes sustainable practices a priority in every aspect of its business and strives to maximize recycled content and recyclability of its packaging. Finally, Tom's donates 10 percent of its pretax profits to charitable organizations. ➤ In all, Tom's "makes uncommonly good products that serve the common good."

Food producers have also found fast-growing markets for natural and organic products. In total, the U.S. organic food market generated nearly $29 billion in sales last year, more than doubling over the past five years. Niche marketers, such as Whole Foods Market, have sprung up to serve this market, and traditional food chains, such as Kroger and Safeway, have added separate natural and organic food sections. Even pet owners are joining the movement as they become more aware of what goes into Fido's food. Almost every major pet food brand now offers several types of natural foods.[42]

People's Views of the Universe. Finally, people vary in their beliefs about the origin of the universe and their place in it. Although most Americans practice religion, religious conviction and practice have been dropping off gradually through the years. According to a recent poll, 16 percent of Americans now say they are not affiliated with any particular faith, almost double the percentage of 18 years earlier. Among Americans ages 18 to 29, 25 percent say they are not currently affiliated with any particular religion.[43]

However, the fact that people are dropping out of organized religion doesn't mean that they are abandoning their faith. Some futurists have noted a renewed interest in spirituality, perhaps as a part of a broader search for a new inner purpose. People have been moving away from materialism and dog-eat-dog ambition to seek more permanent values—family, community, earth, faith—and a more certain grasp of right and wrong. "We are becoming a nation of spiritually anchored people who are not traditionally religious," says one expert.[44] This changing spiritualism affects consumers in everything from the television shows they watch and the books they read to the products and services they buy.

▲ Riding the trend toward all things natural: Tom's of Maine "makes uncommonly good products that serve the common good."

Toms of Maine

SPEED BUMP	LINKING THE CONCEPTS

Slow down and cool your engine. How are all of the environmental factors you've read about in this chapter linked with each other? With a company marketing strategy?

- How are major demographic forces linked with economic changes? With major cultural trends? How are the natural and technological environments linked? Think of an example of a company that has recognized one of these links and turned it into a marketing opportunity.
- Is the marketing environment uncontrollable? How can companies be proactive in changing environmental factors? Think of a good example that makes your point, then read on.

Author Comment ▶
Rather than simply watching and reacting to the marketing environment, companies should take proactive steps.

Responding to the Marketing Environment

Someone once observed, "There are three kinds of companies: those who make things happen, those who watch things happen, and those who wonder what's happened." Many companies view the marketing environment as an uncontrollable element to which they must react and adapt. They passively accept the marketing environment and do not try to change it. They analyze environmental forces and design strategies that will help the company avoid the threats and take advantage of the opportunities the environment provides.

Other companies take a *proactive* stance toward the marketing environment. "Instead of letting the environment define their strategy," advises one marketing expert, "craft a strategy that defines your environment."[45] Rather than assuming that strategic options are bounded by the current environment, these firms develop strategies to change the environment. "Business history . . . reveals plenty of cases in which firms' strategies shape industry structure," says the expert, "from Ford's Model T to Nintendo's Wii."

Even more, rather than simply watching and reacting to environmental events, these firms take aggressive actions to affect the publics and forces in their marketing environment. Such companies hire lobbyists to influence legislation affecting their industries and stage media events to gain favorable press coverage. They run *advertorials* (ads expressing editorial points of view) to shape public opinion. They press lawsuits and file complaints with regulators to keep competitors in line, and they form contractual agreements to better control their distribution channels.

By taking action, companies can often overcome seemingly uncontrollable environmental events. For example, whereas some companies try to hush up negative talk about their products, others proactively counter false information. Taco Bell did this when its brand fell victim to potentially damaging claims about the quality of the beef filling in its tacos.[46]

> When a California woman's class-action suit questioned whether Taco Bell's meat filling could accurately be labeled "beef," the company's reaction was swift and decisive. The suit claimed that Taco Bell's beef filling is 65 percent binders, extenders, preservatives, additives, and other agents. It wanted Taco Bell to stop calling it "beef." But Taco Bell fought back quickly with a major counterattack campaign, in print and on YouTube and Facebook. Full page ads in the *Wall Street Journal*, the *New York Times*, and *USAToday* boldly proclaimed: "Thank you for suing us. Here's the truth about our seasoned beef." In the ad, Taco Bell revealed its not-so-secret recipe. "Start with USDA-inspected quality beef (88%). Then add water to keep it juicy and moist (3%). Mix in Mexican spices and flavors, including salt, chili pepper, onion powder, tomato powder, sugar, garlic powder, and cocoa powder (4%). Combine a little oats, caramelized sugar, yeast, citric acid, and other ingredients that contribute to the flavor, moisture, consistency, and quality of our seasoned beef (5%). The only reason we add anything to our beef is to give the meat flavor and quality." Taco Bell further announced that it would take legal action against those making the false statements. The company's proactive counter campaign quickly squelched the false information in the law suit, which was voluntarily withdrawn only a few months later.

Marketing management cannot always control environmental forces. In many cases, it must settle for simply watching and reacting to the environment. For example, a company would have little success trying to influence geographic population shifts, the economic environment, or major cultural values. But whenever possible, smart marketing managers take a *proactive* rather than *reactive* approach to the marketing environment (see Marketing at Work 3.2).

MARKETING AT WORK   **3.2**

When the Dialog Gets Nasty: Turning Negatives into Positives

Marketers have hailed the Internet as the great new relational medium. Companies use the Web to engage customers, gain insights into their needs, and create customer community. In turn, Web-empowered consumers share their brand experiences with companies and with each other. All of this back-and-forth helps both the company and its customers. But sometimes, the dialog can get nasty. Consider the following examples:

- MSN Money columnist Scott Burns accuses Home Depot of being a "consistent abuser" of customers' time. Within hours, MSN's servers are caving under the weight of 14,000 blistering e-mails and posts from angry Home Depot customers who storm the MSN comment room, taking Home Depot to task for pretty much everything. It is the biggest response in MSN Money's history.
- Blogger Jeff Jarvis posts a series of irate messages to his BuzzMachine blog about the many failings of his Dell computer and his struggles with Dell's customer support. The post quickly draws national attention, and an open letter posted by Jarvis to Dell founder Michael Dell becomes the third most linked-to post on the blogosphere the day after it appears. Jarvis's headline—Dell Hell—becomes shorthand for the ability of a lone blogger to deliver a body blow to an unsuspecting business.
- When 8-year-old Harry Winsor sends a crayon drawing of an airplane he's designed to Boeing with a suggestion that they might want to manufacture it, the company responds with a stern, legal-form letter. "We do not accept unsolicited ideas," the letter states. "We regret to inform you that we have disposed of your message and retain no copies." The embarrassing blunder would probably go unnoticed were it not for the fact that Harry's father—John Winsor, a prominent ad exec—blogs and tweets about the incident, making it instant national news.
- When United Airlines rejects musician Dave Carroll's damage claim after its baggage handlers break his guitar, he produces a catchy music video, "United Breaks Guitars," and posts it on YouTube. "I should've flown with someone else or gone by car," he despairs in the video. "'Cause United breaks guitars." The video becomes one of YouTube's greatest hits—more than 10 million people have now viewed it—and causes an instant media frenzy across major global networks.

Extreme events? Not anymore. The Internet has turned the traditional power relationship between businesses and consumers upside down. In the good old days, disgruntled consumers could do little more than bellow at a company service rep or shout out their complaints from a street corner. Now, armed with only a PC or a smartphone and a broadband connection, they can take it public, airing their gripes to millions on blogs,

chats, online social networks, or even hate sites devoted exclusively to their least favorite corporations.

"I hate" and "sucks" sites are almost commonplace. These sites target some highly respected companies with some highly *dis*respectful labels: PayPalSucks.com (aka NoPayPal); Walmartblows.com; IHateStarbucks.com; DeltaREALLYsucks.com; and UnitedPackageSmashers.com (UPS), to name only a few. "Sucks" videos on YouTube and other video sites also abound. For example, a search of "Apple sucks" on YouTube turns up 5,300 videos; a similar search for Microsoft finds 5,360 videos. An "Apple sucks" search on Facebook links to 540 groups.

Some of these sites, videos, and other Web attacks air legitimate complaints that should be addressed. Others, however, are little more than anonymous, vindictive slurs that unfairly ransack brands and corporate reputations. Some of the attacks are only a passing nuisance; others can draw serious attention and create real headaches.

How should companies react to online attacks? The real quandary for targeted companies is figuring out how far they can go to protect their images without fueling the already raging fire. One point on which all experts seem to agree: Don't try to retaliate in kind. "It's rarely a good idea to lob bombs at the fire starters," says one analyst. "Preemption, engagement, and diplomacy are saner tools."

Some companies have tried to silence the critics through lawsuits, but few have succeeded. The courts have tended to regard such criticism as opinion and, therefore, protected speech. In general, attempts to block, counterattack, or shut down

▲ Today's empowered consumers: Boeing's embarrassing blunder over young Harry Winsor's airplane design made instant national news. However, Boeing quickly took responsibility and turned the potential PR disaster into a positive.

John Winsor

consumer attacks may be shortsighted. Such criticisms are often based on real consumer concerns and unresolved anger. Hence, the best strategy might be to proactively monitor these sites and respond to the concerns they express. "The most obvious thing to do is talk to the customer and try to deal with the problem, instead of putting your fingers in your ears," advises one consultant.

For example, Home Depot CEO Francis Blake drew praise when he heeded the criticisms expressed in the MSN Money onslaught and responded positively. Blake posted a heartfelt letter in which he thanked critic Scott Burns, apologized to angry customers, and promised to make things better. And Boeing quickly took responsibility for mishandling aspiring designer Harry Winsor's drawing, turning a potential PR disaster into a positive. It called and invited young Harry to visit Boeing's facilities. On its corporate Twitter site, it confessed "We're expert at airplanes but novices in social media. We're learning as we go."

United Airlines, however, hasn't fared so well. After Dave Carroll's YouTube video went platinum, United belatedly offered to pay for his ruined guitar. Carroll politely declined but thanked the company for boosting his career—which now boasts two new United videos that air complaints on behalf of other disgruntled customers and call for United to "change in a big way."

Many companies have now created teams of specialists that monitor Web conversations and engage unhappy consumers.

In the years since the Dell Hell incident, Dell has set up a 40-member "communities and conversation team," which does outreach on Twitter and Facebook and communicates with bloggers. The social media team at Southwest Airlines includes a chief Twitter officer who tracks Twitter comments and monitors Facebook groups, an online representative who checks facts and interacts with bloggers, and another person who takes charge of the company's presence on sites such as YouTube, Flickr, and LinkedIn. So if someone posts an online complaint, the company can respond in a personal way.

Thus, by listening and proactively responding to seemingly uncontrollable events in the environment, companies can prevent the negatives from spiraling out of control or even turn them into positives. Who knows? With the right responses, Walmart-blows.com might even become Walmart-rules.com. Then again, probably not.

Source: Quotes, excerpts, and other information from Rupal Parekh and Edmund Lee, "How to Succeed When It's Time to Make Your Social-Media Mea Culpa," *Advertising Age,* May 10, 2010, pp. 5, 25; Michelle Conlin, "Web Attack," *BusinessWeek,* April 16, 2007, pp. 54–56; Christopher L. Marting and Nathan Bennett, "Corporate Reputation; What to Do About Online Attacks," *Wall Street Journal,* March 10, 2008, p. R6; "Boeing's Social Media Lesson," May 3, 2010, http://mediadecoder.blogs.nytimes.com/2010/05/03/boeings-social-media-lesson/; www.youtube.com/watch?v=5YGc4zOqozo, accessed June 2011; and "Corporate Hate Sites," New Media Institute, www.newmedia.org/articles/corporate-hate-sites---nmi-white-paper.html, accessed October 2011.

REST STOP   REVIEWING THE CONCEPTS

MyMarketingLab

Now that you have completed the chapter, return to www.mymktlab.com to experience and apply the concepts and to explore the additional study materials for this chapter.

CHAPTER REVIEW AND KEY TERMS

Objectives Review

In this chapter and the next two chapters, you'll examine the environments of marketing and how companies analyze these environments to better understand the marketplace and consumers. Companies must constantly watch and manage the *marketing environment* to seek opportunities and ward off threats. The marketing environment consists of all the actors and forces influencing the company's ability to transact business effectively with its target market.

OBJECTIVE 1 Describe the environmental forces that affect the company's ability to serve its customers. (pp 67–70)

The company's *microenvironment* consists of actors close to the company that combine to form its value delivery network or that affect its ability to serve its customers. It includes the company's *internal environment*—its several departments and management levels—as it influences marketing decision making. *Marketing channel firms*—suppliers, marketing intermediaries, physical distribution firms, marketing services agencies, and financial intermediaries—cooperate to create customer value. *Competitors* vie with the company in an effort to serve customers better. Various *publics* have an actual or potential interest in or impact on the company's ability to meet its objectives. Finally, five types of customer *markets* exist: consumer, business, reseller, government, and international markets.

The *macroenvironment* consists of larger societal forces that affect the entire microenvironment. The six forces making up the company's macroenvironment are demographic, economic, natural, technological, political/social, and cultural forces. These forces shape opportunities and pose threats to the company.

OBJECTIVE 2 Explain how changes in the demographic and economic environments affect marketing decisions. (pp 70–77)

Demography is the study of the characteristics of human populations. Today's *demographic environment* shows a changing age structure, shifting family profiles, geographic population shifts, a better-educated and more white-collar population, and increasing diversity. The *economic environment* consists of factors that affect buying power and patterns. The economic environment is characterized by more frugal consumers who are seeking greater value—the right combination of good quality and service at a fair price. The distribution of income also is shifting. The rich have grown richer, the middle class has shrunk, and the poor have remained poor, leading to a two-tiered market.

OBJECTIVE 3 Identify the major trends in the firm's natural and technological environments. (pp 77–80)

The *natural environment* shows three major trends: shortages of certain raw materials, higher pollution levels, and more government intervention in natural resource management. Environmental concerns create marketing opportunities for alert companies. The *technological environment* creates both opportunities and challenges. Companies that fail to keep up with technological change will miss out on new product and marketing opportunities.

OBJECTIVE 4 Explain the key changes in the political and cultural environments. (pp 80–88)

The *political environment* consists of laws, agencies, and groups that influence or limit marketing actions. The political environment has undergone changes that affect marketing worldwide: increasing legislation regulating business, strong government agency enforcement, and greater emphasis on ethics and socially responsible actions. The *cultural environment* consists of institutions and forces that affect a society's values, perceptions, preferences, and behaviors. The environment shows trends toward *mass mingling*, a lessening trust of institutions, increasing patriotism, greater appreciation for nature, a changing spiritualism, and the search for more meaningful and enduring values.

OBJECTIVE 5 Discuss how companies can react to the marketing environment. (pp 88–90)

Companies can passively accept the marketing environment as an uncontrollable element to which they must adapt, avoiding threats and taking advantage of opportunities as they arise. Or they can take a *proactive* stance, working to change the environment rather than simply reacting to it. Whenever possible, companies should try to be proactive rather than reactive.

Key Terms

Objective 1
Marketing environment (p 66)
Microenvironment (p 66)
Macroenvironment (p 66)
Marketing intermediaries (p 68)
Public (p 69)

Objective 2
Demography (p 70)
Baby boomers (p 70)

Generation X (p 71)
Millennials (Generation Y) (p 72)
Economic environment (p 76)

Objective 3
Natural environment (p 77)
Environmental sustainability (p 78)
Technological environment (p 79)

Objective 4
Political environment (p 80)
Cultural environment (p 83)

DISCUSSION AND CRITICAL THINKING

Discussion Questions

1. Compare and contrast a company's microenvironment with a company's macroenvironment. (AACSB: Communication)
2. Describe the five types of customer markets. (AACSB: Communication)
3. List some of the demographic trends of interest to marketers in the United States and discuss whether these trends pose opportunities or threats for marketers. (AACSB: Communication; Reflective Thinking)
4. Discuss trends in the natural environment of which marketers must be aware and provide examples of companies' responses to them. (AACSB: Communication)

5. Compare and contrast core beliefs/values and secondary beliefs/values. Provide an example of each and discuss the potential impact marketers have on each. (AACSB: Communication; Reflective Thinking)
6. How should marketers respond to the changing environment? (AACSB: Communication)

Critical Thinking Exercises

1. In a small group, search the Internet for United States population distribution maps and create a PowerPoint presentation illustrating factors such as geographical population shifts, languages spoken, age distributions, and ancestry. Discuss the implications of these factors for marketers. (AACSB: Communication; Use of IT; Diversity)
2. The Wall Street Reform and Consumer Protection Act of 2010 created the Consumer Financial Protection Bureau (CFPB). Learn about this act and the responsibilities of the

CFPB, then write a brief report of how it impacts businesses and consumers. (AACSB: Communication; Use of IT)
3. Cause-related marketing has grown considerably over the past ten years. Visit www.causemarketingforum.com to learn about companies that have won Halo Awards for outstanding cause-related marketing programs. Present an award-winning case study to your class. (AACSB: Communication; Use of IT)

MINICASES AND APPLICATIONS

Marketing Technology   Electric Cars

If you thought that getting 50 miles per gallon driving a Toyota Prius hybrid was good, how about 230 miles per gallon? Or 367 mpg? Well, you are about to see a new breed of automobiles from big and small automakers touting this level of performance. In 2010, look for GM's Volt and Nissan's Leaf, but there will also be offerings from unknown startups such as V-Vehicle, a California-based electric car company backed by billionaire T. Boone Pickens. These automobiles range from hybrids—a combination of gas and electric—to all-electric vehicles. This level of performance comes at a high price, however. Although consumers will receive an expected $7,500 tax credit for purchasing one of these cars, the Volt's expected $40,000 price tag will still cause sticker shock. Also, the lack of public recharging stations poses a significant challenge, especially for all-electric vehicles such as the Leaf, which needs recharging

approximately every 100 miles. And some might question the efficiency claims, especially since the Environmental Protection Agency is still finalizing the methodology that factors in electricity used when making miles-per-gallon equivalency claims.

1. What factors in the marketing environment present opportunities or threats to automakers? (AACSB: Communication; Reflective Thinking)
2. Will it be possible for a startup automaker such as V-Vehicle to compete with big automakers such as Ford, GM, Chrysler, Toyota, Honda, Nissan, Volvo, Hyundai, BMW, and Mercedes? What factors in the marketing environment will enable or inhibit new competitors? (AACSB: Communication; Reflective Thinking)

Marketing Ethics   Small Markets

You've probably heard of heart procedures such as angioplasty and stents that are routinely performed on adults. But such heart procedures, devices, and related medications are not available for infants and children, despite the fact that almost 40,000 children a year are born in the United States with heart defects that oftentimes require repair. This is a life or death situation for many young patients, yet doctors must improvise by using devices designed and tested on adults. For instance, doctors use an adult kidney balloon on an infant's heart because it is the appropriate size for a newborn's aortic valve. However, this device is not approved for the procedure. Why are specific devices and medicines developed for the multibillion-dollar cardiovascular market not also designed for kids? It's a matter of economics—this segment of young consumers is just too small. One leading cardiologist attributed the discrepancy to a "profitability gap" between the children's market and the much more profitable adult market for treating heart disease. While this might make good economic sense for companies, it is little comfort to the parents of these small patients.

1. Discuss the environmental forces acting on medical devices and pharmaceutical companies that are preventing them from meeting the needs of the infant and child market segment. Is it wrong for these companies to not address the needs of this segment? (AACSB: Communication; Reflective Thinking; Ethical Reasoning)
2. Suggest some solutions to this problem. (AACSB: Communication; Reflective Thinking)

Marketing by the Numbers   Estimating Market Demand

China and India are emerging markets that will have a significant impact on the world in coming years. With China's and India's combined population of almost 2.5 billion, they are the two most populous countries, comprising almost 40 percent of the world's population. The economies of both countries are growing at phenomenal rates as well. The term *Chindia* is used to describe the growing power of these two countries, and predictions are that these two will overtake the United States as the largest economies in the world within just a few decades.

1. Discuss a demographic and an economic trend related to Chindia's power and their impact on marketers in the United States. Support your discussion of these trends with statistics. (AACSB: Communication; Reflective Thinking)
2. Using the chain ratio method described in Appendix 3: Marketing by the Numbers, discuss factors to consider when estimating total market demand for automobiles in China or India. (AACSB: Communication, Analytical Reasoning)

Video Case   Ecoist

At least one company has taken the old phrase "One man's trash is another man's treasure" and turned it into a business model. Ecoist uses discarded packaging materials from multinational brands such as Coca-Cola, Frito-Lay, Disney, and Mars to craft high-end handbags that would thrill even the most discriminating fashionistas.

When the company first started in 2004, consumer perceptions of goods made from recycled materials weren't very positive. This video describes how Ecoist found its opportunity in a growing wave of environmentalism. Not only does Ecoist capitalize on low-cost materials and the brand images of some of the world's major brands, it comes out smelling like a rose as it saves tons of trash from landfills.

After viewing the video featuring Ecoist, answer the following questions:

1. How engaged was Ecoist in analyzing the marketing environment before it launched its first company?
2. What trends in the marketing environment have contributed to the success of Ecoist?
3. Is Ecoist's strategy more about recycling or about creating value for customers? Explain.

Company Cases   3 Target / 5 Porsche / 7 Las Vegas

See Appendix 1 for cases appropriate for this chapter. **Case 3, Target: From "Expect More" to "Pay Less."** Changes in the marketing environment lead Target to make big changes in its marketing mix. **Case 5, Porsche: Guarding the Old While Bringing in the New.** Porsche learns that focusing on existing customers doesn't always keep up with market trends, and keeping up with market trends doesn't always please existing customers. **Case 7, Las Vegas: What's Not Happening in Vegas.** The City of Sin makes adjustments to keep its brand relevant and changes in the marketing environment cause big shifts in Las Vegas tourism.

4 Managing Marketing Information
to **Gain Customer Insights**

CHAPTER ROAD MAP

Objective Outline

▷ **OBJECTIVE 1** **Explain the importance of information in gaining insights about the marketplace and customers.** Marketing Information and Customer Insights (96–97)

▷ **OBJECTIVE 2** **Define the marketing information system and discuss its parts.** Assessing Marketing Information Needs (97–98); Developing Marketing Information (98–100)

▷ **OBJECTIVE 3** **Outline the steps in the marketing research process.** Marketing Research (100–115)

▷ **OBJECTIVE 4** **Explain how companies analyze and use marketing information.** Analyzing and Using Marketing Information (115–117)

▷ **OBJECTIVE 5** **Discuss the special issues some marketing researchers face, including public policy and ethics issues.** Other Marketing Information Considerations (117–121)

Previewing the Concepts

In this chapter, we continue our exploration of how marketers gain insights into consumers and the marketplace. We look at how companies develop and manage information about important marketplace elements: customers, competitors, products, and marketing programs. To succeed in today's marketplace, companies must know how to turn mountains of marketing information into fresh customer insights that will help them deliver greater value to customers.

Let's start with a story about marketing research and customer insights in action. Good marketing research can involve a rich variety of sophisticated data collection and analysis techniques. But sometimes research is as simple as just talking with customers directly, listening openly to what they have to say, and using those insights to develop better products and marketing. That's how Domino's Pizza turned a five-year revenue slide into a fresh, hot turnaround.

When online and focus group research showed that pizza lovers thought Domino's pizza "tasted like cardboard" (and worse), the company threw out the recipe and reinvented its pizza from the ground up. "Oh Yes We Did."

Domino's Pizza, Inc.

First Stop

Domino's Pizza: Listening to Consumers and Letting Them Know You Heard Them

After five years of stagnant or declining revenues, in late 2009, Domino's Pizza did something practically unheard of in the business world. "First," says an industry observer, "it asked customers for honest feedback. Second, it actually listened to the painful truth [punctuated by words like "cardboard crust" and "totally devoid of flavor"]. Finally—and here's the most shocking part—the company reinvented its product 'from the crust up.'" What follows is the full story behind Domino's impressive "Pizza Turnaround" campaign.

The turnaround began with marketing research to understand what customers thought and wanted. Industry research showed that although Domino's was tops in service, convenience, and value for the money, it trailed far behind competitors in taste. One taste preference survey placed Domino's dead last, tied with—of all possibilities—Chuck E. Cheese, a competitor not known for culinary excellence.

To gain deeper insights into what consumers really thought about its pizzas, Domino's turned to research using social media channels and focus groups. It monitored consumer online chatter and solicited thousands of direct consumer feedback messages via Facebook, Twitter, and other social media. Then, based on insights it gained online, Domino's launched a wave of good old-fashioned, tried-and-true focus groups to engage customers directly in face-to-face conversations.

The online feedback and focus group results were as difficult to digest as a cold Domino's pizza. The most common complaint: Domino's pizza crust "tasted like cardboard." But that was just the beginning. One after another, pizza lovers panned Domino's pies with biting comments such as "Totally devoid of flavor." "The sauce tastes like ketchup." "Worst excuse for pizza I've ever had." "Processed cheese!!" "Mass-produced, boring, bland pizza." and "Microwave pizza is far superior." One focus group participant concluded: "It doesn't feel like there's much love in Domino's pizza." "They weren't poisoning people," chuckles an analyst, "but taste was [certainly a big] glitch on the radar."

Rather than hiding from these stinging results or waving them off, Domino's executives fessed up to the problems and faced them head on. "We had a focus group webcast to our team," says a Domino's marketing executive. "When somebody's saying something terrible about your pizza, you never get used to it, but for the first time all our executives were face to face with it. They couldn't believe it. We all said: 'we can't just go to the next meeting. We have to do something.'"

Domino's began by completely reinventing its pizzas. It didn't just make improvements to the old product; it threw out the recipe and started over. According to Domino's chief marketing officer, Russell Weiner, "We weren't going to call it 'new and improved' and expect that to break through. We had to blow up the bridge."

Domino's chefs started from scratch with new crusts, sauces, cheese, and other ingredients. The result was an entirely new pizza that Domino's boasts has a "garlic seasoned crust with parsley, baked to a golden brown." The new sauce is "bright, spicy, and robust" with a "little bit

> When consumer research turned up painful truths about its pizza ("cardboard crust," "totally void of flavor"), Domino's completely reformulated its product and launched its startlingly honest, highly successful Pizza Turnaround campaign. Thanks to the research insights, says the CEO, "We're a new Domino's."

of red pepper just to tingle on your tongue." And the new cheese is to die for—mozzarella, shredded not diced, flavored with just a hint of provolone. "We changed everything," says a Domino's product-development chef. "Now it tastes better." Customers seem to agree. Two months after the new pizza was introduced, some 1,800 random pizza consumers from eight U.S. markets did a blind taste test. In head-to-head comparisons, consumers picked Domino's pizzas as tasting better than both Papa John's and Pizza Hut by a wide margin.

To announce the changes and to turn around customer opinions, Domino's launched a daring $75 million "Pizza Turnaround" promotion campaign. In the campaign, the research itself was the message. Self-depreciating TV commercials showed real focus groups describing, in vivid detail, how dreadful the pizza was. In the ads, Domino's CEO Patrick Doyle admits that he's heard what customers had to say and has taken it to heart. "There comes a time," he acknowledges, "when you know you've got to make a change."

The startlingly honest campaign was fully integrated into the brand's Facebook and Twitter pages, where the company posted all the bad along with the good and asked for continuing feedback. The entire turnaround saga—from biting focus group footage to the shocked reactions of Domino's executives and efforts to reformulate the product—was documented for all to see in a forthright four-and-a-half minute behind-the-scenes documentary on the Web site Pizza Turnaround.com. The company even posted a stream of customer comments—good, bad, or indifferent—on a 4,630-square-foot billboard in New York City's Times Square area.

The campaign was risky. When Domino's admitted in its ads that its pizza was gross, some analysts predicted that the approach would be brand suicide. CEO Doyle admits that he had knots in his stomach when the chain launched the campaign. But Domino's wanted to shout out loud and clear: We've heard you! Our pizza was lousy but we fixed the recipe. "We had to be open, honest, and transparent," says CMO Weiner.

As it turns out, the upfront approach worked. In the three months following the start of the Pizza Turnaround campaign, Domino's sales soared 14.3 percent and in-store profits reached new highs. The transparent ads and message grabbed consumer attention and changed opinions. "The advertising itself scored off the charts," says Weiner. And while the ads drew people in, Domino's new pizza kept them coming back. Revenues and profits continued to climb throughout 2010, even as overall revenues for the pizza-delivery industry were declining. The Pizza Turnaround campaign even earned Domino's "marketer of the year" honors from two major marketing publications, *Advertising Age* and *Brandweek*.

The lesson for marketers is that talking to customers, hearing what they have to say, and acting on the insights gained can pay big dividends. Marketing research and really listening to customers, says Doyle, "dramatically changed our momentum, and we can build on this going forward. We feel very good now about our understanding of the brand. We're a new Domino's."[1]

MyMarketingLab

Visit www.mymktlab.com to find activities that help you learn and review in order to succeed in this chapter.

A s the Domino's story highlights, good products and marketing programs begin with good customer information. Companies also need an abundance of information on competitors, resellers, and other actors and marketplace forces. But more than just gathering information, marketers must *use* the information to gain powerful *customer and market insights*.

Author Comment ▶
Marketing information by itself has little value. The value is in the *customer insights* gained from the information and how marketers use these insights to make better decisions.

Marketing Information and Customer Insights

To create value for customers and build meaningful relationships with them, marketers must first gain fresh, deep insights into what customers need and want. Such customer insights come from good marketing information. Companies use these customer insights to develop a competitive advantage.

For example, Apple wasn't the first company to develop a digital music player. However, Apple's research uncovered two key insights: people wanted personal music players that let them take all of their music with them, and they wanted to be able to listen to it unobtrusively. Based on these insights, Apple applied its design and usability magic to create the phenomenally successful iPod. ▶ The expanded iPod and iPod Touch lines now capture a 76 percent share of the U.S. MP3 player market. The iPod insights also spawned other Apple blockbusters such as the iPhone and iPad.[2]

Although customer and market insights are important for building customer value and relationships, these insights can be very difficult to obtain. Customer needs and buying motives are often anything but obvious—consumers themselves usually can't tell you exactly what they need and why they buy. To gain good customer insights, marketers

▲ Key customer insights, plus a dash of Apple's design and usability magic, have made the iPod a blockbuster. It now captures 76 percent of the market and has spawned other Apple blockbusters such as the iPhone and iPad.

Newscom

Customer insights
Fresh understandings of customers and the marketplace derived from marketing information that becomes the basis for creating customer value and relationships.

Marketing information system (MIS)
People and procedures dedicated to assessing information needs, developing the needed information, and helping decision makers to use the information to generate and validate actionable customer and market insights.

Author Comment ▶
The marketing information system begins and ends with users—assessing their information needs and then delivering information that meets those needs.

must effectively manage marketing information from a wide range of sources.

Today's marketers have ready access to plenty of marketing information. With the recent explosion of information technologies, companies can now generate information in great quantities. Moreover, consumers themselves are now generating tons of marketing information. Through e-mail, text messaging, blogging, Facebook, Twitter, and other grassroots digital channels, consumers are now volunteering a tidal wave of bottom-up information to companies and to each other. Companies that tap into such information can gain rich, timely customer insights at lower cost.

Far from lacking information, most marketing managers are overloaded with data and often overwhelmed by it. For example, when a company such as Pepsi monitors online discussions about its brands by searching key words in tweets, blogs, posts, and other sources, its servers take in a stunning six million public conversations a day, more than two billion a year.[3] That's far more information than any manager can digest. Thus, marketers don't need *more* information; they need *better* information. And they need to make better *use* of the information they already have.

The real value of marketing research and marketing information lies in how it is used—in the **customer insights** that it provides. Based on such thinking, many companies are now restructuring their marketing research and information functions. They are creating *customer insights teams*, headed by a vice president of customer insights and composed of representatives from all of the firm's functional areas. For example, Coca-Cola's marketing research group is headed by a vice president of marketing strategy and insights. And at Unilever, marketing research is done by the Consumer and Market Insight division, which helps brand teams harness information and turn it into customer insights.

Customer insights groups collect customer and market information from a wide variety of sources, ranging from traditional marketing research studies to mingling with and observing consumers to monitoring consumer online conversations about the company and its products. Then they *use* this information to develop important customer insights from which the company can create more value for its customers.

Thus, companies must design effective marketing information systems that give managers the right information, in the right form, at the right time and help them to use this information to create customer value and stronger customer relationships. A **marketing information system (MIS)** consists of people and procedures dedicated to assessing information needs, developing the needed information, and helping decision makers use the information to generate and validate actionable customer and market insights.

▶ Figure 4.1 shows that the MIS begins and ends with information users—marketing managers, internal and external partners, and others who need marketing information. First, it interacts with these information users to *assess information needs*. Next, it interacts with the marketing environment to *develop needed information* through internal company databases, marketing intelligence activities, and marketing research. Finally, the MIS helps users to *analyze and use* the information to develop customer insights, make marketing decisions, and manage customer relationships.

Assessing Marketing Information Needs

The marketing information system primarily serves the company's marketing and other managers. However, it may also provide information to external partners, such as suppliers, resellers, or marketing services agencies. For example, Walmart's Retail Link system gives key suppliers access to information on everything from customers' buying patterns and store inventory levels to how many items they've sold in which stores in the past 24 hours.[4]

A good MIS balances the information users would *like* to have against what they really *need* and what is *feasible* to offer. Some managers will ask for whatever information they can get without thinking carefully about what they really need. Too much information can be as harmful as too little. Other managers may omit things they ought to know, or they may not know to ask for some types of information they should have. For example,

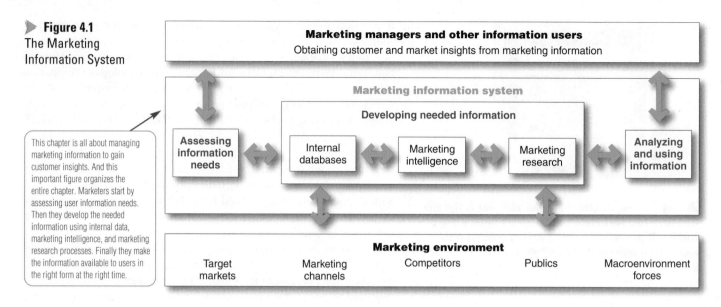

Figure 4.1
The Marketing
Information System

This chapter is all about managing marketing information to gain customer insights. And this important figure organizes the entire chapter. Marketers start by assessing user information needs. Then they develop the needed information using internal data, marketing intelligence, and marketing research processes. Finally they make the information available to users in the right form at the right time.

managers might need to know about surges in favorable or unfavorable consumer discussions about their brands on blogs or online social networks. Because they do not know about these discussions, they do not think to ask about them. The MIS must monitor the marketing environment to provide decision makers with information they should have to better understand customers and make key marketing decisions.

Finally, the costs of obtaining, analyzing, storing, and delivering information can quickly mount. The company must decide whether the value of insights gained from additional information is worth the costs of providing it, and both value and cost are often hard to assess.

Developing Marketing Information

Marketers can obtain the needed information from *internal data*, *marketing intelligence*, and *marketing research*.

Internal Data

Many companies build extensive **internal databases**, electronic collections of consumer and market information obtained from data sources within the company's network. Information in the database can come from many sources. The marketing department furnishes information on customer characteristics, sales transactions, and Web site visits. The customer service department keeps records of customer satisfaction or service problems. The accounting department provides detailed records of sales, costs, and cash flows. Operations reports on production, shipments, and inventories. The sales force reports on reseller reactions and competitor activities, and marketing channel partners provide data on point-of-sale transactions. Harnessing such information can provide powerful customer insights and competitive advantage.

For example, ▶ financial services provider USAA uses its internal database to create an incredibly loyal customer base:[5]

USAA provides financial services to U.S. military personnel and their families, largely through direct marketing via the telephone and Internet. It maintains a huge customer database built from customer purchasing histories and information collected directly through customer surveys, transaction data, and browsing behavior at its Web site. USAA uses the database to tailor direct

Author Comment ▶
The problem isn't *finding* information; the world is bursting with information from a glut of sources. The real challenge is to find the *right* information—from inside and outside sources—and turn it into customer insights.

▲ **Internal data: Financial services provider USAA uses its extensive database to tailor its services to the specific needs of individual customers, creating incredible loyalty.**
Courtney Young

Internal databases
Electronic collections of consumer and market information obtained from data sources within the company network.

marketing offers to the needs of individual customers. For example, for customers looking toward retirement, it sends information on estate planning. If the family has college-age children, USAA sends those children information on how to manage their credit cards.

One delighted reporter, a USAA customer, recounts how USAA even helped him teach his 16-year-old daughter to drive. Just before her birthday, but before she received her driver's license, USAA mailed a "package of materials, backed by research, to help me teach my daughter how to drive, help her practice, and help us find ways to agree on what constitutes safe driving later on, when she gets her license." What's more, marvels the reporter, "USAA didn't try to sell me a thing. My take-away: that USAA is investing in me for the long term." Through such skillful use of its database, USAA serves each customer uniquely, resulting in high customer satisfaction and loyalty. The $18 billion company retains 98 percent of its customers. For the past four years, *Bloomberg BusinessWeek* magazine has ranked USAA among its top two "Customer Service Champs," highlighting its legendary customer service. And MSN Money recently ranked USAA number one on its Customer Service Hall of Fame list.

Internal databases usually can be accessed more quickly and cheaply than other information sources, but they also present some problems. Because internal information is often collected for other purposes, it may be incomplete or in the wrong form for making marketing decisions. Data also ages quickly; keeping the database current requires a major effort. Finally, managing the mountains of information that a large company produces requires highly sophisticated equipment and techniques.

Competitive Marketing Intelligence

Competitive marketing intelligence
The systematic collection and analysis of publicly available information about consumers, competitors, and developments in the marketing environment.

Competitive marketing intelligence is the systematic collection and analysis of publicly available information about consumers, competitors, and developments in the marketplace. The goal of competitive marketing intelligence is to improve strategic decision making by understanding the consumer environment, assessing and tracking competitors' actions, and providing early warnings of opportunities and threats. Marketing intelligence techniques range from observing consumers firsthand to quizzing the company's own employees, benchmarking competitors' products, researching the Internet, and monitoring Internet buzz.

Good marketing intelligence can help marketers gain insights into how consumers talk about and connect with their brands. Many companies send out teams of trained observers to mix and mingle personally with customers as they use and talk about the company's products. Other companies routinely monitor consumers' online chatter. ▶ For example, PepsiCo's Gatorade brand has created an extensive control center to monitor brand-related social media activity.[6]

▲ **Mission control: PepsiCo's Gatorade brand has created an extensive control center to monitor real-time brand-related social media activity.**
Pepsi-Cola North America, Inc.

The Gatorade Mission Control Center, deep within the company's Chicago headquarters, serves as a nerve center in which Gatorade's four-member Mission Control team monitors the brand in real-time across social media. Whenever someone mentions anything related to Gatorade (including competitors, Gatorade athletes, and sports nutrition-related topics) on Twitter, Facebook, a blog, or in other social media, it pops up in various visualizations and dashboards on one of six big screens in Mission Control. Staffers also monitor online-ad and Web site traffic, producing a consolidated picture of the brand's Internet image.

Gatorade uses what it sees and learns at Mission Control to improve its products, marketing, and interactions with customers. For example, while monitoring its "Gatorade Has Evolved" campaign, the team quickly saw that a commercial featuring a song by rap artist

David Banner was being heavily discussed in social media. Within 24 hours, they had worked with Banner to put out a full-length version of the song and distribute it to Gatorade followers and fans on Twitter and Facebook. In another case, the brand knew to bulk up on production of its recovery drinks because of complaints they were selling out. Beyond just monitoring social media conversations, the Mission Control team sometimes joins them, as when staffers recently jumped into a Facebook conversation to answer a poster's questions about where to buy products.

Many companies have even appointed *chief listening officers*, who are charged with sifting through online customer conversations and passing along key insights to marketing decision makers. Dell created a position called *Listening Czar* two years ago. "Our chief listener is critical to making sure that the right people in the organization are aware of what the conversations on the Web are saying about us, so the relevant people in the business can connect with customers," says a Dell marketing executive.[7]

Companies also need to actively monitor competitors' activities. Firms use competitive marketing intelligence to gain early warnings of competitor moves and strategies, new-product launches, new or changing markets, and potential competitive strengths and weaknesses. Much competitor intelligence can be collected from people inside the company—executives, engineers and scientists, purchasing agents, and the sales force. The company can also obtain important intelligence information from suppliers, resellers, and key customers. It can monitor competitors' Web sites and use the Internet to search specific competitor names, events, or trends and see what turns up. And tracking consumer conversations about competing brands is often as revealing as tracking conversations about the company's own brands.

Intelligence seekers can also pour through any of thousands of online databases. Some are free. For example, the U.S. Security and Exchange Commission's database provides a huge stockpile of financial information on public competitors, and the U.S. Patent Office and Trademark database reveals patents that competitors have filed. For a fee, companies can also subscribe to any of the more than 3,000 online databases and information search services, such as Hoover's, LexisNexis, and Dun & Bradstreet. Today's marketers have an almost overwhelming amount of competitor information only a few keystrokes away.

The intelligence game goes both ways. Facing determined competitive marketing intelligence efforts by competitors, most companies are now taking steps to protect their own information. The growing use of marketing intelligence also raises ethical issues. Although the preceding techniques are legal, others may involve questionable ethics. Clearly, companies should take advantage of publicly available information. However, they should not stoop to snoop. With all the legitimate intelligence sources now available, a company does not need to break the law or accepted codes of ethics to get good intelligence.

Marketing Research

In addition to marketing intelligence information about general consumer, competitor, and marketplace happenings, marketers often need formal studies that provide customer and market insights for specific marketing situations and decisions. For example, Budweiser wants to know what appeals will be most effective in its Super Bowl advertising. Yahoo! wants to know how Web searchers will react to a proposed redesign of its site. Or Samsung wants to know how many and what kinds of people will buy its next-generation, ultrathin televisions. In such situations, managers will need marketing research.

Marketing research is the systematic design, collection, analysis, and reporting of data relevant to a specific marketing situation facing an organization. Companies use marketing research in a wide variety of situations. For example, marketing research gives marketers insights into customer motivations, purchase behavior, and satisfaction. It can help them to assess market potential and market share or measure the effectiveness of pricing, product, distribution, and promotion activities.

Some large companies have their own research departments that work with marketing managers on marketing research projects. In addition, these companies—like their smaller counterparts—frequently hire outside research specialists to consult with management on specific marketing problems and to conduct marketing research studies. Sometimes firms simply purchase data collected by outside firms to aid in their decision making.

Author Comment ▶
Whereas marketing intelligence involves actively scanning the general marketing environment, marketing research involves more focused studies to gain customer insights relating to specific marketing decisions.

Marketing research
The systematic design, collection, analysis, and reporting of data relevant to a specific marketing situation facing an organization.

Figure 4.2 The Marketing Research Process

| Defining the problem and research objectives | → | Developing the research plan for collecting information | → | Implementing the research plan—collecting and analyzing the data | → | Interpreting and reporting the findings |

This first step is probably the most difficult but also the most important one. It guides the entire research process. It's frustrating to reach the end of an expensive research project only to learn that you've addressed the wrong problem!

Exploratory research
Marketing research used to gather preliminary information that will help define problems and suggest hypotheses.

Descriptive research
Marketing research used to better describe marketing problems, situations, or markets.

Causal research
Marketing research used to test hypotheses about cause-and-effect relationships.

The marketing research process has four steps (see ▶ **Figure 4.2**): defining the problem and research objectives, developing the research plan, implementing the research plan, and interpreting and reporting the findings.

Defining the Problem and Research Objectives

Marketing managers and researchers must work closely together to define the problem and agree on research objectives. The manager best understands the decision for which information is needed, whereas the researcher best understands marketing research and how to obtain the information. Defining the problem and research objectives is often the hardest step in the research process. The manager may know that something is wrong, without knowing the specific causes.

After the problem has been defined carefully, the manager and the researcher must set the research objectives. A marketing research project might have one of three types of objectives. The objective of **exploratory research** is to gather preliminary information that will help define the problem and suggest hypotheses. The objective of **descriptive research** is to describe things, such as the market potential for a product or the demographics and attitudes of consumers who buy the product. The objective of **causal research** is to test hypotheses about cause-and-effect relationships. For example, would a 10 percent decrease in tuition at a private college result in an enrollment increase sufficient to offset the reduced tuition? Managers often start with exploratory research and later follow with descriptive or causal research.

The statement of the problem and research objectives guides the entire research process. The manager and the researcher should put the statement in writing to be certain that they agree on the purpose and expected results of the research.

Developing the Research Plan

Once researchers have defined the research problem and objectives, they must determine the exact information needed, develop a plan for gathering it efficiently, and present the plan to management. The research plan outlines sources of existing data and spells out the specific research approaches, contact methods, sampling plans, and instruments that researchers will use to gather new data.

Research objectives must be translated into specific information needs. ▶ For example, suppose that Red Bull wants to conduct research on how consumers would react to a proposed new vitamin-enhanced water drink that would be available in several flavors and sold under the Red Bull name. Red Bull currently dominates the worldwide energy drink market with a more than 40 percent market share worldwide.[8] A new line of enhanced waters—akin to Coca Cola's Vitaminwater—might help Red Bull leverage its strong brand position even further. The proposed research might call for the following specific information:

- The demographic, economic, and lifestyle characteristics of current Red Bull customers. (Do current customers also consume

▲ A decision by Red Bull to add a line of enhanced waters to its already successful mix of energy drinks would call for marketing research that provides lots of specific information.

Red Bull North America

enhanced-water products? Are such products consistent with their lifestyles? Or would Red Bull need to target a new segment of consumers?)

- The characteristics and usage patterns of the broader population of enhanced-water users: What do they need and expect from such products, where do they buy them, when and how do they use them, and what existing brands and price points are most popular? (The new Red Bull product would need strong, relevant positioning in the crowded enhanced-water market.)
- Retailer reactions to the proposed new product line: Would they stock and support it? Where would they display it? (Failure to get retailer support would hurt sales of the new drink.)
- Forecasts of sales of both the new and current Red Bull products. (Will the new enhanced waters create new sales or simply take sales away from current Red Bull products? Will the new product increase Red Bull's overall profits?)

Red Bull's marketers will need these and many other types of information to decide whether or not to introduce the new product and, if so, the best way to do it.

The research plan should be presented in a *written proposal*. A written proposal is especially important when the research project is large and complex or when an outside firm carries it out. The proposal should cover the management problems addressed, the research objectives, the information to be obtained, and how the results will help management's decision making. The proposal also should include estimated research costs.

To meet the manager's information needs, the research plan can call for gathering secondary data, primary data, or both. **Secondary data** consist of information that already exists somewhere, having been collected for another purpose. **Primary data** consist of information collected for the specific purpose at hand.

Secondary data
Information that already exists somewhere, having been collected for another purpose.

Primary data
Information collected for the specific purpose at hand.

Gathering Secondary Data

Researchers usually start by gathering secondary data. The company's internal database provides a good starting point. However, the company can also tap into a wide assortment of external information sources.

Companies can buy secondary data from outside suppliers. For example, Nielsen sells shopper insight data from a consumer panel of more than 250,000 households in 25 countries worldwide, with measures of trial and repeat purchasing, brand loyalty, and buyer demographics. ▶ Experian Simmons carries out a full spectrum of consumer studies that provide a comprehensive view of the American consumer. The MONITOR service by Yankelovich sells information on important social and lifestyle trends. These and other firms supply high-quality data to suit a wide variety of marketing information needs.[9]

Using *commercial online databases*, marketing researchers can conduct their own searches of secondary data sources. General database services such as Dialog, ProQuest, and LexisNexis put an incredible wealth of information at the keyboards of marketing decision makers. Beyond commercial Web sites offering information for a fee, almost every industry association, government agency, business publication, and news medium offers free information to those tenacious enough to find their Web sites.

Internet search engines can also be a big help in locating relevant secondary information sources. However, they can also be very frustrating and inefficient. For example, a Red Bull marketer Googling "enhanced water products" would come up with more than 50,000 hits. Still, well-structured, well-designed Web searches can be a good starting point to any marketing research project.

■ Understand
■ Communicate
■ Measure

For over 50 years, marketing professionals have relied on Experian℠ Simmons as the reliable source of marketing information. Experian Simmons provides the most comprehensive view of the American consumer. Our full spectrum of consumer studies includes:

Simmons National Consumer Study
- First syndicated national study launched in the U.S.
- Provides over 60,000 data variables to choose from, and usage behavior for all major media, 450+ product categories and 8,000+ brands on 25,000 U.S. adults
- Media Ratings Council accredited

Simmons National Hispanic Consumer Study
- First syndicated national study for U.S. Hispanic adults
- Surveys over 8,000 Hispanic adults annually providing Hispanic-only information on media, acculturation, language usage and preference, nativity, and country of origin as well as culturally-relevant measures on psychographics, lifestyles, attitudes and opinions
- Media Ratings Council accredited

Simmons Teens Study
- Surveys approximately 2,300 teens between the ages 12 and 17
- Bi-annual release with measures of major media usage, product consumption, demographics, lifestyle/psychographic characteristics as well as information on ownership, purchase, and usage of brands, products and services in the financial, entertainment and consumer package good sectors

Simmons Kids Study
- Surveys approximately 2,200 kids
- Provides insight into the brands and products they prefer and how much of each they consume plus in-depth media information

SimmonsLOCAL℠
the power of Simmons at the local level.
- Reports the unique nuances of all of America's 209 media markets
- Study is integrated into various platforms (i.e. Nielsen Station Index® and Microsoft MapPoint®) which enables users additional ways to analyze data

Simmons Multi-Media Engagement Study
- Provides ratings on the cognitive, behavioral and emotional involvement consumers have with media vehicles
- The only syndicated, cross-channel engagement measurement tool available

Experian Simmons

600 Third Avenue | New York, NY 10016
212.471.2850 | www.ExperianSimmons.com

▲ **Consumer database services such as Experian Simmons sell an incredible wealth of information on everything from the products consumers buy and the brands they prefer to their lifestyles, attitudes, and media preferences. Experian Simmons "provides the most comprehensive view of the American consumer."**
Experian Consumer Research

Secondary data can usually be obtained more quickly and at a lower cost than primary data. Also, secondary sources can sometimes provide data an individual company cannot collect on its own—information that either is not directly available or would be too expensive to collect. For example, it would be too expensive for Red Bull's marketers to conduct a continuing retail store audit to find out about the market shares, prices, and displays of competitors' brands. But those marketers can buy the InfoScan service from SymphonyIRI Group, which provides this information based on scanner and other data from 34,000 retail stores in markets around the nation.[10]

Secondary data can also present problems. Researchers can rarely obtain all the data they need from secondary sources. For example, Red Bull will not find existing information regarding consumer reactions about a new enhanced-water line that it has not yet placed on the market. Even when data can be found, the information might not be very usable. The researcher must evaluate secondary information carefully to make certain it is *relevant* (fits the research project's needs), *accurate* (reliably collected and reported), *current* (up-to-date enough for current decisions), and *impartial* (objectively collected and reported).

Primary Data Collection

Secondary data provide a good starting point for research and often help to define research problems and objectives. In most cases, however, the company must also collect primary data. ▶ **Table 4.1** shows that designing a plan for primary data collection calls for a number of decisions on *research approaches*, *contact methods*, the *sampling plan*, and *research instruments*.

Research Approaches

Research approaches for gathering primary data include observations, surveys, and experiments. We discuss each one in turn.

Observational research

Gathering primary data by observing relevant people, actions, and situations.

Observational Research. **Observational research** involves gathering primary data by observing relevant people, actions, and situations. For example, Trader Joe's might evaluate possible new store locations by checking traffic patterns, neighborhood conditions, and the locations of competing Whole Foods, Fresh Market, and other retail chains.

Researchers often observe consumer behavior to glean customer insights they can't obtain by simply asking customers questions. For instance, Fisher-Price has established an observation lab in which it can observe the reactions little tots have to new toys. The Fisher-Price Play Lab is a sunny, toy-strewn space where lucky kids get to test Fisher-Price prototypes, under the watchful eyes of designers who hope to learn what will get them worked up into a new-toy frenzy.

Marketers not only observe what consumers do but also observe what consumers are saying. As discussed earlier, marketers now routinely listen in on consumer conversations on blogs, social networks, and Web sites. Observing such naturally occurring feedback can provide inputs that simply can't be gained through more structured and formal research approaches.

Ethnographic research

A form of observational research that involves sending trained observers to watch and interact with consumers in their "natural environments."

A wide range of companies now use **ethnographic research**. Ethnographic research involves sending observers to watch and interact with consumers in their "natural environments." The observers might be trained anthropologists and psychologists or company researchers and managers (see Marketing at Work 4.1).

▶ **Table 4.1**	Planning Primary Data Collection		
Research Approaches	**Contact Methods**	**Sampling Plan**	**Research Instruments**
Observation	Mail	Sampling unit	Questionnaire
Survey	Telephone	Sample size	Mechanical instruments
Experiment	Personal	Sampling procedure	
	Online		

MARKETING AT WORK   4.1

Ethnographic Research: Watching What Consumers *Really* Do

A girl walks into a bar and says to the bartender, "Give me a Diet Coke and a clear sight line to those guys drinking Miller Lite in the corner." If you're waiting for a punch line, this is no joke. The "girl" in this situation is Emma Gilding, corporate ethnographer at ad agency Ogilvy & Mather. In this case, her job is to hang out in bars around the country and watch groups of guys knocking back beers with their friends. No kidding. This is honest-to-goodness, cutting-edge marketing research—ethnography style.

As a videographer filmed the action, Gilding kept tabs on how close the guys stood to one another. She eavesdropped on stories and observed how the mantle was passed from one speaker to another, as in a tribe around a campfire. Back at the office, a team of trained anthropologists and psychologists pored over more than 70 hours of footage from five similar nights in bars from San Diego to Philadelphia. One key insight: Miller is favored by groups of drinkers, while its main competitor, Bud Lite, is a beer that sells to individuals. The result was a hilarious series of ads that cut from a Miller Lite drinker's weird experiences in the world—getting caught in the subway taking money from a blind musician's guitar case or hitching a ride in the desert with a deranged trucker—to shots of him regaling friends with tales over a brew. The Miller Lite ads got high marks from audiences for their entertainment value and emotional resonance.

Today's marketers face many difficult questions: What do customers *really* think about a product and what do they say about it to their friends? How do they *really* use it? Will they tell you? *Can* they tell you? All too often, traditional research simply can't provide accurate answers. To get deeper insights, many companies use ethnographic research by watching and interacting with consumers in their "natural environments."

Ethnographers are looking for "consumer truth." In surveys and interviews, customers may state (and fully believe) certain preferences and behaviors, when the reality is actually quite different. Ethnography provides an insider's tour of the customer's world, helping marketers get at what consumers *really* do rather than what they *say* they do. "That might mean catching a heart-disease patient scarfing down a meatball sub and a cream soup while extolling the virtues of healthy eating," observes one ethnographer, "or a diabetic vigorously salting his sausage and eggs after explaining how he refuses jelly for his toast."

By entering the customer's world, ethnographers can scrutinize how customers think and feel as it relates to their products. Here's another example:

Kelly Peña, also known as "the kid whisperer," was digging through a 12-year-old boy's dresser

drawer one recent afternoon. Her undercover mission: to unearth what makes him tick and help the Walt Disney Company reassert itself as a cultural force among boys. Peña, a Disney researcher, heads a team zeroed in on a ratty rock 'n' roll T-shirt. Black Sabbath? "Wearing it makes me feel like I'm going to an R-rated movie," said Dean, the shy redheaded boy under scrutiny. Jackpot! Peña and her team of anthropologists have spent 18 months peering inside the heads of incommunicative boys in search of just that kind of psychological nugget.

Disney is relying on Peña's insights to create new entertainment for boys ages 6 to 14, who account for $50 billion a year in spending worldwide. With the exception of *Cars*, Disney—home to more girl-focused fare such as the "Princesses" merchandising line, "Hannah Montana," and "Pixie Hollow"—has been notably weak on hit entertainment for boys. Peña's research is sometimes conducted in groups; sometimes it involves going shopping with a teenage boy and his mother. Walking through Dean's house, Peña looked for unspoken clues about his likes and dislikes. "What's on the back shelves that he hasn't quite gotten rid of will be telling," she said beforehand. "What's on his walls? How does he interact with his siblings?" One big takeaway from the two-hour visit: Although Dean was trying to sound grown-up and nonchalant in his answers, he still had a lot of little kid in him. He had dinosaur sheets and stuffed animals at the bottom of his bed. "I think he's trying to push a lot of boundaries for the first time," Peña said later.

Children can already see the results of Peña's scrutiny on Disney XD, a new cable channel and Web site. It's no accident, for instance, that the central character on "Aaron Stone" is a mediocre basketball player. Peña told producers that boys identify with protagonists who try hard to grow. "Winning isn't nearly as important to boys as Hollywood thinks," she said.

▲ **Ethnographic research: To better understand the challenges faced by elderly shoppers, this Kimberly-Clark executive tries to shop while wearing vision-impairment glasses and bulky gloves that simulate arthritis.**
Lauren Pond/The Photo Pond

Ethnographic research often yields the kinds of intimate details that just don't emerge from traditional focus groups and surveys. For example, focus groups told the Best Western hotel chain that it's men who decide when to stop for the night and where to stay. But videotapes of couples on cross-country journeys showed it was usually the women. And observation can often uncover problems that customers don't even know they have. By videotaping consumers in the shower, plumbing fixture maker Moen uncovered safety risks that consumers didn't recognize—such as the habit some women have of shaving their legs while holding on to one unit's temperature control. Moen would find it almost impossible to discover such design flaws simply by asking questions.

Experiencing firsthand what customers experience can also provide powerful insights. To that end, consumer products giant Kimberly-Clark even runs a program that puts executives from retail chains such as Walgreens, Rite Aid, and Family Dollar directly into their customers' shoes—literally. The executives shop in their own stores with glasses that blur their vision, unpopped popcorn in their shoes, and bulky rubber gloves on their hands. It's all part of an exercise designed to help marketers understand the physical challenges faced by elderly shoppers, who will represent 20 percent of the total U.S. population by 2030.

The vision-blurring glasses simulate common vision ailments such as cataracts, macular degeneration, and glaucoma. Unpopped popcorn in shoes gives a feel for what it's like to walk with aching joints. And the bulky gloves simulate the limitations to manual dexterity brought on by arthritis. Participants come back from these experiences bursting with ideas for elderly-friendly store changes, such as bigger typefaces and more eye-friendly colors on packaging and fliers, new store lighting and clearer signage, and instant call buttons near heavy merchandise such as bottled water and laundry detergent.

Thus, more and more, marketing researchers are getting up close and personal with consumers—watching them closely as they act and interact in natural settings or stepping in to feel firsthand what they feel. "Knowing the individual consumer on an intimate basis has become a necessity," says one research consultant, "and ethnography is the intimate connection to the consumer."

Sources: Adapted excerpts and other information from Brooks Barnes, "Disney Expert Uses Science to Draw Boy Viewers," *New York Times*, April 14, 2009, p. A1; Linda Tischler, "Every Move You Make," *Fast Company*, April 2004, pp. 73–75; Ellen Byron, "Seeing Store Shelves Through Senior Eyes," *Wall Street Journal*, September 14, 2009, p. B1; and Natasha Singer, "The Fountain of Old Age," *New York Times,* February 6, 2011, p. BU 1.

▲ **Ethnographic research: Kraft Canada sent out its president (above center) and other high-level executives to observe actual family life in diverse Canadian homes. Videos of their experiences helped marketers and others across the company to understand the role Kraft's brands play in people's lives.**

Michael Stuparyk/GetStock.com

Also consider this example:[11]

▶ Kraft Canada recently sent its president and other high-level Kraft executives to observe actual family life in a dozen diverse Canadian homes. "We went out with the purpose of understanding the Canadian family, what's going on in their homes, particularly the kitchen," says Kraft Canada's vice president of consumer insights and strategy. After viewing hours of video of all 12 families visited, the consumer insights group found some unifying themes across Kraft's diverse markets. It learned that almost all families faced the same "mad rush to have something ready to feed the family, a hectic-ness, last-minute decisions, the need to balance the child's needs and different food needs." Kraft shared a compilation of the videos with marketing and sales teams, who used it as a basis for brainstorming sessions, and even put the video on an internal Web site for Kraft's 4,500 employees across Canada to view. The experience of "living with customers" helped Kraft's marketers and others understand how the company's brands help customers by providing more convenient products that reduce the stress of getting meals on the table.

Beyond conducting ethnographic research in physical consumer environments, many companies now routinely conduct *Netnography* research—observing consumers in a natural context on the Internet. Observing people as they interact on and move about the Internet can provide useful insights into both online and offline buying motives and behavior.[12]

Observational and ethnographic research often yield the kinds of details that just don't emerge from traditional research questionnaires or focus groups. Whereas traditional quantitative research approaches seek to test known hypotheses and obtain answers to well-defined product or strategy questions, observational research can generate fresh customer and market insights that people are unwilling or unable to provide. It provides a window into customers' unconscious actions and unexpressed needs and feelings.

In contrast, however, some things simply cannot be observed, such as feelings, attitudes, motives, or private behavior. Long-term or infrequent behavior is also difficult to observe. Finally, observations can be very difficult to interpret. Because of these limitations, researchers often use observation along with other data collection methods.

Survey research

Gathering primary data by asking people questions about their knowledge, attitudes, preferences, and buying behavior.

Survey Research. **Survey research**, the most widely used method for primary data collection, is the approach best suited for gathering descriptive information. A company that wants to know about people's knowledge, attitudes, preferences, or buying behavior can often find out by asking them directly.

The major advantage of survey research is its flexibility; it can be used to obtain many different kinds of information in many different situations. Surveys addressing almost any marketing question or decision can be conducted by phone or mail, in person, or on the Web.

However, survey research also presents some problems. Sometimes people are unable to answer survey questions because they cannot remember or have never thought about what they do and why they do it. People may be unwilling to respond to unknown interviewers or about things they consider private. Respondents may answer survey questions even when they do not know the answer just to appear smarter or more informed. Or they may try to help the interviewer by giving pleasing answers. Finally, busy people may not take the time, or they might resent the intrusion into their privacy.

Experimental research

Gathering primary data by selecting matched groups of subjects, giving them different treatments, controlling related factors, and checking for differences in group responses.

Experimental Research. Whereas observation is best suited for exploratory research and surveys for descriptive research, **experimental research** is best suited for gathering causal information. Experiments involve selecting matched groups of subjects, giving them different treatments, controlling unrelated factors, and checking for differences in group responses. Thus, experimental research tries to explain cause-and-effect relationships.

For example, before adding a new sandwich to its menu, McDonald's might use experiments to test the effects on sales of two different prices it might charge. It could introduce the new sandwich at one price in one city and at another price in another city. If the cities are similar, and if all other marketing efforts for the sandwich are the same, then differences in sales in the two cities could be related to the price charged.

Contact Methods

Information can be collected by mail, telephone, personal interview, or online. ▶ **Table 4.2** shows the strengths and weaknesses of each contact method.

Mail, Telephone, and Personal Interviewing. *Mail questionnaires* can be used to collect large amounts of information at a low cost per respondent. Respondents may give more honest answers to more personal questions on a mail questionnaire than to an unknown interviewer in person or over the phone. Also, no interviewer is involved to bias respondents' answers.

However, mail questionnaires are not very flexible; all respondents answer the same questions in a fixed order. Mail surveys usually take longer to complete, and the response rate—the number of people returning completed questionnaires—is often very low. Finally, the researcher often has little control over the mail questionnaire sample. Even with a good mailing list, it is hard to control *whom* at a particular address fills out the questionnaire. As a result of the shortcomings, more and more marketers are now shifting to faster, more flexible, and lower cost e-mail and online surveys.

▶ **Table 4.2**	Strengths and Weaknesses of Contact Methods			
	Mail	**Telephone**	**Personal**	**Online**
Flexibility	Poor	Good	Excellent	Good
Quantity of data that can be collected	Good	Fair	Excellent	Good
Control of interviewer effects	Excellent	Fair	Poor	Fair
Control of sample	Fair	Excellent	Good	Excellent
Speed of data collection	Poor	Excellent	Good	Excellent
Response rate	Poor	Poor	Good	Good
Cost	Good	Fair	Poor	Excellent

Source: Based on Donald S. Tull and Del I. Hawkins, *Marketing Research: Measurement and Method,* 7th ed. (New York: Macmillan Publishing Company, 1993). Adapted with permission of the authors.

Focus group interviewing
Personal interviewing that involves inviting six to ten people to gather for a few hours with a trained interviewer to talk about a product, service, or organization. The interviewer "focuses" the group discussion on important issues.

Telephone interviewing is one of the best methods for gathering information quickly, and it provides greater flexibility than mail questionnaires. Interviewers can explain difficult questions and, depending on the answers they receive, skip some questions or probe on others. Response rates tend to be higher than with mail questionnaires, and interviewers can ask to speak to respondents with the desired characteristics or even by name.

However, with telephone interviewing, the cost per respondent is higher than with mail or online questionnaires. Also, people may not want to discuss personal questions with an interviewer. The method introduces interviewer bias—the way interviewers talk, how they ask questions, and other differences that may affect respondents' answers. Finally, in this age of do-not-call lists and promotion-harassed consumers, potential survey respondents are increasingly hanging up on telephone interviewers rather than talking with them.

Personal interviewing takes two forms: individual interviewing and group interviewing. *Individual interviewing* involves talking with people in their homes or offices, on the street, or in shopping malls. Such interviewing is flexible. Trained interviewers can guide interviews, explain difficult questions, and explore issues as the situation requires. They can show subjects actual products, advertisements, or packages and observe reactions and behavior. However, individual personal interviews may cost three to four times as much as telephone interviews.

Group interviewing consists of inviting six to ten people to meet with a trained moderator to talk about a product, service, or organization. Participants normally are paid a small sum for attending. A moderator encourages free and easy discussion, hoping that group interactions will bring out actual feelings and thoughts. At the same time, the moderator "focuses" the discussion—hence the name **focus group interviewing**.

In traditional focus groups, researchers and marketers watch the focus group discussions from behind a one-way mirror and record comments in writing or on video for later study. Focus group researchers often use videoconferencing and Internet technology to connect marketers in distant locations with live focus group action. Using cameras and two-way sound systems, marketing executives in a far-off boardroom can look in and listen, using remote controls to zoom in on faces and pan the focus group at will.

Along with observational research, focus group interviewing has become one of the major qualitative marketing research tools for gaining fresh insights into consumer thoughts and feelings. In focus group settings, researchers not only hear consumer ideas and opinions, they can also observe facial expressions, body movements, group interplay, and conversational flows. However, focus group studies present some challenges. They usually employ small samples to keep time and costs down, and it may be hard to generalize from the results. Moreover, consumers in focus groups are not always open and honest about their real feelings, behavior, and intentions in front of other people.

To overcome these problems, many researchers are tinkering with the focus group design. Some companies use *immersion groups*—small groups of consumers who interact directly and informally with product designers without a focus group moderator present. Other researchers are changing the environments in which they conduct focus groups to help consumers relax and elicit more authentic responses. ▶ For example, Lexus recently hosted a series of "An Evening with Lexus" dinners with groups of customers in customers' homes:[13]

▲ **New focus group environments: Lexus general manager Mark Templin hosts "An Evening with Lexus" dinners with luxury car buyers to figure out why they did or didn't become Lexus owners.**

Courtesy of Lexus

Nothing like citrus-cured sardines with Escabeche vegetables or baked halibut with a quail egg to get the conversation flowing. Indeed, Mark Templin, Lexus group vice president and general manager, figures the best way to get up close and personal with customers is to dine with them—in their homes and in style. At the first dinner, held in Beverly Hills, 16 owners of Lexus, Mercedes, BMW, Audi, Land Rover, and other high-end cars traded their perceptions of the Lexus brand. Through lively talk over a sumptuous meal catered by a famous chef, Templin hoped to learn why people did or didn't become Lexus owners.

While feasting on the cuisine, the high-end car consumers gave Templin many actionable insights. For example, he heard that Lexus vehicles often are tagged with being unexciting. "Everyone had driven a Lexus at some point and had a great experience," Templin says. "But the Lexus they [had] wasn't as fun to drive as the car they have now. It's our challenge to show that Lexus is more fun to drive today than it was 15 years ago." Templin was also startled by the extent to which luxury car buyers allow their grown children to decide what car they should purchase. Templin says Lexus marketing in the future also will have to aim at young adults who may not be buying luxury cars but who may strongly influence their parents' decisions.

Individual and focus group interviews can add a personal touch as opposed to more numbers-oriented research. "We get lots of research, and it tells us what we need to run our business, but I get more out of talking one-on-one," says Lexus's Templin. "It really comes to life when I hear people say it."

Online Marketing Research. The growth of the Internet has had a dramatic impact on how marketing research is conducted. Increasingly, researchers are collecting primary data through **online marketing research**: Internet surveys, online panels, experiments, and online focus groups and brand communities.

Online research can take many forms. A company can use the Web as a survey medium: It can include a questionnaire on its Web site or use e-mail to invite people to answer questions, create online panels that provide regular feedback, or conduct live discussions or online focus groups. Researchers can also conduct experiments on the Web. They can experiment with different prices, headlines, or product features on different Web sites or at different times to learn the relative effectiveness of their offers. They can set up virtual shopping environments and use them to test new products and marketing programs. Or a company can learn about the behavior of online customers by following their click streams as they visit the Web site and move to other sites.

The Internet is especially well suited to *quantitative* research—for example, conducting marketing surveys and collecting data. More than three-quarters of all Americans now have access to the Web, making it a fertile channel for reaching a broad cross-section of consumers.[14] As response rates for traditional survey approaches decline and costs increase, the Web is quickly replacing mail and the telephone as the dominant data collection methodology.

Online marketing research
Collecting primary data online through Internet surveys, online focus groups, Web-based experiments, or tracking consumers' online behavior.

Web-based survey research offers many advantages over traditional phone, mail, and personal interviewing approaches. The most obvious advantages are speed and low costs. By going online, researchers can quickly and easily distribute Internet surveys to thousands of respondents simultaneously via e-mail or by posting them on selected Web sites. Responses can be almost instantaneous, and because respondents themselves enter the information, researchers can tabulate, review, and share research data as the information arrives.

Online research also usually costs much less than research conducted through mail, phone, or personal interviews. Using the Internet eliminates most of the postage, phone, interviewer, and data-handling costs associated with the other approaches. Moreover, sample size has little impact on costs. Once the questionnaire is set up, there's little difference in cost between 10 respondents and 10,000 respondents on the Web.

▲ **Online research: Thanks to survey services such as Zoomerang, almost any business, large or small, can create, publish, and distribute its own custom surveys in minutes.**

Zoomerang, a MarketTools Company

Online focus groups
Gathering a small group of people online with a trained moderator to chat about a product, service, or organization and gain qualitative insights about consumer attitudes and behavior.

Its low cost puts online research well within the reach of almost any business, large or small. In fact, with the Internet, what was once the domain of research experts is now available to almost any would-be researcher. ▶ Even smaller, less sophisticated researchers can use online survey services such as Zoomerang (*www.zoomerang.com*) and SurveyMonkey (*www.surveymonkey.com*) to create, publish, and distribute their own custom surveys in minutes.

Web-based surveys also tend to be more interactive and engaging, easier to complete, and less intrusive than traditional phone or mail surveys. As a result, they usually garner higher response rates. The Internet is an excellent medium for reaching the hard-to-reach consumer—for example, the often-elusive teen, single, affluent, and well-educated audiences. It's also good for reaching working mothers and other people who lead busy lives. Such people are well represented online, and they can respond in their own space and at their own convenience.

Just as marketing researchers have rushed to use the Internet for quantitative surveys and data collection, they are now also adopting *qualitative* Internet-based research approaches, such as online focus groups, blogs, and social networks. The Internet can provide a fast, low-cost way to gain qualitative customer insights.

A primary qualitative Web-based research approach is **online focus groups**. Such focus groups offer many advantages over traditional focus groups. Participants can log in from anywhere—all they need is a laptop and a Web connection. Thus, the Internet works well for bringing together people from different parts of the country or world. Also, researchers can conduct and monitor online focus groups from just about anywhere, eliminating travel, lodging, and facility costs. Finally, although online focus groups require some advance scheduling, results are almost immediate.

Online focus groups can take any of several formats. Most occur in real time, in the form of online chat room discussions in which participants and a moderator sit around a virtual table exchanging comments. Alternatively, researchers might set up an online message board on which respondents interact over the course of several days or a few weeks. Participants log in daily and comment on focus group topics.

Although low in cost and easy to administer, online focus groups can lack the real-world dynamics of more personal approaches. To overcome these shortcomings, some researchers are now adding real-time audio and video to their online focus groups. ▶ For example, online research firm Channel M2 "puts the human touch back into online research" by assembling focus group participants in people-friendly "virtual interview rooms." At the appointed time, participants sign on via their webcam-equipped computer, view live video of other participants, and interact in real-time. Researchers can "sit in" on the focus group from anywhere, seeing and hearing every respondent.[15]

▲ **Some researchers have now added real-time audio and video to their online focus groups. For example, Channel M2 "puts the human touch back into online research" by assembling focus group participants in people-friendly "virtual interview rooms."**

Although growing rapidly, both quantitative and qualitative Internet-based research have some drawbacks. One major problem is controlling who's in the online sample. Without seeing respondents, it's difficult to know who they really are. To overcome such sample and context problems, many online research firms use opt-in communities and respondent panels. For example, Zoomerang offers an online consumer and business panel profiled on more than 500 attributes.[16]

Alternatively, many companies are now developing their own custom social networks and using them to gain customer inputs and insights. For example, in addition to picking customers' brains in face-to-face events such as "An Evening with Lexus" dinners in customers' homes, Lexus has built an extensive online research community called the Lexus Advisory Board.[17]

The Lexus Advisory Board consists of 20,000 invitation-only Lexus owners representing a wide range of demographics, psychographics, and model ownership. Lexus surveys the group regularly to obtain owner input on everything from perceptions of the brand and input on new models and features to the Lexus ownership experience and customer relationships with dealers. "As a Lexus owner, your opinion is invaluable to us," says the invitation, "which is why Lexus is inviting you to join our exclusive online research panel. By becoming a member of the Lexus Advisory Board, your feedback will help shape future product development, customer service, and marketing communications." Says a Lexus marketing executive, "This is a great way of listening to customers."

Thus, in recent years, the Internet has become an important tool for conducting research and developing customer insights. But today's marketing researchers are going even further—well beyond structured online surveys, focus groups, and Web communities. Increasingly, they are listening to and watching consumers by actively mining the rich veins of unsolicited, unstructured, "bottom up" customer information already coursing around the Web.

This might be as simple as scanning customer reviews and comments on the company's brand site or on shopping sites such as Amazon.com or BestBuy.com. Or it might mean using sophisticated Web-analysis tools to deeply analyze mountains of consumer comments and messages found in blogs or on social networking sites, such as Facebook or Twitter. Listening to and watching consumers online can provide valuable insights into what consumers are saying or feeling about brands. As one information expert puts it, "The Web knows what you want."[18] (See Marketing at Work 4.2.)

Sampling Plan

Marketing researchers usually draw conclusions about large groups of consumers by studying a small sample of the total consumer population. A **sample** is a segment of the population selected for marketing research to represent the population as a whole. Ideally, the sample should be representative so that the researcher can make accurate estimates of the thoughts and behaviors of the larger population.

Designing the sample requires three decisions. First, *who* is to be studied (what *sampling unit*)? The answer to this question is not always obvious. For example, to learn about the decision-making process for a family automobile purchase, should the subject be the husband, the wife, other family members, dealership salespeople, or all of these? Second, *how many* people should be included (what *sample size*)? Large samples give more reliable results than small samples. However, larger samples usually cost more, and it is not necessary to sample the entire target market or even a large portion to get reliable results.

Sample
A segment of the population selected for marketing research to represent the population as a whole.

MARKETING AT WORK   4.2

Listening Online: The Web Knows What You Want

Thanks to the burgeoning world of blogs, social networks, and other Internet forums, marketers now have near-real-time access to a flood of online consumer information. It's all there for the digging—praise, criticism, recommendations, actions—revealed in what consumers are saying and doing as they ply the Internet. Forward-looking marketers are now mining valuable customer insights from this rich new vein of unprompted, "bottom-up" information.

Whereas traditional marketing research provides insights into the "logical, representative, structured aspect of our consumers," says Kristin Bush, senior manager of consumer and market knowledge at P&G, online listening "provides much more of the intensity, much more of the . . . context and the passion, and more of the spontaneity that consumers are truly giving you [when they offer up their opinions] unsolicited."

Listening online might involve something as simple as scanning customer reviews on the company's brand site or on popular shopping sites such as Amazon.com or BestBuy.com. Such reviews are plentiful, address specific products, and provide unvarnished customer reactions. Amazon.com alone features detailed customer reviews on everything it sells, and its customers rely heavily on these reviews when making purchases. If customers in the market for a company's brands are reading and reacting to such reviews, so should the company's marketers. Many companies are now adding customer review sections to their own brand sites. Both positive and negative feedback can help the company learn what it is doing well and where improvement is needed.

At a deeper level, marketers now employ sophisticated Web-analysis tools to listen in on and mine nuggets from the churning mass of consumer comments and conversations in blogs, in news articles, in online forums, and on social networking sites such as Facebook or Twitter. But beyond monitoring what customers are *saying* about them online, companies are also watching what customers are *doing* online. Marketers scrutinize consumer Web-browsing behavior in precise detail and use the resulting insights to personalize shopping experiences. Consider this example:

A shopper at the retail site FigLeaves.com takes a close look at a silky pair of women's slippers. Next, a recommendation appears for a man's bathrobe. This could seem terribly wrong—unless, of course, it turns out to be precisely what she wanted. Why the bathrobe? Analysis of FigLeaves.com site behavior data—from mouse clicks to search queries—shows that certain types of female shoppers at certain times of the week are likely to be shopping for men.

What a given customer sees at the site might also depend on other behaviors. For example, shoppers who seem pressed for time (say, shopping from work and clicking rapidly from screen to screen) might see more simplified pages with a direct path to the shopping cart and checkout. Alternatively, more leisurely shoppers

(say, those shopping from home or on weekends and browsing product reviews) might receive pages with more features, video clips, and comparison information. The goal of such analysis is to teach Web sites "something close to the savvy of a flesh-and-blood sales clerk," says a Web-analytics expert. "In the first five minutes in a store, the sales guy is observing a customer's body language and tone of voice. We have to teach machines to pick up on those same insights from movements online."

More broadly, information about what consumers do while trolling the vast expanse of the Internet—what searches they make, the sites they visit, what they buy, with whom they connect—is pure gold to marketers. And today's marketers are busy mining that gold.

On the Internet today, everybody knows who you are. In fact, legions of Internet companies know your gender, your age, the neighborhood you live in, who your Facebook and Twitter friends are, that you like pickup trucks, and that you spent, say, three hours and 43 seconds on a Web site for pet lovers on a rainy day in January. All that data streams through myriad computer networks, where it's sorted, cataloged, analyzed, and then used to deliver ads aimed squarely at you, potentially anywhere you travel on the Internet. It's called *behavioral targeting*—tracking consumers' online behavior and using it to target ads to them. So, for example, if you place a cell phone in your Amazon.com shopping cart but don't buy it, you might expect to see some ads for that very type of phone the next time you visit your favorite ESPN site to catch up on the latest sports scores.

That's amazing enough, but the newest wave of Web analytics and targeting takes online eavesdropping even further—from *behavioral* targeting to *social* targeting. Whereas behavioral targeting tracks consumer movements across Web sites,

▲ Marketers watch what consumers say and do online, then use the resulting insights to personalize online shopping experiences. Is it sophisticated Web research or "just a little creepy"?

Andresr/Shutterstock

social targeting also mines individual online social connections. Research shows that consumers shop a lot like their friends and are five times more likely to respond to ads from brands friends use. Social targeting links customer data to social interaction data from social networking sites. So, instead of just having a Zappos.com ad for running shoes pop up because you've recently searched for running shoes (behavioral targeting), an ad for a specific pair of running shoes pops up because a friend that you're connected to via Twitter just bought those shoes from Zappos.com last week (social targeting).

Online listening. Behavioral targeting. Social targeting. All of these are great for marketers as they work to mine customer insights from the massive amounts of consumer information swirling around the Web. The biggest question? You've probably already guessed it. As marketers get more adept at trolling blogs, social networks, and other Web domains, what happens to consumer privacy? Yup, that's the downside. At what point does sophisticated Web research cross the line into consumer stalking?

Proponents claim that behavioral and social targeting benefit more than abuse consumers by feeding back ads and products that are more relevant to their interests. But to many consumers and public advocates, following consumers online and stalking them with ads feels more than just a little creepy. Behavioral targeting, for example, has already been the subject of congressional and regulatory hearings. The FTC has recommended the creation of a "Do Not Track" system (the Internet equivalent to the "Do Not Call" registry), which would let people opt out of having their actions monitored online.

Despite such concerns, however, online listening will continue to grow. And, with appropriate safeguards, it promises benefits for both companies and customers. Tapping into online conversations and behavior lets companies "get the unprompted voice of the consumer, the real sentiments, the real values, and the real points of view that they have of our products and services," says P&G's Bush. "Companies that figure out how to listen and respond . . . in a meaningful, valuable way are going to win in the marketplace." After all, knowing what customers really want is an essential first step in creating customer value. And, as one online information expert puts it, "The Web knows what you want."

Sources: Adapted excerpts, quotes, and other information from Stephen Baker, "The Web Knows What You Want," *BusinessWeek*, July 27, 2009, p. 48; Piet Levy, "The Data Dilemma," *Marketing News,* January 30, 2011, pp. 20–21; Brian Morrissey, "Connect the Thoughts," *Adweek*, June 29, 2009, pp. 10–11; Paul Sloan, "The Quest for the Perfect Online Ad," *Business 2.0*, March 2007, p. 88; David Wiesenfeld, Kristin Bush, and Ronjan Sikdar, "Listen Up: Online Yields New Research Pathway," *Nielsen Consumer Insights*, August 2009, http://en-us.nielsen.com/; Elizabeth A. Sullivan, "10 Minutes with Kristin Bush," *Marketing News*, September 30, 2009, pp. 26–28; Eric Picard, "Why Consumers Think Online Marketing Is Creepy," *iMedia Connection*, December 9, 2010, www.imediaconnection.com/content/28158.asp; and Douglas Karr, "Do Not Track: What Marketers Need to Know," *Marketing Tech Blog,* January 26, 2011, www.marketingtechblog.com/technology/do-not-track/.

Finally, *how* should the people in the sample be *chosen* (what *sampling procedure*)? ▶ **Table 4.3** describes different kinds of samples. Using *probability samples*, each population member has a known chance of being included in the sample, and researchers can calculate confidence limits for sampling error. But when probability sampling costs too much or takes too much time, marketing researchers often take *nonprobability samples*, even though their sampling error cannot be measured. These varied ways of drawing samples have different costs and time limitations as well as different accuracy and statistical properties. Which method is best depends on the needs of the research project.

Research Instruments

In collecting primary data, marketing researchers have a choice of two main research instruments: *questionnaires* and *mechanical devices.*

Questionnaires. The questionnaire is by far the most common instrument, whether administered in person, by phone, by e-mail, or online. Questionnaires are very flexible—there are many ways to ask questions. Closed-end questions include all the possible answers, and subjects make choices among them. Examples include multiple-choice questions and scale questions. Open-end questions allow respondents to answer in their own words. In a survey of airline users, Southwest Airlines might simply ask, "What is your opinion of Southwest Airlines?" Or it might ask people to complete a sentence: "When I choose an airline, the most important consideration is. . . ." These and other kinds of open-end questions often reveal more than closed-end questions because they do not limit respondents' answers.

> **Table 4.3** | Types of Samples

Probability Sample

Simple random sample	Every member of the population has a known and equal chance of selection.
Stratified random sample	The population is divided into mutually exclusive groups (such as age groups), and random samples are drawn from each group.
Cluster (area) sample	The population is divided into mutually exclusive groups (such as blocks), and the researcher draws a sample of the groups to interview.

Nonprobability Sample

Convenience sample	The researcher selects the easiest population members from which to obtain information.
Judgment sample	The researcher uses his or her judgment to select population members who are good prospects for accurate information.
Quota sample	The researcher finds and interviews a prescribed number of people in each of several categories.

Open-end questions are especially useful in exploratory research, when the researcher is trying to find out *what* people think but is not measuring *how many* people think in a certain way. Closed-end questions, on the other hand, provide answers that are easier to interpret and tabulate.

Researchers should also use care in the *wording* and *ordering* of questions. They should use simple, direct, and unbiased wording. Questions should be arranged in a logical order. The first question should create interest if possible, and difficult or personal questions should be asked last so that respondents do not become defensive.

Mechanical Instruments. Although questionnaires are the most common research instrument, researchers also use mechanical instruments to monitor consumer behavior. Nielsen Media Research attaches people meters to television sets, cable boxes, and satellite systems in selected homes to record who watches which programs. Retailers likewise use checkout scanners to record shoppers' purchases.

Other mechanical devices measure subjects' physical responses. For example, ▶ consider Disney Media Networks' new consumer research lab in Austin, Texas:[19]

A technician in a black lab coat gazed at the short, middle-aged man seated inside Disney's secretive new research facility, his face shrouded with eye-tracking goggles. "Read ESPN.com on that BlackBerry," she told him soothingly, like a nurse about to draw blood. "And have fun," she added, leaving the room. In reality, the man's appetite for sports news was not of interest. (The site was a fake version anyway.) Rather, the technician and her fellow researchers from Disney Media Networks—which includes ABC, ESPN, and other networks—were eager to know how the man responded to ads of varying size. How small could the banners become and still draw his attention? A squadron of Disney executives scrutinized the data as it flowed in real time onto television monitors in an adjacent room. "He's not even looking at the banner now," said one researcher. The man clicked to another page. "There we go, that one's drawing his attention." The tools are advanced: In addition to tracking eye movement, the research team uses heart-rate monitors, skin temperature readings, and facial expressions (probes are attached to facial muscles) to gauge reactions. The goal: to learn what works and what does not in the high-stakes game of new media advertising.

Still other researchers are applying *neuromarketing*, measuring brain activity to learn how consumers feel and respond. Marketing scientists using MRI scans and EEG devices

▲ **Mechanical instruments: To find out what ads work and why, Disney researchers have developed an array of devices to track eye movement, monitor heart rates, and measure other physical responses.**

Erich Schlegel/Redux Pictures

have learned that tracking brain electrical activity and blood flow can provide companies with insights into what turns consumers on and off regarding their brands and marketing. "Companies have always aimed for the customer's heart, but the head may make a better target," suggests one neuromarketer. "Neuromarketing is reaching consumers where the action is: the brain."[20]

Companies ranging from PepsiCo and Disney to Google and Microsoft now hire neuromarketing research companies such as NeuroFocus and EmSense to help figure out what people are really thinking. For example, PepsiCo's Frito-Lay unit uses neuromarketing to test commercials, product designs, and packaging. Recent EEG tests showed that, compared with shiny packages showing pictures of potato chips, matte beige bags showing potatoes and other healthy ingredients trigger less activity in an area of the brain associated with feelings of guilt. Needless to say, Frito-Lay quickly switched away from the shiny packaging. And eBay's PayPal began pitching its online payment service as "fast" after brain-wave research showed that speed turns consumers on more than security and safety, earlier themes used in eBay ad campaigns.[21]

Although neuromarketing techniques can measure consumer involvement and emotional responses second by second, such brain responses can be difficult to interpret. Thus, neuromarketing is usually used in combination with other research approaches to gain a more complete picture of what goes on inside consumers' heads.

Implementing the Research Plan

The researcher next puts the marketing research plan into action. This involves collecting, processing, and analyzing the information. Data collection can be carried out by the company's marketing research staff or outside firms. Researchers should watch closely to make sure that the plan is implemented correctly. They must guard against problems created through interacting with respondents, with the quality of participants' responses, and with interviewers who make mistakes or take shortcuts.

Researchers must also process and analyze the collected data to isolate important information and insight. They need to check data for accuracy and completeness and code it for analysis. The researchers then tabulate the results and compute statistical measures.

Interpreting and Reporting the Findings

The market researcher must now interpret the findings, draw conclusions, and report them to management. The researcher should not try to overwhelm managers with numbers and fancy statistical techniques. Rather, the researcher should present important findings and insights that are useful in the major decisions faced by management.

However, interpretation should not be left only to researchers. Although they are often experts in research design and statistics, the marketing manager knows more about the problem and the decisions that must be made. The best research means little if the manager blindly accepts faulty interpretations from the researcher. Similarly, managers may be biased. They might tend to accept research results that show what they expected and reject those that they did not expect or hope for. In many cases, findings can be interpreted in different ways, and discussions between researchers and managers will help point to the best interpretations. Thus, managers and researchers must work together closely when interpreting research results, and both must share responsibility for the research process and resulting decisions.

| **SPEED BUMP** | LINKING THE CONCEPTS |

Whew! We've covered a lot of territory. Hold up a minute, take a breather, and see if you can apply the marketing research process you've just studied.

- What specific kinds of research can Red Bull's brand managers use to learn more about its customers' preferences and buying behaviors? Sketch out a brief research plan for assessing potential reactions to a new Red Bull enhanced-water line.
- Could you use the marketing research process to analyze your own career opportunities and job possibilities? (Think of yourself as a "product" and employers as potential "customers.") What would your research plan look like?

Analyzing and Using Marketing Information

Information gathered in internal databases and through competitive marketing intelligence and marketing research usually requires additional analysis. Managers may need help applying the information to gain customer and market insights that will improve their marketing decisions. This help may include advanced statistical analysis to learn more about the relationships within a set of data. Information analysis might also involve the application of analytical models that will help marketers make better decisions.

Once the information has been processed and analyzed, it must be made available to the right decision makers at the right time. In the following sections, we look deeper into analyzing and using marketing information.

Customer Relationship Management

Customer relationship management (CRM)
Managing detailed information about individual customers and carefully managing customer touch points to maximize customer loyalty.

The question of how best to analyze and use individual customer data presents special problems. Most companies are awash in information about their customers. In fact, smart companies capture information at every possible customer *touch point*. These touch points include customer purchases, sales force contacts, service and support calls, Web site visits, satisfaction surveys, credit and payment interactions, market research studies—every contact between a customer and a company.

Unfortunately, this information is usually scattered widely across the organization. It is buried deep in the separate databases and records of different company departments. To overcome such problems, many companies are now turning to **customer relationship management (CRM)** to manage detailed information about individual customers and carefully manage customer touch points to maximize customer loyalty.

CRM consists of sophisticated software and analytical tools from companies such as Oracle, Microsoft, Salesforce.com, and SAS that integrate customer information from all sources, analyze it in depth, and apply the results to build stronger customer relationships. CRM integrates everything that a company's sales, service, and marketing teams know about individual customers, providing a 360-degree view of the customer relationship.

CRM analysts develop *data warehouses* and use sophisticated *data mining* techniques to unearth the riches hidden in customer data. A data warehouse is a company-wide electronic database of finely detailed customer information that needs to be sifted through for gems. The purpose of a data warehouse is not only to gather information but also to pull it together into a central, accessible location. Then, once the data warehouse brings the data together, the company uses high-powered data mining techniques to sift through the mounds of data and dig out interesting findings about customers.

These findings often lead to marketing opportunities. For example, grocery chain Kroger works with the data mining firm Dunnhumby, which it co-owns with successful London-based retailer Tesco, to dig deeply into data obtained from customer loyalty cards.

It uses the customer insights gained for everything from targeting coupons to locating stores and adjusting inventories to specific locations:[22]

▲ **Grocery chain Kroger works with data mining firm Dunnhumby to dig deeply into data obtained from customer loyalty cards. It uses the customer insights gained for everything from targeting coupons to locating and stocking its stores.**

With permission of The Kroger Co.

Although the recent Great Recession revived penny-pinching, Americans are still redeeming only 1 percent to 3 percent of paper coupons. In contrast, Kroger says as many as *half* the coupons it sends to regular customers do get used. ▶ Kroger digs deep into the reams of information from its more than 55 million shopper cards and uses the resulting insights, augmented with customer interviews, to guide strategies for tailored promotions, pricing, placement, and even stocking variations from store to store. For example, 95 percent of mailings are tailored to specific households, containing coupons for items they usually load into their carts. Such personalization creates more value for customers and makes them feel more appreciated. In turn, Kroger's ability to turn data into insights builds customer loyalty and drives profitable sales. Says Kroger's CEO, "This level of personalization is a direct link to our customers that no other U.S. grocery retailer can [match]."

By using CRM to understand customers better, companies can provide higher levels of customer service and develop deeper customer relationships. They can use CRM to pinpoint high-value customers, target them more effectively, cross-sell the company's products, and create offers tailored to specific customer requirements.

CRM benefits don't come without costs or risk, either in collecting the original customer data or in maintaining and mining it. The most common CRM mistake is to view CRM as a technology and software solution only. Yet technology alone cannot build profitable customer relationships. Companies can't improve customer relationships by simply installing some new software. Instead, CRM is just one part of an effective overall *customer relationship management strategy*. "There's lots of talk about CRM and these days it usually has to do with a software solution," says one analyst. But marketers should start by adhering to "some basic tenets of actual customer relationship management and *then* empower them with high-tech solutions."[23] They should focus first on the R—it's the *relationship* that CRM is all about.

Distributing and Using Marketing Information

Marketing information has no value until it is used to gain customer insights and make better marketing decisions. Thus, the marketing information system must make the information readily available to managers and others who need it. In some cases, this means providing managers with regular performance reports, intelligence updates, and reports on the results of research studies.

But marketing managers may also need nonroutine information for special situations and on-the-spot decisions. For example, a sales manager having trouble with a large customer may want a summary of the account's sales and profitability over the past year. Or a brand manager may want to get a sense of the amount of online buzz surrounding the launch of a recent advertising campaign. These days, therefore, information distribution involves entering information into databases and making it available in a timely, user-friendly way.

Many firms use company *intranet* and internal CRM systems to facilitate this process. These systems provide ready access to research and intelligence information, customer contact information, reports, shared work documents, and more. For example, the CRM system at phone and online gift retailer 1-800-Flowers gives customer-facing employees real-time access to customer information. When a repeat customer calls, the system immediately calls up data on previous transactions and other contacts, helping reps make the customer's

Does Your Business Depend on Key Fleet Information?
We offer a one-stop online fleet management solution.

Full-Service Lease
  Financing and Cost Control
  Maintenance
  Managing Vehicle Lifecycle
  Operational Support
  Safety and Compliance
  Onboard Technology
  Fleet Management Tools
Contract Maintenance

MyFleetAtPenske.com

Fleet Management. Faster. Easier. MyFleetAtPenske.com

▲ **Extranets: Penske Truck Leasing's extranet site, MyFleetAtPenske.com, lets Penske customers access all of the data about their fleets in one spot and provides tools to help fleet managers manage their Penske accounts and maximize efficiency.**

Penske Truck Leasing Co., LP

experience easier and more relevant. For instance, "If a customer usually buys tulips for his wife, we [talk about] our newest and best tulip selections," says the company's vice president of customer knowledge management. "No one else in the business is able to connect customer information with real-time transaction data the way we can."[24]

In addition, companies are increasingly allowing key customers and value-network members to access account, product, and other data on demand through *extranets*. Suppliers, customers, resellers, and select other network members may access a company's extranet to update their accounts, arrange purchases, and check orders against inventories to improve customer service. ▶ For example, Penske Truck Leasing's extranet site, MyFleetAtPenske.com, lets Penske business customers access all the data about their fleets in one spot and provides an array of tools and applications designed to help fleet managers manage their Penske accounts and maximize efficiency.[25]

Thanks to modern technology, today's marketing managers can gain direct access to a company's information system at any time and from virtually anywhere. They can tap into the system from a home office, hotel room, or the local Starbucks—anyplace they can connect on a laptop or smartphone. Such systems allow managers to get the information they need directly and quickly and tailor it to their own needs.

SPEED BUMP | LINKING THE CONCEPTS

Let's stop here for a bit, think back, and be certain that you've got the "big picture" concerning marketing information systems.

- What's the overall goal of an MIS? How are the individual components linked and what does each contribute? Take another look at Figure 4.1—it provides a good organizing framework for the entire chapter.
- Apply the MIS framework to Converse (a Nike company). How might Converse go about assessing marketing managers' information needs, developing the needed information, and helping managers to analyze and use the information to gain actionable customer and market insights?

Author Comment ▶
We finish this chapter by examining three special marketing information topics.

Other Marketing Information Considerations

This section discusses marketing information in two special contexts: marketing research in small businesses and nonprofit organizations and international marketing research. Then, we look at public policy and ethics issues in marketing research.

Marketing Research in Small Businesses and Nonprofit Organizations

Just like larger firms, small organizations need market information and the customer and market insights that it can provide. Managers of small businesses and nonprofit organizations often think that marketing research can be done only by experts in large companies with big research budgets. True, large-scale research studies are beyond the budgets of most small businesses. However, many of the marketing research techniques discussed in this chapter also can be used by smaller organizations in a less formal manner and at little or no expense. ▶ Consider how one small-business owner conducted market research on a shoestring before even opening his doors:[26]

▲ Before opening Bibbentuckers dry cleaner, owner Robert Byerly conducted research to gain insights into what customers wanted. First on the list: quality.
Bibbentuckers

After a string of bad experiences with his local dry cleaner, Robert Byerley decided to open his own dry-cleaning business. But before jumping in, he conducted plenty of market research. He needed a key customer insight: How would he make his business stand out from the others? To start, Byerley spent an entire week in the library and online, researching the dry-cleaning industry. To get input from potential customers, using a marketing firm, Byerley held focus groups on the store's name, look, and brochure. He also took clothes to the 15 best competing cleaners in town and had focus group members critique their work. Based on his research, he made a list of features for his new business. First on his list: quality. His business would stand behind everything it did. Not on the list: cheap prices. Creating the perfect dry-cleaning establishment simply didn't fit with a discount operation.

With his research complete, Byerley opened Bibbentuckers, a high-end dry cleaner positioned on high-quality service and convenience. It featured a banklike drive-through area with curbside delivery. A computerized bar code system read customer cleaning preferences and tracked clothes all the way through the cleaning process. Byerley added other differentiators, such as decorative awnings, TV screens, and refreshments (even "candy for the kids and a doggy treat for your best friend"). "I wanted a place . . . that paired five-star service and quality with an establishment that didn't look like a dry cleaner," he says. The market research yielded results. Today, Bibbentuckers is a thriving six-store operation.

"Too [few] small-business owners have a . . . marketing mind-set," says a small-business consultant. "You have to think like Procter & Gamble. What would they do before launching a new product? They would find out who their customer is and who their competition is."[27]

Thus, small businesses and not-for-profit organizations can obtain good marketing insights through observation or informal surveys using small convenience samples. Also, many associations, local media, and government agencies provide special help to small organizations. For example, the U.S. Small Business Administration offers dozens of free publications and a Web site (*www.sba.gov*) that give advice on topics ranging from starting, financing, and expanding a small business to ordering business cards. Other excellent resources for small businesses include the U.S. Census Bureau (*www.census.gov*) and the Bureau of Economic Analysis (*www.bea.gov*). Finally, small businesses can collect a considerable amount of information at very little cost online. They can scour competitor and customer Web sites and use Internet search engines to research specific companies and issues.

In summary, secondary data collection, observation, surveys, and experiments can all be used effectively by small organizations with small budgets. However, although these informal research methods are less complex and less costly, they still must be conducted with care. Managers must think carefully about the objectives of the research, formulate questions in advance, recognize the biases introduced by smaller samples and less skilled researchers, and conduct the research systematically.[28]

International Marketing Research

International marketing research has grown tremendously over the past decade. International researchers follow the same steps as domestic researchers, from defining the

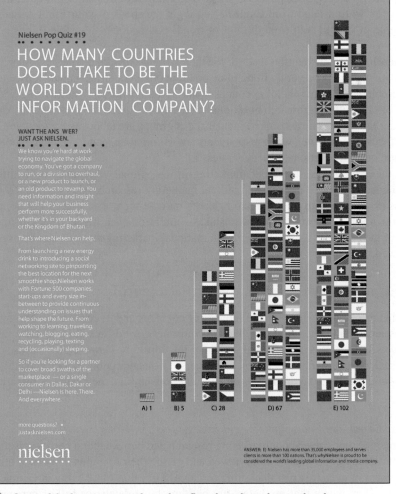

▲ **Some of the largest research services firms have large international organizations. ACNielsen, for example, has offices in more than 100 countries.**

The Nielsen Company

research problem and developing a research plan to interpreting and reporting the results. However, these researchers often face more and different problems. Whereas domestic researchers deal with fairly homogeneous markets within a single country, international researchers deal with diverse markets in many different countries. These markets often vary greatly in their levels of economic development, cultures and customs, and buying patterns.

In many foreign markets, the international researcher may have a difficult time finding good secondary data. Whereas U.S. marketing researchers can obtain reliable secondary data from dozens of domestic research services, many countries have almost no research services at all. Some of the largest international research services operate in many countries. ▶ For example, The Nielsen Company (the world's largest marketing research company) has offices in more than 100 countries, from Schaumburg, Illinois, to Hong Kong to Nicosia, Cyprus. However, most research firms operate in only a relative handful of countries.[29] Thus, even when secondary information is available, it usually must be obtained from many different sources on a country-by-country basis, making the information difficult to combine or compare.

Because of the scarcity of good secondary data, international researchers often must collect their own primary data. However, obtaining primary data may be no easy task. For example, it can be difficult simply to develop good samples. U.S. researchers can use current telephone directories, e-mail lists, census tract data, and any of several sources of socioeconomic data to construct samples. However, such information is largely lacking in many countries.

Once the sample is drawn, the U.S. researcher usually can reach most respondents easily by telephone, by mail, on the Internet, or in person. However, reaching respondents is often not so easy in other parts of the world. Researchers in Mexico cannot rely on telephone, Internet, and mail data collection—most data collection is door-to-door and concentrated in three or four of the largest cities. In some countries, few people have computers, let alone Internet access. For example, whereas there are 76 Internet users per 100 people in the United States, there are only 22 Internet users per 100 people in Mexico. In Kenya, the number drops to 9 Internet users per 100 people. In some countries, the postal system is notoriously unreliable. In Brazil, for instance, an estimated 30 percent of the mail is never delivered. In many developing countries, poor roads and transportation systems make certain areas hard to reach, making personal interviews difficult and expensive.[30]

Cultural differences from country to country cause additional problems for international researchers. Language is the most obvious obstacle. For example, questionnaires must be prepared in one language and then translated into the languages of each country researched. Responses then must be translated back into the original language for analysis and interpretation. This adds to research costs and increases the risks of error.

Translating a questionnaire from one language to another is anything but easy. Many idioms, phrases, and statements mean different things in different cultures. For example, a Danish executive noted, "Check this out by having a different translator put back into English what you've translated from English. You'll get the shock of your life. I remember [an example in which] 'out of sight, out of mind' had become 'invisible things are insane.'"[31]

Consumers in different countries also vary in their attitudes toward marketing research. People in one country may be very willing to respond; in other countries, nonresponse can be a major problem. Customs in some countries may prohibit people from talking with strangers. In certain cultures, research questions often are considered too personal. For example, in many Muslim countries, mixed-gender focus groups are taboo, as is videotaping female-only focus groups. Even when respondents are *willing* to respond, they may not be *able* to because of high functional illiteracy rates.

Despite these problems, as global marketing grows, global companies have little choice but to conduct these types of international marketing research. Although the costs and problems associated with international research may be high, the costs of not doing it—in terms of missed opportunities and mistakes—might be even higher. Once recognized, many of the problems associated with international marketing research can be overcome or avoided.

Public Policy and Ethics in Marketing Research

Most marketing research benefits both the sponsoring company and its consumers. Through marketing research, companies gain insights into consumers' needs, resulting in more satisfying products and services and stronger customer relationships. However, the misuse of marketing research can also harm or annoy consumers. Two major public policy and ethics issues in marketing research are intrusions on consumer privacy and the misuse of research findings.

Intrusions on Consumer Privacy

Many consumers feel positive about marketing research and believe that it serves a useful purpose. Some actually enjoy being interviewed and giving their opinions. However, others strongly resent or even mistrust marketing research. They don't like being interrupted by researchers. They worry that marketers are building huge databases full of personal information about customers. Or they fear that researchers might use sophisticated techniques to probe our deepest feelings, peek over our shoulders as we shop, or track us as we browse and interact on the Internet and then use this knowledge to manipulate our buying.

There are no easy answers when it comes to marketing research and privacy. For example, is it a good or bad thing that marketers track and analyze consumers' Web clicks and target ads to individuals based on their browsing and social networking behavior? Similarly, should we applaud or resent companies that monitor consumer discussions on YouTube, Facebook, Twitter, or other public social networks in an effort to be more responsive? For example, Dell uses Web-monitoring service Radian6 to routinely track social media conversations and often responds quickly. Someone commenting about Dell on a popular blog might be surprised by receiving a response from a Dell representative within only a few hours. Dell views such monitoring as an opportunity to engage consumers in helpful two-way conversations. However, some disconcerted consumers might see it as an intrusion on their privacy.

Increasing consumer privacy concerns have become a major problem for the marketing research industry. Companies face the challenge of unearthing valuable but potentially sensitive consumer data while also maintaining consumer trust. At the same time, consumers wrestle with the trade-offs between personalization and privacy. "The debate over online [privacy] stems from a marketing paradox," says a privacy expert. "Internet shoppers want to receive personalized, timely offers based on their wants and needs but they resent that companies track their online purchase and browsing histories." The key question: "Where is the line between questionable and acceptable customer data gathering activities?"[32] Failure to address such privacy issues could result in angry, less-cooperative consumers and increased government intervention.

The marketing research industry is considering several options for responding to intrusion and privacy issues. One example is the Marketing Research Association's "Your Opinion Counts" and "Respondent Bill of Rights" initiatives to educate consumers about the benefits of marketing research and distinguish it from telephone selling and database building. The industry also has considered adopting broad standards, perhaps based on the International Chamber of Commerce's International Code of Marketing and Social Research Practice. This code outlines researchers' responsibilities to respondents and the general public. For example, it urges that researchers make their names and addresses available to participants and be open about the data they are collecting.[33]

Most major companies—including IBM, Microsoft, Facebook, Citigroup, American Express, and even the U.S. government—have now appointed a chief privacy officer (CPO), whose job is to safeguard the privacy of consumers who do business with the company. In the end, if researchers provide value in exchange for information, customers will gladly provide it. For example, Amazon.com's customers do not mind if the firm builds a database of products they buy as a way to provide future product recommendations. This saves time and provides value. The best approach is for researchers to ask only for the information they need, use it responsibly to provide customer value, and avoid sharing information without the customer's permission.

Misuse of Research Findings

Research studies can be powerful persuasion tools; companies often use study results as claims in their advertising and promotion. Today, however, many research studies appear to be little more than vehicles for pitching the sponsor's products. In fact, in some cases, research surveys appear to have been designed just to produce the intended effect. Few advertisers openly rig their research designs or blatantly misrepresent the findings—most abuses tend to be more subtle "stretches." ▶ Consider the following example:[34]

Based on a scientific study, the Kellogg Company proclaimed in ads and on packaging for Frosted Mini-Wheats that the cereal was "clinically shown to improve kids' attentiveness by nearly 20%." When challenged by the Federal Trade Commission, however, the claims turned out to be a substantial stretch of the study results. Fine print at the bottom of the box revealed the following: "Based upon independent clinical research, kids who ate Kellogg's Frosted Mini-Wheats cereal for breakfast had up to 18 percent better attentiveness three hours after breakfast than kids who ate no breakfast." That is, as one critic noted, "Frosted Mini-Wheats are (up to) 18 percent better than starving." Moreover, according to the FTC complaint, the clinical study referred to by Kellogg actually showed that children who ate the cereal for breakfast *averaged* just under 11 percent better in attentiveness than children who ate no breakfast, and that only about one in nine improved by 20 percent or more. Kellogg settled with the FTC, agreeing to refrain from making unsubstantiated health claims about Frosted Mini-Wheats or other products and from misrepresenting the results of scientific tests.

Recognizing that surveys can be abused, several associations—including the American Marketing Association, the Marketing Research Association, and the Council of American Survey Research Organizations (CASRO)—have developed codes of research ethics and standards of conduct. For example, the CASRO Code of Standards and Ethics for Survey Research outlines researcher responsibilities to respondents, including confidentiality, privacy, and avoidance of harassment. It also outlines major responsibilities in reporting results to clients and the public.[35]

In the end, however, unethical or inappropriate actions cannot simply be regulated away. Each company must accept responsibility for policing the conduct and reporting of its own marketing research to protect consumers' best interests and its own.

▲ **Misuse of research findings:** The Federal Trade Commission recently challenged research-based advertising and packaging claims stating that Kellogg's Frosted Mini-Wheats were "clinically shown to improve kids' attentiveness by nearly 20%."

Eric Meyerson/Rangelife

REST STOP | REVIEWING THE CONCEPTS

MyMarketingLab

Now that you have completed the chapter, return to www.mymktlab.com to experience and apply the concepts and to explore the additional study materials for this chapter.

CHAPTER REVIEW AND KEY TERMS

Objectives Review

To create value for customers and build meaningful relationships with them, marketers must first gain fresh, deep insights into what customers need and want. Such insights come from good marketing information. As a result of the recent explosion of marketing technology, companies can now obtain great quantities of information, sometimes even too much. The challenge is to transform today's vast volume of consumer information into actionable customer and market insights.

> **OBJECTIVE 1   Explain the importance of information in gaining insights about the marketplace and customers. (pp 96–97)**

The marketing process starts with a complete understanding of the marketplace and consumer needs and wants. Thus, the company needs sound information to produce superior value and satisfaction for its customers. The company also requires information on competitors, resellers, and other actors and forces in the marketplace. Increasingly, marketers are viewing information not only as an input for making better decisions but also as an important strategic asset and marketing tool.

> **OBJECTIVE 2   Define the marketing information system and discuss its parts. (pp 97–100)**

The *marketing information system (MIS)* consists of people and procedures for assessing information needs, developing the needed information, and helping decision makers use the information to generate and validate actionable customer and market insights. A well-designed information system begins and ends with users.

The MIS first *assesses information needs*. The MIS primarily serves the company's marketing and other managers, but it may also provide information to external partners. Then the MIS *develops information* from internal databases, marketing intelligence activities, and marketing research. *Internal databases* provide information on the company's own operations and departments. Such data can be obtained quickly and cheaply but often needs to be adapted for marketing decisions. *Marketing intelligence* activities supply everyday information

about developments in the external marketing environment. *Market research* consists of collecting information relevant to a specific marketing problem faced by the company. Lastly, the MIS helps users analyze and use the information to develop customer insights, make marketing decisions, and manage customer relationships.

> **OBJECTIVE 3   Outline the steps in the marketing research process. (pp 100–115)**

The first step in the marketing research process involves *defining the problem and setting the research objectives*, which may be exploratory, descriptive, or causal research. The second step consists of *developing a research plan* for collecting data from primary and secondary sources. The third step calls for *implementing the marketing research plan* by gathering, processing, and analyzing the information. The fourth step consists of *interpreting and reporting the findings*. Additional information analysis helps marketing managers apply the information and provides them with sophisticated statistical procedures and models from which to develop more rigorous findings.

Both *internal* and *external* secondary data sources often provide information more quickly and at a lower cost than primary data sources, and they can sometimes yield information that a company cannot collect by itself. However, needed information might not exist in secondary sources. Researchers must also evaluate secondary information to ensure that it is *relevant*, *accurate*, *current*, and *impartial*.

Primary research must also be evaluated for these features. Each primary data collection method—*observational*, *survey*, and *experimental*—has its own advantages and disadvantages. Similarly, each of the various research contact methods—mail, telephone, personal interview, and online—has its own advantages and drawbacks.

> **OBJECTIVE 4   Explain how companies analyze and use marketing information. (pp 115–117)**

Information gathered in internal databases and through marketing intelligence and marketing research usually requires more analysis. To analyze individual customer data, many companies have now acquired or developed special software and analysis techniques—called *customer relationship management* (*CRM*)—that integrate, analyze, and apply the mountains of individual customer data contained in their databases.

Marketing information has no value until it is used to make better marketing decisions. Thus, the MIS must make the information available to managers and others who make marketing decisions or deal with customers. In some cases, this means providing regular reports and updates; in other cases, it means making nonroutine information available for special situations and on-the-spot decisions. Many firms use company intranets and extranets to facilitate this process. Thanks to modern technology, today's marketing managers can gain direct access to marketing information at any time and from virtually any location.

> **OBJECTIVE 5** Discuss the special issues some marketing researchers face, including public policy and ethics issues. (pp 117–121)

Some marketers face special marketing research situations, such as those conducting research in small business, not-for-profit, or international situations. Marketing research can be conducted effectively by small businesses and nonprofit organizations with limited budgets. International marketing researchers follow the same steps as domestic researchers but often face more and different problems. All organizations need to act responsibly to major public policy and ethical issues surrounding marketing research, including issues of intrusions on consumer privacy and misuse of research findings.

Key Terms

Objective 1
Customer insights (p 97)
Marketing information system (MIS) (p 97)

Objective 2
Internal databases (p 98)
Competitive marketing intelligence (p 99)

Objective 3
Marketing research (p 100)
Exploratory research (p 101)
Descriptive research (p 101)
Causal research (p 101)
Secondary data (p 102)
Primary data (p 102)
Observational research (p 103)
Ethnographic research (p 103)

Survey research (p 106)
Experimental research (p 106)
Focus group interviewing (p 107)
Online marketing research (p 108)
Online focus groups (p 109)
Sample (p 110)

Objective 4
Customer relationship management (CRM) (p 115)

DISCUSSION AND CRITICAL THINKING

Discussion Questions

1. Discuss the real value of marketing research and marketing information and how that value is attained. (AACSB: Communication)
2. Discuss the sources of internal data and the advantages and disadvantages associated with this data. (AACSB: Communication)
3. Explain the role of secondary data in gaining customer insights. Where do marketers obtain secondary data and what are the potential problems in using it? (AACSB: Communication)

4. What are the advantages of Web-based survey research over traditional survey research? (AACSB: Communication)
5. What is *neuromarketing* and how is it useful in marketing research? Why is this research approach usually used with other approaches? (AACSB: Communication)
6. What are the similarities and differences when conducting research in another country versus the domestic market? (AACSB: Communication)

Critical Thinking Exercises

1. In a small group, identify a problem faced by a local business or charitable organization and propose a research project addressing that problem. Develop a research proposal that implements each step of the marketing research process. Discuss how the research results will help the business

or organization. (AACSB: Communication; Reflective Thinking)
2. Want to earn a little extra cash? Businesses use focus groups and surveys to make better marketing decisions, and they might pay for your participation. Visit www.FindFocusGroups

.com and review the opportunities available for research participation. Find two more Web sites that recruit research participants. Write a brief report of what you found and discuss the pros and cons to companies of recruiting research participants this way. (AACSB: Communication; Use of IT; Reflective Thinking)

3. Go to the Strategic Business Insights (SBI) Web site and take the VALS survey (www.strategicbusinessinsights .com/vals/presurvey.shtml). What type of research is being conducted—exploratory, descriptive, or causal? How can marketers use this information? (AACSB: Communication; Use of IT; Reflective Thinking)

MINICASES AND APPLICATIONS

Marketing Technology   EWA Bespoke Communications

In 1996, Marks & Spencer (M&S), the venerable British retailer, launched "lunchtogo"—an online corporate catering service (see www.lunchtogo-e.com/). But M&S found it difficult to develop long-term relationships with corporate customers due to high personnel turnover within customer organizations. Therefore, it turned to EWA Bespoke Communications, a company that uses data mining to "tell you more about your customers." EWA used *propensity modeling* to develop the Critical Lag formula, which identified customers whose last order fell outside of their expected behavior. EWA then developed an automated system to send communications to customers who have not reordered within the maximum allowed order lag determined by the formula. Whereas most customers received e-mails, the system flagged M&S's best corporate catering customers that should receive more personalized phone calls because of their value and importance. EWA also implemented information systems

to improve the company's service. Knowing more about its customers paid off—within a short period of time, the EWA system generated more than €1 million, tripling the operation's revenues, and delivered an almost perfect order accuracy rate.

1. Visit EWA Bespoke Communications at www.ewa.ltd.uk/ to learn more about its Customer Insight services and the types of analyses performed by this company. What is propensity modeling? Review other case studies from this Web site and write a brief report of how data mining technology was used to gain customer insights. (AACSB: Communication; Use of IT)
2. Describe how other organizations can benefit from these types of data mining analyses. Find examples of other companies that can offer such analysis to businesses. (AACSB: Communication; Reflective Thinking)

Marketing Ethics   Tracking Consumers Online

Marketers are hungry for customer information, and the electronic tracking industry is answering the call by gathering consumer Internet behavior data. A recent investigation by the *Wall Street Journal* found that the 50 most popular U.S. Web sites installed more than 3,000 tracking files on the computer used in the study. The total was even higher for the top 50 sites popular with children and teens (4,123 tracking files). Many sites installed more than 100 tracking tools each during the tests. Tracking tools include files placed on users' computers and on Web sites. You probably know about cookies, small files placed on your computer that contain information. Newer technology, such as Web beacons (also known as Web bugs, tracking bugs, pixel tags, and clear GIFs), are invisible graphic files placed on Web sites and in e-mails that, when combined with cookies, can tell a lot about the user. For example, beacons can tell a marketer if a page was viewed and for how long and can even tell if you read the e-mail sent to you. Such tracking has become aggressive to the point where keystrokes can be analyzed for clues about a person and "flash cookies" can re-spawn after a user

deletes them. Although the data do not identify users by name, data-gathering companies can construct consumer profiles that include demographic, geographic, and lifestyle information. Marketers use this information to target online advertisements.

1. Critics claim that Internet tracking infringes on consumer privacy rights. Should marketers have access to such information? Discuss the advantages and disadvantages of this activity for both marketers and consumers. (AACSB: Communication; Ethical Reasoning)
2. Visit the Network Advertising Initiative's Web site at www .networkadvertising.org/ to learn more about behavioral targeting and the advertising industry's efforts to give consumers power to protect their online privacy. Click on the "Consumer Opt-out." How many active cookies have been placed on the computer you are using? After learning more from this Web site, discuss whether you are more or less likely to allow companies to gather your Internet behavior data. (AACSB: Communication; Reflective Thinking)

Marketing by the Numbers   A Big Enough Sample?

Have you ever been disappointed when a television network cancelled one of your favorite television shows because of "low ratings"? The network didn't ask your opinion, did it? It probably didn't ask any of your friends, either. That's because estimates of television audience sizes are based on research done by The Nielsen Company, which uses a sample of only 9,000 households out of the more than 113 million households in the United States to determine national ratings for television programs. That doesn't seem like enough. But as it turns out, statistically, it's many more than enough.

1. Go to www.surveysystem.com/sscalc.htm to determine the appropriate sample size for a population of 113 million households. Assuming a confidence interval of 5, how large should the sample of households be when desiring a 95-percent confidence level? How large for a 99-percent confidence level? Briefly explain what is meant by *confidence interval* and *confidence level*. (AACSB: Communication; Use of IT; Analytical Reasoning)

2. What sample sizes are necessary at population sizes of 1 billion, 10,000, and 100 with a confidence interval of 5 and a 95-percent confidence level? Explain the effect population size has on required sample size. (AACSB: Communication; Use of IT; Analytical Reasoning)

Video Case   Domino's

As a delivery company, no one outdoes Domino's. Its reputation for delivering hot pizza in 30 minutes or less is ingrained in customers' minds. But not long ago, Domino's began hearing negative comments from its customers about its pizza; basically, they felt it was horrible. As a company that has long focused on solid marketing intelligence to make decisions, Domino's went to work on changing consumers' perceptions about its pizza.

Based on its marketing research, Domino's soon realized that it had to take a very risky step and completely recreate the pizza that it had been selling for more than 40 years. This video illustrates how research not only enabled Domino's to come up with a winning recipe, but laid the foundation for a successful promotional campaign that has made fans appreciate Domino's pizza as much as its delivery service.

After viewing the video featuring Domino's, answer the following questions:

1. What role did marketing research play in the creation and launch of Domino's new pizza?
2. Could Domino's have gone about its research process in a more effective way? Explain.
3. Why did it take so long for Domino's to realize that customers didn't like its pizza? Did the company come to this realization accidentally?

Company Cases   4 Meredith / 6 Darden Restaurants / 15 Buick

See Appendix 1 for cases appropriate for this chapter. **Case 4, Meredith: Thanks to Good Marketing Information, Meredith *Knows* Women.** Using its massive database and expertise in managing information, Meredith builds and maintains strong relationships with women. **Case 6, Darden Restaurants: Balancing Standardization and Differentiation.** By listening to customers, Darden finds success by targeting different customers through distinct restaurant formats. **Case 15, Buick: Number One Imported Brand.** Through the information-gathering efforts of its Chinese design team, Buick meets customer needs throughout the world.

5 Understanding **Consumer** and **Business** Buyer Behavior

CHAPTER ROAD MAP

Objective Outline

▷ **OBJECTIVE 1 Understand the consumer market and the major factors that influence consumer buyer behavior.** Consumer Markets and Consumer Buyer Behavior (128); Model of Consumer Behavior (128–129); Characteristics Affecting Consumer Behavior (129–142)

▷ **OBJECTIVE 2 Identify and discuss the stages in the buyer decision process.** The Buyer Decision Process (142–145)

▷ **OBJECTIVE 3 Describe the adoption and diffusion process for new products.** The Buyer Decision Process for New Products (145–147)

▷ **OBJECTIVE 4 Define the business market and identify the major factors that influence business buyer behavior.** Business Markets and Business Buyer Behavior (147); Business Markets (148–149); Business Buyer Behavior (149–154)

▷ **OBJECTIVE 5 List and define the steps in the business buying decision process.** The Business Buying Process (154–156); E-Procurement: Buying on the Internet (156–157)

Previewing the Concepts

You've studied how marketers obtain, analyze, and use information to develop customer insights and assess marketing programs. In this chapter, we continue with a closer look at the most important element of the marketplace—customers. The aim of marketing is to affect how customers think and act. To affect the *whats*, *whens*, and *hows* of buyer behavior, marketers must first understand the *whys*. We first look at *final consumer* buying influences and processes and then at the buyer behavior of *business customers*. You'll see that understanding buyer behavior is an essential but very difficult task.

To get a better sense of the importance of understanding consumer behavior, we begin by first looking at Apple. What makes Apple users so fanatically loyal? Just what is it that makes them buy a Mac computer, an iPod, an iPhone, an iPad, or all of these? Partly, it's the way the equipment works. But at the core, customers buy from Apple because the brand itself is a part of their own self-expression and lifestyle. It's a part of what the loyal Apple customer is.

First Stop

Apple: The Keeper of All Things Cool

▲ **Apple plays to deep-seated customer buying needs in everything it makes and sells. The company has gained a cult-like following because it somehow manages to breathe new life into every category it touches.**

© Michael Nagle/Getty Images

Few brands engender such intense loyalty as that found in the hearts of core Apple buyers. Whether they own a Mac computer, an iPhone, or an iPad, Apple devotees are granite-like in their devotion to the brand. At one end are the quietly satisfied Mac users, folks who own a Mac and use it for e-mail, browsing, and social networking. At the other extreme, however, are the Mac zealots—the so-called MacHeads or Macolytes. The *Urban Dictionary* defines a Macolyte as "one who is fanatically devoted to Apple products," as in "He's a Macolyte; don't even *think* of mentioning Microsoft within earshot."

There's at least a little MacHead in every Apple customer. Mac enthusiasts see late Apple founder Steve Jobs as the Walt Disney of technology. Say the word "Apple" in front of Mac fans and they'll go into rhapsodies about the superiority of the brand. Some MacHeads even tattoo the Apple logo on their bodies. Buy an Apple product and you join a whole community of fervent fellow believers.

What is it that makes Apple buyers so loyal? Why do they buy a Mac instead of an HP or a Dell, or an iPhone instead of a Nokia, LG, or Motorola? Ask the true believers, and they'll tell you simply that Apple's products work better and are simpler to use. But Apple buyer behavior has much deeper roots. Apple puts top priority on understanding its customers and what makes them tick deep down. It knows that, to Apple buyers, a Mac computer or an iPhone is much more than just a piece of electronics equipment. It's a part of buyers' own self-expression and lifestyle—a part of what they are. When you own a Mac, you are anything but mainstream. You're an independent thinker, an innovator, out ahead of the crowd.

Apple plays to these deep-seated customer buying needs and motives in everything it makes and sells. Apple has shown "a marketing and creative genius with a rare ability to get inside the imaginations of consumers and understand what will captivate them," says one analyst. Apple has been "obsessed with the Apple user's experience." Apple's obsession with understanding customers and deepening their Apple experience shows in everything the company does. Many tech companies make products that just occupy space and do work. By contrast, Apple creates "life-feels-good" experiences.

The Apple experience extends well beyond its products. Just peek inside an Apple store. The store design is clean, simple, and just oozing with style—much like an Apple iPad or a featherweight MacBook Air. The bustling stores feel more like community centers than retail outlets. Apple stores encourage a lot of purchasing, to be sure. But they also encourage lingering, with dozens of fully functioning computers, iPods, iPads, and iPhones sitting out for visitors to try—for hours on end. You don't just visit an Apple store, you experience it.

> **Thanks to Apple's deep understanding of consumer behavior, the Apple brand engenders intense loyalty in the hearts of core Apple customers. This consumer love affair with Apple has produced stunning sales and profit results.**

According to one industry expert, "some of the most amazing companies of the coming few years will be businesses that understand how to wrap technology beautifully around human needs so that it matters to people." That's an apt description of Apple and its core segment of enthusiastic disciples. The most recent American Consumer Satisfaction Index gave Apple a market-leading customer-satisfaction score of 86—a full 8 points above the rest of the personal computer industry—with an eye-popping repurchase intent of 81 percent. Those numbers hold for users of other Apple products as well.

This consumer love affair with Apple has produced stunning sales and profit results. In the past five years, despite the worst economic conditions since the Great Depression, Apple sales have nearly tripled to a record $65.2 billion (surpassing rival Microsoft), including a whopping 80 percent revenue increase in just one year. Profits have skyrocketed sevenfold to $14 billion. Apple's iPhone captures more than 25 percent of the U.S. cell phone market; its iPod holds more than 70 percent of the MP3 market. Last year alone, sales of iPads surpassed even Apple's lofty goals and could double this year to account for as much as 15 percent of the company's total revenues. Finally, Apple dominates the high-end personal computing sector, accounting for an amazing 90 percent of dollars spent on computers costing more than $1,000.

There are still plenty of folks who are not Apple customers and don't really want to be. But to the faithful, Apple is what makes them happy. From a consumer behavior perspective, the brand's ability to sculpt an emotional customer experience has made it a benchmark for other companies. Dell wants to be the Apple of business computing; Zipcar the Apple of rental car sharing. Apple has even become a pop culture reference point for excellence. Comedian Bill Maher once asserted that the government would have been better run if Steve Jobs had been elected head of state.

The recent passing of founder and CEO Steve Jobs has cast a small shadow of doubt on the future of the company. Perhaps no large corporation in history has been so strongly tied to the creative genius of its leader. But for now, Apple continues to soar. "To say Apple is hot just doesn't do the company justice," concludes one Apple watcher. "Apple is smoking, searing, blisteringly hot, not to mention hip, with a side order of funky. Gadget geeks around the world have crowned Apple the keeper of all things cool." Just ask your Macolyte friends. In fact, don't bother—they've probably already brought it up.[1]

MyMarketingLab

Visit www.mymktlab.com to find activities that help you learn and review in order to succeed in this chapter.

T he Apple example shows that factors at many levels affect consumer buying behavior. Buying behavior is never simple, yet understanding it is an essential task of marketing management. First we explore the dynamics of the consumer market and the consumer buyer behavior. We then examine business markets and the business buyer process.

Consumer Markets and Consumer Buyer Behavior

Author Comment ▶
In some ways, consumer and business markets are similar in their buyer behavior. But in many other ways, they differ a lot. We start by digging into consumer buyer behavior. Later in the chapter, we'll tackle business buyer behavior.

Consumer buyer behavior refers to the buying behavior of final consumers—individuals and households that buy goods and services for personal consumption. All of these final consumers combine to make up the **consumer market**. The American consumer market consists of more than 310 million people who consume almost $10 trillion worth of goods and services each year, making it one of the most attractive consumer markets in the world.[2]

Consumers around the world vary tremendously in age, income, education level, and tastes. The ways these diverse consumers relate with each other and with other elements of the world around them impact their choices among various products, services, and companies. Here we examine the fascinating array of factors that affect consumer behavior.

Model of Consumer Behavior

Author Comment ▶
Despite the simple-looking model in Figure 5.1, understanding the *whys* of buying behavior is very difficult. Says one expert, "the mind is a whirling, swirling, jumbled mass of neurons bouncing around. . . ."

Consumers make many buying decisions every day, and the buying decision is the focal point of the marketer's effort. Most large companies research consumer buying decisions in great detail to answer questions about what consumers buy, where they buy, how and how much they buy, when they buy, and why they buy. Marketers can study actual consumer purchases to find out what they buy, where, and how much. But learning about the *whys* of consumer buying behavior is not so easy—the answers are often locked deep within the consumer's mind. Often, consumers themselves don't know exactly what influences their purchases.

The central question for marketers is this: How do consumers respond to various marketing efforts the company might use? The starting point is the stimulus-response model of buyer behavior shown in ▶ **Figure 5.1**. This figure shows that marketing and other stimuli enter the consumer's *black box* and produce certain responses. Marketers must figure out what is in the buyer's black box.

Marketing stimuli consist of the four Ps: product, price, place, and promotion. Other stimuli include major forces and events in the buyer's environment: economic, technological, social, and cultural. All these inputs enter the buyer's black box, where they are turned into a set of buyer responses—the buyer's brand and company relationship behavior and what he or she buys, when, where, and how much.

Marketers want to understand how the stimuli are changed into responses inside the consumer's black box, which has two parts. First, the buyer's characteristics influence how he or she perceives and reacts to the stimuli. Second, the buyer's decision process itself affects his or her behavior. We look first at buyer characteristics as they affect buyer behavior and then discuss the buyer decision process.

Characteristics Affecting Consumer Behavior

Consumer purchases are influenced strongly by cultural, social, personal, and psychological characteristics, as shown in ▶ **Figure 5.2**. For the most part, marketers cannot control such factors, but they must take them into account.

Cultural Factors

Cultural factors exert a broad and deep influence on consumer behavior. Marketers need to understand the role played by the buyer's *culture, subculture,* and *social class*.

Culture. **Culture** is the most basic cause of a person's wants and behavior. Human behavior is largely learned. Growing up in a society, a child learns basic values, perceptions, wants, and behaviors from his or her family and other important institutions. A child in the United States normally learns or is exposed to the following values: achievement and success, individualism, freedom, hard work, activity and involvement, efficiency and practicality, material comfort, youthfulness, and fitness and health. Every group or society has a culture, and cultural influences on buying behavior may vary greatly from both county to county and country to country.

Marketers are always trying to spot *cultural shifts* so as to discover new products that might be wanted. For example, the cultural shift toward greater concern about health and fitness has created a huge industry for health-and-fitness services, exercise equipment and clothing, organic foods, and a variety of diets.

Subculture. Each culture contains smaller **subcultures**, or groups of people with shared value systems based on common life experiences and situations. Subcultures include nationalities, religions, racial groups, and geographic regions. Many subcultures make up important market segments, and marketers often design products and marketing programs

---

Consumer buyer behavior
The buying behavior of final consumers—individuals and households that buy goods and services for personal consumption.

Consumer market
All the individuals and households that buy or acquire goods and services for personal consumption.

Author Comment ▶
Many levels of factors affect our buying behavior—from broad cultural and social influences to motivations, beliefs, and attitudes lying deep within us. For example, why *did* you buy *that* specific cell phone you're carrying?

Culture
The set of basic values, perceptions, wants, and behaviors learned by a member of society from family and other important institutions.

We can measure the whats, wheres, and whens of consumerbuying behavior. But it's very difficult to "see" inside the consumer's head and figure out the *whys* of buying behavior (that's why it's called the black box). Marketers spend a lot of time and dollars trying to figure out what makes customers tick.

The environment		Buyer's black box	Buyer responses
Marketing stimuli	**Other**	Buyer's characteristics	Buying attitudes and preferences
Product	Economic	Buyer's decision process	Purchase behavior: what the buyer buys, when, where, and how much
Price	Technological		Brand and company relationship behavior
Place	Social		
Promotion	Cultural		

 Figure 5.1 Model of Buyer Behavior

▶ **Figure 5.2** Factors Influencing Consumer Behavior

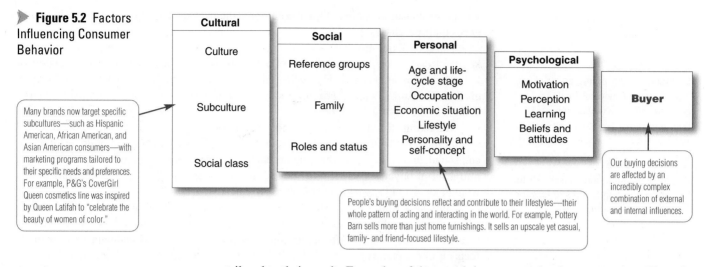

Many brands now target specific subcultures—such as Hispanic American, African American, and Asian American consumers—with marketing programs tailored to their specific needs and preferences. For example, P&G's CoverGirl Queen cosmetics line was inspired by Queen Latifah to "celebrate the beauty of women of color."

People's buying decisions reflect and contribute to their lifestyles—their whole pattern of acting and interacting in the world. For example, Pottery Barn sells more than just home furnishings. It sells an upscale yet casual, family- and friend-focused lifestyle.

Our buying decisions are affected by an incredibly complex combination of external and internal influences.

Subculture
A group of people with shared value systems based on common life experiences and situations.

tailored to their needs. Examples of three such important subculture groups are Hispanic American, African American, and Asian American consumers.

The nation's more than 50 million Hispanic consumers will account for almost 10 percent of the nation's total buying power by 2013.[3] Although Hispanic consumers share many characteristics and behaviors with the mainstream buying public, there are also distinct differences. They tend to be deeply family oriented and make shopping a family affair—children have a big say in what brands they buy. Perhaps more important, Hispanic consumers, particularly first-generation immigrants, are very brand loyal, and they favor brands and sellers who show special interest in them.

Companies such as General Mills, P&G, Verizon, McDonald's, Toyota, Walmart, and many others have developed special targeting efforts for this fast-growing consumer group. For example, General Mills targets Hispanics with its extensive Qué Rica Vida (What a Rich Life) marketing initiative, which communicates with Hispanic mothers about the benefits of General Mills products. The Qué Rica Vida Web site, magazine, and mobile apps offer Spanish-language recipes and a wealth of parenting, family health, lifestyle, and education information. General Mills also targets Hispanics with tailored ads for specific brands. For example, Hispanic advertising for Nature Valley, a popular brand with Hispanic consumers, depicts couples "savoring nature instead of conquering it." Nature Valley sales grew 19 percent in Hispanic markets as a result of the brand's more-targeted approach.[4]

Within the Hispanic market, there exist many distinct subsegments based on nationality, age, income, and other factors. A company's product or message may be more relevant to one nationality over another, such as Mexicans, Costa Ricans, Argentineans, or Cubans. Companies must also vary their pitches across different Hispanic economic segments. For example, Toyota's Tundra full-size pickup truck is a big seller among Mexican immigrants in the Southwest who are characterized as *Jefes*, local heroes considered pillars of strength in their communities. Toyota pitches the Tundra to this segment as a truck that's as tough as the guy who gets behind the wheel. By contrast, Hispanic ads for Toyota's Lexus brand targeting the luxury market in Miami couldn't be more different. That campaign reaches out to affluent Hispanic Americans who appreciate refinement, art, and culture by featuring brightly designed ads placed in local Hispanic lifestyle magazines.[5]

The U.S. African American population is growing in affluence and sophistication. By 2013, the nation's more than 40 million African American consumers will account for more than 13 percent of total U.S. buying power. Although more price conscious than other segments, blacks are also strongly motivated by quality and selection. Brands are important.[6]

In recent years, many companies have developed special products, appeals, and marketing programs for African American consumers. For example, Procter & Gamble has long been the leader in African American advertising, spending nearly twice as much as the second-place spender. P&G also tailors products to the specific needs of black consumers. For example, its CoverGirl Queen Latifah line is specially formulated "to celebrate the beauty of women of color."

In addition to traditional product marketing efforts, P&G also supports a broader. "My Black Is Beautiful" movement.[7]

Procter & Gamble's roots run deep in targeting the African American segment. For example, its "My Black Is Beautiful" movement aims to make black women feel beautiful while also forging a closer relationship between P&G brands and African American consumers.

The Procter & Gamble Company

Created by a group of African American women at P&G, the movement aims "to ignite and support a sustained national conversation by, for, and about black women" and how they are reflected in popular culture. P&G discovered that black women spend three times more than the general market on beauty products yet feel they're portrayed worse than other women in media and advertising. Supported by brands such as Crest, Pantene Pro-V Relaxed & Natural, the CoverGirl Queen Collection, and Olay Definity, the My Black Is Beautiful movement's goal is to empower African American women to embrace their beauty, health, and wellness and, of course, to forge a closer relationship between P&G brands and African American consumers in the process. ▶ With P&G as the main sponsor, My Black Is Beautiful includes a rich Web site, a television talk show on BET, and other venues featuring interviews, vignettes, and style tips on African American beauty.

Asian Americans are the most affluent U.S. demographic segment. They now number more than 16 million and will account for 5.3 percent of U.S. buying power by 2013. Asian Americans are the second-fastest-growing subsegment after Hispanic Americans. And like Hispanic Americans, they are a diverse group. Chinese Americans constitute the largest group, followed by Filipinos, Asian Indians, Vietnamese, Korean Americans, and Japanese Americans. Asian American consumers may be the most tech-savvy segment; more than 90 percent go online regularly and are most comfortable with Internet technologies such as online banking.[8]

As a group, Asian consumers shop frequently and are the most brand conscious of all the ethnic groups. They can be fiercely brand loyal. As a result, many firms now target the Asian American market. For example, State Farm has developed comprehensive advertising, marketing, and public relations campaigns that have helped it to gain significant brand equity and market share among Asian American consumers.[9]

State Farm even recast its familiar "Like a good neighbor, State Farm is there," tagline so that it would retain the spirit of the original line but better resonate with each Asian American market. For example, the Chinese version translates back into English as "With a good neighbor, you are reassured every day." But State Farm's commitment to the Asian American community goes well beyond just slogans. "Being a good neighbor today means investing in tomorrow's leaders," says State Farm's vice president of multicultural business development. Over the years, State Farm has invested in "providing leadership opportunities for [Asian American] youth, teen auto-safety programs, youth and college education-excellence opportunities, financial education for all age groups, and community development."

Beyond targeting segments such as Hispanics, African Americans, and Asian Americans with specially tailored efforts, many marketers now embrace *multicultural marketing*—the practice of including ethnic themes and cross-cultural perspectives within their mainstream marketing. They are finding that insights gleaned from ethnic consumers can influence their broader markets.

For example, today's youth-oriented lifestyle is influenced heavily by Hispanic and African American entertainers. So it follows that consumers expect to see many different cultures and ethnicities represented in the advertising and products they consume. For instance, McDonald's takes cues from African Americans, Hispanics, and Asians to develop menus and advertising in hopes of encouraging mainstream consumers to buy smoothies, mocha drinks, and snack wraps as avidly as they consume hip-hop and rock 'n roll. "The ethnic consumer tends to set trends," says McDonald's chief marketing officer. "So they help set the tone for how we enter the marketplace." Thus, McDonald's might take an ad primarily geared toward African Americans and run it in general-market media. "The reality is that the new mainstream is multicultural," concludes one multicultural marketing expert.[10]

Social class

Relatively permanent and ordered divisions in a society whose members share similar values, interests, and behaviors.

Social Class. Almost every society has some form of social class structure. **Social classes** are society's relatively permanent and ordered divisions whose members share similar values, interests, and behaviors. Social scientists have identified the seven American social classes shown in ▶ **Figure 5.3**.

Social class is not determined by a single factor, such as income, but is measured as a combination of occupation, income, education, wealth, and other variables. In some social systems, members of different classes are reared for certain roles and cannot change their social positions. In the United States, however, the lines between social classes are not fixed and rigid; people can move to a higher social class or drop into a lower one.

Marketers are interested in social class because people within a given social class tend to exhibit similar buying behavior. Social classes show distinct product and brand preferences in areas such as clothing, home furnishings, leisure activity, and automobiles.

Social Factors

A consumer's behavior also is influenced by social factors, such as the consumer's *small groups, family,* and *social roles* and *status.*

Group

Two or more people who interact to accomplish individual or mutual goals.

Groups and Social Networks. Many small **groups** influence a person's behavior. Groups that have a direct influence and to which a person belongs are called membership groups. In contrast, reference groups serve as direct (face-to-face) or indirect points of comparison or reference in forming a person's attitudes or behavior. People often are influenced by reference groups to which they do not belong. For example, an aspirational group is one to

▶ **Figure 5.3** The Major American Social Classes

America's social classes show distinct brand preferences. Social class is not determined by a single factor but by a combination of all of these factors.

(Arrow axis labels, bottom to top: Income, Occupation, Education, Wealth)

Upper Class

Upper Uppers (1 percent): The social elite who live on inherited wealth. They give large sums to charity, own more than one home, and send their children to the finest schools.

Lower Uppers (2 percent): Americans who have earned high income or wealth through exceptional ability. They are active in social and civic affairs and buy expensive homes, educations, and cars.

Middle Class

Upper Middles (12 percent): Professionals, independent businesspersons, and corporate managers who possess neither family status nor unusual wealth. They believe in education, are joiners and highly civic minded, and want the "better things in life."

Middle Class (32 percent): Average-pay white- and blue-collar workers who live on "the better side of town." They buy popular products to keep up with trends. Better living means owning a nice home in a nice neighborhood with good schools.

Working Class

Working Class (38 percent): Those who lead a "working-class lifestyle," whatever their income, school background, or job. They depend heavily on relatives for economic and emotional support, advice on purchases, and assistance in times of trouble.

Lower Class

Upper Lowers (9 percent): The working poor. Although their living standard is just above poverty, they strive toward a higher class. However, they often lack education and are poorly paid for unskilled work.

Lower Lowers (7 percent): Visibly poor, often poorly educated unskilled laborers. They are often out of work, and some depend on public assistance. They tend to live a day-to-day existence.

which the individual wishes to belong, as when a young basketball player hopes to someday emulate basketball star LeBron James and play in the NBA.

Marketers try to identify the reference groups of their target markets. Reference groups expose a person to new behaviors and lifestyles, influence the person's attitudes and self-concept, and create pressures to conform that may affect the person's product and brand choices. The importance of group influence varies across products and brands. It tends to be strongest when the product is visible to others whom the buyer respects.

Word-of-mouth influence

The impact of the personal words and recommendations of trusted friends, associates, and other consumers on buying behavior.

Word-of-mouth influence can have a powerful impact on consumer buying behavior. The personal words and recommendations of trusted friends, associates, and other consumers tend to be more credible than those coming from commercial sources, such as advertisements or salespeople. Most word-of-mouth influence happens naturally: Consumers start chatting about a brand they use or feel strongly about one way or the other. Often, however, rather than leaving it to chance, marketers can help to create positive conversations about their brands.

Opinion leader

A person within a reference group who, because of special skills, knowledge, personality, or other characteristics, exerts social influence on others.

Marketers of brands subjected to strong group influence must figure out how to reach **opinion leaders**—people within a reference group who, because of special skills, knowledge, personality, or other characteristics, exert social influence on others. Some experts call this group *the influentials* or *leading adopters*. When these influentials talk, consumers listen. Marketers try to identify opinion leaders for their products and direct marketing efforts toward them.

Buzz marketing involves enlisting or even creating opinion leaders to serve as "brand ambassadors" who spread the word about a company's products. Many companies now create brand ambassador programs in an attempt to turn influential but everyday customers into brand evangelists. One study found that such programs can increase the effectiveness of word-of-mouth marketing efforts by as much as 50 percent.[11] ▶ For example, JetBlue's CrewBlue program employs real customers to create buzz on college campuses.[12]

Brand ambassadors: JetBlue's CrewBlue program employs real customers to create buzz on college campuses.

Mr. Youth, LLC | the generation of ideas

Over the past few years, the JetBlue CrewBlue program has recruited a small army of college student ambassadors—all loyal JetBlue lovers. CrewBlue representatives advise JetBlue on its campus marketing efforts, talk up the brand to other students, and help organize campus events, such as JetBlue's BlueDay. Held each fall on 21 campuses, the highly successful event urges students to wear outlandish blue costumes (and, on occasion, blue skin and hair). Students with the best costumes are each given a pair of free airline tickets.

The CrewBlue ambassadors are crucial to the success of JetBlue's campus marketing efforts: "Students know what kinds of activities are important to other kids, what we should say to them in our marketing, and how we should say it," says a JetBlue marketing executive. You might think that such brand ambassadors would be perceived as hucksters—or, worse, as annoying evangelists best avoided. Not so, says the executive. "Our brand ambassadors are seen by their college friends as entrepreneurial, creative people." What they aren't, he adds, are the supercool people on campus who are typically thought of as influentials. The best ambassadors, says the executive, are "friendly, everyday brand loyalists who love to talk to people."

Online social networks

Online social communities—blogs, social networking Web sites, and other online communities—where people socialize or exchange information and opinions.

Over the past few years, a new type of social interaction has exploded onto the scene—online social networking. **Online social networks** are online communities where people socialize or exchange information and opinions. Social networking media range from blogs (Gizmodo, Zenhabits) and message boards (Craigslist) to social networking Web sites (Facebook and Twitter) and virtual worlds (Second Life). This new form of consumer-to-consumer and business-to-consumer dialog has big implications for marketers.

Marketers are working to harness the power of these new social networks and other "word-of-Web" opportunities to promote their products and build closer customer relationships. Instead of throwing more one-way commercial messages at consumers, they hope to use the Internet and social networks to *interact* with consumers and become a part of their conversations and lives (see Marketing at Work 5.1).

Word-of-Web: Harnessing the Power of Online Social Influence

People love talking with others about things that make them happy—including their favorite products and brands. Say you really like JetBlue Airways—they fly with flair and get you there at an affordable price. Or you just plain love your new Sony GPS camera—it's too cool to keep to yourself. In the old days, you'd have chatted up these brands with a few friends and family members. But these days, thanks to online technology, anyone can share brand experiences with thousands, even millions, of other consumers via the Web.

In response, marketers are now feverishly working to harness today's newfound technologies and get people interacting with their brands online. Whether it's creating online brand ambassadors, tapping into existing online influentials and social networks, or developing conversation-provoking events and videos, the Internet is awash with marketer attempts to create brand conversations and involvement online.

A company can start by creating its own online brand evangelists. That's what Ford did when it launched its Fiesta subcompact model, targeted heavily toward Millennials.

> Generating buzz for the Fiesta among the incredibly Web-savvy Millennials generation—which includes 70 million drivers—was a must. One study found that 77 percent of Millennials use a social networking site like Facebook or Twitter daily and 28 percent of them have a personal blog. So Ford created the Fiesta Movement campaign, in which it handed Fiestas to 100 influential 20-something Millennials selected from 4,000 applicants. The Fiesta ambassadors lived with the cars for six months, completed monthly "missions" with different themes, and shared their experiences via blogs, tweets, Facebook updates, and YouTube and Flickr posts. Ford didn't tell the ambassadors what to say, nor did it edit their content. "We told them to be completely honest," says Ford's social media manager. The successful Fiesta Movement ambassadors campaign generated 58 percent pre-launch awareness among Fiesta's under-30 target consumers and a 14 percent reservation-to-purchase rate, compared to the company's usual 1 to 2 percent rate.

Beyond creating their own brand ambassadors, companies looking to harness the Web's social power can work with the army of self-made influencers already plying today's Internet—independent bloggers. The blogosphere has exploded onto the scene in recent years. Two-thirds of all U.S. Internet users now read blogs regularly and nearly one-third write one. Believe it or not, there are almost as many people making a living as bloggers as there are lawyers. No matter what the interest area, there are probably hundreds of bloggers covering it. Moreover, research shows that 90 percent of bloggers post about their favorite and least favorite brands.

As a result, most companies try to form relationships with influential bloggers and online personalities. For example, to help build

awareness for its six-year, $3-billion Healthymagination health care innovation initiative, GE tapped well-known social network influentials, such as Justine Ezarik. Known online as iJustine, she has built a passionate, committed, and trusting audience—more than 1 million subscribers to her YouTube channels and 1.2 million Twitter followers. At GE's request, iJustine posted a video on YouTube last year asking viewers how she can live a healthier life. More than 11,000 responded. She produced five videos about those ideas that were viewed more than 2.1 million times. GE's Healthymagination effort received a shout-out in each video. "Justine has tremendous credibility in the space," says GE global advertising chief Judy Hu. "I could not believe the numbers. The views kept going up. It has a life of its own."

The key is to find bloggers who have strong networks of relevant readers, a credible voice, and a good fit with the brand. For example, companies ranging from P&G and Johnson & Johnson to Walmart work closely with influential "mommy bloggers." And you'll no doubt cross paths with the likes of climbers blogging for North Face, bikers blogging for Harley-Davidson, and shoppers blogging for Whole Foods Market or Trader Joe's.

▲ Harnessing online influence: Mountain Dew runs "DEWmocracy" campaigns that invite avid Mountain Dew customers to participate at all levels in launching a new Mountain Dew flavor.
Pepsi-Cola Company

Perhaps the best way to generate brand conversations and social involvement on the Web is simply to do something conversation worthy—to actually involve people with the brand online. Pepsi's Mountain Dew brand runs "DEWmocracy" campaigns that invite avid Mountain Dew customers to participate at all levels in launching a new Mountain Dew flavor, from choosing and naming the flavor to designing the can to submitting and selecting TV commercials and even picking an ad agency and media. Presented through a dedicated Web site, as well as Facebook, Twitter, Flickr, and other public network pages, DEWmocracy has been a perfect forum for getting youthful, socially savvy Dew drinkers talking with each other and the company about the brand. For example, Mountain Dew's Facebook fan page grew fivefold at the launch of the latest DEWmocracy campaign.

Ironically, one of the simplest means of capturing social influence through the Web is one of the oldest—produce a good ad that gets people talking. But in this day and age, both the ads and the media have changed. Almost every brand, large and small, is now creating innovative brand-sponsored videos, posting them online, and hoping they'll go viral. The videos range from traditional 60-second ads to intricate 10- or 12-minute film shorts. Top innovative viral video ads from the past few years, as rated by social media guide Mashable.com, have included everything from a very creative three-minute ad for a small Charlotte, North Carolina, ad agency to a heart-tugging British public service announcement urging people to "Embrace Life" and always wear seatbelts. Such videos can create lots of attention and talk. For example, the Embrace Life video drew more than 13 million YouTube views. One five-minute action video for Inspired Bicycles garnered 15 million rapt views, while a 12-minute love story for Schweppes drew nearly four million views and critical acclaim.

So, whether through online ambassadors, bloggers, social networks, or talked-about videos and events, companies are finding innovative ways to tap social influence online. Called word-of-Web, it's growing fast as *the* place to be—for both consumers and marketers. Last year, the time consumers spent on social networking sites nearly tripled; marketer spending at those sites nearly kept pace. "Social [media] is one of the key trends driving business," says a social marketing executive. "It's more than pure marketing. It's about fast connections with customers and building an ongoing relationship."

Sources: Elisabeth A. Sullivan, "Blog Savvy," *Marketing News*, November 15, 2009, p. 8; Keith Barry, "Ford Bets the Fiesta on Social Networking," *Wired*, April 17, 2009, www.wired.com/autopia/2009/04/how-the-fiesta; Ellen McGirt, "Mr. Social: Ashton Kutcher Plans to Be the Next New-Media Mogul," *Fast Company*, December 1, 2009, accessed at www.fastcompany.com; Josh Warner, "The Ten Most Viral Videos of 2009," December 7, 2009, accessed at www.mashable.com; Warner "The Ten Most Viral Videos of 2010," December 9, 2010, accessed at www.mashable.com; Mark Borden, "The New Influentials," *Fast Company*, November 2010, p. 124; and information from www.dewmocracy.com, accessed August 2011.

For example, Red Bull has an astounding 8.4 million friends on Facebook; Twitter and Facebook are the primary ways it communicates with college students. JetBlue listens in on customers on Twitter and often responds; one consumer recently tweeted "I'm getting on a JetBlue flight" and JetBlue tweeted back "You should try the smoked almonds [on board]." Southwest Airlines employees share stories with each other and customers on the company's "Nuts about Southwest" blog. P&G's Old Spice brand put entertaining spokesman Isaiah Mustafa on the Web recently and invited fans to use Twitter, Facebook, and other social media to pose questions that he would answer. The questions poured in and Mustafa responded quickly in more than 180 Web videos, creating a real-time connection with the brand's community.[13]

Most brands have built a comprehensive social media presence. Eco-conscious outdoor shoe and gear maker Timberland has created an online community (http://community.timberland.com) that connects like-minded "Earthkeepers" with each other and the brand through a network that includes several Web sites, a Facebook page, a YouTube channel, a Bootmakers Blog, an e-mail newsletter, and several Twitter feeds.

Even small brands can leverage the power of the Internet and online social networks. ▶ For example, Blendtec has developed a kind of cult following for its flood of "Will It Blend?" online videos, in which the seemingly indestructible Blendtec Total Blender grinds everything from a hockey puck and a golf club to an iPhone and iPad into dust. The low-cost, simple idea led to a fivefold increase in Blendtec's sales.

But marketers must be careful when tapping into online social networks. Results are difficult to measure and control. Ultimately, the users control the content, so social network marketing attempts can easily backfire. For example, when Skittles designed its Web

▲ **Using online social networks: Blendtec has developed a kind of cult following for its flood of "Will It Blend?" videos on YouTube, resulting in a fivefold increase in Blendtec's sales.**

Blendtec

site to include a live Twitter feed for Skittles-related tweets, pranksters laced Skittles tweets with profanities so they would end up on the candy's Web site. Skittles was forced to abandon the campaign. We will dig deeper into online social networks as a marketing tool in Chapter 14.

Family. Family members can strongly influence buyer behavior. The family is the most important consumer buying organization in society, and it has been researched extensively. Marketers are interested in the roles and influence of the husband, wife, and children on the purchase of different products and services.

Husband-wife involvement varies widely by product category and by stage in the buying process. Buying roles change with evolving consumer lifestyles. For example, in the United States, the wife traditionally has been considered the main purchasing agent for the family in the areas of food, household products, and clothing. But with more women working outside the home and the willingness of husbands to do more of the family's purchasing, all this is changing. A recent survey of men ages 18 to 74 found that more than half now identify themselves as primary grocery shoppers in their households. At the same time, today women account for 50 percent of all technology purchases and influence two-thirds of all new car purchases.[14] Such shifting roles signal a new marketing reality. Marketers in industries that have traditionally sold their products to only women or only men—from groceries and personal care products to cars and consumer electronics—are now courting the opposite sex.

Children may also have a strong influence on family buying decisions. The nation's 36 million children ages 9 to 12 wield an estimated $43 billion in disposable income. They also influence an additional $150 billion that their families spend on them in areas such as food, clothing, entertainment, and personal care items. One study found that kids significantly influence family decisions about everything from what cars they buy to where they eat out and take vacations.[15]

For example, to attract families, casual restaurants reach out to children with everything from sophisticated children's menus and special deals to a wealth of kid-focused activities. At Applebee's, children eat free on Mondays with the purchase of an adult entrée. Carrabba's Italian Grill gives children a ball of dough, pepperoni slices, and cheese so they can make their own pizzas at the table, which are then cooked in the kitchen. And at Roy's Restaurants, as soon as children are seated, the Roy's server learns their names (and addresses them by name throughout the meal). "We want them to get excited and happy immediately," says a Roy's executive. Other kids' perks at Roy's include portable DVD players with movies and headphones on request and sundaes with kids' names written in chocolate. "They love seeing their name in chocolate," says a Roy's executive. Roy's big-hearted commitment to children's happiness is a no-brainer. Happy children equal happy parents.[16]

Roles and Status. A person belongs to many groups—family, clubs, organizations, online communities. The person's position in each group can be defined in terms of both role and status. A role consists of the activities people are expected to perform according to the people around them. Each role carries a status reflecting the general esteem given to it by society.

People usually choose products appropriate to their roles and status. Consider the various roles a working mother plays. In her company, she may play the role of a brand manager; in her family, she plays the role of wife and mother; at her favorite sporting events, she plays the role of avid fan. As a brand manager, she will buy the kind of clothing that reflects her role and status in her company.

Personal Factors

A buyer's decisions also are influenced by personal characteristics such as the buyer's *age and life-cycle stage, occupation, economic situation, lifestyle,* and *personality and self-concept.*

Age and Life-Cycle Stage. People change the goods and services they buy over their lifetimes. Tastes in food, clothes, furniture, and recreation are often age related. Buying is also shaped by the stage of the family life cycle—the stages through which families might pass as they mature over time. Life-stage changes usually result from demographics and life-changing events—marriage, having children, purchasing a home, divorce, children going to college, changes in personal income, moving out of the house, and retirement. Marketers often define their target markets in terms of life-cycle stage and develop appropriate products and marketing plans for each stage.

For example, consumer information giant Acxiom's PersonicX life-stage segmentation system places U.S. households into one of 70 consumer segments and 21 life-stage groups, based on specific consumer behavior and demographic characteristics. ▶ PersonicX includes life-stage groups with names such as *Beginnings, Taking Hold, Cash & Careers, Jumbo Families, Transition Blues, Our Turn, Golden Years,* and *Active Elders.* For example, the *Taking Hold* group consists of young, energetic, well-funded couples and young families who are busy with their careers, social lives, and interests, especially fitness and active recreation. *Transition Blues* are blue-collar, less-educated, mid-income consumers who are transitioning to stable lives and talking about marriage and children.

"Consumers experience many life-stage changes during their lifetimes," says Acxiom. "As their life stages change, so do their behaviors and purchasing preferences." Armed with data about the timing and makeup of life-stage changes, marketers can create targeted, personalized campaigns.[17]

In line with recent tougher economic times, Acxiom has also developed a set of economic life-stage segments, including groups such as *Squeaking By, Eye on Essentials, Tight with a Purpose, It's My Life, Full Speed Ahead,* and *Potential Rebounders.* The *Potential Rebounders* are those more likely to loosen up on spending sooner. This group appears more likely than other segments to use online research before purchasing electronics, appliances, home decor, and jewelry. Thus, home improvement retailers appealing to this segment should have a strong online presence, providing pricing, features and benefits, and product availability.

Occupation. A person's occupation affects the goods and services bought. Blue-collar workers tend to buy more rugged work clothes, whereas executives buy more business suits. Marketers try to identify the occupational groups that have an above-average interest in their products and services. A company can even specialize in making products needed by a given occupational group.

For example, Carhartt makes rugged, durable, no-nonsense work clothes—what it calls "original equipment for the American worker. From coats to jackets, bibs to overalls . . . if the apparel carries the name Carhartt, the performance will be legendary." Its Web site carries real-life testimonials of hard-working Carhartt customers. One electrician, battling the cold in Canada's arctic region, reports wearing Carhartt's lined Arctic bib overalls, Arctic jacket, and other clothing for more than two years without a single "popped button, ripped pocket seam, or stuck zipper." And a railroadman in northern New York, who's spent years walking rough railroad beds, climbing around trains, and switching cars in conditions ranging from extreme heat to frigid cold, calls his trusty brown Carhartt jacket part of his "survival gear—like a bulletproof vest is to a policeman."[18]

Economic Situation. A person's economic situation will affect his or her store and product choices. Marketers watch trends in personal income, savings, and interest rates. Following the Great Recession, most companies took steps to redesign, reposition, and reprice their products. For example, to counter the lingering long-term

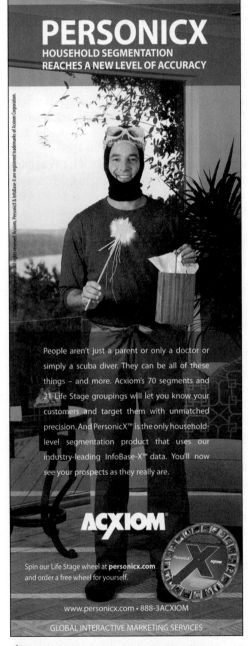

▲ Life-stage segmentation: PersonicX 21 life-stage groupings let marketers see customers as they really are and target them precisely. "People aren't just a parent or only a doctor or simply a scuba diver. They are all of these things."

Acxiom Corporation

effects of the recession, upscale discounter Target has replaced some of its "chic" with "cheap." It has even introduced periodic nationwide "Great Save" events featuring exceptional deals on everyday essentials—a kind of treasure-hunt experience to challenge warehouse retailers such as Sam's and Costco. "Our [tagline] is 'Expect more. Pay less.'" says one Target marketer. These days, "we're putting more emphasis on the pay less promise."[19]

Lifestyle

A person's pattern of living as expressed in his or her activities, interests, and opinions.

Lifestyle. People coming from the same subculture, social class, and occupation may have quite different lifestyles. **Lifestyle** is a person's pattern of living as expressed in his or her psychographics. It involves measuring consumers' major AIO dimensions—activities (work, hobbies, shopping, sports, social events), interests (food, fashion, family, recreation), and opinions (about themselves, social issues, business, products). Lifestyle captures something more than the person's social class or personality. It profiles a person's whole pattern of acting and interacting in the world.

When used carefully, the lifestyle concept can help marketers understand changing consumer values and how they affect buying behavior. Consumers don't just buy products; they buy the values and lifestyles those products represent. For example, Triumph doesn't just sell motorcycles; it sells an independent, "Go your own way" lifestyle. Similarly, Harley-Davidson tells customers to "grab life by the bars." And watchmaker Breitling doesn't sell just sturdy, accurate time pieces. It positions the brand as "instruments for professionals," targeting people who identify with an active, adventurous, rugged lifestyle. One Breitling ad features an airline pilot who spends his spare time setting freediving records beneath the sea. "Whether he's deep beneath the sea or high up in the air," says the ad, "firmly strapped to his wrist is the new Breitling Superocean, an extreme watch cut out for great accomplishments."

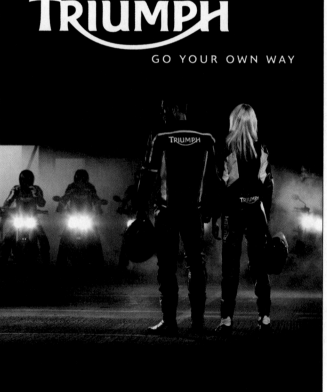

TRIUMPH

GO YOUR OWN WAY

▲ Lifestyle: Triumph doesn't just sell motorcycles; it sells an independent, "Go your own way" lifestyle.

Triumph Motorcycles Ltd.

Personality and Self-Concept. Each person's distinct personality influences his or her buying behavior. **Personality** refers to the unique psychological characteristics that distinguish a person or group. Personality is usually described in terms of traits such as self-confidence, dominance, sociability, autonomy, defensiveness, adaptability, and aggressiveness. Personality can be useful in analyzing consumer behavior for certain product or brand choices.

The idea is that brands also have personalities, and consumers are likely to choose brands with personalities that match their own. A *brand personality* is the specific mix of human traits that may be attributed to a particular brand. One researcher identified five brand personality traits: *sincerity* (down-to-earth, honest, wholesome, and cheerful); *excitement* (daring, spirited, imaginative, and up-to-date); *competence* (reliable, intelligent, and successful); *sophistication* (upper class and charming); and *ruggedness* (outdoorsy and tough). "Your personality determines what you consume, what TV shows you watch, what products you buy, and [most] other decisions you make," says one consumer behavior expert.[20]

Personality

The unique psychological characteristics that distinguish a person or group.

Most well-known brands are strongly associated with one particular trait: Jeep with "ruggedness," Apple with "excitement," the *Washington Post* with "competence," and Dove with "sincerity." Hence, these brands will attract persons who are high on the same personality traits.

Many marketers use a concept related to personality—a person's *self-concept* (also called *self-image*). The idea is that people's possessions contribute to and reflect their identities—that is, "we are what we consume." Thus, to understand consumer behavior, marketers must first understand the relationship between consumer self-concept and possessions.

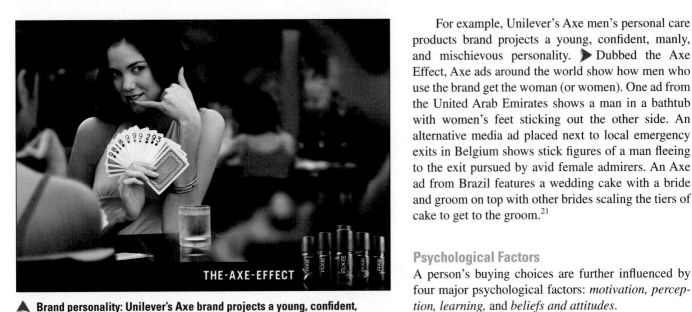

Brand personality: Unilever's Axe brand projects a young, confident, manly, and mischievous personality.

Unilever and Teo Studio Photography Pte Ltd.

Motive (drive)

A need that is sufficiently pressing to direct the person to seek satisfaction of the need.

For example, Unilever's Axe men's personal care products brand projects a young, confident, manly, and mischievous personality. ▶ Dubbed the Axe Effect, Axe ads around the world show how men who use the brand get the woman (or women). One ad from the United Arab Emirates shows a man in a bathtub with women's feet sticking out the other side. An alternative media ad placed next to local emergency exits in Belgium shows stick figures of a man fleeing to the exit pursued by avid female admirers. An Axe ad from Brazil features a wedding cake with a bride and groom on top with other brides scaling the tiers of cake to get to the groom.[21]

Psychological Factors

A person's buying choices are further influenced by four major psychological factors: *motivation, perception, learning,* and *beliefs and attitudes.*

Motivation. A person has many needs at any given time. Some are biological, arising from states of tension such as hunger, thirst, or discomfort. Others are psychological, arising from the need for recognition, esteem, or belonging. A need becomes a motive when it is aroused to a sufficient level of intensity. A **motive** (or **drive**) is a need that is sufficiently pressing to direct the person to seek satisfaction. Psychologists have developed theories of human motivation. Two of the most popular—the theories of Sigmund Freud and Abraham Maslow—carry quite different meanings for consumer analysis and marketing.

Sigmund Freud assumed that people are largely unconscious about the real psychological forces shaping their behavior. He saw the person as growing up and repressing many urges. These urges are never eliminated or under perfect control; they emerge in dreams, in slips of the tongue, in neurotic and obsessive behavior, or, ultimately, in psychoses.

Freud's theory suggests that a person's buying decisions are affected by subconscious motives that even the buyer may not fully understand. Thus, an aging baby boomer who buys a sporty BMW convertible might explain that he simply likes the feel of the wind in his thinning hair. At a deeper level, he may be trying to impress others with his success. At a still deeper level, he may be buying the car to feel young and independent again.

The term *motivation research* refers to qualitative research designed to probe consumers' hidden, subconscious motivations. Consumers often don't know or can't describe why they act as they do. Thus, motivation researchers use a variety of probing techniques to uncover underlying emotions and attitudes toward brands and buying situations.

Many companies employ teams of psychologists, anthropologists, and other social scientists to carry out motivation research. One ad agency routinely conducts one-on-one, therapy-like interviews to delve into the inner workings of consumers. Another company asks consumers to describe their favorite brands as animals or cars (say, Mercedes versus Chevrolets) to assess the prestige associated with various brands. Still others rely on hypnosis, dream therapy, or soft lights and mood music to plumb the murky depths of consumer psyches.

Such projective techniques seem pretty goofy, and some marketers dismiss such motivation research as mumbo jumbo. But many marketers use such touchy-feely approaches, now sometimes called *interpretive consumer research,* to dig deeper into consumer psyches and develop better marketing strategies.

Abraham Maslow sought to explain why people are driven by particular needs at particular times. Why does one person spend a lot of time and energy on personal safety and another on gaining the esteem of others? Maslow's answer is that human needs are

▶ **Figure 5.4** Maslow's Hierarchy of Needs

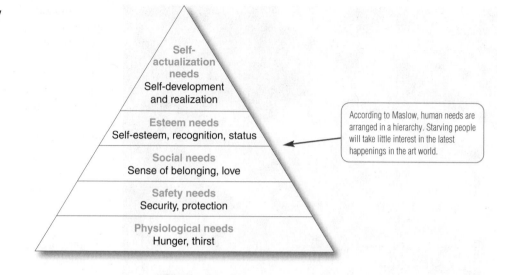

According to Maslow, human needs are arranged in a hierarchy. Starving people will take little interest in the latest happenings in the art world.

arranged in a hierarchy, as shown in ▶ **Figure 5.4**, from the most pressing at the bottom to the least pressing at the top.[22] They include *physiological* needs, *safety* needs, *social* needs, *esteem* needs, and *self-actualization* needs.

A person tries to satisfy the most important need first. When that need is satisfied, it will stop being a motivator, and the person will then try to satisfy the next most important need. For example, starving people (physiological need) will not take an interest in the latest happenings in the art world (self-actualization needs) nor in how they are seen or esteemed by others (social or esteem needs) nor even in whether they are breathing clean air (safety needs). But as each important need is satisfied, the next most important need will come into play.

Perception

The process by which people select, organize, and interpret information to form a meaningful picture of the world.

Perception. A motivated person is ready to act. How the person acts is influenced by his or her own perception of the situation. All of us learn by the flow of information through our five senses: sight, hearing, smell, touch, and taste. However, each of us receives, organizes, and interprets this sensory information in an individual way. **Perception** is the process by which people select, organize, and interpret information to form a meaningful picture of the world.

People can form different perceptions of the same stimulus because of three perceptual processes: selective attention, selective distortion, and selective retention. People are exposed to a great amount of stimuli every day. For example, people are exposed to an estimated 3,000 to 5,000 ad messages every day. It is impossible for a person to pay attention to all these stimuli. *Selective attention*—the tendency for people to screen out most of the information to which they are exposed—means that marketers must work especially hard to attract the consumer's attention.[23]

Even noticed stimuli do not always come across in the intended way. Each person fits incoming information into an existing mind-set. *Selective distortion* describes the tendency of people to interpret information in a way that will support what they already believe. People also will forget much of what they learn. They tend to retain information that supports their attitudes and beliefs. *Selective retention* means that consumers are likely to remember good points made about a brand they favor and forget good points made about competing brands. Because of selective attention, distortion, and retention, marketers must work hard to get their messages through.

Interestingly, although most marketers worry about whether their offers will be perceived at all, some consumers worry that they will be affected by marketing messages without even knowing it—through *subliminal advertising*. More than 50 years ago, a researcher announced that he had flashed the phrases "Eat popcorn" and "Drink Coca-Cola" on a screen in a New Jersey movie theater every five seconds for 1/300th of a second. He reported that although viewers did not consciously recognize these messages, they absorbed them subconsciously and bought 58 percent more popcorn and 18 percent more Coke. Suddenly advertisers and consumer-protection groups became intensely interested

The advertising industry is sometimes charged with sneaking seductive little pictures into ads.

Supposedly, these pictures can get you to buy a product without your even seeing them.

Consider the photograph above. According to some people, there's a pair of female breasts

hidden in the patterns of light refracted by the ice cubes.

Well, if you really searched you probably *could* see the breasts. For that matter, you could also see Millard Fillmore, a stuffed pork chop and a 1946 Dodge.

The point is that so-called "subliminal advertising" simply

doesn't exist. Overactive imaginations, however, most certainly do.

So if anyone claims to see breasts in that drink up there, they aren't in the ice cubes.

They're in the eye of the beholder.

ADVERTISING
ANOTHER WORD FOR FREEDOM OF CHOICE.
American Association of Advertising Agencies

▲ This classic ad from the American Association of Advertising Agencies pokes fun at subliminal advertising. "So-called 'subliminal advertising' simply doesn't exist," says the ad. "Overactive imaginations, however, most certainly do."

American Association of Advertising Agencies

Learning
Changes in an individual's behavior arising from experience.

Belief
A descriptive thought that a person holds about something.

Attitude
A person's consistently favorable or unfavorable evaluations, feelings, and tendencies toward an object or idea.

in subliminal perception. Although the researcher later admitted to making up the data, the issue has not died. Some consumers still fear that they are being manipulated by subliminal messages.

Numerous studies by psychologists and consumer researchers have found little or no link between subliminal messages and consumer behavior. Recent brain wave studies have found that in certain circumstances, our brains may register subliminal messages. ▶ However, it appears that subliminal advertising simply doesn't have the power attributed to it by its critics. Scoffs one industry insider, "Just between us, most [advertisers] have difficulty getting a 2 percent increase in sales with the help of $50 million in media and extremely *liminal* images of sex, money, power, and other [motivators] of human emotion. The very idea of [us] as puppeteers, cruelly pulling the strings of consumer marionettes, is almost too much to bear."[24]

Learning. When people act, they learn. **Learning** describes changes in an individual's behavior arising from experience. Learning theorists say that most human behavior is learned. Learning occurs through the interplay of drives, stimuli, cues, responses, and reinforcement.

A *drive* is a strong internal stimulus that calls for action. A drive becomes a motive when it is directed toward a particular *stimulus object*. For example, a person's drive for self-actualization might motivate him or her to look into buying a camera. The consumer's response to the idea of buying a camera is conditioned by the surrounding cues. *Cues* are minor stimuli that determine when, where, and how the person responds. For example, the person might spot several camera brands in a shop window, hear of a special sale price, or discuss cameras with a friend. These are all cues that might influence a consumer's *response* to his or her interest in buying the product.

Suppose the consumer buys a Nikon camera. If the experience is rewarding, the consumer will probably use the camera more and more, and his or her response will be *reinforced*. Then the next time he or she shops for a camera, or for binoculars or some similar product, the probability is greater that he or she will buy a Nikon product. The practical significance of learning theory for marketers is that they can build up demand for a product by associating it with strong drives, using motivating cues, and providing positive reinforcement.

Beliefs and Attitudes. Through doing and learning, people acquire beliefs and attitudes. These, in turn, influence their buying behavior. A **belief** is a descriptive thought that a person has about something. Beliefs may be based on real knowledge, opinion, or faith and may or may not carry an emotional charge. Marketers are interested in the beliefs that people formulate about specific products and services because these beliefs make up product and brand images that affect buying behavior. If some of the beliefs are wrong and prevent purchase, the marketer will want to launch a campaign to correct them.

People have attitudes regarding religion, politics, clothes, music, food, and almost everything else. **Attitude** describes a person's relatively consistent evaluations, feelings, and tendencies toward an object or idea. Attitudes put people into a frame of mind of liking or disliking things, of moving toward or away from them. Our camera buyer may hold attitudes such as "Buy the best," "The Japanese make the best electronics products in the world," and "Creativity and self-expression are among the most important things in life." If so, the Nikon camera would fit well into the consumer's existing attitudes.

Attitudes are difficult to change. A person's attitudes fit into a pattern; changing one attitude may require difficult adjustments in many others. Thus, a company should usually try to fit its products into existing attitudes rather than attempt to change attitudes. For example, today's beverage marketers now cater to people's new attitudes about health and well-being with drinks that do a lot more than just taste good or quench your thirst. Pepsi's SoBe brand, for example, offers "Lifewater," "elixirs" (juices), and teas—all packed with

▲ **Beliefs and attitudes:** By matching today's attitudes about life and healthful living, the SoBe brand has become a leader in the New Age beverage category.
Pepsi-Cola Company

vitamins, minerals, herbal ingredients, and antioxidants but without artificial preservatives, sweeteners, or colors. SoBe promises drinks that are good tasting (with flavors like YumBerry Pomegranate Purify, Energize Mango Melon, and Orange Cream Tsunami) but are also good for you. ▶ By matching today's attitudes about life and healthful living, the SoBe brand has become a leader in the New Age beverage category.

We can now appreciate the many forces acting on consumer behavior. The consumer's choice results from the complex interplay of cultural, social, personal, and psychological factors.

Author Comment ▶
The actual purchase decision is part of a much larger buying process—starting with need recognition through how you feel after making the purchase. Marketers want to be involved throughout the entire buyer decision process.

The Buyer Decision Process

Now that we have looked at the influences that affect buyers, we are ready to look at how consumers make buying decisions. ▶ **Figure 5.5** shows that the buyer decision process consists of five stages: *need recognition, information search, evaluation of alternatives, purchase decision,* and *postpurchase behavior.* Clearly, the buying process starts long before the actual purchase and continues long after. Marketers need to focus on the entire buying process rather than on the purchase decision only.

Figure 5.5 suggests that consumers pass through all five stages with every purchase in a considered way. But buyers may pass quickly or slowly through the buying decision process. And in more routine purchases, consumers often skip or reverse some of the stages. Much depends on the nature of the buyer, the product, and the buying situation. A woman buying her regular brand of toothpaste would recognize the need and go right to the purchase decision, skipping information search and evaluation. However, we use the model in Figure 5.5 because it shows all the considerations that arise when a consumer faces a new and complex purchase situation.

Need Recognition

The buying process starts with *need recognition*—the buyer recognizes a problem or need. The need can be triggered by *internal stimuli* when one of the person's normal needs—for example, hunger or thirst—rises to a level high enough to become a drive. A need can also be triggered by *external stimuli.* ▶ For example, an advertisement or a discussion with a friend might get you thinking about buying a new car. At this stage, the marketer should research consumers to find out what kinds of needs or problems arise, what brought them about, and how they led the consumer to this particular product.

Information Search

An interested consumer may or may not search for more information. If the consumer's drive is strong and a satisfying product is near at hand, he or she is likely to buy it then. If not, the consumer may store the need in memory or undertake an *information search*

The buying process starts long before the actual purchase and continues long after. In fact, it might result in a decision *not* to buy. Therefore, marketers must focus on the entire buying process, not just the purchase decision.

Need recognition → Information search → Evaluation of alternatives → Purchase decision → Postpurchase behavior

▶ **Figure 5.5** Buyer Decision Process

Inside our NEW **Milano Melts** cookie
is a heart of rich chocolate créme.
One bite and you too will melt.

Milano
melts®

Velvety chocolate créme
centered in a crispy, golden cookie.

PEPPERIDGE FARM

Good is in the details.™

facebook.com/pepperidgefarmmilano

▲ **Need recognition can be triggered by advertising: Time for a snack?**

Campbell Soup Company

related to the need. For example, once you've decided you need a new car, at the least, you will probably pay more attention to car ads, cars owned by friends, and car conversations. Or you may actively search the Web, talk with friends, and gather information in other ways.

Consumers can obtain information from any of several sources. These include *personal sources* (family, friends, neighbors, acquaintances), *commercial sources* (advertising, salespeople, dealer Web sites, packaging, displays), *public sources* (mass media, consumer rating organizations, Internet searches), and *experiential sources* (handling, examining, using the product). The relative influence of these information sources varies with the product and the buyer.

Generally, the consumer receives the most information about a product from commercial sources—those controlled by the marketer. The most effective sources, however, tend to be personal. Commercial sources normally *inform* the buyer, but personal sources *legitimize* or *evaluate* products for the buyer. For example, one recent study found that word of mouth is the number-one influence on consumers' purchasing decisions (76 percent). As one marketer states, "It's rare that an advertising campaign can be as effective as a neighbor leaning over the fence and saying, 'This is a wonderful product.'" Increasingly, that "fence" is a digital one. Another recent study revealed that consumers find sources of user-generated content—discussion forums, blogs, online review sites, and social networking sites—three times more influential when making a purchase decision than conventional marketing methods such as TV advertising.[25]

As more information is obtained, the consumer's awareness and knowledge of the available brands and features increase. In your car information search, you may learn about several brands that are available. The information might also help you to drop certain brands from consideration. A company must design its marketing mix to make prospects aware of and knowledgeable about its brand. It should carefully identify consumers' sources of information and the importance of each source.

Evaluation of Alternatives

We have seen how consumers use information to arrive at a set of final brand choices. How does the consumer choose among alternative brands? Marketers need to know about *alternative evaluation,* that is, how the consumer processes information to arrive at brand choices. Unfortunately, consumers do not use a simple and single evaluation process in all buying situations. Instead, several evaluation processes are at work.

The consumer arrives at attitudes toward different brands through some evaluation procedure. How consumers go about evaluating purchase alternatives depends on the individual consumer and the specific buying situation. In some cases, consumers use careful calculations and logical thinking. At other times, the same consumers do little or no evaluating. Instead they buy on impulse and rely on intuition. Sometimes consumers make buying decisions on their own; sometimes they turn to friends, online reviews, or salespeople for buying advice.

Suppose you've narrowed your car choices to three brands. And suppose that you are primarily interested in four attributes—price, style, operating economy, and warranty. By this time, you've probably formed beliefs about how each brand rates on each attribute. Clearly, if one car rated best on all the attributes, the marketer could predict that you would choose it. However, the brands will no doubt vary in appeal. You might base your buying decision mostly on one attribute, and your choice would be easy to predict. If you wanted style above everything else, you would buy the car that you think has the most style.

But most buyers consider several attributes, each with different importance. By knowing the importance that you assigned to each attribute, the marketer could predict your car choice more reliably.

Marketers should study buyers to find out how they actually evaluate brand alternatives. If marketers know what evaluative processes go on, they can take steps to influence the buyer's decision.

Purchase Decision

In the evaluation stage, the consumer ranks brands and forms purchase intentions. Generally, the consumer's *purchase decision* will be to buy the most preferred brand, but two factors can come between the purchase *intention* and the purchase *decision*. The first factor is the *attitudes of others*. If someone important to you thinks that you should buy the lowest-priced car, then the chances of you buying a more expensive car are reduced.

The second factor is *unexpected situational factors*. The consumer may form a purchase intention based on factors such as expected income, expected price, and expected product benefits. However, unexpected events may change the purchase intention. For example, the economy might take a turn for the worse, a close competitor might drop its price, or a friend might report being disappointed in your preferred car. Thus, preferences and even purchase intentions do not always result in an actual purchase choice.

Postpurchase Behavior

The marketer's job does not end when the product is bought. After purchasing the product, the consumer will either be satisfied or dissatisfied and will engage in *postpurchase behavior* of interest to the marketer. What determines whether the buyer is satisfied or dissatisfied with a purchase? The answer lies in the relationship between the *consumer's expectations* and the product's *perceived performance*. If the product falls short of expectations, the consumer is disappointed; if it meets expectations, the consumer is satisfied; if it exceeds expectations, the consumer is delighted. The larger the gap between expectations and performance, the greater the consumer's dissatisfaction. This suggests that sellers should promise only what their brands can deliver so that buyers are satisfied.

Cognitive dissonance
Buyer discomfort caused by postpurchase conflict.

Almost all major purchases, however, result in **cognitive dissonance**, or discomfort caused by postpurchase conflict. After the purchase, consumers are satisfied with the benefits of the chosen brand and are glad to avoid the drawbacks of the brands not bought. However, every purchase involves compromise. So consumers feel uneasy about acquiring the drawbacks of the chosen brand and about losing the benefits of the brands not purchased. ▶ Thus, consumers feel at least some postpurchase dissonance for every purchase.[26]

Why is it so important to satisfy the customer? Customer satisfaction is a key to building profitable relationships with consumers—to keeping and growing consumers and reaping their customer lifetime value. Satisfied customers buy a product again, talk favorably to others about the product, pay less attention to competing brands and advertising, and buy other products from the company. Many marketers go beyond merely *meeting* the expectations of customers—they aim to *delight* customers.

A dissatisfied consumer responds differently. Bad word of mouth often travels farther

▲ Postpurchase cognitive dissonance: No matter what choice they make, consumers feel at least some postpurchase dissonance for every decision.

Stéphane Bidouze/Shutterstock.com

and faster than good word of mouth. It can quickly damage consumer attitudes about a company and its products. But companies cannot simply rely on dissatisfied customers to volunteer their complaints when they are dissatisfied. Most unhappy customers never tell the company about their problems. Therefore, a company should measure customer satisfaction regularly. It should set up systems that *encourage* customers to complain. In this way, the company can learn how well it is doing and how it can improve.

By studying the overall buyer decision process, marketers may be able to find ways to help consumers move through it. For example, if consumers are not buying a new product because they do not perceive a need for it, marketing might launch advertising messages that trigger the need and show how the product solves customers' problems. If customers know about the product but are not buying because they hold unfavorable attitudes toward it, marketers must find ways to change either the product or consumer perceptions.

Author Comment ▶
Here we look at some special considerations in *new-product* buying decisions.

New product
A good, service, or idea that is perceived by some potential customers as new.

Adoption process
The mental process through which an individual passes from first hearing about an innovation to final adoption.

The Buyer Decision Process for New Products

We now look at how buyers approach the purchase of new products. A **new product** is a good, service, or idea that is perceived by some potential customers as new. It may have been around for a while, but our interest is in how consumers learn about products for the first time and make decisions on whether to adopt them. We define the **adoption process** as the mental process through which an individual passes from first learning about an innovation to final adoption. *Adoption* is the decision by an individual to become a regular user of the product.[27]

Stages in the Adoption Process

Consumers go through five stages in the process of adopting a new product:

Awareness: The consumer becomes aware of the new product but lacks information about it.

Interest: The consumer seeks information about the new product.

Evaluation: The consumer considers whether trying the new product makes sense.

Trial: The consumer tries the new product on a small scale to improve his or her estimate of its value.

Adoption: The consumer decides to make full and regular use of the new product.

This model suggests that new-product marketers should think about how to help consumers move through these stages. For example, Best Buy recently developed a unique way to help concerned customers get past a hurdle in the buying process and make a positive buying decision for new televisions.[28]

Prior to the recent holiday shopping season, to convince buyers to upgrade to new models, television manufacturers offered a flurry of new technologies and loaded their marketing pitches with techie jargon such as 3D, ultrathin, Wi-Fi-capable, widget-equipped, and Internet-ready. However, rather than spurring new purchases, the pitches created a barrier to buying—fear among buyers that whatever they bought might soon be obsolete. In one study, 40 percent of consumers said that concerns about technology becoming outdated were preventing them from buying electronic products such as TVs, mobile phones, and computers. That left electronics retailers like Best Buy with aisles stacked high with unsold electronics.

To help customers past this buying hurdle, Best Buy began offering a Future-Proof Buy Back Program. For an up-front fee of 7 to 20 percent of the price, Best Buy promises customers that, when they're ready for something new, it will redeem purchases in good working order for up to 50 percent of the purchase price, depending on how many months pass before they upgrade. "There is a fair number of consumers on the bubble, not quite willing to make a purchase because they fear some other new thing will come down very quickly," says a Best Buy executive. "We want them to go ahead and make that purchase with confidence."

Figure 5.6 Adopter Categorization on the Basis of Relative Time of Adoption of Innovations

Sources: Based on figures found at http://en.wikipedia.org/wiki/Everett_Rogers, November 2011; and Everett M. Rogers, *Diffusion of Innovations,* 5th ed. (New York: Simon & Schuster, 2003), p. 281.

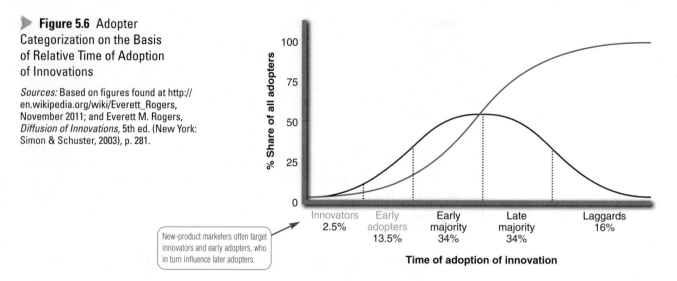

New-product marketers often target innovators and early adopters, who in turn influence later adopters.

Individual Differences in Innovativeness

People differ greatly in their readiness to try new products. In each product area, there are "consumption pioneers" and early adopters. Other individuals adopt new products much later. People can be classified into the adopter categories shown in ▶ **Figure 5.6**. As shown by the black curve, after a slow start, an increasing number of people adopt the new product. The number of adopters reaches a peak and then drops off as fewer nonadopters remain. As successive groups of consumers adopt the innovation (the red curve), it eventually reaches its saturation level. Innovators are defined as the first 2.5 percent of buyers to adopt a new idea (those beyond two standard deviations from mean adoption time); the early adopters are the next 13.5 percent (between one and two standard deviations); and so forth.

The five adopter groups have differing values. *Innovators* are venturesome—they try new ideas at some risk. *Early adopters* are guided by respect—they are opinion leaders in their communities and adopt new ideas early but carefully. The *early majority* is deliberate—although they rarely are leaders, they adopt new ideas before the average person. The *late majority* is skeptical—they adopt an innovation only after a majority of people have tried it. Finally, *laggards* are tradition bound—they are suspicious of changes and adopt the innovation only when it has become something of a tradition itself.

This adopter classification suggests that an innovating firm should research the characteristics of innovators and early adopters in their product categories and direct marketing efforts toward them.

Influence of Product Characteristics on Rate of Adoption

The characteristics of the new product affect its rate of adoption. Some products catch on almost overnight. For example, Apple's iPod, iPhone, and iPad flew off retailers' shelves at an astounding rate from the day they were first introduced. Others take a longer time to gain acceptance. For example, the first HDTVs were introduced in the United States in the 1990s, but the percentage of U.S. households owning a high definition set stood at only 12 percent by 2007 and 61 percent by 2010.[29]

Five characteristics are especially important in influencing an innovation's rate of adoption. For example, consider the characteristics of HDTV in relation to the rate of adoption:

Relative advantage: The degree to which the innovation appears superior to existing products. HDTV offers substantially improved picture quality. This accelerated its rate of adoption.

Compatibility: The degree to which the innovation fits the values and experiences of potential consumers. HDTV, for example, is highly compatible with the lifestyles of the TV-watching public. However, in the early years, HDTV was not yet compatible with programming and broadcasting systems, which slowed adoption. Now, as high definition programs and channels have become the norm, the rate of HDTV adoption has increased rapidly.

Complexity: The degree to which the innovation is difficult to understand or use. HDTVs are not very complex. Therefore, as more programming has become available and prices have fallen, the rate of HDTV adoption has increased faster than that of more complex innovations.

Divisibility: The degree to which the innovation may be tried on a limited basis. Early HDTVs and HD cable and satellite systems were very expensive, which slowed the rate of adoption. As prices have fallen, adoption rates have increased.

Communicability: The degree to which the results of using the innovation can be observed or described to others. Because HDTV lends itself to demonstration and description, its use will spread faster among consumers.

Other characteristics influence the rate of adoption, such as initial and ongoing costs, risk and uncertainty, and social approval. The new-product marketer must research all these factors when developing the new product and its marketing program.

SPEED BUMP | LINKING THE CONCEPTS

Here's a good place to pull over and apply the concepts you've examined in the first part of this chapter.

- Think about a specific major purchase you've made recently. What buying process did you follow? What major factors influenced your decision?
- Pick a company or brand that we've discussed in a previous chapter—Apple, Nike, McDonald's, JetBlue, Domino's, or another. How does the company you chose use its understanding of customers and their buying behavior to build better customer relationships?
- Think about a company like Intel, which sells its products to computer makers and other businesses rather than to final consumers. How would Intel's marketing to business customers differ from Apple's marketing to final consumers? The second part of the chapter deals with this issue.

Author Comment ▶
Now that we've looked at consumer markets and buyer behavior, let's dig into business markets and buyer behavior. Thinking ahead, how are they the same? How are they different?

Business buyer behavior
The buying behavior of organizations that buy goods and services for use in the production of other products and services that are sold, rented, or supplied to others.

Business buying process
The decision process by which business buyers determine which products and services their organizations need to purchase and then find, evaluate, and choose among alternative suppliers and brands.

Business Markets and Business Buyer Behavior

In one way or another, most large companies sell to other organizations. Companies such as Boeing, DuPont, IBM, GE, Caterpillar, and countless other firms sell *most* of their products to other businesses. Even large consumer-products companies, which make products used by final consumers, must first sell their products to other businesses. For example, General Mills makes many familiar consumer brands—Big G cereals (Cheerios, Wheaties, Trix, Chex), baking products (Pillsbury, Betty Crocker, Gold Medal flour), snacks (Nature Valley, Pop Secret, Chex Mix), Yoplait yogurt, Häagen-Dazs ice cream, and others. But to sell these products to consumers, General Mills must first sell them to its wholesaler and retailer customers, who in turn serve the consumer market.

Business buyer behavior refers to the buying behavior of organizations that buy goods and services for use in the production of other products and services that are sold, rented, or supplied to others. It also includes the behavior of retailing and wholesaling firms that acquire goods for the purpose of reselling or renting them to others at a profit. In the **business buying process**, business buyers determine which products and services their organizations need to purchase and then find, evaluate, and choose among alternative suppliers and brands. *Business-to-business (B-to-B) marketers* must do their best to understand business markets and business buyer behavior. Then, like businesses that sell to final buyers, they must build profitable relationships with business customers by creating superior customer value.

Business Markets

The business market is *huge*. In fact, business markets involve far more dollars and items than do consumer markets. For example, think about the large number of business transactions involved in the production and sale of a single set of Goodyear tires. Various suppliers sell Goodyear the rubber, steel, equipment, and other goods that it needs to produce tires. Goodyear then sells the finished tires to retailers, who in turn sell them to consumers. Thus, many sets of *business* purchases were made for only one set of *consumer* purchases. In addition, Goodyear sells tires as original equipment to manufacturers that install them on new vehicles and as replacement tires to companies that maintain their own fleets of company cars, trucks, or other vehicles.

In some ways, business markets are similar to consumer markets. Both involve people who assume buying roles and make purchase decisions to satisfy needs. However, business markets differ in many ways from consumer markets. The main differences are in *market structure and demand,* the *nature of the buying unit,* and the *types of decisions and the decision process* involved.

Market Structure and Demand

The business marketer normally deals with *far fewer but far larger buyers* than the consumer marketer does. Even in large business markets, a few buyers often account for most of the purchasing. For example, when Goodyear sells replacement tires to final consumers, its potential market includes millions of car owners around the world. But its fate in business markets depends on getting orders from only a handful of large automakers.

Further, business demand is **derived demand**—it ultimately derives from the demand for consumer goods. For example, W. L. Gore & Associates sells its Gore-Tex brand to manufacturers who make and sell outdoor apparel brands made from Gore-Tex fabrics. If demand for these brands increases, so does demand for Gore-Tex fabrics. ▶ So to boost demand for Gore-Tex, Gore advertises to final consumers to educate them on the benefits of Gore-Tex fabrics in the brands they buy. It also directly markets brands containing Gore-Tex—from Arc'teryx, Marmot, and The North Face to Burton and L.L. Bean—on its own Web site (*www.gore-tex.com*).

To deepen its direct relationship with outdoor enthusiasts further, Gore even sponsors an "Experience More" online community in which members can share experiences and videos, connect with outdoor experts, and catch exclusive gear offers from partner brands. As a result, consumers around the world have learned to look for the familiar Gore-Tex brand label, and both Gore and its partner brands win. No matter what brand of apparel or footwear you buy, says the label, if it's made with Gore-Tex fabric, it's "guaranteed to keep you dry."

Finally, many business markets have *inelastic and more fluctuating demand.* The total demand for many business products is not much affected by price changes, especially in the short run. A drop in the price of leather will not cause shoe manufacturers to buy much more leather unless it results in lower shoe prices that, in turn, increase consumer demand for shoes. And the demand for many business goods and services tends to change more—and more quickly—than does the demand for consumer goods and services. A small percentage increase in consumer demand can cause large increases in business demand.

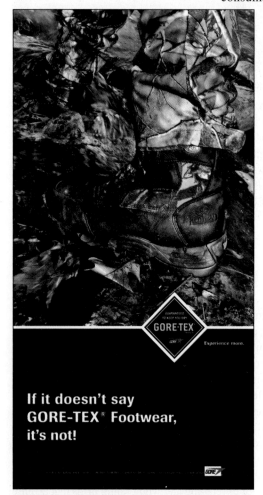

▲ Derived demand: You can't buy anything directly from Gore, but to increase demand for Gore-Tex fabrics, the company markets directly to the buyers of outdoor apparel and other brands made from them. Both Gore and its partner brands win.

Nature of the Buying Unit

Compared with consumer purchases, a business purchase usually involves *more decision participants* and a *more professional purchasing effort.* Often, business buying is done by trained purchasing agents who spend their working lives learning how to buy better. The more complex the purchase, the more

Derived demand
The business demand for products and services that ultimately derives from the demand for consumer goods.

Supplier development
Systematic development of networks of supplier-partners to ensure an appropriate and dependable supply of products and materials exists for use in making products or reselling them to others.

Author Comment ▶
Business buying decisions can range from routine to incredibly complex, involving only a few or very many decision makers and buying influences.

likely it is that several people will participate in the decision-making process. Buying committees composed of technical experts and top management are common in the buying of major goods. Beyond this, B-to-B marketers now face a new breed of higher-level, better-trained supply managers. Therefore, companies must have well-trained marketers and salespeople to deal with these well-trained buyers.

Types of Decisions and the Decision Process

Business buyers usually face *more complex* buying decisions than do consumer buyers. Business purchases often involve large sums of money, complex technical and economic considerations, and interactions among people at many levels of the buyer's organization. The business buying process also tends to be *longer* and *more formalized*. Large business purchases usually call for detailed product specifications, written purchase orders, careful supplier searches, and formal approval.

Finally, in the business buying process, the buyer and seller are often much *more dependent* on each other. B-to-B marketers may roll up their sleeves and work closely with their customers during all stages of the buying process—from helping customers define problems, to finding solutions, to supporting after-sale operation. They often customize their offerings to individual customer needs. In the short run, sales go to suppliers who meet buyers' immediate product and service needs. In the long run, however, business-to-business marketers keep customers by meeting current needs *and* by partnering with them to help solve their problems. For example, Dow Performance Plastics doesn't just sell commodity plastics *to* its industrial customers—it works *with* these customers to help them succeed in their own markets. (See Marketing at Work 5.2.)

In recent years, relationships between customers and suppliers have been changing from downright adversarial to close and chummy. In fact, many customer companies are now practicing **supplier development**, systematically developing networks of supplier-partners to ensure a dependable supply of products and materials that they use in making their own products or reselling to others. For example, Walmart doesn't have a "Purchasing Department"; it has a "Supplier Development Department." The giant retailer knows that it can't just rely on spot suppliers who might be available when needed. Instead, Walmart manages a robust network of supplier-partners that help provide the hundreds of billions of dollars of goods that it sells to its customers each year.

Business Buyer Behavior

At the most basic level, marketers want to know how business buyers will respond to various marketing stimuli. ▶ **Figure 5.7** shows a model of business buyer behavior. In this model, marketing and other stimuli affect the buying organization and produce certain buyer responses. To design good marketing strategies, marketers must understand what happens within the organization to turn stimuli into purchase responses.

▶ **Figure 5.7** A Model of Business Buyer Behavior

In some ways, business markets are similar to consumer markets—this model looks a lot like the model of consumer buyer behavior presented in Figure 5.1. But there are some major differences, especially in the nature of the buying unit, the types of decisions made, and the decision process.

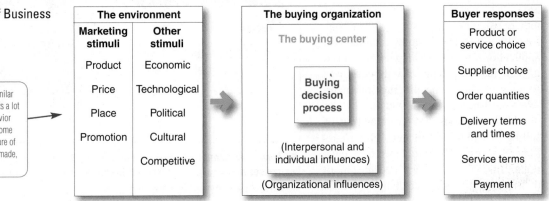

MARKETING AT WORK   5.2

Dow Performance Plastics: "If You Win, We Win"

When you pick up your cell phone to text a friend or hop into your car to head for the mall, you probably don't think much about the plastics that make those state-of-the-art products possible. But at Dow Peformance Plastics, thinking about how plastics can make our lives better is at the very core of its business strategy. What makes that noteworthy is that Dow doesn't sell its products to you and me. Instead, it sells mountains of raw materials to its business customers, who in turn sell parts to companies—such as Nokia and BMW—who sell their products to final users. But Dow Performance Plastics understands that its own success depends heavily on how successfully its business customers use Dow plastic polymers and resins in satisfying final consumer needs. It's not just selling commodity plastics; it's helping the businesses that buy its plastics materials to be heroes with their own customers.

To get a better perspective on this strategy, let's go back a few years. In the late 1980s, The Dow Chemical Company realigned its dozen or so widely varied plastics businesses into a single subsidiary, called Dow Plastics (now Dow Performance Plastics). One of the first things Dow had to do was to decide how to position its new division competitively. Initial research showed that Dow Plastics rated a distant third in customer preference behind industry leaders DuPont and GE Plastics. The research also revealed, however, that customers were unhappy with the service—or lack thereof—that they received from all three suppliers. "Vendors peddled resins as a commodity," said the then head of Dow Plastics' advertising agency. "They competed on price and delivered on time but gave no service."

These findings led to a positioning strategy that went far beyond simply selling good products and delivering them on time. Dow Plastics set out to build deeper relationships with business customers. The organization wasn't just selling products and value-added services; it was partnering with customers to help them win with their own final consumers. Said the agency executive, "Whether they're using Dow's plastics to make bags for Safeway or for complex [automotive] applications, we had to help them succeed in their markets." This new thinking was summed up in the positioning statement, "We don't succeed unless you do."

This new philosophy got Dow out of selling just plastics and into selling customer success. The problems of Dow's organizational customers became more than just engineering challenges. Dow's

business customers sell to somebody else, so the company now faced new challenges of marketing to and helping satisfy customers' customers.

Over the past two decades, the customer success philosophy has come to permeate everything Dow does. Dow doesn't just sell plastics *to* its business customers; it works *with* them to grow and succeed together. Now, whenever Dow people encounter a new plastics product or market, the first question they always ask is, "How does this help our customers succeed?"

For example, carmaker BMW sells to some of the world's most demanding customers. BMW owners want high performance, but they also want reasonable prices and fuel economy. Thus, to help deliver more value to its customers, BMW looks for two important attributes in every vehicle component: cost savings and weight reduction. Lower costs mean more palatable prices for car buyers, and weight reduction yields customer benefits such as improved fuel economy, increased acceleration, and better handling and braking.

So when BMW and its electronic parts supplier Tyco needed an advanced electronics box for the engine compartment of BMW's latest 7 Series models, they looked for something that would not only meet complex performance specifications but also be cost efficient and lightweight. Enter Dow. Working together, the Dow-Tyco team developed a lightweight plastic box that yields "exceptional dimensional stability, low warpage, low weight, and improved hydrolysis resistance," all at a surprisingly economical cost.

That might sound like gibberish to you, but it's sweet music to companies like Tyco and BMW. In the final analysis, of course, the folks at Dow care most about how such parts will help BMW succeed with car buyers. The more cars BMW sells

DOW

Dow Performance Plastics

Think of Dow as the team...
            behind your team.

▲ **Dow Performance Plastics isn't just selling commodity plastics—it's helping the businesses that buy its plastics to be heroes with their own customers.**
Courtesy of The Dow Chemical Company

to final buyers, the more plastics Dow sells to Tyco. Through such innovations, Dow has helped BMW give customers a full-sized 5,100-pound sedan that hits 60 miles per hour from a standstill in 4.4 seconds, blasts through corners like a go-cart, and still gets decent gas mileage.

Selling customer success has turned Dow into a world-leading supplier of plastic resins and material science innovations. Plastics now account for more than 20 percent of Dow Chemical's $54 billion in annual revenues. Dow Performance Plastics doesn't come up with winning solutions for customers by simply dipping into its current product portfolio. It works closely with customers in every stage of product development and production, from material selection through final part testing. Dow Plastics considers itself a partner, not just a supplier. As the company summarized on its Web site:

> Think of Dow as the team behind your team. Dow Performance Plastics' greatest asset, and the one that can make the biggest difference to your business, is our people. Knowledgeable, flexible, and committed to your success, our team puts all our resources together to provide you with a competitive edge. We believe in a simple concept . . . if you win, we win.

Sources: For historical background, see Nancy Arnott, "Getting the Picture: The Grand Design—We Don't Succeed Unless You Do," *Sales & Marketing Management,* June 1994, pp. 74–76. Current quotes and other information from www.omnexus.com/sf/dow/?id=plastics, accessed March 2010; and http://plastics.dow.com/, accessed September 2011.

Within the organization, buying activity consists of two major parts: the buying center, composed of all the people involved in the buying decision, and the buying decision process. The model shows that the buying center and the buying decision process are influenced by internal organizational, interpersonal, and individual factors as well as external environmental factors.

The model in Figure 5.7 suggests four questions about business buyer behavior: What buying decisions do business buyers make? Who participates in the business buying process? What are the major influences on buyers? How do business buyers make their buying decisions?

Major Types of Buying Situations

Straight rebuy

A business buying situation in which the buyer routinely reorders something without any modifications.

Modified rebuy

A business buying situation in which the buyer wants to modify product specifications, prices, terms, or suppliers.

New task

A business buying situation in which the buyer purchases a product or service for the first time.

Systems selling (or solutions selling)

Buying a packaged solution to a problem from a single seller, thus avoiding all the separate decisions involved in a complex buying situation.

There are three major types of buying situations.[30] In a **straight rebuy**, the buyer reorders something without any modifications. It is usually handled on a routine basis by the purchasing department. To keep the business, "in" suppliers try to maintain product and service quality. "Out" suppliers try to find new ways to add value or exploit dissatisfaction so that the buyer will consider them.

In a **modified rebuy**, the buyer wants to modify product specifications, prices, terms, or suppliers. The "in" suppliers may become nervous and feel pressured to put their best foot forward to protect an account. "Out" suppliers may see the modified rebuy situation as an opportunity to make a better offer and gain new business.

A company buying a product or service for the first time faces a **new task** situation. In such cases, the greater the cost or risk, the larger the number of decision participants and the greater the company's efforts to collect information. The new task situation is the marketer's greatest opportunity and challenge. The marketer not only tries to reach as many key buying influences as possible but also provides help and information. The buyer makes the fewest decisions in the straight rebuy and the most in the new task decision.

Many business buyers prefer to buy a complete solution to a problem from a single seller rather than buying separate products and services from several suppliers and putting them together. The sale often goes to the firm that provides the most complete *system* for meeting the customer's needs and solving its problems. Such **systems selling** (or **solutions selling**) is often a key business marketing strategy for winning and holding accounts.

Thus, transportation and logistics giant UPS does more than just ship packages for its business customers; it develops entire solutions to customers' transportation and logistics problems. ▶ For example, UPS bundles a complete system of services that support Nikon's consumer products supply chain—including logistics, transportation, freight, and customs brokerage services—into one smooth-running system.[31]

▲ **Systems selling: UPS bundles a complete system of services that support Nikon's consumer products supply chain—including logistics, transportation, freight, and customs brokerage services.**

Oberhaeuser/Caro/Alamy

When Nikon entered the digital camera market, it decided that it needed an entirely new distribution strategy as well. So it asked transportation and logistics giant UPS to design a complete system for moving its entire electronics product line from its Asian factories to retail stores throughout the United States, Latin America, and the Caribbean. Now products leave Nikon's Asian manufacturing centers and arrive on American retailers' shelves in as few as two days, with UPS handling everything in between. UPS first manages air and ocean freight and related customs brokerage to bring Nikon products from Korea, Japan, and Indonesia to its Louisville, Kentucky, operations center. There, UPS can either "kit" the Nikon merchandise with accessories such as batteries and chargers or repackage it for in-store display. Finally, UPS distributes the products to thousands of retailers across the United States or exports them to Latin American or Caribbean retail outlets and distributors. Along the way, UPS tracks the goods and provides Nikon with a "snapshot" of the entire supply chain, letting Nikon keep retailers informed of delivery times and adjust them as needed.

Participants in the Business Buying Process

Who does the buying of the trillions of dollars' worth of goods and services needed by business organizations? The decision-making unit of a buying organization is called its **buying center**—it consists of all the individuals and units that play a role in the business purchase decision-making process. This group includes the actual users of the product or service, those who make the buying decision, those who influence the buying decision, those who do the actual buying, and those who control buying information.

Buying center

All the individuals and units that play a role in the purchase decision-making process.

The buying center is not a fixed and formally identified unit within the buying organization. It is a set of buying roles assumed by different people for different purchases. Within the organization, the size and makeup of the buying center will vary for different products and for different buying situations. For some routine purchases, one person—say, a purchasing agent—may assume all the buying center roles and serve as the only person involved in the buying decision. For more complex purchases, the buying center may include 20 or 30 people from different levels and departments in the organization.

The buying center concept presents a major marketing challenge. The business marketer must learn who participates in the decision, each participant's relative influence, and what evaluation criteria each decision participant uses. This can be difficult.

The buying center usually includes some obvious participants who are involved formally in the buying decision. For example, the decision to buy a corporate jet will probably involve the company's CEO, the chief pilot, a purchasing agent, some legal staff, a member of top management, and others formally charged with the buying decision. It may also involve less obvious, informal participants, some of whom may actually make or strongly affect the buying decision. Sometimes, even the people in the buying center are not aware of all the buying participants. For example, the decision about which corporate jet to buy may actually be made by a corporate board member who has an interest in flying and who knows a lot about airplanes. This board member may work behind the scenes to sway the decision. Many business buying decisions result from the complex interactions of ever-changing buying center participants.

Major Influences on Business Buyers

Business buyers are subject to many influences when they make their buying decisions. Some marketers assume that the major influences are economic. They think buyers will favor the supplier who offers the lowest price or the best product or the most service. They concentrate on offering strong economic benefits to buyers. Such economic factors are very important to most buyers, especially in a tough economy. However, business buyers actually respond to both economic and personal factors. Far from being cold, calculating, and impersonal, business buyers are human and social as well. They react to both reason and emotion. Today, most B-to-B marketers recognize that emotion plays an important role in business buying decisions. ▶ Consider this example:[32]

▲ **Emotions play an important role in business buying: These emotion-charged images in this B-to-B ad get across the message that Citrix's virtual computing solutions can put computing power back in the hands of companies and their IT departments.**

Citrix creates better ways for people, IT, and business to work, using virtual meetings, desktops, and datacenters. Citrix combines virtualization, networking, and cloud computing technologies into products that let people work and play from anywhere on any device. The company helps businesses consolidate server hardware and centrally manage applications and desktops from the datacenter rather than installing them on individual employee computers. With a tech-savvy audience, you might expect these B-to-B ads to focus entirely on technical features and benefits such as simplicity, productivity, and cost-efficiency. Citrix does promote these benefits, but the ads also pack a decidedly more emotional wallop. Working off the notion that our technology has begun to control us, the Simplicity Is Power campaign from Citrix uses dramatic imagery showing a human hand in complete control of technology. For example, one ad shows a hand crushing servers; another shows laptops and applications dangling from fingers like puppets on springs. These emotionally-charged images convey the message that Citrix virtual computing solutions put unprecedented computing power back into the hands of organizations and their IT departments.

▶ **Figure 5.8** lists various groups of influences on business buyers—environmental, organizational, interpersonal, and individual. *Environmental factors* have the broadest impact. Business buyers are heavily influenced by factors in the current and expected economic environment, such as levels of primary demand and the economic outlook. Business buyers also are affected by supply, technological, political, and competitive developments in the environment. Finally, culture and customs can strongly influence business buyer reactions to the marketer's behavior and strategies, especially in the international marketing environment. The business buyer must watch these factors, determine how they will affect the buyer, and try to turn environmental challenges into opportunities.

Organizational factors are also important. Each buying organization has its own objectives, strategies, structure, systems, and procedures, and the business marketer must understand these factors well. Questions such as these arise: How many people are involved in the buying decision? Who are they? What are their evaluative criteria? What are the company's policies and limits on its buyers?

The buying center usually includes many participants who influence each other, so *interpersonal factors* also influence the business buying process. However, it is often difficult to assess such interpersonal factors and group dynamics. Buying center participants do not wear tags that label them as *key decision maker* or *not influential*. Nor do buying center participants with the highest rank always have the most influence. Participants may influence the buying decision because they control rewards and punishments, are well liked, have special expertise, or have a special relationship with other important participants. Interpersonal factors are often very subtle. Whenever possible, business marketers must try to understand these factors and design strategies that take them into account.

Figure 5.8 Major Influences on Business Buyer Behavior

Like consumer buying decisions in Figure 5.2, business buying decisions are affected by an incredibly complex combination of environmental, interpersonal, and individual influences, but with an extra layer of organizational factors thrown into the mix.

Environmental
The economy
Supply conditions
Technology
Politics/regulation
Competition
Culture and customs

Organizational
Objectives
Strategies
Structure
Systems
Procedures

Interpersonal
Influence
Expertise
Authority
Dynamics

Individual
Age/education
Job position
Motives
Personality
Preferences
Buying style

Buyers

Each participant in the business buying decision process brings in personal motives, perceptions, and preferences. These *individual factors* are affected by personal characteristics such as age, income, education, professional identification, personality, and attitudes toward risk. Also, buyers have different buying styles. Some may be technical types who make in-depth analyses of competitive proposals before choosing a supplier. Other buyers may be intuitive negotiators who are adept at pitting the sellers against one another for the best deal.

The Business Buying Process

Figure 5.9 lists the eight stages of the business buying process.[33] Buyers who face a new task buying situation usually go through all stages of the buying process. Buyers making modified or straight rebuys, in contrast, may skip some of the stages. We will examine these steps for the typical new task buying situation.

The buying process begins with *problem recognition*—when someone in the company recognizes a problem or need that can be met by acquiring a specific product or service. Problem recognition can result from internal or external stimuli. Business marketers use their sales forces or advertising to alert customers to potential problems and then show how their products provide solutions. For example, an award-winning ad from Makino Engineering Services, a leading maker of advanced machining tools, highlights a daunting customer problem: hard-to-machine parts. In the ad, the powerful visual shows a machined part that looks like a scary monster, complete with fangs. The ad's headline then offers the solution: "Our application engineers love the scary parts." The ad goes on to reassure customers that Makino can help them with their most difficult-to-machine parts and urges, "Don't be afraid of the part."

Having recognized a need, the buyer next prepares a *general need description* that describes the characteristics and quantity of the needed items or solutions. For standard purchases, this process presents few problems. For complex items, however, the buyer may need to work with others—engineers, users, consultants—to define what's needed.

Once the buying organization has defined the need, it develops the item's technical *product specifications,* often with the help of a value analysis engineering team. **Product value analysis** is an approach to cost reduction in which the company carefully analyzes a product's or service's components to determine if they can be redesigned and made more effectively and efficiently to provide greater value. The team decides on the best product or service characteristics and specifies them accordingly. Sellers, too, can use value analysis as a tool to help secure new accounts and keep old ones. Improving customer value and helping customers

Problem recognition: Machine tools maker Makino uses ads like this one to alert customers to problems and to reassure them that Makino can help find solutions. "Our application engineers love the scary parts."

Courtesy of Makino, Inc.

Figure 5.9 Stages of the Business Buying Process

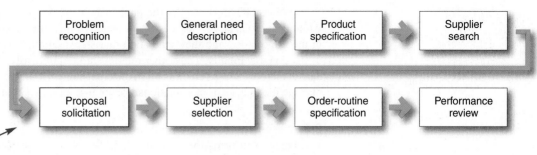

Buyers facing new, complex buying decisions usually go through all of these stages. Those making rebuys often skip some of the stages. Either way, the business buying process is usually much more complicated than this simple flow diagram suggests.

Product value analysis
Carefully analyzing a product's or service's components to determine if they can be redesigned and made more effectively and efficiently to provide greater value.

find more cost-effective solutions gives the business marketer an important edge in keeping current customers loyal and winning new business.

In the next buying process step, the buyer conducts a *supplier search* to find the best vendors. The buyer can locate qualified suppliers through trade directories, computer searches, or recommendations from others. Today, more and more companies are turning to the Internet to find suppliers. For marketers, this has leveled the playing field—the Internet gives smaller suppliers many of the same advantages as larger competitors. The supplier's task is to understand the search process and make certain that their firm is considered.

In the *proposal solicitation* stage of the business buying process, the buyer invites qualified suppliers to submit proposals. When the purchase is complex or expensive, the buyer will usually require detailed written proposals or formal presentations from each potential supplier. In response, business marketers must be skilled in researching, writing, and presenting proposals. The proposals should be marketing documents, not just technical documents. They should spell out how the seller's solution creates greater value for the customer than competing solutions.

The buyer next reviews the proposals and selects a supplier or suppliers. During *supplier selection,* the buyer will consider many supplier attributes and their relative importance. Such attributes include product and service quality, reputation, on-time delivery, ethical corporate behavior, honest communication, and competitive prices. In the end, they may select a single supplier or a few suppliers. Today's supplier development managers often want to develop a full network of supplier-partners that can help the company bring more value to its customers.

The buyer now prepares an *order-routine specification*. It includes the final order with the chosen supplier or suppliers and lists items such as technical specifications, quantity needed, expected time of delivery, return policies, and warranties. Many large buyers now practice *vendor-managed inventory*, in which they turn over ordering and inventory responsibilities to their suppliers. Under such systems, buyers share sales and inventory information directly with key suppliers. The suppliers then monitor inventories and replenish stock automatically as needed. For example, most major suppliers to large retailers such as Walmart, Target, Home Depot, and Lowe's assume vendor-managed inventory responsibilities.

The final stage of the business buying process is the supplier *performance review,* in which the buyer assesses the supplier's performance and provides feedback. For example, Home Depot has issued a set of supplier guidelines and policies and regularly evaluates each supplier in terms of quality, delivery, and other performance variables. It gives suppliers online performance scorecards that provide ongoing feedback that helps them improve their performance.[34] The supplier performance review may lead the buyer to continue, modify, or drop the arrangement. The seller's job is to monitor the same factors used by the buyer to make sure that the seller is giving the expected satisfaction.

The eight-stage buying-process model provides a simple view of the business buying as it might occur in a new task buying situation. The actual process is usually much more complex. In the modified rebuy or straight rebuy situation, some of these stages would be compressed or bypassed. Each organization buys in its own way, and each buying situation has unique requirements.

Different buying center participants may be involved at different stages of the process. Although certain buying-process steps usually do occur, buyers do not always follow them in the same order, and they may add other steps. Often, buyers will repeat certain stages of the process. Finally, a customer relationship might involve many different types of purchases ongoing at a given time, all in different stages of the buying process. The seller must manage the total customer relationship, not just individual purchases.

E-Procurement: Buying on the Internet

Advances in information technology have changed the face of the B-to-B marketing process. Online purchasing, often called **e-procurement**, has grown rapidly in recent years. Virtually unknown a decade and a half ago, online purchasing is standard procedure for most companies today. E-procurement gives buyers access to new suppliers, lowers purchasing costs, and hastens order processing and delivery. In turn, business marketers can connect with customers online to share marketing information, sell products and services, provide customer support services, and maintain ongoing customer relationships.

Companies can do e-procurement in any of several ways. They can conduct *reverse auctions,* in which they put their purchasing requests online and invite suppliers to bid for the business. Or they can engage in online *trading exchanges*, through which companies work collectively to facilitate the trading process. Companies also can conduct e-procurement by setting up their own *company buying sites*. For example, GE operates a company trading site on which it posts its buying needs and invites bids, negotiates terms, and places orders. Or companies can create *extranet links* with key suppliers. For instance, they can create direct procurement accounts with suppliers such as Dell or Office Depot, through which company buyers can purchase equipment, materials, and supplies directly.

B-to-B marketers can help customers online and build stronger customer relationships by creating well-designed, easy-to-use Web sites. For example, *BtoB* magazine recently rated the site of Shaw Floors—a market leader in flooring products—as one of its "10 great B-to-B Web sites." ▶ The site helps Shaw build strong links with its business and trade customers.[35]

E-procurement
Purchasing performed through electronic connections between buyers and sellers—usually online.

▲ **B-to-B Web sites: This Shaw Floors site builds strong links with Shaw's retailers. It provides marketing ideas and tools that make retailers more effective in selling Shaw's products to final customers. Host a pie fight, anyone?**
Shaw Industries, Inc.

At one time, flooring manufacturer Shaw Floors' Web site was nothing more than "brochureware." Today, however, the site is a true interactive experience. At the site, design and construction professionals as well as customers can "see"—virtually—the company's many product lines. At the popular "Try on a Floor" area, designers or retailers can even work with final buyers to upload digital images of an actual floor and put any of the company's many carpets on it to see how they look. They can select various lines and colors immediately without digging through samples. And the extremely detailed images can be rotated and manipulated so a designer, for example, can show a client what the pile of the carpet looks like and how deep it is.

For retailers, Shaw has created a Web site, *www.shawadvantage.com*. This site provides retailers the resources they need to create their own advertising materials and order point of sale materials for their businesses. Retailers can also check their co-op advertising accounts with the company, letting them subsidize or add to their advertising budgets. Retailer-partners can connect to their accounts and search the company's products, make inventory checks, order or reserve products, and track order status for their stores. The Shaw Web Studio lets retailers—many of which are mom-and-pop stores—create their own Web sites in minutes or download photography, catalog engines, and other content to add to their existing Web sites. "So many retailers don't have the time or money to build their own online presence," says Shaw's interactive marketing manager, "so this really helps them."

Business-to-business e-procurement yields many benefits. First, it shaves transaction costs and results in more efficient purchasing for both buyers and suppliers. E-procurement reduces the time between order and delivery. And a Web-powered purchasing program eliminates the paperwork associated with traditional requisition and ordering procedures and helps an organization keep better track of all purchases. Finally, beyond the cost and time savings, e-procurement frees purchasing people from a lot of drudgery and paperwork. In turn, it frees them to focus on more-strategic issues, such as finding better supply sources and working with suppliers to reduce costs and develop new products.

To demonstrate these advantages, consider Kodak. When it remodeled its headquarters facilities in Rochester, New York, it used e-procurement only. From demolition to restoration, the massive project involved managing more than 1,600 contract bids from 150 contractors. Throughout the project, e-procurement reduced paperwork and accelerated review and award times. In the end, the project was completed on time, and Kodak estimates that using e-procurement saved 15 percent on purchasing-process costs (including $186,000 on photocopying expenses alone).[36]

The rapidly expanding use of e-procurement, however, also presents some problems. For example, at the same time that the Internet makes it possible for suppliers and customers to share business data and even collaborate on product design, it can also erode decades-old customer-supplier relationships. Many buyers now use the power of the Internet to pit suppliers against one another and search out better deals, products, and turnaround times on a purchase-by-purchase basis.

E-procurement can also create potential security concerns. Although e-mail and home banking transactions can be protected through basic encryption, the secure environment that businesses need to carry out confidential interactions is sometimes still lacking. Companies are spending millions for research on defensive strategies to keep hackers at bay. Cisco Systems, for example, specifies the types of routers, firewalls, and security procedures that its partners must use to safeguard extranet connections. In fact, the company goes even further; it sends its own security engineers to examine a partner's defenses and holds the partner liable for any security breach that originates from its computers.

REST STOP | REVIEWING THE CONCEPTS

MyMarketingLab

Now that you have completed the chapter, return to www.mymktlab.com to experience and apply the concepts and to explore the additional study materials for this chapter.

CHAPTER REVIEW AND KEY TERMS

Objectives Review

This chapter is the last of three chapters that address understanding the marketplace and consumers. Here, we've looked closely at *consumer* and *business buyer behavior*. The American consumer market consists of more than 310 million people who consume more than $10 trillion worth of goods and services each year, making it one of the most attractive consumer markets in the world. The world consumer market consists of more than 6.9 billion people. The business market involves even more dollars and items than the consumer market. Understanding buyer behavior is one of the biggest challenges marketers face.

▶ OBJECTIVE 1 Understand the consumer market and the major factors that influence consumer buyer behavior. (pp 128–142)

The *consumer market* consists of all the individuals and households who buy or acquire goods and services for personal consumption. A simple model of consumer behavior suggests that marketing stimuli and other major forces enter the consumer's *black box.* This black box has two parts: buyer characteristics and the buyer's decision process. Once in the black box, the inputs result in buyer responses, such as buying attitudes and preferences and purchase behavior.

Consumer buyer behavior is influenced by four key sets of buyer characteristics: cultural, social, personal, and psychological. Understanding these factors can help marketers to identify interested buyers and to shape products and appeals to serve consumer needs better. *Culture* is the most basic determinant of a person's wants and behavior. People in different cultural, subcultural, and social class groups have different product and brand preferences. *Social factors*—such as small group, social network, and family influences—strongly affect product and brand choices, as do *personal characteristics,* such as age, life-cycle stage, occupation, economic circumstances, lifestyle, and personality. Finally, consumer buying behavior is influenced by four major sets of *psychological factors*—motivation, perception, learning, and beliefs and attitudes. Each of these factors provides a different perspective for understanding the workings of the buyer's black box.

▶ OBJECTIVE 2 Identify and discuss the stages in the buyer decision process. (pp 142–145)

When making a purchase, the buyer goes through a decision process consisting of need recognition, information search, evaluation of alternatives, purchase decision, and postpurchase behavior. During *need recognition,* the consumer recognizes a problem or need that could be satisfied by a product or service. Once the need is recognized, the consumer moves into the *information search* stage. With information in hand, the consumer proceeds to *alternative evaluation* and assesses brands in the choice set. From there, the consumer makes a *purchase decision* and actually buys the product. In the final stage of the buyer decision process, *postpurchase behavior,* the consumer takes action based on satisfaction or dissatisfaction. The marketer's job is to understand the buyer's behavior at each stage and the influences that are operating.

▶ OBJECTIVE 3 Describe the adoption and diffusion process for new products. (pp 145–147)

The product *adoption process* is made up of five stages: awareness, interest, evaluation, trial, and adoption. New-product marketers must think about how to help consumers move through these stages. With regard to the *diffusion process* for new products, consumers respond at different rates, depending on consumer and product characteristics. Consumers may be innovators, early adopters, early majority, late majority, or laggards. Each group may require different marketing approaches. Marketers often try to bring their new products to the attention of potential early adopters, especially those who are opinion leaders.

▶ OBJECTIVE 4 Define the business market and identify the major factors that influence business buyer behavior. (pp 147–154)

The *business market* comprises all organizations that buy goods and services for use in the production of other products and services or for the purpose of reselling or renting them to others at a profit. As compared to consumer markets, business markets usually have fewer, larger buyers who are more geographically concentrated. Business demand is derived demand, and the business buying decision usually involves more, and more professional, buyers.

Business buyers make decisions that vary with the three types of *buying situations:* straight rebuys, modified rebuys, and new tasks. The decision-making unit of a buying organization—the *buying center*—can consist of many different persons playing many different roles. The business marketer needs to know the following: Who are the major buying center participants? In what decisions do they exercise influence and to what degree? What evaluation criteria does each decision participant use? The business marketer also needs to understand the major environmental, organizational, interpersonal, and individual influences on the buying process.

▶ OBJECTIVE 5 List and define the steps in the business buying decision process. (pp 154–157)

The *business buying decision process* itself can be quite involved, with eight basic stages: problem recognition, general need description, product specification, supplier search, proposal solicitation, supplier selection, order-routine specification, and performance review. Buyers who face a new-task buying situation usually go through all stages of the buying process. Buyers making modified or straight rebuys, in contrast, may skip some of the stages. Companies must manage the overall customer relationship, which often includes many different buying decisions in various stages of the buying decision process. Recent advances in information technology have given birth to *e-procurement,* by which business buyers are purchasing all kinds of products and services online. Business marketers are increasingly connecting with customers online to share marketing information, sell products and services, provide customer support services, and maintain ongoing customer relationships.

Key Terms

Objective 1
Consumer buyer behavior (p 128)
Consumer market (p 128)

Objective 2
Culture (p 129)
Subculture (p 129)
Social class (p 132)
Group (p 132)
Word-of-mouth influence (p 133)
Opinion leader (p 133)
Online social networks (p 133)
Lifestyle (p 138)
Personality (p 138)

Motive (drive) (p 139)
Perception (p 140)
Learning (p 141)
Belief (p 141)
Attitude (p 141)
Cognitive dissonance (p 144)

Objective 3
New product (p 145)
Adoption process (p 145)

Objective 4
Business buyer behavior (p 147)
Business buying process (p 147)

Derived demand (p 148)
Supplier development (p 149)
Straight rebuy (p 151)
Modified rebuy (p 151)
New task (p 151)
Systems selling
    (or solutions selling) (p 151)
Buying center (p 152)

Objective 5
Product value analysis (p 154)
E-procurement (p 156)

DISCUSSION AND CRITICAL THINKING

Discussion Questions

1. Review the *black box* model of buyer behavior. Which buyer characteristics that affect buyer behavior influence you most when making a clothing purchase decision? Are these the same characteristics that would influence you when making a computer purchase? Explain. (AACSB: Communication; Reflective Thinking)

2. Discuss the stages of the consumer buyer decision process and describe how you or your family used this process to make a purchase. (AACSB: Communication; Reflective Thinking)

3. Describe the five adopter categories for new products. Which group best describes your purchase behavior with

respect to smartphones? (AACSB: Communication; Reflective Thinking)

4. How does the market structure and demand faced by business marketers differ from that faced by consumer marketers? (AACSB: Communication)

5. Name and briefly describe the stages of the business buying process. (AACSB: Communication)

6. Describe how electronic purchasing has changed the business-to-business marketing process and discuss the advantages and disadvantages of electronic purchasing. (AACSB: Communication)

Critical Thinking Exercises

1. Hemopure is a human blood substitute that still has not received Food and Drug Administration approval in the United States, but it has been used to treat surgical anemia in South Africa since 2001. The company has received FDA approval for a similar product, Oxyglobin, in the veterinary market. Visit opkbiotech.com to learn about Hemopure and explain how the product characteristics of relative advantage, compatibility, complexity, divisibility, and communicability will influence the rate of adoption of this product once FDA approval is attained. (AACSB: Communication; Reflective Thinking)

2. Marketers often target consumers before, during, or after a *trigger event*—an event in one's life that triggers change. For example, after having a child, new parents have an increased need for baby furniture, clothes, diapers, car seats,

and lots of other baby-related goods. Consumers who never paid attention to marketing efforts for certain products may now be focused on ones related to their life change. Discuss other trigger events that may provide opportunities to target the right buyer at the right time. (AACSB: Communication; Reflective Thinking)

3. Business buying occurs worldwide, so marketers need to be aware of cultural factors influencing business customers. In a small group, select a country and develop a multimedia presentation on proper business etiquette and manners, including appropriate appearance, behavior, and communication. Include a map showing the location of the country as well as a description of the country in terms of its demographics, culture, and economic history. (AACSB: Communication; Multicultural and Diversity; Use of IT)

MINICASES AND APPLICATIONS

Marketing Technology   Facebook Influences

Have you noticed that some of your Facebook friends like certain advertisements? Marketers know what Facebook users like and are using that knowledge to influence users' friends. *Social-context ads* are based on data collected on the likes and friends of Facebook users. When you click on an ad indicating you like it, you also give Facebook permission to share that "like" with all of your friends. Marketers like this feature because it appears as though you are endorsing the brand to your friends. The more you click on the "Like" button in ads, the greater the chance they will migrate onto your wall and become part of your conversations rather than stay on the perimeter of the page.

1. Which factors are marketers advertising on Facebook using to influence consumers? Would you be influenced by an ad if you saw that your friends liked it? (AACSB: Communication; Use of IT; Reflective Thinking)
2. How would you feel about Facebook using your name in these types of ads or advertising integrating itself in conversations with your friends? (AACSB: Communication; Reflective Thinking)

Marketing Ethics   "Vanity Sizing"

What does an "8" mean to you? Well, if you are a female, then it means a lot, especially if you really are a "12"—size, that is. Marketers know that, too, and the trend is for larger sizes to be labeled with smaller numbers. Sizing was standardized in the 1940s and 1950s when women started purchasing mass-produced clothing. But sizes fluctuated in the following decades and the Department of Commerce abandoned sizing standardization in 1983. Now, the size number can mean anything the marketer wants it to mean. Marketers know that a size-12 woman who finds out she can fit into an 8 will get a self-esteem boost and likely purchase more. This practice, known as *vanity sizing,* has the potential to pay off big for clothing manufacturers. With 34 percent of adults in the United States overweight and another 40 percent obese, that adds up to a sizable market potential. Plus-sized clothing designer Torrid caters to the full-sized woman with sizes ranging from 0–5, where a size 4 is actually a size 26. If a large number on the size label really bothers you, stick to the more expensive brands—they tend to be the ones using vanity sizing most.

1. Which factors are clothing marketers using to influence consumers? Ask five female and five male friends how much the size labeled on clothing influences their behavior. Write a brief report of your findings. (AACSB: Communication; Reflective Thinking)
2. Should manufacturers be allowed to pick whatever measurements they want and attach any size number they want to them? Should the government or business set standardized sizes? (AACSB: Communication; Ethical Reasoning)

Marketing by the Numbers   NAICS Code

The North American Industry Classification System (NAICS) code is very useful for marketers. It is a relatively new coding system that replaces the old product-based Standard Industrial Classification (SIC) system introduced in the 1930s. The NAICS system classifies businesses by production processes, better reflecting changes in the global economy, especially in the service and technology industries. It was developed jointly by the United States, Canada, and Mexico in 1997 in concert with the North American Free Trade Agreement (NAFTA), providing a common classification system for the three countries and better compatibility with the International Standard Industrial Classification (ISIC) system. This six-digit number (in some cases, seven or ten digits) is very useful for understanding business markets.

1. What do the six digits of the NAICS code represent? What industry is represented by the NAICS code 721110? What information can a marketer obtain using this code? (AACSB: Communication; Use of IT; Reflective Thinking)
2. Using the 721110 NAICS code, research and create a report highlighting the trends in this industry. Suggest markets that have the greatest potential. (AACSB: Communication; Use of IT; Reflective Thinking)

Video Case   Goodwill Industries

Since 1902, Goodwill Industries has funded job training and placement programs through its chain of thrift stores. Even though selling used clothing, furniture, and other items may not seem like big business, it amounts to more than $3 billion in annual sales for Goodwill. The company is changing people's perceptions of thrift stores as musty, low-class operations by focusing on concepts of consumer behavior. Like any good marketing company, Goodwill recognizes that not all customers are the same. This video demonstrates how Goodwill caters to different types of customers by recognizing the cultural, social, personal, and psychological factors that affect how customers make buying decisions. In this manner, Goodwill is maximizing customer value by offering the right mix of goods at unbeatable bargain prices.

After viewing the video featuring Goodwill, answer the following questions:

1. How would you describe the different types of Goodwill customers?
2. Which of the four sets of factors affecting consumer behavior do you believe most strongly affects consumers' purchase decisions from Goodwill?
3. How does Goodwill's recognition of consumer behavior principles affect its marketing mix?

Company Cases   1 Converse / 4 Meredith / 10 Porsche

See Appendix 1 for cases appropriate for this chapter. **Case 1, Converse: Shaping the Customer Experience.** Converse continues to provide customers with the authentic experience they desire by allowing them to shape that experience. **Case 4, Meredith: Thanks to Good Marketing Information, Meredith** *Knows* **Women.** Using its massive database and expertise in managing information, Meredith understands what drives the decisions women make. **Case 5, Porsche: Guarding the Old While Bringing in the New.** Over the years, Porsche learns that different factors affect the way customers make purchase decisions.

6 Customer-Driven Marketing Strategy
Creating Value for Target Customers

CHAPTER ROAD MAP

Objective Outline

▷ **OBJECTIVE 1** Define the major steps in designing a customer-driven marketing strategy: market segmentation, targeting, differentiation, and positioning. Customer-Driven Marketing Strategy (162–165)

▷ **OBJECTIVE 2** List and discuss the major bases for segmenting consumer and business markets. Market Segmentation (165–174)

▷ **OBJECTIVE 3** Explain how companies identify attractive market segments and choose a market-targeting strategy. Market Targeting (174–182)

▷ **OBJECTIVE 4** Discuss how companies differentiate and position their products for maximum competitive advantage. Differentiation and Positioning (182–189)

Previewing the Concepts

So far, you've learned what marketing is and about the importance of understanding consumers and the marketplace environment. With that as a background, you're now ready to delve deeper into marketing strategy and tactics. This chapter looks further into key customer-driven marketing strategy decisions—dividing up markets into meaningful customer groups (*segmentation*), choosing which customer groups to serve (*targeting*), creating market offerings that best serve targeted customers (*differentiation*), and positioning the offerings in the minds of consumers (*positioning*). The chapters that follow explore the tactical marketing tools—the four Ps—by which marketers bring these strategies to life.

To open our discussion of segmentation, targeting, differentiation, and positioning, let's look at Dunkin' Donuts. Dunkin' is rapidly expanding into a national powerhouse, on par with Starbucks. But Dunkin' is no Starbucks. In fact, it doesn't want to be. It targets a very different kind of customer with a very different value proposition. Grab yourself a cup of coffee and read on.

Dunkin' Donuts: Targeting the Average Joe

A few years ago, Dunkin' Donuts paid dozens of faithful customers in Phoenix, Chicago, and Charlotte, North Carolina, $100 a week to buy coffee at Starbucks instead. At the same time, the no-frills coffee chain paid Starbucks customers to make the opposite switch. When it later debriefed the two groups, Dunkin' says it found them so polarized that company researchers dubbed them "tribes," each of whom loathed the very things that made the other tribe loyal to their coffee shop. Dunkin' fans viewed Starbucks as pretentious and trendy, whereas Starbucks loyalists saw Dunkin' as plain and unoriginal. "I don't get it," one Dunkin' regular told researchers after visiting Starbucks. "If I want to sit on a couch, I stay at home."

Dunkin' Donuts is rapidly expanding into a national coffee powerhouse, on par with Starbucks, the nation's largest coffee chain. But the

▲ Starbucks is strongly positioned as a sort of high-brow "third place"; Dunkin' Donuts has a decidedly more low-brow, "everyman" kind of positioning. Dunkin's "not going after the Starbucks coffee snob," it's "going after the average Joe."

Bumper DeJesus/Star Ledger/Corbis

research confirmed a simple fact: Dunkin' is not Starbucks. In fact, it doesn't want to be. To succeed, Dunkin' must have its own clear vision of just which customers it wants to serve (what *segments* and *targeting* strategy) and how (what *positioning* or *value proposition*). Dunkin' and Starbucks target very different customers, who want very different things from their favorite coffee shops. Starbucks is strongly positioned as a sort of high-brow "third place"—outside the home and office—featuring couches, eclectic music, wireless Internet access, and art-splashed walls. Dunkin' has a decidedly more low-brow, "everyman" kind of positioning.

Dunkin' Donuts built itself on serving simple fare at a reasonable price to working-class customers. But recently, to broaden its appeal and fuel expansion, the chain has been moving upscale—a bit, but not too far. It's spiffing up its more than 6,700 stores in 36 states and adding new menu items, such as lattes and flatbread sandwiches. Dunkin' has made dozens of store-redesign decisions, big and small, ranging from where to put the espresso machines to how much of its signature pink and orange color scheme to retain and where to display its fresh baked goods.

However, as it inches upscale, Dunkin' Donuts is being careful not to alienate its traditional customer base. There are no couches in the remodeled stores. And Dunkin' renamed a new hot sandwich a "stuffed melt" after customers complained that calling it a "panini" was too fancy; it then dropped it altogether when faithful customers thought it was too messy. "We're walking [a fine] line," says the chain's vice president of consumer insights. "The thing about the Dunkin' tribe is, they see through the hype."

Dunkin' Donuts' research showed that, although loyal customers want nicer stores, they were bewildered and turned off by the atmosphere at Starbucks. They groused that crowds of laptop users made it difficult to find a seat. They didn't like Starbucks' "tall," "grande," and "venti" lingo for small, medium, and large coffees. And they couldn't understand why anyone would pay so much for a cup of coffee. "It was almost as though they were a group of Martians talking about a group of Earthlings," says an executive from Dunkin's ad agency. The Starbucks customers that Dunkin' paid to switch were equally uneasy in Dunkin' shops. "The Starbucks people couldn't bear that they weren't special anymore," says the ad executive.

> **Dunkin' Donuts** has a very clear vision of just which customers it wants to serve and how. It targets the "Dunkin' tribe"—everyday Joes who just don't get what Starbucks is all about.

Such opposing opinions aren't surprising, given the differences in the two stores' customers. Dunkin's customers include more middle-income blue- and white-collar workers across all age, race, and income demographics. By contrast, Starbucks targets a higher-income, more professional group. But Dunkin' researchers concluded that it was more the ideal, rather than income, that set the two tribes apart: Dunkin's tribe members want to be part of a crowd, whereas members of the Starbucks tribe want to stand out as individuals. "You could open a Dunkin' Donuts right next to Starbucks and get two completely different types of consumers," says one retailing expert.

Over the past several years, each targeting its own tribe of customers, both Dunkin' Donuts and Starbucks have grown rapidly, riding the wave of America's growing thirst for coffee. However, the recent recession highlighted differences in the positioning strategies of the two chains. Dunkin' Donuts found itself well-positioned for tougher economic times—Starbucks not so much so. Paying a premium price for the "Starbucks Experience" didn't sell as well in bad times as in good. When the economy drooped, many cash-strapped Starbucks customers cut back or switched to less-expensive brands. Although it has now recovered in an improving economy, after years of sizzling growth, Starbucks sales fell for the first time ever in 2009, down 6 percent for the year.

In contrast, Dunkin' Donuts' positioning seemed to resonate strongly with customers during hard times. Even as competition grew in the superheated coffee category, with everyone from McDonald's to 7-Eleven offering their own premium blends, Dunkin's sales continued to grow. While Starbucks was closing stores, Dunkin' was opening new ones at a rapid pace. And the company aggressively expanded menu options, adding everything from personal pizzas and flatbread sandwiches to smoothies and gourmet cookies.

In refreshing its positioning, Dunkin' Donuts has stayed true to the needs and preferences of the Dunkin' tribe. Dunkin' is "not going after the Starbucks coffee snob," says one analyst, it's "going after the average Joe." So far so good. For five years running, Dunkin' Donuts has ranked number one in the coffee category in a leading customer loyalty survey, ahead of number-two Starbucks. According to the survey, Dunkin' Donuts was the top brand for consistently meeting or exceeding customer expectations with respect to taste, quality, and customer service.

Dunkin' Donuts' positioning and value proposition are pretty well summed up in its popular ad slogan "America Runs on Dunkin'." The latest ads show "everyday Joes," actual customers picked as part of a nationwide casting call, responding to the simple question: "What are you drinkin'?" The answer: "I'm drinkin' Dunkin'." "This campaign celebrates real Dunkin' Donuts customers and their love affair with Dunkin' coffee," says an ad agency executive who helped create the campaign. "It is also an invitation to try Dunkin' Donuts coffee and join the tribe."[1]

MyMarketingLab

Visit www.mymktlab.com to find activities that help you learn and review in order to succeed in this chapter.

Market segmentation
Dividing a market into smaller segments of buyers with distinct needs, characteristics, or behaviors that might require separate marketing strategies or mixes.

Market targeting (targeting)
The process of evaluating each market segment's attractiveness and selecting one or more segments to enter.

Differentiation
Differentiating the market offering to create superior customer value.

Positioning
Arranging for a market offering to occupy a clear, distinctive, and desirable place relative to competing products in the minds of target consumers.

C ompanies today recognize that they cannot appeal to all buyers in the marketplace— or at least not to all buyers in the same way. Buyers are too numerous, widely scattered, and varied in their needs and buying practices. Moreover, companies themselves vary widely in their abilities to serve different market segments. Instead, like Dunkin' Donuts, companies must identify the parts of the market they can serve best and most profitably. They must design customer-driven marketing strategies that build the right relationships with the right customers.

Thus, most companies have moved away from mass marketing and toward *target marketing:* identifying market segments, selecting one or more of them, and developing products and marketing programs tailored to each. Instead of scattering their marketing efforts (the "shotgun" approach), firms are focusing on the buyers who have greater interest in the values they create best (the "rifle" approach).

▶ **Figure 6.1** shows the four major steps in designing a customer-driven marketing strategy. In the first two steps, the company selects the customers that it will serve. **Market segmentation** involves dividing a market into smaller segments of buyers with distinct needs, characteristics, or behaviors that might require separate marketing strategies or mixes. The company identifies different ways to segment the market and develops profiles of the resulting market segments. **Market targeting** (or **targeting**) consists of evaluating each market segment's attractiveness and selecting one or more market segments to enter.

In the final two steps, the company decides on a value proposition—how it will create value for target customers. **Differentiation** involves actually differentiating the firm's

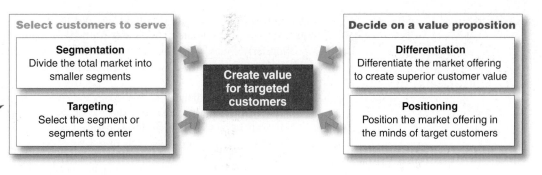

Figure 6.1 Designing a Customer-Driven Marketing Strategy

In concept, marketing boils down to two questions: (1) Which customers will we serve? and (2) How will we serve them? Of course, the tough part is coming up with good answers to these simple-sounding yet difficult questions. The goal is to create more value for the customers we serve than competitors do.

market offering to create superior customer value. **Positioning** consists of arranging for a market offering to occupy a clear, distinctive, and desirable place relative to competing products in the minds of target consumers. We discuss each of these steps in turn.

Market Segmentation

> **Author Comment**
> Market segmentation addresses the first simple-sounding marketing question: What customers will we serve?

Buyers in any market differ in their wants, resources, locations, buying attitudes, and buying practices. Through market segmentation, companies divide large, heterogeneous markets into smaller segments that can be reached more efficiently and effectively with products and services that match their unique needs. In this section, we discuss four important segmentation topics: segmenting consumer markets, segmenting business markets, segmenting international markets, and the requirements for effective segmentation.

Segmenting Consumer Markets

There is no single way to segment a market. A marketer has to try different segmentation variables, alone and in combination, to find the best way to view market structure. **Table 6.1** outlines variables that might be used in segmenting consumer markets. Here we look at the major *geographic*, *demographic*, *psychographic*, and *behavioral* variables.

Geographic Segmentation

> **Geographic segmentation**
> Dividing a market into different geographical units, such as nations, states, regions, counties, cities, or even neighborhoods.

Geographic segmentation calls for dividing the market into different geographical units, such as nations, regions, states, counties, cities, or even neighborhoods. A company may decide to operate in one or a few geographical areas or operate in all areas but pay attention to geographical differences in needs and wants.

Many companies today are localizing their products, advertising, promotion, and sales efforts to fit the needs of individual regions, cities, and neighborhoods. For example, Walmart operates virtually everywhere but has developed special formats tailored to specific types of geographic locations. In strongly Hispanic neighborhoods, Walmart operates Supermercado de Walmart stores, which feature signage, product assortments, and bilingual staff that are more relevant to local Hispanic customers. In markets where full-size

▶ **Table 6.1**	Major Segmentation Variables for Consumer Markets

Segmentation Variable	Examples
Geographic	Nations, regions, states, counties, cities, neighborhoods, population density (urban, suburban, rural), climate
Demographic	Age, life-cycle stage, gender, income, occupation, education, religion, ethnicity, generation
Psychographic	Social class, lifestyle, personality
Behavioral	Occasions, benefits, user status, usage rate, loyalty status

superstores are impractical, Walmart has opened smaller Walmart Market supermarkets and even smaller Walmart Express and Walmart on Campus stores.[2]

Similarly, Macy's, the nation's second-largest department-store chain, lets its 1,600 distant managers around the country customize merchandise in their local stores.[3]

> During the recent holiday season, Macy's shelves were chock-full of Elvis Christmas tree ornaments in the Memphis area, where local shoppers just can't get enough of the King. In Minneapolis, however, an electric *krumkake* baker—used to make those tasty cookies prized by locals of Scandinavian descent—was a hot seller. And in the chain's Brooklyn stores, the Isuma cookware popular in many Hispanic kitchens was displayed prominently. It's all part of the retailer's "My Macy's" strategy to tailor store merchandise to individual markets, making the giant retailer seem smaller and in touch with local shoppers.
>
> At stores around the country, Macy's sales clerks record local requests from shoppers in log books to pass on to the district managers, who then customize the mix of merchandise for their stores. Macy's also draws on data from 2.9 billion transactions to help tailor its wares to local tastes. So all year round, for example, stores in Michigan stock more locally made Sanders chocolate candies. In Orlando, shoppers are offered more twin bedding at stores near condominium rentals, and you'll find more swim suits available in stores near water parks. The chain stocks extra coffee percolators in its Long Island stores, where it sells more of the 1960s must-haves than anywhere else in the country.

Demographic Segmentation

Demographic segmentation

Dividing the market into segments based on variables such as age, life-cycle stage, gender, income, occupation, education, religion, ethnicity, and generation.

Demographic segmentation divides the market into segments based on variables such as age, life-cycle stage, gender, income, occupation, education, religion, ethnicity, and generation. Demographic factors are the most popular bases for segmenting customer groups. One reason is that consumer needs, wants, and usage rates often vary closely with demographic variables. Another is that demographic variables are easier to measure than most other types of variables. Even when marketers first define segments using other bases, such as benefits sought or behavior, they must know a segment's demographic characteristics to assess the size of the target market and reach it efficiently.

Age and life-cycle segmentation

Dividing a market into different age and life-cycle groups.

Age and Life-Cycle Stage. Consumer needs and wants change with age. Some companies use **age and life-cycle segmentation**, offering different products or using different marketing approaches for different age and life-cycle groups. For example, Kraft promotes JELL-O to children as a fun snack, one that "taught the world to wiggle." For adults, it's a tasty, guilt-free indulgence—"the most sweet-tooth satisfaction 10 calories can hold."

Other companies focus on the specific age of life-stage groups. ▶ For example, although consumers in all age segments love Disney cruises, most Disney Cruise Lines destinations and shipboard activities are designed with parents and their children in mind. On board, Disney provides trained counselors who help younger kids join in hands-on activities, teen-only spaces for older children, and family-time or individual-time options for parents and other adults. It's difficult to find a Disney Cruise Lines ad or Web page that doesn't feature a family full of smiling faces. In contrast, Viking River Cruises, the deluxe smaller-boat cruise line that offers tours along the world's great rivers, primarily targets older-adult couples and singles. You won't find a single child in a Viking ad or Web page.

Marketers must be careful to guard against stereotypes when using age and life-cycle segmentation. Although some 80-year-olds fit the doddering stereotypes, others ski and play tennis. Similarly, whereas some 40-year-old couples are sending their children off to college, others are just beginning new families. Thus, age is often a poor predictor of a person's life cycle, health, work or family status, needs, and buying power. Companies marketing to mature consumers usually employ positive images and appeals. For example, a recent Jeep ad in *AARP* magazine features a mature consumer who's nowhere near "elderly," at least in her own view. "I know you're only as old as you feel, and I *still* feel 30. I can text, but I prefer to

▲ **Life-cycle segmentation: Disney Cruise Lines targets primarily families with children, large and small. Most of its destinations and shipboard activities are designed with parents and their children in mind.**

AP Images/PRNewsFoto/Disney Cruise Line

talk. I'll do a bake sale and hit a few trails, too. The grandkids say I'm 'really cool now,' but what they don't know is, I always was." The ad concludes: "I live. I ride. I m. Jeep."

Gender segmentation
Dividing a market into different segments based on gender.

Gender. **Gender segmentation** has long been used in clothing, cosmetics, toiletries, and magazines. For example, P&G was among the first to use gender segmentation with Secret, a brand specially formulated for a woman's chemistry, packaged and advertised to reinforce the female image. More recently, the men's cosmetics industry has exploded, and many cosmetics makers that previously catered primarily to women now successfully market men's lines. Just don't call them "cosmetics."[4]

> L'Oréal's Men's Expert line includes a host of products with decidedly unmanly names such as Men's Expert Vita Lift SPF 15 Anti-Wrinkle & Firming Moisturizer and Men's Expert Hydra-Energetic Ice Cold Eye Roller (for diminishing under-eye dark circles). Other brands, however, try to craft more masculine positions. For example, Menaji promises "Skincare for the Confident Man." Manly men such as Tim McGraw and Kid Rock use it. Menaji products come in discreet packaging such as old cigar boxes, and the line's "undetectable" foundation and concealer (or rather "Camo") come in easy-to-apply Chap Stick-style containers. Menaji founder Michele Probst doesn't call any of it makeup. "The M word is cancer to us," she says. "We are skin care that looks good." Whatever you call it, Menaji sales have grown 70 percent in each of the past 3 years.

An underdeveloped gender segment can offer new opportunities in markets ranging from consumer electronics to motorcycles. For example, Harley-Davidson has traditionally targeted men between 35 and 55 years old, but women are now among its fastest growing customer segments. Female buyers now account for 12 percent of new Harley-Davidson purchases, up from only 2 percent in 1995. ▶ In response, the company is boosting its appeal to women buyers. It recently introduced the SuperLow, a lower-to-the-ground, lighter model geared toward women. And it hired Victoria's Secret and *Sports Illustrated* swimsuit edition model Marisa Miller as a spokesperson. Her riding exploits can be seen in videos at the Harley-Davidson Web site and on YouTube. "It says, look, this is real stuff," says Harley-Davidson CEO Keith Wandell. "A lot of women ride bikes, and here's a Victoria's Secret supermodel riding bikes and doing burnouts."[5]

▲ **Harley-Davidson has boosted its efforts to move women from the back of the bike onto the driver's seat.**
AFP/Getty Images

Income. The marketers of products and services such as automobiles, clothing, cosmetics, financial services, and travel have long used **income segmentation**. Many companies target affluent consumers with luxury goods and convenience services. Other marketers use high-touch marketing programs to court the well-to-do:[6]

Income segmentation
Dividing a market into different income segments.

> Seadream Yacht Club, a small-ship luxury cruise line, calls select guests after every cruise and offers to have the CEO fly out to their home and host, at Seadream's expense, a brunch or reception for a dozen of the couple's best friends. The cruisers tell the story of their cruise. Seadream offers a great rate to their guests and sells several cruises at $1,000 per person per night to the friends (and even friends of friends). Such highly personal marketing creates a community of "brand evangelists" who tell the story to prospective affluent buyers and friends—precisely the right target group. This has been so successful for Seadream that it has abandoned most traditional advertising.

However, not all companies that use income segmentation target the affluent. For example, many retailers—such as the Dollar General, Family Dollar, and Dollar Tree store chains—successfully target low- and middle-income groups. The core market for such stores is represented by families with incomes under $30,000. When Family Dollar real-estate experts scout locations for new stores, they look for lower-middle-class neighborhoods where people wear less-expensive shoes and drive old cars that drip a lot of oil. With their low-income strategies, dollar stores are now the fastest-growing retailers in the nation.

Psychographic Segmentation

Psychographic segmentation
Dividing a market into different segments based on social class, lifestyle, or personality characteristics.

Psychographic segmentation divides buyers into different segments based on social class, lifestyle, or personality characteristics. People in the same demographic group can have very different psychographic characteristics.

In Chapter 5, we discussed how the products people buy reflect their *lifestyles*. As a result, marketers often segment their markets by consumer lifestyles and base their marketing strategies on lifestyle appeals. For example, retailer Anthropologie, with its whimsical, French flea market store atmosphere, sells a Bohemian-chic lifestyle to which its young women customers aspire. And although car-sharing nicher Zipcar rents cars by the hour or the day, it doesn't see itself as a car-rental company. Instead, it sees itself as enhancing its customers' urban lifestyles and targets accordingly. "It's not about cars," says Zipcar's CEO, "it's about urban life." (See Marketing at Work 6.1.)

MARKETING AT WORK | 6.1

Zipcar: "It's Not About Cars—It's About Urban Life"

Imagine a world in which no one owns a car. Cars would still exist, but rather than owning cars, people would just share them. Sounds crazy, right? But Scott Griffith, CEO of Zipcar, the world's largest car-share company, paints a picture of just such an imaginary world. And he has 530,000 passionate customers—or *Zipsters*, as they are called—who will back him up.

Zipcar specializes in renting out cars by the hour or day. The service isn't for everyone—it doesn't try to be. Instead, it zeros in on narrowly defined lifestyle segments, people who live or work in densely populated neighborhoods in New York City, Boston, Atlanta, San Francisco, London, or one of the more than 50 cities in which Zipcar operates (or on more than 225 college campuses across North America). For these customers, owning a car (or a second or third car) is difficult, costly, and environmentally irresponsible. Interestingly, Zipcar doesn't see itself as a car-rental company. Instead, it's selling a lifestyle. "It's not about cars," says CEO Griffith, "it's about urban life. We're creating a lifestyle brand that happens to have a lot of cars."

Initially, Zipcar targeted mostly trendy, young, well-educated, environmentally conscious urbanites. Gradually, however, the Zipster profile is broadening, becoming more mature and mainstream. Still, Zipsters share a number of common urban lifestyle traits. For starters, the lifestyle is rooted in environmental consciousness. At first, Zipcar focused on green-minded customers with promotional pitches such as "We ♥ Earth" and "Imagine a world with a million fewer cars on the road." Zipcar's vibrant green logo reflects this save-the-Earth philosophy. And Zipcar really does deliver on its environmental promises. Studies show that every shared Zipcar takes up to

20 cars off the road and cuts carbon emissions by up to 50 percent per user. On average, Zipsters travel 44 percent fewer miles than when they owned a car.

But if Zipcar was going to grow, it needed to move beyond just being green. So it has broadened its appeals to include other urban lifestyle benefits. One of those benefits is convenience. Owning a car in a densely populated urban area can be a real hassle. Zipcar lets customers focus on driving, not on the complexities of car ownership. It gives them "Wheels when you want them," in four easy steps: "Join. Reserve. Unlock. Drive."

To join, you pay around $60 for an annual membership and receive your personal Zipcard, which unlocks any of the thousands of cars located in urban areas around the world. Then, when you need a car, reserve one—minutes or months in advance—online, by phone, or using a smartphone app. You can choose the car you want, when and where you want it, and drive it for as little as $7 an hour, including gas, insurance, and free miles. When you're ready, walk to the car, hold your Zipcard to the windshield to unlock the doors, and you're good to go. When you're done, you drop the car off at the same parking spot—Zipcar worries about the maintenance and cleaning.

Zipcar not only eliminates the hassle of urban car ownership, it also saves money. By living with less, the average Zipster saves $600 a month on car payments, insurance, gas, maintenance, and other car ownership expenses.

Zipcar's operating system is carefully aligned with its tight urban lifestyle targeting. For starters, Zipcar "pods" (a dozen or so vehicles located in a given neighborhood) are stocked with over 50 different models that trendy urbanites love.

The vehicles are both hip and fuel efficient: Toyota Priuses, Honda CRVs, MINIs, Volvo S60s, BMW 328s, Toyota Tacomas, Toyota Siennas, Subaru Outbacks, and others. And Zipcar is now testing plug-in hybrids and full electric vehicles. Each car has its own personality—a name and profile created by a Zipster. For example, Prius Ping "jogs in the morning; doesn't say much," whereas Civic Carlos "teaches yoga; loves to kayak." Such personal touches make it feel like you're borrowing the car from a friend, rather than being assigned whatever piece of metal happens to be available.

Zipcar's promotion tactics also focus tightly on its narrowly defined urban segments. The company targets urbanites within a 10-minute walk of its car pods—no easy task. "Even with today's highly targeted Web, it's hard to target at that hyper-local level," says Griffith. "So our street teams do it block by block, zip code by zip code." Thus, in addition to local Web ads and transit advertising, Zipcar reps are beating the streets in true guerilla fashion.

For example, in San Francisco, passersby got to swing a sledgehammer at an SUV, while on Harvard's campus, students tried to guess how many frozen IKEA meatballs were stuffed inside a MINI. In Washington, DC, Zipcar street teams planted a couch on a busy sidewalk with the sign "You need a Zipcar to move this." And the company has launched several local "Low-Car Diet" events, in which it asks urban residents to give up their cars and blog about it. Zipcar gave a free bike to a lucky dieter in each of the 69 Zipcar cities. Surveyed dieters reported saving 67 percent on vehicle costs compared to operating their own cars. Nearly half of them also said that they lost weight.

As Zipcar has taken off, it has expanded its targeting to include a different type of urban dweller—businesses and other organizations. Companies such as Google now encourage employees to be environmentally conscious by commuting via a company shuttle and then using Zipcars for both business and personal use during the day. Other companies are using Zipcar as an alternative to black sedans, long taxi rides, and congested parking lots. Government agencies are getting into the game as well. The city of Chicago recently partnered with Zipcar to provide a more efficient and sustainable transportation alternative for city agencies. And Washington, DC, now saves more than $1 million a year using Zipcar. Fleet manager Ralph Burns says that he has departments lining up. "Agencies putting their budgets together for next year are calling me up and saying, 'Ralph, I've got 25 cars I want to get rid of!'"

Zipcar's lifestyle targeting fosters a tight-knit sense of customer community. Zipsters are as fanatically loyal as the hardcore fans of Harley-Davidson or Apple, brands that have been nurturing customer relationships for decades. Loyal Zipsters serve as neighborhood brand ambassadors; 30 percent of new members join up at the recommendation of existing customers. "When I meet another Zipcar member at a party or something, I feel like we have something in common," says one Brooklyn Zipster. "It's like we're both making intelligent choices about our lives."

How is Zipcar's urban lifestyle targeting working? By all accounts, the young car-sharing nicher has the pedal to the metal and its tires are smoking. In just the past six years, Zipcar's annual revenues have rocketed 65-fold, from $2 million to more than $130 million, and it's looking to hit $1 billion in revenues within the next few years.

Zipcar's rapid growth has sounded alarms at the traditional car-rental giants. Enterprise, Hertz, Avis, Thrifty, and even U-Haul now have their own car-sharing operations. But Zipcar has a 10-year head start, cozy relationships in targeted neighborhoods, and an urban hipster cred that corporate giants like Hertz will have trouble matching. To Zipsters, Hertz rents cars, but Zipcar is part of their hectic urban lives.

Sources: "Zipcar Expands Its University Network with the Launch of Eight New Campuses This Winter," February 8, 2011, accessed at http://zipcar.mediaroom.com/index.php?s=43&item=214; Patel, "Zipcar: An America's Hottest Brands Case Study," *Advertising Age*, November 16, 2009, p. 16; Paul Keegan, "Zipcar: The Best New Idea in Business," *Fortune*, August 27, 2009, accessed at www.fortune.com; Elizabeth Olson, "Car Sharing Reinvents the Company Wheels," *New York Times*, May 7, 2009, p. F2; Stephanie Clifford, "How Fast Can This Thing Go, Anyway?" *Inc*, March 2008, accessed at www.inc.com; "Zipcar Partners with City of Chicago to Provide Integrated Car and Featuring Services for Smarter, Streamlined Transportation Alternatives," March 3, 2011, accessed at http://zipcar.mediaroom.com/index.php?s=43&item=216 and www.zipcar.com, accessed November 2011.

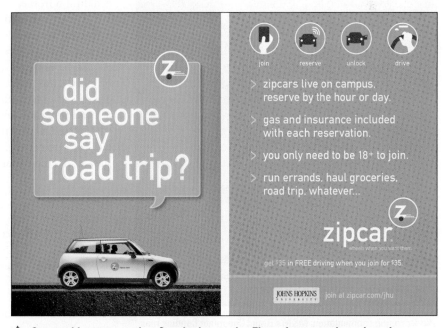

▲ **Geographic segmentation:** Car-sharing service Zipcar focuses only on densely populated metropolitan areas and congested college campuses, positioning itself as a low-cost, low-hassle alternative to owning or driving your own car.
Zipcar, Inc.

VF Corporation offers a closet full of more than 30 premium lifestyle brands which "fit the lives of consumers the world over, from commuters to cowboys, surfers to soccer moms, sports fans to rock bands."[7]

VF is the nation's number-one jeans maker, with brands such as Lee, Riders, Rustler, and Wrangler. But jeans are not the only focus for VF. The company's brands are carefully separated into five major lifestyle segments—Jeans-wear, Imagewear (workwear), Outdoor, Sportswear, and Contemporary Brands. The North Face, part of the Outdoor unit, offers top-of-the-line gear and apparel for diehard outdoor enthusiasts, especially those who prefer cold weather activities. From the Sportswear unit, Nautica focuses on people who enjoy high-end casual apparel inspired by sailing and the sea. Vans began as a skate shoemaker, and Reef features surf-inspired footwear and apparel. In the Contemporary Brands unit, Lucy features upscale active-wear, whereas 7 for All Mankind supplies premium denim and accessories sold in boutiques and high-end department stores such as Saks and Nordstrom. At the other end of the spectrum, Sentinel, part of the Imagewear unit, markets uniforms for security officers. No matter who you are, says the company, "We fit your life."

Marketers also use *personality* variables to segment markets. For example, different soft drinks target different personalities. On the one hand, Mountain Dew projects a youthful, rebellious, adventurous, go-your-own-way personality. Its ads remind customers that "It's different on the Mountain." By contrast, Coca-Cola Zero appears to target more mature, practical, and cerebral but good-humored personality types. Its subtly humorous ads promise "Real Coca-Cola taste and zero calories."

Behavioral Segmentation

Behavioral segmentation divides buyers into segments based on their knowledge, attitudes, uses, or responses to a product. Many marketers believe that behavior variables are the best starting point for building market segments.

Behavioral segmentation
Dividing a market into segments based on consumer knowledge, attitudes, uses, or responses to a product.

Occasion segmentation
Dividing the market into segments according to occasions when buyers get the idea to buy, actually make their purchase, or use the purchased item.

Benefit segmentation
Dividing the market into segments according to the different benefits that consumers seek from the product.

Occasions. Buyers can be grouped according to occasions when they get the idea to buy, actually make their purchase, or use the purchased item. **Occasion segmentation** can help firms build up product usage. For example, most consumers drink orange juice in the morning, but orange growers have promoted drinking orange juice as a cool, healthful refresher at other times of the day. By contrast, Chick-fil-A's "Chikin 4 Brekfust" campaign attempts to increase business by promoting its biscuits and other sandwiches as a great way to start the day.

Some holidays, such as Mother's Day and Father's Day, were originally promoted partly to increase the sales of candy, flowers, cards, and other gifts. And many marketers prepare special offers and ads for holiday occasions. ▶ For example, M&M's Brand Chocolate Candies runs ads throughout the year but prepares special ads and packaging for holidays and events such as Christmas, Easter, and the Super Bowl.

Benefits Sought. A powerful form of segmentation is grouping buyers according to the different *benefits* that they seek from a product. **Benefit segmentation** requires finding the major benefits people look for in a product class, the kinds of people who look for each benefit, and the major brands that deliver each benefit.

For example, Gillette research revealed four distinct benefit segments of women shavers—perfect shave seekers (seeking a close shave with no missed hairs), EZ seekers (fast and convenient shaves), skin pamperers (easy on the skin), and pragmatic functionalists (basic shaves at an affordable price). So Gillette designed a Venus razor for each segment. The Venus Embrace targets perfect

Arriving in time to fill your basket.

Pick up a bag this Easter.

▲ **Occasion segmentation: M&M's Brand Chocolate Candies runs special ads and packaging for holidays and events such as Easter.**

M&M'S is a registered trademark of Mars, Incorporated and its affiliates. This trademark is used with permission. Mars, Incorporated is not associated with Pearson. Advertisment printed with permission of Mars, Incorporated.

shave seekers with five curve-hugging, spring-mounted blades that "hug every curve to get virtually every hair." By contrast, the Venus Breeze is made for EZ seekers—its built-in shave gel bars lather and shave in one step, so there's no need for separate shave gel. The Venus Divine gives skin pamperers "intensive moisture strips for divinely smooth skin." And the Simply Venus, a three-bladed disposable razor, provides pragmatic functionalists with "a close shave at an affordable price."[8]

User Status. Markets can be segmented into nonusers, ex-users, potential users, first-time users, and regular users of a product. Marketers want to reinforce and retain regular users, attract targeted nonusers, and reinvigorate relationships with ex-users. Included in the potential user group are consumers facing life-stage changes—such as new parents and newlyweds—who can be turned into heavy users. For example, to get new parents off to the right start, P&G makes certain its Pampers Swaddlers are the diaper provided for newborns at most U.S. hospitals. And to capture newly engaged couples who will soon be equipping their new kitchens, upscale kitchen and cookware retailer Williams-Sonoma takes the usual bridal registry a step further. Through a program called "The Store Is Yours," it opens its stores after hours, by appointment, exclusively for individual couples to visit and make their wish lists. About half the people who register are new to the Williams-Sonoma brand.

Usage Rate. Markets can also be segmented into light, medium, and heavy product users. Heavy users are often a small percentage of the market but account for a high percentage of total consumption. For instance, a recent study showed that heavy seafood consumers in the United States are a small but hungry bunch. Less than 5 percent of all shoppers buy nearly 64 percent of unbreaded seafood consumed in the United States. Only 2.6 percent of shoppers—mostly mothers buying breaded fish sticks and filets for their families—account for more than 54 percent of breaded seafood sales. Not surprisingly, breaded seafood marketers such as Gortons and Van de Kamps target these heavy users with marketing pitches emphasizing kid appeal, family nutrition, and family meal planning tips and recipes.[9]

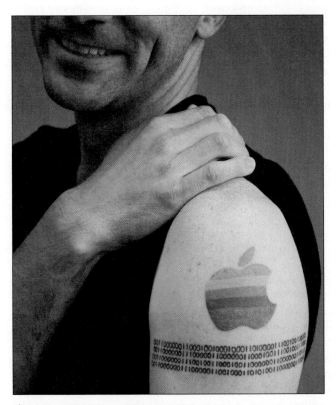

▲ Consumer loyalty: "Mac Fanatics"—fanatically loyal Apple users—helped keep Apple afloat during the lean years, and they are now at the forefront of Apple's burgeoning iPod, iPhone, and iTunes empire.

Doug Hardman

Loyalty Status. A market can also be segmented by consumer loyalty. Consumers can be loyal to brands (Tide), stores (Target), and companies (Apple). Buyers can be divided into groups according to their degree of loyalty.

Some consumers are completely loyal—they buy one brand all the time and can't wait to tell others about it. ▶ For example, as we discussed in the previous chapter, Apple has an almost cult-like following of loyal users. Other consumers are somewhat loyal—they are loyal to two or three brands of a given product or favor one brand while sometimes buying others. Still other buyers show no loyalty to any brand—they either want something different each time they buy, or they buy whatever's on sale.

A company can learn a lot by analyzing loyalty patterns in its market. It should start by studying its own loyal customers. A recent study of highly loyal customers showed that "their passion is contagious," says an analyst. "They promote the brand via blogs, fan Web sites, YouTube videos, and word of mouth." Many companies target diehard fans with special products, appeals, and events. Other companies actually put loyalists to work for the brand. For example, Adidas recently invited devoted fans to spray graffiti on warehouse walls and then used the designs to decorate its shoes. Patagonia relies on its most tried-and-true customers to test products in harsh environments.[10]

In contrast, by studying its less-loyal buyers, the company can detect which brands are most competitive with its own. By looking at customers who are shifting away from its brand, the company can learn about its marketing weaknesses and take actions to correct them.

Using Multiple Segmentation Bases

Marketers rarely limit their segmentation analysis to only one or a few variables. Rather, they often use multiple segmentation bases in an effort to identify smaller, better-defined target groups. Several business information services—such as Nielsen, Acxiom, and Experian—provide multivariable segmentation systems that merge geographic, demographic, lifestyle, and behavioral data to help companies segment their markets down to zip codes, neighborhoods, and even households.

One of the leading segmentation systems is the Nielsen PRIZM system operated by The Nielsen Company. PRIZM classifies every American household based on a host of demographic factors—such as age, educational level, income, occupation, family composition, ethnicity, and housing—and behavioral and lifestyle factors—such as purchases, free-time activities, and media preferences. PRIZM classifies U.S. households into 66 demographically and behaviorally distinct segments, organized into 14 different social groups. PRIZM segments carry such exotic names as "Kids & Cul-de-Sacs," "Gray Power," "Mayberry-ville," "Shotguns & Pickups," "Old Glories," "Multi-Culti Mosaic," "Big City Blues," and "Brite Lites L'il City." The colorful names help to bring the segments to life.[11]

PRIZM and other such systems can help marketers segment people and locations into marketable groups of like-minded consumers. Each segment has its own pattern of likes, dislikes, lifestyles, and purchase behaviors. For example, *Winner's Circle* neighborhoods, part of the Elite Suburbs social group, are suburban areas populated by well-off couples, between the ages of 35 and 54, with large families in new-money neighborhoods. People in this segment are more likely to own a Mercedes GL Class, go jogging, shop at Neiman Marcus, and read the *Wall Street Journal*. In contrast, the *Bedrock America* segment, part of the Rustic Living social group, is populated by young, economically challenged families in small, isolated towns located throughout the nation's heartland. People in this segment are more likely to order from Avon, buy toy cars, and read *Parents Magazine*.

Such segmentation provides a powerful tool for marketers of all kinds. It can help companies identify and better understand key customer segments, reach them more efficiently, and tailor market offerings and messages to their specific needs.

▲ Using Nielsen's PRIZM system, marketers can paint a surprisingly precise picture of who you are, what you watch, and what you might buy. PRIZM segments carry such exotic names as "Brite Lites L'il City," "Kids & Cul-de-Sacs," "Gray Power," and "Big City Blues."

The Nielsen Company

Segmenting Business Markets

Consumer and business marketers use many of the same variables to segment their markets. Business buyers can be segmented geographically, demographically (industry, company size), or by benefits sought, user status, usage rate, and loyalty status. Yet, business marketers also use some additional variables, such as customer *operating characteristics*, *purchasing approaches*, *situational factors*, and *personal characteristics*.

Almost every company serves at least some business markets. For example, American Express targets businesses in three segments: merchants, corporations, and small businesses. It has developed distinct marketing programs for each segment. In the merchants segment, American Express focuses on convincing new merchants to accept the card and managing relationships with those that already do. For larger corporate customers, the company offers a corporate card program, which includes extensive employee expense and travel management services. Finally, for small business customers, American Express has created OPEN: The Small Business Network, a system of small business cards and financial services. It includes credit cards and lines of credit, special usage rewards, financial monitoring and spending report features, and 24/7 customized financial support services.[12]

Many companies establish separate systems for dealing with larger or multiple-location customers. For example, Steelcase, a major producer of office furniture, first divides customers into seven segments: biosciences, higher education, U.S. and Canadian governments, state and local governments, health care, professional services, and retail banking. Next, company salespeople work with independent Steelcase dealers to handle smaller, local, or regional Steelcase customers in each segment. But many national, multiple-location customers, such as ExxonMobil or IBM, have special needs that may reach beyond the scope of individual dealers. Therefore, Steelcase uses national account managers to help its dealer networks handle national accounts.

Segmenting International Markets

Few companies have either the resources or the will to operate in all, or even most, of the countries that dot the globe. Although some large companies, such as Coca-Cola or Sony, sell products in more than 200 countries, most international firms focus on a smaller set. Operating in many countries presents new challenges. Different countries, even those that are close together, can vary greatly in their economic, cultural, and political makeup. Thus, just as they do within their domestic markets, international firms need to group their world markets into segments with distinct buying needs and behaviors.

Companies can segment international markets using one or a combination of several variables. They can segment by *geographic location*, grouping countries by regions such as Western Europe, the Pacific Rim, the Middle East, or Africa. Geographic segmentation assumes that nations close to one another will have many common traits and behaviors. Although this is often the case, there are many exceptions. For example, some U.S. marketers lump all Central and South American countries together. However, the Dominican Republic is no more like Brazil than Italy is like Sweden. Many Central and South Americans don't even speak Spanish, including 200 million Portuguese-speaking Brazilians and the millions in other countries who speak a variety of Indian dialects.

Intermarket (or cross-market) segmentation
Forming segments of consumers who have similar needs and buying behaviors even though they are located in different countries.

World markets can also be segmented on the basis of *economic factors*. Countries might be grouped by population income levels or by their overall level of economic development. A country's economic structure shapes its population's product and service needs and, therefore, the marketing opportunities it offers. For example, many companies are now targeting the BRIC countries—Brazil, Russia, India, and China—which are fast-growing developing economies with rapidly increasing buying power.

Countries can also be segmented by *political and legal factors* such as the type and stability of government, receptivity to foreign firms, monetary regulations, and amount of bureaucracy. *Cultural factors* can also be used, grouping markets according to common languages, religions, values and attitudes, customs, and behavioral patterns.

Segmenting international markets based on geographic, economic, political, cultural, and other factors presumes that segments should consist of clusters of countries. However, as new communications technologies, such as satellite TV and the Internet, connect consumers around the world, marketers can define and reach segments of like-minded consumers no matter where in the world they are. Using **intermarket segmentation** (also called **cross-market segmentation**), they form segments of consumers who have similar needs and buying behaviors even though they are located in different countries.

For example, Lexus targets the world's well-to-do—the "global elite" segment—regardless of their country. Retailer H&M targets fashion-conscious but frugal shoppers in 35 countries with its low-priced, trendy apparel and accessories. ▶ And Coca-Cola creates special programs to target

▲ **Intermarket segmentation: Coca-Cola targets the world's teens no matter where they live, with campaigns such as Coca-Cola Music, which ran in more than 100 markets worldwide.**

age fotostock/SuperStock

teens, core consumers of its soft drinks the world over. By 2020, one-third of the world's population—some 2.5 billion people—will be under 18 years of age. To reach this important global segment, Coca-Cola recently launched the Coca-Cola Music campaign in more than 100 markets. The campaign opened with "24hr Session," in which singing group Maroon 5 holed up in a London studio for 24 hours to create a new original song. Young consumers worldwide attended the studio session virtually, sharing their ideas for lyrics and rhythms. Says Coca-Cola's CEO: "Our success . . . today depends on our ability to grow and connect with teens, the generation of tomorrow."[13]

Requirements for Effective Segmentation

Clearly, there are many ways to segment a market, but not all segmentations are effective. For example, buyers of table salt could be divided into blonde and brunette customers. But hair color obviously does not affect the purchase of salt. Furthermore, if all salt buyers bought the same amount of salt each month, believed that all salt is the same, and wanted to pay the same price, the company would not benefit from segmenting this market.

To be useful, market segments must be

- *Measurable.* The size, purchasing power, and profiles of the segments can be measured.
- *Accessible.* The market segments can be effectively reached and served.
- *Substantial.* The market segments are large or profitable enough to serve. A segment should be the largest possible homogeneous group worth pursuing with a tailored marketing program. It would not pay, for example, for an automobile manufacturer to develop cars especially for people whose height is greater than seven feet.
- *Differentiable.* The segments are conceptually distinguishable and respond differently to different marketing mix elements and programs. If men and women respond similarly to marketing efforts for soft drinks, they do not constitute separate segments.
- *Actionable.* Effective programs can be designed for attracting and serving the segments. For example, although one small airline identified seven market segments, its staff was too small to develop separate marketing programs for each segment.

SPEED BUMP | LINKING THE CONCEPTS

Slow down a bit and enjoy the view. How do the companies you do business with employ the segmentation concepts you're reading about here?

- Can you identify specific companies, other than the examples already mentioned, that practice the different types of segmentation just discussed?
- Using the segmentation bases you've just read about, segment the U.S. footwear market. Describe each of the major segments and subsegments. Keep these segments in mind as you read the next section on market targeting.

Author Comment ▶
After dividing the market into segments, it's time to answer that first seemingly simple marketing strategy question we raised in Figure 6.1: Which customers will the company serve?

Market Targeting

Market segmentation reveals the firm's market segment opportunities. The firm now has to evaluate the various segments and decide how many and which segments it can serve best. We now look at how companies evaluate and select target segments.

Evaluating Market Segments

In evaluating different market segments, a firm must look at three factors: segment size and growth, segment structural attractiveness, and company objectives and resources. First, a company wants to select segments that have the right size and growth characteristics.

But "right size and growth" is a relative matter. The largest, fastest-growing segments are not always the most attractive ones for every company. Smaller companies may lack the skills and resources needed to serve larger segments. Or they may find these segments too competitive. Such companies may target segments that are smaller and less attractive, in an absolute sense, but that are potentially more profitable for them.

The company also needs to examine major structural factors that affect long-run segment attractiveness.[14] For example, a segment is less attractive if it already contains many strong and aggressive *competitors* or if it is easy for *new entrants* to come into the segment. The existence of many actual or potential *substitute products* may limit prices and the profits that can be earned in a segment. The relative *power of buyers* also affects segment attractiveness. Buyers with strong bargaining power relative to sellers will try to force prices down, demand more services, and set competitors against one another—all at the expense of seller profitability. Finally, a segment may be less attractive if it contains *powerful suppliers* who can control prices or reduce the quality or quantity of ordered goods and services.

Even if a segment has the right size and growth and is structurally attractive, the company must consider its own objectives and resources. Some attractive segments can be dismissed quickly because they do not mesh with the company's long-run objectives. Or the company may lack the skills and resources needed to succeed in an attractive segment. For example, the economy segment of the automobile market is large and growing. But given its objectives and resources, it would make little sense for luxury-performance carmaker BMW to enter this segment. A company should only enter segments in which it can create superior customer value and gain advantages over its competitors.

Selecting Target Market Segments

After evaluating different segments, the company must decide which and how many segments it will target. A **target market** consists of a set of buyers who share common needs or characteristics that the company decides to serve. Market targeting can be carried out at several different levels. ▶ **Figure 6.2** shows that companies can target very broadly (*undifferentiated marketing*), very narrowly (*micromarketing*), or somewhere in between (*differentiated or concentrated marketing*).

Undifferentiated Marketing

Using an **undifferentiated marketing** (or **mass marketing**) strategy, a firm might decide to ignore market segment differences and target the whole market with one offer. Such a strategy focuses on what is *common* in the needs of consumers rather than on what is *different*. The company designs a product and a marketing program that will appeal to the largest number of buyers.

As noted earlier in the chapter, most modern marketers have strong doubts about this strategy. Difficulties arise in developing a product or brand that will satisfy all consumers. Moreover, mass marketers often have trouble competing with more-focused firms that do a better job of satisfying the needs of specific segments and niches.

Differentiated Marketing

Using a **differentiated marketing** (or **segmented marketing**) strategy, a firm decides to target several market segments and designs separate offers for each. Toyota Corporation produces several different brands of cars—from Scion to Toyota to Lexus—each targeting

---

Target market
A set of buyers sharing common needs or characteristics that the company decides to serve.

Undifferentiated (mass) marketing
A market-coverage strategy in which a firm decides to ignore market segment differences and go after the whole market with one offer.

Differentiated (segmented) marketing
A market-coverage strategy in which a firm decides to target several market segments and designs separate offers for each.

▶ **Figure 6.2** Market Targeting Strategies

This figure covers a broad range of targeting strategies, from mass marketing (virtually no targeting) to individual marketing (customizing products and programs to individual customers). An example of individual marketing: At mymms.com you can order a batch of M&M's with your face and personal message printed on each little candy.

| Undifferentiated (mass) marketing | Differentiated (segmented) marketing | Concentrated (niche) marketing | Micromarketing (local or individual marketing) |

Targeting broadly → **Targeting narrowly**

▲ **Differentiated marketing: In addition to its broad Hallmark card line, Hallmark has introduced lines targeting a dozen or more specific segments, including its Mahogany, Tree of Life, and Sinceramente Hallmark lines above.**

its own segments of car buyers. And P&G markets six different laundry detergent brands in the United States, which compete with each other on supermarket shelves. Perhaps no brand practices differentiated marketing like Hallmark Cards.[15]

Hallmark vigorously segments the greeting card market. ▶ In addition to its broad Hallmark card line and popular sub-branded lines such as the humorous Shoebox Greetings, Hallmark has introduced lines targeting a dozen or more specific segments. Fresh Ink targets 18- to 39-year-old women. Hallmark Warm Wishes offers hundreds of affordable 99-cent cards. Hallmark's three ethnic lines—Mahogany, Sinceramente Hallmark, and Tree of Life—target African-American, Hispanic, and Jewish consumers, respectively. Hallmark's newer Journeys line of encouragement cards focuses on such challenges as fighting cancer, coming out, and battling depression. Specific greeting cards also benefit charities such as (PRODUCT) RED, UNICEF, and the Susan G. Komen Race for the Cure. Hallmark has also embraced technology. Musical greeting cards incorporate sound clips from popular movies, TV shows, and songs. Online, Hallmark offers e-cards as well as personalized printed greeting cards that it mails for consumers. For business needs, Hallmark Business Expressions offers personalized corporate holiday cards and greeting cards for all occasions and events.

By offering product and marketing variations to segments, companies hope for higher sales and a stronger position within each market segment. Developing a stronger position within several segments creates more total sales than undifferentiated marketing across all segments. Thanks to its differentiated approach, Hallmark's brands account for almost one of every two greeting cards purchased in the United States. Similarly, P&G's multiple detergent brands capture four times the market share of its nearest rival.

But differentiated marketing also increases the costs of doing business. A firm usually finds it more expensive to develop and produce, say, ten units of ten different products than 100 units of a single product. Developing separate marketing plans for separate segments requires extra marketing research, forecasting, sales analysis, promotion planning, and channel management. And trying to reach different market segments with different advertising campaigns increases promotion costs. Thus, the company must weigh increased sales against increased costs when deciding on a differentiated marketing strategy.

Concentrated Marketing

Concentrated (niche) marketing
A market-coverage strategy in which a firm goes after a large share of one or a few segments or niches.

When using a **concentrated marketing** (or **niche marketing**) strategy, instead of going after a small share of a large market, a firm goes after a large share of one or a few smaller segments or niches. For example, Whole Foods Market has about 300 stores and $9 billion in sales, compared with goliaths such as Kroger (more than 3,600 stores and sales of $82 billion) and Walmart (close to 9,000 stores and sales of $419 billion).[16] Yet, over the past five years, the smaller, more upscale retailer has grown faster and more profitably than either of its giant rivals. Whole Foods thrives by catering to affluent customers who the Walmarts of the world can't serve well, offering them "organic, natural, and gourmet foods, all swaddled in Earth Day politics." In fact, a typical Whole Foods customer is more likely to boycott the local Walmart than to shop at it.

Through concentrated marketing, the firm achieves a strong market position because of its greater knowledge of consumer needs in the niches it serves and the special reputation it acquires. It can market more *effectively* by fine-tuning its products, prices, and programs to the needs of carefully defined segments. It can also market more *efficiently*, targeting its products or services, channels, and communications programs toward only consumers that it can serve best and most profitably.

Niching lets smaller companies focus their limited resources on serving niches that may be unimportant to or overlooked by larger competitors. Many companies start as nichers to get a foothold against larger, more-resourceful competitors and then grow into broader competitors. For example, Southwest Airlines began by serving intrastate, no-frills commuters in Texas but is now one of the nation's largest airlines. And Enterprise Rent-A-Car began by building a network of neighborhood offices rather competing with Hertz and Avis in airport locations. Enterprise is now the nation's largest car rental company.

Today, the low cost of setting up shop on the Internet makes it even more profitable to serve seemingly miniscule niches. Small businesses, in particular, are realizing riches from serving small niches on the Web. ▶ Consider Etsy:[17]

Etsy is "The world's handmade marketplace"—selling everything from handmade soaps to Conan O'Brien cufflinks. Sometimes referred to as eBay's funky little sister, the Etsy online crafts fair site is a far cry from the old-fashioned street-corner flea market. Thanks to the reach and power of the Web, Etsy now counts 8 million members and 8.5 million listings in 150 countries. The Web site has 5 million monthly visitors. In just the past three years, Etsy more than tripled its gross sales to $314 million. Etsy's vibrant handmade marketplace is more than an e-commerce site; it's a thriving community. For example, it sponsors actual and virtual meet-ups organized by location (from Syracuse to Saskatchewan and Singapore), medium (papier-mâché, mosaic), and interest area (Chainmailers Guild, Lizards, and Lollipops). Etsy's mission is "to enable people to make a living making things, and to reconnect makers with buyers." It aims "to build a new economy and present a better choice: Buy, Sell, and Live Handmade."

Concentrated marketing: Thanks to the reach and power of the Web, online nicher Etsy—sometimes referred to as eBay's funky little sister—is thriving.

Etsy, Inc. and The Clay Collection

Concentrated marketing can be highly profitable. At the same time, it involves higher-than-normal risks. Companies that rely on one or a few segments for all of their business will suffer greatly if the segment turns sour. Or larger competitors may decide to enter the same segment with greater resources. For these reasons, many companies prefer to diversify in several market segments.

Micromarketing

Micromarketing
Tailoring products and marketing programs to the needs and wants of specific individuals and local customer segments; it includes *local marketing* and *individual marketing*.

Differentiated and concentrated marketers tailor their offers and marketing programs to meet the needs of various market segments and niches. At the same time, however, they do not customize their offers to each individual customer. **Micromarketing** is the practice of tailoring products and marketing programs to suit the tastes of specific individuals and locations. Rather than seeing a customer in every individual, micromarketers see the individual in every customer. Micromarketing includes *local marketing* and *individual marketing*.

Local marketing
Tailoring brands and promotions to the needs and wants of local customer segments—cities, neighborhoods, and even specific stores.

Local Marketing. **Local marketing** involves tailoring brands and promotions to the needs and wants of local customer groups—cities, neighborhoods, and even specific stores. For example, New York City drugstore chain Duane Reade adapts its merchandise assortments to individual neighborhoods. In Manhattan, around Penn Station and the Port Authority, it sells sandwiches and quick lunches to the area's many office workers and commuters. In the Williamsburg neighborhood of Brooklyn—an area short on bars and beer-buying locations—Duane Reade stores sell an abundance of growlers and six-packs of microbrew beer.[18]

Advances in communications technology have given rise to new high-tech versions of location-based marketing. Using location-based social networks such as Foursquare, Gowalla, Shopkick, or Facebook Places and local-marketing deal-of-the-day services such as Groupon or Facebook Deals, retailers can target consumers with local online or mobile phone deals (see Marketing at Work 6.2).

MARKETING AT WORK   6.2

Location-Based Micromarketing Equals Macro Opportunities

Marketers use a host of factors to target customers—from demographics and psychographics to detailed purchase histories. However, today's marketers are increasingly adding an important new targeting variable: location—*where you are, right now*. Thanks to the explosion in net-connected smartphones with GPS capabilities and location-based social networks, companies can now track your whereabouts closely and gear their offers accordingly.

Today's high-tech location-based marketing takes two major forms. One is mobile "check-in" services—such as Foursquare, Gowalla, Whrrl, CheckPoints, and Shopkick—where people check in on their smartphones to reveal their locations and obtain special retail offers. The other is "deal-of-the-day" Web marketers—such as Groupon—that partner with local businesses to offer local shopping deals to subscribers based on where they live and what they like.

The location-based check-in services bridge the gap between the digital world and the real brick-and-mortar world. For example, Foursquare's location-based mobile app lets its more than 6 million users visit participating retail locations such as Starbucks or Gap, check in by pushing buttons on their mobile phones, and reap special rewards. That typically means discount e-coupons. But most check-in services add additional incentives with an addictive game-like twist. For example, Foursquare members compete to become the "mayor" of a given retail location by having the highest number of check-ins there. Scvngr designs smartphone-enabled scavenger hunts, granting discounts for completing certain tasks, such as taking in-store pictures. And members of Gowalla and Stickybits are entered in a lottery for cash or merchandise when checking in at a specified location.

But more than just passing out e-coupons and other rewards, Foursquare and the other check-in services are becoming full-fledged, location-based lifestyle networks. The aim is to enrich people's lives by helping them to learn the whereabouts of friends, share location-related experiences, and discover new places—all while linking them to sponsoring locations that match their interests. For example, Foursquare wants to be the Netflix or Amazon.com of real-world activities, knowing its members so well that it can tell what they individually need at any given moment based on where they are and where they've been. Foursquare cofounder Dennis Crowley suggests this futuristic scenario:

> At 6 P.M., his iPhone alerts him to the evening's plans. It has already checked his friends' [whereabouts and] calendars and knows who's free tonight, so it suggests a nearby restaurant they've all wanted to try. It notes when a table is available and informs him that three other friends are planning to hang out across the street so they can meet up later.

Foursquare is getting closer and closer to making this scenario a reality. At its Web site, it already promises: "Foursquare gives you and your friends new ways to explore. . . . Check-in. Find your friends. Unlock your city." Similarly, competitor Gowalla invites you to "keep up with your friends, share the places you go, and discover the extraordinary in the world around you." Of course, in doing so, you'll reap the rewards. Stickybits invites you to "explore and score." And Facebook Places—the new giant in location-based marketing services—suggests that you "share where you are, connect with friends nearby, *and* find local deals." The check-in networks provide attractive targeting opportunities to retailers, letting them market to people on the go, when they're nearby and ready to eat, shop, and spend.

The second major form of location-based marketing—"deal-of-the-day" Web sites—has become one of the hottest-ever Internet crazes. Among the hundreds of deal-of-the-day services in North America alone, market leader Groupon dominates with more than 70 million subscribers in more than 500 cities worldwide. Groupon partners with retailers in each city to craft attractive offers for area customers. Most local partners are small businesses, attracted to Groupon as an immediate and effective means of promoting their goods and services to local customer bases. But global giants such as Starbucks, Best Buy, Barnes & Noble, and PepsiCo have also gotten into the Groupon act.

Groupon offers subscribers at least one deal each day in their city—such as paying $40 for an $80 voucher at a local restaurant. But the coupon deals kick in only if enough people sign up, encouraging subscribers to spread word of the deal to friends and neighbors and via social media such as Twitter and Facebook. Hence, the name *Groupon*—group plus coupon. When a deal "tips," Groupon shares the revenue roughly 50-50 with the retailer. Nearly all of Groupon's deals tip.

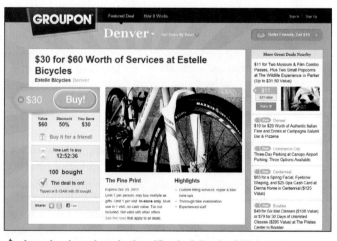

▲ Location-based marketing: "Deal-of-the-day" Web marketers—such as Groupon—partner with local businesses to offer shopping deals to subscribers based on where they live and what they like.
Groupon Inc.

To further personalize its deals, the location-based marketer is now starting to incorporate such factors as gender, age, neighborhood, and buying history through its opt-in Personalized Deals program. It's also testing Groupon Stores, a feature that lets local merchants create their own deals, post them on their own Groupon pages, and send them out to selected Groupon subscribers in their market areas.

Working with Groupon can transform a local business in as little as 24 hours. For example, when the Joffrey Ballet in Chicago offered highly discounted season subscriptions through Groupon, 2,334 people signed up, doubling the performing group's subscription base in a single day. Sometimes, Groupon's deals can work too well. Retailer Gap's server crashed when 445,000 people bought $50 merchandise cards for only $25. And Mission Minis, a small San Francisco gourmet bakery, was reportedly bombarded with an overwhelming 72,000 mini cupcake orders following a Groupon offer. Groupon works to minimize such cases by coaching businesses through the deal process and recommending appropriate deal caps.

During only its third year of operation, Groupon has entered Internet stardom. Its average subscriber is a target marketer's dream: female, between the ages of 18 and 34, single, and making more than $70,000 a year. And Groupon is adding about a million new members every week. Groupon is so hot that—according to some reports—Google recently offered to buy the company for a whopping $6 billion, its biggest buyout offer ever. Groupon supposedly turned Google down flat.

Perhaps the best indicator of the potential of location-based marketing is the arrival of the Web giants, each trying to capture a piece of the burgeoning location-based marketing action. Google is quickly developing its own Groupon-like service, Google Offers. And adding to its Facebook Places check-in service, Facebook recently launched Facebook Deals, which posts Groupon-like offers in partnership with local businesses. Facebook has more than 600 million users, one-third of whom engage through mobile devices. If Facebook Places and Facebook Deals hit it big, Facebook would likely become the world's biggest location-based marketer. And that spells macro potential for location-based micromarketing.

Sources: Brad Stone and Barrett Sheridan, "The Retailer's Clever Little Helper," *BloombergBusinessweek*, August 30–September 6, 2010, pp. 31–32; Diane Brady, "Social Media's New Mantra: Location, Location, Location," *BloombergBusinessweek*, May 10–May 16, pp. 34–36; Bari Weiss, "Groupon's $6 Billion Gambler," *Wall Street Journal*, December 20, 2010, p. 12; Joseph Galante, "Groupon Coupons: The Small Biz Challenge," *BloombergBusinessweek*, June 14, 2010, p. 1; Brian Morrissey, "Location Services: Let the Battle Commence," *Brandweek*, December 12, 2010, pp. 4–5; Erick Schonfeld, "A Sneak Peak at Google Offers," January 25, 2011, accessed at http://techcrunch.com/2011/01/25/sneak-peak-google-offers/; and www.groupon.com, www.facebook.com/places/, www.facebook.com/deals; http://foursquare.com/, and http://gowalla.com/, accessed October 2011.

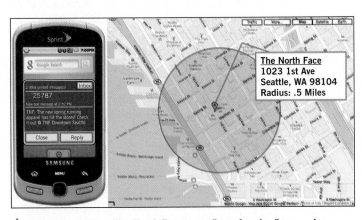

▲ **Local marketing: The North Face uses "geo-fencing" to send localized text messages to consumers who get near one of its stores.**
Yonhap News/YNA/Newscom

For example, the North Face has created "geo-fences" around its stores, and around hiking areas, parks, ski resorts, and other locales popular with its customers. ▶ When customers who have opted-in enter a geo-fenced area, they receive text messages tailored to their whereabouts and predefined interests. If near a store, customers might receive a message about a new merchandise item or promotion. However, a customer at Lake Tahoe who has noted that he or she is a biker might get a message about a great nearby biking trail, along with a report on local weather conditions. Another customer in the same area but with a different preference profile might receive a message about a great swimming spot.[19]

Local marketing has some drawbacks, however. It can drive up manufacturing and marketing costs by reducing the economies of scale. It can also create logistics problems as companies try to meet the varied requirements of different regional and local markets. Still, as companies face increasingly fragmented markets, and as new supporting technologies develop, the advantages of local marketing often outweigh the drawbacks. Local marketing helps a company to market more effectively in the face of pronounced regional and local differences in demographics and lifestyles.

Individual marketing
Tailoring products and marketing programs to the needs and preferences of individual customers.

Individual Marketing. In the extreme, micromarketing becomes **individual marketing**—tailoring products and marketing programs to the needs and preferences of individual customers. Individual marketing has also been labeled *one-to-one marketing*, *mass customization*, and *markets-of-one marketing*.

The widespread use of mass marketing has obscured the fact that for centuries consumers were served as individuals: The tailor custom-made a suit, the cobbler designed shoes for an individual, and the cabinetmaker made furniture to order. Today, new technologies are permitting many companies to return to customized marketing. More detailed databases, robotic production and flexible manufacturing, and interactive communication media such as cell phones and the Internet have combined to foster mass customization. *Mass customization* is the process by which firms interact one-to-one with masses of customers to design products and services tailor-made to individual needs.

Companies these days are hypercustomizing everything from artwork, earphones, and sneakers to yoga mats and food.[20]

▲ **Individual marketing: Companies such as CaféPress are hyper-personalizing everything from artwork, earphones, and sneakers to yoga mats, water bottles, and food.**

Peter Earl McCollough

At mymms.com, candylovers can buy M&Ms embossed with images of their kids or pets. JH Audio in Orlando makes music earphones based on molds of customers' ears to provide optimized fit and better and safer sound. The company even laser prints designs on the tiny ear buds—some people request a kid for each ear; others prefer a dog. Nike's NikeID program lets users choose materials for shoes' tread (say, for trail or street) and upper (Gore-Tex, mesh, or other), pick the color of the swoosh and stitching, and even imprint text on the heels. Different-sized right and left feet? That, too, can be retooled.

"We are so used to customizing the world around us . . . to being able on Facebook to customize our wall and to create who we are," says Amy Maniatis, vice president of marketing at CafePress.com, where visitors can plaster their pictures on a Gaiam yoga mat, Sigg water bottle, or even TomTom GPS navigator. ▶ One recent CafePress.com buyer is Christina Wells, a senior at the University of California, Berkeley who swapped her plain pink yoga mat for a custom tan one with a prominently displayed photo of her boyfriend, Nick, giving her the thumbs-up sign. "He was mocking me for coming to yoga, so now I bring him with me," says Wells. "It's definitely a conversation starter."

Business-to-business marketers are also finding new ways to customize their offerings. For example, John Deere manufactures seeding equipment that can be configured in more than two million versions to individual customer specifications. The seeders are produced one at a time, in any sequence, on a single production line. Mass customization provides a way to stand out against competitors.

Unlike mass production, which eliminates the need for human interaction, individual marketing has made relationships with customers more important than ever. Just as mass production was the marketing principle of the twentieth century, interactive marketing is becoming a marketing principle for the twenty-first century. The world appears to be coming full circle—from the good old days when customers were treated as individuals to mass marketing when nobody knew your name and then back again.

Choosing a Targeting Strategy

Companies need to consider many factors when choosing a market-targeting strategy. Which strategy is best depends on the company's resources. When the firm's resources are limited, concentrated marketing makes the most sense. The best strategy also depends on the degree of product variability. Undifferentiated marketing is more suited for uniform products, such as grapefruit or steel. Products that can vary in design, such as cameras and cars, are more suited to differentiation or concentration. The product's life-cycle stage also must be considered. When a firm introduces a new product, it may be practical to launch one version only, as undifferentiated marketing or concentrated marketing may make the most sense. In the mature stage of the product life cycle (PLC), however, differentiated marketing often makes more sense.

Another factor is *market variability*. If most buyers have the same tastes, buy the same amounts, and react the same way to marketing efforts, undifferentiated marketing is appropriate. Finally, *competitors' marketing strategies* are important. When competitors use differentiated or concentrated marketing, undifferentiated marketing can be suicidal.

Conversely, when competitors use undifferentiated marketing, a firm can gain an advantage by using differentiated or concentrated marketing, focusing on the needs of buyers in specific segments.

Socially Responsible Target Marketing

Smart targeting helps companies become more efficient and effective by focusing on the segments that they can satisfy best and most profitably. Targeting also benefits consumers—companies serve specific groups of consumers with offers carefully tailored to their needs. However, target marketing sometimes generates controversy and concern. The biggest issues usually involve the targeting of vulnerable or disadvantaged consumers with controversial or potentially harmful products.

For example, over the years marketers in a wide range of industries—from cereal, soft drinks, and fast food to toys and fashion—have been heavily criticized for their marketing efforts directed toward children. Critics worry that premium offers and high-powered advertising appeals presented through the mouths of lovable animated characters will overwhelm children's defenses.

Other problems arise when the marketing of adult products spills over into the children's segment—intentionally or unintentionally. For example, Victoria's Secret targets its highly successful Pink line of young, hip, and sexy clothing to young women from 18 to 30 years old. However, critics charge that Pink is now all the rage among girls as young as 11 years old. Responding to Victoria's Secret's designs and marketing messages, tweens are flocking into stores and buying Pink, with or without their mothers. More broadly, critics worry that marketers of everything from lingerie and cosmetics to Barbie dolls are directly or indirectly targeting young girls with provocative products, promoting a premature focus on sex and appearance.[21]

▲ **Socially responsible marketing: Critics worry that marketers of everything from lingerie and cosmetics to Barbie dolls are targeting young girls with provocative products.**

Jarrod Weaton/Weaton Digital, Inc.

Ten-year-old girls can slide their low-cut jeans over "eye-candy" panties. French maid costumes, garter belt included, are available in preteen sizes. ▶ Barbie now comes in a "bling-bling" style, replete with halter top and go-go boots. Abercrombie & Fitch markets a padded "push-up" bikini top for girls as young as 8. Walmart is marketing a make-up line to tweens. And it's not unusual for girls under 12 years old to sing, "Don't cha wish your girlfriend was hot like me?" American girls, say experts, are increasingly being fed a cultural catnip of products and images that promote looking and acting sexy. "The message we're telling our girls is a simple one," laments one reporter about the Victoria's Secret Pink line. "You'll have a great life if people find you sexually attractive. Grown women struggle enough with this ridiculous standard. Do we really need to start worrying about it at 11?" Adds another parenting expert, "The sexualization of teens is bad enough and now this trend is trickling down to our babies."

To encourage responsible advertising, the Children's Advertising Review Unit, the advertising industry's self-regulatory agency, has published extensive children's advertising guidelines that recognize the special needs of child audiences. Still, critics feel that more should been done. Some have even called for a complete ban on advertising to children.

Cigarette, beer, and fast-food marketers have also generated controversy in recent years by their attempts to target inner-city minority consumers. For example, McDonald's and other chains have drawn criticism for pitching their high-fat, salt-laden fare to low-income, urban residents who are much more likely than suburbanites to be heavy consumers. Similarly, big banks and mortgage lenders have been criticized for targeting consumers in poor urban areas with attractive adjustable rate home mortgages that they can't really afford.

The growth of the Internet and other carefully targeted direct media has raised fresh concerns about potential targeting abuses. The Internet allows more precise targeting, letting the makers of questionable products or deceptive advertisers zero in on the most vulnerable audiences. Unscrupulous marketers can now send tailor-made, deceptive messages by e-mail directly to millions of unsuspecting consumers. For example, the FBI's Internet Crime Complaint Center Web site alone received more than 300,000 complaints last year.[22]

Not all attempts to target children, minorities, or other special segments draw such criticism. In fact, most provide benefits to targeted consumers. For example, Pantene markets Relaxed and Natural hair products to women of color. Samsung markets the Jitterbug, an easy-to-use phone, directly to seniors who need a simpler cell phone with bigger buttons, large screen text, and a louder speaker. And Colgate makes a large selection of toothbrush shapes and toothpaste flavors for children—from Colgate SpongeBob SquarePants Mild Bubble Fruit toothpaste to Colgate Dora the Explorer character toothbrushes. Such products help make tooth brushing more fun and get children to brush longer and more often.

Thus, in target marketing, the issue is not really *who* is targeted but rather *how* and for *what*. Controversies arise when marketers attempt to profit at the expense of targeted segments—when they unfairly target vulnerable segments or target them with questionable products or tactics. Socially responsible marketing calls for segmentation and targeting that serve not just the interests of the company but also the interests of those targeted.

SPEED BUMP | LINKING THE CONCEPTS

It's time to pause and take stock.

- At the last Linking the Concepts, you segmented the U.S. footwear market. Refer to Figure 6.2 and select two companies that serve the footwear market. Describe their segmentation and targeting strategies. Can you come up with a company that targets many different segments versus another that focuses on only one or a few segments?
- How does each company you chose differentiate its market offering and image? Has each done a good job of establishing this differentiation in the minds of targeted consumers? The final section in this chapter deals with such positioning issues.

Product position

The way a product is defined by consumers on important attributes—the place the product occupies in consumers' minds relative to competing products.

Author Comment ▶

At the same time that the company is answering the first simple-sounding question (Which customers will we serve?), it must be asking the second question (How will we serve them?). For example, Ritz-Carlton hotels serve the top 5 percent of corporate and leisure travelers. Its parallel value proposition is "The Ritz-Carlton Experience"—one that "enlivens the senses, instills a sense of well-being, and fulfills even the unexpressed wishes and needs of our guests."

Differentiation and Positioning

Beyond deciding which segments of the market it will target, the company must decide on a *value proposition*—how it will create differentiated value for targeted segments and what positions it wants to occupy in those segments. A **product position** is the way a product is *defined by consumers* on important attributes—the place the product occupies in consumers' minds relative to competing products. Products are made in factories, but brands happen in the minds of consumers.

Method laundry detergent is positioned as a smarter, easier, and greener detergent; Dreft is positioned as the gentle detergent for baby clothes. At IHOP, you "Come hungry. Leave happy."; at Olive Garden, "When You're Here, You're Family." In the automobile market, the Nissan Versa and Honda Fit are positioned on economy, Mercedes and Cadillac on luxury, and Porsche and BMW on performance.

Consumers are overloaded with information about products and services. They cannot reevaluate products every time they make a buying decision. To simplify the buying process, consumers organize products, services, and companies into categories and "position" them in their minds. A product's position is the complex set of perceptions, impressions, and feelings that consumers have for the product compared with competing products.

Consumers position products with or without the help of marketers. But marketers do not want to leave their products' positions to chance. They must *plan* positions that will give their products the greatest advantage in selected target markets, and they must design marketing mixes to create these planned positions.

Positioning Maps

In planning their differentiation and positioning strategies, marketers often prepare *perceptual positioning maps* that show consumer perceptions of their brands versus competing products on important buying dimensions. ▶ **Figure 6.3** shows a positioning map for the U.S. large luxury sport utility vehicle (SUV) market.[23] The position of each circle on the map indicates the brand's perceived positioning on two dimensions: price and orientation (luxury versus performance). The size of each circle indicates the brand's relative market share.

Thus, customers view the market-leading Cadillac Escalade as a moderately priced, large, luxury SUV with a balance of luxury and performance. The Escalade is positioned on urban luxury, and, in its case, "performance" probably means power and safety performance. You'll find no mention of off-road adventuring in an Escalade ad.

By contrast, the Range Rover and the Land Cruiser are positioned on luxury with nuances of off-road performance. For example, the Toyota Land Cruiser began in 1951 as a four-wheel drive, Jeep-like vehicle designed to conquer the world's most grueling terrains and climates. In recent years, the Land Cruiser has retained this adventure and performance positioning but with luxury added. Its Web site brags of "legendary off-road capability," with off-road technologies such as downhill assist control and kinetic dynamic suspension systems. "In some parts of the world, it's an essential." Despite its ruggedness, however, the company notes that "its available Bluetooth hands-free technology, DVD entertainment, and a sumptuous interior have softened its edges."

Choosing a Differentiation and Positioning Strategy

Some firms find it easy to choose a differentiation and positioning strategy. For example, a firm well known for quality in certain segments will go after this position in a new segment if there are enough buyers seeking quality. But in many cases, two or more firms will go after the same position. Then each will have to find other ways to set itself apart. Each firm must differentiate its offer by building a unique bundle of benefits that appeals to a substantial group within the segment.

Above all else, a brand's positioning must serve the needs and preferences of well-defined target markets. For example, as noted in the chapter-opening story, although both

▶ **Figure 6.3** Positioning Map: Large Luxury Suvs

Source: Based on data provided by WardsAuto.com and Edmunds.com, 2011.

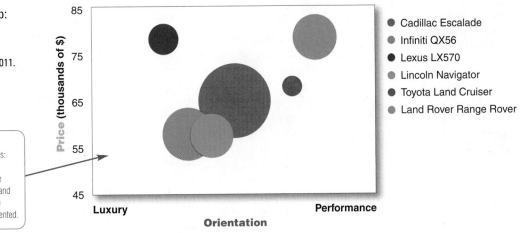

The location of each circle shows where consumers position a brand on two dimensions: price and luxury-performance orientation. The size of each circle indicates the brand's relative market share in the segment. Thus, Toyota's Land Cruiser is a niche brand that is perceived to be relatively affordable and more performance oriented.

Dunkin' Donuts and Starbucks are coffee shops, they offer very different product assortments and store atmospheres. Yet each succeeds because it creates just the right value proposition for its unique mix of customers.

The differentiation and positioning task consists of three steps: identifying a set of differentiating competitive advantages on which to build a position, choosing the right competitive advantages, and selecting an overall positioning strategy. The company must then effectively communicate and deliver the chosen position to the market.

Identifying Possible Value Differences and Competitive Advantages

To build profitable relationships with target customers, marketers must understand customer needs better than competitors do and deliver more customer value. To the extent that a company can differentiate and position itself as providing superior customer value, it gains **competitive advantage**.

Competitive advantage

An advantage over competitors gained by offering greater customer value, either by having lower prices or providing more benefits that justify higher prices.

But solid positions cannot be built on empty promises. If a company positions its product as *offering* the best quality and service, it must actually differentiate the product so that it *delivers* the promised quality and service. Companies must do much more than simply shout out their positions with slogans and taglines. They must first *live* the slogan. For example, when Staples' research revealed that it should differentiate itself on the basis of "an easier shopping experience," the office supply retailer held back its "Staples: That was easy" marketing campaign for more than a year. First, it remade its stores to actually deliver the promised positioning.[24]

> Only a few years ago, things weren't so easy for Staples—or for its customers. The ratio of customer complaints to compliments was running a dreadful eight to one at Staples stores. Weeks of focus groups produced an answer: Customers wanted an easier shopping experience. That simple revelation has resulted in one of the most successful marketing campaigns in recent history, built around the now-familiar "Staples: That was easy" tagline. But Staples' positioning turnaround took a lot more than simply bombarding customers with a new slogan. Before it could promise customers a simplified shopping experience, Staples had to actually deliver one. First, it had to *live* the slogan.
>
> So, for more than a year, Staples worked to revamp the customer experience. It remodeled its stores, streamlined its inventory, retrained employees, and even simplified customer communications. Only when all of the customer-experience pieces were in place did Staples begin communicating its new positioning to customers. The "Staples: That was easy" repositioning campaign has met with striking success, helping to make Staples the runaway leader in office retail. No doubt about it, clever marketing helped. But marketing promises count for little if they are not backed by the reality of the customer experience.

▲ **Product differentiation: Seventh Generation's household products are greener—naturally safe and effective. The brand is "Protecting Planet Home."**

Courtesy of Seventh Generation, Inc.

To find points of differentiation, marketers must think through the customer's entire experience with the company's product or service. An alert company can find ways to differentiate itself at every customer contact point. In what specific ways can a company differentiate itself or its market offer? It can differentiate along the lines of *product*, *services*, *channels*, *people*, or *image*.

Through *product differentiation*, brands can be differentiated on features, performance, or style and design. Thus, Bose positions its speakers on their striking design and sound characteristics. By gaining the approval of the American Heart Association as an approach to a healthy lifestyle, Subway differentiates itself as the healthy fast-food choice. ▶ And Seventh Generation, a maker of household cleaning and laundry supplies, paper products, diapers, and wipes, differentiates itself not so much by how its products perform but by the fact that its products are greener. Seventh Generation products are "Protecting Planet Home."

Beyond differentiating its physical product, a firm can also differentiate the services that accompany the product. Some companies gain *services differentiation* through speedy, convenient, or careful delivery. For example, First Convenience Bank of Texas offers "Real Hours for Real People"; it is open seven days a week, including evenings. Others differentiate their service based on high-quality customer care. In an age where customer satisfaction with airline service is in constant decline, Singapore Airlines sets itself apart through extraordinary customer care and the grace of its flight attendants. "Everyone expects excellence from us," says the international airline. "[So even] in the smallest details of flight, we rise to each occasion and deliver the Singapore Airlines experience."[25]

Firms that practice *channel differentiation* gain competitive advantage through the way they design their channel's coverage, expertise, and performance. Amazon.com and GEICO, for example, set themselves apart with their smooth-functioning direct channels. Companies can also gain a strong competitive advantage through *people differentiation*— hiring and training better people than their competitors do. People differentiation requires that a company select its customer-contact people carefully and train them well. For example, Disney World people are known to be friendly and upbeat. Disney trains its theme park people thoroughly to ensure that they are competent, courteous, and friendly—from the hotel check-in agents, to the monorail drivers, to the ride attendants, to the people who sweep Main Street USA. Each employee is carefully trained to understand customers and to "make people happy."

Even when competing offers look the same, buyers may perceive a difference based on company or brand *image differentiation*. A company or brand image should convey a product's distinctive benefits and positioning. Developing a strong and distinctive image calls for creativity and hard work. A company cannot develop an image in the public's mind overnight by using only a few ads. If Ritz-Carlton means quality, this image must be supported by everything the company says and does.

Symbols, such as the McDonald's golden arches, the red Travelers umbrella, the Nike swoosh, or Apple's "bite mark" logo, can provide strong company or brand recognition and image differentiation. The company might build a brand around a famous person, as Nike did with its Michael Jordan, Kobe Bryant, and LeBron James basketball shoe and apparel collections. Some companies even become associated with colors, such as Coca-Cola (red), IBM (blue), or UPS (brown). The chosen symbols, characters, and other image elements must be communicated through advertising that conveys the company's or brand's personality.

Choosing the Right Competitive Advantages

Suppose a company is fortunate enough to discover several potential differentiations that provide competitive advantages. It now must choose the ones on which it will build its positioning strategy. It must decide how many differences to promote and which ones.

How Many Differences to Promote. Many marketers think that companies should aggressively promote only one benefit to the target market. Advertising executive Rosser Reeves, for example, said a company should develop a *unique selling proposition (USP)* for each brand and stick to it. Each brand should pick an attribute and tout itself as "number one" on that attribute. Buyers tend to remember number one better, especially in this overcommunicated society. Thus, Walmart promotes its unbeatable low prices, and Burger King promotes personal choice—"have it your way."

Other marketers think that companies should position themselves on more than one differentiator. This may be necessary if two or more firms are claiming to be best on the same attribute. Today, in a time when the mass market is fragmenting into many small segments, companies and brands are trying to broaden their positioning strategies to appeal to more segments. ▶ For example, whereas most laundry goods marketers offer separate products for cleaning, softening, and reducing static cling, Henkel's Purex brand recently introduced a product that offers all three benefits in a single sheet: Purex Complete

CLEANS. SOFTENS. REMOVES STATIC.

IF IT COULD ONLY FOLD.

▲ **Purex Complete 3-in-1 is positioned on multiple benefits. The challenge is to convince customers that one brand can do it all.**

Courtesy The Dial Corporation, a Henkel Company

3-in-1 Laundry Sheets. "Cleans. Softens. Removes static. If only it could fold," says one ad. Clearly, many buyers want these multiple benefits. The challenge is to convince them that one brand can do it all.

Which Differences to Promote. Not all brand differences are meaningful or worthwhile, and each difference has the potential to create company costs as well as customer benefits. A difference is worth establishing to the extent that it satisfies the following criteria:

- *Important.* The difference delivers a highly valued benefit to target buyers.
- *Distinctive.* Competitors do not offer the difference, or the company can offer it in a more distinctive way.
- *Superior.* The difference is superior to other ways that customers might obtain the same benefit.
- *Communicable.* The difference is communicable and visible to buyers.
- *Preemptive.* Competitors cannot easily copy the difference.
- *Affordable.* Buyers can afford to pay for the difference.
- *Profitable.* The company can introduce the difference profitably.

Many companies have introduced differentiations that failed one or more of these tests. When the Westin Stamford Hotel in Singapore once advertised that it is the world's tallest hotel, it was a distinction that was not important to most tourists; in fact, it turned many off. Polaroid's Polarvision, which produced instantly developed home movies, bombed too. Although Polarvision was distinctive and even preemptive, it was inferior to another way of capturing motion—namely, camcorders.

Thus, choosing competitive advantages on which to position a product or service can be difficult, yet such choices may be crucial to success. Choosing the right differentiators can help a brand stand out from the pack of competitors. For example, when carmaker Nissan introduced its novel little Cube, it didn't position the car only on attributes shared with competing models, such as affordability and customization. It positioned it as a "mobile device" that fits today's digital lifestyles.

Selecting an Overall Positioning Strategy

Value proposition
The full positioning of a brand—
the full mix of benefits on which
it is positioned.

The full positioning of a brand is called the brand's **value proposition**—the full mix of benefits on which a brand is differentiated and positioned. It is the answer to the customer's question "Why should I buy your brand?" Volvo's value proposition hinges on safety but also includes reliability, roominess, and styling, all for a price that is higher than average but seems fair for this mix of benefits.

▶ **Figure 6.4** shows possible value propositions on which a company might position its products. In the figure, the five green cells represent winning value propositions—differentiation

▶ **Figure 6.4** Possible Value Propostions

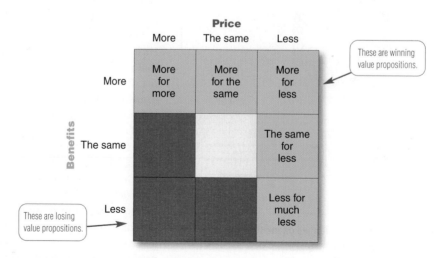

and positioning that gives the company a competitive advantage. The red cells, however, represent losing value propositions. The center yellow cell represents at best a marginal proposition. In the following sections, we discuss the five winning value propositions: more for more, more for the same, the same for less, less for much less, and more for less.

More for More. *More-for-more* positioning involves providing the most upscale product or service and charging a higher price to cover the higher costs. A more-for-more market offering not only offers higher quality, it also gives prestige to the buyer. It symbolizes status and a loftier lifestyle. Four Seasons hotels, Rolex watches, Mercedes automobiles, SubZero appliances—each claims superior quality, craftsmanship, durability, performance, or style and, therefore, charges a higher price. When Apple premiered its iPhone, it offered higher-quality features than a traditional cell phone with a hefty price tag to match.

Similarly, the marketers of Hearts On Fire diamonds have created a more-for-more niche as "The World's Most Perfectly Cut Diamond." Hearts On Fire diamonds have a unique "hearts and arrow" design. When viewed under magnification from the bottom, a perfect ring of eight hearts appears; from the top comes a perfectly formed Fireburst of light. Hearts On Fire diamonds aren't for everyone, says the company. ▶ "Hearts On Fire is for those who expect more and give more in return." The brand commands a 15 to 20 percent price premium over comparable competing diamonds.[26]

Although more-for-more can be profitable, this strategy can also be vulnerable. It often invites imitators who claim the same quality but at a lower price. For example, more-for-more brand Starbucks now faces "gourmet" coffee competitors ranging from Dunkin' Donuts to McDonald's. Also, luxury goods that sell well during good times may be at risk during economic downturns when buyers become more cautious in their spending. The recent gloomy economy hit premium brands, such as Starbucks, the hardest.

The dream is complete when your heart's on fire.

HEARTS ON FIRE®
THE WORLD'S MOST
PERFECTLY CUT DIAMOND®

▲ More-for-more positioning: Hearts On Fire diamonds have created a more-for-more niche as "The World's Most Perfectly Cut Diamond—for those who expect more and give more in return."

Used with permission of Hearts On Fire Company, LLC

More for the Same. Companies can attack a competitor's more-for-more positioning by introducing a brand offering comparable quality at a lower price. For example, Toyota introduced its Lexus line with a *more-for-the-same* value proposition versus Mercedes and BMW. Its first headline read: "Perhaps the first time in history that trading a $72,000 car for a $36,000 car could be considered trading up." It communicated the high quality of its new Lexus through rave reviews in car magazines and a widely distributed videotape showing side-by-side comparisons of Lexus and Mercedes automobiles. It published surveys showing that Lexus dealers were providing customers with better sales and service experiences than were Mercedes dealerships. Many Mercedes owners switched to Lexus, and the Lexus repurchase rate has been 60 percent, twice the industry average.

The Same for Less. Offering *the same for less* can be a powerful value proposition—everyone likes a good deal. Discount stores such as Walmart and "category killers" such as Best Buy, PetSmart, David's Bridal, and DSW Shoes use this positioning. They don't claim to offer different or better products. Instead, they offer many of the same brands as department stores and specialty stores but at deep discounts based on superior purchasing power and lower-cost operations. Other companies develop imitative but lower-priced brands in an effort to lure customers away from the market leader. For example, The Sharper Image makes a less expensive e-reader, the Literati, to compete with the Nook and Kindle.

Less for Much Less. A market almost always exists for products that offer less and therefore cost less. Few people need, want, or can afford "the very best" in everything they buy. In many cases, consumers will gladly settle for less than optimal performance or give up some of the bells and whistles in exchange for a lower price. For example, many travelers seeking lodgings prefer not to pay for what they consider unnecessary extras, such as a pool, an attached restaurant, or mints on the pillow. Hotel chains such as Ramada Limited, Holiday Inn Express, and Motel 6 suspend some of these amenities and charge less accordingly.

Less-for-much-less positioning involves meeting consumers' lower performance or quality requirements at a much lower price. For example, Family Dollar and Dollar General stores offer more affordable goods at very low prices. Costco warehouse stores offer less merchandise selection and consistency and much lower levels of service; as a result, they charge rock-bottom prices.

More for Less. Of course, the winning value proposition would be to offer *more for less.* Many companies claim to do this. And, in the short run, some companies can actually achieve such lofty positions. For example, when it first opened for business, Home Depot had arguably the best product selection, the best service, *and* the lowest prices compared to local hardware stores and other home improvement chains.

Yet in the long run, companies will find it very difficult to sustain such best-of-both positioning. Offering more usually costs more, making it difficult to deliver on the "for-less" promise. Companies that try to deliver both may lose out to more focused competitors. For example, facing determined competition from Lowe's stores, Home Depot must now decide whether it wants to compete primarily on superior service or on lower prices.

All said, each brand must adopt a positioning strategy designed to serve the needs and wants of its target markets. *More for more* will draw one target market, *less for much less* will draw another, and so on. Thus, in any market, there is usually room for many different companies, each successfully occupying different positions. The important thing is that each company must develop its own winning positioning strategy, one that makes the company special to its target consumers.

Developing a Positioning Statement

Positioning statement

A statement that summarizes company or brand positioning using this form: To (target segment and need) our (brand) is (concept) that (point of difference).

Company and brand positioning should be summed up in a **positioning statement**. The statement should follow the form: To (target segment and need) our (brand) is (concept) that (point of difference).[27] Here is an example: "To busy, mobile professionals who need to always be in the loop, the BlackBerry is a wireless business connectivity solution that gives you an easier, more reliable way to stay connected to data, people, and resources while on the go."

Note that the positioning statement first states the product's membership in a category (wireless business connectivity solution) and then shows its point of difference from other members of the category (easier, more reliable connections to data, people, and resources). Placing a brand in a specific category suggests similarities that it might share with other products in the category. But the case for the brand's superiority is made on its points of difference. For example, the U.S. Postal Service ships packages just like UPS and FedEx, but it differentiates its priority mail from competitors with convenient, low-price, flat-rate shipping boxes and envelopes. "If it fits, it ships," promises the Post Office.

Communicating and Delivering the Chosen Position

Once it has chosen a position, the company must take strong steps to deliver and communicate the desired position to its target consumers. All the company's marketing mix efforts must support the positioning strategy.

Positioning the company calls for concrete action, not just talk. If the company decides to build a position on better quality and service, it must first *deliver* that position. Designing the marketing mix—product, price, place, and promotion—involves working out the tactical details of the positioning strategy. Thus, a firm that seizes on a more-for-more position knows that it must produce high-quality products, charge a high price, distribute through high-quality dealers, and advertise in high-quality media. It must hire and train more service people, find retailers who have a good reputation for service, and develop sales and advertising messages that broadcast its superior service. This is the only way to build a consistent and believable more-for-more position.

Companies often find it easier to come up with a good positioning strategy than to implement it. Establishing a position or changing one usually takes a long time. In contrast, positions that have taken years to build can quickly be lost. Once a company has built the desired position, it must take care to maintain the position through consistent performance and communication. It must closely monitor and adapt the position over time to match changes in consumer needs and competitors' strategies. However, the company should avoid abrupt changes that might confuse consumers. Instead, a product's position should evolve gradually as it adapts to the ever-changing marketing environment.

REST STOP | REVIEWING THE CONCEPTS

MyMarketingLab

Now that you have completed the chapter, return to www.mymktlab.com to experience and apply the concepts and to explore the additional study materials for this chapter.

CHAPTER REVIEW AND KEY TERMS

Objectives Review

In this chapter, you learned about the major elements of a customer-driven marketing strategy: segmentation, targeting, differentiation, and positioning. Marketers know that they cannot appeal to all buyers in their markets, or at least not to all buyers in the same way. Therefore, most companies today practice *target marketing*—identifying market segments, selecting one or more of them, and developing products and marketing mixes tailored to each.

 OBJECTIVE 1 Define the major steps in designing a customer-driven marketing strategy: market segmentation, targeting, differentiation, and positioning. (pp 162–165)

A customer-driven marketing strategy begins with selecting which customers to serve and determining a value proposition that best serves the targeted customers. It consists of four steps.

Market segmentation is the act of dividing a market into distinct segments of buyers with different needs, characteristics, or behaviors who might require separate products or marketing mixes. Once the groups have been identified, *market targeting* evaluates each market segment's attractiveness and selects one or more segments to serve. *Differentiation* involves actually differentiating the market offering to create superior customer value. *Positioning* consists of positioning the market offering in the minds of target customers. A customer-driven marketing strategy seeks to build the *right relationships* with the *right customers*.

 OBJECTIVE 2 List and discuss the major bases for segmenting consumer and business markets. (pp 165–174)

There is no single way to segment a market. Therefore, the marketer tries different variables to see which give the best segmentation opportunities. For consumer marketing, the major segmentation variables are geographic, demographic, psychographic, and behavioral. In *geographic segmentation*, the market is divided into different geographical units, such as nations, regions, states, counties, cities, or even neighborhoods. In *demographic segmentation*, the market is divided into groups based on demographic variables, including age, life-cycle stage, gender, income, occupation, education, religion, ethnicity, and generation. In *psychographic segmentation*, the market is divided into different groups based on social class, lifestyle, or personality characteristics. In *behavioral segmentation*, the market is divided into groups based on consumers' knowledge, attitudes, uses, or responses to a product.

Business marketers use many of the same variables to segment their markets. But business markets also can be segmented by business *demographics* (industry, company size), *operating characteristics*, *purchasing approaches*, *situational factors*, and *personal characteristics*. The effectiveness of the segmentation analysis depends on finding segments that are *measurable*, *accessible*, *substantial*, *differentiable*, and *actionable*.

OBJECTIVE 3 Explain how companies identify attractive market segments and choose a market-targeting strategy. (pp 174–182)

To target the best market segments, the company first evaluates each segment's size and growth characteristics, structural attractiveness, and compatibility with company objectives and resources. It then chooses one of four market-targeting strategies—ranging from very broad to very narrow targeting. The seller can ignore segment differences and target broadly using *undifferentiated* (or *mass*) *marketing*. This involves mass producing, mass distributing, and mass promoting about the same product in about the same way to all consumers. Or the seller can adopt *differentiated marketing*—developing different market offers for several segments. *Concentrated marketing* (or *niche marketing*) involves focusing on one or a few market segments only. Finally, *micromarketing* is the practice of tailoring products and marketing programs to suit the tastes of specific individuals and locations. Micromarketing includes *local marketing* and *individual marketing*. Which targeting strategy is best depends on company resources, product variability, the product life-cycle stage, market variability, and competitive marketing strategies.

OBJECTIVE 4 Discuss how companies differentiate and position their products for maximum competitive advantage. (pp 182–189)

Once a company has decided which segments to enter, it must decide on its *differentiation and positioning strategy*. The differentiation and positioning task consists of three steps: identifying a set of possible differentiations that create competitive advantage, choosing advantages on which to build a position, and selecting an overall positioning strategy.

The brand's full positioning is called its *value proposition*—the full mix of benefits on which the brand is positioned. In general, companies can choose from one of five winning value propositions on which to position their products: more for more, more for the same, the same for less, less for much less, or more for less. Company and brand positioning are summarized in positioning statements that state the target segment and need, the positioning concept, and specific points of difference. The company must then effectively communicate and deliver the chosen position to the market.

Key Terms

DISCUSSION AND CRITICAL THINKING

Discussion Questions

1. How does market segmentation differ from market targeting? (AACSB: Communication)
2. Compare and contrast demographic and psychographic segmentation. Which is more useful to marketers? (AACSB: Communication; Reflective Thinking)
3. Explain how companies segment international markets. (AACSB: Communication)
4. Name and describe the levels at which market targeting can be carried out. Give an example of a company using each. (AACSB: Communication; Reflective Thinking)
5. How do marketers use local marketing and individual marketing? Do these terms mean the same thing? (AACSB: Communication; Reflective Thinking)
6. In the context of marketing, what is a product's *position*? How do marketers know what it is? (AACSB: Communication)

Critical Thinking Exercises

1. Visit a grocery store and examine the brands of breakfast cereal. Using the bases for segmenting consumer markets, identify the segmentation variables a specific brand appears to be using. Summarize the segmentation and targeting strategy for each brand. Identify brands with similar positioning strategies. (AACSB: Communication; Reflective Thinking)
2. When Nissan introduced its large Titan pickup truck in the United States and Toyota introduced the Tundra, each thought they would sell around 200,000 vehicles per year and had planned capacity for hundreds of thousands more because of the huge U.S. market potential. After all, the big three American manufacturers averaged sales of almost 2 million trucks per year in this market. But the two Japanese companies missed their sales goals by a wide margin. In a small group, discuss potential reasons for the dismal sales of the Titan and the Tundra in the U.S. market segment. (AACSB: Communication; Reflective Thinking)
3. Create an idea for a new business. Using the steps described in the chapter, develop a customer-driven marketing strategy. Describe your strategy and conclude with a positioning statement for this business. (AACSB: Communication; Reflective Thinking)

MINICASES AND APPLICATIONS

Marketing Technology   *"Net Neutrality"*

Most companies want customers to be heavy users of their products or services. However, when it comes to the Internet and wireless broadband service usage, that's not always the case. Internet providers, such as Comcast, have blocked or slowed down Internet traffic by heavy users, such as those who watch a lot of videos on YouTube. In 2009, the Federal Communications Commission (FCC) banned Comcast from blocking video file sharing, but that ruling was overturned in 2010 by a court ruling that the FCC does not have authority to enforce such *network neutrality* rules. Google, once a champion for unfettered Internet access for all, changed its tune once it found out it could profit from favoring some customers over others in the burgeoning wireless broadband arena. Google and Verizon teamed up to lobby for laws that allow them to favor some Web services over others. The FCC has since adopted new rules to enforce net neutrality principles. The debate is only going to get more heated, particularly since some businesses are relying more and more on the Internet to distribute their products and services. Some of these services, such as movies from Netflix, require considerable bandwidth.

1. Research *net neutrality* and write a report on the pros and cons of this principle from the viewpoint of businesses

providing Internet and wireless broadband services. (AACSB: Communication; Reflective Thinking)

2. What effect does very heavy usage by some customers have on other customers of broadband services? What are marketers of these services doing to counter the effect of heavy users? (AACSB: Communication; Reflective Thinking)

Marketing Ethics   Targeting Young Consumers

You would never know that consumers are more frugal these days if you look at the new children's lines from fashion houses such as Fendi, Versace, and Gucci. Toddler high fashion is not new, but designers are taking it to new levels and extending it beyond special-occasion clothing to everyday wear. In the past, some of the little girls marching down fashion runways carried dolls with matching outfits. But this year, many of the little children's fashions are geared around matching Mom and Dad clothing. Jennifer Lopez and her little ones helped Gucci launch a line for babies and children aged 2 to 8 years old. A Gucci children's outfit with a T-shirt, skinny jeans, a belt with the trademark double-G, a raincoat, and boots will set Mom and

Dad back about $1,000. A Burberry children's double-breasted trench coat for a baby runs $335, a bargain compared to Mom's matching $1,195 trench coat. The CEO of the Young Versace brand sees growth in this market and anticipates this brand making up 10 percent of the company's global sales in only a few years.

1. What segmentation variables are marketers using in this example? (AACSB: Communication; Reflective Thinking)
2. Is it appropriate that marketers focus on such a young market with high-priced clothing? (AACSB: Communication; Reflective Thinking; Ethical Reasoning)

Marketing by the Numbers   Kaplan University Recruits Veterans

For-profit universities, such as Kaplan University, DeVry University, and the University of Phoenix, actively pursue military veterans. In fact, the University of Phoenix has more veterans enrolled than any other college. These schools rely heavily on students receiving federal financial aid, and federal law limits the proportion of for-profit university revenue that can be derived from federal aid to 90 percent. However, enrolling veterans helps them stay below this threshold because the law does not count GI benefits as government assistance. With federal spending on veterans' education more than doubling to almost $10 billion between 2009 and 2010, this market is even more attractive. Kaplan University is one of the most aggressive

in this respect, with a team of 300 representatives focused solely on recruiting military veterans, increasing its enrollment of veterans by almost 30 percent in just one year.

1. Discuss the factors used to evaluate the usefulness of the military veteran segment. (AACSB: Communication; Reflective Thinking)
2. Using the chain ratio method described in Appendix 3: Marketing by the Numbers, estimate the market potential for undergraduate education in the veteran market. Be sure to state any assumptions. (AACSB: Communication; Use of IT; Analytical Reasoning)

Video Case   Boston Harbor Cruises

Since 1926, Boston Harbor Cruises has been providing customers with memorable experiences on ocean-going vessels in and around the Boston area. But these days, the term *cruise* has different meanings to those operating the four-generation family business. To thrive in both strong economic times and

in bad ones, Boston Harbor Cruises has progressively targeted various types of customers with its different boats and different services.

Sight-seeing trips around Boston Harbor, whale-watching tours, fast ferry service to Cape Cod, dinner and wedding cruises, and a high-speed thrill ride are among Boston Harbor Cruises' offerings. It even offers commuter services and off-shore construction support. Targeting this diverse customer base has become even more challenging as Boston Harbor Cruises has further differentiated the market into local customers, domestic vacationers, and international travelers.

After viewing the video featuring Boston Harbor Cruises, answer the following questions:

1. On what main variables has Boston Harbor Cruises mented its markets?
2. Which target marketing strategy best describes Boston Harbor Cruises' efforts? Support your choice.
3. How does Boston Harbor Cruises use the concepts of differentiation and positioning to build the right relationships with the right customers?

Company Cases

5 Porsche / 6 Darden Restaurants / 11 Tesco Fresh & Easy

See Appendix 1 for cases appropriate for this chapter. **Case 5, Porsche: Guarding the Old While Bringing in the New.** Porsche learns that focusing on existing customers doesn't always keep up with market trends, and keeping up with market trends doesn't always please existing customers. **Case 6, Darden Restaurants: Balancing Standardization** **and Differentiation.** By listening to customers, Darden finds success by targeting different customers through distinct restaurant formats. **Case 11, Tesco Fresh & Easy: Another British Invasion.** UK mega-grocer Tesco attempts to penetrate the U.S. market by targeting an underserved customer segment.

MARKETING AND THE MARKETING PROCESS (CHAPTERS 1–2)
NDING THE MARKETPLACE AND CONSUMERS (CHAPTERS 3–5)
A CUSTOMER-DRIVEN STRATEGY AND MIX (CHAPTERS 6–14)
MARKETING (CHAPTERS 15–16)

193

Products, Services, and Brands

Building Customer Value

CHAPTER ROAD MAP

Objective Outline

> **OBJECTIVE 1** Define *product* and the major classifications of products and services. What Is a Product? (196–201)

> **OBJECTIVE 2** Describe the decisions companies make regarding their individual products and services, product lines, and product mixes. Product and Service Decisions (201–208)

> **OBJECTIVE 3** Identify the four characteristics that affect the marketing of services and the additional marketing considerations that services require. Services Marketing (208–214)

> **OBJECTIVE 4** Discuss branding strategy—the decisions companies make in building and managing their brands. Branding Strategy: Building Strong Brands (215–223)

Previewing the Concepts

After examining customer-driven marketing strategy, we now take a deeper look at the marketing mix: the tactical tools that marketers use to implement their strategies and deliver superior customer value. In this and the next chapter, we'll study how companies develop and manage products and brands. Then, in the chapters that follow, we'll look at pricing, distribution, and marketing communication tools. The product and brand are usually the first and most basic marketing consideration. We start with a seemingly simple question: What *is* a product? As it turns out, the answer is not so simple.

Before starting into the chapter, let's look at a good brand story. Marketing is all about creating brands that connect with customers, and few marketers have done that as well as Nike. During the past several decades, Nike has built the Nike swoosh into one of the world's best-known brand symbols. Nike's outstanding success results from much more than just making and selling good sports gear. It's based on a deep-down connection between the iconic Nike brand and its customers.

First Stop

Nike: Building a Deep-Down Brand-Customer Relationship

The Nike "swoosh"—it's everywhere! Just for fun, try counting the swooshes whenever you pick up the sports pages or watch a pickup basketball game or tune into a televised soccer match. Through innovative marketing, Nike has built the ever-present swoosh into one of the best-known brand symbols on the planet.

During the 1980s, Nike revolutionized sports marketing. To build its brand image and market share, Nike lavishly outspent its competitors on big-name endorsements, splashy promotional events, and big-budget, in-your-face "Just Do It" ads. Nike gave customers much more than just good athletic gear. Whereas competitors stressed technical performance, Nike built relationships between the brand and its customers. Beyond shoes, apparel, and equipment, Nike marketed a way of life, a genuine passion for sports, a just-do-it attitude. Customers didn't just *wear* their Nikes, they *experienced* them. As the company stated on its Web page, "Nike has always known the truth—it's not so much the shoes but where they take you."

▲ **Nike's deep connections with customers give it powerful competitive advantage. Nike blurs the line between brand and experience.**

Newscom

Nike powered its way through the early 1990s, aggressively adding products in a dozen new sports, including baseball, golf, skateboarding, wall climbing, bicycling, and hiking. The then-brash young company slapped its familiar brand and swoosh logo on everything from sunglasses and soccer balls to batting gloves and golf clubs. It seemed that things couldn't be going any better.

In the late 1990s, however, Nike stumbled and its sales slipped. As the company grew larger, its creative juices seemed to run a bit dry and buyers seeking a new look switched to competing brands. Looking back, Nike's biggest obstacle may have been its own incredible success. As sales grew, the swoosh may have become too common to be cool. Instead of being *anti*establishment, Nike *was* the establishment, and its hip, once-hot relationship with customers cooled. Nike needed to rekindle the brand's meaning to consumers.

To turn things around, Nike returned to its roots: new-product innovation and a focus on customer relationships. But it set out to forge a new kind of brand-customer connection—an even deeper, more involving one. Its newly minted mission: Nike wants "to bring inspiration and innovation to every athlete* in the world (*if you have a body, you are an athlete.)" This time around, rather than simply outspending competitors on media ads and celebrity endorsers that talk *at* customers, Nike shifted toward cutting-edge marketing tools to interact *with* customers to build brand experiences and brand community.

Nike still invests hundreds of millions of dollars each year on creative advertising. However, it now spends less than one-third of its $593 million annual promotion budget on television and other traditional media, down from 55 percent 10 years ago. These days, behind the bright lights, Nike has developed a host of innovative new relationship-building approaches.

> Nike's outstanding success results from much more than just good sports gear. It's based on a deep-down connection between the iconic Nike brand and its customers.

Using community-oriented, digitally led, social networking tools, Nike is now building communities of customers who talk not just with the company about the brand, but with each other. "Nike's latest masterstroke is social networking, online and off," says one Nike watcher. Whether customers come to know Nike through ads, in-person events at a Niketown store, a local Nike running club, Nike's Facebook page or YouTube channel, or at one of the company's many community

Web sites, more and more people are bonding closely with the Nike brand experience. Consider this example:

> Twice a week, 30 or more people gather at the Nike store in Portland, Oregon, and go for an evening run. Afterward the members of the Niketown running club chat in the store over refreshments. Nike's staff keeps track of their performances and hails members who have logged more than 100 miles. The event is a classic example of up-close-and-personal relationship building with core customers.
>
> Nike augments such events with an online social network aimed at striking up meaningful long-term interactions with even more runners. The Nike+ running Web site lets customers with iPod-linked Nike shoes monitor their performances—the distance, pace, time, and calories burned during their runs. Runners can upload and track their own performances over time, compare them with those of other runners, and even participate in local or worldwide challenges.
>
> Talk about brand involvement. Nike+ can be the next best thing to your own personal trainer or jogging buddy. The Nike+ Web site offers a "Nike Coach" that provides advice and training routines to help you prepare for competitive races. When running, if you have earphones, at the end of every mile a friendly voice tells you how far you've gone and then counts down the final meters. If you hit the wall while running, the push of a button brings up a personally selected "power song" that gives you an extra boost and gets you going again. Back home again, after a quick upload of your running data, Nike+ charts, maps, and helps you analyze your run.
>
> In five years, 2 million Nike+ members have logged some 350 million miles on the site. Collectively, the Nike+ community has run the equivalent of 14,000 trips around the world or 730 journeys to the moon and back. The long-term goal is to have 15 percent of the world's 100 million runners using the system.

Thanks to efforts like Nike+, Nike has built a new kinship and sense of community with and between the brand and its customers. More than just something to buy, Nike products have once again become a part of customers' lives and times. As a result, the world's largest sportswear company is again achieving outstanding results. Over the past five years, even as the faltering economy left most sports apparel and footwear competitors gasping for breath, Nike's global sales and profits raced ahead 38 percent and 35 percent, respectively. During the past three years, Nike's share of the U.S. running shoe market has grown from 48 percent to 61 percent.

As in sports competition, the strongest and best-prepared athlete has the best chance of winning. With deep brand-customer relationships comes powerful competitive advantage. And Nike is once again very close to its customers. As one writer notes, "Nike is blurring the line between brand and experience."[1]

MyMarketingLab

Visit www.mymktlab.com to find activities that help you learn and review in order to succeed in this chapter.

A s the Nike example shows, in their quest to create customer relationships, marketers must build and manage products and brands that connect with customers. This chapter begins with a deceptively simple question: *What is a product?* After addressing this question, we look at ways to classify products in consumer and business markets. Then we discuss the important decisions that marketers make regarding individual products, product lines, and product mixes. Next, we examine the characteristics and marketing requirements of a special form of product—services. Finally, we look into the critically important issue of how marketers build and manage product and service brands.

What Is a Product?

Author Comment ▶
As you'll see, this is a deceptively simple question with a very complex answer.

Product
Anything that can be offered to a market for attention, acquisition, use, or consumption that might satisfy a want or need.

Service
An activity, benefit, or satisfaction offered for sale that is essentially intangible and does not result in the ownership of anything.

We define a **product** as anything that can be offered to a market for attention, acquisition, use, or consumption that might satisfy a want or need. Products include more than just tangible objects, such as cars, computers, or cell phones. Broadly defined, *products* also include services, events, persons, places, organizations, ideas, or a mixture of these. Throughout this text, we use the term *product* broadly to include any or all of these entities. Thus, an Apple iPhone, a Toyota Camry, and a Caffè Mocha at Starbucks are products. But so are a trip to Las Vegas, E*Trade online investment services, and advice from your family doctor.

Because of their importance in the world economy, we give special attention to services. **Services** are a form of product that consists of activities, benefits, or satisfactions offered for sale that are essentially intangible and do not result in the ownership of anything. Examples include banking, hotel services, airline travel, retail, wireless communication, and home-repair services. We will look at services more closely later in this chapter.

Products, Services, and Experiences

Products are a key element in the overall *market offering*. Marketing mix planning begins with building an offering that brings value to target customers. This offering becomes the basis on which the company builds profitable customer relationships.

A company's market offering often includes both tangible goods and services. At one extreme, the market offer may consist of a *pure tangible good*, such as soap, toothpaste, or salt; no services accompany the product. At the other extreme are *pure services*, for which the market offer consists primarily of a service. Examples include a doctor's exam or financial services. Between these two extremes, however, many goods-and-services combinations are possible.

Today, as products and services become more commoditized, many companies are moving to a new level in creating value for their customers. To differentiate their offers, beyond simply making products and delivering services, they are creating and managing customer *experiences* with their brands or company.

Experiences have always been an important part of marketing for some companies. Disney has long manufactured dreams and memories through its movies and theme parks. And Nike has long declared, "It's not so much the shoes but where they take you." Today, however, all kinds of firms are recasting their traditional goods and services to create experiences. ▶ For example, the Olive Garden knows that it's selling more than just Italian food; it's selling a complete dining experience.[2]

▲ **Creating customer experiences: Olive Garden sells more than just Italian food. It serves up an idealized Italian family meal experience. "When you're here, you're family."**

Darden Concepts Inc.

A decade ago, Olive Garden's menu had grown stale, and sales were declining. Research showed that "people missed the emotional comfort and connectivity that comes with family," says Drew Madsen, president and COO of parent company Darden Restaurants. So the Olive Garden set out to recraft its guest dining experience, under the tagline "When you're here, you're family." To actually deliver that guest experience, the Olive Garden began tying everything it did to an idealized Italian family meal. For example, it designed new restaurants to suggest Italian farmhouses, with a large family-style table, modeled on one in a Florentine trattoria. In partnership with Italians, the Olive Garden even founded the Culinary Institute of Tuscany (CIT) in an 11th-century Tuscan village.

Through CIT, hundreds of Olive Garden chefs and restaurant team members have traveled to Italy to gain inspiration and learn the secrets of authentic Italian foods "that you'll enjoy sharing with your friends and family." More than 10 times a year, the company sends restaurant team members, many of whom have never set foot in Italy, to spend a week at CIT, where local experts expose them to everything from how olive oil gets pressed to how to layer flavors in Bolognese. Back home, such inspiring employee experiences translate into an authentic guest experience that's rare for a casual dining restaurant. "People come to a restaurant for both physical and emotional nourishment," says Madsen. "The physical is the food; and the emotional is how you feel when you leave." The now highly successful Olive Garden chain delivers on both.

Companies that market experiences realize that customers are really buying much more than just products and services. They are buying what those offers will *do* for them. A recent BMW ad puts it this way: "We realized a long time ago that what you make people feel is just as important as what you make."

Levels of Product and Services

Product planners need to think about products and services on three levels (see ▶ **Figure 7.1**). Each level adds more customer value. The most basic level is the *core customer value*, which

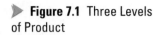

Figure 7.1 Three Levels
of Product

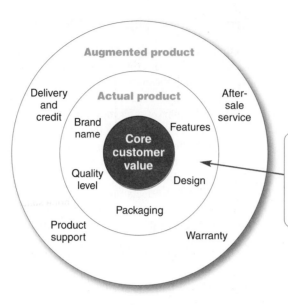

At the most basic level, the company asks, "What is the customer really buying?" For example, people who buy a BlackBerry are buying more than a wireless communications device. They are buying freedom and on-the-go connectivity. Each additional product level helps to build this core value.

▲ Core, actual, and augmented product: People who buy an iPad are buying much more than a tablet computer. They are buying entertainment, self-expression, productivity, and connectivity—a mobile and personal window to the world.

melhi/iStockphoto.com

Consumer product

A product bought by final consumers
for personal consumption.

addresses the question: *What is the buyer really buying?* When designing products, marketers must first define the core, problem-solving benefits or services that consumers seek. A woman buying lipstick buys more than lip color. Charles Revson of Revlon saw this early: "In the factory, we make cosmetics; in the store, we sell hope." And people who buy an Apple iPad are buying much more than just a tablet computer. They are buying entertainment, self-expression, productivity, and connectivity with friends and family—a mobile and personal window to the world.

At the second level, product planners must turn the core benefit into an *actual product*. They need to develop product and service features, a design, a quality level, a brand name, and packaging. For example, the iPad is an actual product. Its name, parts, styling, features, packaging, and other attributes have all been carefully combined to deliver the core customer value of staying connected.

Finally, product planners must build an *augmented product* around the core benefit and actual product by offering additional consumer services and benefits. ▶ The iPad is more than just a digital device. It provides consumers with a complete connectivity solution. Thus, when consumers buy an iPad, Apple and its reseller also might give buyers a warranty on parts and workmanship, instructions on how to use the device, quick repair services when needed, and a Web site to use if they have problems or questions. It also provides access to a huge assortment of apps and accessories.

Consumers see products as complex bundles of benefits that satisfy their needs. When developing products, marketers first must identify the *core customer value* that consumers seek from the product. They must then design the *actual* product and find ways to *augment* it to create this customer value and the most satisfying customer experience.

Product and Service Classifications

Products and services fall into two broad classes based on the types of consumers that use them: *consumer products* and *industrial products*. Broadly defined, products also include other marketable entities such as experiences, organizations, persons, places, and ideas.

Consumer Products

Consumer products are products and services bought by final consumers for personal consumption. Marketers usually classify these products and services further based on how consumers go about buying them. Consumer products include *convenience products*, *shopping products*, *specialty products*, and *unsought products*. These products differ in the ways consumers buy them and, therefore, in how they are marketed (see ▶ **Table 7.1**).

| ▶ **Table 7.1** | Marketing Considerations for Consumer Products |

| | Type of Consumer Product | | | |
Marketing Considerations	**Convenience**	**Shopping**	**Specialty**	**Unsought**
Customer buying behavior	Frequent purchase; little planning, little comparison or shopping effort; low customer involvement	Less frequent purchase; much planning and shopping effort; comparison of brands on price, quality, and style	Strong brand preference and loyalty; special purchase effort; little comparison of brands; low price sensitivity	Little product awareness or knowledge (or, if aware, little or even negative interest)
Price	Low price	Higher price	High price	Varies
Distribution	Widespread distribution; convenient locations	Selective distribution in fewer outlets	Exclusive distribution in only one or a few outlets per market area	Varies
Promotion	Mass promotion by the producer	Advertising and personal selling by both the producer and resellers	More carefully targeted promotion by both the producer and resellers	Aggressive advertising and personal selling by the producer and resellers
Examples	Toothpaste, magazines, and laundry detergent	Major appliances, televisions, furniture, and clothing	Luxury goods, such as Rolex watches or fine crystal	Life insurance and Red Cross blood donations

Convenience product
A consumer product that customers usually buy frequently, immediately, and with minimal comparison and buying effort.

Shopping product
A consumer product that the customer, in the process of selecting and purchasing, usually compares on such attributes as suitability, quality, price, and style.

Specialty product
A consumer product with unique characteristics or brand identification for which a significant group of buyers is willing to make a special purchase effort.

Unsought product
A consumer product that the consumer either does not know about or knows about but does not normally consider buying.

Industrial product
A product bought by individuals and organizations for further processing or for use in conducting a business.

Convenience products are consumer products and services that customers usually buy frequently, immediately, and with minimal comparison and buying effort. Examples include laundry detergent, candy, magazines, and fast food. Convenience products are usually low priced, and marketers place them in many locations to make them readily available when customers need or want them.

Shopping products are less frequently purchased consumer products and services that customers compare carefully on suitability, quality, price, and style. When buying shopping products and services, consumers spend much time and effort in gathering information and making comparisons. Examples include furniture, clothing, used cars, major appliances, and hotel and airline services. Shopping product marketers usually distribute their products through fewer outlets but provide deeper sales support to help customers in their comparison efforts.

Specialty products are consumer products and services with unique characteristics or brand identification for which a significant group of buyers is willing to make a special purchase effort. Examples include specific brands of cars, high-priced photographic equipment, designer clothes, and the services of medical or legal specialists. A Lamborghini automobile, for example, is a specialty product because buyers are usually willing to travel great distances to buy one. Buyers normally do not compare specialty products. They invest only the time needed to reach dealers carrying the wanted products.

Unsought products are consumer products that the consumer either does not know about or knows about but does not normally consider buying. Most major new innovations are unsought until the consumer becomes aware of them through advertising. Classic examples of known but unsought products and services are life insurance, preplanned funeral services, and blood donations to the Red Cross. By their very nature, unsought products require a lot of advertising, personal selling, and other marketing efforts.

Industrial Products

Industrial products are those products purchased for further processing or for use in conducting a business. Thus, the distinction between a consumer product and an industrial product is based on the *purpose* for which the product is purchased. If a consumer buys a lawn mower for use around home, the lawn mower is a consumer product. If the same consumer buys the same lawn mower for use in a landscaping business, the lawn mower is an industrial product.

The three groups of industrial products and services are materials and parts, capital items, and supplies and services. *Materials and parts* include raw materials as well as manufactured materials and parts. Raw materials consist of farm products (wheat, cotton, livestock, fruits, vegetables) and natural products (fish, lumber, crude petroleum, iron ore). Manufactured materials and parts consist of component materials (iron, yarn, cement, wires) and component parts (small motors, tires, castings). Most manufactured materials and parts are sold directly to industrial users. Price and service are the major marketing factors; branding and advertising tend to be less important.

Capital items are industrial products that aid in the buyer's production or operations, including installations and accessory equipment. Installations consist of major purchases such as buildings (factories, offices) and fixed equipment (generators, drill presses, large computer systems, elevators). Accessory equipment includes portable factory equipment and tools (hand tools, lift trucks) and office equipment (computers, fax machines, desks). They have a shorter life than installations and simply aid in the production process.

The final group of industrial products is *supplies and services*. Supplies include operating supplies (lubricants, coal, paper, pencils) and repair and maintenance items (paint, nails, brooms). Supplies are the convenience products of the industrial field because they are usually purchased with a minimum of effort or comparison. Business services include maintenance and repair services (window cleaning, computer repair) and business advisory services (legal, management consulting, advertising). Such services are usually supplied under contract.

Organizations, Persons, Places, and Ideas

In addition to tangible products and services, marketers have broadened the concept of a product to include other market offerings: organizations, persons, places, and ideas.

Organizations often carry out activities to "sell" the organization itself. *Organization marketing* consists of activities undertaken to create, maintain, or change the attitudes and behavior of target consumers toward an organization. Both profit and not-for-profit organizations practice organization marketing. Business firms sponsor public relations or *corporate image marketing* campaigns to market themselves and polish their images. IBM's Smarter Planet campaign, for example, markets IBM as a company that provides innovative solutions that improve the world's IQ. IBM smart solutions span an incredible breadth of industries and processes—from commerce and digital communications to health care, education, and sustainability. For example, one Smarter Planet ad tells how IBM is helping to follow food "from farm to fork" in an effort to reduce the 25 percent of the world's food currently lost to spoilage. At the other extreme, another tells how IBM analytics helped New York State save $889 million by catching tax dodgers.

People can also be thought of as products. *Person marketing* consists of activities undertaken to create, maintain, or change attitudes or behavior toward particular people. People ranging from presidents, entertainers, and sports figures to professionals such as doctors, lawyers, and architects use person marketing to build their reputations. And businesses, charities, and other organizations use well-known personalities to help sell their products or causes. For example, Nike is represented by well-known athletes such as Kobe Bryant, Serena Williams, and hundreds of others around the globe in sports ranging from tennis and basketball to ice hockey and cricket.

The skillful use of marketing can turn a person's name into a powerhouse brand. Consider the chefs on the Food Network, who now approximate rock stars to their many ardent fans. These days it's hard to shop for kitchen products without bumping into goods endorsed by these culinary all-stars. For example, celebrity chef Bobby Flay endorses a kitchen closet full of his own and other

▲ **Organization Marketing: IBM's Smarter Planet campaign markets IBM as a company that helps improve the world's IQ. This ad tells how IBM technologies are helping to create safer food supply chains.**

Reprint Courtesy of International Business Machines Corporation,
© 2011 International Business Machines Corporation

brands of rubs, sauces, and condiments. And if you can find it in the kitchen, department store retailer Kohl's has managed to slap Bobby Flay's name onto it. Similarly, Rachael Ray is a one-woman marketing phenomenon. Beyond her Food Network shows, she landed her own daytime talk show; endorses a litany of orange-colored cookware, bakeware, and cutlery; has her own brand of dog food called Nutrish; and brands her own EVOO (extra virgin olive oil, for those not familiar with Rayisms).

Place marketing involves activities undertaken to create, maintain, or change attitudes or behavior toward particular places. Cities, states, regions, and even entire nations compete to attract tourists, new residents, conventions, and company offices and factories. New York State advertises "I ♥ NY," and California urges you to "Find yourself here." Tourism Ireland, the Irish tourism agency, invites travelers to "Go where Ireland takes you." The Discover Ireland Web site offers information about the country and its attractions, a travel planner, special vacation offers, lists of tour operators, and much more information that makes it easier to say "yes" to visiting Ireland.[3]

Ideas can also be marketed. In one sense, all marketing is the marketing of an idea, whether it is the general idea of brushing your teeth or the specific idea that Crest toothpastes create "healthy, beautiful smiles for life." Here, however, we narrow our focus to the marketing of *social ideas*. This area has been called **social marketing**, defined by the Social Marketing Institute (SMI) as the use of commercial marketing concepts and tools in programs designed to influence individuals' behavior to improve their well-being and that of society.[4]

Social marketing programs cover a wide range of issues. The Ad Council of America (www.adcouncil.org), for example, has developed dozens of social advertising campaigns involving issues ranging from health care, education, and environmental sustainability to human rights and personal safety. But social marketing involves much more than just advertising—the SMI encourages the use of a broad range of marketing tools. "Social marketing goes well beyond the promotional '*P*' of the marketing mix to include every other element to achieve its social change objectives," says the SMI's executive director.[5]

Social marketing
The use of commercial marketing concepts and tools in programs designed to influence individuals' behavior to improve their well-being and that of society.

Product and Service Decisions

Marketers make product and service decisions at three levels: individual product decisions, product line decisions, and product mix decisions. We discuss each in turn.

Individual Product and Service Decisions

Figure 7.2 shows the important decisions in the development and marketing of individual products and services. We will focus on decisions about *product attributes*, *branding*, *packaging*, *labeling*, and *product support services*.

Product and Service Attributes

Developing a product or service involves defining the benefits that it will offer. These benefits are communicated and delivered by product attributes such as *quality*, *features*, and *style and design*.

Product Quality. **Product quality** is one of the marketer's major positioning tools. Quality affects product or service performance; thus, it is closely linked to customer value and satisfaction. In the narrowest sense, quality can be defined as "freedom from defects." But most marketers go beyond this narrow definition. Instead, they define quality in terms of creating customer value and satisfaction. The American Society for Quality defines *quality*

Author Comment ▶
Now that we've answered the "What Is a Product?" question, we dig into the specific decisions that companies must make when designing and marketing products and services.

Product quality
The characteristics of a product or service that bear on its ability to satisfy stated or implied customer needs.

▶ **Figure 7.2** Individual Product Decisions

Don't forget Figure 7.1! The focus of all of these decisions is to create core customer value.

Product attributes → Branding → Packaging → Labeling → Product support services

as the characteristics of a product or service that bear on its ability to satisfy stated or implied customer needs. Similarly, Siemens defines quality this way: "Quality is when our customers come back and our products don't."[6]

Total quality management (*TQM*) is an approach in which all of the company's people are involved in constantly improving the quality of products, services, and business processes. For most top companies, customer-driven quality has become a way of doing business. Today, companies are taking a *return on quality* approach, viewing quality as an investment and holding quality efforts accountable for bottom-line results.

Product quality has two dimensions: level and consistency. In developing a product, the marketer must first choose a *quality level* that will support the product's positioning. Here, product quality means *performance quality*—the product's ability to perform its functions. For example, a Rolls-Royce provides higher performance quality than a Chevrolet: It has a smoother ride, provides more luxury and "creature comforts," and lasts longer. Companies rarely try to offer the highest possible performance quality level; few customers want or can afford the high levels of quality offered in products such as a Rolls-Royce automobile, a Viking range, or a Rolex watch. Instead, companies choose a quality level that matches target market needs and the quality levels of competing products.

Beyond quality level, high quality also can mean high levels of quality consistency. Here, product quality means *conformance quality*—freedom from defects and *consistency* in delivering a targeted level of performance. All companies should strive for high levels of conformance quality. In this sense, a Chevrolet can have just as much quality as a Rolls-Royce. Although a Chevy doesn't perform at the same level as a Rolls-Royce, it can just as consistently deliver the quality that customers pay for and expect.

Product Features. A product can be offered with varying features. A stripped-down model, one without any extras, is the starting point. The company can then create higher-level models by adding more features. Features are a competitive tool for differentiating the company's product from competitors' products. Being the first producer to introduce a valued new feature is one of the most effective ways to compete.

How can a company identify new features and decide which ones to add to its product? It should periodically survey buyers who have used the product and ask these questions: How do you like the product? Which specific features of the product do you like most? Which features could we add to improve the product? The answers to these questions provide the company with a rich list of feature ideas. The company can then assess each feature's *value* to customers versus its *cost* to the company. Features that customers value highly in relation to costs should be added.

Product Style and Design. Another way to add customer value is through distinctive *product style and design*. Design is a larger concept than style. *Style* simply describes the appearance of a product. Styles can be eye catching or yawn producing. A sensational style may grab attention and produce pleasing aesthetics, but it does not necessarily make the product *perform* better. Unlike style, *design* is more than skin deep—it goes to the very heart of a product. Good design contributes to a product's usefulness as well as to its looks.

Good design doesn't start with brainstorming new ideas and making prototypes. Design begins with observing customers, deeply understanding their needs, and shaping their product-use experience. Product designers should think less about technical product specifications and more about how customers will use and benefit from the product. ▶ Consider OXO's outstanding design philosophy and process:[7]

> OXO's uniquely designed kitchen and gardening gadgets look pretty cool. But to OXO, good design means a lot more than good looks. It means that OXO tools work—*really* work—for anyone and everyone. For OXO, design means a salad spinner that can be used with one hand; tools with pressure-absorbing, nonslip handles that make them more efficient; or a watering can with a spout that rotates back toward the body, allowing for easier filling and storing. Ever since it came out with its supereffective Good Grips vegetable peeler in 1990, OXO has been known for clever designs that make everyday living easier. Its eye-catching, super useful houseware designs have even been featured in museum exhibitions, and OXO has now extended its design touch to office supplies, medical devices, and baby products.

We've remodeled the most important parts of your kitchen.

We've remodeled the peeler. We've remodeled the garlic press, the can opener and the wooden spoon. And we didn't stop there. Any kitchen tools that weren't comfortable or easy to use were fair game. The idea isn't to make the old tools

obsolete, it's to make them better. If we can't make them better, we don't make them at all. Pick up OXO Good Grips® and you'll feel what we mean. They're easy to hold, easy to use and easy to love. In fact, they might just change the way you feel about your kitchen.

OXO GOOD GRIPS

For information call 1(800-545-4411)

▲ **Product design: OXO focuses on the desired end-user experience, and then translates its pie-cutter-in-the-sky notions into eminently usable gadgets.**

OXO International Inc.

Brand

A name, term, sign, symbol, or design, or a combination of these, that identifies the products or services of one seller or group of sellers and differentiates them from those of competitors.

Much of OXO's design inspiration comes directly from users. "Every product that we make starts with . . . watching how people use things," says Alex Lee, OXO's president. "Those are the gems—when you pull out a latent problem." For example, after watching people struggle with the traditional Pyrex measuring cup, OXO discovered a critical flaw: You can't tell how full it is without lifting it up to eye level. The resulting OXO measuring cups have markings down the *inside* that can be read from above, big enough to read without glasses. Thus, OXO begins with a desired end-user experience and then translates pie-cutter-in-the-sky notions into eminently usable gadgets.

Branding

Perhaps the most distinctive skill of professional marketers is their ability to build and manage brands. A **brand** is a name, term, sign, symbol, or design, or a combination of these, that identifies the maker or seller of a product or service. Consumers view a brand as an important part of a product, and branding can add value to a consumer's purchase. Customers attach meanings to brands and develop brand relationships. As a result, brands have meaning well beyond a product's physical attributes. For example, consider Coca-Cola:[8]

> In an interesting taste test of Coca-Cola versus Pepsi, 67 subjects were connected to brain-wave-monitoring machines while they consumed both products. When the soft drinks were unmarked, consumer preferences were split down the middle. But when the brands were identified, subjects chose Coke over Pepsi by a margin of 75 percent to 25 percent. When drinking the identified Coke brand, the brain areas that lit up most were those associated with cognitive control and memory—a place where culture concepts are stored. That didn't happen as much when drinking Pepsi. Why? According to one brand strategist, it's because of Coca-Cola's long-established brand imagery—the almost 100-year-old contour bottle and cursive font and its association with iconic images ranging from Mean Joe Greene and the Polar Bears to Santa Claus. Pepsi's imagery isn't quite as deeply rooted. Although people might associate Pepsi with a hot celebrity or the "Pepsi generation" appeal, they probably don't link it to the strong and emotional American icons associated with Coke. The conclusion? Plain and simple: Consumer preference isn't based on taste alone. Coke's iconic brand appears to make a difference.

Branding has become so strong that today hardly anything goes unbranded. Salt is packaged in branded containers, common nuts and bolts are packaged with a distributor's label, and automobile parts—spark plugs, tires, filters—bear brand names that differ from those of the automakers. Even fruits, vegetables, dairy products, and poultry are branded—Sunkist oranges, Dole Classic iceberg salads, Horizon Organic milk, Perdue chickens, Eggland's Best eggs.

Branding helps buyers in many ways. Brand names help consumers identify products that might benefit them. Brands also say something about product quality and consistency—buyers who always buy the same brand know that they will get the same features, benefits, and quality each time they buy. Branding also gives the seller several advantages. The seller's brand name and trademark provide legal protection for unique product features that otherwise might be copied by competitors. Branding helps the seller to segment markets. For example, rather than offering just one general product to all consumers, Toyota can offer the different Lexus, Toyota, and Scion brands, each with numerous sub-brands—such as Camry, Corolla, Prius, Matrix, Yaris, Tundra, and Land Cruiser. Finally, a brand name becomes the basis on which a whole story can be built about a product's special qualities. For example, Eggland's Best sets itself apart from ordinary eggs by promising: "Better Taste. Better Nutrition. Better Eggs."

Building and managing brands are perhaps the marketer's most important tasks. We will discuss branding strategy in more detail later in the chapter.

Packaging

Packaging | The activities of designing and producing the container or wrapper for a product.

Packaging involves designing and producing the container or wrapper for a product. Traditionally, the primary function of the package was to hold and protect the product. In recent times, however, packaging has become an important marketing tool as well. Increased competition and clutter on retail store shelves means that packages must now perform many sales tasks—from attracting buyers, to communicating brand positioning, to closing the sale. As one packaging expert notes, "Not every consumer sees a brand's advertising or is exposed to the exciting social media that your brand is doing. But all of the consumers who buy your product do interact with your humble package."[9]

Companies are realizing the power of good packaging to create immediate consumer recognition of a brand. For example, an average supermarket stocks 48,750 items; the average Walmart supercenter carries 142,000 items. The typical shopper passes by some 300 items per minute, and from 40 percent to 70 percent of all purchase decisions are made in stores. In this highly competitive environment, the package may be the seller's last and best chance to influence buyers. Thus, for many companies, the package itself has become an important promotional medium.[10]

▲ Poorly designed packages can cause frustration for customers and lost sales for companies. "Wrap rage" is the frustration we all feel when trying to free a product from a nearly impenetrable package.

Tktktk/Wikipedia

Poorly designed packages can cause headaches for consumers and lost sales for the company. ▶ Think about all those hard-to-open packages, such as DVD cases sealed with impossibly sticky labels, packaging with finger-splitting wire twist-ties, or sealed plastic clamshell containers that cause "wrap rage" and send about 6,000 people to the hospital each year with lacerations and puncture wounds. Another packaging issue is overpackaging— as when a tiny UBS flash drive in an oversized cardboard and plastic display package is delivered in a giant corrugated shipping carton. Overpackaging creates an incredible amount of waste, frustrating those who care about the environment.[11]

By contrast, innovative packaging can give a company an advantage over competitors and boost sales. For example, Method revolutionized the laundry detergent market last year with its new environmentally friendly, ultra-concentrated detergent (8x concentrated versus the standard 2x). But just as revolutionary was the way Method packaged the product:[12]

The Method laundry detergent package represents a trifecta in great design. First, it's tiny! Less packaging means no more heavy lifting. Second, instead of the traditional jug and measuring cap, the Method container has a nifty pump top that allows accurate, one-handed, no-mess dosing directly into the machine: 4 pumps = 1 load. Finally, the package contains 50 percent recycled materials. Says Method co-founder Eric Ryan, "Our new laundry detergent is transforming the way we do laundry by eliminating heavy, drippy, messy jugs from the laundry room." The new packaging received the International Design Excellence Award last year as well as a Good Housekeeping VIP (Very Innovative Product) award. Such innovations have helped make Method one of the nation's fastest growing companies.

In recent years, product safety has also become a major packaging concern. We have all learned to deal with hard-to-open "childproof" packaging. Due to the rash of product tampering scares in the 1980s, most drug producers and food makers now put their products in tamper-resistant packages. In making packaging decisions, the company also must heed growing environmental concerns. Fortunately, like Method, many companies have gone "green" by reducing their packaging and using environmentally responsible packaging materials.

Labeling

Labels range from simple tags attached to products to complex graphics that are part of the packaging. They perform several functions. At the very least, the label *identifies* the product or brand, such as the name Sunkist stamped on oranges. The label might also *describe* several things about the product—who made it, where it was made, when it was made, its contents, how it is to be used, and how to use it safely. Finally, the label might help to *promote* the brand, support its positioning, and connect with customers. For many companies, labels have become an important element in broader marketing campaigns.

Labels and brand logos can support the brand's positioning and add personality to the brand. For example, Pepsi's recently updated packaging sports a new, more uplifting smiling logo. "It feels like the same Pepsi we know and love," says a brand expert, "but it's more adventurous, more youthful, with a bit more personality to it." It presents a "spirit of optimism and youth," says a Pepsi marketer.[13]

In fact, brand labels and logos can become a crucial element in the brand-customer connection. For example, when PepsiCo recently changed the label design for its Tropicana orange juice packaging, outraged Tropicana loyalists flooded blogs and other online channels for months, calling the new design everything from "ugly" to "stupid" to "generic." PepsiCo conceded and returned to the old packaging—the classic orange with a straw poking out—that customers love. ▶ Similarly, when Gap recently introduced a more contemporary redesign of its familiar old logo—the well-known white text on a blue square—customers went ballistic and imposed intense online pressure. Gap reinstated the old logo after only one week. Such examples "highlight a powerful connection people have to the visual representations of their beloved brands," says an analyst.[14]

▲ **Brand labels and logos: When Gap tried to modernize its familiar old logo, customers went ballistic, highlighting the powerful connection people have to the visual representations of their beloved brands.**

Jean Francois FREY/PHOTOPQR/L'ALSACE/Newscom

Along with the positives, there has been a long history of legal concerns about packaging and labels. The Federal Trade Commission Act of 1914 held that false, misleading, or deceptive labels or packages constitute unfair competition. Labels can mislead customers, fail to describe important ingredients, or fail to include needed safety warnings. As a result, several federal and state laws regulate labeling. The most prominent is the Fair Packaging and Labeling Act of 1966, which set mandatory labeling requirements, encouraged voluntary industry packaging standards, and allowed federal agencies to set packaging regulations in specific industries.

Labeling has been affected in recent times by *unit pricing* (stating the price per unit of a standard measure), *open dating* (stating the expected shelf life of the product), and *nutritional labeling* (stating the nutritional values in the product). The Nutritional Labeling and Educational Act of 1990 requires sellers to provide detailed nutritional information on food products, and recent sweeping actions by the Food and Drug Administration (FDA) regulate the use of health-related terms such as *low fat*, *light*, and *high fiber*. Sellers must ensure that their labels contain all the required information.

Product Support Services

Customer service is another element of product strategy. A company's offer usually includes some support services, which can be a minor part or a major part of the total offering. Later in this chapter, we will discuss services as products in themselves. Here, we discuss services that augment actual products.

Support services are an important part of the customer's overall brand experience. ▶ For example, upscale department store retailer Nordstrom knows that good marketing doesn't stop with making the sale. Keeping customers happy *after* the sale is the key to building lasting relationships. Nordstrom's motto: "Take care of customers, no matter what it takes," before, during, and after the sale.[15]

Nordstrom thrives on stories about its after-sale service heroics, such as employees dropping off orders at customers' homes or warming up cars while customers spend a little more time shopping. In one case, a sales clerk reportedly gave a customer a refund on a tire—Nordstrom doesn't carry tires, but the store prides itself on a no-questions-asked return policy. In another case, a Nordstrom sales clerk stopped a customer in the store and asked if the shoes she was

▲ **Nordstrom thrives on stories about its after-sale service. It wants to "Take care of customers, no matter what it takes," before, during, and after the sale.**

Kelly Redinger/Vibe Images/Alamy

Product line

A group of products that are closely related because they function in a similar manner, are sold to the same customer groups, are marketed through the same types of outlets, or fall within given price ranges.

wearing had been bought there. When a customer said yes, the clerk insisted on replacing them on the spot, saying that they hadn't worn as well as they should. There's even a story about a man whose wife, a loyal Nordstrom customer, died with her Nordstrom account $1,000 in arrears. Not only did Nordstrom settle the account, but it also sent flowers to the funeral. Such service heroics keep Nordstrom customers coming back again and again.

The first step in designing support services is to survey customers periodically to assess the value of current services and obtain ideas for new ones. Once the company has assessed the quality of various support services to customers, it can take steps to fix problems and add new services that will both delight customers and yield profits to the company.

Many companies are now using a sophisticated mix of phone, e-mail, Internet, and interactive voice and data technologies to provide support services that were not possible before. For example, HP offers a complete set of after-sale services for all of its products. It promises "HP Total Care—expert help for every stage of your product's life. From choosing it, to configuring it, to protecting it, to tuning it up—all the way to recycling it." Customers can click on the HP Total Care service portal that offers online resources for HP products and 24/7 tech support, which can be accessed via e-mail, instant online chat, and telephone.[16]

Product Line Decisions

Beyond decisions about individual products and services, product strategy also calls for building a product line. A **product line** is a group of products that are closely related because they function in a similar manner, are sold to the same customer groups, are marketed through the same types of outlets, or fall within given price ranges. For example, Nike produces several lines of athletic shoes and apparel, and Marriott offers several lines of hotels.

The major product line decision involves *product line length*—the number of items in the product line. The line is too short if the manager can increase profits by adding items; the line is too long if the manager can increase profits by dropping items. Managers need to analyze their product lines periodically to assess each item's sales and profits and understand how each item contributes to the line's overall performance.

A company can expand its product line in two ways: by *line filling* or *line stretching*. *Product line filling* involves adding more items within the present range of the line. There are several reasons for product line filling: reaching for extra profits, satisfying dealers, using excess capacity, being the leading full-line company, and plugging holes to keep out competitors. However, line filling is overdone if it results in cannibalization and customer confusion. The company should ensure that new items are noticeably different from existing ones.

Product line stretching occurs when a company lengthens its product line beyond its current range. The company can stretch its line downward, upward, or both ways. Companies located at the upper end of the market can stretch their lines *downward*. A company may stretch downward to plug a market hole that otherwise would attract a new competitor or respond to a competitor's attack on the upper end. Or it may add low-end products because it finds faster growth taking place in the low-end segments. Companies can also stretch their product lines *upward*. Sometimes, companies stretch upward to add prestige to their current products. Or they may be attracted by a faster growth rate or higher margins at the higher end.

To broaden its market appeal and boost growth, BMW has in recent years stretched its line in *both directions* while at the same time filling the gaps in between.[17]

Over the past decade, BMW has morphed from a one-brand, five-model carmaker into a powerhouse with three brands, 14 "Series," and more than 30 distinct models. Not only has the carmaker stretched its product line downward, with MINI Cooper and its compact 1-Series models, but it has also stretched it upward with the addition of Rolls-Royce. The company has filled the gaps in between with Z4 roadsters, 6-Series coupe, X-Series crossovers and sports activity vehicles; and M-Series high-performance models. Next up: a growing selection of hybrids and all-electric cars. As a result, BMW has boosted its appeal to the rich, the super-rich, and the wannabe-rich, all without departing from its pure premium positioning.

Product Mix Decisions

Product mix (or product portfolio)
The set of all product lines and items that a particular seller offers for sale.

An organization with several product lines has a product mix. A **product mix** (or **product portfolio**) consists of all the product lines and items that a particular seller offers for sale. Campbell Soup Company's product mix consists of three major product lines: healthy beverages, baked snacks, and simple meals.[18] Each product line consists of several sublines. For example, the simple meals line consists of soups, sauces, and pastas. Each line and subline has many individual items. Altogether, Campbell's product mix includes hundreds of items.

A company's product mix has four important dimensions: width, length, depth, and consistency. Product mix *width* refers to the number of different product lines the company carries. For example, Campbell Soup Company has a fairly contained product mix that fits its mission of "nourishing people's lives everywhere, every day." By contrast, GE manufactures as many as 250,000 items across a broad range of categories, from light bulbs to jet engines and diesel locomotives.

Product mix *length* refers to the total number of items a company carries within its product lines. Campbell Soup carries several brands within each line. For example, its simple meals line includes Campbell's soups, Wolfgang Puck soups and broths, Prego tomato sauce, Pace salsas, and Swanson broths, plus other international brands.

Product mix *depth* refers to the number of versions offered for each product in the line. Campbell's soups come in seven varieties, ranging from Campbell's Condensed soups and Campbell's Chunky soups to Campbell's Select Harvest soups and Campbell's Healthy Request soups. Each variety offers a number of forms and formulations. For example, you can buy Campbell's Chunky Hearty Beef Noodle soup, Chunky Chicken & Dumplings soup, and Chunky Steak & Potato soup, in either cans or microwavable containers.

Finally, the *consistency* of the product mix refers to how closely related the various product lines are in end use, production requirements, distribution channels, or some other way. Campbell Soup Company's product lines are consistent insofar as they are consumer products and go through the same distribution channels. The lines are less consistent insofar as they perform different functions for buyers.

These product mix dimensions provide the handles for defining the company's product strategy. The company can increase its business in four ways. It can add new product lines, widening its product mix. In this way, its new lines build on the company's reputation in its other lines. The company can lengthen its existing product lines to become a more full-line company. It can add more versions of each product and thus deepen its product mix. Finally, the company can pursue more product line consistency—or less—depending on whether it wants to have a strong reputation in a single field or in several fields.

▲ The product mix: Campbell Soup Company has a nicely contained product line consistent with its mission of "nourishing people's lives everywhere, every day."
Campbell Soup Company

From time to time, a company may also have to streamline its product mix to pare out marginally performing lines and models and to regain its focus. For example, as a central part of its recent turnaround, Ford gave its product mix a major pruning:[19]

Ford culled its herd of nameplates from 97 to fewer than 20. It dropped the Mercury line altogether and sold off the Volvo line. Pruning the company's brands especially thrilled Ford CEO Alan Mulally, who still comes unhinged thinking about how unfocused, how uncool, the Ford brand had become. "I mean, we had 97 of these, for [goodness] sake!" he says, pointing to the list of old models. "How you gonna make 'em all cool? You gonna come in at 8 a.m. and say 'from 8 until noon I'm gonna make No. 64 cool? And then I'll make No. 17 cool after lunch?' It was ridiculous."

SPEED BUMP | LINKING THE CONCEPTS

Slow down for a minute. To get a better sense of how large and complex a company's product offering can become, investigate Procter & Gamble's product mix.

- Using P&G's Web site (www.pg.com), its annual report, or other sources, develop a list of all the company's product lines and individual products. What surprises you about this list of products?
- Is P&G's product mix consistent? What overall strategy or logic appears to have guided the development of this product mix?

Author Comment ▶
As noted at the start of this chapter, services are products, too—intangible ones. So all the product topics we've discussed so far apply to services as well as to physical products. However, in this section, we focus on the special characteristics and marketing needs that set services apart.

Services Marketing

Services have grown dramatically in recent years. Services now account for close to 65 percent of the U.S. gross domestic product (GDP). And the service industry is growing. By 2014, it is estimated that more than four out of five jobs in the United States will be in service industries. Services are growing even faster in the world economy, making up 64 percent of the gross world product.[20]

Service industries vary greatly. *Governments* offer services through courts, employment services, hospitals, military services, police and fire departments, the postal service, and schools. *Private not-for-profit organizations* offer services through museums, charities, churches, colleges, foundations, and hospitals. In addition, a large number of *business organizations* offer services—airlines, banks, hotels, insurance companies, consulting firms, medical and legal practices, entertainment and telecommunications companies, real-estate firms, retailers, and others.

The Nature and Characteristics of a Service

A company must consider four special service characteristics when designing marketing programs: intangibility, inseparability, variability, and perishability (see ▶ **Figure 7.3**).

▶ **Figure 7.3** Four Service Characteristics

Although services are "products" in a general sense, they have special characteristics and marketing needs. The biggest differences come from the fact that services are essentially intangible and that they are created through direct interactions with customers. Think about your experiences with an airline versus Nike or Apple.

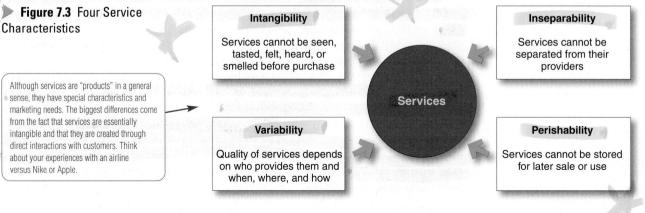

Intangibility
Services cannot be seen, tasted, felt, heard, or smelled before purchase

Inseparability
Services cannot be separated from their providers

Services

Variability
Quality of services depends on who provides them and when, where, and how

Perishability
Services cannot be stored for later sale or use

Service intangibility
The concept that services cannot be seen, tasted, felt, heard, or smelled before they are bought.

Service intangibility means that services cannot be seen, tasted, felt, heard, or smelled before they are bought. For example, people undergoing cosmetic surgery cannot see the result before the purchase. Airline passengers have nothing but a ticket and a promise that they and their luggage will arrive safely at the intended destination, hopefully at the same time. To reduce uncertainty, buyers look for *signals* of service quality. They draw conclusions about quality from the place, people, price, equipment, and communications that they can see.

Therefore, the service provider's task is to make the service tangible in one or more ways and send the right signals about quality. The Mayo Clinic does this well:[21]

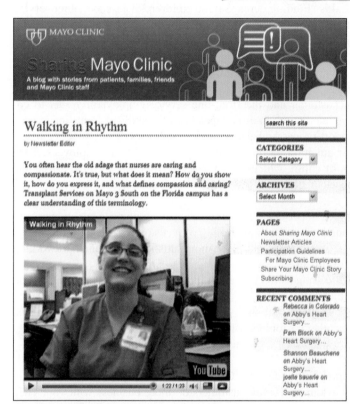

▲ By providing customers with organized, honest evidence of its capabilities, the Mayo Clinic has built one of the most powerful brands in health care. Its Sharing Mayo Clinic blog lets you hear directly from those who have been to the clinic or who work there.

Mayo Foundation for Medical Education and Research

When it comes to hospitals, it's very hard for the average patient to judge the quality of the "product." You can't try it on, you can't return it if you don't like it, and you need an advanced degree to understand it. And so, when considering a medical facility, most of us unconsciously turn into detectives, looking for evidence of competence, caring, and integrity. The Mayo Clinic doesn't leave that evidence to chance. Rather, it offers patients and their families concrete evidence of its strengths and values.

Inside, staff is trained to act in a way that clearly signals Mayo Clinic's patient-first focus. "My doctor calls me at home to check on how I am doing," marvels one patient. "She wants to work with what is best for my schedule." The clinic's physical facilities also send the right signals. They've been carefully designed to offer a place of refuge, convey caring and respect, and signal competence. Looking for external confirmation? Go online and hear directly from those who've been to the clinic or work there. The Mayo Clinic now uses social networking—everything from blogs to Facebook and YouTube—to enhance the patient experience. ▶ For example, on the Sharing Mayo Clinic blog (http://sharing.mayoclinic.org), patients and their families retell their Mayo experiences, and Mayo employees offer behind-the-scenes views. The result? Exceptionally positive word of mouth and abiding customer loyalty have allowed the Mayo Clinic to build what is arguably the most powerful brand in health care.

Physical goods are produced, then stored, then later sold, and then still later consumed. In contrast, services are first sold and then produced and consumed at the same time. **Service inseparability** means that services cannot be separated from their providers, whether the providers are people or machines. If a service employee provides the service, then the employee becomes a part of the service. And customers don't just buy and use a service, they play an active role in its delivery. Customer coproduction makes *provider-customer interaction* a special feature of services marketing. Both the provider and the customer affect the service outcome.

Service inseparability
The concept that services are produced and consumed at the same time and cannot be separated from their providers.

Service variability
The concept that the quality of services may vary greatly depending on who provides them and when, where, and how they are provided.

Service perishability
The concept that services cannot be stored for later sale or use.

Service variability means that the quality of services depends on who provides them as well as when, where, and how they are provided. For example, some hotels—say, Marriott—have reputations for providing better service than others. Still, within a given Marriott hotel, one registration-counter employee may be cheerful and efficient, whereas another standing just a few feet away may be unpleasant and slow. Even the quality of a single Marriott employee's service varies according to his or her energy and frame of mind at the time of each customer encounter.

Service perishability means that services cannot be stored for later sale or use. Some doctors charge patients for missed appointments because the service value existed only at that point and disappeared when the patient did not show up. The perishability of services is not a problem when demand is steady. However, when demand fluctuates, service firms often have difficult problems. For example, because of rush-hour demand, public transportation companies have to own much more equipment than they would if demand were even throughout the day. Thus, service firms often design strategies for producing a better match between demand and supply. Hotels and resorts charge lower prices in the off-season to attract more guests. And restaurants hire part-time employees to serve during peak periods.

Marketing Strategies for Service Firms

Just like manufacturing businesses, good service firms use marketing to position themselves strongly in chosen target markets. JetBlue promises "You above all"; PetSmart says "We love to see healthy, happy pets." At Hampton, "We love having you here." And St. Jude Children's Hospital is "Finding cures. Saving children." These and other service firms establish their positions through traditional marketing mix activities. However, because services differ from tangible products, they often require additional marketing approaches.

The Service Profit Chain

Service profit chain

The chain that links service firm profits with employee and customer satisfaction.

In a service business, the customer and the front-line service employee *interact* to co-create the service. Effective interaction, in turn, depends on the skills of front-line service employees and on the support processes backing these employees. Thus, successful service companies focus their attention on *both* their customers and their employees. They understand the **service profit chain**, which links service firm profits with employee and customer satisfaction. This chain consists of five links:[22]

- *Internal service quality:* superior employee selection and training, a quality work environment, and strong support for those dealing with customers, which results in . . .
- *Satisfied and productive service employees:* more satisfied, loyal, and hardworking employees, which results in . . .
- *Greater service value:* more effective and efficient customer value creation and service delivery, which results in . . .
- *Satisfied and loyal customers:* satisfied customers who remain loyal, make repeat purchases, and refer other customers, which results in . . .
- *Healthy service profits and growth:* superior service firm performance.

As Whole Foods Market cofounder and CEO John Mackey puts it: "Happy team members result in happy customers. Happy customers do more business with you. They become advocates for your enterprise, which results in happy investors."[23] Therefore, all outstanding service companies begin with taking care of those who take care of customers. For example, customer-service all-star Zappos.com—the online shoe, clothing, and accessories retailer—knows that happy customers begin with happy, dedicated, and energetic employees (see Marketing at Work 7.1).

Internal marketing

Orienting and motivating customer-contact employees and service-support people to work as a team to provide customer satisfaction.

Service marketing requires more than just traditional external marketing using the four Ps. ▶ **Figure 7.4** shows that service marketing also requires *internal marketing* and *interactive marketing*. **Internal marketing** means that the service firm must orient and motivate its customer-contact employees and supporting service people to work as a *team* to provide

▶ **Figure 7.4** Three Types of Service Marketing

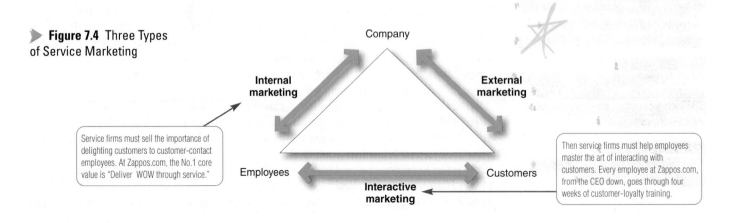

Service firms must sell the importance of delighting customers to customer-contact employees. At Zappos.com, the No.1 core value is "Deliver WOW through service."

Company

Internal marketing

External marketing

Employees

Interactive marketing

Customers

Then service firms must help employees master the art of interacting with customers. Every employee at Zappos.com, from the CEO down, goes through four weeks of customer-loyalty training.

MARKETING AT WORK | 7.1

Zappos.com: Taking Care of Those Who Take Care of Customers

Imagine a retailer with service so good its customers wish it would take over the Internal Revenue Service or start up an airline. It might sound like a marketing fantasy, but this scenario is a reality for customer-service all-star Zappos.com. At Zappos, the customer experience really does come first—it's a daily obsession. Says Zappos' understated CEO, Tony Hsieh (pronounced *shay*), "Our whole goal at Zappos is for the Zappos brand to be about the very best customer service and customer experience." Zappos is "Powered by Service."

Initially launched as a Web site that offered the absolute best selection in shoes—in terms of brands, styles, colors, sizes, and widths—the online retailer now carries many other categories of goods, such as clothing, handbags, and accessories. From the start, the scrappy Web retailer made customer service a cornerstone of its marketing. As a result, Zappos has grown astronomically. It now serves more than 10 million customers annually and gross merchandise sales top $1 billion each year. In fact, Zappos' online success and passion for customers made it an ideal match for another highly successful, customer-obsessed online retailer, Amazon.com, which purchased Zappos in late 2009.

At Zappos, customer care starts with a deep-down, customer-focused culture. As CEO Hsieh is fond of saying, "We are a service company that happens to sell [shoes (or handbags, or clothing, or eventually, anything and everything)]." How does Zappos turn this culture into a customer reality? It all starts with the company's customer-service reps—what the company calls its Customer Loyalty Team. Most of Zappos.com's business is driven by word-of-mouth and customer interactions with company employees. And Zappos knows that happy *customers* begin with happy, dedicated, and energetic *employees*. So the company starts by hiring the right people, training them thoroughly in customer-service basics, and inspiring them to new heights in taking care of customers.

To make sure Zappos' customer obsession permeates the entire organization, each new hire—everyone from the CEO and chief financial officer to the children's footwear buyer—is required to go through four weeks of customer-loyalty training. In fact, in an effort to weed out the half-hearted, Zappos actually bribes people to quit. During the four weeks of customer-service training, it offers employees $2,000 cash, plus payment for the time worked, if they leave the company. The theory goes that those willing to take the money and run aren't right for Zappos' culture anyway.

Hsieh says that originally the incentive was $100, but the amount keeps rising because not enough people take it. On average, only 1 percent take the offer, and Hsieh believes that's too low. Zappos argues that each employee needs to be a great point of contact with customers. "Getting customers excited about the service they had at Zappos has to come naturally," says one Zappos marketing executive. "You can't teach it; you have to hire for it."

Once in place, Zappos treats employees as well as it treats customers. "It's not so much about what the company provides externally," says Hsieh. "It's what the employees ultimately feel internally." The Zappos family culture emphasizes "a satisfying and fulfilling job . . . and a career you can be proud of. Work hard. Play hard. All the time!" Zappos creates a relaxed, fun-loving, and close-knit family atmosphere, complete with free meals, full benefits, profit sharing, a nap room, and even a full-time life coach—all of which make it a great place to work.

The result is what one observer calls "1,550 perpetually chipper employees." Every year, the company publishes a "culture book," filled with unedited, often gushy testimonials from Zapponians about what it's like to work there. "Oh my gosh," says one employee, "this is my home away from home. . . . It's changed my life. . . . Our culture is the best reason to work here." Says another, "The most surprising thing about coming

"A woman just called and asked if we sold dresses. I told her we had hundreds of dresses from the biggest designers. Know what she said? She said, 'I love you.' Actually, she said, 'Thank you,' but I read between the lines."

Zappos
POWERED by SERVICE™

FREE SHIPPING
BOTH WAYS

1.877.927.2330
Happy to help. 24/7.

▲ **Zappos knows that happy customers begin with happy, dedicated, and energetic employees. Zappos is "happy to help, 24/7."**
© 2011 Zappos.com, Inc. or its affiliates

to work here is that there are no limits. So pretty much anything you are passionate about is possible." And what are the things about which Zapponians are most passionate? The Zappos family's No. 1 core value: "Deliver WOW through service."

Such enthusiastic employees, in turn, make outstanding brand ambassadors. Whereas many Web sites bury contact information several links deep because they don't really want to hear from customers, Zappos puts the number at the top of every single Web page and staffs its call center 24/7. Hsieh sees each customer contact as an opportunity: "We actually want to talk to our customers," he says. "If we handle the call well, we have an opportunity to create an emotional impact and lasting memory."

Hsieh insists that reps be helpful with anything that customers might call about—and he really means it. One customer called in search of a pizza joint open after midnight in Santa Monica, CA. Two minutes later, the Zappos rep found him one. And Zappos doesn't hold its reps accountable for call times. Its longest phone call, from a customer who wanted the rep's help while she looked at what seemed like thousands of pairs of shoes, lasted almost 6 hours.

At Zappos, each employee is like a little marketing department. Relationships—inside and outside the company—mean everything at Zappos. Hsieh and many other employees stay in direct touch with customers, with each other, and with just about anyone else interested in the company. They use social networking tools such as Facebook, Twitter, and blogs to share information, both good and bad. Such openness might worry some retailers, but Zappos embraces it.

Zappos even features employees in its marketing. For example, it uses associates in short videos to describe and explain its products. Last year, it turned out 58,000 such videos of staff—not professional models—showing off shoes, bags, and clothing. Zappos found that when the product includes a personal video explanation, purchases rise and returns decrease. And those Zappos ads you see on television showing puppet customers talking with puppet service reps are based on actual customer service encounters, with actual Zappos employees doing the voices.

The moral: Just as the service profit chain suggests, taking good care of customers begins with taking good care of those who take care of customers. Zappos' enthusiasm and culture are infectious. Put Zappos customers and reps together and good things will result. "We've actually had customers ask us if we would please start an airline or run the IRS," Hsieh says, adding, "30 years from now I wouldn't rule out a Zappos airline that's all about the very best service."

Sources: Portions adapted from Natalie Zmuda, "Zappos: Customer Service First—and a Daily Obsession," *Advertising Age,* October 20, 2008, p. 36; and Jeffrey M. O'Brien, "A Perfect Season," *Fortune,* January 22, 2008, pp. 62–66; with additional information and quotes from Jeffrey M. O'Brien, "Zappos Knows How to Kick It," February 2, 2009, p. 54; Masha Zager, "Zappos Delivers Service . . . With Shoes on the Side," *Apparel Magazine,* January 2009, pp. 10–13; Tony Hsieh, "Zappos's CEO on Going to Extremes for Customers," *Harvard Business Review,* July–August 2010, pp. 41–44; Karen J. Bannan, "Fancy Footwork," *Adweek,* September 13, 2010, pp. 48–50; Sarah Nassauer, "A New Sales Model: Employees," *Wall Street Journal,* March 17, 2011, p. D3; and www.youtube.com/users/zappos and www.zappos.com, accessed November 2011.

customer satisfaction. Marketers must get everyone in the organization to be customer centered. In fact, internal marketing must *precede* external marketing. For example, Zappos starts by hiring the right people and carefully orienting and inspiring them to give unparalleled customer service.

Interactive marketing
Training service employees in the fine art of interacting with customers to satisfy their needs.

Interactive marketing means that service quality depends heavily on the quality of the buyer-seller interaction during the service encounter. In product marketing, product quality often depends little on how the product is obtained. But in services marketing, service quality depends on both the service deliverer and the quality of delivery. Service marketers, therefore, have to master interactive marketing skills. Thus, Zappos selects only people with an innate "passion to serve" and instructs them carefully in the fine art of interacting with customers to satisfy their every need. All new hires—at all levels of the company—complete a four-week customer-loyalty training regimen.

Today, as competition and costs increase, and as productivity and quality decrease, more service marketing sophistication is needed. Service companies face three major marketing tasks: They want to increase their *service differentiation,* *service quality,* and *service productivity.*

Managing Service Differentiation

In these days of intense price competition, service marketers often complain about the difficulty of differentiating their services from those of competitors. To the extent that customers view the services of different providers as similar, they care less about the provider than

the price. The solution to price competition is to develop a differentiated offer, delivery, and image.

The *offer* can include innovative features that set one company's offer apart from competitors' offers. For example, some retailers differentiate themselves by offerings that take you well beyond the products they stock. Dick's Sporting Goods has grown from a single bait-and-tackle store in Binghamton, New York, into a 444-store, $4.5-billion sporting goods megaretailer in 42 states by offering interactive services that set it apart from ordinary sporting goods stores. Customers can sample shoes on Dick's indoor footwear track, test golf clubs with an on-site golf swing analyzer and putting green, shoot bows in its archery range, and receive personalized fitness product guidance from an in-store team of fitness trainers. Such differentiated services help make Dick's "the ultimate sporting goods destination store for core athletes and outdoor enthusiasts."[24]

Service companies can differentiate their service *delivery* by having more able and reliable customer-contact people, developing a superior physical environment in which the service product is delivered, or designing a superior delivery process. For example, many grocery chains now offer online shopping and home delivery as a better way to shop than having to drive, park, wait in line, and tote groceries home. And most banks allow you to access your account information from almost anywhere—from the ATM to your cell phone.

Finally, service companies also can work on differentiating their *images* through symbols and branding. Aflac adopted the duck as its advertising symbol. Today, the duck is immortalized through stuffed animals, golf club covers, and free ring tones and screensavers. ▶ The well-known Aflac duck helped make the big but previously unknown insurance company memorable and approachable. Other well-known service characters and symbols include the GEICO gecko, Progressive Insurance's Flo, McDonald's golden arches, Allstate's "good hands," and the Travelers red umbrella.

▲ **Service differentiation: Service companies can differentiate their images using unique characters or symbols, such as the Aflac duck.**
Aflac

Managing Service Quality

A service firm can differentiate itself by delivering consistently higher quality than its competitors provide. Like manufacturers before them, most service industries have now joined the customer-driven quality movement. And like product marketers, service providers need to identify what target customers expect in regard to service quality.

Unfortunately, service quality is harder to define and judge than product quality. For instance, it is harder to agree on the quality of a haircut than on the quality of a hair dryer. Customer retention is perhaps the best measure of quality; a service firm's ability to hang onto its customers depends on how consistently it delivers value to them.

Top service companies set high service-quality standards. They watch service performance closely, both their own and that of competitors. They do not settle for merely good service—they strive for 100 percent defect-free service. A 98 percent performance standard may sound good, but using this standard, the U.S. Postal Service would lose or misdirect 480,000 pieces of mail each hour, and U.S. pharmacists would misfill more than 1.4 million prescriptions each week.[25]

Unlike product manufacturers who can adjust their machinery and inputs until everything is perfect, service quality will always vary, depending on the interactions between employees and customers. As hard as they may try, even the best companies will have an occasional late delivery, burned steak, or grumpy employee. However, good *service recovery* can turn angry customers into loyal ones. In fact, good recovery can win more customer purchasing and loyalty than if things had gone well in the first place. Consider this example:[26]

There are some things that Fred Taylor—senior manager of proactive customer service communications at Southwest Airlines—just cannot explain. For example, there was the female passenger who knelt in front of her middle seat and chewed on the seat cushion, then stripped

▲ **Service recovery: Southwest created a high-level group—headed by Fred Taylor, "senior manager of proactive customer service communications"—that carefully coordinates responses to major flight disruptions, turning wronged customers into even more loyal ones.**

Southwest Airlines, Co.

off her top and ran down the aisle. ▶ But Taylor and others on his customer service team can apologize to the other passengers on that flight and did so, as they've done thousands of other times when something has gone wrong in the air or on the ground. Their job: to find the situations in which something went wrong—a mechanical delay, bad weather, a medical emergency, or a berserk passenger—then apologize to all passengers on that flight quickly and profusely, within 24 hours of their bad experience, if possible.

Their letters to passengers, usually e-mails these days, have three basic components: a sincere apology, a brief explanation of what happened, and a gift to make it up, usually a voucher in dollars that can be used on their next Southwest flight. The team can usually explain a flight delay or other emergency. In the cases like that of the woman who doffed her top after chewing the cushion, however, there isn't much Southwest can say. "We basically say we can't explain the person's behavior," Taylor said. "But what we can do is apologize for the disruption and invite you back for a better experience." Importantly, an apology for a bad flight can actually make a passenger happier than an uneventful flight. Surveys show that when Southwest handles a delay situation well, customers score it 14 to 16 points higher than on regular on-time flights.

Managing Service Productivity

With their costs rising rapidly, service firms are under great pressure to increase service productivity. They can do so in several ways. They can train current employees better or hire new ones who will work harder or more skillfully. Or they can increase the quantity of their service by giving up some quality. Finally, a service provider can harness the power of technology. Although we often think of technology's power to save time and costs in manufacturing companies, it also has great—and often untapped—potential to make service workers more productive.

However, companies must avoid pushing productivity so hard that doing so reduces quality. Attempts to streamline a service or cut costs can make a service company more efficient in the short run. But that can also reduce its longer-run ability to innovate, maintain service quality, or respond to consumer needs and desires. For example, some airlines have learned this lesson the hard way as they attempt to economize in the face of rising costs. They stopped offering even the little things for free—such as in-flight snacks—and began charging extra for everything from curbside luggage check-in to aisle seats. The result is a plane full of resentful customers who avoid the airline whenever they can. In their attempts to improve productivity, these airlines mangled customer service.

Thus, in attempting to improve service productivity, companies must be mindful of how they create and deliver customer value. In short, they should be careful not to take *service* out of the service.

SPEED BUMP | LINKING THE CONCEPTS

Let's pause here for a moment. We've said that although services are *products* in a general sense, they have special characteristics and marketing needs. To get a better grasp of this concept, select a traditional product brand, such as Nike or Honda. Next, select a service brand, such as Southwest Airlines or McDonald's. Then compare the two.

- How are the characteristics and marketing needs of the product and service brands you selected similar?
- How do the characteristics and marketing needs of the two brands differ? How are these differences reflected in each brand's marketing strategy? Keep these differences in mind as we move into the final section of the chapter.

Author Comment ▶
A brand represents everything that a product or service *means* to consumers. As such, brands are valuable assets to a company. For example, when you hear someone say "Coca-Cola," what do you think, feel, or remember? What about "Target"? Or "Google"?

Branding Strategy: Building Strong Brands

Some analysts see brands as *the* major enduring asset of a company, outlasting the company's specific products and facilities. John Stewart, former CEO of Quaker Oats, once said, "If this business were split up, I would give you the land and bricks and mortar, and I would keep the brands and trademarks, and I would fare better than you." A former CEO of McDonald's declared, "If every asset we own, every building, and every piece of equipment were destroyed in a terrible natural disaster, we would be able to borrow all the money to replace it very quickly because of the value of our brand. . . . The brand is more valuable than the totality of all these assets."[27]

Thus, brands are powerful assets that must be carefully developed and managed. In this section, we examine the key strategies for building and managing product and service brands.

Brand Equity

Brands are more than just names and symbols. They are a key element in the company's relationships with consumers. Brands represent consumers' perceptions and feelings about a product and its performance—everything that the product or the service *means* to consumers. In the final analysis, brands exist in the heads of consumers. As one well-respected marketer once said, "Products are created in the factory, but brands are created in the mind." Adds Jason Kilar, CEO of the online video service Hulu, "A brand is what people say about you when you're not in the room."[28]

A powerful brand has high *brand equity*. **Brand equity** is the differential effect that knowing the brand name has on customer response to the product and its marketing. It's a measure of the brand's ability to capture consumer preference and loyalty. A brand has positive brand equity when consumers react more favorably to it than to a generic or unbranded version of the same product. It has negative brand equity if consumers react less favorably than to an unbranded version.

Brands vary in the amount of power and value they hold in the marketplace. Some brands—such as Coca-Cola, Nike, Disney, GE, McDonald's, Harley-Davidson, and others—become larger-than-life icons that maintain their power in the market for years, even generations. Other brands—such as Google, YouTube, Apple, Twitter, and Wikipedia—create fresh consumer excitement and loyalty. These brands win in the marketplace not simply because they deliver unique benefits or reliable service. Rather, they succeed because they forge deep connections with customers. ▶ For example, to a devoted Dunkin' Donuts fan, that cup of coffee from Dunkin isn't just coffee, it's a deeply satisfying experience that no other brand can deliver as well. Dunkin' Donuts regularly beats out Starbucks in customer loyalty ratings.

Ad agency Young & Rubicam's BrandAsset Valuator measures brand strength along four consumer perception dimensions: *differentiation* (what makes the brand stand out), *relevance* (how consumers feel it meets their needs), *knowledge* (how much consumers know about the brand), and *esteem* (how highly consumers regard and respect the brand). Brands with strong brand equity rate high on all four dimensions. The brand must be distinct, or consumers will have no reason to choose it over other brands. However, the fact that a brand is highly differentiated doesn't necessarily mean that consumers will buy it. The brand must stand out in ways that are relevant to consumers' needs. Even a differentiated, relevant brand is far from a shoe-in. Before consumers will respond to the brand, they must

Brand equity
The differential effect that knowing the brand name has on customer response to the product or its marketing.

▲ Consumers sometimes bond very closely with specific brands. To this customer, this isn't just a cup of coffee, it's a deeply satisfying Dunkin' Donuts brand experience.

Amanda Kamen

first know about and understand it. And that familiarity must lead to a strong, positive consumer-brand connection.[29]

Thus, positive brand equity derives from consumer feelings about and connections with a brand. Consumers sometimes bond *very* closely with specific brands. As perhaps the ultimate expression of brand devotion, a surprising number of people—and not just Harley-Davidson fans—have their favorite brand tattooed on their bodies.

A brand with high brand equity is a very valuable asset. *Brand valuation* is the process of estimating the total financial value of a brand. Measuring such value is difficult. However, according to one estimate, the brand value of Apple is a whopping $153 billion, with Google at $112 billion, IBM at $100 billion, McDonald's at $81 billion, Microsoft at $78 billion, and Coca-Cola at $73 billion. Other brands rating among the world's most valuable include AT&T, China Mobile, GE, Walmart, and Amazon.com.[30]

High brand equity provides a company with many competitive advantages. A powerful brand enjoys a high level of consumer brand awareness and loyalty. Because consumers expect stores to carry the particular brand, the company has more leverage in bargaining with resellers. Because a brand name carries high credibility, the company can more easily launch line and brand extensions. A powerful brand also offers the company some defense against fierce price competition.

Above all, however, a powerful brand forms the basis for building strong and profitable customer relationships. The fundamental asset underlying brand equity is *customer equity*— the value of customer relationships that the brand creates. A powerful brand is important, but what it really represents is a profitable set of loyal customers. The proper focus of marketing is building customer equity, with brand management serving as a major marketing tool. Companies need to think of themselves not as portfolios of brands but as portfolios of customers.

Building Strong Brands

Branding poses challenging decisions to the marketer. ▶ **Figure 7.5** shows that the major brand strategy decisions involve *brand positioning*, *brand name selection*, *brand sponsorship*, and *brand development*.

Brand Positioning

Marketers need to position their brands clearly in target customers' minds. They can position brands at any of three levels.[31] At the lowest level, they can position the brand on *product attributes*. For example, P&G invented the disposable diaper category with its Pampers brand. Early Pampers marketing focused on attributes such as fluid absorption, fit, and disposability. In general, however, attributes are the least desirable level for brand positioning. Competitors can easily copy attributes. More importantly, customers are not interested in attributes as such—they are interested in what the attributes will do for them.

A brand can be better positioned by associating its name with a desirable *benefit*. Thus, Pampers can go beyond technical product attributes and talk about the resulting containment and skin-health benefits from dryness. Some successful brands positioned on benefits are FedEx (guaranteed on-time delivery), Nike (performance), Lexus (quality), and Walmart (low prices).

The strongest brands go beyond attribute or benefit positioning. They are positioned on strong *beliefs and values,* engaging customers on a deep, emotional level. For example, to parents, Pampers mean much more than just containment and dryness. The "Pampers village" Web site (www.pampers.com) positions Pampers as a "where we grow together"

Brands are powerful assets that must be carefully developed and managed. As this figure suggests, building strong brands involves many challenging decisions.

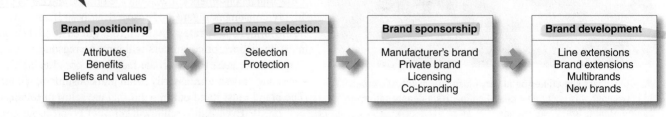

▶ **Figure 7.5** Major Brand Strategy Decisions

SOME PEOPLE THINK THEIR MIND IS THE MOST POWERFUL WEAPON.

TRY LOOSENING THAT RUSTED BOLT WITH YOUR MIND, GENIUS.

WD-40

PENETRATE EVEN THE TOUGHEST CORROSION AND RUST TO REMOVE STUCK PARTS. ONLY WITH WD-40 MULTI-USE PRODUCT.

▲ **Brand positioning: Successful brands engage customers on a deep, emotional level. This ad suggests the deep-down connection that hardcore users have with the WD-40 brand.**

WD-40® is a registered trademark of WD-40 Company

brand that's concerned about happy babies, parent-child relationships, and total baby care. Says a former P&G executive, "Our baby care business didn't start growing aggressively until we changed Pampers from being about dryness to helping mom with her baby's development."[32]

Successful brands engage customers on a deep, emotional level. Advertising agency Saatchi & Saatchi suggests that brands should strive to become *lovemark*s, products or services that "inspire loyalty beyond reason." ▶ Brands ranging from Apple, Google, Disney, and Coca-Cola to Nike, Trader Joe's, Facebook, Wrangler, In-N-Out Burger, and even WD-40 have achieved this status with many of their customers. Lovemark brands pack an emotional wallop. Customers don't just like these brands, they have strong emotional connections with them and love them unconditionally.[33]

When positioning a brand, the marketer should establish a mission for the brand and a vision of what the brand must be and do. A brand is the company's promise to deliver a specific set of features, benefits, services, and experiences consistently to buyers. The brand promise must be simple and honest. Motel 6, for example, offers clean rooms, low prices, and good service but does not promise expensive furnishings or large bathrooms. In contrast, The Ritz-Carlton offers luxurious rooms and a truly memorable experience but does not promise low prices.

Brand Name Selection

A good name can add greatly to a product's success. However, finding the best brand name is a difficult task. It begins with a careful review of the product and its benefits, the target market, and proposed marketing strategies. After that, naming a brand becomes part science, part art, and a measure of instinct.

Desirable qualities for a brand name include the following: (1) It should suggest something about the product's benefits and qualities. Examples: Beautyrest, Acuvue, Lean Cuisine, Mop & Glo. (2) It should be easy to pronounce, recognize, and remember: Tide, Jelly Belly, iPod, Facebook, JetBlue. (3) The brand name should be distinctive: Panera, Flikr, Swiffer. (4) It should be extendable—Amazon.com began as an online bookseller but chose a name that would allow expansion into other categories. (5) The name should translate easily into foreign languages. Before changing its name to Exxon, Standard Oil of New Jersey rejected the name Enco, which it learned meant a stalled engine when pronounced in Japanese. (6) It should be capable of registration and legal protection. A brand name cannot be registered if it infringes on existing brand names.

Choosing a new brand name is hard work. After a decade of choosing quirky names (Yahoo!, Google) or trademark-proof made-up names (Novartis, Aventis, Accenture), today's style is to build brands around names that have real meaning. For example, names like Silk (soy milk), Method (home products), Smartwater (beverages), and Blackboard (school software) are simple and make intuitive sense. But with trademark applications soaring, *available* new names can be hard to find. Try it yourself. Pick a product and see if you can come up with a better name for it. How about Moonshot? Tickle? Vanilla? Treehugger? Simplicity? Google them and you'll find that they're already taken.

Once chosen, the brand name must be protected. Many firms try to build a brand name that will eventually become identified with the product category. Brand names such as Kleenex, Levi's, JELL-O, BAND-AID, Scotch Tape, Formica, and Ziploc have succeeded in this way. However, their very success may threaten the company's rights to the name. Many originally protected brand names—such as cellophane, aspirin, nylon, kerosene, linoleum, yo-yo, trampoline, escalator, thermos, and shredded wheat—are now generic names that any seller can use. To protect their brands, marketers present them carefully using the word *brand* and the registered trademark symbol, as in "BAND-AID® Brand Adhesive Bandages." Even the long-standing "I am stuck on BAND-AID 'cause BAND-AID's stuck on me" jingle has now become "I am stuck on BAND-AID *brand* 'cause BAND-AID's stuck on me."

Brand Sponsorship

A manufacturer has four sponsorship options. The product may be launched as a *national brand* (or *manufacturer's brand*), as when Sony and Kellogg sell their output under their own brand names (Sony Bravia HDTV or Kellogg's Frosted Flakes). Or the manufacturer may sell to resellers who give the product a *private brand* (also called a *store brand* or *distributor brand*). Although most manufacturers create their own brand names, others market *licensed brands*. Finally, two companies can join forces and *co-brand* a product. We discuss each of these options in turn.

National Brands versus Store Brands. National brands (or manufacturers' brands) have long dominated the retail scene. In recent times, however, an increasing number of retailers and wholesalers have created their own **store brands** (or **private brands**). Although store brands have been gaining strength for more than a decade, more frugal economic times have created a store-brand boom. Studies show that consumers are buying more private brands, which on average yield a 30 percent savings. "[Thrifty] times are good times for private labels," says a brand expert. "As consumers become more price-conscious, they also become less brand-conscious."[34] (See Marketing at Work 7.2.)

In fact, store brands are growing much faster than national brands. In all, private label goods account for more than 22 percent of all unit sales. Since 2008, unit sales of private label goods have grown at more than twice the rate of national brands. Private-label apparel, such as Hollister, The Limited, Arizona Jean Company (JCPenney), and Xhilaration (Target), captures a 50 percent share of all U.S. apparel sales, up from 25 percent a decade ago.[35]

Many large retailers skillfully market a deep assortment of store-brand merchandise. For example, Kroger, the nation's largest grocery retailer, stocks some 14,000 store brand items under its own Private Selection, Banner, and Value brands. Store brands now account for more than 27 percent of Kroger's dollar sales and more than one-third of all its unit sales. At the other end of the grocery spectrum, upscale Whole Foods Market offers an array of store brand products under its 365 Everyday Value brand, from organic Canadian maple syrup and frozen chicken Caesar pizza to chewy children's multivitamins and organic whole wheat pasta.[36]

In the so-called *battle of the brands* between national and private brands, retailers have many advantages. They control what products they stock, where they go on the shelf, what prices they charge, and which ones they will feature in local circulars. Retailers often price their store brands lower than comparable national brands, thereby appealing to the budget-conscious shopper in all of us. Although store brands can be hard to establish and costly to stock and promote, they also yield higher profit margins for the reseller. And they give resellers exclusive products that cannot be bought from competitors, resulting in greater store traffic and loyalty. Fast-growing retailer Trader Joe's, which carries 80 percent store brands, began creating its own brands so that "we could put our destiny in our own hands," says the company's president.[37]

To compete with store brands, national brands must sharpen their value propositions, especially when appealing to today's more frugal consumers. In the long run, however, leading brand marketers must invest in R&D to bring out new brands, new features, and continuous quality improvements. They must design strong advertising programs to maintain high awareness and preference. And they must find ways to "partner" with major distributors in a search for distribution economies and improved joint performance.

Licensing. Most manufacturers take years and spend millions to create their own brand names. However, some companies license names or symbols previously created by other manufacturers, names of well-known celebrities, or characters from popular movies and books. For a fee, any of these can provide an instant and proven brand name.

Store brand (or private brand)
A brand created and owned by a reseller of a product or service.

Thrifty Times Are Good Times for Store Brands. But What's a National Brand to Do?

Over the past two years, Elizabeth O'Herron has banished nearly all brand names from her household. So long Pampers, Hefty, and Birds Eye. Instead, the pantry is stocked with cheaper imitations of the same goods: Walmart diapers, BJ's garbage bags, and Stop & Shop's frozen veggies. At the local Walmart, she stocks up on the store's Great Value brand; at Kroger its Private Selection or Kroger Value products. "I'm not loyal to any grocery store or any brand," says O'Herron. "I'm loyal to savings."

These days, more and more consumers have joined O'Herron's way of thinking. In the aftermath of the Great Recession of 2008/2009, even as the economy has recovered, the popularity of store brands continues to soar. From trying cheaper laundry detergents to slipping on a more affordable pair of jeans, Americans have changed their spending habits to save money. "[Thrifty] times are good times for private labels," says one analyst. "As consumers become more price-conscious, they also become less brand-conscious."

It seems that almost every retailer now carries its own store brands. Walmart's private brands account for a whopping 40 percent of its sales: brands such as Great Value food products; Sam's Choice beverages; Equate pharmacy, health, and beauty products; White Cloud brand toilet tissue and diapers; Simple Elegance laundry products; and Canopy outdoor home products. Its private label brands alone generate nearly twice the sales of all P&G brands combined, and Great Value is the nation's largest single food brand. At the other end of the spectrum, even upscale retailer Saks Fifth Avenue carries its own clothing line, which features $98 men's ties, $200 halter tops, and $250 cotton dress shirts.

Once known as "generic" or "no-name" brands, today's store brands are shedding their image as cheap knockoffs of national brands. Store brands now offer much greater selection, and they are rapidly achieving name-brand quality. In fact, retailers such as Target and Trader Joe's are out-innovating many of their national-brand competitors. Rather than simply creating low-end generic brands that offer a low-price alternative to national brands, retailers are now moving toward higher-end private brands that boost both a store's revenues and its image.

As store-brand selection and quality have improved, and as the Great Recession put the brakes on free spending, consumers have shown an ever-increasing openness to store brands. Some 50 percent of U.S. consumers now purchase store brands "all the time" as part of their regular shopping behavior, up from just 12 percent in the early 1990s. And 74 percent say they are more open today to trying store brands than two years ago. Moreover, 34 percent say they don't feel like they're giving anything up (such as flavor or prestige) by using store brands. Only 19 percent believe it's worth paying more for name brand products.

Some retail strategists predict that the slowdown in consumer spending could last for years. The new consumer frugality could "lead to a 'downturn generation' that learns to scrimp and save permanently, including buying more private-label," says one strategist.

Just ask shopper Lisa Dean, whose shopping cart last week was filled with store-brand goods—milk, eggs, tomato sauce, tortilla chips, and trash bags, to name a few. "Once I started trying store brands, and the quality, taste, and price was right, I have continued to purchase store brands and try new things," she says. She estimates that she is saving at least 30 percent on groceries. Will she return to her old favorite brands in the improved economy? No way. "This is absolutely a permanent switch," says Dean.

Does the surge in store brands spell doom for name-brand products? Not likely. But what should national-brand marketers do to thwart the growing competition from store brands? For starters, they need to sharpen their value propositions and do a better job of convincing today's thriftier shoppers that their brands are worth the higher prices. In leaner times and beyond, rather than cheapening their products or lowering their prices, national brands need to distinguish themselves through superior customer value. Long-term national-brand success requires continued investment in product innovation and brand marketing.

When asked whether, in thriftier times, consumers aren't more concerned about lower prices (via store brands) than

▲ The popularity of store brands has soared recently. Walmart's store brands account for a whopping 40 percent of its sales, and its Great Value brand is the nation's largest single food brand.

brand purpose (via national brands), marketing consultant and former P&G global marketing chief Jim Stengel replied:

> I don't think it's an either/or. I think great brands have a strong sense of their meaning, their ideals, their mission—and their ideas represent a tremendous value to consumers. I think great brands have to tell their stories. They have to do great things . . . [bringing] joy, help, and service to people by making them laugh, giving them an idea, or solving a problem. If they do that, [more than just survive,] national brands will thrive.

So, even when the economic pendulum swings downward or upward, national-brand marketers must remain true to their brand stories. "You can have a value proposition that accentuates good value, but you don't want to walk away from the core proposition of the brand," says one marketing executive. "That's the only thing you have to protect yourself" from private labels in the long run. Even some die-hard store-brand buyers prove this important point.

Kalixt Smith has recently given up national brands for bread, milk, toilet paper, and dish detergent, saving up to $50 a month on groceries for her family of four. She's even gone to great lengths to hide some of the changes from her family. "I resorted to buying things like store-brand ketchup, hot sauce, BBQ sauce, and syrup in bulk or large containers and reusing the containers from Heinz, Frank's Red Hot, Kraft, and Mrs. Butterworth's to mask the switch," says Smith. "My kids do not seem to notice the difference." But there're some store-brand items she can't sneak under the family radar, including attempted replacements for Honey Nut Cheerios and Velveeta Shells & Cheese. And, to her surprise, Spam. It turns out that there is no tasty substitute for Spam, at least not for her brood. Thus, despite her tighter spending, Smith still finds many national brands well worth the higher price.

Source: Excerpts adapted from Jenn Abelson, "Seeking Savings, Some Ditch Brand Loyalty," *Boston Globe,* January 29, 2010; Elaine Wong, "Foods OK, But Some Can't Stomach More Increases," *Brandweek,* January 5, 2009, p. 7; and Elaine Wong, "Stengel: Private Label, Digital Change Game," *Brandweek,* April 13, 2009, pp. 7, 37. Also see "Private Label Is Winning Big, Deloitte Survey Finds," *Private Label Buyer,* September 2010, pp. 10–11; "Private Label Gets a Quality Reputation, Causing Consumers to Change Their Buying Habits," *PR Newswire,* January 20, 2011; Ely Portillo, "In Weak Economy, Store Brands Prosper," *McClatchy-Tribune News Service,* March 18, 2011; and http://walmartstores.com/Video/?id=1305, accessed November 2011.

▲ Licensing: Nickelodeon has developed a stable full of hugely popular characters—such as SpongeBob SquarePants—that generate billions of dollars of retail sales each year.

/PRNewsFoto/Nickelodeon

Apparel and accessories sellers pay large royalties to adorn their products—from blouses to ties and linens to luggage—with the names or initials of well-known fashion innovators such as Calvin Klein, Tommy Hilfiger, Gucci, or Armani. Sellers of children's products attach an almost endless list of character names to clothing, toys, school supplies, linens, dolls, lunch boxes, cereals, and other items. Licensed character names range from classics such as Sesame Street, Disney, Barbie, Star Wars, Scooby Doo, Hello Kitty, and Dr. Seuss characters to the more recent Dora the Explorer; Go, Diego, Go!; Little Einsteins; and Hannah Montana. And currently a number of top-selling retail toys are products based on television shows and movies.

Name and character licensing has grown rapidly in recent years. Annual retail sales of licensed products worldwide have grown from only $4 billion in 1977 to $55 billion in 1987 and more than $191 billion today. Licensing can be a highly profitable business for many companies. For example, Disney, the world's biggest licensor, reported more than $27 billion in worldwide merchandise sales last year and plans to double that figure in the next 5 to 7 years. And Nickelodeon has developed a stable full of hugely popular characters, such as Dora the Explorer; Go, Diego, Go!; iCarly; and SpongeBob SquarePants. ▶ SpongeBob alone has generated more than $8 billion in sales and licensing fees over the past decade.[38]

Co-branding. **Co-branding** occurs when two established brand names of different companies are used on the same product. Co-branding offers many advantages. Because each brand dominates in a different category, the combined brands create broader consumer appeal and greater brand equity. Supermarket aisles are

Co-branding

The practice of using the established brand names of two different companies on the same product.

littered with co-branding examples. For example, PepsiCo's Lay's brand joined KC Masterpiece to create Lay's KC Masterpiece Barbeque chips. Pillsbury and Cinnabon joined forces to create Pillsbury Cinnabon cinnamon rolls. And Heinz and TABASCO co-branded Heinz Hot & Spicy Ketchup with a kick of TABASCO pepper sauce.

Co-branding can take advantage of the complementary strengths of two brands. For example, the Tim Hortons coffee chain is establishing co-branded Tim Hortons–Cold Stone Creamery shops. Tim Hortons is strong in the morning and midday periods, with coffee and baked goods, soups, and sandwiches. By contrast, Cold Stone Creamery's ice cream snacks are strongest in the afternoon and evening, which are Tim Hortons's non-peak periods. The co-branded locations offer customers a reason to visit morning, noon, and night.[39]

Co-branding also allows a company to expand its existing brand into a category it might otherwise have difficulty entering alone. For example, Nike and Apple co-branded the Nike+iPod Sport Kit, which lets runners link their Nike shoes with their iPods to track and enhance running performance in real time. "Your iPod Nano [or iPod Touch] becomes your coach. Your personal trainer. Your favorite workout companion." The Nike+iPod arrangement gives Apple a presence in the sports and fitness market. At the same time, it helps Nike bring new value to its customers.[40]

Co-branding can also have limitations. Such relationships usually involve complex legal contracts and licenses. Co-branding partners must carefully coordinate their advertising, sales promotion, and other marketing efforts. Finally, when co-branding, each partner must trust that the other will take good care of its brand. If something damages the reputation of one brand, it can tarnish the co-brand as well.

Brand Development

A company has four choices when it comes to developing brands (see ▶ **Figure 7.6**). It can introduce *line extensions, brand extensions, multibrands,* or *new brands*.

Line extension

Extending an existing brand name to new forms, colors, sizes, ingredients, or flavors of an existing product category.

Line Extensions. **Line extensions** occur when a company extends existing brand names to new forms, colors, sizes, ingredients, or flavors of an existing product category. Thus, the Cheerios line of cereals includes Honey Nut, Frosted, Yogurt Burst, MultiGrain, Banana Nut, and several other variations.

A company might introduce line extensions as a low-cost, low-risk way to introduce new products. Or it might want to meet consumer desires for variety, use excess capacity, or simply command more shelf space from resellers. However, line extensions involve some risks. An overextended brand name might lose some of its specific meaning. Or heavily extended brands can cause consumer confusion or frustration.

> Want a Coke? Okay, but what kind? You can pick from some 20 different varieties. In no-calorie versions alone, Coca-Cola offers two subbrands: Diet Coke and Coke Zero. Throw in flavored and no-caffeine versions—caffeine-free Diet Coke, cherry Diet Coke, black cherry vanilla Diet Coke, Diet Coke with lemon, Diet Coke with lime, vanilla Coke Zero, cherry Coke Zero—and you come up with a head-spinning ten diet colas from Coca-Cola. And that doesn't count Diet Coke with Splenda or Diet Coke Plus (with vitamins B3, B6, and B12 plus minerals zinc and magnesium). Each subbrand has its own marketing spin. But really, are we talking about choices here or just plain confusion? I mean, can you really tell the difference?

▶ **Figure 7.6** Brand Development Strategies

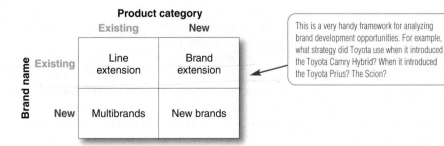

This is a very handy framework for analyzing brand development opportunities. For example, what strategy did Toyota use when it introduced the Toyota Camry Hybrid? When it introduced the Toyota Prius? The Scion?

Another risk is that sales of an extension may come at the expense of other items in the line. For example, how much would yet another Diet Coke extension steal from Coca-Cola's own lines versus Pepsi's? A line extension works best when it takes sales away from competing brands, not when it "cannibalizes" the company's other items.

Brand Extensions. A **brand extension** extends a current brand name to new or modified products in a new category. For example, Kellogg's has extended its Special K cereal brand into a full line of cereals plus lines of crackers, fruit crisps, snack and nutrition bars, breakfast shakes, protein waters, and other health and nutrition products. Victorinox extended its venerable Swiss Army brand from multitool knives to products ranging from cutlery and ballpoint pens to watches, luggage, and apparel. And P&G has leveraged the strength of its Mr. Clean household cleaner brand to launch several new lines: cleaning pads (Magic Eraser), bathroom cleaning tools (Magic Reach), and home auto cleaning kits (Mr. Clean AutoDry). ❯ It even launched Mr. Clean-branded car washes.

Brand extension
Extending an existing brand name to new product categories.

▲ **Brand extensions: P&G has leveraged the strength of its Mr. Clean brand to launch new lines, including Mr. Clean-branded car washes.**
The Procter & Gamble Company

A brand extension gives a new product instant recognition and faster acceptance. It also saves the high advertising costs usually required to build a new brand name. At the same time, a brand extension strategy involves some risk. The extension may confuse the image of the main brand. Brand extensions such as Cheetos lip balm, Heinz pet food, and Life Savers gum met early deaths. And if a brand extension fails, it may harm consumer attitudes toward other products carrying the same brand name. Furthermore, a brand name may not be appropriate to a particular new product, even if it is well made and satisfying—would you consider flying on Hooters Air or wearing an Evian water-filled padded bra (both failed). Thus, before transferring a brand name to a new product, marketers must research how well the product fits the brand's associations.

Multibrands. Companies often market many different brands in a given product category. For example, in the United States, PepsiCo markets at least five brands of soft drinks (Pepsi, Sierra Mist, Slice, Mountain Dew, and Mug root beer), four brands of sports and energy drinks (Gatorade, No Fear, Propel, and AMP Energy), five brands of bottled teas and coffees (Lipton, SoBe, Seattle's Best, Starbucks, and Tazo), two brands of bottled waters (Aquafina and SoBe), and two brands of fruit drinks (Tropicana and Ocean Spray). Each brand includes a long list of subbrands. For instance, SoBe consists of SoBe Teas & Elixers, SoBe Lifewater, SoBe Lean, and SoBe Lifewater with Purevia. Aquafina includes regular Aquafina, Aquafina Flavorsplash, and Aquafina Sparkling.

Multibranding offers a way to establish different features that appeal to different customer segments, lock up more reseller shelf space, and capture a larger market share. For example, although PepsiCo's many brands of beverages compete with one another on supermarket shelves, the combined brands reap a much greater overall market share than any single brand ever could. Similarly, by positioning multiple brands in multiple segments, P&G's five laundry detergent brands combine to capture more than 60 percent of the U.S. laundry detergent market.

A major drawback of multibranding is that each brand might obtain only a small market share, and none may be very profitable. The company may end up spreading its resources over many brands instead of building a few brands to a highly profitable level. These companies should reduce the number of brands they sell in a given category and set up tighter screening procedures for new brands. This happened to GM, which in recent years has cut numerous brands from its portfolio, including Saturn, Oldsmobile, Pontiac, Hummer, and Saab.

New Brands. A company might believe that the power of its existing brand name is waning, so a new brand name is needed. Or it may create a new brand name when it enters a new product category for which none of its current brand names are appropriate. For example, Toyota created the separate Scion brand, targeted toward Millennial consumers.

As with multibranding, offering too many new brands can result in a company spreading its resources too thin. And in some industries, such as consumer packaged goods, consumers and retailers have become concerned that there are already too many brands, with too few differences between them. Thus, P&G, Frito-Lay, Kraft, and other large consumer-product marketers are now pursuing *megabrand* strategies—weeding out weaker or slower-growing brands and focusing their marketing dollars on brands that can achieve the number-one or number-two market share positions with good growth prospects in their categories.

Managing Brands

Companies must manage their brands carefully. First, the brand's positioning must be continuously communicated to consumers. Major brand marketers often spend huge amounts on advertising to create brand awareness and build preference and loyalty. For example, Verizon spends more than $3 billion annually to promote its brand. McDonald's spends more than $1.2 billion.[41]

Such advertising campaigns can help create name recognition, brand knowledge, and perhaps even some brand preference. However, the fact is that brands are not maintained by advertising but by customers' *brand experiences*. Today, customers come to know a brand through a wide range of contacts and touch points. These include advertising but also personal experience with the brand, word of mouth, company Web pages, and many others. The company must put as much care into managing these touch points as it does into producing its ads. "Managing each customer's experience is perhaps the most important ingredient in building [brand] loyalty," states one branding expert. "Every memorable interaction . . . must be completed with excellence and . . . must reinforce your brand essence." ▶ A former Disney top executive agrees: "A brand is a living entity, and it is enriched or undermined cumulatively over time, the product of a thousand small gestures."[42]

The brand's positioning will not take hold fully unless everyone in the company lives the brand. Therefore, the company needs to train its people to be customer centered. Even better, the company should carry on internal brand building to help employees understand and be enthusiastic about the brand promise. Many companies go even further by training and encouraging their distributors and dealers to serve their customers well.

Finally, companies need to periodically audit their brands' strengths and weaknesses. They should ask: Does our brand excel at delivering benefits that consumers truly value? Is the brand properly positioned? Do all of our consumer touch points support the brand's positioning? Do the brand's managers understand what the brand means to consumers? Does the brand receive proper, sustained support? The brand audit may turn up brands that need more support, brands that need to be dropped, or brands that must be rebranded or repositioned because of changing customer preferences or new competitors.

▲ Managing brands requires managing "touch points." Says a former Disney executive: "A brand is a living entity, and it is enriched or undermined cumulatively over time, the product of a thousand small gestures."

Joe Raedle/Getty Images

REST STOP | REVIEWING THE CONCEPTS

MyMarketingLab

Now that you have completed the chapter, return to www.mymktlab.com to experience and apply the concepts and to explore the additional study materials for this chapter.

CHAPTER REVIEW AND KEY TERMS

Objectives Review

A product is more than a simple set of tangible features. Each product or service offered to customers can be viewed on three levels. The *core customer value* consists of the core problem-solving benefits that consumers seek when they buy a product. The *actual product* exists around the core and includes the quality level, features, design, brand name, and packaging. The *augmented product* is the actual product plus the various services and benefits offered with it, such as a warranty, free delivery, installation, and maintenance.

 OBJECTIVE 1 Define *product* and the major classifications of products and services. (pp 196–201)

Broadly defined, a *product* is anything that can be offered to a market for attention, acquisition, use, or consumption that might satisfy a want or need. Products include physical objects but also services, events, persons, places, organizations, ideas, or mixtures of these entities. *Services* are products that consist of activities, benefits, or satisfactions offered for sale that are essentially intangible, such as banking, hotel, tax preparation, and home-repair services.

Products and services fall into two broad classes based on the types of consumers that use them. *Consumer products*—those bought by final consumers—are usually classified according to consumer shopping habits (convenience products, shopping products, specialty products, and unsought products). *Industrial products*—purchased for further processing or for use in conducting a business—include materials and parts, capital items, and supplies and services. Other marketable entities—such as organizations, persons, places, and ideas—can also be thought of as products.

 OBJECTIVE 2 Describe the decisions companies make regarding their individual products and services, product lines, and product mixes. (pp 201–208)

Individual product decisions involve product attributes, branding, packaging, labeling, and product support services. *Product attribute* decisions involve product quality, features, and style

and design. *Branding* decisions include selecting a brand name and developing a brand strategy. *Packaging* provides many key benefits, such as protection, economy, convenience, and promotion. Package decisions often include designing *labels*, which identify, describe, and possibly promote the product. Companies also develop *product support services* that enhance customer service and satisfaction and safeguard against competitors.

Most companies produce a product line rather than a single product. A *product line* is a group of products that are related in function, customer-purchase needs, or distribution channels. All product lines and items offered to customers by a particular seller make up the *product mix*. The mix can be described by four dimensions: width, length, depth, and consistency. These dimensions are the tools for developing the company's product strategy.

 OBJECTIVE 3 Identify the four characteristics that affect the marketing of services and the additional marketing considerations that services require. (pp 208–214)

Services are characterized by four key characteristics: they are *intangible*, *inseparable*, *variable*, and *perishable*. Each characteristic poses problems and marketing requirements. Marketers work to find ways to make the service more tangible, increase the productivity of providers who are inseparable from their products, standardize quality in the face of variability, and improve demand movements and supply capacities in the face of service perishability.

Good service companies focus attention on *both* customers and employees. They understand the *service profit chain*, which links service firm profits with employee and customer satisfaction. Services marketing strategy calls not only for external marketing but also for *internal marketing* to motivate employees and *interactive marketing* to create service delivery skills among service providers. To succeed, service marketers must create *competitive differentiation*, offer high *service quality*, and find ways to increase *service productivity*.

▶ **OBJECTIVE 4 Discuss branding strategy—the decisions companies make in building and managing their brands. (pp 215–223)**

Some analysts see brands as *the* major enduring asset of a company. Brands are more than just names and symbols; they embody everything that the product or the service *means* to consumers. *Brand equity* is the positive differential effect that knowing the brand name has on customer response to the product or the service. A brand with strong brand equity is a very valuable asset.

In building brands, companies need to make decisions about brand positioning, brand name selection, brand sponsorship, and brand development. The most powerful *brand positioning* builds around strong consumer beliefs and values. *Brand name selection* involves finding the best brand name based on a careful review of product benefits, the target market,

and proposed marketing strategies. A manufacturer has four *brand sponsorship* options: it can launch a *national brand* (or manufacturer's brand), sell to resellers who use a *private brand*, market *licensed brands*, or join forces with another company to *co-brand* a product. A company also has four choices when it comes to developing brands. It can introduce *line extensions*, *brand extensions*, *multibrands*, or *new brands*.

Companies must build and manage their brands carefully. The brand's positioning must be continuously communicated to consumers. Advertising can help. However, brands are not maintained by advertising but by customers' *brand experiences*. Customers come to know a brand through a wide range of contacts and interactions. The company must put as much care into managing these touch points as it does into producing its ads. Companies must periodically audit their brands' strengths and weaknesses.

Key Terms

Objective 1
Product (p 196)
Service (p 196)
Consumer product (p 198)
Convenience product (p 199)
Shopping product (p 199)
Specialty product (p 199)
Unsought product (p 199)
Industrial product (p 199)
Social marketing (p 201)

Objective 2
Product quality (p 201)
Brand (p 203)
Packaging (p 204)
Product line (p 206)
Product mix (product portfolio) (p 207)

Objective 3
Service intangibility (p 209)
Service inseparability (p 209)
Service variability (p 209)

Service perishability (p 209)
Service profit chain (p 210)
Internal marketing (p 210)
Interactive marketing (p 212)

Objective 4
Brand equity (p 215)
Store brand (private brand) (p 218)
Co-branding (p 220)
Line extension (p 221)
Brand extension (p 222)

DISCUSSION AND CRITICAL THINKING

Discussion Questions

1. Name and describe the types of consumer products and give an example of each. How does the marketing differ for each product type? (AACSB: Communication; Reflective Thinking)
2. Compare and contrast industrial products and consumer products. (AACSB: Communication; Reflective Thinking)
3. Discuss the product attributes through which benefits are communicated and delivered to customers. (AACSB: Communication)

4. What is a brand? How does branding help both buyers and sellers? (AACSB: Communication)
5. What is a product line? Discuss the various product line decisions marketers make and how a company can expand its product line. (AACSB: Communication)
6. Discuss the four special characteristics of services. In terms of these characteristics, how do the services offered by a doctor's office differ from those offered by a bank? (AACSB: Communication, Reflective Thinking)

Critical Thinking Exercises

1. Branding is not just for products and services—states are getting in on the action, too, as you learned from reading about *place marketing* in the chapter. One of the most recent examples of state branding comes from Michigan with its

"Pure Michigan" campaign, resulting in millions of dollars of tourism revenue. Other famous place branding campaigns include "Virginia is for Lovers," "Florida—the Sunshine State," and "What Happens in Vegas Stays in Vegas."

In a small group, come up with a brand identity proposal for your state. Present your idea to the rest of the class and explain the meaning you are trying to convey. (AACSB: Communication; Reflective Thinking)

2. A product's package is often referred to as a "silent salesperson" and is the last marketing effort before consumers make a selection in the store. One model used to evaluate a product's package is the VIEW model: *V*isibility, *I*nformation, *E*motion, and *W*orkability. Visibility refers to the package's ability to stand out among competing products on the store shelf. Information is the type and amount of data included on the package. Some packages try to simulate an emotional response to influence buyers. Finally, all product packages perform the basic function of protecting and dispensing the product. Select two competing brands in a product category and evaluate each brand's packaging on these dimensions. Which brand's packaging is superior? Suggest ways to improve the other brand's packaging. (AACSB: Communication; Reflective Thinking)

3. Find five examples of service-provider attempts to reduce service intangibility. (AACSB: Communication; Reflective Thinking)

MINICASES AND APPLICATIONS

Marketing Technology   Virtual Goods, Real Money

Who would pay $330,000 for a virtual space station? Or $100,000 for an asteroid space resort? How about $99,000 for a virtual bank license? Players of the massively multiplayer online (MMO) game called Entropia Universe did. Those players are making money, and so are the game developers. There's a new business model—called *freemium*—driving the economics of these games. Under this model, users play for free but can purchase virtual goods with real money. Worldwide sales of virtual goods were $2.2 billion in 2009 and are predicted to reach $6 billion by 2013. Most virtual goods are inexpensive—costing about $1—such as the tractor you can buy in *FarmVille* or a weapon in

World of Warcraft. That doesn't seem like much, but when you consider that game-maker Zynga's *FrontierVille* had 5 million players within one month of launch, we're talking real money!

1. How would you classify virtual goods—a tangible good, an experience, or a service? Discuss the technological factors enabling the growth of virtual goods. (AACSB: Communication; Reflective Thinking)

2. How do players purchase virtual goods? Identify three virtual currencies and their value in U.S. dollars. (AACSB: Communication; Reflective Thinking)

Marketing Ethics   Outsourced Instructors

Have you taken an online course in high school or college? Many students have, but some traditional brick-and-mortar universities are venturing into uncharted territory by outsourcing the teaching function to online providers. Missouri State University is offering its introductory journalism class through Florida-based Poynter Institute, which is a nonprofit journalism training group. Instructional outsourcing is popping up on campuses throughout the country, and most are serviced by for-profit companies such as Academic Partnerships, StraighterLine, and Smarthinking. These partnerships translate into bigger profit margins for both the university and the instructional partner.

1. What is the product offered by a university? Discuss the levels of product offered and how these might change in the next 10 to 20 years due to technology. (AACSB: Communication; Reflective Thinking)

2. Discuss the pros and cons of outsourcing instructors for courses or even entire degrees from the point of view of both the school and the students. Should technology be used in this way to deliver this type of product? (AACSB: Communication; Reflective Thinking; Ethical Reasoning)

Marketing by the Numbers   Brand Value

What is a brand's worth? It depends on who is measuring it. For example, in 2010 Google was valued to be worth $114 billion by one brand valuation company but only $43 billion by another. While this variation is extreme, it is not uncommon

to find valuations of the same brand differ by $20 to $30 billion. Interbrand and BrandZ publish global brand value rankings each year, but a comparison of these two companies' 2010 rankings reveals an overlap of only six of the top ten brands.

1. Compare and contrast the methodologies used by Interbrand (www.interbrand.com) and BrandZ (www.brandz.com) to determine brand value. Explain why there is a discrepancy in the rankings from these two companies. (AACSB: Communication; Reflective Thinking; Analytical Reasoning)

2. In 2008, BrandZ ranked Toyota the number one brand of automobiles, valuing the brand at more than $35 billion. In 2010, however, it valued the Toyota brand under $22 billion. Discuss reasons for the drop in Toyota's brand value. (AACSB: Communication; Reflective Thinking)

Video Case   Life Is Good

You're probably familiar with the Life Is Good apparel brand. The company features its cheerful logo prominently on everything from T-shirts to dog collars and seems to exude a positive vibe. While this company has found considerable success in selling its wares based on a happy brand image, consumers still aren't getting the complete image that the Life Is Good founders intended. This video illustrates the challenges a company faces in balancing the customer's role with that of the company in determining a brand's meaning.

After viewing the video featuring Life Is Good, answer the following questions:

1. What are people buying when they purchase a Life Is Good product?
2. What factors have contributed to the Life Is Good brand image?
3. What recommendations would you make to Life Is Good regarding brand development strategies?

Company Cases   1 Converse / 7 Las Vegas / 8 Samsung

See Appendix 1 for cases appropriate for this chapter. **Case 1, Converse: Shaping the Customer Experience.** Converse continues to provide customers with the authentic experience they desire by allowing them to shape that experience. **Case 7, Las Vegas: What's Not Happening in Vegas.** The Sin City makes adjustments to keep its brand relevant as changes in the marketing environment cause big shifts in Las Vegas tourism. **Case 8, Samsung: From Gallop to Run.** By completely overhauling its business and marketing strategies, Samsung becomes the world's largest consumer electronics manufacturer.

8 Developing New Products
and **Managing** the **Product Life Cycle**

CHAPTER ROAD MAP

Objective Outline

▶ **OBJECTIVE 1   Explain how companies find and develop new-product ideas.** New-Product Development Strategy (230–231)

▶ **OBJECTIVE 2   List and define the steps in the new-product development process and the major considerations in managing this process.** The New-Product Development Process (231–238); Managing New-Product Development (238–242)

▶ **OBJECTIVE 3   Describe the stages of the product life cycle and how marketing strategies change during a product's life cycle.** Product Life-Cycle Strategies (242–248)

▶ **OBJECTIVE 4   Discuss two additional product issues: socially responsible product decisions and international product and services marketing.** Additional Product and Service Considerations (248–250)

Previewing the Concepts

In previous chapters, you've learned how marketers manage and develop products and brands. In this chapter, we examine two additional product topics: developing new products and managing products through their life cycles. New products are the lifeblood of an organization. However, new-product development is risky, and many new products fail. So, the first part of this chapter lays out a process for finding and growing successful new products. Once introduced, marketers then want their products to enjoy long and happy lives. In the second part of this chapter, you'll see that every product passes through several life-cycle stages, and each stage poses new challenges requiring different marketing strategies and tactics. Finally, we wrap up our product discussion by looking at two additional considerations: social responsibility in product decisions and international product and services marketing.

  For openers, consider Google, one of the world's most innovative companies. Google seems to come up with an almost unending flow of knock-your-eye-out new technologies and services. If it has to do with finding, refining, or using information, there's probably an innovative Google solution for it. At Google, innovation isn't just a process—it's in the very spirit of the place.

First Stop

Google: New-Product Innovation at the Speed of Light

▲ Google is spectacularly successful and wildly innovative. Ask the folks who work there and they'll tell you that innovation is more than just a process—it's in the air, in the spirit of the place.

Eric Carr/Alamy

Google is wildly innovative. It recently topped *Fast Company* magazine's list of the world's most innovative companies, and it regularly ranks among everyone else's top two or three innovators. Google is also spectacularly successful. Despite formidable competition from giants like Microsoft and Yahoo!, Google's share in its core business—online search—stands at a decisive 70 percent, more than 2.5 times the combined market shares of its two closest competitors. The company also has a lock on the mobile-search market and captures 83 percent of all search-related advertising revenues.

But Google has grown to become much more than just an Internet search and advertising company. Google's mission is "to organize the world's information and make it universally accessible and useful." In Google's view, information is a kind of natural resource—one to be mined, refined, and universally distributed. That idea unifies what would otherwise appear to be a widely diverse set of Google projects, such as mapping the world, searching the Web on a cell phone screen, or even providing for the early detection of flu epidemics. If it has to do with harnessing and using information, Google's got it covered in some innovative way.

Google knows how to innovate. At many companies, new-product development is a cautious, step-by-step affair that might take a year or two to unfold. In contrast, Google's freewheeling new-product development process moves at the speed of light. The nimble innovator implements major new services in less time than it takes competitors to refine and approve an initial idea. For example, a Google senior project manager describes the lightning-quick development of iGoogle, Google's customizable home page:

> It was clear to Google that there were two groups [of Google users]: people who loved the site's clean, classic look and people who wanted tons of information there—e-mail, news, local weather. [For those who wanted a fuller home page,] iGoogle started out with me and three engineers. I was 22, and I thought, "This is awesome." Six weeks later, we launched the first version in May. The happiness metrics were good, there was healthy growth, and by September, we had [iGoogle fully operational with] a link on Google.com.

Such fast-paced innovation would boggle the minds of product developers at most other companies, but at Google it is standard operating procedure. "That's what we do," says Google's vice president for search products and user experience. "The hardest part about indoctrinating people into our culture is when engineers show me a prototype and I'm like, 'Great, let's go!' They'll say, 'Oh, no, it's not ready.' I tell them, 'The Googly thing is to launch it early on Google Labs [a site where users can try out experimental Google applications] and then to iterate, learning what the market wants—and making it great.'" Adds a Google engineering manager, "We set an operational tempo: When in doubt, do something. If you have two paths and you're not sure which is right, take the fastest path."

When it comes to new-product development at Google, there are no two-year plans. The company's new-product planning looks ahead only four to five months. Google would rather see projects fail quickly than see a carefully planned, long drawn-out project fail.

Google's famously chaotic innovation process has unleashed a seemingly unending flurry of diverse products, ranging from an e-mail service (Gmail), a blog search engine (Google Blog Search), an online payment service (Google Checkout), and a photo sharing service (Google Picasa)

> Google's famously chaotic innovation process has unleashed a seemingly unending flurry of diverse new products. But at Google, innovation is more than a process. It's part of the company's DNA. "Where does innovation happen at Google? It happens everywhere."

229

to a universal platform for mobile-phone applications (Google Android), a cloud-friendly Web browser (Chrome), projects for mapping and exploring the world (Google Maps and Google Earth), and even an early warning system for flu outbreaks in your area (FluTrends). Google claims that FluTrends has identified outbreaks two weeks before the U.S. Centers for Disease Control and Prevention.

Google is open to new-product ideas from about any source. What ties it all together is the company's passion for helping people find and use information. Innovation is the responsibility of every Google employee. Google engineers are encouraged to spend 20 percent of their time developing their own "cool and wacky" new-product ideas. And all new Google ideas are quickly tested in beta form by the ultimate judges—those who will use them. According to one observer:

> Anytime you cram some 20,000 of the world's smartest people into one company, you can expect to grow a garden of unrelated ideas. Especially when you give some of those geniuses one workday a week—Google's famous "20 percent time"—to work on whatever projects fan their passions. And especially when you create Google Labs (www.googlelabs.com), a Web site where the public can kick the

tires on crazy, half-baked Google creations. Some Labs projects go on to become real Google services, and others are quietly snuffed out.

In the end, at Google, innovation is more than a process—it's part of the company's DNA. "Where does innovation happen at Google? It happens everywhere," says a Google research scientist.

Talk to Googlers at various levels and departments, and one powerful theme emerges: Whether they're designing search engines for the blind or preparing meals for their colleagues, these people feel that their work can change the world. The marvel of Google is its ability to continue to instill a sense of creative fearlessness and ambition in its employees. Prospective hires are often asked, "If you could change the world using Google's resources, what would you build?" But here, this isn't a goofy or even theoretical question: Google wants to know because thinking—and building—on that scale is what Google does. This, after all, is the company that wants to make available online every page of every book ever published. Smaller-gauge ideas die of disinterest. When it comes to innovation, Google *is* different. But the difference isn't tangible. It's in the air— in the spirit of the place.[1]

As the Google story suggests, companies that excel at developing and managing new products reap big rewards. Every product seems to go through a life cycle: It is born, goes through several phases, and eventually dies as newer products come along that create new or greater value for customers.

This product life cycle presents two major challenges: First, because all products eventually decline, a firm must be good at developing new products to replace aging ones (the challenge of *new-product development*). Second, a firm must be good at adapting its marketing strategies in the face of changing tastes, technologies, and competition as products pass through stages (the challenge of *product life-cycle strategies*). We first look at the problem of finding and developing new products and then at the problem of managing them successfully over their life cycles.

New-Product Development Strategy

Author Comment ▶
New products are the lifeblood of a company. As old products mature and fade away, companies must develop new ones to take their place. For example, only eight years after it unveiled its first iPod, 66 percent of Apple's revenues come from iPods, iPads, iPhones, and iTunes.

New-product development
The development of original products, product improvements, product modifications, and new brands through the firm's own product development efforts.

A firm can obtain new products in two ways. One is through *acquisition*—by buying a whole company, a patent, or a license to produce someone else's product. The other is through the firm's own **new-product development** efforts. By *new products* we mean original products, product improvements, product modifications, and new brands that the firm develops through its own R&D efforts. In this chapter, we concentrate on new-product development.

New products are important to both customers and the marketers who serve them: They bring new solutions and variety to customers' lives, and they are a key source of growth for companies. Yet innovation can be very expensive and very risky. New products face tough odds. By one estimate, 67 percent of all new products introduced by established companies fail. For new companies, the failure rate soars to 90 percent. Each year, U.S. companies lose an estimated $260 billion on failed new products.[2]

Why do so many new products fail? There are several reasons. Although an idea may be good, the company may overestimate market size. The actual product may be poorly designed. Or it might be incorrectly positioned, launched at the wrong time, priced too high, or poorly advertised. A high-level executive might push a favorite idea despite poor marketing

▲ **Visiting the NewProductWorks Showcase and Learning Center is like finding yourself in some nightmare version of a supermarket. Each product failure represents squandered dollars and hopes.**

Courtesy of NewProductWorks, a division of GFK Strategic Innovation. Used with permission. www.gfkamerica.com/newproductworks.

research findings. Sometimes the costs of product development are higher than expected, and sometimes competitors fight back harder than expected. However, the reasons behind some new-product failures seem pretty obvious. Try the following on for size:[3]

> Strolling the aisles of ASG NewProductWorks collection is like finding yourself in a new-product history museum.
> ▶ Many of the more than 110,000 products on display were quite successful. Others, however, were abject flops. Behind each flop are squandered dollars and hopes and the classic question, "What were they thinking?" Some products failed because they simply didn't bring value to customers—for example, Look of Buttermilk Shampoo, Cucumber antiperspirant spray, or Premier smokeless cigarettes. *Smokeless* cigarettes? What were they thinking? Other companies failed because they attached trusted brand names to something totally out of character. Can you imagine swallowing Ben-Gay aspirin? Or how about Gerber Singles food for adults (perhaps the tasty pureed sweet-and-sour pork or chicken Madeira)? Other misbegotten attempts to stretch a good name include Cracker Jack cereal, Exxon fruit punch, Smucker's premium ketchup, Fruit of the Loom laundry detergent, and Harley-Davidson cake-decorating kits. Really, what were they thinking?

Author Comment ▶
Companies can't just hope that they'll stumble across good new products. Instead, they must develop a systematic new-product development process.

The New-Product Development Process

Companies face a problem: They must develop new products, but the odds weigh heavily against success. To create successful new products, a company must understand its consumers, markets, and competitors and develop products that deliver superior value to customers. It must carry out strong new-product planning and set up a systematic, customer-driven *new-product development process* for finding and growing new products. ▶ **Figure 8.1** shows the eight major steps in this process.

Idea Generation

Idea generation
The systematic search for new-product ideas.

New-product development starts with **idea generation**—the systematic search for new-product ideas. A company typically generates hundreds—even thousands—of ideas to find a few good ones. Major sources of new-product ideas include internal sources and external sources such as customers, competitors, distributors and suppliers, and others.

Internal Idea Sources

Using *internal sources*, the company can find new ideas through formal R&D. However, in one survey, 750 global CEOs reported that only 14 percent of their innovation ideas came from traditional R&D. Instead, 41 percent came from employees, and 36 percent came from customers.[4]

Thus, beyond its internal R&D process, companies can pick the brains of its employees—from executives to salespeople to scientists, engineers, and manufacturing staff. Many

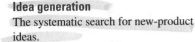

New-product development starts with good new-product ideas—*lots* of them. For example, Cisco's recent I-Prize crowdsourcing challenge attracted 824 ideas from 2,900 innovators representing more than 156 countries.

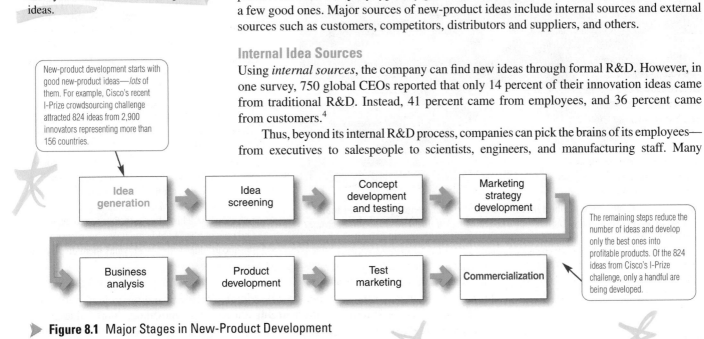

The remaining steps reduce the number of ideas and develop only the best ones into profitable products. Of the 824 ideas from Cisco's I-Prize challenge, only a handful are being developed.

Idea generation → Idea screening → Concept development and testing → Marketing strategy development → Business analysis → Product development → Test marketing → Commercialization

▶ **Figure 8.1** Major Stages in New-Product Development

companies have developed successful *intrapreneurial* programs that encourage employees to envision and develop new-product ideas. For example, the Internet networking company Cisco makes it everybody's business to come up with great ideas. It set up an internal wiki called Idea Zone or I-Zone, through which any Cisco employee can propose an idea for a new product or comment on or modify someone else's proposed idea. Since its inception, I-Zone has generated hundreds of ideas, leading to the formation of four new Cisco business units.[5]

External Idea Sources

Companies can also obtain good new-product ideas from any of a number of external sources. For example, *distributors and suppliers* can contribute ideas. Distributors are close to the market and can pass along information about consumer problems and new-product possibilities. Suppliers can tell the company about new concepts, techniques, and materials that can be used to develop new products. *Competitors* are another important source. Companies watch competitors' ads to get clues about their new products. They buy competing new products, take them apart to see how they work, analyze their sales, and decide whether they should bring out a new product of their own. Other idea sources include trade magazines, shows, and seminars; government agencies; advertising agencies; marketing research firms; university and commercial laboratories; and inventors.

Perhaps the most important sources of new-product ideas are *customers* themselves. The company can analyze customer questions and complaints to find new products that better solve consumer problems. Or it can invite customers to share suggestions and ideas. For example, Starbucks sponsors My Starbucks Idea, a Web site that invites customers to share, discuss, and vote on new product and service ideas. "You know better than anyone else what you want from Starbucks," says the site. "So tell us. What's your Starbucks idea? Revolutionary or simple—we want to hear it."[6]

To harness customer new-product input, 3M has opened nearly two dozen customer innovation centers throughout the world, including sites in the United States, Brazil, Germany, India, China, and Russia. ▶ The innovation centers not only generate plenty of customer-driven new-product ideas but also help 3M establish productive, long-term customer relationships.[7]

▲ Customer-driven new-product ideas: At 3M innovation centers, customer teams meet with 3M marketing and technology experts to spark novel solutions to customer problems.
Courtesy 3M Company

Typically located near company research facilities, the innovation centers engage 3M's corporate customers directly in the innovation process. The idea behind the centers is to gain a richer understanding of customer needs and link these needs to 3M technologies. In a typical customer visit, a customer team meets with 3M marketing and technology experts who pepper them with open-ended questions. Next, together, the customer and 3M teams visit the "World of Innovation" showroom, where they are exposed to more than 40 3M technology platforms—core technologies in areas like optical films, reflective materials, abrasives, and adhesives. This interaction often sparks novel connections and solutions to the customer's needs.

For instance, 3M and customer Visteon Corporation, an automotive supplier, have worked together in the development of a next-generation concept vehicle that incorporates 3M technologies not originally developed for automated applications. Visteon's visit to an innovation center led to the idea of using 3M's 3D technology for navigation displays, Thinsulate materials to reduce noise, and optical films to hide functional elements of the dashboard unless the driver wants them displayed.

Crowdsourcing

More broadly, many companies are now developing *crowdsourcing* or *open-innovation* new-product idea programs. **Crowdsourcing** throws the innovation doors wide open,

Crowdsourcing
Inviting broad communities of people—customers, employees, independent scientists and researchers, and even the public at large—into the new-product innovation process.

inviting broad communities of people—customers, employees, independent scientists and researchers, and even the public at large—into the new-product innovation process. "The first rule of innovation these days is that the most powerful ideas often come from the most unexpected places—the quiet genius of employees inside your company, the hidden genius of customers," says one expert. "Tapping into this hidden genius doesn't require fancy technology or deep pockets—it just requires a leadership mindset that invites outside brainpower into the organization.[8]

For example, when Netflix wanted to improve the accuracy of its Cinematch online recommendation system, which makes movie recommendations to customers based on their ratings of other movies they've rented, it launched a crowdsourcing effort called Netflix Prize.[9]

▲ **Crowdsourcing: When Netflix wanted ideas for improving the accuracy of its Cinematch online recommendation system, it decided to "open it up to the world," promising a $1 million prize for the best solution.**

It was a quest that Netflix scientists and mathematicians have been working on for about a decade. Rather than hiring even more computer scientists to work on the project, Netflix decided to open it up to the world. "We'd like to think that we have smart people bumping around the building, but we don't have anything compared to the worldwide intelligentsia," says Netflix vice president Steve Swasey. ▶The company created a Web site, *NetflixPrize.com*, which issued an open challenge and promised a $1 million prize to whomever submitted the best solution for improving the accuracy of the Cinematch by at least 10 percent. Nearly three years and more than 51,000 participants later, Netflix awarded the prize to BellKors Pragmatic Chaos, a seven-member superteam consisting of engineers, statisticians, and researchers from the United States, Austria, Canada, and Israel. "It was a very innovative way to generate more ideas," says Swasey. "If you think about it, 51,000 scientists" devoted their intelligence, creativity, and man-hours to the project, all for only $1 million.[9]

Rather than creating and managing their own crowdsourcing platforms, companies can use third-party crowdsourcing networks, such as InnoCentive, TopCoder, Hypios, and jo-voto. For example, organizations ranging from Facebook and PayPal to ESPN, NASA, and the Salk Institute tap into TopCoder's network of nearly 300,000 mathematicians, engineers, software developers, and designers for ideas and solutions, offering prizes of $100 to $100,000. PayPal recently posted a challenge to the TopCoder community seeking the development of an innovative Android or iPhone app that would successfully and securely run its checkout process, awarding the winners $5,000 each. After only four weeks of competition and two weeks of review, PayPal had its solutions. The Android app came from a programmer in the United States; the iPhone app from a programmer in Colombia.[10]

Crowdsourcing can produce a flood of innovative ideas. In fact, opening the floodgates to anyone and everyone can overwhelm the company with ideas—some good and some bad. For example, when Cisco Systems sponsored an open-innovation effort called I-Prize, soliciting ideas from external sources, it received more than 820 distinct ideas from more than 2,900 innovators from 156 countries. "The evaluation process was far more labor-intensive than we'd anticipated," says Cisco's chief technology officer. It required "significant investments of time, energy, patience, and imagination . . . to discern the gems hidden within rough stones." In the end, a team of six Cisco people worked full-time for three months to carve out 32 semifinalist ideas, as well as nine teams representing 14 countries in six continents for the final phase of the competition.[11]

Truly innovative companies don't rely only on one source or another for new-product ideas. Instead, they develop extensive innovation networks that capture ideas and inspiration from every possible source, from employees and customers to outside innovators and multiple points beyond.

Idea Screening

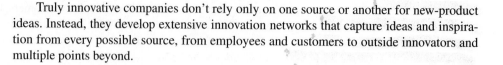

Idea screening
Screening new-product ideas to spot good ideas and drop poor ones as soon as possible.

The purpose of idea generation is to create a large number of ideas. The purpose of the succeeding stages is to *reduce* that number. The first idea-reducing stage is **idea screening**, which helps spot good ideas and drop poor ones as soon as possible. Product development costs rise greatly in later stages, so the company wants to go ahead only with those product ideas that will turn into profitable products.

Many companies require their executives to write up new-product ideas in a standard format that can be reviewed by a new-product committee. The write-up describes the product or the service, the proposed customer value proposition, the target market, and the competition. It makes some rough estimates of market size, product price, development time and costs, manufacturing costs, and rate of return. The committee then evaluates the idea against a set of general criteria.

One marketing expert proposes an R-W-W ("real, win, worth doing") new-product screening framework that asks three questions. First, *Is it real?* Is there a real need and desire for the product and will customers buy it? Is there a clear product concept and will such a product satisfy the market? Second, *Can we win?* Does the product offer a sustainable competitive advantage? Does the company have the resources to make such a product a success? Finally, *Is it worth doing?* Does the product fit the company's overall growth strategy? Does it offer sufficient profit potential? The company should be able to answer yes to all three R-W-W questions before developing the new-product idea further.[12]

Concept Development and Testing

Product concept
A detailed version of the new-product idea stated in meaningful consumer terms.

An attractive idea must then be developed into a **product concept**. It is important to distinguish between a product idea, a product concept, and a product image. A *product idea* is an idea for a possible product that the company can see itself offering to the market. A *product concept* is a detailed version of the idea stated in meaningful consumer terms. A *product image* is the way consumers perceive an actual or potential product.

▲ This is Tesla's initial all-electric roadster. Later, more-affordable mass-market models will travel more than 300 miles on a single charge, recharge in 45 minutes from a normal 120-volt electrical outlet, and cost about one penny per mile to power.

Courtesy of Telsa Motors, Inc.

Concept Development

Suppose a car manufacturer has developed a practical battery-powered, all-electric car. ▶ Its initial prototype is a sleek, sporty roadster convertible that sells for more than $100,000.[13] However, in the near future it plans to introduce more-affordable, mass-market versions that will compete with recently introduced hybrid-electric or all-electric cars such as the Chevy Volt and Nissan Leaf. This 100 percent electric car will accelerate from 0 to 60 miles per hour in 5.6 seconds, travel up to 300 miles on a single charge, recharge in 45 minutes from a normal 120-volt electrical outlet, and cost about one penny per mile to power.

Looking ahead, the marketer's task is to develop this new product into alternative product concepts, find out how attractive each concept is to customers, and choose the best one. It might create the following product concepts for this electric car:

- *Concept 1:* An affordably priced midsize car designed as a second family car to be used around town for running errands and visiting friends.

- *Concept 2:* A mid-priced sporty compact appealing to young singles and couples.
- *Concept 3:* A "green" car appealing to environmentally conscious people who want practical, low-polluting transportation.
- *Concept 4:* A high-end midsize utility vehicle appealing to those who love the space SUVs provide but lament the poor gas mileage.

Concept Testing

Concept testing

Testing new-product concepts with a group of target consumers to find out if the concepts have strong consumer appeal.

Concept testing calls for testing new-product concepts with groups of target consumers. The concepts may be presented to consumers symbolically or physically. Here, in more detail, is concept 3:

> An efficient, fun-to-drive, battery-powered compact car that seats four. This 100 percent electric wonder provides practical and reliable transportation with no pollution. It goes 300 miles on a single charge and costs pennies per mile to operate. It's a sensible, responsible alternative to today's pollution-producing gas-guzzlers. Its fully equipped price is $25,000.

Many firms routinely test new-product concepts with consumers before attempting to turn them into actual new products. For some concept tests, a word or picture description might be sufficient. However, a more concrete and physical presentation of the concept will increase the reliability of the concept test. After being exposed to the concept, consumers then may be asked to react to it by answering questions similar to those in ▶ **Table 8.1**.

The answers to such questions will help the company decide which concept has the strongest appeal. For example, the last question asks about the consumer's intention to buy. Suppose 2 percent of consumers say they "definitely" would buy, and another 5 percent say "probably." The company could project these figures to the full population in this target group to estimate sales volume. Even then, however, the estimate is uncertain because people do not always carry out their stated intentions.

Marketing Strategy Development

Marketing strategy development

Designing an initial marketing strategy for a new product based on the product concept.

Suppose the carmaker finds that concept 3 for the electric car tests best. The next step is **marketing strategy development**, designing an initial marketing strategy for introducing this car to the market.

The *marketing strategy statement* consists of three parts. The first part describes the target market; the planned value proposition; and the sales, market share, and profit goals for the first few years. Thus:

> The target market is younger, well-educated, moderate- to high-income individuals, couples, or small families seeking practical, environmentally responsible transportation. The car will be positioned as more fun to drive and less polluting than today's internal combustion engine or hybrid cars. The company will aim to sell 50,000 cars in the first year, at a loss of not more than $15 million. In the second year, the company will aim for sales of 90,000 cars and a profit of $25 million.

▶ **Table 8.1** | Questions for the All-Electric Car Concept Test

1. Do you understand the concept of a battery-powered electric car?
2. Do you believe the claims about the car's performance?
3. What are the major benefits of an all-electric car compared with a conventional car?
4. What are its advantages compared with a gas-electric hybrid car?
5. What improvements in the car's features would you suggest?
6. For what uses would you prefer an all-electric car to a conventional car?
7. What would be a reasonable price to charge for the car?
8. Who would be involved in your decision to buy such a car? Who would drive it?
9. Would you buy such a car (definitely, probably, probably not, definitely not)?

The second part of the marketing strategy statement outlines the product's planned price, distribution, and marketing budget for the first year:

> The battery-powered electric car will be offered in three colors—red, white, and blue—and will have a full set of accessories as standard features. It will sell at a retail price of $25,000, with 15 percent off the list price to dealers. Dealers who sell more than 10 cars per month will get an additional discount of 5 percent on each car sold that month. A marketing budget of $50 million will be split 50–50 between a national media campaign and local event marketing. Advertising and the Web site will emphasize the car's fun spirit and low emissions. During the first year, $100,000 will be spent on marketing research to find out who is buying the car and what their satisfaction levels are.

The third part of the marketing strategy statement describes the planned long-run sales, profit goals, and marketing mix strategy:

> We intend to capture a 3 percent long-run share of the total auto market and realize an after-tax return on investment of 15 percent. To achieve this, product quality will start high and be improved over time. Price will be raised in the second and third years if competition and the economy permit. The total marketing budget will be raised each year by about 10 percent. Marketing research will be reduced to $60,000 per year after the first year.

Business Analysis

Once management has decided on its product concept and marketing strategy, it can evaluate the business attractiveness of the proposal. **Business analysis** involves a review of the sales, costs, and profit projections for a new product to find out whether they satisfy the company's objectives. If they do, the product can move to the product development stage.

To estimate sales, the company might look at the sales history of similar products and conduct market surveys. It can then estimate minimum and maximum sales to assess the range of risk. After preparing the sales forecast, management can estimate the expected costs and profits for the product, including marketing, R&D, operations, accounting, and finance costs. The company then uses the sales and costs figures to analyze the new product's financial attractiveness.

Business analysis
A review of the sales, costs, and profit projections for a new product to find out whether these factors satisfy the company's objectives.

Product Development

For many new-product concepts, a product may exist only as a word description, a drawing, or perhaps a crude mock-up. If the product concept passes the business test, it moves into **product development**. Here, R&D or engineering develops the product concept into a physical product. The product development step, however, now calls for a huge jump in investment. It will show whether the product idea can be turned into a workable product.

The R&D department will develop and test one or more physical versions of the product concept. R&D hopes to design a prototype that will satisfy and excite consumers and that can be produced quickly and at budgeted costs. Developing a successful prototype can take days, weeks, months, or even years depending on the product and prototype methods.

Often, products undergo rigorous tests to make sure that they perform safely and effectively, or that consumers will find value in them. Companies can do their own product testing or outsource testing to other firms that specialize in testing.

Marketers often involve actual customers in product testing. ▶ For example, HP signs up consumers to evaluate prototype imaging and printing products in their homes and offices. Participants work with prerelease products for periods ranging from a few days to eight weeks and share their experiences about how the products perform in an actual use environment. The product-testing program gives HP a

Product development
Developing the product concept into a physical product to ensure that the product idea can be turned into a workable market offering.

▲ Product testing: HP signs up consumers to evaluate prototype imaging and printing products in their homes and offices to gain insights about their entire "out-of-box experience."

Adrian Sherratt/Alamy

chance to interact with customers and gain insights about their entire "out-of-box experience," from product setup and operation to system compatibility. HP personnel might even visit participants' homes to directly observe installation and first usage of the product.[14]

A new product must have the required functional features and also convey the intended psychological characteristics. The all-electric car, for example, should strike consumers as being well built, comfortable, and safe. Management must learn what makes consumers decide that a car is well built. To some consumers, this means that the car has "solid-sounding" doors. To others, it means that the car is able to withstand a heavy impact in crash tests. Consumer tests are conducted in which consumers test-drive the car and rate its attributes.

Test Marketing

Test marketing
The stage of new-product development in which the product and its proposed marketing program are tested in realistic market settings.

If the product passes both the concept test and the product test, the next step is **test marketing**, the stage at which the product and its proposed marketing program are introduced into realistic market settings. Test marketing gives the marketer experience with marketing a product before going to the great expense of full introduction. It lets the company test the product and its entire marketing program—targeting and positioning strategy, advertising, distribution, pricing, branding and packaging, and budget levels.

The amount of test marketing needed varies with each new product. Test marketing costs can be high, and it takes time that may allow competitors to gain advantages. When the costs of developing and introducing the product are low, or when management is already confident about the new product, the company may do little or no test marketing. In fact, test marketing by consumer-goods firms has been declining in recent years. Companies often do not test-market simple line extensions or copies of competitors' successful products.

However, when introducing a new product requires a big investment, when the risks are high, or when management is not sure of the product or its marketing program, a company may do a lot of test marketing. ▶ For instance, Starbucks VIA instant coffee was one of the company's biggest, most risky product rollouts ever. The company spent 20 years developing the coffee and several months testing the product in Starbucks shops in Chicago and Seattle before releasing the product nationally. In the spring and summer of 2009, Starbucks patrons in the two test markets were offered recession-friendly $1.00 cups of coffee as well as coupons and free samples of VIA to take home with them. In addition, a Taste Challenge was created in Chicago to help drum up interest and induce trial. Performance of VIA exceeded expectations in all three cities and the promotional efforts were applied to the national rollout as well. Said CEO Howard Schultz, "We took a lot of time with it because we knew it could undermine the company if we didn't do it right."[15]

▲ Starbucks tested its VIA instant coffee extensively before launching the new-product nationally. "We knew it could undermine the company if we didn't do it right."

AP Images/Mark Lennihan

As an alternative to extensive and costly standard test markets, companies can use controlled test markets or simulated test markets. In *controlled test markets*, such as SymphonyIRI's BehaviorScan, new products and tactics are tested among controlled panels of shoppers and stores.[16] By combining information on each test consumer's purchases with consumer demographic and TV viewing information, BehaviorScan can provide store-by-store, week-by-week reports on the sales of tested products and the impact of in-store and in-home marketing efforts. Using *simulated test markets*, researchers measure consumer responses to new products and marketing tactics in laboratory stores or simulated online shopping environments. Both controlled test markets and simulated test markets reduce the costs of test marketing and speed up the process.

Commercialization

Commercialization
Introducing a new product into the market.

Test marketing gives management the information needed to make a final decision about whether to launch the new product. If the company goes ahead with **commercialization**— introducing the new product into the market—it will face high costs. For example, the company may need to build or rent a manufacturing facility. And, in the case of a major new consumer product, it may spend hundreds of millions of dollars for advertising, sales promotion, and other marketing efforts in the first year. For instance, to introduce its McCafé coffee in the United States, McDonald's spent $100 million on an advertising blitz that spanned TV, print, radio, outdoor, the Internet, events, public relations, and sampling.[17]

A company launching a new product must first decide on introduction *timing*. If the carmaker's new all-electric car will eat into the sales of its other cars, the introduction may be delayed. If the car can be improved further, or if the economy is down, the company may wait until the following year to launch it. However, if competitors are ready to introduce their own electric models, the company may push to introduce its car sooner.

Next, the company must decide *where* to launch the new product—in a single location, a region, the national market, or the international market. Some companies may quickly introduce new models into the full national market. Companies with international distribution systems may introduce new products through swift global rollouts. Microsoft did this with its Windows Phone 7, using a mammoth $500 million marketing blitz to launch the device simultaneously in more than 30 countries in North America, Europe, Asia-Pacific, and Australia.[18]

Managing New-Product Development

Author Comment ▶
Above all else, new-product development must focus on creating customer value. Says P&G's CEO about the company's new-product development: "We've figured out how to keep the consumer at the center of all our decisions. As a result, we don't go far wrong."

The new-product development process shown in Figure 8.1 highlights the important activities needed to find, develop, and introduce new products. However, new-product development involves more than just going through a set of steps. Companies must take a holistic approach to managing this process. Successful new-product development requires a customer-centered, team-based, and systematic effort.

Customer-Centered New-Product Development

Customer-centered new-product development
New-product development that focuses on finding new ways to solve customer problems and create more customer-satisfying experiences.

Above all else, new-product development must be customer centered. When looking for and developing new products, companies often rely too heavily on technical research in their R&D laboratories. But like everything else in marketing, successful new-product development begins with a thorough understanding of what consumers need and value. **Customer-centered new-product development** focuses on finding new ways to solve customer problems and create more customer-satisfying experiences.

One study found that the most successful new products are ones that are differentiated, solve major customer problems, and offer a compelling customer value proposition. Another study showed that companies that directly engage their customers in the new-product innovation process had twice the return on assets and triple the growth in operating income of firms that did not. Thus, customer involvement has a positive effect on the new-product development process and product success.[19]

For example, whereas the consumer package goods industry's new-product success rate is only about 15 to 20 percent, P&G's success rate is over 50 percent. According to former P&G CEO A. G. Lafley, the most important factor in this success is understanding what consumers want. In the past, says Lafley, P&G tried to push new products down to consumers rather than first understanding their needs. But now, P&G employs an immersion process it calls "Living It," in which researchers go so far as to live with shoppers for several days at a time to envision product ideas based directly on consumer needs. P&Gers also hang out in stores for similar insights, a process they call "Working It." ▶ And at its Connect + Develop crowdsourcing site, P&G urges customers to submit their own ideas and suggestions for new products and services, current product design, and packaging. Its Connect + Develop Program—which includes unsolicited submissions from consumers and innovators plus active searches through global networks—gave birth to such products as the Swiffer Dusters and Olay Regenerist skin cream. "We figured out

▲ **Customer-centered new-product development: P&G's Connect + Develop crowdsourcing site urges customers to submit their own ideas for new products and services.**

The Procter & Gamble Company

Team-based new-product development

An approach to developing new products in which various company departments work closely together, overlapping the steps in the product development process to save time and increase effectiveness.

how to keep the consumer at the center of all our decisions," says Lafley. "As a result, we don't go far wrong."[20]

Thus, today's innovative companies get out of the research lab and connect with customers in search of fresh ways to meet customer needs. Customer-centered new-product development begins and ends with understanding customers and involving them in the process. (See Marketing at Work 8.1 for a great example.)

Team-Based New-Product Development

Good new-product development also requires a total-company, cross-functional effort. Some companies organize their new-product development process into the orderly sequence of steps shown in Figure 8.1, starting with idea generation and ending with commercialization. Under this *sequential product development* approach, one company department works individually to complete its stage of the process before passing the new product along to the next department and stage. This orderly, step-by-step process can help bring control to complex and risky projects. But it can also be dangerously slow. In fast-changing, highly competitive markets, such slow-but-sure product development can result in product failures, lost sales and profits, and crumbling market positions.

To get their new products to market more quickly, many companies use a **team-based new-product development** approach. Under this approach, company departments work closely together in cross-functional teams, overlapping the steps in the product development process to save time and increase effectiveness. Instead of passing the new product from department to department, the company assembles a team of people from various departments that stays with the new product from start to finish. Such teams usually include people from the marketing, finance, design, manufacturing, and legal departments and even supplier and customer companies. In the sequential process, a bottleneck at one phase can seriously slow an entire project. In the team-based approach, however, if one area hits snags, it works to resolve them while the team moves on.

The team-based approach does have some limitations, however. For example, it sometimes creates more organizational tension and confusion than the more orderly sequential approach. However, in rapidly changing industries facing increasingly shorter product life cycles, the rewards of fast and flexible product development far exceed the risks. Companies that combine a customer-centered approach with team-based new-product development gain a big competitive edge by getting the right new products to market faster.

Systematic New-Product Development

Finally, the new-product development process should be holistic and systematic rather than compartmentalized and haphazard. Otherwise, few new ideas will surface, and many good ideas will sputter and die. To avoid these problems, a company can install an *innovation management system* to collect, review, evaluate, and manage new-product ideas.

The company can appoint a respected senior person to be the company's innovation manager. It can set up Web-based idea management software and encourage all company stakeholders—employees, suppliers, distributors, dealers—to become involved in finding and developing new products. It can assign a cross-functional innovation management committee to evaluate proposed new-product ideas and help bring good ideas to market. It can also create recognition programs to reward those who contribute the best ideas.

| **MARKETING AT WORK** | 8.1 |

LEGO Group: Building Customer Relationships, Brick by Brick

Classic LEGO plastic bricks have been fixtures in homes around the world for more than 60 years. A mind-blowing 400 billion LEGO bricks now populate the planet, enough to build a tower to the moon ten times over. In fact, the Danish-based LEGO Group (TLG) now sells seven LEGO sets every second in 130 countries, making it the world's fifth-largest toymaker.

But only seven years ago, TLG was near bankruptcy. Sales were sagging, and the company was losing money at a rate of $300 million a year. The problem: The classic toy company had fallen out of touch with its customers. As a result, its products had fallen out of touch with the times. In the age of the Internet, videogames, iPods, and high-tech playthings, traditional toys such as LEGO bricks had been pushed to the back of the closet. So in 2004, the company set out to rebuild its aging product line—brick by brick.

The LEGO product makeover, however, didn't start with engineers working in design labs. First, TLG had to reconnect with customers. It started by listening to customers, understanding them, and including them in the new-product development process. Then it used the insights it gained to develop new generations of more relevant products. Rather than simply pushing the same old construction sets out to customers, TLG worked *with* customers to co-create new products and concepts.

To get to know its customers better, for instance, LEGO conducted up-close-and-personal ethnographic studies—hanging out with and observing children ages 7 to 9 on their home turf. "We thought we understood our consumers, the children of the world," says a LEGO Group marketer, but it turns out that "we didn't know them as well as we thought." The ethnographic research produced a lot of "Aha! moments" that shattered many of the brand's long-held traditions.

For example, TLG had long held fast to a "keep it simple" mantra. From the beginning, it offered only basic play sets—bricks, building bases, beams, doors, windows, wheels, and slanting roof tiles—with few or no instructions. The philosophy was that giving children unstructured building sets would stimulate their imaginations and foster creativity. But that concept just wasn't cutting it in the modern world. Today's children get bored easily, and in today's fast-moving environment, they are exposed to many more characters and themes.

In response, TLG shifted toward more-specialized, more-structured products. It now churns out some 7,000 unique building pieces each year, which support a seemingly endless assortment of themed product lines and specific building projects. So instead of just buying a set of basic square LEGO bricks and building a house or a car, children can now buy specialized kits to construct anything from a realistic fire engine to a city police helicopter to a working robot. And the LEGO brick lineup

is refreshed regularly; 60 percent of the core LEGO product assortment changes every year.

To add the desired variety and familiarity, TLG now builds plays sets around popular movie and TV themes and characters. It offers an ever-changing assortment of licensed lines based on everything from *Indiana Jones* and *Star Wars* to *Toy Story*. About 60 percent of U.S. LEGO sales are now linked to licenses, more than double that of five years ago. In fact, it's getting harder and harder to find a set of basic LEGO blocks.

TLG's more thematic and structured play sets have given a big boost to sales, but not everyone is thrilled. One industry observer notes, "What LEGO loses is what makes it so special. When you have a less-structured, less-themed set, kids [can] start from scratch. When you have kids playing out Indiana Jones, they're playing out Hollywood's imagination, not their own." But TLG doesn't see this shift as a compromise of values, and most customers agree. For example, one father of two recognizes that LEGO toys have changed since he was a boy, but he thinks that they have retained their innocence. "The most exotic thing I could build when I was a kid was an ambulance," he says. "Now [my kids] can build the Death Star." The fact that "the pieces and the sets are a lot cooler than they were 30 years ago" means that they lure kids away from less imaginative pastimes. "Instead of watching TV or playing computer games, the kids are building something, and [we] build stuff together."

Of course, kids aren't the only ones playing with LEGO bricks. The classic brick sets have a huge fan base of adults that never got over the toys of their youth. TLG estimates that it has

▲ At LEGO, new-product development begins with listening to customers and including them in the design process. LEGO's Design By Me site lets customers download 3D design software, create a LEGO toy, and then order the kit to build it.

as many as 250,000 active AFOLs (adult fans of LEGO) around the globe who spend large sums on LEGO products. These adults maintain thousands of LEGO fan sites and blogs, flock to conventions with names such as BrickFest, and compete with each other to construct "the Biggest LEGO Train Layout Ever (3,343 feet; it ran through an entire LEGO cityscape) or beat the Fastest Time to Build the LEGO Imperial Star Destroyer (3,104 pieces; five builders maximum and no presorting allowed; record: 1 hour 42 minutes 43 seconds)."

In developing new products, TLG actively taps into the AFOL community. It has created a roster of customer ambassadors who provide regular input, and it even invites customers to participate directly in the product-development process. For example, it invited 250 LEGO train-set enthusiasts to visit its New York office to assess new designs. The result was the LEGO Santa Fe Super Chief set, which sold out the first 10,000 units in less than two weeks with virtually no additional marketing. Similarly, TLG used customer co-creation to develop its most popular product ever, LEGO MINDSTORMS:

The LEGO MINDSTORMS build-it-yourself robot was initially an internal effort in partnership with MIT. Within three weeks of its introduction, however, more than 1,000 intrigued customers formed their own Web community to outdo each other in making it better. TLG quickly embraced the co-creation idea. The next generation of LEGO MINDSTORMS featured user-defined parts. Then, LEGO made customer co-creation official by creating the MINDSTORMS Development Program (MDP), through which it selected the most avid MINDSTORMS fans—100 pioneers, inventors, and innovators from across the globe—to play with LEGO MINDSTORMS and create innovative new features and applications. The MDP fans share their ideas with other customers and invite feedback.

Listening to adult customers has also led to the development of the LEGO Design by Me site, which lets customers download 3D design software, create a LEGO toy, and then order the kit to build it. And TLG recently launched LEGO Universe, an MMOG (massively multiplayer online game) in which adults and children alike can act out roles from LEGO sets and build toys from virtual blocks.

Thanks to customer-centered new-product development, TLG is now thriving. In the past five years, even as the overall toy market declined in a weakened economy and as competitors such as Mattel and Hasbro struggled, LEGO's sales have soared 66 percent, and its profits have jumped tenfold. "Kids [including the adult variety] are ruthless," says a senior LEGO executive. "If they don't like the product, then at the end of the day . . . all the rest of it won't make any difference. What counts, all that counts, is that you're at the top of kids' wish lists." Thanks to all that listening and customer involvement, that's where the LEGO Group is again."

Sources: "LEGO Grows by Listening to Customers," *Advertising Age,* November 9, 2009, p. 15; Nelson D. Schwartz, "Beyond the Blocks," *New York Times,* September 6, 2009, p. BU1; Jon Henley, "Toy Story," *Guardian,* March 26, 2009, p. F4; Kevin O'Donnell, "Where Do the Best Ideas Come From? The Unlikeliest Sources," *Advertising Age,* July 14, 2008, p. 15; Lewis Borg Cardona, "LEGO Learns a Lesson," *Change Agent,* June 2008, www.synovate .com/changeagent/index.php/site/full_story/lego_learns_a_lesson/; "Toy Company Lego Reports 69 Percent Rise in Net Profit," *McClatchy-Tribune Business News,* March 3, 2011; and www.lego.com and http://mindstorms.lego.com, accessed November 2011.

The innovation management system approach yields two favorable outcomes. First, it helps create an innovation-oriented company culture. It shows that top management supports, encourages, and rewards innovation. Second, it will yield a larger number of new-product ideas, among which will be found some especially good ones. The good new ideas will be more systematically developed, producing more new-product successes. No longer will good ideas wither for the lack of a sounding board or a senior product advocate.

Thus, new-product success requires more than simply thinking up a few good ideas, turning them into products, and finding customers for them. It requires a holistic approach for finding new ways to create valued customer experiences, from generating and screening new-product ideas to creating and rolling out want-satisfying products to customers.

More than this, successful new-product development requires a whole-company commitment. At companies known for their new-product prowess, such as Google, Apple, 3M, P&G, and GE, the entire culture encourages, supports, and rewards innovation.

New-Product Development in Turbulent Times

When tough economic times hit, or when a company faces financial difficulties, management may be tempted to reduce spending on new-product development. However, such thinking is usually shortsighted. By cutting back on new products, the company may make itself less competitive during or after the downturn. In fact, tough times might call for even greater new-product development, as the company struggles to better align its market offerings with changing consumer needs and tastes. In difficult times, innovation more often helps than hurts in making the company more competitive and positioning it better for the future. Summarizes one analyst:[21]

> Innovation is a messy process—hard to measure and hard to manage. When revenues and earnings decline, executives often conclude that their innovation efforts just aren't worth it. Better to focus on the tried and true than to risk money on untested ideas. The contrary view, of course, is that innovation is both a vaccine against market downturns and an elixir that rejuvenates growth. In today's economy, for example, imagine how much better off General Motors might have fared if it had matched the pace of innovation set by Honda or Toyota. Imagine how much worse off Apple would be had it not—in the midst of previously very difficult times for the company—created the iPod, iTunes, and iPhone.

Thus, rain or shine, good times or bad, a company must continue to innovate and develop new products if it wants to grow and prosper. In fact, says one marketing consultant, "your competitors may be hunkering down, giving you more opportunities."[22]

SPEED BUMP | LINKING THE CONCEPTS

Take a break. Think about new products and how companies find and develop them.

- Suppose that you're on a panel to nominate the "best new products of the year." What products would you nominate and why? See what you can learn about the new-product development process for one of these products.
- Applying the new-product development process you've just studied, develop an idea for an innovative new snack-food product and sketch out a brief plan for bringing it to market. Loosen up and have some fun with this.

Author Comment ▶

A company's products are born, grow, mature, and then decline, just as living things do. To remain vital, the firm must continually develop new products and manage them effectively through their life cycles.

Product life cycle (PLC)
The course of a product's sales and profits over its lifetime.

Product Life-Cycle Strategies

After launching the new product, management wants that product to enjoy a long and happy life. Although it does not expect that product to sell forever, the company wants to earn a decent profit to cover all the effort and risk that went into launching it. Management is aware that each product will have a life cycle, although its exact shape and length is not known in advance.

▶ **Figure 8.2** shows a typical **product life cycle (PLC)**, the course that a product's sales and profits take over its lifetime. The PLC has five distinct stages:

1. *Product development* begins when the company finds and develops a new-product idea. During product development, sales are zero, and the company's investment costs mount.

you have handout

▶ **Figure 8.2** Sales and profits over the Product's Life from Inception to Decline

Some products die quickly; others stay in the mature stage for a long, long time. For example, TABASCO sauce has been around for more than 140 years. Even then, to keep the product young, the company has added a full line of flavors (such as Sweet & Spicy and Chipotle) and a kitchen cabinet full of new TABASCO products (such as spicy beans, a chili mix, and jalapeno nacho slices).

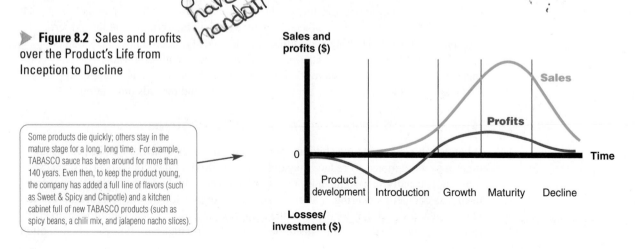

2. *Introduction* is a period of slow sales growth as the product is introduced in the market. Profits are nonexistent in this stage because of the heavy expenses of product introduction.
3. *Growth* is a period of rapid market acceptance and increasing profits.
4. *Maturity* is a period of slowdown in sales growth because the product has achieved acceptance by most potential buyers. Profits level off or decline because of increased marketing outlays to defend the product against competition.
5. *Decline* is the period when sales fall off and profits drop.

Not all products follow all five stages of the product life cycle. Some products are introduced and die quickly; others stay in the mature stage for a long, long time. Some enter the decline stage and are then cycled back into the growth stage through strong promotion or repositioning. It seems that a well-managed brand could live forever. Venerable brands like Coca-Cola, Gillette, Budweiser, Guinness, American Express, Wells Fargo, Kikkoman, Frye, and TABASCO sauce, for instance, are still going strong after more than 100 years. Guinness beer recently celebrated its 250th anniversary; and TABASCO sauce brags that it's "over 140 years old and still able to totally whup your butt!"

The PLC concept can describe a *product class* (gasoline-powered automobiles), a *product form* (SUVs), or a *brand* (the Ford Escape). The PLC concept applies differently in each case. Product classes have the longest life cycles; the sales of many product classes stay in the mature stage for a long time. Product forms, in contrast, tend to have the standard PLC shape. Product forms such as "dial telephones" and "VHS tapes" passed through a regular history of introduction, rapid growth, maturity, and decline.

A specific brand's life cycle can change quickly because of changing competitive attacks and responses. For example, although laundry soaps (product class) and powdered detergents (product form) have enjoyed fairly long life cycles, the life cycles of specific brands have tended to be much shorter. Today's leading brands of powdered laundry soap are Tide and Cheer; the leading brands almost 100 years ago were Fels-Naptha, Octagon, and Kirkman.

The PLC concept also can be applied to what are known as styles, fashions, and fads. Their special life cycles are shown in **Figure 8.3**. A **style** is a basic and distinctive mode of expression. For example, styles appear in homes (colonial, ranch, transitional), clothing (formal, casual), and art (realist, surrealist, abstract). Once a style is invented, it may last for generations, passing in and out of vogue. A style has a cycle showing several periods of renewed interest.

A **fashion** is a currently accepted or popular style in a given field. For example, the more formal "business attire" look of corporate dress of the 1980s and 1990s gave way to the "business casual" look of the 2000s. Fashions tend to grow slowly, remain popular for a while, and then decline slowly.

Fads are temporary periods of unusually high sales driven by consumer enthusiasm and immediate product or brand popularity.[23] A fad may be part of an otherwise normal life cycle, as in the case of recent surges in the sales of poker chips and accessories. Or the fad may comprise a brand's or product's entire life cycle. Pet Rocks are a classic example. Upon hearing his friends complain about how expensive it was to care for their dogs, advertising copywriter Gary Dahl joked about his pet rock. He soon wrote a spoof of a dog-training manual for it, titled "The Care and Training of Your Pet Rock." Soon Dahl was selling some 1.5 million ordinary beach pebbles at $4 a pop. Yet the fad, which broke one October, had sunk like a stone by the next February.[24]

▲ **Product life cycle: Some products die quickly; others stay in the mature stage for a long, long time. TABASCO® sauce is "over 140 years old and yet still able to totally whup your butt!"**

TABASCO® marks, bottle, and label designs are registered trademarks and servicemarks exclusively of McIlhenny Company, Avery Island, LA 70513. www.TABASCO.com.

Style
A basic and distinctive mode of expression.

never goes away.

Fashion
A currently accepted or popular style in a given field.

steady increase decrease.

Fad
A temporary period of unusually high sales driven by consumer enthusiasm and immediate product or brand popularity.

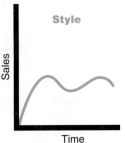
up & down quickly.

▶ **Figure 8.3** Styles, Fashions, and Fads

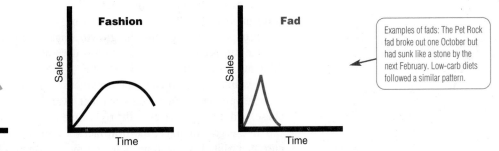

Examples of fads: The Pet Rock fad broke out one October but had sunk like a stone by the next February. Low-carb diets followed a similar pattern.

Marketers can apply the product life-cycle concept as a useful framework for describing how products and markets work. And when used carefully, the PLC concept can help in developing good marketing strategies for its different stages. However, using the PLC concept for forecasting product performance or developing marketing strategies presents some practical problems. For example, in practice, it is difficult to forecast the sales level at each PLC stage, the length of each stage, and the shape of the PLC curve. Using the PLC concept to develop marketing strategy also can be difficult because strategy is both a cause and a result of the PLC. The product's current PLC position suggests the best marketing strategies, and the resulting marketing strategies affect product performance in later stages.

Moreover, marketers should not blindly push products through the traditional product life-cycle stages. Instead, marketers often defy the "rules" of the life cycle and position or reposition their products in unexpected ways. By doing this, they can rescue mature or declining products and return them to the growth phase of the life cycle. Or they can leapfrog obstacles to slow consumer acceptance and propel new products forward into the growth phase.

The moral of the product life cycle is that companies must continually innovate; otherwise, they risk extinction. No matter how successful its current product lineup, a company must skillfully manage the life cycles of existing products for future success. And to grow, the company must develop a steady stream of new products that bring new value to customers.

We looked at the product-development stage of the PLC in the first part of this chapter. We now look at strategies for each of the other life-cycle stages.

Introduction Stage

Introduction stage
The PLC stage in which a new product is first distributed and made available for purchase.

The **introduction stage** starts when a new product is first launched. Introduction takes time, and sales growth is apt to be slow. Well-known products such as frozen foods and HDTVs lingered for many years before they entered a stage of more rapid growth.

In this stage, as compared to other stages, profits are negative or low because of the low sales and high distribution and promotion expenses. Much money is needed to attract distributors and build their inventories. Promotion spending is relatively high to inform consumers of the new product and get them to try it. Because the market is not generally ready for product refinements at this stage, the company and its few competitors produce basic versions of the product. These firms focus their selling on those buyers who are the most ready to buy.

A company, especially the *market pioneer*, must choose a launch strategy that is consistent with the intended product positioning. It should realize that the initial strategy is just the first step in a grander marketing plan for the product's entire life cycle. If the pioneer chooses its launch strategy to make a "killing," it may be sacrificing long-run revenue for the sake of short-run gain. The pioneer has the best chance of building and retaining market leadership if it plays its cards correctly from the start.

Growth Stage

Growth stage
The PLC stage in which a product's sales start climbing quickly.

If the new product satisfies the market, it will enter a **growth stage**, in which sales will start climbing quickly. The early adopters will continue to buy, and later buyers will start following their lead, especially if they hear favorable word of mouth. Attracted by the opportunities for profit, new competitors will enter the market. They will introduce new product features, and the market will expand. The increase in competitors leads to an increase in the number of distribution outlets, and sales jump just to build reseller inventories. Prices remain where they are or decrease only slightly. Companies keep their promotion spending at the same or a slightly higher level. Educating the market remains a goal, but now the company must also meet the competition.

Profits increase during the growth stage as promotion costs are spread over a large volume and as unit manufacturing costs decrease. The firm uses several strategies to sustain rapid market growth as long as possible. It improves product quality and adds new product features and models. It enters new market segments and new distribution channels. It shifts some advertising from building product awareness to building product conviction and purchase, and it lowers prices at the right time to attract more buyers.

In the growth stage, the firm faces a trade-off between high market share and high current profit. By spending a lot of money on product improvement, promotion, and distribution, the company can capture a dominant position. In doing so, however, it gives up maximum current profit, which it hopes to make up in the next stage.

Maturity Stage

Maturity stage
The PLC stage in which a product's sales growth slows or levels off.

At some point, a product's sales growth will slow down, and it will enter the **maturity stage**. This maturity stage normally lasts longer than the previous stages, and it poses strong challenges to marketing management. Most products are in the maturity stage of the life cycle, and therefore most of marketing management deals with the mature product.

The slowdown in sales growth results in many producers with many products to sell. In turn, this overcapacity leads to greater competition. Competitors begin marking down prices, increasing their advertising and sales promotions, and upping their product development budgets to find better versions of the product. These steps lead to a drop in profit. Some of the weaker competitors start dropping out, and the industry eventually contains only well-established competitors.

Although many products in the mature stage appear to remain unchanged for long periods, most successful ones are actually evolving to meet changing consumer needs (see Marketing at Work 8.2). Product managers should do more than simply ride along with or defend their mature products—a good offense is the best defense. They should consider modifying the market, product offering, and marketing mix.

In *modifying the market*, the company tries to increase consumption by finding new users and new market segments for its brands. The company may also look for ways to increase usage among present customers. For example, the Glad Products Company helps customers find new uses for its Press'n Seal wrap, the handy plastic wrap that creates a Tupperware-like seal. As more and more customers contacted the company about alternative uses for the product, Glad set up a special "1000s of Uses. What's Yours?" Web site (www.1000uses.com) at which customers can swap usage tips. Suggested uses for Press'n Seal range from protecting a computer keyboard from dirt and spills and keeping garden seeds fresh to use by soccer moms sitting on damp benches while watching their tykes play. "We just roll out the Glad Press'n Seal over the long benches," says the mom who shared the tip, "and everyone's bottom stays nice and dry."[25]

The company might also try *modifying the product*—changing characteristics such as quality, features, style, or packaging to attract new users and inspire more usage. Thus, makers of consumer food and household products introduce new flavors, colors, scents, ingredients, or packages to revitalize consumer buying. For example, TABASCO pepper sauce may have been around for more than 140 years, but to keep the brand young, the company has added a full line of flavors (such as Garlic, Sweet & Spicy, and Chipotle) and a kitchen cabinet full of new products under the TABASCO name (such as steak sauces, spicy beans, a chili mix, salsas, jalapeno nacho slices, and even spicy chocolate and a TABASCO lollipop).

Finally, the company can try *modifying the marketing mix*—improving sales by changing one or more marketing mix elements. The company can offer new or improved services to buyers. It can cut prices to attract new users and competitors' customers. It can launch a better advertising campaign or use aggressive sales promotions—trade deals, cents-off, premiums, and contests. In addition to pricing and promotion, the company can also move into new marketing channels to help serve new users.

Kellogg used all of these approaches to keep its 55-year-old Special K brand from sinking into decline. Introduced in 1957 as a healthful, high-protein cereal, Special K had matured by the 1990s—sales were flat and the brand had lost its luster. To reinvigorate the brand, Kellogg first extended the cereal line to include a variety of cereal flavors, such as Red Berries, Vanilla Almond, and Chocolatey Delight. ▶ Then, it stretched Special K beyond cereals, turning it into a healthful, slimming lifestyle brand. The expanded line now includes meal and snack bars, protein waters and shakes, crackers and chips, and fruit crisps. To attract new users and more usage, Kellogg promotes the Special K Challenge, a weight management plan built around Special K products. "Whether your goal is to finally slip into those skinny jeans or you're just looking to become a little more fit and fabulous, the Special K Challenge is a great way to kick-start a better you!" The Special K brand-rejuvenation efforts paid off. The Special K line has grown steadily over the past decade and now accounts for more than $2 billion in annual sales.[26]

▲ **Reinvigorating the mature brand: Kellogg kept its 55-year-old Special K brand growing by turning it into a healthful, slimming lifestyle brand.**

mediablitzimages (uk) Limited/Alamy

MARKETING AT WORK   8.2

Managing the PLC: Zippo Keeps the Flame Burning

For nearly 80 years, the Zippo brand has stood for cigarette lighters. Over the years, Zippo Manufacturing Company has sold more than 475 million of its classic windproof, guaranteed-for-life lighters, and the iconic brand holds an amazing 98 percent awareness rate in the United States. The first Zippo lighter—sold in 1933—was designed by the company's founder, George Blaisdell, after he witnessed a man unsuccessfully trying to light a woman's cigarette in the wind. He designed a durable lighter with a unique chimney that would light reliably and stay lit, even in windy conditions. Thus began the long and storied Zippo product life cycle.

Zippo lighter sales really took off in the 1940s as the United States entered World War II. The company shipped hundreds of Zippo lighters to generals and war officials. Recognizing the lighter's durability and dependability, the U.S. government bought up every lighter Zippo produced between 1943 and 1945. Millions of Zippo lighters found their way around the world and sales spread like wildfire. Not only did soldiers love them, but the seeds were sown for global acceptance among everyday consumers. In the post-war years, as smoking increased in popularity, so did Zippo lighters. By 1965, smoking in America had reached an all-time high, and Zippo held the dominant share of the cigarette lighter market.

In the decades that followed, however, as the U.S. antismoking movement took hold and the number of smokers decreased by half, Zippo found itself struggling to capture an increasing share of a declining U.S. market. Zippo lighter sales in the United States peaked in 1998 and then began a slow but steady decline.

Along the way, to bolster sales, Zippo tried an assortment of product extensions, some successful, some not. It introduced promotional items ranging from lighter-shaped tape measures and key holders to belt buckles and money clips. It offered Zippo gift sets and collectible designs. There was the ZipLight, a battery-powered flashlight in a traditional lighter casing. Zippo even considered making golf-ball warmers to increase driving distances, but concluded that the legal liability would be too great if the heated projectiles bounced off people's heads. Other product extensions included everything from cutlery and Swiss watches to leather purses. Such extensions, however, did almost nothing to improve the brand's fortunes. "It was a very frustrating time," says Zippo's vice president of sales and marketing.

By the early 2000s, the declining brand's flame seemed to be flickering. At one point, Zippo's global licensing manager got a serious wake-up call in an elevator when a fellow passenger, spotting her Zippo tote bag, said "Zippo—cool! Are they still in business?" Even as it enjoyed an enviable two-thirds share of the refillable lighter market, said the manager at the time, "the world is not even sure we're alive." Zippo faced a classic product life-cycle problem: how to relight the brand as its core market declined.

Out of that crisis, Zippo developed a new brand-growth logic. The company hasn't given up on cigarette lighters, which still account for 54 percent of sales. It still introduces scores of new designs each year—from lighters with images of Elvis or the Harley logo to the new Zippo BLU Butane Lighter, a higher-end refillable lighter that appeals to cigar smokers. But while it works to increase its share of the declining lighter market, Zippo is also preparing for the post-smoker world.

For starters, Zippo has broadened its focus to selling "all things flame." "Flame is our core competency," says the Zippo marketing executive. First, the company introduced a line of longer, slimmer multipurpose lighters made to handle non-cigarette lighting chores, such as candles, fireplaces, and grills. Next, it developed an entire outdoor line, which includes outdoor utility lighters, hand warmers, an emergency fire starter kit, and campfire starter cedar pucks. Such new products have opened new doors for Zippo by expanding its retailer base, which now includes chains such as Bed Bath & Beyond, Kmart, and Walgreens. Zippo hopes

NEVER, EVER BELIEVE THE WEATHERMAN.

▲ **Managing the PLC: Over its 79-year history, the storied Zippo brand has evolved to meet changing market and customer needs. It's not just a cigarette lighter brand anymore, it's a lifestyle.**

Courtesy of Zippo Manufacturing Company. Zippo® and Zippo BLU® are registered trademarks of Zippo Manufacturing Company.

eventually to provide retailers with in-store boutique *flame centers*, which will feature an array of Zippo products.

At the heart of its brand rekindling strategy, the company wants to turn Zippo into a lifestyle brand. For example, it pitches the outdoor line as "everything you need to make the most of your outdoor adventure." Consistent with its image as a reliable, rugged, durable flame, Zippo is pursuing an ambitious new licensing program that will lend its name to other outdoor products, such as grills, Tiki torches, and patio heaters, followed by camping equipment and other outdoor gear such as cooking stoves and lanterns. Some analysts believe that Zippo could give Coleman a major run for its money.

Consistent with the Zippo lifestyle, the company is even introducing new non-flame products. For example, it recently launched a licensed casual clothing line of hoodies, T-shirts, ball caps, jeans, and belts sold through retailers such as Urban Outfitters. And Zippo will soon bring out a new men's fragrance that is "the ideal companion for the adventures of the day and the passion of the night." "The new cologne doesn't smell anything like lighter fluid," jokes Zippo's global marketing director. Instead, it's "woody" and "spicy."

Thus, as Zippo moves through its life cycle, to grow—even to survive—it must adapt to meet changing market and customer needs. Zippo isn't just a cigarette lighter brand anymore; it's evolving toward a broader mission. "We're turning ourselves into a lifestyle-products company," says president and CEO Greg Booth. "Brand is really the only thing we have. If we think of ourselves as a lighter company, we are nowhere." Booth knows that rekindling the Zippo brand will take patience and skillful product life-cycle management. "We think our brand can go far, but we want to take it one step at a time," he says. "We'll crawl before we run."

Source: Information and quotes from James Hagerty, "Zippo Preps for a Post-Smoker World," *Wall Street Journal*, March 8, 2011, p. B1; Ellen Neuborne, "The Problem: Zippo Has Strong Brand Name, but Stagnant Sales," *Inc.*, September 2004, p. 42; Michael Learmonth, "Zippo Reignites Brand with Social Media, New Products" *Advertising Age*, August 10, 2009, p. 12; and www.zippo.com and www.smokerstuff.com, accessed November 2011.

Decline Stage

The sales of most product forms and brands eventually dip. The decline may be slow, as in the cases of stamps and oatmeal cereal, or rapid, as in the cases of cassette and VHS tapes. Sales may plunge to zero, or they may drop to a low level where they continue for many years. This is the **decline stage**.

Decline stage
The PLC stage in which a product's sales fade away.

Sales decline for many reasons, including technological advances, shifts in consumer tastes, and increased competition. As sales and profits decline, some firms withdraw from the market. Those remaining may prune their product offerings. In addition, they may drop smaller market segments and marginal trade channels, or they may cut the promotion budget and reduce their prices further.

Carrying a weak product can be very costly to a firm, and not just in profit terms. There are many hidden costs. A weak product may take up too much of management's time. It often requires frequent price and inventory adjustments. It requires advertising and sales-force attention that might be better used to make "healthy" products more profitable. A product's failing reputation can cause customer concerns about the company and its other products. The biggest cost may well lie in the future. Keeping weak products delays the search for replacements, creates a lopsided product mix, hurts current profits, and weakens the company's foothold on the future.

For these reasons, companies must identify products in the decline stage and decide whether to maintain, harvest, or drop them. Management may decide to *maintain* its brand, repositioning or reinvigorating it in hopes of moving it back into the growth stage of the product life cycle. P&G has done this with several brands, including Mr. Clean and Old Spice. Management may decide to *harvest* the product, which means reducing various costs (plant and equipment, maintenance, R&D, advertising, sales force), hoping that sales hold up. If successful, harvesting will increase the company's profits in the short run.

Finally, management may decide to *drop* the product from its line. The company can sell the product to another firm or simply liquidate it at salvage value. In recent years, P&G has sold off several lesser or declining brands, such as Folgers coffee, Crisco oil, Comet cleanser, Sure deodorant, Duncan Hines cake mixes, and Jif peanut butter. If the company plans to find a buyer, it will not want to run down the product through harvesting.

▶ **Table 8.2** summarizes the key characteristics of each stage of the PLC. The table also lists the marketing objectives and strategies for each stage.[27]

- maintain
- harvest
- drop.

▶ **Table 8.2**	Summary of Product Life-Cycle Characteristics, Objectives, and Strategies

	Introduction	**Growth**	**Maturity**	**Decline**
Characteristics				
Sales	Low sales	Rapidly rising sales	Peak sales	Declining sales
Costs	High cost per customer	Average cost per customer	Low cost per customer	Low cost per customer
Profits	Negative	Rising profits	High profits	Declining profits
Customers	Innovators	Early adopters	Middle majority	Laggards
Competitors	Few	Growing number	Stable number beginning to decline	Declining number
Marketing Objectives				
	Create product awareness and trial	Maximize market share	Maximize profit while defending market share	Reduce expenditure and milk the brand
Strategies				
Product	Offer a basic product	Offer product extensions, service, and warranty	Diversify brand and models	Phase out weak items
Price	Use cost-plus	Price to penetrate market	Price to match or beat competitors	Cut price
Distribution	Build selective distribution	Build intensive distribution	Build more intensive distribution	Go selective: phase out unprofitable outlets
Advertising	Build product awareness among early adopters and dealers	Build awareness and interest in the mass market	Stress brand differences and benefits	Reduce to level needed to retain hard-core loyals
Sales Promotion	Use heavy sales promotion to entice trial	Reduce to take advantage of heavy consumer demand	Increase to encourage brand switching	Reduce to minimal level

Source: Philip Kotler and Kevin Lane Keller, *Marketing Management,* 14th ed. (Upper Saddle River, NJ: Prentice Hall, 2012), p. 319. © 2012. Printed and electronically reproduced by permission of Pearson Education, Inc., Upper Saddle River, New Jersey.

Author Comment ▶
Let's look at just a few more product topics, including regulatory and social responsibility issues and the special challenges of marketing products internationally.

Additional Product and Service Considerations

We wrap up our discussion of products and services with two additional considerations: social responsibility in product decisions and issues of international product and services marketing.

Product Decisions and Social Responsibility

Marketers should carefully consider public policy issues and regulations regarding acquiring or dropping products, patent protection, product quality and safety, and product warranties.

Regarding new products, the government may prevent companies from adding products through acquisitions if the effect threatens to lessen competition. Companies dropping products must be aware that they have legal obligations, written or implied, to their suppliers, dealers, and customers who have a stake in the dropped product. Companies must also obey U.S. patent laws when developing new products. A company cannot make its product illegally similar to another company's established product.

Manufacturers must comply with specific laws regarding product quality and safety. The Federal Food, Drug, and Cosmetic Act protects consumers from unsafe and adulterated food, drugs, and cosmetics. Various acts provide for the inspection of sanitary conditions in the meat- and poultry-processing industries. Safety legislation has been passed to regulate fabrics, chemical substances, automobiles, toys, and drugs and poisons. The Consumer Product Safety Act of 1972 established the Consumer Product Safety Commission, which has the authority to ban or seize potentially harmful products and set severe penalties for violation of the law.

If consumers have been injured by a product with a defective design, they can sue manufacturers or dealers. A recent survey of manufacturing companies found that product liability was the second-largest litigation concern, behind only labor and employment matters. Product liability suits are now occurring in federal courts at the rate of over 20,000 per year. Although manufacturers are found to be at fault in only 6 percent of all product liability cases, when they are found guilty, the median jury award is $1.5 million, and individual awards can run into the tens or even hundreds of millions of dollars. Class-action suits can run into the billions. For example, after it recalled some seven million vehicles for acceleration pedal-related issues, Toyota will face more than 100 class-action and individual lawsuits beginning in 2013 that could end up costing the company $3 billion or more.[28]

This litigation phenomenon has resulted in huge increases in product liability insurance premiums, causing big problems in some industries. Some companies pass these higher rates along to consumers by raising prices. Others are forced to discontinue high-risk product lines. Some companies are now appointing *product stewards*, whose job is to protect consumers from harm and the company from liability by proactively ferreting out potential product problems.

おばあちゃんの字みると、
なんだか、ほっとするよ。

キット、サクラ、サクラと、よ。

言葉みたいで、声みたいで、顔みたい。
キットメール、発売中
郵便局と〔キット〕は、受験生を応援します。

▲ **The Nestlé Kit Kat chocolate bar in Japan benefits from the coincidental similarity between the bar's name and the Japanese phrase *kitto katsu*, which roughly translates to "You will surely win!" The brand's innovative "May cherries blossom" campaign has turned the Kit Kat bar and logo into national good luck charms.**

NESTLÉ and KIT KAT are registered trademarks of Société des Produits Nestlé S.A., Switzerland and are reproduced with the consent of the trademark owner.

International Product and Services Marketing

International product and services marketers face special challenges. First they must figure out what products and services to introduce and in which countries. Then they must decide how much to standardize or adapt their products and services for world markets.

On the one hand, companies would like to standardize their offerings. Standardization helps a company develop a consistent worldwide image. It also lowers the product design, manufacturing, and marketing costs of offering a large variety of products. On the other hand, markets and consumers around the world differ widely. Companies must usually respond to these differences by adapting their product offerings. For example, Nestlé sells a variety of very popular Kit Kat flavors in Japan that might make the average Western chocolate-lover's stomach turn, such as green tea, red bean, and soy sauce. Beyond taste, Kit Kat's strong following in Japan may also be the result of some unintended cultural factors:[29]

> In recent years, Kit Kat—the world's number two chocolate bar behind Snickers—has become very popular in Japan. Some of this popularity, no doubt, derives from the fact that the notoriously sweet-toothed Japanese love the bar's taste. ▶ But part of the bar's appeal may also be attributed to the coincidental similarity between its name and the Japanese phrase *kitto katsu*, which roughly translates in Japanese as "You will surely win!" Spotting this opportunity, marketers for Nestlé Japan developed an innovative *Juken* (college entrance exam) Kit Kat campaign. The multimedia campaign positions the Kit Kat bar and logo as good luck charms during the highly stressful university entrance exam season. Nestlé even developed a cherry flavored Kit Kat bar in packaging containing the message "May cherries blossom," wishing students luck in achieving their dreams. And it partnered with Japan's postal service to create "Kit Kat Mail," a postcardlike product sold at the post office that could be mailed to students as an edible good-luck charm. The campaign has been such a hit in Japan that it has led to a nationwide social movement to cheer up students for *Juken*.

Service marketers also face special challenges when going global. Some service industries have a long history of international operations. For example, the commercial banking industry was one of the first to grow internationally. Banks had to provide global services to meet the foreign exchange and credit needs of their home country clients who wanted to sell overseas. In recent years, many banks have become truly global. Germany's Deutsche Bank, for example, serves more than 13 million customers through 1,964 branches in 74 countries. For its clients around the world who wish to grow globally, Deutsche Bank can raise money not only in Frankfurt but also in Zurich, London, Paris, Tokyo, and Moscow.[30]

Professional and business services industries, such as accounting, management consulting, and advertising, have also globalized. The international growth of these firms followed the globalization of the client companies they serve. For example, as more clients employ worldwide marketing and advertising strategies, advertising agencies have responded by globalizing their own operations. McCann Worldgroup, a large U.S.-based advertising and marketing services agency, operates in more than 130 countries. It serves international clients such as Coca-Cola, GM, ExxonMobil, Microsoft, MasterCard, Johnson & Johnson, and Unilever in markets ranging from the United States and Canada to Korea and Kazakhstan. Moreover, McCann Worldgroup is one company in the Interpublic Group of Companies, an immense, worldwide network of advertising and marketing services companies.[31]

Retailers are among the latest service businesses to go global. As their home markets become saturated, American retailers such as Walmart, Office Depot, and Saks Fifth Avenue are expanding into faster-growing markets abroad. For example, since 1991, Walmart has entered 15 countries; its international division's sales accounts for almost 25 percent of total sales. Foreign retailers are making similar moves. Asian shoppers can now buy American products in French-owned Carrefour stores. Carrefour, the world's second-largest retailer behind Walmart, now operates more than 15,500 stores in more than 35 countries. It is the leading retailer in Europe, Brazil, and Argentina and the largest foreign retailer in China.[32]

The trend toward growth of global service companies will continue, especially in banking, airlines, telecommunications, and professional services. Today, service firms are no longer simply following their manufacturing customers. Instead, they are taking the lead in international expansion.

REST STOP | REVIEWING THE CONCEPTS

MyMarketingLab

Now that you have completed the chapter, return to www.mymktlab.com to experience and apply the concepts and to explore the additional study materials for this chapter.

CHAPTER REVIEW AND KEY TERMS

Objectives Review

A company's current products face limited life spans and must be replaced by newer products. But new products can fail—the risks of innovation are as great as the rewards. The key to successful innovation lies in a customer-focused, total-company effort; strong planning; and a systematic new-product development process.

▶ **OBJECTIVE 1 Explain how companies find and develop new-product ideas. (pp 230–231)**

Companies find and develop new-product ideas from a variety of sources. Many new-product ideas stem from *internal sources*. Companies conduct formal R&D, or they pick the brains of their employees, urging them to think up and develop new-product ideas. Other ideas come from *external sources.* Companies track *competitors'* offerings and obtain ideas from *distributors and suppliers* who are close to the market and can pass along information about consumer problems and new-product possibilities.

Perhaps the most important sources of new-product ideas are customers themselves. Companies observe customers, invite them to submit their ideas and suggestions, or even involve customers in the new-product development process. Many companies are now developing *crowdsourcing* or *open-innovation* new-product idea programs, which invite broad communities of people—customers, employees, independent scientists and researchers, and even the general public—into the new-product innovation process. Truly innovative companies do not rely only on one source or another for new-product ideas.

> **OBJECTIVE 2 List and define the steps in the new-product development process and the major considerations in managing this process. (pp 231–242)**

The new-product development process consists of eight sequential stages. The process starts with *idea generation.* Next comes *idea screening,* which reduces the number of ideas based on the company's own criteria. Ideas that pass the screening stage continue through *product concept development,* in which a detailed version of the new-product idea is stated in meaningful consumer terms. This stage includes *concept testing,* in which new-product concepts are tested with a group of target consumers to determine whether the concepts have strong consumer appeal. Strong concepts proceed to *marketing strategy development,* in which an initial marketing strategy for the new product is developed from the product concept. In the *business-analysis* stage, a review of the sales, costs, and profit projections for a new product is conducted to determine whether the new product is likely to satisfy the company's objectives. With positive results here, the ide as become more concrete through *product development* and *test marketing* and finally are launched during *commercialization.*

New-product development involves more than just going through a set of steps. Companies must take a systematic, holistic approach to managing this process. Successful new-product development requires a customer-centered, team-based, systematic effort.

> **OBJECTIVE 3 Describe the stages of the product life cycle and how marketing strategies change during a product's life cycle. (pp 242–248)**

Each product has a *life cycle* marked by a changing set of problems and opportunities. The sales of the typical product follow an S-shaped curve made up of five stages. The cycle begins with the *product development* stage in which the company finds and develops a new-product idea. *The introduction stage* is marked by slow growth and low profits as the product is distributed to the market. If successful, the product enters a *growth stage,* which offers rapid sales growth and increasing profits. Next comes a *maturity stage* in which the product's sales growth slows down and profits stabilize. Finally, the product enters a *decline stage* in which sales and profits dwindle. The company's task during this stage is to recognize the decline and decide whether it should maintain, harvest, or drop the product. The different stages of the PLC require different marketing strategies and tactics.

> **OBJECTIVE 4 Discuss two additional product issues: socially responsible product decisions and international product and services marketing. (pp 248–250)**

Marketers must consider two additional product issues. The first is *social responsibility.* This includes public policy issues and regulations involving acquiring or dropping products, patent protection, product quality and safety, and product warranties. The second involves the special challenges facing international product and services marketers. International marketers must decide how much to standardize or adapt their offerings for world markets.

Key Terms

Objective 1
New-product development (p 230)

Objective 2
Idea generation (p 231)
Crowdsourcing (p 232)
Idea screening (p 234)
Product concept (p 234)
Concept testing (p 235)

Marketing strategy development (p 235)
Business analysis (p 236)
Product development (p 236)
Test marketing (p 237)
Commercialization (p 238)
Customer-centered new-product development (p 238)
Team-based new-product development (p 239)

Objective 3
Product life cycle (PLC) (p 242)
Style (p 243)
Fashion (p 243)
Fad (p 243)
Introduction stage (p 244)
Growth stage (p 244)
Maturity stage (p 245)
Decline stage (p 247)

DISCUSSION AND CRITICAL THINKING

Discussion Questions

1. Name and describe the major steps in the new-product development process. (AACSB: Communication)
2. Define *crowdsourcing* and describe an example not already presented in the chapter. (AACSB: Communication; Reflective Thinking)
3. What is test marketing? Explain why companies may or may not test market products and discuss alternatives to full test markets. (AACSB: Communication)

4. Why is it important for companies to continue to focus on new-product development, even in tough economic times? (AACSB: Communication; Reflective Thinking)
5. Briefly describe the five stages of the product life cycle. Identify a product class, form, or brand that is in each stage. (AACSB: Communication; Reflective Thinking)
6. Discuss the special challenges facing international product and services marketers. (AACSB: Communication)

Critical Thinking Exercises

1. Visit the Product Development and Management Association's Web site (www.pdma.org) to learn about this organization. Click on "OCI Award" in the "About PDMA" dropdown menu. Describe this award and the criteria used when granting this award and discuss one company receiving this award. (AACSB: Communication; Use of IT)
2. In a small group, brainstorm an idea for a new product concept. Develop a marketing-strategy statement and describe how you would conduct a business analysis for the new

product based on that concept. (AACSB: Communication; Analytic Skills; Reflective Thinking)
3. To acquire new products, many companies purchase other firms or buy individual brands from other companies. For example, Disney purchased Marvel Entertainment and its portfolio of more than 5,000 characters, such as Spider-Man and Captain America. Discuss two other examples of companies acquiring new products through this means. (AACSB: Communication; Reflective Thinking)

MINICASES AND APPLICATIONS

Marketing Technology   Memrister

If you think the flash-memory chip found in digital cameras and music players is small, wait until you see what's coming next. Researchers at HP have developed a new kind of electronic circuit that could revolutionize computer data storage, making it smaller and more energy-efficient than current memory chip technology. The part is called a memory resistor, or *memrister*, and it allows storage of information on memory chips for long periods of time without electrical current. The theory behind the circuit is not new—it dates back to an electrical engineering professor who worked at the University of California at Berkeley in 1971. Most consumers don't realize that flash chips lose data after a year or so. But with the memrister, the atomic structure is actually changed, allowing for permanent storage

of data. This isn't the only revolutionary change on the horizon. In a joint venture called Numonyx, Intel Corporation and STMicroelectronics are betting on a new technology known as phase-change memory. One thing is for sure, big change is on the way for computers and hand-held devices.

1. What stage of the product life cycle are these products currently in? (AACSB: Communication; Reflective Thinking)
2. Discuss the factors HP and other tech companies should consider when conducting the business analysis for a product such as the *memrister*. How will it add value for customers? (AACSB: Communication; Reflective Thinking)

Marketing Ethics   I Can Find Out Who You Are

Facial recognition is not a new technology, but the way it is being used is new. If you have a criminal record, police can find that out just by looking at you—through their iPhones, that is. Using a device known as Moris, which stands for Mobile Offender Recognition and Information System, a police officer

can snap a picture of a person's face or scan a person's iris and obtain immediate information if there is a match in a criminal database. No more going down to the station and getting inky fingertips—the gadget can collect fingerprints right on the spot. Whereas an iris scan must be conducted with the person's knowledge because of the close range necessary, a picture can be snapped from several feet away without the person knowing it. Facebook uses facial recognition to allow users to identify friends in pictures, and several mobile phone apps allow users to identify Facebook friends with a mere snap of a picture. Google considered a project that would enable mobile phone users to snap a picture of someone and then conduct an image search but rejected the idea because of ethical concerns.

1. Discuss other commercial applications of facial recognition technology. Come up with two new product concepts that employ this technology. (AACSB: Communication; Reflective Thinking)
2. Discuss the ethics of incorporating facial recognition technology in products. (AACSB: Communication; Ethical Reasoning)

Marketing by the Numbers   Cannibalization Assessment

Apple introduced the iPhone 4 in 2010 but still continued to offer the iPhone 3G. The 16GB base version of the iPhone 4 was priced at $199 with unit variable costs equal to $187. The iPhone 3G's price had decreased to $99 by the time the iPhone 4 was introduced and its variable costs were $65.

1. Refer to Appendix 3, Marketing by the Numbers, and calculate the incremental contribution realized by adding the new iPhone 4 if sales during the first six months of launch were 5 million units. Also keep this in mind: The company

estimated that 30 percent of iPhone 4 sales came from customers who would have purchased the iPhone 3G but instead purchased the base model of the iPhone 4. (AACSB: Communication; Analytic Reasoning)
2. Apple also offered a 32GB version of the iPhone 4 at a price of $299. Variable costs for that version were $250. Besides its higher price, explain why Apple would encourage customers to purchase the 32GB over the 16GB version. (AACSB: Communication; Analytic Reasoning; Reflective Reasoning)

Video Case   Subaru

When a company has a winning product, everything else falls into place. Or does it? Subaru is a winning company (one of the few automotive companies to sustain growth and profits in hard economic times) with various winning products, including the Impreza, Legacy, Forester, and Outback. But what happens when any one product starts to decline in popularity?

This video demonstrates how Subaru constantly engages in new-product development as part of its efforts to manage the product life cycle for each of its models. Subaru is focused on both developing the next version of each existing model and developing possible new models to boost its product portfolio.

After viewing the video featuring Subaru, answer the following questions:

1. How would you describe the product life cycle in relation to one Subaru product?
2. How do shifting consumer trends affect Subaru's products?
3. How does Subaru remain customer-oriented in its new product efforts?

Company Cases   2 Trap-Ease / 8 Samsung

See Appendix 1 for cases appropriate for this chapter. **Case 2, Trap-Ease America: The Big Cheese of Mousetraps.** A company creates a "better mousetrap," only to learn that launching a new product takes more than a great product. **Case 8, Samsung:**

From Gallop to Run. By completely overhauling its business and marketing strategies, Samsung becomes the world's largest consumer electronics manufacturer.

9 Pricing

Understanding and Capturing Customer Value

CHAPTER ROAD MAP

Objective Outline

▷ **OBJECTIVE 1   Identify the three major pricing strategies and discuss the importance of understanding customer-value perceptions, company costs, and competitor strategies when setting prices.** What Is a Price? (257); Major Pricing Strategies (257–264)

▷ **OBJECTIVE 2   Identify and define the other important external and internal factors affecting a firm's pricing decisions.** Other Internal and External Considerations Affecting Price Decisions (264–270)

▷ **OBJECTIVE 3   Describe the major strategies for pricing new products.** New-Product Pricing Strategies (270–271)

▷ **OBJECTIVE 4   Explain how companies find a set of prices that maximizes the profits from the total product mix.** Product Mix Pricing Strategies (271–274)

▷ **OBJECTIVE 5   Discuss how companies adjust their prices to take into account different types of customers and situations.** Price Adjustment Strategies (274–280)

▷ **OBJECTIVE 6   Discuss the key issues related to initiating and responding to price changes.** Price Changes (280–283); Public Policy and Pricing (283–285)

Previewing the Concepts

We continue your marketing journey with a look at another major marketing mix tool—pricing. If effective product development, promotion, and distribution sow the seeds of business success, effective pricing is the harvest. Firms successful at creating customer value with the other marketing mix activities must still capture some of this value in the prices they earn. Yet, despite its importance, many firms do not handle pricing well. In this chapter, we begin with the question: *What is a price?* Next, we look at three major pricing strategies—customer value-based, cost-based, and competition-based pricing—and at other factors that affect pricing decisions. Finally, we examine strategies for new-product pricing, product mix pricing, price adjustments, and dealing with price changes.

For openers, let's examine an interesting online pricing story. In case you haven't noticed, there's a war going on—between Walmart, by far the world's largest retailer, and Amazon.com, the world's largest online merchant. The weapon of choice? Prices. Only time will tell who will win on the Web. But for now, the two retailers, especially Walmart, seem determined to fight it out on price.

▲ **Only time will tell who will win on the Web, Walmart or Amazon.com. But for now, the two retail giants, especially Walmart, seem determined to fight it out on price.**

Christopher Schall/Impact Photo

Amazon vs. Walmart: Fighting It Out Online on Price

Walmart to Amazon: "Let's Rumble" read the headline. Ali had Frazier. Coke has Pepsi. The Yankees have the White Sox. Now Walmart, the mightiest retail giant in history, may have met its own worthy adversary: Amazon.com. The two heavyweight retailers are waging a war online. The weapon of choice? Prices—not surprising, given the two combatants' long-held low-cost positions.

The price war between Walmart and Amazon.com began two years ago, with skirmishes over online prices for new books and DVDs. It then escalated quickly to video game consoles, mobile phones, and even toys. At stake: not only the fortunes of the two companies but also those of whole industries whose products they sell, both online and in retail stores. Price can be a potent strategic weapon, but it can also be a double-edged sword.

Amazon.com, its seems, wants to be the "Walmart of the Web"—our digital general store—and it's well on its way to achieving that goal. Although Walmart's overall sales total an incredible $419 billion a year, 12 times Amazon's $34 billion annually, Amazon.com's online sales are nearly 7 times greater than Walmart's online sales. Moreover, Amazon attracts more than 100 million unique U.S. visitors to its Web site monthly, almost triple Walmart's number. One analyst estimates that more than one-half of all U.S. consumers who look online for retail items start their search at Amazon.com.

Why does this worry Walmart? After all, online sales account for only 4 to 5 percent of its overall U.S. retail sales. Walmart captures most of its business by offering affordable prices to middle Americans in its more than 4,000 brick-and-mortar stores. By comparison, according to one analyst, Amazon.com sells mostly to "affluent urbanites who would rather click with their mouse than push around a cart."

But this battle isn't about now—it's about the future. Although still a small market by Walmart's standards, online sales will soar within the next decade to an estimated 15 percent of total U.S. retail sales. And, increasingly, Amazon.com owns the online space. In the fourth quarter of last year, during the holiday season, Amazon.com's sales climbed 36 percent compared to the year prior. Even more importantly, Amazon.com's electronics and general merchandise sales, which compete directly with much of the selection found in Walmart stores, zoomed 60 percent.

Amazon has shown a relentless ambition to offer more of almost everything on the Web. It started by selling only books online, but now it sells everything from books, movies, and musicals to consumer electronics, home and garden products, clothing, jewelry, toys, tools, and even groceries. Its selection expanded further after it purchased online shoe retailer Zappos.com and baby products retailer Diapers.com. It's even beefing up its private-label selection, adding new lines of Amazon-branded goods. If Amazon.com's expansion continues and online sales grow as predicted, the Web seller will eat further and further into Walmart's bread-and-butter store sales.

> Walmart, the world's largest retailer, and Amazon.com, the world's largest online merchant, are at war over the hearts and dollars of online shoppers. The weapon of choice? Prices. However, although price can be a potent strategic weapon, it can also be a double-edged sword.

But Walmart isn't about to let that happen. Instead, it's taking the battle to Amazon.com's home territory—the Web. Through aggressive pricing, it is now fighting for every dollar consumers spend online. Walmart fired the first shot before the 2009 holiday shopping season. It announced that it would take online preorders for ten soon-to-be-released hardback books—all projected best sellers by authors such as John Grisham, Stephen King, Barbara Kingsolver, and James Patterson—at an unprecedented low price of just $10 each. (Actually, the new hardcover prices matched the $9.99 price that Amazon was already charging for e-book versions of bestsellers, downloaded to its Kindle or other readers; Walmart, however, doesn't sell e-books.) To take it a step further, Walmart also cut prices by 50 percent on 200 other best sellers, undercutting Amazon's prices. When Amazon quickly announced that it would match Walmart's $10 price on the 10 best sellers, the price war was on. Walmart dropped its price to $9.00, Amazon.com did likewise, and Walmart lowered its prices yet again, to $8.98.

These low book prices represented a 59 to 74 percent reduction off the list price, much more than the 30 to 40 percent reduction you might expect in traditional retail bookstores such as Barnes & Noble. In fact, Walmart and Amazon.com discounted these best sellers below costs—as so-called *loss leaders*—to lure shoppers to their Web sites in hopes that they would buy other, more profitable items.

Today, the book price war continues. And it's having an impact beyond the two primary combatants, causing collateral damage across the entire book industry. "When your product is treated as a loss leader, it lowers its perceived value," says one publishing executive. In the long run, that's not great for either the companies that publish the books or the retailers who sell them. Price carries messages about customer value, notes another publisher. Companies want to be careful about the messages they send. Moreover, the price war is not just taking place over books. If you compare prices at Walmart.com and Amazon.com, you'll find the price battle raging across a broad range of product categories.

Who will win the online battle for the hearts and dollars of online buyers? Certainly, low prices will be an important factor. And when it comes to low prices, Walmart appears to have the upper hand. With its huge size, it can negotiate better terms with its suppliers. And by combining its online and offline operations, it can provide some unique services, such as free and convenient delivery and returns of Web orders to stores (Walmart's site gives you three buying options: online, in-store, and site-to-store). Walmart is even experimenting with drive-through windows where shoppers can pick up their Internet orders. But Amazon.com also has advantages, including a highly recognizable online brand, a sophisticated distribution network built specifically for Web shopping, a much larger assortment, an unparalleled online customer shopping experience, and fast and free shipping with Amazon Prime. And, of course, Amazon.com is no stranger to low prices.

In the long run, however, reckless price cutting will likely do more damage than good to both Walmart and Amazon.com. Price wars can turn whole product categories into unattractive, low-margin commodities (think DVDs, for example). And buying online is about much more than just getting the best prices, even in today's economy. In the end, winning online consumers will require offering not only the lowest prices but also the best customer value in terms of price *and* product selection, speed, convenience, and overall shopping experience.

For now, the two retailers, especially Walmart, seem determined to fight it out on price. Amazon.com's CEO, Jeff Bezos, has long maintained that there's plenty of room for all competitors in the big world of retailing. However, Paul Vazquez, president and CEO of Walmart.com, says that it's "only a matter of time" before Walmart dominates Web shopping. Pricing, he thinks, will be key. "Our company is based on low prices," says Vazquez, laying down the challenge. "Even in books, we kept going until we were the low-priced leader. And we will do that in every category we need to. Our company is based on low prices." Offering the low price "is in our DNA."[1]

Companies today face a fierce and fast-changing pricing environment. Value-seeking customers have put increased pricing pressure on many companies. Thanks to economic woes in recent years, the pricing power of the Internet, and value-driven retailers such as Walmart, today's more frugal consumers are pursuing spend-less strategies. In response, it seems that almost every company has been looking for ways to cut prices.

Yet, cutting prices is often not the best answer. Reducing prices unnecessarily can lead to lost profits and damaging price wars. It can cheapen a brand by signaling to customers that price is more important than the customer value a brand delivers. ▶ Instead, in both

good economic times and bad, companies should sell value, not price. In some cases, that means selling lesser products at rock-bottom prices. But in most cases, it means persuading customers that paying a higher price for the company's brand is justified by the greater value they gain.

▲ **Pricing: No matter what the state of the economy, companies should sell value, not price.**

magicoven/Shutterstock.com

Price
The amount of money charged for a product or service; the sum of the values that customers exchange for the benefits of having or using the product or service.

Author Comment ▶
Setting the right price is one of the marketer's most difficult tasks. A host of factors come into play. But finding and implementing the right price strategy is critical to success.

What Is a Price?

In the narrowest sense, **price** is the amount of money charged for a product or a service. More broadly, price is the sum of all the values that customers give up to gain the benefits of having or using a product or service. Historically, price has been the major factor affecting buyer choice. In recent decades, however, nonprice factors have gained increasing importance. Even so, price remains one of the most important elements that determines a firm's market share and profitability.

Price is the only element in the marketing mix that produces revenue; all other elements represent costs. Price is also one of the most flexible marketing mix elements. Unlike product features and channel commitments, prices can be changed quickly. At the same time, pricing is the number-one problem facing many marketing executives, and many companies do not handle pricing well. Some managers view pricing as a big headache, preferring instead to focus on other marketing mix elements. However, smart managers treat pricing as a key strategic tool for creating and capturing customer value. Prices have a direct impact on a firm's bottom line. A small percentage improvement in price can generate a large percentage increase in profitability. More importantly, as part of a company's overall value proposition, price plays a key role in creating customer value and building customer relationships. "Instead of running away from pricing," says an expert, "savvy marketers are embracing it."[2]

Major Pricing Strategies

The price the company charges will fall somewhere between one that is too low to produce a profit and one that is too high to produce any demand. ▶ **Figure 9.1** summarizes the major considerations in setting price. Customer perceptions of the product's value set the ceiling for prices. If customers perceive that the product's price is greater than its value, they will not buy the product. Likewise, product costs set the floor for prices. If the company prices the product below its costs, the company's profits will suffer. In setting its price between these two extremes, the company must consider several external and internal factors, including competitors' strategies and prices, the overall marketing strategy and mix, and the nature of the market and demand.

Figure 9.1 suggests three major pricing strategies: customer value-based pricing, cost-based pricing, and competition-based pricing.

▶ **Figure 9.1** Considerations in Setting Price

If customers perceive that a product's price is greater than its value, they won't buy it. If the company prices the product below its costs, profits will suffer. Between the two extremes, the "right" pricing strategy is one that delivers both value to the customer and profits to the company.

Figure 9.2 Value-Based Pricing vs. Cost-Based Pricing

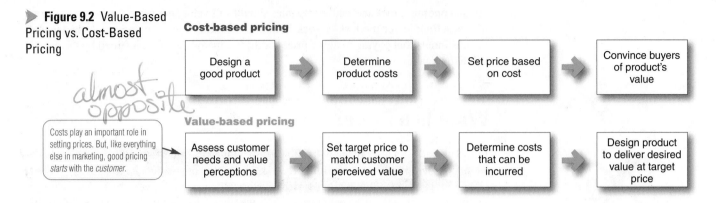

Cost-based pricing

Design a good product → Determine product costs → Set price based on cost → Convince buyers of product's value

almost opposite

Value-based pricing

Costs play an important role in setting prices. But, like everything else in marketing, good pricing *starts* with the *customer*.

Assess customer needs and value perceptions → Set target price to match customer perceived value → Determine costs that can be incurred → Design product to deliver desired value at target price

Author Comment ▶

Like everything else in marketing, good pricing starts with *customers* and their perceptions of value.

Customer value-based pricing

Setting price based on buyers' perceptions of value rather than on the seller's cost.

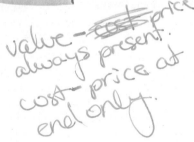
value — cost price always present. cost — price at end only.

Customer Value-Based Pricing

In the end, the customer will decide whether a product's price is right. Pricing decisions, like other marketing mix decisions, must start with customer value. When customers buy a product, they exchange something of value (the price) to get something of value (the benefits of having or using the product). Effective, customer-oriented pricing involves understanding how much value consumers place on the benefits they receive from the product and setting a price that captures that value.

Customer value-based pricing uses buyers' perceptions of value as the key to pricing. Value-based pricing means that the marketer cannot design a product and marketing program and then set the price. Price is considered along with all other marketing mix variables *before* the marketing program is set.

▶ **Figure 9.2** compares value-based pricing with cost-based pricing. Although costs are an important consideration in setting prices, cost-based pricing is often product driven. The company designs what it considers to be a good product, adds up the costs of making the product, and sets a price that covers costs plus a target profit. Marketing must then convince buyers that the product's value at that price justifies its purchase. If the price turns out to be too high, the company must settle for lower markups or lower sales, both resulting in disappointing profits.

Value-based pricing reverses this process. The company first assesses customer needs and value perceptions. It then sets its target price based on customer perceptions of value. The targeted value and price drive decisions about what costs can be incurred and the resulting product design. As a result, pricing begins with analyzing consumer needs and value perceptions, and the price is set to match perceived value.

It's important to remember that "good value" is not the same as "low price." ▶ For example, a Steinway piano—any Steinway piano—costs a lot. But to those who own one, a Steinway is a great value:[3]

A Steinway grand piano typically runs anywhere from $40,000 to $165,000. The most popular model sells for around $72,000. But ask anyone who owns a Steinway grand piano, and they'll tell you that, when it comes to Steinway, price is nothing; the Steinway experience is everything. Steinway makes very high quality pianos—handcrafting each Steinway requires up to one full year. But, more importantly, owners get the Steinway mystique. The Steinway name evokes images of classical concert stages and the celebrities and performers who've owned and played Steinway pianos across more than 155 years.

But Steinways aren't just for world-class pianists and the wealthy. Ninety-nine percent of all Steinway buyers are amateurs who perform only in their dens. To such customers, whatever a Steinway costs, it's a small

▲ **Perceived value: A Steinway piano—any Steinway piano—costs a lot. But to those who own one, price is nothing; the Steinway experience is everything.**

ROBERT CAPLIN/The New York Times/Redux Pictures

price to pay for the value of owning one. "A Steinway takes you places you've never been," says an ad. As one Steinway owner puts it, "My friendship with the Steinway piano is one of the most important and beautiful things in my life." Who can put a price on such feelings?

A company will often find it hard to measure the value customers attach to its product. For example, calculating the cost of ingredients in a meal at a fancy restaurant is relatively easy. But assigning value to other satisfactions such as taste, environment, relaxation, conversation, and status is very hard. Such value is subjective; it varies both for different consumers and different situations.

Still, consumers will use these perceived values to evaluate a product's price, so the company must work to measure them. Sometimes, companies ask consumers how much they would pay for a basic product and for each benefit added to the offer. Or a company might conduct experiments to test the perceived value of different product offers. According to an old Russian proverb, there are two fools in every market—one who asks too much and one who asks too little. If the seller charges more than the buyers' perceived value, the company's sales will suffer. If the seller charges less, its products sell very well, but they produce less revenue than they would if they were priced at the level of perceived value.

We now examine two types of value-based pricing: *good-value pricing* and *value-added pricing*.

Good-Value Pricing

The Great Recession of 2008 to 2009 caused a fundamental and lasting shift in consumer attitudes toward price and quality. In response, many companies have changed their pricing approaches to bring them in line with changing economic conditions and consumer price perceptions. More and more, marketers have adopted **good-value pricing** strategies— offering the right combination of quality and good service at a fair price.

In many cases, this has involved introducing less-expensive versions of established, brand-name products. For example, fast-food restaurants such as Taco Bell and McDonald's offer value menu and dollar menu items. Armani offers the less-expensive, more-casual Armani Exchange fashion line. Alberto-Culver's TRESemmé hair care line promises "A salon look and feel at a fraction of the price." And every car company now offers small, inexpensive models better suited to tighter consumer budgets and thriftier spending habits.

In other cases, good-value pricing has involved redesigning existing brands to offer more quality for a given price or the same quality for less. Some companies even succeed by offering less value but at very low prices. ▶ For example, Snap Fitness is well positioned to take advantage of either good or bad economic conditions:

> Although some gym chains struggled during the recent recession—Bally's Total Fitness filed for bankruptcy twice—24-hour Snap Fitness actually expanded the number of its clubs and its revenues doubled. The franchise chain did all this despite charging members only $35 per month with easy cancellation fees. Its secret? A no-frills approach reinforced by the motto, "Fast, Convenient, Affordable." The small gyms—only 2,500 square feet—typically have five treadmills, two stationary bikes, five elliptical machines, and weight equipment. What's important is what they *don't* have— no classes, spa rooms, on-site childcare, or juice bars. Few clubs have showers, and most are staffed only 25 to 40 hours a week. The sweet spot of their target market is married 35- to 55-year-olds with kids who live nearby and are busy enough that they cannot afford more than an hour a day to go to the gym.[4]

Good-value pricing
Offering the right combination of quality and good service at a fair price.

▲ **Good-value pricing: With its no-frills positioning and low prices, Snap Fitness is well-positioned to take advantage of either good or bad economic conditions.**

Courtesy of Snap Fitness

An important type of good-value pricing at the retail level is *everyday low pricing* (*EDLP*). EDLP involves charging a constant, everyday low price with few or no temporary price discounts. Retailers such as Costco and Lumber Liquidators practice EDLP.

However, the king of EDLP is Walmart, which practically defined the concept. Except for a few sale items every month, Walmart promises everyday low prices on everything it sells. In contrast, *high-low pricing* involves charging higher prices on an everyday basis but running frequent promotions to lower prices temporarily on selected items. Department stores such as Kohl's and Macy's practice high-low pricing by having frequent sale days, early-bird savings, and bonus earnings for store credit-card holders.

Value-Added Pricing

Value-based pricing doesn't mean simply charging what customers want to pay or setting low prices to meet competition. Instead, many companies adopt **value-added pricing** strategies. Rather than cutting prices to match competitors, they attach value-added features and services to differentiate their offers and thus support their higher prices. For example, at a time when competing restaurants have offered a hodgepodge of low-priced value meals and promotional deals, fast-casual chain Panera Bread has prospered by adding value and charging accordingly (see Marketing at Work 9.1).

Similarly, even as recession-era consumer spending habits linger, some movie theater chains are *adding* amenities and charging *more* rather than cutting services to maintain lower admission prices.

> **Value-added pricing**
> Attaching value-added features and services to differentiate a company's offers while charging higher prices.

> **Cost-based pricing**
> Setting prices based on the costs for producing, distributing, and selling the product plus a fair rate of return for effort and risk.

▲ **Value-added pricing: Rather than cutting services to maintain lower admission prices, premium theaters such as AMC's Cinema Suites are adding amenities and charging more. "Once people experience it, . . . they don't want to go anywhere else."**
Courtesy AMC Entertainment. AMC Theatres®, Fork & Screen™, Cinema Suites™ are trademarks of AMC Entertainment.

Some theater chains are turning their multiplexes into smaller, roomier luxury outposts. The new premium theaters offer value-added features such as online reserved seating, high-backed leather executive or rocking chairs with armrests and footrests, the latest in digital sound and super-wide screens, dine-in restaurants serving fine food and drinks, and even valet parking. ▶ For example, AMC Theatres (the second-largest American theater chain) operates more than 50 theaters with some kind of enhanced food and beverage amenities, including Fork & Screen (upgraded leather seating, seat-side service, extensive menu including dinner offerings, beer, wine, and cocktails) and Cinema Suites (additional upscale food offerings in addition to premium cocktails and an extensive wine list, seat-side service, red leather reclining chairs, and eight to nine feet of spacing between rows).

So at the AMC Mainstreet 6 Cinema Suites in Kansas City, Missouri, bring on the mango margaritas! For $9 to $15 a ticket (depending on the time and day), moviegoers are treated to reserved seating, a strict 21-and-over-only policy, reclining leather seats with subwoofers underneath so they feel the vibrations along with the action on the screen, and the opportunity to pay even more to have dinner and drinks brought to their seats. Afterwards, attendants bid guests farewell with a warm towel and a Ghirardelli chocolate mint. Such theaters are so successful that AMC plans to add more. "Once people experience it," says a company spokesperson, "more often than not they don't want to go anywhere else."[5]

> **Author Comment ▶**
> Costs set the floor for price, but the goal isn't always to *minimize* costs. In fact, many firms invest in higher costs so that they can claim higher prices and margins (think about Steinway pianos). The key is to manage the *spread* between costs and prices—how much the company makes for the customer value it delivers.

Cost-Based Pricing

Whereas customer-value perceptions set the price ceiling, costs set the floor for the price that the company can charge. **Cost-based pricing** involves setting prices based on the costs for producing, distributing, and selling the product plus a fair rate of return for its effort and risk. A company's costs may be an important element in its pricing strategy.

Some companies, such as Walmart or Southwest Airlines, work to become the *low-cost producers* in their industries. Companies with lower costs can set lower prices that result in smaller margins but greater sales and profits. However, other companies—such as Apple, BMW, and Steinway—intentionally pay higher costs so that they can claim higher prices and margins. For example, it costs more to make a "handcrafted" Steinway piano

| **MARKETING AT WORK** | 9.1 |

Panera Bread Company: It's Not about Low Prices

In the restaurant business these days, *value* typically means one thing—*cheap*. Today's casual restaurants are offering a seemingly endless hodgepodge of value meals, dollar items, budget sandwiches, and rapid-fire promotional deals that scream "value, value, value." But one everyday eatery—Panera Bread—understands that, even in tight economic times, low prices often aren't the best value. Instead, at Panera, value means wholesome food and fresh-baked bread, served in a warm and inviting environment, even if you have to pay a little more for it. Ronald Shaich, founder and executive chairman of Panera, sums up this value-added concept perfectly. "Give people something of value and they'll happily pay for it," he says.

Shaich realized 30 years ago that people wanted something between fast food and casual dining. He perfected the "fast-casual" dining formula and opened Panera (Spanish for "bread basket"). Today, the bakery-café segment, which Shaich practically created, is the fastest growing sector in the fast-casual market. And Panera does bakery-café better than anyone else. In fact, Panera's $1.5 billion in sales more than doubles the combined sales of its next four competitors.

Why is Panera Bread so successful? Unlike so many competitors in the post-Great Recession era, Panera isn't about having the lowest prices. Instead, it's about the *value* you get for what you pay, and what you get is a full-value dining experience.

At Panera, it all starts with the food, which centers around fresh-baked bread. When customers walk through the door, the first thing they see are massive displays of bread, all hand-formed and baked on-site. Bakers pass out warm bread samples to customers throughout the day. All new employees get "dough training," and even employee meetings start with the staff breaking bread together—literally. Bread is so central to Panera's DNA that the company's R&D team will scrap new dishes if the bread feels like an afterthought.

Of course, the food at Panera goes well beyond bread. Fresh bagels, pastries, egg soufflés, soups, salads, sandwiches and paninis, and coffee drinks and smoothies give customers full meal options at any time of day. Menu items brim with upscale ingredients such as Gorgonzola cheese, fresh basil, chipotle mayonnaise, and applewood-smoked bacon (the kind you'd find at the Four Seasons, not Wendy's). In all, Panera's target audience is more Food Network than fast food. "We hit a chord with people who understand and respond to food," says Scott Davis, chief concept officer. Our profile is "closer to what you'd find in a bistro than a fast-food joint." And to all that good food, Panera adds first-rate customer service. For three years running, Panera has rated among *BusinessWeek's* top 25 "Customer Service Champs."

But good fast-casual food and outstanding service are only part of Panera's value-added proposition. Perhaps even more important is the Panera experience—one so inviting that people don't want to leave. Comfortable booths, leather sofas and chairs, warm lighting, a fireplace, and free Wi-Fi all beg customers to relax and stay awhile. In fact, the local Panera has become a kind of community gathering spot. At any given moment, you'll find a diverse group of customers hanging out together for a variety of reasons. One recent sample included a bride-to-be chatting with her wedding photographer, two businesspeople with laptops, a teacher grading papers, a church group engaged in Bible study, and a baker's dozen of couples and families just enjoying each others' company. Shaich knows that, although the food's important, what he's really selling is an inviting place to be. "In many ways," he says, "we're renting space to people, and the food is the price of admission."

Even during the Great Recession, rather than cutting back on value and lowering prices in difficult times, Panera boosted quality and value while competitors cut back. Freshness remained a driving force. Shaich improved the freshness of lettuce by cutting the time from field to plate in half and using only the hearts of romaine. Store ovens began producing warm bread throughout the day, rather than just in the wee hours of the morning. And the chain's development labs tested a new grill that churned out paninis in half the time. "This was the time to increase the food experience, when the customer least expected it," Shaich insists. "When everyone else pulled back and we did more, the difference between us and our competitors went up."

▲ Panera Bread understands that, even in uncertain economic times, low prices often aren't the best value. Says Panera CEO Ronald Shaich, "Give people something of value and they'll happily pay for it."

AP Images/Tom Gannam

Panera's strategy of adding value and charging accordingly has paid off handsomely, through bad economic times and good. At a time when most chains, including those that slashed their prices, struggled and closed stores, Panera flourished. Over the past five years, its sales have more than tripled, and profits have more than doubled, including six straight quarters of double-digit profit gains through the heart of the recession.

Although everyone wants value, Shaich says, not everyone wants it in the form of a value meal. Anne Skrodzki, a 28-year-old Chicago attorney, agrees. She recently spent $9.72 at Panera on a chicken Caesar salad and frozen lemonade. "I think it's a pretty good value. The portions are generous. The food is high quality . . . I've also gotten used to coming here for the free Wi-Fi."

The Panera Web site spells out the chain's valued-added positioning this way: "We are Panera. We are bakers of bread. We are fresh from the oven. We are a symbol of warmth and welcome. We are a simple pleasure, honest and genuine. We are a life story told over dinner. We are a long lunch with an old friend. We are your weekday morning ritual. We are the kindest gesture of neighbors. We are home. We are family. We are friends." Low prices? Not even on the radar.

Sources: Kate Rockwood, "Rising Dough: Why Panera Bread Is on a Roll," *Fast Company*, October 2009, pp. 69–70; Emily Bryson York, "Panera: An America's Hottest Brands Case Study," *Advertising Age*, November 16, 2009, p. 16; Julie Jargon, "Slicing the Bread But Not the Prices," *Wall Street Journal*, August 18, 2009, p. B1; Ben Steverman, "How Panera Kept Rising Through the Recession," *Bloomberg Businessweek,* November 8, 2010, www.businessweek.com/investor/content/nov2010/pi2010118_183529.htm; "Standouts in Customer Service," *Bloomberg Businessweek,* April 14, 2011, www.businessweek.com/interactive_reports/customer_service_2010.html; and www.panerabread.com, accessed November 2011.

than a Yamaha production model. But the higher costs result in higher quality, justifying that eye-popping $72,000 price. The key is to manage the spread between costs and prices—how much the company makes for the customer value it delivers.

Types of Costs

Fixed costs (overhead)
Costs that do not vary with production or sales level.

Variable costs
Costs that vary directly with the level of production.

Total costs
The sum of the fixed and variable costs for any given level of production.

A company's costs take two forms: fixed and variable. **Fixed costs** (also known as **overhead**) are costs that do not vary with production or sales level. For example, a company must pay each month's bills for rent, heat, interest, and executive salaries regardless of the company's level of output. **Variable costs** vary directly with the level of production. Each PC produced by HP involves a cost of computer chips, wires, plastic, packaging, and other inputs. Although these costs tend to be the same for each unit produced, they are called variable costs because the total varies with the number of units produced. **Total costs** are the sum of the fixed and variable costs for any given level of production. Management wants to charge a price that will at least cover the total production costs at a given level of production.

The company must watch its costs carefully. If it costs the company more than its competitors to produce and sell a similar product, the company will need to charge a higher price or make less profit, putting it at a competitive disadvantage.

Cost-Plus Pricing

Cost-plus pricing (markup pricing)
Adding a standard markup to the cost of the product.

The simplest pricing method is **cost-plus pricing** (or **markup pricing**)—adding a standard markup to the cost of the product. For example, an electronics retailer might pay a manufacturer $20 for a flash drive and mark it up to sell at $30, a 50 percent markup on cost. The retailer's gross margin is $10. If the store's operating costs amount to $8 per flash drive sold, the retailer's profit margin will be $2. The manufacturer that made the flash drive probably used cost-plus pricing, too. If the manufacturer's standard cost of producing the flash drive was $16, it might have added a 25 percent markup, setting the price to the retailers at $20.

Does using standard markups to set prices make sense? Generally, no. Any pricing method that ignores consumer demand and competitor prices is not likely to lead to the best price. Still, cost-plus pricing remains popular for many reasons. First, sellers are more certain about costs than about demand. By tying the price to cost, sellers simplify pricing. Second, when all firms in the industry use this pricing method, prices tend to be similar and price competition is minimized.

Break-even pricing (target return pricing)
Setting price to break even on the costs of making and marketing a product, or setting price to make a target return.

Another cost-oriented pricing approach is **break-even pricing**, or a variation called **target return pricing**. In this method, the firm tries to determine the price at which it will

Figure 9.3 Break-Even Chart for Determining Target Return Price and Break-Even Volume

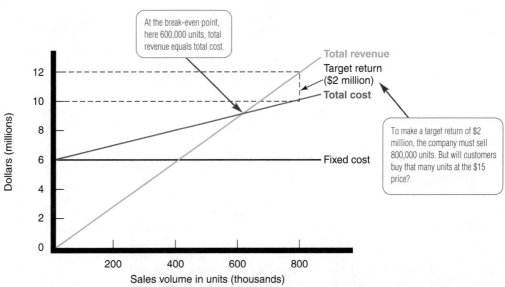

Figure 9.3 Break-Even Chart for Determining Target Return Price and Break-Even Volume

break even or make the target return it is seeking. Target return pricing uses the concept of a *break-even chart*, which shows the total cost and total revenue expected at different sales volume levels. ▶ **Figure 9.3** shows a break-even chart for the flash drive manufacturer discussed previously. Fixed costs are $6 million regardless of sales volume, and variable costs are $5 per unit. Variable costs are added to fixed costs to form total costs, which rise with volume. The slope of the total revenue curve reflects the price. Here, the price is $15 (for example, the company's revenue is $12 million on 800,000 units, or $15 per unit).

At the $15 price, the manufacturer must sell at least 600,000 units to *break even* (break-even volume = fixed costs ÷ (price − variable costs) = $6,000,000 ÷ ($15 − $5) = 600,000). That is, at this level, total revenues will equal total costs of $9 million, producing no profit. If the flash drive manufacturer wants a target return of $2 million, it must sell at least 800,000 units to obtain the $12 million of total revenue needed to cover the costs of $10 million plus the $2 million of target profits. In contrast, if the company charges a higher price, say $20, it will not need to sell as many units to break even or to achieve its target profit. In fact, the higher the price, the lower the manufacturer's break-even point will be.

The major problem with this analysis, however, is that it fails to consider customer value and the relationship between price and demand. As the *price* increases, *demand* decreases. When that happens, the market may not buy even the lower volume needed to break even at the higher price. For example, suppose the flash drive manufacturer calculates that, given its current fixed and variable costs, it must charge a price of $30 for the product in order to earn its desired target profit. But marketing research shows that few consumers will pay more than $25. In this case, the company must trim its costs in order to lower the break-even point so that it can charge the lower price consumers expect.

Thus, although break-even analysis and target return pricing can help the company to determine the minimum prices needed to cover expected costs and profits, they do not take the price-demand relationship into account. When using this method, the company must also consider the impact of price on the sales volume needed to realize target profits and the likelihood that the needed volume will be achieved at each possible price.

Competition-Based Pricing

Competition-based pricing involves setting prices based on competitors' strategies, costs, prices, and market offerings. Consumers will base their judgments of a product's value on the prices that competitors charge for similar products.

In assessing competitors' pricing strategies, the company should ask several questions. First, how does the company's market offering compare with competitors' offerings in terms of customer value? If consumers perceive that the company's product or service provides greater value, the company can charge a higher price. If consumers perceive less

---

Competition-based pricing
Setting prices based on competitors' strategies, prices, costs, and market offerings.

Author Comment ▶

In setting prices, the company must also consider competitors' prices. No matter what price it charges—high, low, or in-between—the company must be certain to give customers superior value for that price.

value relative to competing products, the company must either charge a lower price or change customer perceptions to justify a higher price.

Next, how strong are current competitors and what are their current pricing strategies? If the company faces a host of smaller competitors charging high prices relative to the value they deliver, it might charge lower prices to drive weaker competitors from the market. If the market is dominated by larger, lower-price competitors, the company may decide to target unserved market niches with value-added products at higher prices. ▶ For example, consider Hot Mama, the fast-growing clothing boutique for moms—and their kids:[6]

▲ **Pricing against larger, lower price competitors:** Fast-growing clothing boutique Hot Mama isn't likely to win a price war against giants like Macy's or Kohl's. Instead, it relies on personal service, a mom- and kid-friendly atmosphere, and its knowledgeable staff to turn harried moms into loyal patrons. "It's like shopping with a girlfriend."

Hot Mama

With 20 locations and growing, Hot Mama isn't likely to win a price war against giants Macy's or Kohl's. Instead, the boutique, which sells high-end brands such as Joes Jeans and Free People, relies on its personal approach, mom- and kid-friendly atmosphere, and knowledgeable staff to turn harried moms into a loyal patrons, even if they have to pay a little more. Each Hot Mama location entertains kids with video games, movies, toys, and coloring books—all centrally located to help Mom keep an eye on the little ones. Every aisle is wide enough to accommodate a two-seat stroller, and sales staff double as babysitters. The goal: Give busy mothers 15 minutes of shopping peace (most end up staying nearly an hour). Customers say it's the service, not the prices, that sets Hot Mama apart. Sales employees—or "stylists"—go through three certification programs in their first few months on the floor: denim, body type, and maternity. "Our stylists can outfit any woman, aged 25 to 65, based on her body the minute she walks through the door," says Hot Mama president Kimberly Ritzer, "but they also build personal relationships to find a style that makes her feel comfortable. It's like shopping with a girlfriend."

What principle should guide decisions about what price to charge relative to those of competitors? The answer is simple in concept but often difficult in practice: No matter what price you charge—high, low, or in-between—be certain to give customers superior value for that price.

Author Comment ▶
Now that we've looked at the three general pricing strategies—value-, cost-, and competitor-based pricing—let's dig into some of the many other factors that affect pricing decisions.

Other Internal and External Considerations Affecting Price Decisions

Beyond customer value perceptions, costs, and competitor strategies, the company must consider several additional internal and external factors. Internal factors affecting pricing include the company's overall marketing strategy, objectives, and marketing mix, as well as other organizational considerations. External factors include the nature of the market and demand and other environmental factors.

Overall Marketing Strategy, Objectives, and Mix

Price is only one element of the company's broader marketing strategy. So, before setting price, the company must decide on its overall marketing strategy for the product or service. If the company has selected its target market and positioning carefully, then its marketing mix strategy, including price, will be fairly straightforward. For example, when Honda developed its Acura brand to compete with European luxury-performance cars in the higher-income segment, this required charging a high price. In contrast, when it introduced the Honda Fit model—billed as "a pint-sized fuel miser with feisty giddy up"—this positioning required charging a low price. Thus, pricing strategy is largely determined by decisions on market positioning.

Pricing may play an important role in helping to accomplish company objectives at many levels. A firm can set prices to attract new customers or profitably retain existing ones. It can set prices low to prevent competition from entering the market or set prices at competitors' levels to stabilize the market. It can price to keep the loyalty and support of resellers or avoid government intervention. Prices can be reduced temporarily to create excitement for a brand. Or one product may be priced to help the sales of other products in the company's line.

Price decisions must be coordinated with product design, distribution, and promotion decisions to form a consistent and effective integrated marketing mix program. Decisions made for other marketing mix variables may affect pricing decisions. For example, a decision to position the product on high-performance quality will mean that the seller must charge a higher price to cover higher costs. And producers whose resellers are expected to support and promote their products may have to build larger reseller margins into their prices.

Companies often position their products on price and then tailor other marketing mix decisions to the prices they want to charge. Here, price is a crucial product-positioning factor that defines the product's market, competition, and design. Many firms support such price-positioning strategies with a technique called **target costing**. Target costing reverses the usual process of first designing a new product, determining its cost, and then asking, "Can we sell it for that?" Instead, it starts with an ideal selling price based on customer-value considerations and then targets costs that will ensure that the price is met. For example, when Honda initially designed the Fit, it began with a $13,950 starting price point and highway mileage of 33 miles per gallon firmly in mind. It then designed a stylish, peppy little car with costs that allowed it to give target customers those values.

Target costing
Pricing that starts with an ideal selling price and then targets costs that will ensure that the price is met.

Other companies deemphasize price and use other marketing mix tools to create *nonprice* positions. Often, the best strategy is not to charge the lowest price but rather differentiate the marketing offer to make it worth a higher price. ▶ For example, Bang & Olufsen (B&O)— known for its cutting-edge consumer electronics— builds high value into its products and charges sky-high prices. A B&O 50-inch BeoVision HDTV will cost you $7,500; a 55-inch model runs $18,700, and a 103-inch model goes for almost $100,000. A complete B&O entertainment system? Well, you don't really want to know the price. But target customers recognize B&O's very high quality and are willing to pay more to get it.

Some marketers even position their products on *high* prices, featuring high prices as part of their product's allure. For example, Grand Marnier offers a $225 bottle of Cuvée du Cent Cinquantenaire that's marketed with the tagline "Hard to find, impossible to pronounce, and prohibitively expensive." And advertisements for the Porsche Panamera proudly proclaim: "The Panamera. Starting at $74,400."

▲ **Nonprice positioning:** Cutting-edge consumer electronics maker Bang & Olufsen builds high value into its products and charges sky-high prices. Its 103-inch B&O HDTV goes for almost $100,000.
Bang + Olufsen

Thus, marketers must consider the total marketing strategy and mix when setting prices. But again, even when featuring price, marketers need to remember that customers rarely buy on price alone. Instead, they seek products that give them the best value in terms of benefits received for the prices paid.

Organizational Considerations

Management must decide who within the organization should set prices. Companies handle pricing in a variety of ways. In small companies, prices are often set by top management rather than by the marketing or sales departments. In large companies, pricing is typically handled by divisional or product line managers. In industrial markets, salespeople may be allowed to negotiate with customers within certain price ranges. Even so, top management sets the pricing objectives and policies, and it often approves the prices proposed by lower-level management or salespeople.

In industries in which pricing is a key factor (airlines, aerospace, steel, railroads, oil companies), companies often have pricing departments to set the best prices or help others set them. These departments report to the marketing department or top management. Others who have an influence on pricing include sales managers, production managers, finance managers, and accountants.

The Market and Demand

As noted earlier, good pricing starts with an understanding of how customers' perceptions of value affect the prices they are willing to pay. Both consumer and industrial buyers balance the price of a product or service against the benefits of owning it. Thus, before setting prices, the marketer must understand the relationship between price and demand for the company's product. In this section, we take a deeper look at the price-demand relationship and how it varies for different types of markets. We then discuss methods for analyzing the price-demand relationship.

Pricing in Different Types of Markets

The seller's pricing freedom varies with different types of markets. Economists recognize four types of markets, each presenting a different pricing challenge.

Under *pure competition*, the market consists of many buyers and sellers trading in a uniform commodity, such as wheat, copper, or financial securities. No single buyer or seller has much effect on the going market price. In a purely competitive market, marketing research, product development, pricing, advertising, and sales promotion play little or no role. Thus, sellers in these markets do not spend much time on marketing strategy.

Under *monopolistic competition*, the market consists of many buyers and sellers who trade over a range of prices rather than a single market price. A range of prices occurs because sellers can differentiate their offers to buyers. Because there are many competitors, each firm is less affected by competitors' pricing strategies than in oligopolistic markets. Sellers try to develop differentiated offers for different customer segments and, in addition to price, freely use branding, advertising, and personal selling to set their offers apart. Thus, Honda sets its Odyssey minivan apart through strong branding and advertising, reducing the impact of price. Its tongue-in-cheek "Van of Your Dreams" advertisements tell parents that "the new Odyssey has everything one would dream about in a van, if one had dreams about vans." Beyond the standard utility features you'd expect in a van, Honda tells them, you'll also find yourself surrounded by a dazzling array of technology, a marvel of ingenuity. "Hook up your MP3 player and summon music like a rock god. Call out a song name and it plays through an audio system that can split the heavens!"

Under *oligopolistic competition*, the market consists of only a few large sellers. For example, only four companies—Verizon, AT&T, Sprint, and T-Mobile—control more than 80 percent of the U.S. wireless service provider market. Because there are few sellers, each seller is alert and responsive to competitors' pricing strategies and marketing moves. In a *pure monopoly*, the market is dominated by one seller. The seller may be a government monopoly (the U.S. Postal Service), a private regulated monopoly (a power company), or a private unregulated monopoly (De Beers and diamonds). Pricing is handled differently in each case.

Analyzing the Price-Demand Relationship

Each price the company might charge will lead to a different level of demand. The relationship between the price charged and the resulting demand level is shown in the **demand curve** in ▶ **Figure 9.4**. The demand curve shows the number of units the market will buy in a given time period at different prices that might be charged. In the normal case, demand and price are inversely related—that is, the higher the price, the lower the demand. Thus, the company would sell less if it raised its price from P_1 to P_2. In short, consumers with limited budgets probably will buy less of something if its price is too high.

Demand curve
A curve that shows the number of units the market will buy in a given time period, at different prices that might be charged.

▼ **Figure 9.4** Demand Curve

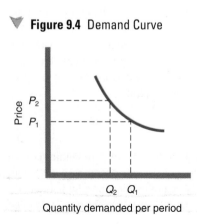

Quantity demanded per period

The price-demand curve: When ConAgra raised prices on its Banquet frozen dinners, sales fell sharply. "The key component . . . is you've got to be at $1," says CEO Gary Rodkin, pictured above. "Everything else pales in comparison to that."

Colby Lysne

Understanding a brand's price-demand curve is crucial to good pricing decisions. ▶ ConAgra Foods learned this lesson when pricing its Banquet frozen dinners.[7]

ConAgra found out the hard way about the perils of pushing up the price of a Banquet frozen dinner. When it tried to recoup high commodity costs by hiking the list price last year, many retailers began charging up to $1.25 a meal. The response from shoppers used to paying $1? The cold shoulder. The resulting sales drop forced ConAgra to peddle excess dinners to discounters and contributed to a 40 percent drop in the company's stock price for the year. It turns out that "the key component for Banquet dinners—the key attribute—is you've got to be at $1," says ConAgra's CEO Gary Rodkin. "Everything else pales in comparison to that." The price is now back to a buck a dinner. To make money at that price, ConAgra is doing a better job of managing costs. It tossed out pricey items such as barbecued chicken and country-fried pork in favor of grilled meat patties and rice and beans. It also shrank portion sizes while swapping in cheaper ingredients, such as mashed potatoes for brownies. Consumers are responding well to the brand's efforts to keep prices down. Where else can you find dinner for $1?

Most companies try to measure their demand curves by estimating demand at different prices. The type of market makes a difference. In a monopoly, the demand curve shows the total market demand resulting from different prices. If the company faces competition, its demand at different prices will depend on whether competitors' prices stay constant or change with the company's own prices.

Price Elasticity of Demand

Price elasticity
A measure of the sensitivity of demand to changes in price.

Marketers also need to know **price elasticity**—how responsive demand will be to a change in price. If demand hardly changes with a small change in price, we say demand is *inelastic*. If demand changes greatly, we say the demand is *elastic*.

If demand is elastic rather than inelastic, sellers will consider lowering their prices. A lower price will produce more total revenue. This practice makes sense as long as the extra costs of producing and selling more do not exceed the extra revenue. At the same time, most firms want to avoid pricing that turns their products into commodities. In recent years, forces such as deregulation and the instant price comparisons afforded by the Internet and other technologies have increased consumer price sensitivity, turning products ranging from telephones and computers to new automobiles into commodities in some consumers' eyes.

The Economy

Economic conditions can have a strong impact on the firm's pricing strategies. Economic factors such as a boom or recession, inflation, and interest rates affect pricing decisions because they affect consumer spending, consumer perceptions of the product's price and value, and the company's costs of producing and selling a product.

In the aftermath of the recent Great Recession, many consumers have rethought the price-value equation. They have tightened their belts and become more value conscious. Consumers will likely continue their thriftier ways well beyond any economic recovery. As a result, many marketers have increased their emphasis on value-for-the-money pricing strategies.

The most obvious response to the new economic realities is to cut prices and offer discounts. Thousands of companies have done just that. Lower prices make products more affordable and help spur short-term sales. However, such price cuts can have undesirable long-term consequences. Lower prices mean lower margins. Deep discounts may cheapen a brand in consumers' eyes. And once a company cuts prices, it's difficult to raise them again when the economy recovers. Consider companies such as Starbucks, Tiffany's, or Whole Foods Market, which have spent years successfully positioning themselves on premium products at premium prices. In adapting to the new pricing environment, such firms face the difficult task of realigning their value propositions while staying true to their longer-term "more-for-more" positioning (see Marketing at Work 9.2).

Rather than cutting prices, many companies have instead shifted their marketing focus to more affordable items in their product mixes. For example, whereas its previous promotions emphasized high-end products and pricey concepts such as creating dream kitchens, Home Depot's more recent advertising pushes items like potting soil and hand tools under the tagline: "More saving. More doing. That's the power of Home Depot." Other companies are holding prices but redefining the "value" in their value propositions. Unilever did this when it repositioned its higher-end Bertolli frozen meals as an eat-at-home brand that's more affordable than eating out. Still others are holding prices but adding value to attract more price-sensitive customers. For instance, to lure back consumers who swapped out higher-end brands for cheaper brands during the recession, many consumer goods are boasting "new and improved" claims on their labels. P&G offered Tide with the ActiLift formula, which "lifts off stains with ease," at the same price as the old Tide.[8]

Remember, even in tough economic times, consumers do not buy based on prices alone. They balance the price they pay against the value they receive. For example, according to one survey, despite selling its shoes for as much as $150 a pair, Nike commands the highest consumer loyalty of any brand in the footwear segment.[9] Customers perceive the value of Nike's products and the Nike ownership experience to be well worth the price. Thus, no matter what price they charge—low or high—companies need to offer great *value for the money*.

▲ Pricing and the economy: Rather than just cutting prices, Home Depot shifted its marketing focus to more affordable items and projects under the tagline: "More saving. More doing."

(logo) Courtesy of The Home Depot, Inc./
(photo) iofoto/Shutterstock.com

Other External Factors

Beyond the market and the economy, the company must consider several other factors in its external environment when setting prices. It must know what impact its prices will have on other parties in its environment. How will *resellers* react to various prices? The company should set prices that give resellers a fair profit, encourage their support, and help them to sell the product effectively. The *government* is another important external influence on pricing decisions. Finally, *social concerns* may need to be taken into account. In setting prices, a company's short-term sales, market share, and profit goals may need to be tempered by broader societal considerations. We will examine public policy issues in pricing later in the chapter.

SPEED BUMP | LINKING THE CONCEPTS

The concept of customer value is critical to good pricing and to successful marketing in general. Pause for a minute and be certain that you appreciate what value really means.

- An earlier example states that, although the most popular Steinway piano model costs $72,000, to those who own one, a Steinway is a great value. Does this fit with your idea of value?
- Pick two competing brands from a familiar product category (watches, perfume, consumer electronics, restaurants)—one low priced and the other high priced. Which, if either, offers the greatest value?
- Does *value* mean the same thing as *low price*? How do these concepts differ?

MARKETING AT WORK | 9.2

Whole Foods Market: Price and Value in a Tighter Economy

Only a few years ago, consumers were flush with cash, and Whole Foods Market was thriving. The upscale grocery retailer was a model "more-for-more" marketer, offering premium value at premium prices. Under its motto, "Whole Foods, Whole People, Whole Planet," it served up a gourmet assortment of high-quality grocery items, including a strong mix of natural and organic foods and health products. Its upscale, health-conscious customers were willing and able to pay higher prices for the extra value they got. Over the previous two decades, Whole Foods Market's sales had soared, and its stock price had grown at an eye-popping compounded annual rate of 25 percent, peaking at almost $80 a share.

Then came the Great Recession of 2008. People in all walks of life began rethinking the price-value equation and looking for ways to save. They asked tough questions, such as the following: "I love the wonderful foods and smells in my Whole Foods Market, but is it worth the extra 30 percent versus shopping at Walmart?" All of a sudden, Whole Foods Market's seemingly perfect premium marketing strategy looked less like a plum and more like a bruised organic banana. Even relatively affluent customers were cutting back and spending less. For the first time in its history, the company faced declines in same-store sales, and its stock price plunged to a shocking low of close to $8. "The company had long touted its premium food offerings in its marketing, and that branding [was] now actually hurting them," observed a retail analyst. Some customers even amended the company's motto, making it "Whole Foods, Whole Paycheck."

Hit hard by the economic downturn, Whole Foods Market faced difficult questions. Should it hold the line on the premium positioning that had won it so much success in the past? Or should it cut prices and reposition itself to fit the leaner times? On the one hand, it could simply batten down the hatches and wait for the economic storm to pass. But a wait-and-see strategy made little sense—the newfound consumer frugality probably will last for years to come. At the other extreme, Whole Foods could reshuffle its product assortment, cut prices, and reposition downward to fit the new times. But that strategy would sacrifice most of what had made the upscale grocer unique over the years.

Faced with these alternatives, Whole Foods Market decided to stick with its core up-market positioning but subtly realign its value proposition to better meet the needs of recession-rattled customers. It set out to downplay the gourmet element of its positioning while playing up the real value of the healthy but exciting food it offers. First, rather than dropping its everyday prices across the board, Whole Foods lowered prices on many basic items that customers demand most and bolstered these savings by offering significant sales on selected other items. It

also started emphasizing its private-label brand, 365 Everyday Value.

Next, Whole Foods Market launched a new marketing program aimed at tempering the chain's high-price reputation, reconnecting with customers, and convincing them that Whole Foods Market was, in fact, an affordable place to shop. To help consumers see the value, it beefed up its communications about private-label and sale items using newsletters, coupons, and its Web site. It assigned workers to serve as "value tour guides" to escort shoppers around stores and point out value items. New ads featured headlines such as "No wallets were harmed in the buying of our 365 Everyday Value products," and "Sticker shock, but in a good way."

The new marketing efforts actually did more than simply promote more affordable merchandise. They worked to convince shoppers that Whole Foods Market's regular products and prices offer good value as well—that when it comes to quality food, price isn't everything. As one tour guide notes, wherever you go, you'll have to pay a premium for organic food. "Value means getting a good exchange for your money." Such conversations helped to shift customers' eyes off of price and back to value.

To strengthen customer relationships further in tighter times, Whole Foods Market also boosted its social media presence. It set up a Facebook page and dozens of Twitter accounts to address specific value and other topics related to every

▲ When the economy dipped, rather than cutting everyday prices, Whole Foods set out to convince shoppers that it was, in fact, an affordable place to shop. It even assigned workers to serve as "value tour guides," like the one above, to escort shoppers around stores pointing out value items.

Librado Romero /The New York Times/Redux Pictures

product category and every store. Videos on its Whole Tube YouTube channel advised customers to "waste not, want not." At the official Whole Foods Market blog—The Whole Story—customers learned about and exchanged views on organic and natural food, recipes, and other topics. Interestingly, customer conversations on this blog tended to focus more heavily on the "what you get" from Whole Foods Market than the "what you pay."

Customers more interested in the value side of the price-value equation could log onto The Whole Deal, an official blog that offers coupons, deals, budget-friendly recipes, and other things that help you make "wiser choices for your budget, the Earth, and your fellow Earthlings." Whole Foods also offered iPhone and iPod apps, providing more than 2,000 recipes using Whole Foods Market natural and organic products and highlighting meals that feed a family of four for less than $15.

How has the Whole Foods Market value realignment worked out? So far, so good. By 2010, sales and earnings were again growing at a healthy clip. By late-2011, stock prices, which hit a low of close to $8 in 2008, had climbed above $65. Regarding the move to value offerings, says Whole Foods Market's COO, "We did it early, we did it strong, and we've done it consistently." Customers now "give us credit for being more competitive and for meeting their needs in these times, and now they can see the better deals, the better pricing, the better choices."

Most important, however, Whole Foods Market has managed to realign its value proposition in a way that preserves all the things that have made it special to its customers through the years. In all, things aren't really much different inside a local Whole Foods Market these days. There are more sale items, and the private-label 365 Everyday Value brand is more prominently presented, but customers can still find the same alluring assortment of high-quality, flavorful, and natural foods wrapped in Whole Foods, Whole People, Whole Planet values. Thanks to the subtle shifts in its value strategy, however, customers might just appreciate the value side of the Whole Foods Market formula a little bit more.

Sources: Quotes and other information from Mike Duff, "Whole Foods Dropping Prices to Raise Its Prospects," *R&FF Retailer,* November 2009, p. 14; David Kesmodel, "Whole Foods Net Falls 31% in Slow Economy," *Wall Street Journal,* August 6, 2008, p. B1; Stuart Elliott, "With Shoppers Pinching Pennies, Some Big Retailers Get the Message," *New York Times,* April 13, 2009, p. B6; "Whole Web," *Progressive Grocer,* June 19, 2009, accessed at http://progressivegrocer.com; Annie Gasparro and Matt Jarzemsky, "Earnings: Whole Foods Boosts View as Net Rises 61%," *Wall Street Journal,* February 10, 2011, p. B4; "What Is It that Only I Can Do?" *Harvard Business Review,* January–February 2011, pp. 119–123; and information from http://blog.wholefoodsmarket.com, www.wholefoodsmarket.com/products/wholedeal/index.php, and www.wholefoodsmarket.com, accessed November 2011.

We've now seen that pricing decisions are subject to a complex array of customer, company, competitive, and environmental forces. To make things even more complex, a company does not set just a single price but rather a *pricing structure* that covers different items in its line. This pricing structure changes over time as products move through their life cycles. The company adjusts its prices to reflect changes in costs and demand and to account for variations in buyers and situations. As the competitive environment changes, the company considers when to initiate price changes and when to respond to them.

We now examine additional pricing approaches used in special pricing situations or to adjust prices to meet changing situations. We look in turn at *new-product pricing* for products in the introductory stage of the product life cycle, *product mix pricing* for related products in the product mix, *price adjustment tactics* that account for customer differences and changing situations, and strategies for initiating and responding to *price changes*.[10]

Author Comment ▶

Pricing new products can be especially challenging. Just think about all the things you'd need to consider in pricing a new cell phone, say the first Apple iPhone. Even more, you need to start thinking about the price—along with many other marketing considerations—at the very beginning of the design process.

New-Product Pricing Strategies

Pricing strategies usually change as the product passes through its life cycle. The introductory stage is especially challenging. Companies bringing out a new product face the challenge of setting prices for the first time. They can choose between two broad strategies: *market-skimming pricing* and *market-penetration pricing*.

Market-Skimming Pricing

Many companies that invent new products set high initial prices to *skim* revenues layer by layer from the market. Apple frequently uses this strategy, called **market-skimming pricing** (or **price skimming**). When Apple first introduced the iPhone, its initial price was

Market-skimming pricing (or price skimming)

Setting a high price for a new product to skim maximum revenues layer by layer from the segments willing to pay the high price; the company makes fewer but more profitable sales.

(apple)

Market skimming conditions

Market-penetration pricing

Setting a low price for a new product to attract a large number of buyers and a large market share.

as much as $599 per phone. The phones were purchased only by customers who really wanted the sleek new gadget and could afford to pay a high price for it. Six months later, Apple dropped the price to $399 for an 8GB model and $499 for the 16GB model to attract new buyers. Within a year, it dropped prices again to $199 and $299, respectively, and you can now buy an 8GB model for $49. In this way, Apple skimmed the maximum amount of revenue from the various segments of the market.

Market skimming makes sense only under certain conditions. First, the product's quality and image must support its higher price, and enough buyers must want the product at that price. Second, the costs of producing a smaller volume cannot be so high that they cancel the advantage of charging more. Finally, competitors should not be able to enter the market easily and undercut the high price.

Market-Penetration Pricing

Rather than setting a high initial price to skim off small but profitable market segments, some companies use **market-penetration pricing**. Companies set a low initial price to *penetrate* the market quickly and deeply—to attract a large number of buyers quickly and win a large market share. The high sales volume results in falling costs, allowing companies to cut their prices even further. For example, the giant Swedish retailer IKEA used penetration pricing to boost its success in the Chinese market:[11]

▲ **Penetration pricing: To lure famously frugal Chinese customers, IKEA slashed its prices. The strategy worked. Weekend crowds at its cavernous Beijing store are so big that employees need to use megaphones to keep them in control.**

Romain Degoul/REA/Redux Pictures

When IKEA first opened stores in China in 2002, people crowded in but not to buy home furnishings. Instead, they came to take advantage of the freebies—air conditioning, clean toilets, and even decorating ideas. Chinese consumers are famously frugal. When it came time to actually buy, they shopped instead at local stores just down the street that offered knockoffs of IKEA's designs at a fraction of the price. So to lure the finicky Chinese customers, IKEA slashed its prices in China to the lowest in the world, the opposite approach of many Western retailers there. By increasingly stocking its Chinese stores with China-made products, the retailer pushed prices on some items as low as 70 percent below prices in IKEA's outlets outside China. The penetration pricing strategy worked. IKEA now captures a 43 percent market share of China's fast-growing home wares market alone, and the sales of its 11 mammoth Chinese stores surged 23 percent last year. One store alone in Beijing draws nearly six million visitors annually. Weekend crowds are so big that employees need to use megaphones to keep them in control.

Several conditions must be met for this low-price strategy to work. First, the market must be highly price sensitive so that a low price produces more market growth. Second, production and distribution costs must decrease as sales volume increases. Finally, the low price must help keep out the competition, and the penetration pricer must maintain its low-price position. Otherwise, the price advantage may be only temporary.

Author Comment ▶

Most individual products are part of a broader product mix and must be priced accordingly. For example, Gillette prices its Fusion razors low. But once you buy the razor, you're a captive customer for its higher-margin replacement cartridges.

Product Mix Pricing Strategies

The strategy for setting a product's price often has to be changed when the product is part of a product mix. In this case, the firm looks for a set of prices that maximizes its profits on the total product mix. Pricing is difficult because the various products have related demand and costs and face different degrees of competition. We now take a closer look at the five product mix pricing situations summarized in ▶ **Table 9.1**: *product line*

▶ **Table 9.1**	Product Mix Pricing
Pricing Situation	**Description**
Product line pricing	Setting prices across an entire product line
Optional product pricing	Pricing optional or accessory products sold with the main product
Captive product pricing	Pricing products that must be used with the main product
By-product pricing	Pricing low-value by-products to get rid of or make money on them
Product bundle pricing	Pricing bundles of products sold together

Product line pricing

Setting the price steps between various products in a product line based on cost differences between the products, customer evaluations of different features, and competitors' prices.

Optional product pricing

The pricing of optional or accessory products along with a main product.

pricing, *optional product pricing*, *captive product pricing*, *by-product pricing*, and *product bundle pricing*.

Product Line Pricing

Companies usually develop product lines rather than single products. For example, Rossignol offers seven different collections of alpine skis of all designs and sizes, at prices that range from $150 for its junior skis, such as Fun Girl, to more than $1,100 for a pair from its Radical racing collection. It also offers lines of Nordic and backcountry skis, snowboards, and ski-related apparel. In **product line pricing**, management must determine the price steps to set between the various products in a line.

The price steps should take into account cost differences between products in the line. More importantly, they should account for differences in customer perceptions of the value of different features. ▶ For example, at a Mr. Clean car wash, you can choose from any of six wash packages, ranging from a basic exterior clean-only "Bronze" wash for $5; to an exterior clean, shine, and protect "Gold" package for $12; to an interior-exterior "Signature Shine" package for $27 that includes the works, from a thorough cleaning inside and out to a tire shine, underbody rust inhibitor, surface protectant, and even air freshener. The car wash's task is to establish perceived value differences that support the price differences.

▲ **Product line pricing:** Mr. Clean car washes offer a complete line of wash packages priced from $5 for the basic Bronze wash to $27 for the feature-loaded Mr. Clean Signature Shine package.

The Procter & Gamble Company

Optional Product Pricing

Many companies use **optional product pricing**—offering to sell optional or accessory products along with the main product. For example, a car buyer may choose to order a GPS navigation system and Bluetooth wireless communication. Refrigerators come with optional ice makers. And when you order a new PC, you can select from a bewildering array of processors, hard drives, docking systems, software options, and service plans. Pricing these options is a sticky problem. Companies must decide which items to include in the base price and which to offer as options.

Captive Product Pricing

Captive product pricing

Setting a price for products that must be used along with a main product, such as blades for a razor and games for a videogame console.

Companies that make products that must be used along with a main product are using **captive product pricing**. Examples of captive products are razor blade cartridges, videogames, and printer cartridges. Producers of the main products (razors, videogame consoles, and printers) often price them low and set high markups on the supplies. For example, when Sony first introduced its PS3 videogame console, priced at $499 and $599 for the regular and premium versions, respectively, it lost as much as $306 per unit sold. Sony hoped to recoup the losses through the sales of more lucrative PS3 games.

However, companies that use captive product pricing must be careful. Finding the right balance between the main product and captive product prices can be tricky. For example, it took more than four years and a major redesign before Sony broke even on the PS3 console.[12] Even more, consumers trapped into buying expensive captive products may come to resent the brand that ensnared them. This happened in the inkjet printer and cartridges industry, providing Kodak with a market opportunity.[13]

Most inkjet printer makers sell their printers at little or no profit. But once you own the printer, you're stuck buying their grossly overpriced, high-margin replacement ink cartridges. The price per ounce of inkjet printer ink can exceed the per-ounce price of an expensive perfume, premium champagne, or even caviar. Enter Kodak—with a unique solution. Kodak recently introduced its EasyShare printers with a revolutionary pricing strategy that has turned the entire inkjet printer industry upside-down. Kodak sells the printers at premium prices with no discounts and then sells the ink cartridges for less. It's a whole new concept in printer pricing and economics.

To reeducate consumers about printer pricing, Kodak launched a "Print and Prosper" marketing campaign, complete with a Web site that lets you calculate how much you're overpaying for ink with your current printer. The successful campaign has sent shockwaves through the inkjet printer industry, and other printer producers are now following Kodak's cheaper-cartridges strategy. As one observer concludes, Kodak's pricing "makes a world-rocking point about the razor-blades model that's lined the coffers of the inkjet industry for years. If you're mad as hell, you don't have to take it anymore."

By-product pricing

Setting a price for by-products to make the main product's price more competitive.

In the case of services, captive product pricing is called *two-part pricing*. The price of the service is broken into a *fixed fee* plus a *variable usage rate*. Thus, at Six Flags and other amusement parks, you pay a daily ticket or season pass charge plus additional fees for food and other in-park features.

By-Product Pricing

Producing products and services often generates by-products. If the by-products have no value and if getting rid of them is costly, this will affect pricing of the main product. Using **by-product pricing**, the company seeks a market for these by-products to help offset the costs of disposing of them and help make the price of the main product more competitive.

The by-products themselves can even turn out to be profitable—turning trash into cash. For example, Seattle's Woodland Park Zoo has learned that one of its major by-products—animal poo—can be an excellent source of extra revenue.[14]

What happens to all that poo at the zoo...

▲ By-product pricing: "There's green and money to be made in animal poop!" exclaims Dan Corum, the Woodland Zoo's enthusiastic Compost and Recycling Coordinator (also known as the Prince of Poo, the Emperor of Excrement, the GM of BM, or just plain Dr. Doo).

Courtesy of Biz Kid$ and Woodland Park Zoo

"What happens to all that poo at the zoo?" asks a recent video about the Woodland Park Zoo. Not long ago, the answer was that it had to be hauled away to the landfill at a cost of about $60,000 a year. But now, the zoo carefully collects all that poo, turns it into compost, and sells it under its Zoo Doo and Bedspread brands, pitched as "the most exotic and highly prized compost in the Pacific Northwest, composed of exotic species feces contributed by the zoo's non-primate herbivores." Customers can buy these coveted compost products by the bucket at the zoo's store. The zoo also sponsors annual Fecal Fests, where lucky lottery winners can buy the processed poo by the trash can or truck full. "There's green *and* money to be made in animal poop!" exclaims Dan Corum, the Woodland Zoo's enthusiastic compost and recycling coordinator (also known as the prince of poo, the emperor of excrement, the GM of BM, or just plain Dr. Doo). Selling Zoo Doo keeps it out of the landfill, so it's good for the planet. It's also good for the zoo, saving disposal costs and generating $15,000 to $20,000 in annual sales.

Product Bundle Pricing

Product bundle pricing
Combining several products and offering the bundle at a reduced price.

Using **product bundle pricing**, sellers often combine several products and offer the bundle at a reduced price. For example, fast-food restaurants bundle a burger, fries, and a soft drink at a "combo" price. Bath & Body Works offers "three-fer" deals on its soaps and lotions (such as three antibacterial soaps for $10). And Comcast, Time Warner, Verizon, and other telecommunications companies bundle TV service, phone service, and high-speed Internet connections at a low combined price. Price bundling can promote the sales of products consumers might not otherwise buy, but the combined price must be low enough to get them to buy the bundle.

Price Adjustment Strategies

Author Comment ▶
Setting the base price for a product is only the start. The company must then adjust the price to account for customer and situational differences. When was the last time you paid the full suggested retail price for something?

Companies usually adjust their basic prices to account for various customer differences and changing situations. Here we examine the seven price adjustment strategies summarized in ▶ **Table 9.2**: *discount and allowance pricing, segmented pricing, psychological pricing, promotional pricing, geographical pricing, dynamic pricing,* and *international pricing.*

Discount and Allowance Pricing

Discount
A straight reduction in price on purchases made during a stated period of time or in larger quantities.

Most companies adjust their basic price to reward customers for certain responses, such as paying bills early, volume purchases, and off-season buying. These price adjustments—called *discounts* and *allowances*—can take many forms.

One form of **discount** is a *cash discount,* a price reduction to buyers who pay their bills promptly. A typical example is "2/10, net 30," which means that although payment

▶ **Table 9.2**	Price Adjustments

Strategy	Description
Discount and allowance pricing	Reducing prices to reward customer responses such as paying early or promoting the product
Segmented pricing	Adjusting prices to allow for differences in customers, products, or locations
Psychological pricing	Adjusting prices for psychological effect
Promotional pricing	Temporarily reducing prices to spur short-run sales
Geographical pricing	Adjusting prices to account for the geographic location of customers
Dynamic pricing	Adjusting prices continually to meet the characteristics and needs of individual customers and situations
International pricing	Adjusting prices for international markets

is due within 30 days, the buyer can deduct 2 percent if the bill is paid within 10 days. A *quantity discount* is a price reduction to buyers who buy large volumes. A seller offers a *functional discount* (also called a *trade discount*) to trade-channel members who perform certain functions, such as selling, storing, and record keeping. A *seasonal discount* is a price reduction to buyers who buy merchandise or services out of season.

Allowance

A reduction from the list price for buyer actions such as trade-ins or promotional and sales support.

almost like a discount but for dealers

Allowances are another type of reduction from the list price. For example, *trade-in allowances* are price reductions given for turning in an old item when buying a new one. Trade-in allowances are most common in the automobile industry but are also given for other durable goods. *Promotional allowances* are payments or price reductions that reward dealers for participating in advertising and sales support programs.

Segmented Pricing

Segmented pricing

Selling a product or service at two or more prices, where the difference in prices is not based on differences in costs.

Companies will often adjust their basic prices to allow for differences in customers, products, and locations. In **segmented pricing**, the company sells a product or service at two or more prices, even though the difference in prices is not based on differences in costs.

Segmented pricing takes several forms. Under *customer-segment* pricing, different customers pay different prices for the same product or service. Museums and movie theaters, for example, may charge a lower admission for students and senior citizens. Under *product-form pricing*, different versions of the product are priced differently but not according to differences in their costs. ▶ For instance, a one-liter bottle (about 34 ounces) of Evian mineral water may cost $1.59 at your local supermarket. But a five-ounce aerosol can of Evian Brumisateur Mineral Water Spray moisturizer sells for a suggested retail price of $11.39 at beauty boutiques and spas. The water is all from the same source in the French Alps, and the aerosol packaging costs little more than the plastic bottles. Yet you pay about 5 cents an ounce for one form and $2.28 an ounce for the other.

local discount

Using *location-based pricing*, a company charges different prices for different locations, even though the cost of offering each location is the same. For instance, state universities charge higher tuition for out-of-state students, and theaters vary their seat prices because of audience preferences for certain locations. Tickets for a Saturday night performance of Green Day's *American Idiot* on Broadway start at $39 for a seat in the rear balcony, whereas orchestra center seats go for $199. Finally, using *time-based pricing*, a firm varies its price by the season, the month, the day, and even the hour. For example, movie theaters charge matinee pricing during the daytime, and resorts give weekend and seasonal discounts.

▲ **Product-form pricing:** Evian water in a one-liter bottle might cost you 5 cents an ounce at your local supermarket, whereas the same water might run $2.28 an ounce when sold in five-ounce aerosol cans as Evian Brumisateur Mineral Water Spray moisturizer.

Christopher Schall/Impact Photo

Psychological Pricing

Price says something about the product. For example, many consumers use price to judge quality. A $100 bottle of perfume may contain only $3 worth of scent, but some people are willing to pay the $100 because this price indicates something special.

In using **psychological pricing**, sellers consider the psychology of prices, not simply the economics. For example, consumers usually perceive higher-priced products as having higher quality. When they can judge the quality of a product by examining it or by calling on past experience with it, they use price less to judge quality. But when they cannot judge quality because they lack the information or skill, price becomes an important quality signal. For example, who's the better lawyer, one who charges $50 per hour or one who charges $500 per hour? You'd have to do a lot of digging into the respective lawyers' credentials to answer this question objectively; even then, you might not be able to judge accurately. Most of us would simply assume that the higher-priced lawyer is better.

Psychological pricing

Pricing that considers the psychology of prices, not simply the economics; the price says something about the product.

Reference prices

Prices that buyers carry in their minds and refer to when they look at a given product.

Another aspect of psychological pricing is **reference prices**—prices that buyers carry in their minds and refer to when looking at a given product. The reference price might be formed by noting current prices, remembering past prices, or assessing the buying situation. Sellers can influence or use these consumers' reference prices when setting price. For example, a grocery retailer might place its store brand of bran flakes and raisins cereal priced at $1.89 next to Kellogg's Raisin Bran priced at $3.20. Or a company might offer more expensive models that don't sell very well to make their less expensive but still-high-priced models look more affordable by comparison:[15]

> In the midst of the recent recession, Ralph Lauren was selling a "Ricky" alligator bag for $14,000, making its Tiffin Bag a steal at just $2,595. And Williams-Sonoma once offered a fancy bread maker for $279. Then it added a $429 model. The costly model flopped, but sales of the cheaper one doubled.

For most purchases, consumers don't have all the skill or information they need to figure out whether they are paying a good price. They don't have the time, ability, or inclination to research different brands or stores, compare prices, and get the best deals. Instead, they may rely on certain cues that signal whether a price is high or low. Interestingly, such pricing cues are often provided by sellers, in the form of sales signs, price-matching guarantees, loss-leader pricing, and other helpful hints.

Even small differences in price can signal product differences. For example, in one study, people were asked how likely they were to choose among LASIK eye surgery providers based only on the prices they charged: $299 or $300. The actual price difference was only $1, but the study found that the psychological difference was much greater. Preference ratings for the providers charging $300 were much higher. Subjects perceived the $299 price as significantly less, but the lower price also raised stronger concerns about quality and risk.[16] Some psychologists even argue that each digit has symbolic and visual qualities that should be considered in pricing. Thus, eight (8) is round and even and creates a soothing effect, whereas seven (7) is angular and creates a jarring effect.

Promotional pricing
Temporarily pricing products below the list price, and sometimes even below cost, to increase short-run sales.

Promotional Pricing

With **promotional pricing**, companies will temporarily price their products below list price—and sometimes even below cost—to create buying excitement and urgency. ▶ Promotional pricing takes several forms. A seller may simply offer *discounts* from normal prices to increase sales and reduce inventories. Sellers also use *special-event pricing* in certain seasons to draw more customers. Thus, large-screen TVs and other consumer electronics are promotionally priced in November and December to attract holiday shoppers into the stores. *Limited-time offers*, such as online *flash sales*, can create buying urgency and make buyers feel lucky to have gotten in on the deal.

Manufacturers sometimes offer *cash rebates* to consumers who buy the product from dealers within a specified time; the manufacturer sends the rebate directly to the customer. Rebates have been popular with automakers and producers of cell phones and small appliances, but they are also used with consumer packaged goods. Some manufacturers offer *low-interest financing*, *longer warranties*, or *free maintenance* to reduce the consumer's "price." This practice has become another favorite of the auto industry.

Promotional pricing, however, can have adverse effects. During most holiday seasons, for example, it's an all-out bargain war. Marketers carpet-bomb consumers with deals, causing buyer wear-out and pricing confusion. Used too frequently, price promotions can create "deal-prone" customers who wait until brands go on sale before buying them. In addition, constantly reduced prices can erode a brand's value in the eyes of customers.

Marketers sometimes become addicted to promotional pricing, especially in difficult economic times. They use price promotions as a quick fix instead of sweating through

▲ **Promotional pricing: Companies offer promotional prices to create buying excitement and urgency.**

(top left) AP Images/David Zalubowski; (top right) AP Images; (bottom left) AP Images/Jim Mone; (bottom right) AP Images/David Zalubowski

the difficult process of developing effective longer-term strategies for building their brands. But companies must be careful to balance short-term sales incentives against long-term brand building. "Companies should be very wary of risking their brands' perceived quality by resorting to deep and frequent price cuts," advises one analyst. "Some discounting is unavoidable, ... but marketers have to find ways to shore up their brand identity and brand equity during times of discount mayhem."[17] The point is that promotional pricing can be an effective means of generating sales for some companies in certain circumstances. But it can be damaging for other companies or if taken as a steady diet.

SPEED BUMP | LINKING THE CONCEPTS

Think about some of the companies and industries you deal with that are "addicted" to promotional pricing.

- Many industries have created "deal-prone" consumers through the heavy use of promotional pricing—fast food, automobiles, cell phones, airlines, tires, furniture, and others. Pick a company in one of these industries and suggest ways that it might deal with this problem.
- How does the concept of value relate to promotional pricing? Does promotional pricing add to or detract from customer value?

Geographical Pricing

A company also must decide how to price its products for customers located in different parts of the United States or the world. Should the company risk losing the business of more-distant customers by charging them higher prices to cover the higher shipping costs? Or should the company charge all customers the same prices regardless of location? We will look at five *geographical pricing* strategies for the following hypothetical situation:

> The Peerless Paper Company is located in Atlanta, Georgia, and sells paper products to customers all over the United States. The cost of freight is high and affects the companies from whom customers buy their paper. Peerless wants to establish a geographical pricing policy. It is trying to determine how to price a $10,000 order to three specific customers: Customer A (Atlanta), Customer B (Bloomington, Indiana), and Customer C (Compton, California).

One option is for Peerless to ask each customer to pay the shipping cost from the Atlanta factory to the customer's location. All three customers would pay the same factory price of $10,000, with Customer A paying, say, $100 for shipping; Customer B, $150; and Customer C, $250. Called *FOB-origin pricing*, this practice means that the goods are placed *free on board* (hence, *FOB*) a carrier. At that point the title and responsibility pass to the customer, who pays the freight from the factory to the destination. Because each customer picks up its own cost, supporters of FOB pricing feel that this is the fairest way to assess freight charges. The disadvantage, however, is that Peerless will be a high-cost firm to distant customers.

Uniform-delivered pricing is the opposite of FOB pricing. Here, the company charges the same price plus freight to all customers, regardless of their location. The freight charge is set at the average freight cost. Suppose this is $150. Uniform-delivered pricing therefore results in a higher charge to the Atlanta customer (who pays $150 freight instead of $100) and a lower charge to the Compton customer (who pays $150 instead of $250). Although the Atlanta customer would prefer to buy paper from another local paper company that uses FOB-origin pricing, Peerless has a better chance of capturing the California customer.

Zone pricing falls between FOB-origin pricing and uniform-delivered pricing. The company sets up two or more zones. All customers within a given zone pay a single total price; the more distant the zone, the higher the price. For example, Peerless might set up an East Zone and charge $100 freight to all customers in this zone, a Midwest Zone in which it charges $150, and a West Zone in which it charges $250. In this way, the customers within a given price zone receive no price advantage from the company. For example, customers in Atlanta and Boston pay the same total price to Peerless. The complaint, however, is that the Atlanta customer is paying part of the Boston customer's freight cost.

Using *basing-point pricing*, the seller selects a given city as a "basing point" and charges all customers the freight cost from that city to the customer location, regardless of the city from which the goods are actually shipped. For example, Peerless might set Chicago as the basing point and charge all customers $10,000 plus the freight from Chicago to their locations. This means that an Atlanta customer pays the freight cost from Chicago to Atlanta, even though the goods may be shipped from Atlanta. If all sellers used the same basing-point city, delivered prices would be the same for all customers, and price competition would be eliminated.

Finally, the seller who is anxious to do business with a certain customer or geographical area might use *freight-absorption pricing*. Using this strategy, the seller absorbs all or part of the actual freight charges to get the desired business. The seller might reason that if it can get more business, its average costs will decrease and more than compensate for its extra freight cost. Freight-absorption pricing is used for market penetration and to hold on to increasingly competitive markets.

Dynamic Pricing

Dynamic pricing
Adjusting prices continually to meet the characteristics and needs of individual customers and situations.

Throughout most of history, prices were set by negotiation between buyers and sellers. *Fixed price* policies—setting one price for all buyers—is a relatively modern idea that arose with the development of large-scale retailing at the end of the nineteenth century. Today, most prices are set this way. However, some companies are now reversing the fixed pricing trend. They are using **dynamic pricing**—adjusting prices continually to meet the characteristics and needs of individual customers and situations.

Dynamic pricing is especially prevalent online. The Internet seems to be taking us back to a new age of fluid pricing. Such pricing offers many advantages for marketers. For example, Internet sellers such as L.L.Bean, Amazon.com, or Dell can mine their databases to gauge a specific shopper's desires, measure his or her means, instantaneously tailor products to fit that shopper's behavior, and price products accordingly. They can change prices on the fly according to changes in demand or costs, adjusting what they charge for specific items on a day-by-day or even hour-by-hour basis. And many direct marketers monitor inventories, costs, and demand at any given moment and adjust prices instantly.

In the extreme, some companies customize their offers and prices based on the specific characteristics and behaviors of individual customers, mined from Web browsing and purchasing histories. These days, online offers and prices might well be based on what specific customers search for and buy, how much they pay for other purchases, and whether they might be willing and able to spend more. Consider this example:[18]

> Gazing online at that BMW might end up costing you. If, for example, you've recently completed online customization of a new BMW, searched for and purchased first class airfare to Paris, surfed for a new Bose Wave Radio, or visited Tiffany & Co.'s Web site, you could later get a somewhat pricier quote for a new sofa. By comparison, your cousin Ralph, who doesn't have a similar upscale online search and purchase history, might get a fire-sale quote when he goes after the same sofa. Or if he considers splurging on that Bose radio, the audio giant might induce him with an offer of five percent off and free shipping.

Although such dynamic pricing practices seem legally questionable, they're not. Dynamic pricing is legal as long as the companies do not discriminate based on age, sex, location, or other similar characteristics. Moreover, the practice goes both ways, and consumers often benefit from the Internet and dynamic pricing. A wealth of price comparison sites—such as Yahoo! Shopping, Bizrate.com, NexTag.com, Epinions.com, PriceGrabber.com, mySimon.com, and PriceScan.com—offer instant product and price comparisons from thousands of vendors. Epinions.com, for instance, lets shoppers browse by category or search for specific products and brands. It then searches the Web and reports back links to sellers offering the best prices along with customer reviews. In addition to simply finding the best product and the vendor with the best price for that product, customers armed with price information can often negotiate lower prices.

Consumers can also negotiate prices at online auction sites and exchanges. Suddenly the centuries-old art of haggling is back in vogue. Want to sell that antique pickle jar that's been collecting dust for generations? Post it on eBay or Craigslist. Want to name your own price for a hotel room or rental car? ▶ Visit Priceline.com or another reverse auction site. Want to bid on a ticket to a show by the rock band Paramore? Check out Ticketmaster.com, which offers an online auction service for concert tickets.

Dynamic pricing makes sense in many contexts—it adjusts prices according to market forces, and it often works to the benefit of the customer. But marketers need to be careful not to use dynamic pricing to take advantage of certain customer groups, thereby damaging important customer relationships.

▲ **Dynamic pricing: The Web seems to be taking us back in time to a new age of fluid pricing. At Priceline.com, you can "name your own price."**

Courtesy of Priceline.com Incorporated

International Pricing

Companies that market their products internationally must decide what prices to charge in different countries. In some cases, a company can set a uniform worldwide price. For example, Boeing sells its jetliners at about the same price everywhere, whether the buyer is in the United States, Europe, or a third-world country. However, most companies adjust their prices to reflect local market conditions and cost considerations.

The price that a company should charge in a specific country depends on many factors, including economic conditions, competitive situations, laws and regulations, and the nature of the wholesaling and retailing system. Consumer perceptions and preferences also may vary from country to country, calling for different prices. Or the company may have different marketing objectives in various world markets, which require changes in pricing strategy. For example, Nokia might introduce sophisticated, feature-rich cell phones into carefully segmented mature markets in highly developed countries—this would call for a market-skimming pricing strategy. By contrast, it might enter sizable but less affluent markets in developing countries with more basic phones, supported by a penetration-pricing strategy.

Costs play an important role in setting international prices. Travelers abroad are often surprised to find that goods that are relatively inexpensive at home may carry outrageously higher price tags in other countries. A pair of Levi's selling for $30 in the United States might go for $63 in Tokyo and $88 in Paris. A McDonald's Big Mac selling for a modest $3.79 in the United States might cost $7.20 in Norway, and an Oral-B toothbrush selling for $2.49 at home may cost $10 in China. Conversely, a Gucci handbag going for only $140 in Milan, Italy, might fetch $240 in the United States. In some cases, such *price escalation* may result from differences in selling strategies or market conditions. In most instances, however, it is simply a result of the higher costs of selling in another country—the additional costs of operations, product modifications, shipping and insurance, import tariffs and taxes, exchange-rate fluctuations, and physical distribution.

Price has become a key element in the international marketing strategies of companies attempting to enter emerging markets, such as China, India, and Brazil. ▶ Consider Unilever's pricing strategy for developing countries:[19]

▲ **International pricing: To lower prices in developing countries, Unilever developed smaller, more affordable packages that put the company's premier brands within the reach of cash-strapped customers.**
AFP/Getty Images

There used to be one way to sell a product in developing markets, if you bothered to sell there at all: Slap on a local label and market at premium prices to the elite. Unilever—the maker of such brands as Dove, Lipton, and Vaseline—changed that. Instead, it built a following among the world's poorest consumers by shrinking packages to set a price that even consumers living on $2 a day could afford. The strategy was forged about 25 years ago when Unilever's Indian subsidiary found its products out of reach for millions of Indians. To lower the price while making a profit, Unilever developed single-use packets for everything from shampoo to laundry detergent, costing just pennies a pack. The small, affordable packages put the company's premier brands within reach of the world's poor. Today, Unilever continues to woo cash-strapped customers with great success.

Thus, international pricing presents some special problems and complexities. We discuss international pricing issues in more detail in Chapter 15.

Author Comment ▶
When and how should a company change its price? What if costs rise, putting the squeeze on profits? What if the economy sags and customers become more price-sensitive? Or what if a major competitor raises or drops its prices? As Figure 9.5 suggests, companies face many price-changing options.

Price Changes

After developing their pricing structures and strategies, companies often face situations in which they must initiate price changes or respond to price changes by competitors.

Initiating Price Changes

In some cases, the company may find it desirable to initiate either a price cut or a price increase. In both cases, it must anticipate possible buyer and competitor reactions.

Initiating Price Cuts

Several situations may lead a firm to consider cutting its price. One such circumstance is excess capacity. Another is falling demand in the face of strong price competition or a weakened economy. In such cases, the firm may aggressively cut prices to boost sales and market share. But as the airline, fast-food, automobile, and other industries have learned in recent years, cutting prices in an industry loaded with excess capacity may lead to price wars as competitors try to hold onto market share.

A company may also cut prices in a drive to dominate the market through lower costs. Either the company starts with lower costs than its competitors, or it cuts prices in the hope of gaining market share that will further cut costs through larger volume. For example, Lenovo uses an aggressive low-cost, low-price strategy to increase its share of the PC market in developing countries.

Initiating Price Increases

A successful price increase can greatly improve profits. For example, if the company's profit margin is 3 percent of sales, a 1 percent price increase will boost profits by 33 percent if the sales volume is unaffected. A major factor in price increases is cost inflation. Rising costs squeeze profit margins and lead companies to pass cost increases along to customers. Another factor leading to price increases is overdemand: When a company cannot supply all that its customers need, it may raise its prices, ration products to customers, or both. Consider today's worldwide oil and gas industry.

▲ **Initiating price increases: When gasoline prices rise rapidly, angry consumers often accuse the major oil companies of enriching themselves by gouging customers.**

Louis DeLuca/Dallas Morning News/Corbis

When raising prices, the company must avoid being perceived as a *price gouger*. ▶ For example, when gasoline prices rise rapidly, angry customers often accuse the major oil companies of enriching themselves at the expense of consumers. Customers have long memories, and they will eventually turn away from companies or even whole industries that they perceive as charging excessive prices. In the extreme, claims of price gouging may even bring about increased government regulation.

There are some techniques for avoiding these problems. One is to maintain a sense of fairness surrounding any price increase. Price increases should be supported by company communications telling customers why prices are being raised.

Wherever possible, the company should consider ways to meet higher costs or demand without raising prices. For example, it might consider more cost-effective ways to produce or distribute its products. It can shrink the product or substitute less-expensive ingredients instead of raising the price, as ConAgra did in an effort to hold its Banquet frozen dinner prices at $1. Or it can "unbundle" its market offering, removing features, packaging, or services and separately pricing elements that were formerly part of the offer.[20]

Buyer Reactions to Price Changes

Customers do not always interpret price changes in a straightforward way. A price *increase*, which would normally lower sales, may have some positive meanings for buyers. For example, what would you think if Rolex *raised* the price of its latest watch model? On the one hand, you might think that the watch is even more exclusive or better made. On the other hand, you might think that Rolex is simply being greedy by charging what the traffic will bear.

Similarly, consumers may view a price *cut* in several ways. For example, what would you think if Rolex were to suddenly cut its prices? You might think that you are getting a better deal on an exclusive product. More likely, however, you'd think that quality had been reduced, and the brand's luxury image might be tarnished. A brand's price and image are often closely linked. A price change, especially a drop in price, can adversely affect how consumers view the brand.

Competitor Reactions to Price Changes

A firm considering a price change must worry about the reactions of its competitors as well as those of its customers. Competitors are most likely to react when the number of firms involved is small, when the product is uniform, and when the buyers are well informed about products and prices.

How can the firm anticipate the likely reactions of its competitors? The problem is complex because, like the customer, the competitor can interpret a company price cut in many ways. It might think the company is trying to grab a larger market share or that it's doing poorly and trying to boost its sales. Or it might think that the company wants the whole industry to cut prices to increase total demand.

The company must guess each competitor's likely reaction. If all competitors behave alike, this amounts to analyzing only a typical competitor. In contrast, if the competitors do not behave alike—perhaps because of differences in size, market shares, or policies—then separate analyses are necessary. However, if some competitors will match the price change, there is good reason to expect that the rest will also match it.

Responding to Price Changes

Here we reverse the question and ask how a firm should respond to a price change by a competitor. The firm needs to consider several issues: Why did the competitor change the price? Is the price change temporary or permanent? What will happen to the company's market share and profits if it does not respond? Are other competitors going to respond?

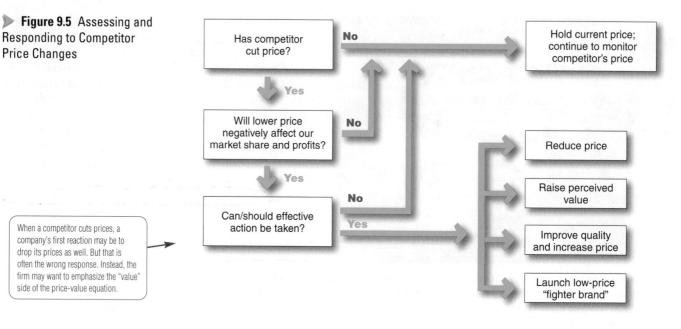

Figure 9.5 Assessing and Responding to Competitor Price Changes

When a competitor cuts prices, a company's first reaction may be to drop its prices as well. But that is often the wrong response. Instead, the firm may want to emphasize the "value" side of the price-value equation.

Besides these issues, the company must also consider its own situation and strategy and possible customer reactions to price changes.

Figure 9.5 shows the ways a company might assess and respond to a competitor's price cut. Suppose the company learns that a competitor has cut its price and decides that this price cut is likely to harm its sales and profits. It might simply decide to hold its current price and profit margin. The company might believe that it will not lose too much market share, or that it would lose too much profit if it reduced its own price. Or it might decide that it should wait and respond when it has more information on the effects of the competitor's price change. However, waiting too long to act might let the competitor get stronger and more confident as its sales increase.

If the company decides that effective action can and should be taken, it might make any of four responses. First, it could *reduce its price* to match the competitor's price. It may decide that the market is price sensitive and that it would lose too much market share to the lower-priced competitor. However, cutting the price will reduce the company's profits in the short run. Some companies might also reduce their product quality, services, and marketing communications to retain profit margins, but this will ultimately hurt long-run market share. The company should try to maintain its quality as it cuts prices.

Alternatively, the company might maintain its price but *raise the perceived value* of its offer. It could improve its communications, stressing the relative value of its product over that of the lower-price competitor. The firm may find it cheaper to maintain price and spend money to improve its perceived value than to cut price and operate at a lower margin. Or, the company might *improve* quality *and increase price*, moving its brand into a higher price-value position. The higher quality creates greater customer value, which justifies the higher price. In turn, the higher price preserves the company's higher margins.

Finally, the company might *launch a low-price "fighter brand"*—adding a lower-price item to the line or creating a separate lower-price brand. This is necessary if the particular market segment being lost is price sensitive and will not respond to arguments of higher quality. Starbucks did this when it acquired Seattle's Best Coffee, a brand positioned with

▲ **Fighter brands:** Starbucks has positioned its Seattle's Best Coffee unit to compete more directly with the "mass-premium" brands sold by Dunkin' Donuts, McDonald's, and other lower-priced competitors.

AP Images/Eric Risberg

"approachable-premium," working class appeal compared to the more full-premium, professional appeal of the main Starbucks brand. Seattle's Best coffee is generally cheaper than the parent Starbucks brand. As such, at retail, it competes more directly with Dunkin' Donuts, McDonald's, and other mass-premium brands through its franchise outlets and through partnerships with Subway, Burger King, Delta, AMC theaters, Royal Caribbean cruise lines, and others. On supermarket shelves, it competes with store brands and other mass-premium coffees such as Folgers Gourmet Selections and Millstone.[21]

To counter store brands and other low-price entrants in a tighter economy, P&G turned a number of its brands into fighter brands. Luvs disposable diapers give parents "premium leakage protection for less than pricier brands." And P&G offers popular budget-priced basic versions of several of its major brands. For example, Charmin Basic "provides the perfect balance of performance and price," and Bounty Basic is "practical, not pricey." However, companies must use caution when introducing fighter brands, as such brands can tarnish the image of the main brand. In addition, although they may attract budget buyers away from lower-priced rivals, they can also take business away from the firm's higher-margin brands.

Public Policy and Pricing

Author Comment ▶
Pricing decisions are often constrained by social and legal issues. For example, think about the pharmaceuticals industry. Are rapidly rising prescription drug prices justified? Or are the drug companies unfairly lining their pockets by gouging consumers who have few alternatives? Should the government step in?

Price competition is a core element of our free-market economy. In setting prices, companies usually are not free to charge whatever prices they wish. Many federal, state, and even local laws govern the rules of fair play in pricing. In addition, companies must consider broader societal pricing concerns. In setting their prices, for example, pharmaceutical firms must balance their development costs and profit objectives against the sometimes life-and-death needs of drug consumers.

The most important pieces of legislation affecting pricing are the Sherman Act, the Clayton Act, and the Robinson-Patman Act, initially adopted to curb the formation of monopolies and regulate business practices that might unfairly restrain trade. Because these federal statutes can be applied only to interstate commerce, some states have adopted similar provisions for companies that operate locally.

▶ **Figure 9.6** shows the major public policy issues in pricing. These include potentially damaging pricing practices within a given level of the channel (price-fixing and predatory pricing) and across levels of the channel (retail price maintenance, discriminatory pricing, and deceptive pricing).[22]

▶ **Figure 9.6** Public Policy Issues in Pricing

Source: Based on Dhruv Grewal and Larry D. Compeau, "Pricing and Public Policy: A Research Agenda and Overview of the Special Issue," *Journal of Public Policy and Marketing*, Spring 1999, pp. 3–10.

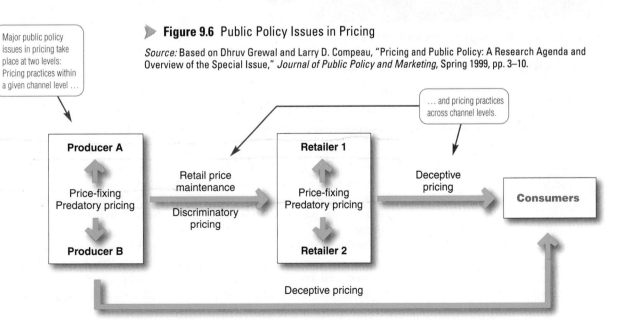

Pricing within Channel Levels

Federal legislation on *price-fixing* states that sellers must set prices without talking to competitors. Otherwise, price collusion is suspected. Price-fixing is illegal per se—that is, the government does not accept any excuses for price-fixing. As such, companies found guilty of these practices can receive heavy fines. Recently, governments at the state and national levels have been aggressively enforcing price-fixing regulations in industries ranging from gasoline, insurance, and concrete to credit cards, CDs, and computer chips. Price-fixing is also prohibited in many international markets. For example, European Union regulators recently fined consumer products giants Unilever and P&G a combined $456 million for fixing laundry detergent prices in eight EU countries. The two competitors agreed not to decrease their prices when making their packages smaller and then later agreed to jointly raise prices.[23]

Sellers are also prohibited from using *predatory pricing*—selling below cost with the intention of punishing a competitor or gaining higher long-run profits by putting competitors out of business. This protects small sellers from larger ones who might sell items below cost temporarily or in a specific locale to drive them out of business. The biggest problem is determining just what constitutes predatory pricing behavior. Selling below cost to unload excess inventory is not considered predatory; selling below cost to drive out competitors is. Thus, the same action may or may not be predatory depending on intent, and intent can be very difficult to determine or prove.

▲ **Predatory pricing: Some critics charge that big-box stores like Best Buy price CDs as loss leaders to drive music competitors out of business. But is it predatory pricing or just plain good marketing?**

AP Images/Reed Saxon

In recent years, several large and powerful companies have been accused of predatory pricing. However, turning an accusation into a lawsuit can be difficult. ▶ For example, many music retailers have accused Walmart and Best Buy of predatory CD pricing. Since 2007 alone, CD sales have plummeted almost 20 percent each year, putting music-only retailers such as Tower Records, Musicland, and a megamall full of small mom-and-pop music shops out of business. Many industry experts attribute slumping CD sales to new music distribution strategies—mainly digital downloads. Others, however, blame the big-box stores for pricing CDs as loss leaders to drive competitors out of business. Low CD prices don't hurt Walmart—it derives less than 2 percent of its sales from CDs, and low-priced CDs pull customers into stores. Once there, they buy other, higher-margin products. Such pricing tactics, however, cut deeply into the profits of music retailers. Still, no predatory pricing charges have ever been filed against Walmart or Best Buy. It would be extremely difficult to prove that such loss-leader CD pricing is purposefully predatory as opposed to just plain good marketing.[24]

Pricing across Channel Levels

The Robinson-Patman Act seeks to prevent unfair *price discrimination* by ensuring that sellers offer the same price terms to customers at a given level of trade. For example, every retailer is entitled to the same price terms from a given manufacturer, whether the retailer is Sears or your local bicycle shop. However, price discrimination is allowed if the seller can prove that its costs are different when selling to different retailers—for example, that it costs less per unit to sell a large volume of bicycles to Sears than to sell a few bicycles to the local dealer.

The seller can also discriminate in its pricing if the seller manufactures different qualities of the same product for different retailers. The seller has to prove that these differences are proportional. Price differentials may also be used to "match competition" in "good faith," provided the price discrimination is temporary, localized, and defensive rather than offensive.

Laws also prohibit *retail (or resale) price maintenance*—a manufacturer cannot require dealers to charge a specified retail price for its product. Although the seller can propose a manufacturer's *suggested* retail price to dealers, it cannot refuse to sell to a dealer that takes independent pricing action nor can it punish the dealer by shipping late or denying advertising allowances. For example, the Florida attorney general's office investigated Nike for allegedly fixing the retail price of its shoes and clothing. It was concerned that Nike might be withholding items from retailers who were not selling its most expensive shoes at prices the company considered suitable.

Deceptive pricing occurs when a seller states prices or price savings that mislead consumers or are not actually available to consumers. This might involve bogus reference or comparison prices, as when a retailer sets artificially high "regular" prices and then announces "sale" prices close to its previous everyday prices. For example, Overstock .com recently came under scrutiny for inaccurately listing manufacturer's suggested retail prices, often quoting them higher than the actual price. Such comparison pricing is widespread.

Although comparison pricing claims are legal if they are truthful, the FTC's *Guides Against Deceptive Pricing* warn sellers not to advertise (1) a price reduction unless it is a savings from the usual retail price, (2) "factory" or "wholesale" prices unless such prices are what they are claimed to be, and (3) comparable value prices on imperfect goods.[25]

Other deceptive pricing issues include *scanner fraud* and price confusion. The widespread use of scanner-based computer checkouts has led to increasing complaints of retailers overcharging their customers. Most of these overcharges result from poor management, such as a failure to enter current or sale prices into the system. Other cases, however, involve intentional overcharges.

Many federal and state statutes regulate against deceptive pricing practices. For example, the Automobile Information Disclosure Act requires automakers to attach a statement on new vehicle windows stating the manufacturer's suggested retail price, the prices of optional equipment, and the dealer's transportation charges. However, reputable sellers go beyond what is required by law. Treating customers fairly and making certain that they fully understand prices and pricing terms is an important part of building strong and lasting customer relationships.

REST STOP | REVIEWING THE CONCEPTS

MyMarketingLab

Now that you have completed the chapter, return to www.mymktlab.com to experience and apply the concepts and to explore the additional study materials for this chapter.

CHAPTER REVIEW AND KEY TERMS

Objectives Review

Before you put pricing in the rearview mirror, let's review the important concepts. *Price* can be defined as the sum of all the values that customers give up in order to gain the benefits of having or using a product or service. Pricing decisions are subject to an incredibly complex array of company, environmental, and competitive forces.

OBJECTIVE 1 **Identify the three major pricing strategies and discuss the importance of understanding customer-value perceptions, company costs, and competitor strategies when setting prices.** (pp 257–264)

A price is the sum of all the values that customers give up in order to gain the benefits of having or using a product or service. The three major pricing strategies are customer value-based pricing, cost-based pricing, and competition-based pricing. Good pricing begins with a complete understanding of the value that a product or service creates for customers and setting a price that captures that value.

Customer perceptions of the product's value set the ceiling for prices. If customers perceive that the price is greater than the product's value, they will not buy the product. At the other extreme, company and product costs set the floor for prices. If the company prices the product below its costs, its profits will suffer. Between these two extremes, consumers will base their judgments of a product's value on the prices that competitors charge for similar products. Thus, in setting prices, companies need to consider all three factors—customer-perceived value, costs, and competitors' pricing strategies.

Costs are an important consideration in setting prices. However, cost-based pricing is often product driven. The company designs what it considers to be a good product and sets a price that covers costs plus a target profit. If the price turns out to be too high, the company must settle for lower markups or lower sales, both resulting in disappointing profits. Value-based pricing reverses this process. The company assesses customer needs and value perceptions and then sets a target price to match targeted value. The targeted value and price then drive decisions about product design and what costs can be incurred. As a result, price is set to match customers' perceived value.

OBJECTIVE 2 **Identify and define the other important external and internal factors affecting a firm's pricing decisions.** (pp 264–270)

Other *internal* factors that influence pricing decisions include the company's overall marketing strategy, objectives, and marketing mix, as well as organizational considerations. Price is only one element of the company's broader marketing strategy. If the company has selected its target market and positioning carefully, then its marketing mix strategy, including price, will be fairly straightforward. Common pricing objectives might include customer retention and building profitable customer relationships, preventing competition, supporting resellers and gaining their support, or avoiding government intervention. Price decisions must be coordinated with product design, distribution, and promotion decisions to form a consistent and effective marketing program. Finally, in order to coordinate pricing goals and decisions, management must decide who within the organization is responsible for setting price.

Other *external* pricing considerations include the nature of the market and demand, as well as environmental factors such as the economy, reseller needs, and government actions. Ultimately, the customer decides whether the company has set the right price. The customer weighs the price against the perceived values of using the product—if the price exceeds the sum of the values, consumers will not buy. So the company must understand concepts like demand curves (the price-demand relationship) and price elasticity (consumer sensitivity to prices).

Economic conditions can have a major impact on pricing decisions. The recent Great Recession caused consumers to rethink the price-value equation. Marketers have responded by increasing their emphasis on value-for-the-money pricing strategies. Even in tough economic times, however, consumers do not buy based on prices alone. Thus, no matter what price they charge—low or high—companies need to offer superior value for the money.

OBJECTIVE 3 **Describe the major strategies for pricing new products.** (pp 270–271)

Pricing is a dynamic process. Companies design a *pricing structure* that covers all their products. They change this structure over time and adjust it to account for different customers and situations. Pricing strategies usually change as a product passes through its life cycle. In pricing innovative new products, a company can use *market-skimming pricing* by initially setting high prices to *skim* the maximum amount of revenue from various segments of the market. Or it can use *market-penetrating pricing* by setting a low initial price to penetrate the market deeply and win a large market share.

OBJECTIVE 4 **Explain how companies find a set of prices that maximizes the profits from the total product mix.** (pp 271–274)

When the product is part of a product mix, the firm searches for a set of prices that will maximize the profits from the total mix. In *product line pricing*, the company decides on price steps for the entire set of products it offers. In addition, the company must set prices for *optional products* (optional or accessory products included with the main product), *captive products* (products that are required for use of the main product), *by-products* (waste or residual products produced when making the main product), and *product bundles* (combinations of products at a reduced price).

OBJECTIVE 5 **Discuss how companies adjust their prices to take into account different types of customers and situations.** (pp 274–280)

Companies apply a variety of *price adjustment strategies* to account for differences in consumer segments and situations. One is *discount and allowance pricing*, whereby the company establishes cash, quantity, functional, or seasonal discounts, or varying types of allowances. A second strategy is *segmented pricing*, where the company sells a product at two or more prices to accommodate different customers, product forms, locations, or times. Sometimes companies consider more than economics in their pricing decisions, such as using *psychological pricing* to better communicate a product's intended position. In *promotional pricing*, a company offers discounts or temporarily sells a product below list price as a special event, sometimes even selling below cost as a loss leader.

Another approach is *geographical pricing*, whereby the company decides how to price to near or distant customers. Finally, *international pricing* means that the company adjusts its price to meet different conditions and expectations in different world markets.

▶ **OBJECTIVE 6 Discuss the key issues related to initiating and responding to price changes.** (pp 280–285)

When a firm considers initiating a *price change*, it must consider customers' and competitors' reactions. There are different implications to *initiating price cuts* and *initiating price increases*. Buyer reactions to price changes are influenced by the meaning customers see in the price change. Competitors' reactions flow from a set reaction policy or a fresh analysis of each situation.

There are also many factors to consider in responding to a competitor's price changes. The company that faces a price change initiated by a competitor must try to understand the competitor's intent as well as the likely duration and impact of the change. If a swift reaction is desirable, the firm should preplan its reactions to different possible price actions by competitors. When facing a competitor's price change, the company might sit tight, reduce its own price, raise perceived quality, improve quality and raise price, or launch a fighting brand.

Key Terms

Objective 1
Price (p 257)
Customer value-based pricing (p 258)
Good-value pricing (p 259)
Value-added pricing (p 260)
Cost-based pricing (p 260)
Fixed costs (overhead) (p 262)
Variable costs (p 262)
Total costs (p 262)
Cost-plus pricing (markup pricing) (p 262)
Break-even pricing (target return pricing) (p 262)
Competition-based pricing (p 263)

Objective 2
Target costing (p 265)
Demand curve (p 266)
Price elasticity (p 267)

Objective 3
Market-skimming pricing (price skimming) (p 270)
Market-penetration pricing (p 271)

Objective 4
Product line pricing (p 272)
Optional product pricing (p 272)

Captive product pricing (p 273)
By-product pricing (p 273)
Product bundle pricing (p 274)

Objective 5
Discount (p 274)
Allowance (p 275)
Segmented pricing (p 275)
Psychological pricing (p 275)
Reference prices (p 275)
Promotional pricing (p 276)
Dynamic pricing (p 278)

DISCUSSION AND CRITICAL THINKING

Discussion Questions

1. What is price? Discuss factors marketers must consider when setting price. (AACSB: Communication; Reflective Thinking)
2. Name and describe the two types of value-based pricing methods. (AACSB: Communication)
3. Discuss the impact of the economy on a company's pricing strategies. (AACSB: Communication)
4. Compare and contrast market-skimming and market-penetration pricing strategies. When would each be appropriate? (AACSB: Communication)

5. Define *captive product pricing* and *two-part pricing* and give examples of each. What should marketers be aware of when using this pricing strategy? (AACSB: Communication; Reflective Thinking)
6. Why do marketers charge customers different prices for the same product or service? Explain how this type of pricing is implemented and the conditions under which it is effective. (AACSB: Communication)

Critical Thinking Exercises

1. In a small group, discuss your perceptions of value and how much you are willing to pay for the following products: automobiles, frozen dinners, jeans, and athletic shoes. Are there differences of opinion among members of your group? Explain why those differences exist. Discuss some examples of brands of these products that are positioned to deliver different value to consumers. (AACSB: Communication; Reflective Thinking)

2. Find estimates of price elasticity for a variety of consumer goods and services. Explain what price elasticities of 0.5 and 2.4 mean (Note: These are absolute values, as price elasticity is usually negative). (AACSB: Communication; Reflective Thinking)

3. In a small group, determine the costs associated with offering an online MBA degree in addition to a traditional MBA degree at a university. Which costs are fixed and which are variable? Determine the tuition (that is, price) to charge for a three-credit course in this degree program. Which pricing method is your group using to determine the price? (AACSB: Communication; Reflective Thinking)

MINICASES AND APPLICATIONS

Marketing Technology   Shop for a Doc

Would you shop around for the best price on a medical procedure? Most patients do not know the price of a medical procedure and many might not care because they think insurance will cover it. But that is not always the case. Many patients are paying out of their own pockets for their health care. However, health care costs and doctors' prices are now more transparent thanks to the Internet. Several Web sites arm patients with cost information and others allow them to make price comparisons in their areas. They might even get a coupon for a price reduction from a participating provider.

1. Try your own hand at health care shopping. For example, go to www.OutOfPocket.com to determine the average cost for a colonoscopy. Using a source such as www.NewChoiceHealth.com, determine the cost for a colonoscopy in your city and in a nearby city. What is the most and least expensive price in each city? Are prices comparable to the national average? Why are there differences or similarities in the range of prices for the two cities? (AACSB: Communication; Use of IT; Reflective Thinking)

2. Health care providers offer price deals through these types of Web sites. Debate the likelihood of consumers taking advantage of Internet price discounts for medical care. (AACSB: Communication; Reflective Thinking)

Marketing Ethics   Telephone Cramming

Have you ever tried to figure out what all those charges are on a phone bill? Not all of them are from your phone service provider. A study by a Congressional committee reported that $2 billion a year in "mystery fees" appear on consumers' landline phone bills—a practice called *cramming*. Although it is illegal for a phone company or a third party to tack unauthorized fees onto landline phone bills, it is still happening. That prompted the Federal Communications Commission to propose new rules requiring companies to disclose charges more clearly so consumers can spot them. The agency would like to see the fees listed in a separate section of customers' bills that will also include the FCC's contact information for filing complaints. In addition, the agency proposed that companies should provide alerts to wireless customers when they are approaching their monthly voice and data limits, as problems are creeping into wireless phone bills as well. Do you remember what happened the first time you exceeded your texting limit? If you don't, and if your parents paid the bill, they do remember!

1. Look at a phone bill for the same service over several months. How does the service provider price this service? Do you see any suspicious charges such as any of those listed by the FCC at *www.ftc.gov/bcp/edu/pubs/consumer/products/pro18.shtm*? Suggest ways to price this service that will make it easier for customers to understand but also allow the company to make a reasonable profit. (AACSB: Communication; Reflective Thinking)

2. How can a third-party vendor place a charge on a phone bill, authorized or unauthorized? Do phone companies benefit from allowing third-party vendor billing? Research this issue and discuss whether or not this should be allowed. (AACSB: Communication; Reflective Thinking; Ethical Reasoning)

Marketing by the Numbers   Is Netflix Crazy or Savvy?

Price increases are always a thorny issue with consumers, and Netflix, the video streaming and DVD-by-mail giant, set off a firestorm by announcing a 60 percent price increase on its most affordable rental plan. Until recently, for $9.99 per month, customers were able to rent one DVD at a time and enjoy unlimited streaming over the Internet. That same service now costs

$15.98 per month, a combination of an existing $7.99-a-month streaming-only plan with a new $7.99-a-month DVD-only plan that allows customers to receive one disc at a time via mail. Because of this change, customers have either had to ante up to continue with the same level of service or step down to one of the more limited services priced at $7.99 per month. Analysts predict that many customers will switch to the streaming-only option, which reduces variable costs for Netflix due to postage savings. However, a Netflix spokesperson indicated that the DVD format will be viable for a while yet. The company better hope that's true because the company needs this product to generate considerable funds to finance its investments in online movie and television show rights.

1. Refer to Appendix 3, Marketing by the Numbers, culate the monthly contribution Netflix realizes fr subscriber at the price of $9.99 per month and $15.98 p month, respectively. Assume average variable costs per customer are $3.50 per month, which do not change with the price increase. How many disgruntled customers can Netflix lose before profitability is affected negatively? For this exercise, assume all of Netflix's 23 million customers are subscribers of the DVD/streaming hybrid plan. (AACSB: Communications; Analytic Reasoning)

2. Is this a smart move by Netflix? Discuss the pros and cons of such a drastic price increase. (AACSB: Communication; Reflective Thinking)

Video Case   Hammerpress

Printing paper goods may not sound like the best business to get into these days, but Hammerpress is nonetheless carving out a niche in this old industry. And they're doing it by returning to old technology. Most of today's printing firms use computer-driven graphic design techniques and printing processes. But Hammerpress creates greeting cards, calendars, and business cards that are hand-crafted by professional artists and printed using traditional letterpress technology.

When it comes to competing, this old-fashioned process presents both opportunities and challenges. While Hammerpress's products certainly stand out as works of art, the cost for producing such goods is considerably higher than the industry average. This video illustrates how Hammerpress employs dynamic pricing techniques to meet the needs of various customer segments and thrive in a competitive environment.

After viewing the video featuring Hammerpress, answer the following questions:

1. How does Hammerpress employ the concept of dynamic pricing?
2. Discuss Hammerpress in relation to the three major pricing strategies. Which of these three strategies is the company's core strategy?
3. Does it make sense for Hammerpress to compete in product categories where the market dictates a price that is not profitable for the company? Explain.

Company Cases   3 Target / 9 Burt's Bees

See Appendix 1 for cases appropriate for this chapter. **Case 3, Target: From "Expect More" to "Pay Less."** Changes in the marketing environment lead Target to make big changes in its marketing mix. **Case 9, Burt's Bees: Willfully Overpriced.** By pricing products above the market average, Burt's Bees gets customers' attention—and business.

10 Marketing Channels

Delivering Customer Value

CHAPTER ROAD MAP

Objective Outline

▷ **OBJECTIVE 1** Explain why companies use marketing channels and discuss the functions these channels perform. Supply Chains and the Value Delivery Network (292–293); The Nature and Importance of Marketing Channels (293–296)

▷ **OBJECTIVE 2** Discuss how channel members interact and how they organize to perform the work of the channel. Channel Behavior and Organization (296–303)

▷ **OBJECTIVE 3** Identify the major channel alternatives open to a company. Channel Design Decisions (303–307)

▷ **OBJECTIVE 4** Explain how companies select, motivate, and evaluate channel members. Channel Management Decisions (307–309)

▷ **OBJECTIVE 5** Discuss the nature and importance of marketing logistics and integrated supply chain management. Marketing Logistics and Supply Chain Management (310–317)

Previewing the Concepts

We now arrive at the third marketing mix tool—distribution. Firms rarely work alone in creating value for customers and building profitable customer relationships. Instead, most are only a single link in a larger supply chain and marketing channel. As such, an individual firm's success depends not only on how well *it* performs but also on how well its *entire marketing channel* competes with competitors' channels. The first part of this chapter explores the nature of marketing channels and the marketer's channel design and management decisions. We then examine physical distribution—or logistics—an area that is growing dramatically in importance and sophistication. In the next chapter, we'll look more closely at two major channel intermediaries: retailers and wholesalers.

We start by looking at a company whose groundbreaking, customer-centered distribution strategy took it to the top of its industry.

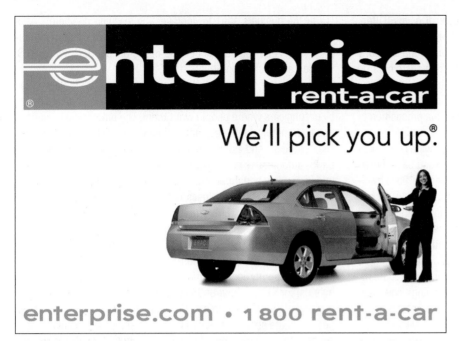

▲ **While competitors such as Hertz and Avis focused on serving travelers at airports, Enterprise opened off-airport, neighborhood locations that provided short-term car-replacement rentals for people whose cars were wrecked, stolen, or being serviced.**

First Stop

Enterprise: Leaving Car-Rental Competitors in the Rearview Mirror

Quick, which rental-car company is number one? Chances are good that you said Hertz. Okay, who's number two? That must be Avis, you say. After all, for years Avis's advertising said, "We're #2, so we try harder!" But if you said Hertz or Avis, you're about to be surprised. By any measure—most revenues, employees, transactions, or number of vehicles—the number-one rental-car company in the world is Enterprise Holdings, which owns and operates the Enterprise Rent-A-Car, Alamo Rent A Car, and National Car Rental brands. Even more, this is no recent development. Enterprise left number-two Hertz in its rearview mirror in the late 1990s and has never looked back.

For many years, the Hertz brand was number one in airport car rentals. However, with all of its combined brands and markets, Enterprise Holdings now captures 48 percent of the total rental-car market, with Hertz a distant second at 20 percent. What's more, by all estimates, the privately owned Enterprise is much more profitable as well.

How did Enterprise become such a powerful industry leader? The company might argue that it was through better prices or better marketing. But what contributed most to Enterprise taking the lead was an industry-changing, customer-driven distribution strategy. While competitors such as Hertz and Avis focused on serving travelers at airports, Enterprise developed a new distribution doorway to a large and untapped segment. It opened off-airport, neighborhood locations that provided short-term car-replacement rentals for people whose cars were wrecked, stolen, or being serviced or for people who simply wanted a different car for a short trip or a special occasion.

It all started more than half a century ago when Enterprise founder Jack Taylor discovered an unmet customer need. He was working at a St. Louis auto dealership, and customers often asked him where they could get a replacement car when theirs was in the shop for repairs or body work. To meet this need, Taylor opened a car-leasing business. But rather than competing head-on with the likes of Hertz and Avis, which served travelers at airports, Taylor located his rental offices in center-city and neighborhood areas, closer to his target customers. These locations also gave Taylor a cost advantage: Property rents were lower, and he didn't have to pay airport taxes and fees.

This groundbreaking distribution strategy worked, and the business grew quickly. As the Taylor family opened multiple locations in St. Louis and other cities, they renamed the business Enterprise Rent-A-Car after the U.S. Navy aircraft carrier on which Jack Taylor had served as a naval aviator. Enterprise continued to focus steadfastly on what it called the "home city" market, primarily serving customers who'd been in wrecks or whose cars were being serviced. Enterprise branch managers developed strong relationships with local auto insurance adjusters, dealership sales and service personnel, and body shops and service garages, making Enterprise a popular neighborhood rental-car provider.

> Thanks to an industry-changing, customer-driven distribution strategy, Enterprise left number-two Hertz in its rearview mirror more than a decade ago and has never looked back.

Customers in the home city market had special needs. Often, they were at the scene of a wreck or at a repair shop and had no way to get to an Enterprise office to pick up a rental car. So the company came up with another game-changing idea—picking customers up wherever they happen to be and bringing them back to the rental office. Hence, the tagline: "Pick Enterprise. We'll Pick You Up," which remains the Enterprise Rent-A-Car brand's main value proposition to this day.

By the late 1980s, Enterprise had a large nationwide network of company-owned, off-airport locations. From this strong base, Enterprise began expanding its distribution system in the mid-1990s by directly challenging Hertz and Avis in the on-airport market. A decade later, it had set up operations in 240 airports in North America and Europe. Then, in late 2007, the Taylor family purchased the Vanguard Car Rental Group, which owned the National and Alamo brands. National focused on the corporate-negotiated airport market, whereas Alamo served primarily the leisure traveler airport market.

With the Vanguard acquisition, Enterprise Holdings now captures a more than 31 percent share of the airport market, putting it ahead of Avis Budget Group and Hertz. That, combined with its share of the off-airport market, makes Enterprise Holdings the runaway leader in overall car rentals. It now operates 7,700 locations in the United States and four other countries.

Another secret to Enterprise's success is its passion for creating customer satisfaction. To measure satisfaction, Enterprise developed what it calls its ESQi (Enterprise Service Quality index). The company calls some two million customers a year and asks a simple question: "Were you completely satisfied with the service?" Enterprise managers don't get promoted unless they keep customers *completely* satisfied. It's as simple as that. If customer feedback is bad, "we call it going to ESQi jail," says an Enterprise human resources manager.

"Until the numbers start to improve, you're going nowhere." As a result, for 11 of the past 12 years, customers have rated the Enterprise Rent-A-Car brand number one in the annual J. D. Power U.S. Car Rental Satisfaction Study.

Looking ahead, rather than resting on its laurels, Enterprise Rent-A-Car continues to seek better ways to keep customers happy by getting cars where people want them. The enterprising company has now motored into yet another innovative distribution venue— "car sharing" and hourly rentals—called WeCar. This operation parks automobiles at convenient locations on college campuses and in densely populated urban areas, where residents often don't own cars and where business commuters would like to have occasional car access. Enterprise is also targeting businesses that want to have WeCar vehicles available in their parking lots for commuting employees to use. WeCar members pay $35 for an annual membership fee, depending on the location. They can then rent conveniently located, fuel-efficient cars (mostly Toyota Prius hybrids) for $10 per hour or $60 to $75 for the day; the rate includes gas and a 200-mile allotment. Renting a WeCar vehicle is a simple get-in-and-go operation. Just pass your member key fob over a sensor to unlock the car, open the glove box, and enter a PIN to release the car key.

Thus, Enterprise Holdings continues to move ahead aggressively with its winning distribution strategy. Says Andy Taylor, founder Jack's son and now long-time CEO, "We own the high ground in this business and we aren't going to give it up. As the dynamics of our industry continue to evolve, it's clear to us that the future belongs to the service providers who offer the broadest array of services for anyone who needs or wants to rent a car." The company intends to distribute cars wherever, whenever, and however customers want them.[1]

MyMarketingLab

Visit www.mymktlab.com to find activities that help you learn and review in order to succeed in this chapter.

As the Enterprise story shows, good distribution strategies can contribute strongly to customer value and create competitive advantage for a firm. But firms cannot bring value to customers by themselves. Instead, they must work closely with other firms in a larger value delivery network.

Supply Chains and the Value Delivery Network

Author Comment ▶
These are pretty hefty terms for a really simple concept: A company can't go it alone in creating customer value. It must work within a broader network of partners to accomplish this task. Individual companies and brands don't compete; their entire value delivery networks do.

Producing a product or service and making it available to buyers requires building relationships not only with customers but also with key suppliers and resellers in the company's *supply chain*. This supply chain consists of upstream and downstream partners. Upstream from the company is the set of firms that supply the raw materials, components, parts, information, finances, and expertise needed to create a product or service. Marketers, however, have traditionally focused on the downstream side of the supply

you know who could use a
car like this? everyone.

the INSiGHT. a new hybrid from Honda. Honda and hybrid. AKA. reliability and efficiency, two
things everyone can use. Other useful things: an innovative battery, split fold-down rear seats and
43 hwy mpg. The hybrid designed and priced for us all. The new Insight. from Honda. for everyone.

insight.honda.com 1-800-33-Honda EX model shown. *Based on 2010 EPA mileage estimates, reflecting new EPA fuel economy methods, beginning with 2008
models. Use for comparison purposes only. Do not compare to models before 2008. Actual mileage will vary. The Eco Assist symbol is a trademark of Honda Motor Co., Ltd.,
and may not be used or reproduced without prior written approval. ©2009 American Honda Motor Co., Inc.

▲ **Value delivery network: In making and marketing its many models, Honda manages a huge network of people within Honda plus thousands of suppliers and dealers outside the company who work together to bring value to final customers.**

Print advertisement provided courtesy of American Honda Motor Co., Inc.

chain—the *marketing channels* (or *distribution channels*) that look toward the customer. Downstream marketing channel partners, such as wholesalers and retailers, form a vital link between the firm and its customers.

The term *supply chain* may be too limited, as it takes a *make-and-sell* view of the business. It suggests that raw materials, productive inputs, and factory capacity should serve as the starting point for market planning. A better term would be *demand chain* because it suggests a *sense-and-respond* view of the market. Under this view, planning starts by identifying the needs of target customers, to which the company responds by organizing a chain of resources and activities with the goal of creating customer value.

Yet, even a demand chain view of a business may be too limited because it takes a step-by-step, linear view of purchase-production-consumption activities. Instead, most large companies today are engaged in building and managing a complex, continuously evolving value delivery network. As defined in Chapter 2, a **value delivery network** is made up of the company, suppliers, distributors, and, ultimately, customers who "partner" with each other to improve the performance of the entire system. ▶ For example, in making and marketing just one of its many models for the global market—say, the Honda Insight hybrid—Honda manages a huge network of people within Honda plus thousands of suppliers and dealers outside the company who work together effectively to give final customers an innovative car "from Honda. for Everyone."

This chapter focuses on marketing channels—on the downstream side of the value delivery network. We examine four major questions concerning marketing channels: What is the nature of marketing channels and why are they important? How do channel firms interact and organize to do the work of the channel? What problems do companies face in designing and managing their channels? What role do physical distribution and supply chain management play in attracting and satisfying customers? In the next chapter, we will look at marketing channel issues from the viewpoints of retailers and wholesalers.

Author Comment ▶

In this section, we look at the downstream side of the value delivery network—the marketing channel organizations that connect the company and its customers. To understand their value, imagine life without retailers—say, without grocery stores or department stores.

Value delivery network
A network composed of the company, suppliers, distributors, and, ultimately, customers who partner to help the entire system deliver better customer value.

The Nature and Importance of Marketing Channels

Few producers sell their goods directly to final users. Instead, most use intermediaries to bring their products to market. They try to forge a **marketing channel** (or **distribution channel**)—a set of interdependent organizations that help make a product or service available for use or consumption by the consumer or business user.

A company's channel decisions directly affect every other marketing decision. Pricing depends on whether the company works with national discount chains, uses high-quality specialty stores, or sells directly to consumers via the Web. The firm's sales force and communications decisions depend on how much persuasion, training, motivation, and support its channel partners need. Whether a company develops or acquires certain new products may depend on how well those products fit the capabilities of its channel members. For example, Kodak initially sold its EasyShare printers only in Best Buy stores because the

**Marketing channel
(or distribution channel)**
A set of interdependent organizations
that help make a product or service
available for use or consumption by
the consumer or business user.

retailer's on-the-floor sales staff was able to educate buyers on the economics of paying a higher initial printer price but lower long-term ink costs.

Companies often pay too little attention to their distribution channels—sometimes with damaging results. In contrast, many companies have used imaginative distribution systems to gain a competitive advantage. Enterprise revolutionized the car-rental business by setting up off-airport rental offices. Apple turned the retail music business on its head by selling music for the iPod via the Internet on iTunes. And FedEx's creative and imposing distribution system made it a leader in express package delivery.

Distribution channel decisions often involve long-term commitments to other firms. For example, companies such as Ford, McDonald's, or HP can easily change their advertising, pricing, or promotion programs. They can scrap old products and introduce new ones as market tastes demand. But when they set up distribution channels through contracts with franchisees, independent dealers, or large retailers, they cannot readily replace these channels with company-owned stores or Web sites if the conditions change. Therefore, management must design its channels carefully, with an eye on both today's likely selling environment and tomorrow's as well.

How Channel Members Add Value

Why do producers give some of the selling job to channel partners? After all, doing so means giving up some control over how and to whom they sell their products. Producers use intermediaries because they create greater efficiency in making goods available to target markets. Through their contacts, experience, specialization, and scale of operation, intermediaries usually offer the firm more than it can achieve on its own.

▶ **Figure 10.1** shows how using intermediaries can provide economies. Figure 10.1A shows three manufacturers, each using direct marketing to reach three customers. This system requires nine different contacts. Figure 10.1B shows the three manufacturers working through one distributor, which contacts the three customers. This system requires only six contacts. In this way, intermediaries reduce the amount of work that must be done by both producers and consumers.

From the economic system's point of view, the role of marketing intermediaries is to transform the assortments of products made by producers into the assortments wanted by consumers. Producers make narrow assortments of products in large quantities, but consumers want broad assortments of products in small quantities. Marketing channel members buy large quantities from many producers and break them down into the smaller quantities and broader assortments desired by consumers.

For example, Unilever makes millions of bars of Lever 2000 hand soap each week. However, you most likely only want to buy a few bars at a time. Therefore, big food, drug, and discount retailers, such as Kroger, Walgreens, and Target, buy Lever 2000 by the truckload and stock it on their stores' shelves. In turn, you can buy a single bar of Lever 2000,

▶ **Figure 10.1** How Adding a Distributor Reduces the Number of Channel Transactions

Marketing channel intermediaries make buying a lot easier for consumers. Again, think about life without grocery retailers. How would you go about buying that 12-pack of Coke or any of the hundreds of other items that you now routinely drop into your shopping cart?

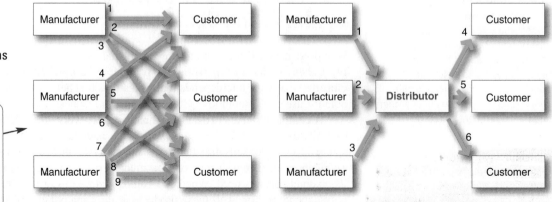

A. Number of contacts without a distributor

B. Number of contacts with a distributor

along with a shopping cart full of small quantities of toothpaste, shampoo, and other related products, as you need them. Thus, intermediaries play an important role in matching supply and demand.

In making products and services available to consumers, channel members add value by bridging the major time, place, and possession gaps that separate goods and services from those who use them. Members of the marketing channel perform many key functions. Some help to complete transactions:

- *Information:* Gathering and distributing information about consumers, producers, and other actors and forces in the marketing environment needed for planning and aiding exchange.
- *Promotion:* Developing and spreading persuasive communications about an offer.
- *Contact:* Finding and communicating with prospective buyers.
- *Matching:* Shaping offers to meet the buyer's needs, including activities such as manufacturing, grading, assembling, and packaging.
- *Negotiation:* Reaching an agreement on price and other terms so that ownership or possession can be transferred.

Others help to fulfill the completed transactions:

- *Physical distribution:* Transporting and storing goods.
- *Financing:* Acquiring and using funds to cover the costs of the channel work.
- *Risk taking:* Assuming the risks of carrying out the channel work.

The question is not *whether* these functions need to be performed—they must be—but rather *who* will perform them. To the extent that the manufacturer performs these functions, its costs go up; therefore, its prices must be higher. When some of these functions are shifted to intermediaries, the producer's costs and prices may be lower, but the intermediaries must charge more to cover the costs of their work. In dividing the work of the channel, the various functions should be assigned to the channel members who can add the most value for the cost.

Number of Channel Levels

Companies can design their distribution channels to make products and services available to customers in different ways. Each layer of marketing intermediaries that performs some work in bringing the product and its ownership closer to the final buyer is a **channel level**. Because both the producer and the final consumer perform some work, they are part of every channel.

The *number of intermediary levels* indicates the *length* of a channel. ▶ **Figure 10.2** shows both consumer and business channels of different lengths. Figure 10.2A shows several common consumer distribution channels. Channel 1, called a **direct marketing channel**, has no intermediary levels—the company sells directly to consumers. For example, Mary Kay Cosmetics and Amway sell their products door-to-door, through home and office sales parties, and on the Internet; GEICO sells insurance directly to customers via the Internet and telephone. The remaining channels in Figure 10.2A are **indirect marketing channels**, containing one or more intermediaries.

Figure 10.2B shows some common business distribution channels. The business marketer can use its own sales force to sell directly to business customers. Or it can sell to various types of intermediaries, who in turn sell to these customers. Although consumer and business marketing channels with even more levels can sometimes be found, these are less common. From the producer's point of view, a greater number of levels means less control and greater channel complexity. Moreover, all the institutions in the channel are connected by several types of *flows*. These include the *physical flow* of products, the *flow of ownership*, the *payment flow*, the *information flow*, and the *promotion flow*. These flows can make even channels with only one or a few levels very complex.

Channel level
A layer of intermediaries that performs some work in bringing the product and its ownership closer to the final buyer.

Direct marketing channel
A marketing channel that has no intermediary levels.

Indirect marketing channel
A marketing channel containing one or more intermediary levels.

Figure 10.2 Consumer and
Business Marketing Channels

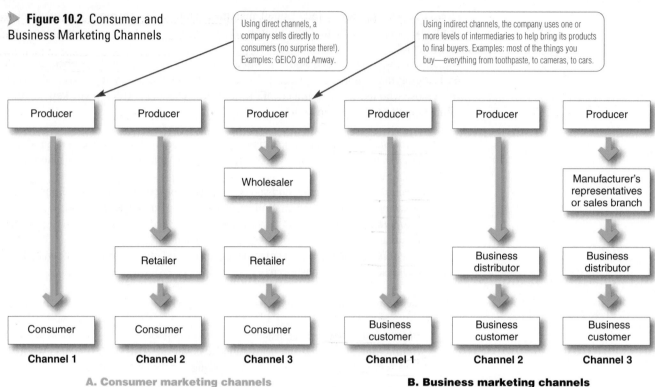

Using direct channels, a company sells directly to consumers (no surprise there!). Examples: GEICO and Amway.

Using indirect channels, the company uses one or more levels of intermediaries to help bring its products to final buyers. Examples: most of the things you buy—everything from toothpaste, to cameras, to cars.

A. Consumer marketing channels   **B. Business marketing channels**

Channel Behavior and Organization

Distribution channels are more than simple collections of firms tied together by various flows. They are complex behavioral systems in which people and companies interact to accomplish individual, company, and channel goals. Some channel systems consist of only informal interactions among loosely organized firms. Others consist of formal interactions guided by strong organizational structures. Moreover, channel systems do not stand still—new types of intermediaries emerge and whole new channel systems evolve. Here we look at channel behavior and how members organize to do the work of the channel.

Channel Behavior

A marketing channel consists of firms that have partnered for their common good. Each channel member depends on the others. For example, a Ford dealer depends on Ford to design cars that meet customer needs. In turn, Ford depends on the dealer to attract customers, persuade them to buy Ford cars, and service the cars after the sale. Each Ford dealer also depends on other dealers to provide good sales and service that will uphold the brand's reputation. In fact, the success of individual Ford dealers depends on how well the entire Ford marketing channel competes with the channels of other auto manufacturers.

Each channel member plays a specialized role in the channel. For example, the role of consumer electronics maker Samsung is to produce electronics products that consumers will like and create demand through national advertising. Best Buy's role is to display these Samsung products in convenient locations, answer buyers' questions, and complete sales. The channel will be most effective when each member assumes the tasks it can do best.

Ideally, because the success of individual channel members depends on the overall channel's success, all channel firms should work together smoothly. They should understand and accept their roles, coordinate their activities, and cooperate to attain overall channel goals. However, individual channel members rarely take such a broad view. Cooperating to achieve overall channel goals sometimes means giving up individual company goals. Although channel members depend on one another, they often act alone in their own short-run best interests. They often disagree on who should do what and for what rewards. Such disagreements over goals, roles, and rewards generate **channel conflict**.

Horizontal conflict occurs among firms at the same level of the channel. For instance, some Ford dealers in Chicago might complain that other dealers in the city steal sales from them by pricing too low or advertising outside their assigned territories. Or Holiday Inn franchisees might complain about other Holiday Inn operators overcharging guests or giving poor service, hurting the overall Holiday Inn image.

Vertical conflict, conflicts between different levels of the same channel, is even more common. ▶ In recent years, for example, Burger King has had a steady stream of conflicts with its franchised dealers over everything from increased ad spending and offensive ads to the prices it charges for cheeseburgers. At issue is the chain's right to dictate policies to franchisees.[2]

Channel conflict

Disagreements among marketing channel members on goals, roles, and rewards—who should do what and for what rewards.

▲ In recent years, Burger King has had a steady stream of conflicts with its franchised dealers over everything from advertising content to the price of its cheeseburgers.

Robyn Lee

The price of a double cheeseburger has generated a lot of heat among Burger King franchisees. In an ongoing dispute, the burger chain insisted that the sandwich be sold for no more than $1—in line with other items on its "Value Menu." Burger King saw the value price as key to competing effectively in the highly competitive fast-food environment. But the company's franchisees claimed that they would lose money at that price. To resolve the dispute, angry franchisees filed a lawsuit (only one of several over the years) asserting that Burger King's franchise agreements don't allow it to dictate prices. (The company had won a separate case in 2008 requiring franchisees to offer the Value Menu, which is core to its efforts to attract price-conscious consumers.) After months of public wrangling, Burger King finally let franchisees have it their way. It introduced a $1 double-patty burger with just one slice of cheese, instead of two, cutting the cost of ingredients. The regular quarter-pound double cheeseburger with two pieces of cheese remained on the Value Menu but was priced at $1.19.

Some conflict in the channel takes the form of healthy competition. However, such competition can be good for the channel; without it, the channel could become passive and non-innovative. For example, Burger King's conflict with its franchisees might represent normal give-and-take over the respective rights of the channel partners. However, severe or prolonged conflict can disrupt channel effectiveness and cause lasting harm to channel relationships. Burger King should manage the channel conflict carefully to keep it from getting out of hand.

Vertical Marketing Systems

For the channel as a whole to perform well, each channel member's role must be specified, and channel conflict must be managed. The channel will perform better if it includes a firm, agency, or mechanism that provides leadership and has the power to assign roles and manage conflict.

Historically, *conventional distribution channels* have lacked such leadership and power, often resulting in damaging conflict and poor performance. One of the biggest channel developments over the years has been the emergence of *vertical marketing systems* that provide channel leadership. ▶ **Figure 10.3** contrasts the two types of channel arrangements.

A **conventional distribution channel** consists of one or more independent producers, wholesalers, and retailers. Each is a separate business seeking to maximize its own profits,

Conventional distribution channel

A channel consisting of one or more independent producers, wholesalers, and retailers, each a separate business seeking to maximize its own profits, perhaps even at the expense of profits for the system as a whole.

Figure 10.3 Comparison of Conventional Distribution Channel with Vertical Marketing System

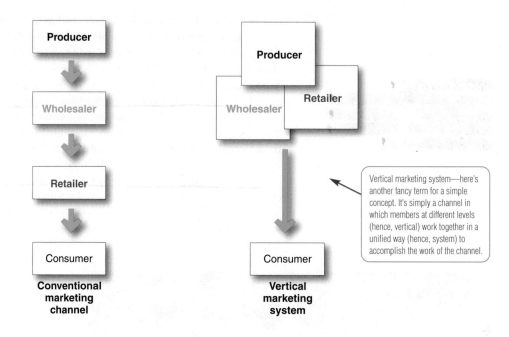

Vertical marketing system—here's another fancy term for a simple concept. It's simply a channel in which members at different levels (hence, vertical) work together in a unified way (hence, system) to accomplish the work of the channel.

perhaps even at the expense of the system as a whole. No channel member has much control over the other members, and no formal means exists for assigning roles and resolving channel conflict.

In contrast, a **vertical marketing system (VMS)** consists of producers, wholesalers, and retailers acting as a unified system. One channel member owns the others, has contracts with them, or wields so much power that they must all cooperate. The VMS can be dominated by the producer, the wholesaler, or the retailer.

We look now at three major types of VMSs: *corporate, contractual*, and *administered*. Each uses a different means for setting up leadership and power in the channel.

Corporate VMS

A **corporate VMS** integrates successive stages of production and distribution under single ownership. Coordination and conflict management are attained through regular organizational channels. For example, the grocery giant Kroger owns and operates 40 manufacturing plants—18 dairies, 10 deli and bakery plants, 10 grocery product plants, and two meat plants—that give it factory-to-store channel control over 40 percent of the more than 11,000 private-label items found on its shelves. And integrating the entire distribution chain—from its own design and manufacturing operations to distribution through its own managed stores—has turned Spanish clothing chain Zara into the world's fastest-growing fashion retailer:[3]

> In recent years, fashion retailer Zara has attracted a near cultlike clientele of shoppers swarming to buy its "cheap chic"—stylish designs that resemble those of big-name fashion houses but at moderate prices. However, Zara's amazing success comes not just from *what* it sells, but from *how fast* its cutting-edge distribution system *delivers* what it sells. Zara delivers fast fashion—*really* fast fashion. Thanks to vertical integration, Zara can take a new fashion concept through design, manufacturing, and store-shelf placement in as little as two weeks, whereas competitors such as Gap, Benetton, or H&M often take six months or more. And the resulting low costs let Zara offer the very latest midmarket chic at downmarket prices.
>
> Speedy design and distribution allows Zara to introduce a copious supply of new fashions—at three times the rate of competitor introductions. Then, Zara's distribution system supplies its stores with small shipments of new merchandise two to three times each week, compared with competing chains' outlets, which get large shipments seasonally, usually just four to six times per year. The combination of a large number of timely new fashions delivered in frequent small batches gives Zara stores a continually updated merchandise mix that brings customers back more often. Fast turnover also results in less outdated and discounted merchandise.

Contractual VMS

A **contractual VMS** consists of independent firms at different levels of production and distribution who join together through contracts to obtain more economies or sales impact

---

Vertical marketing system (VMS)
A channel structure in which producers, wholesalers, and retailers act as a unified system. One channel member owns the others, has contracts with them, or has so much power that they all cooperate.

Corporate VMS
A vertical marketing system that combines successive stages of production and distribution under single ownership—channel leadership is established through common ownership.

Contractual VMS
A vertical marketing system in which independent firms at different levels of production and distribution join together through contracts.

Franchise organization
A contractual vertical marketing system in which a channel member, called a franchisor, links several stages in the production-distribution process.

TURN THIS OVER & SAVE!

Your "To-Do" List
Is No Match For
Mr. Handyman.

Mr. Handyman
On time. Done right.®

See everything Mr. Handyman
can do around your home at
mrhandyman.com.

▲ **Franchising systems: Almost every kind of business has been
franchised—from motels and fast-food restaurants to dating services
and cleaning and handyman companies.**

Mr. Handyman International

than each could achieve alone. Channel members coordinate their activities and manage conflict through contractual agreements.

The **franchise organization** is the most common type of contractual relationship. In this system, a channel member called a *franchisor* links several stages in the production-distribution process. In the United States alone, some 1,500 franchisors and 785,000 franchise outlets account for more than $740 billion of economic output. Industry analysts estimate that a new franchise outlet opens somewhere in the United States every eight minutes and that about one out of every 12 retail business outlets is a franchised business.[4] Almost every kind of business has been franchised—from motels and fast-food restaurants to dental centers and dating services, from wedding consultants and maid services to fitness centers and funeral homes.

There are three types of franchises. The first type is the *manufacturer-sponsored retailer franchise system*—for example, Ford and its network of independent franchised dealers. The second type is the *manufacturer-sponsored wholesaler franchise system*—Coca-Cola licenses bottlers (wholesalers) in various world markets who buy Coca-Cola syrup concentrate and then bottle and sell the finished product to retailers locally. The third type is the *service-firm-sponsored retailer franchise system*—for example, Burger King and its nearly 10,500 franchisee-operated restaurants around the world. ▶ Other examples can be found in everything from auto rentals (Hertz, Avis), apparel retailers (The Athlete's Foot, Plato's Closet), and motels (Holiday Inn, Ramada Inn) to real estate (Century 21) and personal services (Great Clips, Mr. Handyman, Molly Maid).

The fact that most consumers cannot tell the difference between contractual and corporate VMSs shows how successfully the contractual organizations compete with corporate chains. The next chapter presents a fuller discussion of the various contractual VMSs.

Administered VMS

Administered VMS

A vertical marketing system that coordinates successive stages of production and distribution through the size and power of one of the parties.

In an **administered VMS**, leadership is assumed not through common ownership or contractual ties but through the size and power of one or a few dominant channel members. Manufacturers of a top brand can obtain strong trade cooperation and support from resellers. For example, GE, P&G, and Kraft can command unusual cooperation from resellers regarding displays, shelf space, promotions, and price policies. In turn, large retailers such as Walmart, Home Depot, and Barnes & Noble can exert strong influence on the many manufacturers that supply the products they sell.

Horizontal Marketing Systems

Horizontal marketing system

A channel arrangement in which two or more companies at one level join together to follow a new marketing opportunity.

Another channel development is the **horizontal marketing system**, in which two or more companies at one level join together to follow a new marketing opportunity. By working together, companies can combine their financial, production, or marketing resources to accomplish more than any one company could alone.

Companies might join forces with competitors or noncompetitors. They might work with each other on a temporary or permanent basis, or they may create a separate company. For example, Walmart—famous for squeezing costs out of its supply chain—wants to team with PepsiCo's Frito-Lay unit to buy potatoes jointly for a lower price than either company could get alone. That would help both companies to earn more on the spuds and chips they sell in Walmart's

▲ **Horizontal marketing channels:** McDonald's places "express" versions of its restaurants in Walmart stores. McDonald's benefits from Walmart's heavy store traffic and Walmart keeps hungry shoppers from needing to go elsewhere to eat.

stores. ▶ Walmart also partners with McDonald's to place "express" versions of McDonald's restaurants in Walmart stores. McDonald's benefits from Walmart's heavy store traffic, and Walmart keeps hungry shoppers from needing to go elsewhere to eat.[5]

Competitors Microsoft and Yahoo! have joined forces to create a horizontal Internet search alliance. Until 2020, Microsoft's Bing will power Yahoo! searches. In turn, Yahoo! will sell premium search advertising services for both companies. The collaboration, dubbed Bingahoo by industry insiders, has proven beneficial. Because one advertising purchase brings results on both Bing and Yahoo!, advertisers have more incentive to use the combined platform. In the first year, total ad spending climbed 44 percent, making the two companies together a stronger challenger to industry leader Google.[6]

Multichannel Distribution Systems

In the past, many companies used a single channel to sell to a single market or market segment. Today, with the proliferation of customer segments and channel possibilities, more and more companies have adopted **multichannel distribution systems**. Such multichannel marketing occurs when a single firm sets up two or more marketing channels to reach one or more customer segments.

Multichannel distribution system

A distribution system in which a single firm sets up two or more marketing channels to reach one or more customer segments.

▶ **Figure 10.4** shows a multichannel marketing system. In the figure, the producer sells directly to consumer segment 1 using catalogs, telemarketing, and the Internet and reaches consumer segment 2 through retailers. It sells indirectly to business segment 1 through distributors and dealers and to business segment 2 through its own sales force.

These days, almost every large company and many small ones distribute through multiple channels. For example, John Deere sells its familiar green and yellow lawn and garden tractors, mowers, and outdoor power products to consumers and commercial users through several channels, including John Deere retailers, Lowe's home improvement stores, and online. It sells and services its tractors, combines, planters, and other agricultural equipment through its premium John Deere dealer network. And it sells large construction and forestry equipment through selected large, full-service John Deere dealers and their sales forces.

▶ **Figure 10.4** Multichannel Distribution System

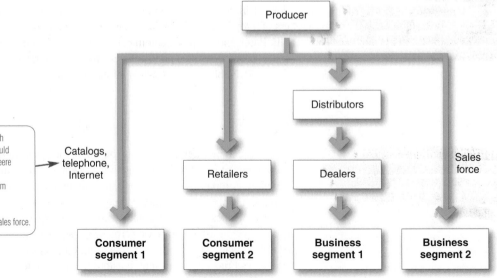

Most large companies distribute through multiple channels. For example, you could buy a familiar green and yellow John Deere lawn tractor from a neighborhood John Deere dealer or from Lowe's. A large farm or forestry business would buy larger John Deere equipment from a premium full-service John Deere dealer and its sales force.

Multichannel distribution systems offer many advantages to companies facing large and complex markets. With each new channel, the company expands its sales and market coverage and gains opportunities to tailor its products and services to the specific needs of diverse customer segments. But such multichannel systems are harder to control, and they generate conflict as more channels compete for customers and sales. For example, when John Deere began selling selected consumer products through Lowe's home improvement stores, many of its dealers complained loudly. To avoid such conflicts in its Internet marketing channels, the company routes all of its Web site sales to John Deere dealers.

Changing Channel Organization

Changes in technology and the explosive growth of direct and online marketing are having a profound impact on the nature and design of marketing channels. One major trend is toward **disintermediation**—a big term with a clear message and important consequences. Disintermediation occurs when product or service producers cut out intermediaries and go directly to final buyers or when radically new types of channel intermediaries displace traditional ones.

Thus, in many industries, traditional intermediaries are dropping by the wayside. For example, Southwest, JetBlue, and other airlines sell tickets directly to final buyers, cutting travel agents from their marketing channels altogether. In other cases, new forms of resellers are displacing traditional intermediaries. For example, online marketers have taken business from traditional brick-and-mortar retailers. Consumers can buy hotel rooms and airline tickets from Expedia.com and Travelocity.com; electronics from Sonystyle.com; clothes and accessories from Bluefly.com; and books, videos, toys, jewelry, sports, consumer electronics, home and garden items, and almost anything else from Amazon.com—all without ever stepping into a traditional retail store. Online music download services such as iTunes and Amazon MP3 are threatening the very existence of traditional music-store retailers. In fact, once-dominant music retailers such as Tower Records have declared bankruptcy and closed their doors for good.

Disintermediation presents both opportunities and problems for producers and resellers. Channel innovators who find new ways to add value in the channel can sweep aside traditional resellers and reap the rewards. In turn, traditional intermediaries must continue to innovate to avoid being swept aside. For example, when Netflix pioneered online video rentals, it sent traditional brick-and-mortar video stores such as Blockbuster into ruin. Then, Netflix faced disintermediation threats from an even hotter channel—digital video downloads and video streaming. But instead of simply watching these developments, Netflix is leading them, disintermediating its own channels before competitors can (see Marketing at Work 10.1).

Similarly, to remain competitive, product and service producers must develop new channel opportunities, such as the Internet and other direct channels. However, developing these new channels often brings them into direct competition with their established channels, resulting in conflict.

To ease this problem, companies often look for ways to make going direct a plus for the entire channel. ▶ For example, guitar and amp maker Fender knows that many customers would prefer to buy its guitars, amps, and accessories online. But selling directly through its Web site would create conflicts with retail partners, from large chains such as Guitar Center, Sam Ash, and Best Buy to small shops scattered throughout the world, such as the Musician's Junkyard

Disintermediation
The cutting out of marketing channel intermediaries by product or service producers or the displacement of traditional resellers by radical new types of intermediaries.

▲ Avoiding disintermediation problems: Fender's Web site provides detailed product information but you can't buy any of the company's products there. Instead, Fender refers you to its resellers' Web sites and stores.

MARKETING AT WORK | 10.1

Netflix: Disintermediate or Be Disintermediated

Baseball great Yogi Berra, known more for his mangled phrasing than for his baseball prowess, once said, "The future ain't what it used to be." For Netflix, the world's largest video subscription service, no matter how you say it, figuring out the future is challenging and a bit scary. Netflix faces dramatic changes in how movies and other video entertainment content will be distributed. The question is: Will Netflix be among the disintermediators or among the disintermediated?

Less than a decade ago, if you wanted to watch a movie at home, your only choice was to roust yourself out of that easy chair and trot down to the local Blockbuster or other neighborhood movie-rental store. At the time, Blockbuster dominated DVD rentals. But all that has changed—abruptly and radically. Facing losses and store closures, once-mighty Blockbuster declared bankruptcy in late 2010. In early 2011, it was bought for a song by Dish Network, which acquired the failed movie-rental chain primarily for its fledgling video-streaming services to complement the Dish's satellite-TV offerings.

The Blockbuster riches-to-rags story underscores the disruption and confusion that typify today's video distribution business. Things are changing quickly and the dust is far from settling. For example, there's Redbox, a company that no one had even heard of just a few years ago, successfully renting discs for a dollar a day through kiosks in more than 26,000 convenience stores, supermarkets, and fast-food restaurants. There's Hulu, which leads the army of start-ups and media veterans that let you view full-length movies, TV shows, and clips on your computer for free, as long as you're willing to watch some ads. And consumers are rapidly snapping up high-tech hardware and Internet technologies that give them instant access to entertainment.

But from the very start, Netflix has met with incredible success by outwitting and out-innovating competitors in the chaotic media distribution business. In the late 1990s, the heyday of brick-and-mortar video-rental retailers, Netflix pioneered a revolutionary new way to rent movies—via the Internet and direct mail. For a monthly subscription fee, members could create a movie wish list online and Netflix would mail out a set of DVDs from that list. Members could keep the DVDs as long as they wanted, then return them in a prepaid return envelope. Netflix automatically sent the next set of DVDs from the member's list.

Thousands, then millions, of subscribers flocked to the Netflix DVD-by-mail model. As Netflix pointed out, there was no hassle of trips to the video store and no worry about late fees. Netflix's selection from more than 100,000 DVD titles dwarfed anything that brick-and-mortar stores could hold. Finding old, rare, documentary, or independent films was easy. And the cost of renting—based on how many DVDs members could check out at one time—was as little as $5 a month. As the

DVD-by-mail model caught on, Netflix's fortunes surged and those of store-rental competitors like Blockbuster sagged.

But no good thing lasts forever. With startling advances in Internet and media-streaming technologies looming, Netflix foresaw even more revolutionary changes in the video distribution race. According to Netflix founder and CEO Reed Hastings, the digital future was scary, but it was also bursting with opportunity. Hastings predicted that physical DVD rental would decline as video-streaming distribution took its place. The key to the future was all in how Netflix defined itself. "If you think of Netflix as a DVD-rental business, you're right to be scared," he said at the time. But "if you think of Netflix as an online movie service with multiple different delivery models, then you're a lot less scared."

So rather than sitting on the success of its still-hot DVD-by-mail business, four years ago, Netflix and Hastings set their sights on a revolutionary new video distribution model: Deliver the Netflix service to every Internet-connected screen, from laptops to Internet-ready TVs to cell phones and other Wi-Fi-enabled devices. Netflix launched its Watch Instantly service, which let Netflix members stream movies instantly via their computers as part of their monthly membership fee, even if it came at the expense of Netflix' still-booming DVD business. At first, selection was slim—only a few thousand movies were available for streaming—and the quality wasn't all that great. But Netflix invested heavily to expand its library of streaming videos and its connecting technologies.

From that fresh start, Netflix has now blossomed into the nation's leading subscription-based digital-streaming service. Now, even as once-formidable competitors such as Blockbuster bite the dust, the transformed Netflix's sales and profits are soaring. Netflix now tops 20 million subscribers (up 47 percent

▲ Netflix faces dramatic changes in how movies and other entertainment content will be distributed. Instead of simply watching the developments, Netflix intends to lead them.

in just the past year) who can choose from more than 20,000 movies to stream, all in high-definition, full-screen splendor. For $7.99 a month, subscribers can stream unlimited movies, TV episodes, and other video content over the Internet to their computers, TVs, or about any other screen. A rising tide of more than 200 devices can now stream from Netflix, including an array of Blu-ray disc players, Internet-connected TVs, home theater systems, DVRs, and Internet video players; Apple's iPhone, iPad, and iPod Touch; Apple TV and Google TV streaming devices; and even Wii, Xbox360, and PS3 videogame consoles.

Although its DVD-by-mail business is still thriving, Netflix appears now to be slowly turning its back on physical DVD rentals. To that end, the company recently began charging separately for its streaming and DVD-by-mail services (a 60 percent price increase to customers who use both) and even tried to split DVD-by-mail into a separate business named Quikster. The abrupt changes caused substantial customer backlash, costing Netflix both customers and some of its brand's previous luster. To repair the damage, Netflix quickly admitted its blunder and reversed its decision to set up a separate Quikster operation. However, it retained the separate, higher pricing for DVDs by mail. Hastings seems determined to speed up the leap from success in DVDs to success in streaming. Our "huge subscriber growth, fueled by the excitement of watching instantly, impressed even us," he says. "The acceptance of on-demand, click-and-watch Internet video . . . has been phenomenal."

Despite its incredible success, Netflix can't rest its innovation machine. The media-distribution industry continues to change at a blurring rate, and resourceful, fast-moving new competitors

have burst onto the scene. For example, Amazon.com recently started its own streaming-video subscription service, available to Amazon Prime members at no additional cost. Internet giant Google is reportedly working on a streaming-video service as well, and Apple is leveraging the popular iTunes store to stream video through its Apple TV device. Upstart Hulu is rumored to be considering launching a virtual cable service, which would offer online access to packages of TV channels similar to those from cable operators, possibly at a lower price.

What's next in the media-distribution industry? No one really knows. But one thing seems certain: Whatever's coming, if Netflix doesn't lead the change, it risks being left behind—and quickly. Netflix must continue to disintermediate its own distribution model before competitors can. As Blockbuster and other slower moving competitors learned the hard way, it's disintermediate or be disintermediated.

Sources: Quotes and other information from Nick Wingfield, "Netflix Sees Surge in Subscribers," *Wall Street Journal*, January 27, 2011, p. B9; Martin Peers, "Competitive Net Tightens around Netflix," *Wall Street Journal*, February 1, 2011, p. C10; Erik Gruenwedel, "Netflix Catches Fire," *Home Media Magazine*, January 31–February 6, 2011, pp. 1, 36; Nick Wingfield, "Netflix Boss Plots Life After the DVD," *Wall Street Journal*, June 23, 2009, p. A1; Nat Worden and Stu Woo, "Amazon Goes after Netflix, Adding New Subscription," *Wall Street Journal*, February 23, 2011, p. B1; "Dish Network Reveals Plans for Blockbuster Retail Stores," *Satellite Today*, April 20, 2011; Charlie Rose, "Charlie Rose Talks to Reed Hastings," *Bloomberg Businessweek*, May 9–May 15, 2011, p. 26; "An Explanation and Some Reflections," and e-mail from Reed Hastings to Netflix customers, September 19, 2011; and www.netflix.com and www.netflix.com/MediaCenter?id=5379, accessed November 2011.

in Windsor, Vermont, or Freddy for Music in Amman, Jordan. So Fender's Web site provides detailed information about the company's products, but you can't buy a new Fender Stratocaster or Acoustasonic guitar there. Instead, the Fender Web site refers you to its resellers' Web sites and stores. Thus, Fender's direct marketing helps both the company and its channel partners.

| **SPEED BUMP** | LINKING THE CONCEPTS |

Stop here for a moment and apply the distribution channel concepts we've discussed so far.

- Compare the Zara and Ford channels. Draw a diagram that shows the types of intermediaries in each channel. What kind of channel system does each company use?
- What are the roles and responsibilities of the members in each channel? How well do these channel members work together toward overall channel success?

Author Comment ▶
Like everything else in marketing, good channel design begins with customers. Marketing channels are really *customer-value delivery networks.*

Channel Design Decisions

We now look at several channel design decisions manufacturers face. In designing marketing channels, manufacturers struggle between what is ideal and what is practical. A new firm with limited capital usually starts by selling in a limited market area. In this case, deciding on the best channels might not be a problem: The problem might simply be how to convince one or a few good intermediaries to handle the line.

If successful, the new firm can branch out to new markets through existing intermediaries. In smaller markets, the firm might sell directly to retailers; in larger markets, it might sell through distributors. In one part of the country, it might grant exclusive franchises; in another, it might sell through all available outlets. Then it might add an Internet store that sells directly to hard-to-reach customers. In this way, channel systems often evolve to meet market opportunities and conditions.

For maximum effectiveness, however, channel analysis and decision making should be more purposeful. **Marketing channel design** calls for analyzing consumer needs, setting channel objectives, identifying major channel alternatives, and evaluating those alternatives.

Analyzing Consumer Needs

As noted previously, marketing channels are part of the overall *customer-value delivery network*. Each channel member and level adds value for the customer. Thus, designing the marketing channel starts with finding out what target consumers want from the channel. Do consumers want to buy from nearby locations or are they willing to travel to more distant and centralized locations? Would customers rather buy in person, by phone, or online? Do they value breadth of assortment or do they prefer specialization? Do consumers want many add-on services (delivery, installation, repairs), or will they obtain these services elsewhere? The faster the delivery, the greater the assortment provided, and the more add-on services supplied, the greater the channel's service level.

Providing the fastest delivery, the greatest assortment, and the most services may not be possible or practical, however. The company and its channel members may not have the resources or skills needed to provide all the desired services. Also, providing higher levels of service results in higher costs for the channel and higher prices for consumers. ▶ For example, your local independent hardware store probably provides more personalized service, a more convenient location, and less shopping hassle than the nearest huge Home Depot or Lowe's store. But it may also charge higher prices. The company must balance consumer needs not only against the feasibility and costs of meeting these needs but also against customer price preferences. The success of discount retailing shows that consumers will often accept lower service levels in exchange for lower prices.

▲ **Meeting customers' channel service needs: Your local hardware store probably provides more personalized service, a more convenient location, and less shopping hassle than a huge Home Depot or Lowe's store. But it may also charge higher prices.**
DAVID WALTER BANKS /The New York Times/Redux Pictures

Setting Channel Objectives

Companies should state their marketing channel objectives in terms of targeted levels of customer service. Usually, a company can identify several segments wanting different levels of service. The company should decide which segments to serve and the best channels to use in each case. In each segment, the company wants to minimize the total channel cost of meeting customer-service requirements.

The company's channel objectives are also influenced by the nature of the company, its products, its marketing intermediaries, its competitors, and the environment. For example, the company's size and financial situation determine which marketing functions it can handle itself and which it must give to intermediaries. Companies selling perishable products, for example, may require more direct marketing to avoid delays and too much handling.

In some cases, a company may want to compete in or near the same outlets that carry competitors' products. For example, Maytag wants its appliances displayed alongside competing brands to facilitate comparison shopping. In other cases, companies may avoid the channels used by competitors. Mary Kay Cosmetics, for example, sells directly to consumers through its corps of more than two million independent beauty consultants in more than 35 markets worldwide rather than going head-to-head with other cosmetics makers for scarce positions in retail stores.[7] GEICO primarily markets auto and homeowner's insurance directly to consumers via the telephone and the Internet rather than through agents.

Finally, environmental factors such as economic conditions and legal constraints may affect channel objectives and design. For example, in a depressed economy, producers will want to distribute their goods in the most economical way, using shorter channels and dropping unneeded services that add to the final price of the goods.

Identifying Major Alternatives

When the company has defined its channel objectives, it should next identify its major channel alternatives in terms of the *types* of intermediaries, the *number* of intermediaries, and the *responsibilities* of each channel member.

Types of Intermediaries

A firm should identify the types of channel members available to carry out its channel work. Most companies face many channel member choices. For example, until recently, Dell sold directly to final consumers and business buyers only through its sophisticated phone and Internet marketing channel. It also sold directly to large corporate, institutional, and government buyers using its direct sales force. However, to reach more consumers and match competitors such as HP, Dell now sells indirectly through retailers such as Best Buy, Staples, and Walmart. It also sells indirectly through value-added resellers, independent distributors and dealers who develop computer systems and applications tailored to the special needs of small- and medium-sized business customers.

Using many types of resellers in a channel provides both benefits and drawbacks. For example, by selling through retailers and value-added resellers in addition to its own direct channels, Dell can reach more and different kinds of buyers. However, the new channels will be more difficult to manage and control. In addition, the direct and indirect channels will compete with each other for many of the same customers, causing potential conflict. In fact, Dell often finds itself "stuck in the middle," with its direct sales reps complaining about competition from retail stores, whereas its value-added resellers complain that the direct sales reps are undercutting their business.

Number of Marketing Intermediaries

Companies must also determine the number of channel members to use at each level. Three strategies are available: intensive distribution, exclusive distribution, and selective distribution. Producers of convenience products and common raw materials typically seek **intensive distribution**—a strategy in which they stock their products in as many outlets as possible. These products must be available where and when consumers want them. For example, toothpaste, candy, and other similar items are sold in millions of outlets to provide maximum brand exposure and consumer convenience. Kraft, Coca-Cola, Kimberly-Clark, and other consumer-goods companies distribute their products in this way.

By contrast, some producers purposely limit the number of intermediaries handling their products. The extreme form of this practice is **exclusive distribution**, in which the producer gives only a limited number of dealers the exclusive right to distribute its products in their territories. Exclusive distribution is often found in the distribution of luxury brands. For example, exclusive Bentley automobiles are typically sold by only a handful of authorized dealers in any given market area. However, some shopping goods producers also practice exclusive distribution. For instance, outdoor power equipment maker STIHL doesn't sell its chain saws, blowers, hedge trimmers, and other products through mass merchandisers such as Lowe's, Home Depot, or Sears. Instead, it sells only through a select corps of independent hardware and lawn and garden dealers. ▶ By granting exclusive distribution, STIHL gains

---

Intensive distribution
Stocking the product in as many outlets as possible.

Exclusive distribution
Giving a limited number of dealers the exclusive right to distribute the company's products in their territories.

[handwritten margin notes:]
convenience or raw materials ↓ intensive distribution

luxury brands ↓ exclusive distribution.

Why is the world's number one selling brand of chain saw not sold at Lowe's or The Home Depot?

We can give you 8,000 reasons, our legion of independent STIHL dealers nationwide. We count on them every day and so can you. To give you a product demonstration, straight talk and genuine advice about STIHL products. To offer fast and expert on-site service. And to stand behind every product they carry, always fully assembled. You see, we won't sell you a chain saw in a box, not even in a big one. **Are you ready for a STIHL?**

To find a dealer: stihlusa.com or call 1-800 GO STIHL.

The Home Depot and Lowe's are registered trademarks of their respective companies.

Number 1 Worldwide **STIHL®**

▲ **Exclusive distribution: STIHL sells its chain saws, blowers, hedge trimmers, and other products only through a select corps of independent hardware and lawn and garden retailers. "We count on them every day and so can you."**

STIHL, Inc., Virginia Beach, VA—headquarters for U.S. operations

stronger dealer selling support. Exclusive distribution also enhances the STIHL brand's image and allows for higher markups resulting from greater value-added dealer service.

Between intensive and exclusive distribution lies **selective distribution**—the use of more than one but fewer than all of the intermediaries who are willing to carry a company's products. Most television, furniture, and home appliance brands are distributed in this manner. For example, Whirlpool and GE sell their major appliances through dealer networks and selected large retailers. By using selective distribution, they can develop good working relationships with selected channel members and expect a better-than-average selling effort. Selective distribution gives producers good market coverage with more control and less cost than does intensive distribution.

Responsibilities of Channel Members

The producer and the intermediaries need to agree on the terms and responsibilities of each channel member. They should agree on price policies, conditions of sale, territory rights, and the specific services to be performed by each party. The producer should establish a list price and a fair set of discounts for the intermediaries. It must define each channel member's territory, and it should be careful about where it places new resellers.

Mutual services and duties need to be spelled out carefully, especially in franchise and exclusive distribution channels. For example, McDonald's provides franchisees with promotional support, a record-keeping system, training at Hamburger University, and general management assistance. In turn, franchisees must meet company standards for physical facilities and food quality, cooperate with new promotion programs, provide requested information, and buy specified food products.

Selective distribution

The use of more than one but fewer than all of the intermediaries who are willing to carry the company's products.

channel criteria
- economic
- adaptable.
- control factor

Evaluating the Major Alternatives

Suppose a company has identified several channel alternatives and wants to select the one that will best satisfy its long-run objectives. Each alternative should be evaluated against economic, control, and adaptability criteria.

Using *economic criteria*, a company compares the likely sales, costs, and profitability of different channel alternatives. What will be the investment required by each channel alternative, and what returns will result? The company must also consider *control issues*. Using intermediaries usually means giving them some control over the marketing of the product, and some intermediaries take more control than others. Other things being equal, the company prefers to keep as much control as possible. Finally, the company must apply *adaptability criteria*. Channels often involve long-term commitments, yet the company wants to keep the channel flexible so that it can adapt to environmental changes. Thus, to be considered, a channel involving long-term commitments should be greatly superior on economic and control grounds.

Designing International Distribution Channels

International marketers face many additional complexities in designing their channels. Each country has its own unique distribution system that has evolved over time and changes very slowly. These channel systems can vary widely from country to country. Thus, global marketers must usually adapt their channel strategies to the existing structures within each country.

In some markets, the distribution system is complex and hard to penetrate, consisting of many layers and large numbers of intermediaries. For example, many Western companies find Japan's distribution system difficult to navigate. It's steeped in tradition and very complex, with many distributors touching the product before it arrives on the store shelf.

At the other extreme, distribution systems in developing countries may be scattered, inefficient, or altogether lacking. For example, China and India are huge markets—each with a population well over one billion people. However, because of inadequate distribution systems, most companies can profitably access only a small portion of the population located in each country's most affluent cities. "China is a very decentralized market," notes a China trade expert. "[It's] made up of two dozen distinct markets sprawling across 2,000 cities. Each has its own culture. . . . It's like operating in an asteroid belt." China's distribution system is so fragmented that logistics costs to wrap, bundle, load, unload, sort, reload, and transport goods amount to more than 15 percent of the nation's GDP, far higher than in most other countries. (U.S. logistics costs account for just under 8 percent of the nation's GDP.) After years of effort, even Walmart executives admit that they have been unable to assemble an efficient supply chain in China.[8]

Sometimes local customs can greatly influence how a company distributes products in global markets. ▶ For example, in low-income neighborhoods in Brazil where consumers have limited access to supermarkets, Nestlé supplements its distribution with thousands of self-employed salespeople who sell Nestlé products door to door. And in Japan, door-to-door salespeople sell nearly one-half of all new cars sold each year.[9]

Because Japanese real estate is so expensive, most auto dealerships are much smaller than their American counterparts, serving more as a base of operations for the sales force. Toyota alone has a 1,000-person sales force—equal to about one-half of the entire U.S. auto sales force for a country the size of California. Toyota's roving salespeople build personal relationships with each of the 3,000 or so households in a typical sales area and make their sales pitches in their customers' living rooms. Because of the door-to-door sales forces, many Japanese car buyers never go to an auto dealership, and most are strongly brand loyal. American car companies selling in Japan need to match these door-to-door selling techniques or risk losing a sizable segment of the market.

▲ **International channel differences: In low-income neighborhoods in Brazil, where consumers have limited access to supermarkets, Nestlé supplements its distribution with thousands of self-employed salespeople who sell Nestlé products door to door.**

Courtesy of Nestlé Brasil Ltda. Photographer: Ricardo Teles.

Thus, international marketers face a wide range of channel alternatives. Designing efficient and effective channel systems between and within various country markets poses a difficult challenge. We discuss international distribution decisions further in Chapter 15.

Channel Management Decisions

Author Comment ▶
Now it's time to implement the chosen channel design and work with selected channel members to manage and motivate them.

Once the company has reviewed its channel alternatives and determined the best channel design, it must implement and manage the chosen channel. **Marketing channel management** calls for selecting, managing, and motivating individual channel members and evaluating their performance over time.

Selecting Channel Members

Marketing channel management
Selecting, managing, and motivating individual channel members and evaluating their performance over time.

Producers vary in their ability to attract qualified marketing intermediaries. Some producers have no trouble signing up channel members. For example, when Toyota first introduced its Lexus line in the United States, it had no trouble attracting new dealers. In fact, it had to turn down many would-be resellers.

At the other extreme are producers who have to work hard to line up enough qualified intermediaries. For example, when Timex first tried to sell its inexpensive watches through regular jewelry stores, most jewelry stores refused to carry them. The company then managed to get its watches into mass-merchandise outlets. This turned out to be a wise decision because of the rapid growth of mass merchandising.

Even established brands may have difficulty gaining and keeping their desired distribution, especially when dealing with powerful resellers. For example, you won't find P&G's Pampers diapers in a Costco store. After P&G declined to manufacture Costco's Kirkland store brand diapers a few years ago, Costco gave Pampers the boot and now only carries Huggies and its own Kirkland brand (manufactured by Huggies maker Kimberly-Clark). The removal by Costco, the number-two diaper retailer after Walmart, has cost P&G an estimated $150 million to $200 million in annual sales.[10]

When selecting intermediaries, the company should determine what characteristics distinguish the better ones. It will want to evaluate each channel member's years in business, other lines carried, location, growth and profit record, cooperativeness, and reputation.

Managing and Motivating Channel Members

Once selected, channel members must be continuously managed and motivated to do their best. The company must sell not only *through* the intermediaries but also *to* and *with* them. Most companies see their intermediaries as first-line customers and partners. They practice strong *partner relationship management* to forge long-term partnerships with channel members. This creates a value delivery system that meets the needs of both the company *and* its marketing partners.

In managing its channels, a company must convince distributors that they can succeed better by working together as a part of a cohesive value delivery system. Thus, P&G works closely with Target to create superior value for final consumers. The two jointly plan merchandising goals and strategies, inventory levels, and advertising and promotion programs.

Similarly, heavy-equipment manufacturer Caterpillar works in close harmony with its worldwide network of independent dealers to find better ways to bring value to customers.[11]

▲ Caterpillar works closely with its worldwide network of independent dealers to find better ways to bring value to customers. When a big piece of CAT equipment breaks down, customers know they can count on Caterpillar and its outstanding dealer network for support.

Reprinted Courtesy of Caterpillar Inc.

One-hundred-year-old Caterpillar produces innovative, high-quality products. Yet the most important reason for Caterpillar's dominance is its distribution network of 220 outstanding independent dealers worldwide. Caterpillar and its dealers work as partners. According to a former Caterpillar CEO: "After the product leaves our door, the dealers take over. They are the ones on the front line. They're the ones who live with the product for its lifetime. They're the ones customers see." ▶ When a big piece of Caterpillar equipment breaks down, customers know that they can count on Caterpillar and its outstanding dealer network for support. Dealers play a vital role in almost every aspect of Caterpillar's operations, from product design and delivery to product service and support.

Caterpillar really knows its dealers and cares about their success. It closely monitors each dealership's sales, market position, service capability, and financial situation. When it sees a problem, it jumps in to help. In addition to more formal business ties, Caterpillar forms close personal ties with dealers in a kind of family relationship. Caterpillar and its dealers feel a deep pride in what they are accomplishing together. As the former CEO puts it, "There's a camaraderie among our dealers around the world that really makes it more than just a financial arrangement. They feel that what they're doing is good for the world because they are part of an organization that makes, sells, and tends to the machines that make the world work."

As a result of its partnership with dealers, Caterpillar dominates the world's markets for heavy construction, mining, and logging equipment. Its familiar yellow tractors, crawlers, loaders, bulldozers, and trucks capture some 40 percent of the worldwide heavy-equipment business, more than twice that of number-two Komatsu.

Many companies are now installing integrated high-tech partnership relationship management (PRM) systems to coordinate their whole-channel marketing efforts. Just as they use CRM software systems to help manage relationships with important customers, companies can now use PRM and supply chain management (SCM) software to help recruit, train, organize, manage, motivate, and evaluate relationships with channel partners.

Evaluating Channel Members

The company must regularly check channel member performance against standards such as sales quotas, average inventory levels, customer delivery time, treatment of damaged and lost goods, cooperation in company promotion and training programs, and services to the customer. The company should recognize and reward intermediaries who are performing well and adding good value for consumers. Those who are performing poorly should be assisted or, as a last resort, replaced.

Finally, companies need to be sensitive to the needs of their channel partners. Those who treat their partners poorly risk not only losing their support but also causing some legal problems. The next section describes various rights and duties pertaining to companies and other channel members.

SPEED BUMP | LINKING THE CONCEPTS

Time for another pause. This time, compare the Caterpillar and Burger King channel systems.

- Diagram the Caterpillar and Burger King channel systems. How do they compare in terms of channel levels, types of intermediaries, channel member roles and responsibilities, and other characteristics? How well is each system designed?
- Assess how well Caterpillar and Burger King have managed and supported their channels. With what results?

Public Policy and Distribution Decisions

For the most part, companies are legally free to develop whatever channel arrangements suit them. In fact, the laws affecting channels seek to prevent the exclusionary tactics of some companies that might keep another company from using a desired channel. Most channel law deals with the mutual rights and duties of channel members once they have formed a relationship.

Many producers and wholesalers like to develop exclusive channels for their products. When the seller allows only certain outlets to carry its products, this strategy is called *exclusive distribution*. When the seller requires that these dealers not handle competitors' products, its strategy is called *exclusive dealing*. Both parties can benefit from exclusive arrangements: The seller obtains more loyal and dependable outlets, and the dealers obtain a steady source of supply and stronger seller support. But exclusive arrangements also exclude other producers from selling to these dealers. This situation brings exclusive dealing contracts under the scope of the Clayton Act of 1914. They are legal as long as they do not substantially lessen competition or tend to create a monopoly and as long as both parties enter into the agreement voluntarily.

Exclusive dealing often includes *exclusive territorial agreements*. The producer may agree not to sell to other dealers in a given area, or the buyer may agree to sell only in its own territory. The first practice is normal under franchise systems as a way to increase dealer enthusiasm and commitment. It is also perfectly legal—a seller has no legal obligation to sell through more outlets than it wishes. The second practice, whereby the producer tries to keep a dealer from selling outside its territory, has become a major legal issue.

Producers of a strong brand sometimes sell it to dealers only if the dealers will take some or all of the rest of its line. This is called *full-line forcing*. Such *tying agreements* are not necessarily illegal, but they violate the Clayton Act if they tend to lessen competition substantially. The practice may prevent consumers from freely choosing among competing suppliers of these other brands.

Finally, producers are free to select their dealers, but their right to terminate dealers is somewhat restricted. In general, sellers can drop dealers "for cause." However, they cannot drop dealers if, for example, the dealers refuse to cooperate in a doubtful legal arrangement, such as exclusive dealing or tying agreements.

Marketing Logistics and Supply Chain Management

In today's global marketplace, selling a product is sometimes easier than getting it to customers. Companies must decide on the best way to store, handle, and move their products and services so that they are available to customers in the right assortments, at the right time, and in the right place. Logistics effectiveness has a major impact on both customer satisfaction and company costs. Here we consider the nature and importance of logistics management in the supply chain, the goals of the logistics system, major logistics functions, and the need for integrated supply chain management.

Nature and Importance of Marketing Logistics

**Marketing logistics
(or physical distribution)**
Planning, implementing, and controlling the physical flow of materials, final goods, and related information from points of origin to points of consumption to meet customer requirements at a profit.

To some managers, marketing logistics means only trucks and warehouses. But modern logistics is much more than this. **Marketing logistics**—also called **physical distribution**—involves planning, implementing, and controlling the physical flow of goods, services, and related information from points of origin to points of consumption to meet customer requirements at a profit. In short, it involves getting the right product to the right customer in the right place at the right time.

In the past, physical distribution planners typically started with products at the plant and then tried to find low-cost solutions to get them to customers. However, today's *customer-centered* logistics starts with the marketplace and works backward to the factory or even to sources of supply. Marketing logistics involves not only *outbound distribution* (moving products from the factory to resellers and ultimately to customers) but also *inbound distribution* (moving products and materials from suppliers to the factory) and *reverse distribution* (reusing, recycling, refurbishing, or disposing of broken, unwanted, or excess products returned by consumers or resellers). That is, it involves entire **supply chain**

Supply chain management
Managing upstream and downstream value-added flows of materials, final goods, and related information among suppliers, the company, resellers, and final consumers.

management—managing upstream and downstream value-added flows of materials, final goods, and related information among suppliers, the company, resellers, and final consumers, as shown in ▶ **Figure 10.5**.

The logistics manager's task is to coordinate the activities of suppliers, purchasing agents, marketers, channel members, and customers. These activities include forecasting, information systems, purchasing, production planning, order processing, inventory, warehousing, and transportation planning.

Companies today are placing greater emphasis on logistics for several reasons. First, companies can gain a powerful competitive advantage by using improved logistics to give customers better service or lower prices. Second, improved logistics can yield tremendous cost savings to both a company and its customers. As much as 20 percent of an average product's price is accounted for by shipping and transport alone. This far exceeds the cost of advertising and many other marketing costs. ▶ American companies spent $1.1 trillion last year—about 7.7 percent of GDP—to wrap, bundle, load, unload, sort, reload, and transport goods. That's more than the national GDPs of all but 13 countries worldwide.[12]

Shaving off even a small fraction of logistics costs can mean substantial savings. For example, Walmart recently undertook a program of logistics improvements through more efficient sourcing, better inventory management, and greater supply chain productivity that will reduce supply chain costs by 5 to15 percent over the next five years—that's a whopping $4 billion to $12 billion.[13]

Third, the explosion in product variety has created a need for improved logistics management. For example, in 1916 the typical Piggly Wiggly grocery store carried only 605 items. Today, a Piggly Wiggly carries a bewildering stock of between 20,000 and 35,000 items, depending on store size. A Walmart Supercenter store carries more than 100,000 products, 30,000 of which are grocery products.[14] Ordering, shipping, stocking, and controlling such a variety of products presents a sizable logistics challenge.

Improvements in information technology have also created opportunities for major gains in distribution efficiency. Today's companies are using sophisticated supply chain management software, Internet-based logistics systems,

▲ Logistics: As this huge stockpile of shipping containers suggests, American companies spent $1.1 trillion last year—7.7 percent of U.S. GDP—to bundle, load, unload, sort, reload, and transport goods.
© Phil Degginger/Alamy

▶ **Figure 10.5** Supply Chain Management

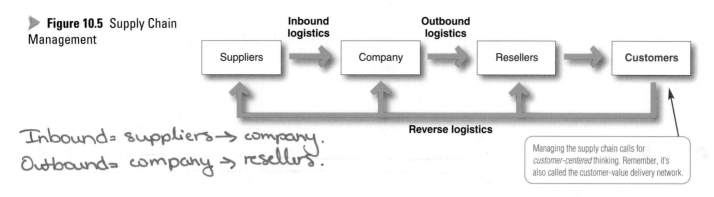

(Handwritten margin note): Inbound= suppliers → company. Outbound= company → resellers.

(Callout in figure): Managing the supply chain calls for *customer-centered* thinking. Remember, it's also called the customer-value delivery network.

(Handwritten margin note): logistics more important because:
— competitive advantage.
— cost savings.
— environmental sustainability.

point-of-sale scanners, RFID tags, satellite tracking, and electronic transfer of order and payment data. Such technology lets them quickly and efficiently manage the flow of goods, information, and finances through the supply chain.

Finally, more than almost any other marketing function, logistics affects the environment and a firm's environmental sustainability efforts. Transportation, warehousing, packaging, and other logistics functions are typically the biggest supply chain contributors to the company's environmental footprint. At the same time, they also provide one of the most fertile areas for cost savings. In other words, developing a *green supply chain* is not only environmentally responsible but can also be profitable. Here's a simple example:[15]

> Consumer package goods maker SC Johnson made a seemingly simple but smart—and profitable—change in the way it packs its trucks. Under the old system, a load of its Ziploc products filled a truck trailer before reaching the maximum weight limit. In contrast, a load of Windex glass cleaner hit the maximum weight before the trailer was full. By strategically mixing the two products, SC Johnson found it could send the same amount of products with 2,098 fewer shipments, while burning 168,000 fewer gallons of diesel fuel and eliminating 1,882 tons of greenhouse gasses. Says the company's director of environmental issues, "Loading a truck may seem simple, but making sure that a truck is truly full is a science. Consistently hitting a trailer's maximum weight provided a huge opportunity to reduce our energy consumption, cut our greenhouse gas emissions, and save money [in the bargain.]" "Sustainability shouldn't be about Washington jamming green stuff down your throat," concludes one supply chain expert. "This is a lot about money, about reducing costs."

Goals of the Logistics System

Some companies state their logistics objective as providing maximum customer service at the least cost. Unfortunately, as nice as this sounds, no logistics system can *both* maximize customer service *and* minimize distribution costs. Maximum customer service implies rapid delivery, large inventories, flexible assortments, liberal returns policies, and other services—all of which raise distribution costs. In contrast, minimum distribution costs imply slower delivery, smaller inventories, and larger shipping lots—which represent a lower level of overall customer service.

The goal of marketing logistics should be to provide a *targeted* level of customer service at the least cost. A company must first research the importance of various distribution services to customers and then set desired service levels for each segment. The objective is to maximize *profits*, not sales. Therefore, the company must weigh the benefits of providing higher levels of service against the costs. Some companies offer less service than their competitors and charge a lower price. Other companies offer more service and charge higher prices to cover higher costs.

Major Logistics Functions

Given a set of logistics objectives, the company designs a logistics system that will minimize the cost of attaining these objectives. The major logistics functions are *warehousing*, *inventory management*, *transportation*, and *logistics information management*.

Warehousing

Production and consumption cycles rarely match, so most companies must store their goods while they wait to be sold. For example, Snapper, Toro, and other lawn mower manufacturers run their factories all year long and store up products for the heavy spring and summer buying seasons. The storage function overcomes differences in needed quantities and timing, ensuring that products are available when customers are ready to buy them.

A company must decide on *how many* and *what types* of warehouses it needs and *where* they will be located. The company might use either *storage warehouses* or *distribution centers*. Storage warehouses store goods for moderate to long periods. In contrast, **distribution centers** are designed to move goods rather than just store them. They are large and highly automated warehouses designed to receive goods from various plants and suppliers, take orders, fill them efficiently, and deliver goods to customers as quickly as possible.

For example, Walmart operates a network of 147 huge distribution centers. A single center, serving the daily needs of 75 to 100 Walmart stores, typically contains some one million square feet of space (about 20 football fields) under a single roof. At a typical center, laser scanners route hundreds of thousands of cases of goods per day along 12 miles of conveyer belts, and the center's 500 to 1,000 associates load or unload some 500 trucks daily. Walmart's Monroe, Georgia, distribution center contains a 127,000-square-foot freezer (that's about 2.5 football fields) that can hold 10,000 pallets—room enough for 58 million Popsicles.[16]

Like almost everything else these days, warehousing has seen dramatic changes in technology in recent years. Outdated materials-handling methods are steadily being replaced by newer, computer-controlled systems requiring few employees. Computers and scanners read orders and direct lift trucks, electric hoists, or robots to gather goods, move them to loading docks, and issue invoices. ▶ For example, office supplies retailer Staples now employs "a team of super-retrievers—in day-glo orange—that keep its warehouse humming":[17]

> **Distribution center**
>
> A large, highly automated warehouse designed to receive goods from various plants and suppliers, take orders, fill them efficiently, and deliver goods to customers as quickly as possible.

▲ **High-tech distribution centers: Staples employs a team of super-retrievers—in day-glo orange—to keep its warehouse humming.**
Brent Humphreys/Redux Pictures

Imagine a team of employees that works 16 hours a day, seven days a week. They never call in sick or show up late. They demand no benefits, require no health insurance, and receive no paychecks. And they never complain. Sounds like a bunch of robots, huh? They are, in fact, robots—and they're dramatically changing the way Staples delivers notepads, pens, and paper clips to its customers. Every day, at Staples' huge Chambersburg, Pennsylvania, distribution center, 150 robots resemble a well-trained breed of working dogs, say, golden retrievers. When orders come in, the robots retrieve racks with the appropriate items and carry them to picking stations, then wait patiently as humans pull the correct products and place them in boxes. When orders are filled, the robots neatly park the racks back among the rest. The robots pretty much take care of themselves. When they run low on power, they head to battery-charging terminals, or, as warehouse personnel say, "They get themselves a drink of water." The robots now run 50 percent of the Chambersburg facility, where average daily output is up 60 percent since they arrived on the scene.

Inventory Management

Inventory management also affects customer satisfaction. Here, managers must maintain the delicate balance between carrying too little inventory and carrying too much. With too little stock, the firm risks not having products when customers want to buy. To remedy this, the firm may need costly emergency shipments or production. Carrying too much inventory results in higher-than-necessary inventory-carrying costs and stock obsolescence. Thus, in managing inventory, firms must balance the costs of carrying larger inventories against resulting sales and profits.

Many companies have greatly reduced their inventories and related costs through *just-in-time* logistics systems. With such systems, producers and retailers carry only small inventories of parts or merchandise, often enough for only a few days of operations. New stock arrives exactly when needed, rather than being stored in inventory until being used. Just-in-time systems require accurate forecasting along with fast, frequent, and flexible delivery so that new supplies will be available when needed. However, these systems result in substantial savings in inventory-carrying and handling costs.

Marketers are always looking for new ways to make inventory management more efficient. In the not-too-distant future, handling inventory might even become fully automated. For example, in Chapter 3 we discussed RFID or "smart tag" technology, by which small transmitter chips are embedded in or placed on products and packaging for everything from flowers and razors to tires. "Smart" products could make the entire supply chain—which accounts for nearly 75 percent of a product's cost—intelligent and automated.

Companies using RFID know, at any time, exactly where a product is located physically within the supply chain. "Smart shelves" would not only tell them when it's time to reorder but also place the order automatically with their suppliers. Such exciting new information technology applications will revolutionize distribution as we know it. Many large and resourceful marketing companies, such as Walmart, P&G, Kraft, IBM, HP, and Best Buy, are investing heavily to make the full use of RFID technology a reality.[18]

Transportation

The choice of transportation carriers affects the pricing of products, delivery performance, and the condition of goods when they arrive—all of which will affect customer satisfaction. In shipping goods to its warehouses, dealers, and customers, the company can choose among five main transportation modes: truck, rail, water, pipeline, and air, along with an alternative mode for digital products—the Internet.

Trucks have increased their share of transportation steadily and now account for 40 percent of total cargo ton-miles moved in the United States. U.S. trucks travel more than 431 billion miles a year—more than double the distance traveled 25 years ago—carrying 10.2 billion tons of freight. According to the American Trucking Association, 80 percent of U.S. communities depend solely on trucks for their goods and commodities. Trucks are highly flexible in their routing and time schedules, and they can usually offer faster service than railroads. They are efficient for short hauls of high-value merchandise. Trucking firms have evolved in recent years to become full-service providers of global transportation services. For example, large trucking firms now offer everything from satellite tracking, Web-based shipment management, and logistics planning software to cross-border shipping operations.[19]

Railroads account for 40 percent of the total cargo ton-miles moved. They are one of the most cost-effective modes for shipping large amounts of bulk products—coal, sand, minerals, and farm and forest products—over long distances. In recent years, railroads have increased their customer services by designing new equipment to handle special categories of goods, providing flatcars for carrying truck trailers by rail (piggyback), and providing in-transit services such as the diversion of shipped goods to other destinations en route and the processing of goods en route.

Water carriers, which account for about 5 percent of the cargo ton-miles, transport large amounts of goods by ships and barges on U.S. coastal and inland waterways. Although the cost of water transportation is very low for shipping bulky, low-value, nonperishable products such as sand, coal, grain, oil, and metallic ores, water transportation is the slowest mode and may be affected by the weather. *Pipelines*, which account for less than 1 percent of the cargo ton-miles, are a specialized means of shipping petroleum, natural gas, and chemicals from sources to markets. Most pipelines are used by their owners to ship their own products.

Although *air* carriers transport less than 1 percent of the cargo ton-miles of the nation's goods, they are an

If you rely on it,

wear it,

consume it,

or depend on it,

Trucks Bring It.

Trucks are essential to deliver everything America needs. Eighty-two percent of U.S. communities depend solely on truck transport for their goods and commodities. Simply put, trucks move America safely, efficiently and on time.

Good stuff.

TRUCKS BRING IT

www.TrucksBringIt.com

▲ **Truck transportation: More than 80 percent of American communities depend solely on the trucking industry for the delivery of their goods. "Good stuff. Trucks bring it."**
American Trucking Association

important transportation mode. Airfreight rates are much higher than rail or truck rates, but airfreight is ideal when speed is needed or distant markets have to be reached. Among the most frequently airfreighted products are perishables (fresh fish, cut flowers) and high-value, low-bulk items (technical instruments, jewelry). Companies find that airfreight also reduces inventory levels, packaging costs, and the number of warehouses needed.

The *Internet* carries digital products from producer to customer via satellite, cable, wireless signal, or phone wire. Software firms, the media, music and video companies, and education all make use of the Internet to transport digital products. The Internet holds the potential for lower product distribution costs. Whereas planes, trucks, and trains move freight and packages, digital technology moves information bits.

Shippers also use **intermodal transportation**—combining two or more modes of transportation. Twelve percent of the total cargo ton-miles are moved via multiple modes. *Piggyback* describes the use of rail and trucks; *fishyback*, water and trucks; *trainship*, water and rail; and *airtruck*, air and trucks. Combining modes provides advantages that no single mode can deliver. Each combination offers advantages to the shipper. For example, not only is piggyback cheaper than trucking alone, but it also provides flexibility and convenience.

In choosing a transportation mode for a product, shippers must balance many considerations: speed, dependability, availability, cost, and others. Thus, if a shipper needs speed, air and truck are the prime choices. If the goal is low cost, then water or rail might be best.

Logistics Information Management

Companies manage their supply chains through information. Channel partners often link up to share information and make better joint logistics decisions. From a logistics perspective, flows of information, such as customer transactions, billing, shipment and inventory levels, and even customer data, are closely linked to channel performance. Companies need simple, accessible, fast, and accurate processes for capturing, processing, and sharing channel information.

Information can be shared and managed in many ways, but most sharing takes place through traditional or Internet-based *electronic data interchange (EDI)*, the digital exchange of data between organizations, which primarily is transmitted via the Internet. Walmart, for example, requires EDI links with its more than 90,000 suppliers. If new suppliers don't have EDI capability, Walmart will work with them to find and implement the needed tools.[20]

In some cases, suppliers might actually be asked to generate orders and arrange deliveries for their customers. Many large retailers—such as Walmart and Home Depot—work closely with major suppliers such as P&G or Moen to set up *vendor-managed inventory (VMI)* systems or *continuous inventory replenishment* systems. Using VMI, the customer shares real-time data on sales and current inventory levels with the supplier. The supplier then takes full responsibility for managing inventories and deliveries. Some retailers even go so far as to shift inventory and delivery costs to the supplier. Such systems require close cooperation between the buyer and seller.

Integrated Logistics Management

Today, more and more companies are adopting the concept of **integrated logistics management**. This concept recognizes that providing better customer service and trimming distribution costs require *teamwork*, both inside the company and among all the marketing channel organizations. Inside, the company's various departments must work closely together to maximize its own logistics performance. Outside, the company must integrate its logistics system with those of its suppliers and customers to maximize the performance of the entire distribution network.

Cross-Functional Teamwork Inside the Company

Most companies assign responsibility for various logistics activities to many different departments—marketing, sales, finance, operations, and purchasing. Too often, each function tries to optimize its own logistics performance without regard for the activities of the other functions. However, transportation, inventory, warehousing, and information management activities interact, often in an inverse way. Lower inventory levels reduce inventory-carrying costs. But they may also reduce customer service and increase costs from stockouts,

---

Intermodal transportation
Combining two or more modes of transportation.

Integrated logistics management
The logistics concept that emphasizes teamwork—both inside the company and among all the marketing channel organizations—to maximize the performance of the entire distribution system.

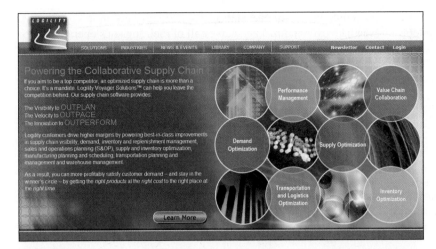

▲ Integrated logistics management: Many companies now employ sophisticated, systemwide supply chain management software, available from companies such as Logility.

Logility, Inc.

back orders, special production runs, and costly fast-freight shipments. Because distribution activities involve strong trade-offs, decisions by different functions must be coordinated to achieve better overall logistics performance.

The goal of integrated supply chain management is to harmonize all of the company's logistics decisions. Close working relationships among departments can be achieved in several ways. Some companies have created permanent logistics committees composed of managers responsible for different physical distribution activities. Companies can also create supply chain manager positions that link the logistics activities of functional areas. For example, P&G has created product supply managers who manage all the supply chain activities for each product category. Many companies have a vice president of logistics with cross-functional authority.

Finally, companies can employ sophisticated, systemwide supply chain management software, now available from a wide range of software enterprises large and small, from SAP and Oracle to Infor and Logility. The important thing is that the company must coordinate its logistics and marketing activities to create high market satisfaction at a reasonable cost.

Building Logistics Partnerships

Companies must do more than improve their own logistics. They must also work with other channel partners to improve whole-channel distribution. The members of a marketing channel are linked closely in creating customer value and building customer relationships. One company's distribution system is another company's supply system. The success of each channel member depends on the performance of the entire supply chain. For example, IKEA can create its stylish but affordable furniture and deliver the "IKEA lifestyle" only if its entire supply chain—consisting of thousands of merchandise designers and suppliers, transport companies, warehouses, and service providers—operates at maximum efficiency and customer-focused effectiveness.

Smart companies coordinate their logistics strategies and forge strong partnerships with suppliers and customers to improve customer service and reduce channel costs. Many companies have created *cross-functional, cross-company teams*. For example, Nestlé's Purina pet food unit has a team of dozens of people working in Bentonville, Arkansas, the home base of Walmart. The Purina Walmart team members work jointly with their counterparts at Walmart to find ways to squeeze costs out of their distribution system. Working together benefits not only Purina and Walmart but also their shared, final consumers.

Other companies partner through *shared projects*. For example, many large retailers conduct joint in-store programs with suppliers. Home Depot allows key suppliers to use its stores as a testing ground for new merchandising programs. The suppliers spend time at Home Depot stores watching how their product sells and how customers relate to it. They then create programs specially tailored to Home Depot and its customers. Clearly, both the supplier and the customer benefit from such partnerships. The point is that all supply chain members must work together in the cause of bringing value to final consumers.

Third-Party Logistics

Third-party logistics (3PL) provider
An independent logistics provider that performs any or all of the functions required to get a client's product to market.

Although most big companies love to make and sell their products, many loathe the associated logistics "grunt work." They detest the bundling, loading, unloading, sorting, storing, reloading, transporting, customs clearing, and tracking required to supply their factories and get products to their customers. They hate it so much that a growing number of firms now outsource some or all of their logistics to **third-party logistics (3PL) providers** such as Ryder, Penske Logistics, BAX Global, DHL Logistics, FedEx Logistics, and UPS

Business Solutions. Outsourced logistics providers can help companies improve their own logistics systems or even take over and manage part or all of their logistics operations (see Marketing at Work 10.2). Here's an example:[21]

> Stonyfield Farm, the world's largest yogurt maker, had a distribution problem. As the company grew, inefficiencies had crept into its distribution system. To help fix the problem, Stonyfield turned to 3PL provider Ryder Supply Chain Solutions. Together, Ryder and Stonyfield designed a new transportation system that cut processing and distribution costs and improved service levels, while at the same time dramatically reducing the company's carbon footprint. After evaluating the Stonyfield network, Ryder identified optimal transportation solutions, including the use of fuel efficient RydeGreen vehicles. It helped Stonyfield set up a small, dedicated truck fleet to make regional deliveries in New England and replaced Stonyfield's national less-than-truckload distribution network with a regional multistop truckload system. As a result, Stonyfield now moves more product in fewer trucks, cutting in half the number of miles traveled. In all, the changes produced a 40 percent reduction in

MARKETING AT WORK   10.2

UPS: "We Love Logistics"—Put UPS to Work for You and You'll Love Logistics Too

Mention UPS and most people envision one of those familiar brown trucks with a friendly driver, rumbling around their neighborhood dropping off parcels. For most of us, seeing a brown UPS truck evokes fond memories of past package deliveries. However, most of UPS's revenue comes not from the residential customers who receive the packages, but from the business customers who send them. And for its business customers, UPS does more than just get Grandma's holiday package there on time.

For most businesses, physical package delivery is just part of a much more complex logistics process that involves purchase orders, inventories, order status checks, invoices, payments, returned merchandise, fleets of delivery vehicles, and even cross-border dealings. Companies need timely information about their outbound and inbound packages—what's in them, where they're now located, to whom they are going, when they'll get there, and how much is owed. UPS knows that, for many companies, logistics can be a real nightmare.

That's where UPS can help. Logistics is exactly what UPS does best. Over the years, UPS has grown to become much more than a neighborhood package delivery service. It is now a $50 billion corporate giant providing a broad range of logistics solutions. Whereas many customers hate dealing with the logistics process, UPS proclaims "We ♥ logistics." To UPS's thinking, "the new logistics" is "the most powerful force in business today" for creating competitive advantage. As the company puts it:

> It's true that logistics is about getting things where they need to be, exactly when they need to be there, and doing it as efficiently as possible. But today's logistics can offer much more than that. Logistics is about using the movement of goods to save money, save time, and become more competitive. It makes running your business easier. It helps you create better customer experiences. It's a whole new way of thinking. It's the new logistics.

If it has to do with logistics, anywhere in the world, UPS can probably do it better than anyone can. UPS offers customers efficient multi-modal package, mail, and freight distribution services. But it can also help customers streamline sourcing, maintain leaner inventories, manage and fulfill orders, warehouse goods, kit or assemble products in response to customer demand, and manage post-sales warranty repair and returns services.

UPS has the resources to handle the logistics needs of just about any size business. It employs more than 400,000 people, owns almost 100,000 delivery vehicles, runs the world's

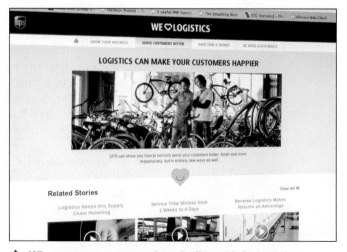

▲ Whereas many customers hate dealing with the logistics process, UPS proclaims "We ♥ logistics." "It makes running your business easier. It helps you create better customer experiences. It's a whole new way of thinking."

Jarrod Weaton/Weaton Digital, Inc.

transportation-related carbon dioxide emissions and knocked an eye-popping 13 percent off Stonyfield's transportation costs.

Ryder, UPS, and other 3PL providers help clients tighten up sluggish, overstuffed supply chains; slash inventories; and get products to customers more quickly and reliably. According to a survey of chief logistics executives at *Fortune 500* companies, 82 percent of these companies use 3PL (also called *outsourced logistics* or *contract logistics*) services. In all, North American shippers spend 47 percent of their logistics budget on outsourced logistics.[22]

Companies use third-party logistics providers for several reasons. First, since getting the product to market is their main focus, using these providers makes the most sense, as they can often do it more efficiently and at lower cost. Outsourcing typically results in a 15 to 30 percent cost savings. Second, outsourcing logistics frees a company to focus more intensely on its core business. Finally, integrated logistics companies understand increasingly complex logistics environments.

ninth-largest airline, and maintains 2,770 operating facilities in 220 countries. Last year, UPS delivered nearly 4 *billion* packages worldwide. The distribution giant is also the world's largest customs broker. With some 815 international flights per day to or from 327 international destinations, UPS can also help businesses to navigate the complexities of international shipping.

At one level, UPS can simply handle a company's package shipments. On a deeper level, however, UPS can advise businesses on how to improve their own overall logistics operations. It can help clients redesign their logistics systems to better synchronize the flow of goods, funds, and information up and down the entire supply chain. At a still deeper level, companies can let UPS take over and manage part or all of their logistics operations.

For example, Zappos.com relies on UPS to help run its efficient, customer-friendly returns process. Returns are key to Zappos' customer satisfaction strategy, and outstanding logistics is key to a smooth-running returns process. Customers can order lots of different styles and sizes from Zappos, try them on, and then return the ones they don't want at no charge. In fact, the company encourages it. Zappos has teamed with UPS on logistics from the start, building its distribution center minutes from UPS's Worldport air hub in Louisville, Kentucky. UPS delivers all of Zappos' packages. Then, to return unwanted items, all customers have to do is put them back in the box, call for pickup, and let UPS handle the rest. This seamless, UPS-run returns process is one reason 75 percent of Zappos.com shoppers are repeat customers. Moreover, by using UPS's integrated shipping and tracking tools, Zappos can monitor incoming returns along with inbound goods from vendors to quickly and efficiently plan and replenish stock for resale.

Consumer electronics maker Toshiba lets UPS handle its entire laptop PC repair process—lock, stock, and barrel:

UPS's logistics prowess was the answer to one of Toshiba's biggest challenges—turnaround time on laptop repairs. According to

Mike Simons, CEO of Toshiba America, "When we started off with UPS, we thought of them [only] as a mover of packages from point A to point B—how to get a PC from the factory floor into the customer's hands. But by sitting down with them and looking at our complete supply chain, talking about our repair process and parts management, we evolved into so much more." Now, customers ship laptops needing repair to a special UPS facility near the Worldport air hub in Louisville. There, UPS employees receive the units, run diagnostics to assess the repairs needed, pick the necessary parts, quickly complete the service, and return the laptops to their owners. UPS can now fix and ship a laptop in a single day, shortening a door-to-door repair process that once took two to three weeks down to four or fewer days. Together, UPS and Toshiba greatly improved the customer repair experience.

So, UPS does much more than just deliver packages. It provides a rich range of logistics services that can help businesses to sharpen their logistics strategies, cut costs, and serve customers better. More than just providing shipping services, UPS becomes a strategic logistics partner. "One of the things we've learned with UPS is their willingness to be a partner," says Toshiba America CEO Simon. "They really understand the overall experience we're trying to create for the customers."

Says a UPS operations manager, "We want to understand the complete supply chain for our customers. When there are issues in the field and you resolve those issues—*quickly* resolve those issues so that you can maintain a high level of customer satisfaction—that's logistics." Letting UPS help with the logistics lets companies focus on what they do best. And it helps take the nightmares out of the logistics process. As one UPS ad concludes: "We love logistics. Put UPS to work for you and you'll love logistics too."

Sources: Quotes, examples, and other information from "How to Level a Playing Field: Why Even the Smallest Companies Should Embrace Logistics," special advertising feature, *Inc.*, June 2011, p. 94; http://thenewlogistics.ups.com/swf#/stories?page=1, accessed October 2011; and www.thenewlogistics.com and www.ups.com/content/us/en/about/facts/worldwide.html, accessed November 2011.

| REST STOP | REVIEWING THE CONCEPTS |

MyMarketingLab

Now that you have completed the chapter, return to www.mymktlab.com to experience and apply the concepts and to explore the additional study materials for this chapter.

CHAPTER REVIEW AND KEY TERMS

Objectives Review

Some companies pay too little attention to their distribution channels; others, however, have used imaginative distribution systems to gain a competitive advantage. A company's channel decisions directly affect every other marketing decision. Management must make channel decisions carefully, incorporating today's needs with tomorrow's likely selling environment.

OBJECTIVE 1 Explain why companies use marketing channels and discuss the functions these channels perform. (pp 292–296)

In creating customer value, a company can't go it alone. It must work within an entire network of partners—a value delivery network—to accomplish this task. Individual companies and brands don't compete, their entire value delivery networks do.

Most producers use intermediaries to bring their products to market. They forge a *marketing channel* (or *distribution channel*)—a set of interdependent organizations involved in the process of making a product or service available for use or consumption by the consumer or business user. Through their contacts, experience, specialization, and scale of operation, intermediaries usually offer the firm more than it can achieve on its own.

Marketing channels perform many key functions. Some help *complete transactions* by gathering and distributing *information* needed for planning and aiding exchange, developing and spreading persuasive *communications* about an offer, performing *contact* work (finding and communicating with prospective buyers), *matching* (shaping and fitting the offer to the buyer's needs), and entering into *negotiation* to reach an agreement on price and other terms of the offer so that ownership can be transferred. Other functions help to *fulfill* the completed transactions by offering *physical distribution* (transporting and storing goods), *financing* (acquiring and using funds to cover the costs of the channel work, and *risk taking* (assuming the risks of carrying out the channel work.

OBJECTIVE 2 Discuss how channel members interact and how they organize to perform the work of the channel. (pp 296–303)

The channel will be most effective when each member assumes the tasks it can do best. Ideally, because the success of individual channel members depends on overall channel success, all channel firms should work together smoothly. They should understand and accept their roles, coordinate their goals and activities, and cooperate to attain overall channel goals. By cooperating, they can more effectively sense, serve, and satisfy the target market.

In a large company, the formal organization structure assigns roles and provides needed leadership. But in a distribution channel composed of independent firms, leadership and power are not formally set. Traditionally, distribution channels have lacked the leadership needed to assign roles and manage conflict. In recent years, however, new types of channel organizations have appeared that provide stronger leadership and improved performance.

OBJECTIVE 3 Identify the major channel alternatives open to a company. (pp 303–307)

Channel alternatives vary from direct selling to using one, two, three, or more intermediary *channel levels*. Marketing channels face continuous and sometimes dramatic change. Three of the most important trends are the growth of *vertical, horizontal,* and *multichannel marketing systems*. These trends affect channel cooperation, conflict, and competition.

Channel design begins with assessing customer channel service needs and company channel objectives and constraints. The company then identifies the major channel alternatives in terms of the *types* of intermediaries, the *number* of intermediaries, and the *channel responsibilities* of each. Each channel alternative must be evaluated according to economic, control, and adaptive criteria. *Channel management* calls for selecting qualified intermediaries and motivating them. Individual channel members must be evaluated regularly.

> **OBJECTIVE 4 Explain how companies select, motivate, and evaluate channel members. (pp 307–309)**

Producers vary in their ability to attract qualified marketing intermediaries. Some producers have no trouble signing up channel members, whereas others have to work hard to line up enough qualified intermediaries. When selecting intermediaries, the company should evaluate each channel member's qualifications and select those that best fit its channel objectives.

Once selected, channel members must be continuously motivated to do their best. The company must sell not only *through* the intermediaries but also *with* them. It should forge strong partnerships with channel members to create a marketing system that meets the needs of both the manufacturer *and* the partners.

> **OBJECTIVE 5 Discuss the nature and importance of marketing logistics and integrated supply chain management. (pp 310–317)**

Marketing logistics (or *physical distribution*) is an area of potentially high cost savings and improved customer satisfaction. Marketing logistics addresses not only *outbound distribution* but also *inbound distribution* and *reverse distribution*. That is, it involves the entire *supply chain management*—managing value-added flows between suppliers, the company, resellers, and final users. No logistics system can both maximize customer service and minimize distribution costs. Instead, the goal of logistics management is to provide a *targeted* level of service at the least cost. The major logistics functions are *warehousing, inventory management, transportation,* and *logistics information management*.

The *integrated supply chain management concept* recognizes that improved logistics requires teamwork in the form of close working relationships across functional areas inside the company and across various organizations in the supply chain. Companies can achieve logistics harmony among functions by creating cross-functional logistics teams, integrative supply manager positions, and senior-level logistics executives with cross-functional authority. Channel partnerships can take the form of cross-company teams, shared projects, and information-sharing systems. Today, some companies are outsourcing their logistics functions to third-party logistics (3PL) providers to save costs, increase efficiency, and gain faster and more effective access to global markets.

Key Terms

Objective 1
Value delivery network (p 293)
Marketing channel (distribution channel) (p 293)
Channel level (p 295)
Direct marketing channel (p 295)
Indirect marketing channel (p 295)

Objective 2
Channel conflict (p 297)
Conventional distribution channel (p 297)
Vertical marketing system (VMS) (p 298)

Corporate VMS (p 298)
Contractual VMS (p 298)
Franchise organization (p 299)
Administered VMS (p 299)
Horizontal marketing system (p 299)
Multichannel distribution system (p 300)
Disintermediation (p 301)

Objective 3
Marketing channel design (p 304)
Intensive distribution (p 305)
Exclusive distribution (p 305)
Selective distribution (p 306)

Objective 4
Marketing channel management (p 307)

Objective 5
Marketing logistics (physical distribution) (p 310)
Supply chain management (p 310)
Distribution center (p 312)
Intermodal transportation (p 314)
Integrated logistics management (p 314)
Third-party logistics (3PL) provider (p 315)

DISCUSSION AND CRITICAL THINKING

Discussion Questions

1. Describe the key functions performed by marketing channel members. (AACSB: Communication)
2. Compare and contrast direct marketing channels and indirect marketing channels. Name the various types of resellers in marketing channels. (AACSB: Communication)
3. Define *disintermediation*. List three industries in which changes in channel systems have resulted in disintermediation. (AACSB: Communication; Reflective Thinking)
4. Describe the three strategies available regarding the number of intermediaries and discuss the types of products for which each is appropriate. (AACSB: Communication; Reflective Thinking)
5. List and briefly describe the major logistics functions. Provide an example of a decision a logistics manager would make for each major function. (AACSB: Communication; Reflective Thinking)
6. Describe intermodal transportation, list the different combinations used to distribute products, and identify the benefits of using this mode of transportation. (AACSB: Communication)

Critical Thinking Exercises

1. In a small group, debate whether or not the Internet will result in disintermediation of the following types of retail stores: (1) video rental stores, (2) music stores, (3) grocery stores, (4) book stores, and (5) clothing stores. (AACSB: Communication; Reflective Thinking)
2. Consumer packaged goods manufacturers typically distribute products to retailers through wholesalers. However, Walmart deals directly with manufacturers—many of whom have offices located in Bentonville, Arkansas—concentrating just on Walmart. Discuss the consequences of manufacturers, such as Kraft and P&G, distributing products directly to one or more large retailers while distributing the same products indirectly to smaller retailers through wholesalers. (AACSB: Communication; Reflective Thinking)
3. Visit www.youtube.com/watch?v=eob532iEpqk and watch "The Future Market" video. What impact will RFID tags have on each of the major logistical functions? What are the biggest current obstacles to adopting this technology? (AACSB: Communication; Use of IT; Reflective Thinking)

MINICASES AND APPLICATIONS

Marketing Technology   Distributing Craft Beer Internationally

Brewing craft beer is both an art and a science, and Sonia Collin, a Belgian researcher, is trying to devise a method to give this highly perishable beer a longer shelf life. If successful, brewers can ship greater amounts of beer over longer distances. Hoping to boost exports of homegrown products, the Belgian government is investing $7 million for research, with $1.7 million of that allocated to Ms. Collins' research. After the $250,000 tasting machine in her laboratory identified the chemical compounds in a sample of beer, researchers were able to recommend using organic ingredients, adjusting the oxygen and yeast levels, and reducing the time the beer spends at high temperatures in the brewing process. Although pasteurization and bottling methods allow giants like Heineken and Anheuser-Busch to export their brews, aficionados prefer the more delicate flavor of craft beers. But craft brews don't travel well—time and sunlight are its worst enemies—so they are limited to local distribution. Most craft beers lose flavor in less than three months.

1. Describe the distribution channel needed for a craft beer to travel from Belgium to your city or town. How many channel levels will be involved? (AACSB: Communication; Reflective Thinking)
2. Discuss the options facing Belgian craft brewers who want to sell their products in the United States if the researchers do not discover a way to sufficiently extend the shelf life of craft beers. (AACSB: Communication; Reflective Thinking)

Marketing Ethics   Supply Chain Demands

Tension is escalating between apparel retailers and suppliers during the economic recovery. Retailers used to place orders almost a year in advance and suppliers produced high volumes cheaply. Now many retailers are placing small initial orders, and if styles take off with consumers, they quickly re-order— a tactic known as *chasing*. Teen retailer Aeropostale has been buying conservatively and chasing for items that are hot with buyers. Appropriate inventory levels in the apparel industry have always been difficult to predict, but it appears that retailers are pushing this worry back onto suppliers.

1. Discuss the concerns of suppliers (that is, garment makers) and retailers in the apparel channel of distribution. Is it fair that retailers should expect suppliers to respond so quickly? Is it fair that suppliers should demand long lead times? (AACSB: Communication; Ethical Reasoning; Reflective Thinking)
2. What type of channel conflict does this represent and are there any benefits resulting from this conflict? (AACSB: Communication; Reflective Thinking)

Marketing by the Numbers   Expanding Distribution

Lightco, Inc. manufactures decorative lighting fixtures sold primarily in the eastern United States. Lightco wants to expand to the Midwest and Southern United States and intends to hire ten new sales representatives to secure distribution for its products. Sales reps will acquire new retail accounts and manage those accounts after acquisition. Each sales rep earns a salary of $50,000 plus 2 percent commission. Each retailer generates an average of $50,000 in revenue for Lightco. Refer to Appendix 3, Marketing by the Numbers, to answer the following questions.

1. If Lightco's contribution margin is 40 percent, what increase in sales will it need to break even on the increase in fixed costs to hire the new sales reps? (AACSB: Communication; Analytical Reasoning)

2. How many new retail accounts must the company acquire break even on this tactic? What average number of accounts must each new rep acquire? (AACSB: Communication; Analytical Reasoning)

Video Case   Gaviña Gourmet Coffee

These days, there seems to be plenty of coffee to go around. So how does a small time coffee roaster like Gaviña succeed in an industry dominated by big players? By carefully crafting a distribution strategy that moves its products into the hands of consumers. Without a big advertising budget, Gaviña has creatively pursued channel partners in the grocery, restaurant, and hospitality industries. Now, major chains such as McDonald's and Publix make Gaviña's coffees available to the public. This video also illustrates the company's distribution strategy's impact on supply chain and product development issues.

After viewing the video featuring Gaviña, answer the following questions:

1. How would you apply the concept of the supply chain to Gaviña?
2. Sketch out as many consumer and business channels for Gaviña as you can. How does each of these channels meet distinct customer needs?
3. How has Gaviña's distribution strategy affected its product mix?

Company Cases   10 Pandora / 11 Tesco Fresh & Easy

See Appendix 1 for cases appropriate for this chapter. **Case 10: Pandora: Disintermediator or Disintermediated?** Pandora's music service gains a huge following by capitalizing on new distribution channels. **Case 11, Tesco Fresh & Easy: Another British Invasion.** UK megagrocer Tesco attempts to penetrate the U.S. market by targeting an underserved customer segment.

11 Retailing and Wholesaling

CHAPTER ROAD MAP

Objective Outline

Previewing the Concepts

We now look more deeply into the two major intermediary marketing channel functions: retailing and wholesaling. You already know something about retailing—retailers of all shapes and sizes serve you every day. However, you probably know much less about the hoard of wholesalers that work behind the scenes. In this chapter, we examine the characteristics of different kinds of retailers and wholesalers, the marketing decisions they make, and trends for the future.

When it comes to retailers, you have to start with Walmart. This megaretailer's phenomenal success has resulted from an unrelenting focus on bringing value to its customers. Day in and day out, Walmart lives up to its promise: "Save money. Live better." That focus on customer value has made Walmart not only the world's largest *retailer* but also the world's largest *company*.

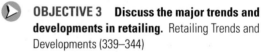

▲ At Walmart: "Save money. Live better." Says Walmart's CEO, "We're obsessed with delivering value to customers."

Beth Hall/Bloomberg via Getty Images

Walmart: The World's Largest Retailer—the World's Largest Company

Walmart is almost unimaginably big. It's the world's largest retailer—the world's largest company. It rang up an incredible $422 billion in sales last year—1.7 times the sales of competitors Costco, Target, Sears/Kmart, Macy's, JCPenney, and Kohl's *combined*.

Walmart is the number-one seller in several categories of consumer products, including groceries, clothing, toys, CDs, and pet care products. It sells well over twice as many groceries as Kroger, the leading grocery-only food retailer, and its clothing and shoe sales alone last year exceeded the total revenues of Macy's Inc., parent of both Macy's and Bloomingdale's department stores. Incredibly, Walmart sells 30 percent of the disposable diapers purchased in the United States each year, 30 percent of the hair care products, 30 percent of all health and beauty products, 26 percent of the toothpaste, and 20 percent of the pet food. On average, worldwide, Walmart serves customers more than 200 million times per week.

It's also hard to fathom Walmart's impact on the U.S. economy. It's the nation's largest employer—one out of every 222 men, women, and children in the United States is a Walmart associate. Its sales of $1.52 billion on a single day in 2003 exceeded the GDPs of 26 countries. According to one study, through its own low prices and impact on competitors' prices, Walmart saves the average American household $2,500 each year, equivalent to more than six months worth of groceries for the average family.

What's behind this spectacular success? First and foremost, Walmart is passionately dedicated to its long-time, low-price value proposition and what its low prices mean to customers: "Save money. Live better." To accomplish this mission, Walmart offers a broad selection of carefully selected goods at "unbeatable low prices." No other retailer has come nearly so close to mastering the concepts of everyday low prices and one-stop shopping. As one analyst put it, "The company gospel . . . is relatively simple: Be an agent for customers—find out what they want and sell it to them for the lowest possible price." Says Walmart's president and CEO, "We're obsessed with delivering value to customers."

How does Walmart make money with such low prices? Walmart is a lean, mean, distribution machine—it has the lowest cost structure in the industry. Low costs let the giant retailer charge lower prices but still reap higher profits. Lower prices attract more shoppers, producing more sales, making the company more efficient, and enabling it to lower prices even more.

Walmart's low costs result in part from superior management and more sophisticated technology. Its Bentonville, Arkansas, headquarters contains an information technology system that the U.S. Department of Defense would envy, giving managers around the country instant access

Day in and day out, giant Walmart lives up to its promise: "Save money. Live better." Its obsession with customer value has made Walmart not only the world's largest *retailer* but also the world's largest *company*.

to sales and operating information. And its huge, fully automated distribution centers employ the latest technology to supply stores efficiently.

Walmart also keeps costs down through good old "tough buying." The company is known for the calculated way it wrings low prices from suppliers. "Don't expect a greeter and don't expect friendly," said one supplier's sales executive after a visit to Walmart's buying offices. "Once you are ushered into one of the spartan little buyers' rooms, expect a steely eye across the table and be prepared to cut your price. They are very, very focused people, and they use their buying power more forcefully than anyone else in America."

Some critics argue that Walmart squeezes its suppliers too hard, driving some out of business. Walmart proponents counter, however, that it is simply acting in its customers' interests by forcing suppliers to be more efficient. And most suppliers seem to agree that although Walmart is tough, it's honest and straightforward in its dealings.

Despite its incredible success over the past four decades, mighty Walmart faces some weighty challenges ahead. Having grown so big, the maturing giant is having difficulty maintaining the rapid growth rates of its youth. To reignite growth, Walmart is pushing into new, faster-growing product and service lines, including organic foods, store brands, in-store health clinics, and consumer financial services. It's also pushing its expansion into international markets and online sales. Still, growth remains a daunting task. Think about this: To grow just 7 percent next year, Walmart will have to add nearly $30 billion in new sales. That's a sales *increase* equivalent to the *total* sales of a Google, a Du-Pont, a Macy's, or more than 1.5 Nikes. That's a lot of growth.

Recently, to refresh its positioning relative to younger, hipper competitors such as Target, Walmart has been giving itself a modest image face-lift. For example, it's spruced up its stores with a cleaner, brighter, more open look and less clutter to make them more shopper-friendly, like Target. It's added some new, higher-quality merchandise: Many urban Walmarts now carry a slew of higher-end consumer electronics products, from Sony plasma televisions to Dell and Toshiba laptops to Apple iPods and iPads. The retailer has also dressed up its apparel racks with more-stylish fashion lines. Finally, Walmart has dropped its old, hard-sell "roll-back prices" advertising in favor of softer, more refined lifestyle ads that better support its "Save money. Live better." slogan.

But don't expect Walmart to try to out-Target Target. In fact, following the recent Great Recession and new consumer spending attitudes, Target has moved more toward Walmart than the other way around. And although Walmart has faced slow U.S. sales growth in the postrecession economy as its mainstay low-income customers have struggled to spend, it remains strongly positioned to serve thriftier consumers in the future. So even as it brushes up its image, Walmart has no intention of ever giving up its core low price value proposition. After all, Walmart is and always will be a discount store. "I don't think Walmart's . . . ever going to be edgy," says a Walmart marketer. "I don't think that fits our brand. Our brand is about saving people money" so that they can live better.[1]

MyMarketingLab

Visit www.mymktlab.com to find activities that help you learn and review in order to succeed in this chapter.

T | he Walmart story sets the stage for examining the fast-changing world of today's resellers. This chapter looks at *retailing* and *wholesaling*. In the first section, we look at the nature and importance of retailing, the major types of store and nonstore retailers, the decisions retailers make, and the future of retailing. In the second section, we discuss these same topics as they apply to wholesalers.

Author Comment ▶
You already know a lot about retailers. You deal with them every day—store retailers, service retailers, online retailers, and others.

Retailing
All the activities involved in selling goods or services directly to final consumers for their personal, nonbusiness use.

Retailing

What is retailing? We all know that Costco, Home Depot, Macy's, Best Buy, and Target are retailers, but so are Amazon.com, the local Hampton Inn, and a doctor seeing patients. **Retailing** includes all the activities involved in selling products or services directly to final consumers for their personal, nonbusiness use. Many institutions—manufacturers, wholesalers, and retailers—do retailing. But most retailing is done by **retailers**, businesses whose sales come *primarily* from retailing.

Retailing plays a very important role in most marketing channels. Each year, retailers account for more than $3.9 trillion of sales to final consumers. They connect brands to consumers in what marketing agency OgilvyAction calls "the last mile"—the final stop in

Retailer

A business whose sales come *primarily* from retailing.

Shopper marketing

Using point-of-sale promotions and advertising to extend brand equity to "the last mile" and encourage favorable in-store purchase decisions.

brand-building from the eyes of the consumer towards the company.

the consumer's path to purchase. It's the "distance a consumer travels between an attitude and an action," explains OgilvyAction's CEO. Some 40 percent of all consumer decisions are made in or near the store. Thus, retailers "reach consumers at key moments of truth, ultimately [influencing] their actions at the point of purchase."[2]

In fact, many marketers are now embracing the concept of **shopper marketing**, using point-of-purchase promotions and advertising to extend brand equity to "the last mile" and encourage favorable point-of-purchase decisions. Shopper marketing involves focusing the entire marketing process—from product and brand development to logistics, promotion, and merchandising—toward turning shoppers into buyers at the point of sale.

Of course, every well-designed marketing effort focuses on customer buying behavior. What differentiates the concept of shopper marketing is the suggestion that these efforts should be coordinated around the shopping process itself. For example, P&G follows a "store back" concept, in which all marketing ideas need to be effective at the store-shelf level and work back from there. "We are now brand-building from the eyes of the consumer toward us," says a P&G executive.[3]

The dramatic growth of digital shopping, or combined digital and in-store shopping, has added a new dimension to shopper marketing. The "last mile" or "point of purchase" no longer takes place only in stores. Most consumers now make at least some of their purchases online, without even setting foot into a retail store. Alternatively, they may research a purchase on the Internet before—or even during—a store visit. ▶ For example, it's not uncommon to see a consumer looking at new TVs in a Best Buy while at the same time using a mobile app to check product reviews and prices at Amazon.com. Thus, shopper marketing isn't just about in-store buying these days. Influencing consumers' buying decisions as they shop involves efforts aimed at in-store, online, and mobile shopping.[4]

▲ Shopper marketing: The dramatic growth of digital shopping has added a new dimension to "point of purchase." Influencing consumers' buying decisions as they shop now involves efforts aimed at in-store, online, and mobile shopping.

x99/ZUMA Press/Newscom

Although most retailing is still done in retail stores, in recent years direct and online retailing have been growing much faster than store retailing. We discuss direct and online retailing in detail in Chapter 14. In this chapter, we will focus on store retailing.

Types of Retailers

Characteristics of Retailers:

- amount of service they offer
- breadth & depth of their product lines.
- prices they charge.
- organization.

Retail stores come in all shapes and sizes—from your local hairstyling salon or family-owned restaurant to national specialty chain retailers such as REI or Williams-Sonoma to megadiscounters such as Costco or Walmart. The most important types of retail stores are described in ▶ **Table 11.1** and discussed in the following sections. They can be classified in terms of several characteristics, including the *amount of service* they offer, the breadth and depth of their *product lines*, the *relative prices* they charge, and how they are *organized*.

Amount of Service

self-service → cheap, convenience goods, DIY,

limited service → some sales assistance, higher prices.

Different types of customers and products require different amounts of service. To meet these varying service needs, retailers may offer one of three service levels: self-service, limited service, and full service.

Self-service retailers serve customers who are willing to perform their own *locate-compare-select* process to save time or money. Self-service is the basis of all discount operations and is typically used by retailers selling convenience goods (such as supermarkets) and nationally branded, fast-moving shopping goods (such as Target or Kohl's). *Limited-service retailers*, such as Sears or JCPenney, provide more sales assistance because they carry more shopping goods about which customers need information. Their increased operating costs result in higher prices.

▶ **Table 11.1**	Major Store Retailer Types	
Type	**Description**	**Examples**
Specialty store	A store that carries a narrow product line with a deep assortment, such as apparel stores, sporting-goods stores, furniture stores, florists, and bookstores.	REI, Radio Shack, Williams-Sonoma
Department store	A store that carries several product lines—typically clothing, home furnishings, and household goods—with each line operated as a separate department managed by specialist buyers or merchandisers.	Macy's, Sears, Neiman Marcus
Supermarket	A relatively large, low-cost, low-margin, high-volume, self-service operation designed to serve the consumer's total needs for grocery and household products.	Kroger, Safeway, SuperValu, Publix
Convenience store	A relatively small store located near residential areas, open long hours seven days a week, and carrying a limited line of high-turnover convenience products at slightly higher prices.	7-Eleven, Stop-N-Go, Circle K, Sheetz
Discount store	A store that carries standard merchandise sold at lower prices with lower margins and higher volumes.	Walmart, Target, Kohl's
Off-price retailer	A store that sells merchandise bought at less-than-regular wholesale prices and sold at less than retail. These include *factory outlets* owned and operated by manufacturers; *independent off-price retailers* owned and run by entrepreneurs or by divisions of larger retail corporations; and *warehouse* (or *wholesale*) *clubs* selling a limited selection of goods at deep discounts to consumers who pay membership fees.	Mikasa (factory outlet); TJ Maxx (independent off-price retailer); Costco, Sam's Club, BJ's (warehouse clubs)
Superstore	A very large store that meets consumers' total needs for routinely purchased food and nonfood items. This includes *supercenters*, combined supermarket and discount stores, and *category killers*, which carry a deep assortment in a particular category.	Walmart Supercenter, SuperTarget, Meijer (discount stores); Best Buy, PetSmart, Staples, Barnes & Noble (category killers)

Full-service retailers, such as high-end specialty stores (for example, Tiffany or Williams-Sonoma) and first-class department stores (such as Nordstrom or Neiman Marcus) assist customers in every phase of the shopping process. Full-service stores usually carry more specialty goods for which customers need or want assistance or advice. They provide more services, which results in much higher operating costs. These higher costs are passed along to customers as higher prices.

Product Line

Retailers can also be classified by the length and breadth of their product assortments. Some retailers, such as **specialty stores**, carry narrow product lines with deep assortments within those lines. Today, specialty stores are flourishing. The increasing use of market segmentation, market targeting, and product specialization has resulted in a greater need for stores that focus on specific products and segments.

By contrast, **department stores** carry a wide variety of product lines. In recent years, department stores have been squeezed between more focused and flexible specialty stores on the one hand and more efficient, lower-priced discounters on the other. In response, many have added promotional pricing to meet the discount threat. Others have stepped up the use of store brands and single-brand *designer shops* to compete with specialty stores. Still others are trying catalog, telephone, and Web selling. Service remains the key differentiating factor. Retailers such as Nordstrom, Saks, Neiman Marcus, and other high-end department stores are doing well by emphasizing exclusive merchandise and high-quality service.

Specialty store
A retail store that carries a narrow product line with a deep assortment within that line.

Department store
A retail store that carries a wide variety of product lines, each operated as a separate department managed by specialist buyers or merchandisers.

Supermarket
A large, low-cost, low-margin, high-volume, self-service store that carries a wide variety of grocery and household products.

Supermarkets are the most frequently visited type of retail store. Today, however, they are facing slow sales growth because of slower population growth and an increase in competition from discounters (Walmart, Costco, Dollar General) on the one hand and specialty food stores (Whole Foods Market, Trader Joe's, Sprouts) on the other. Supermarkets also have been hit hard by the rapid growth of out-of-home eating over the past two decades. In fact, supermarkets' share of the groceries and food market plunged from 66 percent in 2002 to less than 62 percent in 2009. Meanwhile, during the same time period, supercenters boosted their market share from 15.6 percent to 20.6 percent.[5]

In the battle for "share of stomachs," some supermarkets have moved upscale, providing improved store environments and higher-quality food offerings, such as from-scratch bakeries, gourmet deli counters, natural foods, and fresh seafood departments. Others, however, are attempting to compete head-on with food discounters such as Costco and Walmart, the nation's largest grocery seller, by cutting costs, establishing more-efficient operations, and lowering prices. ▶ For example, Kroger, the nation's largest grocery-only retailer, has done this successfully:[6]

▲ Despite a sagging economy that has troubled other supermarkets, leading grocery-only retailer Kroger's sales and market share gains have been the best in the industry thanks to customer-focused pricing. Kroger gives you "more value for the way you live."

Despite the recently sagging economy, while other grocery chains have suffered, Kroger's sales have grown steadily. The chain's eight-year-old strategy of cutting costs and lowering prices has put Kroger in the right position for the times. The food seller's price reductions have been just one part of a four-pronged strategy called "Customer 1st," by which Kroger seeks to continually improve its response to shopper needs through its prices, products, people, and the shopping experience it creates in its stores. The Customer 1st effort began at a time when most other traditional supermarkets were trying to distinguish themselves from discount food retailers by emphasizing higher-level service, quality, and selection. But instead of trying to maintain higher prices, Kroger recognized lower prices as an important part of the changing food-buying experience. Guided by a detailed analysis of customer sales data, it made substantial costs and price cuts, beginning with the most price-sensitive products and categories and then expanding to include additional items each year. To help cost-conscious customers further, Kroger also boosted its private-label offerings. It now offers more than 11,000 private-label items, which account for just under 35 percent of its overall sales. Thanks to customer-focused pricing that promises customers "more value for the way you live," Kroger's recent sales and market-share gains have been the best in the supermarket industry. The food retailer is now well positioned to take advantage of better economic days ahead.

Convenience store
A small store, located near a residential area, that is open long hours seven days a week and carries a limited line of high-turnover convenience goods.

Convenience stores are small stores that carry a limited line of high-turnover convenience goods. After several years of stagnant sales, these stores are now experiencing growth. Many convenience store chains have tried to expand beyond their primary market of young, blue-collar men by redesigning their stores to attract female shoppers. They are shedding the image of a "truck stop" where men go to buy gas, beer, cigarettes, or shriveled hotdogs on a roller grill and are instead offering freshly prepared foods and cleaner, safer, more-upscale environments.

For example, consider Sheetz, widely recognized as one of the nation's top convenience store chains. ▶ Driven by its Total Customer Focus mission and the motto "Feel the Love," Sheetz aims to provide "convenience without compromise while being more than just a convenience store. It's our devotion to your satisfaction that makes the difference."[7]

▲ Convenience stores: Sheetz positions itself as more than just a convenience store. Driven by its Total Customer Focus mission and the motto—"Feel the Love"—Sheetz aims to provide "convenience without compromise."

Sheetz Inc.

Whether it's for road warriors, construction workers, or soccer moms, Sheetz offers "a mecca for people on the go"—fast, friendly service and quality products in clean and convenient locations. "We really care about our customers," says the company. "If you need to refuel your car or refresh your body, . . . Sheetz has what you need, when you need it. And, we're here 24/7/365." Sheetz certainly isn't your run-of-the-mill convenience store operation. The average Sheetz store is nearly twice the size of the average 7-Eleven. Stores offer up a menu of made-to-order cold and toasted subs, sandwiches, and salads, along with hot fries, onion rings, chicken fingers, and burgers—all ordered through touch-screen terminals. Locations feature Sheetz Bros. Coffeez, a full-service espresso bar staffed by a trained barista. Frozen fruit smoothies round out the menu. To help make paying easier, Sheetz was the first chain in the nation to install system-wide MasterCard PayPass, allowing customers to quickly tap their credit cards and go. Sheetz also partnered with M&T Bank to offer ATM services at any Sheetz without a surcharge. Some analysts say that Sheetz aims to become the Walmart of convenience stores, and it just might get there.

Superstore

A store much larger than a regular supermarket that offers a large assortment of routinely purchased food products, nonfood items, and services.

Category killer

A giant specialty store that carries a very deep assortment of a particular line.

Service retailer

A retailer whose product line is actually a service; examples include hotels, airlines, banks, colleges, and many others.

Discount store

A retail operation that sells standard merchandise at lower prices by accepting lower margins and selling at higher volume.

Superstores are much larger than regular supermarkets and offer a large assortment of routinely purchased food products, nonfood items, and services. Walmart, Target, Meijer, and other discount retailers offer *supercenters*, very large combination food and discount stores. Whereas a traditional grocery store brings in about $486,000 a week in sales, a supercenter brings in about $1.5 million a week. Walmart, which opened its first supercenter in 1988, now has almost 3,000 supercenters in North America and is opening new ones at a rate of about 140 per year.[8]

Recent years have also seen the rapid growth of superstores that are actually giant specialty stores, the so-called **category killers** (e.g., Best Buy, Home Depot, and PetSmart). They feature stores the size of airplane hangars that carry a very deep assortment of a particular line. Category killers are found in a wide range of categories, including electronics, home-improvement products, books, baby gear, toys, linens and towels, party goods, sporting goods, and even pet supplies.

Finally, for many retailers, the product line is actually a service. **Service retailers** include hotels and motels, banks, airlines, restaurants, colleges, hospitals, movie theaters, tennis clubs, bowling alleys, repair services, hair salons, and dry cleaners. Service retailers in the United States are growing faster than product retailers.

Relative Prices

Retailers can also be classified according to the prices they charge (see Table 11.1). Most retailers charge regular prices and offer normal-quality goods and customer service. Others offer higher-quality goods and service at higher prices. Retailers that feature low prices are discount stores and "off-price" retailers.

Discount Stores. A **discount store** (for example, Target, Kmart, or Walmart) sells standard merchandise at lower prices by accepting lower margins and selling higher volume. The early discount stores cut expenses by offering few services and operating in warehouse-like facilities in low-rent, heavily traveled districts. Today's discounters have improved their store environments and increased their services, while at the same time keeping prices low through lean, efficient operations.

Leading "big-box" discounters, such as Walmart, Costco, and Target, now dominate the retail scene. However, even "small-box" discounters are thriving in the current economic environment. For example, dollar stores are now today's fastest-growing retail format. Dollar General, the nation's largest small-box discount retailer, makes a powerful value promise for the times: "Save time. Save money. Every day" (see Marketing at Work 11.1).

MARKETING AT WORK | 11.1

Dollar General: Today's Hottest Retailing Format

"Save time. Save money. Every day." Given today's economics, that sounds like a winning proposition. In fact, it's the slogan of discount retailer Dollar General—and it *is* a winning proposition. Dollar stores and other hard discounters are today's hottest retailing format, and Dollar General is the nation's leading dollar store.

Whereas the Walmarts, Costcos, and Targets of the world are *big-box* discounters, Dollar General and the other dollar stores are *small-box* discounters. They remain a relatively small threat to their bigger rivals; for example, the combined annual sales of all dollar stores amount to only about 15 percent of Walmart's annual sales. But they are by far the fastest-growing threat. In the recent down economy, as the big-box discounters struggled, the dollar stores spurted, rapidly adding new stores, customers, and sales.

For example, Dollar General's cash registers are really ringing these days. Over the past 40 years, the retailer's sales have grown from $40 million to more than $13 billion—an average growth rate of 14 percent a year. During the Great Recession, even as the economy withered and competitors' sales suffered, Dollar General's same-store sales grew more than 9 percent each year. The company now operates 9,200 stores in 35 states, and it plans to open 625 new stores this year and overhaul another 550. It plans eventually to grow to more than 12,000 stores (about equivalent to the number of McDonald's restaurants nationwide and more than 20 times the number of Target stores).

What's the story behind Dollar General's success? If you haven't been in a dollar store lately, you might be surprised at what you'll find. Back in the day, dollar stores sold mostly odd-lot assortments of novelties, factory overruns, closeouts, and outdated merchandise—most priced at $1. Not anymore. "Dollar stores have come a long way, baby," says a retail analyst. "The Great Recession accelerated the iconic American chains' transformation from purveyors of kitschy $1 trinkets to discounters in a position to lure shoppers from the likes of supermarkets, drugstores, and Walmart stores." Dollar General now sells a carefully selected assortment of mostly brand-name items. More than two-thirds of its sales come from groceries and household goods. And it isn't really a "dollar store" anymore. Only 25 percent of its merchandise is now priced at a dollar or less.

Dollar General's "Save time. Save money. Every day." slogan isn't just for show. It's a carefully crafted statement of the store's value promise. The company sums up its positioning this way: "Our goal is to provide our customers a better life, and we think our customers are best served when we keep it real and keep it simple. We make shopping for everyday needs simpler and hassle-free by offering a carefully edited assortment of the most popular brands at low everyday prices in small, convenient locations."

Dollar General helps save customers time by keeping things simple. Its carefully edited product assortment includes only about 12,000 core items (compared with 47,000 items in an average supermarket or 142,000 items in a Walmart supercenter). But Dollar General still stocks your favorite sizes and many of your favorite quality brands, such as Coca-Cola, Bounty, Palmolive, Hefty, Kraft, Folgers, and Betty Crocker. Dollar General has even added brands such as Hanes underwear, L'Oréal cosmetics, and Rexall vitamins and herbal supplements.

Keeping it simple also means smaller stores—you could fit more than 25 Dollar General stores inside the average Walmart supercenter. In addition, most stores are located in convenient strip malls, which usually allow customers to park right in front of a store. Once inside, they encounter fewer aisles to navigate, fewer goods to consider, and smaller crowds to out-wrangle than in big-box stores. All that adds up to a quick trip. The average Dollar General customer is in and out of the store in less than 10 minutes. Although Dollar General is experimenting with larger format stores that carry produce, meat, and baked goods, those Super Dollar Generals are still much, much smaller and more manageable than a Walmart supercenter.

As for the "save money" part of the value promise, Dollar General's prices on the brand-name products it carries are an estimated 20 to 40 percent lower than grocery store prices and are roughly in line with those of the big-name discount stores. There are also plenty of savings to be had on dollar items and the increasing selection of Dollar General private-label merchandise. Finally, Dollar General gets a boost from customer perceptions of its dollar store format. Even though only about 25 percent of its goods are priced at $1 or less, almost anything in the store can be had for less than $10. This pricing structure not only draws customers in but also allows them to shop a little more freely than they would elsewhere.

▲ Discounter Dollar General, the nation's largest small-box discount retailer, makes a powerful value promise for the times: "Save time. Save money. Every day."

Keeping things simple for consumers also benefits the company's bottom line. Smaller stores are less expensive to operate, and locating them in smaller markets and less glamorous neighborhoods keeps real estate costs down as well. Dollar General's cost per square foot is as low as one-tenth that of supermarkets. By constructing its stores more cheaply, Dollar General is able to build more of them. In fact, Dollar General now has more stores in the United States than any other discounter.

Dollar General's product mix strategy also contributes to its financial performance. Although it carries top brands, it leans toward brands that are not market leaders. For example, customers are more likely to encounter Gain than Tide. Furthermore, stores don't stock products in all sizes, just the ones that sell the best. Finally, Dollar General's merchandise buyers focus on getting the best deals possible at any given time. This opportunistic buying might mean that the chain stocks Heinz ketchup one month and Hunts the next. Such practices contribute to lower costs and higher margins.

The postrecessionary trend toward more sensible consumer spending has given Dollar General and other dollar stores a real boost. Not only is Dollar General attracting more sales from existing customers, it's also attracting new higher-income customers. A recent survey showed that 65 percent of consumers with incomes under $50,000 had shopped at a dollar store in the past three months. However, 47 percent of households with incomes over $100,000 had done so as well. Although its core customers are still those who make less than $40,000 a year,

Dollar General's fastest-growth segment is those earning more than $75,000 a year.

Put it all together, and things are sizzling right now at the nation's largest small-box discount retailer. Dollar General has the right value proposition for the times. But what will happen to Dollar General and its fellow dollar stores as economic conditions continue to improve? Will newly acquired customers abandon them and return to their previous shopping haunts?

Dollar General doesn't think so. Dollar stores seem to do as well in good times as in bad. The format had already been growing at a healthy rate before the Great Recession hit. And customers who switched over show no signs of relapsing into their old, free-spending ways. We "see signs of a new consumerism," says Dollar General's CEO, as people shift where they shop, switch to lower-cost brands, and stay generally more frugal. And company research shows that 97 percent of new customers plan to continue shopping at Dollar General even as the economy improves, the same percentage as old customers. Low prices and convenience, it seems, will not soon go out of style.

Sources: Jack Neff, "Stuck-in-the-Middle Walmart Starts to Lose Share," *Advertising Age*, March 8, 2010, pp. 1, 23; Kelly Evans, "Dollar General Flexing Its Discount Muscle," *Wall Street Journal*, March 31, 2010, accessed at www.wsj.com; Suzanne Kapner, "The Mighty Dollar," *Fortune*, April 27, 2009, p. 64; Rebecca Tonn, "Dollar General Expansion in Colorado Will Mean 6,000 Jobs," *Colorado Springs Journal*, January 5, 2011; John Jannarone, "Will Dollar General Be Leading Retailers into Battle?" *Wall Street Journal*, June 6, 2011, p. C10; and information from www.dollargeneral.com, accessed November 2011.

Off-price retailer

A retailer that buys at less-than-regular wholesale prices and sells at less than retail.

Independent off-price retailer

An off-price retailer that is either independently owned and run or is a division of a larger retail corporation.

Factory outlet

An off-price retailing operation that is owned and operated by a manufacturer and normally carries the manufacturer's surplus, discontinued, or irregular goods.

Off-Price Retailers. As the major discount stores traded up, a new wave of **off-price retailers** moved in to fill the ultralow-price, high-volume gap. Ordinary discounters buy at regular wholesale prices and accept lower margins to keep prices down. By contrast, off-price retailers buy at less-than-regular wholesale prices and charge consumers less than retail. Off-price retailers can be found in all areas, from food, clothing, and electronics to no-frills banking and discount brokerages.

The three main types of off-price retailers are *independents*, *factory outlets*, and *warehouse clubs*. **Independent off-price retailers** either are independently owned and run or are divisions of larger retail corporations. Although many off-price operations are run by smaller independents, most large off-price retailer operations are owned by bigger retail chains. Examples include store retailers such as TJ Maxx and Marshalls, which are owned by TJX Companies, and Web sellers such as Overstock.com.

Factory outlets—manufacturer-owned and operated stores by firms such as J. Crew, Gap, Levi Strauss, and others—sometimes group together in *factory outlet malls* and *value-retail centers*. At these centers, dozens of outlet stores offer prices as much as 50 percent below retail on a wide range of mostly surplus, discounted, or irregular goods. Whereas outlet malls consist primarily of manufacturers' outlets, value-retail centers combine manufacturers' outlets with off-price retail stores and department store clearance outlets. Factory outlet malls have become one of the hottest growth areas in retailing.

The malls in general are now moving upscale—and even dropping *factory* from their descriptions. A growing number of outlet malls now feature luxury brands such as Coach,

Polo Ralph Lauren, Dolce&Gabbana, Giorgio Armani, Burberry, and Versace. As consumers become more value-minded, even upper-end retailers are accelerating their factory outlet strategies, placing more emphasis on outlets such as Nordstrom Rack, Neiman Marcus Last Call, Bloomingdale's Outlets, and Saks Off 5th. Many companies now regard outlets not simply as a way of disposing of problem merchandise but as an additional way of gaining business for fresh merchandise. The combination of highbrow brands and lowbrow prices found at outlets provides powerful shopper appeal, especially in a postrecession economy.

Warehouse clubs (also known as *wholesale clubs* or *membership warehouses*), such as Costco, Sam's Club, and BJ's, operate in huge, drafty, warehouse-like facilities and offer few frills. However, they offer ultralow prices and surprise deals on selected branded merchandise. Warehouse clubs have grown rapidly in recent years. These retailers appeal not only to low-income consumers seeking bargains on bare-bones products but also to all kinds of customers shopping for a wide range of goods, from necessities to extravagances.

Warehouse club

An off-price retailer that sells a limited selection of brand name grocery items, appliances, clothing, and other goods at deep discounts to members who pay annual membership fees.

Consider Costco, now the nation's third-largest retailer, behind only Walmart and Kroger. Low price is an important part of Costco's equation, but what really sets Costco apart is the products it carries and the sense of urgency that it builds into the Costco shopper's store experience.[9]

▲ **Warehouse clubs: Costco is a retail treasure hunt, where one's shopping cart could contain a $50,000 diamond ring resting on top of a vat of mayonnaise.**

SUZANNE DECHILLO/The New York Times/Redux Pictures

Costco brings flair to an otherwise dreary setting. Alongside the gallon jars of peanut butter and 2,250-count packs of Q-Tips, Costco offers an ever-changing assortment of high-quality products—even luxuries—all at tantalizingly low margins. As one industry analyst puts it, ▶ "Costco is a retail treasure hunt, where one's shopping cart could contain a $50,000 diamond ring resting on top of a vat of mayonnaise." It's the place where high-end products meet deep-discount prices. In just one year, Costco sold more than 93 million hot dog and soda combinations (still only $1.50 as they have been for more than 25 years). At the same time, it sold more than 96,000 carats of diamonds at up to $100,000 per item. It is the nation's biggest baster of poultry (77,000 rotisserie chickens a day at $4.99) but also the country's biggest seller of fine wines (including the likes of a Chateau Cheval Blanc Premier Grand Cru Classe at $1,750 a bottle).

Each Costco store is a theater of retail that creates buying urgency and excitement. Mixed in with its regular stock of staples, Costco features a glittering, constantly shifting array of one-time specials, such as discounted Prada bags, Calloway golf clubs, or Kenneth Cole bags—deals you just won't find anywhere else. In fact, of the 4,000 items that Costco carries, 1,000 are designated as "treasure items" (Costco's words). The changing assortment and great prices keep people coming back, wallets in hand. There was a time when only the great, unwashed masses shopped at off-price retailers, but Costco has changed all that. Now, even people who don't have to pinch pennies shop there.

Organizational Approach

Although many retail stores are independently owned, others band together under some form of corporate or contractual organization. ▶ **Table 11.2** describes four major types of retail organizations—*corporate chains*, *voluntary chains*, *retailer cooperatives*, and *franchise organizations*.

Corporate chains are two or more outlets that are commonly owned and controlled. They have many advantages over independents. Their size allows them to buy in large quantities at lower prices and gain promotional economies. They can hire specialists to deal with areas such as pricing, promotion, merchandising, inventory control, and sales forecasting.

Corporate chains

Two or more outlets that are commonly owned and controlled.

The great success of corporate chains caused many independents to band together in one of two forms of contractual associations. One is the *voluntary chain*—a wholesaler-sponsored group of independent retailers that engages in group buying and common

▶ **Table 11.2**	Major Types of Retail Organizations	
Type	**Description**	**Examples**
Corporate chain	Two or more outlets that are commonly owned and controlled. Corporate chains appear in all types of retailing but they are strongest in department stores, discount stores, food stores, drugstores, and restaurants.	Sears (department stores), Target (discount stores), Kroger (grocery stores), CVS (drugstores)
Voluntary chain	Wholesaler-sponsored group of independent retailers engaged in group buying and merchandising.	Independent Grocers Alliance (IGA), Do It Best (hardware), Western Auto, True Value
Retailer cooperative	Group of independent retailers who jointly establish a central buying organization and conduct joint promotion efforts.	Associated Grocers (groceries), Ace Hardware (hardware)
Franchise organization	Contractual association between a franchisor (a manufacturer, wholesaler, or service organization) and franchisees (independent businesspeople who buy the right to own and operate one or more units in the franchise system).	McDonald's, Subway, Pizza Hut, Jiffy Lube, Meineke Mufflers, 7-Eleven

merchandising. Examples include the Independent Grocers Alliance (IGA), Western Auto, and Do It Best. The other type of contractual association is the *retailer cooperative*—a group of independent retailers that bands together to set up a jointly owned, central wholesale operation and conduct joint merchandising and promotion efforts. Examples are Associated Grocers and Ace Hardware. These organizations give independents the buying and promotion economies they need to meet the prices of corporate chains.

Another form of contractual retail organization is a **franchise**. The main difference between franchise organizations and other contractual systems (voluntary chains and retail cooperatives) is that franchise systems are normally based on some unique product or service; a method of doing business; or the trade name, goodwill, or patent that the franchisor has developed. Franchising has been prominent in fast-food restaurants, motels, health and fitness centers, auto sales and service dealerships, and real estate agencies.

However, franchising covers a lot more than just burger joints and fitness centers. Franchises have sprung up to meet just about any need. For example, Mad Science Group franchisees put on science programs for schools, scout troops, and birthday parties. And Mr. Handyman provides repair services for homeowners, while Merry Maids tidies up their houses.

Once considered upstarts among independent businesses, franchises now command 40 percent of all retail sales in the United States. ▶ These days, it's nearly impossible to stroll down a city block or drive on a city street without seeing a McDonald's, Subway, Jiffy Lube, or Holiday Inn. One of the best-known and most successful franchisers, McDonald's, now has 32,700 stores in 117 countries, including almost 14,000 in the United States. It serves 64 million customers a day and racks up more than $77 billion in annual systemwide sales. More than 80 percent of McDonald's restaurants worldwide are owned and operated by franchisees. Gaining fast is Subway, one of the fastest-growing franchises, with systemwide sales of $15 billion and more than 34,000 shops in 98 countries, including more than 24,000 in the United States.[10]

Franchise
A contractual association between a manufacturer, wholesaler, or service organization (a franchisor) and independent businesspeople (franchisees) who buy the right to own and operate one or more units in the franchise system.

▲ Franchising: These days, it's nearly impossible to stroll down a city block or drive on a suburban street without seeing an abundance of franchise businesses.
SCOTT MCINTYRE/The New York Times/Redux Pictures

SPEED BUMP | LINKING THE CONCEPTS

Slow down here and think about all the different kinds of retailers you deal with regularly, many of which overlap in the products they carry.

- Pick a familiar product: a camera, microwave oven, lawn tool, or something else. Shop for this product at two very different store types, say a discount store or category killer on the one hand, and a department store or smaller specialty store on the other. Then shop for it online. Compare the three shopping outlets on product assortment, services, and prices. If you were going to buy the product, where would you buy it and why?
- What does your shopping trip suggest about the futures of the competing store formats that you sampled?

Retailer Marketing Decisions

Retailers are always searching for new marketing strategies to attract and hold customers. In the past, retailers attracted customers with unique product assortments and more or better services. Today, various retailers' assortments and services are looking more and more alike. You can find most consumer brands not only in department stores but also in mass-merchandise discount stores, off-price discount stores, and all over the Internet. Thus, it's now more difficult for any one retailer to offer exclusive merchandise.

Service differentiation among retailers has also eroded. Many department stores have trimmed their services, whereas discounters have increased theirs. In addition, customers have become smarter and more price sensitive. They see no reason to pay more for identical brands, especially when service differences are shrinking. For all these reasons, many retailers today are rethinking their marketing strategies.

As shown in ▶ **Figure 11.1**, retailers face major marketing decisions about *segmentation and targeting*, *store differentiation and positioning*, and the *retail marketing mix*.

Segmentation, Targeting, Differentiation, and Positioning Decisions

Retailers must first segment and define their target markets and then decide how they will differentiate and position themselves in these markets. Should the store focus on upscale, midscale, or downscale shoppers? Do target shoppers want variety, depth of assortment, convenience, or low prices? Until they define and profile their markets, retailers cannot make consistent decisions about product assortment, services, pricing, advertising, store décor, or any of the other decisions that must support their positions.

Too many retailers, even big ones, fail to clearly define their target markets and positions. For example, what market does the clothing chain Gap target? What is its value

▶ **Figure 11.1** Retailer Marketing Strategy

proposition? If you're having trouble answering those questions, you're not alone—so is Gap's management.[11]

In its heyday in the late 1980s and early 1990s, Gap was solidly positioned on the then-fashionable preppy look and focused on comfortable, casual clothes and easy shopping. But as its core customers aged and moved on, Gap stores didn't. Moving into the 2000s, Gap catered to short-lived fashion trends that alienated its loyal customer base. At the same time, it struggled unsuccessfully to define new positioning that works with today's younger shoppers. As a result, over the past six years, Gap store sales have slipped more than 30 percent. "Right now, Gap could be anything," says one industry expert. "It hasn't got a story." Is it "trying to sell to my wife or my teenage daughter or both," asks another. "I don't think you can do both." To rekindle the brand, Gap needs to "define who the brand's core customers are and be exceptional to them."

By contrast, successful retailers define their target markets well and position themselves strongly. For example, Trader Joe's positions itself strongly with its "cheap gourmet" value proposition (see Marketing at Work 11.2). And Walmart is strongly positioned on low prices and what those always low prices mean to its customers. It promises that customers will "Save money. Live better."

▲ Retail targeting and positioning: Whole Foods Market succeeds by positioning itself strongly away from Walmart and other discounters. "A devoted Whole Foods customer is more likely to boycott the local Walmart than to shop at it."

AP Images/Elise Amendola

With solid targeting and positioning, a retailer can compete effectively against even the strongest competitors. ▶ For example, compare Whole Foods Market to Walmart. (Remember the Whole Foods story in Chapter 9?) Whole Foods Market has about 300 stores and slightly more than $9 billion in sales compared with Walmart's more than 8,400 stores worldwide and sales of $422 billion.[12] How does this smaller grocery chain compete with giant Walmart? It doesn't—at least not directly. Whole Foods Market succeeds by carefully positioning itself *away* from Walmart. It targets a select group of upscale customers and offers them "organic, natural, and gourmet foods, all swaddled in Earth Day politics." In fact, a devoted Whole Foods Market customer is more likely to boycott the local Walmart than to shop at it.

Whole Foods Market can't match Walmart's massive economies of scale, incredible volume purchasing power, ultraefficient logistics, wide selection, and hard-to-beat prices. But then again, it doesn't even try. By positioning itself strongly away from Walmart and other discounters, Whole Foods Market has grown rapidly over the past two decades and is now more than holding its own.

Product Assortment and Services Decision

Retailers must decide on three major product variables: product assortment, services mix, and store atmosphere.

The retailer's product assortment should differentiate the retailer while matching target shoppers' expectations. One strategy is to offer merchandise that no other competitor carries, such as store brands or national brands on which it holds exclusive rights. For example, Saks gets exclusive rights to carry a well-known designer's labels. It also offers its own private-label lines—the Saks Fifth Avenue Signature, Classic, and Sport collections. At JCPenney, private-label and exclusive brands account for 54 percent of its sales.[13]

Another strategy is to feature blockbuster merchandising events. For example, Bloomingdale's is known for running spectacular shows featuring goods from a certain country, such as India or China. Alternatively, the retailer can offer surprise merchandise, as when Costco offers surprise assortments of seconds, overstocks, and closeouts. Finally, the retailer can differentiate itself by offering a highly targeted product assortment: Lane Bryant carries plus-size clothing; Brookstone offers an unusual assortment of gadgets and gifts; and BatteryDepot.com offers about every imaginable kind of replacement battery.

The *services mix* can also help set one retailer apart from another. For example, some retailers invite customers to ask questions or consult service representatives in person or via phone or keyboard. Nordstrom promises to "take care of the customer, no matter what it takes." Home Depot offers a diverse mix of services to do-it-yourselfers, from "how-to" classes and "do-it-herself" and kid workshops to a proprietary credit card.

Trader Joe's Unique Positioning Twist: Cheap Gourmet

It's 7:30 on a July morning, and already a huge crowd has gathered for the opening of Trader Joe's newest outpost, in Manhattan's Chelsea neighborhood. The waiting shoppers chat about their favorite Trader Joe's foods and share their joy over the arrival of the trendy retailer in their neighborhood. Trader Joe's is no ordinary grocery chain. It's an offbeat, fun discovery zone that elevates food shopping from a chore to a cultural experience. It stocks its shelves with a winning combination of low-cost, yuppie-friendly staples (cage-free eggs and organic blue agave sweetener) and exotic, affordable luxuries—Belgian butter waffle cookies or Thai lime-and-chili cashews—that you simply can't find anyplace else. It's little wonder that Trader Joe's is one of the hottest retailers in the United States.

Trader Joe's isn't really a gourmet food store. Then again, it's not a discount food store either. It's actually a bit of both. Trader Joe's has established its own special positioning twist—call it "cheap gourmet." It offers gourmet-caliber, one-of-a-kind products at bargain prices, all served up in a festive, vacation-like atmosphere that makes shopping fun. Trader Joe's inventive positioning has earned it an almost cult-like following of devoted customers who love what they get from Trader Joe's for the prices they pay.

Trader Joe's describes itself as an "island paradise" where "value, adventure, and tasty treasures are discovered, every day." Shoppers bustle and buzz amid cedar-plank-lined walls and fake palm trees as a ship's bell rings out occasionally at checkout alerting them to special announcements. Unfailingly helpful and cheery associates in goofy trademark Hawaiian shirts chat with customers about everything from the weather to menu suggestions for dinner parties. At the Chelsea store opening, workers greeted customers with high-fives and free cookies. Customers don't just shop at Trader Joe's, they experience it.

Shelves bristle with an eclectic assortment of gourmet-quality grocery items. Trader Joe's stocks only a limited assortment of about 4,000 specialty products (compared with the 50,000 items found in a typical grocery store). However, the assortment is uniquely Trader Joe's, including special concoctions of gourmet packaged foods and sauces, ready-to-eat soups, fresh and frozen entrees, snacks, and desserts, all free of artificial colors, flavors, and preservatives. Trader Joe's is a gourmet foodie's delight, featuring everything from wasabi peas, organic strawberry lemonade, dark-chocolate-dipped spiced dry mango, and fair trade coffees to chile lime chicken burgers and triple-ginger ginger snaps.

Another thing that makes Trader Joe's products so special is that you just can't get them elsewhere. More than 80 percent of the store's brands are private-label goods, sold exclusively by Trader Joe's. If asked, almost any customer can tick off a ready list of Trader Joe's favorites that they simply can't live without, a list that

quickly grows. Customers' most common complaint: They came in for one or two things and ended up with a whole cart full of stuff.

A special store atmosphere, exclusive gourmet products, helpful and attentive associates—this all sounds like a recipe for high prices. Not so at Trader Joe's. Whereas upscale competitors such as Whole Foods Market charge upscale prices to match their wares ("Whole Foods, whole paycheck," as the joke went), Trader Joe's amazes customers with its relatively frugal prices. The prices aren't all that low in absolute terms, but they're a real bargain compared with what you'd pay for the same quality and coolness elsewhere. "At Trader Joe's, we're as much about value as we are about great food," says the company. "So you can afford to be adventurous without breaking the bank."

How does Trader Joe's keep its gourmet prices so low? It all starts with lean operations and a near-fanatical focus on saving money. To keep costs down, Trader Joe's typically locates its stores in low-rent, out-of-the-way locations, such as suburban strip malls. Its small store size and limited product assortment result in reduced facilities and inventory costs. Trader Joe's stores save money by eliminating large produce sections and expensive on-site bakery, butcher, deli, and seafood shops. And for its private-label brands, Trader Joe's buys directly from suppliers and negotiates hard on price.

Finally, the frugal retailer saves money by spending almost nothing on advertising. Trader Joe's unique combination of quirky products and low prices produces so much word-of-mouth promotion that the company doesn't really need to advertise. The closest thing to an official promotion is the company's Web site or a newsletter mailed out to people who opt in to receive it.

▲ Trader Joe's unique "cheap gourmet" positioning has earned it an almost cult-like following of devoted customers who love what they get from Trader Joe's for the prices they pay.

Michael Nagle/Stringer/Getty Images

Trader Joe's most potent promotional weapon is its army of faithful followers. Trader Joe's customers have even started their own fan Web site, www.traderjoesfan.com, where they discuss new products and stores, trade recipes, and swap their favorite Trader Joe's stories.

Thus, strong positioning has made Trader Joe's one of the nation's fastest-growing and most popular food stores. Its more than 365 stores in 25 states now reap annual sales of more than $8.5 billion, up more than 75 percent in just the previous five years. Trader Joe's stores pull in an amazing $1,750 per square foot, more than twice the supermarket industry average. *Consumer Reports* recently ranked Trader Joe's, along with Wegmans, as the best supermarket chain in the nation.

It's all about the retailer's unique cheap gourmet positioning. Just ask Trader Joe's regular Chrissi Wright, found early one Friday morning browsing her local Trader Joe's in Bend, Oregon.

Chrissi expects she'll leave Trader Joe's with eight bottles of the popular Charles Shaw wine priced at $2.99 each (known to insiders as "Two-Buck Chuck") tucked under her arms. "I love Trader Joe's because they let me eat like a yuppie without taking all my money," says Wright. "Their products are gourmet, often environmentally conscientious and beautiful . . . and, of course, there's Two-Buck Chuck—possibly the greatest innovation of our time."

Sources: Quotes, extract, and other information from Beth Kowitt, "Inside Trader Joe's," *Fortune,* September 6, 2010, pp. 86–96; Nancy Luna, "Trader Joe's Expanding into Texas," *The Orange County Register,* May 5, 2011, http://fastfood.ocregister.com/2011/05/05/trader-joes-expanding-to-texas/94697/; Anna Sowa, "Trader Joe's: Why the Hype?" *McClatchy-Tribune Business News,* March 27, 2008; "Wegmans, Trader Joe's, Publix Top *Consumer Reports* Supermarket Survey," April 6, 2009, accessed at http://consumeraffairs.com/news04/2009/04/cr_supers.html; "SN's Top 75 Retailers for 2011," *Supermarket News,* http://supermarketnews.com/profiles/top75/2011/; and www.traderjoes.com, November 2011.

The *store's atmosphere* is another important element in the reseller's product arsenal. Retailers want to create a unique store experience, one that suits the target market and moves customers to buy. Many retailers practice *experiential retailing*. For example, outdoor goods retailer Cabela's stores are as much natural history museums for outdoor enthusiasts as they are retail outlets.

Despite Cabela's often remote locations, customers flock to its 31 superstores to buy hunting, fishing, and outdoor gear. A typical Cabela's store draws 4.4 million customers a year; half of Cabela's customers drive 100 miles or more to get there. Just what is it that attracts these hordes of shoppers to Cabela's stores? Part of the answer lies in all the stuff the stores sell. Cabela's huge superstores house a vast assortment of quality merchandise at reasonable prices. ▶ But Cabela's real magic lies in the *experiences* it creates for those who visit. "This is more than a place to go get fishhooks," says a Cabela's spokesperson. "We want to create a sense of wonder" for those who visit.

Mission accomplished! Each Cabela's store creates what amounts to a natural history theme park. Take the store near Fort Worth, Texas, for example. Dominating the center of the store is Conservation Mountain, a two-story mountain replica with two waterfalls and cascading streams. The mountain is divided into four ecosystems and five bioregions: a Texas prairie, an Alaskan habitat, an Arctic icecap, an American woodland, and an Alpine mountaintop. Each bioregion is populated by lifelike, museum-quality taxidermy animals in action poses—everything from prairie dogs, deer, elk, and caribou to brown bears, polar bears, musk oxen, and mountain goats. Getting hungry? Drop by the Mesquite Grill café for an elk, ostrich, or wild boar sandwich—no Big Macs here! The nearby General Store offers old-fashioned candy and snacks. Put it all together and Cabela's is creating total experiences that delight the senses as well as the wallets of its carefully targeted customers.[14]

▲ **Store atmosphere: Cabela's real magic lies in the experiences it creates for those who visit. "This is more than a place to go get fishhooks . . . we wanted to create a sense of wonder."**

IndexStock/PhotoLibrary

Today's successful retailers carefully orchestrate virtually every aspect of the consumer store experience. The next time you step into a retail store—whether it sells consumer electronics, hardware, or high fashion—stop and carefully consider your surroundings. Think about the store's layout and displays. Listen to the background sounds. Smell the smells. Chances are good that everything in the store, from the layout and lighting to the music and even the smells, has been carefully orchestrated to help shape the customers' shopping experiences—and open their wallets. For example, most large retailers have developed signature scents that you smell only in their stores:[15]

Luxury shirtmaker Thomas Pink pipes the smell of clean, pressed shirts into its stores—its signature "line-dried linen" scent. Sheraton Hotels employs Welcoming Warmth, a mix of fig, Jasmine, and freesia; whereas Westin Hotel & Resorts disperses White Tea, which attempts to provide the indefinable "Zen-retreat" experience. Bloomingdale's uses different essences in different departments: the soft scent of baby powder in the baby store, coconut in the swimsuit area, lilacs in intimate apparel, and sugar cookies and evergreen scent during the holiday season. At Abercrombie and Fitch, it's a "woody" aroma—a combination of orange, fir resin, and Brazilian rosewood, among others. Customers have complained that store-bought T-shirts lose the smell after multiple washings, so by popular demand, the retailer now produces the trademark scent in bottle form. Such scents can increase customer "dwell times" and, in turn, buying. Says the founder of ScentAir, a company that produces such scents, "Developing a signature fragrance is much like [developing] a message in print or radio: What do you want to communicate to consumers and how often?"

Such *experiential retailing* confirms that retail stores are much more than simply assortments of goods. They are environments to be experienced by the people who shop in them. Store atmospheres offer a powerful tool by which retailers can differentiate their stores from those of competitors.

In fact, retail establishments sometimes become small communities in themselves—places where people get together. For example, women's sports and fitness chain Title Nine is part women's active apparel shop and part women's gathering spot. Beyond selling apparel for everything from running to rock climbing, it sponsors local fitness events, in-store get-togethers, and an online community for women on the move—called *timeout with Title Nine*—all announced via each store's individual Facebook page. The Portland, Oregon, Title Nine hosts moonlight snowshoe outings, in-store yoga classes, and a weekend cycling series.[16]

Price Decision

A retailer's price policy must fit its target market and positioning, product and service assortment, the competition, and economic factors. All retailers would like to charge high markups and achieve high volume, but the two seldom go together. Most retailers seek *either* high markups on lower volume (most specialty stores) *or* low markups on higher volume (mass merchandisers and discount stores).

Thus, 110-year-old Bergdorf Goodman caters to the upper crust by selling apparel, shoes, and jewelry created by designers such as Chanel, Prada, and Hermes. The up-market retailer pampers its customers with services such as a personal shopper and in-store showings of the upcoming season's trends with cocktails and hors d'oeuvres. By contrast, TJ Maxx sells brand-name clothing at discount prices aimed at Middle Americans. As it stocks new products each week, the discounter provides a treasure hunt for bargain shoppers.

Retailers must also decide on the extent to which they will use sales and other price promotions. Some retailers use no price promotions at all, competing instead on product and service quality rather than on price. For example, it's difficult to imagine Bergdorf Goodman holding a two-for-the-price-of-one sale on Chanel handbags, even in a tight economy. Other retailers—such as Walmart, Costco, and Family Dollar—practice *everyday low pricing (EDLP)*, charging constant, everyday low prices with few sales or discounts.

Still other retailers practice *high-low pricing*—charging higher prices on an everyday basis, coupled with

▲ A retailer's price policy must fit its targeting and positioning. Bergdorf Goodman caters to the upper crust with prices to match.

Deidre Schoo/The New York Times/Redux Pictures

frequent sales and other price promotions, to increase store traffic, create a low-price image, or attract customers who will buy other goods at full prices. The recent economic downturn caused a rash of high-low pricing, as retailers poured on price cuts and promotions to coax bargain-hunting customers into their stores. Which pricing strategy is best depends on the retailer's overall marketing strategy, the pricing approaches of its competitors, and the economic environment.

Promotion Decision

Retailers use any or all of the five promotion tools—advertising, personal selling, sales promotion, public relations (PR), and direct marketing—to reach consumers. They advertise in newspapers and magazines and on radio, television, and the Internet. Advertising may be supported by newspaper inserts and catalogs. Store salespeople greet customers, meet their needs, and build relationships. Sales promotions may include in-store demonstrations, displays, sales, and loyalty programs. PR activities, such as new-store openings, special events, newsletters and blogs, store magazines, and public service activities, are also available to retailers. Most retailers have also created Web sites that offer customers information and other features while selling merchandise directly.

Place Decision

Retailers often point to three critical factors in retailing success: *location*, *location*, and *location*! It's very important that retailers select locations that are accessible to the target market in areas that are consistent with the retailer's positioning. For example, Apple locates its stores in high-end malls and trendy shopping districts—such as the "Magnificent Mile" on Chicago's Michigan Avenue or Fifth Avenue in Manhattan—not low-rent strip malls on the edge of town. By contrast, Trader Joe's places its stores in low-rent, out-of-the-way locations to keep costs down and support its "cheap gourmet" positioning. Small retailers may have to settle for whatever locations they can find or afford. Large retailers, however, usually employ specialists who use advanced methods to select store locations.

Most stores today cluster together to increase their customer pulling power and give consumers the convenience of one-stop shopping. *Central business districts* were the main form of retail cluster until the 1950s. Every large city and town had a central business district with department stores, specialty stores, banks, and movie theaters. When people began moving to the suburbs, however, these central business districts, with their traffic, parking, and crime problems, began to lose business. In recent years, many cities have joined with merchants to revive downtown shopping areas, generally with only mixed success.

A **shopping center** is a group of retail businesses built on a site that is planned, developed, owned, and managed as a unit. A *regional shopping center*, or *regional shopping mall,* the largest and most dramatic shopping center, has from 50 to more than 100 stores, including two or more full-line department stores. It is like a covered mini-downtown and attracts customers from a wide area. A *community shopping center* contains between 15 and 50 retail stores. It normally contains a branch of a department store or variety store, a supermarket, specialty stores, professional offices, and sometimes a bank. Most shopping centers are *neighborhood shopping centers* or *strip malls* that generally contain between 5 and 15 stores. These centers, which are close and convenient for consumers, usually contain a supermarket, perhaps a discount store, and several service stores— dry cleaner, drugstore, hardware store, local restaurant, or other stores.[17]

A newer form of shopping center is the so-called power center. *Power centers* are huge unenclosed shopping centers consisting of a long strip of retail stores, including large, freestanding anchors such as Walmart, Home Depot, Costco, Best Buy, Michaels, PetSmart, and OfficeMax. Each store has its own entrance with parking directly in front for shoppers who wish to visit only one store.

In contrast, *lifestyle centers* are smaller, open-air malls with upscale stores, convenient locations, and nonretail activities, such as a playground, skating rink, hotel, dining establishments, and a movie theater. "Think of lifestyle

Shopping center
A group of retail businesses built on a site that is planned, developed, owned, and managed as a unit.

▲ **Shopping centers: Today's centers are more about "creating places to be rather than just places to buy."**

Andersen Ross/Blend Images/Getty Images

centers as part Main Street and part Fifth Avenue," comments an industry observer. In fact, the original power center and lifestyle center concepts are now morphing into hybrid lifestyle-power centers. "The idea is to combine the hominess and community of an old-time village square with the cachet of fashionable urban stores; the smell and feel of a neighborhood park with the brute convenience of a strip center." ▶ In all, today's centers are more about "creating places to be rather than just places to buy."[18]

The past few years have brought hard times for shopping centers. With more than 100,000 centers in the United States, many experts suggest that the country has been "over-malled." Not surprisingly, the recent Great Recession hit shopping malls hard. Consumer spending cutbacks forced many retailers—small and large—out of business, increasing mall vacancy rates. Power centers were especially hard hit as their big-box retailer tenants suffered during the downturn. Some of the pizzazz has also gone out of lifestyle centers, whose upper-middle-class shoppers suffered most during the recession. Many lifestyle centers are even adding lower-price retailers to replace classier tenants that have folded. "We've learned that lifestyle centers have to adapt to a changing environment to survive," says one mall developer.[19]

Retailing Trends and Developments

Retailers operate in a harsh and fast-changing environment, which offers threats as well as opportunities. Consumer demographics, lifestyles, and spending patterns are changing rapidly, as are retailing technologies. To be successful, retailers need to choose target segments carefully and position themselves strongly. They need to take the following retailing developments into account as they plan and execute their competitive strategies.

A Postrecession Economy and Tighter Consumer Spending

Following many years of good economic times for retailers, the Great Recession turned many retailers' fortunes from boom to bust. Even in a recovered economy, retailers will feel the effects of changed consumer spending patterns well into the future.

Some retailers actually benefit from a down economy. For example, as consumers cut back and looked for ways to spend less on what they bought, big discounters such as Costco scooped up new business from bargain-hungry shoppers. Similarly, lower-priced fast-food chains, such as McDonald's, took business from their pricier eat-out competitors.

For most retailers, however, a sluggish economy means tough times. During and following the recent recession, several large and familiar retailers declared bankruptcy or closed their doors completely—including household names such as Linens 'n Things, Circuit City, KB Toys, Borders Books, and Sharper Image, to name a few. Other retailers, from Macy's and Home Depot to Starbucks, laid off employees, cut their costs, and offered deep price discounts and promotions aimed at luring cash-strapped customers back into their stores.

Beyond cost-cutting and price promotions, many retailers also added new value pitches to their positioning. For example, Home Depot replaced its older "You can do it. We can help." theme with a thriftier one: "More saving. More doing." ▶ Similarly, Whole Foods Market kicked up the promotion of its 365 Everyday Value private-label brand with ads sporting headlines such as "Sticker shock, but in a good way" and "No wallets were harmed in the buying of our 365 Everyday Value products." And following significant declines in same-store sales caused by the recession, Target, for the first time in its history, introduced TV ads featuring price messages. "Our [tagline] is 'Expect more. Pay less.'" a Target marketer said. "We're putting more emphasis on the pay less promise." Even in the postrecession economy, Target's marketing continues to feature more practical price and savings appeals.[20]

▲ **Value pitches from retailers: Even upscale Whole Foods Market has kicked up promotion of its private-label brand, 365 Everyday Value, with ads sporting headlines such as "Sticker shock, but in a good way."**

Courtesy of Whole Foods Market. "Whole Foods Market" is a registered trademark of Whole Foods Market IP, L.P.

When reacting to economic difficulties, retailers must be careful that their short-run actions don't damage their long-run images and positions. For example, drastic price discounting can increase immediate sales but damage brand loyalty. Instead of relying on cost-cutting and price reductions, retailers should focus on building greater customer value within their long-term store positioning strategies. For example, although it makes sense to boost the "Pay less" part of Target's positioning, Target has not abandoned the quality and design that differentiate it from Walmart and other discounters. As the economy has recovered, although it has shifted the balance a bit toward lower prices, Target still asserts its "Target-ness" by continuing to support the "Expect more" side of its value equation as well.

New Retail Forms, Shortening Retail Life Cycles, and Retail Convergence

New retail forms continue to emerge to meet new situations and consumer needs, but the life cycle of new retail forms is getting shorter. Department stores took about 100 years to reach the mature stage of the life cycle; more recent forms, such as warehouse stores, reached maturity in about 10 years. In such an environment, seemingly solid retail positions can crumble quickly. Of the top 10 discount retailers in 1962 (the year that Walmart and Kmart began), not one exists today. Even the most successful retailers can't sit back with a winning formula. To remain successful, they must keep adapting.

Wheel-of-retailing concept

A concept that suggests new types of retailers usually begin as low-margin, low-price, low-status operations but later evolve into higher-priced, higher-service operations, eventually becoming like the conventional retailers they replaced.

Many retailing innovations are partially explained by the **wheel-of-retailing concept**. According to this concept, many new types of retailing forms begin as low-margin, low-price, and low-status operations. They challenge established retailers that have become "fat" by letting their costs and margins increase. The new retailers' success leads them to upgrade their facilities and offer more services. In turn, their costs increase, forcing them to increase their prices. Eventually, the new retailers become like the conventional retailers they replaced. The cycle begins again when still newer types of retailers evolve with lower costs and prices. The wheel-of-retailing concept seems to explain the initial success and later troubles of department stores, supermarkets, and discount stores and the recent success of dollar stores and off-price retailers.

New retail forms are always emerging. For example, many retailers are now experimenting with limited-time *pop-up stores* that let them promote their brands to seasonal shoppers and create buzz in busy areas. ▶ During the 2010 holiday season, for instance, Toys "R" Us set up more than 600 temporary pop-up toy boutiques, many located in malls that formerly housed recently bankrupt KB Toys stores. Likewise, Apple opened a pop-up store in an abandoned store front in Austin, Texas, for two weeks to help handle the flood of demand surrounding the introduction of the iPad 2.[21]

Today's retail forms appear to be converging. Increasingly, different types of retailers now sell the same products at the same prices to the same consumers. For example, you can buy brand-name home appliances at department stores, discount stores, home improvement stores, off-price retailers, electronics superstores, and a slew of Web sites that all compete for the same customers. If you can't find the microwave oven you want at Sears, you can step across the street and find one for a better price at Lowe's or Best Buy—or just order one online from Amazon.com or even RitzCamera.com. This merging of consumers, products, prices, and retailers is called *retail convergence*. Such convergence means greater competition for retailers and greater difficulty in differentiating the product assortments of different types of retailers.

▲ **New retail forms: Many retailers—such as Toys "R" Us—are setting up limited-time "pop-up" stores that let them promote their brands to seasonal shoppers and create buzz in busy areas.**

Courtesy Toys "R" Us, Inc.

The Rise of Megaretailers

The rise of huge mass merchandisers and specialty superstores, the formation of vertical marketing systems, and a rash of retail mergers and acquisitions have created a core of superpower megaretailers. Through their size and buying power, these giant retailers can offer better merchandise selections, good service, and strong price savings to consumers. As a result, they grow even larger by squeezing out their smaller, weaker competitors.

The megaretailers have shifted the balance of power between retailers and producers. A small handful of retailers now control access to enormous numbers of consumers, giving them the upper hand in their dealings with manufacturers. For example, you may never have heard of specialty coatings and sealants manufacturer RPM International, but you've probably used one or more of its many familiar do-it-yourself brands—such as Rust-Oleum paints, Plastic Wood and Dap fillers, Mohawk and Watco finishes, and Testors hobby cements and paints—all of which you can buy at your local Home Depot store. Home Depot is a very important customer to RPM, accounting for a significant share of its consumer sales. However, Home Depot's sales of $68 billion are 20 times RPM's sales of $3.4 billion. As a result, the giant retailer can, and often does, use this power to wring concessions from RPM and thousands of other smaller suppliers.[22]

Growth of Direct and Online Retailing

Many of us still make most of our purchases the old-fashioned way: We go to the store, find what we want, wait patiently in line to plunk down our cash or credit card, and bring home the goods. However, consumers now have a broad array of nonstore alternatives, including direct and online shopping. As we'll discuss in Chapter 14, direct and online marketing are currently the fastest-growing forms of marketing.

Today, thanks to advanced technologies, easier-to-use and enticing Web sites and mobile apps, improved online services, and the increasing sophistication of search technologies, online retailing is thriving. In fact, although it currently accounts for less than 5 percent of total U.S. retail sales, online buying is growing at a much brisker pace than retail buying as a whole. Despite a still-lagging economy, or perhaps because of it, last year's U.S. online retail sales reached an estimated $165 billion and will reach an estimated $279 billion by 2015.[23]

Retailer online sites and mobile apps also influence a large amount of in-store buying. Here are some surprising statistics: 80 percent of shoppers research products online before going to a store to make a purchase; 62 percent of shoppers say that they search for deals online for at least half of their shopping trips; and 62 percent say that they spend at least 30 minutes online every week to help them decide whether and what to buy. Although you'd expect consumers to research expensive products such as consumer electronics, these days they are also researching everyday consumer products. According to one study, more than one-fifth of consumers research food and beverages, nearly one-third research pet products, and 39 percent research baby products before shopping.[24]

Thus, it's no longer a matter of customers deciding whether to shop in the store *or* shop online. Increasingly, customers are merging store and online outlets into a single shopping process. ▶ In fact, the Internet has spawned a whole new breed of shopper and way of shopping. Whether shopping for cars, homes, electronics, consumer products, or medical care, many people just can't buy anything unless they first look it up online and get the lowdown.

All types of retailers now employ direct and online channels. The online sales of large brick-and-mortar retailers, such as Walmart, Sears, Staples, and Best Buy, are increasing rapidly. Many large online-only retailers—Amazon.com, Zappos.com, online travel companies such as Travelocity.com and Expedia.com, and others—have made it big on the Web. At the other extreme, hordes of niche marketers have used the Internet to reach new markets and expand their sales.

▲ The Internet has spawned a whole new breed of shopper—people who just can't buy anything unless they first look it up online and get the lowdown.

Ariwasabi/Shutterstock.com

Still, much of the anticipated growth in online sales will go to multichannel retailers—the click-and-brick marketers who can successfully merge the virtual and physical worlds. In a recent ranking of the top-20 online retail sites, 70 percent were owned by store-based retail chains.[25] For example, thanks largely to rapid growth in online sales, upscale home products retailer Williams-Sonoma now captures more than 40 percent of its total revenues from its direct-to-consumer channel. Like many retailers, Williams-Sonoma has discovered that many of its best customers visit and shop both online and offline. Beyond just offering online shopping, the retailer engages customers through online communities, social media, mobile apps, a blog, and special online programs. "The Internet has changed the way our customers shop," says Williams-Sonoma CEO Laura Alber, "and the online brand experience has to be inspiring and seamless."[26]

Growing Importance of Retail Technology

Retail technologies have become critically important as competitive tools. Progressive retailers are using advanced IT and software systems to produce better forecasts, control inventory costs, interact electronically with suppliers, send information between stores, and even sell to customers within stores. They have adopted sophisticated systems for checkout scanning, RFID inventory tracking, merchandise handling, information sharing, and customer interactions.

Perhaps the most startling advances in retail technology concern the ways in which retailers are connecting with consumers. Today's customers have gotten used to the speed and convenience of buying online and to the control that the Internet gives them over the buying process. The Web lets consumers shop when they like and where they like, with instant access to gobs of information about competing products and prices. No real-world store can do all that.

Increasingly, however, retailers are attempting to meet these new consumer expectations by bringing online-style technologies into their stores. Many retailers now routinely use technologies ranging from touch-screen kiosks, mobile hand-held shopping assistants, and customer-loyalty apps to interactive dressing-room mirrors and virtual sales associates. For example, JCPenney has installed "FindMore" kiosks in select stores, featuring 52-inch touch screens that let customers see the retailer's full range of merchandise, e-mail data about items to themselves or friends, or scan a barcode to learn more about a product and get additional recommendations. The Limited will soon install interactive mirrors in some stores that will allow a shopper to scan a dress and then project that clothing onto her body before going to the dressing room. She can tap the mirror to see different colors, find matching shoes and accessories, and send the image to her Facebook profile. And supermarket chain Stop & Shop now offers hand-held scanners to assist customers as they shop:[27]

> To engage shoppers as they roll their carts down the aisles, speed up checkout, and generally improve the shopping experience, Stop & Shop provides customers with mobile handheld Scan It scanners. Shoppers retrieve a scanner by swiping their loyalty card and then use it to scan and bag products as they shop. The device keeps a running total of purchases. As customers wend their way through the aisles, based on each customer's shopping history and current selections, the Scan It scanners call out sale prices and issue electronic coupons. Customers can even use the scanners to place deli orders while they shop elsewhere in the store. When customers arrive at the deli counter, their order is waiting for them. When done, shoppers pay and go quickly at a dedicated self-checkout lane. The Scan It scanners now process about 10 percent of all Stop & Shop store sales. The new technology not only makes shopping faster, fuller, and more convenient for customers but also reduces store operating costs.

▲ **Retail technology: Stop & Shop uses technology to make shopping faster and more convenient for customers.**

Stop & Shop Supermarket Co.

Green Retailing

Today's retailers are increasingly adopting environmentally sustainable practices. They are greening up their stores and operations, promoting more environmentally responsible products, launching programs to help customers be more responsible, and working with channel partners to reduce their environmental impact.

At the most basic level, most large retailers are making their stores more environmentally friendly through sustainable building design, construction, and operations. For example, new Safeway stores employ extensive recycling and compost programs, wind energy and solar panels for power, and regionally sourced sustainable building materials. ▶ Similarly, McDonald's golden arches are now going green. Its new eco-friendly restaurants are designed from the bottom up with a whole new eco-attitude.[28]

A new "green" McDonald's in Cary, North Carolina, is built and furnished mostly with reclaimed building materials. The parking lot is made with permeable pavers, which absorb and clean storm water and filter it back into the water table. Exterior and interior lighting uses energy-efficient LEDs, which consume as much as 78 percent less energy and last 10 to 20 times longer than traditional lighting. The restaurant is landscaped with hearty, drought-resistant native plants, which require less water. Then, what little water they do need comes from rainwater channeled from the roof and condensation from the super–high-efficiency HVAC system. Inside the restaurant, solartube skylights bring in natural light and reduce energy use. A sophisticated lighting system adjusts indoor illumination based on light entering through the skylights. The dining room is filled with materials made from recycled content (recycled floor tiles, for example, and counters made from recycled glass and concrete), and paints and cleaning chemicals were chosen for their low environmental impact. Other green features include high-efficiency kitchen equipment and water-saving, low-flow faucets and toilets. The restaurant even offers electric vehicle charging stations for customers.

▲ McDonald's golden arches are now going green. Its new eco-friendly restaurants are designed from the bottom up with a whole new eco-attitude.

(bottom) Alexandre Gelebart/REA/Redux Pictures

Retailers are also greening up their product assortments. For example, JCPenney's Simply Green designation identifies store-brand products that are organic, renewable, or made from recycled content. Similarly, Safeway offers its own Bright Green line of home care products, featuring cleaning and laundry soaps made with biodegradable and naturally derived ingredients, energy-efficient light bulbs, and paper products made from 100 percent recycled content. Such products can both boost sales and lift the retailer's image as a responsible company.

Many retailers have also launched programs that help consumers make more environmentally responsible decisions. Staples' EcoEasy program helps customers identify green products sold in its stores and makes it easy to recycle printer cartridges, cell phones, computers, and other office technology products. Staples recycles some 30 million printer cartridges and four million pounds of electronic waste each year. Similarly, Best Buy's "Greener Together" program helps customers select more energy-efficient new products and recycle old ones.[29]

Finally, many large retailers are joining forces with suppliers and distributors to create more sustainable products, packaging, and distribution systems. For example, Amazon.com works closely with the producers of many of the products it sells to reduce and simplify their packaging. And beyond its own substantial sustainability initiatives, Walmart wields its huge buying power to urge its army of suppliers to improve their environmental impact and practices. The retailer has even developed a worldwide Sustainable Product Index, by which it rates suppliers. It plans to translate the index into a simple rating for consumers to help them make more sustainable buying choices.

Green retailing yields both top- and bottom-line benefits. Sustainable practices lift a retailer's top line by attracting consumers looking to support environmentally friendly sellers and products. They also help the bottom line by reducing costs. For example, Amazon.com's reduced-packaging efforts increase customer convenience and eliminate "wrap rage" while at the same time saving packaging costs. And an earth-friendly McDonald's restaurant not only appeals to customers and helps save the planet but costs less to operate.

Global Expansion of Major Retailers

Retailers with unique formats and strong brand positions are increasingly moving into other countries. Many are expanding internationally to escape saturated home markets. Over the years, some giant U.S. retailers, such as McDonald's, have become globally prominent as a result of their marketing prowess. Others, such as Walmart, are rapidly establishing a global presence. Walmart, which now operates more than 4,600 stores in 14 non-U.S. markets, sees exciting global potential. Its international division alone last year racked up sales of more than $109 billion, over 60 percent more than rival Target's *total* sales of $67 billion.[30]

However, most U.S retailers are still significantly behind Europe and Asia when it comes to global expansion. Although nine of the world's top 20 retailers are U.S. companies, only four of these retailers have set up stores outside North America (Walmart, Home Depot, Costco, and Best Buy). Of the 11 non-U.S. retailers in the world's top 20, eight have stores in at least ten countries. Foreign retailers that have gone global include France's Carrefour and Auchan chains, Germany's Metro and Aldi chains, and Britain's Tesco.[31]

French discount retailer Carrefour, the world's second-largest retailer after Walmart, has embarked on an aggressive mission to extend its role as a leading international retailer:

> The Carrefour Group has an interest in almost 16,000 stores in over 30 countries in Europe, Asia, and the Americas. It leads Europe in supermarkets and the world in hypermarkets (supercenters). Carrefour is outpacing Walmart in several emerging markets, including South America, China, and the Pacific Rim. It's the leading retailer in Brazil and Argentina, where it operates more than 1,000 stores, compared to Walmart's 543 units in those two countries. Carrefour is the largest foreign retailer in China, where it operates more than 500 stores versus Walmart's 329. In short, although Walmart has more than three times Carrefour's overall sales, Carrefour is forging ahead of Walmart in most markets outside North America. The only question: Can the French retailer hold its lead? Although no one retailer can safely claim to be in the same league with Walmart as an overall retail presence, Carrefour stands a better chance than most to hold its own in global retailing.[32]

SPEED BUMP | LINKING THE CONCEPTS

Time out! So-called experts have long predicted that online retailing eventually will replace store retailing as our primary way to shop. What do you think?

- Shop for a good book at the Barnes & Noble Web site (www.bn.com), taking time to browse the site and see what it has to offer. Next, shop at a nearby Barnes & Noble or other bookstore. Compare the two shopping experiences. Where would you rather shop? On what occasions? Why?
- A Barnes & Noble store creates an ideal "community" where people can "hang out." How does its Web site compare on this dimension?

Author Comment ▶
Whereas retailers primarily sell goods and services directly to final consumers for personal use, wholesalers sell primarily to those buying for resale or business use.

Wholesaling

Wholesaling includes all the activities involved in selling goods and services to those buying them for resale or business use. Firms engaged *primarily* in wholesaling activities are called **wholesalers**.

Wholesalers buy mostly from producers and sell mostly to retailers, industrial consumers, and other wholesalers. As a result, many of the nation's largest and most important wholesalers are largely unknown to final consumers. ▶ For example, you may never have heard of Grainger, even though it's very well known and much valued by its more than 2 million business and institutional customers in 157 countries.[33]

GRAINGER
FOR THE ONES WHO GET IT DONE

"Service Delivered"

▲ **Wholesaling: Many of the nation's largest and most important wholesalers—like Grainger—are largely unknown to final consumers. But they are very well known and much valued by the business customers they serve.**

W. W. Grainger, Inc.

Grainger may be the biggest market leader you've never heard of. It's a $7.2 billion business that offers more than 1 million maintenance, repair, and operating (MRO) products from 400 manufacturers in 30 countries to 2 million active customers. Through its branch network, service centers, sales reps, catalog, and Web site, Grainger links customers with the supplies they need to keep their facilities running smoothly—everything from light bulbs, cleaners, and display cases to nuts and bolts, motors, valves, power tools, test equipment, and safety supplies. Grainger's 607 branches, 24 strategically located distribution centers, more than 18,500 employees, and innovative Web sites handle more than 115,000 transactions a day. Grainger's customers include organizations ranging from factories, garages, and grocers to schools and military bases.

Grainger operates on a simple value proposition: to make it easier and less costly for customers to find and buy MRO supplies. It starts by acting as a one-stop shop for products needed to maintain facilities. On a broader level, it builds lasting relationships with customers by helping them find *solutions* to their overall MRO problems. Acting as consultants, Grainger sales reps help buyers with everything from improving their supply chain management to reducing inventories and streamlining warehousing operations. So, how come you've never heard of Grainger? Perhaps it's because the company operates in the not-so-glamorous world of MRO supplies, which are important to every business but not so important to consumers. More likely, it's because Grainger is a wholesaler. And like most wholesalers, it operates behind the scenes, selling mostly to other businesses.

Why are wholesalers important to sellers? For example, why would a producer use wholesalers rather than selling directly to retailers or consumers? Simply put, wholesalers add value by performing one or more of the following channel functions:

Wholesaling
All the activities involved in selling goods and services to those buying for resale or business use.

Wholesaler
A firm engaged *primarily* in wholesaling activities.

- *Selling and promoting:* Wholesalers' sales forces help manufacturers reach many small customers at a low cost. The wholesaler has more contacts and is often more trusted by the buyer than the distant manufacturer.
- *Buying and assortment building:* Wholesalers can select items and build assortments needed by their customers, thereby saving much work.
- *Bulk breaking:* Wholesalers save their customers money by buying in carload lots and breaking bulk (breaking large lots into small quantities).
- *Warehousing:* Wholesalers hold inventories, thereby reducing the inventory costs and risks of suppliers and customers.
- *Transportation:* Wholesalers can provide quicker delivery to buyers because they are closer to buyers than are producers.
- *Financing:* Wholesalers finance their customers by giving credit, and they finance their suppliers by ordering early and paying bills on time.
- *Risk bearing:* Wholesalers absorb risk by taking title and bearing the cost of theft, damage, spoilage, and obsolescence.
- *Market information:* Wholesalers give information to suppliers and customers about competitors, new products, and price developments.
- *Management services and advice:* Wholesalers often help retailers train their salesclerks, improve store layouts and displays, and set up accounting and inventory control systems.

Types of Wholesalers

Merchant wholesaler
An independently owned wholesale business that takes title to the merchandise it handles.

Wholesalers fall into three major groups (see ▶ **Table 11.3**): *merchant wholesalers*, *brokers and agents*, and *manufacturers' and retailers' branches and offices*. **Merchant wholesalers** are the largest single group of wholesalers, accounting for roughly 50 percent of

| > **Table 11.3** | Major Types of Wholesalers |

Type	Description
Merchant wholesalers	Independently owned businesses that take title to all merchandise handled. There are *full-service wholesalers* and *limited-service wholesalers*.
Full-service wholesalers	Provide a full line of services: carrying stock, maintaining a sales force, offering credit, making deliveries, and providing management assistance. Full-service wholesalers include wholesale merchants and industrial distributors.
Wholesale merchants	Sell primarily to retailers and provide a full range of services. *General merchandise wholesalers* carry several merchandise lines, whereas *general line wholesalers* carry one or two lines in great depth. *Specialty wholesalers* specialize in carrying only part of a line.
Industrial distributors	Sell to manufacturers rather than to retailers. Provide several services, such as carrying stock, offering credit, and providing delivery. May carry a broad range of merchandise, a general line, or a specialty line.
Limited-service wholesalers	Offer fewer services than full-service wholesalers. Limited-service wholesalers are of several types:
Cash-and-carry wholesalers	Carry a limited line of fast-moving goods and sell to small retailers for cash. Normally do not deliver.
Truck wholesalers (or truck jobbers)	Perform primarily a selling and delivery function. Carry a limited line of semiperishable merchandise (such as milk, bread, snack foods), which is sold for cash as deliveries are made to supermarkets, small groceries, hospitals, restaurants, factory cafeterias, and hotels.
Drop shippers	Do not carry inventory or handle the product. On receiving an order, drop shippers select a manufacturer, who then ships the merchandise directly to the customer. Drop shippers operate in bulk industries, such as coal, lumber, and heavy equipment.
Rack jobbers	Serve grocery and drug retailers, mostly in nonfood items. Rack jobbers send delivery trucks to stores, where the delivery people set up toys, paperbacks, hardware items, health and beauty aids, or other items. Rack jobbers price the goods, keep them fresh, set up point-of-purchase displays, and keep inventory records.
Producers' cooperatives	Farmer-owned members that assemble farm produce for sale in local markets. Producers' cooperatives often attempt to improve product quality and promote a co-op brand name, such as Sun-Maid raisins, Sunkist oranges, or Diamond nuts.
Mail-order or Web wholesalers	Send catalogs to or maintain Web sites for retail, industrial, and institutional customers featuring jewelry, cosmetics, specialty foods, and other small items. Its primary customers are businesses in small outlying areas.
Brokers and agents	Do not take title to goods. Main function is to facilitate buying and selling, for which they earn a commission on the selling price. Generally specialize by product line or customer type.
Brokers	Bring buyers and sellers together and assist in negotiation. Brokers are paid by the party who hired the broker and do not carry inventory, get involved in financing, or assume risk. Examples include food brokers, real estate brokers, insurance brokers, and security brokers.
Agents	Represent either buyers or sellers on a more permanent basis than brokers do. There are four types:
Manufacturers' agents	Represent two or more manufacturers of complementary lines. Often used in such lines as apparel, furniture, and electrical goods. A manufacturer's agent is hired by small manufacturers who cannot afford their own field sales forces and by large manufacturers who use agents to open new territories or cover territories that cannot support full-time salespeople.

▶ **Table 11.3**	Major Types of Wholesalers

Type	Description
Selling agents	Have contractual authority to sell a manufacturer's entire output. The selling agent serves as a sales department and has significant influence over prices, terms, and conditions of sale. Found in product areas such as textiles, industrial machinery and equipment, coal and coke, chemicals, and metals.
Purchasing agents	Generally have a long-term relationship with buyers and make purchases for them, often receiving, inspecting, warehousing, and shipping the merchandise to buyers. Purchasing agents help clients obtain the best goods and prices available.
Commission merchants	Take physical possession of products and negotiate sales. Used most often in agricultural marketing by farmers who do not want to sell their own output. Takes a truckload of commodities to a central market, sells it for the best price, deducts a commission and expenses, and remits the balance to the producers.
Manufacturers' and retailers' branches and offices	Wholesaling operations conducted by sellers or buyers themselves rather than operating through independent wholesalers. Separate branches and offices can be dedicated to either sales or purchasing.
Sales branches and offices	Set up by manufacturers to improve inventory control, selling, and promotion. *Sales branches* carry inventory and are found in industries such as lumber and automotive equipment and parts. *Sales offices* do not carry inventory and are most prominent in the dry goods and notions industries.
Purchasing officers	Perform a role similar to that of brokers or agents but are part of the buyer's organization. Many retailers set up purchasing offices in major market centers, such as New York and Chicago.

all wholesaling. Merchant wholesalers include two broad types: full-service wholesalers and limited-service wholesalers. *Full-service wholesalers* provide a full set of services, whereas the various *limited-service wholesalers* offer fewer services to their suppliers and customers. The different types of limited-service wholesalers perform varied specialized functions in the distribution channel.

Brokers and *agents* differ from merchant wholesalers in two ways: They do not take title to goods, and they perform only a few functions. Like merchant wholesalers, they generally specialize by product line or customer type. A **broker** brings buyers and sellers together and assists in negotiation. **Agents** represent buyers or sellers on a more permanent basis. *Manufacturers' agents* (also called *manufacturers' representatives*) are the most common type of agent wholesaler. The third major type of wholesaling is that done in **manufacturers' sales branches and offices** by sellers or buyers themselves rather than through independent wholesalers.

Wholesaler Marketing Decisions

Wholesalers now face growing competitive pressures, more-demanding customers, new technologies, and more direct-buying programs on the part of large industrial, institutional, and retail buyers. As a result, they have taken a fresh look at their marketing strategies. As with retailers, their marketing decisions include choices of segmentation and targeting, differentiation and positioning, and the marketing mix—product and service assortments, price, promotion, and distribution (see ▶ **Figure 11.2**).

Segmentation, Targeting, Differentiation, and Positioning Decisions

Like retailers, wholesalers must segment and define their target markets and differentiate and position themselves effectively—they cannot serve everyone. They can choose a target

Broker
A wholesaler who does not take title to goods and whose function is to bring buyers and sellers together and assist in negotiation.

Agent
A wholesaler who represents buyers or sellers on a relatively permanent basis, performs only a few functions, and does not take title to goods.

Manufacturers' sales branches and offices
Wholesaling by sellers or buyers themselves rather than through independent wholesalers.

Figure 11.2 Wholesaler Marketing Strategy

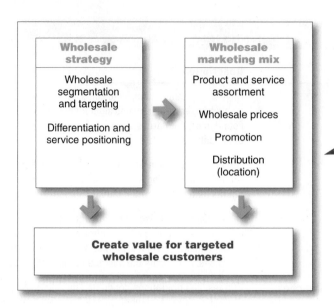

group by size of customer (for example, large retailers only), type of customer (convenience stores only), the need for service (customers who need credit), or other factors. Within the target group, they can identify the more profitable customers, design stronger offers, and build better relationships with them. They can propose automatic reordering systems, establish management-training and advisory systems, or even sponsor a voluntary chain. They can discourage less-profitable customers by requiring larger orders or adding service charges to smaller ones.

Marketing Mix Decisions

Like retailers, wholesalers must decide on product and service assortments, prices, promotion, and place. Wholesalers add customer value though the *products and services* they offer. They are often under great pressure to carry a full line and stock enough for immediate delivery. But this practice can damage profits. Wholesalers today are cutting down on the number of lines they carry, choosing to carry only the more-profitable ones. They are also rethinking which services count most in building strong customer relationships and which should be dropped or paid for by the customer. The key for companies is to find the mix of services most valued by their target customers.

Price is also an important wholesaler decision. Wholesalers usually mark up the cost of goods by a standard percentage—say, 20 percent. Expenses may run 17 percent of the gross margin, leaving a profit margin of 3 percent. In grocery wholesaling, the average profit margin is often less than 2 percent. The recent recession put heavy pressure on wholesalers to cut their costs and prices. As their retail and industrial customers face sales and margin declines, these customers turn to wholesalers looking for lower prices. Wholesalers may, in turn, cut their margins on some lines to keep important customers. They may also ask suppliers for special price breaks in cases when they can turn them into an increase in the supplier's sales.

Although *promotion* can be critical to wholesaler success, most wholesalers are not promotion minded. They use largely scattered and unplanned trade advertising, sales promotion, personal selling, and public relations. Many are behind the times in personal selling; they still see selling as a single salesperson talking to a single customer instead of as a team effort to sell, build, and service major accounts. Wholesalers also need to adopt some of the nonpersonal promotion techniques used by retailers. They need to develop an overall promotion strategy and make greater use of supplier promotion materials and programs.

Finally, *distribution* (location) is important. Wholesalers must choose their locations, facilities, and Web locations carefully. There was a time when wholesalers could locate in low-rent, low-tax areas and invest little money in their buildings, equipment, and systems. Today, however, as technology zooms forward, such behavior results in outdated systems for material handling, order processing, and delivery.

Instead, today's large and progressive wholesalers have reacted to rising costs by investing in automated warehouses and IT systems. Orders are fed from the retailer's information system directly into the wholesaler's, and the items are picked up by mechanical devices and automatically taken to a shipping platform where they are assembled. Most large wholesalers use technology to carry out accounting, billing, inventory control, and forecasting. Modern wholesalers are adapting their services to the needs of target customers and finding cost-reducing methods of doing business. They are also transacting more business online. For example, e-commerce is Grainger's fastest growing sales channel. Online purchasing now accounts for more than 25 percent of the wholesaler's total sales.

Trends in Wholesaling

Today's wholesalers face considerable challenges. The industry remains vulnerable to one of its most enduring trends—the need for ever-greater efficiency. Recent economic conditions have led to demands for even lower prices and the winnowing out of suppliers who are not adding value based on cost and quality. Progressive wholesalers constantly watch for better ways to meet the changing needs of their suppliers and target customers. They recognize that their only reason for existence comes from adding value, which occurs by increasing the efficiency and effectiveness of the entire marketing channel.

As with other types of marketers, the goal is to build value-adding customer relationships. McKesson provides an example of progressive, value-adding wholesaling. The company is a diversified health care services provider and the nation's leading wholesaler of pharmaceuticals, health and beauty care, home health care, and medical supply and equipment products. To survive, especially in a harsh economic environment, McKesson has to be more cost effective than manufacturers' sales branches. Thus, the company has built efficient automated warehouses, established direct computer links with drug manufacturers, and created extensive online supply management and accounts receivable systems for customers. It offers retail pharmacists a wide range of online resources, including supply-management assistance, catalog searches, real-time order tracking, and an account-management system. It has also created solutions such as automated pharmaceutical-dispensing machines that assist pharmacists by reducing costs and improving accuracy. ▶ Retailers can even use the McKesson systems to maintain prescription histories and medical profiles on their customers.

McKesson's medical-surgical supply and equipment customers receive a rich assortment of online solutions and supply management tools, including an online order management system and real-time information on products and pricing, inventory availability, and order status. According to McKesson, it adds value in the channel by providing "supply, information, and health care management products and services designed to reduce costs and improve quality across healthcare."[34]

The distinction between large retailers and large wholesalers continues to blur. Many retailers now operate formats such as wholesale clubs and supercenters that perform many wholesale functions. In return, some large wholesalers are setting up their own retailing operations. For example, until recently, SuperValu was classified as a food wholesaler, with a majority of its business derived from supplying grocery products to independent grocery retailers. However, over the past decade, SuperValu has started or acquired several retail food chains of its own—including Albertsons, Jewel-Osco, Save-A-Lot, Cub Foods, Acme, and others—to become the nation's third-largest food retailer (behind Walmart and Kroger). Thus, even though it remains the country's largest food wholesaler, SuperValu is now classified as a retailer because more than 75 percent of its $40 billion in sales comes from retailing.[35]

▲ **Pharmaceuticals wholesaler McKesson helps its retail pharmacist customers be more efficient by offering a wide range of online resources. Retail pharmacists can even use the McKesson system to maintain medical profiles on their customers.**

Jose Luis Pelaez/Corbis

Wholesalers will continue to increase the services they provide to retailers—retail pricing, cooperative advertising, marketing and management information services, accounting services, online transactions, and others. However, both the recently tight economy and the demand for increased services have put the squeeze on wholesaler profits. Wholesalers who do not find efficient ways to deliver value to their customers will soon drop by the wayside. Fortunately, the increased use of computerized, automated, and Internet-based systems will help wholesalers contain the costs of ordering, shipping, and inventory holding, thus boosting their productivity.

REST STOP | REVIEWING THE CONCEPTS

MyMarketingLab

Now that you have completed the chapter, return to www.mymktlab.com to experience and apply the concepts and to explore the additional study materials for this chapter.

CHAPTER REVIEW AND KEY TERMS

Objectives Review

Retailing and wholesaling consist of many organizations bringing goods and services from the point of production to the point of use. In this chapter, we examined the nature and importance of retailing, the major types of retailers, the decisions retailers make, and the future of retailing. We then examined these same topics for wholesalers.

 OBJECTIVE 1 Explain the role of retailers in the distribution channel and describe the major types of retailers. (pp 324–333)

Retailing includes all the activities involved in selling goods or services directly to final consumers for their personal, non-business use. Retail stores come in all shapes and sizes, and new retail types keep emerging. Store retailers can be classified by the *amount of service* they provide (self-service, limited service, or full service), *product line sold* (specialty stores, department stores, supermarkets, convenience stores, superstores, and service businesses), and *relative prices* (discount stores and off-price retailers). Today, many retailers are banding together in corporate and contractual *retail organizations* (corporate chains, voluntary chains, retailer cooperatives, and franchise organizations).

 OBJECTIVE 2 Describe the major retailer marketing decisions. (pp 333–339)

Retailers are always searching for new marketing strategies to attract and hold customers. They face major marketing decisions about segmentation and targeting, store differentiation and positioning, and the retail marketing mix.

Retailers must first segment and define their target markets and then decide how they will differentiate and position themselves in these markets. Those that try to offer "something for everyone" end up satisfying no market well. By contrast, successful retailers define their target markets well and position themselves strongly.

Guided by strong targeting and positioning, retailers must decide on a retail marketing mix—product and services assortment, price, promotion, and place. Retail stores are much more than simply an assortment of goods. Beyond the products and services they offer, today's successful retailers carefully orchestrate virtually every aspect of the consumer store experience. A retailer's price policy must fit its target market and positioning, products and services assortment, and competition. Retailers use any or all of the five promotion tools—advertising, personal selling, sales promotion, PR, and direct marketing—to reach consumers. Finally, it's very important that retailers select locations that are accessible to the target market in areas that are consistent with the retailer's positioning.

 OBJECTIVE 3 Discuss the major trends and developments in retailing. (pp 339–344)

Retailers operate in a harsh and fast-changing environment, which offers threats as well as opportunities. Following years of good economic times for retailers, the Great Recession turned many retailers' fortunes from boom to bust. New retail forms continue to emerge. At the same time, however, different types of retailers are increasingly serving similar customers with the same products and prices (retail convergence), making differentiation more difficult. Other trends in retailing include the rise of megaretailers, the rapid growth of direct and online retailing, the growing importance of retail technology, a surge in green retailing, and the global expansion of major retailers.

> **OBJECTIVE 4 Explain the major types of wholesalers and their marketing decisions.** (pp 344–350)

Wholesaling includes all the activities involved in selling goods or services to those who are buying for the purpose of resale or business use. Wholesalers fall into three groups. First, *merchant wholesalers* take possession of the goods. They include *full-service wholesalers* (wholesale merchants and industrial distributors) and *limited-service wholesalers* (cash-and-carry

wholesalers, truck wholesalers, drop shippers, rack jobbers, producers' cooperatives, and mail-order wholesalers). Second, *brokers* and *agents* do not take possession of the goods but are paid a commission for aiding companies in buying and selling. Finally, *manufacturers' sales branches and offices* are wholesaling operations conducted by nonwholesalers to bypass the wholesalers.

Like retailers, wholesalers must target carefully and position themselves strongly. And, like retailers, wholesalers must decide on product and service assortments, prices, promotion, and place. Progressive wholesalers constantly watch for better ways to meet the changing needs of their suppliers and target customers. They recognize that, in the long run, their only reason for existence comes from adding value, which occurs by increasing the efficiency and effectiveness of the entire marketing channel. As with other types of marketers, the goal is to build value-adding customer relationships.

Key Terms

Objective 1
Retailing (p 324)
Retailer (p 324)
Shopper marketing (p 325)
Specialty store (p 326)
Department store (p 326)
Supermarket (p 327)
Convenience store (p 327)
Superstore (p 328)
Category killer (p 328)
Service retailer (p 328)

Discount store (p 328)
Off-price retailer (p 330)
Independent off-price retailer (p 330)
Factory outlet (p 330)
Warehouse club (p 331)
Corporate chains (p 331)
Franchise (p 332)

Objective 2
Shopping center (p 338)

Objective 3
Wheel-of-retailing concept (p 340)

Objective 4
Wholesaling (p 344)
Wholesaler (p 344)
Merchant wholesaler (p 345)
Broker (p 347)
Agent (p 347)
Manufacturers' sales branches and offices (p 347)

DISCUSSION AND CRITICAL THINKING

Discussion Questions

1. Discuss how retailers and wholesalers add value to the marketing system. Explain why marketers are embracing the concept of *shopper marketing*. (AACSB: Communication; Reflective Thinking)
2. Name and describe the types of corporate or contractual retail store organizations and the advantages of each. (AACSB: Communication)
3. Suppose that you are a manufacturer's agent for three lines of complementary women's apparel. Discuss what types

   of marketing mix decisions you will be making. (AACSB: Communication; Reflective Thinking)
4. Describe the types of shopping centers and identify specific examples in your community or nearby city. (AACSB: Communication; Reflective Thinking)
5. What is retail convergence? Has it helped or harmed small retailers? (AACSB: Communication; Reflective Thinking)
6. Explain how wholesalers add value in the channel of distribution. (AACSB: Communication)

Critical Thinking Exercises

1. The atmosphere in a retail store is carefully crafted to influence shoppers. Select a retailer that has both a physical store and an online store. Describe the elements of the physical store's atmosphere, such as the colors, lighting, music, scents, and décor. What image is the store's atmosphere projecting? Is that image appropriate given the merchandise assortment and target market of the store? Which elements of the physical store's atmosphere are also part of the online store's atmosphere? Does the retailer integrate the physical store's atmosphere with its online presence? Explain. (AACSB: Communication; Use of IT; Reflective Thinking)

2. Deciding on a target market and positioning are very important marketing decisions for a retail store. In a small group, develop the concept for a new retail store. What is the target market for your store? How is your store positioned? What retail atmospherics will enhance this positioning effectively to attract and satisfy your target market? (AACSB: Communication; Reflective Thinking)

3. Shop for a product of your choice on Amazon.com. Do the consumer reviews influence your perception of a product or brand offered? Many of the product reviews on Amazon.com are submitte d by consumers participating in the Amazon Vine Program. Learn about this program and discuss whether or not a review from a consumer in this program is more useful than one from a consumer not in this program. (AACSB: Communication; Use of IT; Reflective Thinking)

MINICASES AND APPLICATIONS

Marketing Technology   Mirror, Mirror on the Wall

"Who's the fairest of them all?" This is not just a fairy tale feature anymore; it can be found online or at a retailer near you. EZFace, a virtual mirror using augmented reality, is changing the cosmetics aisle in some Walmart stores. A shopper stands in front of the magical mirror, swipes the bar code of the cosmetic she's interested in, and tries it on virtually without opening the package. No more regrets about buying the wrong shade of lipstick! Self-service retailers are interested in this technology because it can reduce damaged inventory from consumers opening a package and then not buying it. This is just one of the interactive digital technologies with which retailers are experimenting—keep an eye out for many more.

1. Visit www.ezface.com or www.ray-ban.com/usa/science/virtual-mirror and use the virtual mirror to try on makeup or sunglasses. Does this technology help you select an appropriate product for your face? (AACSB: Communication; Use of IT; Reflective Thinking)

2. Find other examples of how retailers are using digital technologies, such as digital signage and mobile technologies, to better serve customers. (AACSB: Communication; Use of IT; Reflective Thinking)

Marketing Ethics   Charge!

In the United States, paying for purchases with a credit card is old news. That's not so in much of Asia, however. The United States leads the world in credit cards per capita—2.01—which is much higher than many Asian countries; for example, China has 0.15 cards per capita and India has 0.02. But that's changing dramatically—between 2004 and 2009, Asian credit card transactions grew 158 percent, approaching a quarter of the global transaction volume. Asian governments are encouraging this growth because it stimulates the economy and brings in more tax revenue. Retailers embrace it because consumers spend more when using cards compared to cash. This trend is not without critics, however, given Asians' historical aversion to debt.

1. What are the ethical implications of encouraging electronic payment methods compared to cash payments in Asian countries? (AACSB: Communication; Ethical Reasoning; Reflective Thinking)

2. Most stores have eliminated lay-away options for customers and encourage credit purchases. Should retailers encourage customers to rely heavily on credit? (AACSB: Communication; Reflective Thinking)

Marketing by the Numbers   Mark Up

Consumers typically buy products such as toiletries, food, and clothing from retailers rather than directly from the manufacturer. Likewise, retailers buy from wholesalers. Resellers perform functions for the manufacturer and the consumer and mark up the price to reflect that value. Refer to Appendix 3, Marketing by the Numbers, to answer the following questions.

1. If a manufacturer sells its laundry detergent to a wholesaler for $2.50, at what price will the wholesaler sell it to a retailer if the wholesaler wants a 15 percent margin based on its selling price? (AACSB: Communication; Analytical Reasoning)

2. If a retailer wants a 20 percent margin based on its selling price, at what price will the retailer sell the product to consumers? (AACSB: Communication; Analytical Reasoning)

Video Case   Home Shopping Network

Shopping on television has been around almost as long as television itself. The Home Shopping Network (HSN) made it a full-time endeavor in 1982, giving birth to a new retail channel. Since then, HSN has been a pioneer in products, presentation, and order taking. The company has sold millions of products and has been known for giving an outlet to legitimate products that otherwise would not reach customers.

But what does a company do when the very retail channel that it depends upon starts to fizzle out? This video illustrates how HSN has met the challenges of a changing marketplace and continues to reach its customer base innovatively.

After viewing the video featuring HSN, answer the following questions:

1. How has HSN differentiated itself from other retailers through each element of the retail marketing mix?
2. How does the concept of the retail life cycle relate to HSN?
3. Do you think HSN has a bright future? Why or why not?

Company Cases   6 Darden Restaurants / 11 Tesco Fresh & Easy / 14 eBay

See Appendix 1 for cases appropriate for this chapter. **Case 6, Darden Restaurants: Balancing Standardization and Differentiation.** By listening to customers, Darden finds success by targeting different customers through distinct restaurant formats. **Case 11, Tesco Fresh & Easy: Another British Invasion.** UK megagrocer Tesco attempts to penetrate the U.S. market by targeting an underserved customer segment. **Case 14, eBay: Fixing an Online Marketing Pioneer.** Once the biggest online retailer, eBay alters its marketing strategy to alleviate growing pains.

PART 1: DEFINING MARKETING AND THE MARKETING PROCESS (CHAPTERS 1–2)
PART 2: UNDERSTANDING THE MARKETPLACE AND CONSUMERS (CHAPTERS 3–5)
PART 3: DESIGNING A CUSTOMER-DRIVEN STRATEGY AND MIX (CHAPTERS 6–14)
PART 4: EXTENDING MARKETING (CHAPTERS 15–16)

12 Communicating Customer Value

Advertising and Public Relations

CHAPTER ROAD MAP

Objective Outline

▶ **OBJECTIVE 1** **Define the five promotion mix tools for communicating customer value.** The Promotion Mix (357)

▶ **OBJECTIVE 2** **Discuss the changing communications landscape and the need for integrated marketing communications.** Integrated Marketing Communications (357–362); Shaping the Overall Promotion Mix (362–365)

▶ **OBJECTIVE 3** **Describe and discuss the major decisions involved in developing an advertising program.** Advertising (365–366); Setting Advertising Objectives (366–367); Setting the Advertising Budget (367–369); Developing Advertising Strategy (369–379); Evaluating Advertising Effectiveness and Return on Advertising Investment (379–380); Other Advertising Considerations (380–382)

▶ **OBJECTIVE 4** **Explain how companies use public relations to communicate with their publics.** Public Relations (382–384); Major Public Relations Tools (384–385)

Previewing the Concepts

We'll forge ahead now into the last of the marketing mix tools—promotion. Companies must do more than just create customer value. They must also use promotion to clearly and persuasively communicate that value. Promotion is not a single tool but rather a mix of several tools. Ideally, under the concept of *integrated marketing communications,* the company will carefully coordinate these promotion elements to deliver a clear, consistent, and compelling message about the organization and its products. We'll begin by introducing you to the various promotion mix tools. Next, we'll examine the rapidly changing communications environment and the need for integrated marketing communications. Finally, we'll look more closely at two of the promotion tools—advertising and public relations. In the next chapter, we'll visit two other promotion mix tools—sales promotion and personal selling. Then, in Chapter 14, we'll explore direct and online marketing.

Let's start with the question: Does advertising really make a difference? Microsoft and Apple certainly must think so. Each spends more than a half billion dollars a year on it. Here, we examine the long-running advertising battle between the two computer industry giants. As you read, think about the impact of advertising on each brand's fortunes.

In the long-running advertising battle between Microsoft and Apple, Microsoft's innovative "I'm a PC" campaign has given PC fans everywhere a real boost. Now, it's actually kind of cool to own a PC.

Used with permission from Microsoft Corporation

First Stop

Microsoft vs. Apple: Does Advertising Really Make a Difference?

In 2006, Apple launched its now-famous "Get a Mac" ad campaign, featuring two characters—"Mac" and "PC"—sparring over the advantages of the Apple Mac vs. a Microsoft Windows-based PC. The ads portrayed Mac as a young, hip, laid back guy in a hoodie, whereas PC was a stodgy, befuddled, error-prone, middle-aged nerd in baggie khakis, a brown sport coat, and unfashionable glasses. Not surprisingly, adroit and modern Mac always got the best of outdated and inflexible PC. Over the years, Apple unleashed a nonstop barrage of Mac vs. PC ads that bashed Windows-based machines—and their owners—as outmoded and dysfunctional.

The "Get a Mac" campaign produced results. When the campaign began, Mac held only a 2 to 3 percent share of the U.S. computer market. Less than two years later, its share had more than doubled to 6 to 8 percent and growing. The cool campaign also helped boost customer value perceptions of Apple computers. At one point, even though its computers were widely viewed as more expensive, Apple scored a whopping 70 on the BrandIndex (which tracks daily consumer perceptions of brand value on a scale of −100 to 100). Microsoft, meanwhile, floundered below zero.

Good advertising wasn't the only thing contributing to Apple's success. The popularity of its iPod, iPhone, and other new products was also converting customers to Mac computers. But the smug ads were consistently hitting their mark, and Microsoft needed to do something dramatic to turn the advertising tide. So, two years after the Apple "Get a Mac" onslaught began, conservative Microsoft hired the anything-but-conservative advertising agency Crispin Porter + Bogusky, which is known for its award-winning but cheeky and irreverent campaigns for clients such as Burger King, VW, and Coke Zero. Microsoft and Crispin made for an odd mix of corporate personalities. Even Rob Reilly, executive creative director for Crispin, worried a bit about the partnership. After all, Crispin itself was a Mac shop through and through. Still, Reilly was enthused

about creating a campaign to blunt Apple's attacks and restore Microsoft's image as an innovative industry leader.

To break from the past, Microsoft and Crispin first launched a set of "teaser ads" designed to "get the conversation going." In the ads, comedian Jerry Seinfeld and Microsoft founder Bill Gates spent time together, shopping for shoes, eating ice cream, and exchanging irrelevant banter, all with little or no mention of Microsoft Windows. Although they made few selling points, the humorous, well-received ads put a more human face on the giant software company.

A few weeks later, Microsoft replaced the teaser commercials with a direct counterpunch to Apple's "Get a Mac" ads. It launched its own "I'm a PC" campaign, featuring a dead-on look-alike of Apple's PC character. In the first ad, dressed in PC's dorky outfit, Microsoft's character opened with the line, "I'm a PC. And I've been made into a stereotype." He was followed by a parade of everyday PC users—from environmentalists, political bloggers, mixed martial arts fighters, and mashup DJs to budget-conscious laptop shoppers and remarkably tech-savvy preschoolers—each proclaiming, "I'm a PC."

> After years of PC-bashing by Apple's classic "Get a Mac" campaign, Microsoft is now on equal—and maybe better—footing in the heated advertising battle waged by the two computer-industry giants. Advertising matters, and Microsoft's "I'm a PC" campaign is really working.

The Microsoft "I'm a PC" campaign struck a chord with Windows users. They no longer had to sit back and take Apple's jibes like the clueless drones they were made out to be. "That's where the whole notion of 'I'm a PC' and putting a face on our users came about," said Reilly. Identifying real PC people "was important to do on behalf of our users, who really aren't like that [Mac vs. PC] guy," says a Microsoft brand marketer.

Off to a successful start, Microsoft and Crispin soon extended the "I'm a PC" campaign with a new pitch, one that was more in tune with the then-troubled economy. Part advertising and part reality TV, the new campaign—called "Laptop Hunters"—tagged along with real consumers as they shopped for new computers. The first ad featured an energetic young redhead named Lauren, who wanted a laptop with "comfortable keys and a 17-inch screen" for under $1,000. Stopping first at a Mac store, she learned that Apple offered only one laptop at $1,000, and it had only a 13-inch screen. To get what she wanted from Apple, she figured, "I'd have to double my budget, which isn't feasible. I guess I'm just not cool enough to be a Mac person." Instead, Lauren giddily buys an HP Pavilion laptop for less than $700. "I'm a PC," she concludes, "and I got just what I wanted."

If previous "I'm a PC" ads started a shift in perceptions, the "Laptop Hunters" series really moved the needle. The ads spoke volumes in a difficult economy, portraying Apple as too expensive, "too cool," and out of touch with mainstream consumers. The provocative ads, in tandem with the nation's economic woes, bumped Microsoft's BrandIndex score from near zero to 46.2, while Apple's score dropped from its previous high of 70 to only 12.4. In a sure sign that Microsoft's revitalized advertising was striking a nerve, Apple's lawyers called Microsoft chief operating officer B. Kevin Turner, demanding that he change the ads because Apple was lowering its prices and the ads were no longer accurate. It was "the greatest single phone call" he'd ever taken, said Turner. "I did cartwheels down the hallway."

To maintain momentum, Microsoft and Crispin launched yet another iteration of the "I'm a PC" campaign—this one introducing Microsoft's new Windows 7 operating system. Consistent with the "I'm a PC" theme, the campaign featured testimonials from everyday folks telling how specific Windows 7 features reflected ideas they'd passed along to Microsoft in an eight million-person beta test of the software. At the end of each ad, customers gloated, "I'm a PC, and Windows 7 was my idea."

Once again, Apple responded. It struck back directly with one of its most negative Mac vs. PC ads yet. Called "Broken Promises," it featured a gloating PC telling Mac that Windows 7 wouldn't have any of the problems associated with the old Windows versions. A bewildered Mac notes that he'd heard such claims before, with each previous Windows generation. In the end, PC says, "Trust me." Many analysts felt that the biting tone of the ad suggested that Apple was feeling the heat and getting defensive. Uncharacteristically, Mac seemed to be losing his cool.

In mid-2010, Apple appeared to throw in the towel. It retired its "Get a Mac" campaign in favor of a more straightforward "Why You'll Love a Mac" campaign, which listed the reasons for choosing a Mac rather than a PC. Microsoft, however, showed no signs of letting up. In mid-2011, it and Crispin launched yet another "I'm a PC" campaign, this one featuring "real couples" with outdated PCs. One person in each relationship wants to upgrade; the other is reluctant. In one ad, for example, husband Russell wants a new PC but his wife, Julie, disagrees because "I'm not sure there's something out there better than what I've got right now." So, to come to Russell's aid and show Julie what she's missing, Microsoft builds a PC store right in their house. Of course, after checking out various new PC models, Julie ends up buying one. As Russell gives a gleeful thumbs-up, Julie proudly announces—you guessed it—"I'm a PC."

Thanks to the "I'm a PC" campaign, Microsoft has now put itself on equal—and perhaps better—advertising footing with Apple. Consumer value perceptions for Microsoft and Apple are now running pretty much neck and neck. And the campaign has given PC fans everywhere a real boost. "I've never seen more pride at Microsoft," says one Microsoft employee. "You walk through the campus, and you see people's laptops that have 'I'm a PC' stickers on them. I walk in the company store, and there are these huge banners that say 'I'm a PC' and shirts and ties and mugs." Crispin's Reilly now owns not one but two PC laptops and is thrilled with the impact of his agency's efforts. "You are not so embarrassed to take your PC out of the bag on a plane anymore," he says. "It's actually kind of cool that you do. I know this [campaign] is working."[1]

MyMarketingLab

Visit www.mymktlab.com to find activities that help you learn and review in order to succeed in this chapter.

Building good customer relationships calls for more than just developing a good product, pricing it attractively, and making it available to target customers. Companies must also *communicate* their value propositions to customers, and what they communicate should not be left to chance. All communications must be planned and blended into carefully integrated programs. Just as good communication is important in building and maintaining any other kind of relationship, it is a crucial element in a company's efforts to build profitable customer relationships.

The Promotion Mix

A company's total **promotion mix**—also called its **marketing communications mix**—consists of the specific blend of advertising, public relations, personal selling, sales promotion, and direct-marketing tools that the company uses to persuasively communicate customer value and build customer relationships. The five major promotion tools are defined as follows:[2]

Graski says 4.

- *Advertising:* Any paid form of nonpersonal presentation and promotion of ideas, goods, or services by an identified sponsor.
- *Sales promotion:* Short-term incentives to encourage the purchase or sale of a product or service.
- *Personal selling:* Personal presentation by the firm's sales force for the purpose of making sales and building customer relationships.
- *Public relations:* Building good relations with the company's various publics by obtaining favorable publicity, building up a good corporate image, and handling or heading off unfavorable rumors, stories, and events.
- *Direct marketing:* Direct connections with carefully targeted individual consumers to both obtain an immediate response and cultivate lasting customer relationships.

Each category involves specific promotional tools that are used to communicate with customers. For example, **advertising** includes broadcast, print, Internet, mobile, outdoor, and other forms. **Sales promotion** includes discounts, coupons, displays, and demonstrations. **Personal selling** includes sales presentations, trade shows, and incentive programs. **Public relations (PR)** includes press releases, sponsorships, events, and Web pages. And **direct marketing** includes catalogs, direct-response TV, kiosks, the Internet, mobile marketing, and more.

At the same time, marketing communication goes beyond these specific promotion tools. The product's design, its price, the shape and color of its package, and the stores that sell it *all* communicate something to buyers. Thus, although the promotion mix is the company's primary communications activity, the entire marketing mix—promotion, *as well as* product, price, and place—must be coordinated for greatest impact.

Integrated Marketing Communications

In past decades, marketers perfected the art of mass marketing: selling highly standardized products to masses of customers. In the process, they developed effective mass-media communications techniques to support these strategies. Large companies now routinely invest millions or even billions of dollars in television, magazine, or other mass-media advertising, reaching tens of millions of customers with a single ad. Today, however, marketing managers face some new marketing communications realities. Perhaps no other area of marketing is changing so profoundly as marketing communications, creating both exciting and anxious times for marketing communicators.

The New Marketing Communications Model

Several major factors are changing the face of today's marketing communications. First, *consumers* are changing. In this digital, wireless age, they are better informed and more communications empowered. Rather than relying on marketer-supplied information, they can use the Internet and other technologies to find information on their own. They can connect more easily with other consumers to exchange brand-related information or even create their own marketing messages.

Second, *marketing strategies* are changing. As mass markets have fragmented, marketers are shifting away from mass marketing. More and more, they are developing focused

---

▲ **The new marketing communications model: Sweeping advances in communications technology are causing remarkable changes in the ways in which companies and customers communicate with each other.**

Rido/Shutterstock.com

marketing programs designed to build closer relationships with customers in more narrowly defined micromarkets.

Finally, ▶ sweeping advances in *communications technology* are causing remarkable changes in the ways in which companies and customers communicate with each other. The digital age has spawned a host of new information and communication tools—from smartphones and iPads to satellite and cable television systems to the many faces of the Internet (e-mail, brand Web sites, online social networks, blogs, and so much more). These explosive developments have had a dramatic impact on marketing communications. Just as mass marketing once gave rise to a new generation of mass-media communications, the new digital media have given birth to a new marketing communications model.

Although network television, magazines, newspapers, and other traditional mass media remain very important, their dominance is declining. In their place, advertisers are now adding a broad selection of more-specialized and highly targeted media to reach smaller customer segments with more-personalized, interactive messages. The new media range from specialty cable television channels and made-for-the-Web videos to Internet catalogs, e-mail, blogs, mobile phone content, and online social networks. In all, companies are doing less *broadcasting* and more *narrowcasting*.

Some advertising industry experts even predict that the old mass-media communications model will eventually become obsolete. Mass media costs are rising, audiences are shrinking, ad clutter is increasing, and viewers are gaining control of message exposure through technologies such as video streaming or DVRs that let them skip disruptive television commercials. As a result, they suggest, marketers are shifting ever-larger portions of their marketing budgets away from old-media mainstays and moving them to digital and other new-age media. In recent years, although TV still dominates as an advertising medium, ad spending on the major TV networks has stagnated as ad spending on the Internet and other digital media has surged. Ad spending in magazines, newspapers, and radio, in contrast, has lost considerable ground.[3]

When Kimberly-Clark recently launched its Huggies Pure & Natural line of diapers, for instance, it skipped national TV advertising altogether—something once unthinkable in the consumer products industry. Instead, it targeted new and expectant mothers through mommy blogs, Web sites, print and online ads, e-mail, in-store promotions, and in-hospital TV programming. Similarly, commercials from Heineken's recent "Open your world" campaign debuted first on the brand's YouTube channel and Facebook page before making their way onto TV in 30 countries three months later. The first humorous spot, called "The Entrance," had been watched more than 3.6 million times on YouTube by the time it hit TV. Heineken later brought out 11 video clips, featuring characters from "The Entrance," that ran *only* online.[4]

In the new marketing communications world, rather than using old approaches that interrupt customers and force-feed them mass messages, new media formats let marketers reach smaller groups of consumers in more interactive, engaging ways. For example, think about television viewing these days. Consumers can now watch their favorite programs on just about anything with a screen—on televisions but also laptops, mobile phones, or iPads. And they can choose to watch programs whenever and wherever they wish, often with or without commercials. Increasingly, some programs, ads, and videos are being produced only for Internet viewing.

Despite the shift toward new digital media, however, traditional mass media still capture a lion's share of the promotion budgets of most major marketing firms, a fact that probably won't change quickly. For example, P&G, a leading proponent of digital media, still spends the majority of its huge advertising budget on mass media. Although P&G's digital outlay more than doubled last year to $169 million, digital still accounts for less than 5 percent of the company's annual global advertising budget.[5]

At a broader level, although some may question the future role of TV advertising, it's still very much in use today. Last year, more than 41 percent of U.S. advertising dollars was spent on television advertising vs. 16 percent on Internet advertising. Says one media expert, "Traditional TV [is] still king."[6]

Thus, rather than the old media model rapidly collapsing, most industry insiders see a more gradual blending of new and traditional media. The new marketing communications model will consist of a shifting mix of both traditional mass media and a wide array of exciting, new, more-targeted, and more-personalized media. The challenge is to bridge the "media divide" that too often separates traditional creative and media approaches from new interactive and digital ones. Many advertisers and ad agencies are now grappling with this transition (see Marketing at Work 12.1). In the end, however, regardless of whether it's traditional or digital, the key is to find the mix of media that best communicates the brand message and enhances the customer's brand experience.

The Need for *Integrated* Marketing Communications

The shift toward a richer mix of media and communication approaches poses a problem for marketers. Consumers today are bombarded by commercial messages from a broad range of sources. But consumers don't distinguish between message sources the way marketers do. In the consumer's mind, messages from different media and promotional approaches all become part of a single message about the company. Conflicting messages from these different sources can result in confused company images, brand positions, and customer relationships.

All too often, companies fail to integrate their various communications channels. The result is a hodgepodge of communications to consumers. Mass-media advertisements say one thing, whereas an in-store promotion sends a different signal, and company sales literature creates still another message. Furthermore, the company's Web site, e-mails, Facebook page, or videos posted on YouTube say something altogether different.

The problem is that these communications often come from different parts of the company. Advertising messages are planned and implemented by the advertising department or an ad agency. Personal selling communications are developed by sales management. Other company specialists are responsible for PR, sales promotion events, Internet or social network efforts, and other forms of marketing communications. However, whereas these companies have separated their communications tools, customers don't. Mixed communications from these sources result in blurred brand perceptions by consumers. "This new world of [the Internet, social networks,] tablet computers, smart phones, and apps presents both opportunities and challenges," says one marketing executive. "The biggest issue is complexity and fragmentation . . . the amount of choice out there," he says. The challenge is to "make it come together in an organized way."[7]

Today, more companies are adopting the concept of **integrated marketing communications (IMC)**. Under this concept, as illustrated in ▶ **Figure 12.1**, the company carefully

Integrated marketing communications (IMC)
Carefully integrating and coordinating the company's many communications channels to deliver a clear, consistent, and compelling message about the organization and its products.

▶ **Figure 12.1** Integrated Marketing Communications

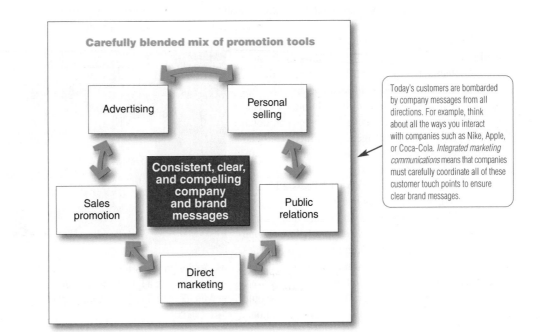

Carefully blended mix of promotion tools

Advertising

Personal selling

Consistent, clear, and compelling company and brand messages

Sales promotion

Public relations

Direct marketing

Today's customers are bombarded by company messages from all directions. For example, think about all the ways you interact with companies such as Nike, Apple, or Coca-Cola. *Integrated marketing communications* means that companies must carefully coordinate all of these customer touch points to ensure clear brand messages.

MARKETING AT WORK 12.1

The Shifting Advertising Universe: SoBe It!

SoBe made a big splash during the 2008 Super Bowl with a big-budget, 60-second commercial produced by the Arnell Group, an old-line Madison Avenue creative ad agency. The ad extravaganza featured supermodel Naomi Campbell and a full troupe of SoBe lizards, energized by colorful droplets of the brand's then-new enhanced water, LifeWater. The computer-generated graphics were stunning, the colors alluring, and Naomi Campbell was, well, Naomi Campbell. However, although the ad drew attention, it was not a viewer favorite. It just didn't connect with consumers.

Not to be denied, for the 2009 Super Bowl, SoBe and its parent company, PepsiCo, assigned the Arnell Group to create an even more elaborate (and even more expensive) commercial, a 3D spectacular featuring pro football players in white tutus performing a ballet, directed by a SoBe lizard. Once the athletes and lizards got a taste of SoBe LifeWater, a DJ cranked up the music, and the dance switched to hip-hop. Once again, although the ad generated a ton of awareness, it simply didn't deliver much in the way of consumer-brand engagement. As one journalist stated bluntly: "The SoBe spots [were] among the biggest wastes of money in Super Bowl history."

Finally the wiser, SoBe stopped running Super Bowl ads. In fact, in a move that sent shivers down the spines of many old-line Madison Avenue agencies, SoBe abandoned its traditional big-media, "TV-first," advertising approach altogether and adopted a more bottom-up, digital, new-media approach. It fired the Arnell Group, replacing the big creative agency with a team of smaller digital, PR, creative, and promotion shops.

SoBe's new advertising model turns the old approach upside down. Instead of starting with mass-market TV and print advertising, SoBe now aims first to hook its 18- to 29-year-old target audience with more focused and involving interactive media. Rather than developing a TV plan and then creating content to fill it, SoBe starts with engaging brand message content and then figures out where to put it to reach customers in the most effective way. In a reverse of past thinking, SoBe now favors a collaborative approach that integrates digital, traditional, and event media. In fact, content often appears online first and then moves to traditional TV. That kind of thinking causes concern for many traditional Madison Avenue creative agencies, which cut their teeth on developing creative ads for big-budget, mostly television and print campaigns.

SoBe's new advertising approach reflects a broader industry trend. In today's splintering advertising universe, in which there are more new places than ever to stick ads—online, on mobile phones, in all places digital and interactive—advertisers and traditional ad agencies alike are scrambling to stay relevant. For decades, the big traditional creative agencies ruled the roost. They were about coming up with strategic Big Ideas that would connect brands emotionally with millions of consumers through large-scale mass-media campaigns. But today, the Small Idea is on the rise. Increasingly, like SoBe, marketers are adding a host of new digital and interactive media—Web sites, viral video, blogs, social networks, street events—that let them target individuals or small communities of consumers rather than the masses.

In this shifting advertising universe, traditional creative agencies, such as the Arnell Group, often find themselves outmaneuvered by smaller, more nimble, and specialized digital, interactive, media, and creative agencies. However, these smaller digital shops sometimes lack experience in leading accounts and driving brand strategy. The competition is fierce, with traditional agencies struggling to become more digital and digital agencies struggling to become more traditional. "We in the ad business are faced with the question of who is going to lead this new world," says an industry analyst. "Will it be digitized traditional agencies or the new breed of digital agencies with big ambitions? The outcome . . . is far from clear."

At SoBe, however, things seem clear enough. Its latest marketing campaign—called "Try Everything"—is a true 360-degree effort developed by a diverse team of agencies including Firstborn (a digital shop), Weber Shandwick (a PR agency), Motive (in-market sampling and events), and Anomaly (advertising). Under the old approach, the SoBe brand team would have developed a "creative brief" that outlined the brand and advertising strategy and then let the Arnell Group take the lead in creating the advertising (usually a traditional television-plus-print campaign). Under the new approach, the SoBe brand team and the team of agencies workshop jointly in an ongoing process to create and distribute engaging message content using an integrated mix of new and old media.

SoBe's "Try Everything" campaign blends TV ads with the brand's Web site, Facebook page, YouTube channel, iPhone app,

▲ Rather than starting with traditional mass-market TV and print ads, SoBe's new bottom-up approach blends interactive digital content with traditional media and hands-on PR to engage customers in the most effective way.
Pepsi-Cola Company

and other digital elements designed to drive home the brand message that "Life is more exciting—and more fun—when you try new things." TV ads draw viewers to the SoBe Web site and other digital elements, which offer a range of virtual experiences inspired by one of SoBe's 31 flavors, from "tickling Kiwis" (inspired by Strawberry Kiwi LifeWater) to "kissing the office hottie" (fueled by SoBe Citrus Energy). The TV and digital efforts are supported by hands-on PR in the form of "Try Everything" street events in New York, Chicago, Los Angeles, Denver, Seattle, and other cities, which encourage locals to experience everything from milking (fake) Orange Cream cows or bowling with melons (Mango Melon) to building sandcastles (SoBe Pina Colada Elixir) or joining in on a rooftop dance party (SoBe Lean Honey Green Tea).

The immersive "Try Everything" effort isn't your traditional "advertising-led" campaign—it's a true team effort. The team's diverse agencies are "all working together to come back with the most compelling approach," says Andrew Katz, SoBe's marketing director. Even the agency that's creating the "Try Everything" ads—Anomaly—prides itself on being anything *but* traditional. Instead, Anomaly is "ideas-led, media-neutral, integrated, and multidisciplinary . . . at its core."

Consumer relevance and interaction seem to be the key to the new approach. For example, go to the SoBe Web site and you'll see customer testimonials from real on-the-street tastings of SoBe flavors or even a "Join the Debate" feature inviting consumers to vote for the next SoBe flavor.

Interestingly, SoBe's shifting communication strategy came at a time when the brand was already doing extremely well. SoBe LifeWater's share of the enhanced and flavored water market grew from 5.9 percent in 2008 to 13.9 percent in 2010. It seems the new advertising approach evolved not to meet a crisis but as a forward-thinking effort to adjust to the new advertising environment.

Thus, for advertisers and their agencies, as oft-misspoken baseball legend Yogi Berra once said, "The future ain't what it used to be." In the fast-changing advertising universe, SoBe and other brands are moving to master the new digital and interactive technologies and merge them effectively with traditional approaches. For advertisers and agencies alike, the message is clear. Says one agency CEO, "We've got to reinvent and transform the way we work."

Sources: Quotes and other information from Ken Wheaton, "Is Pepsi's Pass on Super Bowl an Offensive or Deensive Move?" *Advertising Age*, January 4, 2010, p. 12; Tony Quin, "Race to Relevance: Why the Winners Will Come from Both Sides," *Brandweek*, March 15, 2010, p. 14; Natalie Zmuda, "SoBe Ditches Creative Agency in New Marketing Approach," *Advertising Age*, April 14, 2010, accessed at http://adage.com/agencynews/article?article_id=143303; "Jered Weaver, Kate Upton to Star in New SoBe Ad Campaign," *Advertising Age,* May 17, 2011, http://adage.con/print/227607; "SoBe Celebrates 'Try Everything,'" *PRNewswire*, May 25, 2011; "PepsiCo; SoBe Rallies Millennials to 'Try Everything,'" *Entertainment Newsweekly,* June 3, 2011, p. 139; and www.sobe.com/#/tryeverything, accessed November 2011.

---

integrates its many communications channels to deliver a clear, consistent, and compelling message about the organization and its brands.

Integrated marketing communications calls for recognizing all touch points where the customer may encounter the company and its brands. Each *brand contact* will deliver a message—whether good, bad, or indifferent. The company's goal should be to deliver a consistent and positive message to each contact. IMC leads to a total marketing communications strategy aimed at building strong customer relationships by showing how the company and its products can help customers solve their problems.

Integrated marketing communications ties together all of the company's messages and images. Its television and print ads have the same message, look, and feel as its e-mail and personal selling communications. And its PR materials project the same image as its Web site, online social networks, or mobile marketing efforts. Often, different media play unique roles in attracting, informing, and persuading consumers; these roles must be carefully coordinated under the overall marketing communications plan.

A great example of a well-integrated marketing communications effort comes from premium ice cream maker Häagen-Dazs. To strengthen its emotional connection with consumers, Häagen-Dazs launched the "Häagen-Dazs loves honey bees" campaign, centered on an issue that's important to both the brand and its customers—a mysterious colony-collapse disorder threatening the U.S. honey bee population. Honey bees pollinate one-third of all the natural products we eat and up to 40 percent of the natural flavors used in Häagen-Dazs ice cream, making the "HD loves HB" message a natural for the brand. But perhaps even more important than the "help the honey bees" message itself is the way that Häagen-Dazs communicates that message:[8]

▲ The "HD loves HB" integrated marketing communications campaign uses a rich, well-coordinated blend of promotion elements to successfully deliver Häagen-Dazs' unique message.

Design and Production by InTacto.com - Digital Partner

▶ More than just running a few ads, Häagen-Dazs has created a full-fledged, beautifully integrated marketing communications campaign, using a wide range of media that work harmoniously for the cause. It starts with broadcast and print ads that drive traffic to the campaign's helpthehoneybees.com Web site, a kind of honey bee central where customers can learn about the problem and how to help. At the site, visitors can tap into a news feed called *The Buzz*, turn on "Bee TV," purchase Bee-Ts with phrases like "Long live the queen" and "Bee a hero," send "Bee-mail" messages to friends, or make donations to support honey bee research. To create even more bee buzz, Häagen-Dazs hands out samples of Vanilla Honey Bee ice cream and wildflower seeds at local farmers markets across the country and sponsors fund-raisers by local community and school groups. The campaign also incorporates social networks such as Twitter and Facebook. In all, the rich, well-coordinated blend of communications elements successfully delivers Häagen-Dazs' unique message and positioning. It is now "a brand with a heart and a soul," says the brand's director. "We're not only raising brand awareness," she says, "but making a difference in the world."

In the past, no one person or department was responsible for thinking through the communication roles of the various promotion tools and coordinating the promotion mix. To help implement integrated marketing communications, some companies have appointed a marketing communications director who has overall responsibility for the company's communications efforts. This helps to produce better communications consistency and greater sales impact. It places the responsibility in someone's hands—where none existed before—to unify the company's image as it is shaped by thousands of company activities.

Author Comment ▶
In this section, we'll look at the promotion budget-setting process and how marketers blend the various marketing communication tools into a smooth-functioning integrated promotion mix.

Shaping the Overall Promotion Mix

The concept of integrated marketing communications suggests that the company must blend the promotion tools carefully into a coordinated *promotion mix*. But how does it determine what mix of promotion tools to use? Companies within the same industry differ greatly in the design of their promotion mixes. For example, cosmetics maker Mary Kay spends most of its promotion funds on personal selling and direct marketing, whereas competitor CoverGirl spends heavily on consumer advertising. We now look at factors that influence the marketer's choice of promotion tools.

The Nature of Each Promotion Tool

Each promotion tool has unique characteristics and costs. Marketers must understand these characteristics in shaping the promotion mix.

Advertising

Advertising can reach masses of geographically dispersed buyers at a low cost per exposure, and it enables the seller to repeat a message many times. For example, television advertising can reach huge audiences. An estimated 111 million Americans watched the most recent Super Bowl, more than 37 million people watched at least part of the last Academy Awards broadcast, and 26 million fans tuned in for the kick-off of the tenth season of *American Idol*. For companies that want to reach a mass audience, TV is the place to be.[9]

Beyond its reach, large-scale advertising says something positive about the seller's size, popularity, and success. Because of advertising's public nature, consumers tend to view advertised products as more legitimate. Advertising is also very expressive; it allows the company to dramatize its products through the artful use of visuals, print, sound, and color. On the one hand, advertising can be used to build up a long-term image for a product (such as Coca-Cola ads). On the other hand, advertising can trigger quick sales (as when Kohl's advertises weekend specials).

Advertising also has some shortcomings. Although it reaches many people quickly, advertising is impersonal and lacks the direct persuasiveness of company salespeople. For the most part, advertising can carry on only a one-way communication with an audience, and the audience does not feel that it has to pay attention or respond. In addition, advertising can be very costly. Although some advertising forms, such as newspaper and radio advertising, can be done on smaller budgets, other forms, such as network TV advertising, require very large budgets.

▲ With personal selling, the customer feels a greater need to listen and respond, even if the response is a polite "No thank-you."

Eric Audras/PhotoAlto/Corbis

Personal Selling

Personal selling is the most effective tool at certain stages of the buying process, particularly in building up buyers' preferences, convictions, and actions. It involves personal interaction between two or more people, so each person can observe the other's needs and characteristics and make quick adjustments. Personal selling also allows all kinds of customer relationships to spring up, ranging from matter-of-fact selling relationships to personal friendships. An effective salesperson keeps the customer's interests at heart to build a long-term relationship by solving a customer's problems. ▶ Finally, with personal selling, the buyer usually feels a greater need to listen and respond, even if the response is a polite "No thank-you."

These unique qualities come at a cost, however. A sales force requires a longer-term commitment than does advertising—although advertising can be turned up or down, the size of a sales force is harder to change. Personal selling is also the company's most expensive promotion tool, costing companies on average $350 or more per sales call, depending on the industry.[10] U.S. firms spend up to three times as much on personal selling as they do on advertising.

Sales Promotion

Sales promotion includes a wide assortment of tools—coupons, contests, discounts, premiums, and others—all of which have many unique qualities. They attract consumer attention, offer strong incentives to purchase, and can be used to dramatize product offers and boost sagging sales. Sales promotions invite and reward quick response. Whereas advertising says, "Buy our product," sales promotion says, "Buy it now." Sales promotion effects are often short lived, however, and often are not as effective as advertising or personal selling in building long-run brand preference and customer relationships.

Public Relations

Public relations is very believable—news stories, features, sponsorships, and events seem more real and believable to readers than ads do. PR can also reach many prospects who avoid salespeople and advertisements—the message gets to buyers as "news" rather than as a sales-directed communication. And, as with advertising, PR can dramatize a company or product. Marketers tend to underuse PR or use it as an afterthought. Yet a well-thought-out PR campaign used with other promotion mix elements can be very effective and economical.

Direct Marketing

Although there are many forms of direct marketing—direct mail and catalogs, online marketing, telephone marketing, and others—they all share four distinctive characteristics. Direct marketing is less public: The message is normally directed to a specific person. Direct marketing is immediate and customized: Messages can be prepared very quickly and can be tailored to appeal to specific consumers. Finally, direct marketing is interactive: It allows a dialogue between the marketing team and the consumer, and messages can be altered depending on the consumer's response. Thus, direct marketing is well suited to highly targeted marketing efforts and building one-to-one customer relationships.

Promotion Mix Strategies

Marketers can choose from two basic promotion mix strategies: *push* promotion or *pull* promotion. ▶ **Figure 12.2** contrasts the two strategies. The relative emphasis given to the specific promotion tools differs for push and pull strategies. A **push strategy** involves "pushing" the product through marketing channels to final consumers. The producer directs its marketing activities (primarily personal selling and trade promotion) toward channel members to induce them to carry the product and promote it to final consumers. For example, John Deere does very little promoting of its lawn mowers, garden tractors, and other residential consumer products to final consumers. Instead, John Deere's sales force works with Lowe's, Home Depot, independent dealers, and other channel members, who in turn push John Deere products to final consumers.

Using a **pull strategy**, the producer directs its marketing activities (primarily advertising and consumer promotion) toward final consumers to induce them to buy the product. For example, Unilever promotes its Axe grooming products directly to its young male target market using TV and print ads, a brand Web site, its YouTube channel and Facebook page, and other channels. If the pull strategy is effective, consumers will then demand the brand from retailers, such as CVS, Walgreens, or Walmart, who will in turn demand it from Unilever. Thus, under a pull strategy, consumer demand "pulls" the product through the channels.

Some industrial-goods companies use only push strategies; likewise, some direct-marketing companies use only pull strategies. However, most large companies use some

Push strategy
A promotion strategy in which the sales force and trade promotion are used to *push* the product through channels. The producer promotes the product to channel members who in turn promote it to final consumers.

Pull strategy
A promotion strategy in which a company spends a lot of money on consumer advertising and promotion to induce final consumers to buy the product, creating a demand vacuum that *pulls* the product through the channel.

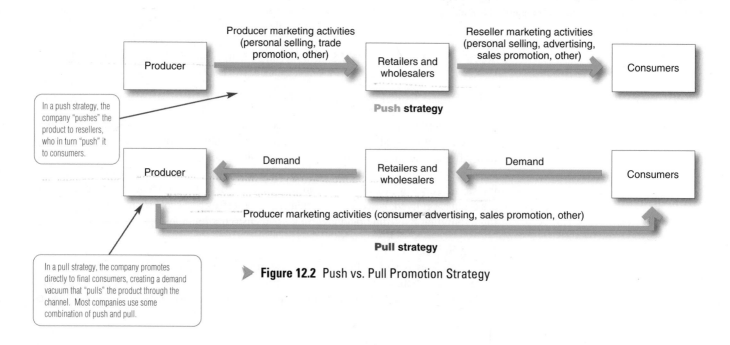

In a push strategy, the company "pushes" the product to resellers, who in turn "push" it to consumers.

In a pull strategy, the company promotes directly to final consumers, creating a demand vacuum that "pulls" the product through the channel. Most companies use some combination of push and pull.

▶ **Figure 12.2** Push vs. Pull Promotion Strategy

combination of both. For example, Unilever spends more than $6 billion worldwide each year on media advertising and consumer sales promotions to create brand preference and pull customers into stores that carry its products. At the same time, it uses its own and distributors' sales forces and trade promotions to push its brands through the channels, so that they will be available on store shelves when consumers come calling.

Companies consider many factors when designing their promotion mix strategies, including the type of product and market. For example, the importance of different promotion tools varies between consumer and business markets. Business-to-consumer companies usually pull more, putting more of their funds into advertising, followed by sales promotion, personal selling, and then PR. In contrast, business-to-business marketers tend to push more, putting more of their funds into personal selling, followed by sales promotion, advertising, and PR.

Now that we've examined the concept of integrated marketing communications and the factors that firms consider when shaping their promotion mixes, let's look more closely at the specific marketing communications tools.

SPEED BUMP | LINKING THE CONCEPTS

Pull over here for a few minutes. Flip back through and link the parts of the chapter you've read so far.

- How do the *integrated marketing communications (IMC)* and *promotion mix* concepts relate to one another?
- How has the changing communications environment affected the ways in which companies communicate with you about their products and services? If you were in the market for a new car, where might you hear about various available models? Where would you *search* for information?

Advertising

Advertising can be traced back to the very beginnings of recorded history. Archaeologists working in countries around the Mediterranean Sea have dug up signs announcing various events and offers. The Romans painted walls to announce gladiator fights and the Phoenicians painted pictures on large rocks to promote their wares along parade routes. During the golden age in Greece, town criers announced the sale of cattle, crafted items, and even cosmetics. An early "singing commercial" went as follows: "For eyes that are shining, for cheeks like the dawn / For beauty that lasts after girlhood is gone / For prices in reason, the woman who knows / Will buy her cosmetics from Aesclyptos."

Modern advertising, however, is a far cry from these early efforts. U.S. advertisers now run up an estimated annual bill of almost $150 billion on measured advertising media; worldwide ad spending exceeds an estimated $500 billion. P&G, the world's largest advertiser, last year spent $4.2 billion on U.S. advertising and $8.7 billion worldwide.[11]

Although advertising is used mostly by business firms, a wide range of not-for-profit organizations, professionals, and social agencies also use advertising to promote their causes to various target publics. In fact, the thirty-third largest advertising spender is a not-for-profit organization—the U.S. government, which advertises in many ways. For example, the federal government recently spent some $300 million on an advertising campaign to motivate Americans to take part in the 2010 Census.[12] Advertising is a good way to inform and persuade, whether the purpose is to sell Coca-Cola worldwide or educate people in developing nations on how to prevent the spread of HIV/AIDS.

Marketing management must make four important decisions when developing an advertising program (see ▶ **Figure 12.3**): *setting advertising objectives*, *setting the advertising budget*, *developing advertising strategy* (*message decisions* and *media decisions*), and *evaluating advertising campaigns*.

Figure 12.3 Major Advertising Decisions

Don't forget—advertising is only part of a broader set of marketing and company decisions. Its job is to help communicate the brand's value proposition to target customers. Advertising must blend well with other promotion and marketing mix decisions.

Setting Advertising Objectives

The first step is to set *advertising objectives*. These objectives should be based on past decisions about the target market, positioning, and the marketing mix, which define the job that advertising must do in the total marketing program. The overall advertising objective is to help build customer relationships by communicating customer value. Here, we discuss specific advertising objectives.

An **advertising objective** is a specific communication *task* to be accomplished with a specific *target* audience during a specific period of *time*. Advertising objectives can be classified by their primary purpose—to *inform, persuade,* or *remind*. ▶ **Table 12.1** lists examples of each of these specific objectives.

Advertising objective
A specific communication *task* to be accomplished with a specific *target* audience during a specific period of *time*.

▶ **Table 12.1**   Possible Advertising Objectives

Informative Advertising

Communicating customer value	Suggesting new uses for a product
Building a brand and company image	Informing the market of a price change
Telling the market about a new product	Describing available services and support
Explaining how a product works	Correcting false impressions

Persuasive Advertising

Building brand preference	Persuading customers to purchase now
Encouraging switching to a brand	Persuading customers to receive a sales call
Changing customer perceptions of product value	Convincing customers to tell others about the brand

Reminder Advertising

Maintaining customer relationships	Reminding consumers where to buy the product
Reminding consumers that the product may be needed in the near future	Keeping the brand in a customer's mind during off-seasons

Informative advertising is used heavily when introducing a new-product category. In this case, the objective is to build primary demand. Thus, early producers of HDTVs first had to inform consumers of the image quality and size benefits of the new product. *Persuasive advertising* becomes more important as competition increases. Here, the company's objective is to build selective demand. For example, once HDTVs became established, Samsung began trying to persuade consumers that *its* brand offered the best quality for their money.

Some persuasive advertising has become *comparative advertising* (or *attack advertising*), in which a company directly or indirectly compares its brand with one or more other brands. You see examples of comparative advertising in almost every product category, ranging from sports drinks, coffee, and soup to computers, car rentals, and credit cards. ▶ For example, over the past few years, Verizon Wireless and AT&T have attacked each other ruthlessly in comparative ads. When Verizon Wireless began offering the iPhone, it used its "Can you hear me now?" slogan to attack AT&T's rumored spotty service. AT&T retaliated with showing that its customers could talk on the phone and surf the Web at the same time, a feature not yet available via Verizon Wireless.

Advertisers should use comparative advertising with caution. All too often, such ads invite competitor responses, resulting in an advertising war that neither competitor can win. Upset competitors might also take more drastic action, such as filing complaints with the self-regulatory National Advertising Division of the Council of Better Business Bureaus or even filing false-advertising lawsuits. For example, recently PepsiCo's Gatorade brand sued Coca-Cola's Powerade over Coca-Cola's claims that Powerade is more "complete." And Sara Lee's Ball Park brand sued Kraft's Oscar Mayer over an advertised taste-test claim.[13]

Reminder advertising is important for mature products; it helps to maintain customer relationships and keep consumers thinking about the product. Expensive Coca-Cola television ads primarily build and maintain the Coca-Cola brand relationship rather than inform consumers or persuade them to buy it in the short run.

Advertising's goal is to help move consumers through the buying process. Some advertising is designed to move people to immediate action. For example, a direct-response television ad by Weight Watchers urges consumers to pick up the phone and sign up right away, and a Best Buy newspaper insert for a weekend sale encourages immediate store visits. However, many ads focus on building or strengthening long-term customer relationships. For example, a Nike television ad in which well-known athletes work through extreme challenges in their Nike gear never directly asks for a sale. Instead, the goal is to somehow change the way the customers think or feel about the brand.

▲ **Comparative advertising: Over the past few years, Verizon Wireless and AT&T have attacked each other ruthlessly in comparative ads.**

(top) AP Images/PRNewsFoto/RealNetworks, Inc.; (bottom) Newscom; (phone) Stephen Krow/iStock

Setting the Advertising Budget

After determining its advertising objectives, the company next sets its **advertising budget** for each product. Here, we look at four common methods used to set the total budget for advertising: the *affordable method*, the *percentage-of-sales method*, the *competitive-parity method*, and the *objective-and-task method*.[14]

Affordable Method

Some companies use the **affordable method**: They set the promotion budget at the level they think the company can afford. Small businesses often use this method, reasoning that a company cannot spend more on advertising than it has. They start with total revenues, deduct operating expenses and capital outlays, and then devote some portion of the remaining funds to advertising.

Advertising budget
The dollars and other resources allocated to a product or a company advertising program.

Affordable method
Setting the promotion budget at the level management thinks the company can afford.

Unfortunately, this method of setting budgets completely ignores the effects of promotion on sales. It tends to place promotion last among spending priorities, even in situations in which advertising is critical to the firm's success. It leads to an uncertain annual promotion budget, which makes long-range market planning difficult. Although the affordable method can result in overspending on advertising, it more often results in underspending.

Percentage-of-Sales Method

Percentage-of-sales method
Setting the promotion budget at a certain percentage of current or forecasted sales or as a percentage of the unit sales price.

Other companies use the **percentage-of-sales method**, setting their promotion budget at a certain percentage of current or forecasted sales. Or they budget a percentage of the unit sales price. The percentage-of-sales method has advantages. It is simple to use and helps management think about the relationships between promotion spending, selling price, and profit per unit.

Despite these claimed advantages, however, the percentage-of-sales method has little to justify it. It wrongly views sales as the *cause* of promotion rather than as the *result*. Although studies have found a positive correlation between promotional spending and brand strength, this relationship often turns out to be effect and cause, not cause and effect. Stronger brands with higher sales can afford the biggest ad budgets.

Thus, the percentage-of-sales budget is based on availability of funds rather than on opportunities. It may prevent the increased spending sometimes needed to turn around falling sales. Because the budget varies with year-to-year sales, long-range planning is difficult. Finally, the method does not provide any basis for choosing a *specific* percentage, except what has been done in the past or what competitors are doing.

Competitive-Parity Method

Competitive-parity method
Setting the promotion budget to match competitors' outlays.

Still other companies use the **competitive-parity method**, setting their promotion budgets to match competitors' outlays. They monitor competitors' advertising or get industry promotion spending estimates from publications or trade associations, and then set their budgets based on the industry average.

Two arguments support this method. First, competitors' budgets represent the collective wisdom of the industry. Second, spending what competitors spend helps prevent promotion wars. Unfortunately, neither argument is valid. There are no grounds for believing that the competition has a better idea of what a company should be spending on promotion than does the company itself. Companies differ greatly, and each has its own special promotion needs. Finally, there is no evidence that budgets based on competitive parity prevent promotion wars.

Objective-and-Task Method

Objective-and-task method
Developing the promotion budget by (1) defining specific objectives, (2) determining the tasks that must be performed to achieve these objectives, and (3) estimating the costs of performing these tasks. The sum of these costs is the proposed promotion budget.

The most logical budget-setting method is the **objective-and-task method**, whereby the company sets its promotion budget based on what it wants to accomplish with promotion. This budgeting method entails (1) defining specific promotion objectives, (2) determining the tasks needed to achieve these objectives, and (3) estimating the costs of performing these tasks. The sum of these costs is the proposed promotion budget.

The advantage of the objective-and-task method is that it forces management to spell out its assumptions about the relationship between dollars spent and promotion results. But it is also the most difficult method to use. Often, it is hard to figure out which specific tasks will achieve stated objectives. For example, suppose Sony wants 95 percent awareness for its latest Blu-ray player during the six-month introductory period. What specific advertising messages and media schedules should Sony use to attain this objective? How much would these messages and media schedules cost? Sony management must consider such questions, even though they are hard to answer.

DOGGIE
DENTURES
Because brushing is just too hard.

Or, there's DENTASTIX:
The treat that's clinically proven to reduce up to 80% of tartar buildup.
Dogsrule.com

▲ **Setting the promotion budget is one of the hardest decisions facing the company. The Pedigree brand spends millions annually on award-winning ads like this one, but is that "half enough or twice too much"?**

Courtesy of Mars, Incorporated. PEDIGREE® and DENTASTIX® are registered trademarks of Mars, Incorporated.

Advertising strategy

The plan by which the company accomplishes its advertising objectives. It consists of two major elements: creating advertising messages and selecting advertising media.

▶ No matter what method is used, setting the advertising budget is no easy task. John Wanamaker, the department store magnate, once said, "I know that half of my advertising is wasted, but I don't know which half. I spent $2 million for advertising, and I don't know if that is half enough or twice too much."

As a result of such thinking, advertising is one of the easiest budget items to cut when economic times get tough. Cuts in brand-building advertising appear to do little short-term harm to sales. For example, in the wake of the recent recession, U.S. advertising expenditures plummeted 12 percent over the previous year. In the long run, however, slashing ad spending may cause long-term damage to a brand's image and market share. In fact, companies that can maintain or even increase their advertising spending while competitors are decreasing theirs can gain competitive advantage.

For example, during the recent Great Recession, while competitors were cutting back, car maker Audi actually increased its marketing and advertising spending. Audi "kept its foot on the pedal while everyone else is pulling back," said an Audi ad executive at the time. "Why would we go backwards now when the industry is generally locking the brakes and cutting spending?" As a result, Audi's brand awareness and buyer consideration reached record levels during the recession, outstripping those of BMW, Mercedes, and Lexus, and positioning Audi strongly for the postrecession era. Audi is now one of the hottest auto brands on the market.[15]

Developing Advertising Strategy

Advertising strategy consists of two major elements: creating advertising *messages* and selecting advertising *media*. In the past, companies often viewed media planning as secondary to the message-creation process. After the creative department created good advertisements, the media department then selected and purchased the best media for carrying those advertisements to the desired target audiences. This often caused friction between creatives and media planners.

Today, however, soaring media costs, more-focused target marketing strategies, and the blizzard of new digital and interactive media have promoted the importance of the media-planning function. The decision about which media to use for an ad campaign—television, newspapers, magazines, a Web site or online social network, mobile phones, or e-mail—is now sometimes more critical than the creative elements of the campaign. As a result, more and more advertisers are orchestrating a closer harmony between their messages and the media that deliver them. In fact, in a really good ad campaign, you often have to ask, "Is that a media idea or a creative idea?"

Creating the Advertising Message

No matter how big the budget, advertising can succeed only if advertisements gain attention and communicate well. Good advertising messages are especially important in today's costly and cluttered advertising environment. In 1950, the average U.S. household received only three network television channels and a handful of major national magazines. Today, the average household receives about 119 channels, and consumers have more than 20,000 magazines from which to choose.[16] Add in the countless radio stations and a continuous barrage of catalogs, direct mail, e-mail and online ads, and out-of-home media, and consumers are being bombarded with ads at home, work, and all points in between. As a result, consumers are exposed to as many as 3,000 to 5,000 commercial messages every day.[17]

Breaking through the Clutter. If all this advertising clutter bothers some consumers, it also causes huge headaches for advertisers. Take the situation facing network television advertisers. They pay an average of $302,000 to make a single 30-second commercial. Then, each time they show it, they pay an average of $122,000 for 30 seconds of advertising time during a popular prime-time program. They pay even more if it's an especially popular program, such as *American Idol* ($468,000), *Sunday Night Football* ($415,000), *Glee* ($273,000), *Family Guy* ($259,000), or a mega-event such as the Super Bowl ($3 million per 30 seconds!).[18]

Then their ads are sandwiched in with a clutter of other commercials, announcements, and network promotions, totaling nearly 20 minutes of nonprogram material per prime-time hour, with commercial breaks coming every six minutes on average. Such clutter in television and other ad media has created an increasingly hostile advertising environment. According to one study, more than 70 percent of Americans think there are too many ads on TV, and 62 percent of national advertisers believe that TV ads have become less effective, citing clutter as the main culprit.[19]

▲ Advertising clutter: Today's consumers, armed with an arsenal of weapons, can choose what they watch and don't watch. Increasingly, they are choosing not to watch ads.

fanelie rosier/iStockphoto.com

Until recently, television viewers were pretty much a captive audience for advertisers. But today's digital wizardry has given consumers a rich new set of information and entertainment choices. With the growth in cable and satellite TV, the Internet, video streaming, and smartphones, today's viewers have many more options.

Digital technology has also armed consumers with an arsenal of weapons for choosing what they watch or don't watch. ▶ Increasingly, thanks to the growth of DVR systems, consumers are choosing *not* to watch ads. Almost 40 percent of American TV households now have DVRs, triple the number reached only four years earlier. One ad agency executive calls these DVR systems "electronic weedwhackers" when it comes to viewing commercials. DVR owners view only about 45 percent of the commercials during DVR playback. At the same time, VOD and video downloads are exploding, letting viewers watch entertainment on their own time—with or without commercials.[20]

Thus, advertisers can no longer force-feed the same old cookie-cutter ad messages to captive consumers through traditional media. Just to gain and hold attention, today's advertising messages must be better planned, more imaginative, more entertaining, and more emotionally engaging. Simply interrupting or disrupting consumers no longer works. Unless ads provide information that is interesting, useful, or entertaining, many consumers will simply skip by them.

Madison & Vine
A term that has come to represent the merging of advertising and entertainment in an effort to break through the clutter and create new avenues for reaching consumers with more engaging messages.

Merging Advertising and Entertainment. To break through the clutter, many marketers have subscribed to a new merging of advertising and entertainment, dubbed "**Madison & Vine**." You've probably heard of Madison Avenue, the New York City street that houses the headquarters of many of the nation's largest advertising agencies. You may also have heard of Hollywood & Vine, the intersection of Hollywood Avenue and Vine Street in Hollywood, California, long the symbolic heart of the U.S. entertainment industry. Now, Madison Avenue and Hollywood & Vine have come together to form a new intersection—Madison & Vine—that represents the merging of advertising and entertainment in an effort to create new avenues for reaching consumers with more engaging messages.

This merging of advertising and entertainment takes one of two forms: advertainment or branded entertainment. The aim of *advertainment* is to make ads themselves so entertaining, or so useful, that people *want* to watch them. There's no chance that you'd watch ads on purpose, you say? Think again. For example, the Super Bowl has become an annual advertainment showcase. Tens of millions of people tune in to the Super Bowl each year, as much to watch the entertaining ads as to see the game.

In fact, DVR systems can actually *improve* viewership of a really *good* ad. For example, most Super Bowl ads last year were viewed more in DVR households than non-DVR households. Rather than zipping past the ads, many people were skipping back to re-watch them during halftime and following the game.[21]

Beyond making their regular ads more entertaining, advertisers are also creating new advertising forms that look less like ads and more like short films or shows. For example, Dove's "Evolution" video wasn't technically an ad, but it drew more—and more meaningful—views than many TV ads do, and the views were initiated by consumers. A range of new brand messaging platforms—from Webisodes and blogs to viral videos and apps—are now blurring the line between ads and entertainment. These days, it's not unusual to see an entertaining ad or other brand message on YouTube before you see it on TV. And you might well seek it out at a friend's suggestion rather than having it forced on you by the advertiser.

Branded entertainment (or *brand integrations*) involves making the brand an inseparable part of some other form of entertainment. The most common form of branded entertainment is product placements—embedding brands as props within other programming. It might be a brief glimpse of the latest LG phone on *Grey's Anatomy,* or the product placement might be scripted into an episode. For example, one entire episode of *Modern Family* centered around the Dunphy family trying to find the recently released, hard-to-find Apple iPad their father, Phil, coveted as his special birthday present. Finally, the placement could be worked into the show's overall storyline. For example, NBC's *The Biggest Loser* and health-club chain 24 Hour Fitness have created a product placement partnership that fully and thematically integrates the brand with the show.[22]

working it into shows ←

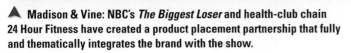

▲ **Madison & Vine: NBC's *The Biggest Loser* and health-club chain 24 Hour Fitness have created a product placement partnership that fully and thematically integrates the brand with the show.**

AP Images/Trae Patton

24 Hour Fitness built and furnished the state-of-the-art gym on the *Loser* set and has been a key integrated brand in the show for nine seasons. On the show, workouts in 24 Hour Fitness are common. Simultaneously, out-of-show marketing has been nearly as extensive. The chain has used the show's contestants in its promotions and the brand outfits every contestant with its branded Bodybugg, so she can calculate her calories in and out. "The fact is, you can tell a great story *and* meet the advertisers' needs," says the show's director.

Originally created with TV in mind, branded entertainment has spread quickly into other sectors of the entertainment industry. For example, it is widely used in movies. Last year's 33 top films contained 592 identifiable brand placements—*Iron Man 2* alone had 64 placements. Morgan Spurlock even created a movie documentary—*POM Wonderful Presents: The Greatest Movie Ever Sold*—which examines the art of the branded entertainment deal and was itself paid for by product placements.[23] If you look carefully, you'll also see product placements in video games, comic books, Broadway musicals, and even pop music. For example, there's a sandwich-making scene featuring Wonder Bread and Miracle Whip in the middle of Lady Gaga's 10-minute "Telephone" video (which captured more than 50 million YouTube views in less than a month).

So, Madison & Vine is now the meeting place for the advertising and entertainment industries. The goal is for brand messages to become a part of the entertainment rather than interrupting it. As advertising agency JWT puts it, "We believe advertising needs to stop *interrupting* what people are interested in and *be* what people are interested in." However, advertisers must be careful that the new intersection itself doesn't become too congested. With all the new ad formats and product placements, Madison & Vine threatens to create even more of the very clutter that it was designed to break through. At that point, consumers might decide to take yet a different route.

Message Strategy. The first step in creating effective advertising messages is to plan a *message strategy*—the general message that will be communicated to consumers. The purpose of advertising is to get consumers to think about or react to the product or company in a certain way. People will react only if they believe they will benefit from doing so. Thus, developing an effective message strategy begins with identifying customer *benefits* that can be used as advertising appeals. Ideally, the message strategy will follow directly from the company's broader positioning and customer value strategies.

Message strategy statements tend to be plain, straightforward outlines of benefits and positioning points that the advertiser wants to stress. The advertiser must next develop a compelling **creative concept**—or *big idea*—that will bring the message strategy to life in a distinctive and memorable way. At this stage, simple message ideas become great ad campaigns. Usually, a copywriter and an art director will team up to generate many creative concepts, hoping that one of these concepts will turn out to be the big idea. The creative concept may emerge as a visualization, a phrase, or a combination of the two.

Creative concept

The compelling *big idea* that will bring the advertising message strategy to life in a distinctive and memorable way.

The creative concept will guide the choice of specific appeals to be used in an advertising campaign. *Advertising appeals* should have three characteristics. First, they should be *meaningful*, pointing out benefits that make the product more desirable or interesting to consumers. Second, appeals must be *believable*. Consumers must believe that the product or service will deliver the promised benefits.

However, the most meaningful and believable benefits may not be the best ones to feature. Appeals should also be *distinctive*. They should tell how the product is better than competing brands. For example, the most meaningful benefit of owning a wristwatch is that it keeps accurate time, yet few watch ads feature this benefit. Instead, based on the distinctive benefits they offer, watch advertisers might select any of a number of advertising themes. For years, Timex has been the affordable watch. Last Father's Day, for example, Timex ads suggested consumers should "Tell Dad more than time this Father's Day. Tell him that you've learned the value of a dollar." Similarly, Rolex ads never talk about keeping time. Instead, they talk about the brand's "obsession with perfection" and the fact that "Rolex has been the preeminent symbol of performance and prestige for more than a century."

▲ **Execution styles: This ad creates a nostalgic mood around the product. "So I baked her the cookies she's loved since she was little."**

Courtesy of Nestlé USA, Inc. Photographer: Stephen Smith/Getty Images

Message Execution. The advertiser now must turn the big idea into an actual ad execution that will capture the target market's attention and interest. The creative team must find the best approach, style, tone, words, and format for executing the message. The message can be presented in various **execution styles**, such as the following:

- *Slice of life:* This style shows one or more "typical" people using the product in a normal setting. For example, a Silk Soymilk "Rise and Shine" ad shows a young professional starting the day with a healthier breakfast and high hopes.
- *Lifestyle:* This style shows how a product fits in with a particular lifestyle. For example, an ad for Athleta active wear shows a woman in a complex yoga pose and states: "If your body is your temple, build it one piece at a time."
- *Fantasy:* This style creates a fantasy around the product or its use. For example, recent IKEA ads show consumers creating fanciful room designs with IKEA furniture, such as "a bedroom for a queen made by Bree and her sister, designed by IKEA."
- *Mood or image:* This style builds a mood or image around the product or service, such as beauty, love, intrigue, or serenity. Few claims are made about the product or service except through suggestion. ▶ For example, a Nestlé Toll House ad shows a daughter hugging her mother after surprising her with an unexpected weekend home from college. The mother responds, "So I baked her the cookies she's loved since she was little."

Execution style

The approach, style, tone, words, and format used for executing (properly conveying) an advertising message.

- *Musical:* This style shows people or cartoon characters singing about the product. For example, Chevrolet recently ran a two-minute-long TV commercial featuring most of the cast of the TV show *Glee* in an elaborate production number set to the 1950s brand jingle, "See the U.S.A. in Your Chevrolet."
- *Personality symbol:* This style creates a character that represents the product. The character might be animated (Mr. Clean, the GEICO Gecko, or the Zappos Zappets) or real (perky Progressive Insurance spokeswoman Flo, the E*TRADE babies, Ronald McDonald).
- *Technical expertise:* This style shows the company's expertise in making the product. Thus, natural foods maker Kashi shows its buyers carefully selecting ingredients for its products, and Jim Koch of the Boston Beer Company tells about his many years of experience in brewing Samuel Adams beer.
- *Scientific evidence:* This style presents survey or scientific evidence that the brand is better or better liked than one or more other brands. For years, Crest toothpaste has used scientific evidence to convince buyers that Crest is better than other brands at fighting cavities.
- *Testimonial evidence or endorsement:* This style features a highly believable or likable source endorsing the product. It could be ordinary people saying how much they like a given product. For example, Subway's spokesman Jared is a customer who lost 245 pounds on a diet of Subway sandwiches. Or it might be a celebrity presenting the product. Olympic gold medal swimmer Michael Phelps also speaks for Subway.

The advertiser also must choose a *tone* for the ad. For example, P&G always uses a positive tone: Its ads say something very positive about its products. Other advertisers now use edgy humor to break through the commercial clutter. Bud Light commercials are famous for this.

The advertiser must use memorable and attention-getting *words* in the ad. For example, rather than claiming simply that its laundry detergent is "superconcentrated," Method asks customers, "Are you jug addicted?" The solution: "Our patent-pending formula that's so fricken' concentrated, 50 loads fits in a teeny bottle….With our help, you can get off the jugs and get clean."

Finally, *format* elements make a difference in an ad's impact as well as in its cost. A small change in an ad's design can make a big difference in its effect. In a print ad, the *illustration* is the first thing the reader notices—it must be strong enough to draw attention. Next, the *headline* must effectively entice the right people to read the copy. Finally, the *copy*—the main block of text in the ad—must be simple but strong and convincing. Moreover, these three elements must effectively work *together* to persuasively present customer value.

Consumer-Generated Messages. Taking advantage of today's interactive technologies, many companies are now tapping consumers for message ideas or actual ads. They are searching existing video sites, setting up their own sites, and sponsoring ad-creation contests and other promotions. Sometimes the results are outstanding; sometimes they are forgettable. If done well, however, user-generated content can incorporate the voice of the customer into brand messages and generate greater consumer brand involvement (see Marketing at Work 12.2).

Many brands hold contests that invite consumers to submit ad message ideas and videos. For example, for the past several years, PepsiCo's Doritos brand has held its annual "Crash the Super Bowl Challenge" contest that invites consumers to create their own video ads about the tasty triangular corn chips. The consumer-generated Doritos ads have been a smashing success. ► At the other end of the size spectrum, online crafts marketplace/community Etsy.com—"Your best place to buy and sell all things

▲ **Consumer-generated advertising: Online crafts marketplace/community Etsy.com ran a contest inviting consumers to tell the Etsy.com story in 30-second videos. The results were "positively remarkable."**

Esty.com

MARKETING AT WORK | 12.2

Consumer-Generated Advertising: When Done Well, It Can Be Really Good

Fueled by the user-generated content craze made popular by the likes of YouTube, Facebook, and other online content-sharing communities, the move toward consumer-generated advertising has spread like wildfire in recent years. Companies large and small—including the likes of PepsiCo, Unilever, P&G, CareerBuilder, and other blue-chip marketers—have fast recognized the benefits (and the drawbacks) of inviting customers to co-create brand messages.

Perhaps no brand has been more successful with user-generated advertising than PepsiCo's Doritos brand. For five years running, the Doritos "Crash the Super Bowl" contest has invited consumers to create their own 30-second video ads featuring the market-leading tortilla chip. A jury of ad pros and Doritos brand managers whittle down the thousands of entries submitted and post the finalists online. Consumers vote for the winners, who receive cash prizes and have their ads run during the Super Bowl. Last year, PepsiCo added its Pepsi Max brand to the contest.

For last year's Super Bowl, PepsiCo threw prize money around like a rich uncle home for the holidays. Six finalists each claimed $25,000, and PepsiCo aired the ads during the game. To put more icing on the cake, Doritos promised to pay a whopping $1 million to any entrant whose ad placed first in the *USA Today* Ad Meter ratings. Second place was good for $600,000, and third place would take home $400,000. If the winners swept the top three Ad Meter spots, each would receive an additional $1 million. Not surprisingly, the contest attracted nearly 5,600 entries.

This year, one of the consumer-made Doritos ads—"Pug goes for the chips"—tied with a Bud Light commercial, the first tie ever in the *USA Today* ratings. Tie or not, the person behind the winning Doritos ad, 31-year-old J. R. Burningham of Utah, took home the $1,000,000 prize—not a bad return for an ad that cost only $500 to produce. In all, three "Crash the Super Bowl" ads finished in *USA Today's* top five. Moreover, the ads finished strongly in virtually every consumer survey. One rating firm judged four of the six consumer-generated ads (two Doritos ads and two Pepsi Max ads) as the top four most effective Super Bowl ads overall. In fact, the ads were a hit before the Super Bowl even began. Prior to the game, PepsiCo aired the ads on YouTube and Facebook and tweeted feverishly about them. By game day, the videos already had 3 million-plus views each.

It seems that many other companies are also getting into the consumer-generated content act. According to one global report that ranks the world's top creative work, nine of last year's top ten campaigns involved some kind of consumer input.

"This is a big seismic shift in our business," says the former ad agency executive who assembled the report. "We've had 100 years of business-to-consumer advertising, but now the Web has enabled us to get people actively involved in talking to each other. If the idea is interesting enough, consumers will do the work for you." Even more, they'll work for little or no pay.

That kind of talk makes some ad agencies nervous. However, the idea isn't that companies should fire their ad agencies and have consumers create their ads instead. In fact, most consumer-generated ad campaigns are coordinated by ad agencies. For example, Unilever is expanding its crowdsourcing efforts with a video ad contest that involves 13 of its brands, including Ben & Jerry's, Dove, Lipton, and Vaseline. However, the company is quick to clarify the role of its user-generated content strategy.

> This in no way is a replacement for our ad agencies. The real reason for it is to offer more participation for our consumers, to get closer to consumers, and allow them to be more involved with our brands. It will help them become advocates, help them have more of a connection with the brands if they've been a part of helping to create it. It's not one of our objectives to save money. I mean it's a nice benefit, if we can get great stuff. But it's not really the objective. We believe that marketing will be much more participatory in the next few years and we want to be at the leading edge of that.

Although most consumer-generated content efforts are limited to ad and video messages, PepsiCo's award-winning Mountain Dew crowdsourcing campaign—called "Dewmocracy"—has involved consumers in decisions across the entire range of marketing for the brand. Dewmocracy seeks

▲ Consumer-generated messages: Last year, three Doritos "Crash the Super Bowl" ads finished in USA Today's top five. This "Pug goes for the chips" ad tied for first place.
Frito-Lay, Inc.

inputs from ardent brand fans on everything from product development to ad messages and ad agency selection.

At the start of the most recent Dewmocracy campaign, Mountain Dew asked loyal fans to submit ideas for three new flavors. It sent 50 finalists home-tasting kits and Flip video cameras and encouraged them to upload videos about their experience to YouTube. With three finalists selected, Mountain Dew asked consumers to pick names (Typhoon, Distortion, and White Out rose to the top), colors, and package designs for the new flavors on the Dewmocracy Web site, Facebook, Twitter, and other social media sites. The three flavors were rolled out over the summer, and fans were asked to try them and vote for a favorite, which became a permanent addition to the Mountain Dew lineup.

As for advertising, rather than having consumers submit their own video ads, Mountain Dew invited fans to help choose the ad agencies that would do the job. Consumers "built these products and had a clear idea of the products," said Mountain Dew's director of marketing. They "challenged us to say, who is going to do our advertising, and how do we get some new thinking?" Ad agencies and individuals submitted more than 200 12-second videos outlining their ideas for promoting the three new flavors. Consumers cast 15,000 votes. In the end, three small ad shops landed the jobs.

The Dewmocracy consumer-generated marketing campaigns have produced successful new, customer-approved Mountain Dew flavors at very little cost (the brand didn't spend a dollar on media throughout the process). But they met an even bigger objective. They have "allowed us to have as rich a dialogue as we could with consumers," says the brand's marketing director. The average loyal Mountain Dew drinker is male, between the ages of 18 and 39, with 92 percent on Facebook and 50 percent using YouTube. The digital Dewmocracy campaigns have been incredibly successful at engaging this group and giving them an ownership stake in the brand.

There are downsides to consumer-generated ads, of course. Although it might seem "free," the process of wading through hundreds—or even thousands—of entries can be difficult, costly, and time consuming. In dealing with user-created content, copyright issues, poor production quality, offensive themes, and even attacks on the brand are all par for the course. And in the end, you never know what you're going to get. For every hit Doritos ad, there are hundreds that are uninspired or just plain dreadful. Many Madison Avenue advertising pros write off consumer-generated efforts as mostly amateurish, crudely produced, and ineffective.

But when it's done well, it can be very good. Despite "a lot of advertising people" playing it down as "a seventh-grader in his backyard with a video camera," says one advertising expert, "it complements efforts by marketers to engage and involve consumers. Consumer-generated content really can work."

Sources: Extracts, quotes, and other information from Stuart Elliott, "Do-It Yourself Super Ads," *New York Times*, February 9, 2010, p. B3; Andrew McMains, "Unilever Embraces UGC," *Adweek*, April 20, 2010, accessed at www.adweek.com; Emma Hall, "Most Winning Creative Work Involves Consumer Participation," *Advertising Age*, January 6, 2010, accessed at http://adage.com/print/141329; Natalie Zmuda, "Why Mountain Dew Let Skater Dudes Take Control of Its Marketing," *Advertising Age*, February 22, 2010, p. 30; "Doritos and Pepsi Max's '*Crash the Super Bowl* Contest' Delivered Top 4 Most Effective Super Bowl Ads," *BusinessWire*, February 8, 2011; Bruce Horovitz, "Admeter First: A Doggone Tie," *USA Today*, February 7, 2011, p. 6B; Bruce Horovitz, "Super Bowl Ads Win with Social-Media Play," *USA Today*, February 8, 2011, p. 3B; and "Mtn Dew Thanks Fans by Name in New Campaign," *Advertising Age*, June 14, 2011, http://adage.com/print/228189.

handmade"—ran a contest inviting consumers to tell the Etsy.com story in 30-second videos. The results were what one well-known former advertising critic called "positively remarkable."[24]

> The 10 semifinalists are, as a group, better thought-out and realized than any 10 random commercials running on TV anywhere in the world. The best user-created Etsy ad features a simple, sad, animated robot, consigned to a life of soul-crushing assembly-line production. "See, there's a lot of robots out there," says the voice of the unseen Etsy craftswomen who crafted him. "A lot of these robots are sad because they're stuck making these boring, mass-produced things. Me, I really can believe all that great stuff about how it helps the environment and microeconomics and feeling special about getting something handmade by someone else. But the real reason I make handmade goods is because every time somebody buys something handmade, a robot gets its wings." The user-made ad "is simply magnificent," concludes the ad critic, "in a way that the agency business had better take note of."

Not all consumer-generated advertising efforts, however, are so successful. As many big companies have learned, ads made by amateurs can be . . . well, pretty amateurish. If done well, however, consumer-generated advertising efforts can produce new creative ideas and fresh perspectives on the brand from consumers who actually experience it. Such campaigns can boost consumer involvement and get consumers talking and thinking about a brand and its value to them.[25]

Selecting Advertising Media

The major steps in **advertising media** selection are (1) determining *reach*, *frequency*, and *impact*; (2) choosing among major *media types*; (3) selecting specific *media vehicles*; and (4) choosing *media timing*.

Advertising media
The vehicles through which advertising messages are delivered to their intended audiences.

Determining Reach, Frequency, and Impact. To select media, the advertiser must determine the reach and frequency needed to achieve the advertising objectives. *Reach* is a measure of the *percentage* of people in the target market who are exposed to the ad campaign during a given period of time. For example, the advertiser might try to reach 70 percent of the target market during the first three months of the campaign. *Frequency* is a measure of how many *times* the average person in the target market is exposed to the message. For example, the advertiser might want an average exposure frequency of three.

But advertisers want to do more than just reach a given number of consumers a specific number of times. The advertiser also must determine the desired *media impact*—the *qualitative value* of message exposure through a given medium. For example, the same message in one magazine (say, *Newsweek*) may be more believable than in another (say, the *National Enquirer*). For products that need to be demonstrated, messages on television may have more impact than messages on radio because television uses sight *and* sound. Products for which consumers provide input on design or features might be better promoted at an interactive Web site than in a direct mailing.

More generally, the advertiser wants to choose media that will *engage* consumers rather than simply reach them. In any medium, how relevant an ad is for its audience is often much more important than how many people it reaches. ▶ For example, in an effort to make every advertising dollar count, Ford has recently been selecting TV programs based on viewer engagement ratings:[26]

▲ **Viewer engagement:** Viewers most deeply engaged in the Discovery Channel's *Dirty Jobs* series turned out to be truck-buying men, a ripe demographic for Ford's F-Series pickups.

Fordimages.com and Mike Rowe/MikeRoweWorks.com

Ford had little apparent reason to advertise on the Discovery Channel's *Dirty Jobs* series, which stars Mike Rowe. The show delivers puny Nielsen ratings. But when engagement metrics were applied to the program, the viewers most deeply absorbed in the show turned out to be truck-buying men between the ages of 18 and 49—a ripe demographic for Ford. That prompted Ford to advertise heavily and hire Rowe to appear in highly successful Web videos demonstrating the durability of the F-Series pickup.

Although Nielsen is beginning to measure the levels of television *media engagement*, such measures are hard to come by for most media. Current media measures are things such as ratings, readership, listenership, and click-through rates. However, engagement happens inside the consumer. Notes one expert, "Just measuring the number of eyeballs in front of a television set is hard enough without trying to measure the intensity of those eyeballs doing the viewing."[27] Still, marketers need to know how customers connect with an ad and brand idea as a part of the broader brand relationship.

Engaged consumers are more likely to act upon brand messages and even share them with others. Thus, rather than simply tracking *consumer impressions* for a media placement—how many people see, hear, or read an ad—Coca-Cola now also tracks the *consumer expressions* that result, such as a comment, a "like," uploading a photo or video, or passing content onto their networks. Today's empowered consumers often generate more messages about a brand than a company can. Through engagement, "instead of having to always pay for their message to run somewhere, [marketers] can 'earn' media for free, via consumer spreading YouTube clips, Groupons, and tweets," says an advertising consultant.[28]

For example, Coca-Cola estimates that on YouTube there are about 146 million views of content related to Coca-Cola. However, only about 26 million of those are of content that Coca-Cola created. The other 120 million are of content created by engaged consumers. "We can't match the volume of our consumers' output," says Coca-Cola's chief marketing officer, "but we can spark it with the right type [and placement] of content."[29]

Choosing among Major Media Types. As summarized in ▶ **Table 12.2**, the major media types are television, newspapers, the Internet, direct mail, magazines, radio, and outdoor. Advertisers can also choose from a wide array of new digital media, such as mobile phones and other digital devices, which reach consumers directly. Each medium has its advantages and its limitations.

Media planners want to choose media that will effectively and efficiently present the advertising message to target customers. Thus, they must consider each medium's impact, message effectiveness, and cost. Typically, it's not a question of which one medium to use. Rather, the advertiser selects a mix of media and blends them into a fully integrated marketing communications campaign.

The mix of media must be reexamined regularly. For a long time, television and magazines dominated the media mixes of national advertisers, with other media often neglected. However, as discussed previously, the media mix appears to be shifting. As mass-media costs rise, audiences shrink, and exciting new digital and interactive media emerge, many advertisers are finding new ways to reach consumers. They are supplementing the traditional mass media with more-specialized and highly targeted media that cost less, target more effectively, and engage consumers more fully.

In addition to the explosion of online media, cable and satellite television systems are thriving. Such systems allow narrow programming formats, such as all sports, all news, nutrition, arts, home improvement and gardening, cooking, travel, history, finance, and others that target select groups. Time Warner, Comcast, and other cable operators are even testing systems that will let them target specific types of ads to TVs in specific neighborhoods or individually to specific types of customers. For example, ads for a Spanish-language channel would run in only Hispanic neighborhoods, or only pet owners would see ads from pet food companies. Advertisers can take advantage of such *narrowcasting* to "rifle in" on special market segments rather than use the "shotgun" approach offered by network broadcasting.

▶ Table 12.2 — Profiles of Major Media Types

Medium	Advantages	Limitations
Television	Good mass-marketing coverage; low cost per exposure; combines sight, sound, and motion; appealing to the senses	High absolute costs; high clutter; fleeting exposure; less audience selectivity
Newspapers	Flexibility; timeliness; good local market coverage; broad acceptability; high believability	Short life; poor reproduction quality; small pass-along audience
The Internet	High selectivity; low cost; immediacy; interactive capabilities	Potentially low impact; the audience controls exposure
Direct mail	High audience selectivity; flexibility; no ad competition within the same medium; allows personalization	Relatively high cost per exposure; "junk mail" image
Magazines	High geographic and demographic selectivity; credibility and prestige; high-quality reproduction; long life and good pass-along readership	Long ad purchase lead time; high cost; no guarantee of position
Radio	Good local acceptance; high geographic and demographic selectivity; low cost	Audio only; fleeting exposure; low attention ("the half-heard" medium); fragmented audiences
Outdoor	Flexibility; high repeat exposure; low cost; low message competition; good positional selectivity	Little audience selectivity; creative limitations

Finally, in their efforts to find less-costly and more-highly targeted ways to reach consumers, advertisers have discovered a dazzling collection of *alternative media*. These days, no matter where you go or what you do, you will probably run into some new form of advertising.

⚠ Marketers have discovered a dazzling array of alternative media, like this heated Caribou Coffee bus shelter.

Caribou Coffee

Tiny billboards attached to shopping carts urge you to buy JELL-O Pudding Pops or Pampers, while ads roll by on the store's checkout conveyor touting your local Chevy dealer. Step outside and there goes a city trash truck sporting an ad for Glad trash bags or a school bus displaying a Little Caesar's pizza ad. A nearby fire hydrant is emblazoned with advertising for KFC's "fiery" chicken wings. You escape to the ballpark, only to find billboard-size video screens running Budweiser ads while a blimp with an electronic message board circles lazily overhead. ▶ In mid-winter, you wait in a city bus shelter that looks like an oven—with heat coming from the coils—introducing Caribou Coffee's line-up of hot breakfast sandwiches. How about a quiet trip in the country? Sorry—you find an enterprising farmer using his milk cows as four-legged billboards mounted with ads for Ben & Jerry's ice cream.

These days, you're likely to find ads—well—anywhere. Taxi cabs sport electronic messaging signs tied to GPS location sensors that can pitch local stores and restaurants wherever they roam. Ad space is being sold on DVD cases, parking-lot tickets, airline boarding passes, subway turnstiles, golf scorecards, ATMs, municipal garbage cans, and even police cars, doctors' examining tables, and church bulletins. One agency even leases space on the shaved heads of college students for temporary advertising tattoos ("cranial advertising").

Such alternative media seem a bit far-fetched, and they sometimes irritate consumers who resent it all as "ad nauseam." But for many marketers, these media can save money and provide a way to hit selected consumers where they live, shop, work, and play. Of course, all this may leave you wondering if there are any commercial-free havens remaining for ad-weary consumers. Public elevators, perhaps, or stalls in a public restroom? Forget it! Each has already been invaded by innovative marketers.

Another important trend affecting media selection is the rapid growth in the number of *media multitaskers*, people who absorb more than one medium at a time. For example, it's not uncommon to find someone watching TV with a smartphone in hand, posting on Facebook, texting friends, and chasing down product information on Google. One recent survey found that a whopping 86 percent of U.S. mobile Internet users watch TV with their devices in hand. Another study found that 60 percent of TV viewers go online via their smartphones, tablets, or PCs during their TV viewing time. Still another study found that a majority of these multitaskers "are 'primarily focused' on the Internet rather than TV, and their online viewing is overwhelmingly unrelated to the TV programs or commercials they are watching." Marketers need to take such media interactions into account when selecting the types of media they will use.[30]

Selecting Specific Media Vehicles. Media planners must also choose the best media vehicles—specific media within each general media type. For example, television vehicles include *30 Rock* and *ABC World News Tonight*. Magazine vehicles include *Newsweek*, *Real Simple*, and *ESPN The Magazine*.

Media planners must compute the cost per 1,000 persons reached by a vehicle. For example, if a full-page, four-color advertisement in the U.S. national edition of *Newsweek* costs $168,300 and *Newsweek's* readership is 1.5 million people, the cost of reaching each group of 1,000 persons is about $112. The same advertisement in *Bloomberg BusinessWeek* may cost only $139,500 but reach only 900,000 people—at a cost per 1,000 of about $155. The media planner ranks each magazine by cost per 1,000 and favors those magazines with the lower cost per 1,000 for reaching target consumers.[31]

Media planners must also consider the costs of producing ads for different media. Whereas newspaper ads may cost very little to produce, flashy television ads can be very costly. Many online ads cost little to produce, but costs can climb when producing made-for-the-Web videos and ad series.

In selecting specific media vehicles, media planners must balance media costs against several media effectiveness factors. First, the planner should evaluate the media vehicle's audience quality. For a Huggies disposable diapers advertisement, for example, *Parents* magazine would have a high exposure value; *Maxim* would have a low exposure value. Second, the media planner should consider audience engagement. Readers of *Vogue*, for example, typically pay more attention to ads than do *Newsweek* readers. Third, the planner should assess the vehicle's editorial quality. *Time* and the *Wall Street Journal* are more believable and prestigious than *Star* or the *National Enquirer*.

Deciding on Media Timing. An advertiser must also decide how to schedule the advertising over the course of a year. Suppose sales of a product peak in December and drop in March (for winter sports gear, for instance). The firm can vary its advertising to follow the seasonal pattern, oppose the seasonal pattern, or be the same all year. Most firms do some seasonal advertising. For example, Mars currently runs M&M's special ads for almost every holiday and "season," from Easter, Fourth of July, and Halloween to the Super Bowl season and the Oscar season. The Picture People, the national chain of portrait studios, advertises more heavily before major holidays, such as Christmas, Easter, Valentine's Day, and Halloween. Some marketers do *only* seasonal advertising: ➤ For instance, P&G advertises its Vicks NyQuil only during the cold and flu season.

Finally, the advertiser must choose the pattern of the ads. *Continuity* means scheduling ads evenly within a given period. *Pulsing* means scheduling ads unevenly over a given time period. Thus, 52 ads could either be scheduled at one per week during the year or pulsed in several bursts. The idea behind pulsing is to advertise heavily for a short period to build awareness that carries over to the next advertising period. Those who favor pulsing feel that it can be used to achieve the same impact as a steady schedule but at a much lower cost. However, some media planners believe that although pulsing achieves minimal awareness, it sacrifices depth of advertising communications.

FOR A BETTER-LOOKING TOMORROW.

Vicks NyQuil. The nighttime, sniffling, sneezing, coughing, aching, fever, best sleep you ever got with a cold... medicine.

VICKS breathe life in™

▲ **Media timing: Vicks NyQuil runs ads like this only during the cold and flu season.**

The Procter & Gamble Company

Return on advertising investment
The net return on advertising investment divided by the costs of the advertising investment.

Evaluating Advertising Effectiveness and the Return on Advertising Investment

Measuring advertising effectiveness and the **return on advertising investment** has become a hot issue for most companies, especially in a tighter economic environment. A less friendly economy "has obligated us all to pinch pennies all the more tightly and squeeze blood from a rock," says one advertising executive.[32] That leaves top management at many companies asking their marketing managers, "How do we know that we're spending the right amount on advertising?" and "What return are we getting on our advertising investment?"

Advertisers should regularly evaluate two types of advertising results: the communication effects and the sales and profit effects. Measuring the *communication effects* of an ad or ad campaign tells whether the ads and media are communicating the ad message well. Individual ads can be tested before or after they are run. Before an ad is placed, the advertiser can show it to consumers, ask how they like it, and measure message recall or attitude changes resulting from it. After an ad is run, the advertiser can measure how the ad affected consumer recall or product awareness, knowledge, and preference. Pre- and postevaluations of communication effects can be made for entire advertising campaigns as well.

Advertisers have gotten pretty good at measuring the communication effects of their ads and ad campaigns. However, *sales and profit* effects of advertising are often much harder to measure. For example, what sales and profits are produced by an ad campaign that increases brand awareness by 20 percent and brand preference by 10 percent? Sales and profits are affected by many factors other than advertising—such as product features, price, and availability.

One way to measure the sales and profit effects of advertising is to compare past sales and profits with past advertising expenditures. Another way is through experiments. For example, to test the effects of different advertising spending levels, Coca-Cola could vary the amount it spends on advertising in different market areas and measure the differences in the resulting sales and profit levels. More complex experiments could be designed to include other variables, such as differences in the ads or media used.

However, because so many factors affect advertising effectiveness, some controllable and others not, measuring the results of advertising spending remains an inexact science. Managers often must rely on large doses of judgment along with quantitative analysis when assessing advertising performance.

Other Advertising Considerations

In developing advertising strategies and programs, the company must address two additional questions. First, how will the company organize its advertising function—who will perform which advertising tasks? Second, how will the company adapt its advertising strategies and programs to the complexities of international markets?

Organizing for Advertising

Different companies organize in different ways to handle advertising. In small companies, advertising might be handled by someone in the sales department. Large companies have advertising departments whose job it is to set the advertising budget, work with the ad agency, and handle other advertising not done by the agency. However, most large companies use outside advertising agencies because they offer several advantages.

Advertising agency

A marketing services firm that assists companies in planning, preparing, implementing, and evaluating all or portions of their advertising programs.

How does an **advertising agency** work? Advertising agencies originated in the mid- to late-1800s by salespeople and brokers who worked for the media and received a commission for selling advertising space to companies. As time passed, the salespeople began to help customers prepare their ads. Eventually, they formed agencies and grew closer to the advertisers than to the media.

Today's agencies employ specialists who can often perform advertising tasks better than the company's own staff can. Agencies also bring an outside point of view to solving the company's problems, along with lots of experience from working with different clients and situations. So, today, even companies with strong advertising departments of their own use advertising agencies.

Some ad agencies are huge; the largest U.S. agency, McCann Erickson Worldwide, has annual gross U.S. revenues of more than $457 million. In recent years, many agencies have grown by gobbling up other agencies, thus creating huge agency holding companies. The largest of these megagroups, WPP, includes several large advertising, PR, and promotion agencies with combined worldwide revenues of $14.4 billion.[33] Most large advertising agencies have the staff and resources to handle all phases of an advertising campaign for their clients, from creating a marketing plan to developing ad campaigns and preparing, placing, and evaluating ads.

International Advertising Decisions

International advertisers face many complexities not encountered by domestic advertisers. The most basic issue concerns the degree to which global advertising should be adapted to the unique characteristics of various country markets.

Some advertisers have attempted to support their global brands with highly standardized worldwide advertising, with campaigns that work as well in Bangkok as they do in Baltimore. For example, McDonald's unifies its creative elements and brand presentation under the familiar "i'm lovin' it" theme in all its 100-plus markets worldwide. Visa coordinates worldwide advertising for its debit and credit cards under the "more people go with Visa" creative platform, which works as well in Korea as it does in the United States or Brazil. And ads from Brazilian flip-flops maker Havaianas make the same outrageously colorful splash worldwide, no matter what the country.

In recent years, the increased popularity of online social networks and video sharing has boosted the need for advertising standardization for global brands. Most big marketing and advertising campaigns include a large online presence. Connected consumers can now zip easily across borders via the Internet, making it difficult for advertisers to roll out adapted campaigns in a controlled, orderly fashion. As a result, at the very least, most global consumer brands coordinate their Web sites internationally. For example, check out the McDonald's Web sites from Germany to Jordan to China. You'll find the golden arches logo, the "i'm lovin' it" logo and jingle, a Big Mac equivalent, and maybe even Ronald McDonald himself.

Standardization produces many benefits—lower advertising costs, greater global advertising coordination, and a more consistent worldwide image. But it also has drawbacks. Most importantly, it ignores the fact that country markets differ greatly in their cultures, demographics, and economic conditions. Thus, most international advertisers "think globally but act locally." They develop global advertising *strategies* that make their worldwide efforts more efficient and consistent. Then they adapt their advertising *programs* to make them more responsive to consumer needs and expectations within local markets. ▶ For example, although Visa employs its "more people go with Visa" theme globally, ads in specific locales employ local language and inspiring local imagery that make the theme relevant to the local markets in which they appear.

Global advertisers face several special problems. For instance, advertising media costs and availability differ vastly from country to country. Countries also differ in the extent to which they regulate advertising practices. Many countries have extensive systems of laws restricting how much a company can spend on advertising, the media used, the nature of advertising claims, and other aspects of the advertising program. Such restrictions often require advertisers to adapt their campaigns from country to country.

For example, alcohol products cannot be advertised in India or in Muslim countries. In many countries, such as Sweden and Canada, junk food ads are banned from children's television programming. To play it safe, McDonald's advertises itself as a family restaurant in Sweden. Comparative ads, although acceptable and even common in the United States and Canada, are less commonly used in the United Kingdom and are illegal in India and Brazil. China bans sending e-mail for advertising purposes to people without their permission, and all advertising e-mail that is sent must be titled "advertisement."

China also has restrictive censorship rules for TV and radio advertising; for example, the words *the best* are banned, as are ads that "violate social customs" or present women in "improper ways." McDonald's once avoided government sanctions in China by publicly apologizing for an ad that crossed cultural norms by showing a

▲ Standardized global advertising: VISA coordinates its worldwide advertising under the theme "more people go with VISA," a theme that works as well in Brazil (bottom) as it does in the United States (top).

Courtesy of Visa International

customer begging for a discount. Similarly, Coca-Cola's Indian subsidiary was forced to end a promotion that offered prizes, such as a trip to Hollywood, because it violated India's established trade practices by encouraging customers to "gamble."

Thus, although advertisers may develop global strategies to guide their overall advertising efforts, specific advertising programs must usually be adapted to meet local cultures and customs, media characteristics, and regulations.

SPEED BUMP | LINKING THE CONCEPTS

Think about what goes on behind the scenes for the ads we all tend to take for granted.

- Pick a favorite print or television ad. Why do you like it? Do you think that it's effective? Can you think of an ad that people like that may not be effective?
- Dig a little deeper and learn about the campaign *behind* your ad. What are the campaign's objectives? What is its budget? Assess the campaign's message and media strategies. Looking beyond your own feelings about the ad, is the campaign likely to be effective?

Author Comment ▶

Not long ago, public relations was considered a marketing stepchild because of its limited marketing use. That situation is changing fast, however, as more marketers recognize PR's brand-building power.

Public Relations

Another major mass-promotion tool, public relations, consists of activities designed to build good relations with the company's various publics. PR departments may perform any or all of the following functions:[34]

- *Press relations or press agency:* Creating and placing newsworthy information in the news media to attract attention to a person, product, or service.
- *Product publicity:* Publicizing specific products.
- *Public affairs:* Building and maintaining national or local community relationships.
- *Lobbying:* Building and maintaining relationships with legislators and government officials to influence legislation and regulation.
- *Investor relations:* Maintaining relationships with shareholders and others in the financial community.
- *Development:* Working with donors or members of nonprofit organizations to gain financial or volunteer support.

Public relations is used to promote products, people, places, ideas, activities, organizations, and even nations. Companies use PR to build good relations with consumers, investors, the media, and their communities. Trade associations have used PR to rebuild interest in commodities, such as eggs, apples, potatoes, milk, and even onions. For example, the Vidalia Onion Committee built a PR campaign around the DreamWorks character Shrek—complete with Shrek images on packaging and in-store displays with giant inflatable Shreks—that successfully promoted onions to children. Even government organizations use PR to build awareness. For example, the National Heart, Lung, and Blood Institute (NHLBI) of the National Institutes of Health sponsors a long-running PR campaign that builds awareness of heart disease in women:[35]

> Heart disease is the number one killer of women; it kills more women each year than all forms of cancer combined. But a 2000 survey by the NHLBI showed that only 34 percent of women knew this, and that most people thought of heart disease as a problem mostly affecting men. So with the help of Ogilvy Public Relations Worldwide, the NHLBI set out to "create a personal and urgent wakeup call to American women." In 2002, it launched a national PR campaign—"The Heart Truth"—to raise awareness of heart disease among women and get women to discuss the issue with their doctors.

▲ **Public relations campaigns: NHLBI's "The Heart Truth" campaign has produced impressive results in raising awareness of the risks of heart disease in women.**

Courtesy of the National Heart, Lung, and Blood Institute

▶ The centerpiece of the campaign is the Red Dress, now the national symbol for women and heart disease awareness. The campaign creates awareness through an interactive Web site, mass media placements, and campaign materials—everything from brochures, DVDs, and posters to speaker's kits and airport dioramas. It also sponsors several major national events, such as the National Wear Red Day, an annual Red Dress Collection Fashion Show, and The Heart Truth Road Show, featuring heart disease risk factor screenings in major U.S. cities. Finally, the campaign works with more than three-dozen corporate sponsors, such as Diet Coke, St. Joseph aspirin, Tylenol, Cheerios, CVS Pharmacy, Swarovski, and Bobbi Brown Cosmetics. So far, some 2.65 billion product packages have carried the Red Dress symbol.

The results are impressive: Awareness among American women of heart disease as the number one killer of women has increased to 57 percent, and the number of heart disease deaths in women has declined steadily from one in three women to one in four. The American Heart Association has also adopted the Red Dress symbol and introduced its own complementary campaign.

The Role and Impact of PR

Public relations can have a strong impact on public awareness at a much lower cost than advertising can. When using public relations, the company does not pay for the space or time in the media. Rather, it pays for a staff to develop and circulate information and manage events. If the company develops an interesting story or event, it could be picked up by several different media and have the same effect as advertising that would cost millions of dollars. What's more, it would have more credibility than advertising.

PR results can sometimes be spectacular. ▶ Consider the launches of Apple's iPad and iPad 2:[36]

Apple's iPad was one of the most successful new-product launches in history. The funny thing: Whereas most big product launches are accompanied by huge prelaunch advertising campaigns, Apple pulled this one off with no advertising. None at all. Instead, it simply fed the PR fire. It built buzz months in advance by distributing iPads for early reviews, feeding the offline and online press with tempting tidbits, and offering fans an early online peek at thousands of new iPad apps that would be available. At launch time, it fanned the flames with a cameo on the TV sitcom *Modern Family*, a flurry of launch-day appearances on TV talk shows, and other launch-day events. In the process, through PR alone, the iPad launch generated unbounded consumer excitement, a media frenzy, and long lines outside retail stores on launch day. Apple sold more than 300,000 of the sleek gadgets on the first day alone and more than two million in the first two months—even as demand outstripped supply. Apple repeated the feat a year later with the equally successful launch of iPad 2, which sold close to one million devices the weekend of its launch.

▲ **The power of PR: Apple's iPad and iPad 2 launches created unbounded consumer excitement, a media frenzy, and long lines outside retail stores—all with no advertising, just PR.**

AP Images/BEHAR ANTHONY/SIPA

Despite its potential strengths, public relations is occasionally described as a marketing stepchild because of its sometimes limited and scattered use. The PR department is often located at corporate headquarters or handled by a third-party agency. Its staff is so busy dealing with various publics—stockholders, employees, legislators, and the press—that PR programs to support product marketing objectives may be ignored. Moreover, marketing managers and PR practitioners do not always speak the same language. Whereas many PR practitioners see their jobs as simply communicating, marketing managers tend to be much more interested in how advertising and PR affect brand building, sales and profits, and customer involvement and relationships.

This situation is changing, however. Although public relations still captures only a small portion of the overall marketing budgets of most firms, PR can be a powerful brand-building tool. And in this digital age, the lines between advertising and PR are becoming more and more blurred. For example, are brand Web sites, blogs, online social networks, and viral brand videos advertising efforts or PR efforts? All are both. The point is that PR should work hand in hand with advertising within an integrated marketing communications program to help build brands and customer relationships.

"This is PR's time to shine," says P&G's global marketing and brand building officer. "PR is going to grow its impact on the future [of] marketing because it is a great amplifier, builds relationships and invites consumer participation," he says. "PR [gives] our big ideas a megaphone that we used to spur participation [leading] to spontaneous combustion."[37]

Major Public Relations Tools

Public relations uses several tools. One of the major tools is *news*. PR professionals find or create favorable news about the company and its products or people. Sometimes news stories occur naturally; sometimes the PR person can suggest events or activities that would create news. Another common PR tool is *special events*, ranging from news conferences and speeches, press tours, grand openings, and fireworks displays to laser light shows, hot air balloon releases, multimedia presentations, or educational programs designed to reach and interest target publics.

Public relations people also prepare *written materials* to reach and influence their target markets. These materials include annual reports, brochures, articles, and company newsletters and magazines. *Audiovisual materials*, such as DVDs and online videos, are being used increasingly as communication tools. *Corporate identity materials* can also help create a corporate identity that the public immediately recognizes. Logos, stationery, brochures, signs, business forms, business cards, buildings, uniforms, and company cars and trucks all become marketing tools when they are attractive, distinctive, and memorable. Finally, companies can improve public goodwill by contributing money and time to *public service activities*.

As previously discussed, the Web is also an important PR channel. Web sites, blogs, and social networks such as YouTube, Facebook, and Twitter are providing new ways to reach more people. "The core strengths of public relations—the ability to tell a story and spark conversation—play well into the nature of such social media," says a PR expert. ▶ Consider the recent Papa John's twenty-fifth anniversary "Camaro Search" PR campaign:[38]

▲ **Papa John's "Camaro Search" campaign used traditional PR media plus a host of new social media.**
Papa John's International, Inc.

During a road trip last summer to find his long-lost Camaro, John Schnatter, the "Papa John" of Papa John's pizza, set a record for the world's highest pizza delivery (at the Willis Tower's Skydeck in Chicago), rang the closing bell at the Nasdaq stock exchange, and visited a children's hospital. The road trip got solid pickup in the media, with stories in the *New York Times*, the *Wall Street Journal*, and *USA Today*. ABC World News Tonight, CNBC, and CNN also covered the story, which included a $250,000 reward for the person reuniting Schnatter with his beloved Camaro Z28. These were all traditional pre-Web kinds of PR moves.

But unlike the old days, online social media was a key to getting the word out about this Papa John's journey. A Web site dedicated to the trip drew 660,000 unique visitors. On the day of the media conference announcing Schnatter's reunion with his old Chevy classic—Kentuckian Jeff Robinson turned up with the car and took home the cash—there were more than 1,000 tweets about him finding his car, with links galore. In addition, hundreds of people posted photos of themselves on Facebook (in their own Camaros) picking up the free pizza Papa John offered to all Camaro owners as part of the celebration. In all, the Web was buzzing about the Camaro Search story. Pre-Web, "there were different techniques used for [PR]—speeches, publicity, awards," says a PR executive. "Now we're applying the same mindset to social media to build relationships that are critical to any corporate entity."

By itself, a company's Web site is an important PR vehicle. Consumers and other publics often visit Web sites for information or entertainment. Web sites can also be ideal for handling crisis situations. For example, when several bottles of Odwalla apple juice sold on the West Coast were found to contain *E. coli* bacteria, Odwalla initiated a massive product recall. Within only three hours, it set up a Web site laden with information about the crisis and Odwalla's response. Company staffers also combed the Internet looking for newsgroups discussing Odwalla and posted links to the site. In this age where "it's easier to disseminate information through e-mail marketing, blogs, and online chat," notes an analyst, "public relations is becoming a valuable part of doing business in a digital world."[39]

As with the other promotion tools, in considering when and how to use product public relations, management should set PR objectives, choose the PR messages and vehicles, implement the PR plan, and evaluate the results. The firm's PR should be blended smoothly with other promotion activities within the company's overall integrated marketing communications effort.

REST STOP REVIEWING THE CONCEPTS

MyMarketingLab

Now that you have completed the chapter, return to www.mymktlab.com to experience and apply the concepts and to explore the additional study materials for this chapter.

CHAPTER REVIEW AND KEY TERMS

Objectives Review

In this chapter, you've learned how companies use integrated marketing communications (IMC) to communicate customer value. You've also explored two of the major marketing communications mix elements—advertising and public relations. Modern marketing calls for more than just creating customer value by developing a good product, pricing it attractively, and making it available to target customers. Companies also must clearly and persuasively *communicate* that value to current and prospective customers. To do this, they must blend five communication-mix tools, guided by a well-designed and implemented IMC strategy.

 OBJECTIVE 1 Define the five promotion mix tools for communicating customer value. (p 357)

A company's total *promotion mix*—also called its *marketing communications mix*—consists of the specific blend of *advertising, personal selling, sales promotion, public relations,* and *direct-marketing* tools that the company uses to persuasively communicate customer value and build customer relationships. Advertising includes any paid form of nonpersonal presentation and promotion of ideas, goods, or services by an identified sponsor. In contrast, public relations focuses on building good relations with the company's various publics. Personal selling is personal presentation by the firm's sales force for the purpose of making sales and building customer relationships. Firms use sales promotion to provide short-term incentives to encourage the purchase or sale of a product or service. Finally, firms seeking immediate response from targeted individual customers use direct-marketing tools to communicate with customers and cultivate relationships with them.

> **OBJECTIVE 2** **Discuss the changing communications landscape and the need for integrated marketing communications.** (pp 357–365)

The explosive developments in communications technology and changes in marketer and customer communication strategies have had a dramatic impact on marketing communications. Advertisers are now adding a broad selection of more-specialized and highly targeted media—including digital media—to reach smaller customer segments with more-personalized, interactive messages. As they adopt richer but more fragmented media and promotion mixes to reach their diverse markets, they risk creating a communications hodge-podge for consumers. To prevent this, companies are adopting the concept of *integrated marketing communications (IMC)*. Guided by an overall IMC strategy, the company works out the roles that the various promotional tools will play and the extent to which each will be used. It carefully coordinates the promotional activities and the timing of when major campaigns take place.

> **OBJECTIVE 3** **Describe and discuss the major decisions involved in developing an advertising program.** (pp 365–382)

Advertising—the use of paid media by a seller to inform, persuade, and remind about its products or organization—is a strong promotion tool that takes many forms and has many uses. *Advertising decision making* involves decisions about the objectives, the budget, the message, the media, and, finally, the evaluation of results. Advertisers should set clear *objectives* as to whether the advertising is supposed to inform, persuade, or remind buyers. The advertising *budget* can be based on what is affordable, on sales, on competitors' spending, or on advertising objectives and tasks. The *message decision* calls for planning a message strategy and executing it effectively. The *media decision* involves defining reach, frequency, and impact goals; choosing major media types; selecting media vehicles; and deciding on media timing. Message and media decisions must be closely coordinated for maximum campaign effectiveness. Finally, *evaluation* calls for evaluating the communication and sales effects of advertising before, during, and after the advertising is placed and measuring advertising's return on investment.

> **OBJECTIVE 4** **Explain how companies use public relations to communicate with their publics.** (pp 382–385)

Public relations involves building good relations with the company's various publics. Its functions include *press agentry, product publicity, public affairs, lobbying, investor relations,* and *development*. Public relations can have a strong impact on public awareness at a much lower cost than advertising can, and PR results can sometimes be spectacular. Despite its potential strengths, however, PR sometimes sees only limited and scattered use. Public relations tools include *news, special events, written materials, audiovisual materials, corporate identity materials,* and *public service activities*. A company's Web site and online social networking can be good PR vehicles. In considering when and how to use product PR, management should set PR objectives, choose the PR messages and vehicles, implement the PR plan, and evaluate the results. Public relations should be blended smoothly with other promotion activities within the company's overall IMC effort.

Key Terms

Objective 1

Promotion mix (marketing
    communications mix) (p 357)
Advertising (p 357)
Sales promotion (p 357)
Personal selling (p 357)
Public relations (PR) (p 357)
Direct marketing (p 357)

Objective 2

Integrated marketing communications
    (IMC) (p 359)

Push strategy (p 364)
Pull strategy (p 364)

Objective 3

Advertising objective (p 366)
Advertising budget (p 367)
Affordable method (p 368)
Percentage-of-sales method (p 368)
Competitive-parity method (p 368)

Objective-and-task method (p 368)
Advertising strategy (p 369)
Madison & Vine (p 370)
Creative concept (p 372)
Execution style (p 372)
Advertising media (p 376)
Return on advertising investment
    (p 379)
Advertising agency (p 380)

DISCUSSION AND CRITICAL THINKING

Discussion Questions

1. Name and define the five promotion mix tools for communicating customer value. (AACSB: Communication)
2. Compare and contrast pull and push promotion strategies. Which promotion tools are most effective in each? (AACSB: Communication)
3. Discuss the major advertising objectives and describe an advertisement that is attempting to achieve each objective. (AACSB: Communication; Reflective Thinking)
4. Why is it important that the advertising creative and media departments work closely together? (AACSB: Communication)
5. How do marketers measure the effectiveness of advertising? (AACSB: Communication)
6. What are the role and functions of public relations within an organization? (AACSB: Communication)

Critical Thinking Exercises

1. Any message can be presented using different execution styles. Select a brand and target audience and design two advertisements, each using a different execution style to deliver the same message to the target audience but in a different way. Identify the types of execution styles you are using and present your advertisements. (AACSB: Communication; Reflective Thinking)
2. Marketers are developing branded Web series to get consumers involved with their brands. One successful series is "The Real Women of Philadelphia" from Kraft (www.realwomenofphiladelphia.com). Fans can watch videos of professionals making delicious, simple recipes with one common ingredient—Philadelphia Cream Cheese, of course! The site features a recipe contest, and entrants even get training on how to photograph their entries to make them look as yummy as possible. Visit this Web site and find two other branded Web series. Critique the sites and describe how viewers interact with the Web sites. (AACSB: Communication; Use of IT; Reflective Thinking)
3. In a small group, discuss the major public relations tools and develop three public relations items for each of the following: (a) your school, (b) a frozen yogurt store, (c) a dentist, (d) a bank, and (e) a church. (AACSB: Communication; Reflective Thinking).

MINICASES AND APPLICATIONS

Marketing Technology   MerchantCircle

Small businesses account for 90 percent of all companies in the United States and many do not have resources to spare for promoting their businesses. Although newspaper, radio, and the Yellow Pages have been the mainstay media for local businesses, they can be expensive. As a result, many businesses are tuning into the Internet. One survey found that more than half of all small businesses using the Internet are creating or maintaining a social-networking presence on sites such as Facebook, Twitter, and Foursquare. However, social-networking media can be daunting to a small business owner, so MerchantCircle offers a network that brings customers and local businesses together. Founded in 2005, MerchantCircle is now the largest online network of local business owners, with 1.3 million members. Consumers can go to the site to search for local businesses, or they can ask questions and get input from any of MerchantCircle's business members. MerchantCircle business members can interact with each other to help grow their businesses.

1. Visit www.MerchantCircle.com and search for a jeweler in your city or some other city. What information is provided from your search? Are any jewelers in your city members of MerchantCircle? Search for other products and services and describe the benefits this network provides to you as a consumer. (AACSB: Communication; Use of IT; Reflective Thinking)
2. Explore the MerchantCircle site to learn the benefits and costs for local businesses. Write a brief report of what you find. (AACSB: Communication; Use of IT; Reflective Thinking)

Marketing Ethics   Bad Ad Program

The Food and Drug Administration (FDA) is enlisting doctors in its battle against misleading and deceptive prescription drug advertisements targeted toward consumers (called direct-to-consumer or DTC ads) and other promotional activities directed at medical professionals. You've probably seen the TV commercials for Viagra, Lipitor, Chantix, and other prescription drugs. Since the FDA relaxed the rules regarding broadcast prescription drug advertising in the late 1990s, DTC advertising has increased more than 300 percent, with $4.5 billion spent in 2009. That's actually down from the peak of $5.5 billion in 2006 because of the recession. It's difficult for the FDA to monitor DTC ads and other promotional activity aimed at medical professionals, so it created the "Bad Ad Program" and spent most of 2010 educating doctors about why it exists.

1. Visit www.fda.gov and search for "Bad Ad Program" to learn more about it. What is the FDA asking medical professionals to look for in DTC ads and other promotional activities directed toward them? How might this program be abused by the pharmaceutical industry? (AACSB: Communication; Ethical Reasoning; Reflective Thinking)

2. Many consumers are not aware of the FDA's regulations regarding DTC advertising. The agency has a parallel program—called EthicAd—to educate consumers and to encourage them to report violations. Search the FDA's Web site for this program, look at the examples of correct and incorrect ads, and evaluate two prescription drug advertisements using these guidelines. (AACSB: Communication; Ethical Reasoning; Reflective Thinking)

Marketing by the Numbers   Television Audience Ratings

Nielsen ratings are very important to both advertisers and television programmers because the cost of television advertising time is based on this rating. A show's *rating* is the number of households in Nielsen's sample tuned to that program divided by the number of television-owning households— 115 million in the United States. A show's *share* of the viewing audience is the number of households watching that show divided by the number of households using TV at that time. That is, ratings consider all TV-owning households whereas share considers only households that actually have the television turned on at the time. Ratings and share are usually given together. For example, suppose that one hour on Sunday evening showed the following ratings/shares for the major broadcast networks:

Network	Program	Rating/Share
NBC	Sunday Night Football (played on Thursday)	13.6/22
CBS	Big Brother 12	4.6/8
ABC	Wipeout	3.1/5
FOX	Bones	2.9/5
The CW	The Vampire Diaries	2.0/3

1. If one rating point represents 1 percent of TV households, how many households were watching football that evening? How many households were tuned into *The Vampire Diaries*? (AACSB: Communication; Analytical Reasoning)

2. What total share of the viewing audience was captured by all five networks? Explain why share is higher than the rating for a given program. (AACSB: Communication; Analytical Reasoning; Reflective Thinking)

Video Case   OXO

For over 20 years, OXO has put its well-known kitchen gadgets into almost every home in the United States through word-of-mouth, product placement, and other forms of non-traditional promotional techniques. While OXO is a leading national brand, it competes in product categories that are small in size. With its tight advertising budgets, mass-media promotions are not feasible.

This video demonstrates how OXO is moving forward with its promotional mix through online and social media campaigns. For its Good Grips, SteeL, Candela, Tot, and Staples/OXO brands, OXO is making extensive use of the major social

networks, expanding into the blogosphere, developing online ad campaigns, and more.

After viewing the video featuring OXO, answer the following questions:

1. How would you describe OXO's overall advertising strategy?

2. Why has OXO chosen to change its promotional strategy at this time?

3. Is OXO abandoning its old promotional methods? How is OXO blending a new advertising strategy with the promotional techniques that have made it a success?

Company Cases   7 Las Vegas/ 12 Ogilvy

See Appendix 1 for cases appropriate for this chapter. **Case 7, Las Vegas: What's Not Happening in Vegas** (pp A12–A14). The Sin City makes adjustments to keep its brand relevant and changes in the marketing environment cause big shifts in Las Vegas tourism. **Case 12, Ogilvy: It's Not Creative Unless It Sells** (pp A22–A24). With an online contest, a veteran agency returns to the roots of advertising—selling.

13 Personal Selling and Sales Promotion

CHAPTER ROAD MAP

Objective Outline

▷ **OBJECTIVE 1** Discuss the role of a company's salespeople in creating value for customers and building customer relationships. Personal Selling (392–394)

▷ **OBJECTIVE 2** Identify and explain the six major sales force management steps. Managing the Sales Force (395–405)

▷ **OBJECTIVE 3** Discuss the personal selling process, distinguishing between transaction-oriented marketing and relationship marketing. The Personal Selling Process (405–409)

▷ **OBJECTIVE 4** Explain how sales promotion campaigns are developed and implemented. Sales Promotion (409–415)

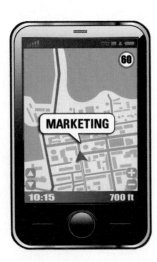

Previewing the Concepts

In the previous chapter, you learned about communicating customer value through integrated marketing communications (IMC) as well as two elements of the promotion mix: advertising and public relations. In this chapter, we examine two more IMC elements: personal selling and sales promotion. Personal selling is the interpersonal arm of marketing communications, in which the sales force interacts with customers and prospects to build relationships and make sales. Sales promotion consists of short-term incentives to encourage the purchase or sale of a product or service. As you read, remember that although this chapter presents personal selling and sales promotion as separate tools, they must be carefully integrated with the other elements of the promotion mix.

To start, what is your first reaction when you think of a salesperson or a sales force? Perhaps you think of pushy retail sales clerks, "yell and sell" TV pitchmen, or the stereotypical glad-handing "used-car salesman." In reality, however, such stereotypes simply don't fit most of today's salespeople—sales professionals who succeed not by taking advantage of customers but by listening to their needs and helping them to forge solutions. For most companies, personal selling plays an important role in building profitable customer relationships. Consider Procter & Gamble, whose customer-focused sales force has long been considered one of the nation's best.

▲ **P&G Customer Business Development managers know that to grow P&G's business, they must first help their retail partners to sell P&G's brands.**

Jin Lee/Bloomberg/Getty Images

First Stop

P&G: It's Not Sales, It's Customer Business Development

For decades, Procter & Gamble has been at the top of almost every expert's A-list of outstanding marketing companies. The experts point to P&G's stable of top-selling consumer brands, or that, year in and year out, P&G is the world's largest advertiser. Consumers seem to agree. You'll find at least one of P&G's blockbuster brands in 99 percent of all American households; in many homes, you'll find a dozen or more familiar P&G products. But P&G is also highly respected for something else—its top-notch, customer-focused sales force.

P&G's sales force has long been an American icon for selling at its very best. When it comes to selecting, training, and managing salespeople, P&G sets the gold standard. The company employs a massive sales force of more than 5,000 salespeople worldwide. At P&G, however, they rarely call it *sales*. Instead, it's *Customer Business Development (CBD)*. And P&G sales reps aren't *salespeople*—they're *CBD managers* or *CBD account executives*. All this might seem like just so much "corp-speak," but at P&G the distinction goes to the very core of how selling works.

P&G understands that if its customers don't do well, neither will the company. To grow its own business, therefore, P&G must first grow the business of the retailers that sell its brands to final consumers. And at P&G, the primary responsibility for helping customers grow falls to the sales force. Rather than just selling *to* its retail and wholesale customers, CBD managers partner strategically *with* customers to help develop their business in P&G's product categories. "We depend on them as much as they depend on us," says one CBD manager. By partnering with each other, P&G and its customers create "win–win" relationships that help both to prosper.

Most P&G customers are huge and complex businesses—such as Walgreens, Walmart, or Dollar General—with thousands of stores and billions of dollars in revenues. Working with and selling to such customers can be a very complex undertaking, more than any single salesperson or sales team could accomplish. Instead, P&G assigns a full CBD team to every large customer account. Each CBD team contains not only salespeople but also a full complement of specialists in every aspect of selling P&G's consumer brands at the retail level.

CBD teams vary in size depending on the customer. For example, P&G's largest customer, Walmart—which accounts for an amazing 20 percent of the company's sales—commands a 350-person CBD team. By contrast, the P&G Dollar General team consists of about 30 people. Regardless of size, every CBD team constitutes a complete, multifunctional customer-service unit. Each team includes a CBD manager and several CBD account executives (each responsible for a specific P&G product category), supported by specialists in marketing strategy, product development, operations, information systems, logistics, finance, and human resources.

To deal effectively with large accounts, P&G salespeople must be smart, well trained, and strategically grounded. They deal daily with high-level retail category buyers who may purchase hundreds of millions of dollars worth of P&G and competing brands annually. It takes a lot more

> P&G's sales force has long been an American icon for selling at its very best. But at P&G they rarely call it *sales*. Instead, it's *Customer Business Development*.

than a friendly smile and a firm handshake to interact with such buyers. Yet, individual P&G salespeople can't know everything, and thanks to the CBD sales structure, they don't have to. Instead, as members of a full CBD team, P&G salespeople have at hand all the resources they need to resolve even the most challenging customer problems. "I have everything I need right here," says a household care account executive. "If my customer needs help from us with in-store promotions, I can go right down the hall and talk with someone on my team in marketing about doing some kind of promotional deal. It's that simple."

Customer Business Development involves partnering with customers to jointly identify strategies that create shopper value and satisfaction and drive profitable sales at the store level. When it comes to profitably moving Tide, Pampers, Gillette, or other P&G brands off store shelves and into consumers' shopping carts, P&G reps and their teams often know more than the retail buyers they advise. In fact, P&G's retail partners often rely on CBD teams to help them manage not only the P&G brands on their shelves but also entire product categories, including competing brands.

Wait a minute. Does it make sense to let P&G advise on the stocking and placement of competitors' brands as well as its own? Would a P&G CBD rep ever tell a retail buyer to stock fewer P&G products and more of a competing brand? Believe it or not, it happens all the time. The CBD team's primary goal is to help the customer win in each product category. Sometimes, analysis shows that the best solution for the customer is "more of the other guy's product." For P&G, that's okay. It knows that creating the best situation for the retailer ultimately pulls in more customer traffic, which in turn will likely lead to increased sales for other P&G products in the same category. Because most of P&G's brands are market share leaders, it stands to benefit more from the increased traffic than competitors do. Again, what's good for the customer is good for P&G—it's a win–win situation.

Honest and open dealings also help to build long-term customer relationships. P&G salespeople become trusted advisors to their retailer-partners, a status they work hard to maintain. "It took me four years to build the trust I now have with my buyer," says a veteran CBD account executive. "If I talk her into buying P&G products that she can't sell or out of stocking competing brands that she should be selling, I could lose that trust in a heartbeat."

Finally, collaboration is usually a two-way street—P&G gives and customers give back in return. "We'll help customers run a set of commercials or do some merchandising events, but there's usually a return-on-investment," explains another CBD manager. "Maybe it's helping us with distribution of a new product or increasing space for fabric care. We're very willing if the effort creates value for us as well as for the customer and the final consumer."

According to P&G, "Customer Business Development is selling and a whole lot more. It's a P&G-specific approach [that lets us] grow business by working as a 'strategic partner' with our accounts, focusing on mutually beneficial business building opportunities. All customers want to improve their business; it's [our] role to help them identify the biggest opportunities."

Thus, P&G salespeople aren't the stereotypical glad-handers that some people have come to expect when they think of selling. In fact, they aren't even called *salespeople*. They are *Customer Business Development managers*—talented, well-educated, well-trained sales professionals who do all they can to help customers succeed. They know that good selling involves working with customers to solve their problems for mutual gain. They know that if customers succeed, they succeed.[1]

MyMarketingLab

Visit www.mymktlab.com to find activities that help you learn and review in order to succeed in this chapter.

I n this chapter, we examine two more promotion mix tools: *personal selling* and *sales promotion*. Personal selling consists of interpersonal interactions with customers and prospects to make sales and maintain customer relationships. Sales promotion involves using short-term incentives to encourage customer purchasing, reseller support, and sales force efforts.

Author Comment ▶
Personal selling is the interpersonal arm of the promotion mix. A company's sales force creates and communicates customer value through personal interactions with customers.

Personal Selling

Robert Louis Stevenson once noted, "Everyone lives by selling something." Companies around the world use sales forces to sell products and services to business customers and final consumers. But sales forces are also found in many other kinds of organizations. For example, colleges use recruiters to attract new students, and churches use membership committees to attract new members. Museums and fine arts organizations use fund-raisers to contact donors and raise money. Even governments use sales forces. The U.S. Postal Service, for instance, uses a sales force to sell Express Mail and other services to corporate customers. In the first part of this chapter, we examine personal selling's role in the organization, sales force management decisions, and the personal selling process.

The Nature of Personal Selling

Personal selling

Personal presentations by the firm's sales force for the purpose of making sales and building customer relationships.

Salesperson

An individual representing a company to customers by performing one or more of the following activities: prospecting, communicating, selling, servicing, information gathering, and relationship building.

Personal selling is one of the oldest professions in the world. The people who do the selling go by many names, including salespeople, sales representatives, agents, district managers, account executives, sales consultants, and sales engineers.

People hold many stereotypes of salespeople—including some unfavorable ones. *Salesman* may bring to mind the image of Dwight Schrute, the opinionated Dunder Mifflin paper salesman from the TV show *The Office*, who lacks both common sense and social skills. Or they may think of the real-life "yell-and-sell" TV pitchmen, who hawk everything from the ShamWow to the Swivel Sweeper and Point 'n Paint in infomercials. However, the majority of salespeople are a far cry from these unfortunate stereotypes.

As the opening P&G story shows, most salespeople are well-educated and well-trained professionals who add value for customers and maintain long-term customer relationships. They listen to their customers, assess customer needs, and organize the company's efforts to solve customer problems. The best salespeople are the ones who work closely with customers for mutual gain.

▲ **Professional selling: It takes more than fast talk and a warm smile to sell high-tech diesel locomotives. GE's real challenge is to win buyers' business by building day-in, day-out, year-in, year-out partnerships with customers.**
GE Transportation

Consider GE's diesel locomotive business. ▶ It takes more than fast talk and a warm smile to sell a batch of $2-million high-tech locomotives. A single big sale can easily run into the hundreds of millions of dollars. GE salespeople head up an extensive team of company specialists—all dedicated to finding ways to satisfy the needs of large customers. The selling process can take years from the first sales presentation to the day the sale is announced. The real challenge is to win buyers' business by building day-in, day-out, year-in, year-out partnerships with them based on superior products and close collaboration.

The term **salesperson** covers a wide range of positions. At one extreme, a salesperson might be largely an *order taker*, such as the department store salesperson standing behind the counter. At the other extreme are *order getters*, whose positions demand *creative selling* and *relationship building* for products and services ranging from appliances, industrial equipment, and locomotives to insurance and information technology services. In this chapter, we focus on the more creative types of selling and the process of building and managing an effective sales force.

The Role of the Sales Force

Personal selling is the interpersonal arm of the promotion mix. Advertising consists largely of nonpersonal communication with large groups of consumers. By contrast, personal selling involves interpersonal interactions between salespeople and individual customers—whether face-to-face, by telephone, via e-mail, through video or Web conferences, or by other means. Personal selling can be more effective than advertising in more complex selling situations. Salespeople can probe customers to learn more about their problems and then adjust the marketing offer and presentation to fit each customer's special needs.

The role of personal selling varies from company to company. Some firms have no salespeople at all—for example, companies that sell only online or through catalogs, or companies that sell through manufacturer's reps, sales agents, or brokers. In most firms, however, the sales force plays a major role. In companies that sell business products and services, such as IBM, DuPont, or Boeing, salespeople work directly with customers. In consumer product companies such as Nestlé or Nike, the sales force plays an important behind-the-scenes role. It works with wholesalers and retailers to gain their support and help them be more effective in selling the company's products.

Linking the Company with Its Customers

The sales force serves as a critical link between a company and its customers. ▶ In many cases, salespeople serve two masters—the seller and the buyer. First, they *represent the company to customers*. They find and develop new customers and communicate information about the company's products and services. They sell products by approaching customers, presenting their offerings, answering objections, negotiating prices and terms, closing sales, and servicing accounts.

▲ **Salespeople link the company with its customers. To many customers, the salesperson is the company.**

yellowdog/cultura/Corbis

At the same time, salespeople *represent customers to the company*, acting inside the firm as "champions" of customers' interests and managing the buyer-seller relationship. Salespeople relay customer concerns about company products and actions back inside to those who can handle them. They learn about customer needs and work with other marketing and nonmarketing people in the company to develop greater customer value.

In fact, to many customers, the salesperson *is* the company—the only tangible manifestation of the company that they see. Hence, customers may become loyal to salespeople as well as to the companies and products they represent. This concept of *salesperson-owned loyalty* lends even more importance to the salesperson's customer relationship-building abilities. Strong relationships with the salesperson will result in strong relationships with the company and its products. Conversely, poor relationships will probably result in poor company and product relationships.

Given its role in linking the company with its customers, the sales force must be strongly customer-solutions focused. In fact, such a customer-solutions focus is a must not only for the sales force but also for the entire organization. Says Anne Mulcahy, successful former CEO and chairman of Xerox, who started her career in sales, a strong customer-service focus "has to be the center of your universe, the heartland of how you run your company."[2]

Coordinating Marketing and Sales

Ideally, the sales force and other marketing functions (marketing planners, brand managers, and researchers) should work together closely to jointly create value for customers. Unfortunately, however, some companies still treat sales and marketing as separate functions. When this happens, the separate sales and marketing groups may not get along well. When things go wrong, marketers blame the sales force for its poor execution of what they see as an otherwise splendid strategy. In turn, the sales team blames the marketers for being out of touch with what's really going on with customers. Neither group fully values the other's contributions. However, if not repaired, such disconnects between marketing and sales can damage customer relationships and company performance.

A company can take several actions to help bring its marketing and sales functions closer together. At the most basic level, it can increase communications between the two groups by arranging joint meetings and spelling out communications channels. It can create opportunities for salespeople and marketers to work together. Brand managers and researchers can tag along on sales calls or sit in on sales planning sessions. In turn, salespeople can sit in on marketing planning sessions and share their firsthand customer knowledge.

A company can also create joint objectives and reward systems for sales and marketing teams or appoint marketing-sales liaisons—people from marketing who "live with the sales force" and help coordinate marketing and sales force programs and efforts. Finally, it can appoint a high-level marketing executive to oversee both marketing and sales. Such a person can help infuse marketing and sales with the common goal of creating value for customers to capture value in return.[3]

Managing the Sales Force

Author Comment ▶
Here's another definition of sales force management: "Planning, organizing, leading, and controlling personal contact programs designed to achieve profitable customer relationships." Once again, the goal of every marketing activity is to create customer value and build customer relationships.

Sales force management
Analyzing, planning, implementing, and controlling sales force activities.

We define **sales force management** as analyzing, planning, implementing, and controlling sales force activities. It includes designing sales force strategy and structure, as well as recruiting, selecting, training, compensating, supervising, and evaluating the firm's salespeople. These major sales force management decisions are shown in ▶ **Figure 13.1** and discussed in the following sections.

Designing the Sales Force Strategy and Structure

Marketing managers face several sales force strategy and design questions. How should salespeople and their tasks be structured? How big should the sales force be? Should salespeople sell alone or work in teams with other people in the company? Should they sell in the field, by telephone, or on the Web? We address these issues next.

The Sales Force Structure

A company can divide sales responsibilities along any of several lines. The structure decision is simple if the company sells only one product line to one industry with customers in many locations. In that case the company would use a *territorial sales force structure*. However, if the company sells many products to many types of customers, it might need a *product sales force structure*, a *customer sales force structure*, or a combination of the two.

Territorial sales force structure
A sales force organization that assigns each salesperson to an exclusive geographic territory in which that salesperson sells the company's full line.

In the **territorial sales force structure**, each salesperson is assigned to an exclusive geographic area and sells the company's full line of products or services to all customers in that territory. This organization clearly defines each salesperson's job and fixes accountability. It also increases the salesperson's desire to build local customer relationships that, in turn, improve selling effectiveness. Finally, because each salesperson travels within a limited geographic area, travel expenses are relatively small. A territorial sales organization is often supported by many levels of sales management positions. For example, individual territory sales reps may report to area managers, who in turn report to regional managers who report to a director of sales.

Product sales force structure
A sales force organization in which salespeople specialize in selling only a portion of the company's products or lines.

If a company has numerous and complex products, it can adopt a **product sales force structure**, in which the sales force specializes along product lines. For example, GE employs different sales forces within different product and service divisions of its major businesses. Within GE Infrastructure, for instance, the company has separate sales forces for aviation, energy, transportation, and water processing products and technologies. No single salesperson can become expert in all of these product categories, so product specialization is required. Similarly, GE Healthcare employs different sales forces for diagnostic imaging, life sciences, and integrated IT products and services. In all, a company as large and complex as GE might have dozens of separate sales forces serving its diverse product and service portfolio.

Customer (or market) sales force structure
A sales force organization in which salespeople specialize in selling only to certain customers or industries.

Using a **customer** (or **market**) **sales force structure**, a company organizes its sales force along customer or industry lines. Separate sales forces may be set up for different industries, serving current customers versus finding new ones, and serving major accounts versus regular accounts.[4] Organizing the sales force around customers can help a company build closer relationships with important customers. Many companies even have special sales forces to handle the needs of individual large customers. For example, appliance maker Whirlpool assigns individual teams of salespeople to big retail customers such as Sears, Lowe's, Best Buy, and Home Depot. Each Whirlpool sales team aligns with the large customer's buying team.

▶ **Figure 13.1** Major Steps in Sales Force Management

The goal of this process? You guessed it! The company wants to build a skilled and motivated sales team that will help to create customer value and build strong customer relationships.

| Designing sales force strategy and structure | Recruiting and selecting salespeople | Training salespeople | Compensating salespeople | Supervising salespeople | Evaluating salespeople |

▲ **Sales force structure: Whirlpool specializes its sales force by customer and by territory for each key customer group.**

AP Images/ Paul Sancya

When a company sells a wide variety of products to many types of customers over a broad geographic area, it often employs a *complex sales force structure,* which combines several types of organization. Salespeople can be specialized by customer and territory; product and territory; product and customer; or territory, product, and customer. ▶ For example, Whirlpool specializes its sales force by customer (with different sales teams for Sears, Lowe's, Best Buy, Home Depot, and smaller independent retailers) *and* by territory for each key customer group (territory representatives, territory managers, regional managers, and so on). No single structure is best for all companies and situations. Each company should select a sales force structure that best serves the needs of its customers and fits its overall marketing strategy.

Sales Force Size

Once the company has set its structure, it is ready to consider *sales force size.* Sales forces may range in size from only a few salespeople to tens of thousands. Some sales forces are huge—for example, PepsiCo employs 36,000 salespeople; American Express, 23,400; GE, 16,400; and Xerox, 15,000.[5] Salespeople constitute one of the company's most productive—and most expensive—assets. Therefore, increasing their numbers will increase both sales and costs.

Many companies use some form of *workload approach* to set sales force size. Using this approach, a company first groups accounts into different classes according to size, account status, or other factors related to the amount of effort required to maintain the account. It then determines the number of salespeople needed to call on each class of accounts the desired number of times.

The company might think as follows: Suppose we have 1,000 A-level accounts and 2,000 B-level accounts. A-level accounts require 36 calls per year, and B-level accounts require 12 calls per year. In this case, the sales force's *workload*—the number of calls it must make per year—is 60,000 calls [(1,000 × 36) + (2,000 × 12) = 36,000 + 24,000 = 60,000]. Suppose our average salesperson can make 1,000 calls a year. Thus, we need 60 salespeople (60,000 ÷ 1,000).

Other Sales Force Strategy and Structure Issues

Sales management must also determine who will be involved in the selling effort and how various sales and sales support people will work together.

Outside sales force (or field sales force)

Salespeople who travel to call on customers in the field.

Inside sales force

Salespeople who conduct business from their offices via telephone, the Internet, or visits from prospective buyers.

Outside and Inside Sales Forces. The company may have an **outside sales force** (or **field sales force**), an **inside sales force**, or both. Outside salespeople travel to call on customers in the field. In contrast, inside salespeople conduct business from their offices via telephone, the Internet, or visits from buyers.

Some inside salespeople provide support for the outside sales force, freeing them to spend more time selling to major accounts and finding new prospects. For example, *technical sales support people* provide technical information and answers to customers' questions. *Sales assistants* provide administrative backup for outside salespeople. They call ahead and confirm appointments, follow up on deliveries, and answer customers' questions when outside salespeople cannot be reached. Using such combinations of inside and outside salespeople can help serve important customers better. The inside rep provides daily access and support, whereas the outside rep provides face-to-face collaboration and relationship building.

Other inside salespeople do more than just provide support. *Telemarketers* and *Internet sellers* use the phone and Internet to find new leads and qualify their prospects or sell and service accounts directly. Telemarketing and Internet selling can be very effective, less costly ways to sell to smaller, harder-to-reach customers. Depending on the complexity of the product and customer, for example, a telemarketer can make from 20 to 33 decision-maker contacts a day, compared to the average of four that an outside salesperson can make. In addition, whereas an average business-to-business field sales call can cost $350 or more, a routine industrial telemarketing call costs only about $5; a complex call costs about $20.[6]

Although the federal government's Do Not Call Registry put a dent in telephone sales to consumers, telemarketing remains a vital tool for many B-to-B marketers. For some smaller companies, telephone and Internet selling may be the primary sales approaches. However, larger companies also use these tactics, either to sell directly to small and mid-size customers or help out with larger ones. Especially in the leaner times following the recent recession, many companies reduced their in-person customer visits in favor of more telephone, e-mail, and Internet selling.

▶ For many types of products and selling situations, phone or Internet selling can be as effective as a personal sales call:

▲ For many types of selling situations, phone or Web selling can be as effective as a personal sales call. At Climax Portable Machine Tools, phone reps build surprisingly strong and personal customer relationships.

Helen King / Corbis

Climax Portable Machine Tools, which manufactures portable maintenance tools for the metal cutting industry, has proven that telemarketing can save money and still lavish attention on buyers. Under the old system, Climax sales engineers spent one-third of their time on the road, training distributor salespeople and accompanying them on calls. They could make about four contacts a day. Now, each of five sales engineers on Climax's inside sales team calls about 30 prospects a day, following up on leads generated by ads and e-mails. Because it takes about five calls to close a sale, the sales engineers update a prospect's profile after each contact, noting the degree of commitment, requirements, next call date, and personal comments. "If anyone mentions he's going on a fishing trip, our sales engineer enters that in the sales information system and uses it to personalize the next phone call," says Climax's president, noting that this is one way to build good relations.

Another is that the first contact with a prospect includes the sales engineer's business card with his or her picture on it. Climax's customer information system also gives inside reps instant access to customer information entered by the outside sales force and service people. Armed with all the information, inside reps can build surprisingly strong and personal customer relationships. Of course, it takes more than friendliness to sell $15,000 machine tools over the phone (special orders may run $200,000), but the telemarketing approach works well. When Climax customers were asked, "Do you see the sales engineer often enough?" the response was overwhelmingly positive. Obviously, many people didn't realize that the only contact they had with Climax had been on the phone.[7]

Team Selling. As products become more complex, and as customers grow larger and more demanding, a single salesperson simply can't handle all of a large customer's needs. Instead, most companies now use **team selling** to service large, complex accounts. Sales teams can unearth problems, solutions, and sales opportunities that no individual salesperson could. Such teams might include experts from any area or level of the selling firm—sales, marketing, technical and support services, R&D, engineering, operations, finance, and others.

In many cases, the move to team selling mirrors similar changes in customers' buying organizations. Many large customer companies have implemented team-based purchasing, requiring marketers to employ equivalent team-based selling. When dealing with large, complex accounts, one salesperson can't be an expert in everything the customer needs. Instead, selling is done by strategic account teams, quarterbacked by senior account managers or customer business managers.

Some companies, such as IBM, Xerox, and P&G, have used teams for a long time. In the chapter-opening story, we learned that P&G sales reps are organized into Customer

Team selling

Using teams of people from sales, marketing, engineering, finance, technical support, and even upper management to service large, complex accounts.

Business Development (CBD) teams. Each CBD team is assigned to a major P&G customer, such as Walmart, Safeway, or CVS Pharmacy. The CBD organization places the focus on serving the complete needs of each major customer. It lets P&G "grow business by working as a 'strategic partner' with our accounts," not just as a supplier.[8]

Team selling does have some pitfalls, however. For example, salespeople are by nature competitive and have often been trained and rewarded for outstanding individual performance. Salespeople who are used to having customers all to themselves may have trouble learning to work with and trust others on a team. In addition, selling teams can confuse or overwhelm customers who are used to working with only one salesperson. Finally, difficulties in evaluating individual contributions to the team selling effort can create some sticky compensation issues.

Recruiting and Selecting Salespeople

At the heart of any successful sales force operation is the recruitment and selection of good salespeople. The performance difference between an average salesperson and a top salesperson can be substantial. In a typical sales force, the top 30 percent of the salespeople might bring in 60 percent of the sales. Thus, careful salesperson selection can greatly increase overall sales force performance. Beyond the differences in sales performance, poor selection results in costly turnover. When a salesperson quits, the costs of finding and training a new salesperson—plus the costs of lost sales—can be very high. Also, a sales force with many new people is less productive, and turnover disrupts important customer relationships.

What sets great salespeople apart from all the rest? In an effort to profile top sales performers, Gallup Consulting, a division of the well-known Gallup polling organization, has interviewed hundreds of thousands of salespeople. ▶ Its research suggests that the best salespeople possess four key talents: intrinsic motivation, a disciplined work style, the ability to close a sale, and, perhaps most important, the ability to build relationships with customers.[9]

▲ **Great salespeople: The best salespeople possess intrinsic motivation, a disciplined work style, the ability to close a sale, and, perhaps most important, the ability to build relationships with customers.**
Sigrid Olsson/Corbis

Super salespeople are motivated from within—they have an unrelenting drive to excel. Some salespeople are driven by money, a desire for recognition, or the satisfaction of competing and winning. Others are driven by the desire to provide service and build relationships. The best salespeople possess some of each of these motivations. They also have a disciplined work style. They lay out detailed, organized plans and then follow through in a timely way.

But motivation and discipline mean little unless they result in closing more sales and building better customer relationships. Super salespeople build the skills and knowledge they need to get the job done. Perhaps most important, top salespeople are excellent customer problem solvers and relationship builders. They understand their customers' needs. Talk to sales executives and they'll describe top performers in these terms: good listeners, empathetic, patient, caring, and responsive. Top performers can put themselves on the buyer's side of the desk and see the world through their customers' eyes. They don't want just to be liked; they want to add value for their customers.

That said, there is no one right way to sell. Each successful salesperson uses a different approach, one that best applies his or her unique strengths and talents. For example, some salespeople enjoy the thrill of a harder sell in confronting challenges and winning people over. Others might apply "softer" talents to reach the same goal. "The key is for sales reps to understand and nurture their innate talents so they can develop their own personal approach and win business *their* way," says a selling expert.[10]

When recruiting, a company should analyze the sales job itself and the characteristics of its most successful salespeople to identify the traits needed by a successful salesperson in their industry. Then it must recruit the right salespeople. The human resources department looks for applicants by getting names from current salespeople, using employment agencies, searching the Internet, placing classified ads, and working through college placement services. Another source is to attract top salespeople from other companies. Proven salespeople need less training and can be productive immediately.

Recruiting will attract many applicants from which the company must select the best. The selection procedure can vary from a single informal interview to lengthy testing and interviewing. Many companies give formal tests to sales applicants. Tests typically measure sales aptitude, analytical and organizational skills, personality traits, and other characteristics. But test scores provide only one piece of information in a set that includes personal characteristics, references, past employment history, and interviewer reactions.

Training Salespeople

New salespeople may spend anywhere from a few weeks or months to a year or more in training. After the initial training ends, most companies provide continuing sales training via seminars, sales meetings, and Internet e-learning throughout the salesperson's career. In all, U.S. companies spend billions of dollars annually on training salespeople, and sales training typically captures the largest share of the training budget. Although training can be expensive, it can also yield dramatic returns. For instance, one recent study showed that sales training conducted by ADP, an administrative services firm, resulted in an ROI of nearly 338 percent in only 90 days.[11]

Training programs have several goals. First, salespeople need to know about customers and how to build relationships with them. Therefore, the training program must teach them about different types of customers and their needs, buying motives, and buying habits. It must also teach them how to sell effectively and train them in the basics of the selling process. Salespeople also need to know and identify with the company, its products, and its competitors. Therefore, an effective training program teaches them about the company's objectives, organization, products, and the strategies of major competitors.

Today, many companies are adding e-learning to their sales training programs. Online training may range from simple text-based product training and Internet-based sales exercises that build sales skills to sophisticated simulations that re-create the dynamics of real-life sales calls. Training online instead of on-site can cut travel and other training costs, and it takes up less of a salesperson's selling time. It also makes on-demand training available to salespeople, letting them train as little or as much as needed, whenever and wherever needed. Although most e-learning is Web-based, many companies now offer on-demand training from anywhere via almost any digital device.

Many companies are now using imaginative and sophisticated e-learning techniques to make sales training more efficient—and sometimes even more fun. For example, Bayer HealthCare Pharmaceuticals worked with Concentric Pharma Advertising, a health care marketing agency, to create a role-playing simulation video game to train its sales force on a new drug marketing program:[12]

Most people don't usually associate fast-paced rock music and flashy graphics with online sales training tools. ▶ But Concentric Pharma Advertising's innovative role-playing video game—Rep Race: The Battle for Office Supremacy—has all that and a lot more. Rep Race gives Bayer sales reps far more entertainment than the staid old multiple-choice skills tests it replaces. The game was created to help breathe new life into a mature Bayer product—Betaseron, an 18-year-old multiple sclerosis (MS) therapy treatment. The aim was to find a fresh, more active way to help Bayer

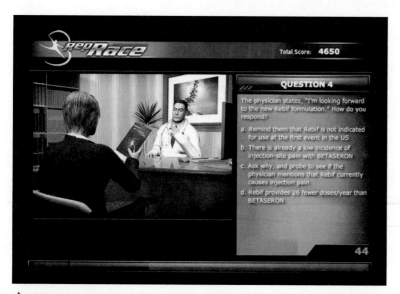

▲ **E-Training can make sales training more efficient—and more fun. Bayer HealthCare Pharmaceuticals' role-playing video game—Rep Race—helped improve sales rep effectiveness by 20 percent.**
Concentric Pharma Advertising

sales reps apply the in-depth information they learned about Betaseron to actual selling and objections-handling situations. Bayer also wanted to increase rep engagement through interactive learning and feedback through real-time results. Bayer reps liked Rep Race from the start. According to Bayer, when the game was first launched, reps played it as many as 30 times. In addition to its educational and motivational value, Rep Race allowed Bayer to measure sales reps' individual and collective performance. In the end, Bayer calculated that the Rep Race simulation helped improve the Betaseron sales team's effectiveness by 20 percent.

Compensating Salespeople

To attract good salespeople, a company must have an appealing compensation plan. Compensation consists of four elements: a fixed amount, a variable amount, expenses, and fringe benefits. The fixed amount, usually a salary, gives the salesperson some stable income. The variable amount, which might be commissions or bonuses based on sales performance, rewards the salesperson for greater effort and success.

Management must determine what *mix* of these compensation elements makes the most sense for each sales job. Different combinations of fixed and variable compensation give rise to four basic types of compensation plans: straight salary, straight commission, salary plus bonus, and salary plus commission. According to one study of sales force compensation, 18 percent of companies pay straight salary, 19 percent pay straight commission, and 63 percent pay a combination of salary plus incentives. A study showed that the average salesperson's pay consists of about 67 percent salary and 33 percent incentive pay.[13]

A sales force compensation plan can both motivate salespeople and direct their activities. Compensation should direct salespeople toward activities that are consistent with the overall sales force and marketing objectives. For example, if the strategy is to acquire new business, grow rapidly, and gain market share, the compensation plan might include a larger commission component, coupled with a new-account bonus to encourage high sales performance and new account development. In contrast, if the goal is to maximize current account profitability, the compensation plan might contain a larger base-salary component with additional incentives for current account sales or customer satisfaction.

In fact, more and more companies are moving away from high commission plans that may drive salespeople to make short-term grabs for business. They worry that a salesperson who is pushing too hard to close a deal may ruin the customer relationship. Instead, companies are designing compensation plans that reward salespeople for building customer relationships and growing the long-run value of each customer.

When times get tough economically, some companies are tempted to cut costs by reducing sales compensation. However, although some cost-cutting measures make sense when business is sluggish, cutting sales force compensation across the board is usually a "don't-go-there, last-of-the-last-resorts" action, says one sales compensation expert. "Keep in mind that if you burn the salesperson, you might burn the customer relationship." If the company must reduce its compensation expenses, says the expert, a better strategy than across-the-board cuts is to "keep the pay up for top performers and turn the [low performers] loose."[14]

Supervising and Motivating Salespeople

New salespeople need more than a territory, compensation, and training—they need supervision and motivation. The goal of *supervision* is to help salespeople "work smart" by doing the right things in the right ways. The goal of *motivation* is to encourage salespeople to "work hard" and energetically toward sales force goals. If salespeople work smart and work hard, they will realize their full potential—to their own and the company's benefit.

Supervising Salespeople

Companies vary in how closely they supervise their salespeople. Many help salespeople identify target customers and set call objectives. Some may also specify how much time the sales force should spend prospecting for new accounts and set other time management

▶ **Figure 13.2** How Salespeople
Spend Their Time

Source: Proudfoot Consulting. Data used
with permission.

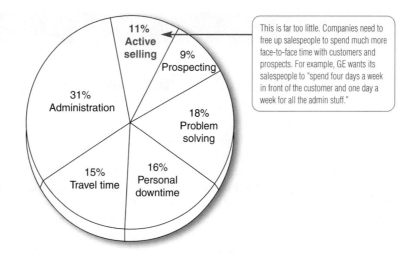

This is far too little. Companies need to free up salespeople to spend much more face-to-face time with customers and prospects. For example, GE wants its salespeople to "spend four days a week in front of the customer and one day a week for all the admin stuff."

priorities. One tool is the weekly, monthly, or annual *call plan* that shows which customers and prospects to call on and which activities to carry out. Another tool is *time-and-duty analysis*. In addition to time spent selling, the salesperson spends time traveling, waiting, taking breaks, and doing administrative chores.

▶ **Figure 13.2** shows how salespeople spend their time. On average, active selling time accounts for only 11 percent of total working time! If selling time could be raised from 11 percent to 33 percent, this would triple the time spent selling.[15] Companies are always looking for ways to save time—simplifying administrative duties, developing better sales-call and routing plans, supplying more and better customer information, and using phone, e-mail, or Internet conferencing instead of traveling.

Many firms have adopted *sales force automation systems*: computerized, digitized sales force operations that let salespeople work more effectively anytime, anywhere. Companies now routinely equip their salespeople with technologies such as laptops or tablets, smartphones, wireless connections, videoconferencing technologies, and customer-contact and relationship management software. Armed with these technologies, salespeople can more effectively and efficiently profile customers and prospects, analyze and forecast sales, schedule sales calls, make presentations, prepare sales and expense reports, and manage account relationships. The result is better time management, improved customer service, lower sales costs, and higher sales performance. ▶ In all, technology has reshaped the ways in which salespeople carry out their duties and engage customers.

▲ **Sales force automation: Technology has reshaped the ways in which salespeople carry out their duties and engage customers.**
Courtesy of Cisco

Selling and the Internet

Perhaps the fastest-growing sales technology tool is the Internet. The Internet offers explosive potential for conducting sales operations and interacting with and serving customers. Some analysts even predict that the Internet will mean the death of person-to-person selling, as salespeople are ultimately replaced by Web sites, online social networking, mobile apps, and other tools that allow direct customer contact. "Don't believe it," says one sales expert (see Marketing at Work 13.1). Sales organizations are now both enhancing their effectiveness and saving time and money by using a host of innovative Internet approaches to train sales reps, hold sales meetings, service accounts, and conduct sales meetings with customers:[16]

With the Internet as a new business platform, all stakeholders—prospects, customers, salespeople, and marketers—can now connect, learn, plan, analyze, engage, collaborate, and conduct business together in ways that were not even imaginable a few years ago. The Internet supports

MARKETING AT WORK | 13.1

B-to-B Salespeople: Who Needs Them Anymore?

It's hard to imagine a world without salespeople. But according to some analysts, there will be a lot fewer of them a decade from now. With the explosion of the Internet, mobile devices, and other technologies that link customers directly with companies, they reason, who needs face-to-face selling anymore? According to the doubters, salespeople are rapidly being replaced by Web sites, e-mail, blogs, mobile apps, video sharing, virtual trade shows, social networks like Facebook and LinkedIn, and a host of other new-age interaction tools.

Research firm Gartner predicts that by 2020, 85 percent of all interactions between businesses will be executed without human intervention, requiring fewer salespeople. Of the 18 million salespeople now employed in the United States, the firm says, there will be only about 4 million left. "The world no longer needs salespeople," one doomsayer boldly proclaims. "Sales is a dying profession and soon will be as outmoded as oil lamps and the rotary phone." Says another, "If we don't find and fill a need faster than a computer, we won't be needed."

So, is business-to-business selling really dying? Will the Internet, mobile technologies, and online networks replace the age-old art of selling face to face? To answer these questions, *SellingPower* magazine called together a panel of five sales experts and asked them to weigh in on the future of B-to-B sales. The panel members agreed that technology is radically transforming the selling profession. Today's revolutionary changes in how people communicate are affecting every aspect of business, and selling is no exception.

But is B-to-B selling dead in this Internet age? Don't believe it, says the *SellingPower* panel. "The assumption that technology, especially the Internet, will replace person-to-person buying and selling is . . . ridiculous" declares one panelist. "Has selling changed? Of course. But when it comes to B-to-B sales, the profession is only going to become more valuable . . . in the future." Other panelists agreed: "The Internet can take orders and disseminate content, but what it can't do is discover customer needs," says one. "It can't build relationships, and it can't prospect on its own." Adds another panelist, "Someone must define the company's value proposition and unique message and communicate it to the market, and that person is the sales rep."

What is dying, however, is what one panelist calls the account-maintenance role—the order taker who stops by the customer's office on Friday and says, "Hey, got anything for me?" Such salespeople are not creating value and can easily be replaced by automation. However, salespeople who excel at new-customer acquisition, relationship management, and account growth with existing customers will always be in high demand.

There's no doubt about it—technology is transforming the profession of selling. Instead of relying on salespeople for basic information and education, customers can now do much of their own pre-purchase research via Web sites, Internet searches, online-community contacts, and other venues. "The conversation with the customer starts online," says a panelist. "Customers often come to the initial meeting already having done their homework about you, your products, and your competitors. They're ready to go deeper. [So] instead of focusing on educating, the salesperson needs to move into the discovery and relationship-building phase, uncovering pain points and focusing on the prospect's business."

Rather than replacing salespeople, however, technology is augmenting them. "We're really not doing anything fundamentally different than what we and our predecessors have been doing for decades," observes a sales executive. Selling has always involved buyers and sellers doing research and social networking. Only now, we're "doing it on steroids" with a wider range of tools and applications.

For example, many companies are moving rapidly into online community-based selling. Case in point: enterprise-software company SAP, which has set up EcoHub, its own online, community-powered marketplace consisting of customers, partners, and almost anyone else who wants to join. The EcoHub community (ecohub.sap.com) has two million users in 200 countries and extends across a broad Internet spectrum—a dedicated Web site, Twitter channels, LinkedIn groups, Facebook fan pages, YouTube

▲ Online selling tools, such as SAP's EcoHub online community-based marketplace, are coming into their own in helping to build customer awareness and generate consideration, purchase interest, and sales. But rather than replacing salespeople, such efforts extend their reach and effectiveness.

channels, Flickr groups, mobile apps, and more. It includes 600 "solution storefronts" where visitors can "easily discover, evaluate, and initiate the purchase of software solutions and services from SAP and its partners." EcoHub also lets users rate the solutions and advice they get from other community members.

SAP was surprised to learn that what it had originally seen as a place for customers to discuss issues, problems, and solutions has turned into a significant point of sale. The information, give-and-take discussions, and conversations at the site draw in customers, even for big-ticket sales. "Some customers are spending $20 to $30 million due to EcoHub," says the SAP vice president who heads up the community.

However, although EcoHub draws in new potential customers and takes them through many of the initial stages of product discovery and evaluation, it doesn't replace SAP's or its partners' salespeople. Instead, it extends their reach and effectiveness. The real value of EcoHub is the flood of sales leads it creates for the SAP and partner sales forces. Once prospective customers have discovered, discussed, and evaluated SAP solutions on EcoHub, SAP invites them to "initiate contact, request a proposal, or start the negotiation process." That's where the person-to-person selling begins.

All this suggests that B-to-B selling isn't dying, it's just changing. "It may take on a different appearance, employ different tools and techniques, and adapt to the changes in the marketplace," concludes one of the *SellingPower* panelists, "but I don't think you can ever replace the value of a strong sales team, particularly in a B-to-B environment." Salespeople who can discover customer needs, solve customer problems, and build relationships will be needed and successful, regardless of what else changes. Especially for those big-ticket B-to-B sales, "all the new technology may make it easier to sell by building strong ties to customers even before the first sit-down, but when the signature hits the dotted line, there will be a sales rep there."

Sources: Quotes and other information from Robert McGarvey, "All About Us," *SellingPower,* March 7, 2011, p. 48; Lain Chroust Ehmann, "Sales Up!" *SellingPower,* January/February, 2011, p. 40; James Ledbetter, "Death of a Salesman. Of Lots of Them, Actually," *Slate,* September 21, 2010, www .slate.com/id/2268122/; Sean Callahan, "Is B-to-B Marketing Really Obsolete," *BtoB,* January 17, 2011, p. 1; Gerhared Gschwandtner, "How Many Salespeople Will Be Left by 2020?" *SellingPower,* May/June 2011, p. 7; and "Getting Started with SAP EcoHub," http://ecohub.sap.com/getting-started, accessed November 2011.

customer-focused methodologies and productivity-enhancing technologies that transform selling from an art to an interactive science. It has forever changed the process by which people buy and companies sell. Will all this new sales technology reduce the role of face-to-face selling? The good news is that the Internet will not make salespeople obsolete. It will make them a lot more productive and effective.

Internet-based technologies can produce big organizational benefits for sales forces. They help conserve salespeople's valuable time, save travel dollars, and give salespeople a new vehicle for selling and servicing accounts. Over the past decade, customer buying patterns have changed. In today's digital world, customers often know almost as much about a company's products as their salespeople do. This gives customers more control over the sales process than they had in the days when brochures and pricing were only available from a sales rep. New sales force technologies recognize and take advantage of these buying process changes, creating new avenues for connecting with customers in the Internet age.

For example, sales organizations now generate lists of prospective customers from online databases and networking sites, such as Hoovers and LinkedIn. They create dialogs when prospective customers visit their Web sites through live chats with the sales team. They use Web conferencing tools such as WebEx, GoToMeeting, or TelePresence to talk live with customers about products and services. Other digital tools allow salespeople to monitor Internet interactions between customers about how they would like to buy, how they feel about a vendor, and what it would take to make a sale.

Today's sales forces are also ramping up their use of social networking media, from proprietary online customer communities to webinars and even Twitter, Facebook, and YouTube applications. A recent survey of business-to-business marketers found that, although they have recently cut back on traditional media and event spending, 68 percent are investing more in social media. ▶ Consider Makino, a leading manufacturer of metal cutting and machining technology:[17]

▲ **Selling on the Internet: Machinery manufacturer Makino makes extensive use of online social networking—everything from proprietary online communities and webinars to Twitter, Facebook, and YouTube.**

Courtesy of Makino, Inc.

Makino complements its sales force efforts through a wide variety of social media initiatives that inform customers and enhance customer relationships. For example, it hosts an ongoing series of industry-specific webinars that position the company as an industry thought leader. Makino produces about three webinars each month and has archived more than 100 on topics ranging from how to get the most out of your machine tools to how metal-cutting processes are done. Webinar content is tailored to specific industries, such as aerospace or medical, and is promoted through carefully targeted banner ads and e-mail invitations. The webinars help to build Makino's customer database, generate leads, build customer relationships, and prepare the way for salespeople by serving up relevant information and educating customers online. Makino even uses Twitter, Facebook, and YouTube to inform customers and prospects about the latest Makino innovations and events and dramatically demonstrate the company's machines in action. "We've shifted dramatically into the electronic marketing area," says Makino's marketing manager. "It speeds up the sales cycle and makes it more efficient—for both the company and the customer. The results have been 'outstanding.'"

Ultimately, digital technologies are "delivering instant information that builds relationships and enables sales to be more efficient and cost-effective and more productive," says one sales technology analyst. "Think of it as . . . doing what the best reps always did but doing it better, faster, and cheaper," says another.[18]

However, the technologies also have some drawbacks. For starters, they're not cheap. In addition, such systems can intimidate low-tech salespeople or clients. Even more, there are some things you just can't present or teach via the Internet—things that require personal interactions. For these reasons, some high-tech experts recommend that sales executives use Internet technologies to supplement training, sales meetings, and preliminary client sales presentations but resort to old-fashioned, face-to-face meetings when the time draws near to close the deal.

Motivating Salespeople

Beyond directing salespeople, sales managers must also motivate them. Some salespeople will do their best without any special urging from management. To them, selling may be the most fascinating job in the world. But selling can also be frustrating. Salespeople often work alone, and they must sometimes travel away from home. They may also face aggressive competing salespeople and difficult customers. Therefore, salespeople often need special encouragement to do their best.

Management can boost sales force morale and performance through its organizational climate, sales quotas, and positive incentives. *Organizational climate* describes the feeling that salespeople have about their opportunities, value, and rewards for a good performance. Some companies treat salespeople as if they are not very important, so performance suffers accordingly. Other companies treat their salespeople as valued contributors and allow virtually unlimited opportunity for income and promotion. Not surprisingly, these companies enjoy higher sales force performance and less turnover.

Many companies motivate their salespeople by setting **sales quotas**—standards stating the amount they should sell and how sales should be divided among the company's products. Compensation is often related to how well salespeople meet their quotas. Companies also use various *positive incentives* to increase the sales force effort. *Sales meetings* provide social occasions, breaks from the routine, chances to meet and talk with "company brass," and opportunities to air feelings and identify with a larger group. Companies also sponsor *sales contests* to spur the sales force to make a selling effort above and beyond what is normally expected. Other incentives include honors, merchandise and cash awards, trips, and profit-sharing plans.

Sales quota
A standard that states the amount a salesperson should sell and how sales should be divided among the company's products.

Evaluating Salespeople and Sales Force Performance

We have thus far described how management communicates what salespeople should be doing and how it motivates them to do it. This process requires good feedback, which means getting regular information about salespeople to evaluate their performance.

Management gets information about its salespeople in several ways. The most important source is *sales reports*, including weekly or monthly work plans and longer-term territory marketing plans. Salespeople also write up their completed activities on *call reports* and turn in *expense reports* for which they are partly or wholly reimbursed. The company can also monitor the sales and profit performance data in the salesperson's territory. Additional information comes from personal observation, customer surveys, and talks with other salespeople.

Using various sales force reports and other information, sales management evaluates the members of the sales force. It evaluates salespeople on their ability to "plan their work and work their plan." Formal evaluation forces management to develop and communicate clear standards for judging performance. It also provides salespeople with constructive feedback and motivates them to perform well.

On a broader level, management should evaluate the performance of the sales force as a whole. Is the sales force accomplishing its customer relationship, sales, and profit objectives? Is it working well with other areas of the marketing and company organization? Are sales force costs in line with outcomes? As with other marketing activities, the company wants to measure its *return on sales investment*.

SPEED BUMP	LINKING THE CONCEPTS

Take a break and reexamine your thoughts about salespeople and sales management.

- Again, when someone says "salesperson," what image comes to mind? Have your perceptions of salespeople changed after what you've read in the chapter so far? How? Be specific.
- Find someone employed in professional sales and ask about how this salesperson's company designs its sales force and recruits, selects, trains, compensates, supervises, and evaluates its salespeople. Report your findings. Would you like to work as a salesperson for this company?

Author Comment ▶
So far, we've examined how sales management develops and implements overall sales force strategies and programs. In this section, we'll look at how individual salespeople and sales teams sell to customers and build relationships with them.

The Personal Selling Process

We now turn from designing and managing a sales force to the personal selling process. The **selling process** consists of several steps that salespeople must master. These steps focus on the goal of getting new customers and obtaining orders from them. However, most salespeople spend much of their time maintaining existing accounts and building long-term customer *relationships*. We will discuss the relationship aspect of the personal selling process in a later section.

Steps in the Selling Process

As shown in ▶ **Figure 13.3**, the selling process consists of seven steps: prospecting and qualifying, preapproach, approach, presentation and demonstration, handling objections, closing, and follow-up.

Prospecting and Qualifying

The first step in the selling process is **prospecting**—identifying qualified potential customers. Approaching the right customers is crucial selling success. Salespeople don't want

Selling process
The steps that salespeople follow when selling, which include prospecting and qualifying, preapproach, approach, presentation and demonstration, handling objections, closing, and follow-up.

Figure 13.3 Steps in the Selling Process

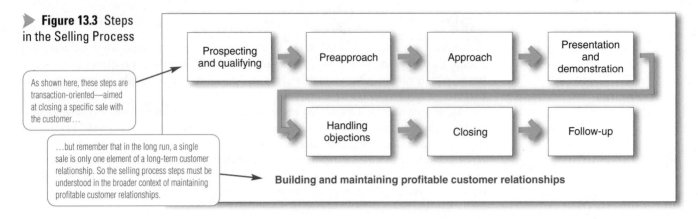

As shown here, these steps are transaction-oriented—aimed at closing a specific sale with the customer...

...but remember that in the long run, a single sale is only one element of a long-term customer relationship. So the selling process steps must be understood in the broader context of maintaining profitable customer relationships.

Building and maintaining profitable customer relationships

Prospecting

Prospecting
The sales step in which a salesperson or company identifies qualified potential customers.

to call on just any potential customers. They want to call on those who are most likely to appreciate and respond to the company's value proposition—those the company can serve well and profitably.

A salesperson must often approach many prospects to get only a few sales. Although the company supplies some leads, salespeople need skill in finding their own. The best source is referrals. Salespeople can ask current customers for referrals and cultivate other referral sources, such as suppliers, dealers, noncompeting salespeople, and Web or other social network contacts. They can also search for prospects in directories or on the Internet and track down leads using the telephone and e-mail. Or, as a last resort, they can drop in unannounced on various offices (a practice known as *cold calling*).

Salespeople also need to know how to *qualify* leads—that is, how to identify the good ones and screen out the poor ones. Prospects can be qualified by looking at their financial ability, volume of business, special needs, location, and possibilities for growth.

Preapproach

Preapproach
The sales step in which a salesperson learns as much as possible about a prospective customer before making a sales call.

Before calling on a prospect, the salesperson should learn as much as possible about the organization (what it needs, who is involved in the buying) and its buyers (their characteristics and buying styles). This step is known as **preapproach**. A successful sale begins long before the salesperson sets foot into a prospect's office. Preapproach begins with good research and preparation. The salesperson can consult standard industry and online sources, acquaintances, and others to learn about the company. Then the salesperson must apply the research gathered to develop a customer strategy.

The salesperson should set *call objectives*, which may be to qualify the prospect, gather information, or make an immediate sale. Another task is to determine the best approach, which might be a personal visit, a phone call, a letter, or an e-mail. The ideal timing should be considered carefully because many prospects are busiest at certain times of the day or week. Finally, the salesperson should give thought to an overall sales strategy for the account.

Approach

Approach
The sales step in which a salesperson meets the customer for the first time.

During the **approach** step, the salesperson should know how to meet and greet the buyer and get the relationship off to a good start. This step involves the salesperson's appearance, opening lines, and follow-up remarks. The opening lines should be positive to build goodwill from the outset. This opening might be followed by some key questions to learn more about the customer's needs or by showing a display or sample to attract the buyer's attention and curiosity. As in all stages of the selling process, listening to the customer is crucial.

Presentation and Demonstration

During the **presentation** step of the selling process, the salesperson tells the "value story" to the buyer, showing how the company's offer solves the customer's problems. The *customer-solution approach* fits better with today's relationship marketing focus than does a hard sell or glad-handing approach. "Stop selling and start helping," advises one sales consultant. "Your goal should be to sell your customers exactly what will benefit them most," says another.[19] Buyers today want answers, not smiles; results, not razzle-dazzle. Moreover, they don't want just products. More than ever in today's economic climate, buyers want to know how those products will add value to their businesses. They want salespeople who listen to their concerns, understand their needs, and respond with the right products and services.

But before salespeople can *present* customer solutions, they must *develop* solutions to present. The solutions approach calls for good listening and problem-solving skills. The qualities that buyers *dislike most* in salespeople include being pushy, late, deceitful, unprepared, disorganized, or overly talkative. The qualities they *value most* include good listening, empathy, honesty, dependability, thoroughness, and follow-through. Great salespeople know how to sell, but more importantly they know how to listen and build strong customer relationships. According to an old sales adage, "You have two ears and one mouth. Use them proportionally." ▶ A classic ad from office products maker Boise Cascade makes the listening point. It shows a Boise salesperson with huge ears drawn on. "With Boise, you'll notice a difference right away, especially with our sales force," says the ad. "At Boise . . . our account representatives have the unique ability to listen to your needs."

Finally, salespeople must also plan their presentation methods. Good interpersonal communication skills count when it comes to making effective sales presentations. However, today's media-rich and cluttered communications environment presents many new challenges for sales presenters. Today's information-overloaded customers demand richer presentation experiences. For their part, presenters now face multiple distractions during presentations from cell phones, text messages, and mobile Internet devices. As a result, salespeople must deliver their messages in more engaging and compelling ways.

Thus, today's salespeople are employing advanced presentation technologies that allow for full multimedia presentations to only one or a few people. The venerable old flip chart has been replaced with sophisticated presentation software, online presentation technologies, interactive whiteboards, tablet computers, and digital projectors.

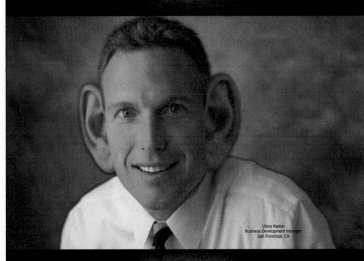

With Boise, you'll notice a difference right away.

Vince Keelan
Business Development Manager
San Francisco, CA

Especially with our sales force.

Boise Cascade Office Products At Boise Cascade Office Products, our account representatives have the unique ability to listen to your
www.bcop.com   needs beyond the obvious office supplies and furniture items. Sure, the product selection and pricing
are outstanding. But the dialogue helps us determine a custom ordering and billing solution to suit your corporate needs. As
long as you're a happy Boise customer, that's music to our ears. Call **888-BOISE-88** — we can't wait to hear from you.

BOISE. IT COULDN'T BE EASIER.™

OFFICE SUPPLIES • TECHNOLOGY PRODUCTS • FURNITURE • BUSINESS SERVICES

▲ **This classic ad from Boise makes the point that good selling starts with listening. "Our account representatives have the unique ability to listen to your needs."**
Courtesy of OfficeMax Incorporated

Handling Objections

Customers almost always have objections during the presentation or when asked to place an order. The objections can be either logical or psychological, and are often unspoken. In **handling objections**, the salesperson should use a positive approach, seek out hidden objections, ask the buyer to clarify any objections, take objections as opportunities to provide more information, and turn the objections into reasons for buying. Every salesperson needs training in the skills of handling objections.

Closing

After handling the prospect's objections, the salesperson next tries to close the sale. However, some salespeople do not get around to **closing** or handle it well. They may lack confidence, feel guilty about asking for the order, or fail to recognize the right moment to close the sale. Salespeople should know how to recognize closing signals from the buyer, including physical actions, comments, and questions. For example, the customer might sit forward and nod approvingly or ask about prices and credit terms.

Salespeople can use any of several closing techniques. They can ask for the order, review points of agreement, offer to help write up the order, ask whether the buyer wants this model or that one, or note that the buyer will lose out if the order is not placed now. The salesperson may offer the buyer special reasons to close, such as a lower price or an extra quantity at no charge.

Follow-Up

Follow-up

The sales step in which a salesperson follows up after the sale to ensure customer satisfaction and repeat business.

The last step in the selling process—**follow-up**—is necessary if the salesperson wants to ensure customer satisfaction and repeat business. Right after closing, the salesperson should complete any details on delivery time, purchase terms, and other matters. The salesperson then should schedule a follow-up call after the buyer receives the initial order to make sure proper installation, instruction, and servicing occur. This visit would reveal any problems, assure the buyer of the salesperson's interest, and reduce any buyer concerns that might have arisen since the sale.

Personal Selling and Managing Customer Relationships

The steps in the just-described selling process are *transaction oriented*—their aim is to help salespeople close a specific sale with a customer. But in most cases, the company is not simply seeking a sale. Rather, it wants to serve the customer over the long haul in a mutually profitable *relationship*. The sales force usually plays an important role in customer relationship building. Thus, as shown in Figure 13.3, the selling process must be understood in the context of building and maintaining profitable customer relationships.

Successful sales organizations recognize that winning and keeping accounts requires more than making good products and directing the sales force to close lots of sales. If the company wishes only to close sales and capture short-term business, it can do this by simply slashing its prices to meet or beat those of competitors. Instead, most companies want their salespeople to practice *value selling*—demonstrating and delivering superior customer value and capturing a return on that value that is fair for both the customer and the company.

Unfortunately, in the heat of closing sales—especially in a tight economy—salespeople too often take the easy way out by cutting prices rather than selling value. Sales management's challenge is to transform salespeople from customer advocates for price cuts into company advocates for value. Here's how Rockwell Automation sells value and relationships rather than price:[20]

Facing pressure from Walmart to lower its prices, a condiment producer hastily summoned several competing supplier representatives—including Rockwell Automation sales rep Jeff Policicchio—who were given full access to the plant for one day and asked to find ways to dramatically reduce the customer's operating costs. Policicchio quickly learned that a major problem stemmed from lost production and down time due to poorly performing pumps on 32 huge condiment tanks. Policicchio gathered relevant cost and usage data and then used a Rockwell Automation laptop value-assessment tool to construct the best pump solution for the customer.

The next day, Policicchio and the competing reps presented their solutions to plant management. Policicchio's value proposition: "With this Rockwell Automation pump solution, through less downtime, reduced administrative costs in procurement, and lower spending on repair parts, your company will save at least $16,268 per pump—on up to 32 pumps—relative to our best competitor's solution." It turns out the Policicchio was the only rep to demonstrate tangible cost savings for his proposed solution. Everyone else made fuzzy promises about possible benefits or offered to save the customer money by simply shaving their prices.

The plant managers were so impressed with Policicchio's value proposition that—despite its higher initial price—they immediately purchased one Rockwell Automation pump solution for a trial. When the actual savings were even better than predicted, they placed orders for the remaining pumps. Thus, Policicchio's value-selling approach rather than price-cutting approach not only landed the initial sale but also provided the basis for a profitable long-term relationship with the customer.

Sales promotion
Short-term incentives to encourage the purchase or sales of a product or a service.

Value selling requires listening to customers, understanding their needs, and carefully coordinating the whole company's efforts to create lasting relationships based on customer value.

Author Comment ▶
Sales promotion is the most short-term of the promotion mix tools. Whereas advertising or personal selling says "buy," sales promotions say "buy now."

Sales Promotion

Personal selling and advertising often work closely with another promotion tool, sales promotion. **Sales promotion** consists of short-term incentives to encourage the purchase or sales of a product or service. Whereas advertising offers reasons to buy a product or service, sales promotion offers reasons to buy *now*.

Examples of sales promotions are found everywhere. A freestanding insert in the Sunday newspaper contains a coupon offering $1 off PEDIGREE GoodBites treats for your dog. ▶A Bed Bath & Beyond ad in your favorite magazine offers 20 percent off on any single item. The end-of-the-aisle display in the local supermarket tempts impulse buyers with a wall of Coca-Cola cases—four 12-packs for $12. Buy a new HP laptop and get a free memory upgrade. A hardware store chain receives a 10 percent discount on selected Stihl power lawn and garden tools if it agrees to advertise them in local newspapers. Sales promotion includes a wide variety of promotion tools designed to stimulate earlier or stronger market response.

▲ Sales promotions are found everywhere. For example, your favorite magazine is loaded with offers like this one that promote a strong and immediate response.
Bed Bath & Beyond Inc.

The Rapid Growth of Sales Promotion

Sales promotion tools are used by most organizations, including manufacturers, distributors, retailers, and not-for-profit institutions. They are targeted toward final buyers (*consumer promotions*), retailers and wholesalers (*trade promotions*), business customers (*business promotions*), and members of the sales force (*sales force promotions*). Today, in the average consumer packaged-goods company, sales promotion accounts for 77 percent of all marketing expenditures.[21]

Several factors have contributed to the rapid growth of sales promotion, particularly in consumer markets. First, inside the company, product managers face greater pressures to increase current sales, and they view promotion as an effective short-run sales tool. Second, externally, the company faces more competition, and competing brands are less differentiated. Increasingly, competitors are using sales promotion to help differentiate their offers. Third, advertising efficiency has declined because of rising costs, media clutter, and legal restraints. Finally, consumers have become more deal oriented. In the current economy, consumers are demanding lower prices and better deals. Sales promotions can help attract today's more thrift-oriented consumers.

The growing use of sales promotion has resulted in *promotion clutter*, which is similar to advertising clutter. According to one recent study, for example, in 70 percent of packaged-goods categories last year, 30 percent of all merchandise was sold with some sort of promotional support.[22] A given promotion runs the risk of being lost in a sea of other promotions, weakening its ability to trigger an immediate purchase. Manufacturers are now searching for ways to rise above the clutter, such as offering larger coupon values, creating more dramatic point-of-purchase displays, or delivering promotions through new interactive media—such as the Internet or mobile phones.

In developing a sales promotion program, a company must first set sales promotion objectives and then select the best tools for accomplishing these objectives.

Sales Promotion Objectives

Sales promotion objectives vary widely. Sellers may use *consumer promotions* to urge short-term customer buying or enhance customer brand involvement. Objectives for *trade promotions* include getting retailers to carry new items and more inventory, buy ahead, or promote the company's products and give them more shelf space. *Business promotions* are used to generate business leads, stimulate purchases, reward customers, and motivate salespeople. For the sales force, objectives include getting more sales force support for current or new products or getting salespeople to sign up new accounts.

Sales promotions are usually used together with advertising, personal selling, direct marketing, or other promotion mix tools. Consumer promotions must usually be advertised and can add excitement and pulling power to ads. Trade and sales business promotions support the firm's personal selling process.

▲ **Customer loyalty programs: Kroger keeps its Plus Card holders coming back by linking food purchases to discounts on gasoline prices.**

When the economy tightens and sales lag, it's tempting to offer deep promotional discounts to spur consumer spending. In general, however, rather than creating only short-term sales or temporary brand switching, sales promotions should help to reinforce the product's position and build long-term *customer relationships*. If properly designed, every sales promotion tool has the potential to build both short-term excitement and long-term consumer relationships. Marketers should avoid "quick fix," price-only promotions in favor of promotions that are designed to build brand equity. Examples include the various *frequency marketing programs* and loyalty cards that have mushroomed in popularity in recent years. Most hotels, supermarkets, and airlines offer frequent-guest/buyer/flyer programs that give rewards to regular customers to keep them coming back. All kinds of companies now offer rewards programs. Such promotional programs can build loyalty through added value rather than discounted prices.

For example, Kroger Plus Card holders receive the usual frequent shopper perks—special in-store discounts on selected items, exclusive e-mail offers and coupons, and the ability to create and save their shopping lists online. ▶ But the grocery chain also keeps customers coming back by linking cumulative food purchases to discounts on gasoline prices. Shoppers who use the company's loyalty card when they shop can accrue 10 cents off each gallon of gas for every $100 spent in the store, up to a $1-per-gallon discount when they fill up their tanks. "With gas prices taking a bigger chunk of household budgets, our customers appreciate being able to save where they can," says Kroger.[23]

Major Sales Promotion Tools

Many tools can be used to accomplish sales promotion objectives. Descriptions of the main consumer, trade, and business promotion tools follow.

Consumer Promotions

Consumer promotions include a wide range of tools—from samples, coupons, refunds, premiums, and point-of-purchase displays to contests, sweepstakes, and event sponsorships.

Samples are offers of a trial amount of a product. Sampling is the most effective—but most expensive—way to introduce a new product or create new excitement for an existing one. Some samples are free; for others, the company charges a small amount to offset its cost. The sample might be sent by mail, handed out in a store or at a kiosk, attached to another product, or featured in an ad or an e-mail. Samples are sometimes combined into sample packs, which can then be used to promote other products and services. Sampling can be a powerful promotional tool.

Coupons are certificates that save buyers money when they purchase specified products. Most consumers love coupons. U.S. packaged-goods companies distributed more than 332 billion coupons last year with an average face value of $1.46. Consumers redeemed more than 3.3 billion of them for a total savings of about $3.7 billion.[24] Coupons can promote early trial of a new brand or stimulate sales of a mature brand. However, as a result of coupon clutter, redemption rates have been declining in recent years. Thus, most major consumer-goods companies are issuing fewer coupons and targeting them more carefully.

Marketers are also cultivating new outlets for distributing coupons, such as supermarket shelf dispensers, electronic point-of-sale coupon printers, and online and mobile coupon programs. According to a recent study, digital coupons now outpace printed newspaper coupons by 10 to 1. Almost one-third of all U.S. coupon users are digital coupon users who only get coupons online or by phone via sites such as Coupons.com, Groupon, LivingSocial, and Cellfire (see Marketing at Work 13.2).

Cash refunds (or *rebates*) are like coupons except that the price reduction occurs after the purchase rather than at the retail outlet. The customer sends proof of purchase to the manufacturer, which then refunds part of the purchase price by mail. For example, Toro ran a clever preseason promotion on some of its snowblower models, offering a rebate if the snowfall in the buyer's market area turned out to be below average. Competitors were not able to match this offer on such short notice, and the promotion was very successful.

Price packs (also called *cents-off deals*) offer consumers savings off the regular price of a product. The producer marks the reduced prices directly on the label or package. Price packs can be single packages sold at a reduced price (such as two for the price of one) or two related products banded together (such as a toothbrush and toothpaste). Price packs are very effective—even more so than coupons—in stimulating short-term sales.

Premiums are goods offered either free or at low cost as an incentive to buy a product, ranging from toys included with kids' products to phone cards and DVDs. A premium may come inside the package (in-pack), outside the package (on-pack), or through the mail. For example, over the years, McDonald's has offered a variety of premiums in its Happy Meals—from *Kung Fu Panda* characters to *My Little Pony* and *Pokémon* toy figures. Customers can visit www.happymeal.com to play games and watch commercials associated with the current Happy Meal sponsor.[25]

Advertising specialties, also called *promotional products*, are useful articles imprinted with an advertiser's name, logo, or message that are given as gifts to consumers. Typical items include T-shirts and other apparel, pens, coffee mugs, calendars, key rings, mouse pads, matches, tote bags, coolers, golf balls, and caps. U.S. marketers spent nearly $17 billion on advertising specialties last year. Such items can be very effective. The "best of them stick around for months, subtly burning a brand name into a user's brain," notes a promotional products expert.[26]

MARKETING AT WORK | 13.2

Mobile Coupons: Reaching Customers Where They Are—Now

As mobile phones become appendages that many people can't live without, businesses are increasingly eyeing them as prime real estate for marketing messages. Whether it's to build a brand, boost business, or reward loyalty, more merchants are using mobile marketing to tap into the mobile phone's power of immediacy.

"It's cool," said Kristen Palestis at her local Jamba Juice recently after she opted in to receive a 20-percent-off coupon on her mobile phone. "I'm spending less money and it was real easy," she said after she used the coupon to buy a smoothie. Palestis received the coupon within seconds of texting a special five-digit code from her mobile phone.

Retailers' mobile marketing messages can include text messages with numeric "short codes" that customers dial to receive a promotion, bar-coded digital coupons, Web site links, and display advertisements. "We know the most effective way to reach the customer is to be where they are," says a marketer at Jamba Juice, a national chain that sells smoothies and other "better-for-you" beverages and foods. "For our customers this means both on the Internet and on their mobiles."

Jamba Juice and a growing host of other retailers want to get special offers quickly into the hands of the consumers who are most apt to use them. These mobile social users—as they're called—represent 11 percent of online adults in the United States, but their ranks are growing. They're more likely to respond to ads on their mobile phones, buy mobile content and services, and access the mobile Web.

Mobile marketing can be very effective. For example, Fresh Encounter Community Markets, an Ohio grocery chain, uses mobile messages to help customers plan their meals. When Fresh Encounter sends out an urgent same-day offer, as in a chicken promotion, redemptions can exceed 30 percent.

Companies that embrace mobile marketing know they have to be careful not to abuse the access consumers have granted, so permission-based offers are becoming the standard. Trade groups, such as the Mobile Marketing Association in New York, have set guidelines for marketers that are designed to protect the consumer, including opt-in, opt-out, and message-delivery frequency standards.

Coupons by phone offer an alluring opportunity. Worldwide, the number of mobile coupon users is forecast to triple by 2014 to more than 300 million people. In the United States alone last year, 49 million consumers used digital coupons, up 10 percent over the previous year. Of that group, almost one-third used *only* digital coupons, meaning that they didn't clip coupons from newspapers or magazines. Use of digital coupons is so widespread that seven out of ten shoppers have now used coupon Web sites.

Still, mobile coupons aren't for everyone. Some consumers just don't want marketing messages delivered to their phones.

Therefore, many digital coupon marketers include print and e-mail delivery options as well. Challenges aside, companies ranging from Sears and Target to Wendy's, Chick-Fil-A, and Enterprise Rent-A-Car are testing the digital couponing waters. For example, Dunkin' Donuts recently sent out free iced coffee coupons to customers living near several Florida stores who'd already opted-in for promotional text messages. The digital promotion generated buzz and also let Dunkin' Donuts learn more about area customers' demographics and shopping psyche.

Over the past few years, a growing list of online coupon sites—such as Coupons.com, MyCoupster, Groupon, Living-Social, and Cellfire—have sprung up. These sites allow consumers to find coupons online and download them to mobile devices, print them out at home, or transfer them to store loyalty cards for later redemption at stores.

▲ As mobile phones become appendages that many people can't live without, companies ranging from Target and Sears to Chick-fil-A and Enterprise Rent-A-Car are testing the mobile couponing waters.

m42/ZUMA Press/Newscom

Mobile coupons offer distinct advantages to both consumers and marketers. Consumers don't have to find and clip paper coupons or print out Web coupons and bring them along when they shop. They always have their cell phone coupons with them. To use the coupons, users simply call up stored digital coupons on their phones and present them at a retail location for scanning. For marketers, mobile coupons allow more careful targeting and eliminate the costs of printing and distributing paper coupons. The redemption rates can be dazzling—as high as 20 percent—whereas the industry average paper coupon response is less than 1 percent.

Thus, when properly used, mobile coupons can both cost less and be more immediate and effective. When it comes to digital couponing, marketers are increasingly echoing the sentiments of Jamba Juice customer Kristen Palestis. "It's cool."

Sources: Portions adapted from Arlene Satchel, "More Merchants Embrace Mobile Coupons," *McClatchy-Tribune News Service,* February 10, 2010; with information from Erik Sass, "Is Digital Coupons' Rise Print Inserts' Demise?" *MediaDailyNews,* February 17, 2010, accessed at http://tinyurl.com/25vh966; and "Digital Coupons Overtaking Print Coupons," *Business-Wire,* February 8, 2011, www.businesswire.com/news/home/20110208007022/en/Digital-Coupons-Represent-Fastest-Growing-Coupon-Segment.

Point-of-purchase (POP) promotions include displays and demonstrations that take place at the point of sale. Think of your last visit to the local Safeway, Costco, CVS, or Bed Bath & Beyond. Chances are good that you were tripping over aisle displays, promotional signs, "shelf talkers," or demonstrators offering free tastes of featured food products. Unfortunately, many retailers do not like to handle the hundreds of displays, signs, and posters they receive from manufacturers each year. Manufacturers have therefore responded by offering better POP materials, offering to set them up, and tying them in with television, print, or online messages.

Contests, _sweepstakes_, and _games_ give consumers the chance to win something, such as cash, trips, or goods, by luck or through extra effort. A *contest* calls for consumers to submit an entry—a jingle, guess, suggestion—to be judged by a panel that will select the best entries. A *sweepstakes* calls for consumers to submit their names for a drawing. A *game* presents consumers with something—bingo numbers, missing letters—every time they buy, which may or may not help them win a prize.

All kinds of companies use sweepstakes and contests to create brand attention and boost consumer involvement. For example, Outback's Kick Back with the Guys Sweepstakes offers chances to win a dinner for four of "crave-able appetizers and juicy steaks." The O'Reilly Auto Parts Win Free Gas for a Year Giveaway promises to let you "forget about gas prices for a year." Enter the Coleman Great American Family Vacation Sweepstakes and you could win a family trip to Yellowstone and a Coleman camping package. ▶ And next Father's Day, submit the winning entry in the Sears "Dads Making a Difference Contest," showing "how your dad

▲ Companies use sweepstakes and contests to create brand attention and boost consumer involvement. Enter this year's "Dads Making a Difference Contest" and you could win your dad up to $30,000 in support of a community project.

is using his tools and talents for the greater good of the community," and you could win him up to $30,000 in project support.

Finally, marketers can promote their brands through **event marketing** (or **event sponsorships**). They can create their own brand-marketing events or serve as sole or participating sponsors of events created by others. The events might include anything from mobile brand tours to festivals, reunions, marathons, concerts, or other sponsored gatherings. Event marketing is huge, and it may be the fastest-growing area of promotion.

Event marketing (or event sponsorships)
Creating a brand-marketing event or serving as a sole or participating sponsor of events created by others.

Effective event marketing links events and sponsorships to a brand's value proposition. For example, to help build awareness of its new LEAF electric vehicle, Nissan signed on to a two-year sponsorship as the official vehicle of the Amgen Tour of California, an 800-mile, eight-day cycling road race. Last year, Nissan supplied 40 LEAFs to serve as lead, support, medical, and VIP vehicles for the event. The Amgen event links well with the brand's positioning; sponsoring an event for people living healthy lifestyles is a no-brainer for a car that promises "100% electric. zero gas. zero tailpipe." According to a senior Nissan marketer, "This event offers a unique opportunity to not only participate in America's largest cycling event but to also reaffirm the company's commitment to supporting healthy lifestyles." In addition to such sponsorships, Nissan fields its own national event, the Nissan LEAF Drive Electric Tour. The tour takes the LEAF to the streets in major U.S. cities, giving prospective buyers an opportunity to learn about the innovative car, kick the tires, and sign up for test drives.[27]

Trade Promotions

Manufacturers direct more sales promotion dollars toward retailers and wholesalers (81 percent) than to final consumers (16 percent).[28] **Trade promotions** can persuade resellers to carry a brand, give it shelf space, promote it in advertising, and push it to consumers. Shelf space is so scarce these days that manufacturers often have to offer price-offs, allowances, buy-back guarantees, or free goods to retailers and wholesalers to get products on the shelf and, once there, to keep them on it.

Trade promotions
Sales promotion tools used to persuade resellers to carry a brand, give it shelf space, promote it in advertising, and push it to consumers.

Manufacturers use several trade promotion tools. Many of the tools used for consumer promotions—contests, premiums, displays—can also be used as trade promotions. Or the manufacturer may offer a straight *discount* off the list price on each case purchased during a stated period of time (also called a *price-off*, *off-invoice*, or *off-list*). Manufacturers also may offer an *allowance* (usually so much off per case) in return for the retailer's agreement to feature the manufacturer's products in some way. For example, an advertising allowance compensates retailers for advertising the product, whereas a display allowance compensates them for using special displays.

Manufacturers may offer *free goods*, which are extra cases of merchandise, to resellers who buy a certain quantity or who feature a certain flavor or size. They may also offer *push money*—cash or gifts to dealers or their sales forces to "push" the manufacturer's goods. Manufacturers may give retailers free *specialty advertising items* that carry the company's name, such as pens, calendars, memo pads, flashlights, and tote bags.

Business Promotions

Companies spend billions of dollars each year on promotion geared toward industrial customers. **Business promotions** are used to generate business leads, stimulate purchases, reward customers, and motivate salespeople. Business promotions include many of the same tools used for consumer or trade promotions. Here, we focus on two additional major business promotion tools: conventions and trade shows and sales contests.

Business promotions
Sales promotion tools used to generate business leads, stimulate purchases, reward customers, and motivate salespeople.

Many companies and trade associations organize *conventions and trade shows* to promote their products. Firms selling to the industry show their products at the trade show. Vendors at these shows receive many benefits, such as opportunities to find

▲ **Some trade shows are huge. At this year's International Consumer Electronics Show 2,700 exhibitors attracted more than 150,000 professional visitors.**
Consumer Electronics Association (CEA)

new sales leads, contact customers, introduce new products, meet new customers, sell more to present customers, and educate customers with publications and audiovisual materials. Trade shows also help companies reach many prospects that are not reached through their sales forces.

Some trade shows are huge. ▶ For example, at this year's International Consumer Electronics Show, 2,700 exhibitors attracted some 150,000 professional visitors. Even more impressive, at the BAUMA mining and construction equipment trade show in Munich, Germany, more than 3,200 exhibitors from 53 countries presented their latest product innovations to more than 420,000 attendees from more than 200 countries. Total exhibition space equaled about 5.9 million square feet (more than 124 football fields).[29]

A *sales contest* is a contest for salespeople or dealers to motivate them to increase their sales performance over a given period. Sales contests motivate and recognize good company performers, who may receive trips, cash prizes, or other gifts. Some companies award points for performance, which the receiver can turn in for any of a variety of prizes. Sales contests work best when they are tied to measurable and achievable sales objectives (such as finding new accounts, reviving old accounts, or increasing account profitability).

Developing the Sales Promotion Program

Beyond selecting the types of promotions to use, marketers must make several other decisions in designing the full sales promotion program. First, they must determine the *size of the incentive*. A certain minimum incentive is necessary if the promotion is to succeed; a larger incentive will produce more sales response. The marketer also must set *conditions for participation*. Incentives might be offered to everyone or only to select groups.

Marketers must determine how to *promote and distribute the promotion* program itself. For example, a $2-off coupon could be given out in a package, at the store, via the Internet, or in an advertisement. Each distribution method involves a different level of reach and cost. Increasingly, marketers are blending several media into a total campaign concept. The *length of the promotion* is also important. If the sales promotion period is too short, many prospects (who may not be buying during that time) will miss it. If the promotion runs too long, the deal will lose some of its "act now" force.

Evaluation is also very important. Marketers should work to measure the returns on their sales promotion investments, just as they should seek to assess the returns on other marketing activities. The most common evaluation method is to compare sales before, during, and after a promotion. Marketers should ask: Did the promotion attract new customers or more purchasing from current customers? Can we hold onto these new customers and purchases? Will the long-run customer relationship and sales gains from the promotion justify its costs?

Clearly, sales promotion plays an important role in the total promotion mix. To use it well, the marketer must define the sales promotion objectives, select the best tools, design the sales promotion program, implement the program, and evaluate the results. Moreover, sales promotion must be coordinated carefully with other promotion mix elements within the overall IMC program.

REST STOP | REVIEWING THE CONCEPTS

MyMarketingLab

Now that you have completed the chapter, return to www.mymktlab.com to experience and apply the concepts and to explore the additional study materials for this chapter.

CHAPTER REVIEW AND KEY TERMS

Objectives Review

This chapter is the second of three chapters covering the final marketing mix element—promotion. The previous chapter dealt with overall integrated marketing communications and with advertising and public relations. This one investigates personal selling and sales promotion. Personal selling is the interpersonal arm of the communications mix. Sales promotion consists of short-term incentives to encourage the purchase or sale of a product or service.

▶ **OBJECTIVE 1   Discuss the role of a company's salespeople in creating value for customers and building customer relationships.** (pp 392–394)

Most companies use salespeople, and many companies assign them an important role in the marketing mix. For companies selling business products, the firm's sales force works directly with customers. Often, the sales force is the customer's only direct contact with the company and therefore may be viewed by customers as representing the company itself. In contrast, for consumer-product companies that sell through intermediaries, consumers usually do not meet salespeople or even know about them. The sales force works behind the scenes, dealing with wholesalers and retailers to obtain their support and helping them become more effective in selling the firm's products.

As an element of the promotion mix, the sales force is very effective in achieving certain marketing objectives and carrying out such activities as prospecting, communicating, selling and servicing, and information gathering. But with companies becoming more market oriented, a customer-focused sales force also works to produce both customer satisfaction and company profit. The sales force plays a key role in developing and managing profitable customer relationships.

▶ **OBJECTIVE 2   Identify and explain the six major sales force management steps.** (pp 395–405)

High sales force costs necessitate an effective sales management process consisting of six steps: designing sales force strategy and structure, recruiting and selecting, training, compensating, supervising, and evaluating salespeople and sales force performance.

In designing a sales force, sales management must address various issues, including what type of sales force structure will work best (territorial, product, customer, or complex structure), sales force size, who will be involved in selling, and how various sales and sales-support people will work together (inside or outside sales forces and team selling).

Salespeople must be recruited and selected carefully. In recruiting salespeople, a company may look to the job duties and the characteristics of its most successful salespeople to suggest the traits it wants in new salespeople. It must then look for applicants through recommendations of current salespeople, ads, and the Internet and other social networks, as well as college recruitment/placement centers. In the selection process, the procedure may vary from a single informal interview to lengthy testing and interviewing. After the selection process is complete, training programs familiarize new salespeople not only with the art of selling but also with the company's history, its products and policies, and the characteristics of its customers and competitors.

The sales force compensation system helps to reward, motivate, and direct salespeople. In addition to compensation, all salespeople need supervision, and many need continuous encouragement because they must make many decisions and face many frustrations. Periodically, the company must evaluate their performance to help them do a better job. In evaluating salespeople, the company relies on information gathered from sales reports, personal observations, customer surveys, and conversations with other salespeople.

▶ **OBJECTIVE 3   Discuss the personal selling process, distinguishing between transaction-oriented marketing and relationship marketing.** (pp 405–409)

Selling involves a seven-step process: prospecting and qualifying, preapproach, approach, presentation and demonstration, handling objections, closing, and follow-up. These steps help marketers close a specific sale and, as such, are transaction oriented. However, a seller's dealings with customers should be guided by the larger concept of relationship marketing. The company's sales force should help to orchestrate a whole-company effort to develop profitable long-term relationships with key customers based on superior customer value and satisfaction.

> **OBJECTIVE 4   Explain how sales promotion campaigns are developed and implemented.** (pp 409–415)

Sales promotion campaigns call for setting sales promotions objectives (in general, sales promotions should be *consumer relationship building*); selecting tools; and developing and implementing the sales promotion program by using *consumer promotion tools* (from coupons, refunds, premiums, and point-of-purchase promotions to contests, sweepstakes, and events), *trade promotion tools* (from discounts and allowances to free goods and push money), and *business promotion tools* (conventions, trade shows, and sales contests), as well as determining such things as the size of the incentive, the conditions for participation, how to promote and distribute the promotion package, and the length of the promotion. After this process is completed, the company must evaluate its sales promotion results.

Key Terms

Objective 1
Personal selling (p 393)
Salesperson (p 393)

Objective 2
Sales force management (p 395)
Territorial sales force structure (p 395)
Product sales force structure (p 395)
Customer (or market) sales force structure (p 395)
Outside sales force (or field sales force) (p 396)

Inside sales force (p 396)
Team selling (p 397)
Sales quota (p 404)

Objective 3
Selling process (p 405)
Prospecting (p 405)
Preapproach (p 406)
Approach (p 406)
Presentation (p 407)
Handling objections (p 407)

Closing (p 407)
Follow-up (p 408)

Objective 4
Sales promotion (p 409)
Consumer promotions (p 411)
Event marketing (or event sponsorships) (p 414)
Trade promotions (p 414)
Business promotions (p 414)

DISCUSSION AND CRITICAL THINKING

Discussion Questions

1. Discuss how the salesperson is a critical link between the company and the customer. (AACSB: Communication; Reflective Thinking)
2. Compare and contrast the three sales force structures outlined in the chapter. Which structure is most effective? (AACSB: Communication; Reflective Thinking)
3. Discuss the activities involved in sales force management. (AACSB: Communication)

4. Define *sales promotion* and discuss its objectives. (AACSB: Communication)
5. Name and describe the types of consumer promotions. (AACSB: Communication; Reflective Thinking)
6. Discuss the different types of trade sales promotions and distinguish these types of promotions from business promotions. (AACSB: Communication)

Critical Thinking Exercises

1. Interview a salesperson. Is this salesperson an *order taker* or an *order getter*? How much training did he or she receive to perform the sales job? Write a report of what you learned. (AACSB: Communication; Reflective Thinking)
2. Select a product or service and role-play a sales call—from the approach to the close—with another student. Have one member of the team act as the salesperson with the other member acting as the customer, raising at least three objections. Select another product or service and perform this

exercise again with your roles reversed. (AACSB: Communication; Reflective Thinking)
3. Suppose your company is planning the launch of a new brand of energy drink sold in supermarkets. You are the marketing coordinator responsible for recommending the sales promotion plan for this product. What promotional tools would you consider for this task and what decisions must be made? (AACSB: Communications; Reflective Thinking)

MINICASES AND APPLICATIONS

Marketing Technology   Another Day, Another Deal

The humble coupon has gotten a boost from social media. Groupon, the group deal-of-the-day coupon service that started in late 2008 and is exceeding even Google's and Facebook's phenomenal early growth rates, now offers about 1,000 deals every day to more than 70 million subscribers in almost 50 countries. The business model is simple. A business sets up a deal through Groupon, such as offering $50 worth of merchandise for $25, but the deal is only honored if enough people sign up for it. Groupon typically takes a 50 percent cut of all the revenue generated on the deal (that is, $12.50 of the $25 the consumer pays for the Groupon). In return, the business gets a lot of store traffic from the deal. Because the business model is so simple and the entry barriers so small, there are now more than 600 of these digital daily-deal Web sites.

1. Debate the pros and cons of offering coupons through digital deal-of-the-day Web sites such as Groupon from the perspective of the businesses offering the deal. (AACSB: Communication; Use of IT; Reflective Thinking)
2. Create an idea for a local group-buying promotional service based on Groupon's model as a class project or as a fundraiser for a student organization at your school. Students will be the target market of this digital deal Web site. Develop a sales plan to recruit local businesses to offer deals as well as the promotion plan to attract students to the Web site. Present your plans to the class. (AACSB: Communication; Reflective Thinking)

Marketing Ethics   Ethical Selling

Hank is a sales representative for a customer relationship management (CRM) software company and makes several cold calls each day prospecting for customers. He usually starts his call to a technology professional in a company by introducing himself and asking the person if he or she would take a few moments to participate in a survey on technology needs in companies. After a few questions, however, it becomes obvious that Hank is trying to sell software solutions to the potential customer.

1. Is Hank being ethical? Discuss other sales tactics that might be unethical. (AACSB: Communication; Ethical Reasoning; Reflective Thinking)
2. What traits and behaviors characterize an ethical salesperson? What role does the sales manager play in ethical selling behavior? (AACSB: Communication; Ethical Reasoning; Reflective Thinking)

Marketing by the Numbers   Sales Force Calculations

FireSpot, Inc. is a manufacturer of drop-in household fireplaces sold primarily in the eastern United States. The company has its own sales force that does more than just sell products and services—it manages relationships with retail customers to enable them to better meet consumers' needs. FireSpot's sales reps visit customers several times per year—often for hours at a time. Thus, sales managers must ensure that they have enough salespeople to adequately deliver value to customers. Refer to Appendix 3, Marketing by the Numbers, to answer the following questions.

1. Determine the number of salespeople FireSpot needs if it has 1,000 retail customer accounts that need to be called on five times per year. Each sales call lasts approximately

2.5 hours, and each sales rep has approximately 1,250 hours per year to devote to customers. (AACSB: Communication; Analytical Reasoning)
2. FireSpot wants to expand to the Midwest and Western United States and intends to hire ten new sales representatives to secure distribution for its products. Each sales rep earns a salary of $50,000 plus commission. Each retailer generates an average $50,000 in revenue for FireSpot. If FireSpot's contribution margin is 40 percent, what increase in sales will it need to break even on the increase in fixed costs to hire the new sales reps? How many new retail accounts must the company acquire to break even on this tactic? What average number of accounts must each new rep acquire? (AACSB: Communication; Analytical Reasoning)

Video Case   MedTronic

Many companies sell products that most customers can live without. But MedTronic's devices are literally a matter of life and death. Patient well-being depends upon the insulin delivery devices, implantable defibrillators, and cardiac pacemakers designed and manufactured by MedTronic. In some markets, seven out of eight medical devices in use are MedTronic devices.

But what happens when MedTronics has a product that it knows will help a given business or institutional customer in terms of cost, time, and end-user well-being, but it can't get a foot in the door to communicate that information? This video demonstrates how MedTronic sales representatives maintain a customer-centered approach to the personal selling process as a means for effectively communicating their product benefits.

After viewing the video featuring MedTronic, answer the following questions:

1. How is the sales force at MedTronic structured?
2. Can you identify the selling process for MedTronic? Give an example of each step.
3. Is MedTronic effective at building long-term customer relationships through its sales force? How?

Company Cases   12 Ogilvy / 13 HP

See Appendix 1 for cases appropriate for this chapter. **Case 12, Ogilvy: It's Not Creative Unless It Sells.** With an online contest, a veteran agency returns to the roots of advertising—selling.

Case 13, HP: Overhauling a Vast Corporate Sales Force. A new CEO puts a huge industrial corporation back in touch with its corporate customers by overhauling its sales force.

14 Direct and Online Marketing
Building Direct Customer Relationships

CHAPTER ROAD MAP

Objective Outline

▷ **OBJECTIVE 1 Define direct marketing and discuss its benefits to customers and companies.** The New Direct Marketing Model (423); Growth and Benefits of Direct Marketing (423–426); Customer Databases and Direct Marketing (426–427)

▷ **OBJECTIVE 2 Identify and discuss the major forms of direct marketing.** Forms of Direct Marketing (427–432)

▷ **OBJECTIVE 3 Explain how companies have responded to the Internet and other powerful new technologies with online marketing strategies.** Online Marketing (432–436)

▷ **OBJECTIVE 4 Discuss how companies go about conducting online marketing to profitably deliver more value to customers.** Setting Up an Online Marketing Presence (436–443)

▷ **OBJECTIVE 5 Overview the public policy and ethical issues presented by direct marketing.** Public Policy Issues in Direct Marketing (443–446)

Previewing the Concepts

In the previous two chapters, you learned about communicating customer value through integrated marketing communication and about four elements of the marketing communications mix: advertising, publicity, personal selling, and sales promotion. In this chapter, we examine direct marketing and its fastest-growing form, online marketing. Actually, direct marketing can be viewed as more than just a communications tool. In many ways it constitutes an overall marketing approach—a blend of communication and distribution channels all rolled into one. As you read this chapter, remember that although direct marketing is presented as a separate tool, it must be carefully integrated with the other elements of the promotion mix.

Let's start by looking at Facebook, a company that exists only online. The giant online social network promises to become one of the world's most powerful and profitable online marketers. Yet, as a marketing company, Facebook is just getting started.

▲ The burgeoning young Facebook online social network is only now beginning to realize its staggering marketing potential. It "helps you connect and share with the people in your life."

Justin Sullivan/Getty Images

First Stop

Facebook: "We Are One Percent Done with Our Mission"

The world is rapidly going social and online. And no company is more social or more online than Facebook. The huge online social network has a deep and daily impact on the lives of hundreds of millions of members around the world. Yet Facebook is now grappling with a crucial question: How can it profitably tap the marketing potential of its massive community to make money without driving off its legions of loyal users?

Facebook is humongous. In little more than seven years, it has signed up more than 720 million members—one-tenth of the world's population. It recently passed Google to become the most visited site on the Internet. Every 60 seconds, Facebook users send 230,000 messages, update 95,000 statuses, write 80,000 wall posts, tag 65,000 photos, share 50,000 links, and write a half-million comments affirming or disparaging all that activity.

With that many eyeballs glued to one virtual space, Facebook has tremendous impact and influence, not just as a sharing community but also as an Internet gateway. It is the default home page for many users, and some users have it on their screens 24-7. But Facebook's power comes not just from its size and omnipresence. Rather, it lies in the deep social connections between users. Facebook's mission is "Giving people the power to share." It's a place where friends and family meet, share their stories, display their photos, and chronicle their lives. Hordes of people have made Facebook their digital home.

By wielding all of that influence, Facebook has the potential to become one of the world's most powerful and profitable online marketers. Yet the burgeoning social network is only now beginning to realize that potential. Although Facebook's membership exploded from the very start, CEO Mark Zuckerberg and the network's other idealistic young co-founders gave little thought to making money. They actually opposed running ads or other forms of marketing, worried that marketing might damage Facebook's free (and commercial-free) sharing culture. So instead they focused on simply trying to manage the online revolution they'd begun.

In fact, without any help from Facebook, companies themselves were first to discover the network's commercial value. Most brands—small and large—have now built their own Facebook pages, gaining free and relatively easy access to the gigantic community's word-of-Web promise. Today, people "like" a Facebook brand page 50 million times every day. At one extreme, little Café Poca Cosa in Tucson, Arizona, has 166 Facebook fans. At the other extreme, the Los Angeles Dodgers have 682,000 fans. Coca-Cola has 21.6 million.

As the company has matured, however, Zuckerberg has come to realize that Facebook must make its own marketing and moneymaking moves. If Facebook doesn't make money, it can't continue to serve its members. As a first step, Facebook changed its philosophy on advertising. Today, for a fee, companies can place display or video ads on users' home, profile, or photo pages. The ads are carefully targeted based on user profile data. Or brands can pay Facebook to promote "sponsored stories," by which one member's interactions with a brand (check-ins, recommendations, likes) appear in the news feeds on their friends' Facebook pages. For example, if you see an item that says "Harry Gold: Second time today

> Online social network Facebook is grappling with a crucial question: How can it profitably tap into its massive marketing potential to make money without driving off its legions of loyal users?

at Starbucks with Jenny Novak," followed by a Starbucks logo and link, Starbucks paid a fee for the placement. The organic feel of these sponsored stories increases user involvement by making the ad feels like just another part of the Facebook experience.

Advertising is proving to be a real moneymaker for Facebook. The company generated an estimated $4.1 billion in advertising revenues last year, more than double the prior year's total. But advertising revenues are only the tip of the marketing iceberg for Facebook. As a global gathering place where people spend time with friends, Facebook is also a natural for selling entertainment. For example, recognizing that members often exit the Facebook environment to listen to music or watch movies, the company is now moving to provide these services. For instance, Facebook has partnered with music-streaming service Spotify to integrate a Pandora-like listening function into the site. Similarly, Facebook is now entering the movie rental business. With 42 million viewers, Facebook is already the sixth-most popular video site in the United States. Until recently, however, that included only user-generated and music videos. Now, Facebook is partnering with content providers—such as Warner Bros. Entertainment—to make streamed movies available within the Facebook community.

Beyond entertainment, Facebook is also entering the location-based and deal-of-the-day online markets. Its Facebook Places feature takes on Foursquare and other check-in services. Although Foursquare had a two-year head start and became the undisputed market leader with 9.5 million users, Facebook passed it with a flip of the switch. Almost immediately after its 2011 release, Facebook Places was registering more check-ins than Foursquare. Facebook next fired a shot over the bow of deal-of-the-day merchants such as Groupon and LivingSocial by launching Facebook Deals. True to Facebook form, Deals not only lets users buy deals, it also employs its vast referral power in letting users share deals and see what deals friends have grabbed for themselves.

If Facebook can market digital entertainment and coupons, can it do the same with tangible goods? Many companies think so. Procter & Gamble sells Pampers via Facebook, and 1-800 Flowers has made a selection of floral bouquets available there as well. But more telling, JCPenney recently put its entire catalog on Facebook—not just for browsing, but also for buying. The veteran catalog retailer hopes that as users see any of its 250,000 items in their friends' news feeds, referral power will kick in to boost sales. In all, e-commerce offers huge revenue potential: Facebook takes as much as a 30 percent cut for every song, movie download, diaper, or flower bouquet sold.

In line with its goal to keep everything within the community, Facebook has even entered the banking business. That's right, banking. Facebook users can now exchange any of 15 world currencies for Facebook Credits, then use those credits to purchase anything sold within the Facebook universe. Facebook will soon require that all transactions within Facebook use its Facebook Credits currency. With Facebook's massive membership and growing e-commerce presence, it could soon pass PayPal as the online payments leader. Perhaps more impressive, Facebook Credits could become a powerful global currency all by itself.

Will increased marketing on Facebook alienate loyal Facebook fans? Not if it's done right. Research shows that online users readily accept—even welcome—well-targeted online advertising and marketing. Tasteful and appropriately targeted offers can enhance rather than detract from the Facebook user experience. "We've found, frankly, that users are getting more value [because of our marketing efforts]," says a Facebook marketing executive, so that companies are "getting value putting more [marketing] in."

It's too soon to say whether Facebook will eventually challenge the likes of Google in online advertising or Amazon.com in selling all things online. But its immense, closely knit social network gives Facebook staggering potential. As a marketing company, Facebook is just getting started. Carolyn Everson, Facebook's vice president of global sales, sums up Facebook's growth potential this way: "I'm not sure the marketing community understands our story yet. We evolve so quickly. We have a saying here: 'We are one percent done with our mission.'"[1]

MyMarketingLab

Visit www.mymktlab.com to find activities that help you learn and review in order to succeed in this chapter.

Many of the marketing and promotion tools that we've examined in previous chapters were developed in the context of *mass marketing*: targeting broad markets with standardized messages and offers distributed through intermediaries. Today, however, with the trend toward narrower targeting and the surge in digital technologies, many companies are adopting *direct marketing*, either as a primary marketing approach or as a supplement to other approaches. In this section, we explore the exploding world of direct marketing.

Direct marketing
Connecting directly with carefully targeted segments or individual consumers, often on a one-to-one, interactive basis.

Direct marketing consists of connecting directly with carefully targeted consumers, often on a one-to-one, interactive basis. Using detailed databases, companies tailor their marketing offers and communications to the needs of narrowly defined segments or individual buyers.

Beyond brand and relationship building, direct marketers usually seek a direct, immediate, and measurable consumer response. For example, Amazon.com interacts directly with customers via its Web site or mobile app to help them discover and buy almost anything and everything on the Internet. Similarly, GEICO interacts directly with customers—by telephone, through its Web site, or even on its Facebook, Twitter, and YouTube pages, as well as any of several iPhone and Android apps—to build individual brand relationships, give insurance quotes, sell policies, or service customer accounts.

The New Direct Marketing Model

Early direct marketers—catalog companies, direct mailers, and telemarketers—gathered customer names and sold goods mainly by mail and telephone. Today, however, spurred by rapid advances in database technologies and new interactive media—especially the Internet—direct marketing has undergone a dramatic transformation.

In previous chapters, we discussed direct marketing as direct distribution—as marketing channels that contain no intermediaries. We also included direct marketing as one element of the promotion mix—as an approach for communicating directly with consumers. In actuality, direct marketing is both of these things and more.

Most companies still use direct marketing as a supplementary channel or medium. Thus, Lexus markets mostly through mass-media advertising and its high-quality dealer network. However, it also supplements these channels with direct marketing, such as promotional DVDs and other materials mailed directly to prospective buyers and a Web page (www.lexus.com) that provides prospective customers with information about various models, competitive comparisons, financing, and dealer locations. Its Lexus Drivers Web site assists and builds community among current Lexus owners. Similarly, most department stores, such as Sears or Macy's, sell the majority of their merchandise off their store shelves, but they also sell through direct mail and online catalogs.

However, for many companies today, direct marketing is more than just a supplementary channel or advertising medium—it constitutes a complete model for doing business. ▶ Firms employing this *direct model* use it as the *only* approach. Companies such as Amazon, eBay, Priceline, Netflix, and GEICO have built their entire approach to the marketplace around direct marketing. Many, like Amazon.com, have employed this model with tremendous success (see Marketing at Work 14.1).

▲ The new direct marketing model: Companies such as GEICO have built their entire approach to the marketplace around direct marketing—just visit geico.com or call 1-800-947-auto.
GEICO

Growth and Benefits of Direct Marketing

Direct marketing has become the fastest-growing form of marketing. According to the Direct Marketing Association (DMA), U.S. companies spent almost $155 billion on direct and digital marketing last year. As a result, direct marketing sales now account for about 8 percent of total sales in the U.S. economy. The DMA estimates that direct marketing sales will grow 5.3 percent annually through 2013, compared with a projected 4.1 percent annual growth for total U.S. sales.[2]

Direct marketing continues to become more Internet-based, and Internet marketing is claiming a fast-growing share of marketing spending and sales. For example, U.S. marketers spent an estimated $26 billion on online advertising last year, a whopping 15 percent increase over the previous year. These efforts generated nearly $300 billion in online consumer spending.[3]

Benefits to Buyers

For buyers, direct marketing is convenient, easy, and private. Direct marketers never close their doors, and customers don't have to trek to and through stores to find products. From their homes, offices, or almost anywhere else, customers can shop the Internet at any time

Amazon.com: *The* Model for Direct Marketing in the Digital Age

When you think of shopping online, chances are good that you think first of Amazon. The online pioneer first opened its virtual doors in 1995, selling books out of founder Jeff Bezos's garage in suburban Seattle. Amazon still sells books—*lots and lots* of books. But it now sells just about everything else as well, from music, videos, electronics, tools, housewares, apparel, mobile phones, and groceries to loose diamonds and Maine lobsters. Many analysts view Amazon.com as *the* model for direct marketing in the digital age.

From the start, Amazon has grown explosively. Its annual sales have rocketed from a modest $150 million in 1997 to more than $34 billion today. In the past five years, despite the shaky economy, its sales have more than quadrupled. Although it took the company eight years to turn its first full-year profit in 2003, Amazon's profits have since surged more than 30-fold. Last year alone, sales grew 40 percent; profits popped nearly 28 percent. This past holiday season, at one point, the online store's more than 120 million active customers worldwide were purchasing 110 items per second.

What has made Amazon one of the world's premier direct marketers? To its core, the company is relentlessly customer driven. "The thing that drives everything is creating genuine value for customers," says Bezos. The company starts with the customer and works backward. "Rather than ask what are we good at and what else can we do with that skill," says Bezos, "we ask, who are our customers? What do they need? And then [we] learn those skills."

For example, when Amazon saw an opportunity to serve its book-buying customers better through access to e-books and other e-content, it developed its own product for the first time ever—the innovative Kindle, a wireless reading device for downloading books, blogs, magazines, newspapers, and other matter. The Kindle took more than four years and a whole new set of skills to develop. But Amazon's start-with-the-customer thinking paid off handsomely. The Kindle is now the company's number one selling product, and Amazon.com currently sells more e-books than hardcovers and paperbacks combined. The Kindle Store now offers more than 550,000 e-books, including new releases and bestsellers, at $11.99 or less. And various Kindle apps let customers enjoy e-books on devices ranging from BlackBerrys and Droids to iPhones and iPads.

Perhaps more important than *what* Amazon sells is *how* it sells. The company wants to do much more than just sell books, DVDs, or digital cameras. It wants to deliver a special *experience* to every customer. "The customer experience really matters," says Bezos. "We've focused on just having a better store, where it's easier to shop, where you can learn more about the products, where you have a bigger selection, and where you have the lowest prices."

Most Amazon.com regulars feel a surprisingly strong relationship with the company, especially given the almost complete lack of actual human interaction. Amazon obsesses over making each customer's experience uniquely personal. For example, the Web site greets customers with their very own personalized home pages, and its "Recommendations for You"

feature offers personalized product recommendations. Amazon was the first company to use "collaborative filtering" technology, which sifts through each customer's past purchases and the purchasing patterns of customers with similar profiles to come up with personalized site content. "We want Amazon.com to be the right store for you as an individual," says Bezos. "If we have 120 million customers, we should have 120 million stores."

Visitors to Amazon.com receive a unique blend of benefits: huge selection, good value, and convenience. But it's the "discovery" factor that makes the buying experience really special. Once on the Amazon.com site, you're compelled to stay for a while—looking, learning, and discovering. Amazon.com has become a kind of online community in which customers can browse for products, research purchase alternatives, share opinions and reviews with other visitors, and chat online with authors and experts. In this way, Amazon does much more than just sell goods online. It creates direct, personalized customer

▲ Online pioneer Amazon.com does much more than just sell goods on the Web. It creates direct, personalized online customer experiences. "The thing that drives everything is creating genuine value for customers," says founder and CEO Jeff Bezos, pictured above.
AP Images/Andy Rogers

relationships and satisfying online experiences. Year after year, Amazon comes in number one or number two on the American Customer Satisfaction Index, regardless of industry.

To create even greater selection and discovery for customers, Amazon.com allows competing retailers—from mom-and-pop operations to Marks & Spencer department stores—to offer their products on Amazon.com, creating a virtual shopping mall of incredible proportions. It even encourages customers to sell used items on the site. The broader selection attracts more customers, and everyone benefits. "We are becoming increasingly important in the lives of our customers," says an Amazon marketing executive.

Based on its powerful growth, many have speculated that Amazon.com will become the Walmart of the Web. In fact, some argue, it already is. As pointed out in Chapter 9, although Walmart's total sales of more than $419 billion dwarf Amazon's $34 billion in sales, Amazon's Internet sales are 12 times greater than Walmart's. So it's Walmart that's chasing Amazon on the Web. Put another way, Walmart wants to become the Amazon.com of the Web, not the other way around. However, despite its mammoth proportions,

to catch Amazon online, Walmart will have to match the superb Amazon customer experience, and that won't be easy.

Whatever the eventual outcome, Amazon has forever changed the face of direct marketing. Most importantly, the innovative direct retailer has set a very high bar for the online customer experience. "The reason I'm so obsessed with . . . the customer experience is that I believe [our success] has been driven exclusively by that experience," says Bezos. "We are not great advertisers. So we start with customers, figure out what they want, and figure out how to get it to them."

Sources: See Daniel Lyons, "The Customer Is Always Right," *Newsweek*, January 4, 2010, p. 85; Brad Stone, "Can Amazon Be the Walmart of the Web?" *New York Times*, September 20, 2009, p. BU1; Joe Nocera, "Putting Buyers First? What a Concept," *New York Times*, January 5, 2008, www.nytimes.com; Scott Cendrowski, "How Amazon Keeps Cranking," *Fortune*, February 28, 2011, p. 18; Andrew Edgecliffe-Johnson, "Amazon's Electronic Book Sales Beat Print," *Financial Times*, May 20, 2011, p. 22; and annual reports and other information found at www.amazon.com and http://local.amazon.com/businesses, accessed October 2011.

of the day or night. Likewise, business buyers can learn about products and services without tying up time with salespeople.

Direct marketing gives buyers ready access to a wealth of products. Direct marketers can offer an almost unlimited selection to customers almost anywhere in the world. Just compare the huge selections offered by many online merchants to the more meager assortments of their brick-and-mortar counterparts. For instance, go to Bulbs.com, the Internet's number one light bulb superstore, and you'll have instant access to every imaginable kind of light bulb or lamp—incandescent bulbs, fluorescent bulbs, projection bulbs, surgical bulbs, automotive bulbs—you name it. Similarly, direct retailer Zappos.com stocks more than 3 million shoes, handbags, clothing items, and accessories from more than 1,300 brands. No physical store could offer handy access to such vast selections.

Direct marketing channels also give buyers access to a wealth of comparative information about companies, products, and competitors. Good catalogs or Web sites often provide more information in more useful forms than even the most helpful retail salesperson can provide. For example, Amazon.com offers more information than most of us can digest, ranging from top-ten product lists, extensive product descriptions, and expert and user product reviews to recommendations based on customers' previous purchases. Catalogs from Sears offer a treasure trove of information about the store's merchandise and services. In fact, you probably wouldn't think it strange to see a Sears' salesperson referring to a catalog in the store for more detailed product information while trying to advise a customer.

Finally, direct marketing is immediate and interactive: Buyers can interact with sellers by phone or on the seller's Web site to create exactly the configuration of information, products, or services they desire and then order them on the spot. Moreover, direct marketing gives consumers a greater measure of control. Consumers decide which catalogs they will browse and which Web sites they will visit.

Benefits to Sellers

For sellers, direct marketing is a powerful tool for building customer relationships. Today's direct marketers can target small groups or individual customers. Because of the one-to-one nature of direct marketing, companies can interact with customers by phone or online, learn more about their needs, and personalize products and services to specific customer tastes. In turn, customers can ask questions and volunteer feedback.

Direct marketing also offers sellers a low-cost, efficient, speedy alternative for reaching their markets. Direct marketing has grown rapidly in business-to-business marketing, partly in response to the ever-increasing costs of marketing through the sales force. When personal sales calls cost an average of $350 or more per contact, they should be made only when necessary and to high-potential customers and prospects.[4] Lower-cost-per-contact media—such as B-to-B telemarketing, direct mail, and company Web sites—often prove more cost effective.

Similarly, online direct marketing results in lower costs, improved efficiencies, and speedier handling of channel and logistics functions, such as order processing, inventory handling, and delivery. Direct marketers such as Amazon.com or Netflix also avoid the expense of maintaining stores and the related costs of rent, insurance, and utilities, passing the savings along to customers.

Direct marketing can also offer greater flexibility. It allows marketers to make ongoing adjustments to prices and programs or make immediate, timely, and personal announcements and offers. ▶ For example, Southwest Airlines uses techie direct marketing tools—including a widget (DING!), a blog (Nuts about Southwest), and smartphone apps—to inject itself directly into customers' everyday lives, at their invitation:[5]

▲ **Southwest Airlines uses techie direct marketing tools—including a blog, DING! widget, and smartphone app—to inject itself directly into customers' everyday lives—at their invitation.**
Southwest Airlines, Co.

The Nuts about Southwest blog, written by Southwest employees, creates a two-way customer-employee dialogue that gives customers a look inside the company's culture and operations. At the same time, it lets Southwest talk directly with and get feedback from customers. Southwest's smartphone apps provide customers with direct and convenient anytime access to Southwest ticket, check-in, and flight information and purchasing. And DING!, available as a desktop widget or via the phone app, offers exclusive, limited-time air fare deals. When an enticing new deal becomes available, DING! emits the familiar in-flight seatbelt-light bell dinging sound. The deep discounts last only 6 to 12 hours and can be accessed only online through the application. DING! lets Southwest Airlines bypass the reservations system and pass bargain fares directly to interested customers. Eventually, DING! may even allow Southwest Airlines to customize fare offers based on each customer's unique characteristics and travel preferences.

Finally, direct marketing gives sellers access to buyers that they could not reach through other channels. Smaller firms can mail catalogs to customers outside their local markets and post toll-free telephone numbers to handle orders and inquiries. Internet marketing is a truly global medium that allows buyers and sellers to click from one country to another in seconds. A Web user from Paris or Istanbul can access an L.L. Bean online catalog as easily as someone living in Freeport, Maine, the direct retailer's hometown. Even small marketers find that they have ready access to global markets.

Customer Databases and Direct Marketing

Author Comment ▶
Direct marketing begins with a good customer database. A company is no better than what it knows about its customers.

Customer database
An organized collection of comprehensive data about individual customers or prospects, including geographic, demographic, psychographic, and behavioral data.

Effective direct marketing begins with a good customer database. A **customer database** is an organized collection of comprehensive data about individual customers or prospects. A good customer database can be a potent relationship-building tool. The database gives companies a 360-degree view of their customers and how they behave. A company is no better than what it knows about its customers.

In consumer marketing, the customer database might contain a customer's geographic data (address, region), demographic data (age, income, family members, birthdays), psychographic data (activities, interests, and opinions), and buying behavior (buying preferences and the recency, frequency, and monetary value [RFM] of past purchases). In B-to-B marketing, the customer profile might contain the products and services the customer has bought, past volumes and prices, key contacts, competing suppliers, the status of current contracts, estimated future spending, and competitive strengths and weaknesses in selling and servicing the account.

Some of these databases are huge. For example, casino operator Harrah's Entertainment has built a customer database containing 700 terabytes worth of customer information, roughly 70 times the amount of the printed collection in the Library of Congress, which it uses to create special customer experiences. Similarly, Walmart captures data on every item, for every customer, for every store, every day. Its database contains more than 2.5 petabytes of data—that's equivalent to two billion copies of *Moby Dick*.[6]

Companies use their databases in many ways. They use databases to locate good potential customers and generate sales leads. They also mine their databases to learn about customers in detail and then fine-tune their market offerings and communications to the special preferences and behaviors of target segments or individuals. In all, a company's database can be an important tool for building stronger long-term customer relationships.

For example, ▶ retailer Best Buy mines its huge customer database to glean actionable insights, which it uses to personalize promotional messages and offers:[7]

▲ **Customer databases: Best Buy mines its huge database to glean actionable insights on customer interests, lifestyles, passions, and likely next purchases. It uses this information to develop personalized, customer-triggered promotional messages and offers.**

m42/ZUMA Press/Newscom

Best Buy's 15-plus terabyte customer database contains seven years of data on more than 75 million customer households. The retail chain captures every scrap of store and online interaction data—from purchase transactions to phone calls and mouse clicks to delivery and rebate check addresses—and merges it with third-party and publicly available data to create multidimensional customer profiles. Then, sophisticated match-and-merge algorithms score individual customers in terms of their interests, lifestyles, and passions, and use this information to identify their likely next purchases.

Through such analysis, Best Buy categorizes three-quarters of its customers—more than 100 million individuals—into segments with names like Buzz (the young tech enthusiast), Jill (the suburban soccer mom), Larry (the wealthy professional guy), Ray (the family man), and Charlie and Helen (empty nesters with money to spend). Based on these profiles and individual transaction information, Best Buy then develops personalized, customer-triggered promotional messages and offers. So if your previous interactions suggest that you are a young Buzz assembling a home entertainment system, and you recently used Best Buy's smartphone app to look up product details and customer ratings on a specific component, you might soon receive a spot-on mobile coupon offering discounts on that and related products.

Like many other marketing tools, database marketing requires a special investment. Companies must invest in computer hardware, database software, analytical programs, communication links, and skilled personnel. The database system must be user-friendly and available to various marketing groups, including those in product and brand management, new-product development, advertising and promotion, direct mail, Internet marketing, field sales, order fulfillment, and customer service. However, a well-managed database usually results in sales and customer-relationship gains that more than cover these costs.

Author Comment ▶
Direct marketing is rich in tools, from traditional old favorites such as direct mail, catalogs, and telemarketing to the Internet and other new digital approaches.

Forms of Direct Marketing

The major forms of direct marketing—as shown in ▶ **Figure 14.1**—are face-to-face or personal selling, direct-mail marketing, catalog marketing, telemarketing, direct-response television (DRTV) marketing, kiosk marketing, and online marketing. We examined personal selling in depth in Chapter 13. Here, we look into the other forms of direct marketing.

▶ **Figure 14.1** Forms of Direct Marketing

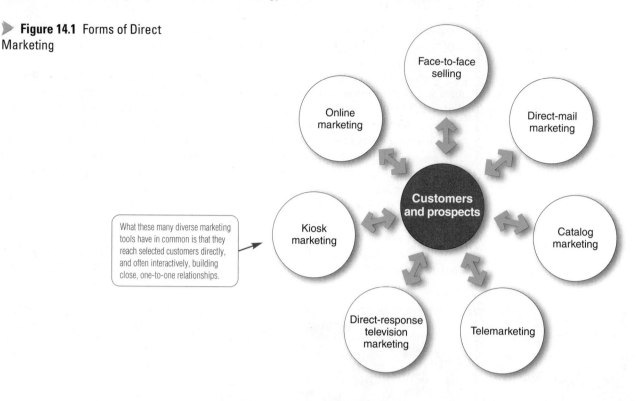

Face-to-face selling

Direct-mail marketing

Online marketing

Customers and prospects

Catalog marketing

Kiosk marketing

What these many diverse marketing tools have in common is that they reach selected customers directly, and often interactively, building close, one-to-one relationships.

Direct-response television marketing

Telemarketing

Direct-Mail Marketing

Direct-mail marketing

Marketing that occurs by sending an offer, announcement, reminder, or other item directly to a person at a particular address.

Direct-mail marketing involves sending an offer, announcement, reminder, or other item to a person at a particular address. Using highly selective mailing lists, direct marketers send out millions of mail pieces each year—letters, catalogs, ads, brochures, samples, DVDs, and other "salespeople with wings." Direct mail is by far the largest direct marketing medium. The DMA reports that U.S. marketers spent $45 billion on direct mail last year (including both catalog and noncatalog mail), which accounted for 29 percent of all direct marketing spending and generated nearly a third of all direct marketing sales. According to the DMA, every dollar spent on direct mail generates $12.57 in sales.[8]

Direct mail is well suited to direct, one-to-one communication. It permits high target-market selectivity, can be personalized, is flexible, and allows the easy measurement of results. Although direct mail costs more per thousand people reached than mass media such as television or magazines, the people it reaches are much better prospects. Direct mail has proved successful in promoting all kinds of products, from books, insurance, travel, gift items, gourmet foods, clothing, and other consumer goods to industrial products of all kinds. Charities also use direct mail heavily to raise billions of dollars each year.

Some analysts predict a decline in the use of traditional forms of direct mail in coming years, as marketers switch to newer digital forms, such as e-mail and mobile marketing. E-mail, mobile, and other newer forms of direct marketing deliver messages at incredible speeds and lower costs compared to the U.S. Post Office's "snail mail" pace. We will discuss e-mail and mobile marketing in more detail later in the chapter.

However, even though the new digital forms of direct marketing are gaining popularity, traditional direct mail is still by far the most widely used method. Mail marketing offers some distinct advantages over digital forms. It provides something tangible for people to hold and keep and it can be used to send samples. "Mail makes it real," says one analyst. It "creates an emotional connection with customers that digital cannot. They hold it, view it, and engage with it in a manner entirely different from their online experiences." In contrast, e-mail is easily screened or trashed. "[With] spam filters and spam folders to keep our messaging away from consumers' inboxes," says a direct marketer, "sometimes you have to lick a few stamps."[9]

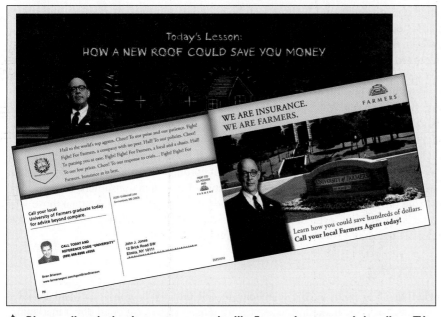

▲ **Direct mail marketing: Insurance companies like Farmers Insurance rely heavily on TV advertising to establish broad customer awareness. However, they also use lots of good old direct mail to communicate with consumers in a more direct and personalized way.**
Farmers Group, Inc.

Traditional direct mail can be an effective component of a broader integrated marketing campaign. For example, most large insurance companies rely heavily on TV advertising to establish broad customer awareness and positioning. However, the insurance companies also use lots of good old direct mail to break through the glut of insurance advertising on TV. ▶ Consider Farmers Insurance:[10]

"It might shock people to know how much money is spent in promoting [insurance] on television," says John Ingersoll, vice president of marketing communications for Farmers Insurance. "In the middle of all that clutter, there's a lot of messaging and a lot of competition to find the consumer. Broadcast, by definition, is broad—you're trying to talk to everybody. And e-mail has been difficult to manage because of spam filtering. We're always looking to communicate with consumers in a more direct and personalized way." Enter direct mail. "Mail is a channel that allows all of us to find the consumer with a very targeted, very specific message that you can't do in broadcast," says Ingersoll. And "most people are still amenable to getting marketing communications in their mailbox, which is why I think direct mail will grow."

Direct mail may be resented as *junk mail* or *spam* if sent to people who have no interest in it. For this reason, smart marketers are targeting their direct mail carefully so as not to waste their money and recipients' time. They are designing permission-based programs that send e-mail and mobile ads only to those who want to receive them.

Catalog marketing
Direct marketing through print, video, or digital catalogs that are mailed to select customers, made available in stores, or presented online.

Catalog Marketing

Advances in technology, along with the move toward personalized, one-to-one marketing, have resulted in exciting changes in **catalog marketing**. *Catalog Age* magazine used to define a *catalog* as "a printed, bound piece of at least eight pages, selling multiple products, and offering a direct ordering mechanism." Today, this definition is sadly out of date.

With the stampede to the Internet, more and more catalogs are going digital. A variety of Web-only catalogers have emerged, and most print catalogers have added Web-based catalogs and smartphone catalog shopping apps to their marketing mixes. For example, apps such as Catalog Spree put a mall full of classic catalogs from retailers such as Hammacher Schlemmer, Coldwater Creek, or Wine Enthusiast only a swipe of the finger away on an iPad. ▶ And days before the latest Lands' End catalog arrives in the mail, customers can access it digitally at landsend.com, at social media outlets such as Facebook, or via the Lands' End mobile app for their iPad, iPhone, or Android phone. With Lands' End Mobile, says the company, "You're carrying every item we carry."[11]

Digital catalogs eliminate printing and mailing costs. And whereas space is limited in a print catalog, online catalogs can offer an almost unlimited amount of merchandise. They also offer a broader assortment of presentation formats, including search and video. Finally, online catalogs allow real-time

▲ **Digital catalogs: Days before the latest Lands' End catalog arrives in the mail, customers can access it digitally at landsend.com, at Facebook, or via the Lands' End mobile app.**

merchandising; products and features can be added or removed as needed, and prices can be adjusted instantly to match demand.

However, despite the advantages of Web-based catalogs, as your overstuffed mailbox may suggest, printed catalogs are still thriving. U.S. direct marketers mail out some 20 billion catalogs each year—about 64 per American. Why aren't companies ditching their old-fashioned paper catalogs in this new digital era? For one thing, paper catalogs create emotional connections with customers that Web-based sales spaces simply can't. "Glossy catalog pages still entice buyers in a way that computer images don't," says an analyst. "Among retailers who rely mainly on direct sales, 62 percent say their biggest revenue generator is a paper catalog."[12]

In addition, printed catalogs are one of the best ways to drive online sales, making them more important than ever in the digital era. According to a recent study, 70 percent of Web purchases are driven by catalogs. Another study found that consumers who received catalogs from the retailer spent 28 percent more on that retailer's Web site than those who didn't get a catalog. Thus, even dedicated online-only retailers, such as Zappos.com, have started producing catalogs with the hopes of driving online sales.[13]

Telemarketing

Telemarketing
Using the telephone to sell directly to customers.

Telemarketing involves using the telephone to sell directly to consumers and business customers. Last year, telemarketing accounted for almost 19 percent of all direct marketing-driven sales. We're all familiar with telephone marketing directed toward consumers, but B-to-B marketers also use telemarketing extensively, accounting for more than 55 percent of all telephone marketing sales.[14] Marketers use *outbound* telephone marketing to sell directly to consumers and businesses. ▶ They also use *inbound* toll-free numbers to receive orders from television and print ads, direct mail, or catalogs.

Properly designed and targeted telemarketing provides many benefits, including purchasing convenience and increased product and service information. However, the explosion in unsolicited outbound telephone marketing over the years has annoyed many consumers, who object to the almost daily "junk phone calls."

In 2003, U.S. lawmakers responded with the National Do Not Call Registry, which is managed by the FTC. The legislation bans most telemarketing calls to registered phone numbers (although people can still receive calls from nonprofit groups, politicians, and companies with which they have recently done business). Consumers responded enthusiastically. To date, more than 191 million home and mobile phone numbers have been registered at www.donotcall.gov or by calling 888-382-1222. Businesses that break do-not-call laws can be fined up to $16,000 per violation. As a result, reports an FTC spokesperson, the program "has been exceptionally successful."[15]

Do-not-call legislation has hurt the consumer telemarketing industry. However, two major forms of telemarketing—inbound consumer telemarketing and outbound B-to-B telemarketing—remain strong and growing. Telemarketing also remains a major fund-raising tool for nonprofit and political groups. Interestingly, do-not-call regulations appear to be helping many direct marketers more than it's hurting them. Rather than making unwanted calls, many of these marketers are developing "opt-in" calling systems, in which they provide useful information and offers to customers who have invited the company to contact them by phone or e-mail. The opt-in model provides better returns for marketers than the formerly invasive one.

Meanwhile, marketers who violate do-not-call regulations have increasingly become the targets of crusading consumer activist groups, who return the favor by flooding the violating company's phone system with return calls and messages.[16]

▲ Marketers use inbound toll-free 800 numbers to receive orders from television and print ads, direct mail, or catalogs. Here, the Carolina Cookie Company urges, "Don't wait another day. Call now to place an order or request a catalog."
Carolina Cookie Company

Direct-Response Television Marketing

Direct-response television (DRTV) marketing
Direct marketing via television, including direct-response television advertising (or infomercials) and interactive television (iTV) advertising.

Direct-response television (DRTV) marketing takes one of two major forms: direct-response television advertising and interactive TV (iTV) advertising. Using *direct-response television advertising*, direct marketers air television spots, often 60 or 120 seconds in length, which persuasively describe a product and give customers a toll-free number or a Web site for ordering. It also includes full 30-minute or longer advertising programs, called *infomercials*, for a single product.

Successful direct-response advertising campaigns can ring up big sales. For example, little-known infomercial maker Guthy-Renker has helped propel its Proactiv Solution acne treatment and other "transformational" products into power brands that pull in $1.5 billion in sales annually to five million active customers (compare that to only about $150 million in annual drugstore sales of acne products in the United States).[17]

DRTV ads are often associated with somewhat loud or questionable pitches for cleaners, stain removers, kitchen gadgets, and nifty ways to stay in shape without working very hard at it. For example, over the past few years yell-and-sell TV pitchmen like Anthony Sullivan (Swivel Sweeper, Awesome Auger) and Vince Offer (ShamWow, SlapChop) have racked up billions of dollars in sales of "As Seen on TV" products. Brands like OxiClean, ShamWow, and the Snuggie (a blanket with sleeves) have become DRTV cult classics. And infomercial viral sensation Shake Weight created buzz on everything from YouTube to *Late Night with Jimmy Fallon*, selling more than 2 million units for $40 million in revenues in less than a year.[18]

In recent years, however, a number of large companies—from P&G, Disney, Revlon, Apple, and Kodak to Coca-Cola, Anheuser-Busch, and even the U.S. Navy—have begun using infomercials to sell their wares, refer customers to retailers, recruit members, or attract buyers to their Web sites. For example, Kodak uses direct-response TV to get its message out directly to customers.[19]

▲ Large, well-known companies—such as Kodak—are now using direct-response TV to get the message out directly to customers.

With permission by Eastman Kodak Company

The phrase "As Seen on TV" might bring to mind Snuggie, Sham-Wow, and PedEgg but probably not a venerable American brand that invites you to share the most important moments of your life. Yet for Kodak, DRTV has become an effective and preferred way to reach consumers. ▶ Short and long infomercials for Kodak printers and low-priced ink, which last two minutes and nearly a half-hour, respectively, focus on the value message Kodak uses in its traditional brand advertising. However, the ads also spell out specific savings, provide testimonials and examples, and even include the tone of a more typical infomercial. One short spot opens with the line "Are you sick of paying ridiculous prices for printer ink?" The Kodak infomercials have produced outstanding results, especially in slower economic times—printer and ink sales increased 20 percent after the first airing. "Everybody else in the market [was] down 20 percent, [we were] up 44 percent . . . on both equipment and ink," says Kodak's chief marketing officer. "Talking directly to consumers like that is not a bad idea."

A more recent form of direct-response television marketing is *interactive TV (iTV)* marketing. It lets viewers interact with television programming and advertising using their remote controls. Interactive TV gives marketers an opportunity to reach targeted audiences in an interactive, more involved way.

In the past, iTV has been slow to catch on. However, the technology now appears poised to take off as a direct marketing medium. Research shows that the level of viewer engagement with iTV is much higher than with regular 30-second spots. A recent poll indicated that 66 percent of viewers would be "very interested" in interacting with commercials that piqued their interest. And broadcasting systems such as DIRECTV, EchoStar, and Time Warner are now offering iTV capabilities.[20]

New York area cable provider Cablevision offers an iTV service by which advertisers can run interactive 30-second spots.[21]

During the ads, a bar at the bottom of the screen lets viewers use their remotes to choose additional content and offers, such as on-demand free product samples, brand channels, video showcases, or e-mailed brochures or coupons. For example, a Gillette ad offered to send free samples of its body

▲ **Kiosk marketing: Redbox operates more than 27,000 DVD rental kiosks in supermarkets and fast-food outlets nationwide.**
Redbox Automated Retail

wash product, Benjamin Moore offered coupons for paint color samples, and Century 21 offered $10 gift cards. Advertisers such as Mattel Barbie and the U.S. Navy invited viewers to select their branded Cablevision channels for optional information and entertainment. So far, response rates for the interactive content have been impressive. For example, in an early test last year, the Disney Travel Channel allowed subscribers to browse information about Disney theme parks and then request a call from an agent. The booking rate for people requesting a call was an amazing 25 percent.

Kiosk Marketing

As consumers become more and more comfortable with digital and touch-screen technologies, many companies are placing information and ordering machines—called *kiosks* (good old-fashioned vending machines but so much more)—in stores, airports, hotels, college campuses, and other locations. Kiosks are everywhere these days, from self-service hotel and airline check-in devices to in-store ordering devices that let you order merchandise not carried in the store. "Flashy and futuristic, souped-up machines are popping up everywhere," says one analyst. "They have touch screens instead of buttons, facades that glow and pulse . . . [they] bridge the gap between old-fashioned stores and online shopping."[22]

In-store Kodak, Fuji, and HP kiosks let customers transfer pictures from memory sticks, mobile phones, and other digital storage devices; edit them; and make high-quality color prints. Kiosks in Hilton hotel lobbies let guests view their reservations, get room keys, view prearrival messages, check in and out, and even change seat assignments and print boarding passes for flights on any of 18 airlines. At JetBlue's Terminal Five in New York's John F. Kennedy airport, more than 200 screens throughout the terminal let travelers order food and beverages to be delivered to their respective gate. ▶ And Redbox operates more than 27,000 DVD rental kiosks in McDonald's, Walmart, Walgreens, CVS, and other retail outlets. Customers make their selections on a touch screen, then swipe a credit or debit card to rent DVDs at $1 a day. Customers can even prereserve DVDs online to ensure that their trip to the kiosk will not be a wasted one. The market share for stand-alone kiosk movie rentals surpassed that of traditional retail store rentals in the United States last year.[23]

SPEED BUMP | LINKING THE CONCEPTS

Hold up a moment and think about the impact of direct marketing on your life.

- When was the last time that you *bought* something via direct marketing? What did you buy and why did you buy it direct? When was the last time that you *rejected* a direct marketing offer? Why did you reject it? Based on these experiences, what advice would you give to direct marketers?
- For the next week, keep track of all the direct marketing offers that come your way via direct mail and catalogs, telephone, direct-response television, and the Internet. Then analyze the offers by type, source, and what you liked or disliked about each offer and the way it was delivered. Which offer best hit its target (you)? Which missed by the widest margin?

Author Comment ▶
Online direct marketing is growing at a blistering pace. By one estimate, the Internet now influences a staggering 50 percent of total retail sales.

Online Marketing

As noted earlier, **online marketing** is the fastest-growing form of direct marketing. Widespread use of the Internet is having a dramatic impact on both buyers and the marketers who serve them. In this section, we examine how marketing strategy and practice are changing to take advantage of today's Internet technologies.

Marketing and the Internet

Online marketing
Efforts to market products and services and build customer relationships over the Internet.

Internet
A vast public web of computer networks that connects users of all types around the world to each other and an amazingly large information repository.

Much of the world's business today is carried out over digital networks that connect people and companies. The **Internet**, a vast public web of computer networks, connects users of all types all around the world to each other and an amazingly large information repository. These days, people connect with the Internet at almost any time and from almost anywhere using their computers, smartphones, tablets, or even TVs. The Internet has fundamentally changed customers' notions of convenience, speed, price, product information, and service. As a result, it has given marketers a whole new way to create value for customers and build relationships with them.

Internet usage and impact continues to grow steadily. Last year, 77 percent of the U.S. population had access to the Internet, and the average U.S. Internet user spent some 32 hours a month surfing the Web. Moreover, more than 63 million people in the United States access the Internet via their smartphones. Worldwide, more than 2 billion people now have Internet access. And last year, half a billion people around the globe accessed the mobile Internet, a number that's expected to double over the next five years as mobile becomes an ever-more popular way to get online.[24]

Click-only companies
The so-called dot-coms, which operate online only and have no brick-and-mortar market presence.

To reach this burgeoning market, all kinds of companies now market online. **Click-only companies** operate on the Internet only. They include a wide array of firms, from *e-tailers* such as Amazon.com and Expedia.com that sell products and services directly to final buyers via the Internet to *search engines and portals* (such as Yahoo!, Google, and MSN), *transaction sites* (eBay, Craigslist), *content sites* (the *New York Times* on the Web, ESPN.com, and *Encyclopædia Britannica*), and *online social networks* (Facebook, YouTube, Twitter, and Flickr).

Click-and-mortar companies
Traditional brick-and-mortar companies that have added online marketing to their operations.

The success of the dot-coms has caused existing *brick-and-mortar* manufacturers and retailers to reexamine how they serve their markets. Now, almost all of these traditional companies have created their own online sales and communications channels, becoming **click-and-mortar companies**. It's hard to find a company today that doesn't have a substantial online presence.

In fact, many click-and-mortar companies are now having more online success than their click-only competitors. A recent ranking of the world's ten largest online retail sites contained only one click-only retailer (Amazon.com, which was ranked number one).[25] ▶ For example, number two on the list was Staples, the $24.5 billion office supply retailer. Staples operates more than 2,280 superstores worldwide. But you might be surprised to learn that more than half of Staples' North American sales and profits come from its online and direct marketing operations.[26]

Selling on the Web lets Staples build deeper, more personalized relationships with customers large and small. A large customer, such as GE or P&G, can create lists of approved office products at discount prices and then let company departments or even individuals do their own online purchasing. This reduces ordering costs, cuts through the red tape, and speeds up the ordering process for customers. At the same time, it encourages companies to use Staples as a sole source for office supplies. Even the smallest companies and individual consumers find 24-hour-a-day online ordering via the Web of Staples mobile phone app easier and more efficient.

In addition, Staples' Web operations complement store sales. The Staples.com site and smartphone app build store traffic by offering hot deals and by helping customers find a local store and check stock and prices. In return, the local store promotes the Web site through in-store kiosks. If customers don't find what they need on the shelves, they can quickly order it via the kiosk. Thus, Staples backs its "that was easy" positioning by offering a full range of contact points and delivery modes—online, catalogs, phone, and in the store. No click-only or brick-only seller can match that kind of call, click, or visit convenience and support.

▲ Click-and-mortar marketing: Staples backs its "that was easy" positioning by offering a full range of contact points and delivery modes.
Courtesy of Staples the Office Superstore, LLC & Staples, Inc.

Online Marketing Domains

The four major online marketing domains are shown in ▶ **Figure 14.2**: business-to-consumer (B-to-C), business-to-business (B-to-B), consumer-to-consumer (C-to-C), and consumer-to-business (C-to-B).

> **Figure 14.2**
> Online Marketing Domains

	Targeted to consumers	**Targeted to businesses**
Initiated by business	B-to-C (business-to-consumer)	B-to-B (business-to-business)
Initiated by consumer	C-to-C (consumer-to-consumer)	C-to-B (consumer-to-business)

Online marketing can be classified by who initiates it and to whom it is targeted. As consumers, we're most familiar with B-to-C and C-to-C, but B-to-B is also flourishing.

Business-to-Consumer

Business-to-consumer (B-to-C) online marketing
Businesses selling goods and services online to final consumers.

The popular press has paid the most attention to **business-to-consumer (B-to-C) online marketing**—businesses selling goods and services online to final consumers. Today's consumers can buy almost anything online. More than half of all U.S. households now regularly shop online, and online consumer buying continues to grow at a healthy double-digit rate. U.S. online retail sales were an estimated $176 billion last year and are expected to grow at 10 percent a year over the next four years as consumers shift their spending from physical stores to online stores.[27]

Perhaps even more important, although online shopping currently captures less than 10 percent of total U.S. retail sales, by one estimate, the Internet influences a staggering 50 percent of those sales—including sales transacted online plus those made in stores but encouraged by online research. Some 97 percent of Web-goers now use the Internet to research products before making purchases.[28] And a growing number of consumers armed with smartphones use them while shopping to find better deals and score price-matching offers. Thus, smart marketers are employing integrated multichannel strategies that use the Internet to drive sales to other marketing channels.

Online buyers differ from traditional offline consumers in their approaches to buying and their responses to marketing. In the online exchange process, customers initiate and control the contact. Traditional marketing targets a somewhat passive audience. In contrast, online marketing targets people who actively select which Web sites and shopping apps they will use and what marketing information they will receive about which products. Thus, online marketing requires new marketing approaches.

Business-to-Business

Business-to-business (B-to-B) online marketing
Businesses using online marketing to reach new business customers, serve current customers more effectively, and obtain buying efficiencies and better prices.

Although the popular press has given the most attention to B-to-C Web sites, **business-to-business (B-to-B) online marketing** is also flourishing. B-to-B marketers use Web sites, e-mail, online product catalogs, online trading networks, mobile apps, and other online resources to reach new business customers, sell to current customers, and serve customers more efficiently and effectively. Beyond simply selling their products and services online, companies can use the Internet to build stronger relationships with important business customers.

Most major B-to-B marketers now offer product information, customer purchasing, and customer-support services online. For example, corporate buyers can visit networking equipment and software maker Cisco Systems' Web site (www.cisco.com), select detailed descriptions of Cisco's products and service solutions, request sales and service information, attend events and training seminars, view videos on a wide range of topics, have live chats with Cisco staff, and place orders. Some major companies conduct almost all of their business online. For example, Cisco Systems takes more than 80 percent of its orders over the Internet.

Consumer-to-Consumer

Consumer-to-consumer (C-to-C) online marketing
Online exchanges of goods and information between final consumers.

Considerable **consumer-to-consumer (C-to-C) online marketing** and communication occurs online between interested parties over a wide range of products and subjects. In some cases, the Internet provides an excellent means by which consumers can buy or exchange goods or information directly with one another. For example, eBay, Overstock.com Auctions, Craigslist.com, and other auction sites offer popular market spaces for displaying and selling almost anything, from art and antiques, coins and stamps, and jewelry to computers and consumer electronics. eBay's C-to-C online trading community of more than 94 million active users worldwide (that's more than the total populations of Great Britain, Egypt, or Turkey) transacted some $62 billion in trades last year—more than $2,000 every second.[29]

In other cases, C-to-C involves interchanges of information through Internet forums that appeal to specific special-interest groups. Such activities may be organized for

Blogs

Online journals where people post their thoughts, usually on a narrowly defined topic.

commercial or noncommercial purposes. Web logs, or **blogs**, are online journals where people post their thoughts, usually on a narrow topic. Blogs can be about anything, from politics or baseball to haiku, car repair, or the latest television series. According to Nielsen, there are now more than 163 million blogs. Many bloggers use social networks such as Twitter and Facebook to promote their blogs, giving them huge reach. Such numbers give blogs—especially those with large and devoted followings—substantial influence.[30]

Many marketers are now tapping into the blogosphere as a medium for reaching carefully targeted consumers. For example, many companies have set up their own blogs. Sony has a PlayStation Blog, where fans can exchange views and submit and vote on ideas for improving PlayStation products. The Disney Parks Blog is a place to learn about and discuss all things Disney, including a Behind the Scenes area with posts about dance rehearsals, sneak peeks at new construction sites, interviews with employees, and more.[31]

Dell has a dozen or more blogs that facilitate "a direct exchange with Dell customers about the technology that connects us all." The blogs include Direct2Dell (the official Dell corporate blog), Dell TechCenter (IT brought into focus), DellShares (insights for investor relations), Health Care (about health care technology that connects us all), and Education (insights on using technology to enhance teaching, learning, and educational administration). Dell also has a very active and successful YouTube presence which it calls Dell Vlog, with 750 videos and more than 5 million video views. Dell bloggers often embed these YouTube videos into blog posts.

Companies can also advertise on existing blogs or influence content there. Alternatively, they might encourage "sponsored conversations" by influential bloggers. For example, IZEA's SocialSpark is an online marketplace that helps marketers and bloggers get together to create sponsored posts relevant to both the brand's customers and the blog's fans.[32]

▲ Using the blogosphere to reach carefully targeted consumers: Purex used SocialSpark to help introduce its Purex Complete 3-in-1 Laundry Sheets via blogs such as Freaky Frugalite, Bargain Briana, 3 Kids and Us, and others that reach homemakers.
Rebecca Mecomber, www.FreakyFrugalite.com

Brands ranging from Bloomingdale's, British Airways, Coldwell Banker, and HP to Kraft Foods and Purex have used SocialSpark to place sponsored messages about their brands and promotions on blogs that reach targeted consumers. ▶ For instance, Purex used SocialSpark to help introduce its Purex Complete 3-in-1 Laundry Sheets via blogs such as Bargain Briana, Freaky Frugalite, 3 Kids and Us, and others that reach homemakers. The blog posts, written by the bloggers with IZEA's help, were clearly identified as being sponsored by Purex. They described the new Complete 3-in-1 Laundry Sheets product and analyzed in detail its convenience versus cost benefits—complete with photos and links to free sample offers from Purex. "I'm a mom with four kids and five pets and a husband who works with mail and newspapers all day," wrote enthusiastic Freaky Frugalite blogger Rebecca Mecomber. "I am basically doomed to a life of laundry. The amazing dudes at Purex recognized my plight; and when they offered to make my life EASIER, . . . I grabbed at the chance."

As a marketing tool, blogs offer some advantages. They can offer a fresh, original, personal, and cheap way to enter into consumer online conversations. However, the blogosphere is cluttered and difficult to control. Blogs remain largely a C-to-C medium. Although companies can sometimes leverage blogs to engage in meaningful customer relationships, consumers remain largely in control.

Whether or not they actively participate in the blogosphere or other C-to-C conversations, companies should monitor and listen to them. C-to-C means that online buyers don't just consume product information—increasingly, they create it. As a result, *word of Web* is joining *word of mouth* as an important buying influence. Marketers should use insights from consumer online conversations to improve their marketing programs.

Consumer to Business

Consumer-to-business (C-to-B) online marketing
Online exchanges in which consumers search out sellers, learn about their offers, initiate purchases, and sometimes even drive transaction terms.

The final online marketing domain is **consumer-to-business (C-to-B) online marketing**. Thanks to the Internet, today's consumers are finding it easier to communicate with companies. Most companies now invite prospects and customers to submit suggestions and questions via company Web sites. Beyond this, rather than waiting for an invitation, consumers can search out sellers on the Web, learn about their offers, initiate purchases, and give feedback. Using the Web, consumers can even drive transactions with businesses, rather than the other way around. For example, at Priceline.com, would-be buyers can bid for airline tickets, hotel rooms, rental cars, cruises, and vacation packages, leaving the sellers to decide whether to accept their offers.

Consumers can also use Web sites such as GetSatisfaction.com, Complaints.com, and PlanetFeedback.com to ask questions, offer suggestions, lodge complaints, or deliver compliments to companies. GetSatisfaction.com provides "people-powered customer service" by creating a user-driven customer service community. The site provides forums where customers ask questions, share ideas, give praise, or report problems they're having with the products and services of 48,000 companies—from Microsoft and P&G to Google and Zappos.com—whether the company participates or not. GetSatisfaction.com also provides tools by which companies can adopt GetSatisfaction.com as an official customer service resource.[33]

SPEED BUMP | LINKING THE CONCEPTS

Pause here and cool your engine. Think about the relative advantages of *click-only, brick-and-mortar-only,* and *click-and-mortar* retailers.

- Visit Amazon.com. Search for a specific book or DVD—perhaps one that's not too well known—and go through the buying process.
- Now visit www.bn.com and shop for the same book or video. Then visit a Barnes & Noble store and shop for the item.
- What advantages does Amazon.com have over Barnes & Noble? What disadvantages? How does your local independent bookstore, with its store-only operations, fare against these two competitors?

Setting Up an Online Marketing Presence

In one way or another, most companies have now moved online. Companies conduct online marketing in any or all of the five ways shown in ▶ **Figure 14.3**: creating Web sites, placing ads and promotions online, setting up or participating in online social networks, sending e-mail, or using mobile marketing.

▶ **Figure 14.3** Setting Up for Online Marketing

It's hard to find a company today that doesn't have a substantial Web presence. The first step is one or more Web sites. But most large companies use all of these approaches. Don't forget, they all need to be integrated—with each other and with the rest of the promotion mix.

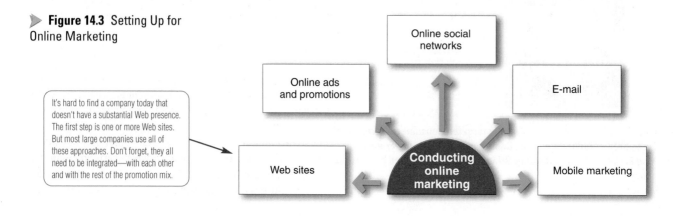

Creating Web Sites

For most companies, the first step in conducting online marketing is to create a Web site. However, beyond simply creating a Web site, marketers must design an attractive site and find ways to get consumers to visit the site, stay around, and come back often.

Corporate (or brand) Web site
A Web site designed to build customer goodwill, collect customer feedback, and supplement other sales channels rather than sell the company's products directly.

Web sites vary greatly in purpose and content. The most basic type is a **corporate** (or **brand**) **Web site**. This type of site is designed to build customer goodwill, collect customer feedback, and supplement other sales channels rather than to sell the company's products directly. It typically offers a rich variety of information and other features in an effort to answer customer questions, build closer customer relationships, and generate excitement about the company or brand.

▶ For example, you can't buy anything at Nestlé's colorful Wonka.com site, but you can learn about different Nestlé candy products, enter the latest contest, or hang around a while and doodle with Nerds, "paint your dreams" with the Wonka imaginator, or post Wonka-inspired digital art. Similarly, you can't buy anything at GE's corporate Web site. Instead, the site serves as a global public face for the huge company. It presents a massive amount of product, service, and company information to a diverse audience of customers, investors, journalists, and employees. It's both a B-to-B site and a portal for consumers, whether it's a U.S. consumer researching a microwave, an Indonesian business buyer checking into eco-friendly locomotives, or a German investor looking for shareholder information.

▲ Corporate Web sites: You can't buy anything at Nestlé's colorful Wonka.com site, but you can learn about different Nestlé candy products or just hang around for a while and "feed your imagination."
Screen capture courtesy of Nestlé

Marketing Web site
A Web site that interacts with consumers to move them closer to a direct purchase or other marketing outcome.

Other companies create a **marketing Web site**. These sites interact with consumers to move them closer to a direct purchase or other marketing outcome. For example, MINI USA operates a marketing Web site at www.miniusa.com. Once a potential customer clicks in, the carmaker wastes no time trying to turn the inquiry into a sale and then into a long-term relationship. The site offers a garage full of useful information and interactive selling features, including detailed and fun descriptions of current MINI models, tools for designing your very own MINI, information on dealer locations and services, and even tools for tracking your new MINI from factory to delivery.

Creating a Web site is one thing; getting people to *visit* the site is another. To attract visitors, companies aggressively promote their Web sites in offline print and broadcast advertising and through ads and links on other sites. But today's Web users are quick to abandon any Web site that doesn't measure up. The key is to create enough value and excitement to get consumers who come to the site to stick around and come back again. At the very least, a Web site should be easy to use, professional looking, and physically attractive. Ultimately, however, Web sites must also be *useful*. When it comes to Web browsing and shopping, most people prefer substance over style and function over flash. Thus, effective Web sites contain deep and useful information, interactive tools that help buyers find and evaluate products of interest, links to other related sites, changing promotional offers, and entertaining features that lend relevant excitement.

Placing Ads and Promotions Online

Online advertising
Advertising that appears while consumers are browsing the Web, including display ads, search-related ads, online classifieds, and other forms.

As consumers spend more and more time on the Internet, companies are shifting more of their marketing dollars to **online advertising** to build their brands or attract visitors to their Web sites. Online advertising has become a major medium. Total U.S. Internet advertising spending will reach an estimated $31 billion this year and is expected to approach $50 billion by 2015, making it the second largest medium behind TV—ahead of even newspapers and magazines.[34]

The major forms of online advertising are search-related ads, display ads, and online classifieds. Online display ads might appear anywhere on an Internet user's screen and are often related to the information being viewed. For instance, while browsing vacation packages on Travelocity.com, you might encounter a display ad offering a free upgrade on a rental car from Enterprise Rent-A-Car. Or while visiting the Yahoo! Finance site, a flashing E*TRADE ad might promise a free BlackBerry smartphone when you open a new account. Internet display ads have come a long way in recent years in terms of attracting and holding consumer attention. New *rich media* ads now incorporate animation, video, sound, and interactivity.

The largest form of online advertising is *search-related ads* (or *contextual advertising*), which accounted for 46 percent of all online advertising spending last year. In search advertising, text-based ads and links appear alongside search engine results on sites such as Yahoo! and Google. For example, search Google for "LCD TVs." At the top and side of the resulting search list, you'll see inconspicuous ads for ten or more advertisers, ranging from Samsung and Dell to Best Buy, Sears, Amazon.com, Walmart.com, and Nextag.com. Nearly all of Google's $29 billion in revenues last year came from ad sales. Search is an always-on kind of medium. And in today's tight economy, the results are easily measured.[35]

A search advertiser buys search terms from the search site and pays only if consumers click through to its site. For instance, type "Coke" or "Coca-Cola" or even just "soft drinks" or "rewards" into your Google or Yahoo! search engine and almost without fail "My Coke Rewards" comes up as one of the top options. This is no coincidence. Coca-Cola supports its popular online loyalty program largely through search buys. The soft drink giant started first with traditional TV and print advertising but quickly learned that search was the most effective way to bring consumers to its www.mycokerewards.com Web site to register. Now, any of dozens of purchased search terms will return MyCokeRewards.com at or near the top of the search list.

Other forms of online promotions include content sponsorships and viral advertising. Using content sponsorships, companies gain name exposure on the Internet by sponsoring special content on various Web sites, such as news or financial information or special interest topics. For example, Alamo sponsors the "Vacation and Travel Planner and Guides" on Weather.com. And Marriott sponsors a "Summer to the Rescue!" microsite at Travelocity.com. Sponsorships are best placed in carefully targeted sites where they can offer relevant information or service to the audience.

Viral marketing

The Internet version of word-of-mouth marketing: a Web site, video, e-mail message, or other marketing event that is so infectious that customers will seek it out or pass it along to friends.

Finally, online marketers use **viral marketing**, the Internet version of word-of-mouth marketing. Viral marketing involves creating a Web site, video, e-mail, mobile message, advertisement, or other marketing event that is so infectious that customers will seek it out or pass it along to their friends. Because customers find and pass along the message or promotion, viral marketing can be very inexpensive. And when the information comes from a friend, the recipient is much more likely to view or read it.

For example, P&G's Old Spice brand created a viral sensation with its "Smell like a man, man" campaign featuring Isaiah Mustafa. The campaign consisted of TV ads and made-for-the-Web videos designed to go viral on YouTube, Facebook, and other social media. The initial campaign garnered tens of millions of viral views. A second campaign, which consisted of nearly 200 videos in which Mustafa responded personally to digital inquiries from users including Ellen DeGeneres and Alyssa Milano, scored 21 million views in only its first week. It increased the brand's Facebook interaction by 800 percent and OldSpice.com traffic by 300 percent. After the introduction of these videos, Old Spice's YouTube page became the all-time-most-viewed channel on the site.[36]

Sometimes a well-made regular ad can go viral with the help of targeted "seeding." ▶ For example, Volkswagen's clever "The Force" Super Bowl ad, featuring a pint-sized Darth Vader using The Force to start a VW Passat, turned viral after a team at VW's ad agency seeded it to selected auto, pop culture, and Star Wars sites the week before the sporting event. By the time the ad aired during the Super Bowl, it had received more than 18 million hits online.

▲ Viral marketing: Sometimes a well-made regular ad can go viral. For example, Volkswagen's clever "The Force" Super Bowl ad, featuring a pint-sized Darth Vader, received more than 18 million online hits the week before it aired on TV during the Super Bowl.
LUCASFILM/MCT/Newscom

However, marketers usually have little control over where their viral messages end up. They can seed messages online, but that does little good unless the message itself strikes a chord with consumers. For example, why did the seeded VW Darth Vader ad explode virally? Because the sentimental ad appeals to parents—the car's target demographic—who want a responsible suburban family ride. And it appeals to the child inside the parent, who may have once been wowed by *Star Wars* and now wants a car with a little bit of magic. Says one creative director, "you hope that the creative is at a high enough mark where the seeds grow into mighty oaks. If they don't like it, it ain't gonna move. If they like it, it'll move a little bit; and if they love it, it's gonna move like a fast-burning fire through the Hollywood hills."[37]

Creating or Participating in Online Social Networks

Online social networks

Online communities where people congregate, socialize, and exchange views and information.

As we discussed in Chapters 1 and 5, the popularity of the Internet has resulted in a rash of **online social networks** or *Web communities*. Countless independent and commercial Web sites have arisen that give consumers online places to congregate, socialize, and exchange views and information. These days, it seems, almost everyone is buddying up on Facebook, checking in with Twitter, tuning into the day's hottest videos at YouTube, or checking out photos on Flickr. And, of course, wherever consumers congregate, marketers will surely follow. Most marketers are now riding the huge social networking wave.

Marketers can engage in online communities in two ways: They can participate in existing Web communities or they can set up their own. Joining existing networks seems the easiest. Thus, most major brands—from Dunkin' Donuts and Harley-Davidson to Nissan and Victoria's Secret—have created YouTube channels. GM and other companies have posted visual content on Flickr. Coca-Cola's Facebook page has 26 million fans.

Some of the major social networks are huge. The largest social network—Facebook—by itself commands 70 percent of all social network traffic. Forty-seven percent of the online population visits Facebook every day. That rivals the 55 percent who watch any TV channel and trounces the percentage listening to radio (37 percent) and reading newspapers (22 percent) daily. Now at more than 720 million members, Facebook aims to reach one billion members by 2012.[38]

Although large online social networks such as Facebook, YouTube, and Twitter have grabbed most of the headlines, a new breed of more focused niche networks has emerged. These networks cater to the needs of smaller communities of like-minded people, making them ideal vehicles for marketers who want to target special interest groups. There's at least one social network for just about every interest or hobby.[39]

▲ Thousands of social networking sites have popped up to cater to specific interests, backgrounds, professions, and age groups. At Dogster, 700,000 members set up profiles of their four-legged friends, read doggy diaries, or just give a dog a bone.

Dogster.com

Yub.com and kaboodle.com I are for shopaholics, moms advise and commiserate at CafeMom.com, and PassportStamp.com is one of several sites for avid travelers. GoFISHn, a community of 4,000 anglers, features maps that pinpoint where fish are biting and a photo gallery where members can show off their catches. ▶ At Dogster, 700,000 members set up profiles of their four-legged friends, read doggy diaries, or just give a dog a bone. On Ravelry.com, 1.4 million registered knitters, crocheters, designers, spinners, and dyers share information about yarn, patterns, methods, and tools.

Some niche sites cater to the obscure. Passions Network is an "online dating niche social network" with 600,000 members and 145 groups for specific interests, including Star Trek fans, truckers, atheists, and people who are shy. Others reach more technical communities: More than a million scientists use ResearchGATE to coordinate research in areas such as artificial intelligence and cancer biology. And at myTransponder.com, pilots find work, students locate flight instructors, and trade-specific advertisers—such as aviation software maker ForeFlight—hone in on a hard-to-reach audience of more than 2,000 people who love aviation. The myTransponder community aims to "make aviation more social."

But participating successfully in existing online social networks presents challenges. First, most companies are still experimenting with how to use them effectively, and results are hard to measure. Second, such online networks are largely user controlled. The company's goal is to make the brand a part of consumers' conversations and their lives. However, marketers can't simply muscle their way into consumers' online interactions—they need to earn the right to be there. A brand has no right to be there unless the conversation is already about that brand. Rather than intruding, marketers must learn to become a valued part of the online experience.

To avoid the mysteries and challenges of building a presence on existing online social networks, many companies have created their own targeted Web communities. For example, on Nike's Nike+ Web site, more than 4 million runners with more than 375 million miles logged in 243 countries join together online to upload, track, and compare their performances. Nike plans eventually to have 15 percent or more of the world's 100 million runners actively participating in the Nike+ online community.[40]

Similarly, *Men's Health* magazine created a Web community in conjunction with its Belly Off! program (http://my.menshealth.com/bellyoff/). The magazine's long-running program helps readers develop a solid plan for exercise and diet over a set schedule. The community Web site incorporates user-generated content and offers workout and eating plans, reports on progress, how-to videos, and success stories. In all, the Belly Off! site serves a community of nearly 125,000 members who share similar weight-loss and fitness goals. Since 2001, the program has helped 400,000 people lose nearly 2 million pounds.[41]

Sending E-Mail

E-mail marketing

Sending highly targeted, tightly personalized, relationship-building marketing messages via e-mail.

E-mail marketing is an important and growing online marketing tool. E-mail is a much-used communication tool; by one estimate, the number of worldwide e-mail accounts will grow from the current 2.9 billion to more than 3.8 billion over the next five years. Not surprisingly, then, a recent study by the DMA found that 79 percent of all direct marketing campaigns employ e-mail. U.S. companies now spend more than $660 million a year on e-mail marketing, and this spending will grow by an estimated 13.6 percent annually through 2014.[42]

When used properly, e-mail can be the ultimate direct marketing medium. Most blue-chip marketers use it regularly and with great success. E-mail lets these marketers send highly targeted, tightly personalized, relationship-building messages. For example, the National Hockey League (NHL) sends hypertargeted e-newsletters to fans based on their team affiliations and locations. It sends 62 versions of the e-newsletter weekly—two for each of the 30 teams, tailored to fans in the United States and Canada, respectively, and two generic league e-newsletters for the two countries. Another NHL e-mail campaign promoting the start of single-game ticket sales had 930 versions.[43]

Spam

Unsolicited, unwanted commercial e-mail messages.

But there's a dark side to the growing use of e-mail marketing. ▶ The explosion of **spam**—unsolicited, unwanted commercial e-mail messages that clog up our e-mailboxes—has produced consumer irritation and frustration. According to one research company, spam now accounts for almost 75 percent of all e-mail sent.[44] E-mail marketers walk a fine line between adding value for consumers and being intrusive.

To address these concerns, most legitimate marketers now practice *permission-based e-mail marketing*, sending e-mail pitches only to customers who "opt in." Many companies use configurable e-mail systems that let customers choose what they want to get. Amazon.com targets opt-in customers with a limited number of helpful "we thought you'd like to know" messages

▲ E-mail can be an effective marketing tool. But there's a dark side—spam, unwanted commercial e-mail that clogs up our inboxes and causes frustration.

(left) iStockphoto International; (right) ICP/incamerastock/Alamy

based on their expressed preferences and previous purchases. Few customers object, and many actually welcome such promotional messages. Similarly, StubHub redesigned its e-mail system to make certain that its e-mails go only to consumers who actually *want* to receive them:

> As a start-up almost a decade ago, online ticket merchant StubHub ran "batch-and-blast" e-mail campaigns focused on building awareness. For years, sheer volume far outweighed e-mail relevancy. But StubHub has now learned the value of carefully targeted, relevant e-mail messages. It now lets customers opt in for e-mail at registration, during purchases, and at sign-up modules throughout the StubHub site. Using opt-in customer data, StubHub targets designated consumer segments with ticket and event information closely aligned with their interests. Incorporating customer data produced immediate and stunning results. E-mail click-through rates quickly jumped 30 percent, and the company saw a 79 percent year-over-year increase in ticket sales despite having sent fewer e-mails. "The results speak for themselves," says a StubHub marketer. "These [new targeted campaigns] are driving 2,500 percent more revenue per e-mail than [our] average marketing campaigns."[45]

Given its targeting effectiveness and low costs, e-mail can be an outstanding marketing investment. According to the DMA, e-mail marketing produces the greatest return on investment of all direct marketing media.[46]

Using Mobile Marketing

Mobile marketing

Marketing to on-the-go consumers through mobile phones, smartphones, tablets, and other mobile communication devices.

Mobile marketing features marketing messages and promotions delivered to on-the-go consumers through their mobile devices. Marketers use mobile marketing to reach and interact with customers anywhere, anytime during the buying and relationship-building processes. The widespread adoption of mobile devices and the surge in mobile Web traffic have made mobile marketing a must for most brands.

With the recent proliferation of mobile phones, smartphone devices, and tablet PCs, more than 96 percent of U.S. households own some sort of mobile device. Nearly 27 percent of U.S. households are currently mobile-only households; this means they have no landline and instead depend on mobile devices to make and receive all calls. Furthermore, about 63 million people in the United States own a smartphone device, and about 35 percent of smartphone users use it to access the mobile Internet. They not only browse the mobile Web but are also avid mobile application users. The mobile apps market is exploding: The Apple App Store offers 425,000 iPhone apps plus another 90,000 iPad apps. Android Market offers upwards of 150,00 apps.[47]

A recent study estimates that mobile advertising spending in the United States will grow from $743 million in 2010 to $2.5 billion by 2014. Marketers of all kinds—from Pepsi and Nordstrom to nonprofits such as the ASPCA to the local bank or supermarket—are now integrating mobile platforms into their direct marketing. Sixty percent of mobile users currently click on a mobile ad at least once a week.[48]

A mobile marketing campaign might involve placing display ads, search ads, or videos on relevant mobile Web sites and online communities such as Facebook or YouTube. Today's rich media mobile ads can create substantial impact and involvement. For example, HBO ran engaging mobile ads for the season premiere of its *True Blood* series:[49]

> Imagine browsing through the Flixter app looking for a movie or browsing the Variety app, and the first touch of the screen turns into a bloody fingerprint. Touch again and get another fingerprint, then the blood pours down and takes over the screen and the activation pops up, a tap-to-watch-trailer call-to-action screen with a banner ad at the bottom. HBO's *True Blood* mobile ad campaign sent chills down consumers' spines and increased viewership 38 percent; 5.1 million viewers tuned in to view the season premiere.

A mobile marketing effort might be as simple as inviting people to text a number, such as when the Red Cross asked for Japan earthquake and tsunami relief donations (text "JAPAN" to 90999 to donate $10). It might involve texting promotions to consumers—anything from retailer announcements of discounts, brand coupons, and gift suggestions to mobile games and contests. Many marketers have also created their own mobile Web sites, optimized for specific phones and mobile service providers. Others have created useful or entertaining mobile apps to engage customers with their brands and help them shop (see Marketing at Work 14.2). For example, Nike gained unprecedented direct access to runners with a Nike+ GPS iPhone app for real-time tracking of runs and bike rides.

MARKETING AT WORK   14.2

Mobile Marketing: Customers Come Calling

You're at the local Best Buy checking out portable GPS navigation systems. You've narrowed it down to the latest Garmin nüvi versus a less-expensive competing model, but you're not certain that Best Buy has the best prices. Also, you'd love to know how other consumers rate the two brands. No problem. Just pull out your smartphone and launch your Amazon Mobile app, which lets you browse the brands you're considering, read customer reviews, and compare prices of portable GPS systems sold by Amazon.com and its retail partners. The application even lets you snap a photo or scan a barcode from an item; Amazon.com employees will then search for a similar item available from Amazon. If Amazon.com offers a better deal, you can make the purchase directly from the application.

Welcome to the new world of mobile marketing. Today's new smartphones are changing the way we live—including the way we shop. And as they change how we shop, they also change how marketers sell to us.

A growing number of consumers—especially younger ones—are using their mobile phones as a "third screen" for texting, browsing the mobile Web, watching videos and shows, and checking e-mail. According to one expert, "the mobile phone . . . is morphing into a content device, a kind of digital Swiss army knife with the capability of filling its owner's every spare minute with games, music, live and on-demand TV, Web browsing, and, oh yes, advertising." Says the president of the Mobile Marketing Association, "It's only a matter of time before mobile is the 'first screen.'" According to another industry insider:

Mobile phones, iPads, and other mobile devices have quietly become the hottest new frontier for marketers, especially those targeting the coveted 18- to 34-year-old set. TV networks are prodding viewers to send text messages to vote for their favorite reality TV character. Wireless Web sites are lacing sports scores and news digests with banner ads for Lexus, Burger King, and Sheraton. A few companies are even customizing 10-second video ads for short, TV-style episodes that are edging their way onto mobile phones. For advertisers, the young audience is just one selling point. Mobile gadgets are always-on, ever-present accessories. The fact that a phone or other device is tethered to an individual means that ads can be targeted. And users can respond instantly to time-sensitive offers. The mobile phone is very personal, and it's always with you.

Marketers large and small are weaving mobile marketing into their direct marketing mixes. For example, Walmart uses text message alerts to spread the news about sales; once you receive a text, you can click on links within the messages to go to the retailer's mobile Web site and check on details. Unilever

phones out mobile coupons for Ragu pasta sauce, Dove body wash, Breyers ice cream, and its other brands: Just hold up your mobile phone at the checkout, and the cashier will scan the barcode off the screen. Tide's Stain Brain app helps customers find ways to remove stains. A Sit or Squat app that directs people to nearby public restrooms opens with a splash page for Charmin bathroom tissue.

Beyond helping you buy, other mobile marketing applications provide helpful services, useful information, and entertainment. USAA's mobile banking app lets you check your balance, transfer funds, and even deposit a check via phone by taking a photo of the front and back of the check and hitting "send." Zipcar's app lets members find and reserve a Zipcar, honk the horn (so they can find it in a crowd), and even lock and unlock the doors—all from their phones. REI's The Snow and Ski Report app gives ski slope information for locations throughout the United States and Canada, such as snow depth, snow conditions, and the number of open lifts. The app also links you to "Shop REI," for times "when you decide you can't live without a new set of K2 skis or a two-man Hoo-Doo tent."

For entertainment, carmaker Audi offers the Audi A4 Driving Challenge game for the iPhone, iPod, and iPod Touch, which features a tiny A4 that maneuvers its way through different driving courses—to steer, you tilt your phone right or left. Similarly, Audi's

▲ **Mobile marketing:** Zipcar's iPhone app lets members find and book a Zipcar, honk the horn (so they can find it in a crowd), and even lock and unlock the doors—all from their iPhone.

Copyright Zipcar, Inc.

"Truth in 24" app lets you in on the action behind the notorious 24 Hours of Le Mans Audi auto race, including an iPhone game that "puts the excitement of LeMans racing right in the palm of your hand." For customers interested in reviewing Audi's cars, Audi A4 and A8 "Experience" apps let you explore these models interactively inside and out. Audi claims that such apps have been downloaded millions of times, drawing hundreds of thousands of visitors to its mobile Web sites.

One of the most effective mobile marketing applications is Kraft's iFood Assistant, which provides easy-to-prepare recipes for food shoppers on the go, how-to videos, a recipe box, and a built-in shopping list. iFood Assistant supplies advice on how to prepare some 7,000 simple but satisfying meals—at three meals a day, that's almost 20 years worth of recipes. The iFood Assistant will even give you directions to local stores. Of course, most of the meals call for ingredients that just happen to be Kraft brands. The iFood Assistant app cost Kraft less than $100,000 to create but has engaged millions of shoppers, providing great marketing opportunities for Kraft and its brands.

Increasingly, consumers are using their phones as in-store shopping aids, and retailers are responding accordingly. For example, while strolling among the bookshelves at the local Barnes & Noble store, you can now snap a photo of any book cover that strikes your interest and use a Barnes & Noble app to learn more

about it. The app uses image-recognition software to recognize the book and then almost instantly pulls up user reviews from barnesandnoble.com to help shoppers decide whether to buy. "We've seen a huge uplift in reservations of books for purchase in physical stores, as well as buying, from the . . . app since we launched it," says the chain's vice president for digital devices.

Many consumers are initially skeptical about mobile marketing. But they often change their minds if mobile marketers deliver value in the form of useful brand and shopping information, entertaining content, or discounted prices and coupons for their favorite products and services. Most mobile marketing efforts target only consumers who voluntarily opt in or who download apps. In the increasingly cluttered mobile marketing space, customers just won't do that unless they see real value in it. The challenge for marketers: Develop useful and engaging mobile marketing apps that make customers come calling.

Sources: Adapted extract, quotes, and other information from Christine Birkner, "Mobile Marketing: This Time It's Different," *Marketing News,* January 30, 2011, pp. 17–18; Richard Westlund, "Mobile on Fast Forward," *Brandweek*, March 15, 2010, pp. M1–M5; Todd Wasserman, "I'm on the Phone!" *Adweek*, February 23, 2009, pp. 6–7; Alice Z. Cuneo, "Scramble for Content Drives Mobile," *Advertising Age*, October 24, 2005, p. S6; Jen Arnoff, "Wising Up to Smart Phones," *News & Observer* (Raleigh), April 22, 2009, p. 5B; Carol Angrisani, "Priced to Cell," *Supermarket News*, June 1, 2009, p. 28; Reena Jana, "Retailers Are Learning to Love Smartphones," *Businessweek*, October 26, 2009, p. 49; and www .usaa.com/inet/pages/usaa_mobile_main, accessed August 2011.

As with other forms of direct marketing, however, companies must use mobile marketing responsibly or risk angering already ad-weary consumers. "If you were interrupted every two minutes by advertising, not many people want that," says a mobile marketing expert. "The industry needs to work out smart and clever ways to engage people on mobiles." The key is to provide genuinely useful information and offers that will make consumers want to opt in or call in. One study found that 42 percent of cell phone users are open to mobile advertising if it's relevant.[50]

In all, online marketing continues to offer both great promise and many challenges for the future. Its most ardent apostles still envision a time when the Internet and online marketing will replace magazines, newspapers, and even stores as sources for information and buying. Most marketers, however, hold a more realistic view. To be sure, online marketing has become a successful business model for some companies—Internet firms such as Amazon .com, Facebook, and Google, as well as direct marketing companies such as GEICO and Netflix. However, for most companies, online marketing will remain just one important approach to the marketplace that works alongside other approaches in a fully integrated marketing mix.

Public Policy Issues in Direct Marketing

Author Comment ▶

Although we mostly benefit from direct marketing, like most other things in life, it has its dark side as well. Marketers and customers alike must guard against irritating or harmful direct marketing practices.

Direct marketers and their customers usually enjoy mutually rewarding relationships. Occasionally, however, a darker side emerges. The aggressive and sometimes shady tactics of a few direct marketers can bother or harm consumers, giving the entire industry a black eye. Abuses range from simple excesses that irritate consumers to instances of unfair practices or even outright deception and fraud. The direct marketing industry has also faced growing privacy concerns, and online marketers must deal with Internet security issues.

Irritation, Unfairness, Deception, and Fraud

Direct marketing excesses sometimes annoy or offend consumers. For example, most of us dislike direct-response TV commercials that are too loud, long, and insistent. Our mailboxes fill up with unwanted junk mail, our e-mailboxes bulge with unwanted spam, and our computer screens flash with unwanted display or pop-up ads.

Beyond irritating consumers, some direct marketers have been accused of taking unfair advantage of impulsive or less-sophisticated buyers. Television shopping channels and program-long infomercials targeting television-addicted shoppers seem to be the worst culprits. They feature smooth-talking hosts, elaborately staged demonstrations, claims of drastic price reductions, "while they last" time limitations, and unequaled ease of purchase to inflame buyers who have low sales resistance. Worse yet, so-called heat merchants design mailers and write copy intended to mislead buyers.

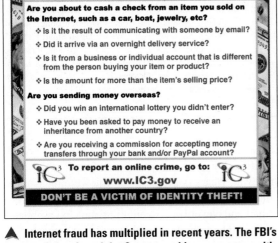

▲ **Internet fraud has multiplied in recent years. The FBI's Internet Crime Complaint Center provides consumers with a convenient way to alert authorities to suspected violations.**

FBI

Fraudulent schemes, such as investment scams or phony collections for charity, have also multiplied in recent years. *Internet fraud*, including identity theft and financial scams, has become a serious problem. ▶ Last year alone, the FBI's Internet Crime Complaint Center (IC3) received nearly 304,000 complaints related to Internet fraud involving monetary loss.[51]

One common form of Internet fraud is *phishing*, a type of identity theft that uses deceptive e-mails and fraudulent Web sites to fool users into divulging their personal data. For example, consumers may receive an e-mail, supposedly from their bank or credit card company, saying that their account's security has been compromised. The sender asks them to log onto a provided Web address and confirm their account number, password, and perhaps even their social security number. If they follow the instructions, they are actually turning this sensitive information over to scam artists. Although many consumers are now aware of such schemes, phishing can be extremely costly to those caught in the net. It also damages the brand identities of legitimate online marketers who have worked to build user confidence in Web and e-mail transactions.

Many consumers also worry about *online security*. They fear that unscrupulous snoopers will eavesdrop on their online transactions, picking up personal information or intercepting credit and debit card numbers. Although online shopping has grown rapidly, 75 percent of participants in one survey said they still do not like sending personal or credit card information over the Internet.[52] Internet shoppers are also concerned about contracting annoying or harmful viruses, spyware, and other malware (malicious software).

Another Internet marketing concern is that of *access by vulnerable or unauthorized groups*. For example, marketers of adult-oriented materials and sites have found it difficult to restrict access by minors. A survey by *Consumer Reports* found 5 million U.S. children under age 10 on Facebook, which supposedly allows no children under age 13 to have a profile. It found another 2.5 million 11- and 12-year-old Facebook subscribers. And it's not just Facebook. Young users are logging onto social networks such as Formspring, tweeting their location to the Web, and making friends out of strangers on Disney and other games sites. Concerned state and national lawmakers are currently debating bills that would help better protect children online. Unfortunately, this requires the development of technology solutions, and as Facebook puts it, "That's not so easy."[53]

Consumer Privacy

Invasion of privacy is perhaps the toughest public policy issue now confronting the direct marketing industry. Consumers often benefit from database marketing; they receive more offers that are closely matched to their interests. However, many critics worry that marketers may know *too* much about consumers' lives and that they may use this knowledge to take unfair advantage of consumers. At some point, they claim, the extensive use of databases intrudes on consumer privacy.

These days, it seems that almost every time consumers enter a sweepstakes; apply for a credit card; visit a Web site; or order products by mail, telephone, or the Internet, their names are entered into some company's already bulging database. Using sophisticated computer technologies, direct marketers can use these databases to "microtarget" their selling efforts. Most marketers have become highly skilled at collecting and analyzing detailed consumer information. Even the experts are sometimes surprised by how much marketers can learn. Consider this account by one *Advertising Age* reporter:[54]

> I'm no neophyte when it comes to targeting—not only do I work at *Ad Age*, but I cover direct marketing. Yet even I was taken aback when, as an experiment, we asked the database-marketing company to come up with a demographic and psychographic profile of me. Was it ever spot-on. Using only publicly available information, it concluded my date of birth, home phone number, and political-party affiliation. It gleamed that I was a college graduate, that I was married, and that one of my parents had passed away. It found that I have several bank, credit, and retail cards at "low-end" department stores. It knew not just how long I've lived at my house but how much it costs, how much it was worth, the type of mortgage that's on it, and—within a really close ballpark guess—how much is left to pay on it. It estimated my household income—again nearly perfectly—and determined that I am of British descent.
>
> But that was just the beginning. The company also nailed my psychographic profile. It correctly placed me into various groupings such as: someone who relies more on their own opinions than the recommendations of others when making a purchase; someone who is turned off by loud and aggressive advertising; someone who is family-oriented and has an interest in music, running, sports, computers, and is an avid concert-goer; someone who is never far from a Web connection, generally used to peruse sports and general news updates; and someone who sees health as a core value. Scary? Certainly.

Some consumers and policy makers worry that the ready availability of information may leave consumers open to abuse. For example, they ask, should Web sellers be allowed to plant cookies in the browsers of consumers who visit their sites and use tracking information to target ads and other marketing efforts? Should credit card companies be allowed to make data on their millions of cardholders worldwide available to merchants who accept their cards? Or is it right for states to sell the names and addresses of driver's license holders, along with height, weight, and gender information, allowing apparel retailers to target tall or overweight people with special clothing offers?

A Need for Action

To curb direct marketing excesses, various government agencies are investigating not only do-not-call lists but also do-not-mail lists, do-not-track lists, and Can Spam legislation. In response to online privacy and security concerns, the federal government has considered numerous legislative actions to regulate how Web operators obtain and use consumer information. For example, Congress is drafting legislation that would give consumers more control over how Web information is used. In addition, the FTC is taking a more active role in policing online privacy.

All of these concerns call for strong actions by marketers to prevent privacy abuses before legislators step in to do it for them. For example, to head off increased government regulation, four advertiser groups—the American Association of Advertising Agencies, the Association of National Advertisers, the DMA, and the Interactive Advertising Bureau—recently issued new guidelines for Web sites. Among other measures, the guidelines call for Web marketers to alert consumers if their activities are being tracked. The ad industry has agreed on an *advertising option icon*—a little "i" inside a triangle—that it will add to most behaviorally targeted online ads to tell consumers why they are seeing a particular ad and allowing them to opt out.[55]

Of special concern are the privacy rights of children. In 2000, Congress passed the Children's Online Privacy Protection Act (COPPA), which requires Web site operators targeting children to post privacy policies on their sites. They must also notify parents about any information they're gathering and obtain parental consent before collecting personal information from children under age 13. With the subsequent advent of online social networks, mobile phones, and other new technologies, privacy groups are now urging the U.S.

▲ Consumer privacy: By clicking on the little AdChoices advertising option icon in the upper right of this online ad, consumers can learn why they are seeing the ad and opt out if they wish.

Senate to extend COPPA to include both the new technologies and teenagers. The main concern is the amount of data mined by third parties from social networks as well as the social networks' own hazy privacy policies.[56]

Many companies have responded to consumer privacy and security concerns with actions of their own. Still others are taking an industry-wide approach. For example, TRUSTe, a nonprofit self-regulatory organization, works with many large corporate sponsors, including Microsoft, Yahoo!, AT&T, Facebook, Disney, and Apple, to audit privacy and security measures and help consumers navigate the Web safely. According to the company's Web site, "TRUSTe believes that an environment of mutual trust and openness will help make and keep the Internet a free, comfortable, and richly diverse community for everyone." To reassure consumers, the company lends its TRUSTe privacy seal to Web sites that meet its privacy and security standards.[57]

The direct marketing industry as a whole is also addressing public policy issues. For example, in an effort to build consumer confidence in shopping direct, the DMA—the largest association for businesses practicing direct, database, and interactive marketing, including nearly half of the Fortune 100 companies—launched a "Privacy Promise to American Consumers." The Privacy Promise requires that all DMA members adhere to a carefully developed set of consumer privacy rules. Members must agree to notify customers when any personal information is rented, sold, or exchanged with others. They must also honor consumer requests to opt out of receiving further solicitations or having their contact information transferred to other marketers. Finally, they must abide by the DMA's Preference Service by removing the names of consumers who do not wish to receive mail, telephone, or e-mail offers.[58]

Direct marketers know that, if left untended, such direct marketing abuses will lead to increasingly negative consumer attitudes, lower response rates, and calls for more restrictive state and federal legislation. Most direct marketers want the same things that consumers want: honest and well-designed marketing offers targeted only toward consumers who will appreciate and respond to them. Direct marketing is just too expensive to waste on consumers who don't want it.

REST STOP · REVIEWING THE CONCEPTS

MyMarketingLab

Now that you have completed the chapter, return to www.mymktlab.com to experience and apply the concepts and to explore the additional study materials for this chapter.

CHAPTER REVIEW AND KEY TERMS

Objectives Review

This chapter is the last of three chapters covering the final marketing mix element—promotion. The previous chapters dealt with advertising, public relations, personal selling, and sales promotion. This one investigates the burgeoning field of direct and online marketing.

 OBJECTIVE 1 Define direct marketing and discuss its benefits to customers and companies. (pp 423–427)

Direct marketing consists of direct connections with carefully targeted segments or individual consumers. Beyond brand and

relationship building, direct marketers usually seek a direct, immediate, and measurable consumer response. Using detailed databases, direct marketers tailor their offers and communications to the needs of narrowly defined segments or even individual buyers.

For buyers, direct marketing is convenient, easy to use, and private. It gives buyers ready access to a wealth of products and information, at home and around the globe. Direct marketing is also immediate and interactive, allowing buyers to create exactly the configuration of information, products, or services they desire and then order them on the spot. For sellers, direct marketing is a powerful tool for building customer relationships. Using database marketing, today's marketers can target small groups or individual customers, tailor offers to individual needs, and promote these offers through personalized communications. It also offers them a low-cost, efficient alternative for reaching their markets. As a result of these advantages to both buyers and sellers, direct marketing has become the fastest-growing form of marketing.

 OBJECTIVE 2 Identify and discuss the major forms of direct marketing. (pp 427–432)

The main forms of direct marketing are *personal face-to-face selling, direct-mail marketing, catalog marketing, telemarketing, DRTV marketing, kiosk marketing*, and *online marketing*. We discussed personal selling in the previous chapter.

Direct-mail marketing, the largest form of direct marketing, consists of the company sending an offer, announcement, reminder, or other item to a person at a specific address. Some marketers rely on catalog marketing—selling through catalogs mailed to a select list of customers, made available in stores, or accessed on the Web. Telemarketing consists of using the telephone to sell directly to consumers. DRTV marketing has two forms: direct-response advertising (or infomercials) and interactive television (iTV) marketing. Kiosks are information and ordering machines that direct marketers place in stores, airports, hotels, and other locations. Online marketing involves online channels that digitally link sellers with consumers.

 OBJECTIVE 3 Explain how companies have responded to the Internet and other powerful new technologies with online marketing strategies. (pp 432–436)

Online marketing is the fastest-growing form of direct marketing. The *Internet* enables consumers and companies to access and share huge amounts of information through their computers, smartphones, tablets, and other devices. In turn, the Internet has given marketers a whole new way to create value for customers and build customer relationships. It's hard to find a company today that doesn't have a substantial online marketing presence.

Online consumer buying continues to grow at a healthy rate. Most American online users now use the Internet to shop. Perhaps more importantly, the Internet influences offline shopping as well. Thus, smart marketers are employing integrated multichannel strategies that use the Internet to drive sales to other marketing channels.

 OBJECTIVE 4 Discuss how companies go about conducting online marketing to profitably deliver more value to customers. (pp 436–443)

Companies of all types are now engaged in online marketing. The Internet gave birth to the *click-only companies* that operate online only. In addition, many traditional brick-and-mortar companies have added online marketing operations, transforming themselves into *click-and-mortar companies*. Many click-and-mortar companies are now having more online success than the click-only companies.

Companies can conduct online marketing in any or all of these five ways: creating Web sites, placing ads and promotions online, setting up or participating in Web communities and online social networks, sending e-mail, or using mobile marketing. The first step typically is to create a Web site. Beyond simply creating a site, however, companies must make their sites engaging, easy to use, and useful to attract visitors, hold them, and bring them back again.

Online marketers can use various forms of online advertising and promotion to build their Internet brands or attract visitors to their Web sites. Forms of online promotion include online display advertising, search-related advertising, content sponsorships, and *viral marketing*, the Internet version of word-of-mouth marketing. Online marketers can also participate in online social networks and other Web communities, which take advantage of the *C-to-C* properties of the Web. Finally, e-mail and mobile marketing have become a fast-growing tool for both *B-to-C* and *B-to-B* marketers. Whatever direct marketing tools they use, marketers must work hard to integrate them into a cohesive marketing effort.

 OBJECTIVE 5 Overview the public policy and ethical issues presented by direct marketing. (pp 443–446)

Direct marketers and their customers usually enjoy mutually rewarding relationships. Sometimes, however, direct marketing presents a darker side. The aggressive and sometimes shady tactics of a few direct marketers can bother or harm consumers, giving the entire industry a black eye. Abuses range from simple excesses that irritate consumers to instances of unfair practices or even outright deception and fraud. The direct marketing industry has also faced growing concerns about invasion-of-privacy and Internet security issues. Such concerns call for strong action by marketers and public policy makers to curb direct marketing abuses. In the end, most direct marketers want the same things that consumers want: honest and well-designed marketing offers targeted only toward consumers who will appreciate and respond to them.

Key Terms

Objective 1
Direct marketing (p 422)
Customer database (p 426)

Objective 2
Direct-mail marketing (p 428)
Catalog marketing (p 429)

Telemarketing (p 430)
Direct-response television (DRTV)
  marketing (p 430)

Objective 3

Online marketing (p 432)
Internet (p 433)
Click-only companies (p 433)
Click-and-mortar companies (p 433)
Business-to-consumer (B-to-C) online
marketing (p 434)
Business-to business (B-to-B) online
marketing (p 434)

Consumer-to-consumer (C-to-C) online
marketing (p 434)
Blogs (p 435)
Consumer-to-business (C-to-B) online
marketing (p 436)

Objective 4

Corporate (or brand) Web site (p 437)
Marketing Web site (p 437)

Online advertising (p 437)
Viral marketing (p 438)
Online social networks (p 439)
E-mail marketing (p 440)
Spam (p 440)
Mobile marketing (p 441)

DISCUSSION AND CRITICAL THINKING

Discussion Questions

1. Discuss the benefits of direct marketing for both buyers and sellers. (AACSB: Communication)
2. List and briefly describe the various forms of direct marketing. (AACSB: Communication)
3. Describe the four major e-marketing domains and provide an example of each. (AACSB: Communication)
4. Explain the ways in which companies can set up an online marketing presence. (AACSB: Communication)

5. Compare and contrast the different forms of online advertising. What factors should a company consider in deciding among these different forms? (AACSB: Communication)
6. What is *phishing* and how does it harm consumers and marketers? (AACSB: Communication; Reflective Thinking)

Critical Thinking Exercises

1. In a small group, design and deliver a direct-response television ad (DRTV) for a national brand not normally associated with this type of promotion, such as an athletic shoe, automobile, or food product. (AACSB: Communication; Reflective Thinking)
2. Review the FTC's guidelines on sponsored conversations (www.ftc.gov/os/2009/10/091005revisedendorsementguides.pdf) and visit the Word of Mouth Marketing Association's

Web site (womma.org) and IZEA's Web site (IZEA.com). Write a report on how marketers can effectively use sponsored conversations within the FTC's guidelines. (AACSB: Communication; Reflective Thinking)
3. Find articles about two data security breaches in the news. How did the breaches occur and who is potentially affected by them? (AACSB: Communication; Reflective Thinking)

MINICASES AND APPLICATIONS

Marketing Technology: Marketing to Those on the Go

Your smartphone might someday be the only thing you'll need for locking your door, starting a car, paying for purchases, or even simply paying your friend the $20 you owe him. Mobile technologies allow users to do almost anything remotely and allow marketers to target services and promotions directly to consumers based on where they are. You may have noticed some Starbucks customers just wave their phones in front of a scanner—no wallet, cash, or card required. Those customers may have gotten discount offers that lured them to Starbucks

because their phone tipped the marketer off that they were nearby.

1. What mobile applications currently exist and what's on the horizon? How many of these applications do you or someone you know use? (AACSB: Communication; Use of IT; Reflective Thinking)
2. What are the barriers to adoption of mobile applications? (AACSB: Communication; Reflective Thinking)

Marketing Ethics   Online Tax Battle

Online retailing is experiencing phenomenal growth, but struggling states are not reaping the spoils—in taxes, that is. One study estimates lost state and local revenue at upwards of $10 billion a year on nontaxed e-commerce. Amazon.com is the biggest beneficiary. States are battling back by introducing, and sometimes successfully passing, laws informally dubbed "Amazon laws" that require online retailers to collect state sales taxes. These taxation efforts have the support of rivals such as Walmart and Target. To counter them, Amazon strategically seeks to minimize sales tax collection across the country by using legal loopholes and even limiting employees' activities when traveling to certain states deemed "bad states" because of their efforts to enact tax laws to grab a piece of Amazon's profits.

It's worth the effort to Amazon to fight tax initiatives, however, as Credit Suisse estimated Amazon would lose $653 million in sales if it had to collect sales taxes in all states.

1. Debate whether or not online retailers should be required to collect state sales taxes. Suggest an equitable solution to this issue. (AACSB: Communication; Ethical Reasoning)
2. Research online tax rules. Look specifically at the 1992 Supreme Court ruling in *Quill Corp. v. North Dakota* on which the rules are based. Is this rule still relevant? Are Amazon and other online retailers being ethical by using this rule to their advantage? (AACSB: Communication; Reflective Thinking; Ethical Reasoning)

Marketing by the Numbers   The Power of "Like"

Marketers know that Facebook is a force to be reckoned with, but until now they have not been able to measure that force and compare it to traditional media. Whereas traditional media have established metrics, such as ratings, to measure what marketers are getting for their money, an entirely new set of metrics—such as *click-through rates* and *impressions*—has evolved for online media. Unfortunately, the two metrics are not comparable. ComScore and Nielsen are two companies attempting to rectify that situation by developing a rating system based on *gross rating points* to show the power of Facebook as a marketing tool.

1. Research marketing expenditure trends in social media marketing as well as other forms of online advertising. Compare these trends with traditional advertising media expenditures. Develop a presentation illustrating those trends. (AACSB: Communication; Analytical Reasoning; Reflective Thinking)
2. Visit www.comScore.com and www.Nielsen.com to learn more about the measures these companies have developed for measuring the marketing exposure of brands on Facebook. How do these metrics differ from those that have been used with regard to measuring online advertising impact? (AACSB: Communication; Use of IT; Reflective Thinking)

Video Case   Home Shopping Network

Long ago, television marketing was associated with low-quality commercials broadcast in the wee hours of the morning that offered obscure merchandise. But Home Shopping Network (HSN) has played an instrumental role in making television shopping a legitimate outlet. Around the clock, top-quality programming featuring name-brand merchandise is now the norm.

But just like any retailer, HSN has had its share of challenges. This video illustrates how HSN has focused on principles of direct marketing in order to overcome these challenges and form strong customer relationships. As market conditions continue to shift, HSN explores new ways to form and strengthen direct relationships with customers.

After viewing the video featuring HSN, answer the following questions:

1. What are the different ways that HSN engages in direct marketing?
2. What advantages does HSN specifically have over brick-and-mortar retailers?
3. What recommendations would you suggest for how HSN could make better use of its role as a direct marketer?

Company Cases   10 Pandora / 14 eBay

See Appendix 1 for cases appropriate for this chapter. **Case 10: Pandora: Disintermediator or Disintermediated?** Using an ingenious mathematical algorithm, music service Pandora knows exactly what customers want to hear. **Case 14, eBay: Fixing an Online Marketing Pioneer.** Once the biggest online retailer, eBay alters its marketing strategy to alleviate growing pains.

15 The Global Marketplace

CHAPTER ROAD MAP

Objective Outline

▶ **OBJECTIVE 1** **Discuss how the international trade system and the economic, political-legal, and cultural environments affect a company's international marketing decisions.** Global Marketing Today (452–454); Looking at the Global Marketing Environment (454–460); Deciding Whether to Go Global (461); Deciding Which Markets to Enter (461–463)

▶ **OBJECTIVE 2** **Describe three key approaches to entering international markets.** Deciding How to Enter the Market (463–467)

▶ **OBJECTIVE 3** **Explain how companies adapt their marketing strategies and mixes for international markets.** Deciding on the Global Marketing Program (467–472)

▶ **OBJECTIVE 4** **Identify the three major forms of international marketing organization.** Deciding on the Global Marketing Organization (472–473)

Previewing the Concepts

You've now learned the fundamentals of how companies develop competitive marketing strategies to create customer value and build lasting customer relationships. In this chapter, we extend these fundamentals to global marketing. Although we discussed global topics in each previous chapter—it's difficult to find an area of marketing that doesn't contain at least some international applications—here we'll focus on special considerations that companies face when they market their brands globally. Advances in communication, transportation, and other technologies have made the world a much smaller place. Today, almost every firm, large or small, faces international marketing issues. In this chapter, we will examine six major decisions marketers make in going global.

To start our exploration of global marketing, let's look again at Google. Google is a truly global operation. It is accessible just about anywhere in the world and in hundreds of different languages. But just as international markets provide opportunities, they sometimes present daunting challenges. Here, we examine Google's odyssey into mainland China—and back out again.

▲ **The challenges of global marketing: After a long-running feud with the Chinese government over censorship, Google pulled out of mainland China.**

AP Images/Vincent Thian

Google in China: Running the Global Marketing Gauntlet

Google's mission is "to organize the world's information and make it universally accessible and useful." Almost by definition, this suggests that Google needs to operate internationally. What's more, international markets are a key to Google's expansion, as growth slows in domestic search advertising, Google's strongest business.

True to its mission and growth model, Google has, in fact, gone global. International markets now make up about 52 percent of the company's revenues. Whereas Google controls 60 percent of the U.S. Internet search market, it controls an even more impressive 80 percent of the European market. Google is available in 146 languages—from Korean to Arabic to Zulu—almost anywhere in the world. Anywhere, that is, except China. After a long-running feud with the Chinese government over censorship and other issues, Google has all but shut down—at least for now—its operations in mainland China and its Google.cn search engine.

Google's experiences in China vividly illustrate the prospects and perils of going global. As the world's most populous country and second-largest economy, China represents a huge potential market for Google. The number of Internet users in China passed 450 million last year, an amount almost one-and-one-half times the entire population of the United States. The Internet in China, especially for young people, offers an outlet to satisfy their enormous pent-up demand for entertainment, amusement, and social interaction. More than 70 percent of Chinese Internet users are under 30 years old. The Internet also holds financial keys, as online advertising in China will generate an estimated $7 billion in annual revenues in 2012.

To access all that potential, however, Google has had to run against a gauntlet of local competitors and government restrictions. Google began in early 2000 by building a Chinese language version of its search engine, one that mirrored the English language content on Google.com. In 2002, however, the Chinese government shut down Google's site in China, claiming that people were using it to access forbidden content. To the disappointment of many, Google revised the site to self-censor content deemed taboo by the Chinese government. It argued that it was blocking only a small proportion of the sites that Chinese users visit. Users still would be able to get uncensored information on most important topics.

By early 2006, Google had received Chinese government approval to launch Google.cn. The company wanted to locate its own servers in China—inside the so-called "Great Firewall of China," the government's system of censoring electronic information that enters or leaves the country. Although Chinese Internet users could access Google.com, having servers inside the country would help Google to compete more effectively with Chinese-owned market leader Baidu and with Yahoo and Microsoft's MSN, which had already established local Chinese operations.

Google was especially interested in providing services for the potentially lucrative Chinese mobile phone market. China has more than 910 million mobile phone users—many more than the United States, Japan, Germany, and the United Kingdom combined. The Chinese use their phones to buy ringtones, pictures, and other content from Internet portals such as KongZhong and TOM Online. Although such downloads sell for only a few cents each, when multiplied by hundreds of millions, the revenues add up quickly. Mobile users also like to play online multiplayer games, providing their creators with substantial subscription and accessories revenues.

> Just as international markets provide opportunities, they sometimes present challenges. Google's odyssey into mainland China—and back out again—vividly illustrates the prospects and perils of going global.

With Google.cn established, Google began a bruising competitive battle for the hearts, minds, and wallets of Chinese consumers. Its most formidable rival was Baidu, which successfully targeted less-educated, lower-income users, the fastest-growing Chinese subscriber segment. It was an uphill climb for Google. Baidu had a six-year head start in China and, as a local company, had a better understanding of the nuances of the Chinese market and language. Mandarin Chinese is a character-based language in which characters can have multiple meanings. Google had to learn how to "talk" to users—how to interpret the correct meaning of characters in search requests. Still, by late 2009, Google's share of the China search market had increased to 35.6 percent, while Baidu's share had fallen to 58 percent.

Despite this success, however, Google was growing increasingly uncomfortable with China's censorship restrictions. Chinese law banned the spread of "content subverting State power, undermining national unity, infringing upon national honor and interest, inciting ethnic hatred and secession," or supporting pornography or terrorism. By 2010, the Chinese government was enforcing strict interpretations of these laws on foreign IT companies operating in China. But knuckling under to government censorship just didn't fit well with Google's culture of free and open expression. To top things off, while Google was struggling with self-censorship issues, it suffered what it called a "highly sophisticated" cyber attack by Chinese hackers who stole some proprietary code and infiltrated the Google e-mail accounts of Chinese human-rights activists.

In early 2010, Google had seen enough of what it viewed as the Chinese government's heavy-handed tactics. The company announced that it planned to remove all technical operations from mainland China and route www.google.com.cn users to an uncensored version of its www.google.com.hk site in Hong Kong, which was not subject to the restrictions. Despite the Chinese government's displeasure with Google's evasive action, in mid-2010 it renewed Google's operating license, allowing Google to continue serving Chinese users by letting them click through the Google.cn site to the uncensored Hong Kong service. Still, the cat-and-mouse game continued, and Google's Chinese connection remained shaky.

In pulling its search operations out of mainland China, Google doesn't lose all that much current business—analysts estimate that Google earns only 1 to 2 percent of its global revenue from China. And about 30 to 40 percent of that revenue comes from Chinese companies that place ads on Google sites outside China, which will likely continue. However, leaving mainland China cedes the country's huge search advertising potential to competitors. For example, by mid-2011, Baidu's share of China's search market by revenue had grown to 76 percent versus Google's 19 percent. Pulling out also threatens Google's mobile phone business in China. Thus, many analysts think that Google will eventually resolve its feud with the Chinese government and once again enter this important market directly. By the time you read this, Google's return might already have happened.

For now, however, Google's mainland China pullout has won praise on moral grounds. Beyond its mission to make the world's information universally accessible, Google was founded on a simple code of conduct: "Don't be evil." According to Google founders Larry Page and Sergey Brin, that means "we believe strongly that in the long term, we will be better served—as shareholders and in all other ways—by a company that does good things for the world, even if we forego some short-term gains." In the eyes of many Google fans—even those in China—the company's strong stand against censorship is simply the right thing to do. Says one prominent Chinese blogger, it was "high time to change [Google's policy in China] back to the right track."[1]

MyMarketingLab

Visit www.mymktlab.com to find activities that help you learn and review in order to succeed in this chapter.

I n the past, U.S. companies paid little attention to international trade. If they could pick up some extra sales via exports, that was fine. But the big market was at home, and it teemed with opportunities. The home market was also much safer. Managers did not need to learn other languages, deal with strange and changing currencies, face political and legal uncertainties, or adapt their products to different customer needs and expectations. Today, however, the situation is much different. Organizations of all kinds, from Google, Coca-Cola, and HP to MTV and even the NBA, have gone global.

Author Comment ▶
The rapidly changing global environment provides both opportunities and threats. It's difficult to find a marketer today that isn't affected in some way by global developments.

Global Marketing Today

The world is shrinking rapidly with the advent of faster communication, transportation, and financial flows. Products developed in one country—Samsung electronics, McDonald's hamburgers, Zara fashions, Caterpillar construction equipment, Japanese sushi, German BMWs—have found enthusiastic acceptance in other countries. It would not be surprising to hear about a German businessman wearing an Italian suit meeting an English friend at a Japanese restaurant who later returns home to drink Russian vodka and watch *American Idol* on TV.

International trade has boomed over the past three decades. Since 1990, the number of multinational corporations in the world has grown from 30,000 to more than 63,000. Some of these multinationals are true giants. In fact, of the largest 150 economies in the world, only 83 are countries. The remaining 67 are multinational corporations. Walmart, the world's largest company, has annual revenues greater than the GDP of all but the world's 24 largest countries.[2]

Between 2000 and 2008, total world trade grew more than 7 percent per year, easily outstripping GDP output, which was about 3 percent. Despite a dip in world trade caused by the recent worldwide recession, the world trade of products and services last year was valued at more than $18.9 trillion, about 29 percent of GDP worldwide.[3]

▲ **Many American companies have now made the world their market, as this Niketown storefront in China featuring NBA star Kobe Bryant suggests. Quintessentially American Nike draws 65 percent of its sales from non-U.S. markets.**

Dorothea Schmid/laif/Redux Pictures

Many U.S. companies have long been successful at international marketing: McDonald's, Coca-Cola, Nike, Starbucks, GE, IBM, Colgate, Caterpillar, Boeing, and dozens of other American firms have made the world their market. In the United States, names such as Toyota, Nestlé, IKEA, Canon, LG, and Nokia have become household words. Other products and services that appear to be American are, in fact, produced or owned by foreign companies, such as Bantam books, Baskin-Robbins ice cream, GE and RCA televisions, Carnation milk, Universal Studios, and Motel 6. Michelin, the oh-so-French tire manufacturer, now does 34 percent of its business in North America; J&J, the maker of quintessentially all-American products such as BAND-AIDs and Johnson's Baby Shampoo, does 52 percent of its business abroad. And America's own Caterpillar belongs more to the wider world, with 68 percent of its sales coming from outside the United States.[4]

But as global trade grows, global competition is also intensifying. Foreign firms are expanding aggressively into new international markets, and home markets are no longer as rich in opportunity. Few industries are currently safe from foreign competition. If companies delay taking steps toward internationalizing, they risk being shut out of growing markets in western and eastern Europe, China and the Pacific Rim, Russia, India, Brazil, and elsewhere. Firms that stay at home to play it safe might not only lose their chances to enter other markets but also risk losing their home markets. Domestic companies that never thought about foreign competitors suddenly find these competitors in their own backyards.

Ironically, although the need for companies to go abroad is greater today than in the past, so are the risks. Companies that go global may face highly unstable governments and currencies, restrictive government policies and regulations, and high trade barriers. The recently dampened global economic environment has also created big global challenges. In addition, corruption is an increasing problem; officials in several countries often award business not to the best bidder but to the highest briber.

A **global firm** is one that, by operating in more than one country, gains marketing, production, R&D, and financial advantages that are not available to purely domestic competitors. Since the global company sees the world as one market, it minimizes the importance of national boundaries and develops global brands. The global company raises capital, obtains materials and components, and manufactures and markets its goods wherever it can do the best job.

For example, U.S.-based Otis Elevator, the world's largest elevator maker, is headquartered in Farmington, Connecticut. However, it offers products in more than 200 countries and achieves more than 80 percent of its sales from outside the United States. It gets elevator door systems from France, small geared parts from Spain, electronics from Germany, and special motor drives from Japan. It operates manufacturing facilities in the

Global firm

A firm that, by operating in more than one country, gains R&D, production, marketing, and financial advantages in its costs and reputation that are not available to purely domestic competitors.

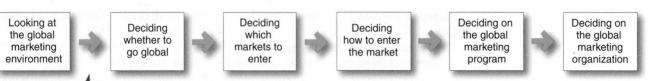

Figure 15.1 Major International Marketing Decisions

It's a big and beautiful but threatening world out there for marketers! Most large American firms have made the world their market. For example, once all-American McDonald's now captures 66 percent of its sales from outside the United States.

Americas, Europe, and Asia, and engineering and test centers in the United States, Austria, Brazil, China, Czech Republic, France, Germany, India, Italy, Japan, Korea, and Spain. In turn, Otis Elevator is a wholly owned subsidiary of global commercial and aerospace giant United Technologies Corporation.[5] Many of today's global corporations—both large and small—have become truly borderless.

This does not mean, however, that every firm must operate in a dozen countries to succeed. Smaller firms can practice global niching. But the world is becoming smaller, and every company operating in a global industry—whether large or small—must assess and establish its place in world markets.

The rapid move toward globalization means that all companies will have to answer some basic questions: What market position should we try to establish in our country, in our economic region, and globally? Who will our global competitors be and what are their strategies and resources? Where should we produce or source our products? What strategic alliances should we form with other firms around the world?

As shown in ▶ **Figure 15.1**, a company faces six major decisions in international marketing. We discuss each decision in detail in this chapter.

Looking at the Global Marketing Environment

Author Comment ▶
As if operating within a company's own borders wasn't difficult enough, going global adds many layers of complexities. For example, Coca-Cola markets its products in hundreds of countries around the globe. It must therefore understand the varying trade, economic, cultural, and political environments in each market.

Before deciding whether to operate internationally, a company must understand the international marketing environment. That environment has changed a great deal in recent decades, creating both new opportunities and new problems.

The International Trade System

U.S. companies looking abroad must start by understanding the international *trade system*. When selling to another country, a firm may face restrictions on trade between nations. Governments may charge *tariffs*, taxes on certain imported products designed to raise revenue or protect domestic firms. Tariffs are often used to force favorable trade behaviors from other nations. For example, the United States recently threatened high tariffs on—of all things—Roquefort cheese in retaliation to a European Union (EU) ban on U.S. hormone-treated beef. The EU's French-led refusal to import hormone-treated U.S. beef resulted in threatened U.S. tariffs of 100 to 300 percent on Roquefort and dozens of other European gourmet food delights ranging from Italian mineral water to Irish oatmeal and French chestnuts. The United States dropped the threatened tariff increases after the EU agreed to quadruple its U.S. non-hormone-treated beef imports over the next four years.[6]

Countries may set *quotas*, limits on the amount of foreign imports that they will accept in certain product categories. The purpose of a quota is to conserve on foreign exchange and protect local industry and employment. Firms may also face *exchange controls*, which limit the amount of foreign exchange and the exchange rate against other currencies.

A company also may face *nontariff trade barriers*, such as biases against its bids, restrictive product standards, or excessive host-country regulations. ▶ For example, as we learned in the chapter-opening story, the Chinese government has set up a "great firewall of China"—electronic and censorship barriers that limit or keep out foreign Web sites such as Google. These barriers, however, have created a safe haven within which Chinese copycat Web sites can thrive.[7]

▲ Trade barriers: The Chinese government has set up a "great firewall of China"—electronic and censorship barriers that limit or keep out foreign Web sites such as Google and YouTube, while creating safe havens within which Chinese copycat Web sites such as Baidu and Youku can thrive.

With Google's hands tied in China, local competitor Baidu is thriving in China. Similarly, YouTube has been blocked in China for nearly two years, leaving the field wide open for Chinese copycats Tudou and Youku. Twitter was blocked in China in 2009, following Twitter-fed ethnic riots in the western region of Xinjaing. Shortly after, one of China's mammoth portals, Sina, launched a Twitter-like microblog service called Weibo, which now has 50 million users. Similarly, China has copycat versions of Amazon.com (Dangdang.com), eBay (Taobao), Wikipedia (Hudong, Baidu Baike), Expedia (Ctrip), and Yelp (Dianping)—all comfortably sheltered behind the Great Firewall of China.

At the same time, certain other forces can *help* trade between nations. Examples include the World Trade Organization (WTO) and various regional free trade agreements.

The World Trade Organization

The General Agreement on Tariffs and Trade (GATT), established in 1947 and modified in 1994, was designed to promote world trade by reducing tariffs and other international trade barriers. ▶ It established the World Trade Organization (WTO), which replaced GATT in 1995 and now oversees the original GATT provisions. WTO and GATT member nations (currently numbering 153) have met in eight rounds of negotiations to reassess trade barriers and establish new rules for international trade. The WTO also imposes international trade sanctions and mediates global trade disputes. Their actions have been productive. The first seven rounds of negotiations reduced the average worldwide tariffs on manufactured goods from 45 percent to just 5 percent.[8]

The most recently completed negotiations, dubbed the Uruguay Round, dragged on for seven long years before concluding in 1994. The benefits of the Uruguay Round will be felt for many years as the accord promoted long-term global trade growth, reduced the world's remaining merchandise tariffs by 30 percent, extended the WTO to cover trade in agriculture and a wide range of services, and toughened the international protection of copyrights, patents, trademarks, and other intellectual property. A new round of global WTO trade talks, the Doha Round, began in Doha, Qatar, in late 2001 and was set to conclude in 2005; however, the discussions still continued through 2011.[9]

▲ The WTO promotes trade by reducing tariffs and other international trade barriers.

(left) Corbis; (right) AP Images/Donald Stampfli

Regional Free Trade Zones

Certain countries have formed *free trade zones* or **economic communities**. These are groups of nations organized to work toward common goals in the regulation of international trade. One such community is the *European Union (EU)*. Formed in 1957, the EU set out to create a single European market by reducing barriers to the free flow of products, services, finances, and labor among member countries and developing policies on trade with nonmember nations. Today, the EU represents one of the world's largest single markets. Currently, it has 27 member countries containing more than half a billion consumers and accounting for more than 20 percent of the world's exports.[10]

▲ **Economic communities: The European Union represents one of the world's single largest markets. Its current member countries contain more than half a billion consumers and account for 20 percent of the world's exports.**
© European Union, 2011

Economic community
A group of nations organized to work toward common goals in the regulation of international trade.

▶ The EU offers tremendous trade opportunities for U.S. and other non-European firms. However, it also poses threats. As a result of increased unification, European companies have grown bigger and more competitive. Perhaps an even greater concern, however, is that lower barriers *inside* Europe will create only thicker *outside* walls. Some observers envision a "Fortress Europe" that heaps favors on firms from EU countries but hinders outsiders by imposing obstacles.

Progress toward European unification has been slow. In recent years, however, 17 member nations have taken a significant step toward unification by adopting the euro as a common currency. Widespread adoption of the euro has decreased much of the currency risk associated with doing business in Europe, making member countries with previously weak currencies more attractive markets. However, the adoption of a common currency has also caused problems as European economic powers such as Germany and France have had to step in recently to prop up weaker economies such as Greece and Portugal.[11]

Even with the adoption of the euro, it is unlikely that the EU will ever go against 2,000 years of tradition and become the "United States of Europe." A community with more than two-dozen different languages and cultures will always have difficulty coming together and acting as a single entity. Still, with a combined annual GDP of more than $16 trillion, the EU has become a potent economic force.[12]

In 1994, the *North American Free Trade Agreement (NAFTA)* established a free trade zone among the United States, Mexico, and Canada. The agreement created a single market of 457 million people who produce and consume over $17 trillion worth of goods and services annually. Over the past 15 years, NAFTA has eliminated trade barriers and investment restrictions among the three countries. According to the International Monetary Fund, total trade among the three countries has nearly tripled from $306 billion in 1993 to $846 billion in 2010.[13]

Following the apparent success of NAFTA, in 2005 the Central American Free Trade Agreement (CAFTA-DR) established a free trade zone between the United States and Costa Rica, the Dominican Republic, El Salvador, Guatemala, Honduras, and Nicaragua. Other free trade areas have formed in Latin America and South America. For example, the Union of South American Nations (UNASUR), modeled after the EU, was formed in 2004 and formalized by a constitutional treaty in 2008. Consisting of 12 countries, UNASUR makes up the largest trading bloc after NAFTA and the EU, with a population of 388 million, a combined economy of more than $973 billion, and exports worth $182 billion. Similar to NAFTA and the EU, UNASUR aims to eliminate all tariffs between nations by 2019.[14]

Each nation has unique features that must be understood. A nation's readiness for different products and services and its attractiveness as a market to foreign firms depend on its economic, political-legal, and cultural environments.

Economic Environment

The international marketer must study each country's economy. Two economic factors reflect the country's attractiveness as a market: its industrial structure and its income distribution.

The country's *industrial structure* shapes its product and service needs, income levels, and employment levels. The four types of industrial structures are as follows:

- *Subsistence economies:* In a subsistence economy, the vast majority of people engage in simple agriculture. They consume most of their output and barter the rest for simple goods and services. They offer few market opportunities.
- *Raw material exporting economies:* These economies are rich in one or more natural resources but poor in other ways. Much of their revenue comes from

exporting these resources. Some examples are Chile (tin and copper) and the Democratic Republic of the Congo (copper, cobalt, and coffee). These countries are good markets for large equipment, tools and supplies, and trucks. If there are many foreign residents and a wealthy upper class, they are also a market for luxury goods.

- *Emerging economies (industrializing economies):* In an emerging economy, fast growth in manufacturing results in rapid overall economic growth. Examples include the BRIC countries—Brazil, Russia, India, and China. As manufacturing increases, the country needs more imports of raw textile materials, steel, and heavy machinery, and fewer imports of finished textiles, paper products, and automobiles. Industrialization typically creates a new rich class and a small but growing middle class, both demanding new types of imported goods.

- *Industrial economies:* Industrial economies are major exporters of manufactured goods, services, and investment funds. They trade goods among themselves and also export them to other types of economies for raw materials and semifinished goods. The varied manufacturing activities of these industrial nations and their large middle class make them rich markets for all sorts of goods. Examples include the United States, Japan, and Norway.

The second economic factor is the country's *income distribution*. Industrialized nations may have low-, medium-, and high-income households. In contrast, countries with subsistence economies consist mostly of households with very low family incomes. Still other countries may have households with either very low or very high incomes. Even poor or emerging economies may be attractive markets for all kinds of goods. These days, companies in a wide range of industries—from cars to computers to candy—are increasingly targeting even low- and middle-income consumers in emerging economies. ▶ For example, in India, Ford recently introduced a new model targeted to consumers who are only now able to afford their first car:[15]

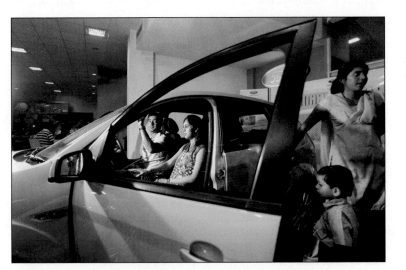

▲ **Economic environment: In India, Ford's $7,700 Figo targets low- to middle-income consumers who are only now able to afford their first car.**
Namas Bhojani/Namas Bhojani Photography

In an effort to boost its presence in Asia's third-largest auto market behind Japan and China, Ford introduced the Figo, a successful new $7,700 hatchback design for a hypothetical twenty-something Indian named Sandeep. He works in IT, finance, or another service industry and tools around on a motorcycle. But now that he's enjoying the first fruits of affluence, Sandeep wants four wheels. "There are huge numbers of people wanting to move off their motorbikes," says Ford's India general manager. Some 70 percent of cars sold in India are in the Figo's size and price range. The Figo is now also selling well in other emerging markets across Asia and Africa.

Political-Legal Environment

Nations differ greatly in their political-legal environments. In considering whether to do business in a given country, a company should consider factors such as the country's attitudes toward international buying, government bureaucracy, political stability, and monetary regulations.

Some nations are very receptive to foreign firms; others are less accommodating. For example, India has tended to bother foreign businesses with import quotas, currency restrictions, and other limitations that make operating there a challenge. In contrast, neighboring Asian countries, such as Singapore and Thailand, court foreign investors and shower them with incentives and favorable operating conditions. Political and regulatory stability is another issue. For example, Venezuela's government is notoriously volatile—due to economic factors such as inflation and steep public spending—which increases the risk of doing business there. Although most international marketers still find the Venezuelan market attractive, the unstable political and regulatory situation will affect how they handle business and financial matters.[16]

Companies must also consider a country's monetary regulations. Sellers want to take their profits in a currency of value to them. Ideally, the buyer can pay in the seller's currency or in other world currencies. Short of this, sellers might accept a blocked currency—one whose removal from the country is restricted by the buyer's government—if they can buy other goods in that country that they need or can sell elsewhere for a needed currency. In addition to currency limits, a changing exchange rate also creates high risks for the seller.

Most international trade involves cash transactions. Yet many nations have too little hard currency to pay for their purchases from other countries. They may want to pay with other items instead of cash. *Barter* involves the direct exchange of goods or services: for example, China agreed to help the Democratic Republic of Congo develop $6 billion of desperately needed infrastructure—2,400 miles of roads, 2,000 miles of railways, 32 hospitals, 145 health centers, and two universities—in exchange for natural resources needed to feed China's booming industries—10 million tons of copper and 400,000 tons of cobalt.[17]

Cultural Environment

Each country has its own folkways, norms, and taboos. When designing global marketing strategies, companies must understand how culture affects consumer reactions in each of its world markets. In turn, they must also understand how their strategies affect local cultures.

The Impact of Culture on Marketing Strategy

Sellers must understand the ways that consumers in different countries think about and use certain products before planning a marketing program. There are often surprises. For example, the average French man uses almost twice as many cosmetics and grooming aids as his wife. The Germans and the French eat more packaged, branded spaghetti than Italians do. Some 49 percent of Chinese eat on the way to work. Most American women let down their hair and take off makeup at bedtime, whereas 15 percent of Chinese women style their hair at bedtime and 11 percent put *on* makeup.[18]

Companies that ignore cultural norms and differences can make some very expensive and embarrassing mistakes. Here are two examples:

> Nike inadvertently offended Chinese officials when it ran an ad featuring LeBron James crushing a number of culturally revered Chinese figures in a kung fu–themed television ad. The Chinese government found that the ad violated regulations to uphold national dignity and respect the "motherland's culture" and yanked the multimillion-dollar campaign. With egg on its face, Nike released a formal apology.
>
> Burger King made a similar mistake when it created in-store ads in Spain showing Hindu goddess Lakshmi atop a ham sandwich with the caption "a snack that is sacred." Cultural and religious groups worldwide objected strenuously—Hindus are vegetarian. Burger King apologized and pulled the ads.[19]

Business norms and behaviors also vary from country to country. For example, American executives like to get right down to business and engage in fast and tough face-to-face bargaining. However, Japanese and other Asian businesspeople often find this behavior offensive. They prefer to start with polite conversation, and they rarely say no in face-to-face conversations. As another example, handshakes are a common and expected greeting in most Western countries; in some Middle Eastern countries, however, handshakes might be refused if offered. In some countries, when being entertained at a meal, not finishing all the food implies that it was somehow substandard. In other countries, in contrast, wolfing down every last bite might be taken as a mild insult, suggesting that the host didn't supply enough quantity.[20] American business executives need to understand these kinds of cultural nuances before conducting business in another country.

▲ **The impact of culture on marketing strategy: IKEA customers in China want a lot more from its stores than just affordable Scandinavian-design furniture.**
Lou Linwei/Alamy

By the same token, companies that understand cultural nuances can use them to their advantage in the global markets. ❯ For example, furniture retailer IKEA's stores are a big draw for up-and-coming Chinese consumers. But IKEA has learned that customers in China want a lot more from its stores then just affordable Scandinavian-design furniture:[21]

> Yang Shuqi paces the aisles of an IKEA store in Beijing, looking for a "small bed with toys." She's not planning to buy one—her grandson Beibei just needs to take a nap. Unfortunately on this Saturday afternoon, every bed in the huge store is occupied, with some children and adults fast asleep under the covers. In China, IKEA stores have become a popular destination—a respite from the hustle and smog and a place to get a reliable lunch. Customers come on family outings, hop into display beds and nap, pose for snapshots with the décor, and hang out for hours to enjoy the air conditioning and free soda refills.
>
> Eager to build their brand, managers at the Swedish furniture retailer don't mind. They figure that the more customers choose to relax in its Western-style showrooms or grab a cheap snack at the in-store restaurants, the more likely they'll be to make a purchase once their incomes catch up with their aspirations. "Maybe if you've been visiting IKEA, eating meatballs, hot dogs, or ice cream for 10 years, then maybe you will consider IKEA when you get yourself a sofa," says the company's Asia-Pacific president. Thanks to such cultural understandings, IKEA already captures about 7 percent of the surging Chinese home-furnishings market.

Thus, understanding cultural traditions, preferences, and behaviors can help companies not only avoid embarrassing mistakes but also take advantage of cross-cultural opportunities.

The Impact of Marketing Strategy on Cultures

Whereas marketers worry about the impact of culture on their global marketing strategies, others may worry about the impact of marketing strategies on global cultures. For example, social critics contend that large American multinationals, such as McDonald's, Coca-Cola, Starbucks, Nike, Microsoft, Disney, and MTV, aren't just globalizing their brands; they are Americanizing the world's cultures.[22]

> There are now as many people studying English in China (or playing basketball, for that matter) as there are people in the United States. Seven of the 10 most watched TV shows around the world are American, *Avatar* is the top-grossing film of all time in China, and the world is as fixated on U.S. brands as ever, which is why U.S. multinationals from McDonald's to Nike book more than half their revenues overseas. If you bring together teenagers from Nigeria, Sweden, South Korea, and Argentina—to pick a random foursome—what binds these kids together in some kind of community is American culture—the music, the Hollywood fare, the electronic games, Google, American consumer brands. The only thing they will likely have in common that doesn't revolve around the United States is an interest in soccer. The . . . rest of the world is becoming [evermore] like us—in ways good and bad.

"Today, globalization often wears Mickey Mouse ears, eats Big Macs, drinks Coke or Pepsi, and does its computing with Windows," says Thomas Friedman in his book *The Lexus and the Olive Tree: Understanding Globalization*.[23] Critics worry that, under such "McDomination," countries around the globe are losing their individual cultural identities. Teens in India watch MTV and ask their parents for more westernized clothes and other symbols of American pop culture and values. Grandmothers in small European villas no longer spend each morning visiting local meat, bread, and produce markets to gather the ingredients for dinner. Instead, they now shop at Walmart Supercenters. Women in Saudi Arabia see American films and question their societal roles. In China, most people never drank coffee before Starbucks entered the market. Now Chinese consumers rush to Starbucks stores "because it's a symbol of a new kind of lifestyle." Similarly, in China, where McDonald's operates more than 80 restaurants in Beijing alone, nearly half of all children identify the chain as a domestic brand.

Such concerns have sometimes led to a backlash against American globalization. Well-known U.S. brands have become the targets of boycotts and protests in some international markets. As symbols of American capitalism, companies such as Coca-Cola, McDonald's, Nike, and KFC have been singled out by antiglobalization protestors in hot spots around the world, especially when anti-American sentiment peaks.

Despite such problems, defenders of globalization argue that concerns of Americanization and the potential damage to American brands are overblown. U.S. brands are doing very well internationally. In the most recent Millward Brown Optimor brand value survey of global consumer brands, 16 of the top 20 brands were American owned, including megabrands such as Apple, Google, IBM, McDonald's, Microsoft, Coca-Cola, GE, Amazon.com, and Walmart.[24] ▶ Many iconic American brands are prospering globally, even in some of the most unlikely places:[25]

▲ Many iconic American brands are prospering globally, even in some of the most unlikely places. At this Tehran restaurant, American colas are the drink of choice. Coke and Pepsi have grabbed about half the national soft drink sales in Iran. (Also, did you notice the familiar TABASCO hot sauce bottle?)
Shahpari Sohaie/Redux Pictures

It's lunchtime in Tehran's tiny northern suburbs, and around the crowded tables at Nayeb Restaurant, elegant Iranian women in Jackie O sunglasses and designer jeans let their table chatter glide effortlessly between French, English, and their native Farsi. The only visual clues that these lunching ladies aren't dining at some smart New York City eatery but in the heart of Washington's axis of evil are the expensive Hermès scarves covering their blonde-tipped hair in deference to the mullahs. And the drink of choice? This being revolutionary Iran, where alcohol is banned, the women are making do with Coca-Cola. Yes, Coca-Cola. It's a hard fact for some of Iran's theocrats to swallow. They want Iranians to shun "Great Satan" brands like Coke and Pepsi, and the Iranian government has recently pressured Iranian soft drink companies to clarify their "ties with the Zionist company Coca-Cola." Yet, Coke and Pepsi have grabbed about half the national soft drink sales in Iran, one of the Middle East's biggest drink markets. "I joke with customers not to buy this stuff because it's American," says a Tehran storekeeper, "but they don't care. That only makes them want to buy it more."

More fundamentally, the cultural exchange goes both ways: America gets as well as gives cultural influence. True, Hollywood dominates the global movie market, but British TV originated the programming that was Americanized into such hits as *The Office*, *American Idol*, and *Dancing with the Stars*. Although Chinese and Russian youth are donning NBA superstar jerseys, the increasing popularity of American soccer has deep international roots. Even American childhood has been increasingly influenced by European and Asian cultural imports. Most kids know all about imports such as Hello Kitty, the Bakugan Battle Brawler, or any of a host of Nintendo or Sega game characters. And J. K. Rowling's so-very-British Harry Potter books have shaped the thinking of a generation of American youngsters, not to mention the millions of American oldsters who've fallen under their spell as well. For the moment, English remains the dominant language of the Internet, and having Web access often means that third-world youth have greater exposure to American popular culture. Yet these same technologies let Eastern European students studying in the United States hear Webcast news and music from Poland, Romania, or Belarus.

Thus, globalization is a two-way street. If globalization has Mickey Mouse ears, it is also talking on a Nokia cell phone, buying furniture at IKEA, driving a Toyota Camry, and watching a British-inspired show on a Samsung HDTV.

Deciding Whether to Go Global

Not all companies need to venture into international markets to survive. For example, most local businesses need to market well only in their local marketplace. Operating domestically is easier and safer. Managers don't need to learn another country's language and laws. They don't have to deal with unstable currencies, face political and legal uncertainties, or redesign their products to suit different customer expectations. However, companies that operate in global industries, where their strategic positions in specific markets are affected strongly by their overall global positions, must compete on a regional or worldwide basis to succeed.

Any of several factors might draw a company into the international arena. For example, global competitors might attack the company's home market by offering better products or lower prices. The company might want to counterattack these competitors in their home markets to tie up their resources. The company's customers might be expanding abroad and require international servicing. Or, most likely, international markets might simply provide better opportunities for growth. For example, Coca-Cola has emphasized international growth in recent years to offset stagnant or declining U.S. soft drink sales. Today, nearly 80 percent of Coca-Cola's sales come from outside the United States, and the company is making major pushes into emerging markets such as China, India, and now Africa (see Marketing at Work 15.1).[26]

Before going abroad, the company must weigh several risks and answer many questions about its ability to operate globally. Can the company learn to understand the preferences and buyer behavior of consumers in other countries? Can it offer competitively attractive products? Will it be able to adapt to other countries' business cultures and deal effectively with foreign nationals? Do the company's managers have the necessary international experience? Has management considered the impact of regulations and the political environments of other countries?

Deciding Which Markets to Enter

Before going abroad, the company should try to define its international *marketing objectives and policies*. It should decide what *volume* of foreign sales it wants. Most companies start small when they go abroad. Some plan to stay small, seeing international sales as a small part of their business. Other companies have bigger plans, however, seeing international business as equal to, or even more important than, their domestic business.

The company also needs to choose in *how many* countries it wants to market. Companies must be careful not to spread themselves too thin or expand beyond their capabilities by operating in too many countries too soon. Next, the company needs to decide on the *types* of countries to enter. A country's attractiveness depends on the product, geographical factors, income and population, political climate, and other factors. In recent years, many major new markets have emerged, offering both substantial opportunities and daunting challenges.

After listing possible international markets, the company must carefully evaluate each one. It must consider many factors. For example, Walmart's decision to enter Africa seems like a no-brainer: Taken as a whole, the African market is three times the size of China and is home to more than 1 billion people and six of the world's ten fastest growing economies. In fact, Walmart recently gained a toehold in Africa by acquiring a majority stake in South African retailer Massmart, which operates its Makro, Game, and other discount and warehouse stores mostly in South Africa but also in 13 other African countries.

However, as Walmart considers expanding into African markets, it must ask some important questions. Can it compete effectively on a country-by-country basis with hundreds of local competitors? Will the various African governments be stable and supportive? Does Africa provide for the needed logistics technologies? Can Walmart master the varied and vastly different cultural and buying differences of African consumers?

Coca-Cola in Africa: "Everything Is Right There to Have It Happen"

Coca-Cola is one of the world's truly iconic brands—a $35-billion global powerhouse. It puts Coke products within "an arm's length" of 98 percent of the world's population. Already the world's number one soft drink maker, Coca-Cola still plans to double its global system revenues by 2020.

But achieving such growth won't be easy. The major problem: Soft drink-sales growth has lost its fizz in North America and Europe, two of Coca-Cola's largest and most profitable markets. In North America in 1989, for example, consumers gulped $2.6 billion worth of Coke. Twenty years later, that figure was only $2.9 billion, which means that, adjusted for inflation, Coke's North American sales actually declined. In fact, the U.S. soft drink market has shrunk for five straight years. With sales stagnating in its mature markets, Coca-Cola must look elsewhere to meet its ambitious growth goals.

In recent years, Coca-Cola has sought growth primarily in developing global markets such as China and India, which boast large emerging middle classes but relatively low per-capita consumption of Coke. However, both China and India are now crowded with competitors and notoriously difficult for outsiders to navigate. So while Coca-Cola will continue to compete heavily in those countries, it has set its sights on an even more promising long-term growth opportunity—Africa.

Many Western companies view Africa as an untamed final frontier—a kind of no man's land plagued by poverty, political corruption and instability, unreliable transportation, and shortages of fresh water and other essential resources. But Coca-Cola sees plenty of opportunity in Africa to justify the risks. Africa has a growing population of more than 1 billion people and a just-emerging middle class. The number of African households earning at least $5,000—the income level where families begin to spend at least half their income on non-food items—is expected to double to more than 106 million by 2014. "You've got an incredibly young population, a dynamic population," says Coca-Cola CEO Muhtar Kent. "[And] huge disposable income. I mean $1.6 trillion of GDP, which is bigger than Russia, bigger than India."

Coca-Cola is no stranger to Africa. It has operated there since 1929, and it's the only multinational that offers its products in every African country. In fact, Coca-Cola is Africa's largest employer, with 65,000 employees and 160 plants. The company has a dominant 29 percent market share in Africa and the Middle East, as compared with Pepsi's 15 percent share. Africa now contributes 6 to 7 percent of Coca-Cola's global revenues.

But there's still plenty of room for Coca-Cola to grow in Africa. For example, annual per capita consumption of Coke in Kenya is just 39 servings, compared with more developed countries like Mexico, where consumption

runs at an eye-popping 665 servings per year. So the stage is set for Coca-Cola to up the ante on the African continent, not just for its flagship Coke brand but also for its large stable of other soft drinks, waters, and juices. Whereas the beverage giant invested $6 billion in the African market over the past decade, it plans to invest twice that amount during the next 10 years.

Marketing in Africa is a very different proposition from marketing in more developed regions. "Africa . . . is not Atlanta," observes one analyst, "and Coke is, in a sense, sticking its hand into a bees' nest to get some honey." To grow its sales in Africa, beyond just marketing through traditional channels in larger African cities, Coca-Cola is now invading smaller communities with more grassroots tactics. "[Just] being in a country is very easy; you can go and set up a depot in every capital city," says CEO Kent. But in Africa, "that's not what we're about. There's nowhere in Africa that we don't go. We go to every town, every village, every community, every township." In Africa, every small shop in every back alley has become important, as Coca-Cola launches what another analyst describes as "a street-by-street campaign to win drinkers . . . not yet used to guzzling Coke by the gallon."

For example, take the Mamakamau Shop in Uthiru, a poor community outside Nairobi, Kenya. Piles of trash burn outside the shop and sewage trickles by in an open trench. Besides Coca-Cola products, the shop—known as a *duka*—also carries everything from mattresses to plastic buckets, all in a room about the size of a small bedroom. Still, proprietor Mamakamau Kingori has earned Coca-Cola's "Gold" vendor status, its highest level, for selling about 72 cola products a day, priced at 30 Kenyan

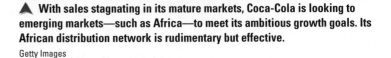

▲ With sales stagnating in its mature markets, Coca-Cola is looking to emerging markets—such as Africa—to meet its ambitious growth goals. Its African distribution network is rudimentary but effective.

Getty Images

shillings (37 U.S. cents) for a 500 milliliter bottle. Most customers drink the soda in the store while sitting on overturned red crates—they can't afford to pay the bottle deposit. Coca-Cola's Kenyan bottler will reuse the glass bottles up to 70 times.

To earn her "Gold" status, Kingori follows carefully prescribed selling techniques. She uses a red, Coke-provided, refrigerated cooler by the front entrance, protected by a blue cage. Like other mom-and-pop stores in her area, she keeps the cooler fully stocked with Coke on top, Fanta in the middle, and large bottles on the bottom. Inside the store, she posts red menu signs provided by Coca-Cola that push combo meals, such as a 300 milliliter Coke and a *ndazi*, a type of local donut, for 25 Kenyan shillings.

In Kabira, another poor Nairobi neighborhood, the crowded streets are lined with shops painted Coke red. The local bottler hires an artist to paint the shops with logos and Swahili phrases like "Burudika na Coke Baridi," meaning "enjoy Coke cold." In countless communities across Africa, whether it's the *dukas* in Nairobi or *tuck shops* in Johannesburg, South Africa, small stores play a big role in helping Coca-Cola grow.

Such shops are supplied by a rudimentary but effective network of Coca-Cola distributors. For example, in downtown Nairobi, men in red lab coats load hand-pulled trolleys with 22 to 40 crates of Coke and other soft drinks from Rosinje Distributors, one of 3,000 Manual Distribution Centers that Coca-Cola operates in Africa. These centers are the spine of Coca-Cola's African distribution network. The Nairobi crews hustle Coke, Fanta, Stoney Ginger Beer, and other Coca-Cola brands—sometimes a case at a time carried on their heads—to 345 local shops and beverage kiosks. Because of the poor roads crowded with traffic, moving drinks by hand is often the best method. The Manual Distribution Centers help Coca-Cola to get its products into remote areas, making them available as people develop a taste for soft drinks and have the income to buy them.

Despite their elemental nature, Coca-Cola's marketing approaches in Africa are proving effective. In Alexandra, a densely populated suburb of Johannesburg with a 65 percent unemployment rate, Coca-Cola's coolers and signs are everywhere. The company's first rule is to get its products "cold and close." "If they don't have roads to move products long distances on trucks, we will use boats, canoes, or trolleys," says the president of Coca-Cola South Africa.

There's little doubt that Coca-Cola's increased commitment to Africa will be key to its achieving its global goals. As CEO Muhtar Kent concludes: "Africa is the untold story and could be the big story of the next decade, like India and China were this past decade. . . . Everything is right there to have it happen."

Sources: Portions based on Duane Stanford, "Africa: Coke's Last Round," *Bloomberg Businessweek,* November 1, 2010, pp. 54–61; with additional information from Annaleigh Vallie, "Coke Turns 125 and Has Much Life Ahead," *Business Day,* May 16, 2011, www.businessday.co.za/articles/Content .aspx?id=142848; and Michelle Russell, "Comment—Soft Drinks Competition to Intensify in Africa," *Just-Drinks Global News,* April 8, 2011, www .just-drinks.com/comment/comment-soft-drinks-competition-to-intensify-in-africa_id103532.aspx.

Walmart's expansion in Africa will likely be a slow process, as it confronts many unfamiliar cultural, political, and logistical challenges. Along with the huge opportunities, many African countries rank among the world's most difficult places to do business. "You see a market like Nigeria [with a population of more than 150 million] and it feels like a big opportunity," says the chief executive of Walmart International. "But we've learned [that] we really need to think about it a city at a time as opposed to a country at a time."[27]

Possible global markets should be ranked on several factors, including market size, market growth, the cost of doing business, competitive advantage, and risk level. The goal is to determine the potential of each market, using indicators such as those shown in ▶ **Table 15.1**. Then the marketer must decide which markets offer the greatest long-run return on investment.

Author Comment ▶
A company has many options for entering an international market, from simply exporting its products to working jointly with foreign companies to holding its own foreign-based operations.

Deciding How to Enter the Market

Once a company has decided to sell in a foreign country, it must determine the best mode of entry. Its choices are *exporting*, *joint venturing*, and *direct investment*. ▶ **Figure 15.2** shows three market entry strategies, along with the options each one offers. As the figure shows, each succeeding strategy involves more commitment and risk but also more control and potential profits.

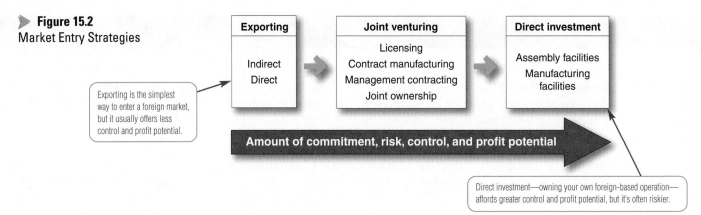

Figure 15.2
Market Entry Strategies

Exporting

Exporting
Entering foreign markets by selling goods produced in the company's home country, often with little modification.

The simplest way to enter a foreign market is through **exporting**. The company may passively export its surpluses from time to time, or it may make an active commitment to expand exports to a particular market. In either case, the company produces all its goods in its home country. It may or may not modify them for the export market. Exporting involves the least change in the company's product lines, organization, investments, or mission.

Companies typically start with *indirect exporting*, working through independent international marketing intermediaries. Indirect exporting involves less investment because the firm does not require an overseas marketing organization or network. It also involves less risk. International marketing intermediaries bring know-how and services to the relationship, so the seller normally makes fewer mistakes. Sellers may eventually move into *direct exporting*, whereby they handle their own exports. The investment and risk are somewhat greater in this strategy, but so is the potential return.

Table 15.1	Indicators of Market Potential

Demographic Characteristics	**Sociocultural Factors**
Education	Consumer lifestyles, beliefs, and values
Population size and growth	Business norms and approaches
Population age composition	Cultural and social norms
	Languages

Geographic Characteristics	**Political and Legal Factors**
Climate	National priorities
Country size	Political stability
Population density—urban, rural	Government attitudes toward global trade
Transportation structure and market accessibility	Government bureaucracy
	Monetary and trade regulations

Economic Factors

GDP size and growth
Income distribution
Industrial infrastructure
Natural resources
Financial and human resources

Joint Venturing

Joint venturing
Entering foreign markets by joining with foreign companies to produce or market a product or service.

Licensing
Entering foreign markets through developing an agreement with a licensee in the foreign market.

Contract manufacturing
A joint venture in which a company contracts with manufacturers in a foreign market to produce the product or provide its service.

A second method of entering a foreign market is by **joint venturing**—joining with foreign companies to produce or market products or services. Joint venturing differs from exporting in that the company joins with a host country partner to sell or market abroad. It differs from direct investment in that an association is formed with someone in the foreign country. There are four types of joint ventures: licensing, contract manufacturing, management contracting, and joint ownership.

Licensing

Licensing is a simple way for a manufacturer to enter international marketing. The company enters into an agreement with a licensee in the foreign market. For a fee or royalty payments, the licensee buys the right to use the company's manufacturing process, trademark, patent, trade secret, or other item of value. The company thus gains entry into a foreign market at little risk; at the same time, the licensee gains production expertise or a well-known product or name without having to start from scratch.

In Japan, Budweiser beer flows from Kirin breweries, and Moringa Milk Company produces ▶ Sunkist fruit juice, drinks, and dessert items. Coca-Cola markets internationally by licensing bottlers around the world and supplying them with the syrup needed to produce the product. Its global bottling partners range from the Coca-Cola Bottling Company of Saudi Arabia to Europe-based Coca-Cola Hellenic, which bottles and markets Coca-Cola products to 560 million people in 30 countries, from Italy and Greece to Nigeria and Russia.

Licensing has potential disadvantages, however. The firm has less control over the licensee than it would over its own operations. Furthermore, if the licensee is very successful, the firm has given up these profits, and if and when the contract ends, it may find it has created a competitor.

▲ Licensing: In Japan, Sunkist fruit juices, drinks, and dessert items are produced by Moringa Milk Company.

Management contracting
A joint venture in which the domestic firm supplies the management know-how to a foreign company that supplies the capital; the domestic firm exports management services rather than products.

Contract Manufacturing

Another option is **contract manufacturing**, in which the company makes agreements with manufacturers in the foreign market to produce its product or provide its service. Sears used this method in opening up department stores in Mexico and Spain, where it found qualified local manufacturers to produce many of the products it sells. The drawbacks of contract manufacturing are decreased control over the manufacturing process and loss of potential profits on manufacturing. The benefits are the chance to start faster, with less risk, and the later opportunity either to form a partnership with or buy out the local manufacturer.

Management Contracting

Under **management contracting**, the domestic firm provides the management know-how to a foreign company that supplies the capital. In other words, the domestic firm exports management services rather than products. Hilton uses this arrangement in managing hotels around the world. For example, the hotel chain recently opened a Doubletree by Hilton in Jordan. The property is locally owned, but Hilton manages the hotel with its world-renowned hospitality expertise.[28]

Management contracting is a low-risk method of getting into a foreign market, and it yields income from the beginning. The arrangement is even more attractive if the contracting firm has an option to buy some share in the managed company later on. The arrangement is not sensible, however, if the company can put its scarce management talent to better uses or if it can make greater profits by undertaking the whole venture. Management contracting also prevents the company from setting up its own operations for a period of time.

Joint Ownership

Joint ownership
A cooperative venture in which a company creates a local business with investors in a foreign market, who share ownership and control.

Joint ownership ventures consist of one company joining forces with foreign investors to create a local business in which they share possession and control. A company may buy an interest in a local firm, or the two parties may form a new business venture. Joint ownership may be needed for economic or political reasons. For example, the firm may lack the financial, physical, or managerial resources to undertake the venture alone. Alternatively, a foreign government may require joint ownership as a condition for entry.

Often, companies form joint ownership ventures to merge their complementary strengths in developing a global marketing opportunity. ▶ For example, Campbell Soup Company recently formed a 60/40 joint venture with Hong Kong-based Swire Pacific— called Campbell Swire—to help distribute the company's soups better in China.[29]

▲ Joint ventures: Campbell Soup Company and Hong Kong-based Swire Pacific formed a joint venture—Campbell Swire—to market Campbell brands in the vast Chinese market.
Campbell Soup Company and John Swire & Sons (H.K.) Ltd.

China represents a tremendous opportunity for Campbell: The Chinese population consumes about 355 billion servings of soup annually, but nearly all of them are homemade. Campbell Swire will be responsible for manufacturing, packaging, branding, marketing, selling, and distributing Campbell's soups in China. Each company brings unique strengths to the partnership. Campbell is a global leader in marketing and manufacturing soup; Swire Pacific has long experience in food distribution in China and a deep understanding of the Chinese market. Together, each can accomplish more than either could alone. "We've made great strides in understanding the market and refining our products to appeal to Chinese consumers," says the president of Campbell International. "This partnership will help unlock the potential of the soup market in China by pairing Campbell's brands, recipes, and consumer insights with Swire's sales force, logistics capabilities, and overall market knowledge."

Joint ownership has certain drawbacks, however. The partners may disagree over investment, marketing, or other policies. Whereas many U.S. firms like to reinvest earnings for growth, local firms often prefer to take out these earnings; whereas U.S. firms emphasize the role of marketing, local investors may rely on selling.

Direct Investment

Direct investment
Entering a foreign market by developing foreign-based assembly or manufacturing facilities.

The biggest involvement in a foreign market comes through **direct investment**—the development of foreign-based assembly or manufacturing facilities. For example, HP has made direct investments in several major markets abroad, including India. It has opened two factories that make PCs for the Indian market, along with HP-owned retail outlets in 150 Indian cities. Thanks to such commitments, HP is a market leader in India and now controls more than 17 percent of the market in India.[30]

If a company has gained experience in exporting and if the foreign market is large enough, foreign production facilities offer many advantages. The firm may have lower costs in the form of cheaper labor or raw materials, foreign government investment incentives, and freight savings. The firm may also improve its image in the host country because it creates jobs. Generally, a firm develops a deeper relationship with the government, customers, local suppliers, and distributors, allowing it to adapt its products to the local market better. Finally, the firm keeps full control over the investment and therefore can develop manufacturing and marketing policies that serve its long-term international objectives.

The main disadvantage of direct investment is that the firm faces many risks, such as restricted or devalued currencies, falling markets, or government changes. In some cases, a firm has no choice but to accept these risks if it wants to operate in the host country.

SPEED BUMP | LINKING THE CONCEPTS

Slow down here and think about McDonald's global marketing issues.

- To what extent can McDonald's standardize for the Chinese market? What marketing strategy and program elements can be similar to those used in the United States and other parts of the Western world? Which ones must be adapted? Be specific.
- To what extent can McDonald's standardize its strategy, products, and programs for the Canadian market? What elements can be standardized and which must be adapted?
- To what extent are McDonald's globalization efforts contributing to the Americanization of countries and cultures around the world? What are the positives and negatives of such cultural developments?

Author Comment ▶
The major global marketing decision usually boils down to this: How much, if at all, should a company adapt its marketing strategy and programs to local markets? How might the answer differ for Boeing versus McDonald's?

Standardized global marketing
An international marketing strategy that basically uses the same marketing strategy and mix in all of the company's international markets.

Adapted global marketing
An international marketing approach that adjusts the marketing strategy and mix elements to each international target market, which creates more costs but hopefully produces a larger market share and return.

Deciding on the Global Marketing Program

Companies that operate in one or more foreign markets must decide how much, if at all, to adapt their marketing strategies and programs to local conditions. At one extreme are global companies that use **standardized global marketing**, essentially using the same marketing strategy approaches and marketing mix worldwide. At the other extreme is **adapted global marketing**. In this case, the producer adjusts the marketing strategy and mix elements to each target market, resulting in more costs but hopefully producing a larger market share and return.

The question of whether to adapt or standardize the marketing strategy and program has been much debated over the years. On the one hand, some global marketers believe that technology is making the world a smaller place, and consumer needs around the world are becoming more similar. This paves the way for global brands and standardized global marketing. Global branding and standardization, in turn, result in greater brand power and reduced costs from economies of scale.

On the other hand, the marketing concept holds that marketing programs will be more effective if tailored to the unique needs of each targeted customer group. If this concept applies within a country, it should apply even more across international markets. Despite global convergence, consumers in different countries still have widely varied cultural backgrounds. They still differ significantly in their needs and wants, spending power, product preferences, and shopping patterns. Because these differences are hard to change, most marketers today adapt their products, prices, channels, and promotions to fit consumer desires in each country.

However, global standardization is not an all-or-nothing proposition. It's a matter of degree. Most international marketers suggest that companies should "think globally but act locally"—that they should seek a balance between standardization and adaptation. The company's overall strategy should provide global strategic direction. Then regional or local units should focus on adapting the strategy to specific local markets.

Collectively, local brands still account for the overwhelming majority of consumers' purchases. "The vast majority of people still lead very local lives," says a global analyst. "By all means go global, but the first thing you have to do is win on the ground. You have to go local." Another analyst agrees: "You need to respect local culture and become part of it." A global brand must "engage with consumers in a way that feels local to them." Simon Clift, head of marketing for global consumer-goods giant Unilever, puts it this way: "We're trying to strike a balance between being mindlessly global and hopelessly local."[31]

▲ **Marketing mix adaptation: In India, McDonald's serves chicken, fish, and vegetable burgers, and the Maharja Mac—two all-mutton patties, special sauce, lettuce, cheese, pickles, onions, on a sesame-seed bun.**

Douglas E. CURRAN Agence France Presse/Newscom

Straight product extension

Marketing a product in a foreign market without making any changes to the product.

Product adaptation

Adapting a product to meet local conditions or wants in foreign markets.

McDonald's operates this way: It uses the same basic fast-food look, layout, and operating model in its restaurants around the world but adapts its menu to local tastes. In Japan, it offers Ebi Filet-O-Shrimp burgers and fancy Salad Macs salad plates. In Korea it sells the Bulgogi Burger, a grilled pork patty on a bun with a garlicky soy sauce. ▶ In India, where cows are considered sacred, McDonald's serves McChicken, Filet-O-Fish, McVeggie (a vegetable burger), Pizza McPuffs, McAloo Tikki (a spiced-potato burger), and the Maharaja Mac—two all-chicken patties, special sauce, lettuce, cheese, pickles, onions on a sesame-seed bun. In all, McDonald's serves local markets with a global brand.

Product

Five strategies are used for adapting product and marketing communication strategies to a global market (see ▶ **Figure 15.3**).[32] We first discuss the three product strategies and then turn to the two communication strategies.

Straight product extension means marketing a product in a foreign market without making any changes to the product. Top management tells its marketing people, "Take the product as is and find customers for it." The first step, however, should be to find out whether foreign consumers use that product and what form they prefer.

Straight extension has been successful in some cases and disastrous in others. Apple iPads, Gillette razors, Black & Decker tools, and even 7-Eleven Slurpees are all sold successfully in about the same form around the world. But when General Foods introduced its standard powdered JELL-O in the British market, it discovered that British consumers prefer a solid wafer or cake form. Likewise, Philips began to make a profit in Japan only after it reduced the size of its coffeemakers to fit into smaller Japanese kitchens and its shavers to fit smaller Japanese hands. Straight extension is tempting because it involves no additional product development costs, manufacturing changes, or new promotion. But it can be costly in the long run if products fail to satisfy consumers in specific global markets.

Product adaptation involves changing the product to meet local requirements, conditions, or wants. For example, although the U.S. and European versions of the feisty little Fiat 500 might look a lot alike, Fiat has made stem-to-stern adaptations in the U.S. model to meet U.S. safety standards and American buyer expectations. To name just a few modifications, the U.S. Fiat 500 has a redesigned engine that offers the power demanded by U.S. consumers while simultaneously providing the better gas mileage and lower emissions required by the country's regulations. The gas tank is 40 percent larger to accommodate the longer driving distances that are typical in the United States, and there's lots more insulation in the U.S. car to keep it quiet enough for Americans. Another big difference—the cupholders:[33]

> A silly matter to Europeans, but vital to Americans, the U.S. Fiat 500 has an enlarged pod of holders up front to fit U.S.-size drinks, instead of the small European holders, plus two additional holders at the rear of the floor console. The in-car beverage concept is so foreign to Europeans that the 500 design team didn't understand the need for more and bigger holders—until one engineer drew a cartoon of an American wearing one of those gimmick hats that hold two beer cans and have long tubes at straws. Then everybody said, "Ah, yes."

▶ **Figure 15.3** Five Global Product and Communications Strategies

The real question buried in this figure is this: How much should a company standardize or adapt its products and marketing across global markets?

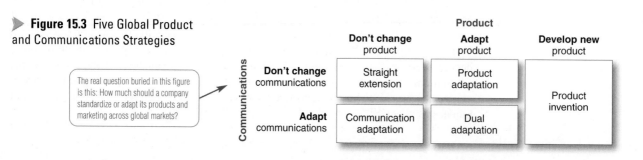

	Product		
Communications	**Don't change** product	**Adapt** product	**Develop new** product
Don't change communications	Straight extension	Product adaptation	Product invention
Adapt communications	Communication adaptation	Dual adaptation	

Product invention
Creating new products or services for foreign markets.

Product invention consists of creating something new to meet the needs of consumers in a given country. As markets have gone global, companies ranging from appliance manufacturers and carmakers to candy and soft drink producers have developed products that meet the special purchasing needs of low-income consumers in developing economies. For example, Ford developed the economical, low-priced Figo model especially for entry-level consumers in India; GM created the inexpensive Baojun for China (the name means "treasured horse"). Chinese appliance producer Haier developed sturdier washing machines for rural users in emerging markets, where it found that lighter-duty machines often became clogged with mud when farmers used them to clean vegetables as well as clothes.[34]

Similarly, Finnish mobile phone maker Nokia has created full-featured but rugged and low-cost phones especially designed for the harsher living conditions faced by less-affluent consumers in large developing countries such as India, China, and Kenya. For instance, it developed dustproof keypads, which are crucial in dry, hot countries with many unpaved roads. Some phones have built-in radio antennas for areas where radio is the main source of entertainment. And after learning that poor people often share their phones, the company developed handsets with multiple address books. Thanks to such innovation, Nokia is the market leader in Africa, the Middle East, Eastern Europe, and Asia.[35]

Promotion

Companies can either adopt the same communication strategy they use in the home market or change it for each local market. Consider advertising messages. Some global companies use a standardized advertising theme around the world. For example, Apple sold millions of iPods with a single global campaign featuring silhouetted figures dancing against a colorful background. And other than for language, the Apple Web site looks about the same for any of the more than 70 countries in which Apple markets its products, from Australia to Senegal to the Czech Republic.

Of course, even in highly standardized communications campaigns, some adjustments might be required for language and cultural differences. Global companies often have difficulty crossing the language barrier, with results ranging from mild embarrassment to outright failure. Seemingly innocuous brand names and advertising phrases can take on unintended or hidden meanings when translated into other languages. For example, an Italian company's Traficante mineral water received an interesting reception in Spain, where the name translates as "drug dealer." And Motorola's Hellomoto ring tone sounds like "Hello, Fatty" in India. (See Marketing at Work 15.2 for more language blunders in international marketing.) Marketers must be watchful to avoid such mistakes.

Communication adaptation
A global communication strategy of fully adapting advertising messages to local markets.

Other companies follow a strategy of **communication adaptation**, fully adapting their advertising messages to local markets. Consumer products marketer Unilever does this for many of its brands. For example, whereas ads for Unilever toothpaste brands in Western markets might emphasize anything from whiter teeth or fresher breath to greater sex appeal, ads in Africa take a more basic educational approach, emphasizing the importance of brushing twice a day. And Unilever adapts the positioning, formulation, and appeals for its Sunsilk Lively Clean & Fresh shampoo to serve the varying needs of consumers in different markets. Consider this example:[36]

Thick waves of hair cascade over a woman's shoulder. She gives a flirtatious flick of her locks and tells viewers that they too can get such a luxurious mane—if they buy the shampoo she is holding up to the camera. That is the script for your standard shampoo commercial. Cut to the television spot for Sunsilk's Lively Clean & Fresh shampoo. Another young, smiling woman is the star, but there is not a strand of hair in sight. Her tresses are completely covered by a tudung, the head scarf worn by many Muslim women in Malaysia. The pitch? Lively Clean & Fresh helps remove excess oil from the scalp and hair—a common problem among wearers of tudungs. Unilever says the product is the first shampoo to speak directly to the "lifestyle of a tudung wearer." The ad begins with the young woman saying that now she can do what she wants without worrying about her hair, before she goes on to kick a goal in a coed soccer game. As the Islamic population has grown in size and affluence—there are now 1.57 billion Muslims worldwide—Unilever and other multinationals are seeking to tap into the market.

MARKETING AT WORK 15.2

Global Marketing: Watch Your Language!

Many global companies have had difficulty crossing the language barrier, with results ranging from mild embarrassment to outright failure. Seemingly innocuous brand names and advertising phrases can take on unintended or hidden meanings when translated into other languages. Careless translations can make a marketer look downright foolish to foreign consumers.

The classic language blunders involve standardized brand names that do not translate well. When Coca-Cola first marketed Coke in China in the 1920s, it developed a group of Chinese characters that, when pronounced, sounded like the product name. Unfortunately, the characters actually translated as "bite the wax tadpole." Now the characters on Chinese Coke bottles translate as "happiness in the mouth."

Several modern-day marketers have had similar problems when their brand names crashed into the language barrier. Chevy's Nova translated into Spanish as *no va*—"it doesn't go." GM changed the name to Caribe (Spanish for Caribbean), and sales increased. Rolls-Royce avoided the name Silver Mist in German markets, where *mist* means "manure." Sunbeam, however, entered the German market with its Mist Stick hair-curling iron. As should have been expected, the Germans had little use for a "manure wand." IKEA marketed a children's workbench named FARTFULL (the word means "speedy" in Swedish); it soon discontinued the product.

Interbrand of London, the firm that created household names such as Prozac and Acura, recently developed a brand name "hall of shame" list, which contained these and other foreign brand names you're never likely to see inside the local Kroger supermarket: Krapp toilet paper (Denmark), Plopp chocolate (Scandinavia), Crapsy Fruit cereal (France), Poo curry powder (Argentina), and Pschitt lemonade (France).

Travelers often encounter well-intentioned advice from service firms that takes on meanings very different from those intended. The menu in one Swiss restaurant proudly stated, "Our wines leave you nothing to hope for." Signs in a Japanese hotel pronounced, "You are invited to take advantage of the chambermaid." At a laundry in Rome, it was, "Ladies, leave your clothes here and spend the afternoon having a good time."

Advertising themes often lose—or gain—something in the translation. The Coors beer slogan "get loose with Coors" in Spanish came out as "get the runs with Coors." Coca-Cola's "Coke adds life" theme in Japanese translated into "Coke brings your ancestors back from the dead." The milk industry learned too late that its American advertising question "Got Milk?" translated in Mexico as a more provocative "Are you lactating?" In Chinese, the KFC slogan "finger-lickin' good" came out as "eat your fingers off." And Motorola's Hellomoto ringtone sounds like "Hello, Fatty" in India. Even when the language is the same, word usage may differ from country to country. Thus, the classic British ad line for Electrolux vacuum cleaners—"Nothing sucks like an Electrolux"—would capture few customers in the United States.

So, crossing the language barrier involves much more than simply translating names and slogans into other languages. Beyond just word meanings and nuances, international marketers must also consider things such as phonetic appeal and even associations with historical figures, legends, and other factors. "You can't uproot a concept and just translate it and put it into another market," says one translation consultant. "It's not really about translating word for word, but actually adapting a certain meaning." Says another, "If you fail to review what your brand is saying to a foreign market, you may wish you stayed home."

Sources: Quotes, examples, and other information from Neil Payne, "Cross-Cultural Marketing Blunders," July 28, 2008, accessed at www.proz.com/translation-articles/articles/1909/1/Cross-Cultural-Marketing-Blunders-; Randall Frost, "Lost in Translation," *Brandchannel.com*, November 13, 2006, www.brandchannel.com/features_effect.asp?pf_id=340; David A. Ricks, "Perspectives: Translation Blunders in International Business," *Journal of Language for International Business,* Vol. 7, No. 2, 1996, pp. 50–55; Mark Young, "Don't Let Your Brand Get Lost in Translation," *Brandweek*, February 8, 2010, p. 34; and Pete Wise, "International Marketing and Advertising Translation—The Top 20 Blunders, Mistakes, and Failures," http://ezinearticles.com/?International-Marketing-and-Advertising-Translation---The-Top-20-Blunders,-Mistakes-and-Failures&id=3999831, accessed November 2011.

▲ Global language barriers: Some standardized names do not translate well globally. You won't likely find this French lemonade brand at your local Kroger store.

Malias/Flickr.com

Media also need to be adapted internationally because media availability and regulations vary from country to country. TV advertising time is very limited in Europe, for instance, ranging from four hours a day in France to none in Scandinavian countries. Advertisers must buy time months in advance, and they have little control over airtimes. However, cell phone ads are much more widely accepted in Europe and Asia than in the United States. Magazines also vary in effectiveness. For example, magazines are a major medium in Italy but a minor one in Austria. Newspapers are national in the United Kingdom but only local in Spain.[37]

Price

Companies also face many considerations in setting their international prices. For example, how might Stanley Black & Decker price its tools globally? It could set a uniform price globally, but this amount would be too high a price in poor countries and not high enough in rich ones. It could charge what consumers in each country would bear, but this strategy ignores differences in the actual costs from country to country. Finally, the company could use a standard markup of its costs everywhere, but this approach might price Stanley Black & Decker out of the market in some countries where costs are high.

Regardless of how companies go about pricing their products, their foreign prices probably will be higher than their domestic prices for comparable products. An Apple iPad that sells for $600 in the United States goes for $750 in the United Kingdom. Why? Apple faces a *price escalation* problem. It must add the cost of transportation, tariffs, importer margin, wholesaler margin, and retailer margin to its factory price. Depending on these added costs, the product may have to sell for two to five times as much in another country to make the same profit.

▲ **International pricing: Levi Strauss recently launched the Denizen brand, created for teens and young adults in emerging markets such as China, India, and Brazil who cannot afford Levi's-branded jeans.**
Bloomberg via Getty Images

To overcome this problem when selling to less-affluent consumers in developing countries, many companies make simpler or smaller versions of their products that can be sold at lower prices. Others have introduced new, more affordable brands in emerging markets. For example, Levi recently launched the Denizen brand, created for teens and young adults in emerging markets such as China, India, and Brazil who cannot afford Levi's-branded jeans. The name combines the first four letters of *denim* with *zen*, a word with Japanese and Chinese roots that means "meditative state" or "escape from the hustle and bustle of everyday life."[38]

Recent economic and technological forces have had an impact on global pricing. For example, the Internet is making global price differences more obvious. When firms sell their wares over the Internet, customers can see how much products sell for in different countries. They can even order a given product directly from the company location or dealer offering the lowest price. This is forcing companies toward more standardized international pricing.

Distribution Channels

Whole-channel view
Designing international channels that take into account the entire global supply chain and marketing channel, forging an effective global value delivery network.

An international company must take a **whole-channel view** of the problem of distributing products to final consumers. ▶ **Figure 15.4** shows the two major links between the seller and the final buyer. The first link, *channels between nations*, moves company products from points of production to the borders of countries within which they are sold. The second link, *channels within nations*, moves products from their market entry points to the final consumers. The whole-channel view takes into account the entire global supply chain and marketing channel. It recognizes that to compete well internationally, the company must effectively design and manage an entire *global value delivery network*.

> **Figure 15.4** Whole-Channel
Concept for International Marketing

Distribution channels between and within nations can vary dramatically around the world. For example, in the United States, Nokia distributes phones through a network of sophisticated retailers. In rural India, it maintains a fleet of Nokia-branded vans that prowl the rutted country roads.

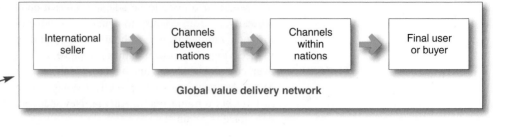

| International seller | → | Channels between nations | → | Channels within nations | → | Final user or buyer |

Global value delivery network

Channels of distribution within countries vary greatly from nation to nation. There are large differences in the numbers and types of intermediaries serving each country market and in the transportation infrastructure serving these intermediaries. For example, whereas large-scale retail chains dominate the U.S. scene, most of the retailing in other countries is done by small, independent retailers. In India, millions of retailers operate tiny shops or sell in open markets. Thus, in its efforts to sell those rugged, affordable phones discussed earlier to Indian consumers, Nokia has had to forge its own distribution structure.[39]

▲ **Distribution channels vary greatly from nation to nation. In its efforts to sell rugged, affordable phones to Indian consumers, Nokia forged its own distribution structure, including a fleet of distinctive blue Nokia-branded vans that prowl rutted country roads to visit remote villages.**

Atul Loke/Panos Pictures

In India, Nokia has a presence in almost 90 percent of retail outlets selling mobile phones. It estimates there are 90,000 points-of-sale for its phones, ranging from modern stores to makeshift kiosks. That makes it difficult to control how products are displayed and pitched to consumers. "You have to understand where people live, what the shopping patterns are," says a Nokia executive. "You have to work with local means to reach people—even bicycles or rickshaws." ▶ To reach rural India, Nokia has outfitted its own fleet of distinctive blue Nokia-branded vans that prowl the rutted country roads. Staffers park these advertisements-on-wheels in villages, often on market or festival days. There, with crowds clustering around, Nokia reps explain the basics of how the phones work and how to buy them. Nokia has extended the concept to minivans, which can reach even more remote places. Thanks to smart product development and innovative channels, Nokia now owns an astounding 30 percent share of India's mobile device market.

Similarly, as we learned in the story about its ventures in Africa, Coca-Cola adapts its distribution methods to meet local challenges in global markets. For example, in Montevideo, Uruguay, where larger vehicles are challenged by traffic, parking, and pollution difficulties, Coca-Cola purchased 30 small, efficient three-wheeled ZAP alternative transportation trucks. The little trucks average about one-fifth the fuel consumption and scoot around congested city streets with greater ease. In rural areas, Coca-Cola uses a manual delivery process. In China, an army of more than 10,000 Coca-Cola sales reps make regular visits to small retailers, often on foot or bicycle. To reach the most isolated spots, the company even relies on teams of delivery donkeys. In Tanzania, 93 percent of Coca-Cola's products are manually delivered via pushcarts and bicycles.[40]

Author Comment ▶
Many large companies, regardless of their "home country," now think of themselves as truly global organizations. They view the entire world as a single borderless market. For example, although headquartered in Chicago, Boeing is as comfortable selling planes to Lufthansa or Air China as to American Airlines.

Deciding on the Global Marketing Organization

Companies manage their international marketing activities in at least three different ways: Most companies first organize an export department, then create an international division, and finally become a global organization.

A firm normally gets into international marketing by simply shipping out its goods. If its international sales expand, the company will establish an *export department* with a sales manager and a few assistants. As sales increase, the export department can expand to include various marketing services so that it can actively go after business. If the firm moves into joint ventures or direct investment, the export department will no longer be adequate.

Many companies get involved in several international markets and ventures. A company may export to one country, license to another, have a joint ownership venture in a third, and own a subsidiary in a fourth. Sooner or later it will create *international divisions* or subsidiaries to handle all its international activity.

International divisions are organized in a variety of ways. An international division's corporate staff consists of marketing, manufacturing, research, finance, planning, and personnel specialists. It plans for and provides services to various operating units, which can be organized in one of three ways. They can be *geographical organizations*, with country managers who are responsible for salespeople, sales branches, distributors, and licensees in their respective countries. Or the operating units can be *world product groups*, each responsible for worldwide sales of different product groups. Finally, operating units can be *international subsidiaries*, each responsible for their own sales and profits.

Many firms have passed beyond the international division stage and are truly *global organizations*. ▶ For example, consider Reckitt Benckiser (RB), a $12 billion European producer of household, health, and personal care products and consumer goods with a stable full of familiar brands (Air Wick, Lysol, Woolite, Calgon, Mucinex, Clearasil, French's, and many others—see www.rb.com):[41]

▲ European household, health, and consumer goods producer Reckitt Benckiser has a truly global organization. "Most of our top managers . . . view themselves as global citizens rather than as citizens of any given nation."

Reckitt Benckiser plc.

RB has operations in more than 60 countries. Its top 400 managers represent 53 different nationalities. Although headquartered in the United Kingdom, an Italian runs its UK business, an American runs the German business, and a Dutchman runs the U.S. business. An Indian runs the Chinese business, a Belgian the Brazilian business, a Frenchman the Russian business, an Argentine the Japanese business, a Brit the Middle East North Africa business, and a Czech the South Africa business. "Most of our top managers . . . view themselves as global citizens rather than as citizens of any given nation," says RB's chief executive officer.

The company has spent the past decade building a culture of global mobility because it thinks that's one of the best ways to generate new ideas and create global entrepreneurs. And it has paid off. Products launched in the past three years—all the result of global cross-fertilization—account for 35–40 percent of net revenue. Over the past few years, even during the economic downturn, the company has outperformed its rivals—P&G, Unilever, and Colgate—in growth.

Global organizations don't think of themselves as national marketers who sell abroad but as global marketers. The top corporate management and staff plan worldwide manufacturing facilities, marketing policies, financial flows, and logistical systems. The global operating units report directly to the chief executive or the executive committee of the organization, not to the head of an international division. Executives are trained in worldwide operations, not just domestic *or* international operations. Global companies recruit management from many countries, buy components and supplies where they cost the least, and invest where the expected returns are greatest.

Today, major companies must become more global if they hope to compete. As foreign companies successfully invade their domestic markets, companies must move more aggressively into foreign markets. They will have to change from companies that treat their international operations as secondary to companies that view the entire world as a single borderless market.

REST STOP | REVIEWING THE CONCEPTS

MyMarketingLab

Now that you have completed the chapter, return to www.mymktlab.com to experience and apply the concepts and to explore the additional study materials for this chapter.

CHAPTER REVIEW AND KEY TERMS

Objectives Review

Companies today can no longer afford to pay attention only to their domestic market, regardless of its size. Many industries are global industries, and firms that operate globally achieve lower costs and higher brand awareness. At the same time, global marketing is risky because of variable exchange rates, unstable governments, tariffs and trade barriers, and several other factors. Given the potential gains and risks of international marketing, companies need a systematic way to make their global marketing decisions.

> **OBJECTIVE 1 Discuss how the international trade system and the economic, political-legal, and cultural environments affect a company's international marketing decisions. (pp 452–463)**

A company must understand the *global marketing environment*, especially the international trade system. It must assess each foreign market's *economic*, *political-legal*, and *cultural characteristics*. The company must then decide whether it wants to go abroad and consider the potential risks and benefits. It must decide on the volume of international sales it wants, how many countries it wants to market in, and which specific markets it wants to enter. These decisions call for weighing the probable returns against the level of risk.

> **OBJECTIVE 2 Describe three key approaches to entering international markets. (pp 463–467)**

The company must decide how to enter each chosen market—whether through *exporting*, *joint venturing*, or *direct investment*. Many companies start as exporters, move to joint ventures, and finally make a direct investment in foreign markets. In *exporting*, the company enters a foreign market by sending and selling products through international marketing intermediaries (indirect exporting) or the company's own

department, branch, or sales representative or agents (direct exporting). When establishing a *joint venture*, a company enters foreign markets by joining with foreign companies to produce or market a product or service. In *licensing*, the company enters a foreign market by contracting with a licensee in the foreign market and offering the right to use a manufacturing process, trademark, patent, trade secret, or other item of value for a fee or royalty.

> **OBJECTIVE 3 Explain how companies adapt their marketing strategies and mixes for international markets. (pp 467–472)**

Companies must also decide how much their marketing strategies and their products, promotion, price, and channels should be adapted for each foreign market. At one extreme, global companies use *standardized global marketing* worldwide. Others use *adapted global marketing*, in which they adjust the marketing strategy and mix to each target market, bearing more costs but hoping for a larger market share and return. However, global standardization is not an all-or-nothing proposition. It's a matter of degree. Most international marketers suggest that companies should "think globally but act locally"—that they should seek a balance between globally standardized strategies and locally adapted marketing mix tactics.

> **OBJECTIVE 4 Identify the three major forms of international marketing organization. (pp 472–473)**

The company must develop an effective organization for international marketing. Most firms start with an *export department* and graduate to an *international division*. A few become *global organizations*, with worldwide marketing planned and managed by the top officers of the company. Global organizations view the entire world as a single, borderless market.

Key Terms

Objective 1
Global firm (p 453)
Economic community (p 455)

Objective 2
Exporting (p 464)
Joint venturing (p 465)
Licensing (p 465)

Contract manufacturing (p 465)
Management contracting (p 465)
Joint ownership (p 466)
Direct investment (p 466)

Objective 3
Standardized global marketing (p 467)
Adapted global marketing (p 467)

Straight product extension (p 468)
Product adaptation (p 468)
Product invention (p 469)
Communication adaptation (p 469)
Whole-channel view (p 471)

DISCUSSION AND CRITICAL THINKING

Discussion Questions

1. Explain what is meant by the term *global firm* and list the six major decisions involved in international marketing. (AACSB: Communication)
2. Discuss the types of restrictions governments might impose on trade between nations. (AACSB: Communication)
3. Discuss the four types of country industrial structures and the opportunities each offers to international marketers. (AACSB: Communication)
4. Name and describe the advantages and disadvantages of the different types of joint venturing when entering a foreign market. (AACSB: Communication; Reflective Thinking)
5. Discuss the strategies used for adapting products to a global market. Which strategy is best? (AACSB: Communication)
6. Discuss how global distribution channels differ from domestic channels. (AACSB: Communication)

Critical Thinking Exercises

1. Visit www.transparency.org and click on "corruption perception index." What is the most recent CPI for the following countries: Denmark, Jamaica, Malaysia, Myanmar, New Zealand, Somali, and the United States? What are the implications of this index for U.S.-based companies doing business in these countries? (AACSB: Communication; Use of IT; Reflective Thinking)
2. Selling a product in a foreign country is difficult and many companies make mistakes. Find and report on two examples of companies making marketing mistakes when entering a foreign country. (AACSB: Communication; Reflective Thinking)
3. One way to analyze the cultural differences among countries is to conduct a Hofstede analysis. Visit www.geert-hofstede.com/ to learn what this analysis considers. Develop a presentation explaining how three countries of your choice differ from the United States. (AACSB: Communication; Use of IT; Reflective Thinking)

MINICASES AND APPLICATIONS

Marketing Technology   Reverse Innovation

Reverse innovation, innovation blowback, and *trickle-up innovation* are terms used to describe the process by which innovations have developed to meet the needs of emerging markets as they make their way into developed markets. Traditionally, innovations are birthed in developed countries with older models later offered in lower-income markets such as India and China. But things are now changing. Although many "bottom of the pyramid" emerging markets are low on the economic food chain, they have large populations, providing opportunities for businesses that meet growing needs at an affordable price. GE, the dominant maker of expensive electrocardiograph (ECG) machines sold to hospitals, developed a lower-priced, small, battery-powered ECG machine for use in India and China. GE then marketed this product to primary care doctors, visiting nurses, and rural hospitals and clinics in the United States. Reverse innovation is not limited to technological products—it can apply to products as basic as yogurt.

1. Learn more about how GE used reverse innovation to capitalize on opportunities in the United States. Find two other examples of reverse innovation for technological products. (AACSB: Communication; Reflective Thinking)
2. Discuss two examples of reverse innovation for nontechnology products. (AACSB: Communication; Reflective Thinking)

Marketing Ethics   Trade Incentives

The U.S. apparel industry is fiercely competitive; as a result, marketers often need to keep prices low to survive. Many apparel manufacturers have shuttered their U.S. factories in favor of cheaper labor across the globe, and the U.S. government is encouraging this behavior. For example, the African Growth and Opportunity Act (AGOA) was signed into law in 2000 to foster economic growth in Sub-Saharan Africa countries. Consequently, several clothing manufacturers have located in Africa to take advantage of the cheap labor and liberal U.S. market access to these countries. The AGOA allows poorly developed African countries to export items to the United States duty free. There has been an unintended consequence, however, as more developed African countries such as South Africa, which must pay regular duties to export to the United States, are seeing their textile industry suffer. One factor is rising labor costs—65 cents per hour in South Africa but only 19 cents in neighboring African countries such as Lesotho, Swaziland, and

Mozambique. Another significant factor is the ability of these countries to export to the United States duty-free as allowed by the AGOA. As a result, the South African textile industry saw 52 factories closed in the first half of 2011 alone, 8,000 jobs lost, and a reduction of $1.5 billion in direct investment. While regulations enacted in the United States are not completely responsible for this decline, critics argue that the AGOA played a major role.

1. Should the U.S. government be able to make laws that favor some countries and impact the United States and other countries so dramatically? (AACSB: Communication; Ethical Reasoning)
2. Find another example of a U.S. law or trade agreement that encourages or discourages trade with foreign countries. Discuss the positive and negative consequences of the law. (AACSB: Communication; Reflective Thinking)

Marketing by the Numbers   Balance of Trade

The United States exported almost $2 trillion worth of goods and services in 2010 yet realized a trade deficit of more than $500 million, meaning it imported more than it exported. That has been the case for decades, and some Americans believe this is harming the country.

1. Visit www.bea.gov and find the U.S. trade in goods and services. Create a line chart showing the change in this number from 1992 to 2010. (AACSB: Communication; Use of IT; Reflective Thinking)
2. Debate the pros and cons of the United States having trade deficits consistently year after year. (AACSB: Communication; Reflective Thinking)

Video Case   The U.S. Film Industry

If you like movies, you've no doubt seen a foreign film at some point. But did you know that American films are some of the biggest and most anticipated foreign films in the world? In fact, foreign box office and DVD sales account for nearly 70 percent of all revenues for the U.S. film industry. With that much financial impact, foreign markets are playing a bigger and bigger role not only in the pricing, distribution, and promotion of U.S. films, but in developing the product itself.

This video illustrates the challenges faced by the U.S. film industry stemming from differences in the marketing environment in different international markets. The result is that this industry is now like any other export industry. The marketing mix must be adapted at an optimum level in order to meet the needs of global markets while still maintaining the benefits of standardization.

After viewing the video featuring the U.S. film industry, answer the following questions:

1. Which part of the marketing environment seems to be having the greatest impact on U.S. films abroad?

2. Which of the five strategies for adapting products and promotion for the global market is most relevant to the U.S. film industry?

3. Is the U.S. film industry now dependent upon foreign markets for success? Compare this to other U.S. exports.

Company Cases   11 Tesco Fresh & Easy / 15 Buick

See Appendix 1 for cases appropriate for this chapter. **Case 11, Tesco Fresh & Easy: Another British Invasion.** UK mega-grocer Tesco attempts to penetrate the U.S. market by targeting an underserved customer segment. **Case 15, Buick: Number One Imported Brand.** Through the information-gathering efforts of its Chinese design team, Buick meets customer needs throughout the world.

16 Sustainable Marketing

Social Responsibility and Ethics

CHAPTER ROAD MAP

Objective Outline

Previewing the Concepts

In this final chapter, we'll examine the concepts of sustainable marketing, meeting the needs of consumers, businesses, and society—now and in the future—through socially and environmentally responsible marketing actions. We'll start by defining sustainable marketing and then look at some common criticisms of marketing as it impacts individual consumers, as well as public actions that promote sustainable marketing. Finally, we'll see how companies themselves can benefit from proactively pursuing sustainable marketing practices that bring value to not only individual customers but also society as a whole. Sustainable marketing actions are more than just the right thing to do; they're also good for business.

First, let's look at an example of sustainable marketing in action at Unilever, the world's third-largest consumer products company. For 12 years running, Unilever has been named sustainability leader in the food and beverage industry by the Dow Jones Sustainability Indexes. The company recently launched its Sustainable Living Plan, by which it intends to double its size by 2020 while at the same time reducing its impact on the planet and increasing the social benefits arising from its activities. That's an ambitious goal.

▲ As part of its Sustainable Living Plan, Unilever is working with its more than 2 billion customers worldwide to improve the social and environmental impact of its products in use. "Small actions. Big difference."

Reproduced with kind permission of Unilever PLC and group companies

First Stop

Sustainability at Unilever: Creating a Better Future Every Day

When Paul Polman took over as CEO of Unilever in 2009, the home and personal care products company was a slumbering giant. Despite its stable of star-studded brands—including the likes of Dove, Axe, Noxema, Sunsilk, VO5, Hellmann's, Lipton, and Ben & Jerry's—Unilever had experienced a decade of stagnant sales and profits. The company needed renewed energy and purpose. "To drag the world back to sanity, we need to know why we are here," said Polman.

To answer the "why are we here" question and find a more energizing mission, Polman looked beyond the usual corporate goals of growing sales, profits, and shareholder value. Instead, he asserted, growth results from accomplishing a broader social and environmental mission. Unilever exists "for consumers, not shareholders," he said. "If we are in sync with consumer needs and the environment in which we operate, and take responsibility for our [societal impact], then the shareholder will also be rewarded."

As a result of such thinking, in late 2010 Unilever launched its Sustainable Living Plan. Under this plan, the company set out to "create a better future every day for people around the world: the people who work for us, those we do business with, the billions of people who use our products, and future generations whose quality of life depends on the way we protect the environment today." According to Polman, Unilever's long-run *commercial* success depends on how well it manages the *social* and *environmental* impact of its actions.

The Sustainable Living Plan sets out three major social and environmental objectives to be accomplished by 2020: "(1) To help more than one billion people take action to improve their health and well-being; (2) to halve the environmental footprint of the making and use of our products; and (3) to source 100 percent of our agricultural raw materials sustainably."

Evaluating and working on societal and environmental impact is nothing new at Unilever. The company already had multiple programs in place to manage the impact of its products and operations. For example, over the past five years, the company's Nutrition Enhancement Program has reviewed Unilever's entire portfolio of foods—some 30,000 products—resulting in reductions in saturated and trans fat, sugar, and salt in thousands of items. And over the past decade, the company's factories have reduced CO_2 emissions by 44 percent, water use by 66 percent, and total waste disposal by 73 percent. However, the Sustainable Living Plan pulls together all of the work the company has been doing and sets ambitious new sustainability goals.

Unilever's sustainability efforts span the entire value chain, from how the company sources raw materials to how customers use and dispose of its products. "The world faces enormous environmental pressures," says the company. "Our aim is to make our activities more sustainable and also encourage our customers, suppliers, and others to do the same." On the "upstream supply side," more than two-thirds of Unilever's raw materials come from agriculture, so the company is helping suppliers develop sustainable farming practices that meet its own high expectations for environmental and social impact. Unilever assesses suppliers against two sets of standards. The first is the Unilever Supplier Code, which calls for socially responsible actions regarding human rights, labor practices, product safety, and care for the environment. The second is the Unilever Sustainable Agriculture Code, which details Unilever's expectations for sustainable agriculture practices, so that it and its suppliers "can commit to the sustainability journey together." Unilever also collaborates closely with its commercial and trade customers, such as Walmart and other large retailers, many of whom have their own ambitious goals in areas such as energy use, greenhouse gas emissions, and recycling and waste reduction.

> Under its Sustainable Living Plan, consumer goods giant Unilever has set out to "create a better future every day for people around the world." Unilever's long-run *commercial* success depends on how well it manages the *social* and *environmental* impact of its actions.

But Unilever's Sustainable Living Plan goes far beyond simply creating more responsible supply and distribution chains. Unilever is also working with final consumers to improve the social and environmental impact of its products in use. More than 2 billion customers in 178 countries use a Unilever product on any given day. Therefore, small everyday customer actions can add up to a big difference. Unilever sums it up with this equation: "Unilever brands × small everyday events × billions of consumers = big difference."

For example, almost one-third of households worldwide use Unilever laundry products to do their washing—approximately 125 billion washes every year. Up to 70 percent of the total greenhouse gas footprint of Unilever's laundry products, and 95 percent of the water footprint, occur during consumer use. Therefore, under its Sustainable Living Plan, Unilever is both creating more eco-friendly laundry products and motivating consumers to improve their laundry habits.

For example, around the world, Unilever is encouraging consumers to wash clothes at lower temperatures and use the correct dosage of detergent. One Unilever product, Persil Small & Mighty laundry detergent, is a concentrated detergent that uses less packaging, making it cheaper and less polluting to transport. More importantly, it washes better at lower temperatures and uses less energy. Another Unilever product, Comfort One Rinse fabric conditioner, was created for handwashing clothes in developing and emerging markets where water is often in short supply. The innovative product requires only one bucket of water for rinsing rather than three, saving customers time, effort, and 30 liters of water per wash. Such energy and water savings don't show up on Unilever's income statement, but they will be extremely important to the people and the planet. Similarly, small changes in product nutrition and customer eating habits can have a surprisingly big impact on human health. "In all," says the company, "we will inspire people to take small, everyday actions that can add up to a big difference for the world."

Will Unilever's Sustainable Living Plan produce results for the company? It is still too soon to tell, but so far, so good. Last year, Unilever's revenues grew 11 percent while profits grew 26 percent. The sustainability plan is not just the right thing to do for people and the environment, claims Polman, it's also right for Unilever. The quest for sustainability saves money by reducing energy use and minimizing waste. It fuels innovation, resulting in new products and new customer benefits. And it creates new market opportunities: More than half of Unilever's sales are from developing countries, the very places which face the greatest sustainability challenges.

In all, Polman predicts, the sustainability plan will help Unilever double in size by 2020, while also creating a better future for billions of people without increasing the environmental footprint. "We do not believe there is a conflict between sustainability and profitable growth," he concludes. "The daily act of making and selling consumer goods drives economic and social progress. There are billions of people around the world who deserve the better quality of life that everyday products like soap, shampoo, and tea can provide. Sustainable living is not a pipedream. It can be done, and there is very little downside."[1]

 esponsible marketers discover what consumers want and respond with market offerings that create value for buyers and capture value in return. The marketing concept is a philosophy of customer value and mutual gain. Its practice leads the economy by an invisible hand to satisfy the many and changing needs of millions of consumers.

Not all marketers follow the marketing concept, however. In fact, some companies use questionable marketing practices that serve their own rather than consumers' interests. Moreover, even well-intentioned marketing actions that meet the current needs of some consumers may cause immediate or future harm to other consumers or the larger society. Responsible marketers must consider whether their actions are sustainable in the longer run.

This chapter examines sustainable marketing and the social and environmental effects of private marketing practices. First, we address the question: What is sustainable marketing and why is it important?

Sustainable marketing
Socially and environmentally responsible marketing that meets the present needs of consumers and businesses while also preserving or enhancing the ability of future generations to meet their needs.

Author Comment ▶
Marketers must think beyond immediate customer satisfaction and business performance toward strategies that preserve the world for future generations.

Sustainable Marketing

Sustainable marketing calls for socially and environmentally responsible actions that meet the present needs of consumers and businesses while also preserving or enhancing the ability of future generations to meet their needs. ▶ **Figure 16.1** compares the sustainable marketing concept with marketing concepts we studied in earlier chapters.[2]

The *marketing concept* recognizes that organizations thrive from day to day by determining the current needs and wants of target customers and fulfilling those needs and wants

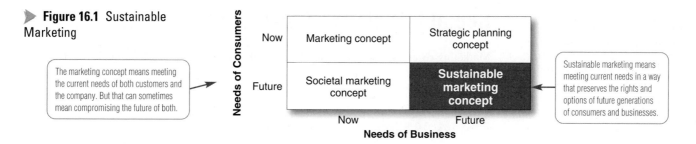

▶ **Figure 16.1** Sustainable Marketing

The marketing concept means meeting the current needs of both customers and the company. But that can sometimes mean compromising the future of both.

Sustainable marketing means meeting current needs in a way that preserves the rights and options of future generations of consumers and businesses.

more effectively and efficiently than competitors do. It focuses on meeting the company's short-term sales, growth, and profit needs by giving customers what they want now. However, satisfying consumers' immediate needs and desires doesn't always serve the future best interests of either customers or the business.

For example, McDonald's early decisions to market tasty but fat- and salt-laden fast foods created immediate satisfaction for customers, as well as sales and profits for the company. However, critics assert that McDonald's and other fast-food chains contributed to a longer-term national obesity epidemic, damaging consumer health and burdening the national health system. In turn, many consumers began looking for healthier eating options, causing a slump in the sales and profits of the fast-food industry. Beyond issues of ethical behavior and social welfare, McDonald's was also criticized for the sizable environmental footprint of its vast global operations, everything from wasteful packaging and solid waste creation to inefficient energy use in its stores. Thus, McDonald's strategy was not sustainable in terms of either consumer or company benefit.

Whereas the *societal marketing concept* identified in Figure 16.1 considers the future welfare of consumers and the *strategic planning concept* considers future company needs, the *sustainable marketing concept* considers both. Sustainable marketing calls for socially and environmentally responsible actions that meet both the immediate and future needs of customers and the company.

For example, as we discussed in Chapter 2, McDonald's has responded to these challenges in recent years with a more sustainable "Plan to Win" strategy of diversifying into salads, fruits, grilled chicken, low-fat milk, and other healthy fare. Also, after a seven-year search for healthier cooking oil, McDonald's phased out traditional artery-clogging trans fats without compromising the taste of its french fries. The company also launched a major multi-faceted education campaign—called "it's what i eat and what i do . . . i'm lovin' it"—to help consumers better understand the keys to living balanced, active lifestyles.

▶ The McDonald's "Plan to Win" strategy also addresses environmental issues. For example, it calls for food-supply sustainability, reduced and environmentally sustainable packaging, reuse and recycling, and more responsible store designs. McDonald's has even developed an environmental scorecard that rates its suppliers' performance in areas such as water use, energy use, and solid waste management.

McDonald's more sustainable strategy is benefiting the company as well as its customers. Since announcing its "Plan to Win" strategy, McDonald's sales have increased by more than 40 percent, and profits have more than tripled. Thus, McDonald's is well positioned for a sustainably profitable future.[3]

▲ **Sustainable marketing: McDonald's "Plan to Win" strategy has both created sustainable value for customers and positioned the company for a profitable future.**

Alexandre Gelebart/REA/Redux Pictures

Truly sustainable marketing requires a smooth-functioning marketing system in which consumers, companies, public policy makers, and others work together to ensure socially and environmentally responsible marketing actions. Unfortunately, however, the marketing system doesn't always work smoothly. The following sections examine several sustainability questions: What are the most frequent social criticisms of marketing? What steps have private citizens taken to curb marketing ills? What steps have legislators and government agencies taken to promote sustainable marketing? What steps have enlightened companies taken to carry out socially responsible and ethical marketing that creates sustainable value for both individual customers and society as a whole?

Author Comment ▶
In most ways, we all benefit greatly from marketing activities. However, like most other human endeavors, marketing has its flaws. Here we present both sides of some of the most common criticisms of marketing.

Social Criticisms of Marketing

Marketing receives much criticism. Some of this criticism is justified; much is not. Social critics claim that certain marketing practices hurt individual consumers, society as a whole, and other business firms.

Marketing's Impact on Individual Consumers

Consumers have many concerns about how well the American marketing system serves their interests. Surveys usually show that consumers hold mixed or even slightly unfavorable attitudes toward marketing practices. Consumer advocates, government agencies, and other critics have accused marketing of harming consumers through high prices, deceptive practices, high-pressure selling, shoddy or unsafe products, planned obsolescence, and poor service to disadvantaged consumers. Such questionable marketing practices are not sustainable in terms of long-term consumer or business welfare.

High Prices

Many critics charge that the American marketing system causes prices to be higher than they would be under more "sensible" systems. Such high prices are hard to swallow, especially when the economy takes a downturn. Critics point to three factors—*high costs of distribution*, *high advertising and promotion costs*, and *excessive markups*.

High Costs of Distribution. A long-standing charge is that greedy channel intermediaries mark up prices beyond the value of their services. Critics charge that there are too many intermediaries, that intermediaries are inefficient, or that they provide unnecessary or duplicate services. As a result, distribution costs too much, and consumers pay for these excessive costs in the form of higher prices.

How do resellers answer these charges? They argue that intermediaries do work that would otherwise have to be done by manufacturers or consumers. Markups reflect services that consumers themselves want—more convenience, larger stores and assortments, more service, longer store hours, return privileges, and others. In fact, they argue, retail competition is so intense that margins are actually quite low. If some resellers try to charge too much relative to the value they add, other resellers will step in with lower prices. Low-price stores such as Walmart, Costco, and other discounters pressure their competitors to operate efficiently and keep their prices down. In fact, in the wake of the recent recession, only the most efficient retailers have survived profitably.

High Advertising and Promotion Costs. Modern marketing is also accused of pushing up prices to finance heavy advertising and sales promotion. ▶ For example, a heavily promoted national brand sells for much more than a virtually identical non-branded or store-branded product. Differentiated products—cosmetics, detergents, toiletries—include promotion and packaging costs that can amount to 40 percent or more of the manufacturer's price to the retailer. Critics charge that much of this packaging and promotion adds only psychological, not functional, value to the product.

Marketers respond that although advertising adds to product costs, it also adds value by informing potential buyers of the availability and merits of a brand. Brand name products may cost more, but branding gives buyers assurances of consistent quality. Moreover, although consumers can usually buy functional versions of products at lower prices, they *want* and are willing to pay more for products that also provide

▲ A heavily promoted brand sells for much more than a virtually identical non-branded or store-branded product. Critics charge that promotion adds only psychological value to the product rather than functional value.

psychological benefits—that make them feel wealthy, attractive, or special. In addition, heavy advertising and promotion may be necessary for a firm to match competitors' efforts; the business would lose "share of mind" if it did not match competitive spending.

At the same time, companies are cost conscious about promotion and try to spend their funds wisely. Today's more frugal consumers are demanding genuine value for the prices they pay. The continuing shift toward buying store brands and generics suggests that when it comes to value, consumers want action, not just talk.

Excessive Markups. Critics also charge that some companies mark up goods excessively. They point to the drug industry, where a pill costing five cents to make may cost the consumer $2 to buy. They point to the pricing tactics of funeral homes that prey on the confused emotions of bereaved relatives and the high charges for auto repairs and other services.

Marketers respond that most businesses try to deal fairly with consumers because they want to build customer relationships and repeat business, and that most consumer abuses are unintentional. When shady marketers take advantage of consumers, they should be reported to Better Business Bureaus and state and federal agencies. Marketers also respond that consumers often don't understand the reasons for high markups. For example, pharmaceutical markups must cover the costs of purchasing, promoting, and distributing existing medicines plus the high R&D costs of formulating and testing new medicines. As pharmaceuticals company GlaxoSmithKline has stated in its ads, "Today's medicines finance tomorrow's miracles."

Deceptive Practices

Marketers are sometimes accused of deceptive practices that lead consumers to believe they will get more value than they actually do. Deceptive practices fall into three groups: pricing, promotion, and packaging. *Deceptive pricing* includes practices such as falsely advertising "factory" or "wholesale" prices or a large price reduction from a phony high retail list price. *Deceptive promotion* includes practices such as misrepresenting the product's features or performance or luring customers to the store for a bargain that is out of stock. *Deceptive packaging* includes exaggerating package contents through subtle design, using misleading labeling, or describing size in misleading terms.

Deceptive practices have led to legislation and other consumer protection actions. For example, in 1938 Congress enacted the Wheeler-Lea Act, which gave the Federal Trade Commission power to regulate "unfair or deceptive acts or practices." The FTC has since published several guidelines listing deceptive practices. Despite regulations, however, some critics argue that deceptive claims are still common, even for well-known brands. ▶ For example, several consumer groups recently complained that Coca-Cola's vitaminwater brand made deceptive and unsubstantiated—even "outlandish"— health claims for its products.[4]

▲ Deceptive practices: Critics argue that deceptive claims are still common, even for well-known brands. Coca-Cola's vitaminwater brand recently faced allegations of deceptive and unsubstantiated—even "outlandish"— health claims for its products.

Coco-Cola's vitaminwater is marketed as a super-healthy alternative to regular H2O, but critics say the claims don't hold water. The National Consumers League (NCL) and other consumer groups recently filed complaints with the FTC and lawsuits alleging that the brand made "dangerously misleading" claims. Among the claims cited by the NCL were one print ad that suggested that vitaminwater served as a viable substitute for a seasonal flu shot; a television ad that implied that vitaminwater boosts the immune system and helps fend off garden-variety sickness; and language on the label reading, "vitamins + water = all you need." For instance, one TV ad depicted a woman who had so many unused sick days at work that she could take them to stay home and watch movies with her boyfriend. The ad stated: "One of my secrets? vitaminwater power-c. It's got vitamin C and zinc to help support a healthy immune system. So I can stay home with my boyfriend—who's also playing hooky."

"These advertising claims are not only untrue; they constitute a public health menace," says NCL's executive director. Although vitaminwater implies that it contains only vitamins and water, it packs 125 calories per bottle. "Two-thirds of Americans are overweight or obese; the last thing people need is sugar water with vitamins you could get from eating a healthy diet, or by taking a vitamin pill," says the NCL. Britain's Advertising Standards Authority appears to agree. It recently banned as deceptive a vitaminwater ad claiming that the drink is "nutritious," saying that the public would not expect a nutritious drink to have the equivalent of up to five teaspoons of added sugar.

The toughest problem is defining what is "deceptive." For instance, an advertiser's claim that its chewing gum will "rock your world" isn't intended to be taken literally. Instead, the advertiser might claim, it is "puffery"—innocent exaggeration for effect. However, others claim that puffery and alluring imagery can harm consumers in subtle ways. Think about the popular and long-running MasterCard Priceless commercials that painted pictures of consumers fulfilling their priceless dreams despite the costs. The ads suggested that your credit card can make it happen. But critics charge that such imagery by credit card companies encouraged a spend-now-pay-later attitude that caused many consumers to *over*use their cards, contributing heavily to the nation's recent financial crisis.

Marketers argue that most companies avoid deceptive practices. Because such practices harm a company's business in the long run, they simply aren't sustainable. Profitable customer relationships are built on a foundation of value and trust. If consumers do not get what they expect, they will switch to more reliable products. In addition, consumers usually protect themselves from deception. Most consumers recognize a marketer's selling intent and are careful when they buy, sometimes even to the point of not believing completely true product claims.

High-Pressure Selling

Salespeople are sometimes accused of high-pressure selling that persuades people to buy goods they had no thought of buying. It is often said that insurance, real estate, and used cars are *sold*, not *bought*. Salespeople are trained to deliver smooth, canned talks to entice purchases. They sell hard because sales contests promise big prizes to those who sell the most. Similarly, TV infomercial pitchmen use "yell and sell" presentations that create a sense of consumer urgency that only those with the strongest willpower can resist.

But in most cases, marketers have little to gain from high-pressure selling. Although such tactics may work in one-time selling situations for short-term gain, most selling involves building long-term relationships with valued customers. High-pressure or deceptive selling can seriously damage such relationships. For example, imagine a P&G account manager trying to pressure a Walmart buyer or an IBM salesperson trying to browbeat an information technology manager at GE. It simply wouldn't work.

Shoddy, Harmful, or Unsafe Products

Another criticism concerns poor product quality or function. One complaint is that, too often, products and services are not made or performed well. A second complaint concerns product safety. Product safety has been a problem for several reasons, including company indifference, increased product complexity, and poor quality control. A third complaint is that many products deliver little benefit, or may even be harmful.

For example, think again about the fast-food industry.  Many critics blame the plentiful supply of fat-laden, high calorie, fast-food fare for the nation's rapidly growing obesity epidemic. Studies show that some two-thirds of American adults are either obese or overweight. In addition, one-third of American children are obese. This national weight issue continues despite repeated medical studies showing that excess weight brings increased risks for heart disease, diabetes, and other maladies, even cancer.[5] The critics are quick to fault what they see as greedy food marketers who are cashing in on vulnerable consumers, turning us into a nation of overeaters.

▲ Harmful products: Is the fast-food industry being socially responsible by promoting overindulgence to ill-informed consumers? Or is it simply serving the wants of customers while letting them make their own eating choices?

Tiplyashin Anatoly/Shutterstock.com

Is the fast-food industry being socially irresponsible by aggressively promoting overindulgence to ill-informed or unwary consumers? Or is it simply serving the wants of customers by offering food that pings their taste buds while letting consumers make their own eating choices? Is it the industry's job to police public tastes? The fast-food merchants claim that they offer plenty of healthy menu choices but that many consumers turn up their noses at them. As in many matters of social responsibility, what's right and wrong may be a matter of opinion.

Most manufacturers *want* to produce quality goods. After all, the way a company deals with product quality and safety problems can damage or help its reputation. Companies selling poor-quality or unsafe products risk damaging conflicts with consumer groups and regulators. Unsafe products can result in product liability suits and large awards for damages. More fundamentally, consumers who are unhappy with a firm's products may avoid future purchases and talk other consumers into doing the same. Thus, quality missteps are not consistent with sustainable marketing. Today's marketers know that good quality results in customer value and satisfaction, which in turn creates sustainable customer relationships.

Planned Obsolescence

Critics also have charged that some companies practice *planned obsolescence*, causing their products to become obsolete before they actually should need replacement. They accuse some producers of using materials and components that will break, wear, rust, or rot sooner than they should. And if the products themselves don't wear out fast enough, other companies are charged with *perceived obsolescence*—continually changing consumer concepts of acceptable styles to encourage more and earlier buying.[6] An obvious example is constantly changing clothing fashions.

Still others are accused of introducing planned streams of new products that make older models obsolete. Critics claim that this occurs in the consumer electronics and computer industries. If you're like most people, you probably have a drawer full of yesterday's hottest technological gadgets—from mobile phones and cameras to iPods and flash drives—now reduced to the status of fossils. It seems that anything more than a year or two old is hopelessly out of date. For example, here's one critic's tongue-in-cheek take on Apple's practice of frequent product releases that get customers to ditch the old iPod, iPhone, or iPad and buy the latest and greatest version:[7]

> Apple has probably already developed iPods that double as jetpacks that allow you to orbit the moon. But you won't see those anytime soon. And when they come out, they'll first just have iPods that can fly you to your neighbor's house. Then a few months later they'll introduce ones that can fly you across the country. And that'll seem pretty amazing compared to the ones that could only go down the street, but they won't be amazing three months later, when the iPod Sputnik hits the market.

Marketers respond that consumers *like* style changes; they get tired of the old goods and want a new look in fashion. Or they *want* the latest high-tech innovations, even if older models still work. No one has to buy the new product, and if too few people like it, it will simply fail. Finally, most companies do not design their products to break down earlier because they do not want to lose customers to other brands. Instead, they seek constant improvement to ensure that products will consistently meet or exceed customer expectations. Much of the so-called planned obsolescence is the working of the competitive and technological forces in a free society—forces that lead to ever-improving goods and services.

Poor Service to Disadvantaged Consumers

Finally, the American marketing system has been accused of poorly serving disadvantaged consumers. For example, critics claim that the urban poor often have to shop in smaller stores that carry inferior goods and charge higher prices. The presence of large national chain stores in low-income neighborhoods would help to keep prices down. However, the critics accuse major chain retailers of *redlining*, drawing a red line around disadvantaged neighborhoods and avoiding placing stores there.

▲ **Underserved consumers:** Because of the lack of supermarkets in low-income areas, many disadvantaged consumers find themselves in *food deserts,* with little or no access to healthy, affordable fresh foods.

© dbimages/Alamy

For example, the nation's poor areas have 30 percent fewer supermarkets than affluent areas do. ▶ As a result, many low-income consumers find themselves in *food deserts*, which are awash with small markets offering frozen pizzas, Cheetos, Twinkies, and Cokes, but where fruits and vegetables or fresh fish or chicken are out of reach. Currently, some 23.5 million Americans—including 6.5 million children—live in low-income areas that lack stores selling affordable and nutritious foods. In such areas, "you can go for miles without being able to find a fresh apple or a piece of broccoli," says the executive director of The Food Trust, a group that's trying to tackle the problem. In turn, the lack of access to healthy, affordable fresh foods has a negative impact on the health of underserved consumers in these areas. Many national chains, such as Walmart, Walgreens, and SuperValu, have recently agreed to open or expand more stores that bring nutritious and fresh foods to underserved communities.[8]

Clearly, better marketing systems must be built to service disadvantaged consumers. In fact, many marketers profitably target such consumers with legitimate goods and services that create real value. In cases in which marketers do not step in to fill the void, the government likely will. For example, the FTC has taken action against sellers who advertise false values, wrongfully deny services, or charge disadvantaged customers too much.

SPEED BUMP | LINKING THE CONCEPTS

Hit the brakes for a moment. Few marketers *want* to abuse or anger consumers—it's simply not good business. Still, some marketing abuses do occur.

- Think back over the past three months or so and list any instances in which you've suffered a marketing abuse such as those just discussed. Analyze your list: What kinds of companies were involved? Were the abuses intentional? What did the situations have in common?
- Pick one of the instances you listed and describe it in detail. How might you go about righting this wrong? Write out an action plan and then do something to remedy the abuse. If we all took such actions when wronged, there would be far fewer wrongs to right!

Marketing's Impact on Society as a Whole

The American marketing system has been accused of adding to several "evils" in American society at large, such as creating too much materialism, too few social goods, and a glut of cultural pollution.

False Wants and Too Much Materialism

Critics have charged that the marketing system urges too much interest in material possessions, and America's love affair with worldly possessions is not sustainable. Too often, people are judged by what they *own* rather than by who they *are*. The critics do not view this interest in material things as a natural state of mind but rather as a matter of false wants created by marketing. Marketers, they claim, stimulate people's desires for goods and create materialistic models of the good life. Thus, marketers have created an endless cycle of mass consumption based on a distorted interpretation of the "American Dream."

In this view, marketing's purpose is to promote consumption, and the inevitable outcome of successful marketing is unsustainable *over*consumption. Says one critic: "For most of us, our basic material needs are satisfied, so we seek in ever-growing consumption

▲ Materialism: Consumer activist Annie Leonard's *The Story of Stuff* video about the social and environmental consequences of America's love affair with stuff has been viewed more than 1.2 million times online and in thousands of schools and community centers around the world.

Handout/MCT/Newscom

the satisfaction of wants, which consumption cannot possibly deliver. More is not always better; it is often worse."[9] Some critics have taken their concerns straight to the public. ► For example, consumer activist Annie Leonard founded *The Story of Stuff* project with a 20-minute Web video about the social and environmental consequences of America's love affair with stuff—"How our obsession with stuff is trashing the planet, our communities, and our health." The video has been viewed more than 1.2 million times online and in thousands of schools and community centers around the world.[10]

Marketers respond that such criticisms overstate the power of business to create needs. They claim people have strong defenses against advertising and other marketing tools. Marketers are most effective when they appeal to existing wants rather than when they attempt to create new ones. Furthermore, people seek information when making important purchases and often do not rely on single sources. Even minor purchases that may be affected by advertising messages lead to repeat purchases only if the product delivers the promised customer value. Finally, the high failure rate of new products shows that companies are not able to control demand.

On a deeper level, our wants and values are influenced not only by marketers but also by family, peer groups, religion, cultural background, and education. If Americans are highly materialistic, these values arose out of basic socialization processes that go much deeper than business and mass media could produce alone.

Moreover, consumption patterns and attitudes are also subject to larger forces, such as the economy. As discussed in Chapter 1, the recent Great Recession put a damper on materialism and conspicuous spending. Many observers predict a new age of more sensible consumption. "The [materialistic] American dream is on pause," says one analyst. Says another, shoppers "now are taking pride in their newfound financial discipline." As a result, far from encouraging today's more sensible consumers to overspend their means, marketers are working to help them find greater value with less.[11]

Too Few Social Goods

Business has been accused of overselling private goods at the expense of public goods. As private goods increase, they require more public services that are usually not forthcoming. For example, an increase in automobile ownership (private good) requires more highways, traffic control, parking spaces, and police services (public goods). The overselling of private goods results in social costs. For cars, some of the social costs include traffic congestion, gasoline shortages, and air pollution. For example, American travelers lose, on average, 34 hours a year in traffic jams, costing the United States more than $115 billion a year. In the process, they waste 3.9 billion gallons of fuel and emit millions of tons of greenhouse gases.[12]

A way must be found to restore a balance between private and public goods. One option is to make producers bear the full social costs of their operations. For example, the government is requiring automobile manufacturers to build cars with more efficient engines and better pollution-control systems. Auto makers will then raise their prices to cover the extra costs. If buyers find the price of some car models too high, however, these models will disappear. Demand will then move to those producers that can support the sum of the private and social costs.

A second option is to make consumers pay the social costs. For example, many cities around the world are now charging congestion tolls in an effort to reduce traffic congestion. ► To unclog its streets, the city of London levies a congestion charge of £10 per day per car to drive in an eight-square-mile area downtown. The charge has not only reduced traffic congestion within the zone and increased bicycling and bus ridership, it also raises money to shore up London's public transportation system.[13]

▲ Balancing private and public goods: In response to lane-clogging traffic congestion like that above, London now levies a congestion charge. The charge has not only reduced traffic congestion, it also raises money to shore up the city's public transportation system.

(left) National Pictures/Topham/The Image Works

Cultural Pollution

Critics charge the marketing system with creating *cultural pollution*. They feel our senses are being constantly assaulted by marketing and advertising. Commercials interrupt serious programs; pages of ads obscure magazines; billboards mar beautiful scenery; spam fills our e-mailboxes. What's more, the critics claim, these interruptions continually pollute people's minds with messages of materialism, sex, power, or status. Some critics call for sweeping changes.

Marketers answer the charges of commercial noise with these arguments: First, they hope that their ads primarily reach the target audience. But because of mass-communication channels, some ads are bound to reach people who have no interest in the product and are therefore bored or annoyed. People who buy magazines addressed to their interests—such as *Vogue* or *Fortune*—rarely complain about the ads because the magazines advertise products of interest.

Second, because of ads, many television, radio, and online sites are free to users. Ads also help keep down the costs of magazines and newspapers. Many people think commercials are a small price to pay for these benefits. In addition, consumers find many television commercials entertaining and seek them out; for example, ad viewership during the Super Bowl usually equals or exceeds game viewership. Finally, today's consumers have alternatives. For example, they can zip or zap TV commercials on recorded programs or avoid them altogether on many paid cable, satellite, and online channels. Thus, to hold consumer attention, advertisers are making their ads more entertaining and informative.

Marketing's Impact on Other Businesses

Critics also charge that a company's marketing practices can harm other companies and reduce competition. They identify three problems: acquisitions of competitors, marketing practices that create barriers to entry, and unfair competitive marketing practices.

Critics claim that firms are harmed and competition reduced when companies expand by acquiring competitors rather than by developing their own new products. The large number of acquisitions and the rapid pace of industry consolidation over the past several decades have caused concern that vigorous young competitors will be absorbed, thereby reducing competition. In virtually every major industry—retailing, entertainment, financial services, utilities, transportation, automobiles, telecommunications, health care—the number of major competitors is shrinking.

Acquisition is a complex subject. In some cases, acquisitions can be good for society. The acquiring company may gain economies of scale that lead to lower costs and lower prices. In addition, a well-managed company may take over a poorly managed company and improve its efficiency. An industry that was not very competitive might become more competitive after the acquisition. But acquisitions can also be harmful and, therefore, are closely regulated by the government.

Critics have also charged that marketing practices bar new companies from entering an industry. Large marketing companies can use patents and heavy promotion spending or tie up suppliers or dealers to keep out or drive out competitors. Those concerned with antitrust regulation recognize that some barriers are the natural result of the economic advantages of doing business on a large scale. Existing and new laws can challenge other barriers. For example, some critics have proposed a progressive tax on advertising spending to reduce the role of selling costs as a major barrier to entry.

Finally, some firms have, in fact, used unfair competitive marketing practices with the intention of hurting or destroying other firms. They may set their prices below costs, threaten to cut off business with suppliers, or discourage the buying of a competitor's products. Although various laws work to prevent such predatory competition, it is often difficult to prove that the intent or action was really predatory.

In recent years, Walmart has been accused of using predatory pricing in selected market areas to drive smaller, mom-and-pop retailers out of business. Walmart has become a lightning rod for protests by citizens in dozens of towns who worry that the megaretailer's unfair practices will choke out local businesses. However, whereas critics charge that Walmart's actions are predatory, others assert that its actions are just the healthy

▲ **Walmart prescription pricing: Is it predatory pricing or is it just good business?**

AP Images

competition of a more-efficient company against less-efficient ones.

For instance, ▶ when Walmart began a program to sell generic drugs at $4 a prescription, local pharmacists complained of predatory pricing. They charged that at those low prices, Walmart must be selling under cost to drive them out of business. But Walmart claimed that, given its substantial buying power and efficient operations, it could make a profit at those prices. The $4 pricing program, the retailer claimed, was not aimed at putting competitors out of business. Rather, it was simply a good competitive move that served customers better and brought more of them in the door. Moreover, Walmart's program drove down prescription prices at the pharmacies of other supermarkets and discount stores, such as Kroger and Target. Currently more than 300 prescription drugs are available for $4 at the various chains, and Walmart claims that the program has saved its customers more than $3 billion.[14]

<table>
<tr><td>

Author Comment ▶

Sustainable marketing isn't the province of businesses and governments only. Through consumerism and environmentalism, consumers themselves can play an important role.

</td><td>

Consumer Actions to Promote Sustainable Marketing

Sustainable marketing calls for more responsible actions by both businesses and consumers. Because some people view businesses as the cause of many economic and social ills, grassroots movements have arisen from time to time to keep businesses in line. Two major movements have been *consumerism* and *environmentalism*.

Consumerism

</td></tr>
<tr><td>

Consumerism

An organized movement of citizens and government agencies designed to improve the rights and power of buyers in relation to sellers.

</td><td>

Consumerism is an organized movement of citizens and government agencies to improve the rights and power of buyers in relation to sellers. Traditional *sellers' rights* include the following:

- The right to introduce any product in any size and style, provided it is not hazardous to personal health or safety, or, if it is, to include proper warnings and controls
- The right to charge any price for the product, provided no discrimination exists among similar kinds of buyers
- The right to spend any amount to promote the product, provided it is not defined as unfair competition
- The right to use any product message, provided it is not misleading or dishonest in content or execution
- The right to use buying incentive programs, provided they are not unfair or misleading

Traditional *buyers' rights* include the following:

- The right not to buy a product that is offered for sale
- The right to expect the product to be safe
- The right to expect the product to perform as claimed

Comparing these rights, many believe that the balance of power lies on the seller's side. True, the buyer can refuse to buy. But critics feel that the buyer has too little information,

</td></tr>
</table>

education, and protection to make wise decisions when facing sophisticated sellers. Consumer advocates call for the following additional consumer rights:

● The right to be well informed about important aspects of the product
● The right to be protected against questionable products and marketing practices
● The right to influence products and marketing practices in ways that will improve "quality of life"
● The right to consume now in a way that will preserve the world for future generations of consumers

Each proposed right has led to more specific proposals by consumerists and consumer protection actions by the government. ▶ The right to be informed includes the right to know the true interest on a loan (truth in lending), the true cost per unit of a brand (unit pricing), the ingredients in a product (ingredient labeling), the nutritional value of foods (nutritional labeling), product freshness (open dating), and the true benefits of a product (truth in advertising). Proposals related to consumer protection include strengthening consumer rights in cases of business fraud and financial protection, requiring greater product safety, ensuring information privacy, and giving more power to government agencies. Proposals relating to quality of life include controlling the ingredients that go into certain products and packaging and reducing the level of advertising "noise." Proposals for preserving the world for future consumption include promoting the use of sustainable ingredients, recycling and reducing solid wastes, and managing energy consumption.

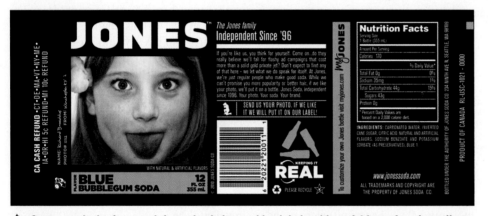
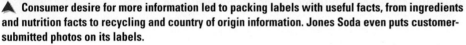

▲ Consumer desire for more information led to packing labels with useful facts, from ingredients and nutrition facts to recycling and country of origin information. Jones Soda even puts customer-submitted photos on its labels.

Courtesy of Jones Soda Co.

Sustainable marketing applies not only to businesses and governments but also to consumers. Consumers have not only the *right* but also the *responsibility* to protect themselves instead of leaving this function to the government or someone else. Consumers who believe they got a bad deal have several remedies available, including contacting the company or the media; contacting federal, state, or local agencies; and going to small-claims courts. Consumers should also make good consumption choices, rewarding companies that act responsibly while punishing those that don't. Ultimately, the move from irresponsible consumption to sustainable consumption is in the hands of consumers.

Environmentalism

Environmentalism
An organized movement of concerned citizens and government agencies designed to protect and improve people's current and future living environment.

Whereas consumerists consider whether the marketing system is efficiently serving consumer wants, environmentalists are concerned with marketing's effects on the environment and the environmental costs of serving consumer needs and wants. **Environmentalism** is an organized movement of concerned citizens, businesses, and government agencies designed to protect and improve people's current and future living environment.

Environmentalists are not against marketing and consumption; they simply want people and organizations to operate with more care for the environment. "Too often the environment is seen as one small piece of the economy," says one activist. "But it's not just one little thing; it's what every single thing in our life depends upon."[15] The marketing system's goal, the environmentalists assert, should not be to maximize consumption, consumer choice, or consumer satisfaction but rather maximize life quality. Life quality means not only the quantity and quality of consumer goods and services but also the quality of the environment.

Figure 16.2 The Environmental Sustainability Portfolio

Sources: Stuart L. Hart, "Innovation, Creative Destruction, and Sustainability," *Research Technology Management*, September–October 2005, pp. 21–27.

	Today: Greening	**Tomorrow: Beyond Greening**
Internal	**Pollution prevention** Eliminating or reducing waste before it is created	**New clean technology** Developing new sets of environmental skills and capabilities
External	**Product stewardship** Minimizing environmental impact throughout the entire product life cycle	**Sustainability vision** Creating a strategic framework for future sustainability

How does "environmental sustainability" relate to "marketing sustainability"? Environmental sustainability involves preserving the natural environment, whereas marketing sustainability is a broader concept that involves both the natural and social environments—pretty much everything in this chapter.

Environmental sustainability

A management approach that involves developing strategies that both sustain the environment and produce profits for the company.

Environmentalism is concerned with damage to the ecosystem caused by global warming, resource depletion, toxic and solid wastes, litter, and other problems. Other issues include the loss of recreational areas and the increase in health problems caused by bad air, polluted water, and chemically treated food.

Over the past several decades, such concerns have resulted in federal and state laws and regulations governing industrial commercial practices impacting the environment. Some companies have strongly resented and resisted such environmental regulations, claiming that they are too costly and have made their industries less competitive. These companies responded to consumer environmental concerns by doing only what was required to avert new regulations or keep environmentalists quiet.

In recent years, however, most companies have accepted responsibility for doing no harm to the environment. They are shifting from protest to prevention and from regulation to responsibility. More and more companies are now adopting policies of **environmental sustainability**. Simply put, environmental sustainability is about generating profits while helping to save the planet. Today's enlightened companies are taking action not because someone is forcing them to or to reap short-run profits but because it's the right thing to do—for both the company's well-being and the planet's environmental future.

Figure 16.2 shows a grid that companies can use to gauge their progress toward environmental sustainability. It includes both internal and external *greening* activities that will pay off for the firm and environment in the short run, and *beyond greening* activities that will pay off in the longer term. At the most basic level, a company can practice *pollution prevention*. This involves more than pollution control—cleaning up waste after it has been created. Pollution prevention means eliminating or minimizing waste *before* it is created. Companies emphasizing prevention have responded with internal green marketing programs—designing and developing ecologically safer products, recyclable and biodegradable packaging, better pollution controls, and more energy-efficient operations.

For example, Nike makes shoes out of "environmentally preferred materials," recycles old sneakers, and educates young people about conservation, reuse, and recycling. UPS has been developing its green fleet, which now boasts more than 2,000 low-carbon-emissions vehicles, including electric, hybrid-electric, compressed natural gas, liquefied natural gas, and propane trucks. Intel is installing solar power systems at four of its offices; the new solar panels for just one office will reduce carbon dioxide emissions by 32.8 million pounds.[16]

Subaru of Indiana (SIA), which manufactures all North American Subarus and some Toyota Camrys, brags that its entire plant now sends less trash to the landfill each year than the average American family. "Whenever we look at plant efficiency and quality, we also look to see if we [can] reduce waste, recycle materials, and cut back gas, water, and energy use," says SIA's safety and environmental compliance manager.

As it turns out... It is easy to be green.

On May 4, 2004, Subaru of Indiana Automotive became the first auto manufacturing plant in the U.S. to become zero landfill. And we did it two years ahead of schedule.

As it turns out, being a good steward of the environment isn't that hard to do. And if a big auto plant can do it...so can you. For more information, log onto www.subaru-earth.com

SUBARU of INDIANA AUTOMOTIVE, INC.
www.subaru-sia.com

Pollution prevention: Subaru of Indiana claims that it now sends less trash to the landfill each year than the average American family.

Courtesy of Subaru of Indiana Automotive, Inc.

That's great news for the Earth and it's also great for SIA's bottom line. "This is not [just] about recycling, or a nice marketing to-do," says an analyst. "This is a strict dollars-and-cents, moneymaking-and-savings calculation that also drives better safety and quality." Last year the plant saved $5.3 million by obsessively reducing, recycling, composting, and incinerating.[17]

At the next level, companies can practice *product stewardship*—minimizing not only pollution from production and product design but also all environmental impacts throughout the full product life cycle, while at the same time reducing costs. Many companies are adopting *design for environment (DFE)* and *cradle-to-cradle* practices. This involves thinking ahead to design products that are easier to recover, reuse, recycle, or safely return to nature after usage, thus becoming part of the ecological cycle. Design for environment and cradle-to-cradle practices not only help to sustain the environment, but they can also be highly profitable for the company.

For example, more than a decade ago, IBM started a business—IBM Global Asset Recovery Services—designed to reuse and recycle parts from returned mainframe computers and other equipment. Last year, IBM processed more than 36,600 metric tons of end-of-life products and product waste worldwide, stripping down old equipment to recover chips and valuable metals. It finds uses for more than 99 percent of what it takes in, sending less than 1 percent to landfills and incineration facilities. What started out as an environmental effort has now grown into a multibillion dollar IBM business that profitably recycles electronic equipment at 22 sites worldwide.[18]

Today's *greening* activities focus on improving what companies already do to protect the environment. The *beyond greening* activities identified in Figure 16.2 look to the future. First, internally, companies can plan for *new clean technology*. Many organizations that have made good sustainability headway are still limited by existing technologies. To create fully sustainable strategies, they will need to develop innovative new technologies.

For example, by 2020, Coca-Cola has committed to reclaiming and recycling the equivalent of all the packaging it uses around the world. It has also pledged to dramatically reduce its overall environmental footprint. To accomplish these goals, the company invests heavily in new clean technologies that address a host of environmental issues, such as recycling, resource usage, distribution, and even outdoor advertising:[19]

▲ **New clean technologies: Coca-Cola is investing heavily to develop new solutions to environmental issues—from eco-friendly packaging to this billboard in the Philippines covered in pollution-absorbing Fukien tea plants.**
The Philippine STAR/Joven Cagande

First, to attack the solid waste problem caused by its plastic bottles, Coca-Cola invested heavily to build the world's largest state-of-the-art plastic-bottle-to-bottle recycling plant. As a more permanent solution, Coke is researching and testing new bottles made from aluminum, corn, or bioplastics. It is also designing more eco-friendly distribution alternatives. Currently, some 10 million vending machines and refrigerated coolers gobble up energy and use potent greenhouse gases called hydrofluorocarbons (HFCs) to keep Cokes cold. To eliminate them, the company invested $40 million in research and recently began installing sleek new HFC-free coolers that use 30 to 40 percent less energy. Coca-Cola also aims to become "water neutral" by researching ways to help its bottlers add back all the fresh water they extract during the production of Coca-Cola beverages.

▶ In the Philippines, Coca-Cola has even worked with the World Wildlife Fund to create a 60-by-60-foot billboard that's covered in Fukien tea plants, which absorb air pollution. The plant-covered billboard absorbs an estimated 46,800 pounds of carbon dioxide a year from the air. The rest of the billboard is just as environmentally friendly. The plants are contained in 3,600 pots made from old Coke bottles, the potting mixture was made from industrial byproducts and organic fertilizers, and a drip irrigation system saves water and fertilizer. The innovative billboard "is an embodiment of our company's 'Live Positively' commitment to making a positive difference in the world by incorporating sustainability into everything we do," says the president of Coca-Cola Philippines. In all, concludes one analyst, "Coke is literally more important, when it comes to sustainability, than the United Nations."

Finally, companies can develop a *sustainability vision*, which serves as a guide to the future. It shows how the company's products and services, processes, and policies must evolve and what new technologies must be developed to get there. This vision of sustainability provides a framework for pollution control, product stewardship, and new environmental technology for the company and others to follow.

Most companies today focus on the upper-left quadrant of the grid in Figure 16.2, investing most heavily in pollution prevention. Some forward-looking companies practice product stewardship and are developing new environmental technologies. However, emphasizing only one or two quadrants in the environmental sustainability grid can be shortsighted. Investing only in the left half of the grid puts a company in a good position today but leaves it vulnerable in the future. In contrast, a heavy emphasis on the right half suggests that a company has good environmental vision but lacks the skills needed to implement it. Thus, companies should work at developing all four dimensions of environmental sustainability.

Walmart, for example, is doing just that. Through its own environmental sustainability actions and its impact on the actions of suppliers, Walmart has emerged in recent years as the world's super "eco-nanny" (see Marketing at Work 16.1). Johnson & Johnson is also setting a high sustainability standard. It recently ranked as the number-two most sustainable corporation in the annual "Global 100 Most Sustainable Corporations in the World" ranking. J & J has multiple programs in place to manage the environmental impacts of its own operations:[20]

> Johnson & Johnson's concern for societal interests is summarized in a document called "Our Credo," which stresses putting people before profits. The company's stated purpose is to "improve the health and well-being of families everywhere." To fulfill that goal, says the company, "we have a responsibility to take care of our planet and preserve its beauty, resources, and strength for future generations. A healthy planet and healthy community go hand-in-hand. Accordingly, J & J has accomplished a long list of "Healthy Planet" goals, from reducing water and energy use, CO_2 emissions, and hazardous and non-hazardous waste to improving the environmental footprint of its products. And its "Healthy Communities, Healthy Ecosystems" partnership with the World Wildlife Fund links healthy environment and the health of local people around the globe. Over the years, Johnson & Johnson's dedication to the wellbeing of its customers and communities has made it one of America's most admired companies—and one of the most profitable.

Environmentalism creates some special challenges for global marketers. As international trade barriers come down and global markets expand, environmental issues are having an ever-greater impact on international trade. Countries in North America, Western Europe, and other developed regions are generating strict environmental standards. In the United States, for example, more than two dozen major pieces of environmental legislation have been enacted since 1970, and recent events suggest that more regulation is on the way. A side accord to the North American Free Trade Agreement established the Commission for Environmental Cooperation for resolving environmental matters. And the European Union's Eco-Management and Audit Scheme (EMAS) provides guidelines for environmental self-regulation.[21]

However, environmental policies still vary widely from country to country. Countries such as Denmark, Germany, Japan, and the United States have fully developed environmental policies and high public expectations. But major developing countries such as China, India, Brazil, and Russia are only in the early stages of developing such policies. Moreover, environmental factors that motivate consumers in one country may have no impact on consumers in another. For example, PVC soft-drink bottles cannot be used in Switzerland or Germany. However, they are preferred in France, which has an extensive recycling process for them. Thus, international companies have found it difficult to develop standard environmental practices that work globally. Instead, they are creating general policies and then translating these policies into tailored programs that meet local regulations and expectations.

MARKETING AT WORK | 16.1

Walmart: The World's Super Eco-Nanny

When you think of the corporate "good guys"—companies that are helping to save the world through sustainable actions—you probably think of names like Patagonia, Timberland, Ben & Jerry's, Whole Foods Market, or Stonyfield Farm. But hold onto your seat. When it comes to sustainability, perhaps no company in the world is doing more good these days than Walmart. That's right—big, bad Walmart. Notes one incredulous reporter: "The company whose 3,000 supercenters take up at least 53,000 acres of earth, whose 135 square miles of asphalt parking lots add up to the size of Tampa, Florida, and who in 2004 faced fines for violating environmental laws in nine states, has . . . found green religion."

Critics have long bashed Walmart for a broad range of alleged social misdeeds, from unfair labor practices to destroying small communities. So, many consumers are surprised to learn that the world's largest company is also the world's biggest crusader for the cause of saving the world for future generations. When it comes to sustainability, Walmart has emerged as the world's super "eco-nanny." In the long run, Walmart's stated environmental goals are to use 100 percent renewable energy, create zero waste, and sell only products that sustain people and the world's environment. Toward that goal, Walmart is not only greening up its own operations but also working with its vast networks of 100,000 suppliers, 2 million employees, and the 200 million customers who walk through its doors every week to get them to do the same.

Walmart operates almost 8,400 stores around the world, and its huge stores are gluttons for energy and other resources. Because of this, even small steps toward making stores more efficient can add up to huge environmental savings. For example, just removing the lights from vending machines across Walmart stores saves $1.4 million worth of energy per year. But Walmart isn't settling for small steps; it's moving in large leaps to develop new eco-technologies. In 2005, the giant retailer opened two experimental superstores in McKinney, Texas, and Aurora, Colorado, that were designed to test dozens of environmentally friendly and energy-efficient technologies:

A 143-foot-tall wind turbine stands outside a Walmart Supercenter in Aurora, Colorado. Incongruous as it might seem, it's a clear sign that something about this particular store is different. On the outside, the store's façade features row after row of windows to allow in as much natural light as possible. The landscaping uses native, drought-tolerant plants well adapted to the hot, dry Colorado summers, cutting down on watering, mowing, and the amount of fertilizer and other chemicals needed. Inside the store, an efficient high-output linear fluorescent lighting system saves enough electricity annually from this store alone to supply the needs of 52 single-family homes. The store's heating system burns recovered cooking oil from the deli's fryers; the oil is collected, mixed with waste engine oil from the store's Tire and Lube Express, and burned in the waste-oil boiler. All organic waste, including produce, meats, and paper, is placed in an organic waste compactor, which is then hauled off to a company that turns it into mulch for the garden. These and dozens more technological touches make the supercenter a laboratory for efficient and Earth-friendly retail operations.

After evaluating these experimental stores, Walmart is now rolling out new high-efficiency stores, each one saving more energy than the last. A recently opened Las Vegas store uses 45 percent less energy than a standard Walmart. Moreover, Walmart is eagerly spreading the word by encouraging visitors and sharing what it learns—even with competing companies such as Target and Home Depot.

At the same time that Walmart presses forward with its own sustainability initiatives, it's also affecting the environmental behaviors of its customers, employees, and suppliers. For example, it puts its marketing muscle behind eco-friendly products, regularly promoting brands such as Sun Chips, PUR water filters, and GE fluorescent bulbs. "If Walmart can galvanize its regular shopper base into green purchasing and eco-friendly habits, it's succeeded in reducing the ecological footprint of 200 million people," says one analyst. The giant retailer has also launched an employee program called the "personal sustainability project" (PSP), in which employees commit to responsible acts in front of their coworkers—anything from quitting smoking to converting the lights in their house to energy-efficient bulbs. The company now has more than 200,000 PSPs.

▲ For Walmart, sustainability is about more than just doing the right thing. Above all, it makes good business sense—"driving out hidden costs, conserving our natural resources for future generations, and providing sustainable and affordable products for our customers so they can save money and live better."

(logo) AP Images/PRNewsFoto/Walmart; © Bebay/iStockphoto

Walmart is also laying down the eco-law to suppliers. It recently announced plans to cut some 20 million metric tons of greenhouse gas emissions from its supply chain by the end of 2015—the equivalent of removing more than 3.8 million cars from the road for a year. To accomplish this and other sustainability goals, Walmart is asking its huge corps of suppliers to examine the carbon life cycles of their products and rethink how they source, manufacture, package, and transport these goods.

Walmart is even developing a Sustainability Index—based on information provided by suppliers—that tracks the life cycle of every product it sells, measuring it on everything from water use and greenhouse gas emissions to fair labor practices. Within a few years, Walmart wants to place a Sustainability Index tag on all its goods that details each product's eco-friendliness and social impact. High-scoring products will earn preferential treatment—and likely more shelf space—in Walmart stores.

Because of Walmart's size, even small supplier product and packaging changes have a substantial environmental impact. For example, to meet Walmart's requests, P&G developed a mega roll technology for its Charmin brand, which combines the sheets of four regular toilet paper rolls into one small roll. The seemingly minor change saves 89.5 million cardboard rolls and 360,000 pounds of plastic packaging wrap a year. It also allows Walmart to ship 42 percent more units on its trucks, saving about 54,000 gallons of fuel a year.

Although some suppliers are grumbling about Walmart's heavy-handed sustainability requirements, most are joining in. With its immense buying power, Walmart can humble even the mightiest supplier. When imposing its environmental demands on suppliers, Walmart "has morphed into . . . a sort of privatized Environmental Protection Agency, only with a lot more clout," says an industry observer. "The EPA can levy [only] a seven-figure fine; Walmart can wipe out more than a quarter of a business in one fell swoop."

So there you have it—Walmart the eco-nanny. Walmart's sustainability efforts have earned praise from even its harshest critics. As one skeptic begrudgingly admits, "Walmart has more green clout than anyone." But for Walmart, leading the eco-charge is about more than just doing the right thing. Above all, it also makes good business sense. More efficient operations and less wasteful products are not only good for the environment but also save Walmart money. Lower costs, in turn, let Walmart do more of what it has always done best—save customers money.

Says a Walmart executive, "We've laid the foundation for a long-term effort that will transform our business by driving out hidden costs, conserving our natural resources for future generations, and providing sustainable and affordable products for our customers so they can save money and live better."

Sources: Quotes, adapted extract, and other information from "Walmart," *Fast Company*, March 2010, p. 66; "Walmart Eliminates More Than 80 Percent of Its Waste in California That Would Otherwise Go to Landfills," March 17, 2011, http://walmartstores.com/pressroom/news/10553.aspx; Jack Neff, "Why Walmart Has More Green Clout Than Anyone," *Advertising Age*, October 15, 2007, p. 1; Denise Lee Yohn, "A Big, Green, Reluctant Hug for Retailing's 800-lb. Gorilla," *Brandweek*, May 5, 2008, p. 61; Edward Humes, *Force of Nature: The Unlikely Story of Walmart's Green Revolution* (New York: HarperCollins, 2011); and "Sustainability," http://walmartstores.com/sustainability/, accessed November 2011.

Public Actions to Regulate Marketing

Citizen concerns about marketing practices will usually lead to public attention and legislative proposals. Many of the laws that affect marketing were identified in Chapter 3. The task is to translate these laws into a language that marketing executives understand as they make decisions about competitive relations, products, price, promotion, and distribution channels. ▶ **Figure 16.3** illustrates the major legal issues facing marketing management.

Author Comment ▶
In the end, marketers themselves must take responsibility for sustainable marketing. That means operating in a responsible and ethical way to bring both immediate and future value to customers.

Business Actions toward Sustainable Marketing

At first, many companies opposed consumerism, environmentalism, and other elements of sustainable marketing. They thought the criticisms were either unfair or unimportant. But by now, most companies have grown to embrace sustainability marketing principles as a way to create both immediate and future customer value and strengthen customer relationships.

Sustainable Marketing Principles

Under the sustainable marketing concept, a company's marketing should support the best long-run performance of the marketing system. It should be guided by five sustainable marketing principles: *consumer-oriented marketing*, *customer-value marketing*, *innovative marketing*, *sense-of-mission marketing*, and *societal marketing*.

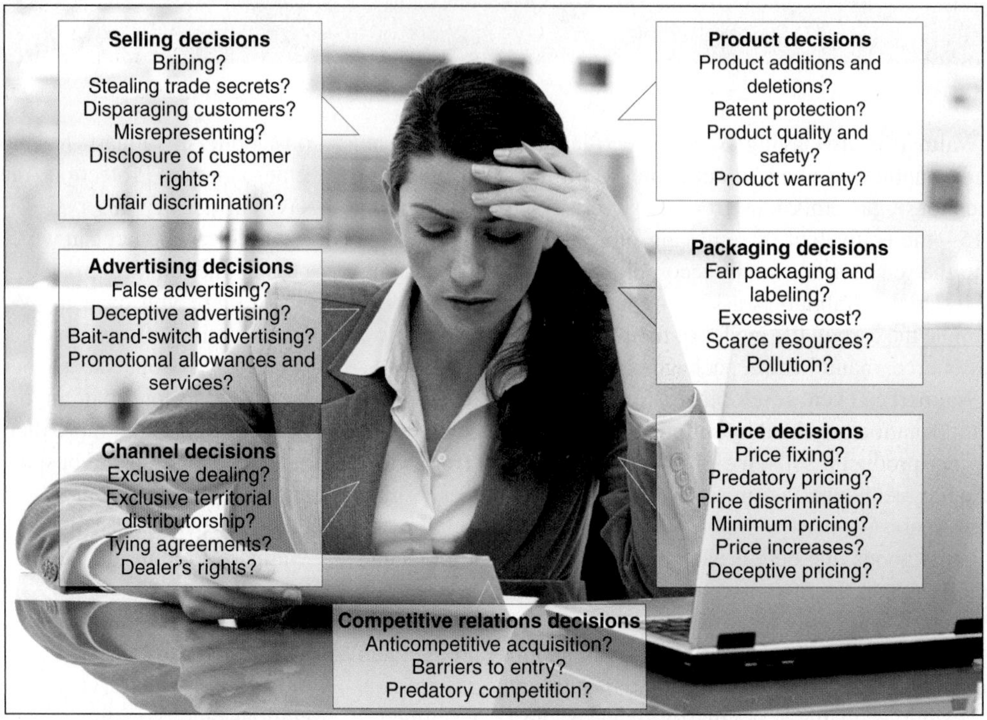

Figure 16.3 Major Marketing Decision Areas That May Be Called into Question under the Law

(photo) wavebreakmedia ltd/ Shutterstock.com

Selling decisions
Bribing?
Stealing trade secrets?
Disparaging customers?
Misrepresenting?
Disclosure of customer rights?
Unfair discrimination?

Advertising decisions
False advertising?
Deceptive advertising?
Bait-and-switch advertising?
Promotional allowances and services?

Channel decisions
Exclusive dealing?
Exclusive territorial distributorship?
Tying agreements?
Dealer's rights?

Product decisions
Product additions and deletions?
Patent protection?
Product quality and safety?
Product warranty?

Packaging decisions
Fair packaging and labeling?
Excessive cost?
Scarce resources?
Pollution?

Price decisions
Price fixing?
Predatory pricing?
Price discrimination?
Minimum pricing?
Price increases?
Deceptive pricing?

Competitive relations decisions
Anticompetitive acquisition?
Barriers to entry?
Predatory competition?

Consumer-Oriented Marketing

Consumer-oriented marketing
A principle of sustainable marketing that holds a company should view and organize its marketing activities from the consumer's point of view.

Consumer-oriented marketing means that the company should view and organize its marketing activities from the consumer's point of view. It should work hard to sense, serve, and satisfy the needs of a defined group of customers—both now and in the future. The good marketing companies that we've discussed throughout this text have had this in common: an all-consuming passion for delivering superior value to carefully chosen customers. Only by seeing the world through its customers' eyes can the company build sustainable and profitable customer relationships.

Customer-Value Marketing

Customer-value marketing
A principle of sustainable marketing that holds a company should put most of its resources into customer-value-building marketing investments.

According to the principle of **customer-value marketing**, the company should put most of its resources into customer-value-building marketing investments. Many things marketers do—one-shot sales promotions, cosmetic product changes, direct-response advertising—may raise sales in the short run but add less *value* than would actual improvements in the product's quality, features, or convenience. Enlightened marketing calls for building long-run consumer loyalty and relationships by continually improving the value consumers receive from the firm's market offering. By creating value *for* consumers, the company can capture value *from* consumers in return.

Innovative Marketing

Innovative marketing
A principle of sustainable marketing that requires a company to seek real product and marketing improvements.

The principle of **innovative marketing** requires that the company continuously seek real product and marketing improvements. The company that overlooks new and better ways to do things will eventually lose customers to another company that has found a better way. An excellent example of an innovative marketer is Samsung:[22]

Not too many years ago, Samsung was a copycat consumer electronics brand you bought if you couldn't afford Sony. But today, the brand holds a high-end, cutting-edge aura. In 1996, Samsung Electronics turned its back on making cheap knock-offs and set out to overtake rival Sony, not just in size but also in style and innovation. It hired a crop of fresh, young designers who unleashed a torrent of sleek, bold, and beautiful new products targeted to high-end users. Samsung called them "lifestyle works of art"—from brightly colored mobile phones to large-screen TVs that hung on walls like paintings. Every new product had to pass the "Wow!" test: if it didn't get a "Wow!" reaction during market testing, it went straight back to the design studio. Thanks to its strategy

Sense-of-mission marketing
A principle of sustainable marketing that holds a company should define its mission in broad social terms rather than narrow product terms.

of innovation, the company quickly surpassed its lofty goals—and more. Samsung Electronics is now, by far, the world's largest consumer electronics company, with 50 percent greater sales than Sony. It's the world's largest TV manufacturer and second-largest mobile phone producer. And its designs are coveted by consumers. Says a Samsung designer, "We are not el cheapo anymore."[23]

Sense-of-Mission Marketing

Sense-of-mission marketing means that the company should define its mission in broad *social* terms rather than narrow *product* terms. When a company defines a social mission, employees feel better about their work and have a clearer sense of direction. Brands linked with broader missions can serve the best long-run interests of both the brand and consumers.

Meet Echo.

Echo lives in a shelter.
She was the loser in a divorce.
Echo isn't used to her new home—
the cement feels strange on her paws.
When people walk past, she runs
to the front of her cage and smiles.
Then they move on. And Echo
doesn't understand where they went.
When you buy Pedigree, we make
a donation to help dogs like Echo
find loving homes.
Help us help dogs.
The PEDIGREE Adoption Drive

Dogsrule.com

▲ **Sense-of-mission marketing: The PEDIGREE Brand's "dogs rule" mission has helped to make it the world's number-one dog food brand. "Everything we do is because we love dogs, because dogs rule. It's just so simple."**

Courtesy of Mars, Incorporated. PEDIGREE® and "Dogs Rule®" are registered trademarks of Mars. Incorporated.

For example, the PEDIGREE Brand makes good dog food, but that's not what the brand is really all about. Instead, the brand came up with the tagline "Dogs rule." The tagline "is the perfect encapsulation of everything we stand for," says a PEDIGREE marketer. "Everything that we do is because we love dogs, because dogs rule. It's just so simple." This mission-focused positioning drives everything the brand does—internally and externally. ▶ One look at a PEDIGREE ad or a visit to the pedigree.com Web site confirms that the people behind the PEDIGREE Brand really do believe the "Dogs rule" mission. An internal manifesto called "Dogma" even encourages employees to take their dogs to work and on sales calls. To further fulfill the "Dogs rule" brand promise, the company created The PEDIGREE Foundation, which, along with the PEDIGREE Adoption Drive campaign, has raised millions of dollars for helping "shelter dogs" find good homes. Sense-of-mission marketing has made PEDIGREE the world's number one dog food brand.[24]

Some companies define their overall corporate missions in broad societal terms. For example, defined in narrow product terms, the mission of outdoor gear and apparel maker Patagonia might be "to sell clothes and outdoor equipment." However, Patagonia states its mission more broadly, as one of producing the highest quality products while doing the least harm to the environment. From the start, Patagonia has pursued a passionately held social responsibility mission:[25]

> For us at Patagonia, "a love of wild and beautiful places demands participation in the fight to save them, and to help reverse the steep decline in the overall environmental health of our planet." Our reason for being is to "build the best product and cause no unnecessary harm—to use business to inspire and implement solutions to the environmental crisis." Yet we're keenly aware that everything we do as a business—or have done in our name—leaves its mark on the environment. As yet, there is no such thing as a sustainable business, but every day we take steps to lighten our footprint and do less harm.

Each year since 1985, the company has given away 10 percent of its pretax profits to support environmental causes. Today, it donates its time, services, and at least 1 percent of sales or 10 percent pretax profits to hundreds of grassroots environmental groups all over the world who work to help reverse the environmental tide.

However, having a *double bottom line* of values and profits isn't easy. Over the years, companies such as Patagonia, Ben & Jerry's, The Body Shop, and Burt's Bees—all known and respected for putting "principles before profits"—have at times struggled with less-than-stellar financial returns. In recent years, however, a new generation of social entrepreneurs has emerged, well-trained business managers who know that to *do good*, they must first *do well* in terms of profitable business operations. Moreover, today, socially responsible business is no longer the sole province of small, socially conscious entrepreneurs. Many large, established companies and brands—from Walmart and Nike to PepsiCo—have adopted substantial social and environmental responsibility missions (see Marketing at Work 16.2).

| MARKETING AT WORK | 16.2 |

Socially Responsible Marketing: Making the World a Better Place

Chances are, when you hear the term *socially responsible business*, a handful of companies leap to mind, companies such as Ben & Jerry's, The Body Shop, Burt's Bees, Stonyfield Farms, Patagonia, Timberland, and TOMS Shoes, to name a few. Such companies pioneered the concept of *values-led business* or *caring capitalism*. Their mission: Use business to make the world a better place.

The classic "do good" pioneer is Ben & Jerry's. Ben Cohen and Jerry Greenfield founded the company in 1978 as a firm that cared deeply about its social and environmental responsibilities. Ben & Jerry's bought only hormone-free milk and cream and used only organic fruits and nuts to make its ice cream, which it sold in environmentally friendly containers. It went to great lengths to buy from minority and disadvantaged suppliers. From its early Rainforest Crunch to its more recent Chocolate Macadamia (made with sustainably-sourced macadamias and fair trade certified cocoa and vanilla), Ben & Jerry's has championed a host of social and environmental causes over the years. From the start, Ben & Jerry's donated a whopping 7.5 percent of pretax profits to support projects that exhibited "creative problem solving and hopefulness . . . relating to children and families, disadvantaged groups, and the environment." By the mid-1990s, Ben & Jerry's had become the nation's number two superpremium ice cream brand.

However, as competitors not shackled by Ben & Jerry's "principles before profits" mission invaded its markets, growth and profits flattened. After several years of lackluster financial returns, Ben & Jerry's was acquired by consumer goods giant Unilever. What happened to the founders' lofty ideals of caring capitalism? Looking back, Ben & Jerry's may have focused too much on social issues at the expense of sound business management. Ben Cohen never really wanted to be a businessperson, and he saw profits as a dirty word. Cohen once commented, "There came a time [when I had to admit] 'I'm a businessman.' And I had a hard time mouthing those words."

Having a "double bottom line" of values and profits is no easy proposition. Operating a business is tough enough. Adding social goals to the demands of serving customers and making a profit can be daunting and distracting. You can't take good intentions to the bank. In fact, many of the pioneering values-led businesses have since been acquired by bigger companies. For example, Unilever absorbed Ben & Jerry's, Clorox bought out Burt's Bees, L'Oréal acquired The Body Shop, Dannon ate up Stonyfield Farms, and VFC acquired Timberland.

The experiences of pioneers like Ben & Jerry's, however, taught the socially responsible business movement some hard lessons. As a result, a new generation of mission-driven entrepreneurs emerged—not social activists with big hearts who hate capitalism but well-trained business managers and company builders with a passion for a cause. These new

double-bottom-line devotees know that to *do good*, they must first *do well* in terms of viable and profitable business operations.

For example, home and cleaning products company Method is on a mission to "inspire a happy, healthy home revolution." All of Method's products are derived from natural ingredients, such as soy, coconut, and palm oils. The products come in environmentally responsible, biodegradable packaging. But Method knows that just doing good things won't make it successful. In fact, it's the other way around—being successful will let it do good things. "Business is the most powerful agent for positive change on the planet," says Method co-founder and "chief greenskeeper" Adam Lowry. "Mere sustainability is not our goal. We want to go much farther than that. We want to become restorative and enriching in everything we do so that the bigger we get, the more good we can create. We are striving for sustainable abundance. That's why at Method, we are always looking for ways to not just make our products greener, but our company better."

Beyond its social responsibility mission, Method is a well-run business and savvy marketer. Instead of touting the eco-friendly properties of its products, Method emphasizes product performance and innovation. Its products really work. And Method's marketing is on par with that of large blue chip competitors, such as P&G or Unilever. For example, through solid marketing, Method has attained mainstream distribution in Kroger, Safeway, Target, Whole Foods Market, Bed Bath & Beyond, Staples, Amazon.com, and a growing list of other big retailers. In only a few short years, through smart business practices, Method has become one of the nation's

▲ Method's mission is to inspire a happy, healthy home revolution. Says Method co-founder and "chief greenskeeper" Adam Lowry, "business is the most powerful agent for positive change on the planet."

Christopher Schall/Impact Photo

fastest growing companies, with more than $100 million in annual revenues. In the process, it's achieving its broader social goals.

Small companies with big social goals are one thing. However, today, socially responsible missions are no longer the exclusive domain of well-intentioned startups. Social responsibility has gone mainstream, with large corporations—from Walmart and Nike to Starbucks, Mars, and PepsiCo—adopting broad-based "change the world" initiatives. For example, Walmart is fast becoming the world's leading eco-nanny. Likewise, Starbucks created C.A.F.E. Practices, guidelines for achieving product quality, economic accountability, social responsibility, and environmental leadership.

Nike supports a broad social and environmental responsibility agenda, everything from eco-friendly product designs and manufacturing processes to improving conditions for the nearly 800,000 workers in its global supply chain to programs that engage the world's youth in the fight against AIDS in Africa. Sounding more like Ben & Jerry's or Method than a large, uncaring corporation, Nike states "We can use the power of our brand, the energy and passion of our people, and the scale of our business to create meaningful change." Says one Nike manager, "Our customers expect this from us. It's not about two or three green shoes—it's about changing the way our company does things in general."

Some brands are building their very identities around social responsibility missions. For example, as previously discussed, Mars Inc.'s PEDIGREE Brand is on a "Dogs rule" mission to urge people to adopt homeless dogs and support the care of these animals in shelters. Since 2008, The PEDIGREE Foundation

has raised and donated more than $5 million to thousands of animal shelters. It also donates its own dog food. For example, for every social media engagement (Facebook like or post, Twitter feed) describing "what every dog deserves" during the month of June, Pedigree donates one pound of dog food to shelters. Last June, that added up to more than 10,000 pounds of dog food.

Similarly, through its Pepsi Refresh campaign, PepsiCo redefines its flagship brand as not just a soft drink but as an agent for world change. Last year, the Pepsi Refresh Project awarded $20 million in grants to hundreds of individuals and organizations in local communities that propose ideas that will "make the world a better place." Pepsi has backed the project with a big-budget traditional and social marketing campaign. The Pepsi Refresh Project is no mere cause-related marketing effort: It makes "doing good" a major element of Pepsi's mission and positioning. Says Pepsi's director of marketing, "We want people to be aware that every time you drink a Pepsi you are actually supporting the Pepsi Refresh Project and ideas that are going to move this country forward."

Sources: Quotes and other information from Bob Liodice, "10 Companies with Social Responsibility at the Core," *Advertising Age*, April 19, 2010, p. 88; Mike Hoffman, "Ben Cohen: Ben & Jerry's Homemade, Established in 1978," *Inc*, April 30, 2001, p. 68; Sindya N. Bhanoo, "Products That Are Earth-and-Profit Friendly," *New York Times*, June 12, 2010, p. B3; Jessica Shambora, "David vs. Goliath," *Fortune,* November 15, 2010, p. 55; Zmuda, "Who Are the Big Pepsi Refresh Winners? Local Bottlers and Community Groups," *Advertising Age*, November 1, 2010, p. 2; and www.methodhome.com/behind-the-bottle/, www.benjerry.com/company/history/, www.nikebiz.com/responsibility/, www.pedigreefoundation.org/, and www.refresheverything.com, accessed October 2011.

Societal marketing

A principle of sustainable marketing that holds a company should make marketing decisions by considering consumers' wants, the company's requirements, consumers' long-run interests, and society's long-run interests.

Deficient products

Products that have neither immediate appeal nor long-run benefits.

Pleasing products

Products that give high immediate satisfaction but may hurt consumers in the long run.

Salutary products

Products that have low immediate appeal but may benefit consumers in the long run.

Societal Marketing

Following the principle of **societal marketing**, a company makes marketing decisions by considering consumers' wants, the company's requirements, consumers' long-run interests, and society's long-run interests. Companies should be aware that neglecting consumer and societal long-run interests is a disservice to consumers and society. Alert companies view societal problems as opportunities.

Sustainable marketing calls for products that are not only pleasing but also beneficial. The difference is shown in ▶ **Figure 16.4**. Products can be classified according to their degree of immediate consumer satisfaction and long-run consumer benefit.

Deficient products, such as bad-tasting and ineffective medicine, have neither immediate appeal nor long-run benefits. **Pleasing products** give high immediate satisfaction but may hurt consumers in the long run. Examples include cigarettes and junk food. **Salutary products** have low immediate appeal but may benefit consumers in the long run; for instance, bicycle helmets or some insurance products. **Desirable products** give both high immediate satisfaction and high long-run benefits, such as a tasty *and* nutritious breakfast food.

Examples of desirable products abound. GE's Energy Smart compact fluorescent light bulb provides good lighting at the same time that it gives long life and energy savings. Envirosax reusable shopping bags are stylish and affordable while also eliminating the need for less eco-friendly disposable paper and plastic store bags. Toggery organic clothing combines

▶ **Figure 16.4** Societal
Classification of Products

IMMEDIATE SATISFACTION

The goal? Create desirable products—those that create both immediate customer satisfaction and a long-run customer benefit. An example is Haworth's Zody office chair, which is both good for your body and good for the environment.

Desirable products
Products that give both high immediate satisfaction and high long-run benefits.

contemporary design with environmentally conscious fabrics, such as cotton, bamboo, and modal (made from recycled beech wood), all manufactured in the United States. And Haworth's Zody office chair is not only attractive and functional but also environmentally responsible. It's made without PVC, chlorofluorocarbons (CFCs), chrome, or any other toxic materials. Ninety-eight percent of the chair can be recycled; some 50 percent of it already has been. The energy used in the manufacturing process is completely offset by wind-power credits. When the chair is ready to be retired, the company will take it back and reuse its components.[26]

Companies should try to turn all of their products into desirable products. The challenge posed by pleasing products is that they sell very well but may end up hurting the consumer. The product opportunity, therefore, is to add long-run benefits without reducing the product's pleasing qualities. The challenge posed by salutary products is to add some pleasing qualities so that they will become more desirable in consumers' minds.

For example, PepsiCo recently hired a team of "idealistic scientists," headed by a former director of the World Health Organization, to help the company create attractive new healthy product options while "making the bad stuff less bad." PepsiCo wants healthy products to be a $30 billion business for the company by 2020.[27] The group of physicians, PhDs, and other health advocates, under the direction of PepsiCo's vice president for global health policy, looks for healthier ingredients that can go into multiple products. ▶ For example, their efforts led to an all-natural zero-calorie sweetener now featured in several new PepsiCo brands, including the $100 million Trop50 brand, a Tropicana orange juice variation that contains no artificial sweeteners and half the sugar and calories.

Marketing Ethics

Good ethics are a cornerstone of sustainable marketing. In the long run, unethical marketing harms customers and society as a whole. Further, it eventually damages a company's reputation and effectiveness, jeopardizing its very survival. Thus, the sustainable marketing goals of long-term consumer and business welfare can be achieved only through ethical marketing conduct.

Conscientious marketers face many moral dilemmas. The best thing to do is often unclear. Because not all managers have fine moral sensitivity, companies need to develop *corporate marketing ethics policies*—broad guidelines that everyone in the organization must follow. These policies should cover distributor relations, advertising standards, customer service, pricing, product development, and general ethical standards.

The finest guidelines cannot resolve all the difficult ethical situations the marketer faces. ▶ **Table 16.1** lists some difficult ethical issues marketers could face during their careers. If marketers choose immediate sales-producing actions in all these cases, their marketing

▲ **Desirable products: PepsiCo has hired a team of scientists to help it develop a larger portfolio of healthy product options, such as the Trop50 brand.**
AP Images/PR NEWSWIRE

▶ **Table 16.1**	Some Morally Difficult Situations in Marketing

1. Your R&D department has slightly changed one of your company's products. It is not really "new and improved," but you know that putting this statement on the package and in advertising will increase sales. What would you do?

2. You have been asked to add a stripped-down model to your line that could be advertised to pull customers into the store. The product won't be very good, but salespeople will be able to switch buyers who come into the store up to higher-priced units. You are asked to give the green light for the stripped-down version. What would you do?

3. You are thinking of hiring a product manager who has just left a competitor's company. She would be more than happy to tell you all the competitor's plans for the coming year. What would you do?

4. One of your top dealers in an important territory recently has had family troubles, and his sales have slipped. It looks like it will take him a while to straighten out his family trouble. Meanwhile, you are losing many sales. Legally, on performance grounds, you can terminate the dealer's franchise and replace him. What would you do?

5. You have a chance to win a big account that will mean a lot to you and your company. The purchasing agent hints that a "gift" would influence the decision. Your assistant recommends sending a large-screen television to the buyer's home. What would you do?

6. You have heard that a competitor has a new product feature that will make a big difference in sales. The competitor will demonstrate the feature in a private dealer meeting at the annual trade show. You can easily send a snooper to this meeting to learn about the new feature. What would you do?

7. You have to choose between three advertising campaigns outlined by your agency. The first (a) is a soft-sell, honest, straight-information campaign. The second (b) uses sex-loaded emotional appeals and exaggerates the product's benefits. The third (c) involves a noisy, somewhat irritating commercial that is sure to gain audience attention. Pretests show that the campaigns are effective in the following order: c, b, and a. What would you do?

8. You are interviewing a capable female applicant for a job as salesperson. She is better qualified than the men who have been interviewed. Nevertheless, you know that in your industry some important customers prefer dealing with men, and you will lose some sales if you hire her. What would you do?

---

behavior might well be described as immoral or even amoral. If they refuse to go along with *any* of the actions, they might be ineffective as marketing managers and unhappy because of the constant moral tension. Managers need a set of principles that will help them figure out the moral importance of each situation and decide how far they can go in good conscience.

But *what* principle should guide companies and marketing managers on issues of ethics and social responsibility? One philosophy is that the free market and the legal system should decide such issues. Under this principle, companies and their managers are not responsible for making moral judgments. Companies can in good conscience do whatever the market and legal systems allow.

A second philosophy puts responsibility not on the system but in the hands of individual companies and managers. This more enlightened philosophy suggests that a company should have a social conscience. Companies and managers should apply high standards of ethics and morality when making corporate decisions, regardless of "what the system allows." History provides an endless list of examples of company actions that were legal but highly irresponsible.

Each company and marketing manager must work out a philosophy of socially responsible and ethical behavior. Under the societal marketing concept, each manager must look beyond what is legal and allowed and develop standards based on personal integrity, corporate conscience, and long-run consumer welfare.

Dealing with issues of ethics and social responsibility in an open and forthright way helps to build strong customer relationships based on honesty and trust. In fact, many companies now routinely include consumers in the social responsibility process. Consider toy maker Mattel:[28]

In fall 2007, the discovery of lead paint on several of its best-selling products forced Mattel to make worldwide recalls on millions of toys. Threatening as this was, rather than hesitating or hiding the incident, the company's brand advisors were up to the challenge. Their quick, decisive response helped to maintain consumer confidence in the Mattel brand, even contributing to a 6 percent sales increase over the same period from the year before. Just who were these masterful "brand advisors"? They were the 400 moms with kids ages 3 to 10 who constitute The Playground community, a private online network launched by Mattel's worldwide consumer insights department in June 2007 to "listen to and gain insight from moms' lives and needs." Throughout the crisis, The Playground community members kept in touch with Mattel regarding the product recalls and the company's forthright response plan, even helping to shape the postrecall promotional strategy for one of the affected product lines. Even in times of crisis, "brands that engage in a two-way conversation with their customers create stronger, more trusting relationships," says a Mattel executive.

As with environmentalism, the issue of ethics presents special challenges for international marketers. Business standards and practices vary a great deal from one country to the next. For example, bribes and kickbacks are illegal for U.S. firms, and a variety of treaties against bribery and corruption have been signed and ratified by more than 60 countries. Yet these are still standard business practices in many countries. The World Bank estimates that bribes totaling more than $1 trillion per year are paid out worldwide. One study showed that the most flagrant bribe-paying firms were from India, Mexico, China, and Russia. Other countries where corruption is common include Iraq, Myanmar, and Haiti. The least corrupt were companies from Belgium, Canada, and the Netherlands.[29] The question arises as to whether a company must lower its ethical standards to compete effectively in countries with lower standards. The answer is no. Companies should make a commitment to a common set of shared standards worldwide.

Many industrial and professional associations have suggested codes of ethics, and many companies are now adopting their own codes. For example, the American Marketing Association, an international association of marketing managers and scholars, developed the code of ethics that calls on marketers to adopt the following ethical norms:[30]

- ***Do no harm.*** This means consciously avoiding harmful actions or omissions by embodying high ethical standards and adhering to all applicable laws and regulations in the choices we make.
- ***Foster trust in the marketing system.*** This means striving for good faith and fair dealing so as to contribute toward the efficacy of the exchange process as well as avoiding deception in product design, pricing, communication, and delivery of distribution.
- ***Embrace ethical values.*** This means building relationships and enhancing consumer confidence in the integrity of marketing by affirming these core values: honesty, responsibility, fairness, respect, transparency, and citizenship.

Companies are also developing programs to teach managers about important ethical issues and help them find the proper responses. They hold ethics workshops and seminars and create ethics committees. Furthermore, most major U.S. companies have appointed high-level ethics officers to champion ethical issues and help resolve ethics problems and concerns facing employees.

PricewaterhouseCoopers (PwC) is a good example. In 2002, PwC established a global ethics office and comprehensive ethics program, headed by a high-level global ethics officer. The ethics program begins with a code of conduct called "Doing the Right Thing— the PwC Way." PwC employees learn about the code of conduct and about how to handle thorny ethics issues in comprehensive ethics training programs, which start when the employee joins the company and continue throughout the employee's career. The program also includes *ethics champions* around the world and channels such programs as ethics helplines to enable people to raise concerns. "It is obviously not enough to distribute a document," says PwC's former CEO, Samuel DiPiazza. "Ethics is in everything we say and do."[31]

Still, written codes and ethics programs do not ensure ethical behavior. Ethics and social responsibility require a total corporate commitment. They must be a component of the overall corporate culture. According to DiPiazza, "I see ethics as a mission-critical issue . . . deeply embedded in who we are and what we do. It's just as important as our product development cycle or our distribution system. . . . It's about creating a culture based on integrity and respect, not a culture based on dealing with the crisis of the day. . . . We ask ourselves every day, 'Are we doing the right things?'"[32]

The Sustainable Company

At the foundation of marketing is the belief that companies that fulfill the needs and wants of customers will thrive. Companies that fail to meet customer needs or that intentionally or unintentionally harm customers, others in society, or future generations will decline.

Says one observer, "Sustainability is an emerging business megatrend, like electrification and mass production, that will profoundly affect companies' competitiveness and even their survival." Says another, "increasingly, companies and leaders will be assessed not only on immediate results but also on . . . the ultimate effects their actions have on societal wellbeing. This trend has been coming in small ways for years but now is surging. So pick up your recycled cup of fair-trade coffee, and get ready."[33]

Sustainable companies are those that create value for customers through socially, environmentally, and ethically responsible actions. Sustainable marketing goes beyond caring for the needs and wants of today's customers. It means having concern for tomorrow's customers in assuring the survival and success of the business, shareholders, employees, and the broader world in which they all live. Sustainable marketing provides the context in which companies can build profitable customer relationships by creating value *for* customers in order to capture value *from* customers in return—now and in the future.

REST STOP | REVIEWING THE CONCEPTS

MyMarketingLab

Now that you have completed the chapter, return to www.mymktlab.com to experience and apply the concepts and to explore the additional study materials for this chapter.

CHAPTER REVIEW AND KEY TERMS

Objectives Review

In this chapter, we addressed many of the important *sustainable marketing* concepts related to marketing's sweeping impact on individual consumers, other businesses, and society as a whole. Sustainable marketing requires socially, environmentally, and ethically responsible actions that bring value to not only present-day consumers and businesses but also future generations and society as a whole. Sustainable companies are those that act responsibly to create value for customers in order to capture value from customers in return—now and in the future.

> **OBJECTIVE 1 Define sustainable marketing and discuss its importance. (pp 480–481)**

Sustainable marketing calls for meeting the present needs of consumers and businesses while preserving or enhancing the ability of future generations to meet their needs. Whereas the marketing concept recognizes that companies thrive by fulfilling the day-to-day needs of customers, sustainable marketing calls for socially and environmentally responsible actions that meet both the

immediate and future needs of customers and the company. Truly sustainable marketing requires a smooth-functioning marketing system in which consumers, companies, public policymakers, and others work together to ensure responsible marketing actions.

> **OBJECTIVE 2 Identify the major social criticisms of marketing. (pp 482–489)**

Marketing's *impact on individual consumer welfare* has been criticized for its high prices, deceptive practices, high-pressure selling, shoddy or unsafe products, planned obsolescence, and poor service to disadvantaged consumers. Marketing's *impact on society* has been criticized for creating false wants and too much materialism, too few social goods, and cultural pollution. Critics have also denounced marketing's *impact on other businesses* for harming competitors and reducing competition through acquisitions, practices that create barriers to entry, and unfair competitive marketing practices. Some of these concerns are justified; some are not.

> **OBJECTIVE 3** **Define consumerism and environmentalism and explain how they affect marketing strategies.** (pp 489–495)

Concerns about the marketing system have led to citizen action movements. *Consumerism* is an organized social movement intended to strengthen the rights and power of consumers relative to sellers. Alert marketers view it as an opportunity to serve consumers better by providing more consumer information, education, and protection. *Environmentalism* is an organized social movement seeking to minimize the harm done to the environment and quality of life by marketing practices. Most companies are now accepting responsibility for doing no environmental harm. They are adopting policies of *environmental sustainability*—developing strategies that both sustain the environment and produce profits for the company. Both consumerism and environmentalism are important components of sustainable marketing.

> **OBJECTIVE 4** **Describe the principles of sustainable marketing.** (pp 495–500)

Many companies originally resisted these social movements and laws, but most now recognize a need for positive consumer

information, education, and protection. Under the sustainable marketing concept, a company's marketing should support the best long-run performance of the marketing system. It should be guided by five sustainable marketing principles: *consumer-oriented marketing*, *customer-value marketing*, *innovative marketing*, *sense-of-mission marketing*, and *societal marketing*.

> **OBJECTIVE 5** **Explain the role of ethics in marketing.** (pp 500–503)

Increasingly, companies are responding to the need to provide company policies and guidelines to help their managers deal with questions of *marketing ethics*. Of course, even the best guidelines cannot resolve all the difficult ethical decisions that individuals and firms must make. But there are some principles from which marketers can choose. One principle states that the free market and the legal system should decide such issues. A second and more enlightened principle puts responsibility not on the system but in the hands of individual companies and managers. Each firm and marketing manager must work out a philosophy of socially responsible and ethical behavior. Under the sustainable marketing concept, managers must look beyond what is legal and allowable and develop standards based on personal integrity, corporate conscience, and long-term consumer welfare.

Key Terms

Objective 1
Sustainable marketing (p 480)

Objective 3
Consumerism (p 489)
Environmentalism (p 490)
Environmental sustainability (p 491)

Objective 4
Consumer-oriented marketing (p 496)
Customer-value marketing (p 496)
Innovative marketing (p 496)
Sense-of-mission marketing (p 497)
Societal marketing (p 499)
Deficient products (p 499)

Pleasing products (p 499)
Salutary products (p 499)
Desirable products (p 499)

DISCUSSION AND CRITICAL THINKING

Discussion Questions

1. What is sustainable marketing? Explain how the sustainable marketing concept differs from the marketing concept and the societal marketing concept. (AACSB: Communication)
2. Critics claim that marketing results in higher prices for consumers. Discuss the bases for this claim and how marketers refute them. (AACSB: Communication)
3. Discuss the types of harmful impact that marketing practices can have on competition and the associated problems. (AACSB: Communication)

4. Can an organization focus on both consumerism and environmentalism at the same time? Explain. (AACSB: Communication; Reflective Thinking)
5. Discuss the challenges environmentalism creates for global marketers and how marketers are dealing with these challenges. (AACSB: Communication)
6. Discuss the philosophies that might guide marketers facing ethical issues. (AACSB: Communication)

Critical Thinking Exercises

1. Some cultures are more accepting than others of corrupt practices such as bribery. Although corruption is not tolerated in the United States or by U.S. firms operating abroad, it's the price of entry in some countries for many foreign firms. Visit www.transparency.org and look at the Corruption Perception Index (CPI) report. The CPI can range from 0 to 10, where a low index score means a country is perceived as highly corrupt and a higher score means highly ethical. Pick three countries that are rated as least corrupt and three that are highly corrupt and explain why you think they may be that way. (AACSB: Communication; Use of IT)

2. Watch *The Story of Stuff* video at www.youtube.com/story ofstuffproject#p/u/22/9GorqroigqM or one of the other videos, such as *The Story of Bottled Water*, *The Story of Electronics*, or *The Story of Cosmetics*. In a small group, critique the message in the video and develop an argument to counter this point of view. (AACSB: Communication; Reflective Thinking)

3. Google "green awards" to learn about the various awards programs recognizing environmental consciousness and sustainable practices. Select one that recognized a business for a sustainable marketing practice and develop a brief presentation explaining why the company received the award. (AACSB: Communication; Use of IT; Reflective Thinking)

MINICASES AND APPLICATIONS

Marketing Technology   Compostable Packaging

Corn-based packaging is hitting the shelves for everything from bottles to bags. But one such endeavor had unintended consequences. Frito-Lay came out with a 100 percent compostable bag for its Sun Chip line of chips. The package, made from 100 percent polylactic acid (PLA), which is a corn-based biopolymer that fully decomposes within 14 weeks, had one drawback—it was terribly noisy. An Air Force pilot posted a video on YouTube showing the sound reaching 95 decibels when the bag was touched, leading him to claim it was "louder than the cockpit of my jet." Others likened the sound to "revving motorcycles" or "glass breaking." The package soon became the butt of jokes, even resulting in a Facebook group called "Sorry But I Can't Hear You Over This Sun Chips Bag." Frito-Lay relented and reintroduced a less-noisy bag.

1. Search the Internet for more examples of compostable packaging. Discuss three of them. (AACSB: Communication; Use of IT)

2. Is corn-based compostable packaging a sustainable solution to replace petroleum-based plastic packaging? Discuss the pros and cons of this alternative. (AACSB: Communication; Reflective Thinking)

Marketing Ethics   Eco Index

Many companies, such as Timberland, Patagonia, and others described in this chapter, take sustainable marketing seriously. Consumers might soon be able to use the Outdoor Industry Association's (OIA) *Eco Index* to help them identify such companies. The OIA has guided brand manufacturers and retailers, such as Nike, Levi Strauss, Timberland, Target, Patagonia, and many others in developing a software tool to measure the eco-impact of their products. A product as simple as a pair of jeans has considerable environmental impact. A pair of Levi's jeans moves from cotton grown in Louisiana; to fabric woven in North Carolina; to jeans cut in the Dominican Republic, sewn in Haiti, and finished in Jamaica; to final products distributed to the store where you purchase them. And that's just for jeans sold in the United States—Levi's are sold all over the world. The Eco Index takes all this and more into account. It factors in other environmental things, such as washing methods, the amount of water used in the life of the jeans, and the disposal of the product. The holdup on the Eco Index, however, is that all the information is self-reported, and manufacturers have to obtain information from their suppliers as well.

1. Learn more about this initiative by visiting the Outdoor Industry's Web site at www.outdoorindustry.org. If implemented, will this index help marketers who score well on it develop a sustainable competitive advantage? Would you be more willing to purchase a product from a company that scores well on this index? (AACSB: Communication; Use of IT; Reflective Thinking)

2. The Eco Index is an industry-led initiative and all information is self-reported with no substantiation required. Does the potential exist to abuse the system and possibly deceive consumers? Explain. (AACSB: Communication; Ethical Reasoning; Reflective Thinking)

Marketing by the Numbers   The Cost of Sustainability

One element of sustainability is organic farming. However, if you've priced organic foods, you know they are more expensive. Organic farming costs much more than conventional farming, and those costs are passed on to consumers. For example, a dozen conventionally farmed eggs costs consumers $1.50, whereas a dozen organic eggs costs $2.80. However, if prices get too high, consumers will not purchase the organic eggs. Suppose that the average fixed costs per year for conventionally farmed eggs are $1 million per year but they are twice that amount for organic eggs. Organic farmers' variable costs per dozen are twice as much as well, costing $1.80 per dozen. Refer to Appendix 3, Marketing by the Numbers, to answer the following questions.

1. Most large egg farmers sell eggs directly to retailers. What is the farmer's price per dozen to the retailer for conventional and organic eggs if the retailer's margin is 20 percent based on the retail price? (AACSB: Communication; Analytical Reasoning)
2. How many dozen eggs does a conventional farmer need to sell to break even? How many does an organic farmer need to sell to break even? (AACSB: Communication; Analytical Reasoning)

Video Case   Life Is Good

Most companies these days are looking for ways to be more socially responsible in manufacturing and marketing the goods and services they produce. But only a few companies produce goods and services with the primary purpose of making the world a better place. Life Is Good is one of those companies. Most people are familiar with the cheerful logo on Life Is Good products. But few are aware of what the company does with its profits behind the scenes.

This video focuses on Life Is Good Playmakers, a nonprofit organization dedicated to helping children overcome life-threatening challenges. From the time Life Is Good started selling T-shirts in the early 1990s, its founders supported

Playmakers. The relationship between the two organizations became progressively stronger, ultimately leading Life Is Good to make Playmakers an official branch of the company.

After viewing the video featuring Life Is Good, answer the following questions:

1. How many examples can you provide showing how Life Is Good defies the common social criticisms of marketing?
2. How does Life Is Good practice sustainable marketing principles?
3. With all its efforts to do *good*, can Life Is Good continue to do *well*? Explain.

Company Cases   9 Burt's Bees / 16 International Paper

See Appendix 1 for cases appropriate for this chapter. **Case 9, Burt's Bees: Willfully Overpriced.** By pricing products above the market average, Burt's Bees gets customers' attention—and business. **Case 16, International Paper: Combining Industry**

and Social Responsibility. A leader in one of the oldest manufacturing industries becomes a leading example of social responsibility.

Appendix 1 Company Cases

Company Case 1

Converse: Shaping the Customer Experience

They dominated the basketball courts—both amateur and professional—for more than 40 years. The first U.S. Olympic basketball team wore them, and Dr. J made them famous in the NBA. Punk rocker Joey Ramone made them standard issue for cult musicians; indeed, Kurt Cobain even donned a pair when he committed suicide. Today, a broad range of consumers, from the nerdiest of high school students to A-list celebrities, claim them as their own. What are they? Converse All Stars—more particularly, the famous Chuck Taylor All Stars known throughout the world as Cons, Connies, Convics, Verses, Chuckers, Chuckies, Chucks, and a host of other nicknames.

The cool quotient of the iconic Converse brand is unquestionable. However, you might wonder just how the brand has maintained its status decade after decade. The answer is this: by doing nothing. That may seem an oversimplification, but the folks who run the Converse brand understand that in order to provide a meaningful customer experience, sometimes they just need to stand back and leave customers alone.

The Rise and Fall of a Legend

Converse has been around a long time, perhaps longer than you realize. Founded in 1908 in Massachusetts, Converse introduced the canvas high top All Star in 1917. In 1923, it renamed the shoe the Chuck Taylor, after a semiprofessional basketball player from Akron, Ohio. When his basketball career ended, Charles "Chuck" Taylor became an aggressive member of the Converse sales force. He drove throughout the Midwest, stopping at playgrounds to hawk the high tops to players. Some consider Taylor to be the original Phil Knight, Nike's CEO, who also started out by selling his shoes at track meets from the back of his van. From the 1930s to the 1960s, Chuck Taylor All Stars were *the* shoes to wear, even though they only came in basic black or white until 1969. At that time, 70 to 80 percent of all basketball players wore Converse.

There's no question that Converse invented basketball shoes. You might even say that Converse's pioneering efforts paved the way for the success of athletic shoes of all kinds. And the popularity of All Stars on the court played an instrumental role in making athletic shoes everyday footwear. But as the sneaker market began to explode in the 1970s and 1980s, shoes became more specialized, more high tech, and more expensive. As Nike, Adidas, and Reebok took over the market, Converse experienced a financial roller coaster ride. The company ultimately declared bankruptcy in 2001 as its market share bottomed out at 2 percent of the athletic shoe market, a small fraction of its prior position.

Yet, even as Converse fell from market dominance, something interesting happened in the marketplace. Emerging artists, designers, and musicians began wearing Chucks because of their affordability, simplicity, and classic look. Young people caught on and adopted them as an expression of individuality. In fact, Converse's shrinking market share and ad budget made its shoes a favorite of the anti-establishment, anti-corporate crowd who were tired of trendy fashions. These people would take a cheap pair of comfy Converse All Stars and thrash them, scribble on them, and customize them as a canvas for personal expression. Perhaps the most intriguing aspect of consumers adopting Converse as a counter-culture icon is that Converse itself never promoted the brand as anything but basketball shoes.

Despite its emergence as a niche counter-culture brand, Converse continued to struggle. In 2003, however, Nike came to the rescue by acquiring Converse and making it part of the Nike corporate family. Many analysts speculated that this acquisition by a big-brand corporation would ruin Converse's cult caché as a "non-brand." However, although Nike buoyed Converse with an infusion of cash and access to its product-development labs, it left Converse management pretty much alone to implement its own strategy. It kept an arms-length distance between Converse and the Nike swoosh. In fact, to this day, few consumers know that Nike owns Converse.

In the years since Nike acquired Converse, sales have improved; however, the company's market share has gone up very little. Although Converse has added different styles of shoes during the past decade (think Dwayne Wade), its primary focus has been on the original Chuck Taylor All Stars. However, Converse has branched out from that original design. For example, the Converse One Star is a low-priced line available at Target. The company has developed thousands of higher-priced versions of All Stars created by fashion designers and sold through upscale retailers such as Saks and Bloomingdales. And its Rock Collaborations line has featured designs created by rock legends Pink Floyd, Ozzy Osbourne, and The Who.

While some analysts worry that all these variations might detract from the authenticity of the original All Stars, so far that doesn't seem to be the case. Even the most hard-core music fans turn giddy when they see a pair of All Star high tops designed by their rock idol. Now, anti-establishment rock fans beg Converse to feature a shoe by their favorite artist.

In certain respects, the Converse brand seems to be more popular than ever. In fact, despite low market share, Converse is the most popular sneaker brand on Facebook, with more than 19 million fans—almost four times as many as market leader Nike. Converse brings in 20,000 Likes a day, versus just a few thousand for Nike. All this popularity comes from a brand that grabs less than 3 percent of the total athletic shoe market.

The Customer Is in Charge

How did Converse become the biggest little sneaker brand on Facebook? Its approach was simple: leave the brand in the hands of the customers. In fact, when Geoff Cottrill, Converse's chief marketing officer, discovered that the brand had achieved number one status on Facebook and was asked what the brand should do about it, he replied, "Nothing." By that, Cottrill explained, he meant that the brand should do nothing that would mess up Converse's valuable customer-brand relationship.

Even before Converse rose to Facebook dominance, the company had already embraced the social media. Today, Converse spends 90 percent of its marketing dollars on emerging digital media rather than traditional media. This allocation of promotional spending reflects a philosophy that customers, not companies, control brands. Although a company can influence the way its customers think, those customers ultimately decide what the brand means and how they interact with it.

As the various social media outlets emerged, Cottrill developed what he calls a "good party guest" approach to managing customer relationships. "Our philosophy in social media has been to bring our voice to the medium, which includes acting like a good party guest—we bring something to the table and we listen more than we talk." This philosophy rests on the notion of "letting go." Converse sees its role as one of making great products that its customers want to wear. Beyond that, it participates in consumer discussions rather than dictating them.

This is a dramatic shift from the old methods of one-way promotional brand communication. In this manner, Converse shows that it respects and trusts its customers. In turn, it fosters an emotional bond between the customer and the brand. When purchase time comes around, the strong relationship pays off. "I believe [the] brand benefits via strong advocacy—having millions of advocates can be a powerful thing," Cottrill says.

To be sure, Converse is very strategic about its "stand-back" approach. The brand sponsors planned communications such as posts about products, content, and questions of the day. But it also remains flexible and ready to talk about lots of topics as they arise—just like at a dinner party. For example, when the YouTube "Yosemitebear Mountain Giant Double Rainbow" video was exploding, that inspired the Converse "Design-Your-Own Shoe" contest.

One of the planned elements of Converse's promotional strategy was joining forces with the (RED) Global Fund, which raises money to fight AIDS, tuberculosis, and malaria. Through the (RED) initiative, Converse has developed more than 110 artist-, designer-, and musician-designed All Stars, including limited editions by The Edge, Lupe Fiasco, Terence Koh, and Vena Cava. Up to 100 percent of the profits from the (RED) All Stars go to the Global Fund. In the five years since Converse joined forces with (RED), it has sent $160 million to the fund—no small venture. Its next five-year goal is even bigger: to deliver the first generation of babies born without HIV in nearly three decades.

In another strategic move that earned Converse a spot on *Fast Company*'s Most Innovative Companies list, the company built a music studio in Brooklyn called Converse Rubber Tracks. Although Converse is not trying to get into the music business per se, this effort keeps its brand associations with music strong. Converse offers emerging artists free recording time in exchange for agreeing to do future promotions with the brand. Converse doesn't demand anything in the way of rights or royalties to the music. Rather, the logic is that by investing in lots of unknown bands, it will have a foot in the door with those that become hits.

Converse rides a fine line: How many limited editions and upscale designs can the brand produce without losing its image as a non-marketing marketer? How popular can the brand become without losing the core customers who love it precisely because it isn't popular? In growing the brand, Converse has been very careful in all that it does to remember one very important thing. For a brand like Converse, where authenticity is the most important trait, the customer experience should be driven by the customer.

Questions for Discussion

1. What are some examples of the needs, wants, and demands that Converse customers demonstrate? Differentiate these three concepts.

2. What are Converse and customers exchanging in the purchase transaction? Describe in detail all the facets of Converse's product and its relationship with customers.

3. Which of the five marketing management concepts best applies to Converse?

4. What are the benefits and drawbacks of Converse's "stand-back" approach?

5. How can Converse continue to grow its brand while at the same time maintaining its authentic image?

Sources: Edmund Lee, "Major Marketers Shift More Dollars Toward Social Media," *Advertising Age*, April 6, 2011, http://adage.com/article/226838/; Austin Carr, "Converse: I'm with the Brand," *Fast Company*, October 7, 2010, www.fastcompany.com/1693621/; Geoff Cottrill, "Our Five-Year Plan: An AIDS-Free Generation in 2015," *Advertising Age*, December 1, 2010, http://adage.com/article/147384/; Todd Wasserman, "How Converse Became the Biggest Little Sneaker Brand on Facebook," Mashable.com, May 4, 2011, http://mashable.com/2011/05/04/converse-facebook/.

Company Case 2

Trap-Ease America: The Big Cheese of Mousetraps

Conventional Wisdom

One April morning, Martha House, president of Trap-Ease America, entered her office in Costa Mesa, California. She paused for a moment to contemplate the Ralph Waldo Emerson quote that she had framed and hung near her desk:

> If a man [can] . . . make a better mousetrap than his neighbor . . . the world will make a beaten path to his door.

Perhaps, she mused, Emerson knew something that she didn't. She *had* the better mousetrap—Trap-Ease—but the world didn't seem all that excited about it.

Martha had just returned from the National Hardware Show in Chicago. Standing in the trade show display booth for long hours and answering the same questions hundreds of times had been tiring. Yet, all the hard work had paid off. Each year, National Hardware Show officials held a contest to select the best new product introduced at that year's show. The Trap-Ease had won the contest this year, beating out over 300 new products.

Such notoriety was not new for the Trap-Ease mousetrap, however. *People* magazine had run a feature article on the trap, which had also been discussed on numerous talk shows. Trap-Ease was also the subject of numerous articles in various popular press and trade publications.

Despite all of this attention, however, the expected demand for the trap had not materialized. Martha hoped that this award might stimulate increased interest and sales.

Background

A group of investors had formed Trap-Ease America in January after it had obtained worldwide rights to market the innovative mousetrap. In return for marketing rights, the group agreed to pay the inventor and patent holder, a retired rancher, a royalty fee for each trap sold. The group then hired Martha to serve as president and to develop and manage the Trap-Ease America organization.

Trap-Ease America contracted with a plastics-manufacturing firm to produce the traps. The mousetrap consisted of a square, plastic tube measuring about 6 inches long and 1-1/2 inches in diameter. The tube bent in the middle at a 30-degree angle, so that when the front part of the tube rested on a flat surface, the other end was elevated. The elevated end held a removable cap into which the user placed bait (cheese, dog food, or some other aromatic tidbit). The front end of the tube had a hinged door. When the trap was "open," this door rested on two narrow "stilts" attached to the two bottom corners of the door. (See Exhibit.)

The simple trap worked very efficiently. A mouse, smelling the bait, entered the tube through the open end. As it walked up the angled bottom toward the bait, its weight made the elevated

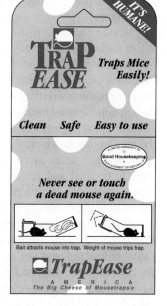

end of the trap drop downward. This action elevated the open end, allowing the hinged door to swing closed, trapping the mouse. Small teeth on the ends of the stilts caught in a groove on the bottom of the trap, locking the door closed. The user could then dispose of the mouse while it was still alive or leave it alone for a few hours to suffocate in the trap.

Martha believed the trap had many advantages for the consumer when compared with traditional spring-loaded traps or poisons. Consumers could use it safely and easily with no risk of catching their fingers while loading it. It posed no injury or poisoning threat to children or pets. Furthermore, with Trap-Ease, consumers avoided the unpleasant "mess" they often encountered with the violent spring-loaded traps. The Trap-Ease created no "clean-up" problem. Finally, the user could reuse the trap or simply throw it away.

Martha's early research suggested that women were the best target market for the Trap-Ease. Men, it seemed, were more willing to buy and use the traditional, spring-loaded trap. In contrast, the targeted women did not like the traditional trap. These women often stayed at home and took care of their children. Thus, they wanted a means of dealing with the mouse problem that avoided the unpleasantness and risks that the standard trap created in the home.

To reach this target market, Martha decided to distribute Trap-Ease through national grocery, hardware, and discount chains. She sold the trap directly to these large retailers, avoiding any wholesalers or other middlemen.

The traps sold in packages of two, with a suggested retail price of $5.99. Although this price made the Trap-Ease about five times more expensive than smaller, standard traps, consumers appeared to offer little initial price resistance. The manufacturing cost for the Trap-Ease, including freight and packaging costs, was about 59 cents per unit. The company paid an additional 19 cents per unit in royalty fees. Martha priced the traps to retailers at $2.38 per unit (two units to a package) and estimated that, after sales and volume discounts, Trap-Ease would produce net revenue from retailers of $1.50 per unit.

Martha budgeted approximately $145,000 for Trap-Ease promotion during the first year. She planned to use $100,000 of this amount for travel costs to visit trade shows and to make sales calls on retailers. The remaining $45,000 was earmarked for advertising. Since the mousetrap had generated so much publicity, however, Martha did not feel the need to do much advertising. Still, she had placed advertising in *Good Housekeeping* (after all, the trap had earned the *Good Housekeeping* Seal of Approval) and in other "home and shelter" magazines.

Martha was the company's only salesperson, but she intended to hire more salespeople soon.

Martha had initially forecasted Trap-Ease's first-year sales at five million units. Through April, however, the company had only sold several hundred thousand units. Martha wondered if most new products got off to such a slow start, or if she was doing something wrong. She had detected some problems, although none seemed overly serious. For one, there had not been enough repeat buying. For another, she had noted that many of the retailers upon whom she called kept their sample mouse-traps on their desks as conversation pieces—she wanted the traps to be used and demonstrated. Martha wondered if consumers were also buying the traps as novelties rather than as solutions to their mouse problems.

Martha knew that the investor group believed that Trap-Ease America had a "once-in-a-lifetime chance" with its innovative mousetrap, and she sensed the group's impatience with the company's progress so far. She had budgeted approximately $500,000 in administrative and fixed costs for the first year (not including marketing costs). To keep the investors happy, the company needed to sell enough traps to cover those costs and make a reasonable profit.

Back to the Drawing Board

In the first few months of the Trap-Ease launch, Martha learned that marketing a new product was not an easy task. Some customers were very demanding. For example, one national retailer placed a large order with instructions that Trap-Ease America was to deliver the order to the loading dock at one of the retailer's warehouses between 1:00 and 3:00 p.m. on a specified day. When the truck delivering the order arrived after 3:00 p.m., the retailer refused to accept the shipment. The retailer told Martha it would be a year before she got another chance.

As Martha sat down at her desk, she realized she needed to rethink her marketing strategy. Perhaps she had missed something or made some mistake that was causing sales to be so slow. Glancing at the quotation again, she thought that perhaps she should send the picky retailer and other customers a copy of Emerson's famous quote.

Questions for Discussion

1. Martha and the Trap-Ease America investors believe they face a once-in-a-lifetime opportunity. What information do they need to evaluate this opportunity? How do you think the group would write its mission statement? How would *you* write it?

2. Has Martha identified the best target market for Trap-Ease? What other market segments might the firm target?

3. How has the company positioned the Trap-Ease for the chosen target market? Could it position the product in other ways?

4. How would you describe the current marketing mix for Trap-Ease? Do you see any problems with this mix?

5. Who is Trap-Ease America's competition?

6. How would you change Trap-Ease's marketing strategy? What kinds of control procedures would you establish for this strategy?

Company Case 3

Target: From "Expect More" to "Pay Less"

When you hear the term *discount retail*, two names usually come to mind: Walmart and Target. The two competitors have been compared so much that the press rarely covers one without at least mentioning the other. The reasons for the comparisons are fairly obvious. These corporations are two of the largest discount retailers in the United States. Category-for-category, they offer very similar merchandise. And they tend to build their stores in close proximity to one another, often even facing each other across major boulevards.

But even with such strong similarities, ask any consumer if there's a difference between the two and they won't even hesitate in offering a reply. Walmart is all about low prices; Target is about style and fashion. The "upscale discounter" label applied by consumers and the media over the years perfectly captures Target's long-standing positioning: "Expect More. Pay Less." With its numerous designer product lines,

Target has been so successful with its brand positioning that for many years it has slowly chipped away at Walmart's massive market share lead. Granted, the difference in the scale of the two companies has always been huge. Walmart's most recent annual revenues of $419 billion are more than six times Target's $67 billion. But for many years, Target's grew at a much faster pace than Walmart's.

In fact, as Walmart's same-store sales began to lag in the mid-2000s, the world's largest retailer unabashedly attempted to become more like Target. It spruced up its store environment, added more fashionable clothing and housewares, and stocked organic and gourmet foods in its grocery aisles. Walmart even experimented with luxury brands. After 19 years of promoting the slogan, "Always Low Prices. Always.", Walmart replaced it with the very Target-esque tagline, "Save Money. Live Better." However, none of those efforts seemed to speed up Walmart's revenue growth or slow down Target's.

But as the global recession began to tighten its grip on the world's retailers in 2008, the dynamics between the two retail giants reversed almost overnight. As unemployment rose and consumers began pinching their pennies, Walmart's familiar price "rollbacks" resonated with consumers, whereas Target's image of slightly better stuff for slightly higher prices did not. Target's well-cultivated upscale discount image was turning away customers who believed that its fashionable products and trendy advertising meant steeper prices. By mid-2008, Target had experienced three straight quarters of flat same-store sales growth and a slight dip in store traffic. At the same time, Walmart was defying the economic slowdown, posting quarterly increases in same-store sales of close to 5 percent along with substantial jumps in profits.

Same Slogan, Different Emphasis

In the fall of 2008, Target acknowledged the slide and announced its intentions to do something about it. CEO Gregg Steinhafel succinctly summarized the company's new strategy: "The customer is very cash strapped right now. And in some ways, our greatest strength has become somewhat of a challenge. So, we're still trying to define and find the right balance between 'Expect More. Pay Less.' The current environment means that the focus is squarely on the 'Pay Less' side of it."

In the few years since Steinhafel unveiled the new strategic plan, Target has gone through some drastic changes. The executives at Target challenged every assumption about the brand and the business model that had formerly brought Target so much success. While this adjustment certainly meant cutting costs and prices, Walmart's decades-long lead in that department meant that Target would have to do more.

According to Michael Francis, Target's chief marketing officer, doing more is exactly what happened. "There was more innovation happening within Target during the recession than in any time in my 25 years with the corporation." For starters, Target began a massive effort to redesign its stores. This included redesigning departments and making updates to store signage and lighting. But the biggest change to store design came from the PFresh concept, an expansion of the grocery section in regular Target stores to include fresh produce, meat, and dairy products. This new "mini-grocery store" was design to provide a narrow selection of 90 percent of the food categories found in full-size grocery stores while occupying only a corner of an existing Target store.

Target's intention was to create mini-grocery stores to provide customers with a one-stop shopping experience. One shopper's reaction was just what Target was hoping for. A Wisconsin housewife and mother of two stopped by her local Target to buy deodorant and laundry detergent before heading to the local grocery store. But as she worked her way through the fresh-food aisles, she found everything on her list. "I'm done," she said, as she grabbed for a 99-cent green pepper. "I just saved myself a trip."

While the PFresh concept demonstrated promise for increasing store traffic, groceries are a low-margin category. That's why Target's second major operational change focused on stronger sales of higher margin goods. Target surprised many analysts by unveiling a new package for its main store brand . . . one without the familiar Target bulls-eye! Instead, the new Target store brand, "up & up," featured big, colorful, upward-pointing arrows on a white background. The total number of products under the store label was expanded from 730 to 800 and promotional efforts for the store brand were increased in weekly newspaper circulars. Kathryn Tesija, Target's vice president of merchandising, stated, "We believe that it will stand out on the shelf, and it is so distinctive that we'll get new guests that will want to try it that maybe didn't even notice the Target brand before."

The design changes to Target stores required a major shift in the company's store growth plan. In fact, Target opened only 10 new stores in 2010, the lowest number in its history. "It will be a long time before we approach the development pace of several years ago," said Doug Scovanner, Target's chief financial officer. Meanwhile, Target continues to put its money into remodeling existing stores to better accommodate the shifts in inventory.

As its product portfolio and prices began to reflect the "Pay Less" part of its slogan, Target also shifted its advertising strategy. For years, the company had featured ads that projected the "Expect More" part of its slogan. But even as it turned the stated message of its ads toward price, trendy and stylish visual imagery continued to strike customers as "expensive." Therefore, Target put all its advertising in the hands of Wieden & Kennedy as its first-ever lead advertising agency. Wieden went to work, fine-tuning the marketing message in an effort to convince consumers that Target was just as committed to bargains as Walmart.

Target's most recent campaign, "Life's A Moving Target," is spot on. The campaign has produced in excess of 70 spots, each 15 seconds long and highlighting a specific product, ranging from flu shots to pants to cheese. The overall message that "the pace of life is complex" is much more in line with the reality that middle America faces. In addition, each ad ultimately shows that Target is there to fill consumers' daily needs. For example, one clever shot shows a young boy at the table, sliding his Brussells sprouts under the table to the dog. But the dog won't have them and leaves, just as a bag of PEDIGREE dog food flashes on the screen, followed by the campaign's tag line. The campaign also brings in co-op dollars from vendors who are even petitioning Target to be part of the campaign.

Signs of Life

Although Steinhafel's "Pay Less" strategy was aggressive, Target's sales and profits were slow to respond. In fact, sales initially fell, at one point dropping by 10 percent from the previous year. Target's profits suffered even more. It didn't help matters that as Target's financials suffered, Walmart bucked the recessionary retail trend by posting revenue increases.

But Target's journey over the past few years demonstrates that changing the direction of a large corporation is like trying to reverse a moving freight train. It has to slow down before going the other way. It now appears that consumers may have finally gotten the message. During 2010, Target's same-store sales rose by as much as 5 percent while profits shot up 16 percent. Both the amount spent per visit and number of store visits increased. In a sign that Target's efforts are truly paying off, Walmart's fortunes reversed as well. The retail giant saw same-store sales decline for seven straight quarters.

Steinhafel makes it clear that Target is viewing the new signs of life with cautious optimism. "Clearly the economy and consumer sentiment have improved since their weakest point in 2009," says the Target CEO. "But we believe that both are still somewhat unstable and fragile and will likely continue to experience occasional setbacks as the year progresses." Steinhafel's comments reflect an understanding that even as the recession showed signs of ending, research indicated that consumers everywhere have adopted a new-found sense of frugality and monetary responsibility. Although economic growth may have improved, inflation is on the rise and unemployment remains high.

Some Wall Street analysts have expressed concern that Target's recent value strategy may weaken the brand as customers lose sight of the distinctive features that set it apart from Walmart. But the words of one shopper are a good indication that, despite having emphasized the "Pay Less" part of its image, Target still retains the "Expect More" part: "Target is a nice place to go. Walmart may have good prices, but I would rather tell my friends that I came back from shopping at Target."

Questions for Discussion

1. What microenvironmental factors have affected Target's performance over the past few years?

2. What macroenvironmental factors have affected Target's performance during that period?

3. By focusing on the "Pay Less" part of its slogan, has Target pursued the best strategy? Why or why not?

4. What alternative strategy might Target have followed in responding to the first signs of declining revenues and profits?

5. Given Target's current situation, what recommendations would you make to CEO Steinhafel for the company's future?

Sources: Natalie Zmuda, "Why the Bad Economy Has Been Good for Target," *Advertising Age,* October 4, 2010, accessed at www.adage .com; Rita Trichur and Marina Strauss, "Target Knows What They Are; Clean, Bright, and Well-Organized," *Globe and Mail,* January 14, 2011, p. B4; Karen Talley, "Target Profit Rises on Strong Sales, Improved Credit-Card Operations," *Wall Street Journal,* May 20, 2010, accessed at www.wsj.com; Ann Zimmerman, "Target Believes a Rebound Recipe Is in Grocery Aisle," *Wall Street Journal,* May 12, 2009, p. B1; Nicole Maestri, "Target Revamps Its Target Brand as 'up & up'," *Reuters,* May 19, 2009, accessed at www.reuters.com.

Company Case 4

Meredith: Thanks to Good Marketing Information, Meredith *Knows* Women

You may not recognize the name Meredith Corporation but you have certainly heard of the magazines it publishes. *Better Homes and Gardens*, *Ladies' Home Journal,* and *Family Circle* are some of its oldest and best-known titles. Meredith has been publishing magazines for more than 100 years and maintains many top-ten titles, both by category and overall. With a total of 21 subscription magazines, Meredith is also the creator of *American Baby, Parents, Fitness, Midwest Living,* and *MORE.* This powerhouse publisher also produces 150 special interest publications—the kind that are available only at retail outlets. Meredith's magazines have a combined circulation of 30 million—*Better Homes and Gardens* alone reaches nearly 8 million paid readers each month.

If Meredith's magazines sound like something your mom would read, that's intentional. Meredith caters to women. In fact, Meredith has become the undisputed leading media and marketing company focused on women, a reputation earned by developing an expertise in managing deep relationships with female customers. With core categories of home, health, family, and personal development, Meredith's goal is to touch every life stage of women, from young adults and new parents to established families and empty nesters.

Print media is hardly a growth industry—in fact, it's been declining in recent years. But building an empire on magazines doesn't mean that Meredith has painted itself into a corner. In fact, Meredith no longer describes itself as a magazine publisher. It claims to be a creator of "content," delivered to women "whenever, wherever, and however [they want] it." Long before print media began its decline, Meredith expanded into television stations, cable programming, and Web sites. Today, Meredith has a strong foundation on the Web, with more than 50 Web sites that reach an average of 20 million unique visitors each month. Its Web empire includes BHG.com, Parents .com, DivineCaroline.com, and FitnessMagazine.com, to name just a few. This network allows Meredith to do more than just distribute content; the company has also become proficient in social networking. With so many brands available through print, television, online, mobile, and video, Meredith plans to continue to touch women's lives in meaningful ways for a long, long time.

How has Meredith been able to achieve success as the leading expert on women? In short, Meredith *knows* women. The company knows women through a continual strategic effort to manage marketing information about them. In fact, Meredith's marketing information system is its core competency. That system produces customer insights that allow the company to understand women's needs and desires and maintain strong relationships with them.

It Starts with Data

Although there are lots of different ways that companies gather and manage marketing information, Meredith's core strength lies in its massive database. Meredith's database is the largest collection of customer information of any U.S. media company. With more than 85 million unduplicated names, it contains information on 80 percent of U.S. home-owning households as well as a good portion of non-home-owning households. Beyond its breadth, Meredith's database also has unsurpassed depth. On average, each name in the database has more than

700 data points attached to it. If that doesn't impress you, think about how many pieces of information you could write down about your family members, best friends, or even yourself. Those 700 data points allow Meredith to truly know each person on an intimate level.

The basic information in Meredith's database comes from typical internal company sources. Information gathered through sales transactions alone is huge. This includes not only descriptive and demographic information, but also information on which magazines customers buy, to which magazines they subscribe, what kinds of incentive offers they like, and how they have responded to particular creative executions. The database also incorporates additional internal information from product shipments, customer satisfaction surveys, and Web site visits for each specific customer. Although most companies have no idea how to process and handle all that information, Meredith effectively puts it all into one place so that managers throughout the company can access it.

Beyond gathering information from internal sources, Meredith also conducts marketing research. Online and traditional surveys allow Meredith to dig deeper into attitudinal information. One of the focal points is questions about customers' life events. "Are you having a baby, are your kids about to go to school, are your oldest kids about to graduate, are you thinking about retiring?" explains Cheryl Dahlquist, director of database marketing services at Meredith. "As much as we can, we'd like to know that information because we feel like those are the things that influence really what's happening with someone." Knowing a single life event can tell a lot about a person's needs and wants. However, possessing updated information on dozens of life events for a given person becomes very powerful.

Yet, all the information in the world means little unless you can make sense of it. Fortunately, Meredith is as skilled at analyzing and using database information as it is collecting it. Through complex statistical analysis, Meredith learns about each customer's interests and how those interests evolve throughout the customer's life. Through a concept Meredith calls "passion points," the company computes scores for numerous different interest areas, such as cooking, fitness, and gardening. It then segments each interest area into specifics, such that fitness becomes running, yoga, and hiking, to name just a few. Multiple data points feed into each score.

In this manner, Meredith not only knows what your primary interests are, it also knows how your interest levels compare to those of everyone else in the database. "We've developed through our statistical group the ability to say when somebody reaches a certain score, that's when they're really hot to trot in [say] cooking, and they're ready to respond to just about all the offers that come their way around the cooking category." Meredith employs 20 predictive analytical models, each designed to rank the order of a person's interests. All 20 models are scored and ranked each week. That's how Meredith gets to know women.

Putting Customer Insights to Use

Based on the valuable insights that it extracts from its database, Meredith manages relationships with its customers through various means. For starters, customer insights not only drive the content of its media products, they drive the development of new products. For example, over the years, *Better Homes and Gardens* has spawned spin-offs such as *Country Home* and *Traditional Home*, not to mention BHG.com and the cable program *Better*.

But the insights that come from Meredith's marketing information system also tell the company which products are the most relevant to a given individual. And with its large and holistic portfolio of products, there is something for almost everyone. David Ball, vice president of consumer marketing for Meredith, explains how this works: "We had *American Baby* at the very early stages of a woman going into the homeowning and child rearing years. We filled in with *Parents* and *Family Circle*. *American Baby* is prenatal, *Parents* is postnatal, *Family Circle* is teens and tweens. And so now we're able to take someone who subscribes to *American Baby* and really graduate them into our other products."

The fruits of managing customer information don't stop at matching the right product to the customer. Rich customer insights allow Meredith to meet customer needs when it comes to promotion and pricing as well. Because Meredith has so many media products, almost all of its promotional efforts are either through direct mail and e-mail or cross-promoting across titles. Based on what it knows about specific customers, Meredith customizes the types of offers and messages contained in its promotions, often in real time. This makes promotional efforts much more effective and much less costly. "I don't want to be sending out a million pieces of direct mail if I could send out a hundred thousand pieces of direct mail only to the people who really want it," says Ball. If you think about it, this is marketing at its finest. When customers and potential customers aren't bothered by irrelevant messages and products, but are approached only with offers that actually interest them, everyone wins.

Meredith's ability to manage marketing information has opened other doors for the company. Given its vast database and its skill at managing information, Meredith can sell marketing research to other companies that need insights on women. Its strength in managing marketing information has also resulted in numerous partnerships with leading companies such as Home Depot, DirectTV, Chrysler, and Carnival Cruise Lines. In addition, Meredith's database and research efforts have resulted in something else that may be a first: The Meredith Engagement Dividend, a program that guarantees Meredith advertisers an increase in sales. Meredith can make such a guarantee because, based on information in its database, advertisers are able to increase their product sales by an average of 10 percent over a one-year period.

As a whole, magazine advertising has been decreasing for years, and the decline is projected to continue in the coming years. Meredith's flat revenues over the past five years suggest that, as a company, it is still heavily tied to print media for distributing its content. But with a consistent profit margin of 8 to 10 percent of sales, Meredith is holding its own. More importantly, Meredith's core competency of managing customer information is not exclusive to print. It is something that will fuel the company's expansion into other, faster growing media. As

Meredith maintains its marketing information system strategy, it will continue to develop the right products, price, distribution methods, and promotions for each and every woman in its database.

Questions for Discussion

1. Analyze Meredith's marketing information system. What are its strengths and weaknesses?

2. Can impersonal data points really result in meaningful relationships? Explain.

3. Does Meredith's marketing information expertise transfer into other media and products?

4. As a company still heavily rooted in print, what does Meredith's future hold?

5. What recommendations would you make to Meredith's executives?

Sources: Officials at Meredith Corporation contributed to and supported the development of this case. Additional information comes from www.meredith.com, August 2011.

Company Case 5

Porsche: Guarding the Old While Bringing in the New

Porsche (pronounced *Porsh*-uh) is a unique company. It has always been a niche brand that makes cars for a small and distinctive segment of automobile buyers. Porsche recently had annual sales of only 27,717 cars among the five models it sells in the United States. By comparison, Honda sold about 10 times that many Accords alone. But Porsche owners are as rare as their vehicles. For that reason, top managers at Porsche spend a great deal of time thinking about customers. They want to know who their customers are, what they think, and how they feel. They want to know why they buy a Porsche rather than a Jaguar, or a Ferrari, or a big Mercedes Coupe. These are challenging questions to answer—even Porsche owners themselves don't know exactly what motivates their buying. But given Porsche's low volume and the increasingly fragmented auto market, it is imperative that management understand its customers and what gets their motors running.

Profile of a Porsche Owner

Porsche was founded in 1931 by Ferdinand Porsche, the man credited for designing the original Volkswagen Beetle, known as Adolf Hitler's "people's car" and one of the most successful car designs of all time. For most of its first two decades, the company built Volkswagen Beetles for German citizens while making tanks and Beetles for the military. As Porsche AG began to sell cars under its own nameplate in the 1950s and 1960s, a few constants developed. The company sold very few models, creating an image of exclusivity. Those models had a rounded, bubble shape that had its roots in the original Beetle but evolved into something more Porsche-like with the world famous 356 and 911 models. Finally, Porsche's automobiles featured air-cooled four- and six-cylinder "boxer" motors (cylinders in an opposed configuration) in the rear of the car. This gave the cars a unique and often dangerous characteristic—a tendency for the rear-end to swing out when cornering hard. That's one of the reasons that Porsche owners were drawn to them: since they were challenging to drive, most people stayed away.

Since its early days, Porsche has appealed to a very narrow segment of financially successful people. These are achievers who see themselves as entrepreneurial, even if they work for a corporation. They set very high goals for themselves and then work doggedly to meet them. These people expect no less from the clothes they wear, the restaurants they go to, or the cars they drive. They see themselves not as a part of the regular world, but as exceptions to it. They buy Porsches because the car mirrors their self-image—it stands for the things owners like to see in themselves and in their lives.

Most of us buy what Porsche executives call utility vehicles. That is, we buy cars to go to work, to deliver the kids, and to run errands. Because we have to use our cars to accomplish these daily tasks, we base buying decisions on features such as price, size, fuel economy, and other practical considerations. But Porsche is more than a utility car. Its owners see it as a car to be enjoyed, not just used. Most Porsche buyers are not moved by information, but by feelings. A Porsche is like a piece of clothing, something the owner "wears" and is seen in. Owners develop a personal relationship with their cars, one that has more to do with the way the car sounds, vibrates, and feels than how many cup holders it has or how much cargo it can hold in the trunk. They admire their Porsche because it is a competent performance machine without being flashy or phony.

People buy Porsches because they enjoy driving. If all they needed was something to get them from point A to point B, they could find something much less expensive. And while many Porsche owners are car enthusiasts, some of them are not. One successful businesswoman and owner of a high-end Porsche said, "When I drive this car to the high school to pickup my daughter, I end up with five youngsters in the car. If I drive any other car, I can't even find her; she doesn't want to come home."

From Niche to Numerous

For the first few decades, Porsche AG lived by the philosophy of Ferry Porsche, Ferdinand's son. Ferry created the Porsche 356 because no one else made a car like the one he wanted. "We did not market research, we had no sales forecasts, no return-on-investment calculations. None of that. I very simply built my dream car and figured that there would be other people who share that dream." So really, Porsche AG from the beginning was very much like its customers: an achiever that set out to make the very best.

But as the years rolled on, Porsche management became concerned with a significant issue: Were there enough Porsche buyers to keep the company afloat? Granted, the company never had illusions of churning out the number of cars produced by Chevrolet or Toyota. But to fund innovation, even a niche manufacturer has to grow a little. And Porsche began to worry that the quirky nature of the people who buy Porsches might just run out on them.

This led Porsche to extend its brand outside the box. In the early 1970s, Porsche introduced the 914, a square-ish, mid-engine, two-seater that was much cheaper than the 911. This meant that a different class of people could afford a Porsche. It was no surprise that the 914 became Porsche's top selling model. By the late 1970s, Porsche replaced the 914 with a hatchback coupe that had something no other regular Porsche model had ever had: an engine in the front. At less than $20,000, more than $10,000 less than the 911, the 924 and later 944 models were once again Porsche's pitch to affordability. At one point, Porsche increased its sales goal by nearly 50 percent to 60,000 cars a year.

Although these cars were in many respects sales successes, the Porsche faithful cried foul. They considered these entry-level models to be cheap and underperforming. Most loyalists never really accepted these models as "real" Porsches. In fact, they were not at all happy that they had to share their brand with a customer who didn't fit the Porsche owner profile. They were turned off by what they saw as a corporate strategy that had focused on *mass* over *class* marketing. This tarnished image was compounded by the fact that Nissan, Toyota, BMW, and other car makers had ramped up high-end sports car offerings, creating some fierce competition. In fact, both the Datsun 280-ZX and the Toyota Supra were not only cheaper than Porsche's 944, they were faster. A struggling economy threw more sand in Porsche's tank. By 1990, Porsche sales had plummeted and the company flirted with bankruptcy.

Return to Its Roots?

But Porsche wasn't going down without a fight. It quickly recognized the error of its ways and halted production of the entry-level models. It rebuilt its damaged image by revamping its higher-end model lines with more race-bred technology. In an effort to regain rapport with customers, Porsche once again targeted the high end of the market in both price and performance. It set modest sales goals and decided that moderate growth with higher margins would be more profitable in the long term. The company set out to make one less Porsche than the public demanded. According to one executive, "We're not looking for volume, we're searching for exclusivity."

Porsche's efforts had the desired effect. By the late 1990s, the brand was once again favored by the same type of achiever who had so deeply loved the car for decades. The cars were once again exclusive, and the company was once again profitable. But by the early 2000s, Porsche management was asking itself a familiar question: To have a sustainable future, could

Porsche rely on only the Porsche faithful? According to then CEO Wendelin Wiedeking, "For Porsche to remain independent, it can't be dependent on the most fickle segment in the market. We don't want to become just a marketing department of some giant. We have to make sure we're profitable enough to pay for future development ourselves."

So in 2002, Porsche did the unthinkable. It became one of the last car companies to jump into the insatiable SUV market. At roughly 5,000 pounds, the new Porsche Cayenne was heavier than anything that Porsche had ever made with the exception of some prototype tanks it made during World War II. Once again, the new model featured an engine up front. And it was the first Porsche to ever be equipped with seatbelts for five. As news spread about the car's development, howls could be heard from Porsche's customer base.

This time, however, Porsche did not seem too concerned that the loyalists would be put off. Could it be that the company had already forgotten what happened the last time it deviated from the mold? After driving one of the first Cayenne's off the assembly line, one journalist stated, "A day at the wheel of the 444 horsepower Cayenne Turbo leaves two overwhelming impressions. First, the Cayenne doesn't behave or feel like an SUV, and second, it drives like a Porsche." This was no entry-level car. Porsche had created a two-and-a-half ton beast that could accelerate to 60 miles per hour in just over five seconds, corner like it was on rails, and hit 165 miles per hour, all while coddling five adults in sumptuous leather seats with almost no wind noise from the outside world. On top of that, it could keep up with a Land Rover when the pavement ended. Indeed, Porsche had created the Porsche of SUVs.

Last year, Porsche upped the ante one more time by unveiling another large vehicle. But this time, it was a low-slung, five-door luxury sedan. The Porsche faithful and the automotive press again gasped in disbelief. But by the time the Panamera hit the pavement, Porsche had proven once again that Porsche customers could have their cake and eat it, too. The Panamera is almost as big as the Cayenne but can move four adults down the road at speeds of up to 188 miles per hour and accelerate from a standstill to 60 miles per hour in four seconds flat.

Although some Porsche traditionalists would never be caught dead driving a front engine Porsche that has more than two doors, Porsche insists that two trends will sustain these new models. First, a category of Porsche buyers has moved into life stages that have them facing inescapable needs—they need to haul more people and stuff. This not only applies to certain regular Porsche buyers, but also to new buyers entering its dealerships who otherwise wouldn't have considered a Porsche. This time, the price points of the new vehicles are drawing only the well-healed, allowing Porsche to maintain its exclusivity. These buyers also seem to fit the achiever profile of regular Porsche buyers.

The second trend is the growth of emerging economies. Whereas the United States has long been the world's biggest consumer of Porsches, the company expects China to become its biggest customer before too long. Twenty years ago, the United States accounted for about 50 percent of Porsche's worldwide sales. Now, it only buys about 26 percent. In China, many people who can afford to buy a car as expensive as a Porsche also hire a chauffer. The Cayenne and the Panamera are perfect for those who want to be driven around in style but who may also want to make a quick getaway if necessary.

The most recent economic downturn has brought down the sales of just about every maker of premium automobiles. When times are tough, buying a car like a Porsche is the ultimate deferrable purchase. But as this downturn turns back up, Porsche is better poised than it has ever been to meet the needs of its customer base. It is also in better shape than ever to maintain its brand image with the Porsche faithful, and with others as well. Sure, understanding Porsche buyers is still a difficult task. But one former chief executive of Porsche summed it up this way: "If you really want to understand our customers, you have to understand the phrase, 'If I were going to be a car, I'd be a Porsche.'"

Questions for Discussion

1. Analyze the buyer decision process of a traditional Porsche customer. What conclusions can you draw?

2. How does the traditional Porsche customer decision process contrast with the decision process for a Cayenne or Panamera customer?

3. Which concepts from the chapter explain why Porsche sold so many lower-priced models in the 1970s and 1980s?

4. Explain how both positive and negative attitudes toward a brand like Porsche develop. How might Porsche change consumer attitudes toward the brand?

5. What role does the Porsche brand play in the self-concept of its buyers?

Sources: Christoph Rauwald, "Porsche Raises Outlook," *Wall Street Journal*, June 18, 2010, accessed at www.wsj.com; Jonathan Welsh, "Porsche Relies Increasingly on Sales in China," *Wall Street Journal*, April 2, 2010, accessed at www.wsj.com; David Gumpert, "Porsche on Nichemanship," *Harvard Business Review*, March/April 1986, pp. 98–106; Peter Robinson, "Porsche Cayenne—Driving Impression," *Car and Driver*, January 2003, accessed at www.caranddriver.com; Jens Meiners, "2010 Porsche Panamera S/4S/Turbo—First Drive Review," *Car and Driver*, June 2009, accessed at www.caranddriver.com.

Company Case 6

Darden Restaurants: Balancing Standardization and Differentiation

You may have never heard of Darden Restaurants, but you've probably eaten one of the more than 400 million meals it serves up every year in its more than 1,800 restaurants. Darden Restaurants includes niche-type brands such as The Capital Grille, Bahama Breeze, and Seasons 52. But you're probably more familiar with Olive Garden, Red Lobster, and LongHorn Steakhouse. Together, these chains account for more than $7 billion a year in revenues, making Darden Restaurants the largest full-service restaurant operation in the United States. Darden isn't just big, however. It is also a pioneer of what is now known as *casual dining*, a category that has become so popular that it accounts for 39 percent of all sit-down restaurant meals.

Darden has become a dominant industry force by forging a strategy of standardization and collaboration. Tearing a page from the Walmart playbook, Darden employs leading-edge technology across multiple brands to make the notoriously unpredictable restaurant business more efficient. At the $100 million state-of-the-art Darden corporate headquarters in Orlando, Florida, executives and support staff for all Darden brands work under the same roof. Test kitchens for each brand operate side by side. Darden encourages and expects employees from each chain to share information and best practices.

At the operating level, each individual Darden restaurant is a just-in-time manufacturing plant, using standardized preparation and service methods. This allows each restaurant to create a wide range of products in minutes that are selected, consumed, and judged by customers who show up unannounced. An order-processing program called "meal pacing" helps restaurant personnel turn tables around faster. That has not only generated higher revenues but also higher chain-wide guest-satisfaction scores. Darden's forecasting software is also the best in the business. Each restaurant, no matter what the brand, can pull up a forecast for any hour of any day that is within 1 to 4 percent of actual turnout. This has enabled Darden to reduce unplanned workforce hours by 40 percent and trim excess food costs by 10 percent.

In addition to these standardized practices, Darden chains also share a seafood-sourcing network that contracts directly with fish farms in more than 32 countries. This system, put into place by founder Bill Darden, gives Darden an advantage in setting prices and ensuring supply. Darden Restaurants also benefit from corporate initiatives that protect and enhance sea life ecosystems. This isn't just an effort to save the world. Each of its chains would suffer without a steady flow of affordable seafood.

Thus, standardized practices have played a key role in Darden's rise to dominance. But perhaps the biggest secret to Darden's success doesn't lie in its ability to standardize its operations. Rather, it lies in the company's ability to make brands with similar underlying operations distinct. Darden has spent decades segmenting and targeting dining patrons. Much like P&G, Darden's brands are so well differentiated and positioned—with its corporate name so low-profile—that the vast majority of patrons have no idea that the chains have a common owner. According to CEO Clarence Otis, that's because Darden doesn't leave anything to chance. "You hear people in the restaurant industry say, 'I have a feel for the business.'" But Otis is not one of those people. Instead, as his predecessors did before him, Otis guides the Darden brands by making use of marketing intelligence and analytics. "The direction of our business is based on understanding customers." That understanding contributes to the distinct positioning of each of the company's major chains.

Olive Garden: "When You're Here, You're Family."

With its heaping bowls of pasta and all-you-can-eat breadsticks, Olive Garden contributes half of Darden's revenues. Olive Garden was launched in the early 1980s as an affordable Italian restaurant—a safe choice, but nothing particularly notable. By the 1990s, it had hundreds of locations, a stale menu, and declining sales. But it didn't take long for Darden to turn Olive Garden into a hot concept. According to Drew Madsen, chief operating officer for the nation's biggest Italian restaurant chain, the key customer insight gleaned from Olive Garden's research was that people go to a restaurant for emotional as well as physical nourishment. In fact, emotional nourishment is most important; it stays with people much longer after they walk out the door.

Today, Olive Garden builds its strategy around the concept of a mythical Italian family. No doubt you've seen some of Olive Garden's "When you're here, you're family" commercials, showing Italian family members enjoying a meal together. Olive Garden locations are designed to suggest an Italian farmhouse with a large family-style table. And the menu at Olive Garden has been cultivated through a partnership with real Italians at Olive Garden's Culinary Institute of Tuscany. That's where corporate and restaurant chefs are exposed to authentic Italian recipes and cooking techniques.

All this has led to an authentic Italian eating experience that is rare for a large chain. Hard-core foodies might scoff at the suggestion that Olive Garden is authentic Italian. But the chain has made staples of Chianti-braised short ribs, portobello mushrooms, and risotto. A decade ago, most of middle America had never heard of such culinary ingredients. And when compared to former Olive Garden menu items like Italian nachos, the current fare demonstrates the improved and authentic focus of today's Olive Garden.

Red Lobster: "The Taste of Wood-Grilled Seafood."

The second-biggest brand in Darden's portfolio is also the oldest. Founder Bill Darden opened the first Red Lobster in Lakeland, Florida, in 1968 after 30 years in the restaurant business. He saw a gap in the market between the still-young fast-food concept and upscale white-tablecloth restaurants. His new seafood restaurant filled the niche. And while Bill Darden had seen success as a restaurateur, Red Lobster was the breakthrough concept for expanding to a regional, then national level. In fact, the company is credited with introducing middle America to the wonders of fried shrimp.

But after more than 35 years of expansion and growth, Red Lobster's sales began to flounder. In 2004, quarterly same-store sales dropped for the first time in five years. Darden had taken its eye off the fish market, sticking to the way it had always done things even as consumer trends shifted. At that point, Darden's research indicated that consumers regarded Red Lobster as an out-of-date fried-fish shack.

To turn things around, even at the risk of alienating its core customers, management made substantial changes to Red Lobster's positioning, changes even more extensive than those made to turn Olive Garden around. At the center of these changes was a concept called "stealth health." The chain developed a new menu around wood-fired grilling, which required extensive investments in equipment and training. Classic Red Lobster fans needn't have worried too much, though—they can still get fried scallops and popcorn shrimp. But grilled items now make up one-third of the offerings. Red Lobster's new pitch is: "The taste of wood-grilled seafood." And each restaurant prints a new fresh-fish menu twice a day. Combined with an extensive remodeling plan, the strategic changes will cost Red Lobster more than $350 million. But as an indication that its new healthy strategy is more than just talk, the chain was recently dubbed "best sit-down chain in America" by *Men's Health* magazine.

LongHorn Steakhouse: "The Flavor of the West."

With about $1 billion in annual revenues, LongHorn Steakhouse is Darden's third-largest and newest brand, acquired as part of a 2007 purchase. The chain is still in the process of being "Dardenized." But Darden CEO Clarence Otis and LongHorn Steakhouse president Dave George see it as the concept with the most potential. They expect that sales could double in only a few more years. Steak is the second-biggest casual dining sector. LongHorn Steakhouse already has just over 350 restaurants, making it the perfect challenger to the market leader, Outback Steakhouse. Moreover, until just recently, all LongHorn Steakhouse restaurants were in the eastern half of the United States, giving it plenty of room for westward expansion.

Darden has infused LongHorn Steakhouse with the same authenticity and hospitality that have served its other brands so well. Proclaiming itself as "The Flavor of the West," it welcomes "guests into a warm, relaxing atmosphere reminiscent of a Western rancher's home, where friendly, attentive servers help them unwind and savor a great steakhouse meal." Darden has added a touch of class to the old LongHorn Steakhouse. It serves only fresh steaks, chicken, and fish, and the menu has been dressed up with variations on common steakhouse themes, such as steak stuffed with fontina cheese and wild mushrooms. The burgers have been stripped of unwieldy garnishes. In addition, changes to the dining room include replacing musty old deer heads with cowboy sculptures by Frederic Remington. As a result, LongHorn Steakhouse customer traffic is sizzling, even more than at Olive Garden or Red Lobster.

Achieving the Perfect Balance

Although the performance of Darden's big three chains has been historically strong, like most restaurants today, it faces new challenges. The economic environment of the past few years has tightened consumer dining-out budgets. Even more troubling to the industry, sit-down dining has been on the decline for some 17 years. Today, the average American eats 16 percent fewer sit-down meals. At the same time, the number of casual-dining restaurants has grown twice as fast as the U.S. population. Although the restaurant industry as a whole is showing signs of recovery, projected growth is expected is be much more moderate than the rapid growth they experienced during the 1990s. All this means that Darden's future growth will have to come primarily through taking market share from competitors.

Darden outperformed the rest of the industry throughout the recent Great Recession, with same-store sales at Olive Garden and LongHorn Steakhouse growing and Red Lobster sales dropping only slightly. But the gap between Darden's and competitors' same-store sales is narrowing, an indication that competitors are stepping up their games. Darden also faces rising food and energy costs, an issue that will have to be carefully balanced with price increases so as not to frighten off customers.

Still, Darden Restaurants hold a competitive advantage based on scale, standardization across brands, and expertise in market segmentation and targeting. Darden is constantly tweaking its formula to achieve the best mix of independence and collaboration among its brands. Darden's different chains may use the same technologies to pace cooking and predict dinner traffic, and they may all serve salmon from the same Norwegian fish farms. But COO Madsen knows that each brand must retain its distinctive positioning. "It's all about balance. There's an art and science to this." For Darden, that means that whatever collaboration takes place across its brands, no one is messing with Olive Garden's breadsticks or Red Lobster's cheese biscuits.

Questions for Discussion

1. How does Darden segment and target the sit-down dining market? Use the full spectrum of segmentation variables in your response.

2. Has Darden differentiated and positioned its brands effectively? Explain.

3. Although Darden's efforts to standardize across brands have contributed to its success, how might such practices backfire?

4. Given current conditions, will Darden Restaurants continue to dominate the market? Why or why not?

5. What recommendations would you make that will help Darden's future growth?

Sources: Shobhana Chandra and Anthony Feld, "Dining Out Is in as Tax Cuts Lift Darden, Texas Roadhouse Sales," *Bloomberg Businessweek*, March 15, 2011, accessed at www.businessweek.com; Kelly Evans, "After a Few Lean Years, Darden Looks to Feast," *Wall Street Journal*, December 20, 2010, p. C1; Joan E. Solsman, "New Restaurants Lift Darden Profits," *Wall Street Journal*, December 21, 2010, p. B5; Chuck Salter, "Why America Is Addicted to Olive Garden," *Fast Company*, July 1, 2009, p. 102; and quotes and other information are from www.darden.com, November 2011.

Company Case 7

Las Vegas: What's Not Happening in Vegas

When you hear someone mention Las Vegas, what comes to mind? Sin City? Wholesome entertainment for the entire family? An indulgent luxury vacation? Or perhaps a value-oriented reward for hard-working Americans? If you answered "all of the above," you wouldn't necessarily be wrong. The truth is, all of these have been characteristics associated with Las Vegas over the years. In recent times, the Las Vegas Convention and Visitors Authority (LVCVA) fielded several national ad campaigns. Tourism is Vegas's biggest industry, and the LVCVA is charged with maintaining the city's brand image and keeping the visitors coming to one of the world's most famous cities.

Although the positioning of the Vegas brand has changed from time to time, the town will probably never entirely lose the "Sin City" label. That title was born when Las Vegas was young—an anything-goes gambling town full of smoke-filled casinos, bawdy all-girl revues, all-you-can-eat buffets, Elvis impersonators, and no-wait weddings on the Vegas Strip. This was the Vegas epitomized by the Rat Pack, when Frank Sinatra, Dean Martin, Sammy Davis Jr., and the rest of the crew appeared nightly on stage to standing room only crowds at the Sands Hotel. Sinatra was even known for referring to anywhere that wasn't Las Vegas as "dullsville."

But as the 1990s rolled around, many Las Vegas officials felt that the town needed to broaden its target audience. So they set out to appeal to—of all things—families. Some of the biggest casinos on the strip built roller coasters and other thrill rides, world-class water parks, and family-friendly shows like Treasure Island's live-action swashbuckler spectacle, visible to everyone passing by on the street. Although this strategy seemed effective for a brief time, Vegas marketers came to realize that the family image just didn't sync well with the classic vices that were still alive and well in Vegas.

As the LVCVA started to consider its options, the terrorist attacks of September 11, 2001, dealt Las Vegas tourism one of its worst blows ever. Declining tourism led to 15,000 lost jobs. The LVCVA decided that it was time to unabashedly proclaim that Las Vegas was a destination for adults. That didn't just mean a return to the classic vices. The LVCVA engineered an image of Vegas as a luxury destination oozing with excess and indulgence. Gone were the theme parks, replaced by five-star resorts, high-rise condos, expansive shopping malls filled with the world's top luxury brands, and restaurants bearing the names of world-renowned chefs. Family-friendly entertainment was replaced by a new breed of high-dollar stage shows for adult audiences. This change of strategy worked. Even as Las Vegas struggled through economic recovery in the post 9-11 world, visitors returned in record numbers.

However, to Rossi Ralenkotter, CEO of the LVCVA, it soon became apparent that the town was much more than just an assortment of facilities and amenities. "We talked to old customers and new customers to determine the essence of the brand of Las Vegas," he said. The LVCVA found that to the nearly

40 million who flocked to the city each year, Vegas is an emotional connection, a total brand experience.

And just what *is* the "Las Vegas experience"? Research shows that when people come to Las Vegas, they're a little naughtier—a little less inhibited. They stay out longer, eat more, do some gambling, and spend more on shopping and dining. "We found that [the Las Vegas experience] centered on adult freedom," says Ralenkotter. "People could stay up all night and do things they wouldn't normally do in their own towns."

Based on these customer insights, the LVCVA coined the now-familiar catchphrase—"Only Vegas: What happens here, stays here." The phrase captured the essence of the Las Vegas experience—that it's okay to be a little naughty in Vegas. That simple phrase became the centerpiece of what is now deemed one of the most successful tourism campaigns in history. The campaign transformed Las Vegas's image from one of the down-and-dirty "Sin City" to the enticing and luxurious "Only Vegas."

The $75 million ad campaign showed the naughty nature of people once they arrive in Las Vegas. In one ad, a woman spontaneously married a visibly younger man in a Las Vegas wedding chapel. Then, ignoring his ardent pleas, she kissed him goodbye and pulled herself away, insisting that she had to get back to her business convention. In another ad, an outgoing young woman is shown introducing herself to various men, each time giving a different name. In a third ad, a sexy woman hops into a limo, flirts with the driver, and emerges from the car at the airport for her trip home as a conservative business woman. At the end of each ad was the simple reminder, "What happens here, stays here."

The LVCVA continued investing heavily in the bold and provocative campaign and in a variation on the theme, "Your Vegas is showing." All the while, Las Vegas experienced its biggest growth boom in history. Hotel occupancy rates hovered at an incredible 90 percent, visitors came in ever-increasing numbers, and there was seemingly no end to the construction of lavish new luxury properties. To top it all off, Las Vegas was dubbed the number two hottest brand by respected brand consultancy Landor Associates, right behind Google. It seemed that the LVCVA had found the magic formula and that Vegas had found its true identity. With everything going so well, what could possibly go wrong?

The city found out in 2008, when Las Vegas suffered another one-two punch. First, the worst recession since the Great Depression had consumers scaling back on unnecessary expenses. Second, in the wake of government bailouts and a collapsing financial industry, company CEOs and executives everywhere came under scrutiny for lavish expenses. Suddenly, Las Vegas's carefully nurtured, naughty, indulgent image made even prudent, serious company conferences held there look bad. It didn't help matters when President Obama delivered a statement that Las Vegas mayor, Oscar Goodman, perceived as the straw that broke the camel's back. Obama scolded Wall Street executives by saying, "You can't get corporate jets, you can't go take a trip to Las Vegas or go down to the Super Bowl on the taxpayer's dime." Whether or not the president's comment actually affected tourism in Vegas, Goodman took the statement as a direct hit on the Las Vegas economy. As a result of the new economic realities, both leisure travel and the convention industry—two staples in Las Vegas's success—took a big hit.

As a result, 2008 and 2009 were some of the worst years ever for Las Vegas. For 2009, the total number of visitors dropped to 36.4 million, 7 percent less than the 2007 peak of 39.1 million. This translated into a 24 percent decrease in convention attendance, a 22 percent drop in room occupancy, and a 10 percent decline in gambling revenues. "People aren't coming in the numbers they used to, and those that are bet on the cheaper tables" said Steven Kent, an analyst for Goldman Sachs. Nevada's unemployment rate climbed to one of the highest levels in the United States. The Las Vegas hospitality industry responded by chopping prices. Rooms on the strip could be had for as cheaply as $25 a night. Gourmet meals were touted for half-price. The town was practically begging for visitors.

After years of successfully pedaling Vegas naughtiness as the primary selling point, the LVCVA realized it had to make a shift. So in the midst of the economic carnage, with so much to offer and great deals to be had, it focused on the value and affordability of a Vegas vacation. A new ad campaign, "Vegas Bound," urged hard-working Americans to take a well-deserved break in Las Vegas to recharge their batteries before returning home to brave the tough economy. A series of "Vegas Bound" ads and online mini-documentaries showed average Americans in high-end nightclubs, spas, and restaurants. One grinning 81-year-old woman was even shown giving a thumbs-up after an indoor skydiving session.

"We had to think how we should address our customers during this financial crisis when they're reluctant to make big financial commitments," said the LVCVA's Ralenkotter at the start of the campaign. "We're appealing to Americans saying, 'You're working hard. It's OK to take a break.'" The campaign didn't eliminate glamour and luxury. Rather, it repackaged these traits in an "affordable" and "well-deserved" wrapper.

But after so many years of hearing about Las Vegas as a guilt-free adult playground, no matter what the ad campaign said, consumers had a hard time seeing Vegas as prudent. Research showed that even in a painful recession, consumers still saw Vegas for what it was: a place they could go to sample pleasures not available at home. It took the LVCVA only five months to pull the plug on "Vegas Bound" and to resurrect "What happens here, stays here." In a near 180-degree flip, Ralenkotter said, "We feel it is time to get back to our brand messaging."

Although there is rarely a magic bullet in a situation like the one Las Vegas faced, the LVCVA's return to its core brand message seems to be working. In the last couple of years, Las Vegas tourism is up. The LVCVA shows that the number of visitors increased by 9 percent in the most recent year. "I think there's pent-up demand," said Cathy Tull, senior vice president of marketing for the authority. "People want to travel, they want to escape, and Vegas works very well for that."

Just as the needle started to budge, MGM Resorts International opened the most ambitious project Las Vegas had ever seen. In fact, its $8.5 billion CityCenter was said to be the largest privately funded construction project in U.S. history. A pedestrian-friendly resort, CityCenter was designed as a small city in and of itself with four luxury hotels, two residential condo towers, and a 500,000-square-foot high-end shopping and dining center.

Adding 6,000 rooms and 12,000 jobs to the Las Vegas strip has met with mixed reactions. Some speculate that this game-changing property will put an exclamation point on Las Vegas's image and provide additional oomph in a time of crisis. "History has shown that new properties increase visitation across the board," said Ralenkotter. But others see the introduction of such a large property as hazardous to recovery. "Will it cannibalize other properties?" asked Tony Henthorne, professor and chair of tourism and convention administration at the University of Nevada at Las Vegas. "Probably so, within a short-term period."

But even as such major signs of life are sprouting up along the Vegas strip, there's an air of caution. Jim Murren, CEO for MGM, believes his company is not yet out of the woods. When asked if he thought CityCenter was in the clear, he responded emphatically, "Absolutely not. We're not declaring victory at all. We are a year or two away from even having a chance to consider that." That is probably the best attitude to take. After all, the Las Vegas Monorail just filed for bankruptcy. Two other major projects that were expected to boost the Vegas economy have also been shelved. You can still get a room on the strip for cheap. And in spite of the fact that the tourist visits are on the rise, they are still down from the 2007 peak. Although visitors are returning, they aren't spending as much, resulting in a slight decrease in spending on areas like gaming.

Las Vegas has certainly had its share of ups and downs. Times may be brightening now, but the city will face many challenges in the months and years to come. Goldman analyst

Kent expresses confidence in the brand. "For the long-term, we believe in Vegas and its ability to transform itself and attract more customers." R&R Partners, the ad agency handling the Las Vegas marketing campaigns, made an important discovery that supports Kent's point-of-view. It found through its research that, especially during hard economic times, people wanted to know that the same Vegas they've known and loved is still there.

Questions for Discussion

1. Given all the changes in the branding strategy for Las Vegas over the years, has the Vegas brand had a consistent meaning to consumers? Is this a benefit or a detriment as the city moves forward?

2. What is Las Vegas selling? What are visitors really buying? Discuss these questions in terms of the core benefit, actual product, and augmented product levels.

3. Will the most recent efforts by the LVCVA continue to work? Why or why not?

4. What recommendations would you make to the managers at the LVCVA for Las Vegas's future?

Sources: Ashley Powers and Jessica Gelt, "Another Part of Old Las Vegas Vanishes," *Los Angeles Times*, March 12, 2011, p. A1; Jeff Delong, "After a Down Year, Vegas Hoping for a Rebound," *USA Today*, May 21, 2010, p. 2A; Nancy Trejos, "Las Vegas Bets the Future on a Game-Changing New Hotel Complex," *Washington Post*, January 31, 2010, p. F01; John King, "Luck Running Low in Las Vegas," CNN .com, May 22, 2009, accessed at www.cnn.com; Tamara Audi, "Vegas Tries Luck with Old Slogan," *Wall Street Journal*, May 13, 2009, p. B5; and Tamara Audi, "Las Vegas Touts Its Affordability," *Wall Street Journal*, February 4, 2009, p. B5.

Company Case 8

Samsung: From Gallop to Run

In the world of consumer electronics, copycat brands are a dime a dozen. These are the brands consumers turn to if they don't want to pay the price for the high-end market leaders. Therefore, if consumers want a top-tier television, they'll probably look at one from Sony or LG. If they want something cheaper that's probably not quite as good, they'll look at brands such as Insignia, Dynex, or Vizio.

But what about Samsung? Believe it or not, Samsung Electronics was a maker of cheap consumer electronic knock-offs from the time it started making calculators and black-and-white TVs in 1969 through the mid-1990s. Today, however, Samsung is the world's largest television manufacturer and offers the most cutting-edge models around.

Putting the brand in context, Samsung Electronics is part of the world's largest conglomerate, South Korea's Samsung Group. Founded in 1938, the huge Samsung Group also owns

the world's second largest shipbuilder, a major global construction company, and the largest life insurance company in Korea. The conglomerate is so big that it accounts for 25 percent of all corporate profits in South Korea, well ahead of the number two Hyundai-Kia Automotive Group at 6.4 percent. Under the direction of CEO and chairman Lee Kun-hee, the third son of founder Lee Byung-Chull, Samsung Electronics has made major strides.

The New Management Strategy

In 1993, CEO Lee unveiled what he called "new management," a top-to-bottom strategy for the entire company. As part of Lee's new management, he took Samsung Electronics in a very ambitious new direction. The goal: He wanted Samsung to become a premier brand that would dethrone Sony as the biggest consumer electronics firm in the world. Instead of being a copycat, Samsung was to become a cutting-edge product leader. The company hired a new crop of fresh, young designers who unleashed a torrent of new products—not humdrum, me-too products, but sleek, bold, and beautiful products targeting high-end users. Samsung called them "lifestyle works of art." Every new product had to pass the "Wow!" test: If it didn't get a "Wow!" reaction during market testing, it went straight back to the design studio.

As part of Samsung's revamped strategy and positioning, along with developing stylish and innovative new products, the company altered distribution to match. It abandoned low-end distributors such as Walmart and Kmart, and instead built strong relationships with specialty retailers such as Best Buy and Circuit City. "We're not el cheapo anymore," said one Samsung designer.

In less than two decades, Samsung Electronics has achieved its lofty goals—and much more. Last year, the company rang up revenues of $143 billion with profits of $15 billion. Compare that to Sony at $88 billion in revenues and a net loss of almost $3.2 billion. Interbrand crowned Samsung as the world's fastest growing brand over one five-year period. Recently, Samsung hit number 19 on Interbrand's list of most valuable global brands as Sony fell to number 34.

Samsung is now by far the largest consumer electronics company in the world and has been since 2005. It's the world's largest TV manufacturer and second-largest cell phone producer. Samsung competes strongly in the markets for DVD players, home theaters, digital cameras and camcorders, home appliances, and laser printers. But more than just making finished consumer products, Samsung Electronics is also the world's largest technology electronic components company. It makes a sizable share of the LCD and LED panels, mobile displays, and telecommunication used in other company's products. It's also the world's largest manufacturer of flash memory.

Works of Art

Most impressive, Samsung has become more than just big. It has also achieved its goal to become a producer of state-of-the-art products. In fact, both *Fast Company* and *BusinessWeek* recently placed Samsung high on their lists of most innovative companies. As evidence of its design prowess, Samsung took home eight prizes at the International Design Excellence Awards (IDEA), where entries are judged based on appearance, functionality, and the thinking behind each one. Design darling Apple took home only seven awards.

Consider some of this year's winners. A Samsung "Touch of Color" Blu-ray DVD player featuring a hint of red tone blended naturally into a piano black frame had the judges ogling. Comments indicated that, with color and appearance that changed in different lighting, the DVD player looked like a work of art made of glass. Samsung's Luxia LED TV series also packed "Wow!" appeal. With specs that exceed anything on the market, a 55-inch model is a mere one-inch thick and weighs just 49 pounds. Samsung's EcoFit monitors feature a transparent stand that gives the appearance of floating in the air. The Samsung YP-S2 Pebble is part MP3 player, part fashion item. Designed to conjure up images of nature with its pebble-shape and stunning colors, it can be worn around the neck and sports five tactile keys that make it simple enough for Grandma to use. And the Samsung Kiwi mini notebook PC is a 10-inch laptop that is high-tech, convenient, cute, and familiar all at once. These and the other Samsung winners at last year's IDEA

Awards earned Samsung the designation of "a company that's hitting its design stride."

Samsung is moving many of its product categories forward. For example, as the mobile phone industry moves from "dumbphones" to smartphones, Samsung aims to double its share of the higher-end market from 5 to 10 percent. With the release of its latest high-tech communication phone, the Galaxy S, Samsung no doubt has a shot. One industry analyst says, "Samsung may easily meet [its] target as the handset market is sharply transferring to smartphones and the hardware features of the Galaxy S are pretty competitive in the market." Running on Google's new Android operating system, the phone features a four-inch screen, an e-book reader, a five-megapixel camera, and a high-definition video recorder and player. But perhaps the best thing going for it is the fact that it will not be tied exclusively to any single carrier, as are many of the top smartphones. The Galaxy S will be offered by more than 100 mobile operators around the world.

Mabuljungje

Lee was recently named top CEO of the Decade by *Fortune* Korea. True to that title, he has just recently announced that the "new management" is now old news. After 17 years of remarkable success, Lee admitted that the world's largest technology firm's current main products may likely become obsolete within the next ten years. That forward thinking has him again in reform mode. He has dubbed Samsung's newest strategy *mabuljungje*, a Chinese axiom that means "horse that does not stop." In a memo to Samsung employees, Lee said, "The 'new management' doctrine for the past 17 years helped catapult the company into being one of the world's best electronics makers. Now is not a time to be complacent but a time to run."

As with any truly forward thinking, innovative company, Samsung doesn't claim to know what will replace today's products as they become obsolete. Rather, it is investing heavily to ensure that it is the company that develops them. Samsung recently unveiled a $23 billion investment plan, its biggest to date. That amount is three times the one that Samsung discarded only months earlier. It's also bigger than the combined investment budgets of Intel, IBM, and Sony. Much of this year's budget is earmarked for capital expenditures, new equipment, and plants to ensure that Samsung stays ahead of the game. The rest is for research and development. At a groundbreaking ceremony for a new chip plant outside of Seoul, Lee announced that, despite Samsung's past success, the company risked losing market share if it did not completely overhaul its business model.

According to Timothy Baxter, president of Samsung Electronics America, as a major pillar of mabuljungje, Samsung will capitalize on interactivity—as in mobile phones with TVs and TVs with the Internet. Samsung's future will bring many products that will talk to each other. At a recent expo, Baxter stared at a pair of aces displayed on his Samsung Omnia II mobile phone. After tapping a few phone buttons, up popped a poker table on a Samsung big-screen TV with a pile of cards held by his opponent—a poker buddy in another city. "There's no reason these phones can't interact with the TV," Baxter said, indicating that if he has his way, Texas Hold 'em is just the first in a series of such synergistic exchanges.

But such advances in product interactivity go beyond just presenting consumers with flashy hardware features. They will take Samsung into a competition for consumer eyeballs with companies such as Apple. Samsung knows that it cannot thrive in the long term by merely offering sharper colors or better sound quality. Pricing power comes only from unique features or control over content. Samsung is putting plenty of resources into discovering the unique features. But its investment strategy will also position Samsung as somewhat of a broker between advertisers and the devices that carry the ads. Although Samsung is now hush-hush about its plans, it has announced its intention to unveil a tablet computer and an app store similar to Apple's that will give Samsung control over that content. Samsung sees apps as an advertising vehicle of the future.

In its favor, Samsung has access to a piece of the puzzle that Apple doesn't—big screens. Thus, as its small devices interact with its Web-enabled TVs, Samsung could bring in lots of ad dollars from companies eager to pitch their products on screens 25 times the size of an iPhone's. If successful, Samsung will pose a threat not only to Apple but to cable companies as well. That's because the type of network that Samsung has planned will also make it a data collector, privy to insight about the kinds of applications its TV owners like so that it can help suggest what ads they should receive.

Questions for Discussion

1. How was Samsung able to go from copycat brand to product leader?

2. Is Samsung's product development process customer-centered? Team-based? Systematic?

3. Based on the product life cycle, what challenges does Samsung face in managing its high-tech products?

4. Will Samsung likely achieve its goals in markets where it does not dominate, such as smartphones? Why or why not?

Sources: Mark Borden, "The World's 50 Most Innovative Companies: #36: Samsung," *Fast Company*, February 17, 2010, p. 90; Shinhye Kang, "Samsung Aims to Double Its Smartphone Market Share," *Bloomberg Businessweek*, June 21, 2010, accessed online at www.businessweek.com; Laurie Burkitt, "Samsung Courts Consumers, Marketers," *Forbes*, June 7, 2010, accessed online at www.forbes.com; Choi He-suk, "Samsung Renews Resolve to Reform," *Korea Herald*, June 8, 2010, accessed online at www.koreaherald.com.

Company Case 9

Burt's Bees: Willfully Overpriced

How much are you willing to pay for a standard-sized tube of lip balm? The market leader charges just a bit more than $1. But would you pay $2 for a comparable product? How about $3? When it comes to price, your first thought might be, "The lower the better." Many companies follow this reasoning and try to out-do each other by providing the cheapest option. But such a strategy can lead to razor thin margins and even losses. Although low price might seem to be the most attractive way to lure customers into purchasing goods and services, when it comes to actually creating value for customers, that's not always the case.

Burt's Bees understands that sometimes it pays to charge more. Just 10 years ago, the popular maker of natural personal care products was a niche brand, distributed only in boutiques and natural foods stores. But Burt's Bees' sales exploded when major supermarket and discount retail chains started carrying the small company's line. Although Walmart and other national chains are known for pressuring manufacturers to cut costs and lower prices, Burt's Bees achieved its distribution victory through a strategy that has been called "willful overpricing." In Burt's Bees' case, that means charging price premiums of 80 percent or more over comparable non-natural brands. Case in point: Burt's Bees lip balm, the brand's best-selling product, sells for $2.99 a tube, while market-leading ChapStick can be had for about a third of that price. To understand how Burt's Bees has succeeded with this pricing strategy, let's look at what makes the brand so special.

From Humble Beginnings

Burt's Bees started like many entrepreneurial ventures, with founders that had a good idea but not a penny to their names. In the late 1980s, Burt Shavitz was a beekeeper in northern Maine selling honey out of his pickup truck and living in a modified turkey coop. Roxanne Quimby, a wife and mother looking for a way to supplement the family income, had the idea to buy Burt's surplus beeswax to make and sell candles. Her first venture at a craft fair yielded $200 in sales.

A few years later, Roxanne happened upon a nineteenth-century book of homemade personal care recipes and acquired a secondhand industrial mixer from a university cafeteria. That's when the Burt's Bees brand that so many people now know and love began to take shape. The main product line of natural beeswax candles was slowly replaced by personal care products, including the brand's famous lip balm made with beeswax, coconut and sunflower oils, and other ingredients that you could just as easily eat as put on your lips.

As Burt's Bees grew, it automated its manufacturing processes one piece of machinery at a time. Yet the products that rolled off those automated lines maintained the quality and feel of natural homemade goods. Burt's Bees developed body lotions featuring natural milk and sugar enzymes, bath products made with sea ingredients, shampoos derived from soy protein and pomegranate extract, and toothpaste infused with spearmint oil and cranberry extract. The company can't claim that all of its 150 different products are 100 percent natural. But with more than half its products meeting the 100-percent mark and the rest coming very close, Burt's Bees boasts that its product lines are, on average, 99-percent natural, and the company maintains a commitment to what it calls *The Natural Standard.*

With natural ingredients as its main point of differentiation and core values oriented around environmental conservation and social responsibility, Burt's Bees grew very quickly. The company's sales grew by an average of 30 percent every year from 2003 to 2007, when sales topped $250 million across 30,000 outlets. That's quite a jump in just a decade and a half.

Value versus Price

In certain respects, cross-comparing personal care products is problematic because there is so much variation on both features and price. But consider some popular Burt's Bees products. Its standard shampoos and conditioners run $7.99 for a 12-ounce bottle, whereas you can pick up a same-size bottle with a Pantene label on it for only $3.99. Burt's body lotion runs $9.99 for a 12-ounce bottle, whereas a slightly larger bottle of Nivea body lotion only costs $5.99. Like various brands, Burt's Bees offers a line of anti-aging creams. But at $24.99 for any one of them, the price is almost double that of similar Oil of Olay products priced at only $12.99.

When making such comparisons, the choice seems obvious. That leads to the question: How has Burt's Bees achieved such success with this pricing strategy? You might think that it does so despite higher prices. However, a closer examination suggests that success might actually be the result of that pricing. In some cases, higher prices merely serve as an indicator of quality level. But more important to Burt's Bees, higher prices can also peak customer curiosity. When people compare brands, a moderately higher-priced option causes them to take notice and look a little deeper to understand why a certain brand is more expensive. They may learn that the product contains features that justify the higher price—features they may not have even considered before. Customers then ask themselves, "Do I need this benefit or not?" Some studies show that in such situations, customers recall nearly twice as much product information and can cite more arguments in favor of buying the products. If the price premium charged is too high or too low, however, shoppers ignore the option.

Fortunately for Burt's Bees, its strategy of willful overpricing coincided with a trend of growing consumer preference toward natural products and environmentally friendly goods. Thus, Burt's Bees' natural ingredients and company values were enough to justify the brand's higher prices for many. But can a pricing strategy that relies on trends in consumer preferences work forever?

Eco-Brands in Hard Times

On Earth Day, 2011, the front page of the *New York Times* featured the headline, "As Consumers Cut Spending, 'Green Products' Lose Allure." The article pointed out that during the Great Recession, the mainstream consumer's love affair with green products faded like a cheap T-shirt. When times are tough, the very features that seem to justify paying a higher price during fat times lose their importance as budgets tighten. But within that economic dynamic, researchers found an interesting exception. "Dark Green" consumers—who are more educated, committed, and affluent—don't drop higher-priced green products as quickly as "light green" consumers do. As a result, sales of brands perceived to be less authentic when it comes to eco-friendliness decreased, whereas sales of brands deemed more authentic remained firm. It's a perception of value *and* values. Brands such as Method and Seventh Generation are top on the list of those benefiting from this "authenticity gap," whereas S. C. Johnson's *Nature's Source* and Clorox's *Green Works* are at the bottom.

This phenomenon creates complicated issues for Burt's Bees. The well-known creator of natural products has been a hard-core eco-brand from its beginnings. But while Burt Shavitz's earthy image still adorns the package of many Burt's Bees products, the beekeeper sold his share of the company to Roxanne Quimby more than a decade ago and returned to beekeeping and his turkey coop. Quimby bowed out in 2007 as part of an even bigger shakeup. Clorox purchased Burt's Bees for a whopping $925 million as part of its comprehensive strategy to become more environmentally friendly and to free itself of a chemical polluting image. Clorox followed in the footsteps of Unilever (which purchased Ben & Jerry's in 2000), Colgate-Palmolive (which bought Tom's of Maine in 2006), and PepsiCo (which acquired Naked Juice in 2006). Major global players have paid big money for the image and the customer base of good green brands.

After buying Burt's Bees, Clorox immediately ran magazine ads comparing natural ingredients in Burt's Bees to chemical ingredients found in other products. At the same time, Burt's Bees executives claimed that the brand's quality and standards would only improve. For all intents and purposes, Clorox allows Burt's Bees to operate as an independent division, remaining true to its original mission and values.

Still, many viewed the Burt's Bees acquisition as a big sellout. Fans vented their frustrations online as they created new names for the company like "Burt's Bleach" and "Clorox's Bees." Comments such as "I use lots of Burt's Bees products. I won't be buying them anymore," and "I think I'm going to have to stock up now before Clorox ruins it," indicated the potential fallout of the merger. Burt's Bees risked losing some of its authenticity as an eco-brand, thus becoming more susceptible to the effects of consumer frugality.

Beyond value perceptions of green brands, the recession has had a lingering impact on personal care products in general, regardless of their shade of green. This trend runs contrary to the *lipstick index*, a term invented by Leonard Lauder, chairman of Estée Lauder. Lauder's company data reflected an inverse relationship between cosmetics sales (particularly lipstick) and the health of the economy. He hypothesized that, in tighter times, women cut back on higher-priced items, such as clothing and handbags, but actually bought more cosmetics. However, Lauder's intriguing index has since been discredited; overall cosmetic sales increased during the strong economic times of the mid-2000s, followed by an industry decline that coincided with the recession of the late 2000s.

Pressing on with Price Premiums

Recently, almost four years after the Burt's Bees acquisition, Clorox announced that it was writing off almost $250 million—about 25 percent—of the price it paid for the brand due to overvaluation at the time of the deal. You might take this as a sign that Burt's Bees isn't doing so well these days. However, Clorox chief financial officer Dan Heinrich suggests just the opposite:

> The Burt's Bees business remains a very solid contributor to Clorox's results, with sales growth and profit margins above the company average. . . . Despite the impairment, Burt's Bees remains the fastest growing business unit in the company, with double-digit fiscal-year-to-date sales growth, and our revised estimates continue to project low double-digit sales growth for this business over the next several years.

If Burt's Bees' Facebook fan base is any indication, Heinrich can be taken at his word. In little more than a year's time, Burt's Bees went from about 100,000 fans to more than 650,000. The corporate buyout and economic trends appear to have had little impact on the brand. In the end, it just may be that Burt's Bees' pricing strategy is proof that, by leveraging a brand's strengths, customers will continue to buy on value, not just on price.

Questions for Discussion

1. Does Burt's Bees' pricing strategy truly differentiate it from the competition?
2. Has Burt's Bees executed value-based pricing, cost-based pricing, or competition-based pricing? Explain.
3. How has Burt's Bees implemented product-mix pricing strategies?
4. Could Burt's Bees have been successful as a natural product marketer had it employed a low-price strategy? Explain.
5. Is Burt's Bees pricing strategy sustainable? Explain.

Sources: Tess Stynes and Paul Ziobro, "Clorox Forecasts Profit, Sales Below Expectations," *Wall Street Journal*, January 3, 2011, http://online.wsj.com/article/SB10001424052748704111504576059583589187332.html; Tim Donnelly, "How to Sell on Value Rather Than Price," *Inc.*, July 20, 2011, www.inc.com/guides/201107/how-to-sell-on-value-rather-than-price.html; Marco Bertini and Luc Wathieu, "How to Stop Customers from Fixating on Price," *Harvard Business Review*, May 2010, pp. 85–91; Mitch Maranowski, "The Triple Value Proposition: Why Inauthentic Green Brands Are Doomed to Fail," *Fast Company*, May 18, 2011, www.fastcompany.com/1754132/the-triple-value-proposition-why-inauthentic-green-brands-are-doomed-to-fail; and quotes and other information from www.burtsbees.com, August 2011.

Company Case 10

Pandora: Disintermediator or Disintermediated?

For Pandora, one of the biggest players in Internet radio, figuring out the future is both challenging and intimidating. If the regular challenges of growing a new company aren't enough, Pandora also faces a market that is reeling in turmoil. In the new digital world, the way people listen to music continues to change dramatically. It seems likely that Pandora will either lead the changes or fall victim to them.

Pandora was founded just over a decade ago. At that time, a vast majority of music listeners were still getting their groove on in one of two ways: They either popped a CD into their home, car, or personal CD player or they turned on the old AM/FM radio. But the advent of digital formats like MP3s has had a huge impact on CD sales and has drawn people away from what is now called "terrestrial radio." Moreover, like the music business, the radio business has faced major changes of its own. The Telecommunications Act of 1996 reduced limitations on the number of stations that one owner could hold. This led to huge ownership groups that consolidated and standardized listening formats. The result is less diversity on the radio, with shorter playlists and fewer artists represented. From one city to the next, all across the United States, radio stations have started to sound more alike.

Both these trends—combined with the explosion of Internet usage and changes in online technologies—have led to a deluge of companies trying to capitalize on the future of music distribution. This includes download services such as iTunes, subscription services such as Rhapsody and eMusic, an endless number of Internet radio stations, and even satellite radio network SiriusXM. Today, with an ever-growing list of listening devices and cloud music services that store personal music libraries so they can be accessed anywhere by any device, listening trends continue to evolve. But one thing about the future is certain: The business of listening to music is full of disruption and confusion. Things are changing fast and the winning products and services—indeed, the survivors—are yet to be determined.

The Power of People

Amid the chaos, Pandora has carved out its own niche, setting itself apart as an automated music recommendation service. It isn't a play-on-demand service, where members can simply choose the exact song and artist they want. Rather, listeners enter an artist or song suggestion. The playlist starts with a track by the requested artist and inserts additional songs by that artist every once in a while. But in between, Pandora cues up songs by other artists similar in nature to the requested material. If an unliked or unwanted song plays, the listener can click the "thumbs down" icon or just skip the song and it will be removed from the list. Users can also create stations by browsing artists alphabetically, or they can tune in to pre-made genre stations or to other users' stations. Listeners can create as many stations as they wish, each oriented around the initial input.

Lots of online services employ similar recommendation features (think Netflix and Amazon). But Pandora has set a precedent by the predictive power of its recommendation software. The Pandora software is amazingly precise at choosing material that fits with what the user wants. According to Tim Westergren, founder and chief strategy officer for Pandora, the secret sauce is the people behind the software. Behind this digitized, automated, software-driven machine, Westergren says, "You need a human ear to discern. It's true that the algorithms mathematically match songs, but the math, all it's doing is translating what a human being is actually measuring."

Each of the 850,000 songs from 80,000 different artists in Pandora's library has been analyzed and coded by a professional musician. Each song is rated on as many as 500 different musical attributes or "genes." Each gene corresponds to a music characteristic, such as gender of the lead vocalist, level of distortion on the electric guitar, syncopation, and vocal harmonies, to name just a few. Pandora's music analysts must pass application tests. As junior analysts, they are required to sit in the same room with other analysts so they can regularly peel back their headphones and engage the others about the music they're coding. Senior analysts can take their work on the road—often dissecting songs between gigs as they play on tour. "That is the magic bullet for us," Westergren says of the company's human element. "I can't overstate it. It's been the most important part of Pandora. It defines us in so many ways."

Pandora takes this unmatched competency for coding music and adds features and options that further differentiate its service. For starters, listeners can choose from two subscription plans. On the free plan, listeners hear an advertisement every now and then, but far fewer ads than are heard on terrestrial radio. This plan also sets certain user limits, such as a 40 hour-per-month listening maximum and 12 total skips every 24 hours. For $36 a year, the subscription-based plan provides members with unlimited listening hours, higher-quality audio, a desktop player, and no ads.

Once a user selects a plan, Pandora's brain takes in all the listener's inputs and marks them as unique to that person's musical tastes. With each indication of "likes" and "dislikes," Pandora gets smarter. Listeners can further empower Pandora's guru-like prowess with such responses as "I'm tired of this song," "Why was this song selected?", "Move song to another station," "New station," and "Bookmark." No rewinding or repeating is available (just like terrestrial radio). But further customization occurs when users modify their preference settings for additions like not allowing explicit lyrics. And blurring the line between radio service and music ownership, a "buy" button is located at the top of each song that takes listeners directly to iTunes or Amazon.com.

From Net Radio to Everywhere Radio

At first, the only way you could listen to Pandora was via Pandora's Web page on a computer. But Pandora's "Anytime, anywhere," mantra has guided its distribution strategy. As music enthusiasts have become more mobile, Pandora

has followed. By forging strategic partnerships, Pandora has pushed the music service into a variety of channels, including apps for smartphones and tablets as well as through home entertainment systems such as video game players, DVD players, and Internet radios. Pandora has also pioneered one of the hottest trends—providing alternatives to terrestrial radio in new vehicles. "Half of radio listing happens in cars," Westergren points out. "It's an important place for us to be." Systems in new Fords, Mercedes, Buicks, Toyotas, and Minis allow people to access Pandora on the car's sound system via Web-connected smartphone apps. Similar integrations with Alpine and Pioneer after-market systems make access available in virtually any vehicle.

All this access and the allure of cool features have allowed Pandora to dominate Internet radio with a 51 percent share of the market. Its 94 million members (over one in every four Americans) dwarf SiriusXM's 30 million subscribers. And unlike SiriusXM, Pandora's base is rapidly growing and progressively eroding the listenership of terrestrial radio. In addition, Pandora members—especially young ones—listen longer on average than listeners of terrestrial radio or satellite radio.

Not out of the Woods

Although a large and growing member base is certainly nothing to frown at, Pandora is far from declaring financial success. True, its revenues of $138 million for 2011 were about 38 percent higher than the previous year. An IPO filed during 2011 raised $100 million and gave Pandora a valuation of nearly $2.6 billion. But to date, Pandora has seen profits during only one quarter and the company is not expected to be rolling in profits any time soon. In fact, Pandora's own projections don't forecast an annual profit. In addition, other substantial threats have some investors worried. To name a few:

- **Cost structure:** Pandora pays royalties for every song played. Thus, as it increases its membership and listening hours, royalty expenses increase at a linear rate, unlike the decreasing rate for most producers of goods and services. Because Internet radio is new, royalty rates have been volatile as the music industry tries to arrive at a fair value. Only a few short years ago, Pandora was on the verge of collapse because royalties doubled. But Pandora was successful in renegotiating lower royalty rates. Further, any given music label could decide to end its contract with Pandora, thus reducing the volume of content. The future on this matter is uncertain, especially as international options are considered. (Pandora is currently available only in the United States because of royalty issues.)

- **Fees for advertising dollars:** Pandora derives 86 percent of its revenues from advertising dollars. Therefore, it must convince advertisers of the benefits of advertising on Pandora or it will not be able to create sustainable profits. This issue is complicated by Pandora's growth on mobile devices as the value for mobile advertising is even less certain than that of standard Web advertising.

- **Competition:** While competition is always a threat, the shifting nature of technology and consumer preference in the music industry makes competitive threats even more dangerous. Just take a look at all the competitive services noted earlier. Then, consider that changes in the marketing environment could lead to competitive threats not yet considered that could potentially upend the entire market.

- *Dependence on devices:* Pandora's ability to grow depends entirely on its ability to establish and maintain relationships with makers of connected devices—especially mobile devices. Such manufacturers may have reasons to contract with other services under exclusive conditions. This also puts a burden on Pandora to make and keep its technologies compatible with the many platforms used in the device field.

The digital world is full of failed dreams. Pets.com shipped a lot of 50-pound bags of dog food before realizing that its business model simply wasn't cost effective. Myspace signed up over 200 million members before crashing to its current membership of less than 20 million, leading News Corp to sell it for pennies on the dollar after just six short years. In addition, a host of other dot-coms have achieved high levels of Web traffic and huge stock valuations, only to fall because of

threats similar to those previously noted. Will that be Pandora's fate? Or will the Internet radio giant ultimately declare, "Let the music play?"

Questions for Discussion

1. How would you sketch the value chain for Pandora from the production of content to the listener? Be as complete as possible.

2. How do horizontal and vertical conflict impact Pandora?

3. How does Pandora add value for customers through its distribution functions?

4. Will Pandora be successful in the long term? Why or why not?

Sources: Matther Lasar, "Are the Likes of Pandora Poised to Kill AM/FM Radio?", *Wired*, November 2, 2010; Tyler Gray, "Pandora Pulls Back the Curtain on Its Magic Music Machine," *Fast Company*, January 21, 2011, accessed at www.fastcompany.com; Austin Carr, "Pandora, Innovative Internet Radio Station, Files for $100 Million IPO," *Fast Company*, February 11, 2011, accessed at www.fastcompany.com.

Company Case 11

Tesco Fresh & Easy: Another British Invasion

One beautiful autumn morning in Ontario, California, a long line of people waited anxiously with shopping carts. The occasion? The grand opening of a Fresh & Easy Neighborhood Market. This was big news for a community starving for decent retail outlets. "The residents have been screaming for this," said Mayor Paul Leon. "For years residents have been asking for more choices in the south Ontario area," a growing suburb populated in the past more by cows than people.

Introducing Tesco

What is Fresh & Easy? To answer that question, let's step back and look at the company behind the new Fresh & Easy grocery chain—Tesco. You may not have heard of Tesco, but it's one of the world's hottest retailers. The first Tesco opened its doors in London in 1919, selling surplus groceries. In the decades that followed, it developed into a traditional grocery store chain and one of the biggest in the United Kingdom, selling 15 percent of the country's groceries.

But in 1997, new CEO Terry Leahy performed a truly amazing feat. Under Leahy's direction, Tesco became the third-largest retailer in the world, trailing only Walmart and France's Carrefour. In just 13 years, Leahy opened more than 4,000 stores, bringing Tesco's current total to over 4,800. Under Leahy's leadership, Tesco grew from selling mostly groceries

to becoming a major force in general merchandise. The mega-retailer's portfolio now includes Walmart-style supercenters, full-sized supermarkets, Walgreens-style stores, and even non-food discount stores. With 94 million total square feet of retail space, the company employs 472,000 people. During Leahy's tenure, Tesco's UK market share doubled to 30 percent as it expanded from 6 to 14 countries, gaining a presence in the emerging economies of Asia, the Middle East, and Eastern Europe. Revenue soared to $93 billion for 2010 while profits hit $4.7 billion, figures that both grew even during the recent recession.

With everything seemingly going the company's way, Leahy surprisingly announced his retirement in the summer of 2010 at the age of 55. "My work here is done," he claimed. The accolades came pouring in. "He must surely be written up as one of Britain's greatest businessmen," proclaimed analyst Darren Shirley. "The way that the Tesco brand has been developed, extended, and enhanced by geography and category has been a textbook exercise." In addition to expanding the company, Leahy was known for bringing the business of grocery and discount retailing closer to the shopper with the Tesco Clubcard, an incentive-based loyalty program.

Sizing Up the U.S. Market

With Tesco's resources and momentum, it was only a matter of time before it made a move to crack the U.S. market. In 2007, Tesco made that move with a fat $2-billion commitment and a goal of 1,000 U.S. stores in the first five years. In the years leading up to Tesco's 2007 debut, the U.S. economy was still riding high. Housing developments were spreading like wildfire, and all those new homes needed retailers to feed them. As far as Tesco was concerned, it couldn't have picked a better time.

But Tesco also knew that it would face heavily entrenched competition. Walmart dominated the retail landscape, and other entrenched U.S. chains such as Kroger, Safeway, and Super-Valu all had strong market shares as well. Then there were the countless regional chains that provided the allure of supporting local and state economies.

Tesco spent lots of time, effort, and money researching the U.S. markets and making decisions on what approach it would take. It examined 20 years worth of data. But it didn't just rely on numbers. "We went into people's houses, talked to them about food and food shopping," said Simon Uwins, Tesco's marketing director. "We went into their kitchens and poked around pantries." In this manner, Tesco videotaped and monitored every habit of American families.

Tesco's research led to some important conclusions. For starters, it chose to focus its U.S. rollout on California, with some outlets spilling over into Arizona and Nevada. One of the biggest reasons was that Walmart actually had a minimal presence in California, a state with a GDP big enough to make it the eighth largest country in the world. Despite Walmart's worldwide dominance, the megaretailer had only opened 22 grocery-selling Supercenters in the golden state, compared to 279 in Texas.

Big box stores became a dominant force in the United States. Aside from Walmart Supercenters, the success of retailers such as Best Buy, Bed Bath & Beyond, and Home Depot suggested that growth in just about every category was dominated by superstores. Tesco, however, decided that it would buck this trend and differentiate itself from existing superstore choices. Tim Mason, CEO of Fresh & Easy, revealed the insights that helped Tesco reach that conclusion.

> Probably the most surprising thing to me was the number of different stores that an American family uses to shop. They shop in up to 20 different stores—many more than the equivalent [family] would in the UK. They will use different types of shops for their food, for their cleaning products, and for their personal care products. What I discovered is that you just can't get everything that you want in one place. The main retail brands in Britain have much higher levels of loyalty and genuinely do fulfill the notion of a one-stop shop. That's less of the case here. People will wait for flyers and coupons and indeed, people who have time but not money will actually take their shopping list and walk to two or three big players and then decide what to buy.

Introducing Fresh & Easy

With that, Tesco decided to not even try the one-stop super-center approach. Instead, Fresh & Easy was designed from the beginning as a smaller neighborhood style store positioned between convenience stores and full-sized supermarkets. Tesco calls this an "express" mini-supermarket. The average size of a Fresh & Easy Neighborhood Market is 15,000 square feet. Compare that to a full-sized supermarket at 50,000 to 60,000 square feet or a Walmart Supercenter that reaches up to 260,000 square feet.

With the smaller size, a Fresh & Easy clearly can't carry everything. Therefore, the chain focuses on fresh, prepared, and ready-to-eat foods with a bit of emphasis on gourmet items—think bags of pomegranates, rose-gold apples, watercress,

Japanese shrimp dumplings, and Indian samosas. The stores carry a big selection of store-labeled products with a good balance of premium brands. If you're thinking that sounds like Trader Joe's, that's exactly the comparison which is often made.

Fresh & Easy promises "big box discounts without the big box." In another Web site headline, Tesco takes a direct shot at Whole Foods: "Wholesome food, not whole paycheck." With this combination of benefits, store openings often play out like the one in Ontario. Customers are greeted by a brightly painted store-front and a green logo in lowercase letters. Inside, cheerful employees in green shirts move about a bright, clean store with wide uncluttered aisles. Every food item in Fresh & Easy, even produce, has an expiration date. The stores tout another distinguishing feature—no cashiers. Instead, shoppers are met at a self-checkout aisle by an animated female avatar who guides them through the process.

Fresh & Easy is betting on another strong point of differentiation. The green logo and shirts are intentional. Fresh & Easy has positioned itself as a chain with sustainability in its DNA. All stores are designed with energy-efficient lighting and refrigerators. Most of the meats, vegetables, and other fresh foods arrive in reusable plastic containers rather than disposable cardboard. Some stores offer reserved parking for hybrids. And one California Fresh & Easy store has even received the coveted seal of approval from the Leadership in Energy and Environmental Design (LEED). The company's Southern California distribution center hosts the largest solar roof array in the state. And all products reach stores in hybrid electric-diesel semis. Fresh & Easy even plans to roll out carbon labels, a simple calculation of the amount of greenhouse gases emitted from an item's production, distribution, use, and disposal.

Not Quite a Hit

This kind of venture seems like a no-brainer; one that can't fail. In fact, many predicted that Fresh & Easy would be a category killer. But initial results have given Tesco cause for concern. For starters, the first Fresh & Easy store openings coincided with the beginning of the subprime-mortgage crisis. California, Arizona, and Nevada were among the states hardest hit. As foreclosures multiplied, houses sat vacant in the very developments where Fresh & Easy stores were expected to make a big splash.

Fresh & Easy may also have missed the mark on meeting consumer needs. One observer stated harshly, "It's as if the place purports to solve all kinds of vexing marketing 'problems' while failing to address the most basic real world problem. Namely, why would anyone even want to come here to begin with?" After her initial visit to a Fresh & Easy, one Trader Joe's loyalist said, "I'm sure the food here is tasty. But we are going to have to find more useful things if we are going to shop here much." To compound this problem, initial perceptions of everyday low prices left a lot to be desired.

Tesco claims to be responsive to customer feedback. Indeed, it moved quickly to make some changes after the feedback it received from its first store openings. It hit pricing harder with reductions and increased use of coupons, including regular coupons for $5 off a $20 shopping bill. In addition, it put higher shelves in stores to add 1,000 new products without taking any items away.

Although Tesco asserts that it is exceeding sales targets, the company also slowed its rate of store openings. Whereas it had initially planned to open 100 new stores in the first year and then increase that rate, after three years there are now just over 150 Fresh & Easy stores. Given the high sunk cost of its distribution system, Tesco needs bigger store numbers in order to defray that expense across more stores. Indeed, the U.S. arm of Tesco posted huge losses in its first years of operation.

Many analysts now speculate as to what will happen with Fresh & Easy as the economy shows signs of improvement. Tesco continues to invest in store format tweaks and updates. Fresh & Easy management now predicts that the chain will break even sometime in 2012 or 2013.

However, the economic environment has been complicated. Additionally, many economists and analysts aren't optimistic about what the future holds for the grocery business. Dave McCarthy, a Citigroup managing director and former Tesco employee, provides cautionary advice for Tesco. "The sector is heading for its most difficult time in many years. Opening programs are doubling, industry like-for-likes are currently negative, and discretionary income is falling. And there's uncertainty on how Tesco will deal with the changing industry environment. It will be interesting to see if [Tesco] maintains long term commitment to the United States if it continues to drain profits."

Questions for Discussion

1. How would you describe Fresh & Easy according to the different types of retailers discussed in the chapter?

2. As a retail brand, how would you assess the Fresh & Easy retail strategy with respect to segmentation, targeting, differentiation, and positioning?

3. Evaluate Tesco's research efforts for the U.S. market. Did this research help or hurt?

4. Will Fresh & Easy succeed or fail in the long term? Support your answer.

5. What recommendations would you make to Tesco for Fresh & Easy?

Sources: Andrea Felsted, "Fresh Assault on U.S. Market After Far from Easy Start," *Financial Times*, July 20, 2011, p. 19; Simon Zekaria, "Leahy's Work Not Yet Done," *Wall Street Journal*, June 8, 2010, accessed online at www.wsj.com; Paul Sonne, "Tesco's CEO-to-Be Unfolds Map for Global Expansion," *Wall Street Journal*, June 9, 2010, p. B1; Jeffrey Ball, "Tesco to Launch U.S. 'Green' Grocer," *Wall Street Journal*, September 24, 2009, p. B4; Liset Marquez, "Customers Line Up at South Ontario Fresh and Easy," *Inland Valley Daily Bulletin*, December 2, 2009, accessed at www.dailybulletin.com.

Company Case 12

OgilvyOne: It's Not Creative Unless It Sells

These days, there are some extremely creative ads fighting for our attention. Television spots are often on par with feature films in terms of artistic quality. Print ads and billboards rival works of art. Such ads can move our emotions powerfully. They can make us laugh, cry, or sing; they can produce feelings of guilt, fear, or joy. Ads themselves are often as entertaining as the programming in which they appear. However, although highly creative ads might dazzle us and even win awards from advertising critics, they sometimes overlook a very important fundamental truth: Truly creative advertising is advertising that creates sales.

Not all ads have forgotten this truth. But too often, advertisers become so enamored with the artistry of advertising that they forget about the selling part. After all, the ultimate objective of advertising is not to win awards or even to make people like an ad. It's to get people to think, feel, or *act* in some way after being exposed to an ad. Ultimately, no matter how entertaining or artistic an ad, it's not creative unless it sells.

This thinking prompted one of the world's premiere advertising agencies—OgilvyOne Worldwide—to run a unique contest. Part of Ogilvy & Mather Worldwide, OgilvyOne launched a contest to search for the World's Greatest Salesperson. According to Rory Sutherland, vice chairman for the British operations of Ogilvy & Mather, the goal of the contest was "recreating the noble art of ka-ching. There's an interesting case to be made that advertising has strayed too far from the business of salesmanship."

"Salesmanship has been lost in the pursuit of art or the dazzle of technology," said Brian Fetherstonhaugh, chairman and CEO at OgilvyOne. "It needs to be rekindled in this postrecession environment, as consumers are making more informed and deliberate choices." But as Fetherstonhaugh also points out, the return to selling through advertising is more challenging today than ever. Technologies such as TiVo, SPAM filters, and viewing-on-demand through the Internet have put consumers in control of the media more than ever. For this reason, advertisers not only need to become great salespeople, they need to be salespeople that get invited into the consumer's environment. According to Fetherstonhaugh, advertising needs to be "less about intrusion and repetition and more about engagement and evangelizing."

The Contest

OgilvyOne chose a popular format for its "World's Greatest Salesperson" contest. Entrants prepared one- to two-minute video clips selling the assigned product and submitted them via YouTube. Viewers voted for their favorite videos and a panel of judges winnowed the field down to a set of finalists.

However, the product that contestants were assigned to sell was anything but the usual. They weren't asked to sell a glitzy new smartphone or super-thin large-screen TV. Instead, they had to make a pitch for a brick. That's right, a common, everyday red brick. Why a brick? "If you can sell a red brick, maybe you can sell anything," said Mat Zucker, executive creative director for OgilvyOne and the creator of the contest. Some people at Ogilvy pushed for a more exciting product. But Mish Fletcher, worldwide marketing director at OgilvyOne, pointed out that perhaps those exciting products don't need "the World's Greatest Salesperson" as much.

A Heritage in Sales

The "World's Greatest Salesperson" contest was a nod to advertising legend David Ogilvy, who founded Ogilvy & Mather more than 60 years ago. Prior to entering the advertising world, Ogilvy sold stoves door-to-door in Scotland. He sold so many stoves, the company asked him to write a manual for other salesmen. That manual was dubbed "the finest sales instruction manual ever written" by the editors of *Fortune* magazine, who still used it as a resource guide 30 years after Ogilvy wrote it. Ogilvy once revealed the secret to his success as a stove salesman: "No sale, no commission. No commission, no eat. That made an impression on me." That notion forms the basis for Ogilvy's credo, "We sell, or else."

David Ogilvy left sales, but sales never left him. He founded Ogilvy & Mather in 1949 based on the principles that the function of advertising is to sell and that successful advertising for any product is based on customer information. Ogilvy's principles worked for major corporation after major corporation. In 1962, *Time* magazine called Ogilvy "the most sought-after wizard in today's advertising industry." He was so successful at expanding the bounds of creativity in advertising that he has often been called "The Father of Advertising." The list of iconic advertising campaigns that he developed is as long as anyone's in the business.

Based on this heritage, Zucker came up with the idea for the "World's Greatest Salesperson" contest. "If we believe in selling, and our founder was a salesman, we have a special responsibility to reassert the importance of sales," Zucker said.

Creative Pitches

More than 230 videos from entrants in 12 countries were uploaded to Ogilvy's YouTube contest site. Ogilvy eventually narrowed the entrants down to three finalists. The first finalist was Todd Herman, an international performance coaching and training expert from Edmonton, Canada. Herman pitched a single brick as a symbol of something that can be used as the first step in building something great. He started his video with a brick in hand, saying "The story of a simple, red brick is one filled with power, struggle, and romance. And now you have the chance to capture some of its magic." From there, Herman summarized various ways that bricks have been used throughout history to build and connect civilizations. His pitch was based on the idea that a red brick is not just a common object but a symbol of a dream that was acted upon.

Eric Polins, managing partner of a marketing consulting firm in Tampa, Florida, was the second finalist. Polins, who left broadcast news because of extreme stage fright every time he stepped in front of a camera, sold his brick as an intangible asset—a good luck charm. In a clever way, he pointed out that the classic good luck charms all have problems. A rabbit's foot is too morbid. A four-leaf clover is too hard to come by in a paved-over world. The "knock on wood" gesture is outdated as hardly anything is made out of wood anymore. And a horseshoe . . . who can afford a horse?

The third finalist was Lee Abbas, a former Panasonic marketing executive from Japan. She organized her approach around a reinvention of the classic old brick—a must-have purse with chrome steel handles. She demonstrated this new product from a brick factory and maker of high-strength, lightweight bricks. She then related how a friend of hers was mugged. Rather than reaching into her purse for a can of pepper spray, she simply whacked her assailant over the head with a brick, knocking him out cold.

All three finalists were winners in one respect. Each received an all-expense paid trip to Cannes, France, for the 57th annual Cannes Lions International Advertising Festival. There, each had to make a live presentation for a second product in front of a studio audience and panel of judges. This time, the finalists had to sell a Motorola Droid phone. They made their presentations, the audience voted, and Todd Herman emerged as the "World's Greatest Salesperson."

"I honestly can't believe I'm standing here with the World's Greatest Salesperson award," Herman stated. "[I]t's such an honor to be working with a company whose founder has been such a huge influence on my business philosophy." Perhaps the biggest part of the prize was a job with OgilvyOne. Herman was given the opportunity to fulfill a three-month fellowship with the agency with the express purpose of crafting a sales guide to the twenty-first century. The principles in the guide will be presented at the Direct Marketing Association's annual conference.

As would be expected of the World's Greatest Salesperson, Fetherstonhaugh pointed out, Herman "is a true student of persuasion and motivation. It shone through at every stage of the World's Greatest Salesperson competition." Herman's own words seem to reflect the principles of David Ogilvy and the true nature of advertising. "People always think of sales as the in-your-face-used-car salesman. But selling happens all the time. Really great selling is never noticed. You should feel like you just bought something, not like you just got sold."

Questions for Discussion

1. Do you agree with David Ogilvy that the primary function of advertising is selling? How does that fit with the three advertising objectives of informing, persuading, and reminding?

2. If the primary purpose of advertising is to sell, are there any message execution techniques that seem best predisposed to this purpose?

3. As a creator of advertising, what kind of return on investment did OgilvyOne get out of this promotional contest?

4. Do you agree or disagree with the premise that the primary function of advertising is to sell? Give examples of ad campaigns to support your position.

Sources: Stuart Elliott, "In a Test of Sales Savvy, Selling a Red Brick on YouTube," *New York Times*, March 29, 2010, p. B3; "Todd Herman Voted World's Greatest Salesperson," accessed at prnewswire.com, July 2010; Robert Trigaux, "To Be 'Greatest Salesperson,' Just Sell a Measly Red Brick," *St. Petersburg Times*, June 15, 2010, p. 1B; Florence Loyie, "Patter to Sell Brick Wins Trip to Cannes," *Edmonton Journal*, June 10, 2010, p. A3.

Company Case 13

Hewlett-Packard: Overhauling a Vast Corporate Sales Force

Imagine this scenario: You need a new digital camera. You're not sure which one to buy or even what features you need, so you visit your nearest electronics superstore to talk with a salesperson. You walk through the camera section but can't find anyone to help you. When you finally find a salesperson, he yawns and tells you that he's responsible for selling all the products in the store, so he doesn't really know all that much about cameras. Then, he reads some information from the box of one of the models that you ask about, as if he is telling you something that you can't figure out for yourself. He then suggests that you should talk to someone else. You finally find a camera-savvy salesperson. However, after answering a few questions, she disappears to handle some other task, handing you off to someone new. And the new salesperson seems to contradict what the first salesperson said, even quoting different prices on a couple of models you like.

That imaginary situation may actually have happened to you. If so, then you can understand what many business buyers face when attempting to buy from a large corporate supplier. This was the case with business customers of technology giant Hewlett-Packard before Mark Hurd took over as HP's CEO a few years ago. Prior to Hurd assuming command, HP's revenues and profits had flattened and its stock price had plummeted. To find out why, Hurd first talked directly with 400 corporate customers. Mostly what he heard were gripes about HP's corporate sales force.

Customers complained that they had to deal with too many salespeople, and that HP's confusing management layers made it hard to figure out whom to call. They had trouble tracking down HP sales representatives. And once found, the reps often came across as apathetic, leaving the customer to take the initiative. HP reps were responsible for a broad range of complex products, so they sometimes lacked the needed depth of knowledge on any subset of them. Customers grumbled that they received varying price quotes from different sales reps, and that it often took weeks for reps to respond to seemingly simple requests. In all, HP's corporate customers were frustrated, not a happy circumstance for a company that gets more than 70 percent of its revenues from businesses.

But customers weren't the only ones frustrated by HP's unwieldy and unresponsive sales force structure. HP was organized into three main product divisions: the Personal Systems Group (PSG), the Technology Solutions Group (TSG), and the Image and Printing Group (IPG). However, HP's corporate sales force was housed in a fourth division, the Customer Sales Group (CSG). All salespeople reported directly to the CSG and were responsible for selling products from all three product divisions. To make matters worse, the CSG was bloated and underperforming. According to one reporter, "Of the 17,000 people working in HP's corporate sales, only around 10,000 sold directly to customers. The rest were support staff or in management." HP division executives were frustrated by the CSG structure. They complained that they had little or no direct control over the salespeople who sold their products. Furthermore, the multiple layers of management slowed sales force decision making and customer responsiveness.

Finally, salespeople themselves were frustrated by the structure. They weren't being given the time and support they needed to serve their customers well. Burdened with administrative tasks and bureaucratic red tape, they were spending less than a third of their time with customers. In addition, they had to work through multiple layers of bureaucracy to get price quotes and sample products for customers. "The customer focus was lacking," says an HP sales vice president. "Trying to navigate inside HP was difficult. It was unacceptable."

As CEO Mark Hurd peeled back the layers, it became apparent that HP's organizational problems went deeper than the sales force. The entire company had become so centralized, with so many layers of management, that it was unresponsive and out of touch with customers. Hurd had come to HP with a reputation for cost-cutting and ruthless efficiency. Prior to his new position, he spent 25 years at NCR where he ultimately headed the company. Although it was a considerably smaller company than HP, Hurd had it running like a well-oiled machine. Nothing bothered him more than the discoveries he made about HP's inefficient structure.

Thus began what one observer called "one of Hurd's biggest management challenges: overhauling HP's vast corporate sales force." For starters, Hurd eliminated the CSG division, instead assigning salespeople directly to the three product divisions. He also did away with three layers of management and cut hundreds of unproductive sales workers. This move gave divisional marketing and sales executives direct control over a leaner, more efficient sales process, resulting in speedier sales decisions and quicker market response.

Hurd also took steps to reduce salesperson and customer frustrations. Eliminating the CSG meant that each salesperson was responsible for selling a smaller number of products and was able to develop expertise in a specific product area. Hurd urged sales managers to cut back on salesperson administrative requirements and to improve sales support so that salespeople could spend more quality time with customers. As a result, salespeople now spend more than 40 percent of their time with customers, up from just 30 percent before. And HP salespeople are noticing big changes in the sales support they receive:

> Salesman Richard Ditucci began noticing some of the changes late last year. At the time, Ditucci was trying to sell computer servers to Staples. As part of the process, Staples had asked him to provide a sample server for the company to evaluate. In the past, such requests typically took two to three weeks to fulfill because of HP's bureaucracy. This time, Ditucci got the server he needed within three days. The quick turnaround helped him win the contract, valued at several million dollars.

To ensure that important customers are carefully tended, HP assigned each salesperson three or fewer accounts. The top 2,000 accounts were assigned just one salesperson—"so they'll always know whom to contact." Because of this change, customers are noticing differences in the attention that they get from HP salespeople:

> James Farris, a senior technology executive at Staples, says HP has freed up his salesman to drop by Staples at least twice a month instead of about once a month before. The extra face time enabled the HP salesman to create more valuable interactions, such as arranging a workshop recently for Staples to explain HP's technology to the retailer's executives. As a result, Farris says he is planning to send more business HP's way. Similarly, Keith Morrow, chief information officer of convenience-store chain 7-Eleven, says his HP sales representative is now "here all the time," and has been more knowledgeable in pitching products tailored to his business. As a result, last October, 7-Eleven began deploying in its U.S. stores 10,000 HP pen pads—a mobile device that helps 7-Eleven workers on the sales floor.

A Salesman at Heart

Once the new sales force started to take shape, Hurd began to focus on the client's role in the sales process. The fact that HP refers to its business buyers as "partners" says a lot about its philosophy. "We heavily rely on [our partners]. We look at them as an extension of the HP sales force," Hurd said. To strengthen the relationship between HP and its partners, HP has partners participating in account planning and strategy development, an activity that teams the partners with HP sales reps and its top executive team.

Because Hurd wants the sales force to have strong relationships with its partners, he practices what he preaches. He spends up to 60 percent of the year on the road with various channel partners and *their* customers. Part of his time is funneled through HP's Executive Connections program, roundtable meetings that take place all over the world. But many of Hurd's interactions with HP partners take place outside that program as well. This demonstration of customer commitment

at the highest level has created some fierce customer loyalty toward HP.

"I've probably met Mark Hurd more times in the last three or four years than all the CEOs of our other vendors combined," said Simon Palmer, president of California-based STA, one of HP's fastest growing solution provider partners. "There's no other CEO of any company that size that's even close. He's such a down-to-earth guy. He presents the HP story in very simple-to-understand terms." Mark Sarazin, executive vice president of AdvizeX Technologies, an HP partner for 25 years, sings similar praises. "He spent two-and-a-half hours with our customers. He talked in terms they could relate with, about his own relationship with HP IT. He knocked the ball out of the park with our 25-plus CIOs who were in the room. One said it was the best event he'd been to in his career."

In the four years since Hurd took over as CEO, HP's revenues, profits, and stock price have increased by 44 percent, 123 percent, and 50 percent, respectively. Still, with HP's markets as volatile as they've been, Hurd has taken HP into new equipment markets as well as gaining a substantial presence in service solutions. Each time the company enters a new market and faces new competitors, the HP sales force is at the center of the activity. In an effort to capture market share from Dell, Cisco, and Lexmark in the server market, HP opened a new sales operation in New Mexico called the SMB Exchange. It combines a call center, inside sales, and channel sales teams. Observers have noted that, whereas HP's sales force was known for being more passive in the past, it is now much more aggressive—like Cisco's.

Hurd knows that because of HP's enormous size, it walks a fine line. In fact, he refers to the company's size as a "strange friend." On the one hand, it allows the company to offer a tremendous portfolio of products and services with support from a massive sales force. On the other hand, multiple organizational layers can make it more difficult to create solutions for partners and customers. Hurd is doing everything he can to make HP leaner and meaner so that it can operate with the nimbleness and energy of a much smaller company.

The changes that have taken place at HP have made most everyone more satisfied. And happier salespeople are more productive, resulting in happier customers. That should mean a bright future for HP. However, CEO Hurd knows that there's still much more work to be done. But with a continued focus on the sales force and the sales process, HP is developing a structure that creates better value for its business customers. Now, if your local electronics superstore could only do the same for you. . . .

Questions for Discussion

1. Which of the sales force structures described in the text best describes HP's structure?

2. What are the positive and negative aspects of HP's new sales force structure?

3. How would you describe some of the differences in the selling process steps that an HP sales rep might face in

selling to a long-term established customer versus a prospective customer?

4. Given that Hurd has an effective sales force, does he really need to meet with HP partners as much as he does?

5. Is it possible for HP to function like a smaller company? Why or why not?

Sources: Quotes and adapted examples from Pui-Wing Tam, "System Reboot: Hurd's Big Challenge at HP: Overhauling Corporate Sales," *Wall Street Journal*, April 3, 2006, p. A1; Damon Poeter, "Never Enough," *Computer Reseller News*, April 1, 2010, p. 24; and Steven Burke, "HP Vs. Cisco: It's Personal," *Computer Reseller News*, November 1, 2009, p. 8.

Company Case 14

eBay: Fixing an Online Marketing Pioneer

Pop quiz: Name the high-tech company that got its start in someone's living room, grew from zero revenue to a multi-billion-dollar corporation in less than a decade, and pioneered the model for an entire industry to follow. If you're thinking that the list of companies that fit this description is a mile long, you're right. But in this case, we're talking about eBay.

eBay is one of the biggest Web success stories in the history of, well, the World Wide Web. But sooner or later, every high-growth company hits a speed bump and experiences growing pains. After amazing growth for its first 15 years, eBay has hit that speed bump. Current CEO John Donahoe is faced with the difficult challenge of putting eBay back on the superhighway to prosperity.

eBay started in 1995 as an auction house. Unlike most dot-coms, eBay was based on a model that produced profits, not just revenue. Whenever a user posted an item for auction, eBay collected a fee. The more products that went up for auction, the more money eBay made. eBay has tinkered with its fee structure over the years, but the basic idea has remained the same. The online auction formula took off like wildfire and eBay dominated the industry. eBay's revenue, stock price, profits, and number of employees soared. By the year 2000, eBay was the number one e-commerce site in the world by sales revenue.

The Changing Face of a Growing Company

With explosive growth, change is inevitable. According to many industry observers, the face of eBay slowly began to change based on two dynamics. The first was expansion. eBay's list of categories and subcategories grew into the hundreds. The e-commerce giant also added international sites for different countries. And it began to launch sub-sites (such as eBay Motors) and to acquire other dot-coms relevant to its business. Such acquisitions ultimately included Half.com, PayPal, StubHub, Shopping.com, and Skype.

The second dynamic driving change in eBay was the addition of fixed-price selling options. During its early years, open auction was the only option buyers and sellers had. Sellers put up an item for sale with a designated starting price for a period of one to ten days and sold to the highest bidder. In 1999, eBay augmented

that core method with a fixed-price, "Buy It Now" option. Two years later, it took that concept much further with the introduction of eBay stores. With eBay stores, a seller could create an online "storefront" within eBay. The feature allowed sellers to post items more quickly, making it easier for high-volume sellers to do business. It also gave fixed-price options with no bidding whatsoever and virtually eliminated the sales period for an item.

Both of these dynamics continued to fuel eBay's steady, strong growth for years. For 2006, $52.5 billion worth of goods were sold on eBay. Those sales were generated by 222 million users posting 610 million new listings. eBay's take was $5.97 billion in revenue and $1.12 billion in net income. These numbers were tremendous for a company that had only been doing business for a single decade. They also marked a zenith for the company.

In 2007, however, eBay began to show signs of slowing down. In early 2008, John Donahoe took over as CEO, replacing Meg Whitman, the mastermind behind the company's success for 10 of its 12 years. Donahoe acknowledged that eBay faced issues, including the fact that it had been resting on its laurels. "We were the biggest and the best. eBay has a storied past. But frankly, it's a past we've held onto too much." Consumer behavior was shifting. When eBay was new, many users were thrilled by the uncertainty of bidding against other buyers for a bargain. But as online shopping went mainstream, more people opted for the tried-and-true method of finding the best price on a new piece of merchandise and buying it from a reputable retailer.

The consumer shift to buying new products at fixed prices was evident in the growth experienced by online retailers such as Amazon.com, Buy.com, and Walmart.com, companies that eBay had previously refused to recognize as competitors. Amazon had passed eBay as the largest online retailer a number of years earlier by continuing to expand its selection of fixed-price items, often with free shipping.

Shortly after taking over from Whitman, Donahoe said at a public event, "We need to redo our playbook, we need to redo it fast, and we need to take bold actions." He unveiled the details of a new strategy for eBay's turnaround, one that focused on changing the identity of the eBay marketplace. Donahoe specified that the new strategy would focus on building the site's business in the secondary market, the $500-billion-a-year slice of retail that included out-of-season and overstock items as well as the used and antique items for which eBay had always been known.

Core to Donahoe's strategy, eBay changed its fee structure, search-engine algorithm, and feedback rating system in ways that favored highly rated sellers, fixed-price listings, and sellers offering free shipping. Donahoe claimed that all these tactics helped align eBay's interests with those of its best sellers. But the moves also created tension among two groups of sellers that had been growing apart for years. The traditional eBay seller sold typical flea market wares including used, vintage, antique, and homemade items. These sellers typically included mom-and-pop operations that dealt in low to moderate volumes. These merchants gave eBay its start and continued to be a sizable portion of eBay's business. Such sellers were a sharp contrast to eBay's high-volume PowerSellers. These sellers were often major operations employing dozens if not hundreds of people. They most often sold new, refurbished, or overstock items in bulk. High-volume sellers sold tens of thousands, hundreds of thousands, and even millions of items on eBay every year.

In light of the site's changes, the traditional eBay sellers cried foul, asserting that the company's new strategy made it harder for them to do business profitably while favoring the high-volume sellers. Donahoe responded that the managers at eBay knew there would be growing pains, but that the transformation was essential. "We have to create a marketplace where we're helping our sellers give our buyers what they want," he said. He added that he strongly believed that buyers wanted a fixed price, quick service, and free shipping. For eBay to not focus on market demands would ultimately be bad for everyone.

From Bad to Worse

All that may have ended well had eBay's numbers turned around. Instead, eBay's financials slid badly. In the last quarter of 2008, typically eBay's strongest period with holiday shopping, eBay experienced its first ever quarterly decline. For its core marketplace, revenue was down 16 percent from the previous year, while net income dropped a whopping 31 percent. It would have been very easy for Donahoe and his team to blame the company's woes on the economic downturn. But as eBay experienced a drop in traffic, competitors Amazon.com and Walmart.com enjoyed increases.

Still, Donahoe moved forward with even greater resolve. "The 'buyer beware' experience has run its course," he said. He reiterated eBay's plans to focus on the secondary market. "We're going to focus where we can win," Donahoe said, indicating that the shift away from new merchandise where its biggest competitors dominated would give eBay a strong point of differentiation. "We have begun significant change. The eBay you knew is not the eBay we are, or the eBay we will become." As these changes began to take root, eBay's financials began to stabilize. But with total e-commerce growth in the low double digits and the likes of Amazon.com growing considerably faster, it was clear that eBay would continue to lag behind for the foreseeable future.

eBay could take some solace in the strength of its non-marketplace division, PayPal. PayPal had been growing at a considerably faster rate than the core eBay site for a number of years. As the demand for secure online payment services exploded, PayPal was optimally poised as the market leader to take advantage. In fact, as eBay executives forecasted 5 to 7 percent growth for its core marketplace through 2013, it was estimated that PayPal's revenue would double to a whopping

$7 billion. Based on those growth dynamics, PayPal would shortly account for more than half of eBay's corporate revenues.

A New Point of Differentiation

Even with the strength of PayPal, eBay is not turning its back on the eBay brand. As Donahoe's initial turnaround strategy plays out, eBay is working to stimulate stronger marketplace growth. Under Donahoe's direction, eBay's focus is, and will continue to be, on enhancing the shopping experience. To this end, the e-commerce pioneer is once again braving new frontiers, only this time it is capitalizing on the explosive growth of mobile communications.

eBay is exploring several initiatives for making shopping on mobile devices easier and more fulfilling. eBay's RedLaser bar-code scanning tool lets users scan just about any product on a shelf for immediate comparison with online sources. It even suggests nearby stores that have the product in stock. Soon, eBay will enable shoppers to tap into the same shopping tools by merely taking a photo of a product, on or off the shelf. If you like the shoes your friend is wearing, you can buy them and have them on the way to you within seconds.

The idea is to engage consumers even when they aren't thinking about buying something. To this end, eBay is also creating some big app innovations. To make its array of product categories less daunting, eBay has launched specialty apps such as eBay Fashion. This app emphasizes browsing over buying, featuring a style guide and a shared virtual closet where users can mix, match, and model different outfits with friends. But even though the focus is on browsing, eBay knows that browsers will buy. Users spend an average of 10 minutes browsing on the eBay Fashion app—40 percent longer than they spend on the main eBay app. In the Fashion app's first year, eBay mobile fashion sales tripled.

eBay hopes to carry the niche app success into other areas, including automotive, electronics, and home-and-garden sales. And although Amazon is still way ahead in terms of total sales and sales growth, eBay now has the jump in mobile commerce. Last year, eBay sold almost $2 billion worth of goods via smartphones and tablets, more than double its total from the year before. Amazon claims just over $1 billion in mobile sales, including Kindle e-books. Given that expert projections suggest that mobile commerce will top $119 billion by 2015, being on top of this trend is a great place to be.

With the developments in eBay's marketplace, mobile commerce, and online payments, Donahoe's confidence is becoming more credible. "We have gone from turnaround to offensive," the CEO states. "Our purpose is to bring consumers the best experience to find what they want, how they want, and when they want it, whether it's on eBay or otherwise." As e-commerce continues to evolve at a blistering pace, only time will tell if Donahoe's strategy will pay off.

Questions for Discussion

1. Analyze the marketing environment and the forces shaping eBay's business over the years. What conclusions can you draw?

2. How has the change in the nature of eBay sellers affected the creation of value for buyers?

3. Do you agree or disagree with CEO Donahoe that eBay's turnaround strategy is the best way to go?

4. Based on eBay's current developments with PayPal and mobile apps, what do you predict the outcome for the company will be in five years?

Sources: Dan Macsai, "eBay Dials M for Makeover," *Fast Company*, November 16, 2010, accessed at www.fastcompany.com; Geoffrey Fowler, "Auctions Fade in eBay's Bid for Growth," *Wall Street Journal*, May 26, 2009, p. A1; Peter Burrows, "eBay Outlines Three-Year Revival Plan," *BusinessWeek*, March 12, 2009, accessed at www.businessweek.com; Max Colchester and Ruth Bender, "eBay CEO Continues to Seek Acquisitions," *Wall Street Journal*, May 23, 2011, accessed at www.wsj.com.

Company Case 15

Buick: Number One Imported Brand

There's an old joke that goes something like this: A certain Buick dealer went broke as the popularity of imported cars finally took its toll and forced him out of business. One day he found a bottle from which a genie emerged, offering to grant him one wish. He wished for a foreign car dealership in a major city. Instantly, he found himself smack dab in the showroom of his old Buick dealership—but in Tokyo!

Most Americans perceive Buick as a brand that sells only in the United States. But there has always been one big exception to that—China. In fact, if the dealer in the previous tale had found his dealership in Shanghai or Beijing, he truly would have gotten his wish. You see, Buick sells more premium vehicles in China than any other brand—even BMW or Mercedes-Benz. Moreover, Buick is one of the best-selling auto brands in China period, luxury or otherwise.

Buick's success in China makes for an interesting story. But perhaps more important than how the brand got there is what General Motors is doing now to take advantage of it. GM is not only embracing the Chinese market for Buick (and for some of its other brands), it's using the Chinese market as a key driver for Buick products in the United States and other countries. Globalization for Buick no longer means exporting the domestic product. Rather, GM is looking to China for key customer insights into creating a truly global product.

A Car for Royalty

Folks in the United States might think that American products in China today are a relatively recent phenomenon. However, Buick's place at the top of the Chinese market has a history almost as old as the brand itself. Buick first hung out its shingle in 1899, making it the oldest American automotive brand still in existence. Soon after, Chinese government officials began showing an interest in introducing the vehicle to China. The first Buicks arrived on the streets of Shanghai in 1912.

Buick immediately became associated with Chinese political leaders. Pu Yi, China's last emperor, owned a Buick in the 1920s, and provincial presidents were also known for choosing Buicks over brands such as Rolls-Royce and Mercedes-Benz. That led Buick to open a sales office in Shanghai in 1929 and start advertising there. Some early examples of advertising copy included, "One out of every six cars [in China] is a Buick," and "Buick owners are mostly the leading men in China."

Over the years, Buick's image as the vehicle of choice for China's elite burned itself into the minds of the Chinese people. As China's market economy began to take off in the late 1900s, its exploding middle class fueled the demand for cars. Buick was poised to ride the trend to the top. In 1997, GM formed a joint venture with Shanghai Automotive Industry Corporation—Shanghai GM—to build GM cars in China. The first Chinese-made Buick rolled off the assembly line in 1998. Shanghai GM would go on to become the first Chinese auto manufacturer to sell more than 1 million vehicles in a single year. Around that time, Buick enjoyed a brand familiarity rating of more than 85 percent in China.

An Evolving Global Strategy

For decades, GM's international marketing strategy was largely characterized by exporting products made for the U.S. market. In GM's thinking, what worked in America would work globally. This included selling left-hand-drive cars in right-hand-drive countries like Japan and Great Britain. The strategy made sense at a time when the United States was far and away the biggest car market in the world and GM was selling far more cars in the United States than anywhere else.

But U.S. automotive sales matured years ago at a time when growth in other markets took off. China is now the world's largest passenger car market, and with over 1.3 billion people, it has a way to go before the market is saturated. Fortunately for GM, Buick had rubber on the road in China before that market started accelerating. When the Chinese market took off, GM put things into overdrive. As a result, GM sold 2.35 million cars in China in 2010, marking the first time ever that a U.S. automaker sold more cars in another country than it did in the domestic market. That also marked the sixth consecutive year for GM as China's number one automaker.

As GM's overall growth dynamics shifted, Buick was ahead of the curve. The year 2000 was one of Buick's best years ever in the United States, with sales of more than 400,000 vehicles. But that began a steady and steep decline for the brand. As GM worked its way through the recession, bankruptcy, and a government bailout, it considered eliminating Buick entirely. But in China, Buick sales were rising as fast as they were sinking in the United States. In 2009, the same year that Buick's U.S. sales hit an all-time low of just 102,000 units, the brand sold 450,000 cars in China. No doubt about it, China saved Buick from the fate that befell discontinued GM brands like Oldsmobile, Pontiac, and Saturn.

As Buick's sales have shifted, so has its Chinese portfolio of models. Currently at the bottom of Buick's Chinese line is the Excelle—the company's best-seller, which is based on a Korean Daewoo but dressed up to look like a Buick. That car is not to be confused with the top-trim Excelle GT, which is based on an entirely different vehicle, the German-designed Opel Astra. China's Regal and LaCrosse models are assembled at Shanghai GM, but share their designs with the same models assembled at other GM plants. The Enclave SUV is built in Lansing, Michigan. And the top-of-the line Park Avenue is built on a platform from GM's Australian division, Holden. Buick China also sells a minivan—a vehicle class that still enjoys popularity in the Land of the Rising Sun. And if the electric Chevy Volt makes it to China, it is rumored that it will be branded as a Buick.

China Takes the Lead

Buick's Chinese lineup seems like a better international product strategy than the old approach of selling only domestic U.S. models. But in many respects, it's a hodgepodge of cars from GM's world operations that have little in common other than the trademark three-shield emblem. What isn't apparent from the description of these models alone is the extent to which the Chinese market is influencing the design not only of future Buick vehicles for China, but also for the rest of world. Enter car designer Joe Qiu.

> Joe Qiu doesn't own a car. He doesn't even have a driver's license. His favorite vehicle, actually, is a go-kart with a top speed of 75 miles per hour. His distressed leather bomber jacket, which he rarely takes off, betrays his fascination with airplanes and all things military. His jeans, the hems unfashionably turned up, and a brush-like crewcut, are pure 21st-century China. His TAG Heuer watch: a nod to the international uniform of designers. At 31, Qiu still lives with his parents. But he spends much of his time drinking in the vibes at the expensive high-end clubs, over-the-top shopping malls, and elegant, luxurious hotels where Shanghai's burgeoning middle class gathers. "I'm just a piece of white paper," he says, collecting insights into China's skyrocketing consumer culture. He has an uncanny knack for divining Chinese tastes and whims, what it is they'll buy.

Joe Qiu is also a designer for Shanghai GM's Pan Asia Technical Automotive Center (PATAC). A few years ago, Qiu and a team of PATAC designers won a competition with other GM design centers throughout the world to take charge of designing what is now the current model Buick LaCrosse. As one of the smallest and least known GM design houses, this was akin to a high school basketball team competing in the NBA playoffs and winning the finals. As Qiu and his colleagues considered the rounded-exterior and plain-vanilla interior of the original LaCrosse, they knew that Chinese consumers would sneer at such frumpy wheels that were meant to appeal to Buick's aging U.S. consumers. Buick's Chinese customers were in their mid-30s, successful, entrepreneurial, fashionable, and much more discerning—a demographic profile that made the bosses back in Michigan drool.

The PATAC team rethought and reshaped every piece of sheet metal on the LaCrosse. What came out was a glamorous, elegant sedan, with enough bling to turn heads of status-conscious young Shanghai buyers. Qui was in charge of the interior. With Shanghai's trendy clubs in mind, Qui stated, "I looked at where people lived, where they hung out, and then I tried to create that same feeling inside the car." The result feels more like a beautifully designed living room than the stoic interiors common to other Buicks. Soft buttery-colored ambient light glows from the instrument panel as well as from hidden lights in the rear. The front and back seats are well-padded and feature power massage.

PATAC's LaCrosse sold more than 110,000 units in China during its second year of production. That's more cars than all the Buicks sold in the United States during that same year. The LaCrosse was instrumental in pushing Buick's 2010 total Chinese sales to 550,000 units. "Our LaCrosse pushed the expectations," says Raymond Bierzynski, president of PATAC. "Our Buick is what the brand wants to be everywhere in the world." The move to incorporate PATAC's designs into a vehicle that would sell in all of Buick's markets signals that GM is recognizing that the world is bigger than North America. PATAC is taking the lead on creative strategy. "We aren't the little voice at the end of the phone anymore," Bierzynski says. "China commands 8 million units a year. We're GM's [biggest] market. We are the experts."

The big question is this: How will Chinese-influenced designs be received in the United States and other markets? While the LaCrosse is never expected to be as successful in the United States as it is in China, 2010 was Buick's best year in the United States in over a decade. Total sales increased by 52 percent over the previous year, making Buick the fastest-growing mainstream car brand in the country.

Perhaps more important are changes in consumer perceptions of the brand that indicate the potential for future growth. During 2010, public opinion of Buick improved by 125 percent while purchase consideration went up 65 percent. That's not all because of the LaCrosse, mind you. But it is worth noting that automotive journalists gave PATAC's redesign rave reviews. In fact, the LaCrosse was one of *Car and Driver* magazine's three finalists for "Car of the Year." The magazine proclaimed it, "Easily the best Buick sedan in a long time." The outcome of PATAC's LaCrosse has earned the design studio other projects that will sell in multiple world markets.

Buick will be introducing 12 new models to China in the near future as GM has its sights set on big targets. Its goal is to double its Chinese sales by 2015, putting its tally at nearly 5 million vehicles, with Buick accounting for more than 1 million of that. Ford is struggling to break 500,000 units in China in a single year and Chrysler isn't even on the radar. However, some financial analysts aren't so optimistic, estimating that GM will grow to only 3.3 million units in China by 2015 and will actually lose market share in the rapidly growing Chinese market. Whatever the outcome, it's clear that Buick is a global brand with momentum in the right place.

Questions for Discussion

1. Does Buick have a truly global strategy, or just a series of regional strategies? Explain.

2. Do GM's global manufacturing facilities, such as Shanghai GM, solidify a global strategy? Why or why not?

3. What is Buick's global strategy in terms of the five global product and communications strategies?

4. Can competitors easily replicate Buick's strategy in China? Why or why not?

5. Based on Buick's goals as discussed in the case, what do you predict for Buick in the coming years in China? In the United States?

Sources: Jens Meiners, "Ford and GM Battle for Sales in China," *Car and Driver*, September 2010, accessed at www.caranddriver .com; Steve Shannon, "Buick Is Popular in China?" accessed at www.gmblogs.com; Fara Warner, "Made in China," *Fast Company*, December 2007, accessed at www.fastcompany.com; Ken Zino, "Buick Sales in China Surpass 3 Million," May 2011, accessed at www.autoinformed.com.

Company Case 16

International Paper: Combining Industry and Social Responsibility

What image comes to mind when you hear the term *industrial corporation*? Pollution-belching smoke stacks? Strip-mined landscapes? Chemicals seeping into water supplies? Now think about the term *environmental steward*. Although that label might not seem compatible, the truth is that changes in regulations, combined with pressure from environmental and consumer groups, have forced most industrial companies to be more socially responsible. But at least one company has had social responsibility as a core value since it started business more than 110 years ago: International Paper (IP). Today, IP is considered by many to be the most socially responsible company in the world.

You may not know much about International Paper, but it makes products that you use every day: paper for printers, envelopes for mail, cardboard clamshells and paper bags for fast food, and the boxes that hold your cold cereal, to name just a few. IP makes lots of those products. Last year, it sold over $25 billion worth of paper, packaging, and wood products, placing it in the number 105 slot on the Fortune 500. With operations all over the world, IP employs more than 60,000 people. Those are pretty big numbers for a company that most people know little about.

In addition to receiving notice for its size and scope, International Paper has also ranked consistently among *Fortune* magazine's most admired companies. Not only did it grab the number-one spot on that list in its industry six years in a row, but out of more than 600 contending companies from all industries, IP recently ranked number one in social responsibility. That's right—a paper and lumber company leading in initiatives to make the world a better place.

At the heart of International Paper's admirable actions, we have to look at the comprehensive, integrated plan that the company labels *sustainability*. The company sums up the program with the slogan, "Sustaining a better world for generations, the IP way." That's not just a catch phrase. It lies at the heart of IP's corporate mission statement and has created a culture based on a set of supporting principles. According to company literature, "We have always taken a sustainable approach to business that balances environmental, social, and economic needs. This approach has served our company and society well." IP constantly maintains this balance by adhering to three key pillars that transform the concepts into action: managing natural resources, reducing the environmental footprint, and building strategic partnerships.

Managing Natural Resources

According to David Liebetreu, IP's vice president of global sourcing, "Sustainability means that we can take care of the environment and our businesses—those two concepts are not mutually exclusive." By taking care of the environment, Liebetreu refers to the systems that IP has in place to ensure that every phase of the corporate global supply chain—manufacturing, distribution, sales, and recycling—is carried out in a way that safely and responsibly cares for natural resources.

For example, International Paper has been a leader in promoting the planting and growing of trees. It believes that if forest resources are properly managed, they provide an infinite supply of raw materials for the company's products while supporting clean water, diverse wildlife habitats, recreational opportunities, and aesthetic beauty. To this end, the company actively supports research, innovation, and third-party certification to improve the management of forest resources.

Another way that International Paper manages natural resources is through conservation. But it has proven time and time again that conservation doesn't have to be a sunk cost. It can be an investment that provides cost savings for a company.

Pulp and paper mills are complex, energy intensive operations. Finding ways to reduce, reuse and recycle energy at each of its facilities reduces the consumption of fossil fuels and reduces air emissions, including carbon dioxide.

Typically gas, coal or bark fuels are fired in boilers to produce steam to power operations throughout the mill. Capturing steam in one area and reusing it in another reduces the amount of fresh steam required and reduces the amount of fuel needed to power the plant.

[The IP] mill in Vicksburg, Mississippi, is recovering and reusing 38,000 pounds of steam per hour. A one-time investment of $2.8 million in capital improvements will save an estimated $2.4 million in fuel costs annually. At [an IP] mill in Savannah, Georgia, an investment of $900,000 in capital improvements reduced the demand for steam, and consequently the coal needed to produce it, by 25,000 pounds per hour. The annual savings are estimated at more than $600,000.

Reducing the Environmental Footprint

When it refers to reducing its environmental footprint, International Paper means that it is committed to transparently reporting its activities to the public for any of its activities that impact the environment, health, or safety. "At International Paper, we've been routinely sharing our environmental, economic, and social performance with the public for over a decade," said David Struhs, vice president of environment, health, and safety. "Over the years, these reports have offered a level of transparency unmatched in our industry." This reporting philosophy applies to any company activity that leaves a footprint, including air emissions, environmental performance, health and safety, solid waste, and environmental certifications.

With transparency comes accountability. Because of its reporting practices, International Paper is more motivated to reduce its environmental footprint. Over a recent two-year period, the company cut its hazardous waste by almost 8 percent. It reduced the amount that it put in landfills by 10 percent by finding beneficial ways to recycle those materials. It made similar improvements in virtually every company footprint area. A recent account of company activities in Brazil illustrates this concept well.

Nature, once tamed, is again growing wild along Brazil's Mogi Guacu River, which means "large river of snakes" in the native language of Tupi. This year, seven constructed lagoons running along the banks of the Mogi Guacu designed to filter used water from the nearby International Paper plant were replaced by a more modern wastewater facility.

Although the lagoons are no longer needed for water treatment, International Paper recognized their potential environmental benefits. Five of the ponds were restored with native vegetation to establish a vast expanse of natural wetland habitat. Two of the ponds were preserved to sustain wildlife that had made their home in the area—snakes included.

To better manage the future impact of mill operations on the lush tropical landscape, the mill also installed technology at the river's edge to continuously measure and report water quality. The results are monitored remotely by facility managers as well as by government regulators. This unprecedented access to information on environmental performance has set a standard for other industries along this large river of snakes.

Building Strategic Partnerships

In order to most efficiently carry out its sustainability efforts, International Paper must enlist the help of numerous organizations. Building strategic partnerships is, therefore, critical. International Paper has a long tradition of partnering with a broad range of governmental, academic, environmental, and customer organizations. These partnerships are guided by the objectives of making progress in sustainability, providing solutions for customers, making a positive impact on the environment, and supporting social responsibility.

International Paper has partnered with some of the biggest sustainability organizations to make big differences. Partners include the National Park Foundation, the National Recycling Coalition, and the Conservation Fund. But the following story from a company press release illustrates how even a minor partnership oriented around a small product can make a "latte" difference in the world.

Coffee is one of the world's most popular drinks. Coffee houses—long a fixture in cultures and countries around the globe—sprang up across America during the last 20 years. Every year, as many as 15 billion "cups of joe" are served on the go in paper cups and that number is expected to grow to 23 billion by the end of the decade.

While coffee connoisseurs savored the flavors of new varieties of beans and brews, engineers and scientists at International Paper were thinking about how to improve the cup. Though cups are made of fiber grown and harvested from sustainable forests, conventional paper cups are lined with a petroleum-based plastic. The plastic lining is a small part of the cup but is made from nonrenewable resources and inhibits the decomposition of the underlying paper. As a result, disposable cups once filled with coffee are filling up our landfills.

But what if disposable coffee cups could join coffee grounds in the compost heap? To achieve that vision, International Paper, with partners DaniMer Scientific and NatureWorks LLC, developed a new type of cup lining made from plants instead of petro-chemicals. The revolutionary new cup, dubbed the ecotainer, is coated with a resin made from modified biopolymer. When discarded in commercial and municipal operations, cups with the new lining become compost, which can then be used for gardening, landscaping, and farming.

Since the launch of the ecotainer with Green Mountain Coffee Roasters in 2006, large and small companies alike have adopted this new cup. More than half a billion cups have eliminated over a million pounds of petrochemical plastic from the marketplace—enough petroleum to heat more than 32,000 homes for one year.

Coffee cups are just the beginning. International Paper is exploring opportunities to expand the technology to other products used in foodservice disposable packaging. So next time you order an espresso with steamed milk, ask for one in an ecotainer and you too can make a "latte" difference in the world.

International Paper hasn't been one of the high-growth juggernauts of the corporate world. Then again, it operates in a very mature industry. Nonetheless, IP makes innovative products that meet the needs of consumers. It employs tens of thousands of people throughout the world, contributing substantially to the communities in which it does business. It has grown in size to become one of the largest companies in the United States, and has been consistently profitable. It does all these things while sustaining the world for future generations. Indeed, International Paper proves that good business and good corporate citizenship can go hand in hand.

Questions for Discussion

1. How does International Paper defy the common social criticisms of marketing? Give as many examples as you can.

2. Why is International Paper successful in applying concepts of sustainability?

3. Analyze International Paper according to the Environmental Sustainability Portfolio in Figure 16.2. What conclusions can you draw?

4. Does International Paper practice enlightened marketing? Support your answer with as many examples as possible.

5. Would International Paper be more financially successful if it were not so focused on social responsibility? Explain.

Sources: Extracts and other case information are from International Paper's corporate Web site, accessed at www.internationalpaper.com/US/EN/Company/Sustainability/index.html, August 2011; with additional information from money.cnn.com/magazines/fortune/mostadmired/.

Appendix 2 Marketing Plan

The Marketing Plan: An Introduction

As a marketer, you will need a good marketing plan to provide direction and focus for your brand, product, or company. With a detailed plan, any business will be better prepared to launch a new product or build sales for existing products. Nonprofit organizations also use marketing plans to guide their fund-raising and outreach efforts. Even government agencies put together marketing plans for initiatives such as building public awareness of proper nutrition and stimulating area tourism.

The Purpose and Content of a Marketing Plan

Unlike a business plan, which offers a broad overview of the entire organization's mission, objectives, strategy, and resource allocation, a marketing plan has a more limited scope. It serves to document how the organization's strategic objectives will be achieved through specific marketing strategies and tactics, with the customer as the starting point. It is also linked to the plans of other departments within the organization. Suppose, for example, a marketing plan calls for selling 200,000 units annually. The production department must gear up to make that many units, the finance department must arrange funding to cover the expenses, the human resources department must be ready to hire and train staff, and so on. Without the appropriate level of organizational support and resources, no marketing plan can succeed.

Although the exact length and layout will vary from company to company, a marketing plan usually contains the sections described in Chapter 2. Smaller businesses may create shorter or less formal marketing plans whereas corporations frequently require highly structured marketing plans. To guide implementation effectively, every part of the plan must be described in considerable detail. Sometimes a company will post its marketing plans on an internal Web site, which allows managers and employees in different locations to consult specific sections and collaborate on additions or changes.

The Role of Research

Marketing plans are not created in a vacuum. To develop successful strategies and action programs, marketers need up-to-date information about the environment, the competition, and the market segments to be served. Often, analysis of internal data is the starting point for assessing the current marketing situation, supplemented by marketing intelligence and research investigating the overall market, the competition, key issues, and threats and opportunities. As the plan is put into effect, marketers use a variety of research techniques to measure progress toward objectives and identify areas for improvement if results fall short of projections.

Finally, marketing research helps marketers learn more about their customers' requirements, expectations, perceptions, and satisfaction levels. This deeper understanding provides a foundation for building competitive advantage through well-informed segmenting, targeting, differentiating, and positioning decisions. Thus, the marketing plan should outline what marketing research will be conducted and how the findings will be applied.

The Role of Relationships

The marketing plan shows how the company will establish and maintain profitable customer relationships. In the process, however, it also shapes a number of internal and external relationships. First, it affects how marketing personnel work with each other and with other departments to deliver value and satisfy customers. Second, it affects how the company works with suppliers, distributors, and strategic alliance partners to achieve the objectives listed in the plan. Third, it influences the company's dealings with other stakeholders, including government regulators, the media, and the community at large. All of these relationships are important to the organization's success, so they should be considered when a marketing plan is being developed.

From Marketing Plan to Marketing Action

Companies generally create yearly marketing plans, although some plans cover a longer period. Marketers start planning well in advance of the implementation date to allow time for marketing research, thorough analysis, management review, and coordination between departments. Then, after each action program begins, marketers monitor ongoing results, compare them with projections, analyze any differences, and take corrective steps as needed. Some marketers also prepare contingency plans for implementation if certain conditions emerge. Because of inevitable and sometimes unpredictable environmental changes, marketers must be ready to update and adapt marketing plans at any time.

For effective implementation and control, the marketing plan should define how progress toward objectives will be measured. Managers typically use budgets, schedules, and performance standards for monitoring and evaluating results. With budgets, they can compare planned expenditures with actual expenditures for a given week, month, or other period. Schedules allow management to see when tasks were supposed to be completed—and when they were actually completed. Performance standards track the outcomes of marketing programs to see whether the company is moving toward its objectives. Some examples of performance standards are market share, sales volume, product profitability, and customer satisfaction.

Sample Marketing Plan: Chill Beverage Company

Executive Summary

The Chill Beverage Company is preparing to launch a new line of vitamin-enhanced water called NutriWater. Although the bottled water market is maturing, the vitamin-enhanced water category is still growing. NutriWater will be positioned by the slogan "Expect more"—indicating that the brand offers more in the way of desirable product features and benefits at a competitive price. Chill Beverage is taking advantage of its existing experience and brand equity among its loyal current customer base of Millennials who consume its Chill Soda soft drink. NutriWater will target similar Millennials who are maturing and looking for an alternative to soft drinks and high-calorie sugared beverages.

The primary marketing objective is to achieve first-year U.S. sales of $30 million, roughly 2 percent of the enhanced water market. Based on this market share goal, the company expects to sell more than 17 million units the first year and break even in the final period of the year.

Current Marketing Situation

The Chill Beverage Company was founded in 2001 by an entrepreneur who had successfully built a company that primarily distributed niche and emerging products in the beverage industry. Its Chill Soda soft drink brand hit the market with six unique flavors in glass bottles. A few years later, the Chill Soda brand introduced an energy drink as well as a line of natural juice drinks. The company now markets dozens of Chill Soda flavors, many unique to the brand. Chill Beverage has grown its business every year since it was founded. In the most recent year, it achieved $185 million in revenue and net profits of $14.5 million.

As part of its future growth strategy, Chill Beverage is currently preparing to enter a new beverage category with a line of vitamin-enhanced waters.

As a beverage category, bottled water experienced tremendous growth during the 1990s and 2000s. Currently, the average person in the United States consumes more than 28 gallons of bottled water every year, a number that has increased 20-fold in just 30 years. Bottled water consumption is second only to soft drink consumption, ahead of milk, beer, and coffee. Although bottled water growth has tapered off somewhat in recent years, it is still moderately strong at approximately 3 percent growth annually. Most other beverage categories have experienced declines. In the most recent year, 8.75 billion gallons of bottled water were sold in the United States with a value of more than $7.6 billion.

Competition is more intense now than ever as demand slows, industry consolidation continues, and new types of bottled water emerge. The U.S. market is dominated by three global corporations. With a portfolio of 12 brands (including Poland Spring, Nestlé Pure Life, and Arrowhead), Nestlé leads the market for "plain" bottled water. However, when all subcategories of bottled water are included (enhanced water, flavored water, etc.), Coca-Cola leads the U.S. market with a 22.9 percent share. Nestlé markets only plain waters but is number two at 21.5 percent of the total bottled water market. PepsiCo is third with 16.2 percent of the market. To demonstrate the strength of the vitamin-enhanced water segment, Coca-Cola's vitaminwater has higher annual sales than any other bottled water brand.

To break into this market, dominated by huge global corporations and littered with dozens of other small players, Chill Beverage must carefully target specific segments with features and benefits valued by those segments.

Market Description

The bottled water market consists of many different types of water. Varieties of plain water include spring, purified, mineral, and distilled. Although these different types of water are sold as consumer products, they also serve as the core ingredient for other types of bottled waters including enhanced water, flavored water, sparkling water, or any combination of those categories.

Although some consumers may not perceive much of a difference between brands, others are drawn to specific product features and benefits provided by different brands. For example, some consumers may perceive spring water as healthier than other types of water. Some may look for water that is optimized for hydration. Others seek additional nutritional benefits claimed by bottlers that enhance their brands with vitamins, minerals, herbs, and other additives. Still other consumers make selections based on flavor. The industry as a whole has positioned bottled water of all kinds as a low-calorie, healthy alternative to soft drinks, sports drinks, energy drinks, and other types of beverages.

Bottled water brands also distinguish themselves by size and type of container, multipacks, and refrigeration at point-of-sale. Chill Beverage's market for NutriWater consists of consumers of single-serving-sized bottled beverages who are looking for a healthy yet flavorful alternative. "Healthy" in this context means both low-calorie and enhanced nutritional content. This market includes traditional soft drink consumers who want to improve their health as well as non-soft drink consumers who want an option other than plain bottled water. Specific segments that Chill Beverage will target during the first year include athletes, the health conscious, the socially responsible, and Millennials who favor independent corporations. The Chill Soda brand has established a strong base of loyal customers, primarily among Millennials. This generational segment is becoming a prime target as it matures and seeks alternatives to full-calorie soft drinks. ▶ **Table A2.1** shows how NutriWater addresses the needs of targeted consumer segments.

Product Review

Chill Beverage's new line of vitamin-enhanced water—called NutriWater—offers the following features:

- Six new-age flavors including Peach Mango, Berry Pomegranate, Kiwi Dragonfruit, Mandarin Orange, Blueberry Grape, and Key Lime.
- Single-serving size, 20-ounce, PET recyclable bottles.

> **Table A2.1**   Segment Needs and Corresponding Features/Benefits of NutriWater

Targeted Segment	Customer Need	Corresponding Features/Benefits
Athletes	• Hydration and replenishment of essential minerals • Energy to maximize performance	• Electrolytes and carbohydrates • B vitamins, carbohydrates
Health conscious	• Maintain optimum weight • Optimize nutrition levels • Avoid harmful chemicals and additives • Desire to consume a tastier beverage than water	• Half the calories of fully sugared beverages • Higher levels of vitamins A, B, C, E, Zinc, Chromium, and Folic Acid than other products; vitamins unavailable in other products • All natural ingredients • Six new-age flavors
Socially conscious	• Support causes that help solve world's social problems	• 25 cent donation from each purchase to Vitamin Angels
Millennials	• Aversion to mass-media advertising/technologically savvy • Counter-culture attitude • Diet enhancement due to fast-paced lifestyle	• Less-invasive online and social networking promotional tactics • Small, privately held company • Full RDA levels of essential vitamins and minerals

- Formulated for wellness, replenishment, and optimum energy.
- Full Recommended Daily Allowance (RDA) of essential vitamins and minerals (including electrolytes).
- Higher vitamin concentration—vitamin levels are two to ten times higher than market-leading products, with more vitamins and minerals than any other brand.
- Additional vitamins—vitamins include A, E, and B2, as well as Folic Acid—none of which are contained in the market-leading products.
- All natural—no artificial flavors, colors, or preservatives.
- Sweetened with pure cane sugar and Stevia, a natural zero-calorie sweetener.
- Twenty-five cents from each purchase will be donated to Vitamin Angels, a nonprofit organization with a mission to prevent vitamin deficiency in at-risk children.

Competitive Review

As sales of bottled waters entered a strong growth phase in the 1990s, the category began to expand. In addition to the various types of plain water, new categories emerged. These included flavored waters—such as Aquafina's Flavorsplash—as well as enhanced waters. Enhanced waters emerged to bridge the gap between soft drinks and waters, appealing to people who knew they should drink more water and less soft drinks but still wanted flavor. Development of brands for this product variation has occurred primarily in startup and boutique beverage companies. In the 2000s, major beverage corporations acquired the most successful smaller brands, providing the bigger firms with a solid market position in this category and diversification in bottled waters in general. Currently, enhanced water sales account for approximately 18 percent of the total bottled water market.

The fragmentation of this category, combined with domination by the market leaders, has created a severely competitive environment. Although there is indirect competition posed by all types of bottled waters and even other types of beverages (soft drinks, energy drinks, juices, teas), this competitive analysis focuses on direct competition from enhanced water brands. For the purposes of this analysis, enhanced water is bottled water with additives that are intended to provide health and wellness benefits. The most common additives include vitamins, minerals (including electrolytes), and herbs. Most commonly, enhanced waters are sweetened, flavored, and colored. This definition distinguishes enhanced water from sports drinks that have the primary purpose of maximizing hydration by replenishing electrolytes.

Enhanced water brands are typically sweetened with a combination of some kind of sugar and a zero-calorie sweetener, resulting in about half the sugar content, carbohydrates, and calories of regular soft drinks and other sweetened beverages. The types of sweeteners used create a point of differentiation. Many brands, including the market leaders, sell both regular and zero-calorie varieties.

Pricing for this product is consistent across brands and varies by type of retail outlet, with convenience stores typically charging more than grocery stores. The price for a 20-ounce bottle ranges from $1.00 to $1.89, with some niche brands costing slightly more. Key competitors to Chill Beverage's NutriWater line include the following:

- *Coca-Cola's vitaminwater:* Created in 2000 as a new product for Energy Brands' Glacéau, which was also the developer of Smartwater (distilled water with electrolytes). Coca-Cola purchased Energy Brands for $4.1 billion in 2007. Coca-Cola's vitaminwater is sold in regular and zero-calorie versions. With 28 varieties, vitaminwater offers more options than any brand on the market. Whereas vitaminwater varieties are distinguished by flavor, they are named according to functional benefits such as Stur-D (healthy bones), Defense (strengthens immune system), Focus (mental clarity), and Restore (post work-out recovery). The brand's current slogan is "Hydration for every occasion—morning, noon, and night." vitaminwater is vapor distilled, de-ionized, and/or filtered and is sweetened with crystalline fructose (corn syrup) and erythritol all-natural sweetener. Available in 20-ounce PET bottles and multipacks, vitaminwater exceeds $830 million in annual sales and commands 61 percent of the enhanced waters market. More notably, it outsells all other bottled water brands, enhanced or otherwise, including Coca-Cola's own Dasani.

- *SoBe Lifewater:* PepsiCo bought SoBe in 2000. SoBe introduced Lifewater in 2008 with a hit Super Bowl ad as an answer to Coca-Cola's vitaminwater. The Lifewater line includes 17 regular and zero-calorie varieties. Each bottle of Lifewater is designated by flavor and one of six different functional categories: Electrolytes, Lean Machine, B-Energy, C-Boost, Antioxidants, and Pure. Each variety is infused with a formulation of vitamins, minerals, and herbs designed to provide the claimed benefit. The most recent line—Pure—contains only water, a hint of flavor, and electrolytes. Sweetened with a combination of sugar and erythritol, Lifewater makes the claim to be "all natural." It contains no artificial flavors or colors. However, some analysts debate the "natural" designation for erythritol. Lifewater is sold in 20-ounce PET bottles and multipacks as well as one-liter PET bottles. With more than $269 million in annual revenues, Lifewater is the number two enhanced water brand, capturing 20 percent of the market.

- *Propel Zero:* Gatorade created Propel in 2000, just one year prior to PepsiCo's purchase of this leading sports drink marketer. Originally marketed and labeled as "fitness water," it is now available only as Propel Zero. Although the fitness water designation has been dropped, Propel Zero still leans toward that positioning with the label stating "REPLENISH + ENERGIZE + PROTECT." Propel Zero comes in seven flavors, each containing the same blend of B vitamins, vitamin C, vitamin E, antioxidants, and electrolytes. It is sweetened with sucralose. Propel Zero is available in a wider variety of sizes, with 16.9-, 20-, and 24-ounce PET bottles and multipacks. Propel Zero is also marketed in powder form to be added to bottled water. With $165 million in revenues, Propel Zero is the number three enhanced water brand with a 12 percent share of the enhanced waters market.

- *RESCUE Water:* The Arizona Beverage Company is best known as the number one producer of ready-to-drink bottled teas. However, it also bottles a variety of other beverages including smoothies, sports drinks, energy drinks, and juice blends. Its newest brand is RESCUE Water, introduced to the U.S. market in 2010. It sets itself apart from other enhanced waters with green tea extract added to a blend of vitamins and minerals. This provides a significant point of differentiation for those desiring green tea, but rules the brand out for the majority of customers who do not want it. It comes in five flavors, each with its own functional benefit. RESCUE Water touts other points of distinction as well, including branded Twinlab vitamins, all-natural ingredients, and a high-tech plastic bottle that resembles glass and maximizes freshness. Its Blueberry Coconut Hydrate variety contains real coconut water, an emerging alternative beverage category. Although RESCUE Water sales and market share figures are not yet known because of the product's newness, the Arizona Beverage Company is a multibillion dollar corporation with a long history of successful new product introductions.

- *Niche brands:* The market for enhanced waters includes at least four companies that market their wares on a small scale through independent retailers: Assure, Ex Aqua Vitamins, Ayala Herbal Water, and Skinny Water. Some brands feature exotic additives and/or artistic glass bottles.

Despite the strong competition, NutriWater believes it can create a relevant brand image and gain recognition among the targeted segments. The brand offers strong points of differentiation with higher and unique vitamin content, all-natural ingredients, and support for a relevant social cause. With other strategic assets, Chill Beverage is confident that it can establish a competitive advantage that will allow NutriWater to grow in the market. ▶ **Table A2.2** shows a sample of competing products.

Channels and Logistics Review

The purchase of vitaminwater by Coca-Cola left a huge hole in the independent distributor system. NutriWater will be distributed through an independent distributor to a network of retailers in the United States. This strategy will avoid some of the head-on competition for shelf space with the Coca-Cola and PepsiCo brands and will also directly target likely NutriWater customers. As with the rollout of the core Chill Soda brand, this strategy will focus on placing coolers in retail locations that will exclusively hold NutriWater. These retailers include:

- *Grocery chains:* Regional grocery chains such as HyVee in the Midwest, Wegman's in the east, and WinCo in the west.
- *Health and natural food stores:* Chains such as Whole Foods, as well as local health food co-ops.
- *Fitness centers:* National fitness center chains such as 24 Hour Fitness, Gold's Gym, and other regional chains.

As the brand gains acceptance, channels will expand into larger grocery chains, convenience stores, and unique locations relevant to the target customer segment.

Strengths, Weaknesses, Opportunities, and Threat Analysis

NutriWater has several powerful strengths on which to build, but its major weakness is lack of brand awareness and image. Major opportunities include a growing market and consumer

▶ **Table A2.2**	Sample of Competing Products	
Competitor	**Brand**	**Features**
Coca-Cola	vitaminwater	Regular and zero-calorie versions; 28 varieties; each flavor provides a different function based on blend of vitamins and minerals; vapor distilled, de-ionized, and/or filtered; sweetened with crystalline fructose and erythritol; 20-ounce single-serve or multi-pack.
PepsiCo	SoBe Lifewater	Regular and zero-calorie versions; 17 varieties; six different functional categories; vitamins, minerals, and herbs; Pure—mildly flavored, unsweetened water; sweetened with sugar and erythritol; "all natural"; 20-ounce single-serve and multi-packs as well as one-liter bottles.
PepsiCo	Propel Zero	Zero-calorie only; seven flavors; fitness positioning based on "Replenish + Energize + Protect"; B vitamins, vitamin C, vitamin E, antioxidants, and electrolytes; sweetened with sucralose; 16.9-ounce, 20-ounce, and 24-ounce PET bottles and multipacks; powdered packets.
Arizona Beverage	RESCUE Water	Full calorie only; five flavors, each with its own blend of vitamins and minerals; green tea extract (caffeine included); only brand with coconut water; Twinlab branded vitamins; high-tech plastic bottle.

trends targeted by NutriWater's product traits. Threats include barriers to entry posed by limited retail space, as well as image issues for the bottled water industry. ▶ **Table A2.3** summarizes NutriWater's main strengths, weaknesses, opportunities, and threats.

Strengths

NutriWater can rely on the following important strengths:

1. *Superior quality:* NutriWater boasts the highest levels of added vitamins of any enhanced water, including full RDA levels of many vitamins. It is all natural with no artificial flavors, colors, or preservatives. It is sweetened with both pure cane sugar and the natural zero-calorie sweetener, Stevia.
2. *Expertise in alternative beverage marketing:* The Chill Soda brand went from nothing to a successful and rapidly growing soft drink brand with fiercely loyal customers in a matter of only one decade. This success was achieved by starting small and focusing on gaps in the marketplace.
3. *Social responsibility:* Every customer will have the added benefit of helping malnourished children throughout the world. Although the price of NutriWater is in line with other competitors, low promotional costs allow for the substantial charitable donation of 25 cents per bottle while maintaining profitability.
4. *Anti-establishment image:* The big brands have decent products and strong distribution relationships. But they also carry the image of the large, corporate establishments. Chill Beverage has achieved success with an underdog image while remaining privately held. Coca-Cola's vitaminwater and PepsiCo's SoBe were built on this same image, but both are now owned by major multinational corporations.

Weaknesses

1. *Lack of brand awareness:* As an entirely new brand, NutriWater will enter the market with limited or no brand awareness. The affiliation with Chill Soda will be kept at a minimum in order to prevent associations between NutriWater and soft drinks. This issue will be addressed through promotion and distribution strategies.
2. *Limited budget:* As a smaller company, Chill Beverage has much smaller funds available for promotional and research activities.

Opportunities

1. *Growing market:* Although growth in the overall market for bottled water has slowed to some extent, its current rate of growth in the 3 percent range is relatively

| ▶ **Table A2.3** | NutriWater's Strengths, Weaknesses, Opportunities, and Threats |

Strengths	**Weaknesses**
● Superior quality	● Lack of brand awareness
● Expertise in alternative beverage marketing	● Limited budget
● Social responsibility	
● Anti-establishment image	

Opportunities	**Threats**
● Growing market	● Limited shelf space
● Gap in the distribution network	● Image of enhanced waters
● Health trends	● Environmental issues
● Anti-establishment image	

strong among beverage categories. Of the top six beverage categories, soft drinks, beer, milk, and fruit drinks experienced declines. The growth for coffee was less than 1 percent. More important than the growth of bottled waters in general, the enhanced water category is experiencing growth in the high single and low double digits.

2. *Gap in the distribution network:* The market leaders distribute directly to retailers. This gives them an advantage in large national chains. However, no major enhanced water brands are currently being sold through independent distributors.

3. *Health trends:* Weight and nutrition continue to be issues for consumers in the United States. The country has the highest obesity rate for developed countries at 34 percent, with well over 60 percent of the population officially "overweight." Those numbers continue to rise. Additionally, Americans get 21 percent of their daily calories from beverages, a number that has tripled in the last three decades. Consumers still desire flavored beverages but look for lower calorie alternatives.

4. *Anti-establishment image.* Millennials (born between 1977 and 2000) maintain a higher aversion to mass marketing messages and global corporations than do Gen Xers and baby boomers.

Threats

1. *Limited shelf space:* Whereas competition is generally a threat for any type of product, competition in retail beverages is particularly high because of limited retail space. Carrying a new beverage product requires retailers to reduce shelf or cooler space already occupied by other brands.

2. *Image of enhanced waters:* The image of enhanced waters is currently in question as Coca-Cola fights a class-action lawsuit accusing it of violating FDA regulations by promoting the health benefits of its vitaminwater brand. The lawsuit exposed the number one bottled water brand as basically sugar water with minimal nutritional value.

3. *Environmental issues:* Environmental groups continue to educate the public on the environmental costs of bottled water, including landfill waste, carbon emissions from production and transportation, and harmful effects of chemicals in plastics.

Objectives and Issues

Chill Beverage has set aggressive but achievable objectives for NutriWater for the first and second years of market entry.

First-Year Objectives

During the initial year on the market, Chill Beverage aims for NutriWater to achieve a 2 percent share of the enhanced water market, or approximately $30 million in sales, with break even achieved in the final period of the year. With an average retail price of $1.69, that equates with a sales goal of 17,751,480 bottles.

Second-Year Objectives

During the second year, Chill Beverage will unveil additional NutriWater flavors, including zero-calorie varieties. The second-year objective is to double sales from the first year, to $60 million.

Issues

In launching this new brand, the main issue is the ability to establish brand awareness and a meaningful brand image based on positioning that is relevant to target customer segments. Chill Beverage will invest in nontraditional means of promotion to accomplish these goals and to spark word-of-mouth. Establishing distributor and retailer relationships will also be critical in order to make the product available and provide point-of-purchase communications. Brand awareness and knowledge will be measured in order to adjust marketing efforts as necessary.

Marketing Strategy

NutriWater's marketing strategy will involve developing a "more for the same" positioning based on extra benefits for the price. The brand will also establish channel differentiation, as it will be available in locations where major competing brands are not. The primary target segment is Millennials. This segment is comprised of tweens (ages 10 to 12), teens (13 to 18), and young adults (19 to 33). NutriWater will focus specifically on the young adult market. Subsets of this generational segment include athletes, the health conscious, and the socially responsible.

Positioning

NutriWater will be positioned on an "Expect more" value proposition. This will allow for differentiating the brand based on product features (expect more vitamin content and all natural ingredients), desirable benefits (expect greater nutritional benefits), and values (do more for a social cause). Marketing will focus on conveying that NutriWater is more than just a beverage: It gives customers much more for their money in a variety of ways.

Product Strategy

NutriWater will be sold with all the features described in the Product Review section. As awareness takes hold and retail availability increases, more varieties will be made available. A zero-calorie version will be added to the product line, providing a solid fit with the health benefits sought by consumers. Chill Beverage's considerable experience in brand-building will be applied as an integral part of the product strategy for NutriWater. All aspects of the marketing mix will be consistent with the brand.

Pricing

There is little price variation in the enhanced waters category, particularly among leading brands. For this reason, NutriWater will follow a competition-based pricing strategy. Given that NutriWater claims superior quality, it must be careful not to position itself as a lower-cost alternative. Manufacturers do not quote list prices on this type of beverage, and prices vary considerably based on type of retail outlet and whether or not the product is refrigerated. Regular prices for single 20-ounce bottles of competing products are as low as $1.00 in discount-retailer stores and as high as $1.89 in convenience stores. Because NutriWater will not be targeting discount retailers and convenience stores initially, this will allow Chill Beverage to set prices at the average to higher end of the range for similar products in the same outlets. For grocery chains, this should be approximately $1.49 per bottle, with that price rising to $1.89 at health food stores and fitness centers, where prices tend to be higher.

Distribution Strategy

Based on the information in the Channels and Logistics Review, NutriWater will employ a selective distribution strategy with well-known regional grocers, health and natural food stores, and fitness centers. This distribution strategy will be executed through a network of independent beverage distributors, as there are no other major brands of enhanced water following this strategy. Chill Beverage gained success for its core Chill Soda soft drink line using this method. It also placed coolers with the brand logo in truly unique venues such as skate, surf, and snowboarding shops; tattoo and piercing parlors; fashion stores; and music stores—places that would expose the brand to target customers. Then, the soft drink brand expanded by getting contracts with retailers such as Panera, Barnes & Noble, Target, and Starbucks. This same approach will be taken with NutriWater by starting small, then expanding into larger chains. NutriWater will not target all the same stores used originally by Chill Soda, as many of those outlets were unique to the positioning and target customer for the Chill Soda soft drink brand.

Marketing Communication Strategy

As with the core Chill Soda brand, the marketing communication strategy for NutriWater will not follow a strategy based on traditional mass-communication advertising. Initially, there will be no broadcast or print advertising. Promotional resources for NutriWater will focus on three areas:

- *Online and mobile marketing:* The typical target customer for NutriWater spends more time online than with traditional media channels. A core component for this strategy will be building a brand Web site and driving traffic to that Web site by creating a presence on social networks, including Facebook, Google+, and Twitter. The NutriWater brand will also incorporate location-based services such as Foursquare and Facebook Places to help drive traffic to retail locations. A mobile phone ad campaign will provide additional support to the Web efforts.
- *Trade promotions:* Like the core Chill Soda brand, NutriWater's success will rely on relationships with retailers to create product availability. Primary incentives to retailers will include point-of-purchase displays, branded coolers, and volume incentives and contests. This push marketing strategy will combine with the other pull strategies.
- *Event marketing:* NutriWater will deploy teams in brand-labeled RVs to distribute product samples at events such as skiing and snowboarding competitions, golf tournaments, and concerts.

Marketing Research

To remain consistent with the online promotional approach, as well as using research methods that will effectively reach target customers, Chill Beverage will monitor online discussions via services such as Radian6. In this manner, the company will gauge customer perceptions of the brand, the products, and general satisfaction. For future development of the product and new distribution outlets, crowdsourcing methods will be utilized.

Action Programs

NutriWater will be introduced in February. The following are summaries of action programs that will be used during the first six months of the year to achieve the stated objectives.

January: Chill Beverage representatives will work with both independent distributors and retailers to educate them on the trade promotional campaign, incentives, and advantages for selling NutriWater. Representatives will also ensure that distributors and retailers are educated on product features and benefits as well as instructions for displaying point-of-purchase materials and coolers. The brand Web site and other sites such as Facebook will present teaser information about the product as well as availability dates and locations. Buzz will be enhanced by providing product samples to selected product reviewers, opinion leaders, influential bloggers, and celebrities.

February: On the date of availability, product coolers and point-of-purchase displays will be placed in retail locations. The full brand Web site and social network campaign will launch with full efforts on Facebook, Google+, and Twitter. This campaign will drive the "Expect more" slogan, as well as illustrate the ways that NutriWater delivers more than expected on product features, desirable benefits, and values by donating to Vitamin Angels and the social cause of battling vitamin deficiency in children.

March: To enhance the online and social marketing campaign, location-based services Foursquare and Facebook Places will be employed to drive traffic to retailers. Point-of-purchase displays and signage will be updated to support these efforts and to continue supporting retailers. The message of this campaign will focus on all aspects of "Expect more."

April: A mobile phone ad campaign will provide additional support, driving Web traffic to the brand Web site and social network sites, as well as driving traffic to retailers.

May: A trade sales contest will offer additional incentives and prizes to the distributors and retailers that sell the most NutriWater during a four-week period.

June: An event marketing campaign will mobilize a team of NutriWater representatives in NutriWater RVs to concerts and sports events. This will provide additional visibility for the brand as well as giving customers and potential customers the opportunity to sample products.

Budgets

Chill Beverage has set a first-year retail sales goal of $30 million with a projected average retail price of $1.69 per unit for a total of 17,751,480 units sold. With an average wholesale price of 85 cents per unit, this provides revenues of just over $15 million. Chill Beverage expects to break even during the final period of the first year. A break-even analysis assumes per-unit wholesale revenue of 85 cents per unit, a variable cost per unit of 14 cents, and estimated first-year fixed costs of $12,500,000. Based on these assumptions, the break-even calculation is:

$$\frac{\$12,500,000}{\$0.85/\text{unit} - \$0.14/\text{unit}} = 17,605,634$$

Controls

Chill Beverage is planning tight control measures to closely monitor product quality, brand awareness, brand image, and customer satisfaction. This will enable the company to react quickly in correcting any problems that may occur. Other early warning signals that will be monitored for signs of deviation from the plan include monthly sales (by segment and channel) and monthly expenses. Given the market's volatility, contingency plans are also in place to address fast-moving environmental changes such as shifting consumer preferences, new products, and new competition.

Sources: Jeffrey Klineman, "Restoring an Icon," *Beverage Spectrum Magazine,* December 2010, pp. 16–18; Ryan Underwood, "Jonesing for Soda," *Fast Company*, December 19, 2007, accessed at www.fastcompany.com; "New Playbook at Jones Soda," *Beverage Spectrum Magazine*, March 2008; Matt Casey, "Enhanced Options Divide a Category," *Beverage Spectrum Magazine*, December 2008, p. 74; product and market information obtained from www.sobe.com, www.vitaminwater.com, www.nestle-waters.com, www.drinkarizona.com, and www.jonessoda.com, September 2011.

Appendix 3 Marketing by the Numbers

Marketing managers are facing increased accountability for the financial implications of their actions. This appendix provides a basic introduction to measuring marketing financial performance. Such financial analysis guides marketers in making sound marketing decisions and in assessing the outcomes of those decisions.

The appendix is built around a hypothetical manufacturer of consumer electronics products—HD. The company is introducing an Internet TV Blu-ray disc player that plays Blu-ray and 3-D video discs as well as videos and television programming streamed over the Internet on high-definition and 3-D televisions. In this appendix, we will analyze the various decisions HD's marketing managers must make before and after the new-product launch.

The appendix is organized into three sections. The *first section* introduces pricing, break-even, and margin analysis assessments that will guide the introduction of HD's new product. The *second section* discusses demand estimates, the marketing budget, and marketing performance measures. It begins with a discussion of estimating market potential and company sales. It then introduces the marketing budget, as illustrated through a *pro forma* profit-and-loss statement followed by the actual profit-and-loss statement. Next, we discuss marketing performance measures, with a focus on helping marketing managers to better defend their decisions from a financial perspective. In the *third section,* we analyze the financial implications of various marketing tactics.

Each of the three sections ends with a set of quantitative exercises that provide you with an opportunity to apply the concepts you learned to situations beyond HD.

Pricing, Break-Even, and Margin Analysis

Pricing Considerations

Determining price is one of the most important marketing-mix decisions. The limiting factors are demand and costs. Demand factors, such as buyer-perceived value, set the price ceiling. The company's costs set the price floor. In between these two factors, marketers must consider competitors' prices and other factors such as reseller requirements, government regulations, and company objectives.

Most current competing Internet TV Blu-ray disc player products sell at retail prices between $100 and $600, some are over $1,000. We first consider HD's pricing decision from a cost perspective. Then, we consider consumer value, the competitive environment, and reseller requirements.

Determining Costs

Fixed costs
Costs that do not vary with production or sales level.

Variable costs
Costs that vary directly with the level of production.

Recall from Chapter 10 that there are different types of costs. **Fixed costs** do not vary with production or sales level and include costs such as rent, interest, depreciation, and clerical and management salaries. Regardless of the level of output, the company must pay these costs. Whereas total fixed costs remain constant as output increases, the fixed cost per unit (or average fixed cost) will decrease as output increases because the total fixed costs are spread across more units of output. **Variable costs** vary directly with the level of production and include costs related to the direct production of the product (such as costs of goods sold—COGS) and many of the marketing costs associated with selling it. Although these costs tend to be uniform for each unit produced, they are called variable because their total

Total costs
The sum of the fixed and variable costs for any given level of production.

varies with the number of units produced. **Total costs** are the sum of the fixed and variable costs for any given level of production.

HD has invested $10 million in refurbishing an existing facility to manufacture the new media phone product. Once production begins, the company estimates that it will incur fixed costs of $20 million per year. The variable cost to produce each device is estimated to be $125 and is expected to remain at that level for the output capacity of the facility.

Setting Price Based on Costs

Cost-plus pricing (or markup pricing)
A standard markup to the cost of the product.

HD starts with the cost-based approach to pricing discussed in Chapter 10. Recall that the simplest method, **cost-plus pricing** (or **markup pricing**), simply adds a standard markup to the cost of the product. To use this method, however, HD must specify expected unit sales so that total unit costs can be determined. Unit variable costs will remain constant regardless of the output, but *average unit fixed costs* will decrease as output increases.

To illustrate this method, suppose HD has fixed costs of $20 million, variable costs of $125 per unit, and expects unit sales of 1 million players. Thus, the cost per unit is given by:

$$\text{Unit cost} = \text{variable cost} + \frac{\text{fixed costs}}{\text{unit sales}} = \$125 + \frac{\$20,000,000}{1,000,000} = \$145$$

Relevant costs
Costs that will occur in the future and that will vary across the alternatives being considered.

Note that we do *not* include the initial investment of $10 million in the total fixed cost figure. It is not considered a fixed cost because it is not a *relevant* cost. **Relevant costs** are those that will occur in the future and that will vary across the alternatives being considered. HD's investment to refurbish the manufacturing facility was a one-time cost that will not reoccur in the future. Such past costs are *sunk costs* and should not be considered in future analyses.

Break-even price
The price at which total revenue equals total cost and profit is zero.

Also notice that if HD sells its product for $145, the price is equal to the total cost per unit. This is the **break-even price**—the price at which unit revenue (price) equals unit cost and profit is zero.

Suppose HD does not want to merely break even but rather wants to earn a 25 percent markup on sales. HD's markup price is:[1]

$$\text{Markup price} = \frac{\text{unit cost}}{(1 - \text{desired return on sales})} = \frac{\$145}{1 - 0.25} = \$193.33$$

This is the price at which HD would sell the product to resellers such as wholesalers or retailers to earn a 25 percent profit on sales.

Return on investment (ROI) pricing (or target-return pricing)
A cost-based pricing method that determines price based on a specified rate of return on investment.

Another approach HD could use is called **return on investment (ROI) pricing** (or **target-return pricing**). In this case, the company *would* consider the initial $10 million investment, but only to determine the dollar profit goal. Suppose the company wants a 30 percent return on its investment. The price necessary to satisfy this requirement can be determined by:

$$\text{ROI price} = \text{unit cost} + \frac{\text{ROI} \times \text{investment}}{\text{unit sales}} = \$145 + \frac{0.3 \times \$10,000,000}{1,000,000} = \$148$$

That is, if HD sells its product for $148, it will realize a 30 percent return on its initial investment of $10 million.

In these pricing calculations, unit cost is a function of the expected sales, which were estimated to be 1 million units. But what if actual sales were lower? Then the unit cost would be higher because the fixed costs would be spread over fewer units, and the realized percentage markup on sales or ROI would be lower. Alternatively, if sales are higher than the estimated 1 million units, unit costs would be lower than $145, so a lower price would produce the desired markup on sales or ROI. It's important to note that these cost-based pricing methods are *internally* focused and do not consider demand, competitors' prices, or reseller requirements. Because HD will be selling this product to consumers through wholesalers and retailers offering competing brands, the company must consider markup pricing from this perspective.

Setting Price Based on External Factors

Whereas costs determine the price floor, HD also must consider external factors when setting price. HD does not have the final say concerning the final price of its product to consumers—retailers do. So it must start with its suggested retail price and work back. In doing so, HD must consider the markups required by resellers that sell the product to consumers.

Markup
The difference between a company's selling price for a product and its cost to manufacture or purchase it.

In general, a dollar **markup** is the difference between a company's selling price for a product and its cost to manufacture or purchase it. For a retailer, then, the markup is the difference between the price it charges consumers and the cost the retailer must pay for the product. Thus, for any level of reseller:

$$\text{Dollar markup} = \text{selling price} - \text{cost}$$

Markups are usually expressed as a percentage, and there are two different ways to compute markups—on *cost* or on *selling price*:

$$\text{Markup percentage on cost} = \frac{\text{dollar markup}}{\text{cost}}$$

$$\text{Markup percentage on selling price} = \frac{\text{dollar markup}}{\text{selling price}}$$

To apply reseller margin analysis, HD must first set the suggested retail price and then work back to the price at which it must sell the product to a wholesaler. Suppose retailers expect a 30 percent margin and wholesalers want a 20 percent margin based on their respective selling prices. In addition, suppose that HD sets a manufacturer's suggested retail price (MSRP) of $299.99 for its product.

Value-based pricing
Offering just the right combination of quality and good service at a fair price.

HD selected the $299.99 MSRP because it is lower than most competitors' prices but is not so low that consumers might perceive it to be of poor quality. In addition, the company's research shows that it is below the threshold at which more consumers are willing to purchase the product. By using buyers' perceptions of value and not the seller's cost to determine the MSRP, HD is using **value-based pricing**. For simplicity, we will use an MSRP of $300 in further analyses.

Markup chain
The sequence of markups used by firms at each level in a channel.

To determine the price HD will charge wholesalers, we must first subtract the retailer's margin from the retail price to determine the retailer's cost ($300 − ($300 × 0.30) = $210). The retailer's cost is the wholesaler's price, so HD next subtracts the wholesaler's margin ($210 − ($210 × 0.20) = $168). Thus, the **markup chain** representing the sequence of markups used by firms at each level in a channel for HD's new product is:

Suggested retail price:	$300
minus retail margin (30%):	−$ 90
Retailer's cost/wholesaler's price:	$210
minus wholesaler's margin (20%):	−$ 42
Wholesaler's cost/HD's price:	$168

By deducting the markups for each level in the markup chain, HD arrives at a price for the product to wholesalers of $168.

Break-Even and Margin Analysis

The previous analyses derived a value-based price of $168 for HD's product. Although this price is higher than the break-even price of $145 and covers costs, that price assumed a demand of 1 million units. But how many units and what level of dollar sales must HD achieve to break even at the $168 price? And what level of sales must be achieved to realize various profit goals? These questions can be answered through break-even and margin analysis.

Determining Break-Even Unit Volume and Dollar Sales

Based on an understanding of costs, consumer value, the competitive environment, and reseller requirements, HD has decided to set its price to wholesalers at $168. At that price, what sales level will be needed for HD to break even or make a profit on its product? **Break-even analysis** determines the unit volume and dollar sales needed to be profitable given a particular price and cost structure. At the break-even point, total revenue equals total costs and profit is zero. Above this point, the company will make a profit; below it, the company will lose money. HD can calculate break-even volume using the following formula:

$$\text{Break-even volume} = \frac{\text{fixed costs}}{\text{price} - \text{unit variable cost}}$$

Break-even analysis

Analysis to determine the unit volume and dollar sales needed to be profitable given a particular price and cost structure.

The denominator (price − unit variable cost) is called **unit contribution** (sometimes called contribution margin). It represents the amount that each unit contributes to covering fixed costs. Break-even volume represents the level of output at which all (variable and fixed) costs are covered. In HD's case, break-even unit volume is:

$$\text{Break-even volume} = \frac{\text{fixed cost}}{\text{price} - \text{variable cost}} = \frac{\$20,000,000}{\$168 - \$125} = 465,116.2 \text{ units}$$

Unit contribution

The amount that each unit contributes to covering fixed costs—the difference between price and variable costs.

Thus, at the given cost and pricing structure, HD will break even at 465,117 units.

To determine the break-even dollar sales, simply multiply the unit break-even volume by the selling price:

$$\text{BE sales} = \text{BE}_{\text{vol}} \times \text{price} = 465,117 \times \$168 = \$78,139,656$$

Another way to calculate dollar break-even sales is to use the percentage contribution margin (hereafter referred to as **contribution margin**), which is the unit contribution divided by the selling price:

Contribution margin

The unit contribution divided by the selling price.

$$\text{Contribution margin} = \frac{\text{price} - \text{variable cost}}{\text{price}} = \frac{\$168 - \$125}{\$168} = 0.256 \text{ or } 25.6\%$$

Then,

$$\text{Break-even sales} = \frac{\text{fixed costs}}{\text{contribution margin}} = \frac{\$20,000,000}{0.256} = \$78,125,000$$

Note that the difference between the two break-even sales calculations is due to rounding.

Such break-even analysis helps HD by showing the unit volume needed to cover costs. If production capacity cannot attain this level of output, then the company should not launch this product. However, the unit break-even volume is well within HD's capacity. Of course, the bigger question concerns whether HD can sell this volume at the $168 price. We'll address that issue a little later.

Understanding contribution margin is useful in other types of analyses as well, particularly if unit prices and unit variable costs are unknown or if a company (say, a retailer) sells many products at different prices and knows the percentage of total sales variable costs represent. Whereas *unit contribution* is the difference between unit price and unit variable costs, *total contribution* is the difference between total sales and total variable costs. The overall contribution margin can be calculated by:

$$\text{Contribution margin} = \frac{\text{total sales} - \text{total variable costs}}{\text{total sales}}$$

Regardless of the actual level of sales, if the company knows what percentage of sales is represented by variable costs, it can calculate the contribution margin. For example, HD's unit variable cost is $125, or 74 percent of the selling price ($125 ÷ $168 = 0.74). That means for every $1 of sales revenue for HD, $0.74 represents variable costs, and the difference ($0.26) represents contribution to fixed costs. But even if the company doesn't know its unit price and unit variable cost, it can calculate the contribution margin from total sales and total variable costs or from knowledge of the total cost structure. It can set total sales equal to 100 percent regardless of the actual absolute amount and determine the contribution margin:

$$\text{Contribution margin} = \frac{100\% - 74\%}{100\%} = \frac{1 - 0.74}{1} = 1 - 0.74 = 0.26 \text{ or } 26\%$$

Note that this matches the percentage calculated from the unit price and unit variable cost information. This alternative calculation will be very useful later when analyzing various marketing decisions.

Determining "Break Even" for Profit Goals

Although it is useful to know the break-even point, most companies are more interested in making a profit. Assume HD would like to realize a $5 million profit in the first year. How many units must it sell at the $168 price to cover fixed costs and produce this profit? To determine this amount, HD can simply add the profit figure to fixed costs and again divide by the unit contribution to determine unit sales:

$$\text{Unit volume} = \frac{\text{fixed cost} + \text{profit goal}}{\text{price} - \text{variable cost}} = \frac{\$20,000,000 + \$5,000,000}{\$168 - \$125} = 581,395.3 \text{ units}$$

Thus, to earn a $5 million profit, HD must sell 581,396 units. Multiply this amount by price to determine the dollar sales needed to achieve a $5 million profit:

$$\text{Dollar sales} = 581,396 \text{ units} \times \$168 = \$97,674,528$$

Or use the contribution margin:

$$\text{Sales} = \frac{\text{fixed cost} + \text{profit goal}}{\text{contribution margin}} = \frac{\$20,000,000 + \$5,000,000}{0.256} = \$97,656,250$$

Again, note that the difference between the two break-even sales calculations is due to rounding.

As we saw previously, a profit goal can also be stated as a return on investment goal. For example, recall that HD wants a 30 percent return on its $10 million investment. Thus, its absolute profit goal is $3 million ($10,000,000 × 0.30). This profit goal is treated the same way as in the previous example:[2]

$$\text{Unit volume} = \frac{\text{fixed cost} + \text{profit goal}}{\text{price} - \text{variable cost}} = \frac{\$20,000,000 + \$3,000,000}{\$168 - \$125} = 534,884 \text{ units}$$

$$\text{Dollars sales} = 534,884 \text{ units} \times \$168 = \$89,860,512$$

Or

$$\text{Dollar sales} = \frac{\text{fixed cost} + \text{profit goal}}{\text{contribution margin}} = \frac{\$20,000,000 + \$3,000,000}{0.256} = \$89,843,750$$

Finally, HD can express its profit goal as a percentage of sales, which we also saw in previous pricing analyses. Assume HD desires a 25 percent return on sales. To determine the unit and sales volume necessary to achieve this goal, the calculation is a little different from the previous two examples. In this case, we incorporate the profit goal into the unit contribution as an additional variable cost. Look at it this way: If 25 percent of each sale must go toward profits, that leaves only 75 percent of the selling price to cover fixed costs. Thus, the equation becomes:

$$\text{Unit volume} = \frac{\text{fixed cost}}{\text{price} - \text{variable cost} - (0.25 \times \text{price})} \text{ or } \frac{\text{fixed cost}}{(0.75 \times \text{price}) - \text{variable cost}}$$

So,

$$\text{Unit volume} = \frac{\$20,000,000}{(0.75 \times \$168) - \$125} = 20,000,000 \text{ units}$$

$$\text{Dollar sales necessary} = 20,000,000 \times \text{units} \times \$168 = \$3,360,000,000$$

Thus, HD would need more than \$3 billion in sales to realize a 25 percent return on sales given its current price and cost structure! Could it possibly achieve this level of sales? The major point is this: Although break-even analysis can be useful in determining the level of sales needed to cover costs or to achieve a stated profit goal, it does not tell the company whether it is *possible* to achieve that level of sales at the specified price. To address this issue, HD needs to estimate demand for this product.

Before moving on, however, let's stop here and practice applying the concepts covered so far. Now that you have seen pricing and break-even concepts in action as they relate to HD's new product, here are several exercises for you to apply what you have learned in other contexts.

Marketing by the Numbers Exercise Set One

1.1 Sanborn, a manufacturer of electric roof vents, realizes a cost of \$55 for every unit it produces. Its total fixed costs equal \$2 million. If the company manufactures 500,000 units, compute the following:
  a. unit cost
  b. markup price if the company desires a 10 percent return on sales
  c. ROI price if the company desires a 25 percent return on an investment of \$1 million

1.2 An interior decorator purchases items to sell in her store. She purchases a lamp for \$125 and sells it for \$225. Determine the following:
  a. dollar markup
  b. markup percentage on cost
  c. markup percentage on selling price

1.3 A consumer purchases a toaster from a retailer for \$60. The retailer's markup is 20 percent, and the wholesaler's markup is 15 percent, both based on selling price. For what price does the manufacturer sell the product to the wholesaler?

1.4 A vacuum manufacturer has a unit cost of \$50 and wishes to achieve a margin of 30 percent based on selling price. If the manufacturer sells directly to a retailer who then adds a set margin of 40 percent based on selling price, determine the retail price charged to consumers.

1.5 Advanced Electronics manufactures DVDs and sells them directly to retailers who typically sell them for \$20. Retailers take a 40 percent margin based on the retail selling price. Advanced's cost information is as follows:

DVD package and disc	\$2.50/DVD
Royalties	\$2.25/DVD
Advertising and promotion	\$500,000
Overhead	\$200,000

▶ **Table A3.1**	Pro Forma Profit-and-Loss Statement for the 12-Month Period Ended December 31, 2012		

			% of Sales
Net Sales		$125,000,000	100%
Cost of Goods Sold		62,500,000	50%
Gross Margin		$62,500,000	50%
Marketing Expenses			
Sales expenses	$17,500,000		
Promotion expenses	15,000,000		
Freight	12,500,000	45,000,000	36%
General and Administrative Expenses			
Managerial salaries and expenses	$2,000,000		
Indirect overhead	3,000,000	5,000,000	4%
Net Profit before Income Tax		$12,500,000	10%

Operating expenses can be presented in total or broken down in detail. Here, HD's estimated operating expenses include *marketing expenses* and *general and administrative expenses*.

- *Marketing expenses:* include sales expenses, promotion expenses, and distribution expenses. The new product will be sold through HD's sales force, so the company budgets $5 million for sales salaries. However, because sales representatives earn a 10 percent commission on sales, HD must also add a variable component to sales expenses of $12.5 million (10 percent of $125 million net sales), for a total budgeted sales expense of $17.5 million. HD sets its advertising and promotion to launch this product at $10 million. However, the company also budgets 4 percent of sales, or $5 million, for cooperative advertising allowances to retailers who promote HD's new product in their advertising. Thus, the total budgeted advertising and promotion expenses are $15 million ($10 million for advertising plus $5 million in co-op allowances). Finally, HD budgets 10 percent of net sales, or $12.5 million, for freight and delivery charges. In all, total marketing expenses are estimated to be $17.5 million + $15 million + $12.5 million = $45 million.
- *General and administrative expenses:* are estimated at $5 million, broken down into $2 million for managerial salaries and expenses for the marketing function and $3 million of indirect overhead allocated to this product by the corporate accountants (such as depreciation, interest, maintenance, and insurance). Total expenses for the year, then, are estimated to be $50 million ($45 million marketing expenses + $5 million in general and administrative expenses).
- *Net profit before taxes:* profit earned after all costs are deducted. HD's estimated net profit before taxes is $12.5 million.

In all, as Table A3.1 shows, HD expects to earn a profit on its new product of $12.5 million in 2012. Also note that the percentage of sales that each component of the profit-and-loss statement represents is given in the right-hand column. These percentages are determined by dividing the cost figure by net sales (that is, marketing expenses represent 36 percent of net sales determined by $45 million ÷ $125 million). As can be seen, HD projects a net profit return on sales of 10 percent in the first year after launching this product.

Marketing Performance Measures

Profit-and-loss statement (or income statement or operating statement)
A statement that shows actual revenues less expenses and net profit for an organization, product, or brand during a specific planning period, typically a year.

Now let's fast-forward a year. HD's product has been on the market for one year and management wants to assess its sales and profit performance. One way to assess this performance is to compute performance ratios derived from HD's **profit-and-loss statement** (or **income statement** or **operating statement**).

Whereas the pro forma profit-and-loss statement shows *projected* financial performance, the statement given in ▶ **Table A3.2** shows HD's *actual* financial performance based on actual sales, cost of goods sold, and expenses during the past year. By comparing the profit-and-loss statement from one period to the next, HD can gauge performance against goals, spot favorable or unfavorable trends, and take appropriate corrective action.

The profit-and-loss statement shows that HD lost $1 million rather than making the $12.5 million profit projected in the pro forma statement. Why? One obvious reason is that net sales fell $25 million short of estimated sales. Lower sales translated into lower variable costs associated with marketing the product. However, both fixed costs and the cost of goods sold as a percentage of sales exceeded expectations. Hence, the product's contribution margin was 21 percent rather than the estimated 26 percent. That is, variable costs represented 79 percent of sales (55 percent for cost of goods sold, 10 percent for sales commissions, 10 percent for freight, and 4 percent for co-op allowances). Recall that contribution margin can be calculated by subtracting that fraction from one $(1 - 0.79 = 0.21)$. Total fixed costs were $22 million, $2 million more than estimated. Thus, the sales that HD needed to break even given this cost structure can be calculated as:

$$\text{Break-even sales} = \frac{\text{fixed costs}}{\text{contribution margin}} = \frac{\$22,000,000}{0.21} = \$104,761,905$$

If HD had achieved another $5 million in sales, it would have earned a profit.

Although HD's sales fell short of the forecasted sales, so did overall industry sales for this product. Overall industry sales were only $2.5 billion. That means that HD's **market share** was 4 percent ($100 million ÷ $2.5 billion =0.04 = 4 percent), which

Market share
Company sales divided by market sales.

▶ **Table A3.2**   Profit-and-Loss Statement for the 12-Month Period Ended December 31, 2012

			% of Sales
Net Sales		$100,000,000	100%
Cost of Goods Sold		<u>55,000,000</u>	<u>55%</u>
Gross Margin		$45,000,000	45%
Marketing Expenses			
Sales expenses	$15,000,000		
Promotion expenses	14,000,000		
Freight	<u>10,000,000</u>	39,000,000	39%
General and Administrative Expenses			
Managerial salaries and expenses	$2,000,000		
Indirect overhead	<u>5,000,000</u>	<u>7,000,000</u>	<u>7%</u>
Net Profit Before Income Tax		($1,000,000)	(−1%)

was higher than forecasted. Thus, HD attained a higher-than-expected market share but the overall market sales were not as high as estimated.

Analytic Ratios

Operating ratios
The ratios of selected operating statement items to net sales.

The profit-and-loss statement provides the figures needed to compute some crucial **operating ratios**—the ratios of selected operating statement items to net sales. These ratios let marketers compare the firm's performance in one year to that in previous years (or with industry standards and competitors' performance in that year). The most commonly used operating ratios are the gross margin percentage, the net profit percentage, and the operating expense percentage. The inventory turnover rate and return on investment (ROI) are often used to measure managerial effectiveness and efficiency.

Gross margin percentage
The percentage of net sales remaining after cost of goods sold—calculated by dividing gross margin by net sales.

The **gross margin percentage** indicates the percentage of net sales remaining after cost of goods sold that can contribute to operating expenses and net profit before taxes. The higher this ratio, the more a firm has left to cover expenses and generate profit. HD's gross margin ratio was 45 percent:

$$\text{Gross margin percentage} = \frac{\text{gross margin}}{\text{net sales}} = \frac{\$45,000,000}{\$100,000,000} = 0.45 = 45\%$$

Note that this percentage is lower than estimated, and this ratio is seen easily in the percentage of sales column in Table A3.2. Stating items in the profit-and-loss statement as a percent of sales allows managers to quickly spot abnormal changes in costs over time. If there was a previous history for this product and this ratio was declining, management should examine it more closely to determine why it has decreased (that is, because of a decrease in sales volume or price, an increase in costs, or a combination of these). In HD's case, net sales were $25 million lower than estimated, and cost of goods sold was higher than estimated (55 percent rather than the estimated 50 percent).

Net profit percentage
The percentage of each sales dollar going to profit—calculated by dividing net profits by net sales.

The **net profit percentage** shows the percentage of each sales dollar going to profit. It is calculated by dividing net profits by net sales:

$$\text{Net profit percentage} = \frac{\text{net profit}}{\text{net sales}} = \frac{-\$1,000,000}{\$100,000,000} = -0.01 = -1.0\%$$

This ratio is easily seen in the percent of sales column. HD's new product generated negative profits in the first year, which is not a good situation given that net profits before taxes were estimated at more than $12 million before the product launch. Later in this appendix, we will discuss further analyses the marketing manager should conduct to defend the product.

Operating expense percentage
The portion of net sales going to operating expenses—calculated by dividing total expenses by net sales.

The **operating expense percentage** indicates the portion of net sales going to operating expenses. Operating expenses include marketing and other expenses not directly related to marketing the product, such as indirect overhead assigned to this product. It is calculated by:

$$\text{Operating expense percentage} = \frac{\text{total expenses}}{\text{net sales}} = \frac{\$46,000,000}{\$100,000,000} = 0.46 = 46\%$$

This ratio can also be quickly determined from the percent of sales column in the profit-and-loss statement by adding the percentages for marketing expenses and general and administrative expenses (39 percent + 7 percent). Thus, 46 cents of every sales dollar went for operations. Although HD wants this ratio to be as low as possible, and 46 percent is not an alarming amount, it is of concern if it is increasing over time or if a loss is realized.

Inventory turnover rate
(or stockturn rate)
The number of times an inventory turns over or is sold during a specified time period (often one year)—calculated based on costs, selling price, or units.

Another useful ratio is the **inventory turnover rate** (also called the **stockturn rate** for resellers). The inventory turnover rate is the number of times an inventory turns over or is sold during a specified time period (often one year). This rate tells how quickly a business is moving inventory through the organization. Higher rates indicate that lower investments in inventory are made, thus freeing up funds for other investments. It may be computed on a cost, selling price, or unit basis. The formula based on cost is:

$$\text{Inventory turnover rate} = \frac{\text{cost of goods sold}}{\text{average inventory at cost}}$$

Assuming HD's beginning and ending inventories were $30 million and $20 million, respectively, the inventory turnover rate is:

$$\text{Inventory turnover rate} = \frac{\$55,000,000}{(\$30,000,000 + \$20,000,000)/2} = \frac{\$55,000,000}{\$25,000,000} = 2.2$$

That is, HD's inventory turned over 2.2 times in 2012. Normally, the higher the turnover rate, the higher the management efficiency and company profitability. However, this rate should be compared to industry averages, competitors' rates, and past performance to determine if HD is doing well. A competitor with similar sales but a higher inventory turnover rate will have fewer resources tied up in inventory, allowing it to invest in other areas of the business.

Return on investment (ROI)
A measure of managerial effectiveness and efficiency—net profit before taxes divided by total investment.

Companies frequently use **return on investment (ROI)** to measure managerial effectiveness and efficiency. For HD, ROI is the ratio of net profits to total investment required to manufacture the new product. This investment includes capital investments in land, buildings, and equipment (here, the initial $10 million to refurbish the manufacturing facility) plus inventory costs (HD's average inventory totaled $25 million), for a total of $35 million. Thus, HD's ROI for this product is:

$$\text{Return on investment} = \frac{\text{net profit before taxes}}{\text{investment}} = \frac{-\$1,000,000}{\$35,000,000} = -.0286 = -2.86\%$$

ROI is often used to compare alternatives, and a positive ROI is desired. The alternative with the highest ROI is preferred to other alternatives. HD needs to be concerned with the ROI realized. One obvious way HD can increase ROI is to increase net profit by reducing expenses. Another way is to reduce its investment, perhaps by investing less in inventory and turning it over more frequently.

Marketing Profitability Metrics

Given the previous financial results, you may be thinking that HD should drop this new product. But what arguments can marketers make for keeping or dropping this product? The obvious arguments for dropping the product are that first-year sales were well below expected levels and the product lost money, resulting in a negative return on investment.

So what would happen if HD did drop this product? Surprisingly, if the company drops the product, the profits for the total organization will decrease by $4 million! How can that be? Marketing managers need to look closely at the numbers in the profit-and-loss statement to determine the *net marketing contribution* for this product. In HD's case, the net marketing contribution for the product is $4 million; if the company drops this product, that contribution will disappear as well. Let's look more closely at this concept to illustrate how marketing managers can better assess and defend their marketing strategies and programs.

Net Marketing Contribution

Net marketing contribution (NMC)
A measure of marketing profitability that includes only components of profitability controlled by marketing.

Net marketing contribution (NMC), along with other marketing metrics derived from it, measures *marketing* profitability. It includes only components of profitability that are controlled by marketing. Whereas the previous calculation of net profit before taxes from the profit-and-loss statement includes operating expenses not under marketing's control,

NMC does not. Referring back to HD's profit-and-loss statement given in Table A3.2, we can calculate net marketing contribution for the product as:

$$NMC = \text{net sales} - \text{cost of goods sold} - \text{marketing expenses}$$
$$= \$100 \text{ million} - \$55 \text{ million} - \$41 \text{ million} = \$4 \text{ million}$$

The marketing expenses include sales expenses ($15 million), promotion expenses ($14 million), freight expenses ($10 million), and the managerial salaries and expenses of the marketing function ($2 million), which total $41 million.

Thus, the product actually contributed $4 million to HD's profits. It was the $5 million of indirect overhead allocated to this product that caused the negative profit. Further, the amount allocated was $2 million more than estimated in the pro forma profit-and-loss statement. Indeed, if only the estimated amount had been allocated, the product would have earned a *profit* of $1 million rather than losing $1 million. If HD drops the product, the $5 million in fixed overhead expenses will not disappear—it will simply have to be allocated elsewhere. However, the $4 million in net marketing contribution *will* disappear.

Marketing Return on Sales and Investment

To get an even deeper understanding of the profit impact of the marketing strategy, we'll now examine two measures of marketing efficiency—*marketing return on sales* (marketing ROS) and *marketing return on investment* (marketing ROI).[4]

Marketing return on sales (or **marketing ROS**) shows the percent of net sales attributable to the net marketing contribution. For our product, ROS is:

Marketing return on sales (or marketing ROS)

The percent of net sales attributable to the net marketing contribution—calculated by dividing net marketing contribution by net sales.

$$\text{Marketing ROS} = \frac{\text{net marketing contribution}}{\text{net sales}} = \frac{\$4,000,000}{\$100,000,000} = 0.04 = 4\%$$

Thus, out of every $100 of sales, the product returns $4 to HD's bottom line. A high marketing ROS is desirable. But to assess whether this is a good level of performance, HD must compare this figure to previous marketing ROS levels for the product, the ROSs of other products in the company's portfolio, and the ROSs of competing products.

Marketing return on investment (or **marketing ROI**) measures the marketing productivity of a marketing investment. In HD's case, the marketing investment is represented by $41 million of the total expenses. Thus, marketing ROI is:

Marketing return on investment (or marketing ROI)

A measure of the marketing productivity of a marketing investment—calculated by dividing net marketing contribution by marketing expenses.

$$\text{Marketing ROI} = \frac{\text{net marketing contribution}}{\text{marketing expenses}} = \frac{\$4,000,000}{\$41,000,000} = 0.0976 = 9.76\%$$

As with marketing ROS, a high value is desirable, but this figure should be compared with previous levels for the given product and with the marketing ROIs of competitors' products. Note from this equation that marketing ROI could be greater than 100 percent. This can be achieved by attaining a higher net marketing contribution and/or a lower total marketing expense.

In this section, we estimated market potential and sales, developed profit-and-loss statements, and examined financial measures of performance. In the next section, we discuss methods for analyzing the impact of various marketing tactics. However, before moving on to those analyses, here's another set of quantitative exercises to help you apply what you've learned to other situations.

Marketing by the Numbers Exercise Set Two

2.1 Determine the market potential for a product that has 50 million prospective buyers who purchase an average of three per year if the product's price averages $25. How many units must a company sell if it desires a 10 percent share of this market?

2.2 Develop a profit-and-loss statement for the Westgate division of North Industries. This division manufactures light fixtures sold to consumers through home improvement and hardware stores. Cost of goods sold represents 40 percent of net sales. Marketing expenses include selling expenses, promotion expenses, and freight. Selling expenses include sales salaries totaling $3 million per year and sales commissions (5 percent of sales). The company spent $3 million on advertising last year, and freight costs were 10 percent of sales. Other costs include $2 million for managerial salaries and expenses for the marketing function and another $3 million for indirect overhead allocated to the division.

   a. Develop the profit-and-loss statement if net sales were $20 million last year.
   b. Develop the profit-and-loss statement if net sales were $40 million last year.
   c. Calculate Westgate's break-even sales.

2.3 Using the profit-and-loss statement you developed in question 2.2b, and assuming that Westgate's beginning inventory was $11 million, ending inventory was $7 million, and total investment was $20 million including inventory, determine the following:

   a. gross margin percentage
   b. net profit percentage
   c. operating expense percentage
   d. inventory turnover rate
   e. return on investment (ROI)
   f. net marketing contribution
   g. marketing return on sales (marketing ROS)
   h. marketing return on investment (marketing ROI)
   i. Is the Westgate division doing well? Explain your answer.

Financial Analysis of Marketing Tactics

Although the first-year profit performance for HD's new product was less than desired, management feels that this attractive market has excellent growth opportunities. Although the sales of HD's product were lower than initially projected, they were not unreasonable given the size of the current market. Thus, HD wants to explore new marketing tactics to help grow the market for this product and increase sales for the company.

For example, the company could increase advertising to promote more awareness of the new product and its category. It could add salespeople to secure greater product distribution. HD could decrease prices so that more consumers could afford its product. Finally, to expand the market, HD could introduce a lower-priced model in addition to the higher-priced original offering. Before pursuing any of these tactics, however, HD must analyze the financial implications of each.

Increase Advertising Expenditures

HD is considering boosting its advertising to make more people aware of the benefits of this device in general and of its own brand in particular. What if HD's marketers recommend increasing national advertising by 50 percent to $15 million (assume no change in the variable cooperative component of promotional expenditures)? This represents an increase in fixed costs of $5 million. What increase in sales will be needed to break even on this $5 million increase in fixed costs?

A quick way to answer this question is to divide the increase in fixed costs by the contribution margin, which we found in a previous analysis to be 21 percent:

$$\text{Increase in sales} = \frac{\text{increase in fixed cost}}{\text{contribution margin}} = \frac{\$5,000,000}{0.21} = \$23,809,524$$

Thus, a 50 percent increase in advertising expenditures must produce a sales increase of almost $24 million to just break even. That $24 million sales increase translates into an almost 1 percentage point increase in market share (1 percent of the $2.5 billion overall market equals $25 million). That is, to break even on the increased advertising expenditure, HD would have to increase its market share from 4 percent to 4.95 percent ($123,809,524 ÷ $2.5 billion = 0.0495 or 4.95 percent market share). All of this assumes that the total market will not grow, which might or might not be a reasonable assumption.

Increase Distribution Coverage

HD also wants to consider hiring more salespeople in order to call on new retailer accounts and increase distribution through more outlets. Even though HD sells directly to wholesalers, its sales representatives call on retail accounts to perform other functions in addition to selling, such as training retail salespeople. Currently, HD employs 60 sales reps who earn an average of $50,000 in salary plus 10 percent commission on sales. The product is currently sold to consumers through 1,875 retail outlets. Suppose HD wants to increase that number of outlets to 2,500, an increase of 625 retail outlets. How many additional salespeople will HD need, and what sales will be necessary to break even on the increased cost?

One method for determining what size sales force HD will need is the **workload method**. The workload method uses the following formula to determine the sales force size:

Workload method
An approach to determining sales force size based on the workload required and the time available for selling.

$$NS = \frac{NC \times FC \times LC}{TA}$$

Where

NS = number of salespeople
NC = number of customers
FC = average frequency of customer calls per customer
LC = average length of customer call
TA = time an average salesperson has available for selling per year

HD's sales reps typically call on accounts an average of 20 times per year for about 2 hours per call. Although each sales rep works 2,000 hours per year (50 weeks per year × 40 hours per week), they spend about 15 hours per week on nonselling activities such as administrative duties and travel. Thus, the average annual available selling time per sales rep per year is 1,250 hours (50 weeks × 25 hours per week). We can now calculate how many sales reps HD will need to cover the anticipated 2,500 retail outlets:

$$NS = \frac{2,500 \times 20 \times 2}{1,250} = 80 \text{ salespeople}$$

Therefore, HD will need to hire 20 more salespeople. The cost to hire these reps will be $1 million (20 salespeople × $50,000 salary per salesperson).

What increase in sales will be required to break even on this increase in fixed costs? The 10 percent commission is already accounted for in the contribution margin, so the contribution margin remains unchanged at 21 percent. Thus, the increase in sales needed to cover this increase in fixed costs can be calculated by:

$$\text{Increase in sales} = \frac{\text{increase in fixed cost}}{\text{contribution margin}} = \frac{\$1,000,000}{0.21} = \$4,761,905$$

That is, HD's sales must increase almost $5 million to break even on this tactic. So, how many new retail outlets will the company need to secure to achieve this sales increase? The average revenue generated per current outlet is $53,333 ($100 million in sales divided by 1,875 outlets). To achieve the nearly $5 million sales increase needed to break even, HD would need about 90 new outlets ($4,761,905 ÷ $53,333 = 89.3 outlets), or about 4.5 outlets per new rep. Given that current reps cover about 31 outlets apiece (1,875 outlets ÷ 60 reps), this seems very reasonable.

Decrease Price

HD is also considering lowering its price to increase sales revenue through increased volume. The company's research has shown that demand for most types of consumer electronics products is elastic—that is, the percentage increase in the quantity demanded is greater than the percentage decrease in price.

What increase in sales would be necessary to break even on a 10 percent decrease in price? That is, what increase in sales will be needed to maintain the total contribution that HD realized at the higher price? The current total contribution can be determined by multiplying the contribution margin by total sales:[5]

$$\text{Current total contribution} = \text{contribution margin} \times \text{sales}$$
$$= 0.21 \times \$100 \text{ million} = \$21 \text{ million}$$

Price changes result in changes in unit contribution and contribution margin. Recall that the contribution margin of 21 percent was based on variable costs representing 79 percent of sales. Therefore, unit variable costs can be determined by multiplying the original price by this percentage: $168 × 0.79 = $132.72 per unit. If price is decreased by 10 percent, the new price is $151.20. However, variable costs do not change just because the price decreased, so the contribution and contribution margin decrease as follows:

	Old	New (reduced 10 percent)
Price	$168	$151.20
− Unit variable cost	$132.72	$132.72
=Unit contribution	$35.28	$18.48
Contribution margin	$35.28/$168 = 0.21 or 21%	$18.48/$151.20 = 0.12 or 12%

So, a 10 percent reduction in price results in a decrease in the contribution margin from 21 percent to 12 percent.[6] To determine the sales level needed to break even on this price reduction, we calculate the level of sales that must be attained at the new contribution margin to achieve the original total contribution of $21 million:

$$\text{New contribution margin} \times \text{new sales level} = \text{original total contribution}$$

So,

$$\text{New sales level} = \frac{\text{original contribution}}{\text{new contribution margin}} = \frac{\$21,000,000}{0.12} = \$175,000,000$$

Thus, sales must increase by $75 million ($175 million − $100 million) just to break even on a 10 percent price reduction. This means that HD must increase market share to 7 percent ($175 million ÷ $2.5 billion) to achieve the current level of profits (assuming no increase in the total market sales). The marketing manager must assess whether or not this is a reasonable goal.

Extend the Product Line

Cannibalization
The situation in which one product sold by a company takes a portion of its sales from other company products.

As a final option, HD is considering extending its product line by offering a lower-priced model. Of course, the new, lower-priced product would steal some sales from the higher-priced model. This is called **cannibalization**—the situation in which one product sold by a company takes a portion of its sales from other company products. If the new product has a lower contribution than the original product, the company's total contribution will decrease on the cannibalized sales. However, if the new product can generate enough new volume, it is worth considering.

To assess cannibalization, HD must look at the incremental contribution gained by having both products available. In the previous analysis, we determined that unit variable costs were $132.72 and unit contribution was just over $35. Assuming costs remain the same next year, HD can expect to realize a contribution per unit of approximately $35 for every unit of the original product sold.

Assume that the first model offered by HD is called HD1 and the new, lower-priced model is called HD2. HD2 will retail for $250, and resellers will take the same markup percentages on price as they do with the higher-priced model. Therefore, HD2's price to wholesalers will be $140 as follows:

Retail price:	$250
minus retail margin (30 percent):	−$ 75
Retailer's cost/wholesaler's price:	$175
minus wholesaler's margin (20 percent):	−$ 35
Wholesaler's cost/HD's price	$140

If HD2's variable costs are estimated to be $120, then its contribution per unit will equal $20 ($140 − $120 = $20). That means for every unit that HD2 cannibalizes from HD1, HD will *lose* $15 in contribution toward fixed costs and profit (that is, contribution$_{HD2}$ − contribution$_{HD1}$ = $20 − $35 = −$15). You might conclude that HD should not pursue this tactic because it appears as though the company will be worse off if it introduces the lower-priced model. However, if HD2 captures enough *additional* sales, HD will be better off even though some HD1 sales are cannibalized. The company must examine what will happen to *total* contribution, which requires estimates of unit volume for both products.

Originally, HD estimated that next year's sales of HD1 would be 600,000 units. However, with the introduction of HD2, it now estimates that 200,000 of those sales will be cannibalized by the new model. If HD sells only 200,000 units of the new HD2 model (all cannibalized from HD1), the company would lose $3 million in total contribution (200,000 units × −$15 per cannibalized unit = −$3 million)—not a good outcome. However, HD estimates that HD2 will generate the 200,000 of cannibalized sales plus an *additional* 500,000 unit sales. Thus, the contribution on these additional HD2 units will be $10 million (i.e., 500,000 units × $20 per unit = $10 million). The net effect is that HD will gain $7 million in total contribution by introducing HD2.

The following table compares HD's total contribution with and without the introduction of HD2:

	HD1 Only	HD1 and HD2
HD1 contribution	600,000 units × $35 = $21,000,000	400,000 units × $35 = $14,000,000
HD2 contribution	0	700,000 units × $20 = $14,000,000
Total contribution	$21,000,000	$28,000,000

The difference in the total contribution is a net gain of $7 million ($28 million − $21 million). Based on this analysis, HD should introduce the HD2 model because it results in a positive incremental contribution. However, if fixed costs will increase by more than $7 million as a result of adding this model, then the net effect will be negative and HD should not pursue this tactic.

Now that you have seen these marketing tactic analysis concepts in action as they relate to HD's new product, here are several exercises that will allow you to apply what you have learned in this section to other contexts.

Marketing by the Numbers Exercise Set Three

3.1 Kingsford, Inc. sells small plumbing components to consumers through retail outlets. Total industry sales for Kingsford's relevant market last year were $80 million, with Kingsford's sales representing 10 percent of that total. Contribution margin is 25 percent. Kingsford's sales force calls on retail outlets and each sales rep earns $45,000 per year plus 1 percent commission on all sales. Retailers receive a 40 percent margin on selling price and generate average revenue of $10,000 per outlet for Kingsford.

   a. The marketing manager has suggested increasing consumer advertising by $300,000. By how much would dollar sales need to increase to break even on this expenditure? What increase in overall market share does this represent?

   b. Another suggestion is to hire three more sales representatives to gain new consumer retail accounts. How many new retail outlets would be necessary to break even on the increased cost of adding three sales reps?

   c. A final suggestion is to make a 20 percent across-the-board price reduction. By how much would dollar sales need to increase to maintain Kingsford's current contribution? (See endnote 6 to calculate the new contribution margin.)

   d. Which suggestion do you think Kingsford should implement? Explain your recommendation.

3.2 PepsiCo sells its soft drinks in approximately 400,000 retail establishments, such as supermarkets, discount stores, and convenience stores. Sales representatives call on each retail account weekly, which means each account is called on by a sales rep 52 times per year. The average length of a sales call is 75 minutes (or 1.25 hours). An average salesperson works 2,000 hours per year (50 weeks per year × 40 hours per week), but each spends 10 hours a week on nonselling activities, such as administrative tasks and travel. How many salespeople does PepsiCo need?

3.3 Hair Zone manufactures a brand of hair-styling gel. It is considering adding a modified version of the product—a foam that provides stronger hold. Hair Zone's variable costs and prices to wholesalers are:

	Current Hair Gel	New Foam Product
Unit selling price	2.00	2.25
Unit variable costs	0.85	1.25

Hair Zone expects to sell 1 million units of the new styling foam in the first year after introduction, but it expects that 60 percent of those sales will come from buyers who normally purchase Hair Zone's styling gel. Hair Zone estimates that it would sell 1.5 million units of the gel if it did not introduce the foam. If the fixed cost of launching the new foam will be $100,000 during the first year, should Hair Zone add the new product to its line? Why or why not?

References

Chapter 1

1. See "The American Customer Satisfaction Index: Scores by Industry," www.theacsi.org/index.php?option=com_content&view=article&id=148&Itemid=213, accessed June 2011; Stuart Elliott, "JetBlue Asks Its Fliers to Keep Spreading the Word," *New York Times*, May 10, 2010, p. B7; Kevin Randall, "Red, Hot, and Blue: The Hottest American Brand Is Not Apple," *Fast Company*, June 3, 2010, accessed at www.fastcompany.com/1656066/apple-jetblue-social-currency-twitter; "JetBlue Airways Leads Airline Industry in Customer Loyalty for Second Consecutive Year in Satmetrix 2011 Net Promoter Benchmark Study," *PR Newswire*, February 17, 2011; and http://jetblue.com/experience/ and www.jetblue.com/about/, accessed September 2011.

2. See "U.S. Market Leaders," *Advertising Age*, December 10, 2010, p. 14.

3. See Philip Kotler and Kevin Lane Keller, *Marketing Management*, 14th ed. (Upper Saddle River, NJ: Prentice Hall, 2012), p. 5.

4. The American Marketing Association offers the following definition: "Marketing is an organizational function and a set of processes for creating, communicating, and delivering value to customers and for managing customer relationships in ways that benefit the organization and its stakeholders." See www.marketingpower.com/_layouts/Dictionary.aspx?dLetter=M, accessed November 2011.

5. See Dan Sewell, "Kroger CEO Often Roams Aisles, Wielding Carte Blanche," *Journal Gazette* (Fort Wayne, IN), November 15, 2010, www.journalgazette.net/article/20101115/BIZ/311159958/-1/BIZ09.

6. See www.michigan.org and www.adcouncil.org/default.aspx?id=602, accessed September 2011.

7. See Theodore Levitt's classic article, "Marketing Myopia," *Harvard Business Review*, July–August 1960, pp. 45–56. For more recent discussions, see "What Business Are You In?" *Harvard Business Review*, October 2006, pp. 127–137; Lance A. Bettencourt, "Debunking Myths about Customer Needs," *Marketing Management*, January/February 2009, pp. 46–51; here p. 50; and N. Craig Smith, Minette E. Drumright, and Mary C. Gentile, "The New Marketing Myopia," *Journal of Public Policy & Marketing*, Spring 2010, pp. 4–11.

8. Information from HP's recent "The Computer Is Personal Again" and "Everybody On" marketing campaigns. See www.hp.com/united-states/personal_again/index.html and www.hp.com/global/us/en/everybody-on/ribbons/passionTVSpot.html, accessed September 2011.

9. "Henry Ford, Faster Horses and Market Research," *Research Arts*, January 25, 2011, www.researcharts.com/2011/01/henry-ford-faster-horses-and-market-research/.

10. Adapted from information found in Michael E. Porter and Mark R. Kramer, "Creating Shared Value," *Harvard Business Review*, January–February 2011, pp. 63-77; and Michael Krauss, "Evolution of an Academic: Kotler on Marketing 3.0," *Marketing News*, January 30, 2011, p. 12.

11. Based on information from www.responsibility.ups.com/Sustainability; and www.responsibility.ups.com/community/Static%20Files/sustainability/Highlights.pdf, accessed September 2011.

12. Based on information from www.weber.com, accessed September 2011.

13. Based on information from Michael Bush, "Why You Should Be Putting on the Ritz," *Advertising Age*, June 21, 2010, p. 1; Julie Barker, "Power to the People," *Incentive*, February 2008, p. 34; and Carmine Gallo, "Employee Motivation the Ritz-Carlton Way," *BusinessWeek*, February 29, 2008, accessed at www.businessweek.com/smallbiz/content/feb2008/sb20080229_347490.htm; and Philip Kotler and Kevin Lane Keller, *Marketing Management,* 14th ed. (Upper Saddle River, NJ: Prentice Hall, 2012), p. 381. Also see http://corporate.ritzcarlton.com/en/About/Awards.htm#Hotel, accessed September 2011.

14. Matthew Dixon, Karen Freeman, and Nicholas Toman, "Stop Trying to Delight Your Customers," *Harvard Business Review*, July–August 2010, pp. 116–122. Also see Chris Morran, "Stop Treating Customers Like Liabilities, Start Treating Them Like People," *Advertising Age,* February 14, 2011, p. 10.

15. Information about Weber Nation from www.webernation.com, accessed September 2011.

16. Elizabeth A. Sullivan, "Just Say No," *Marketing News*, April 15, 2008, p. 17. Also see Raymund Flandez, "It Just Isn't Working? Some File for Customer Divorce," *Wall Street Journal*, November 16, 2009, p. B7.

17. Sullivan, "Just Say No," p. 17.

18. The following example is adapted from information found in Vikas Mittal, Matthew Sarkees, and Feisal Murshed, "The Right Way to Manage Unprofitable Customers," *Harvard Business Review*, April 2008, pp. 95–102. Quotes from http://whitneyhess.com/blog/2010/02/21/fire-your-worst-customers/; and Jeff Schmidt, "Save Your Company by Firing Your Customers," *Bloomberg Businessweek*, April 5, 2011, www.businessweek.com/managing/content/apr2011/ca2011045_952921.htm?campaign_id=rss_topStories.

19. Quotes from Andrew Walmsley, "The Year of Consumer Empowerment," *Marketing*, December 20, 2006, p. 9; and Jeff Heilman, "Rules of Engagement: During a Recession, Marketers Need to Have *Their* Keenest Listening-to-Customers Strategy in Place," *The Magazine of Branded Content*, Winter 2009, p. 7. Also see Frank's Striefler, "5 Marketing Principles Brands Should Embrace in 2010," *Adweek*, January 13, 2010, accessed at www.adweek.com.

20. See Brian Morrissey, "Brand Sweepstakes Get Twitterized," *Adweek*, November 22, 2009, accessed at www.adweek.com; Alicia Wallace, "Owing Social: Businesses Dial in to Facebook, Twitter to Build Business," *McClatchy-Tribune Business News*, April 26, 2010; Judah Schiller, "Social Medias Isn't the Problem, It's Your Culture," The Employee Engagement Group, February 22, 2011, http://employeeengagement.com/2011/02/social-media-isnt-the-problem-its-your-culture/; and Mark Milian, "The App Maker Said to Be Planning Twitter Competitor," *CNN*, April 13, 2011, http://articles.cnn.com/2011-04-13/tech/ubermedia.twitter_1_tweetdeck-twitter-blackberry-app?_s=PM:TECH.

21. Casey Hibbard, "Cold Stone Transforms the Ice Cream Social with Facebook," *Social Media Examiner*, November 22, 2010, www.socialmediaexaminer.com/cold-stone-transforms-the-ice-cream-social-with-facebook/; Heba Hornsby, "Social Media

Success Stories: See How Cold Stone Ice Cream Became So 'Hot' on Facebook," *Garious Blog*, February 10, 2011, http://garious .com/blog/2011/02/cold-stone-creamery-success-story/; and www .facebook.com/coldstonecreamery, accessed August 2011.

22. Elizabeth A. Sullivan, "We Were Right!" *Marketing News*, December 15, 2008, p. 17.

23. Joel Rubenstein, "Marketers, Researchers, and Your Ears," *Brandweek*, February 15, 2010, p. 34. For other discussion and examples, see Venkat Ramaswamy and Francis Gouillart, "Building the Co-Creative Enterprise," *Harvard Business Review,* October 2010, pp. 100–109.

24. Tim Nudd, "Doritos 'Pug Attack' Director Wins $1 Million," *Ad Freak,* February 7, 2011, http://adweek.blogs.com/adfreak/ 2011/02/doritos-pug-attack-director-wins-1-million.html; Bruce Horowitz, "Ad Meter 1st: A Doggone Tie," *USA Today,* February 7, 2011, p. 68; and www.crashthesuperbowl.com, accessed April 2011.

25. Gavin O'Malley, "Entries Pour in for Heinz Ketchup Commercial Contest," August 13, 2007, accessed at http://publications .mediapost.com.

26. Teaching Brands New Tricks," *Adweek,* April 4, 2011, pp. 12–13. Also see Steven Rosenbaum, *Curator Nation: How to Win in the World Where Consumers Are Creators* (New York: McGraw-Hill, 2011).

27. "Consumer 'New Frugality' May Be an Enduring Feature of Post-Recession Economy, Finds Booz & Company Survey," *Business Wire*, February 24, 2010; "Private Label Gets a Quality Reputation, Causing Consumers to Change Their Buying Habits," *PR Newswire,* January 20, 2011; and Ely Portillo, "In Weak Economy, Store Brands Prosper," *McClatchy-Tribune News Service,* March 18, 2011.

28. "Stew Leonard's," *Hoover's Company Records*, July 15, 2011, http://subscriber.hoovers.com/H/company360/overview.html ?companyId=104226000000000; and www.stew-leonards.com/ html/about.cfm, accessed November 2011.

29. Graham Brown, "Mobile Youth Key Statistics," March 28, 2008, www.mobileyouth.org/?s=MobileYouth+ Key+ Statistics. For interesting discussions of customer lifetime value, see Sunil Gupta et al., "Modeling Customer Lifetime Value," *Journal of Service Research*, November 2006, pp. 139–146; Jason Q. Zhang, Ashutosh Dixit, and Roberto Friedman, "Customer Loyalty and Lifetime Value: An Empirical Investigation of Consumer Packaged Goods," *Journal of Marketing Theory and Practice*, Spring 2010, p. 127; and Norman W. Marshall, "Commitment, Loyalty, and Customer Lifetime Value: Investigating the Relationships among Key Determinants," *Journal of Business & Economics Research,* August 2010, pp. 67–85.

30. Based on quotes and information from Heather Green, "How Amazon Aims to Keep You Clicking," *BusinessWeek*, March 2, 2009, pp. 34–40; Geoffrey A. Fowler, "Corporate News: Amazon's Sales Soar, Lifting Profit," *Wall Street Journal*, April 23, 2010, p. B3; and Brad Stone, "What's in the Box? Instant Gratification," *Bloomberg Businessweek*, November 29–December 5, 2010, pp. 39-40.

31. For more discussion on customer equity, see Roland T. Rust, Valerie A. Zeithaml, and Katherine A. Lemon, *Driving Customer Equity* (New York: Free Press 2000); Rust, Lemon, and Zeithaml, "Return on Marketing: Using Customer Equity to Focus Marketing Strategy," *Journal of Marketing*, January 2004, pp. 109–127; Dominique M. Hanssens, Daniel Thorpe, and Carl Finkbeiner, "Marketing When Customer Equity Matters," *Harvard Business Review*, May 2008, pp. 117–124; V. Kumar and Denish Shaw,

"Expanding the Role of Marketing: From Customer Equity to Market Capitalization," *Journal of Marketing*, November 2009, p. 119; and Philip E. Pfeifer, "On Estimating Current-Customer Equity Using Company Summary Data," *Journal of Interactive Marketing*, February 2011, p. 1.

32. This example is adapted from information found in Rust, Lemon, and Zeithaml, "Where Should the Next Marketing Dollar Go?" *Marketing Management*, September–October 2001, pp. 24–28; with information from Grace Hamulic, "Audi, Cadillac, Lexus Buyer Demographics Exhibit Most Changes," *Motorway America*, May 2010, www.motorwayamerica.com/editorial/ audi-cadillac-lexus-buyer-demographics-exhibit-most-changes.

33. Based on Werner Reinartz and V. Kumar, "The Mismanagement of Customer Loyalty," *Harvard Business Review*, July 2002, pp. 86–94. Also see Stanley F. Slater, Jakki J. Mohr, and Sanjit Sengupta, "Know Your Customer," *Marketing Management,* February 2009, pp. 37–44.

34. Natalie Zmuda, "Why the Bad Economy Has Been Good for Target," *Advertising Age*, October 4, 2010, p. 1; and Sharon Edelson, "Target Eying $100 Billion in Sales," *WWD,* February 25, 2011, p. 2.

35. Emily Thornton, "The New Rules," *BusinessWeek*, January 19, 2009, pp. 30–34.

36. Adapted from information in Brad Stone, "Breakfast Can Wait. Today's First Stop Is Online," *New York Times*, August 10, 2009, p. A1. Also see Rich Gagnon, "2011: A Pivotal Year for Marketing," *Adweek,* January 17, 2011, www.adweek.com/news/ advertising-branding/2011-pivotal-year-marketing-125424.

37. Internet usage stats from www.internetworldstats.com/stats .htm, accessed June 2011; Pew/Internet, "The Future of the Internet III," December 14, 2008, accessed at www.pewinternet .org/Reports/2008/The-Future-of-the-Internet-III.aspx; "Digital Hotlist: By the Numbers," *Adweek,* October 11, 2010, p. 20; and James Lewin, "Pew Internet and the American Life Project: Trend *Data,*" www.pewinternet.org/Trend-Data.aspx, accessed June 2011.

38. "Pew Internet and the American Life Project: Trend Data," and "comScore Reports Record-Breaking $43.4 Billion in Q4 2010 U.S. Retail E-Commerce Spending, Up 11 Percent vs. Year Ago," *PR Newswire*, February 8, 2011.

39. For examples and for a good review of nonprofit marketing, see Philip Kotler and Alan R. Andreasen, *Strategic Marketing for Nonprofit Organizations*, 7th ed. (Upper Saddle River, NJ: Prentice Hall, 2008); Philip Kotler and Karen Fox, *Strategic Marketing for Educational Institutions* (Upper Saddle River, NJ: Prentice Hall, 1995); Philip Kotler, John Bowen, and James Makens, *Marketing for Hospitality and Tourism*, 4th ed. (Upper Saddle River, NJ: Prentice Hall, 2006); and Philip Kotler and Nancy Lee, *Marketing in the Public Sector: A Roadmap for Improved Performance* (Philadelphia: Wharton School Publishing, 2007).

40. Adapted from information found in Natalie Zmuda, "St. Jude's Goes from Humble Beginnings to Media Ubiquity," *Advertising Age,* February 14, 2011, p. 37; and various pages at www.stjude .org, accessed September 2011.

41. "Leading National Advertisers," *Advertising Age*, June 21, 2010, pp. 10–12. For more on social marketing, see Philip Kotler, Ned Roberto, and Nancy R. Lee, *Social Marketing: Improving the Quality of Life*, 2nd ed. (Thousand Oaks, CA: Sage Publications, 2002).

42. www.aboutmcdonalds.com/mcd and www.nikebiz.com, accessed June 2011.

43. Quotes and information found at www.patagonia.com/web/us/ contribution/patagonia.go?assetid=2329, accessed August 2011.

Chapter 2

1. Based on information found in Andrew Martin, "McDonald's Maintains Momentum in Bad Times," *New York Times*, January 11, 2009; "McDonald's Posts Another Year of Stellar Store Growth in 2010," January 24, 2011, http://retailsails.com/2011/01/24/mcdonalds-posts-another-year-of-stellar-growth-in-2010/; Julie Jargon, "On McDonald's Menu: Variety, Caution," *Wall Street Journal,* December 27, 2010, p. A1; and John Cloud, "McDonald's Has a Chef?" *Time*, February 22, 2010, pp. 88–91. Financial and other company information and facts from www.aboutmcdonalds.com/mcd/media_center.html/invest.html and www.aboutmcdonalds.com/mcd, accessed November 2011.

2. Various mission statements in the text and table are from www.nasa.gov/about/highlights/what_does_nasa_do.html; www.facebook.com; and www.chipotle.com, accessed December 2011.

3. Jack and Suzy Welch, "State Your Business; Too Many Mission Statements Are Loaded with Fatheaded Jargon. Play It Straight," *BusinessWeek*, January 14, 2008, p. 80. For more examples of mission statements, both good and bad, see Piet Levy, ""Mission vs. Vision," *Marketing News,* February 28, 2011, p. 10; and www.missionstatements.com/fortune_500_mission_statements.html, accessed September 2011.

4. Information from www.heinz.com, accessed September 2011.

5. The following discussion is based in part on information found at www.bcg.com/documents/file13904.pdf, accessed December 2011.

6. Jason Garcia, "Disney Profit Leaps 54 Percent," *McClatchy-Tribune Business News*, the boring nine, 2011; and http://corporate.disney.go.com/investors/annual_reports.html, accessed September 2011.

7. H. Igor Ansoff, "Strategies for Diversification," *Harvard Business Review*, September–October 1957, pp. 113–124.

8. Information about Under Armour in this section is from Matt Townsend, "Under Armour Advances After Raising Sales Forecast," *Bloomberg Businessweek,* January 27, 2011, www.businessweek.com/news/2011-01-27/under-armour-advances-after-raising-sales-forecast.html; Kyle Stack, "How Under Armour Learned to Love Cotton Fiber," *Wired*, February 9, 2011, www.wired.com/playbook/2011/02/under-armour-cotton-fiber/; and Under Armour annual reports and other documents, www.underarmour.com, accessed September 2011.

9. See Michael E. Porter, *Competitive Advantage: Creating and Sustaining Superior Performance* (New York: Free Press, 1985); and Michael E. Porter, "What Is Strategy?" *Harvard Business Review*, November–December 1996, pp. 61–78. Also see "The Value Chain," www.quickmba.com/strategy/value-chain, accessed July 2010; and Philip Kotler and Kevin Lane Keller, *Marketing Management*, 14th ed. (Upper Saddle River, NJ: Prentice Hall, 2012), pp. 34–35 and pp. 203–204.

10. Nirmalya Kumar, "The CEO's Marketing Manifesto," *Marketing Management*, November–December 2008, pp. 24–29.

11. See www.nikebiz.com/company_overview/, accessed July 2011.

12. "100 Leading National Advertisers," *Advertising Age*, June 21, 2010, p. 10.

13. The four Ps classification was first suggested by E. Jerome McCarthy, *Basic Marketing: A Managerial Approach* (Homewood, IL: Irwin, 1960). For the four Cs, other proposed classifications, and more discussion, see Robert Lauterborn, "New Marketing Litany: 4P's Passé C-Words Take Over," *Advertising Age*, October 1, 1990, p. 26; Phillip Kotler, "Alphabet Soup," *Marketing Management*, March–April 2006, p. 51; Nirmalya Kumer, "The CEO's Marketing Manifesto," *Marketing Management*, November/December 2008, pp. 24–29; and Roy McClean, "Marketing 101—4 C's versus the 4 P's of Marketing," www.customfitfocus.com/marketing-1.htm, accessed September 2011.

14. For more discussion of the chief marketing officer position, see Philip Kotler and Kevin Lane Keller, *Marketing Management*, 14th ed. (Upper Saddle River, NJ: Prentice Hall, 2012), p. 17; and John Obrecht, "CMO Summit: Driving Corporate Culture," *BtoB*, January 17, 2011, p. 3.

15. Adapted from information found in Diane Brady, "Making Marketing Measure Up," *BusinessWeek*, December 13, 2004, pp. 112–113; and J. Mark Carr and Richard Schreuer, "Connecting the Dots," *Marketing Management*, Summer 2010, pp. 26–32.

16. Carr and Schreuer, "Connecting the Dots," p. 28. Also see "Measurement and Accountability Are More Important than Ever for Marketers," *Business Wire*, July 28, 2010; Ken Cook, "A Practical Look at Marketing Accountability," *Rural Telecommunications*, September–October 2010, p. 36; and Michael Barnett, "Marketing Metrics: True Measure of Performances Bottom Line," *Marketing Week*, September 16, 2010, p. 24.

17. See Lawrence A. Crosby, "Getting Serious about Marketing ROI," *Marketing Management*, May/June 2009, pp. 10–11; and Carr and Schreuer, "Connecting the Dots," p. 28.

18. See "We Believe Research Should Lead to Action," *Marketing News*, November 15, 2009, p. 30.

19. For a full discussion of this model and details on customer-centered measures of return on marketing investment, see Roland T. Rust, Katherine N. Lemon, and Valerie A. Zeithaml, "Return on Marketing: Using Customer Equity to Focus Marketing Strategy," *Journal of Marketing*, January 2004, pp. 109–127; Roland T. Rust, Katherine N. Lemon, and Das Narayandas, *Customer Equity Management* (Upper Saddle River, NJ: Prentice Hall, 2005); Roland T. Rust, "Seeking Higher ROI? Base Strategy on Customer Equity," *Advertising Age*, September 10, 2007, pp. 26–27; Thorsen Wiesel, Bernd Skiera, and Julián Villanueva, "Customer Equity: An Integral Part of Financial Reporting," *Journal of Marketing*, March 2008, pp. 1–14; and Andreas Persson and Lynette Ryals, "Customer Assets and Customer Equity: Management and Measurement Issues," *Marketing Theory*, December 2010, pp. 417–436.

20. Elizabeth A. Sullivan, "Measure Up," *Marketing News*, May 30, 2009, pp. 8–17; and "Marketing Strategy: Diageo CMO: 'Workers Must Be Able to Count,'" *Marketing Week*, June 3, 2010, p. 5.

Chapter 3

1. Danielle Sacks, "How YouTube's Global Platform Is Redefining the Entertainment Business," *Fast Company*, February 2011, p. 58; Jessica E. Vascellaro, Amir Efrati, and Ethan Smith, "YouTube Recasts for New Viewers," *Wall Street Journal*, April 7, 2011, p. B1; and www.youtube.com/t/about_youtube, www.youtube.com/shows, www.youtube.com/partners, and www.realwomenofphiladelphia.com/, accessed July 2011.

2. "Asia: L'Oréal's Long-Term Commitment," *Premium Beauty News,* April 12, 2011, www.premiumbeautynews.com/Asia-L-Oreal-s-long-term,2918; Rebecca Ellinor, "Crowd Pleaser," *Supply Management*, December 13, 2007, pp. 26–29; and information from www.loreal.com/_en/_ww/html/suppliers/index.aspx, accessed December 2011.

3. Information from Robert J. Benes, Abbie Jarman, and Ashley Williams, "2007 NRA Sets Records," at www.chefmagazine.com,

accessed September 2007; and www.thecoca-colacompany.com/presscenter/presskit_fs.html and www.cokesolutions.com, accessed November 2011.

4. See "About Tide Loads of Hope," www.tide.com/en-US/loads-of-hope/about.jspx, accessed November 2011.

5. World POPClock, U.S. Census Bureau, at www.census.gov/main/www/popclock.html, accessed July 2011. This Web site provides continuously updated projections of the U.S. and world populations.

6. U.S. Census Bureau projections and POPClock Projection, at www.census.gov/main/www/popclock.html, accessed November 2011.

7. Emily Brandon, "Planning to Retire: 10 Things You Didn't Know about Baby Boomers," *USNews.com,* January 15, 2009, http://money.usnews.com; Rick Ferguson and Bill Brohaugh, "The Aging of Core Areas," *Journal of Consumer Marketing*, Vol. 27, No. 1, 2010, p. 76; Suzanne Wilson, "Baby Boomers Thrown a Curve Ball," *Daily Hampshire Gazette,* February 14, 2011, p. D1; and Piet Levy, "Segmentation by Generation," *Marketing News,* May 15, 2011, pp. 20–23.

8. See Simon Hudson, "Wooing Zoomers: Marketing to the Mature Traveler," *Marketing Intelligence & Planning*, Vol. 28, No. 4, 2010, pp. 444–461; and Gavin O'Malley, "Boomers Value Brands They Champion 'Youthful' Style," *MediaPostNews*, April 12, 2011, www.mediapost.com.

9. Based on information from Todd Wasserman, "Merrill Lynch Asks Jittery Boomers to Vent Via Text," *Brandweek*, January 25, 2010, www.brandweek.com; Tanya Irwin, "Merrill Lynch Launches $20 Million Effort," *MediaPostNews*, January 27, 2010, accessed at www.mediapost.com/publications/?fa=Articles.showArticle&art_aid=121313; and www.totalmerrill.com/TotalMerrill/Pages/help2retire.aspx?mb=1#/homepage, accessed June 2011.

10. For more discussion, see R. K. Miller and Kelli Washington, *Consumer Behavior 2009* (Atlanta, GA: Richard K. Miller & Associates, 2009), Chapter 27; Bernadette Turner, "Generation X . . . . . . Let's GO!" *New Pittsburgh Courier,* March 2–March 8, 2011, p. A11; and Piet Levy, "Segmentation by Generation," *Marketing News*, May 15, 2011, pp. 20–23.

11. Based on information found in Donna C. Gregory, "Virginia Tourism Corp. Marketing to Generation X," December 29, 2009, www.virginiabusiness.com/index.php/news/article/romancing-generation-x. Also see www.virginia.org/home.asp, accessed December 2011.

12. Piet Levy, "Segmentation by Generation," p. 22; and Jon Lafayette, "Marketers Targeting Generation of Millennial's," *Broadcasting Cable*, April 11, 2011, p. 28.

13. Piet Levy, "Segmentation by Generation," p. 23.

14. Tanzina Vega, "A Campaign to Introduce Keds to a New Generation," *New York Times*, February 22, 2011, www.nytimes.com/2011/02/23/business/media/23adco.html; and http://hdyd.keds.com/, accessed December 2011.

15. See U.S. Census Bureau, "Families and Living Arrangements: 2010," at www.census.gov/population/www/socdemo/hh-fam.html, accessed May 2011.

16. U.S. Census Bureau, "Facts for Features," March 2011, accessed at www.census.gov/newsroom/releases/archives/facts_for_features_special_editions/cb11-ff04.html; and Hope Yen, "As More Women Earn Degrees, More Men Stay Home," *The News and Observer (Raleigh),* April 27, 2011, p. A1.

17. See Marissa Miley and Ann Mack, "The New Female Consumer: The Rise of the Real Mom," *Advertising Age*, November 16, 2009, p. A1; and Christine Birkner, "Mom's the Word," *Marketing News*, May 15, 2011, p. 8.

18. U.S. Census Bureau, "Geographical Mobility/Migration," at www.census.gov/population/www/socdemo/migrate.html, accessed April 2011.

19. See U.S. Census Bureau, "Metropolitan and Micropolitan Statistical Areas," www.census.gov/population/www/metroareas/metroarea.html, accessed June 2011; and "Population of 576 U.S. Micropower Areas—2010 Senses," *The Business Journals*, April 5, 2011, www.census.gov/population/www/metroareas/metroarea.html.

20. "Table 1: Selected Demographic Characteristics of Employed People by Work-at-Home Status: 2005," www.census.gov/population/www/socdemo/workathome.html#dc accessed June 2011.

21. See "WebEx Overview," at www.webex.com/overview/index.html, accessed December 2011.

22. U.S. Census Bureau, "Educational Attainment," at www.census.gov/population/www/socdemo/educ-attn.html, accessed June 2011.

23. See U.S. Census Bureau, *The 2011 Statistical Abstract: Labor Force, Employment, and Earnings,*" Table 605, accessed at www.census.gov/compendia/statab/cats/labor_force_employment_earnings.html; and U.S. Department of Labor, *Occupational Outlook Handbook, 2010–11 Edition*, accessed at www.bls.gov/oco/.

24. See U.S. Census Bureau, "U.S. Population Projections," www.census.gov/population/www/projections/summarytables.html, accessed August 2011; and "Characteristics of the Foreign-Born Population by Nativity and US Citizenship Status," www.census.gov/population/www/socdemo/foreign/cps2008.html.

25. See www.harlistasfilm.com/ and www.harley-davidson.com/en_US/Content/Pages/harlistas/harlista.html, accessed June 2011.

26. Witeck-Combs Communications, "America's Disability Market at a Glance," Andrew Adam Newman, "Web Marketing to a Segment Too Big to Be a Niche," *New York Times*, October 30, 2007, p. 9; Kenneth Hein, "The Invisible Demographic," *Brandweek*, March 3, 2008, p. 20; Tanya Mohn, "Smoothing the Way," *New York Times*, April 26, 2010, www.nytimes.com; and www.disability-marketing.com/facts/, accessed May 2011.

27. Witeck-Combs Communications, "America's Gay 2010 Buying Power Projected at $743 Billion," *Cause + Effect,* July 20, 2010, http://cause-pr.com/2010/07/america%E2%80%99s-gay-2010-buying-power-projected-at-743-billion/.

28. See Brandon Miller, "And the Winner Is . . ." *Out Traveler*, Winter 2008, pp. 64–65; Bradley Johnson, "Why (and How) You Should Go after the Gay Dollar," *Advertising Age,* October 11, 2010, p. 22; and www.aa.com/rainbow, accessed June 2011.

29. Gavin Rabinowitz, "India's Tata Motors Unveils $2,500 Car, Bringing Car Ownership within Reach of Millions," *Associated Press*, January 10, 2008; Jessica Scanlon, "What Can Tata's Nano Teach Detroit?" *BusinessWeek*, March 19, 2009, accessed at www.businessweek.com/innovate/content/mar2009/id20090318_012120.htm; Mark Phelan, "Engineers Study the Magic Behind Tata Nano," *Pittsburgh Tribune Review*, April 17, 2010, www.pittsburghlive.com; and http://tatanano.inservices.tatamotors.com/tatamotors/nano_brochure.pdf, accessed August 2011.

30. U.S. Census Bureau, "Income, Poverty, and Health Insurance Coverage in the United States: 2009," September 2010, table 3, www.census.gov/prod/2010pubs/p60-238.pdf.

31. The 2030 Water Resources Group, "Charting Our Water Future: Executive Summary," 2009, www.mckinsey.com/clientservice/water/charting_our_water_future.aspx.

32. Facts from www.pepsico.com/Purpose/Environmental-Sustainability.html, accessed June 2011.

33. See "American Apparel RFID Case Study," accessed at www.apparel.averydennison.com/solutions/american-apparel-rfid.asp,

June 2011; and Mary Catherine O'Connor, "American Apparel Adding 50 More Stores in Aggressive RFID Rollout," *RFID Journal*, April 26, 2011, www.rfidjournal.com/article/view/8374.

34. See Tamara Schweitzer, "The Way I Work," *Inc.*, June 2010, pp. 112–116; Christina Binkley, "Style—On Style: Charity Gives Shoe Brand Extra Shine," *Wall Street Journal*, April 1, 2010, p. D7; and www.toms.com, accessed June 2011.

35. Emily Steel, "Cause-Tied Marketing Requires Care," *Wall Street Journal*, March 21, 2011, p. B4.

36. See "The Growth of Cause Marketing," at www.causemarketingforum.com/page.asp?ID=188, accessed June 2011.

37. See "10 Crucial Consumer Trends for 2010," Trendwatching.com, http://trendwatching.com/trends/pdf/trendwatching%20 2009-12%2010trends.pdf; and "The F-Factor," Trendingwatching.com, May 2011, http://trendwatching.com/trends/pdf/trendwatching%202009-12%2010trends.pdf.

38. "The F-Factor," Trendingwatching.com, p. 1.

39. Laura Feldmann, "After 9/11 Highs, America's Back to Good Ol' Patriotism," *Christian Science Monitor*, July 5, 2006, p. 1; Leon F. Dube and Gregory S. Black, "Impact of National Traumatic Events on Consumer Purchasing," *International Journal of Consumer Studies*, May 2010, p. 333; and "Lifestyle Statistics: Very Proud of Their Nationality," at www.nationmaster.com, accessed June 2011.

40. Sarah Mahoney, "Report: LOHAS Market Nears $300 Billion," *Marketing Daily*, April 26, 2010, www.mediapost.com/publications/?art_aid=126836&fa=Articles.showArticle; and www.lohas.com, accessed November 2011.

41. See www.tomsofmaine.com/home, accessed June 2011.

42. "Organic Farming Grows to $29-Billion Industry," *Western Farm Press*, April 26, 2011.

43. The Pew Forum on Religion & Public Life, "U.S. Religious Landscape Survey," http://religions.pewforum.org/reports#, accessed November 2011.

44. Dan Harris, "America Is Becoming Less Christian, Less Religious," *ABC News*, March 9, 2009, accessed at http://abcnews.go.com.

45. W. Chan Kim and Renée Mauborgne, "How Strategy Shaped Structure," *Harvard Business Review*, September 2009, pp. 73–80.

46. Paula Forbes, "Taco Bell Ad: Thank You for Suing Us," January 28, 2011, *Eater,* http://eater.com/archives/2011/01/28/taco-bell-ad-thanks-firm-for-law-suit.php; Courtney Hutchinson and Katie Moisse, "Taco Bell Fights 'Where's the Beef' Lawsuit," January 28, 2011, http://abcnews.go.com/Health/Wellness/taco-bell-defends-beef-legal-action/story?id=12785818; and "Law Firm Voluntarily Withdraws Class-Action Lawsuit against Taco Bell," April 19, 2011, http://money.msn.com/business-news/article.aspx?feed=BW&date=20110419&id=13327023.

Chapter 4

1. Excerpts, quotes, and other information from T. L. Stanley, "Easy As Pie: How Russell Weiner Turned Sabotage Into Satisfaction," *Adweek*, September 13, 2010, p. 40; "Lessons from the Domino's Turnaround," *Restaurant Hospitality,* June 2010, p. 30; Rupal Parekh, "Marketer of the Year," *Advertising Age*, October 18, 2010, p. 19; Emily Bryson York, "Domino's Claims Victory with New Strategy: Pizza Wasn't Good, We Fixed It," *Advertising Age,* May 10, 2010, p. 4; Mark Brandau, "Domino's Do-Over," *Nation's Restaurant News,* March 8, 2010, p. 44; "Domino's Puts Customer Feedback on Times Square Billboard," *Detroit News,* July 26, 2011; and annual reports and other information from www.dominosbiz.com and www.pizzaturnaround.com, accessed December 2011.

2. Dan Frommer, "Apple iPod Still Obliterating Microsoft Zune," *Business Insider*, July 12, 2010, http://read.bi/axUYCO.

3. Carey Toane, "Listening: The New Metric," *Strategy*, September 2009, p. 45.

4. Warren Thayer and Michael Sansolo, "Walmart: Our Retailer of the Year," *R&FF Retailer*, June 2009, pp. 14–20; and information from http://walmartstores.com/Suppliers/248.aspx, accessed December 2011.

5. See Scott Horstein, "Use Care with That Database," *Sales & Marketing Management*, May 2006, p. 22; "USAA Announces Mobile RDC App for Android Phones," *TechWeb*, January 27, 2010; "USAA," *Hoover's Company Records*, June 15, 2010; Jean McGregor, "Customer Service Champs: USAA's Battle Plan," *Bloomberg Businessweek,* March 1, 2010, pp. 40–43; "Largest U.S. Corporations," *Fortune,* May 3, 2010, p. F7; and www.usaa.com, accessed September 2011.

6. Based on information from Adam Ostrow, "Inside the Gatorade's Social Media Command Center," June 6, 2010, accessed at http://mashable.com/2010/06/15/gatorade-sical-media-mission-control/; and Valery Bauerlein, "Gatorade's 'Mission': Using Social Media to Boost Sales," *Wall Street Journal Asia*, September 15, 2010, p. 8.

7. Irena Slutsky, "'Chief Listeners Use Technology to Track, Sort Company Mentioned," *Advertising Age*, August 30, 2010, accessed at http://adage.com/digital/article?article_id=145618.

8. See http://biz.yahoo.com/ic/101/101316.html, accessed September 2011.

9. For more on research firms that supply marketing information, see Jack Honomichl, "2010 Honomichl Top 50," special section, *Marketing News*, June 17, 2010. Other information from www.nielsen.com/us/en/measurement/retail-measurement.html and www.yankelovich.com, accessed September 2011.

10. See http://symphonyiri.com/?TabId=159&productid=84, accessed September 2011.

11. Example adapted from Dana Flavelle, "Kraft Goes Inside the Kitchen of the Canadian Family," *Toronto Star*, January 16, 2010, www.thestar.com/business/article/751507. For other examples, see Philip Kotler and Kevin Lane Keller, *Marketing Management,* 14th ed. (Upper Saddle River, NJ: Prentice Hall, 2012), p. 101.

12. For more discussion of online ethnography, see Pradeep K. Tyagi, "Webnography: A New Tool to Conduct Marketing Research," *Journal of American Academy of Business*, March 2010, pp. 262–268; Robert V. Kozinets, "Netnography: The Marketer's Secret Weapon," March 2010, accessed at http://info.netbase.com/rs/netbase/images/Netnography_WP.; and http://en.wikipedia.org/wiki/Online_ethnography, accessed September 2011.

13. Example adapted from information found in "My Dinner with Lexus," *Automotive News,* November 29, 2010, accessed at www.autonews.com/apps/pbcs.dll/article?AID=/20101129/RETAIL03/311299949/1292.

14. See www.internetworldstats.com/stats14.htm, accessed July 2011.

15. Based on information found at www.channelm2.com/How OnlineQualitativeResearch.html, accessed December 2011.

16. See "Online Panel," www.zoomerang.com/online-panel/, accessed December 2011.

17. Derek Kreindler, "Lexus Soliciting Customer Feedback with Lexus Advisory Board," August 24, 2010, accessed at www.autoguide.com/auto-news/2010/08/lexus-soliciting-customer-feedback-with-lexus-advisory-board.html; and "20,000 Customers Sign up for the Lexus Advisory Board," August 30, 2010, accessed at www.4wheelsnews.com/20000-customers-signed-up-for-the-lexus-advisory-board/.

18. Stephen Baker, "The Web Knows What You Want," *Business-Week*, July 27, 2009, p. 48.

19. Adapted from Brooks Barnes, "Lab Watches Web Surfers to See Which Ads Work," *New York Times*, July 26, 2009; and "Walt Disney Company's Media Networks to Develop Emerging Media and Advertising Research Lab," accessed at http://corporate .disney.go.com/corporate/moreinfo/media_advertising_research_ lab.html, August 2011.

20. Jessica Tsai, "Are You Smarter Than a Neuromarketer?" *Customer Relationship Management*, January 2010, pp. 19–20.

21. For these and other neuromarketing examples and discussion, see Laurie Burkitt, "Neuromarketing: Companies Use Neuroscience for Consumer Insights," *Forbes*, November 16, 2009, www.forbes.com; Ilan Brat, "The Emotional Quotient of Soup Shopping," *Wall Street Journal*, February 17, 2010, p. B6; Natasha Singer, "Making Ads That Will Spur the Brain," *New York Times*, November 14, 2010, p. BU4; and Deena Diggs, "Emotional Marketing," *Editor & Publisher*, January 2010, p. 7.

22. Example adapted from information found in Dan Sewell, "Kroger Uses Shopper Data to Target Coupons," *Huffington Post*, January 6, 2009, www.huffingtonpost.com/2009/01/06/ kroger-uses-shopper-data_n_155667.html; and Dan Sewell, "Kroger CEO Often Roams Aisles, Wielding Carte Blanche," *Journal-Gazette* (Ft. Wayne, IN), November 15, 2010, p. C4.

23. Gillian S. Ambroz, "Is This Just: Getting Back to Basics," *Folio*, January 2010, p. 97.

24. "SAS helps 1-800-Flowers.com Grow Deep Roots with Customers," www.sas.com/success/1800flowers.html, accessed September 2011.

25. See www.pensketruckleasing.com/leasing/precision/precision_ features.html, accessed September 2011.

26. Adapted from information in Ann Zimmerman, "Small Business; Do the Research," *Wall Street Journal*, May 9, 2005, p. R3; with information from John Tozzi, "Market Research on the Cheap," *BusinessWeek*, January 9, 2008, www.businessweek.com/ smallbiz/content/jan2008/sb2008019_352779.htm; and www .bibbentuckers.com, accessed September 2011.

27. Zimmerman, "Small Business; Do the Research," *Wall Street Journal*, p. R3.

28. For some good advice on conducting market research in a small business, see "Conducting Market Research," www.sba.gov/ content/conducting-market-research, accessed August 2011; and "Researching Your Market," *Entrepreneur*, accessed at www .entrepreneur.com/article/43024-1, March 2011.

29. See "Top 25 Global Market Research Organizations," *Marketing News*, August 30, 2010, p. 16; and www.nielsen.com/us/en/ about-us.html, accessed September 2011.

30. Internet stats are from http://data.worldbank.org/indicator/ IT.NET.USER.P2, accessed March 2011.

31. Subhash C. Jain, *International Marketing Management*, 3rd ed. (Boston: PWS-Kent, 1990), p. 338. For more discussion on international marketing research issues and solutions, see Warren J. Keegan and Mark C. Green, *Global Marketing*, 6th ed. (Upper Saddle River, NJ: Prentice Hall, 2011), pp. 170–201.

32. For these quotes and excellent discussions of online privacy, see Juan Martinez, "Marketing Marauders or Consumer Counselors?" *CRM Magazine*, January 2011, accessed at www.destinationcrm .com; and Lauren McKay, "Eye on Customers: Are Consumers Comfortable with or Creeped out by Online Data Collection Tactics?" *CRM Magazine*, January 2011, accessed at www .destinationcrm.com.

33. "ICC/ESOMAR International Code of Marketing and Social Research Practice," www.esomar.org/index.php/codes-guidelines .html, accessed July 2011. Also see "Respondent Bill of Rights," www.mra-net.org/ga/billofrights.cfm, accessed November 2011.

34. Federal Trade Commission, "Kellogg Settles FTC Charges That Ads for Frosted Mini-Wheats Were False," April 20, 2009, www.ftc.gov/opa/2009/04/kellogg.shtm; "Kellogg's Frosted Mini-Wheats Neuroscience: The FTC Reckoning," http:// rangelife.typepad.com/rangelife/2009/04/kelloggs-frosted- miniwheats-neuroscience-the-ftc-reckoning.html, April 21, 2009; Todd Wasserman, "New FTC Asserts Itself," *Brandweek*, April 27, 2009, p. 8; and "FTC Investigation of Ad Claims that Rice Krispies Benefits Children's Immunity Leads to Stronger Order Against Kellogg," *US Fed News Service*, June 4, 2010.

35. Information at www.casro.org/codeofstandards.cfm#intro, accessed December 2011.

Chapter 5

1. "Macolyte," *Urban Dictionary*, accessed at www.urbandictionary .com, October 2011; "Apple," the American Consumer Satisfaction Index, accessed at www.theacsi.org, March 2011; Steve Maich, "Nowhere to Go But Down," *Maclean's*, May 9, 2005, p. 32; Steven H. Wildstrom, "The Stubborn Luxury of Apple," *BusinessWeek*, November 23, 2009, p. 82; Jim Joseph, "How Do I Love Thee, Apple? Let Me Count the Ways," *Brandweek*, May 24, 2010, p. 30; Farad Manjoo, "Apple Nation," *Fast Company*, July/August, 2010, pp. 68–76, 110; Henrik Werdelin, "Three Things Google Can Learn from Apple," *Fast Company*, July 13, 2010, accessed at www .fastcompany.com/1669457/3-things-google-can-learn-from-apple; "Apple: for Dominating the Business Landscape, in 101 Ways," *Fast Company*, March 2011, pp. 68–74; and financial information found at www.apple.com, September 2011.

2. Consumer expenditure figures from http://en.wikipedia.org/wiki/ Gross_domestic_product. Population figures from the World POPClock, U.S. Census Bureau, www.census.gov/main/www/ popclock.html, accessed May 2011. This Web site provides continuously updated projections of U.S. and world populations.

3. See "Many Cultures, Many Numbers," *Adweek*, September 27, 2010, p. 16; and Sam Fahmy, "Despite Recession, Hispanic and Asian Buying Power Expected to Surge in U.S.," November 4, 2010, accessed at www.terry.uga.edu/news/releases/2010/ minority-buying-power-report.html.

4. See Emily Bryson York, "General Mills Targets Three Groups to Fuel Growth," *Advertising Age*, February 16, 2010, accessed at http://adage.com/print?article_id=142138; "General Mills Launches Its First Spanish-Language App for Apple IPad," *Marketing Weekly News*, October 30, 2010, p. 220; and "PR Best Practices and Nation's Biggest Names in Hispanic Marketing to Take Center Stage at Hispanicize 2011," *PR Newswire*, February 9, 2011.

5. See Della de Lafuente, "The New Weave," *Adweek*, March 3, 2008, pp. 26–28; and "Latino Subcultures: A Rising Force of Cultural Inspiration," Conill, http://conill.com/#/white-papers, accessed March 2011. For lots of other good examples, see "Hispanic Creative Advertising Awards," *Advertising Age*, October 9, 2010, pp. 36–45.

6. See "Many Cultures, Many Numbers," *Brandweek*, September 27, 2010, p. 16; Sam Fahmy, "Despite Recession, Hispanic and Asian Buying Power Expected to Surge in U.S.," accessed at www.terry.uga.edu/news/releases/2010/minority-buying- power-report.html; and U.S. Census Bureau reports, www .census.gov, accessed October 2011.

7. "Procter & Gamble; P&G's My Black Is Beautiful TV Series Celebrates Another Successful Season on BET Networks," *Marketing Weekly News,* January 1, 2011, p. 76; "Procter & Gamble's My Black Is Beautiful Honored with City of Cincinnati Proclamation," *PR Newswire,* May 21, 2010; and information from www.myblackisbeautiful.com, accessed October 2011.

8. See "Many Cultures, Many Numbers," p. 16; Sam Fahmy, "Despite Recession, Hispanic and Asian Buying Power Expected to Surge in U.S."; and U.S. Census Bureau reports www.census.gov, accessed October 2011.

9. Bill Imada, "Why State Farm Tries to Be a Good Neighbor to Asian American Community," *Advertising Age,* September 1, 2009, http://adage.com/bigtent/post?article_id=138735; Imada, "Top 10 Corporate Marketers in the U.S. Asian Market in 2009," *Advertising Age,* January 20, 2010, http://adage.com/bigtent/post?article_id=141595; and Imada, "Don't Be So Quick to Dismiss Power of Asian Consumers," *Advertising Age,* October 11, 2010, p. 14.

10. Eleftheria Parpis, "Goodbye Color Codes," *Adweek,* September 27, 2010, pp. 24–25; and "Ethnic Marketing: McDonald's Is Lovin' It," *Bloomberg Businessweek,* July 18, 2010, pp. 22–23.

11. "Research Reveals Word-of-Mouth Campaigns on Customer Networks Double Marketing Results," *Business Wire,* October 27, 2009.

12. See "JetBlue Lovers Unite to Share Brand Perks with Peers," WOOMA Case, www.womma.org/casestudy/examples/archive2008/jetblue-lovers-unite-to-share/, accessed March 2011; Joan Voigt, "The New Brand Ambassadors," *Adweek,* December 31, 2007, pp. 18–19, 26; Rebecca Nelson, "A Citizen Marketer Talks," *Adweek,* December 31, 2007, p. 19; Holly Shaw, "Buzzing Influencers," *National Post,* March 13, 2009, p. FP 12; and information from www.repnation.com, accessed October 2011.

13. Victoria Taylor, "The Best-Ever Social Media Campaign," *Forbes,* August 17, 2010, accessed at www.forbes.com; Bruce Horovitz, "Marketers: Inside Job on College Campuses," *USA Today,* October 4, 2010, p. B1; and "Old Spice Guide Isaiah Mustafa Says Fans Love to Smell Him," *TV Replay,* February 2, 2011, accessed at www.tvsquad.com/2011/02/02/old-spice-guy-isaiah-mustafa-says-fans-love-to-smell-him-video/.

14. See Eleftheria Parpis, "She's in Charge," *Adweek,* October 6–13, 2008, p. 38; Abigail Posner, "Why Package-Goods Companies Should Market to Men," *Advertising Age,* February 9, 2009, http://adage.com/print?article_id=134473; and Marissa Miley and Ann Mark, "The New Female Consumer: The Rise of the Real Mom," *Advertising Age,* November 16, 2009, pp. A1–A27.

15. Laura A. Flurry, "Children's Influence in Family Decision Making: Examining the Impact of the Changing American Family," *Journal of Business Research,* April 2007, pp. 322–330; and "Tween Years Prove to Be Rewarding for Toymakers," *USA Today,* December 22, 2010, p. 1B.

16. See Ron Ruggless, "Casual Chains Cater to Kids as Way to Lure *Back* Families," *Nation's Restaurant News,* July 13, 2009, pp. 1, 29–30; and information from www.roysrestaurant.com, accessed October 2011.

17. For information on Acxiom's PersonicX segmentation system, see "PersonicX Interactive Wheel," accessed at www.acxiom.com/products_and_services/Consumer%20Insight%20Products/segmentation/Pages/index.html, October 2011.

18. Quotes and examples from www.carhartt.com, September 2011.

19. See "Target Introduces the Great Save," *Business Wire,* January 4, 2010; and John Ewold, "How Does Target's Great Save Compare to Costco and Sam's?" *Star Tribune* (Minneapolis-St. Paul),

January 7, 2011, accessed at www.startribune.com/lifestyle/yourmoney/blogs/113095249.html.

20. See Jennifer Aaker, "Dimensions of Measuring Brand Personality," *Journal of Marketing Research,* August 1997, pp. 347–356; Kevin Lane Keller, *Strategic Brand Management,* 3rd ed. (Upper Saddle River, New Jersey, 2008), pp. 66–67; Beth Snyder Bulik, "You Want to Watch, Market Data Suggests," *Advertising Age,* November 1, 2010, p. 12; and Michael R. Solomon, *Consumer Behavior,* 9th ed. (Upper Saddle River, NJ: Prentice Hall, 2011), pp. 221–226.

21. "Axe: Let Me Entertain You," *Brand Strategy,* October 9, 2007, 20; and www.unilever.com/brands/personalcarebrands/axe/index.aspx, accessed September 2011.

22. See Abraham H. Maslow, "A Theory of Human Motivation," *Psychological Review,* 50 (1943), pp. 370–396. Also see Maslow, *Motivation and Personality,* 3rd ed. (New York: HarperCollins Publishers, 1987); and Leon G. Schiffman and Leslie Lazar Kanuk, *Consumer Behavior* (Upper Saddle River, NJ: Prentice Hall, 2010), pp. 98–106.

23. See Louise Story, "Anywhere the Eye Can See, It's Likely to See an Ad," *New York Times,* January 15, 2007, www.nytimes.com/2007/01/15/business/media/15everywhere.html; Matthew Creamer, "Caught in the Clutter Crossfire: Your Brand," *Advertising Age,* April 1, 2007, p. 35; and Ruth Mortimer, "Consumer Awareness: Getting the Right Attention," *Brand Strategy,* December 10, 2008, p. 55.

24. See Bob Garfield, "'Subliminal' Seduction and Other Urban Myths," *Advertising Age,* September 18, 2000, pp. 4, 105; Cahal Milmo, "Power of the Hidden Message Is Revealed," *Independent* (London), September 28, 2009, p. 8; "50 Great Myths of Popular Psychology," *McClatchy-Tribune Business News,* May 3, 2010; and Michael R. Solomon, *Consumer Behavior,* 9th ed. (Upper Saddle River, NJ: Prentice Hall, 2011), pp. 73–75.

25. Quotes and information from Yubo Chen and Jinhong Xie, "Online Consumer Review: Word-of-Mouth as a New Element of Marketing Communication Mix," *Management Science,* March 2008, pp. 477–491; "Leo J. Shapiro & Associates: User-Generated Content Three Times More Influential Than TV Advertising on Consumer Purchase Decisions," *Marketing Business Weekly,* December 28, 2008, p. 34; and *Customer Experience Report, North America, 2010,* RightNow Technologies, October 13, 2010, www.rightnow.com/cx-news-16097.php#.

26. See Leon Festinger, *A Theory of Cognitive Dissonance* (Stanford, CA: Stanford University Press, 1957); Cynthia Crossen, "'Cognitive Dissonance' Became a Milestone in the 1950s Psychology," *Wall Street Journal,* December 12, 2006, p. B1; and Anupam Bawa and Purva Kansal, "Cognitive Dissonance and the Marketing of Services: Some Issues," *Journal of Services Research,* October 2008–March 2009, p. 31.

27. The following discussion draws from the work of Everett M. Rogers. See his *Diffusion of Innovations,* 5th ed. (New York: Free Press, 2003).

28. Jackie Crosbie, "Best Buy Launches Gadget Buyback," *Star Tribune* (Minneapolis-St. Paul), January 10, 2011; "How Marketing Missteps Stalled TV Sales," *Bloomberg Businessweek,* January 30, 2011, pp. 24–25; and www.bestbuy.com/site/Misc/Buy-Back-Program/pcmcat230000050010.c?id=pcmcat230000050010&DCMP=rdr2161, accessed August 2011.

29. "HDTV Households Now Dominate U.S. Viewing Landscape, According to LRG Study," *Broadcast Engineering,* December 30, 2010, http://broadcastengineering.com/hdtv/hdtv-households-dominate-viewing-landscape-according-to-lrg-study-20110104/.

30. This classic categorization was first introduced in Patrick J. Robinson, Charles W. Faris, and Yoram Wind, *Industrial Buying Behavior and Creative Marketing* (Boston: Allyn & Bacon, 1967). Also see James C. Anderson, James A. Narus, and Das Narayandas, *Business Market Management*, 3rd ed. (Upper Saddle River, NJ: Prentice Hall, 2009), Chapter 3; and Philip Kotler and Kevin Lane Keller, *Marketing Management*, 14th ed. (Upper Saddle River, NJ: Prentice Hall, 2012), Chapter 7.

31. Example adapted from information found in "Nikon Focuses on Supply Chain Innovation—and Makes New Product Distribution a Snap," UPS case study, www.ups-scs.com/solutions/case_studies/cs_on.pdf, accessed November 2011.

32. Based on "Citrix Systems: Integrated Campaign—Honorable Mention," *BtoB*, August 2009, accessed at www.btobonline.com/apps/pbcs.dll/article?AID=/20101011/FREE/101019997; and information provided by Citrix, July 2011.

33. Robinson, Faris, and Wind, *Industrial Buying Behavior*, p. 14. Also see Philip Kotler and Kevin Lane Keller, *Marketing Management*, pp. 197–203.

34. See https://suppliercenter.homedepot.com/wps/portal, accessed October 2011.

35. For this and other examples, see "10 Great Web Sites," *BtoB Online*, September 13, 2010. Other information from www.shawfloors.com/About-Shaw/Retailer-Support, accessed October 2011.

36. See William J. Angelo, "E-Procurement Process Delivers Best Value for Kodak," *Engineering News-Record*, March 17, 2008, p. 22. Also see Gareth Griffiths and Hamad Payab, "Supply on the Heels of Demand: Issues of e-Procurement," *Journal of Global Business Issues*, Summer 2010, pp. 29–37; and "Markets and Research: Effective e-Procurement: Assessing Options for the New 'Economic Normal,'" *Business Wire*, February 22, 2011.

Chapter 6

1. Quotes and other information from "High-Five! Dunkin' Donuts Is Number One in Customer Loyalty for Fifth Straight Year," February 16, 2011, accessed at http://news.dunkindonuts.com/dunkin+donuts/dunkin+donuts+news/dunkin+donuts+customer+loyalty.htm; "Dunkin Brands Announces Robust 2010 Development Growth," *PR Newswire*, February 3, 2011; Janet Adamy, "Battle Brewing: Dunkin' Donuts Tries to Go Upscale, But Not Too Far," *Wall Street Journal*, April 8, 2006, p. A1; "Dunkin Donuts Launches New Advertising Campaign to Celebrate the Passion of Real Fans: 'I'm Drinkin' Dunkin'!'" *Entertainment Business Newsweekly*, January 23, 2011, p. 33; and www.starbucks.com, www.dunkindonuts.com, and www.dunkinbrands.com, accessed September 2011.

2. See Sarah Mahoney, "Walmart to Launch Campaign, Expand Small Stores," *MediaPost News*, March 10, 2010; Margaret Rhodes, "Mini-(Wal)Mart vs. Micro-Target," *Fast Company*, January 12, 2011, p. 32; Jonathan Birchall, "Walmart Looks to Hispanic Market in Expansion Drive," *Financial Times*, March 13, 2009, p. 18; and http://walmartstores.com/AboutUs/7606.aspx, accessed September 2011.

3. Adapted from Cotton Timberlake, "With Stores Nationwide, Macy's Goes Local," *Bloomberg Businessweek*, October 4, 2010–October 10, 2010, pp. 21–22; and Robert Klara, "For the New Macy's, All Marketing Is Local," *Adweek*, June 7, 2010, p. 25–26. For other examples, see Philip Kotler and Kevin Lane Keller, *Marketing Management*, 14th ed. (Upper Saddle River, NJ: Prentice Hall, 2012), pp. 234–235.

4. Joel Stein, "The Men's 'Skin Care' Product Boom," *Time*, October 30, 2010, www.time.com/time/magazine/article/0,9171,2025576,00.html; and Joyce V. Harrison, "Men Invade Female Turf of Cosmetics," Associated Content from Yahoo!, November 2, 2010, www.associatedcontent.com/article/5922774/men_invade_female_turf_of_cosmetics_pg2.html?cat=69.

5. Mark Clothier, "Hardly Shows Its Feminine Side," *Bloomberg Businessweek*, October 4, 2010–October 10, 2010, pp. 25–26; and www.harley-davidson.com/en_US/Content/Pages/2010c/ss/start-something.html and www.harley-davidson.com/wcm/Content/Pages/women_riders/landing.jsp, accessed September 2011.

6. Example from Richard Baker, "Retail Trends—Luxury Marketing: The End of a Mega-Trend," *Retail*, June/July 2009, pp. 8–12.

7. See Suzanne Kapner, "How Fashion's VF Supercharges Its Brands," *Fortune*, April 14, 2008, pp. 108–110; and www.vfc.com, accessed December 2011.

8. See Philip Kotler and Kevin Lane Keller, *Marketing Management*, 14th ed. (Upper Saddle River, NJ: Prentice Hall, 2012), p. 98; and Jenn Abelson, "Gillette Sharpens Its Focus on Women," *Boston Globe*, January 4, 2009. Venus product descriptions from www.gillettevenus.com/en_US/products/index.jsp, accessed September 2011.

9. See Carolyn Chapin, "Seafood Nets Loyal Consumers," *Refrigerated & Frozen Foods*, June 2009, p. 42; and "Tracking Consumer Attitudes toward Seafood Safety Resulting from the Gulf of Oil Spill," December 2010, accessed at http://louisianaseafood.com/pdf/LSPMBSeafoodPhaseI-FinalVersion.pdf.

10. See these and other examples in Andreas B. Eisenerich and others, "Behold the Extreme Consumers…," *Harvard Business Review*, April 2010, pp. 30–31.

11. For more on the PRIZM Lifestyle Segmentation System, see www.MyBestSegments.com, accessed December 2011.

12. Information from www201.americanexpress.com/sbsapp/FMACServlet?request_type=alternateChannels&lpid=246_open&ccsgeep=40600&openeep=30212&ccsgeep2=40604, accessed August 2011.

13. "Coca-Cola Launches Global Music Effort to Connect with Teens," *Advertising Age*, March 3, 2011, accessed at http://adage.com/print/149204.

14. See Michael Porter, *Competitive Advantage* (New York: Free Press, 1985), pp. 4–8, 234–236. For more recent discussions, see Kenneth Sawka and Bill Fiora, "The Four Analytical Techniques Every Analyst Must Know: 2. Porter's Five Forces Analysis," *Competitive Intelligence Magazine*, May–June 2003, p. 57; and Philip Kotler and Kevin Lane Keller, *Marketing Management*, 14th ed. (Upper Saddle River, NJ: Prentice Hall, 2012), p. 232.

15. Example adapted from Philip Kotler and Kevin Lane Keller, *Marketing Management*, 14th ed., p. 235. Also see Barry Silverstein, "Hallmark—Calling Card," June 15, 2009, www.brandchannel.com; Brad van Auken, "Leveraging the Brand: Hallmark Case Study," January 11, 2008, www.brandstrategyinsider.com; and www.hallmark.com, accessed September 2011.

16. Store information found at www.walmartstores.com, www.wholefoodsmarket.com, and www.kroger.com, accessed September 2011.

17. Adapted from information found in Linda Tischler, "The Fast Company 50 – 2009: Etsy," *Fast Company*, February 11, 2009, www.fastcompany.com/fast50_09/profile/list/etsy; Max Chafkin, "Rob's World," *Inc.*, April 2011, pp. 56–64; and www.etsy.com/press/kit/, accessed October 2011.

18. Stephanie Clifford, "Drug Chain's Beer Bar Serves a Neighborhood," *New York Times*, January 14, 2011, p. B. 1.

19. Jennifer Van Grove, "Location-Based Text Message Ads Get a Major Boom," Mashable.com, August 18, 2010, http://mashable.com/2010/08/18/shopalerts/.

20. Adapted from portions of Gwendolyn Bounds, "The Rise of Holiday Me-tailers," *Wall Street Journal,* December 8, 2010, p. D1.

21. Based on quotes and information from Fae Goodman, "Lingerie Is Luscious and Lovely," *Chicago Sun-Times,* February 19, 2006, p. B2; Stacy Weiner, "Goodbye to Girlhood," *Washington Post,* February 20, 2007, p. HE01; India Knight, "Relax: Girls Will Be Girls," *Sunday Times* (London), February 21, 2010, p. 4; and "Abercrombie & Fitch Removes 'Push-Up' From Girls' Bikini Description Following Outcry," *Fox News,* March 30, 2011, accessed at www.foxnews.com.

22. See "IC3 2010 Annual Report on Internet Crime Released," February 24, 2011, www.ic3.gov/media/2011/110224.aspx.

23. SUV sales data furnished by www.WardsAuto.com, accessed March 2011. Price data from www.edmunds.com, accessed March 2011.

24. Based on information found in Michael Myser, "Marketing Made Easy," *Business 2.0,* June 2006, pp. 43–44; "Staples, Inc." *Hoover's Company Records,* http://premium.hoovers.com/subscribe/co/factsheet.xhtml?ID=rcksfrhrfjcxtr, April 2011; and www.staples.com, accessed August 2011.

25. Quote from "Singapore Airlines: Company Information," accessed at www.singaporeair.com, November 2011.

26. Based on information from Philip Kotler and Kevin Lane Keller, *Marketing Management,* 14th ed., p. 336; and www.heartsonfire.com/Learn-About-Our-Diamonds.asp, accessed October 2011.

27. See Bobby J. Calder and Steven J. Reagan, "Brand Design," in Dawn Iacobucci, ed., *Kellogg on Marketing* (New York: John Wiley & Sons, 2001), p. 61. For more discussion, see Philip Kotler and Kevin Lane Keller, *Marketing Management,* 14th ed., Chapter 10.

Chapter 7

1. Quotes and other information from "Nike, Inc. Reports Fiscal 2011 Third-Quarter Results," *Business Wire,* March 17, 2011; Barbara Lippert, "Game Changers," *Adweek,* November 17–24, 2008, p. 20; Mark Borden, "Nike," *Fast Company,* March 2008, p. 93; Jonathon Birchall, "Nike Seeks 'Opportunities' in Turmoil," *Financial Times,* March 16, 2009, p. 20; Brian Morrissey, "Nike Plus Starts to Open Up to Web," *Adweek,* July 20–July 27, 2009, p. 8; "Nike," *Campaign,* December 10, 2010, p. 17; and annual reports and other sources at www.nikebiz.com, accessed September 2011.

2. Adapted from information found in Chuck Salter, "Why America Is Addicted to Olive Garden," *Fast Company,* July–August 2009, pp. 102–106; and "Culinary Institute of Tuscany," www.olivegarden.com/culinary/cit/, accessed November 2011.

3. Information from www.discoverireland.com/us, accessed May 2011. Also see www.iloveny.com and www.visitcalifornia.com, accessed May 2011.

4. Accessed at www.social-marketing.org/aboutus.html, November 2011.

5. For more on social marketing, see Alan R. Andreasen, *Social Marketing in the 21st Century* (Thousand Oaks, CA: Sage Publications, 2006); Philip Kotler and Nancy Lee, *Social Marketing: Improving the Quality of Life,* 3rd ed. (Thousand Oaks, CA: Sage Publications, 2008); and www.adcouncil.com and www.socialmarketing.org, accessed September 2011.

6. Quotes and definitions from Philip Kotler, *Kotler on Marketing* (New York: Free Press, 1999), p. 17; and www.asq.org/glossary/q.html, accessed November 2011.

7. Quotes and other information from Regina Schrambling, "Tool Department; The Sharpest Knives in the Drawer," *Los Angeles Times,* March 8, 2006, p. F1; "Alex Lee at Gel 2008," video and commentary at http://vimeo.com/3200945, accessed June 2009; Reena Jana and Helen Walters, "OXO Gets a Grip on New Markets," *BusinessWeek,* October 5, 2009, p. 71; and www.oxo.com/about.jsp, accessed August 2011.

8. Andy Goldsmith, "Coke vs. Pepsi: The Taste They Don't Want You to Know About," *The 60-Second Marketer,* www.60secondmarketer.com/60SecondArticles/Branding/cokevs.pepsitast.html, accessed September 2011.

9. James Black, "What Is Your Product Saying to Consumers? *Advertising Age,* January 18, 2011, http://adage.com/print?article_id=148283.

10. See "FMI—Supermarketfacts," www.fmi.org/facts_figs/?fuseaction=superfact, accessed May 2011; "Walmart Facts," www.walmartfacts.com/StateByState/?id=2, accessed May 2011; and "Shopper Decisions Made In-Store by OgilvyAction," www.wpp.com, accessed May 2011.

11. See Collin Dunn, "Packaging Design at Its Worst," *Treehugger.com,* July 6, 2009, www.treehugger.com/galleries/2009/07/packaging-design-at-its-worst.php.

12. Leonora Oppenhei, "Method Laundry Detergent's Radical Innovation Wins International Design Excellence Award," *Treehugger.com,* July 20, 2010, www.treehugger.com/files/2010/07/methodlaundry-detergent-wins-international-design-excellence-award.php; and www.methodhome.com, accessed August 2011.

13. Natalie Zmuda, "What Went into the Updated Pepsi Logo," *Advertising Age,* October 27, 2008, p. 6; Natalie Zmuda, "Pepsi, Coke Tried to Outdo Each Other with Rays of Sunshine," *Advertising Age,* January 19, 2009, p. 6; "New Pepsi Logo Kicks off Campaign," *McClatchy-Tribune Business News,* January 15, 2010.

14. Linda Tischler, "Never Mind! Pepsi Pulls Much-Loathed Tropicana Packaging," *Fast Company,* February 23, 2009, www.fastcompany.com/blog/linda-tischler/design-times/never-mind-pepsi-pulls-much-loathed-tropicana-packaging; "Leggo Your Logo," *Adweek,* December 6, 2010, p. 12; "New Gap Logo a Neural Failure," October 10, 2010, www.newscientist.com/blogs/shortsharpscience/2010/10/-normal-0-false-false-2.html; and "Marketer in the News," *Marketing,* February 9, 2011, p. 8.

15. For these and other stories, see Bob Janet, "Customers Never Tire of Great Service," *Dealerscope,* July 2008, p. 40; and Greta Schulz, "Nordstrom Makes Customer Service Look Easy," December 11, 2009, http://amazingserviceguy.com/2370/2370/.

16. See the HP Total Care site at http://h71036.www7.hp.com/hho/cache/309717-0-0-225-121.html, accessed November 2011.

17. Based on an example from Philip Kotler and Kevin Lane Keller, *Marketing Management,* 14th ed. (Upper Saddle River, NJ: Prentice Hall, 2012), p. 343, with additional information from http://en.wikipedia.org/wiki/BMW and www.bmwusa.com/standard/content/byo/default.aspx, accessed September 2011.

18. Information on Campbell Soup Company's product mix from http://investor.campbellsoupcompany.com/phoenix.zhtml?c=88650&p=irol-reportsannual, accessed May 2011.

19. Paul Hochman, "Ford's Big Reveal," *Fast Company,* April 2010, pp. 90–95.

20. See "GDP and the Economy," U.S. Bureau of Economic Analysis, February 2011, accessed at www.bea.gov/scb/pdf/2011/02%20

February/0211_gdpecon.pdf; and information from the Bureau of Labor Statistics, www.bls.gov, accessed May 2011.

21. Portions adapted from information in Leonard Berry and Neeli Bendapudi, "Clueing in Customers," *Harvard Business Review*, February 2003, pp. 100–106; with additional information and quotes from Jeff Hansel, "Mayo Hits the Blogosphere," *McClatchy-Tribune Business News*, January 22, 2009; and www.mayoclinic.org, accessed August 2011.

22. See James L. Heskett, W. Earl Sasser, Jr., and Leonard A. Schlesinger, *The Service Profit Chain: How Leading Companies Link Profit and Growth to Loyalty, Satisfaction, and Value* (New York: Free Press, 1997); Heskett, Sasser, and Schlesinger, *The Value Profit Chain: Treat Employees Like Customers and Customers Like Employees* (New York: Free Press, 2003); and Rachael W. Y. Yee and others, "The Service-Profit Chain: An Empirical Analysis in High-Contact Service Industries," *International Journal of Production Economics*, April 2011, p. 36.

23. Justin Fox, "What Is It That Only I Can Do?" *Harvard Business Review,* January–February 2011, pp. 119–123.

24. See annual reports and information accessed at http://phx.corporate-ir.net/phoenix.zhtml?c=132215&p=irol-irhome, May 2011.

25. See "United States: Prescription Drugs," www.statehealthfacts.org/profileind.jsp?sub=66&rgn=1&cat=5, accessed April 2011; and "Postal Facts," www.usps.com/communications/newsroom/postalfacts.htm, accessed August 2011.

26. Adapted from information found in Terry Maxon, "Horrible Flight? Airlines' Apology Experts Will Make It Up to You," *McClatchy-Tribune News Service*, August 24, 2010.

27. See "McAtlas Shrugged," *Foreign Policy*, May–June 2001, pp. 26–37; and Philip Kotler and Kevin Lane Keller, *Marketing Management*, 14th ed. (Upper Saddle River, NJ: Prentice Hall, 2012), p. 256.

28. Quotes from Jack Trout, "'Branding' Simplified," *Forbes*, April 19, 2007, www.forbes.com; and a presentation by Jason Kilar at the Kenan-Flagler Business School, University of North Carolina at Chapel Hill, Fall 2009.

29. For more on Young & Rubicam's BrandAsset Valuator, see "Brand Asset Valuator," *Value Based Management.net*, www.valuebasedmanagement.net/methods_brand_asset_valuator.html, accessed May 2011; www.brandassetconsulting.com, accessed May 2011; and W. Ronald Lane, Karen Whitehill King, and Tom Reichert, *Kleppner's Advertising Procedure*, 18th ed. (Upper Saddle River, NJ: Pearson Prentice Hall, 2011), pp. 83–84.

30. See MillwardBrown Optimor, "BrandZ Top 100 Most Valuable Global Brands 2011," www.millwardbrown.com/brandz/.

31. See Scott Davis, *Brand Asset Management*, 2nd ed. (San Francisco: Jossey-Bass, 2002). For more on brand positioning, see Philip Kotler and Kevin Lane Keller, *Marketing Management*, 14th ed., Chapter 10.

32. See "For P&G, Success Lies in More Than Merely a Dryer Diaper," *Advertising Age*, October 15, 2007, p. 20; and Jack Neff, "Stengel Discusses Transition at P&G," *Advertising Age*, July 21, 2008, p. 17.

33. See www.saatchi.com/the_lovemarks_company and www.lovemarks.com/, accessed December 2011.

34. Susan Wong, "Foods OK, But Some Can't Stomach More Ad Increases," *Brandweek*, January 5, 2009, p. 7. Also see "Brand Names Need to Reward Consumers to Keep Them According to Study," *PR Newswire*, October 23, 2009; "IDDBA Study Shows Store Brands Spiking," *Dairy Foods*, January 2010, p. 38; "Consumers Praise Store Brands," *Adweek*, April 8, 2010, www.adweek.com; and "Store Brands Save Us Up to 52 Percent," *Consumer Reports*, October 2010, p. 16.

35. See Jack Neff, "Private Label Winning Battle of Brands," *Advertising Age*, February 23, 2009, p. 1; Jenn Abelson, "Seeking Savings, Some Ditch Brand Loyalty," *Boston Globe*, January 29, 2010, p. B1; Todd Hale, "Store Brands Flex Muscle in Weak Economy," *NielsenWire*, May 3, 2010, http://blog.nielsen.com/nielsenwire/consumer/store-brands-flex-muscle-in-weak-economy/; and Trefis, "Private Label Surge Threatens Polo Ralph Lauren," *The Street*, July 8, 2010, www.thestreet.com/story/10801997/private-label-surge-threatens-polo-ralph-lauren.html.

36. See information from www.thekrogerco.com and www.wholefoodsmarket.com/products/365-everyday-value.php, accessed May 2011.

37. Nirmalya Kumar and Jan-Benedict E. M. Steenkamp, *Private Label Strategy* (Boston, MA: Harvard Business School Press, 2007), p. 5.

38. Andy Fixmer, "Disney Aims to Double Merchandise Sales, Moony Says," June 2, 2010, accessed at www.businessweek.com/news/2010-06-02/disney-aims-to-double-merchandise-sales-mooney-says-update1-.html; Adam Bluestein, "Unleash the Merch-inator," *Fast Company,* November 2010, pp. 44–48; and www.licensingexpo.com, accessed May 2011.

39. For this and other examples, see "Tim Hortons and Cold Stone: Co-Branding Strategies," *BusinessWeek*, July 10, 2009, www.businessweek.com/smallbiz/content/jul2009/sb20090710_574574.htm; and Dan Beem, "The Case for Co-Branding," *Forbes*, March 16, 2010, accessed at www.forbes.com.

40. Quote from www.apple.com/ipod/nike/, accessed June 2011.

41. "Advertising Spending," *Advertising Age*, December 20, 2010, p. 10.

42. Quotes from Stephen Cole, "Value of the Brand," *CA Magazine*, May 2005, pp. 39–40; and Lawrence A. Crosby and Sheree L. Johnson, "Experience Required," *Marketing Management*, July/August 2007, pp. 21–27.

Chapter 8

1. Extracts, quotes, and other information from or adapted from Gary Johnson, "Google vs Bing: Marketing Share and 2011 Expectations," *PR Product Reviews,* February 3, 2011, accessed at www.product-reviews.net/2011/02/03/bing-vs-google-market-share-and-2011-expectations/; "Google Search Advertising Revenue Grows 20.2% in 2010," *Telecompaper,* January 20, 2011, accessed at www.telecompaper.com/news/google-search-advertising-revenue-grows-202-in-2010; Chuck Salter, "Google: The Faces and Voices of the World's Most Innovative Company," *Fast Company,* March 2008, pp. 74–88; David Pogue, "Geniuses at Play, On the Job," *New York Times,* February 26, 2009, p. B1; Quentin Hardy, "When Google Runs Your Life," *Forbes,* December 28, 2009, pp. 88–93; "World's Most Admired Companies," *Fortune,* March 21, 2011, pp. 110–112; "World's 50 Most Innovative Companies," *Fast Company,* March 2011, p. 66; Laura Gordon-Mumane, "Innovation Labs: A Window Into the Cutting Edge of Search," *Online,* March–April 2011, p. 14; and www.google.com and www.googlelabs.com, accessed September 2011.

2. Rob Adams, "Market Validation: Why Ready, Aim, Fire Beats Ready, Fire, Fire, Fire, Aim," *Inc.,* April 27, 2010, accessed at www.inc.com/rob-adams/market-validation-new-book.html.

3. Information and examples from Robert M. McMath and Thom Forbes, *What Were They Thinking? Money-Saving, Time-Saving, Face-Saving Marketing Lessons You Can Learn from Products That Flopped* (New York: Times Business, 1999), various pages; Beatriz Cholo, "Living with Your 'Ex': A Brand New World," *Brandweek,*

December 5, 2005, p. 4; "Top 25 Biggest Product Flops of All Time," *WalletPop,* accessed at http://www.walletpop.com/photos/top-25-biggest-product-flops-of-all-time/, February 2011; and www.gfkamerica.com/newproductworks, accessed October 2011.

4. John Peppers and Martha Rogers, "The Buzz on Customer-Driven Innovation," *Sales & Marketing Management,* June 2007, p. 13.

5. See Richard Martin, "Collaboration Cisco Style," *InformationWeek,* January 28, 2008, p. 30; Guido Jouret, "Inside Cisco's Search for the Next Big Idea," *Harvard Business Review,* September 2009, pp. 43–45; and Philip Kotler and Kevin Lane Keller, *Marketing Management,* 14th ed. (Upper Saddle River, NJ: Prentice Hall, 2012), p. 577.

6. See http://mystarbucksidea.force.com/ideaHome, accessed November 2011.

7. Mary Tripsas, "Seeing Customers as Partners in Invention," *New York Times,* December 26, 2009, accessed at www.nytimes.com/2009/12/27/business/27proto.html; and James Anderson, "3M Opens Innovation Center in Dubai," *Minneapolis/St. Paul Business Journal,* January 27, 2011.

8. Bill Taylor, "John Fluevog: Ideas with Sole—In Tough Times, Tap the 'Hidden Genius' of Your Customers," March 2009, http://blogs.hbr.org/taylor/2009/03/fluevogs_opensource_footwear.html. Also see "Entrepreneurs Seek Input from Outsiders," *Wall Street Journal (Online),* December 22, 2010, http://online.wsj.com/article/SB10001424052748704774604576036013767458044.html.

9. Adapted from Elizabeth A. Sullivan, "A Group Effort: More Companies Are Turning to the Wisdom of the Crowd to Find Ways to Innovate," *Marketing News,*" February 28, 2010, pp. 22–29. Also see www.netflixprize.com/, accessed June 2011.

10. See Andrew Abbott, "Announcing the PayPal Mobile App Challenge Winners!" February 8, 2011, http://topcoder.com/home/x/2011/02/08/announcing-the-paypal-mobile-app-challenges-winners/; and www.topcoder.com and https://www.x.com, accessed March 2011.

11. Guido Jouret, "Inside Cisco's Search for the Next Big Idea," *Harvard Business Review,* September 2009, pp. 43–45; and www.cisco.com/web/solutions/iprize/index.html, accessed June 2011.

12. See George S. Day, "Is It Real? Can We Win? Is It Worth Doing?" *Harvard Business Review,* December 2007, pp. 110–120.

13. This example is based on Tesla Motors and information obtained from www.teslamotors.com, accessed June 2011. For more on competitors in this industry, see "Charged for Battle," *Bloomberg Businessweek,* January 3–January 9, 2011, pp. 49–55.

14. Information from www.hpproducttest.com/index.cfm, accessed November 2011.

15. Susan Berfield, "Baristas, Patrons Steaming Over Starbucks VIA," *Bloomberg Businessweek,* November 13, 2009; and Jodi Westbury, "Starbucks VIA—A Success to Build On," www.jodiwestbury.com/2011/01/28/starbucks-via-a-success-to-build-on/, January 28, 2011.

16. For information on BehaviorScan Rx, see www.symphony-iri.com/ProductsSolutions/AllProducts/AllProductsDetail/tabid/159/productid/75/Default.aspx, accessed October 2011.

17. See Emily Bryson York, "McD's Serves Up $100M McCafé Ad Blitz," *Crain's Chicago Business,* May 4, 2009, www.chicagobusiness.com.

18. Jared Newman, "Windows Phone 7 to Get Half a Billion Dollar Marketing Blitz," *PCWorld,* August 27, 2010, accessed at www.pcworld.com; and Joel Evans, "Microsoft Reboots with Windows Phone 7 Global Launch—Will People Buy?" *ZDNet,* October 11, 2010, accessed at www.zdnet.com.

19. See Robert G. Cooper, "Formula for Success," *Marketing Management,* March–April 2006, pp. 19–23; Barry Jaruzelski and Kevin Dehoff, "The Global Innovation of 1000," *Strategy + Business,* Issue 49, fourth quarter, 2007, pp. 68–83; Shu-Hua Chien and Jyh-jye Chen, "Supplier Involvement and Customer Involvement Effect on New Product Development Success in the Financial Service Industry," *Service Industries Journal,* February 2010, p. 185; and Christoph Fuchs and Martin Schreier, "Customer Empowerment in New Product Development," *Product Innovation Management,* January 2011, pp. 17–32.

20. Robert Berner, "How P&G Pampers New Thinking," *BusinessWeek,* April 14, 2008, pp. 73–74; "How P&G Plans to Clean Up," *BusinessWeek,* April 13, 2009, pp. 44–45; and "Procter & Gamble Company," www.wikinvest.com/stock/Procter_&_Gamble_Company_(PG), accessed April 2011. For P&G Connect+Develop, see https://secure3.verticali.net/pg-connection-portal/ctx/noauth/PortalHome.do and https://secure3.verticali.net/pg-connection-portal/ctx/noauth/0_0_1_4_83_4_15.do, accessed February 2011.

21. Adapted from Darrell K. Rigby, Karen Gruver, and James Allen, "Innovation in Turbulent Times," *Harvard Business Review,* June 2009, pp. 79–86. Also see John Hayes, "In a Tough Economy, Innovation Is King," *Marketing News,* April 15, 2009, pp. 14–17.

22. Ibid.; and Judann Pollock, "Now's the Time to Reset Marketing for Post-Recession," *Advertising Age,* February 1, 2010, p. 1.

23. This definition is based on one found in Bryan Lilly and Tammy R. Nelson, "Fads: Segmenting the Fad-Buyer Market," *Journal of Consumer Marketing,* Vol. 20, No. 3, 2003, pp. 252–265.

24. See Katya Kazakina and Robert Johnson, "A Fad's Father Seeks a Sequel," *New York Times,* May 30, 2004, www.nytimes.com; John Schwartz, "The Joy of Silly," *New York Times,* January 20, 2008, p. 5; and www.crazyfads.com, accessed November 2011.

25. See www.1000uses.com, accessed September 2011.

26. Elaine Wong, "Kellogg Makes Special K a Way of Life," *Adweek,* June 7, 2010, p. 18; and www.kellogg.com and www.specialk.com, accessed October 2011.

27. For a more comprehensive discussion of marketing strategies over the course of the PLC, see Philip Kotler and Kevin Lane Keller, *Marketing Management,* 13th ed. (Upper Saddle River, NJ: Prentice Hall, 2009), pp. 278–290.

28. See "Year-by-Year Analysis Reveals an Overall Compensatory Award of $1,500,000 for Products Liability Cases," *Personal Injury Verdict Reviews,* July 3, 2006; Administrative Office of the U.S. Courts, "Judicial Facts and Figures: Multi-Year Statistical Compilations on the Federal Judiciary's Caseload Through Fiscal Year 2008," September 2009, www.uscourts.gov/judicialfactsfigures/2008/all2008judicialfactsfigures.pdf; and Christy Tierney, "Toyota Recalls 2.2M More Vehicles," *Detroit News,* February 25, 2011, A10.

29. Example based on information provided by Nestlé Japan Ltd., May 2008; with additional information from Laurel Wentz, "Kit Kat Wins Cannes Media Grand Prix for Edible Postcard," *Advertising Age,* June 23, 2009, http://adage.com/cannes09/article?article_id=137520; Tucker S. Cummings, "Japan's Strangest Kit Kat Flavors," March 18, 2010, accessed at www.weirdasianews.com/2010/03/18/japans-strangest-kit-kat-flavors/; and http://en.wikipedia.org/wiki/Kit_Kat; and the Japanese Wikipedia discussion of Kit Kat at http://ja.wikipedia.org, accessed November 2011.

30. Information accessed online at www.db.com, September 2011.

31. Information accessed online at www.interpublic.com and www.mccann.com, accessed September 2011.

32. See "Global Powers of Retailing 2011," www.deloitte.com; "Walmart Corporate International," http://walmartstores.com/AboutUs/246.aspx, October 2011; and information accessed at www.carrefour.com, October 2011.

Chapter 9

1. Quotes and extracts from Brad Stone and Stephanie Rosenbloom, "The Gloves Come Off at Amazon and Walmart," *New York Times*, November 24, 2009, p. 1; Gayle Feldman, "Behind the US Price War," *Bookseller*, November 13, 2009, p. 16; Jeffrey A. Trachtenberg and Miguel Bustillo, "Amazon, Walmart Cut Deeper in Book Duel," *Wall Street Journal*, October 19, 2009, p. B1; and Josh Smith, "2010 Marks Return of Price Wars Between Amazon, Best Buy, and Walmart," January 19, 2010, accessed at www.walletpop.com/2010/01/19/2010-marks-return-of-price-wars-between-amazon-best-buy-and-wal/. Also see Brad Stone, "Can Amazon Be Walmart of the Web," *New York Times*, September 20, 2009, p. 1; Jonathan Birchall, "Walmart Tweaks Price in Amazon Battle," *Financial Times*, October 17, 2009, www.ft.com; Curt Woodward, "Amazon: Feds OK Diapers.com Deal," *Xconomy*, March 24, 2011, accessed at www.xconomy.com; Matthew Boyle and Douglas MacMillan, "Walmart's Rocky Path from Bricks to Clicks," *Bloomberg Businessweek*, July 25-July 31, 1022, pp. 31-33; and information from www.walmart.com and www.amazon.com, accessed October 2011.

2. For more on the importance of sound pricing strategy, see Thomas T. Nagle, John Hogan, and Joseph Zale, *The Strategy and Tactics of Pricing: A Guide to Growing More Profitably*, 5th ed. (Upper Saddle River, NJ: Prentice Hall, 2011), Chapter 1.

3. Based on information from Anne Marie Chaker, "For a Steinway, I Did It My Way," *Wall Street Journal*, May 22, 2008, www.wsj.com; and www.steinway.com/steinway and www.steinway.com/steinway/quotes.shtml, accessed November 2011.

4. See Philip Kotler and Kevin Lane Keller, *Marketing Management,* 14th ed. (Upper Saddle River, NJ: Prentice Hall, 2012), p. 158.

5. Maria Puente, "Theaters Turn Up the Luxury," *USA Today*, March 12, 2010, p. 1A; and information from www.amctheatres.com/dinein/cinemasuites/, accessed July 2011.

6. Stephanie Schomer, "How Retailer Hot Mama Is Rethinking Shopping for Moms," *Fast Company*, February 2011, pp. 40–41; and www.shopmama.com, accessed September 2011.

7. Adapted from information found in Joseph Weber, "Over a Buck for Dinner? Outrageous," *BusinessWeek*, March 9, 2009, p. 57; and Tom Mulier and Matthew Boyle, "Dollar Dinners from ConAgra's Threatened by Costs," *Bloomberg Businessweek*, August 19, 2010, accessed at www.businessweek.com.

8. See Brad Tuttle, "Why You'll See Tons of 'New and Improved' Products Soon," *Time*, April 12, 2010, http://money.blogs.time.com/2010/04/12/why-youll-see-tons-of-new-and-improved-products-soon; and Rafi Mohammed, "Ditch the Discounts," *Harvard Business Review,* January–February 2011, pp. 23–25.

9. Kenneth Hein, "Study: Value Trumps Price among Shoppers," *Brandweek*, March 2, 2009, p. 6.

10. For comprehensive discussions of pricing strategies, see Thomas T. Nagle, John E. Hogan, and Joseph Zale, *The Strategy and Tactics of Pricing*, 5th ed. (Upper Saddle River, NJ: Prentice Hall, 2011).

11. Adapted from information found in Mei Fong, "IKEA Hits Home in China; The Swedish Design Giant, Unlike Other Retailers, Slashes Prices for the Chinese," *Wall Street Journal*, March 3,

2006, p. B1; "Beijing Loves IKEA—But Not for Shopping," *Los Angeles Times*, http://articles.latimes.com/2009/aug/25/business/fi-china-ikea25; Michael Wei, "In IKEA's China Stores, Loitering Is Encouraged," *Bloomberg Businessweek,* November 1, 2010, p. 1; and www.ikea.com/ms/en_US/about_ikea/facts_and_figures/index.html, accessed September 2011.

12. Joe Martin, "Sony: PS3 Is Breaking Even," *bit-gamer.net*, June 30, 2010, www.bit-tech.net/news/gaming/2010/06/30/sony-ps3-is-breaking-even/1.

13. Quote and other information from David Pogue, "Paying More for Printer, But Less for Ink," '*New York Times*, May 17, 2007, p. C1; "Kodak Stages 'Preintervention,'" *DMNews*, October 2010, p. 60; and www.kodak.com/global/mul/consumer/print/en_ca/index.html, accessed October 2011.

14. Information from "What Happens to All That Poo at the Zoo . . .," www.youtube.com/watch?v=kjfNVEvRI3w&feature=player_embedded#, accessed November 2011; "Zoo Doo® at Woodland Park Zoo," www.zoo.org/zoo-doo, accessed November 2011.

15. Peter Coy, "Why the Price Is Rarely Right," *Bloomberg Businessweek*, February 1 & 8, 2010, pp. 77–78.

16. Anthony Allred, E. K. Valentin, and Goutam Chakraborty, "Pricing Risky Services: Preference and Quality Considerations," *Journal of Product and Brand Management*, Vol. 19, No. 1, 2010, p. 54. Also see Kenneth C. Manning and David E. Sprott, "Price Endings, Left-Digit Effects, and Choice," *Journal of Consumer Research*, August 2009, pp. 328–336; and Carl Bialik, Elizabeth Holmes, and Ray Smith, "Many Discounts, Few Deals," *Wall Street Journal,* December 15, 2010, p. D12.

17. Elizabeth A. Sullivan, "Stay on Course," *Marketing News,* February 15, 2009, pp. 11–13. Also see Rafi Mohammed, "Ditch the Discounts," *Harvard Business Review,* January–February 2011, pp. 23–25.

18. Adapted from Justin D. Martin, "Dynamic Pricing: Internet Retailers Are Treating Us Like Foreign Tourists in Egypt," *Christian Science Monitor*, January 7, 2011. See also Annie Lowrey, "How Online Retailers Stay a Step Ahead of Comparison Shoppers," *Washington Post*, December 11, 2010, www.washingtonpost.com/wp-dyn/content/article/2010/12/11/AR2010121102435.html?hpid=sec-business.

19. Based on information found in "The World's Most Influential Companies: Unilever," *BusinessWeek*, December 22, 2008, p. 47; and www.unilever.com/sustainability/, accessed November 2009. Also see Ashish Karamchandani, Mike Kubzansky, and Nishant Lalwani, "Is the Bottom of the Pyramid Really for You?" *Harvard Business Review,* March 2011, pp. 107–112.

20. For more discussion of these strategies, see Stephanie Clifford and Catherine Rampell, "Smaller Bags Hide Surge in Food Costs," *New York Times,* March 29, 2011, p. A1.

21. Information from Maureen Morrison, "Seattle's Best Launches First Major Ad Campaign," *Advertising Age*, January 10, 2011, http://adage.com/article/news/seattle-s-coffee-launches-ad-campaign/148118/; "Starbuck's Kid Brother Grows Up Fast," *Bloomberg Businessweek,* April 25-May 1, 2011, pp. 26-27; and www.starbucks.com, accessed May 2011.

22. For discussions of these issues, see Dhruv Grewel and Larry D. Compeau, "Pricing and Public Policy: A Research Agenda and Overview of the Special Issue," *Journal of Public Policy and Marketing*, Spring 1999, pp. 3–10; Michael V. Marn, Eric V. Roegner, and Craig C. Zawada, *The Price Advantage* (Hoboken, New Jersey: John Wiley & Sons, 2004), Appendix 2; and Thomas T. Nagle, John E. Hogan, and Joseph Zale, *The Strategy and Tactics of Pricing*, 5th ed. (Upper Saddle River, NJ: Prentice Hall, 2011).

23. Foo Yun Chee, "Unilever, P&G Fined 315 Million Euros for Price Fixing," *Reuters,* April 13, 2011, www.reuters.com/article/2011/04/13/us-eu-cartel-idUSTRE73C1XV20110413.

24. See Mark A. Fox, "Market Power in Music Retailing: The Case of Wal-Mart," *Popular Music and Society,* October 2005, pp. 501–519; Ed Christman, "Blue Christmas," *Billboard,* January 6, 2007, www.billboard.com; and Ed Christman, "Solutions for Sale," *Billboard,* January 23, 2010, www.billboard.com.

25. "FTC Guides Against Deceptive Pricing," www.ftc.gov/bcp/guides/decptprc.htm, accessed December 2011.

Chapter 10

1. The "e" logo, Enterprise, and "We'll Pick You Up" are registered trademarks of Enterprise Rent-A-Car Company. Quotes and other information from "Enter Enterprise," *Business Travel News,* April 23, 2007; Carol J. Loomis, "Enterprise Pulls Up at the Airport," *Fortune,* July 23, 2007, p. 50; "The Global Car Rental Industry Begins Showing Signs of Recovery," *Standard & Poor's,* June 21, 2010, www2.standardandpoors.com/spf/pdf/events/airport102610art4.pdf; "Market Data: [U.S. Car Rental Market]," *ANR Fact Book 2011,* www.autorentalnews.com/fc_resources/ARN-6.pdf, accessed June 2011; and www.enterprise.com, www.enterpriseholdings.com, www.wecar.com, and http://aboutus.enterprise.com/press_room/fact_sheets.html, accessed October 2011.

2. Example adapted from Richard Gibson, "Burger King Franchisees Can't Have It *Their* Own Way," *Wall Street Journal,* January 21, 2010, p. B1; with additional information from Emily Bryson York, "BK Swears Off Sex in Ads to Quell Franchisee Freak Out," *Advertising Age,* July 13, 2009, p. 1; York, "Burger King, Franchisees Start Making Nice," *Advertising Age,* February 17, 2010, http://adage.com/article?article_id=142158; and Gibson, "Franchising—Franchisee vs. Franchiser: What's New on the Legal Front," *Wall Street Journal,* February 14, 2011, p. R3.

3. Rohwedder, "Turbocharged Supply Chain May Speed Zara Past Gap as Top Clothing Retailer," *Globe and Mail,* March 26, 2009, p. B12; Felipe Caro and Jeremie Gallien, "Inventory Management of a Fast-Fashion Retail Network," *Operations Research,* March–April 2010, pp. 257–273; and information from the Inditex Press Dossier, www.inditex.com/en/press/information/press_kit, accessed October 2011.

4. Franchising facts from *2011 Economic Outlook Fact Sheet,* January 3, 2011, www.franchise.org/uploadedFiles/EconOutlook%20FactSheet11(1).pdf; and www.azfranchises.com/franchisefacts.htm, accessed May 2011.

5. "To Boost Buying Power, Walmart Woos Partners," *Bloomberg Businessweek,* October 11–October 17, 2010, p. 23.

6. Brent Kendall and Scott Morrison, "Regulators Clear Microsoft-Yahoo Alliance," *Wall Street Journal,* February 19, 2010, p. B5; and Loren Baker, "Bing Yahoo 'Bingahoo' Alliance Shows a Payoff," *Search Engine Journal,* February 2, 2011, www.searchenginejournal.com/bing-yahoo-bingahoo-alliance-shows-a-payoff/27606/.

7. Information from www.marykay.com/company/default.aspx, accessed October 2011.

8. Quotes and information from Normandy Madden, "Two Chinas," *Advertising Age,* August 16, 2004, pp. 1, 22; Russell Flannery, "China: The Slow Boat," *Forbes,* April 12, 2004, p. 76; Jeff Berman, "U.S. Providers Say Logistics in China on the Right Track," *Logistics Management,* March 2007, p. 22; Jamie Bolton, "China: The Infrastructure Imperative," *Logistics Management,* July 2007, p. 63; and China trade facts from http://cscmp.org/press/fastfacts.asp, accessed April 2011.

9. For more discussion, see Warren J. Keegan and Mark C. Green, *Global Marketing,* 6th ed. (Upper Saddle River, NJ: Prentice Hall, 2011), p. 367.

10. Mark Ritson, "Why Retailers Call the Shots," *Marketing,* February 18, 2009, p. 24.

11. Quotes and other information from Alex Taylor III, "Caterpillar," *Fortune,* August 20, 2007, pp. 48–54; Donald V. Fites, "Make Your Dealers Your Partners," *Harvard Business Review,* March–April 1996, pp. 84–95; and information at www.cat.com, accessed October 2011.

12. Stephanie Clifford, "Shipping Slowdown Puts Retailers in a Jam," *International Herald Tribune,* July 28, 2010, p. 13; "State of Logistics 2010: Business Logistics Costs Fall 18.2 Percent," *Modern Materials Handling,* June 9, 2010, www.mmh.com/article/state_of_logistics_2010_business_logistics_costs_fall_18.2_percent/; and supply chain facts from http://cscmp.org/press/fastfacts.asp, accessed September 2011.

13. William B. Cassidy, "Walmart Squeezes Costs from Supply Chain," *Journal of Commerce,* January 5, 2010; and "Walmart Vows to 'Drive Unnecessary Costs Out of Supply Chain'," *Procurement Leaders,* January 24, 2011, www.procurementleaders.com/news/latestnews/0401-walmart-drives-supply-chain/.

14. Andy Brack, "Piggly Wiggly Center Offers Info-Packed Field Trip," *Charleston Currents,* January 4, 2010, www.charlestoncurrents.com/issue/10_issues/10.0104.html; and information from http://en.wikipedia.org/wiki/Piggly_wiggly and http://walmartstores.com, accessed September 2011.

15. Bill Mongrelluzzo, "Supply Chain Expert Sees Profits in Sustainability," *Journal of Commerce,* March 11, 2010, www.joc.com/logistics-economy/sustainability-can-lead-profits-says-expert. SC Johnson example from "SC Johnson Reduces Greenhouse Gasses by the Truckload," *CRS Press Release,* www.csrwire.com/press_releases/22882-SC-Johnson-Reduces-Greenhouse-Gases-by-the-Truckload. Also see Hau L. Lee, "Don't Tweak Your Supply Chain—Rethink It End to End," *Harvard Business Review,* October 2010, pp. 62–72.

16. Facts from http://walmartstores.com/pressroom/FactSheets/, accessed September 2011.

17. Example adapted from Evan West, "These Robots Play Fetch," *Fast Company,* July/August 2007, pp. 49–50. See also "Rise of the Orange Machines," *Bloomberg Businessweek,* November 15–November 21, 2010, p. 47; and www.kivasystems.com/video.htm, accessed February 2011.

18. See David Blanchard, "The Five Stages of RFID," *Industry Week,* January 1, 2009, p. 50; Maida Napolitano, "RFID Revisited," *Modern Materials Handling,* February 2010, p. 45; and Nick Hughes, "Printed RFID: Why the Radio Heads Are Receiving Static," *Printweek,* February 25, 2011, p. 21.

19. Michael Margreta, Chester Ford, and M. Adhi Dipo, "U.S. Freight on the Move: Highlights from the 2007 Commodity Flow Survey Preliminary Data," September 30, 2009, www.bts.gov/publications/bts_special_report/2009_09_30/html/entire.html; Bureau of Transportation Statistics, "Pocket Guide to Transportation 2011," January 2011, www.bts.gov/publications/pocket_guide_to_transportation/2011/; and American Trucking Association, www.truckline.com, accessed September 2011.

20. See Walmart's supplier requirements at http://walmartstores.com/Suppliers/248.aspx, accessed October 2011.

21. "Stonyfield Farm: Ringer Supply Chain Accelerates Profit and Carbon Footprint Reduction," www.ryder.com/supplychain_casestudies_stonyfield.shtml, accessed October 2011.

22. Jeff Berman, "2009 3PL Revenue Down 15.2 Percent Year-Over-Year," *Logistics Management*, February 2010, p. 21; and David Biederman, "3PL Slowdown Goes Global," *Journal of Commerce*, February 8, 2010, www.joc.com/logistics-economy/3pl-slowdown-goes-global.

Chapter 11

1. Quotes and other information from "The Fortune 500," *Fortune*, May 23, 2011, pp. F1–F51; John Jannarone, "Walmart Stores' Giant Disadvantage," *Wall Street Journal*, May 18, 2011, p. C20; Jack Neff, "Why Walmart Is Getting Serious about Marketing," *Advertising Age*, June 8, 2009, p. 1; Miguel Bustillo, "Walmart to Tout Goods Returning to Shelves," *Wall Street Journal*, April 11, 2011, p. B3; and various fact sheets and other reports found at www.walmartstores.com, accessed November 2011.

2. See Katy Bachman, "Suit Your Shelf," *AdweekMedia*, January 19, 2009, pp. 10–12; "OgilvyAction Takes Regional Marketers to the Last Mile," January 23, 2008, accessed at www.entrepreneur.com/tradejournals/article/173710015.html; and Jack Neff, "Trouble in Store for Shopper Marketing," *Advertising Age*, March 2, 2009, pp. 3–4. Retail sales statistics from "Monthly and Annual Retail Trade," U.S. Census Bureau, www.census.gov/retail/, accessed June 2011.

3. Jack Neff, "P&G Pushes Design in Brand-Building Strategy," April 12, 2010, accessed at http://adage.com/print?article_id=143211.

4. For more on digital aspects of shopper marketing, see Ken Schept, "Digital and Mobile Disrupt Traditional Shopping Path," *Advertising Age*, May 2, 2011, p. 92; and Ellen Byron, "In-Store Sales Begin at Home," *Wall Street Journal*, April 25, 2011, www.wsj.com.

5. David Rogers, "Grocery Market Share Trends," *Progressive Grocer*, September 16, 2010, www.progressivegrocer.*com*/top-stories/special-features/industry-intelligence/id30449/grocery-market-share-trends/.

6. Mark Hamstra, "In Tune," *Supermarket News*, October 13, 2008, p. 14; "Kroger Profits as It Woos Shoppers," *Los Angeles Times*, March 10, 2010, p. B2; David Kaplan, "For Kroger, Upgrades Are in Store," *McClatchy-Tribune Business News*, January 1, 2011; and www.thekrogerco.com, accessed September 2011.

7. See "Stan Sheetz Recognized among Most Influential Retail Leaders in the World," *PR Newswire*, January 29, 2008; Alan J. Liddle, "Sheetz Highlights Value, Convenience to Build Sales," *Nation's Restaurant News,* July 21, 2010, www.nrn.com/article/sheetz-highlights-value-convenience-build-sales;andwww.sheetz.com/main/about/definition.cfm, accessed October 2011.

8. Statistics based on information from "SN Top 75 2011," http://supermarketnews.com/profiles/top75/walmart_stores11/, accessed April 2011; Elliot Zwiebach, "Wal-Mart Trims HQ Office Staff," *Supermarket News*, February 16, 2009, p. 4; and "Supermarket Facts," www.fmi.org/facts_figs/?fuseaction=superfact, accessed June 2011.

9. Quotes and other information from "Costco Outshines the Rest," *Consumer Reports*, May 2009, p. 8; Matthew Boyle, "Why Costco Is So Addictive," *Fortune*, October 25, 2006, pp. 126–132; Andrew Bary, "Everybody's Store," *Barron's*, February 12, 2007, pp. 29–32; Jeff Chu and Kate Rockwood, "Thinking Outside the Big Box," *Fast Company*, November 2008, pp. 128–131; "America's Top Stores," *Consumer Reports,* July 2010, p. 16; and www.costco.com, accessed October 2011.

10. Company information from Mark Brandau, "Subway May Have More Units, but Mcd Holds More Cash," *Nation's Restaurant News,* March 9, 2011, www.nrn.com/article/subway-may-have-more-units-mcd-holds-more-cash; and www.aboutmcdonalds.com/mcd and www.subway.com/subwayroot/AboutSubway/index.aspx, accessed June 2011.

11. Stephanie Clifford, "New President for Struggling Gap Inc. Unit," *New York Times,* February 2, 2011, p. B3; Natalie Zmuda, "Under New Management, Gap Must Figure Out Way to Fix a Faded Icon," *Advertising Age*, February 7, 2011, pp. 2–3; and www.gapinc.com/public/Investors/inv_financials.shtml, accessed June 2011.

12. "Whole Foods Market, Inc.," *Hoover's Company Records*, March 25, 2011, p. 10952, p.1; "First: Planet Walmart," *Fortune,* May 3, 2010, p. 27; and www.wholefoodsmarket.com, accessed October 2011.

13. See www.wikinvest.com/stock/J.C._Penney_(JCP), accessed October 2011.

14. Based on information from "Cabela's Has Lived Up to Its Hype," *McClatchy-Tribune Business News,* March 31, 2010; Zach Benoit, "New Cabela's Packs Them In," *McClatchy-Tribune Business News*, May 15, 2009; "Bargain Hunting," *Fortune*, November 24, 2008, p. 16; Jan Falstad, "Outdoor Retailer Adds New Dynamic to Local Marketplace," *McClatchy-Tribune Business News*, May 10, 2009; Diane Dietz, "Rush to Cabela's," *McClatchy-Tribune Business News*, May 6, 2011; and information from www.cabelas.com, accessed October 2011.

15. See Sandy Smith, "Scents and Sellability," *Stores*, July 2009, www.stores.org/stores-magazine-july-2009/scents-and-sellability; Spencer Morgan, "The Sweet Smell of Excess," *Bloomberg Businessweek,* June 21–June 27, 2010, pp. 85–87; and www.scentair.com, accessed October 2011.

16. See www.titlenine.com and https://www.facebook.com/pages/Title-Nine-Portland/62987646947, accessed October 2011.

17. For definitions of these and other types of shopping centers, see "Dictionary," American Marketing Association, www.marketingpower.com/_layouts/Dictionary.aspx, accessed November 2011.

18. Paul Grimaldi, "Shopping for a New Look: Lifestyle Centers Are Replacing Enclosed Malls," *Providence Journal* (*Rhode Island*), April 29, 2007, p. F10; Neil Nisperos, "Lifestyle Centers Offer More Than Fresh Air," *Inland Valley Daily Bulletin*, January 5, 2009; and Courtenay Edelhart, "Malls Can't Take Customers for Granted As New Outdoor Centers Pop Up," *McClatchy-Tribune Business News*, January 16, 2010.

19. See H. Lee Murphy, "Life Ebbs Out of Many Lifestyle Centers," *National Real Estate Investor,* May 1, 2011, p. 31; and Elaine Misonzhnik, "Borders Bankruptcy Shines Light on Continued Weakness of Power Centers" *Retail Traffic,* February 16, 2011.

20. Kenneth Hein, "Target Tries First Price Point Driven TV Ads," *Brandweek*, January 14, 2009, accessed at www.brandweek.com; Natalie Zmuda, "Why the Bad Economy Has Been Good for Target," *Advertising Age*, October 4, 2010, p. 1; and Sharon Edelson, "Target Eying $100 Billion in Sales," *WWD*, February 25, 2011, p. 2.

21. See Matt Townsend, "The Staying Power of Pop-Ups," *Bloomberg Businessweek,* November 15–November 21, 2010, p. 26; and Philip Elmer-DeWitt, "Apple's iPad Pop-Up Shop," March 10, 2011, http://tech.fortune.cnn.com/2011/03/10/apples-ipad-pop-up-shop/.

22. See www.rpminc.com/consumer.asp, accessed October 2011.

23. U.S. Census Bureau News, "Quarterly Retail E-Commerce Sales, 4th Quarter 2010," February 17, 2011, accessed at www.census.gov/retail/mrts/www/data/pdf/ec_current.pdf; and Robin Wauters, "Forrester: Online Retail Industry in the US Will Be

Worth $279 Billion in 2015," *TechCrunch*, February 28, 2011, http://techcrunch.com/2011/02/28/forrester-online-retail-industry-in-the-us-will-be-worth-279-billion-in-2015/.

24. Mark Penn, "New Info Shoppers," *Wall Street Journal*, January 8, 2009, accessed at http://online.wsj.com/article/SB123144483005365353.html; and Ellen Byron, "In-Store Sales Begin at Home," *Wall Street Journal*, April 25, 2011, p. B7.

25. "Top 500 Guide," *Internet Retailer*, www.internetretailer.com/top500/list/, accessed June 2011.

26. Adam Blair, "Williams-Sonoma Invests $75M in Fast-Growing, Profitable E-Commerce," *RIS*, March 22, 2011, http://risnews.edgl.com/retail-best-practices/Williams-Sonoma-Invests-$75M-in-Fast-Growing,-Profitable-E-Commerce71523.

27. See Deena M. Amato McCoy, "Connecting with Customers," *Grocery Headquarters*, December 1, 2009, http://groceryheadquarters.com/articles/2009-12-01/Connecting-with-customers; and Bob Greenberg, "Reinventing Retail," *Brandweek*, February 15, 2010, p. 16.

28. See Jordan Cooke, "McDonald's Gets Eco-Friendly Seal," *McClatchy-Tribune Business News*, January 13, 2010; "The Golden Arches Go Green: McDonald's First LEED Certified Restaurant," December 11, 2008, accessed at www.greenbeanchicago.com; "McDonald's Green Prototype Uses 25 Percent Less Energy," *Environmental Leader*, April 8, 2009, accessed at www.environmentalleader.com; Kiri Tannenbaum, "The Green Arches?" *Delish*, October 20, 2010, www.delish.com/food/recalls-reviews/sustainable-green-practices-mcdonalds; www.aboutmcdonalds.com/mcd/csr/about/environmental_responsibility.html, accessed October 2011.

29. See www.staples.com and www.bestbuy.com, accessed October 2011.

30. See "Walmart: International Data Sheet," http://walmartstores.com/AboutUs/246.aspx and http://walmartstores.com/sites/annualreport/2011/financials/2011_Financials.pdf, accessed June 2011; and http://investors.target.com/phoenix.zhtml?c=65828&p=irol-IRHome, accessed June 2011.

31. See "Emerging from the Downturn: Global Powers of Retailing 2011," *Stores*, January 2011, accessed at www.deloitte.com/assets/Dcom-Global/Local%20Assets/Documents/Consumer%20Business/GlobPowDELOITTE_14%20Jan.pdf.

32. Information from http://walmartstores.com//default.aspx and www.carrefour.com, accessed October 2011.

33. Grainger facts and other information are from the *Grainger 2011 Fact Book* accessed at http://phx.corporate-ir.net/External.File?item=UGFyZW50SUQ9ODgzOTB8Q2hpbGRJRD0tMXxUeEXBIPTM=&t=1 and www.grainger.com.

34. Information from "About Us," www.mckesson.com; and "Supply Management Online," www.mckesson.com/en_us/McKesson.com/For+Pharmacies/Retail+National+Chains/Ordering+and+Inventory+Management/Supply+Management+Online.html, accessed June 2011.

35. Facts from www.supervalu.com, accessed October 2011.

Chapter 12

1. See Devin Leonard, "Hey, PC, Who Taught You to Fight Back?" *New York Times*, August 30, 2009, p. BU1; Noreen O'Leary, "Amid Transition, Rivals Are Descending on Apple," *Brandweek*, November 7, 2009, p. 4; Abbey Klaassen, "In Mac vs. PC Battle, Microsoft Winning in Value Perception," *Advertising Age*, May 18, 2009, http://adage.com/digital/article?article_id=136731; Rupal Parekh, "Microsoft vs. Apple Fight Enters New Round,"

Advertising Age, September 18, 2008, accessed at http://adage.com/article?article_id=131102; Janet Stilson, "Open Up the Window," *Adweek*, September 13, 2010, pp. 32–34; and Don Reisinger, "Microsoft Launching New Ad Campaign Tonight," *CNET News*, May 9, 2011, http://news.cnet.com/8301-13506_3-20061134-17.html.

2. For other definitions, see www.marketingpower.com/_layouts/Dictionary.aspx, accessed November 2011.

3. See Martin Peers, "Television's Fuzzy Ad Picture," *Wall Street Journal*, May 10, 2011, p. C22; and Lisa Waananen, "How Agencies Are Spending Online Media Budgets," *Mashable.com*, June 9, 2011, http://mashable.com/2011/06/09/media-agency-budgets/.

4. Elizabeth A. Sullivan, "Targeting to the Extreme," *Marketing News*, June 15, 2009, pp. 17–19; and Stuart Elliott, "Heineken Aims Ads at Young Digital Devotees," *New York Times*, May 26, 2011, p. B6.

5. Jim Edwards, "P&G's $1 Billion Problem: Is Its Ad Budget Too Big?" *BNET*, August 4, 2010, www.bnet.com/blog/advertising-business/p-g-8217s-1-billion-problem-is-its-ad-budget-too-big/5368; and "Procter & Gamble Names New Top Digital Marketer," *The Ratti Report*, May 2, 2011, www.the-ratti-report.com/blog/622492-procter-gamble-names-new-top-digital-marketer/.

6. Quote from Michael Schneider, "Nielsen: Traditional TV Still King," *Variety*, December 7, 2009. TV and Internet advertising stats from Lisa Waananen, "How Agencies Are Spending Online Media Budgets," *Mashable.com*, June 9, 2011, http://mashable.com/2011/06/09/media-agency-budgets/.

7. Jon Lafayette, "4A's Conference: Agencies Urged to Embrace New Technologies," *Broadcasting & Cable*, March 8, 2011, www.broadcastingcable.com/article/464951-4A_s_Conference_Agencies_Urged_To_Embrace_New_Technologies.php.

8. See "Integrated Campaigns: Häagen-Dazs," *Communication Arts Advertising Annual 2009*, pp. 158–159; Tiffany Meyers, "Marketing 50: Häagen-Dazs, Katty Pien," *Advertising Age*, November 17, 2008, p. S15; "Häagen-Dazs Loves Honey Bees," April 28, 2010, a summary video accessed at http://limeshot.com/2010/haagen-dazs-loves-honey-bees-titanium-silver-lion-cannes-2009; Alan Bjerga, "U.S. Queen Bees Work Overtime to Save Hives," *Bloomberg Businessweek*, April 3, 2011, pp. 27–28; and information from www.helpthehoneybees.com, accessed October 2011.

9. See David Barron, "Super Bowl XLV Most-Watched Show Ever," *McClatchy-Tribune Business News*, February 8, 2011; Sam Schechner, "Oscar's Big Night Comes Up Short," *Wall Street Journal*, March 1, 2011, p. B1; and Sam Schechner, "'Idol' Retains Crown, but Audience Falls," *Wall Street Journal*, January 21, 2011, p. B8.

10. See discussions at "What Is the Real Cost of a B2B Sales Call?" accessed at www.marketing-playbook.com/sales-marketing-strategy/what-is-the-real-cost-of-a-b2b-sales-call, June 2011; and "The Costs of Personal Selling," April 13, 2011, www.seekarticle.com/business-sales/personal-selling.html.

11. Adam Smith, "GroupM Forecasts Global Ad Spending to Surpass $500 Billion in 2011," December 6, 2010, www.aaaa.org/news/agency/Pages/120610_groupm_forecast.aspx; "Top 100 Global Advertisers See World of Opportunity," *Advertising Age*, December 6, 2010, http://adage.com/print?article_id=147436; "Advertising Spending," *Advertising Age*, December 20, 2010, p. 10; and "Which Marketer Has the Deepest Pockets? Ask the DataCenter," special promotional supplement, *Advertising Age*, February 14, 2011, p. 3.

12. See http://2010.census.gov/mediacenter/paid-ad-campaign/new-ads/index.php?vn11, accessed June 2010.

13. For these and other examples of comparative advertising, see Emily Bryson York and Natalie Zmuda, "So Sue Me: Why Big Brands Are Taking Claims to Court," *Advertising Age*, January 4, 2010, pp. 1, 23; "Pepsi Suing Coca-Cola Over Powerade Ads," *New York Times*, April 13, 2009, accessed at www.nytimes.com; and Fred Beard, "Comparative Advertising Wars: An Historical Analysis of Their Causes and Consequences," *Journal of Macromarketing*, September 2010, pp. 270–286.

14. For more on setting promotion budgets, see W. Ronald Lane, Karen Whitehill King, and J. Thomas Russell, *Kleppner's Advertising Procedure*, 18th ed. (Upper Saddle River, NJ: Prentice Hall, 2011), Chapter 6.

15. See Jean Halliday, "Thinking Big Takes Audi from Obscure to Awesome," *Advertising Age*, February 2, 2009, accessed at http://adage.com/print?article_id=134234; Chad Thomas and Andreas Cremer, "Audi Feels a Need for Speed in the U.S.," *Bloomberg Businessweek*, November 22, 2010, p. 1; and Tito F. Hermoso, "Watch Out for Audi," *BusinessWorld*, June 15, 2011, p. 1.

16. "Average U.S. Home Now Receives a Record 118.6 TV Channels, According to Nielsen," June 6, 2008, http://en-us.nielsen.com/content/nielsen/en_us/news/news_releases/2008/june/average_u_s__home.html; and "Number of Magazines Titles," www.magazine.org/ASME/EDITORIAL_TRENDS/1093.aspx, accessed July 2011.

17. Louise Story, "Anywhere the Eye Can See, It's Likely to See an Ad," *New York Times*, January 15, 2007, p. A12; and James Othmer, "Persuasion Gives Way to Engagement," *Vancouver Sun*, August 20, 2009, p. A13.

18. "Executive Summary of the 4A's Television Production Cost Survey," December 15, 2009, www.aaaa.org/news/bulletins/Documents/2008TVPCSExecSumcosts.pdf; "Prime Time Programs & 30 Second Ad Costs: Historical Look 2000–2011," www.frankwbaker.com/prime_time_programs_30_sec_ad_costs.htm, accessed July 2011; and Aaron Smith "Super Bowl Ad: Is $3 Million Worth It?" *CNNMoney.com*, February 3, 2011.

19. "Advertising in the U.S.: Synovate Global Survey Shows Internet, Innovation and Online Privacy a Must," December 3, 2009, accessed at www.synovate.com/news/article/2009/12/advertising-in-the-us-synovate-global-survey-shows-internet-innovation-and-online-privacy-a-must.html; and Katy Bachman, "Survey: Clutter Causing TV Ads to Lack Effectiveness," *MediaWeek*, February 8, 2010.

20. Wayne Freedman, "Nielsen: DVR Playback Doubles, More Ads Watch," *MediaPostNews*, August 5, 2010, www.mediapost.com/publications/?fa=Articles.showArticle&art_aid=133321; Robert Seidman, "DVR Penetration Grows to 39.7% of Households, 42.2% of Viewers," *TV by the Numbers*, March 23, 2011, http://tvbythenumbers.zap2it.com/2011/03/23/dvr-penetration-grows-to-39-7-of-households-42-2-of-viewers/86819.

21. "Rentrak Reports That Many Super Bowl Commercials Are Watched Over and Over Via Viewers' DVR," February 21, 2011, www.rentrak.com/section/corporate/press_room/press_release_detail.html?release_no=1803.

22. T. L. Stanley, "A Place for Everything," *Brandweek*, March 1, 2010, p. 12.

23. Wayne Friedman, "Lights, Camera, Apple! Tech Giant Product Placement King," *MediaPostNews*, February 22, 2011, www.mediapost.com/publications/?fa=Articles.showArticle&art_aid=145480; and Stuart Elliott, "Film on Branded Content Examines a Blurred Line," *New York Times*, April 22, 2011, p. B3.

24. Adapted from information found in Bob Garfield, "How Etsy Made Us Rethink Consumer-Generated Ads," *Advertising Age*, September 21, 2009, p. 4.

25. For more on consumer-generated advertising, see Emma Hall, "Most Winning Creative Work Involves Consumer Participation," *Advertising Age*, January 6, 2010, accessed at http://adage.com/print?article_id=141329; Stuart Elliott, "Do-It-Yourself Super Ads," *New York Times*, February 8, 2010, www.nytimes.com; Rich Thomaselli, "If Consumer Is Your Agency, It's Time for Review," *Advertising Age*, May 17, 2010, p. 2; and Colin Campbell et al., "Understanding Consumer Conversations around Ads in Web 2.0 World," *Journal of Advertising*, Spring 2011, p. 87.

26. See David Kiley, "Paying for Viewers Who Pay Attention," *BusinessWeek*, May 18, 2009, p. 56.

27. Brian Steinberg, "Viewer-Engagement Rankings Signal Change for TV Industry," *Advertising Age*, May 10, 2010, p. 12.

28. Tavis Coburn, "Mayhem on Madison Avenue," *Fast Company*, January 2011, pp. 110–115.

29. Joe Tripoti, "Coca-Cola Marketing Shifts from Impressions to Expressions," April 27, 2011, http://blogs.hbr.org/cs/2011/04/coca-colas_marketing_shift_fro.html.

30. See Jon Swartz, "Multitasking at Home: Internet and TV Viewing," *USA Today*, July 6, 2010, www.usatoday.com; Dan Zigmond and Horst Stipp, "Vision Statement: Multitaskers May Be Advertisers' Best Audience," *Harvard Business Review*, January–February 2011, http://hbr.org/2011/01/vision-statement-multi-taskers-may-be-advertisers-best-audience/ar/1; and Kunar Patel, "When's Prime Time in Mobile? Same as TV," *Advertising Age*, July 5, 2011, www.adage.com/print/228536.

31. *Newsweek* and *BusinessWeek* cost and circulation data online at www.bloombergmedia.com/magazine/businessweek/ and www.newsweekmediakit.com, accessed October 2010.

32. Kate Maddox, "Optimism, Accountability, Social Media Top Trends," *BtoB*, January 18, 2010, p. 1.

33. Information on advertising agency revenues from "Agency Report," *Advertising Age*, April 25, 2011, pp. 24–41.

34. Adapted from Scott Cutlip, Allen Center, and Glen Broom, *Effective Public Relations*, 10th ed. (Upper Saddle River, NJ: Prentice Hall, 2009), Chapter 1.

35. Information from "The Heart Truth: Making Healthy Hearts Fashionable," Ogilvy Public Relations Worldwide, www.ogilvypr.com/en/case-study/heart-truth?page=0, www.goredforwomen.org/; and www.nhlbi.nih.gov/educational/hearttruth/about/index.htm, accessed October 2011.

36. See Geoffrey Fowler and Ben Worthen, "Buzz Powers iPad Launch," *Wall Street Journal*, April 2, 2010; "Apple iPad Sales Top 2 Million Since Launch," *Tribune-Review* (Pittsburgh), June 2, 2010; "PR Pros Must Be Apple's iPad as a True Game-Changer," *PRweek*, May 2010, p. 23; and Yukari Iwatani Kane, "Apple's iPad 2 Chalks Up Strong Sales in Weekend Debut," *Wall Street Journal*, March 14, 2011, http://online.wsj.com/article/SB10001424052748704027504576198832667732862.html.

37. Michael Bush, "P&G's Marc Pritchard Touts Value of PR," *Advertising Age*, October 27, 2010, http://adage.com/article/news/p-g-s-marc-pritchard-touts-pr/146749/.

38. Adapted from information in "PR in the Driver's Seat," *Advertising Age*, October 26, 2009, pp. S6–S7.

39. Paul Holmes, "Senior Marketers Are Sharply Divided about the Role of PR in the Overall Mix," *Advertising Age*, January 24, 2005, pp. C1–C2. For another example, see Jack Neff, "How Pampers Battled Diaper Debacle," *Advertising Age*, May 10, 2010, accessed at http://adage.com/article?article_id=143777.

Chapter 13

1. Based on information from numerous P&G managers; with information from "500 Largest Sales Forces in America," *Selling Power*, October 2010, pp. 39–56; and www.experiencepg.com/jobs/customer-business-development-sales.aspx, accessed November 2011.

2. See Henry Canaday, "Sales Rep to CEO: Anne Mulcahy and the Xerox Revolution," *Selling Power*, November/December 2008, pp. 53–57.

3. See Philip Kotler, Neil Rackham, and Suj Krishnaswamy, "Ending the War Between Sales and Marketing," *Harvard Business Review*, July–August 2006, pp. 68–78; Elizabeth A. Sullivan, "The Ties That Bind," *Marketing News*, May 15, 2010; Alan Edwards, "On the Road to Know-How," *Marketing*, March 23, 2011, p. 19; and Philip Kotler and Kevin Lane Keller, *Marketing Management*, 14th ed. (Upper Saddle River, NJ: Prentice Hall, 2012), p. 554.

4. See Henry Canaday, "Give It a Whirl," *Selling Power*, May/June 2010, pp. 22–24.

5. "Selling Power 500: The Largest Sales Force in America," *Selling Power*, September/October 2010, pp. 44–56.

6. See discussions at "What Is the Real Cost of a B2B Sales Call?" accessed at www.marketing-playbook.com/sales-marketing-strategy/what-is-the-real-cost-of-a-b2b-sales-call, June 2011; and "The Costs of Personal Selling," April 13, 2011, www.seekarticle.com/business-sales/personal-selling.html.

7. See "Case Study: Climax Portable Machine Tools," www.selltis.com/productSalesCaseStudyClimax.aspx, accessed November 2011.

8. "Customer Business Development," www.experiencepg.com/jobs/customer-business-development-sales.aspx, accessed November 2011.

9. For this and more information and discussion, see www.gallup.com/consulting/1477/Sales-Force-Effectiveness.aspx, accessed October 2010; "The 10 Skills of 'Super' Salespeople," www.businesspartnerships.ca/articles/the_10_skills_of_super_salespeople.phtml, accessed May 2010; and Lynette Ryals and Iain Davies, "Do You Really Know Who Your Best Salespeople Are?" *Harvard Business Review*, December 2010, pp. 34–35.

10. Barbara Hendricks, "Strengths-Based Selling," February 8, 2011, www.gallup.com/press/146246/Strengths-Based-Selling.aspx.

11. "ADP Case Study," Corporate Visions, Inc., http://win.corporatevisions.com/caseStudy_ADP.html, accessed July 2011.

12. Based on information found in Sara Donnelly, "Staying in the Game," *Pharmaceutical Executive*, May 2008, pp. 158–159; "Improving Sales Force Effectiveness: Bayer's Experiment with New Technology," Bayer Healthcare Pharmaceuticals, Inc., 2008, www.icmrindia.org/casestudies/catalogue/Marketing/MKTG200.htm; and Tanya Lewis, "Concentric," *Medical Marketing and Media*, July 2008, p. 59. For more on e-learning, see "Logging On for Sales School," *CustomRetailer*, November 2009, p. 30; and Sarah Boehle, "Global Sales Training's Balancing Act," *Training*, January 2010, p. 29.

13. See Joseph Kornak, "'07 Compensation Survey: What's It All Worth?" *Sales & Marketing Management*, May 2007, pp. 28–39; William L. Cron and Thomas E. DeCarlo, *Dalrymple's Sales Management*, 10th ed. (New York: John Wiley & Sons Inc., 2009), p. 303; and Alexander Group, "2011 Sales Compensation Trends Survey Results," January 5, 2011, http://salescompsolutions.com/downloads/2011SCTExecSummFinal.pdf.

14. Susan Greco, "How to Reduce Your Cost of Sales," *Inc.*, March 5, 2010, www.inc.com/guide/reducing-cost-of-sales.html. Also see Robert McGarvey, "Pay for Performance," *Selling Power*, February 2011, p. 54.

15. See Charles Fifield, "Necessary Condition #3—The Right Day-to-Day Operational Focus," December 2010, www.baylor.edu/content/services/document.php/127101.pdf. For another summary, see Gerhard Gschwandtner, "How Much Time Do Your Salespeople Spend Selling?" *Selling Power*, March/April 2011, p. 8.

16. Quote above from Lain Chroust Ehmann, "Sales Up!" *Selling Power*, January/February 2011, p. 40. Extract adapted from information found in Pelin Wood Thorogood, "Sales 2.0: How Soon Will It Improve Your Business?" *Selling Power*, November/December 2008, pp. 58–61; Gerhard Gschwandtner, "What Is Sales 2.0, and Why Should You Care?" *Selling Power*, March/April 2010, p. 9. Also see Michael Brenner, "The State of the Union in B2B Marketing," January 25, 2011, www.b2bmarketinginsider.com/strategy/the-state-of-the-union-in-b2b-marketing.

17. Adapted from information in Elizabeth A. Sullivan, "B-to-B Marketers: One-to-One Marketing," *Marketing News*, May 15, 2009, pp. 11–13. Also see "Social Media to Lead Growth in Online B2B Marketing," *Min's b2b*, February 8, 2010, accessed at www.minonline.com/b2b/13441.html; and Robert McGarvey, "All About Us: How the Social-Community Phenomenon Has Affected B2B Sales," *Selling Power*, November/December 2010, p. 48.

18. Quotes from David Thompson, "Embracing the Future: A Step by Step Overview of Sales 2.0," *Sales and Marketing Management*, July/August 2008, p. 21; and "Ahead of the Curve: How Sales 2.0 Will Affect Your Sales Process—For the Better," *Selling Power*, March/April 2010, pp. 14–17. Also see Robert McGarvey, "All About Us," *Selling Power*, March 7, 2011, p. 48; and Lain Chroust Ehmann, "Sales Up!" *Selling Power*, January/February 2011, p. 40.

19. John Graham, "Salespeople under Siege: The Profession Redefined," *Agency Sales*, January 2010, pp. 20–25; Rick Phillips, "Don't Pressure, Persuade," *Selling Power*, January/February 2010, p. 22; and Bill Farquharson and T. J. Tedesco, "How to 'Build' a Sales Rep," *Printing Impressions*, April 2011, p. 38.

20. Example based on information from James C. Anderson, Nirmalya Kumar, and James A. Narus, "Become a Value Merchant," *Sales & Marketing Management*, May 6, 2008, pp. 20–23; and "Business Market Value Merchants," *Marketing Management*, March/April 2008, pp. 31+. For another value selling example, see Heather Baldwin, "Deeper Value Delivery," *Selling Power*, September/October 2010, p. 16.

21. *Transforming Trade Promotion/Shopper-Centric Approach* (Wilton, CT: Kantar Retail, June 2010), p. 8.

22. Jack Neff, "Why Promotion May End Up a Bad Deal for Packaged Goods," *Advertising Age*, January 31, 2011, p. 11.

23. "Kroger Expands Fuel Discount Program," May 31, 2011, www.csnews.com/top-story-kroger_expands_fuel_discount_program-58803.html.

24. See "Value-Centric Shoppers Save $3.7 Billion in 2010 Using Coupons," *PR Newswire*, January 20, 2011.

25. See www.happymeal.com/en_US/, accessed July 2011.

26. See "2010 Estimate of Promotional Products Distributor Sales," www.ppai.org/inside-ppai/research/Documents/2010%20Sales%20Volume%20Sheet.pdf, accessed June 2011.

27. "Nissan Returns as Official Automotive Sponsor of the 2011 Amgen Tour of California," May 11, 2011, www.amgentourofcalifornia.com/news/press/Nissan-returns-as-official-automotive-sponsor-of-the-2011-Amgen-Tour-of-California.html; and www.nissanusa.com/leaf-electric-car/events/index#/leaf-electric-car/events/index, accessed July 2011.

28. *Transforming Trade Promotion/Shopper-Centric Approach*, p. 8.

29. See "2011 International CES: Attendee Audit Summary Results," accessed at www.cesweb.org/docs/2011AuditSummary.pdf, June 2011; and "Bauma 2010 Closing Report," www.bauma.de/en/Press/Closingreport, accessed October 2011.

Chapter 14

1. Leah Fabel, "The Business of Facebook," *Fast Company*, April 1, 2011, www.fastcompany.com; E. B. Boyd, "Facebook Deals Out-Groups Groupon," *Fast Company*, April 26, 2011, www.fastcompany.com; Michelle Kung and Geoffrey A. Fowler, "Warner 'Likes' Facebook Rentals," *Wall Street Journal*, March 9, 2011, p. B4; Parmy Olson, "Facebook to Launch Music Service with Spotify," *Forbes*, May 25, 2011, http://blogs.forbes.com/parmyolson/2011/05/25/facebook-to-launch-music-service-with-spotify/; Venessa Miemis, "The Bank of Facebook: Currency, Identify, Reputation," *Forbes*, April 4, 2011, http://blogs.forbes.com/venessamiemis/2011/04/04/the-bank-of-facebook-currency-identity-reputation/; "Facebook's Sales Chief: Madison Avenue Doesn't Understand Us Yet," *Advertising Age*, April 29, 2011, http://adage.com/print/227314/; Brian Womack, "Facebook Ad Rates Hold as Inventory Rises," *Bloomberg Businessweek*, July 6, 2011, www.bloomberg.com; and information from www.facebook.com, accessed October 2011.

2. For these and other direct marketing statistics in this section, see Direct Marketing Association, *The DMA 2011 Statistical Fact Book*, 33rd ed., February 2011; Direct Marketing Association, *The Power of Direct Marketing: 2008–2009 Edition*, June 2009; Juan Martinez, "Direct, Digital 2010 Ad Spend Up 2.7%," *Direct Marketing News*, January 13, 2011, www.dmnews.com/direct-digital-2010-ad-spend-up-27-winterberry-group/article/194185/; and a wealth of other information at www.the-dma.org, accessed October 2011.

3. Erik Sass, "Online Ad Revenue to Grow 10% in 2011, S&P Predicts," *MediaPostNews*, December 29, 2010; Nat Worden, "Ads for Web Surpassed Newspapers in 2010," *Wall Street Journal*, April 14, 2011, p. B9.

4. See discussions at "What Is the Real Cost of a B2B Sales Call?" accessed at www.marketing-playbook.com/sales-marketing-strategy/what-is-the-real-cost-of-a-b2b-sales-call, June 2011; and "The Costs of Personal Selling," April 13, 2011, www.seekarticle.com/business-sales/personal-selling.html.

5. Information from Nuts about Southwest, www.blogsouthwest.com; "What Is DING!?" www.southwest.com/ding; and www.southwest.com/iphone/; all accessed November 2011.

6. Mike Freeman, "Data Company Helps Wal-Mart, Casinos, Airlines Analyze Data," *Knight Ridder Business Tribune News*, February 24, 2006, p. 1; Eric Lai, "Teradata Creates Elite Club for Petabyte-Plus Data Warehouse Customers," *Computer World*, October 14, 2008, www.computerworld.com/s/article/9117159/Teradata_creates_elite_club_for_petabyte_plus_data_warehouse_customers; and "Data, Data Everywhere," *Economist*, February 27, 2010, p. 3.

7. See "Best Buy Plugs into the Power of Customer Centricity," *FICO.com*, 2009, www.fico.com/en/FIResourcesLibrary/Best_Buy_Success_2271CS_EN.pdf; and Philip Kotler and Kevin Lane Keller, *Marketing Management*, 14th ed. (Upper Saddle River, NJ: Prentice Hall, 2012), p. 71.

8. See DMA, *The Power of Direct Marketing*, 2009–2010 Edition; and "It's Never Been Easier to Send Direct Mail," *PRNewswire*, June 8, 2011.

9. Julie Liesse, "When Times Are Hard, Mail Works," *Advertising Age*, March 30, 2009, p. 14; and Paul Vogel, "Marketers Are Rediscovering the Value of Mail," *Deliver Magazine*, January 11, 2011, www.delivermagazine.com/2011/01/marketers-are-rediscovering-the-value-of-mail/.

10. Bruce Britt, "Marketing Leaders Discuss the Resurgence of Direct Mail," *Deliver Magazine*, January 18, 2011, www.delivermagazine.com/2011/01/marketing-leaders-discuss-resurgence-of-direct-mail/.

11. See "Catalog Spree; Over a Dozen Classic Retailers Added to Catalog Spree iPad Shopping App," *Marketing Weekly News*, July 2, 2011, p. 944; and www.landsend.com/mobile/index.html and http://catalogspree.com/, accessed October 2011.

12. Jeffrey Ball, "Power Shift: In Digital Era, Marketers Still Prefer a Paper Trail," *Wall Street Journal*, October 16, 2009, p. A3; and Jennifer Valentino-DeVries, "With Catalogs, Opt-Out Policies Vary," *Wall Street Journal*, April 13, 2011, p. B7.

13. Ball, "Power Shift: In Digital Era, Marketers Still Prefer a Paper Trail"; and "Report: Catalogs Increasingly Drive Online Sales," RetailCustomerExperience.com, March 17, 2010, www.retailcustomerexperience.com/article/21521/Report-Catalogs-increasingly-drive-online-sales.

14. DMA, *The Power of Direct Marketing*, 2009–2010 Edition.

15. Jeff Gelles, "Consumer 10.0: Calls Persist Despite List," *Philadelphia Inquirer*, January 24, 2010, p. D2; and www.donotcall.gov, accessed October 2011.

16. See Geoffrey A. Fowler, "Peeved at Auto Warranty Calls, a Web Posse Strikes Back," *Wall Street Journal*, May 15, 2009, A1.

17. See Rachel Brown, "Perry, Fischer, Lavigne Tapped for Proactiv," *WWD*, January 13, 2010, p. 3; www.proactiv.com, accessed July 2011.

18. Darren Rovell, "The Shake Weight Hits $40 Million in Sales," August 2010, www.cnbc.com/id/38788941/The_Shake_Weight_Hits_40_Million_In_Sales; and "Sporting Activities, Baseball; Shake Weight Gets Serious," *Entertainment Newsweekly*, June 10, 2011, p. 126.

19. Example adapted from Beth Snyder Bulik, "Act Now, and We'll Double Your Market Share!" *Advertising Age*, August 27, 2009, accessed at http://adage.com/article?article_id=138693.

20. Shahnaz Mahmud, "Survey: Viewers Crave TV Ad Fusion," Adweek.com, January 25, 2008, www.adweek.com; Hampp, "Scorecard: Were We Wrong or Almost Right on ITV?" *Advertising Age*, April 12, 2010, http://adage.com/cabletv10/article?article_id=143163; John M. Smart, "Tomorrow's Interactive Television," *The Futurist*, November/December 2010, p. 41; and David Verklin, "Boost Sales with Interactive TV," *DM News*, February 23, 2011, p. 24.

21. Adapted from information in Zachary Rodgers, "Cablevision's Interactive TV Ads Pay Off for Gillette," *ClickZ*, October 21, 2009, accessed at www.clickz.com/3635413/print; David Goetzl, "Interactive Ads Pay Off for Cablevision," *MediaPost News*, January 12, 2010, accessed at www.mediapost.com/publications; and "Cable Television Companies; Advertisers Embrace New Feature of Optimum Select RFI to Immediately Deliver Brochures, Coupons, Offers, and Other Information to Consumers Via E-Mail," *Marketing Weekly News*, July 2, 2011, p. 158.

22. Stephanie Rosenbloom, "The New Touch-Face of Vending Machines," *New York Times*, May 25, 2010, accessed at www.nytimes.com/2010/05/26/business/26vending.html.

23. Rebecca Troyer, "Redbox DVD Rental Kiosks Now at CVS Store in Bloomington," *McClatchy-Tribune Business News*, May 14, 2011; and www.redbox.com, accessed October 2011.

24. See "Study Finds Internet More Important Than TV," *Radio Business Report*, March 25, 2010, www.rbr.com/media-news/research/22765.html; Jack Marshall, "U.S. Smart Phone Penetration Up 60 Percent in Q4 2010," *ClickZ*, February 8, 2011, www.clickz.com/clickz/stats/2024999/smartphone-penetration-percent-q4-2010; and "Global Mobile Statistics," *MobiThinking,* June 2011, http://mobithinking.com/stats-corner/global-mobile-statistics-2011-all-quality-mobile-marketing-research-mobile-web-stats-su.

25. See "Internet Retailer: Top 500 Guide," www.internetretailer.com/top500/list, accessed July 2011.

26. Staples data from annual reports and other information found at www.staples.com, accessed October 2011.

27. See Stu Woo, "E-Commerce Will Keep Rolling, Research Firm Says," *WSJ Blogs*, February 27, 2011, http://blogs.wsj.com/digits/2011/02/27/e-commerce-will-keep-rolling-research-firm-says/?mod=dist_smartbrief.

28. Anna Johnson, "Local Marketing: 97 Percent of Consumers Use Online Media for Local Shopping," *Kikabink News*, March 17, 2010, accessed at www.kikabink.com/news/local-marketing-97-percent-of-consumers-use-online-media-for-local-shopping/; and "Web Influence on Retail Sales," *South Carolina Business Blog*, January 5, 2011, www.framelegal.com/blog/articletype/articleview/articleid/306/2011-web-influence-on-retail-sales.aspx.

29. See facts from eBay annual reports and other information at www.ebayinc.com, accessed July 2011.

30. Jon Sobel, "State of the Blogosphere 2010," Technorati, November 3, 2010, accessed at http://technorati.com/blogging/article/state-of-the-blogosphere-2010-introduction/; and www.blogpulse.com/, accessed July 2011.

31. For these and other examples, see Erica Swallow, "15 Excellent Corporate Blogs to Learn From," August 13, 2010, http://mashable.com/2010/08/13/great-corporate-blogs/; and http://share.blog.us.playstation.com/, http://disneyparks.disney.go.com/blog/, and http://en.community.dell.com/dell-blogs/default.aspx, accessed October 2011.

32. See "IZEA and ImageShack Partner to Form Largest Global Social Media Sponsorship Network," *The Pak Banker,* March 27, 2011; and http://socialspark.com/advertisers/sample-campaigns/, accessed October 2011.

33. See "Get Satisfaction Connects Customer Support and the Social Web," *PRNewswire*, April 21, 2010; and www.getsatisfaction.com, accessed October 2011.

34. "Search, Display Trends Push Online Ad Spend Past $31 Billion," *eMarketer*, July 5, 2011, www.emarketer.com/Article.aspx?R=1008476.

35. Internet Advertising Bureau, *IAB Internet Advertising Revenue Report*, May 26, 2011, www.iab.net/media/file/IAB_Full_year_2010_0413_Final.pdf; and Google annual reports, Annual Report, http://investor.google.com/proxy.html.

36. See "Campaigns Creativity Liked," *Advertising Age*, December 13, 2010, p. 18; Thomas Pardee, "Think the Old Spice Guy Is So 2010? Think Again," *Advertising Age*, February 16, 2011, http://adage.com/print/148911; and Dan Sewell, "Old Spice Teases Its Sexy New Ad Campaign," *USA Today*, January 26, 2011, www.usatoday.com/money/advertising/2011-01-26-old-spice-mustafa-ad_N.htm.

37. David Gelles, "The Public Image: Volkswagen's 'The Force' Campaign," *Financial Times*, February 22, 2011, p. 14; and Troy Dreier, "The Force Was Strong with This One," *Streaming Media Magazine*, April/May 2011, pp. 66–68.

38. Brian Morrissey, "Social Media Use Becomes Pervasive," *Adweek*, April 15, 2010, accessed at www.adweek.com; and www.checkfacebook.com/, accessed July 2011.

39. For these and other examples, see Douglas MacMillan, "With Friends Like This, Who Needs Facebook?" *Bloomberg Businessweek*, September 13–September 19, 2010, pp. 35–37; and www.mytransponder.com/home.php, www.gofishn.com, www.ravelry.com, www.dogster.com, www.researchgate.net, www.passionsnetwork.com, www.passportstamp.com/welcome, and www.cafemom.com, all accessed October 2011.

40. "Happy Birthday to Nike+," *Run247,* May 23, 2011, www.run247.com/articles/article-1337-happy-birthday-to-nike%2B.html.

41. See http://my.menshealth.com/bellyoff/, accessed July 2011.

42. See Ken Magill, "E-mail ROI Still Stunning, Still Slipping: DMA," *Direct Magazine*, October 20, 2009, accessed at http://directmag.com/magilla/1020-e-mail-roi-still-slipping/; "E-Mail," *Advertising Age's Digital Marketing Facts 2010* section, February 22, 2010; and "Think E-Mail Marketing Is Dying? Think Again," *PR Newswire,* May 3, 2011.

43. Elizabeth A. Sullivan, "Targeting to the Extreme," *Marketing News*, June 15, 2010, pp. 17–19.

44. Symantec, *The State of Spam and Phishing: Home of the Monthly Report—May 2011*, accessed at http://go.symantec.com/spam_report/.

45. Jessica Tsai, "How Much Marketing Is Too Much?" *DestinationCRM.com*, October 1, 2008, www.destinationcrm.com; "StubHub Increases Revenue Per E-Mail by Over 2,500 Percent with Responsys Interact and Omniture Recommendations," February 18, 2009, www.responsys.com/company/press/2009_02_18.php.

46. Carroll Trosclair, "Direct Marketing, Advertising and ROI: Commercial E-Mail Delivers Highest DM Return on Investment," *Suite101.com*, April 2, 2010, http://advertising.suite101.com/article.cfm/direct-marketing-advertising-and-roi. For examples of outstanding e-mail marketing campaigns, see "MarketingSherpa Email Awards 2011," *MarketingSherpa*, www.marketingsherpa.com/EmailAwards2011/EmailAwards2011Winners.pdf.

47. Facts in this paragraph are from *State of Mobile Advertising 2011, Mobile Marketer*, June 2011, www.mobilemarketer.com/cms/lib/12311.pdf; and www.apple.com/ipad/from-the-app-store/ and www.apple.com/iphone/apps-for-iphone/, accessed October 2011.

48. *State of Mobile Advertising 2011,* p. 4; Dan Frommer, "The Future of Mobile Advertising," *Business Insider,* June 8, 2011, www.sfgate.com/cgi-bin/article.cgi?f=/g/a/2011/06/08/businessinsider-future-of-mobile-advertising-2011-6.DTL; and Giselle Tsirulnik, "In-App Mobile Ad Spend to Reach $685M in 2011," *Mobile Marketer*, September 21, 2010, www.mobilemarketer.com/cms/news/research/7424.html.

49. Adapted from Giselle Tsirulnik, "Most Impressive Mobile Advertising Campaigns in 2010," December 29, 2010, www.mobilemarketer.com/cms/news/advertising/8617.html.

50. See Emily Burg, "Acceptance of Mobile Ads on the Rise," *MediaPost Publications*, March 16, 2007, accessed at www.mediapost.com/publications; Steve Miller and Mike Beirne, "The iPhone Effect," Adweek.com, April 28, 2008, www.adweek.com; Altmeyer, "Smart Phones, Social Networks to Boost Mobile Advertising," *Reuters.com*, June 29, 2009; and Richard Westlund, "Mobile on Fast Forward," *Brandweek*, March 15, 2010, pp. M1–M5.

51. See Internet Crime Complaint Center, "IC3 2010 Annual Report on Internet Crime Released," February 24, 2011, www.ic3.gov/media/2011/110224.aspx.

52. See Greg Sterling, "Pew: Americans Increasingly Shop Online But Still Fear Identity Theft," *SearchEngineLand.com*, February 14, 2008, accessed at http://searchengineland.com/

pew-americans-increasingly-shop-online-but-still-fear-identity-theft-13366. See also www.ftc.gov/bcp/edu/microsites/idtheft/ and www.spendonlife.com/guide/identity-theft-statistics, accessed November 2011.

53. See Cecilia Kang, "Underage and on Facebook," *Washington Post*, June 13, 2011, www.washingtonpost.com/blogs/post-tech/post/underage-and-on-facebook/2011/06/12/AGHKHySH_blog.html.

54. Adapted from information in Michael Bush, "My Life, Seen through the Eyes of Marketers," *Advertising Age,* April 26, 2010, http://adage.com/print/143479.

55. See "Digital Advertising Alliance Announces First 100 Companies Participating in Self-Regulatory Program for Online Behavioral Advertising," June 7, 2011, www.the-dma.org/cgi/dispann-ouncements?article=1558; and www.aboutads.info/, accessed July 2011.

56. See Mark Rotenberg, "An Examination of Children's Privacy: New Technologies and the Children's Online Privacy Protection Act (COPPA)," April 29, 2010, http://epic.org/privacy/kids/EPIC_COPPA_Testimony_042910.pdf; "FTC to Study Children's Online Privacy Protection Act," April 21, 2010, www.aaaa.org/advocacy/gov/news/Pages/042110_children.aspx; and Wendy Davis, "Rockefeller Urges FTC to Move Faster on COPPA Rules," *Daily Online Examiner*, May 19, 2011, www.mediapost.com/publications/?fa=Articles.showArticle&art_aid=150867.

57. Information on TRUSTe at www.truste.com, accessed October 2011.

58. Information on the DMA Privacy Promise at www.the-dma.org/cgi/dispissue? article=129, accessed October 2011.

Chapter 15

1. Quotes and other information from Matthew Fomey and Arthur Kroeber, "Google's Business Reason for Leaving China," *Wall Street Journal*, April 6, 2010, p. 15; Aaron Back and Loretta Chao, "Google Weaves a Tangled Chinese Web," *Wall Street Journal*, March 25, 2010, http://online.wsj.com; Jessica E. Vascellaro, "Brin Drove Google's Pullback," *Wall Street Journal*, March 25, 2010, p. A1; Bruce Einhorn, "Google in China: A Win for Liberty—and Strategy," *Bloomberg Businessweek*, January 25, 2010, p. 35; Calum MacLeod, "China Agency Aims to Police Healthy Internet Growth," *USA Today*, May 10, 2011, p. A6; Chen Limin, "Online Ad Revenue to Beat Newspapers," *China Daily*, January 8, 2011, www.chinadaily.com.cn/bizchina/2011-01/08/content_11812626.htm; "China's Mobile Phone Users Continue to Rise," *China Business News,* June 27, 2011; Li Woke, "Baidu Wins Top 100 Branding Accolade," *McClatchy-Tribune Business News,* May 10, 2011; and "Google and Its Ordeal in China," *Fortune,* May 2, 2011, pp. 94–98.

2. Data from Michael V. Copeland, "The Mighty Micro-Multinational," *Business 2.0*, July 28, 2006, accessed at http://cnnmoney.com; "List of Countries by GDP: List by the CIA World Factbook," *Wikipedia*, http://en.wikipedia.org/wiki/List_of_countries_by_GDP_(nominal), accessed July 2011; and "Fortune 500," *Fortune*, May 23, 2011, pp. F1–F26.

3. "Global Economic Prospects 2010: Crisis, Finance, and Growth," *World Bank*, January 21, 2010, accessed at http://tinyurl.com/2bfgrd6; and "World Trade 2010, Prospects for 2011," World Trade Organization, April 7, 2011, www.wto.org/english/news_e/pres11_e/pr628_e.pdf.

4. Information from www.michelin.com/corporate, www.jnj.com, and www.caterpillar.com, accessed October 2011.

5. See www.otisworldwide.com/d1-about.html, accessed October 2011.

6. Frank Greve, "International Food Fight Could Spell End to Roquefort Dressing," *McClatchy-Tribune Business News*, April 9, 2009; James Hagengruber, "A Victory for Cheese Eaters?" *Christian Science Monitor*, May 7, 2009, www.csmonitor.com.

7. See Jeremy Goldkorn, "Behind the Great Firewall of China," *Fast Company*, February 2011, p. 73.

8. "What Is the WTO?" www.wto.org/english/thewto_e/whatis_e/whatis_e.htm, accessed October 2011.

9. See Alan Beattie, "WTO Scrambles to Salvage Doha Talks," *FT.com*, June 12, 2011, www.ft.com/cms/s/0/eed080f6-9510-11e0-a648-00144feab49a.html#axzz1RpakqSrp; *WTO Annual Report 2011*, www.wto.org/english/res_e/publications_e/anrep11_e.htm, accessed August 2011; and World Trade Organization, "10 Benefits of the WTO Trading System," www.wto.org/english/thewto_e/whatis_e/10ben_e/10b00_e.htm, accessed October 2011.

10. "The EU at a Glance," http://europa.eu/abc/index_en.htm; and "EU Statistics and Opinion Polls," http://europa.eu/documentation/statistics-polls/index_en.htm; accessed September 2011.

11. "Economic and Monetary Affairs," http://europa.eu/pol/emu/index_en.htm, accessed October 2011.

12. CIA, *The World Factbook*, https://www.cia.gov/library/publications/the-world-factbook, accessed August 2011.

13. Statistics and other information from CIA, *The World Factbook*, https://www.cia.gov/library/publications/the-world-factbook/, accessed June 2011; and "Trilateral Trade Between the NAFTA Partners," www.economia-snci.gob.mx/sic_php/pages/files_varios/.../Can_Mar11.pdf, May 2011, p. 5.

14. See CIA, *The World Factbook*, https://www.cia.gov/library/publications/the-world-factbook/, accessed June 2011; and www.comunidadandina.org/ingles/sudamerican.htm, accessed July 2011.

15. Adapted from information found in Bruce Einhorn, "Alan Mulally's Asian Sales Call," *Bloomberg Businessweek*, April 12, 2010, pp. 41–43; and "Ford, Volkswagen Eye Up North India to Set Up New Facilities," *Businessline*, December 8, 2010, p. 1. See also, "India's Hottest Selling Cars in May," *Rediff.com*, June 21, 2011, www.rediff.com/business/slide-show/slide-show-1-auto-a-look-at-top-selling-cars-in-may/20110621.htm.

16. See "Venezuela: Key Developments," *EIU ViewsWire,* July 1, 2011; Leticia Lozano, "Trade Disputes Roil South American Nations," *Journal of Commerce*, January 18, 2010, www.joc.com/breakbulk/trade-disputes-roil-south-american-nations; and "Welcome to the U.S. Commercial Service Venezuela," www.buyusa.gov/venezuela/en/, accessed October 2011.

17. See "$9 Billion Barter Deal," *BarterNews.com*, April 19, 2008, accessed at www.barternews.com/9_billion_dollar_barter_deal.htm; David Pilling, "Africa Builds as Beijing Scrambles to Invest," *Financial Times*, December 10, 2009, p. 11; and International Reciprocal Trade Association, www.irta.com/modern-trade-a-barter.html, accessed June 2011.

18. For these and other examples, see Emma Hall, "Do You Know Your Rites? BBDO Does," *Advertising Age*, May 21, 2007, p. 22.

19. Jamie Bryan, "The Mintz Dynasty," *Fast Company*, April 2006, pp. 56–61; Viji Sundaram, "Offensive Durga Display Dropped," *India-West*, February 2006, p. A1; and Emily Bryson York and Rupal Parekh, "Burger King's MO: Offend, Earn Media, Apologize, Repeat," *Advertising Age*, July 8, 2009, accessed at http://adage.com/print?article_id=137801.

20. For these and other examples, see "Managing Quality Across the (Global) Organization, Its Stakeholders, Suppliers, and

Customers," Chartered Quality Institute, www.thecqi.org/ Knowledge-Hub/Knowledge-portal/Corporate-strategy/ Managing-quality-globally/, accessed August 2011.

21. Adapted from information found in David Pierson, "A Beijing Theme Park with Futons," *Los Angeles Times,* August 25, 2009, p. A1; and Michael Wei, "In IKEA's China Stores, Loitering Is Encouraged," *Bloomberg Businessweek,* November 1, 2010, pp. 22–23.

22. Andres Martinez, "The Next American Century," *Time*, March 22, 2010, p. 1.

23. Thomas L. Friedman, *The Lexus and the Olive Tree: Understanding Globalization* (New York: Anchor Books, 2000).

24. "BrandZ Top Global Brands 2011," Millward Brown Optimor, www.millwardbrown.com/Libraries/Optimor_BrandZ_Files/2011_ BrandZ_Top100_Chart.sflb.ashx, accessed August 2011.

25. Eric Ellis, "Iran's Cola War," *Fortune*, March 5, 2007, pp. 35–38; and Herb Keinon, "Iran Launches Campaign to Boycott 'Zionist' Brands, Coca-Cola, IBM and Intel Are on Ahmadinejad's No-Buy List," *Jerusalem Post,* July 1, 2010, p. 1.

26. Duane Stanford, "Can Coke Surpass Its Record High of $88 a Share?" *Bloomberg Businessweek,* June 2, 2011, p. 1.

27. Barney Jopson and Andrew England, "Walmart to Apply 'Sweat and Muscle' to Africa," *Financial Times,* June 5, 2011, p. 18; and Emma Hall, "Marketers, Agencies Eye Booming Africa for Expansion," *Advertising Age,* June 13, 2011, p. 28.

28. "Doubletree by Hilton Expands M.E. Portfolio with Jordan Deal," *Hotel Interactive,* June 4, 2010, www.hotelinteractive.com/ article.aspx?articleid=17191.

29. Example adapted from "Campbell Soup Company and Swire Pacific Form Joint Venture in China," *BusinessWire,* January 12, 2011, www.businesswire.com/news/home/20110112005834/en/ Campbell-Soup-Company-Swire-Pacific-Form-Joint.

30. John Riberio, "HP Regains Top Position in India's PC Market," *Computerworld*, February 17, 2011, www.computerworld.com .au/article/377104/hp_regains_top_position_india_pc_market/.

31. Quotes from Andrew McMains, "To Compete Globally, Brands Must Adapt," *Adweek*, September 25, 2008, accessed at www .adweek.com; Pankaj Ghemawat, "Regional Strategies for Global Leadership," *Harvard Business Review*, December 2005, pp. 97–108; Eric Pfanner, "The Myth of the Global Brand," *New York Times*, January 11, 2009, www.nytimes.com. Also see Pankej Ghemawat, "Finding Your Strategy in the New Landscape," *Harvard Business Review*, March 2010, pp. 54–60.

32. See Warren J. Keegan and Mark C. Green, *Global Marketing*, 6th ed. (Upper Saddle River, NJ: Prentice Hall, 2011), pp. 314–321.

33. James R. Healey, "Fiat 500: Little Car Shoulders Huge Responsibility in U.S.; Retro Cutie Had to Be Redone from Inside Out for Sale Here," *USA Today*, June 1, 2011, p. B1.

34. See "Easier Said Than Done," *The Economist*, April 15, 2010, www.economist.com/node/15879299; and Normandy Madden, "In China, Multinationals Forgo Adaptation for New-Brand Creation," *Advertising Age*, January 17, 2011, p. 10.

35. "Nokia Still Dominant in Africa in Market Share," *Celebrating Progress Africa*, June 12, 2011, www.cp-africa.com/2011/06/12/ nokia-still-dominant-in-africa-in-market-share-ad-impressions; and "Nokia Still a Hot Brand among Indian Consumers: Survey," *The Press Trust of India,* July 10, 2011.

36. Emma Hall, "Marketers, Agencies Eye Booming Africa for Expansion," *Advertising Age,* June 13, 2011, p. 28; and Liz Gooch, "The Biggest Thing Since China: Global Companies Awake to the Muslim Consumer, and Marketers Follow Suit," *International Herald Tribune,* August 12, 2010, p. 1.

37. See George E. Belch and Michael A. Belch, *Advertising and Promotion: An Integrated Marketing Communications Perspective,* 7th ed. (New York: McGraw Hill, 2007), Chapter 20; Shintero Okazaki and Charles R. Taylor, "What Is SMS Advertising and Why Do Multinationals Adopt It?" *Journal of Business Research*, January 2008, pp. 4–12; and Warren J. Keegan and Mark C. Green, *Global Marketing*, 6th ed. (Upper Saddle River, NJ: Prentice Hall, 2011), pp. 413–415.

38. For these and other examples, see Normandy Madden, "In China, Multinationals Forgo Adaptation for New-Brand Creation," *Advertising Age,* January 17, 2011, p. 10; and Cristina Drafta, "Levi Strauss Targets Asia with Denizen," *EverythingPR,* May 16, 2011, www.pamil-visions.net/denizen/228239/.

39. Adapted from Jack Ewing, "First Mover in Mobile: How It's Selling Cell Phones to the Developing World," *BusinessWeek*, May 14, 2007, p. 60; with information from "Nokia's Market Share Troubles to Hit Profits," *Reuters*, January 19, 2011, www.reuters .com/article/2011/01/19/us-nokia-idUSTRE70I25P20110119.

40. See "Coca-Cola Rolls Out New Distribution Model with ZAP," *ZAP*, January 23, 2008, www.zapworld.com/zap-coca-cola-truck; and Jane Nelson, Eriko Ishikawa, and Alexis Geaneotes, "Developing Inclusive Business Models: A Review of Coca-Cola's Manual Distribution Centers in Ethiopia and Tanzania," Harvard Kennedy School, 2009, www.hks.harvard.edu/m-rcbg/CSRI/ publications/other_10_MDC_report.pdf. For some interesting photos of Coca-Cola distribution methods in third-world and emerging markets, see www.flickr.com/photos/73509998@N00/ sets/72157594299144032/, accessed October 2011.

41. Adapted from information found in Bart Becht, "Building a Company without Borders," *Harvard Business Review*, April 2010, p. 103–106; and www.rb.com/Investors-media/Investor-information, accessed October 2011.

Chapter 16

1. Quotes and other information from or adapted from Andrew Saunders, "Paul Polman of Unilever," *Management Today*, March 2011, pp. 42–47; "Our Sustainability Strategy," www .unilever.com/sustainability/introduction/vision/index.aspx, accessed August 2011; "Sustainable Development Report," www.unilever .com/sustainability/introduction/?WT.LHNAV=Sustainability_at_ Unilever, accessed August 2011; and various annual reports and other documents found at www.unilever.com, accessed October 2011.

2. The figure and the discussion in this section are adapted from Philip Kotler, Gary Armstrong, Veronica Wong, and John Saunders, *Principles of Marketing: European Edition*, 5th ed. (London: Pearson Publishing, 2009), Chapter 2.

3. McDonald's financial information and other facts from www.aboutmcdonalds.com/mcd/investors.html and www .aboutmcdonalds.com/mcd, accessed October 2011.

4. Adapted from information in Patrick Corcoran, "Vitaminwater Awash in Accusations of Deceptive Advertising," *FairWarning,* February 14, 2011, www.fairwarning.org/2011/02/vitaminwater-awash-in-accusations-of-deceptive-advertising/; and "Consumer Group Urges FTC to Halt Vitamin Water Is Outlandish Claims," *International Business Times*, February 4, 2011, http://m.ibtimes .com/coca-cola-vitaminwater-advertising-national-washington-consumers-league-ftc-flu-shots-108891.html.

5. See Jennifer Corbett Dooren, "One-Third of American Adults Are Obese, but Rate Slows," *Wall Street Journal*, February 8, 2010; and "Overweight and Obesity," Centers for Disease Control and

Prevention, www.cdc.gov/nccdphp/dnpa/obesity/trend/index.htm, accessed July 2011.

6. For more on perceived obsolescence, see Annie Leonard, *The Story of Stuff* (New York: Free Press, 2010), pp. 162–163; and www.storyofstuff.com, accessed September 2011.

7. Dan Pashman, "Planned Obsolescence-Induced Insanity (Or: Damn You Steve Jobs! Why Must You Torment Me?!)," *National Public Radio*, September 6, 2007, www.npr.org/blogs/bryantpark/2007/09/planned_obsolescenceinduced_in_1.html. For more discussion, see "Apple's Latest 'Innovation' Is Turning Planned Obsolescence into Planned Failure," *iFixIt.com*, January 20, 2011, www.ifixit.com/blog/blog/2011/01/20/apples-latest-innovation-is-turning-planned-obsolescence-into-planned-failure/.

8. See Karen Auge, "Planting Seed in Food Deserts: Neighborhood Gardens, Produce in Corner Stores," *Denver Post*, April 18, 2010, p. 1; Nanci Hellmich and Melanie Eversley, "First Lady Teams Up with Grocers Nationwide," *USA Today*, July 13, 2011; and "Supermarket Campaign: Improving Access to Supermarkets in Underserved Communities," *The Food Trust*, www.thefoodtrust.org/php/programs/super.market.campaign.php, accessed August 2011.

9. Richard J. Varey, "Marketing Means and Ends for a Sustainable Society: A Welfare Agenda for Transformative Change," *Journal of Macromarketing*, June 2010, pp. 112–126.

10. See "The Story of Stuff," www.storyofstuff.com, accessed October 2011.

11. "The American Dream Has Been Revised Not Reversed," *Business Wire*, March 9, 2009; Connor Dougherty and Elizabeth Holmes, "Consumer Spending Perks Up Economy," *Wall Street Journal*, March 13, 2010, p. A1; and John Gerzema, "How U.S. Consumers Are Steering the Spend Shift," *Advertising Age*, October 11, 2010, p. 26.

12. See "Economic Recovery Bringing Renewed Congestion Growth," *Texas Transportation Institute*, January 20, 2011, http://mobility.tamu.edu/ums/media_information/press_release.stm.

13. See www.tfl.gov.uk/roadusers/congestioncharging/6710.aspx, accessed October 2011.

14. See Martin Sipkoff, "Four-Dollar Pricing Considered Boom or Bust," *Drug Topics*, August 2008, p. 4S; and Sarah Bruyn Jones, "Economic Survival Guide: Drug Discounts Common Now," *McClatchy-Tribune Business News*, February 23, 2009; and http://i.walmartimages.com/i/if/hmp/fusion/customer_list.pdf, accessed October 2011.

15. Celia Cole, "Overconsumption Is Costing Us the Earth and Human Happiness," *The Guardian*, June 21, 2010, www.guardian.co.uk/environment/2010/jun/21/overconsumption-environment-relationships-annie-leonard.

16. See Jack Neff, "Green-Marketing Revolution Defies Economic Downturn," *Advertising Age*, April 20, 2009, p. 2; Ben Jacklet, "Energy Hog Intel Hones Green-Power Strategy," *Oregon Business*, March 2010, p. 14; and "UPS Corporate Responsibility: Alternative Fuels," http://responsibility.ups.com/Environment/Alternative+Fuels, accessed August 2011.

17. See Sara Snow, "Green Eyes On: A Visit to a Zero Landfill Subaru Plant," *Treehugger*, May 4, 2010, accessed at www.treehugger.com/files/2010/05/green-eyes-on-subaru-plant.php; and Roben Farzad, "Subaru of Indiana, America's Scrappiest Carmaker," *Bloomberg Businessweek*, June 6, 2011, p. 68.

18. See Alan S. Brown, "The Many Shades of Green," *Mechanical Engineering*, January 2009, http://memagazine.asme.org/Articles/2009/January/Many_Shades_Green.cfm; and www.ibm.com/ibm/environment/products/recycling.shtml, accessed October 2011.

19. Based on information from Simon Houpt, "Beyond the Bottle: Coke Trumpets Its Green Initiatives," *Globe and Mail (Toronto)*, January 13, 2011; Marc Gunther, "Coca-Cola's Green Crusader," *Fortune*, April 28, 2008, p. 150; "Coca-Cola to Install 1,800 CO_2 Coolers in North America," April 30, 2009, www.r744.com/articles/2009-04-30-coca-cola-to-install-1800-co2-coolers-in-north-america.php; Tim Nudd, "Coca-Cola's Green Billboard Made of Plants That Absorb Air Pollution," *Adweek*, June 27, 2011, www.adweek.com/adfreak/coca-colas-green-billboard-made-plants-absorb-air-pollution-132966; and "The Business of Recycling," www.thecoca-colacompany.com/citizenship/environment_case_studies.html, accessed October 2011.

20. See "2011 Global 100 Most Sustainable Companies," www.global100.org, accessed August 2011; and www.jnj.com/connect/about-jnj/jnj-credo/ and www.jnj.com/connect/caring/environment-protection/, accessed October 2011.

21. See Geoffrey Garver and Aranka Podhora, "Transboundary Environmental Impact Assessment as Part of the North American Agreement on Environmental Cooperation," *Impact Assessment & Project Appraisal*, December 2008, pp. 253–263; http://ec.europa.eu/environment/index_en.htm, accessed August 2011; and "What Is EMAS?" http://ec.europa.eu/environment/emas/index_en.htm, accessed October 2011.

22. Based on information found in Chuck Salter, "Fast 50: The World's Most Innovative Companies," *Fast Company*, March 2008, pp. 73+. Also see Yukari Iwatani Kane and Daisuke Wakabayashi, "Nintendo Looks Outside the Box," *Wall Street Journal*, May 27, 2009, p. B5.

23. Information from Mark Borden, "The World's 50 Most Innovative Companies: #36: Samsung," *Fast Company*, February 17, 2010, p. 90; Laurie Burkitt, "Samsung's Big Spend," *Forbes*, June 7, 2010, p. 60; and Tarun Khanna, Jaeyong Song, and Kyungmook Lee, "The Paradox of Samsung's Rise," *Harvard Business Review*, July–August 2011, pp. 142–147.

24. Information from Eleftheria Parpis, "Must Love Dogs," *Adweek*, February 18, 2008, accessed at www.adweek.com; and www.pedigree.com and www.mars.com/global/global-brands/pedigree.aspx, accessed October 2011.

25. See "Our Reason for Being," www.patagonia.com/web/us/patagonia.go?slc=en_US&sct=US&assetid=2047, accessed November 2011.

26. Information from www.toggerycollection.com/about/ and www.haworth.com/en-us/Products/Furniture/Seating/Desk/Pages/Zody.aspx, accessed August 2011.

27. Nanette Byrnes, "Pepsi Brings in the Health Police," *Bloomberg Businessweek*, January 25, 2010, pp. 50–51; and Mike Esterl, "You Put What in This Chip?" *Wall Street Journal*, March 24, 2011, p. D1.

28. Adapted from material found in Jeff Heilman, "Rules of Engagement," *The Magazine of Branded Engagement*, Winter 2009, pp. 7–8; and "Mattel's The Playground Community Created by Communispace Helps Them Weather Recall," accessed at www.communispace.com/uploadedFiles/Clients_Section/Forrester_Groundswell/Groundswell_Mattel.pdf, August 2011.

29. See The World Bank, "The Costs of Corruption," April 8, 2004, accessed at http://tinyurl.com/ytavm; "Bribe Payers Index 2008," *Transparency International*, www.transparency.org/policy_research/surveys_indices/bpi; and "Global Corruption Barometer 2010," *Transparency International*, www.transparency.org/policy_research/surveys_indices/gcb/2010. Also see Michael Montgomery, "The Cost of Corruption," *American RadioWorks*, http://americanradioworks.publicradio.org/features/corruption/, accessed June 2011.

30. See www.marketingpower.com/AboutAMA/Pages/Statement%20of%20Ethics.aspx, accessed November 2011.

31. See Samuel A. DiPiazza, Jr., "Ethics in Action," *Executive Excellence*, January 2002, pp. 15–16; "Interview: Why Have a Code?" accessed at www.pwc.com/gx/en/ethics-business-conduct/why-have-a-code-interview.jhtml, August 2011; Samuel A. DiPiazza Jr., "It's All Down to Personal Values," August 2003, accessed at www.hollywoodreporter.com/hr/search/article_display.jsp?vnu_content_id=2000910; and "Ethics and Business Conduct," www.pwc.com/ethics, accessed November 2011.

32. DiPiazza, "Ethics in Action," p. 15.

33. David A. Lubin and Daniel C. Esty, "The Sustainability Imperative," *Harvard Business Review*, May 2010, pp. 41–50; and Roasbeth Moss Kanter, "It's Time to Take Full Responsibility," *Harvard Business Review*, October 2010, p. 42.

Appendix 3

1. This is derived by rearranging the following equation and solving for price: Percentage markup = (price − cost) ÷ price.

2. Again, using the basic profit equation, we set profit equal to ROI × I: $ROI \times I = (P \times Q) - TFC - (Q \times UVC)$. Solving for Q gives $Q = (TFC + (ROI \times I)) \div (P - UVC)$.

3. U.S. Census Bureau, available at www.census.gov/prod/1/pop/p25-1129.pdf, accessed October 26, 2009.

4. See Roger J. Best, *Market-Based Management,* 4th ed. (Upper Saddle River, NJ: Prentice Hall, 2005).

5. Total contribution can also be determined from the unit contribution and unit volume: Total contribution = unit contribution × unit sales. Total units sold in 2012 were 595,238 units, which can be determined by dividing total sales by price per unit ($100 million ÷ $168). Total contribution = $35.28 contribution per unit × 595,238 units = $20,999,996.64 (difference due to rounding).

6. Recall that the contribution margin of 21 percent was based on variable costs representing 79 percent of sales. Therefore, if we do not know price, we can set it equal to $1.00. If price equals $1.00, 79 cents represents variable costs and 21 cents represents unit contribution. If price is decreased by 10 percent, the new price is $0.90. However, variable costs do not change just because price decreased, so the unit contribution and contribution margin decrease as follows:

	Old	New (reduced 10 percent)
Price	$1. 00	$0.90
− Unit variable cost	$0.79	$0.79
= Unit contribution	$0.21	$0.11
Contribution margin	$0.21/$1.00 = 0.21 or 21%	$0.11/$0.90 = 0.12 or 12%

Glossary

Adapted global marketing An international marketing approach that adjusts the marketing strategy and mix elements to each international target market, which creates more costs but hopefully produces a larger market share and return.

Administered VMS A vertical marketing system that coordinates successive stages of production and distribution through the size and power of one of the parties.

Adoption process The mental process through which an individual passes from first hearing about an innovation to final adoption.

Advertising Any paid form of nonpersonal presentation and promotion of ideas, goods, or services by an identified sponsor.

Advertising agency A marketing services firm that assists companies in planning, preparing, implementing, and evaluating all or portions of their advertising programs.

Advertising budget The dollars and other resources allocated to a product or a company advertising program.

Advertising media The vehicles through which advertising messages are delivered to their intended audiences.

Advertising objective A specific communication *task* to be accomplished with a specific *target* audience during a specific period of *time*.

Advertising strategy The plan by which the company accomplishes its advertising objectives. It consists of two major elements: creating advertising messages and selecting advertising media.

Affordable method Setting the promotion budget at the level management thinks the company can afford.

Age and life-cycle segmentation Dividing a market into different age and life-cycle groups.

Agent A wholesaler who represents buyers or sellers on a relatively permanent basis, performs only a few functions, and does not take title to goods.

Allowance A reduction from the list price for buyer actions such as trade-ins or promotional and sales support.

Approach The sales step in which a salesperson meets the customer for the first time.

Attitude A person's consistently favorable or unfavorable evaluations, feelings, and tendencies toward an object or idea.

Baby boomers The 78 million people born during the years following World War II and lasting until 1964.

Behavioral segmentation Dividing a market into segments based on consumer knowledge, attitudes, uses, or responses to a product.

Belief A descriptive thought that a person holds about something.

Benefit segmentation Dividing the market into segments according to the different benefits that consumers seek from the product.

Blogs Online journals where people post their thoughts, usually on a narrowly defined topic.

Brand A name, term, sign, symbol, or design, or a combination of these, that identifies the products or services of one seller or group of sellers and differentiates them from those of competitors.

Brand equity The differential effect that knowing the brand name has on customer response to the product or its marketing.

Brand extension Extending an existing brand name to new product categories.

Break-even analysis Analysis to determine the unit volume and dollar sales needed to be profitable given a particular price and cost structure.

Break-even price The price at which total revenue equals total cost and profit is zero.

Break-even pricing (target return pricing) Setting price to break even on the costs of making and marketing a product, or setting price to make a target return.

Broker A wholesaler who does not take title to goods and whose function is to bring buyers and sellers together and assist in negotiation.

Business analysis A review of the sales, costs, and profit projections for a new product to find out whether these factors satisfy the company's objectives.

Business buyer behavior The buying behavior of organizations that buy goods and services for use in the production of other products and services that are sold, rented, or supplied to others.

Business buying process The decision process by which business buyers determine which products and services their organizations need to purchase and then find, evaluate, and choose among alternative suppliers and brands.

Business portfolio The collection of businesses and products that make up the company.

Business promotions Sales promotion tools used to generate business leads, stimulate purchases, reward customers, and motivate salespeople.

Business-to-business (B-to-B) online marketing Businesses using online marketing to reach new business customers, serve current customers more effectively, and obtain buying efficiencies and better prices.

Business-to-consumer (B-to-C) online marketing Businesses selling goods and services online to final consumers.

Buying center All the individuals and units that play a role in the purchase decision-making process.

By-product pricing Setting a price for by-products to make the main product's price more competitive.

Cannibalization The situation in which one product sold by a company takes a portion of its sales from other company products.

Captive product pricing Setting a price for products that must be used along with a main product, such as blades for a razor and games for a videogame console.

Catalog marketing Direct marketing through print, video, or digital catalogs that are mailed to select customers, made available in stores, or presented online.

Category killer A giant specialty store that carries a very deep assortment of a particular line.

Causal research Marketing research used to test hypotheses about cause-and-effect relationships.

Chain ratio method Estimating market demand by multiplying a base number by a chain of adjusting percentages.

Channel conflict Disagreements among marketing channel members on goals, roles, and rewards—who should do what and for what rewards.

Channel level A layer of intermediaries that performs some work in bringing the product and its ownership closer to the final buyer.

Click-and-mortar companies Traditional brick-and-mortar companies that have added online marketing to their operations.

Click-only companies The so-called dot-coms, which operate online only and have no brick-and-mortar market presence.

Closing The sales step in which a salesperson asks the customer for an order.

Co-branding The practice of using the established brand names of two different companies on the same product.

Cognitive dissonance Buyer discomfort caused by postpurchase conflict.

Commercialization Introducing a new product into the market.

Communication adaptation A global communication strategy of fully adapting advertising messages to local markets.

Competition-based pricing Setting prices based on competitors' strategies, prices, costs, and market offerings.

Competitive advantage An advantage over competitors gained by offering greater customer value, either by having lower prices or providing more benefits that justify higher prices.

Competitive marketing intelligence The systematic collection and analysis of publicly available information about consumers, competitors, and developments in the marketing environment.

Competitive-parity method Setting the promotion budget to match competitors' outlays.

Concentrated (niche) marketing A market-coverage strategy in which a firm goes after a large share of one or a few segments or niches.

Concept testing Testing new-product concepts with a group of target consumers to find out if the concepts have strong consumer appeal.

Consumer buyer behavior The buying behavior of final consumers—individuals and households that buy goods and services for personal consumption.

Consumer-generated marketing Brand exchanges created by consumers themselves—both invited and uninvited—by which consumers are playing an increasing role in shaping their own brand experiences and those of other consumers.

Consumerism An organized movement of citizens and government agencies designed to improve the rights and power of buyers in relation to sellers.

Consumer-oriented marketing A principle of sustainable marketing that holds a company should view and organize its marketing activities from the consumer's point of view.

Consumer market All the individuals and households that buy or acquire goods and services for personal consumption.

Consumer product A product bought by final consumers for personal consumption.

Consumer promotions Sales promotion tools used to boost short-term customer buying and involvement or enhance long-term customer relationships.

Consumer-to-business (C-to-B) online marketing Online exchanges in which consumers search out sellers, learn about their offers, initiate purchases, and sometimes even drive transaction terms.

Consumer-to-consumer (C-to-C) online marketing Online exchanges of goods and information between final consumers.

Contract manufacturing A joint venture in which a company contracts with manufacturers in a foreign market to produce the product or provide its service.

Contractual VMS A vertical marketing system in which independent firms at different levels of production and distribution join together through contracts.

Contribution margin The unit contribution divided by the selling price.

Convenience product A consumer product that customers usually buy frequently, immediately, and with minimal comparison and buying effort.

Convenience store A small store, located near a residential area, that is open long hours seven days a week and carries a limited line of high-turnover convenience goods.

Conventional distribution channel A channel consisting of one or more independent producers, wholesalers, and retailers, each a separate business seeking to maximize its own profits, perhaps even at the expense of profits for the system as a whole.

Corporate (or brand) Web site A Web site designed to build customer goodwill, collect customer feedback, and supplement other sales channels rather than sell the company's products directly.

Corporate chains Two or more outlets that are commonly owned and controlled.

Corporate VMS A vertical marketing system that combines successive stages of production and distribution under single ownership—channel leadership is established through common ownership.

Cost-based pricing Setting prices based on the costs for producing, distributing, and selling the product plus a fair rate of return for effort and risk.

Cost-plus pricing (or markup pricing) A standard markup to the cost of the product.

Creative concept The compelling *big idea* that will bring the advertising message strategy to life in a distinctive and memorable way.

Crowdsourcing Inviting broad communities of people—customers, employees, independent scientists and researchers, and even the public at large—into the new-product innovation process.

Cultural environment Institutions and other forces that affect society's basic values, perceptions, preferences, and behaviors.

Culture The set of basic values, perceptions, wants, and behaviors learned by a member of society from family and other important institutions.

Customer database An organized collection of comprehensive data about individual customers or prospects, including geographic, demographic, psychographic, and behavioral data.

Customer equity The total combined customer lifetime values of all of the company's customers.

Customer insights Fresh understandings of customers and the marketplace derived from marketing information that becomes the basis for creating customer value and relationships.

Customer lifetime value The value of the entire stream of purchases a customer makes over a lifetime of patronage.

Customer relationship management The overall process of building and maintaining profitable customer relationships by delivering superior customer value and satisfaction.

Customer relationship management (CRM) Managing detailed information about individual customers and carefully managing customer touch points to maximize customer loyalty.

Customer (or market) sales force structure A sales force organization in which salespeople specialize in selling only to certain customers or industries.

Customer satisfaction The extent to which a product's perceived performance matches a buyer's expectations.

Customer value-based pricing Setting price based on buyers' perceptions of value rather than on the seller's cost.

Customer-centered new-product development New-product development that focuses on finding new ways to solve customer problems and create more customer-satisfying experiences.

Customer-managed relationships Marketing relationships in which customers, empowered by today's new digital technologies, interact with companies and with each other to shape their relationships with brands.

Customer-perceived value The customer's evaluation of the difference between all the benefits and all the costs of a marketing offer relative to those of competing offers.

Customer-value marketing A principle of sustainable marketing that holds a company should put most of its resources into customer-value-building marketing investments.

Decline stage The PLC stage in which a product's sales fade away.

Deficient products Products that have neither immediate appeal nor long-run benefits.

Demand curve A curve that shows the number of units the market will buy in a given time period, at different prices that might be charged.

Demands Human wants that are backed up by buying power.

Demographic segmentation Dividing the market into segments based on variables such as age, life-cycle stage, gender, income, occupation, education, religion, ethnicity, and generation.

Demography The study of human populations in terms of size, density, location, age, gender, race, occupation, and other statistics.

Department store A retail store that carries a wide variety of product lines, each operated as a separate department managed by specialist buyers or merchandisers.

Derived demand   The business demand for products and services that ultimately derives from the demand for consumer goods.

Descriptive research   Marketing research used to better describe marketing problems, situations, or markets.

Desirable products   Products that give both high immediate satisfaction and high long-run benefits.

Differentiated (segmented) marketing   A market-coverage strategy in which a firm decides to target several market segments and designs separate offers for each.

Differentiation   Actually differentiating the market offering to create superior customer value.

Direct investment   Entering a foreign market by developing foreign-based assembly or manufacturing facilities.

Direct-mail marketing   Marketing that occurs by sending an offer, announcement, reminder, or other item directly to a person at a particular address.

Direct marketing   Connecting directly with carefully targeted segments or individual consumers, often on a one-to-one, interactive basis.

Direct marketing channel   A marketing channel that has no intermediary levels.

Direct-response television (DRTV) marketing   Direct marketing via television, including direct-response television advertising (or infomercials) and interactive television (iTV) advertising.

Discount   A straight reduction in price on purchases made during a stated period of time or in larger quantities.

Discount store   A retail operation that sells standard merchandise at lower prices by accepting lower margins and selling at higher volume.

Disintermediation   The cutting out of marketing channel intermediaries by product or service producers or the displacement of traditional resellers by radical new types of intermediaries.

Distribution center   A large, highly automated warehouse designed to receive goods from various plants and suppliers, take orders, fill them efficiently, and deliver goods to customers as quickly as possible.

Diversification   Company growth through starting up or acquiring businesses outside the company's current products and markets.

Dynamic pricing   Adjusting prices continually to meet the characteristics and needs of individual customers and situations.

E-mail marketing   Sending highly targeted, tightly personalized, relationship-building marketing messages via e-mail.

E-procurement   Purchasing performed through electronic connections between buyers and sellers—usually online.

Economic community   A group of nations organized to work toward common goals in the regulation of international trade.

Economic environment   Economic factors that affect consumer purchasing power and spending patterns.

Environmental sustainability   A management approach that involves developing strategies that both sustain the environment and produce profits for the company.

Environmental sustainability   Developing strategies and practices that create a world economy that the planet can support indefinitely.

Environmentalism   An organized movement of concerned citizens and government agencies designed to protect and improve people's current and future living environment.

Ethnographic research   A form of observational research that involves sending trained observers to watch and interact with consumers in their "natural environments."

Event marketing (or event sponsorships)   Creating a brand-marketing event or serving as a sole or participating sponsor of events created by others.

Exchange   The act of obtaining a desired object from someone by offering something in return.

Exclusive distribution   Giving a limited number of dealers the exclusive right to distribute the company's products in their territories.

Execution style   The approach, style, tone, words, and format used for executing (properly conveying) an advertising message.

Experimental research   Gathering primary data by selecting matched groups of subjects, giving them different treatments, controlling related factors, and checking for differences in group responses.

Exploratory research   Marketing research used to gather preliminary information that will help define problems and suggest hypotheses.

Exporting   Entering foreign markets by selling goods produced in the company's home country, often with little modification.

Factory outlet   An off-price retailing operation that is owned and operated by a manufacturer and normally carries the manufacturer's surplus, discontinued, or irregular goods.

Fad   A temporary period of unusually high sales driven by consumer enthusiasm and immediate product or brand popularity.

Fashion   A currently accepted or popular style in a given field.

Fixed costs (overhead)   Costs that do not vary with production or sales level.

Focus group interviewing   Personal interviewing that involves inviting six to ten people to gather for a few hours with a trained interviewer to talk about a product, service, or organization. The interviewer "focuses" the group discussion on important issues.

Follow-up The sales step in which a salesperson follows up after the sale to ensure customer satisfaction and repeat business.

Franchise A contractual association between a manufacturer, wholesaler, or service organization (a franchisor) and independent businesspeople (franchisees) who buy the right to own and operate one or more units in the franchise system.

Franchise organization A contractual vertical marketing system in which a channel member, called a franchisor, links several stages in the production-distribution process.

Gender segmentation Dividing a market into different segments based on gender.

Generation X The 49 million people born between 1965 and 1976 in the "birth dearth" following the baby boom.

Geographic segmentation Dividing a market into different geographical units, such as nations, states, regions, counties, cities, or even neighborhoods.

Global firm A firm that, by operating in more than one country, gains R&D, production, marketing, and financial advantages in its costs and reputation that are not available to purely domestic competitors.

Good-value pricing Offering the right combination of quality and good service at a fair price.

Gross margin percentage The percentage of net sales remaining after cost of goods sold—calculated by dividing gross margin by net sales.

Group Two or more people who interact to accomplish individual or mutual goals.

Growth-share matrix A portfolio-planning method that evaluates a company's SBUs in terms of its market growth rate and relative market share.

Growth stage The PLC stage in which a product's sales start climbing quickly.

Handling objections The sales step in which a salesperson seeks out, clarifies, and overcomes any customer objections to buying.

Horizontal marketing system A channel arrangement in which two or more companies at one level join together to follow a new marketing opportunity.

Idea generation The systematic search for new-product ideas.

Idea screening Screening new-product ideas to spot good ideas and drop poor ones as soon as possible.

Income segmentation Dividing a market into different income segments.

Independent off-price retailer An off-price retailer that is either independently owned and run or is a division of a larger retail corporation.

Indirect marketing channel A marketing channel containing one or more intermediary levels.

Individual marketing Tailoring products and marketing programs to the needs and preferences of individual customers.

Industrial product A product bought by individuals and organizations for further processing or for use in conducting a business.

Innovative marketing A principle of sustainable marketing that requires a company to seek real product and marketing improvements.

Inside sales force Salespeople who conduct business from their offices via telephone, the Internet, or visits from prospective buyers.

Integrated logistics management The logistics concept that emphasizes teamwork—both inside the company and among all the marketing channel organizations—to maximize the performance of the entire distribution system.

Integrated marketing communications (IMC) Carefully integrating and coordinating the company's many communications channels to deliver a clear, consistent, and compelling message about the organization and its products.

Intensive distribution Stocking the product in as many outlets as possible.

Interactive marketing Training service employees in the fine art of interacting with customers to satisfy their needs.

Intermarket (or cross market) segmentation Forming segments of consumers who have similar needs and buying behaviors even though they are located in different countries.

Intermodal transportation Combining two or more modes of transportation.

Internal databases Electronic collections of consumer and market information obtained from data sources within the company network.

Internal marketing Orienting and motivating customer-contact employees and service-support people to work as a team to provide customer satisfaction.

Internet A vast public web of computer networks that connects users of all types all around the world to each other and to an amazingly large information repository.

Introduction stage The PLC stage in which a new product is first distributed and made available for purchase.

Inventory turnover rate (or stockturn rate) The number of times an inventory turns over or is sold during a specified time period (often one year)—calculated based on costs, selling price, or units.

Joint ownership   A cooperative venture in which a company creates a local business with investors in a foreign market, who share ownership and control.

Joint venturing   Entering foreign markets by joining with foreign companies to produce or market a product or service.

Learning   Changes in an individual's behavior arising from experience.

Licensing   Entering foreign markets through developing an agreement with a licensee in the foreign market.

Lifestyle   A person's pattern of living as expressed in his or her activities, interests, and opinions.

Line extension   Extending an existing brand name to new forms, colors, sizes, ingredients, or flavors of an existing product category.

Local marketing   Tailoring brands and promotions to the needs and wants of local customer segments—cities, neighborhoods, and even specific stores.

Macroenvironment   The larger societal forces that affect the microenvironment—demographic, economic, natural, technological, political, and cultural forces.

Madison & Vine   A term that has come to represent the merging of advertising and entertainment in an effort to break through the clutter and create new avenues for reaching consumers with more engaging messages.

Management contracting   A joint venture in which the domestic firm supplies the management know-how to a foreign company that supplies the capital; the domestic firm exports management services rather than products.

Manufacturers' sales branches and offices   Wholesaling by sellers or buyers themselves rather than through independent wholesalers.

Market   The set of all actual and potential buyers of a product or service.

Market development   Company growth by identifying and developing new market segments for current company products.

Market offerings   Some combination of products, services, information, or experiences offered to a market to satisfy a need or want.

Market penetration   Company growth by increasing sales of current products to current market segments without changing the product.

Market-penetration pricing   Setting a low price for a new product to attract a large number of buyers and a large market share.

Market potential   The upper limit of market demand.

Market segment   A group of consumers who respond in a similar way to a given set of marketing efforts.

Market segmentation   Dividing a market into distinct groups of buyers who have different needs, characteristics, or behaviors, and who might require separate products or marketing programs.

Market share   Company sales divided by market sales.

Market-skimming pricing (or price skimming)   Setting a high price for a new product to skim maximum revenues layer by layer from the segments willing to pay the high price; the company makes fewer but more profitable sales.

Market targeting (or targeting)   The process of evaluating each market segment's attractiveness and selecting one or more segments to enter.

Marketing   The process by which companies create value for customers and build strong customer relationships in order to capture value from customers in return.

Marketing channel (or distribution channel)   A set of interdependent organizations that help make a product or service available for use or consumption by the consumer or business user.

Marketing channel design   Designing effective marketing channels by analyzing customer needs, setting channel objectives, identifying major channel alternatives, and evaluating those alternatives.

Marketing channel management   Selecting, managing, and motivating individual channel members and evaluating their performance over time.

Marketing concept   A philosophy in which achieving organizational goals depends on knowing the needs and wants of target markets and delivering the desired satisfactions better than competitors do.

Marketing control   Measuring and evaluating the results of marketing strategies and plans and taking corrective action to ensure that the objectives are achieved.

Marketing environment   The actors and forces outside marketing that affect marketing management's ability to build and maintain successful relationships with target customers.

Marketing implementation   Turning marketing strategies and plans into marketing actions to accomplish strategic marketing objectives.

Marketing information system (MIS)   People and procedures dedicated to assessing information needs, developing the needed information, and helping decision makers to use the information to generate and validate actionable customer and market insights.

Marketing intermediaries   Firms that help the company to promote, sell, and distribute its goods to final buyers.

Marketing logistics (or physical distribution)   Planning, implementing, and controlling the physical flow of materials, final goods, and related information from points of origin to points of consumption to meet customer requirements at a profit.

Marketing management   The art and science of choosing target markets and building profitable relationships with them.

Marketing mix   The set of tactical marketing tools—product, price, place, and promotion—that the firm blends to produce the response it wants in the target market.

Marketing myopia   The mistake of paying more attention to the specific products a company offers than to the benefits and experiences produced by these products.

Marketing research   The systematic design, collection, analysis, and reporting of data relevant to a specific marketing situation facing an organization.

Marketing return on investment (or marketing ROI)   A measure of the marketing productivity of a marketing investment—calculated by dividing net marketing contribution by marketing expenses.

Marketing return on sales (or marketing ROS)   The percent of net sales attributable to the net marketing contribution—calculated by dividing net marketing contribution by net sales.

Marketing strategy   The marketing logic by which the company hopes to create customer value and achieve profitable customer relationships.

Marketing strategy development   Designing an initial marketing strategy for a new product based on the product concept.

Marketing Web site   A Web site that interacts with consumers to move them closer to a direct purchase or other marketing outcome.

Markup   The difference between a company's selling price for a product and its cost to manufacture or purchase it.

Markup chain   The sequence of markups used by firms at each level in a channel.

Maturity stage   The PLC stage in which a product's sales growth slows or levels off.

Merchant wholesaler   An independently owned wholesale business that takes title to the merchandise it handles.

Microenvironment   The actors close to the company that affect its ability to serve its customers—the company, suppliers, marketing intermediaries, customer markets, competitors, and publics.

Micromarketing   Tailoring products and marketing programs to the needs and wants of specific individuals and local customer segments; it includes *local marketing* and *individual marketing*.

Millennials (or Generation Y)   The 83 million children of the baby boomers born between 1977 and 2000.

Mission statement   A statement of the organization's purpose—what it wants to accomplish in the larger environment.

Mobile marketing   Marketing to on-the-go consumers through mobile phones, smartphones, tablets, and other mobile communication devices.

Modified rebuy   A business buying situation in which the buyer wants to modify product specifications, prices, terms, or suppliers.

Motive (drive)   A need that is sufficiently pressing to direct the person to seek satisfaction of the need.

Multichannel distribution system   A distribution system in which a single firm sets up two or more marketing channels to reach one or more customer segments.

Natural environment   Natural resources that are needed as inputs by marketers or that are affected by marketing activities.

Needs   States of felt deprivation.

Net marketing contribution (NMC)   A measure of marketing profitability that includes only components of profitability controlled by marketing.

Net profit percentage   The percentage of each sales dollar going to profit—calculated by dividing net profits by net sales.

New product   A good, service, or idea that is perceived by some potential customers as new.

New-product development   The development of original products, product improvements, product modifications, and new brands through the firm's own product development efforts.

New task   A business buying situation in which the buyer purchases a product or service for the first time.

Objective-and-task method   Developing the promotion budget by (1) defining specific objectives, (2) determining the tasks that must be performed to achieve these objectives, and (3) estimating the costs of performing these tasks. The sum of these costs is the proposed promotion budget.

Observational research   Gathering primary data by observing relevant people, actions, and situations.

Occasion segmentation   Dividing the market into segments according to occasions when buyers get the idea to buy, actually make their purchase, or use the purchased item.

Off-price retailer   A retailer that buys at less-than-regular wholesale prices and sells at less than retail.

Online advertising   Advertising that appears while consumers are browsing the Web, including display ads, search-related ads, online classifieds, and other forms.

Online focus groups   Gathering a small group of people online with a trained moderator to chat about a product, service, or organization and gain qualitative insights about consumer attitudes and behavior.

Online marketing   Efforts to market products and services and build customer relationships over the Internet.

Online marketing research   Collecting primary data online through Internet surveys, online focus groups, Web-based experiments, or tracking consumers' online behavior.

Online social networks   Online communities where people congregate, socialize, and exchange views and information.

Operating expense percentage The portion of net sales going to operating expenses—calculated by dividing total expenses by net sales.

Operating ratios The ratios of selected operating statement items to net sales.

Opinion leader A person within a reference group who, because of special skills, knowledge, personality, or other characteristics, exerts social influence on others.

Optional product pricing The pricing of optional or accessory products along with a main product.

Outside sales force (or field sales force) Salespeople who travel to call on customers in the field.

Packaging The activities of designing and producing the container or wrapper for a product.

Partner relationship management Working closely with partners in other company departments and outside the company to jointly bring greater value to customers.

Percentage-of-sales method Setting the promotion budget at a certain percentage of current or forecasted sales or as a percentage of the unit sales price.

Perception The process by which people select, organize, and interpret information to form a meaningful picture of the world.

Personal selling Personal presentations by the firm's sales force for the purpose of making sales and building customer relationships.

Personality The unique psychological characteristics that distinguish a person or group.

Pleasing products Products that give high immediate satisfaction but may hurt consumers in the long run.

Political environment Laws, government agencies, and pressure groups that influence and limit various organizations and individuals in a given society.

Portfolio analysis The process by which management evaluates the products and businesses that make up the company.

Positioning Arranging for a market offering to occupy a clear, distinctive, and desirable place relative to competing products in the minds of target consumers.

Positioning statement A statement that summarizes company or brand positioning using this form: To (target segment and need) our (brand) is (concept) that (point of difference).

Preapproach The sales step in which a salesperson learns as much as possible about a prospective customer before making a sales call.

Presentation The sales step in which a salesperson tells the "value story" to the buyer, showing how the company's offer solves the customer's problems.

Price The amount of money charged for a product or service; the sum of the values that customers exchange for the benefits of having or using the product or service.

Price elasticity A measure of the sensitivity of demand to changes in price.

Primary data Information collected for the specific purpose at hand.

Pro forma (or projected) profit-and-loss statement (or income statement or operating statement) A statement that shows projected revenues less budgeted expenses and estimates the projected net profit for an organization, product, or brand during a specific planning period, typically a year.

Product Anything that can be offered to a market for attention, acquisition, use, or consumption that might satisfy a want or need.

Product adaptation Adapting a product to meet local conditions or wants in foreign markets.

Product bundle pricing Combining several products and offering the bundle at a reduced price.

Product concept A detailed version of the new-product idea stated in meaningful consumer terms.

Product concept The idea that consumers will favor products that offer the most quality, performance, and features; therefore, the organization should devote its energy to making continuous product improvements.

Product development Company growth by offering modified or new products to current market segments.

Product development Developing the product concept into a physical product to ensure that the product idea can be turned into a workable market offering.

Product invention Creating new products or services for foreign markets.

Product life cycle (PLC) The course of a product's sales and profits over its lifetime.

Product line A group of products that are closely related because they function in a similar manner, are sold to the same customer groups, are marketed through the same types of outlets, or fall within given price ranges.

Product line pricing Setting the price steps between various products in a product line based on cost differences between the products, customer evaluations of different features, and competitors' prices.

Product mix (or product portfolio) The set of all product lines and items that a particular seller offers for sale.

Product position The way a product is defined by consumers on important attributes—the place the product occupies in consumers' minds relative to competing products.

Product quality The characteristics of a product or service that bear on its ability to satisfy stated or implied customer needs.

Product sales force structure A sales force organization in which salespeople specialize in selling only a portion of the company's products or lines.

Product value analysis Carefully analyzing a product's or service's components to determine if they can be redesigned and made more effectively and efficiently to provide greater value.

Product/market expansion grid A portfolio-planning tool for identifying company growth opportunities through market penetration, market development, product development, or diversification.

Production concept The idea that consumers will favor products that are available and highly affordable; therefore, the organization should focus on improving production and distribution efficiency.

Profit-and-loss statement (or income statement or operating statement) A statement that shows actual revenues less expenses and net profit for an organization, product, or brand during a specific planning period, typically a year.

Promotion mix (or marketing communications mix) The specific blend of promotion tools that the company uses to persuasively communicate customer value and build customer relationships.

Promotional pricing Temporarily pricing products below the list price, and sometimes even below cost, to increase short-run sales.

Prospecting The sales step in which a salesperson or company identifies qualified potential customers.

Psychographic segmentation Dividing a market into different segments based on social class, lifestyle, or personality characteristics.

Psychological pricing Pricing that considers the psychology of prices, not simply the economics; the price says something about the product.

Public Any group that has an actual or potential interest in or impact on an organization's ability to achieve its objectives.

Public relations (PR) Building good relations with the company's various publics by obtaining favorable publicity, building up a good corporate image, and handling or heading off unfavorable rumors, stories, and events.

Pull strategy A promotion strategy in which a company spends a lot of money on consumer advertising and promotion to induce final consumers to buy the product, creating a demand vacuum that *pulls* the product through the channel.

Push strategy A promotion strategy in which the sales force and trade promotion are used to *push* the product through

channels. The producer promotes the product to channel members who in turn promote it to final consumers.

Reference prices Prices that buyers carry in their minds and refer to when they look at a given product.

Relevant costs Costs that will occur in the future and that will vary across the alternatives being considered.

Retailer A business whose sales come *primarily* from retailing.

Retailing All the activities involved in selling goods or services directly to final consumers for their personal, nonbusiness use.

Return on advertising investment The net return on advertising investment divided by the costs of the advertising investment.

Return on investment (ROI) A measure of managerial effectiveness and efficiency—net profit before taxes divided by total investment.

Return on investment (ROI) pricing (or target-return pricing) A cost-based pricing method that determines price based on a specified rate of return on investment.

Return on marketing investment (or marketing ROI) The net return from a marketing investment divided by the costs of the marketing investment.

Sales force management Analyzing, planning, implementing, and controlling sales force activities.

Sales promotion Short-term incentives to encourage the purchase or sales of a product or service.

Sales quota A standard that states the amount a salesperson should sell and how sales should be divided among the company's products.

Salesperson An individual representing a company to customers by performing one or more of the following activities: prospecting, communicating, selling, servicing, information gathering, and relationship building.

Salutary products Products that have low immediate appeal but may benefit consumers in the long run.

Sample A segment of the population selected for marketing research to represent the population as a whole.

Secondary data Information that already exists somewhere, having been collected for another purpose.

Segmented pricing Selling a product or service at two or more prices, where the difference in prices is not based on differences in costs.

Selective distribution The use of more than one but fewer than all of the intermediaries who are willing to carry the company's products.

Selling concept   The idea that consumers will not buy enough of the firm's products unless the firm undertakes a large-scale selling and promotion effort.

Selling process   The steps that salespeople follow when selling, which include prospecting and qualifying, preapproach, approach, presentation and demonstration, handling objections, closing, and follow-up.

Sense-of-mission marketing   A principle of sustainable marketing that holds a company should define its mission in broad social terms rather than narrow product terms.

Service   An activity, benefit, or satisfaction offered for sale that is essentially intangible and does not result in the ownership of anything.

Service inseparability   The concept that services are produced and consumed at the same time and cannot be separated from their providers.

Service intangibility   The concept that services cannot be seen, tasted, felt, heard, or smelled before they are bought.

Service perishability   The concept that services cannot be stored for later sale or use.

Service profit chain   The chain that links service firm profits with employee and customer satisfaction.

Service retailer   A retailer whose product line is actually a service; examples include hotels, airlines, banks, colleges, and many others.

Service variability   The concept that the quality of services may vary greatly depending on who provides them and when, where, and how they are provided.

Share of customer   The portion of the customer's purchasing that a company gets in its product categories.

Shopper marketing   Using point-of-sale promotions and advertising to extend brand equity to "the last mile" and encourage favorable in-store purchase decisions.

Shopping center   A group of retail businesses built on a site that is planned, developed, owned, and managed as a unit.

Shopping product   A consumer product that the customer, in the process of selecting and purchasing, usually compares on such attributes as suitability, quality, price, and style.

Social class   Relatively permanent and ordered divisions in a society whose members share similar values, interests, and behaviors.

Social marketing   The use of commercial marketing concepts and tools in programs designed to influence individuals' behavior to improve their well-being and that of society.

Societal marketing   A principle of sustainable marketing that holds a company should make marketing decisions by considering consumers' wants, the company's requirements, consumers' long-run interests, and society's long-run interests.

Societal marketing concept   The idea that a company's marketing decisions should consider consumers' wants, the company's requirements, consumers' long-run interests, and society's long-run interests.

Spam   Unsolicited, unwanted commercial e-mail messages.

Specialty product   A consumer product with unique characteristics or brand identification for which a significant group of buyers is willing to make a special purchase effort.

Specialty store   A retail store that carries a narrow product line with a deep assortment within that line.

Standardized global marketing   An international marketing strategy that basically uses the same marketing strategy and mix in all of the company's international markets.

Store brand (or private brand)   A brand created and owned by a reseller of a product or service.

Straight product extension   Marketing a product in a foreign market without making any changes to the product.

Straight rebuy   A business buying situation in which the buyer routinely reorders something without any modifications.

Strategic planning   The process of developing and maintaining a strategic fit between the organization's goals and capabilities and its changing marketing opportunities.

Style   A basic and distinctive mode of expression.

Subculture   A group of people with shared value systems based on common life experiences and situations.

Supermarket   A large, low-cost, low-margin, high-volume, self-service store that carries a wide variety of grocery and household products.

Superstore   A store much larger than a regular supermarket that offers a large assortment of routinely purchased food products, nonfood items, and services.

Supplier development   Systematic development of networks of supplier-partners to ensure an appropriate and dependable supply of products and materials exists for use in making products or reselling them to others.

Supply chain management   Managing upstream and downstream value-added flows of materials, final goods, and related information among suppliers, the company, resellers, and final consumers.

Survey research   Gathering primary data by asking people questions about their knowledge, attitudes, preferences, and buying behavior.

Sustainable marketing   Socially and environmentally responsible marketing that meets the present needs of consumers and businesses while also preserving or enhancing the ability of future generations to meet their needs.

SWOT analysis   An overall evaluation of the company's strengths (S), weaknesses (W), opportunities (O), and threats (T).

Systems selling (or solutions selling) Buying a packaged solution to a problem from a single seller, thus avoiding all the separate decisions involved in a complex buying situation.

Target costing Pricing that starts with an ideal selling price and then targets costs that will ensure that the price is met.

Target market A set of buyers sharing common needs or characteristics that the company decides to serve.

Team-based new-product development An approach to developing new products in which various company departments work closely together, overlapping the steps in the product development process to save time and increase effectiveness.

Team selling Using teams of people from sales, marketing, engineering, finance, technical support, and even upper management to service large, complex accounts.

Technological environment Forces that create new technologies, creating new product and market opportunities.

Telemarketing Using the telephone to sell directly to customers.

Territorial sales force structure A sales force organization that assigns each salesperson to an exclusive geographic territory in which that salesperson sells the company's full line.

Test marketing The stage of new-product development in which the product and its proposed marketing program are tested in realistic market settings.

Third-party logistics (3PL) provider An independent logistics provider that performs any or all of the functions required to get a client's product to market.

Total costs The sum of the fixed and variable costs for any given level of production.

Total market demand The total volume that would be bought by a defined consumer group in a defined geographic area in a defined time period in a defined marketing environment under a defined level and mix of industry marketing effort.

Trade promotions Sales promotion tools used to persuade resellers to carry a brand, give it shelf space, promote it in advertising, and push it to consumers.

Undifferentiated (mass) marketing A market-coverage strategy in which a firm decides to ignore market segment differences and go after the whole market with one offer.

Unit contribution The amount that each unit contributes to covering fixed costs—the difference between price and variable costs.

Unsought product A consumer product that the consumer either does not know about or knows about but does not normally consider buying.

Value-added pricing Attaching value-added features and services to differentiate a company's offers while charging higher prices.

Value-based pricing Offering just the right combination of quality and good service at a fair price.

Value chain The series of internal departments that carry out value-creating activities to design, produce, market, deliver, and support a firm's products.

Value delivery network A network composed of the company, suppliers, distributors, and, ultimately, customers who partner with each other to improve the performance of the entire system in delivering customer value.

Value proposition The full positioning of a brand—the full mix of benefits on which it is positioned.

Variable costs Costs that vary directly with the level of production.

Vertical marketing system (VMS) A channel structure in which producers, wholesalers, and retailers act as a unified system. One channel member owns the others, has contracts with them, or has so much power that they all cooperate.

Viral marketing The Internet version of word-of-mouth marketing: a Web site, video, e-mail message, or other marketing event that is so infectious that customers will seek it out or pass it along to friends.

Wants The form human needs take as they are shaped by culture and individual personality.

Warehouse club An off-price retailer that sells a limited selection of brand name grocery items, appliances, clothing, and other goods at deep discounts to members who pay annual membership fees.

Wheel-of-retailing concept A concept that suggests new types of retailers usually begin as low-margin, low-price, low-status operations but later evolve into higher-priced, higher-service operations, eventually becoming like the conventional retailers they replaced.

Whole-channel view Designing international channels that take into account the entire global supply chain and marketing channel, forging an effective global value delivery network.

Wholesaler A firm engaged *primarily* in wholesaling activities.

Wholesaling All the activities involved in selling goods and services to those buying for resale or business use.

Word-of-mouth influence The impact of the personal words and recommendations of trusted friends, associates, and other consumers on buying behavior.

Workload method An approach to determining sales force size based on the workload required and the time available for selling.

Indexes

Name, Company, Brand, and Organization

OTHER MARKETING TITLES OF INTEREST

PRINCIPLES OF MARKETING

Marketing: An Introduction 11/E
Armstrong & Kotler
ISBN-10: 0132744031 | ISBN-13: 9780132744034

Marketing Plan Handbook and Marketing Plan Pro Package, 4/E
Wood
ISBN-10: 0138020876 | ISBN-13: 9780138020873

Principles of Marketing, 14/E
Kotler & Armstrong
ISBN-10: 0132167123 | ISBN-13: 9780132167123

Marketing: Real People, Real Choices, 7/E
Solomon, Marshall & Stuart
ISBN-10: 013217684X | ISBN-13: 9780132176842

Marketing: Defined, Explained, Applied, 2e
Levens
ISBN-10: 0132177153 | ISBN-13: 9780132177153

Hasselback Marketing Faculty Guide, 13e
Hasselback
ISBN-10: 0136010024 | ISBN-13: 9780136010029

Marketing Ethics: Cases and Readings, 1/E
Murphy & Laczniak
ISBN-10: 0131330888 | ISBN-13: 9780131330887

CONSUMER BEHAVIOR

Consumer Behavior, 10/E
Solomon
ISBN-10: 0132671840 | ISBN-13: 9780132671842

Consumer Behavior, 10/E
Schiffman & Kanuk
ISBN-10: 0135053013 | ISBN-13: 9780135053010

Critical Thinking in Consumer Behavior: Cases and Experiential Exercises, 2/E
Graham
ISBN-10: 0136027164 | ISBN-13: 9780136027164

Consumer Behavior and Managerial Decision Making, 2/E
Kardes
ISBN-10: 0130916021 | ISBN-13: 9780130916020

MARKETING RESEARCH

Basic Marketing Research Using Microsoft Excel Data Analysis, 3/E
Burns & Bush
ISBN-10: 0135078229 | ISBN-13: 9780135078228

Basic Marketing Research: A Decision-Making Approach 4/E
Malhotra
ISBN-10: 0132544482 | ISBN-13: 9780132544481

Marketing Research, 6/E
Burns & Bush
ISBN-10: 0136027040 | ISBN-13: 9780136027041

Multivariate Data Analysis, 7/E
Hair, Black, Babin & Anderson
ISBN-10: 0138132631 | ISBN-13: 9780138132637

INTERNATIONAL MARKETING

Global Marketing, 7/E
Keegan & Green
ISBN-10: 0132719150 | ISBN-13: 9780132719155

Global Marketing Management, 7/E
Keegan
ISBN-10: 0132719150 | ISBN-13: 9780132719155

International Marketing Research, 1/E
Kumar
ISBN-10: 0130453862 | ISBN-13: 9780130453860

MARKETING MANAGEMENT

Marketing Management, 14/E
Kotler & Keller
ISBN-10: 0132102927 | ISBN-13: 9780132102926

A Framework for Marketing Management, 5/E
Kotler & Keller
ISBN-10: 0132539306 | ISBN-13: 9780132539302

A Framework for Marketing Management Integrated with PharmaSim, 4/E
Kotler & Keller
ISBN-10: 0136083447 | ISBN-13: 9780136083443

Market-Based Management, 6/E
Best
ISBN-10: 0130387754 | ISBN-13: 9780130387752

Marketing Management, 4/E
Winer
ISBN-10: 0136074898 | ISBN-13: 9780136074892

Strategic Marketing Problems: Cases and Comments, 12/E
Kerin & Peterson
ISBN-10: 0136107060 | ISBN-13: 9780136107064

Strategic Marketing, 1e
Mooradian, Matzler, & Ring
ISBN-10: 0136028047 | ISBN-13: 9780136028048

Marketing Planning: Where Strategy Meets Action, 1e
Sorger
ISBN-10: 0132544709 | ISBN-13: 9780132544702

SELLING

Selling Today: Creating Customer Value, 12/E
Manning, Reece & Ahearne
ISBN-10: 0132109867 | ISBN-13: 9780132109864

Selling Financial Products, 1e
Bexley
ISBN-10: 0132752131 | ISBN-13: 9780132752138

SALES MANAGEMENT

Sales Management: Shaping Future Sales Leaders, 1/E
Tanner, Honeycutt & Erffmeyer
ISBN-10: 0132324121 | ISBN-13: 9780132324120

RETAILING

Retail Management: A Strategic Approach, 11/E
Berman & Evans
ISBN-10: 0136087582 | ISBN-13: 9780136087588